Baker's
POCKET
COMMENTARY
on the
NEW
TESTAMENT

Baker's
POCKET
COMMENTARY
on the
NEW
TESTAMENT

BAKER BOOK HOUSE
Grand Rapids, Michigan

Originally printed in 1912 by
Thomas Nelson and Sons
under the title
Teachers' Testament With Notes and Helps
Reprinted with permission in 1964 by
Baker Book House
under the title
Compact Commentary on the New Testament
Paperback edition issued 1974 by
Baker Book House
ISBN: 0-8010-0617-1
Printed in the United States of America

INTRODUCTION

Here is an excellent tool to put into the hands of laymen, church people, and teachers. It is serviceable, stimulating, and concise. As a handy size, pocket edition of a commentary it is outstanding.

First, *it is a commentary*. Those who have contributed have done their exegesis well. In the light of the hermeneutical principles of their day the interpretations are sound. Without being technical for the scholar, they have yet embodied the results of scholarship in their suggestive notes. Second, *it is a compact commentary*. Nothing verbose or wordy is here. Words are used succinctly and practically. Without elaboration there is good condensation and exposition within the limits of the space available. Third, *it is a compact commentary for the general reader*. There are exhaustive commentaries for the specialist, but this seeks to provide adequate help for the person whose time is limited and who needs assistance to find the meaning of the text. For private devotion and Sunday School teaching nothing could be better.

Their work remains vigorous and relevant, even though new light through archaelogy has been thrown upon the text since the editors and contributors wrote their notes. They were among the best interpreters of the New Testament in their knowledge, faith, and devotion. The text of the American Standard Version is still used as one of the best to communicate the message of the New Testament.

It is a pleasure to recommend this commentary. We trust that by means of it "more light will yet break forth from God's holy Word."

RALPH G. TURNBULL

NOTE BY THE PUBLISHERS

To meet the many demands for a Testament with Notes and Comments that will make the text clear and plain to everyone, we have prepared NELSON'S EXPLANATORY TESTAMENT, using the American Standard Version, which is acknowledged by all the leading scholars to be the best version in any language.

The Text of this Testament is printed from large easy reading type, with the words of Christ emphasized in black letters and all the proper names have been divided into syllables and accented, thus making it possible for anyone to pronounce them correctly.

Special care has been exercised in the selection and preparation of the Notes and Comments on the text of NELSON'S EXPLANATORY TESTAMENT, so as to give a full and complete explanation of all the difficult passages, with entire freedom from theological and denominational bias. With this object in view, the Notes and Comments have been revised and approved by noted scholars representing the different evangelical denominations and acting as associate editors.

The Introductions contain a wealth of accurate information concerning the books of the New Testament, in concise language and compact form. In addition to an introduction to each book by an eminent scholar, there is an article of great interest and value on the Language and Text of the New Testament.

NELSON'S EXPLANATORY TESTAMENT

with

COPIOUS NOTES AND COMMENTS

and an

INTRODUCTION TO EACH BOOK

JOHN WILLIAM RUSSELL, M.A., Editor-in-Chief and Writer of the Notes and Comments.

Associate Editors

REV. J. R. MILLER, D.D., LL.D., Editorial Superintendent of the Presbyterian Board of Publication and Sunday School Work; Author of many Devotional and Religious Books.

M. C. HAZARD, PH.D., Editor Emeritus of the Sunday School Periodicals of the Congregational Church; Editor of Walker's Concordance; formerly Assistant Editor of "The Sunday School Times."

REV. JOHN McNAUGHER, D.D., Professor of the New Testament, Allegheny Theological Seminary of the United Presbyterian Church.

REV. J. T. McFARLAND, D.D., Editor of the Sunday School Literature of the Methodist Episcopal Church.

REV. C. R. BLACKALL, D.D., Editor of the Periodicals of the American Baptist Publication Society.

REV. J. B. REMENSNYDER, D.D., LL.D., Pastor of St. James' Lutheran Church, New York; Author of "Work and Personality of Luther," "The Post-Apostolic Age and Current Religious Problems" and other books.

REV. SAMUEL HART, D.D., LL.D., Custodian of The Standard Book of Common Prayer; Dean and Professor of Doctrinal Theology, Berkeley Divinity School (Protestant Episcopal).

REV. H. M. HAMILL, D.D., Superintendent of the General Sunday School Work of the Methodist Episcopal Church, South; Author of several books on The Bible and Sunday Schools.

REV. HAROLD E. MONSER, B.A., Editor of the Cross-Reference Bible; General Evangelist, The Disciples.

REV. H. H. FOUT, D.D., Editor of the Sunday School Periodicals of the United Brethren Church.

REV. I. J. VAN NESS, D.D., Editorial Secretary of the Sunday School Board of the Southern Baptist Church; formerly President of the Sunday School Editors' Association of the United States and Canada.

REV. RUFUS W. MILLER, D.D., Secretary of the Sunday School Board of the Reformed Church in the United States.

Each Book of Nelson's Explanatory Testament is preceded by an Introduction Prepared by one of the following Biblical Scholars:

JAMES RENDEL HARRIS, M.A., LL.D., Director of Studies at the Friends' Settlement for Social and Religious Study, Woodbrooke, near Birmingham, England; formerly Lecturer in Cambridge University and Professor of Theology in the University of Leyden.

REV. MARCUS DODS, D.D., Professor in the Free Church College, Edinburgh.

REV. MATTHEW B. RIDDLE, D.D., Professor of New Testament Exegesis, Western Theological Seminary.

SIR WILLIAM MITCHELL RAMSAY, D.C.L., LL.D., Professor of Humanity, University of Aberdeen.

REV. THOMAS C. EDWARDS, D.D., Professor in Wyoming Seminary; formerly Editor of "The Missionary."

REV. JAMES DENNEY, D.D., Professor of New Testament Language, Literature and Theology, United Free Church College, Glasgow.

REV. TALBOT W. CHAMBERS, D.D., Professor in Rutgers Theological Seminary.

REV. BENJAMIN B. WARFIELD, D.D., LL.D., Professor of Didactic and Polemical Theology, Princeton Theological Seminary.

INTRODUCTION TO THE NEW TESTAMENT

BY PROFESSOR M. B. RIDDLE, D.D., LL.D.

Unity.—The New Testament is a collection of twenty-seven distinct writings, from eight (or nine) different hands. Of these writers, four were apostles—Matthew, John, Paul, and Peter; two were companions of the apostles—Mark and Luke; two were our Lord's brothers, probably not apostles—James and Jude. The books are usually classed as Historical (five), Didactic (twenty-one), Prophetical (one); though the writings of the first class include much more than one-half of the entire matter. The unity of the whole is remarkable; all the books find their centre in Jesus Christ our Lord. The four Gospels narrate His life on earth; the fifth historical book tells how the new life, that came from Him through the Holy Spirit, passed from Jerusalem to Rome. The epistles, written by men of varied personal character and temperament, set forth the significance of the Gospel facts, as revealed to them, according to our Lord's promise (John 16.12, 13). The single prophetical book, however it is to be interpreted, shows the Lamb as King, to become Victor on earth, where His church is preparing through conflict to share His triumph.

Order.—In our English Bible the order is not chronological. In ancient manuscripts there was much variation in position; the seven General Epistles were usually placed immediately after Acts, the Gospels coming first, though not always in the order now universal. The Pauline Epistles seem to have been arranged according to length, so that the earliest and the latest stand together (1 and 2 Thes., with 1 and 2 Tim. and Titus).

Progress of Doctrine.—There is evident in these writings an advance of Christian thought toward maturity; but the progress is not along divergent lines, nor can all the books be classified according to assumed types of doctrine. Biblical Theology properly discusses the theology of the several writings; but the theology of the New Testament is one, whatever progress is discernible. Moreover, the advance in Paul's teaching, as indicated by a comparison of Thessalonians with Ephesians, is almost as marked as that between the General Epistles of James and John, which are regarded as presenting the respective extremes in the progress of doctrine. The Gospels cannot be classified by any such principle; for while John, from its purpose, presents the most mature statements, there is no appreciable advance in doctrine from Matthew to Luke. The same Lord Jesus Christ was apprehended by all the writers in substantially the same way.

THE GOSPELS

The four Gospels were written primarily for different circles of readers; each has its peculiar design, and each evangelist has his distinctive method. Only by a comparison of all four can a complete view be obtained of the history of our Lord's life on earth, and thus of His person and work. One fact should be noted: the four Gospels place the emphasis on the closing events. More than one-half of all the narratives describes the events of the last year—one of conflict; more than one-third is devoted to the few weeks which closed with the death and resurrection of our Lord. A comparison of the methods employed by the evangelists confirms the view of Godet: Matthew gives long discourses—he writes as a preacher; Mark depicts events as they occurred, one after the other—he is a chronicler: Luke arranges the incidents with reference to their relations—he is a historian; while John selects such facts and discourses as prove a given truth—he is a theologian. The Gospel according to John, evidently written last, is properly distinguished from the others, which resemble each other more closely.

SYNOPTIC GOSPELS

The Gospels according to Matthew, Mark, and Luke have been termed "Synoptic," and the writers "Synoptists," because a common outline is pursued. Much of the matter throughout is common to all three; but there are many points of difference. The arrangement is rarely the same in all three, even when the events of the same period are narrated, except in the accounts of Passion Week. In language the differences are remarkable. When the same incident is given by all, they rarely agree exactly for ten consecutive words (in the Greek). So that, whatever be the source of the common matter, there is *literary independence*.

How are these agreements and differences to be accounted for? The safest view is: that the common matter represents in general the story of Jesus Christ as it was at first preached by the apostles and others; that when written Gospels were needed, these three writers, each with added material, wrote the accounts we now have. Matthew had his own knowledge of the events; Mark learned from Peter; Luke gathered material when in Palestine (58-60 A.D.), while eye-witnesses were living, probably using, for the parts peculiar to his narrative (especially ch. 1, 2), some written documents or memoranda. But many hold that there was a common document or documents on which all three Gospels were based.

By many the "double source" theory is now accepted. This assumes that there were two original documents referred to by Papias (died 163 A.D.): one, by Matthew, containing the Ora-

cles (Logia) in the Hebrew dialect; the other, by Mark, derived
from Peter. The one consisted mainly of discourses; the other, of
narratives. But there is no agreement as to the extent of these assumed documents. The one, it is asserted by some, contained only
discourses; according to others, it also included narratives. The
other is held by some to be a briefer form of Mark's Gospel; by
others, to be that Gospel as we now have it. Luke's Gospel is regarded as the last composite result of the combinations. But none
of these theories accounts satisfactorily for the obvious literary independence of the Synoptic Gospels.

The faithful use of a common document or documents would
have led to greater similarity both in order and in language. If
the writers purposely deviated from the common source or sources,
valid reasons must be discovered for the modifications. The reasons
assigned often assume that these writers had the literary habits of
modern authors or reporters; too often they imply, though in
smoother phrase, that the changes were purposed corruptions.
That the reasons are not valid is rendered highly probable by the
fact that two critics of equal ability, both holding the "double
source" theory, frequently reach conclusions diametrically opposed
to each other, in applying the theory to most of the sections containing common matter. The problem is an interesting one; but
prolonged discussion has not as yet yielded any positive result. At
least, there is no prospect of obtaining in this way a more faithful
portrayal of our Lord's person and of His work than that derived
from the canonical Gospels, which, from the days preceding Justin
Martyr, have been read in Christian assemblies, cited by Christian
authors, and cherished by Christian hearts.

The independence of the Synoptic Gospels involves the probability that they were written within a few years of each other, and that
the testimony they present is that of three distinct witnesses to the
main facts respecting our Lord's life on earth.

LANGUAGE AND TEXT OF THE NEW TESTAMENT

BY PROFESSOR J. RENDEL HARRIS, M.A., LL.D.

Language.—The New Testament is written entirely in the Greek language.

Text.—The existence of a number of various readings in the text of the New Testament necessitates an inquiry into the materials from which the text is derived, and into the causes which have produced the divergent readings. Most of these divergences are mere trifles, caused by careless copying and insufficient correction.

The materials of textual criticism are usually reckoned under the heads of Copies, Versions, and Fathers, which might be perhaps better grouped as:—

1. Copies + Patristic Citations from Copies.
2. Versions + Patristic Citations from Versions.

Copies may be classified according to the materials upon which they are written—Papyrus, Vellum, and Paper; or according to the hands in which they are written—*Uncials* (large letters) and *Cursives* (running hand).

Uncial MSS. are usually denoted by capital letters borrowed from the Latin, Greek, and Hebrew alphabets; and Cursives, by Arabic numerals.

But the same sign may mean different MSS. in different parts of the New Testament. For convenience the books are grouped under the heads of Gospels, Acts and Catholic Epistles, Pauline Epistles, and Apocalypse; and the enumeration of authorities is made *de novo* with each group. Sometimes this is indicated by writing a few letters above the sign representing the MS., as D ^{Paul}, E ^{Act}, or by adding a subscript numeral, as D_2, E_2.

Only a few fragments of the New Testament exist written on papyrus. It is, however, almost certain that that was the primitive material upon which the Apostolic documents were written (*cf.* 2 John 12: "I would not write them with paper and ink"). Of MSS. written on vellum, the most important are those belonging to the fourth, fifth, and sixth centuries, which pass under the name of the "Five Great Uncials." They are as follows:—

1. ℵ (Aleph; fourth century)—the Codex Sinaiticus, discovered by Tischendorf in 1844 (and 1859) in the monastery of St. Catherine, on Mount Sinai. The greater part of this MS. is now in St. Petersburg. It contains the whole of the New Testament complete, together with the Epistle of Barnabas, and a large part of the Shepherd of Hermas. The last twelve verses of Mark are wanting; but it is suspicious that the page where they should occur appears to be a cancel.

2. B (Vaticanus; fourth century) is in the Vatican Library at

Rome. It contains the New Testament as far as the middle of Heb. 9.14; but the rest of Hebrews, as well as the Pastoral Epistles and the Apocalypse, are wanting. Whether these later books were ever contained in the Codex is uncertain. A modern Cursive hand has completed the Hebrews and has added the Apocalypse. ℵ and B probably proceeded from a common workshop, perhaps the library at Cæsarea; and this may explain why both lack the last twelve verses of Mark. (On the other hand, it may be regarded as reasonably certain that these twelve verses are not part of the primitive text.)

3. A (Alexandrinus; fifth century) is now in the British Museum, where it is exposed to view in one of the show cases. It came to England in 1628 as a present from Cyril Lucar, the Patriarch of Constantinople, to King Charles the First. There seems no reason to doubt the tradition which assigns the Codex to Alexandria. This MS. contains the first Epistle of Clement and a part of the second Epistle.

4. C (Ephræmi Syri rescriptus; fifth century) derives its name from the fact that the original text of its Greek Bible was washed out in the twelfth century in order to make room for a Greek translation of some works of St. Ephrem the Syrian. The MS. is now in Paris, but almost nothing is known of its origin and history. It is suspected that the MS. needs to be re-read. About three-fifths of the New Testament have been recovered from its pages.

5. D (Codex Bezæ; sixth century) derives its name from Beza the Reformer, who presented it in 1581 to the University of Cambridge, in whose public library it is exposed to view. Beza obtained it from some monastery in the south-east of France. This MS. is a bilingual, and contains, besides the Greek text of the Gospels and Acts, a parallel Latin version of great antiquity.

This is probably the most remarkable of all Greek MSS. of the New Testament, in the number and peculiar character of its textual variations. It has at least one passage in the Gospels to which no parallel can be found anywhere else. It is an insertion in the text after Luke 6.5 as follows:—"And on the same day" (*i.e.* the Sabbath), "seeing some one working on the Sabbath, he said to him, 'Man, if thou knowest what thou doest, blessed art thou; but if thou knowest not, thou art accursed, and a transgressor of the law.'"

Closely related to the text of D in the Acts is E ᴬᶜᵗ, or Codex Laudianus (sixth century), a Græco-Latin Codex presented to the University of Oxford by Archbishop Laud. This MS. is also interesting from the fact that it is the very copy employed by the Venerable Bede when writing his *Retractations* on the Acts.

A number of Uncial MSS. and some Cursives also are written with gold and silver inks upon vellum which has been stained purple. These magnificent books were probably prepared for royal hands. One of the most valuable is Codex N (sixth century), of which scattered leaves exist in Rome, London, Vienna, and in the convent of St. John in Patmos.

The whole number of Uncial MSS. known to the critical world is estimated at something over 120; but in this enumeration a number of MSS. are counted more than once, on account of their appearing in the different classes (Evan., Acts—Cath., Paul., and Apoc.) described above. The Codex Sinaiticus counts for four in such an enumeration.

The Cursive MSS. are, as might be expected on account of their later dates, much more numerous; probably we might set their number at between 2400 and 2500 (the enumeration being repeated for the different groups of books as before). Of all this number, only a very few have been rendered available for criticism by exact collation; a fact which is much to be regretted, as there are preserved in Cursive MSS. many rare and curious readings which are of great antiquity, and yet have no attestation in Uncial MSS. It is not meant that all Cursive MSS. deserve complete and exhaustive collation, but most of them deserve a more careful study than they have hitherto received. It is also readily to be admitted that they are, relatively to the Uncial MSS. and the versions, of much less value in the determination of the text. But we must bear in mind that the texts of Cursive MSS. are merely the descendants of lost Uncial MSS., and that the maxim that "all various readings are early" applies to them as well as to the more imposing Uncial MSS. Where a number of Cursive MSS. can be proved to come from a common lost original, it is often possible to restore the lost (Uncial) ancestor by a critical comparison of the texts that are descended from it.

Lectionaries.—A word must be said in passing of Lectionaries, or copies of the Gospels, or the Acts and Epistles, arranged for reading in churches. They are very numerous, and almost unknown as to text; but enough is known to enable us to affirm with certainty that they often contain fragments of very early texts. When the lectionary is made up out of lessons from the Gospels, it is commonly called an *Evangelistarium;* when the lessons are taken from the Acts and Epistles, it is known as an *Apostolos* or *Praxapostolos*.

Versions.—We come now to versions, a class of witnesses to which greater weight is continually being assigned in the determination of the text. The great value of the versions lies in the evidence which they furnish as to the state of the New Testament text at the time when it was translated. Many of the versions are of the highest antiquity—in fact, three of them are commonly credited to the second century—and this means that, if their evidence had come down to us unchanged from the time of the first translation, we should have the equivalent of three Greek MSS. which would be at least 150 years older than any existing copies. Unfortunately versions are only copies in a different language, and are subject to the same tendencies to revision and textual change as are ordinary Greek MSS. It becomes, therefore, of the first importance to edit the versions as nearly as possible in the forms in which they stood when first made. A polished Vulgate must be carried back to the rough and probably barbaric ancestor from which it is derived, and the evidence of the ancestral translation will be of the highest value. It is, for textual purposes, *the* evidence of the version.

We may divide the earliest versions into the following groups:

1. SYRIAC VERSIONS.
2. LATIN VERSIONS.
3. EGYPTIAN VERSIONS.

Each of these versions is believed to go back in some form to the second century; and this may be taken as proved for the first two groups. The third group has not yet been adequately studied.

Fathers.—As we have already said, the Greek copies of the New Testament, as well as the versions made from the Greek, derive great collateral confirmation from the citations made by the Fathers of the church. And here we have the advantage that almost every quotation made by a Patristic writer is a dated landmark in the history of the text; so that from a study of Origen's works we recover large portions of the MSS. which he used in the third century; from a study of Cyprian's works we restore the Latin Bible of Carthage in the same century; from the quotations of Aphrahat, the fourth-century Persian father, we derive great accessions to our knowledge of the old Syriac version, and so on.

It need hardly be said that the importance of such examinations of the texts underlying Patristic writings is very great. Yet we are still quite at the beginning of the studies which enable us to make a proper use of these valuable materials.

Printed Text.—The first printed text of the Greek New Testament was brought out by Cardinal Ximenes in the Bible which is known as the Complutensian Polyglot. This splendid work is named after the University of Alcala in Spain, whose Latin name is Complutum. Although this is the first printed New Testament (1514 A.D.), it is not the first published; for the issue of it was delayed, and the cardinal was anticipated by Erasmus, who brought out in 1516 an edition which was published by Froben, the printer of Basle. The work of Erasmus was done too hastily, and in one passage at the end of the Apocalypse, his MS. being defective, he supplied the defect by retranslating from the Vulgate.

Of later editions, the most famous are those which bear the name of Beza the Reformer, of Stephen, the Paris printer and scholar, and of the Elzevir brothers of Leyden in Holland. The folio edition of Stephen in 1550 has become the standard text in many of the countries of Europe. On the other hand, the Elzevir edition of 1624 was characterized by its printers, in their second edition of 1633, as *textum ab omnibus receptum*, "text received by everybody," and hence is commonly known as the Textus Receptus.

Of recent editions the most important are those of Tischendorf, Tregelles, and Westcott-Hort, and the text that underlies the Revised Version.

THE NAMES AND ORDER

OF THE

BOOKS OF THE NEW TESTAMENT

THE GOSPEL ACCORDING TO MATTHEW

INTRODUCTION BY PROFESSOR M. B. RIDDLE, D.D., LL.D.

The Writer.—The apostle Matthew, also called "Levi the son of Alphæus" (Mark 2.14; *cf.* Luke 5. 27-29), was, when called, a publican, or tax-gatherer, probably a collector of tolls and custom duties in the traffic across the Sea of Galilee. His office was odious to the Jews, yet the list of the twelve in this Gospel (10.3) designates him "Matthew the publican." The name Matthew, which was probably adopted in consequence of his new relation to our Lord, is akin to Matthias—that is, "gift of God." His call is narrated in the three Gospels, but while he refers to the feast which Mark and Luke distinctly place at his house, he makes no allusion to that fact. Tradition says he was murdered in Ethiopia, while at prayer; but according to an earlier statement by Clement of Alexandria, he died a natural death.

The Original Language.—Papias and Irenæus, both of whom lived in the second century, state that Matthew wrote in the Hebrew dialect (Aramaic). The former uses the word "Logia," or Oracles, which was certainly used of writings containing more than discourses, and applied very early to books of Scripture. But the earliest citations from the Gospels, some of them in works of the earlier half of the second century, give the exact words of the Greek Gospel we now have. No certain traces of a previous Aramaic Gospel have been discovered, nor does the Greek Gospel show any marks of being a translation. It is therefore probable either that there was no Aramaic original, or that it was superseded very soon by a Greek narrative which the apostle made, or caused to be made. As Greek was extensively spoken in Palestine, and a publican would necessarily be familiar with that language, a Greek original is not improbable. At all events, we now have a well-attested Greek Gospel; and we are not likely to discover in it, or anterior to it, traces of an Aramaic original written by Matthew.

Design.—The Gospel seems to have been written in Palestine, and primarily for Jewish Christians. It presents Jesus of Nazareth as the last and greatest Prophet and Lawgiver, fulfilling the predictions of the Old Testament, because He was the Messiah of God, the King of the true Israel. This design seems to have modified the arrangement to some extent, especially in ch. 5-13.

The historical facts and discourses furnish the proof that Jesus of Nazareth is the Messiah from His words and works. Hence there are many citations from the Old Testament, to show how He fulfilled its predictions. The discourses in the earlier part of the Gospel stand in close relation to "the training of the twelve." They present the law of the Kingdom (the Sermon on the Mount), the service

1

of the Kingdom (the mission of the twelve, ch. 10), the progress of the Kingdom (the discourse in parables, ch. 13). The main design gives prominence to "the kingdom of heaven," and many details peculiar to this Gospel set forth our Lord as the promised King.

Time of Writing.— From the Gospel itself it is plain that it was written before the destruction of Jerusalem, but a number of years after the resurrection (27.7; 28.15). Irenæus says it was written "when Peter and Paul were preaching at Rome," which was certainly after 61 A.D. All the Synoptic Gospels were probably written between 60 and 64 A.D. Some scholars think the time should be extended beyond the latter date, and that the Gospel according to Matthew was written later than 64 A.D.

Summary.—While the contents of this Gospel may be analyzed as a succession of historical proofs that Jesus is the Messiah promised in the Old Testament, it will facilitate a comparison with the other narratives to divide it into periods.

1. The genealogy, birth, and infancy of Jesus (1, 2). Most of these incidents are peculiar to this Gospel.

2. The ministry of John the Baptist; the baptism and temptation of Jesus (3 to 4.11).

3. The Galilæan ministry, until the death of John the Baptist (4.12 to 13.53). As already indicated, three important discourses are reported (5-7, 10, 13); the other events being grouped without reference to chronological order.

4. The later Galilæan ministry, largely a period of conflict, including several journeys (14-18).

5. The close of the Peræan ministry, and the final journey to Jerusalem (19, 20). A period of several months, spent by our Lord in Peræa and Jerusalem, is passed over in silence by Matthew and Mark.

6. The final conflicts at Jerusalem (21-25).

7. The Passover, the agony in Gethsemane, the betrayal, the trials before the Jewish rulers and before Pilate, the crucifixion and burial (26, 27).

8. The resurrection, the appearance of the Risen Lord, the great commission to preach the gospel. Closing promise (28).

THE GOSPEL:—

ACCORDING TO

MATTHEW

Genealogy of Jesus

1 ^aThe book of the ^bgeneration of Je'sus Christ, the son of David, the son of Abraham.

2 Abraham begat I'saac; and I'saac begat Jacob; and Jacob begat Ju'dah and his brethren; 3 and Ju'dah begat Pe'rez and Ze'rah of Ta'mar; and Pe'rez begat Hez'ron; and Hez'ron begat ^cRam; 4 and ^cRam begat Am-min'a-dab; and Am-min'a-dab begat Nah'shon; and Nah'shon begat Sal'mon; 5 and Sal'mon begat Bo'az of Ra'hab; and Bo'az begat O'bed of Ruth; and O'bed begat Jes'se; 6 and Jes'se begat David the king.

And David begat Sol'o-mon of her *that had been the wife of* U-ri'ah; 7 and Sol o-mon begat

---

a Or, *The genealogy of Jesus Christ* *b* Or, *birth*: as in ver. 18. *c* Gr. *Aram.*

CHAPTER 1

1. *Son of David.* Matthew, writing specially for the Jews, naturally emphasized the descent of Jesus from Abraham, through David. No one claiming to be the Messiah could obtain a hearing unless he was able to prove his Davidic descent. Our Lord's derivation from the royal line was not doubted by the Jews. Modern popular notions on this subject have been confused by ignoring the distinction between descent and condition. These two may apparently contradict each other. Jesus was born in a stable, yet he came of the stock of the kings of Israel. He was called 'the carpenter's son,' and wrought at his trade in the obscure village of Nazareth, yet his ancestors were surrounded with royal pomp. These facts seem incongruous to us; but they did not seem so to the people from whom he sprang. With the Jews the different kinds of occupations did not so closely indicate corresponding degrees of social condition and consideration as they do with us. Paul, a man of position and influence, was a tent-maker. The Jews thought more of a man's recorded and attested descent than of his trade or profession. It was more important for them to know who a man was than how he earned his living.

3. *Tamar.* The first of four women—the other three being Rahab, Ruth, and Bathsheba—mentioned by Matthew in his lineage of Jesus. Two things are to be learned from this: Matthew meant to remind the Jews that two Gentiles, Rahab and Ruth, were among the ancestors of our Lord; and the sins of Tamar, Rahab, and Bathsheba did not exclude them from this list. Jesus did not scorn to number the foreigner and the sinner in the line of his descent.

3

Re-ho-bo'am; and Re-ho-bo'am begat A-bi'jah; and A-bi'jah begat ^{d}A'sa; 8 and ^{d}A'sa begat Je-hosh'a-phat; and Je-hosh'a-phat begat Jo'ram; and Jo'ram begat Uz-zi'ah; 9 and Uz-zi'ah begat Jo'tham; and Jo'tham begat A'haz; and A'haz begat Hez-e-ki'ah; 10 and Hez-e-ki'ah begat Ma-nas'seh; and Ma-nas'-seh begat ^{e}A'mon; and ^{e}A'mon begat Jo-si'ah; 11 and Jo-si'ah begat Jech-o-ni'ah and his brethren, at the time of the ^{f}carrying away to Bab'y-lon.

12 And after the ^{f}carrying away to Bab'y-lon, Jech-o-ni'ah begat ^{g}She-al'ti-el; and ^{g}She-al'ti-el begat Ze-rub'ba-bel; 13 and Ze-rub'ba-bel begat A-bi'ud; and A-bi'ud begat E-li'a-kim; and E-li'a-kim begat A-zor; 14 and A'zor begat Sa'doc; and Sa'doc begat A'chim; and A'chim begat E-li'ud; 15 and E-li'ud begat E-le-a'zar; and E-le-a'zar begat Mat'than; and Mat'than begat Jacob; 16 and Jacob begat Joseph the husband of Mary, of whom was born Je'sus, who is called Christ.

17 So all the generations from Abraham unto David are fourteen generations; and from David unto the ^{f}carrying away to Bab'y-lon fourteen generations; and from the ^{f}carrying away to Bab'y-lon unto the Christ fourteen generations:

18 Now the ^{h}birth ^{i}of Je'sus Christ was on this wise: When his mother Mary had been betrothed to Joseph, before they came together she was found with child of the Holy Spirit. 19 And Joseph her husband, being a righteous man, and not willing to make her a public example, was minded to put her away privily. 20 But when he thought on these things, behold, an angel of the Lord appeared unto him in a dream, saying, Joseph, thou son of David, fear not to take unto thee Mary thy wife: for that which is ^{k}conceived in her is of the Holy Spirit. 21 And she shall bring forth a son; and thou shalt call his name JE'SUS; for it is he that shall save his people from their sins. 22 Now all this is come to pass, that it might be fulfilled which was spoken by the Lord through the prophet, saying,

23 ^{l}Behold, the virgin shall be
    with child, and shall bring
    forth a son,
And they shall call his name
    ^{m}Im-man'u-el;

---

^{d} Gr. *Asaph.* ^{e} Gr. *Amos.* ^{f} Or, *removal to Babylon* ^{g} Gr. *Salathiel.* ^{h} Or, *generation:* as in ver 1.

^{i} Some ancient authorities read *of the Christ.* ^{k} Gr. *begotten.* ^{l} Is. vii. 14. ^{m} Gr. *Emmanuel.*

---

16. *Joseph the husband of Mary.* It is the lineage of Joseph that is traced here, as Jewish genealogies did not mention women. Jesus, as son of Mary, wife of Joseph, was the latter's son according to Jewish law. In order to establish the Messiahship of Jesus, Matthew had to prove his legal descent through Joseph.

18. *Jesus Christ.* 'Jesus' means

Saviour; 'Christ' means Anointed. The title 'Anointed' was given to those who attained the office of a priest, a prophet, or a king.

21. *Save his people from their sins.* The true mission of the Messiah is here made clear. He was to be the spiritual saviour of his people. The traditional expectation of a national or political deliverer from the Romans is ignored.

which is, being interpreted, God with us. 24 And Joseph arose from his sleep, and did as the angel of the Lord commanded him, and took unto him his wife; 25 and knew her not till she had brought forth a son: and he called his name JE′SUS.

2 Now when Je′sus was born in Beth′le-hem of Ju-dæ′a in the days of Her′od the king, behold, *a*Wise-men from the east came to Je-ru′sa-lem, saying, 2 *b*Where is he that is born King of the Jews? for we saw his star in the east, and are come to *c*worship him. 3 And when Her′od the king heard it,

he was troubled, and all Je-ru′-sa-lem with him. 4 And gathering together all the chief priests and scribes of the people, he inquired of them where the Christ should be born. 5 And they said unto him, In Beth′le-hem of Ju-dæ′a: for thus it is written through the prophet,

6 *d*And thou Beth′le-hem, land of Ju′dah,
　Art in no wise least among the princes of Ju′dah:
For out of thee shall come forth a governor,
　Who shall be shepherd of my people Is′ra-el.

7 Then Her′od privily called the

---

a Gr. *Magi.* Compare Esther 1.13; Dan. 2.12; Acts 13.6, 8. *b* Or, *Where is the King of the Jews that is born?* *c* The Greek word denotes an act of reverence

whether paid to a creature (see ch. 4.9; 18. 26), or to the Creator (see ch. 4.10). *d* Mic. v. 2.

CHAPTER 2

1. *Bethlehem* (house of bread). The village is five miles south of Jerusalem. Its modern name is Beit Lahm. The traditional place of Jesus' birth is a cave hewn from rock, over which a church, now known as the Church of the Nativity, was built about 330 A. D. by Empress Helena, mother of Constantine the Great. Part of the original church still stands. Bethlehem was the birthplace of David as well as of him who was called the Son of David. *Herod.* Later known as Herod the Great. He was an Idumæan by birth, was made king by favor of the Romans and firmly supported their rule. He was a fierce and unscrupulous though able ruler and was easily angered by any threat or prospect of interference with his power or with the succession to his throne. Hence his jealous alarm when he heard about the birth of a king of the Jews.

2. *His star in the east.* Apart from the plain statement that it was intended to guide the Wise-men to Bethlehem, the most probable explanation of the star is that of some planetary conjunction which led the

Wise-men, who were students of astronomy and astrology, to connect it with the predicted birth of a king of the Jews.

3. *Troubled.* His fears were aroused that his own children might be excluded from his throne.

4. *All the chief priests and scribes.* One way of designating the Sanhedrin, the supreme Jewish council of seventy-one members. It governed according to Jewish law, and in religious and moral affairs its influence and decisions were potent throughout the whole Jewish world. In the time of Christ its legislative, judicial and administrative authority extended over all Judæa. It was composed of chief priests, elders and scribes. See note on Acts 4.5.

The Christ. Herod had in mind the promised Messiah of the Jews, who was expected to be a political deliverer. His coming meant the end of Herod and his kingdom.

5. *Bethlehem of Judæa.* Not to be mistaken for another Bethlehem in the tribe of Zebulun (Josh. 19.15).

7. *Privily called the Wise-men.* This summons, unlike that to the Sanhedrin, was part of a plot to use the Wise-men as aids in the search

ᵉWise-men, and learned of them exactly ᶠwhat time the star appeared. 8 And he sent them to Beth′le-hem, and said, Go and search out exactly concerning the young child; and when ye have found *him*, bring me word, that I also may come and ᵃworship him. 9 And they, having heard the king, went their way; and lo, the star, which they saw in the east, went before them, till it came and stood over where the young child was. 10 And when they saw the star, they rejoiced with exceeding great joy. 11 And they came into the house and saw the young child with Mary his mother; and they fell down and worshipped him; and opening their treasures they offered unto him gifts, gold and frankincense and myrrh. 12 And being warned *of God* in a dream

that they should not return to Her′od, they departed into their own country another way.

13 Now when they were departed, behold, an angel of the Lord appeareth to Joseph in a dream, saying, Arise and take the young child and his mother, and flee into E′gypt, and be thou there until I tell thee: for Her′od will seek the young child to destroy him. 14 And he arose and took the young child and his mother by night, and departed into E′gypt; 15 and was there until the death of Her′od: that it might be fulfilled which was spoken by the Lord through the prophet, saying, ᵍOut of E′gypt did I call my son.

16 Then Her′od, when he saw that he was mocked of the ᵉWise-men, was exceeding wroth, and sent forth, and slew all the male

e Gr. *Maqi.* Compare Esther 1.13; Dan. 2.12; Acts 13.6, 8.   *f* Gr, *the time of the*   *star that appeared*   *g* Hos. xi. 1.

for the infant Jesus. Herod at first took all steps openly to assist the Wise-men, who were members either of the Persian or of the Babylonian priestly caste, revered for their knowledge, by asking the opinion of the Sanhedrin as to where the Christ was to be born; but this secret call had a deadly purpose behind it. It meant murder. The King relied upon the Wise-men to find out the exact date of the Messiah's birth.

11. *Fell down and worshipped him.* Blending the reverence due to their spiritual ruler, the Messiah, with the homage due to an earthly king. *Frankincense and myrrh.* Odorous gum resins obtained from shrubs found in tropical countries of the East.

12. *Warned of God in a dream.* Here was a divine direction and interference beyond the knowledge or power of the Wise-men. It saved both the infant Jesus and them from Herod's wrath.

13. *Egypt.* The safest land for shelter, as Egypt then contained hundreds of thousands of Jews. It was a Roman province.

14. *By night.* The flight was hurried and secret to avoid Herod's vengeance.

15. *Until the death of Herod.* The best authorities agree that the time was not many months. *Through the prophet.* Hos. 11.1 is not a prophecy but a historical fact, and Matthew means to compare the call of Jesus out of Egypt with the call of Israel out of Egypt in the former time.

16. *All the male children.* The number was probably between twenty and forty. The absence of mention of the massacre by historians is accounted for by its unimportance among greater cruelties of Herod. *From two years old and under.* So as to include all the male infants born since the appearance of the star.

6

children that were in Beth'le-hem, and in all the borders thereof, from two years old and under, according to the time which he had exactly learned of the *h*Wise-men. 17 Then was fulfilled that which was spoken through Jer-e-mi'ah the prophet, saying,

18 *i*A voice was heard in Ra'mah,
Weeping and great mourning,
Ra'chel weeping for her children;
And she would not be comforted, because they are not.

19 But when Her'od was dead, behold, an angel of the Lord appeareth in a dream to Joseph in E'gypt, saying, 20 Arise and take the young child and his mother, and go into the land of Is'ra-el: for they are dead that sought the young child's life. 21 And he arose and took the young child and his mother, and came into the land of Is'ra-el. 22 But when he heard that Ar-che-la'us was reigning over Ju-dæ'a in the room of his father Her'od, he was afraid to go thither; and being warned *of God* in a dream, he withdrew into the parts of Gal'i-lee, 23 and came and dwelt in a city called Naz'a-reth; that it might be fulfilled which was spoken through the prophets, *k*that he should be called a Naz-a-rene'.

3 And in those days cometh John the Bap'tist, preaching in the wilderness of Ju-dæ'a, saying, 2 Repent ye; for the kingdom of heaven is at hand. 3 For this is he that was spoken of through I-sa'iah the prophet, saying,
*a*The voice of one crying in the wilderness,
Make ye ready the way of the Lord,
Make his paths straight.
4 Now John himself had his raiment of camel's hair, and a leathern girdle about his loins; and his food was locusts and

---

h Gr. *Magi.* Compare Esther 1.13; Dan. 2.12; Acts 13.6, 8.   *i* Jer. xxxi. 15.   *k* Isa. xi. 1 in the Heb.?   *a* Isa. xl. 3.

---

18. *Rachel.* Her tomb, according to tradition, is near Bethlehem. See Gen. 35.19.

19. *When Herod was dead.* At the time of his death Herod was seventy years old. He had reigned from 37 B.C. to 4 A.D.

22. *Archelaus.* As this king was almost as cruel as his father Herod, Joseph could expect no mercy.

23. *Nazareth.* This village, less known than Bethlehem, is not mentioned in the Old Testament or in Josephus. Its modern name is En-Nasira. It is situated in a valley not far north of the Esdraelon plain.

CHAPTER 3

1. *In those days.* In the fifteenth year of the reign of the Emperor Tiberius. See Luke 3.1. *John the*

Baptist. Mark and Luke also call him by this name, because of the ordinance of baptism administered by him. Baptism was not a new custom among the Jews.

2. *Repent ye.* Meaning a complete change in the motives of life, a spiritual revolution. *Kingdom of heaven.* A phrase peculiar to Matthew. In ancient Jewish usage it was equivalent to 'kingdom of God,' and was bound up with the belief in the coming Messiah. In the New Testament it signifies the kingdom of Christ, hence the rule of holiness in the inner life.

3. *For this is he.* These are Matthew's words to identify John.

4. *Raiment.* A loose robe of camel's hair cloth. *Locusts and wild honey.* Both are used as food in the East at the present time.

7

wild honey. 5 Then went out unto him Je-ru'sa-lem, and all Ju-dæ'a, and all the region round about the Jordan; 6 and they were baptized of him in the river Jordan, confessing their sins. 7 But when he saw many of the Phar'i-sees and Sad'du-cees coming *b*to his baptism, he said unto them, Ye offspring of vipers, who warned you to flee from the wrath to come? 8 Bring forth therefore fruit worthy of *c*repentance: 9 and think not to say within yourselves, We have Abraham to our father: for I say unto you, that God is able of these stones to raise up children unto Abraham. 10 And even now the axe lieth at the root of the trees: every tree therefore that bringeth not forth good fruit is hewn down, and cast into the fire. 11 I in-

deed baptize you *d*in water unto repentance: but he that cometh after me is mightier than I, whose shoes I am not *e*worthy to bear: he shall baptize you *d*in the Holy Spirit and *in* fire: 12 whose fan is in his hand, and he will thoroughly cleanse his threshing-floor; and he will gather his wheat into the garner, but the chaff he will burn up with unquenchable fire.

13 Then cometh Je'sus from Gal'i-lee to the Jordan unto John, to be baptized of him. 14 But John would have hindered him, saying, I have need to be baptized of thee, and comest thou to me? 15 But Je'sus answering said unto him, **Suffer** *f it* now: **for this it becometh us to fulfil all righteousness.** Then he suffereth him. 16 And Je'sus, when he was baptized, went

---

b Or, *for baptism*   *c* Or, *your repentance*

d Or, *with*   *e* Gr. *sufficient.*   *f* Or, *me*

---

6. *Were baptized.* A sign of repentance and a public confession of their sins.

7. *Pharisees and Sadducees.* The Pharisees, or, according to the meaning of the name, the Separatists, were the religious, popular and patriotic party among the Jews. They believed in angels and spirits, the resurrection of the dead, and in eternal retribution in the future life. They hated Roman rule and were always ready to conspire against it. They cherished the hope of a Messiah who would deliver the Jews from the political sway of Rome. In religion they considered the traditions of the elders as of equal authority with the Mosaic law. The Sadducees, named after Zadok, one of the two chief priests in David's time, were religious and political opponents of the Pharisees. They denied the future life, the existence of angels and the authority of tradition. They accepted and obeyed literally the written law. They

were a small, but a wealthy and influential party, and practically controlled the appointment of the high priest, the presiding officer of the Sanhedrin. They were friendly to Rome. *Ye offspring of vipers.* The Pharisees and Sadducees came to see John in a spirit of insolent curiosity. They were fiercely rebuked and their insincerity exposed. *The wrath to come.* Referring to the expected judgment at the coming of the Messiah. John here implies punishment upon all the wicked, both Jews and Gentiles.

11. *Baptize you in the Holy Spirit.* John here refers to the spiritual life which acceptance of Christ would impart.

15. *Becometh us to fulfil all righteousness.* Jesus, by coming to be baptized, admitted John to be his true forerunner and ordained by God to that purpose. It was therefore a fulfilling of all righteousness to receive baptism at John's hands.

16. *He saw the Spirit of God de-*

up straightway from the water: and lo, the heavens were opened *g*unto him, and he saw the Spirit of God descending as a dove, and coming upon him; 17 and lo, a voice out of the heavens, saying, *h*This is my beloved Son, in whom I am well pleased.

4 Then was Je'sus led up of the Spirit into the wilderness to be tempted of the devil. 2 And when he had fasted forty days and forty nights, he afterward hungered. 3 And the tempter came and said unto him, If thou art the Son of God, command that these stones become *a*bread. 4 But he answered and said, It is written, *b*Man shall not live by bread alone, but by every word that proceedeth out of the mouth of God. 5 Then the devil taketh him into the holy city; and he set him on the *c*pinnacle of the temple, 6 and saith unto him, If thou art the

Son of God, cast thyself down: for it is written,

*d*He shall give his angels charge concerning thee:

and,

On their hands they shall bear thee up,

Lest haply thou dash thy foot against a stone.

7 Je'sus said unto him, **Again it is written, *e*Thou shalt not make trial of the Lord thy God.** 8 Again, the devil taketh him unto an exceeding high mountain, and showeth him all the kingdoms of the world, and the glory of them; 9 and he said unto him, All these things will I give thee, if thou wilt fall down and *f*worship me. 10 Then saith Je'sus unto him, **Get thee hence, Satan: for it is written, *g*Thou shalt worship the Lord thy God, and him only shalt thou serve.** 11 Then the devil leaveth him; and behold, angels came and ministered unto him.

g Some ancient authorities omit *unto him.* *h* Or, *This is my Son; my beloved in whom I am well pleased.* See ch. 12.18.

a Gr. *loaves.* *b* Dt. viii. 3. *c* Gr. *wing.* *d* Ps. xci. 11, 12. *e* Dt. vi. 16. *f* See marginal note on ch. 2.2. *g* Dt. vi. 13.

scending, etc. The vision and the voice, according to the text, were for Jesus only; but that the Baptist also saw the vision is said in John 1.32.

CHAPTER 4

1. *Led up of the Spirit.* Matthew, Mark and Luke affirm the agency of the Spirit of God in the temptation of Jesus. The Spirit ordained that Jesus through temptation should become the sympathizing friend and victorious Saviour of men. *Wilderness.* The actual place is unknown. *The devil.* Or 'slanderer.'

2. *Fasted forty days and forty nights.* Some modern instances of fasting have exceeded this in length of time.

3. *Become bread.* The first temptation was to the lust of the flesh, to work a miracle to relieve the hunger of the body.

5. *The holy city.* Jerusalem. The pinnacle mentioned in the next clause most likely overlooked the Temple courts and the deep valley of the Kidron below.

6. *Cast thyself down.* A suggestion to do a vulgarly spectacular act to astonish the multitude. These two temptations were direct challenges to Jesus to prove his divinity by wonder-working.

8. *An exceeding high mountain.* A figurative expression, as no physical elevation could be sufficient.

9. *All these things will I give thee.* The earthly lure, the false glory of the things of the world. This temptation had point from the apparently resistless force of the rulers of that day. The Roman emperors were as gods to the ignorant multitudes who feared and obeyed them.

12 Now when he heard that John was delivered up, he withdrew into Gal'i-lee; 13 and leaving Naz'a-reth, he came and dwelt in Ca-per'na-um, which is by the sea, in the borders of Zeb-u-lun and Naph'ta-li: 14 that it might be fulfilled which was spoken through I-sa'iah the prophet, saying,

15 *h* The land of Zeb'u-lun and the land of Naph'ta-li,

i Toward the sea, beyond the Jordan,

Gal'i-lee of the *k* Gen'tiles,

16 The people that sat in darkness

Saw a great light,

And to them that sat in the region and shadow of death,

To them did light spring up.

17 From that time began Je'sus to preach, and to say, **Repent**

ye; **for the kingdom of heaven is at hand.**

18 And walking by the sea of Gal'i-lee, he saw two brethren, Si'mon who is called Peter, and Andrew his brother, casting a net into the sea; for they were fishers. 19 And he saith unto them, **Come ye after me, and I will make you fishers of men.** 20 And they straightway left the nets, and followed him. 21 And going on from thence he saw two other brethren, *l* James the *son* of Zeb'e-dee, and John his brother, in the boat with Zeb'e-dee their father, mending their nets: and he called them. 22 And they straightway left the boat and their father, and followed him.

23 And *m* Je'sus went about in all Gal'i-lee, teaching in their

---

h Is. ix. 1, 2.   *i* Gr. *The way of the sea.*
k Gr. *nations:* and so elsewhere.

l Or, *Jacob*   *m* Some ancient authorities read *he.*

---

12. *Was delivered up.* See ch. 14.3–5. *Withdrew into Galilee.* Jesus left Judæa most probably on account of the hatred of the Pharisees and began his ministry in Galilee. It is not known how long his Judæan ministry lasted. A few authorities say about a month, but most of them eight months. His way led through Samaria. 'Galilee' means a circle or region, which originally contained the twenty cities given by Solomon to Hiram, King of Tyre. Afterwards the name was applied to larger districts, until it included the country southward to the Esdraelon plain.

13. *Capernaum.* On the northwest coast of the Sea of Galilee. Some writers think it was at the north end of the Sea and on the same site as the modern Tell Hûm. The remains of a synagogue have been found there.

16. *The people that sat in darkness.* Those who suffered most from the Assyrian invasions.

17. *The kingdom of heaven.* The

phrase as spoken by our Lord has its deepest spiritual meaning from his own life and teaching. Its use in the Old Testament and by John the Baptist is merged in its final and personal application by Jesus to the individual: 'The kingdom of heaven is within you.'

22. *And their father.* Mark adds 'with the hired servants' (1.20). The common notion that all the apostles were men of the humblest station in life is not well-founded. The sons of Zebedee certainly were not, nor is it likely that their two partners, Simon Peter and Andrew, were. Manual labor was not a social reproach among the Jews. Paul, a man of learning and position, was a maker of tents.

23. *All Galilee.* The country was about sixty-five miles long and twenty-five wide, and thickly populated, containing more than two hundred towns and villages. *Synagogues.* Jewish places of worship, also used as local courts of law and public schools. Jewish theology

synagogues, and preaching the [n]gospel of the kingdom, and healing all manner of disease and all manner of sickness among the people. 24 And the report of him went forth into all Syr′i-a: and they brought unto him all that were sick, holden with divers diseases and torments, [o]possessed with demons, and epileptic, and palsied; and he healed them. 25 And there followed him great multitudes from Gal′-i-lee and De-cap′o-lis and Je-ru′sa-lem and Ju-dæ′a and *from* beyond the Jordan.

5 And seeing the multitudes, he went up into the mountain: and when he had sat down, his disciples came unto him: 2

---

n Or, *good tidings*: and so elsewhere.
o Or, *demoniacs*

---

and he opened his mouth and taught them, saying,

3 Blessed are the poor in spirit: for theirs is the kingdom of heaven.

4 [a]Blessed are they that mourn: for they shall be comforted.

5 Blessed are the meek: for they shall inherit the earth.

6 Blessed are they that hunger and thirst after righteousness: for they shall be filled.

7 Blessed are the merciful: for they shall obtain mercy.

8 Blessed are the pure in heart: for they shall see God.

9 Blessed are the peacemakers: for they shall be called sons of God.

10 Blessed are they that have

---

a Some ancient authorities transpose ver. 4 and 5.

---

was taught in them. The members elected a governing body of elders, over whom was the ruler of the synagogue. The service, held on the Sabbath and on the second and fifth day of the week, consisted of reading of the Law and Prophets, a sermon by some member appointed by the ruler, and prayers.

25. *Decapolis.* A group of ten cities in a district south and east of the Sea of Galilee. See note on Mk. 5.20.

CHAPTER 5

1. *Into the mountain.* The Sermon on the Mount which begins in ver. 3 of this chapter is the same as that in briefer form in Luke 6.20–49. It is Christ's exposition of the kingdom of heaven. It was delivered after choosing the twelve apostles.

3. *Poor in spirit.* Poverty of spirit is the humility which leads to communion with and faith in God. This is the first of the nine beatitudes. The word 'beatitude,' signifying a special inward blessedness, comes from 'beati' (blessed), which begins the Vulgate, the revision of the Old Latin Bible by Jerome.

4. *Mourn.* Godly repentance for

sin, and sympathy with others in their sorrow.

5. *Meek.* Christian humility, a virtue unknown to Jewish, Roman and Greek practice of that time.

6. *Hunger and thirst after righteousness.* The longing for holiness of life, harmony of Christian character.

7. *They shall obtain mercy.* Love in thought, speech and act shall be repaid in kind.

8. *Pure in heart.* A contrast to the ceremonial purity of the Pharisees and scribes. *Shall see God.* Purity of heart and soul is as necessary for clear vision of God, for insight of the truth of God, as an eye free from defects is necessary for the perfect sight of a physical object.

9. *Peacemakers.* Who make peace by appealing to the righteousness and results of peace. There is a deeper meaning not to be overlooked. He cannot well make peace with or among others who has not first tried to make peace for and within himself. This is founded on the 'peace of God,' Phil. 4.7; the 'peace of Christ,' Col. 3.15.

10. *Persecuted for righteousness' sake.* Only the righteous share this

been persecuted for righteousness' sake: for theirs is the kingdom of heaven. 11 Blessed are ye when *men* shall reproach you, and persecute you, and say all manner of evil against you falsely, for my sake. 12 Rejoice, and be exceeding glad: for great is your reward in heaven: for so persecuted they the prophets that were before you.

13 Ye are the salt of the earth: but if the salt have lost its savor, wherewith shall it be salted? it is thenceforth good for nothing, but to be cast out and trodden under foot of men. 14 Ye are the light of the world. A city set on a hill cannot be hid. 15 Neither do *men* light a lamp, and put it under the bushel, but on the stand; and it shineth unto all that are in the house. 16 Even so let your light shine before men; that they may see your good works, and glorify your Father who is in heaven.

17 Think not that I came to destroy the law or the prophets: I came not to destroy, but to fulfil. 18 For verily I say unto you, Till heaven and earth pass away, one jot or one tittle shall in no wise pass away from the law, till all things be accomplished. 19 Whosoever therefore shall break one of these least commandments, and shall teach men so, shall be called least in the kingdom of heaven: but whosoever shall do and teach them, he shall be called great in the kingdom of heaven. 20 For I say unto you, that except your righteousness shall exceed *the righteousness* of the scribes and Phar'i-sees, ye shall in no wise enter into the kingdom of heaven.

21 Ye have heard that it was said to them of old time, *b*Thou shalt not kill; and whosoever

---

b Ex. xx. 13; Dt. v. 17.

---

blessing, which is a warning against misguided zeal.

13. *Ye are the salt of the earth.* The apostles and disciples. *Lost its savor.* Its distinctive and essential quality as a preservative. The disciples were to be the salt that preserves society from corruption.

14. *A city set on a hill.* A shining example to lead the people to Christ.

15. *A lamp.* In ancient times a vessel shaped somewhat like a modern pitcher, but much lower and shallower. It contained oil in which was immersed a flax wick whose lighted end rested upon the lip of the vessel. *The bushel.* Whose capacity was about equal to that of a peck of our measure.

17. *I came not to destroy, but to fulfil.* This was a solemn promise that nothing of value would be slighted or taken away, and a solemn denial that either the law or the prophets would be repudiated. But on the other hand our Lord assuredly implied that the law and the prophets were not perfect as they stood, and that their perfection, that is, their fulfilment, could be found only in him.

19. *Whosoever therefore shall break,* etc. A warning that any disobedience of the law, or even any disloyalty to it in thought, would lessen the spiritual power of the offender and reduce his rank to that of the least in the spiritual kingdom. Such was the strict loyalty of Christ to the law and the prophets that preceded him.

20. *Ye shall in no wise enter.* Although our Lord had just upheld the commandments of the law, he at once repudiated the false ideal of righteousness by which the scribes and Pharisees had sanctioned their imperfect practice of the law.

21. *The judgment.* The village and town courts of seven or more elders.

shall kill shall be in danger of the judgment: 22 but I say unto you, that every one who is angry with his brother[c] shall be in danger of the judgment; and whosoever shall say to his brother, [d]Ra′ca, shall be in danger of the council; and whosoever shall say, [e]Thou fool, shall be in danger [f]of the [g]hell of fire. 23 If therefore thou art offering thy gift at the altar, and there rememberest that thy brother hath aught against thee, 24 leave there thy gift before the altar, and go thy way, first be reconciled to thy brother, and then come and offer thy gift. 25 Agree with thine adversary quickly, while thou art with him in the way; lest haply the adversary deliver thee to the judge, and the judge [h]deliver thee to the officer, and thou be cast into prison. 26 Verily I say unto thee, Thou shalt by no means come out thence, till thou have paid the last farthing.

27 Ye have heard that it was said, [i]Thou shalt not commit adultery: 28 but I say unto you, that every one that looketh on a woman to lust after her hath committed adultery with her already in his heart. 29 And if thy right eye causeth thee to stumble, pluck it out, and cast it from thee: for it is profitable for thee that one of thy members should perish, and not thy whole body be cast into [k]hell. 30 And if thy right hand causeth thee to stumble, cut it off, and cast it from thee: for it is profitable for thee that one of thy members should perish, and not thy whole body go into [k]hell. 31 It was said also, [l]Whosoever shall put away his wife, let him give her a writing of divorce-

---

c Many ancient authorities insert without cause. d An expression of contempt. e Or, Moreh, a Hebrew expression of condemnation. f Gr. unto or into.. g Gr. Gehenna of fire. h Some ancient authorities omit deliver thee. i Ex. xx. 14; Dt. v. 18. k Gr. Gehenna. l Dt. xxiv. 1, 3.

---

22. But I say unto you. An assertion of his divine authority and power to perfect the commandment of the law by forbidding murder in its source, the feeling of anger. The council. The Sanhedrin. See note on ch. 2.4.

24. Leave there thy gift. Instantly put aside for the moment the lesser duty of offering thy gift, and attend first to the greater duty of making peace with thy brother.

25. Agree with thine adversary quickly. A command to seize the precious opportunity of coming to terms with any one with whom a dispute may arise, before an appeal to the law causes a contest, financial loss to one party or both, a deeper enmity between the contending parties, and the penalty imposed by the judge.

27. Ye have heard that it was said.

Jesus in this manner prepares his hearers for the contrast between the commandments of the Mosaic law and the new truth of his gospel.

28. Every one that looketh. This sin is to be traced and condemned in its origin, lack of chastity of mind and soul.

29. If thy right eye causeth thee to stumble. The meaning of ver. 29, 30 is that friends, pleasures, habits and associations that endanger inward purity and goodness must be cast off, even if they seem as necessary and useful as the eye and the hand.

31. A writing of divorcement. According to Jewish custom a man could divorce his wife by giving her a written document in the presence of witnesses, without specifying the cause. This practice became a cover for divorce on the slightest grounds, and became a flagrant abuse.

ment: 32 but I say unto you, that every one that putteth away his wife, saving for the cause of fornication, maketh her an adulteress: and whosoever shall marry her when she is put away committeth adultery.

33 Again, ye have heard that it was said to them of old time, *m*Thou shalt not forswear thyself, but shalt perform unto the Lord thine oaths: 34 but I say unto you, Swear not at all; neither by the heaven, for it is the throne of God; 35 nor by the earth, for it is the footstool of his feet; nor *n*by Je-ru'sa-lem, for it is the city of the great King. 36 Neither shalt thou swear by thy head, for thou canst not make one hair white or black. 37 *o*But let your speech be, Yea, yea; Nay, nay: and whatsoever is more than these is of *p*the evil *one*.

38 Ye have heard that it was said, An *q*eye for an eye, and a tooth for a tooth: 39 but I say unto you, Resist not *r*him that is evil: but whosoever smiteth thee on thy right cheek, turn to him the other also. 40 And if any man would go to law with thee, and take away thy coat, let him have thy cloak also. 41 And whosoever shall *s*compel thee to go one mile, go with him two. 42 Give to him that asketh thee, and from him that would borrow of thee turn not thou away.

43 Ye have heard that it was said, *t*Thou shalt love thy neighbor, and hate thine enemy: 44 but I say unto you, Love your enemies, and pray for them that persecute you; 45 that ye may be sons of your Father who is in heaven: for he maketh his sun to rise on the evil and the good, and sendeth rain on the just and the unjust. 46 For if ye love them that love you, what reward

m Lev. xix. 12; Num. xxx. 2; Dt. xxiii. 21. *n* Or, *toward*   *o* Some ancient authorities read *But your speech shall be.*   *p* Or, *evil*: as in ver. 39; vi. 13.   *q* Ex. xxi. 24; Lev. xxiv. 20; Dt. xix. 21.   *r* Or, *evil*   *s* Gr. *impress.*   *t* Lev. xix. 18.

32. *Maketh her.* Forces his wife into the temptation to commit this sin. Jesus does not here speak of the remarriage of an innocent party when the offending one has been divorced.

34. *Swear not at all.* This prohibition can only be taken as having in view a state of society in which a man's word is as good as his oath. Judicial oaths, in so far as they help to make men truthful in speech, tend to do away with swearing of every kind.

39. *Resist not.* Jesus here condemns the Mosaic law of retaliation in terms which plainly imply forgiveness of injuries instead of personal vengeance taken for them. The words are not to be taken literally, but their meaning is none the less clear.

40. *Cloak.* To give the cloak, a long outer garment, was a proof of greater self-denial and forgiveness than to give the coat, which was an undergarment.

42. *Turn not thou away.* Jesus does not mean us to lend without knowing what we do. It is the right attitude of mind and heart which he insists upon. He leaves it to us to apply his law of kindness to each case as it arises.

44. *Love your enemies.* This strikes at the root of all false distinctions as to those who are worthy of our affection. The word 'love' in this sentence has a meaning which implies that, however difficult it may be to love our enemies, grace will be given us to do so. *Pray for them that persecute you.* As he did on the cross (Luke 23.34).

14

have ye? do not even the *pub-licans the same? 47 And if ye salute your brethren only, what do ye more *than others?* do not even the Gen'tiles the same? 48 Ye therefore shall be perfect, as your heavenly Father is perfect.

6 Take heed that ye do not your righteousness before men, to be seen of them: else ye have no reward with your Father who is in heaven.

2 When therefore thou doest alms, sound not a trumpet before thee, as the hypocrites do in the synagogues and in the streets, that they may have glory of men. Verily I say unto you, They have received their reward. 3 But when thou doest alms, let not thy left hand know what thy right hand doeth: 4 that thine alms may be in secret: and thy Father who seeth in secret shall recompense thee.

5 And when ye pray, ye shall not be as the hypocrites: for they love to stand and pray in the synagogues and in the corners of the streets, that they may be seen of men. Verily I say unto you, They have received their reward. 6 But thou, when thou prayest, enter into thine inner chamber, and having shut thy door, pray to thy Father who is in secret, and thy Father who seeth in secret shall recompense thee. 7 And in praying use not vain repetitions, as the Gen'tiles do: for thy think that they shall be heard for their much speaking. 8 Be not therefore like unto them: for *your Father knoweth what things ye have need of, before ye ask him. 9 After this manner therefore pray ye: Our Father who art in heaven, Hallowed be thy name. 10 Thy kingdom come. Thy will be done, as in heaven, so on

---

u That is, *collectors or renters of Roman taxes.*

a Some ancient authorities read *God your Father.*

---

48. *As your heavenly Father.* That is, ye shall be perfect in love as is your heavenly Father, loving your enemies as well as your neighbors and friends, in this respect being like Him who sends rain upon the just and the unjust.

CHAPTER 6

1. *To be seen of them.* Jesus here implies the worthlessness of human praise, apart from the righteousness approved by God.

2. *They have received their reward.* The acts done to earn the applause of men have no reward beyond that.

5. *Hypocrites.* From a Greek word meaning the acting of a part on the stage; hence pretenders, deceivers.

6. *Pray to thy Father who is in secret.* Our Lord here contrasts the praying hypocrite with the sincere

believer. He does not say that secret prayer as such is better than public prayer; but commands his hearers to shun the habits of those whose prayers in public are no better than mockery. It is not a question of place. Sincerity is the test, whether prayer is public or private.

7. *Vain repetitions.* 'Vain' because the mere sound of pious words is thought to have some merit.

9. *Our Father.* The fatherhood of God and the brotherhood of man are taught in these two words. *Hallowed be thy name.* Reverence for the name of God must precede any petition to Him.

10. *Thy kingdom come.* The Jews were always looking for a kingdom. This expectant habit of the Jewish mind is here recognized, but what is meant is the spiritual kingdom in which righteousness and truth shall prevail. *Thy will be done.* A prayer

earth. 11 Give us this day [b]our daily bread. 12 And forgive us our debts, as we also have forgiven our debtors. 13 And bring us not into temptation, but deliver us from [c]the evil one[d]. 14 For if ye forgive men their trespasses, your heavenly Father will also forgive you. 15 But if ye forgive not men their trespasses, neither will your Father forgive your trespasses.

16 Moreover when ye fast, be not, as the hypocrites, of a sad countenance: for they disfigure their faces, that they may be seen of men to fast. Verily I say unto you, They have received their reward. 17 But thou, when thou fastest, anoint thy head, and wash thy face; 18 that thou be not seen of men to fast, but of thy Father who is in secret: and thy Father, who seeth in secret, shall recompense thee.

19 Lay not up for yourselves treasures upon the earth, where moth and rust consume, and where thieves [e]break through and steal: 20 but lay up for yourselves treasures in heaven, where neither moth nor rust doth consume, and where thieves do not [e]break through nor steal: 21 for where thy treasure is, there will thy heart be also. 22 The lamp of the body is the eye: if therefore thine eye be single, thy whole body shall be full of light. 23 But if thine eye be evil, thy whole body shall be full of darkness. If therefore the light that is in thee be darkness, how great is the darkness! 24 No man can serve two masters: for either he will hate the one, and love the other; or else he will hold to one, and despise the other. Ye cannot serve God and mammon. 25 Therefore I say unto you Be not anxious for your life,

---

b Gr. our bread for the coming day. Or, our needful bread   c Or, evil   d Many authorities, some ancient, but with variations, add *For thine is the kingdom, and the power, and the glory, for ever. Amen.* e Gr. *dig through.*

---

that faith in God may be realized in entire submission to Him.

11. *Daily bread.* But the daily needs of the body may not be met without foresight and work by him who prays. The truth taught is the need of daily conscious dependence upon God.

12. *As we also have forgiven.* Our debts, or sins, will not be forgiven us by God unless we are forgiving. All through this prayer it is taken for granted that we can not ask for ourselves what we deny to others.

13. *Bring us not into temptation.* When God permits temptation, He provides a way of escape.

16. *As the hypocrites, of a sad countenance.* Here the warning to the insincere is repeated. It is not the manner of fasting which counts, but the motive which prompts it.

19. *Moth and rust.* In the East a

large part of riches consisted in costly garments especially liable to destruction by moths.

21. *There will thy heart be also.* One whose treasures are his earthly hopes and desires will have a heart for nothing else. One whose mind is centered on holiness of life, will be moulded in the image of the Master.

24. *No man can serve two masters.* This and the two preceding verses illustrate the need of singleness, that is, whole-hearted devotion, in the service of God. As a diseased eye admits no light or at least an imperfect light to the body, so a diseased conscience, ' the light that is in thee,' darkens or blinds the soul. No man can serve both God and the world. *Mammon.* Riches.

25. *Be not anxious.* A reproof of believers who worry.

what ye shall eat, or what ye shall drink; nor yet for your body, what ye shall put on. Is not the life more than the food, and the body than the raiment? 26 Behold the birds of the heaven, that they sow not, neither do they reap, nor gather into barns; and your heavenly Father feedeth them. Are not ye of much more value than they? 27 And which of you by being anxious can add one cubit unto *the measure of his life? 28 And why are ye anxious concerning raiment? Consider the lilies of the field, how they grow; they toil not, neither do they spin: 29 yet I say unto you, that even Sol'o-mon in all his glory was not arrayed like one of these 30 But if God doth so clothe the grass of the field, which to-day is, and to-morrow is cast into the oven, *shall he* not much more *clothe* you, O ye of little faith? 31 Be not therefore anxious, saying, What shall we eat? or, What shall we drink? or, Wherewithal shall we be clothed? 32 For after all these things do the Gen'tiles seek; for your heavenly Father knoweth that ye have need of all these things. 33 But seek ye first his kingdom, and his righteousness; and all these things shall be added unto you. 34 Be not therefore anxious for the morrow: for the morrow will be anxious for itself. Sufficient unto the day is the evil thereof.

7 Judge not, that ye be not judged. 2 For with what judgment ye judge, ye shall be judged: and with what measure ye mete, it shall be measured unto you. 3 And why beholdest thou the mote that is in thy brother's eye, but considerest not the beam that is in thine own eye? 4 Or how wilt thou say to thy brother, Let me cast out the mote out of thine eye; and lo, the beam is in thine own eye? 5 Thou hypocrite, cast out

---

f Or, *his stature*

27. *One cubit.* A foot and a half. Here it is used figuratively and may be taken to mean any arbitrary amount or measure.

28. *Consider the lilies.* Think of their beauty and how perfectly they have been clothed, although not troubled or anxious about their raiment.

30. *Cast into the oven.* In the East dried grass is often burned to heat the ovens of baked clay.

32. *Your heavenly Father knoweth.* A fact sufficient to remove from believers all anxiety about bodily needs.

33. *Seek ye first his kingdom, and his righteousness.* Having sought and found this kingdom, which is within us, all lesser blessings follow.

34. *Be not therefore anxious.* The Master's disciples are to be cheerful and confident. Christianity has too often been thought of as a religion of sadness. Among the most precious words of Jesus are these: 'Be of good cheer; I have overcome the world.' (Jn. 16:33.)

CHAPTER 7

1. *Judge not,* etc. Those who would escape criticism must not be fault-finders. *Mete.* That is, measure.

3. *Mote.* Literally, a small particle of dust, cloth, or a splinter or small twig. *Beam.* A stick of large timber. The mote and the beam were often figuratively used in Jewish controversy. The mote stood for a small fault, the beam for a serious sin. Jesus here means by it want of charity in thought and speech.

17

first the beam out of thine own eye; and then shalt thou see clearly to cast out the mote out of thy brother's eye.

6 Give not that which is holy unto the dogs, neither cast your pearls before the swine, lest haply they trample them under their feet, and turn and rend you.

7 Ask, and it shall be given you; seek, and ye shall find; knock, and it shall be opened unto you: 8 for every one that asketh receiveth; and he that seeketh findeth; and to him that knocketh it shall be opened. 9 Or what man is there of you, who, if his son shall ask him for a loaf, will give him a stone; 10 or if he shall ask for a fish, will give him a serpent? 11 If ye then,

being evil, know how to give good gifts unto your children, how much more shall your Father who is in heaven give good things to them that ask him? 12 All things therefore whatsoever ye would that men should do unto you, even so do ye also unto them: for this is the law and the prophets.

13 Enter ye in by the narrow gate: for wide *a*is the gate, and broad is the way, that leadeth to destruction, and many are they that enter in thereby. 14 *b*For narrow is the gate, and straitened the way, that leadeth unto life, and few are they that find it.

15 Beware of false prophets, who come to you in sheep's clothing, but inwardly are raven-

---

a Some ancient authorities omit *is the gate.*

b Many ancient authorities read *How narrow is the gate, &c.*

6. *That which is holy.* Literally, the meat offerings in the Jewish sacrifices. Here are meant the truths of religion. *Dogs . . . swine.* While reproving fault-finding, our Lord commands that we should not err in the opposite direction. We are not to praise men indiscriminately, or without discretion to offer them the pearls of religious truth, for among those thus praised and favored will be the brutal, the blasphemous and the cruel.

7. *Ask, seek, knock.* A series of increasingly patient and aggressive attempts to realize the relation of the soul to God, to gain his favor and direction. We are never to despair, for the victory is promised to those who persevere.

12. *All things therefore.* The Golden Rule is the one great light needed to be thrown upon the dark problems of society. Other great religious teachers announce it in negative form or limit its application. Jesus alone makes it positive, constructive and universal. He takes it beyond the narrow range of

relatives, friends, neighbors, or of the tribe and nation. He makes it the foundation of the personal life in society. 'Do not do unto others that which you would not have them do unto you,' is only good advice, a maxim of precaution, a preparation for doing good. Jesus goes far beyond this. He speaks to individual men and women and at once makes them active contributors to the justice, kindness and happiness of the world.

13. *Narrow gate.* Eastern cities were usually surrounded by walls. The gates in the walls were generally narrow and difficult to pass through. Hence the saying about the broad and the narrow way, which was in common use among the Jews. Few are willing to practice self-denial, to accept the rule of the Spirit which leads to life, while the way of the world is broad and easy, and agrees with the natural inclinations. It leads to destruction.

15. *Beware of false prophets.* Those who knew the way of life, but were not sincere in their motives and in-

The Two Foundations — MATTHEW 7.16—7.29

ing wolves. 16 By their fruits ye shall know them. Do *men* gather grapes of thorns, or figs of thistles? 17 Even so every good tree bringeth forth good fruit; but the corrupt tree bringeth forth evil fruit. 18 A good tree cannot bring forth evil fruit, neither can a corrupt tree bring forth good fruit. 19 Every tree that bringeth not forth good fruit is hewn down, and cast into the fire. 20 Therefore by their fruits ye shall know them. 21 Not every one that saith unto me, Lord, Lord, shall enter into the kingdom of heaven; but he that doeth the will of my Father who is in heaven. 22 Many will say to me in that day, Lord, Lord, did we not prophesy by thy name, and by thy name cast out demons, and by thy name do many *mighty works?* 23 And then will I profess unto them, I never knew you: depart from me, ye that work iniquity.

24 Every one therefore that heareth these words of mine, and doeth them, shall be likened unto a wise man, who built his house upon the rock: 25 and the rain descended, and the floods came, and the winds blew, and beat upon that house; and it fell not: for it was founded upon the rock. 26 And every one that heareth these words of mine, and doeth them not, shall be likened unto a foolish man, who built his house upon the sand: 27 and the rain descended, and the floods came, and the winds blew, and smote upon that house; and it fell: and great was the fall thereof.

28 And it came to pass, when Je′sus had finished these words, the multitudes were astonished at his teaching: 29 for he taught them as *one* having authority, and not as their scribes.

c Gr. *powers.*

tentions. They were professed believers in Christ (ver. 22).

16. *Fruits.* Their acts; their moral conduct (ch. 12.33; Lk. 6. 43–45).

19. *Is hewn down,* etc. This is still a custom in the East.

21. *Lord.* Taken in connection with the clause following, the title which Jesus here applies to himself can only mean that he is Lord of the universe, the ruler of the kingdom of heaven of which he speaks. *He that doeth.* Again in this discourse he brings all professions to the test of obedience.

22. *That day.* Jesus here speaks of a future when his life and teaching shall be in control, when it will be worth while, in fact a protection, to profess belief in him.

23. *I never knew you.* This implies the omniscience of Christ, one of its manifestations being the power to know the true spiritual condition of all who come before him. *Iniquity.* Literally, what is contrary to law.

24. *A wise man, who built his house upon the rock.* The hearing and the doing of Christ's words, taken together, are the highest wisdom, the only sure foundation. The first step in the doing is the first stone in that foundation, built upon the rock, which is Christ himself.

26. *And doeth them not.* The emphasis of Jesus upon the uselessness of hearing without doing suggests the great warning of this parable. Indifference and inaction after hearing are the chief dangers.

29. *Not as their scribes.* The great contrast was this: the scribes were accurate copyists and narrow expounders of the Mosaic law and were constantly appealing to its authority; Jesus spoke as the source of authority, with power to revise and amend the law.

19

8 And when he was come down from the mountain, great multitudes followed him. 2 And behold, there came to him a leper and ^aworshipped him, saying, Lord, if thou wilt, thou canst make me clean. 3 And he stretched forth his hand, and touched him, saying, **I will; be thou made clean.** And straightway his leprosy was cleansed. 4 And Je'sus saith unto him, ^bSee thou tell no man; but go, show thyself to the priest, and offer the gift that Mo'ses commanded, for a testimony unto them.

5 And when he was entered into Ca-per'na-um, there came unto him a centurion, beseeching him, 6 and saying, Lord, my ^cservant lieth in the house sick of the palsy, grievously tormented. 7 And he saith unto him, **I will come and heal him.** 8 And the centurion answered and said, Lord, I am not ^dworthy that thou shouldest come under my roof; but only say ^ethe word, and my ^cservant shall be healed. 9 For I also am a man ^funder authority, having under myself soldiers: and I say to this one, Go, and he goeth; and to another, Come, and he cometh; and to my ^gservant, Do this, and he doeth it. 10 And when Je'sus heard it, he marvelled, and said to them that followed, **Verily I say unto you,** ^h**I have not found so great faith, no, not in Is'ra-el. 11 And I say unto you, that many shall come from the east and the west, and shall** ⁱ**sit down with Abraham, and I'saac, and Jacob, in the kingdom of heaven: 12 but the sons of the kingdom shall be cast forth into the outer darkness: there shall be the weeping and the gnashing of teeth.** 13 And Je'sus said unto the centurion, **Go thy way; as thou hast believed,** *so* **be it done unto thee.** And the ^cservant was healed in that hour.

14 And when Je'sus was come

---

^a See marginal note on ch. 2.2.   ^b Lev. xiii. 49; xiv. 2 ff.   ^c Or, *boy*   ^d Gr. *sufficient.*   ^e Gr. *with a word.*   ^f Some ancient authorities insert *set*: as in Lk. 7.8.   ^g Gr. *bondservant.*   ^h Many ancient authorities read *With no man in Israel have I found so great faith.*   ⁱ Gr. *recline.*

CHAPTER 8

2. *Lord, if thou wilt, thou canst make me clean.* To cleanse the leper meant not only to cure him but to free him from the disability of defilement under the Levitical law.

3. *I will; be thou made clean.* The same authority and power that marked his words were in his healing.

4. *Offer the gift that Moses commanded* (Lev. 14.3, 4). As a proof of the cure which the priest, after due precaution to test its genuineness, would be bound to accept. It was to be done quietly so as to avoid popular clamor.

5. *A centurion.* A Roman army officer in command of from fifty to a hundred men.

6. *My servant.* A favorite slave. This miracle is the first recorded experience of Jesus with slavery.

8. *Only say the word.* Probably his complete faith was caused by having witnessed or heard of some other miracle by Jesus.

11. *Many shall come from the east and the west.* A declaration by Jesus that Gentiles of all kinds would be admitted, by reason of their faith, into the joys of the true Messianic kingdom. It was a rebuke to the exclusiveness of the Jews.

12. *Sons of the kingdom.* The Jews. *Outer darkness.* Bitter disappointment and sorrow.

into Peter's house, he saw his wife's mother lying sick of a fever. 15 And he touched her hand, and the fever left her; and she arose, and ministered unto him. 16 And when even was come, they brought unto him many [k]possessed with demons: and he cast out the spirits with a word, and healed all that were sick: 17 that it might be fulfilled which was spoken through I-sa'iah the prophet, saying, [l]Himself took our infirmities, and bare our diseases.

18 Now when Je'sus saw great multitudes about him, he gave commandment to depart unto the other side. 19 And there came [m]a scribe, and said unto him, Teacher, I will follow thee whithersoever thou goest. 20 And Je'sus saith unto him, The foxes have holes, and the birds of the heaven *have* [n]nests; but the Son of man hath not where to lay his head. 21 And another of the disciples said unto him, Lord, suffer me first to go and bury my father. 22 But Je'sus saith unto him, **Follow me; and leave the dead to bury their own dead.**

23 And when he was entered into a boat, his disciples followed him. 24 And behold, there arose a great tempest in the sea, insomuch that the boat was covered with the waves: but he was asleep. 25 And they came to him, and awoke him, saying, Save, Lord; we perish. 26 And he saith unto them, **Why are ye fearful, O ye of little faith?** Then he arose, and rebuked the winds and the sea; and there was a great calm. 27 And the men marvelled, saying, What manner of man is this, that even the winds and the sea obey him?

28 And when he was come to the other side into the country of the Gad-a-renes', there met him two [k]possessed with demons,

---

[k] Or, *demoniacs* [l] Is. liii. 4. [m] Gr. *one scribe.* [n] Gr. *lodging-places.*

15. *The fever left her.* She was healed immediately, according to Mark. *Ministered.* Waited upon him.

16. *With a word.* Contrast with the healing of the leper and Peter's wife's mother by touch.

19. *Teacher, I will follow thee.* This offer of the scribe to follow Jesus whithersoever he went was quickly put to the test by the reply, which denied all prosperity and worldly honors to the applicant.

20. *The Son of man.* The expression most frequently used by Jesus to describe himself. The reason for so doing was probably to divert attention from any immediate claim to be the Messiah, as that would disturb the results of his teaching. 'Son of man' is best taken to mean the representative man, the man in whom all that is greatest and noblest in human nature is summed up and embodied.

22. *Leave the dead to bury their own dead.* Among different interpretations of this saying one meaning is clear: Leave lesser duties without delay to follow Christ.

25. *Save, Lord.* The miracle of calming the tempest was a new experience for the disciples. The words 'or we perish' seem to show that there was some doubt as to the Master's power. They had seen him heal disease and cast out evil spirits, but now he was called upon to command the forces of physical nature.

28. *The Gadarenes.* The inhabitants of the city, or of the surrounding district, of Gadara, the capital of Peræa. It has been identified as the modern Umm Keis, about five and a half English miles southeast of the southern extremity of the Sea

coming forth out of the tombs, exceeding fierce, so that no man could pass by that way. 29 And behold, they cried out, saying, What have we to do with thee, thou Son of God? art thou come hither to torment us before the time? 30 Now there was afar off from them a herd of many swine feeding. 31 And the demons besought him, saying, If thou cast us out, send us away into the herd of swine. 32 And he said unto them, Go. And they came out, and went into the swine: and behold, the whole herd rushed down the steep into the sea, and perished in the waters. 33 And they that fed them fled, and went away into the city, and told everything, and what was befallen to them that were *possessed with demons. 34 And behold, all the city came out to meet Je'sus: and when they saw him, they besought *him* that he would depart from their borders.

9 And he entered into a boat, and crossed over, and came into his own city. 2 And behold, they brought to him a man sick of the palsy, lying on a bed: and Je'sus seeing their faith said unto the sick of the palsy, *a*Son, be of good cheer; **thy sins are forgiven.** 3 And behold, certain of the scribes said within themselves, This man blasphemeth. 4 And Je'sus *b*knowing their thoughts said, **Wherefore think ye evil in your hearts? 5 For which is easier, to say, Thy sins are forgiven; or to say, Arise, and walk? 6 But that ye may know that the Son of man hath authority on earth to forgive sins** (then saith he to the sick of the palsy), **Arise, and take up thy bed, and go unto thy house.** 7 And he arose, and departed to his house. 8 But when the multitudes saw it, they were afraid, and glorified God, who had given such authority unto men.

9 And as Je'sus passed by from thence, he saw a man, called Mat'thew, sitting at the place of toll: and he saith unto him, **Follow me.** And he arose, and followed him.

---

o Or, demoniacs *a Gr. Child.* | *b Many ancient authorities read seeing.*

of Galilee. *Out of the tombs.* Modern travelers have noticed maniacs in the cemeteries of Palestine.

29. *Thou Son of God.* A similar confession by demons is found in Mk. 3.11 and Lk. 4.41. *To torment us before the time.* They knew when their hour of punishment would return.

CHAPTER 9

2. *Thy sins are forgiven.* Those who looked on evidently expected that Jesus would speak first of this paralytic's body, but instead he forgives the sick man's sins.

3. *This man blasphemeth.* The

listening scribes eagerly caught at the utterance and charged Jesus with blasphemy, thereby raising an issue of the utmost possible moment, namely, Had he power to forgive sins?

5. *Which is easier,* etc. Jesus accepts the challenge and performs a physical miracle in order to prove his power to forgive. He knew that the scribes would regard the healing of the sick man as the greater wonder of the two. They were caught in their own trap and put to shame.

9. *Matthew.* Otherwise known as Levi (Lk. 5.27). Matthew was a publican or tax collector.

22

10 And it came to pass, as he ᶜsat at meat in the house, behold, many ᵈpublicans and sinners came and sat down with Je'sus and his disciples. 11 And when the Phar'i-sees saw it, they said unto his disciples, Why eateth your Teacher with the ᵈpublicans and sinners? 12 But when he heard it, he said, They that are ᵉwhole have no need of a physician, but they that are sick. 13 But go ye and learn what *this* meaneth, ᶠI desire mercy, and not sacrifice: for I came not to call the righteous, but sinners.

14 Then come to him the disciples of John, saying, Why do we and the Phar'i-sees fast ᵍoft, but thy disciples fast not? 15 And Je'sus said unto them, Can the ʰsons of the bridechamber mourn, as long as the bridegroom is with them? but the days will come, when the bridegroom shall be taken away from them, and then will they fast. 16 And no man putteth a piece of undressed cloth upon an old garment; for that which should fill it up taketh from the garment, and a worse rent is made. 17 Neither do *men* put new wine into old ᶦwine-skins: else the skins burst, and the wine is spilled, and the skins perish: but they put new wine into fresh wine-skins, and both are preserved.

18 While he spake these things unto them, behold, there came ᵏa ruler, and ᶥworshipped him, saying, My daughter is even now dead: but come and lay thy hand upon her, and she shall live. 19 And Je'sus arose, and followed him, and *so did* his

---

c Gr. *reclined*: and so always.   d See marginal note on ch. 5.46.   e Gr. *strong*. f Hos. vi. 6.   g Some ancient authorities omit *oft*.   h That is, *companions of the* bridegroom.   i That is, *skins used as bottles*. k Gr. *one ruler*.   Compare Mk. 5.22. l See marginal note on ch. 2.2.

---

10. *In the house.* In Matthew's house.

12. *They that are whole.* A rebuke to the self-sufficient Pharisees, followed by a word of sympathy for the publicans and sinners.

13. *But go ye and learn,* etc. A difficult command for the Pharisees to obey. For them to prefer mercy to sacrifice, or in other words, love to formal observances, would have been to uproot their whole doctrine and manner of life.

14. *The disciples of John.* John the Baptist was at this time in prison; hence without their leader his disciples, who had already shown jealousy because of the success of Jesus, were the more easily beguiled to take sides with the Pharisees against our Lord on the question of fasting. The Pharisees were plotting to make it appear that Jesus was not living up to the character and mission which John had ascribed to him.

15. *The bridegroom.* Jesus is the bridegroom, figuratively speaking; the Christian Church, the bride; and his disciples the 'sons of the bridechamber.' These latter, according to Jewish custom, were the bridegroom's friends who went to lead the bride forth from her father's house. Mourning and fasting were out of place so long as Christ was with his disciples. *Then will they fast.* After Christ's death on the cross.

16. *Undressed cloth.* Undressed cloth, like new wine and fresh wine-skins, represents the freedom which the new doctrine of Jesus gave, and the old garment and old wine-skins are the narrow decaying beliefs and prejudices of Judaism which could not be reconciled with the life of the gospel.

18. *Ruler.* Jaïrus, chief ruler of the synagogue (Mk. 5.22).

disciples. 20 And behold, a woman, who had an issue of blood twelve years, came behind him, and touched the border of his garment: 21 for she said within herself, If I do but touch his garment, I shall be *made* whole. 22 But Je'sus turning and seeing her said, **Daughter, be of good cheer; thy faith hath** *made* **thee whole.** And the woman was *made* whole from that hour. 23 And when Je'sus came into the ruler's house, and saw the flute-players, and the crowd making a tumult, 24 he said, **Give place: for the damsel is not dead, but sleepeth.** And they laughed him to scorn. 25 But when the crowd was put forth, he entered in, and took her by the hand; and the damsel arose. 26 And *the* fame hereof went forth into all that land.

27 And as Je'sus passed by from thence, two blind men followed him, crying out, and saying, Have mercy on us, thou son of David. 28 And when he was come into the house, the blind men came to him: and Je'sus saith unto them, **Believe ye that I am able to do this?** They say unto him, Yea, Lord. 29 Then touched he their eyes, saying, **According to your faith be it done unto you.** 30 And their eyes were opened. And Je'sus *strictly* charged them, saying, **See that no man know it.** But they went forth, and spread abroad his fame in all that land.

32 And as they went forth, behold, there was brought to him a dumb man possessed with a demon. 33 And when the demon was cast out, the dumb man spake: and the multitudes marvelled, saying, It was never so seen in Is'ra-el. 34 But the Phar'i-sees said, *By the prince of the demons casteth he out demons.

35 And Je'sus went about all the cities and the villages, teaching in their synagogues, and preaching the 'gospel of the kingdom, and healing all manner

---

m Or, *saved*   *n* Or, *saved thee*   *o* Gr. *this fame.*   *p* Or, *sternly*   *q* Or, *In*

r See marginal note on ch. 4.23.

---

20. *A woman, who,* etc. This miracle was performed while Jesus was on the way to perform another.

23. *The flute-players.* Hired mourners.

24. *They laughed him to scorn.* A proof that they were insolently sure the damsel was dead.

27. *Two blind men.* Exposure to the burning sun, the dust and sand by day and to dews by night make blindness very common in the East. Several miracles of this kind are mentioned in the Gospels. *Thou Son of David.* Jesus is here addressed for the first time in the evangelists by the title then associated with the coming Messiah.

28. *Believe ye.* Jesus usually looked for faith in the individual before he cured him. He loved especially to heal those who believed. See ch. 13.58.

29. *According to your faith.* Not only as illustrated in this miracle, but generally in all the work of life, the degree of faith measures the amount of success.

32. *A dumb man.* The word 'dumb' here may mean also a deaf mute.

34. *But the Pharisees said,* etc. The Pharisees, at first scornful and patronizing, then curious, became afterward jealous and fearful, and in this verse they were plainly malicious. The reply to their accusation that Jesus by the prince of demons cast out demons is given in ch. 12.25–30.

of disease and all manner of sickness. 36 But when he saw the multitudes, he was moved with compassion for them, because they were distressed and scattered, as sheep not having a shepherd. 37 Then saith he unto his disciples, The harvest indeed is plenteous, but the laborers are few. 38 Pray ye therefore the Lord of the harvest, that he send forth laborers into his harvest.

10 And he called unto him his twelve disciples, and gave them authority over unclean spirits, to cast them out, and to heal all manner of disease and all manner of sickness.

2 Now the names of the twelve apostles are these: The first, Si'mon, who is called Peter, and Andrew his brother; [a]James the *son* of Zeb'e-dee, and John his brother; 3 Philip, and Bar-thol'o-mew; Thomas, and Mat'-thew the [b]publican; [a]James the *son* of Al-phæ'us, and Thad-

dæ'us; 4 Si'mon the [c]Ca-na-næ'an, and Ju'das Is-car'i-ot, who also [d]betrayed him.

5 These twelve Je'sus sent forth, and charged them, saying, Go not into *any* way of the Gen'tiles, and enter not into any city of the Sa-mar'i-tans: 6 but go rather to the lost sheep of the house of Is'ra-el. 7 And as ye go, preach, saying, The kingdom of heaven is at hand. 8 Heal the sick, raise the dead, cleanse the lepers, cast out demons: freely ye received, freely give. 9 Get you no gold, nor silver, nor brass in your [e]purses; 10 no wallet for *your* journey, neither two coats, nor shoes, nor staff: for the laborer is worthy of his food. 11 And into whatsoever city or village ye shall enter, search out who in it is worthy; and there abide till ye go forth. 12 And as ye enter into the house, salute it. 13 And if the house be worthy, let your peace come upon it: but if it be not worthy,

---

a Or, *Jacob* *b* See marginal note on ch. 5.46. *c* Or, *Zealot* See Lk. 6. 15; Acts 1.13. *d* Or, *delivered him up* *e* Gr. *girdles.*

---

36. As sheep not having a shepherd. The Pharisees and scribes and doctors of the law had not been true shepherds of the people. Their flocks were distressed and scattered.

37. The laborers are few. A fact which called for missionary work by the twelve disciples under the direction of the Master.

CHAPTER 10

1. Gave them authority, etc. The disciples were not only to teach, but to exercise in their appointed measure the miraculous power of the Master.

2. Apostles. Messengers, envoys, those sent forth.

5. These twelve. In all four evangelists as well as in Acts there

is a list of the twelve apostles, but in no two is the order in which they are mentioned exactly the same.

6. Go rather to the lost sheep of the house of Israel. The Gentiles and the cities of the Samaritans were temporarily excluded from the mission work of the twelve; preaching and healing among them were postponed.

7. The kingdom of heaven is at hand. The saying implied an appeal and warning to prepare for it.

8. Freely ye received, freely give. They were to be gladly willing and self-sacrificing in their service.

11. Who in it is worthy. Whosoever received the disciples kindly and entertained them.

12. Salute it. The usual form was 'peace be to this house.'

let your peace return to you. 14 And whosoever shall not receive you, nor hear your words, as ye go forth out of that house or that city, shake off the dust of your feet. 15 Verily I say unto you, It shall be more tolerable for the land of Sod'om and Go-mor'rah in the day of judgment, than for that city.

16 Behold, I send you forth as sheep in the midst of wolves: be ye therefore wise as serpents, and *f*harmless as doves. 17 But beware of men: for they will deliver you up to councils, and in their synagogues they will scourge you; 18 yea and before governors and kings shall ye be brought for my sake, for a testimony to them and to the Gen'-tiles. 19 But when they deliver you up, be not anxious how or what ye shall speak: for it shall be given you in that hour what ye shall speak. 20 For it is not ye that speak, but the Spirit of your Father that speaketh in you. 21 And brother shall deliver up brother to death, and the father his child: and children

shall rise up against parents, and *g*cause them to be put to death. 22 And ye shall be hated of all men for my name's sake: but he that endureth to the end, the same shall be saved. 23 But when they persecute you in this city, flee into the next: for verily I say unto you, Ye shall not have gone through the cities of Is'ra-el, till the Son of man be come.

24 A disciple is not above his teacher, nor a *h*servant above his lord. 25 It is enough for the disciple that he be as his teacher, and the *h*servant as his lord. If they have called the master of the house *i*Be-el'ze-bub, how much more them of his household! 26 Fear them not therefore: for there is nothing covered, that shall not be revealed; and hid, that shall not be known. 27 What I tell you in the darkness, speak ye in the light; and what ye hear in the ear, proclaim upon the house-tops. 28 And be not afraid of them that kill the body, but are not able to kill the soul: but rather fear

---

f Or, *simple*   *g* Or, *put them to death*   *h* Gr. *bondservant.*   *i* Gr. *Beelzebul.*

---

14. *Shake off the dust of your feet.* It was a common saying among the Jews that the dust of heathen lands defiled the feet. In this case rejection of the doctrine of Jesus by the Jews was to receive the same sign of condemnation as if they were heathens.

15. *Shall be more tolerable.* Sins of weakness and ignorance are more worthy of pardon than deliberate, wilful sins against a clear conscience.

16. *Wise as serpents*, etc. Tactful, quiet, without offence to those among whom they preached and worked.

17. *Beware of men.* They were warned to watch the moods and

schemes of those who would hinder and destroy their usefulness.

18. *Governors and kings.* As Paul was brought before Festus and Agrippa (Acts 25.6, 23).

22. *Hated of all men for my name's sake.* The natural hatred of the world and the flesh for the rule of the Spirit, which was demanded in the name of Jesus.

25. *As his teacher.* The disciple should be expected to endure all the persecution that befalls his teacher.

27. *In the darkness.* Jesus began in an obscure corner of the earth, despised Galilee; the work was carried by his disciples to the great cities of the world.

26

him who is able to destroy both soul and body in *k*hell. 29 Are not two sparrows sold for a penny? and not one of them shall fall on the ground without your Father: 30 but the very hairs of your head are all numbered. 31 Fear not therefore: ye are of more value than many sparrows. 32 Every one therefore who shall confess *l* me before men, *m* him will I also confess before my Father who is in heaven. 33 But whosoever shall deny me before men, him will I also deny before my Father who is in heaven.

34 Think not that I came to *n* send peace on the earth: I came not to *n* send peace, but a sword. 35 For I came to set a man at variance against his father, and the daughter against her mother, and the daughter in law against her mother in law: 36 and a man's foes *shall be* they of his own household. 37 He that loveth father or mother more than me is not worthy of me; and he that loveth son or daughter more than me is not worthy of me. 38 And he that doth not take his cross and follow after me, is not worthy of me. 39 He that *o* findeth his life shall lose it; and he that *p* loseth his life for my sake shall find it.

40 He that receiveth you receiveth me, and he that receiveth me receiveth him that sent me. 41 He that receiveth a prophet in the name of a prophet shall receive a prophet's reward: and he that receiveth a righteous man in the name of a righteous man shall receive a righteous man's reward. 42 And whosoever shall give to drink unto one of these little ones a cup of cold water only, in the name of a disciple, verily I say unto you he shall in no wise lose his reward.

11 And it came to pass when Je′sus had finished commanding his twelve disciples, he departed thence to teach and preach in their cities.

2 Now when John heard in the prison the works of the

---

k Gr. *Gehenna.*   *l* Gr *in me.*   *m* Gr. *in*   *him.*   *n* Gr. *cast.*   *o* Or, *found*   *p* Or, *lost*

---

34. *I came not to send peace, but a sword.* He who accepts as his guide and inspiration the words and life of Christ must expect to endure the consequences.

37. *More than me.* The most sacred family ties are to be sundered if they conflict with the supreme claim of Christ's love. Comp. Lk. 14.26.

38. *Take his cross.* A still costlier sacrifice is demanded. The true believer must even take and bear his cross, as Christ did, to the scene of his death. Jesus may have referred to his coming crucifixion.

39. *Shall lose it.* Shall lose the higher, larger life by being contented with the lower and smaller. *Shall find it.* Shall find the spiritual,

eternal life through loss of the life of earthly ambitions and pleasures. Christ's aim is to impress by means of striking contrasts the true meaning of life and of love and the self-denial each calls for.

40. *Receiveth me.* The welcome given to the messenger or representative of Christ is accounted as given to Christ himself.

41. *In the name of a prophet.* Out of respect to the office and work of a prophet.

42. *These little ones.* The apostles.

CHAPTER 11

2. *In the prison.* At Machærus, a fortified place about five miles east of the Dead Sea.

27

Christ, he sent by his disciples 3 and said unto him, Art thou he that cometh, or look we for another? 4 And Je′sus answered and said unto them, Go and tell John the things which ye hear and see: 5 the blind receive their sight, and the lame walk, the lepers are cleansed, and the deaf hear, and the dead are raised up, and the poor have [a]good tidings preached to them. 6 And blessed is he, whosoever shall find no occasion of stumbling in me.

7 And as these went their way, Je′sus began to say unto the multitudes concerning John, What went ye out into the wilderness to behold? a reed shaken with the wind? 8 But what went ye out to see? a man clothed in soft *raiment*? Behold, they that wear soft *raiment* are in kings' houses. 9 [b]But wherefore went ye out? to see a prophet? Yea, I say unto you, and much more than a prophet. 10 This is he, of whom it is written,

[c]Behold, I send my messenger before thy face,
Who shall prepare thy way before thee.

11 Verily I say unto you, Among them that are born of women there hath not arisen a greater than John the Bap′tist: yet he that is [d]but little in the kingdom of heaven is greater than he. 12 And from the days of John the Bap′tist until now the kingdom of heaven suffereth violence, and men of violence take it by force. 13 For all the prophets and the law prophesied until John. 14 And if ye are willing to receive [e]it, this is E-li′jah, that is to come. 15 He that hath ears [f]to hear, let him hear. 16 But whereunto shall I liken this generation? It is like unto children sitting in the marketplaces, who call unto their fellows 17 and say, We piped unto you, and ye did not dance; we wailed, and ye did not [g]mourn. 18 For John came neither eating nor drinking, and they say, He hath a demon.

---

a Or, *the gospel*   b Many ancient authorities read *But what went ye out to see? a prophet?*   c Mal. iii. 1.   d Gr. *lesser.*

e Or, him   f Some ancient authorities omit *to hear.*   g Gr. *beat the breast.*

---

3. *He that cometh.* The Messiah. Perhaps it was not John himself who was doubtful but his disciples, and he wished them to know that Jesus was really the Messiah. Or through his disappointment he may have come to have doubts.

6. *Blessed is he*, etc. Blessed is he who clearly sees in these miracles proofs that I am the Messiah.

7. *What went ye out into the wilderness to behold?* Jesus defends John in ver. 7–11 from any reproach of luxury or of weakness of faith and character, yet in the last clause of ver. 11 he that is but little in the kingdom of heaven is declared to be greater than the Bap-

tist. This refers to the new order or dispensation brought in by Jesus himself. In that order the least surpassed the greatest in the old.

12. *Suffereth violence.* The most eager and sincere pursuit of righteousness wins the highest reward in the spiritual life. This truth was strikingly illustrated by the aggressive enthusiasm of John as the herald of the kingdom of heaven. Such men take the kingdom, as it were, by force.

16. *Like unto children.* By this comparison with children playing games is meant that the Jews were too frivolous and insincere to take either Jesus or John seriously.

28

19 The Son of man came eating and drinking, and they say, Behold, a gluttonous man and a winebibber, a friend of *h*publicans and sinners! And wisdom *i*is justified by her *k*works.

20 Then began he to upbraid the cities wherein most of his *l*mighty works were done, because they repented not. 21 Woe unto thee, Cho-ra'zin! woe unto thee, Beth-sa'i-da! for if the *l*mighty works had been done in Tyre and Si'don which were done in you, they would have repented long ago in sackcloth and ashes. 22 But· I say unto you, it shall be more tolerable for Tyre and Si'don in the day of judgment, than for you. 23 And thou, Ca-per'na-um, shalt thou be exalted unto heaven? thou shalt *m*go down unto Ha'des: for if the *l*mighty works had been done in Sod'om

which were done in thee, it would have remained until this day. 24 But I say unto you that it shall be more tolerable for the land of Sod'om in the day of judgment, than for thee.

25 At that season Je'sus answered and said, I *n*thank thee, O Father, Lord of heaven and earth, that thou didst hide these things from the wise and understanding, and didst reveal them unto babes: 26 yea, Father, *o*for so it was well-pleasing in thy sight. 27 All things have been delivered unto me of my Father: and no one knoweth the Son, save the Father; neither doth any know the Father, save the Son, and he to whomsoever the Son willeth to reveal *him*. 28 Come unto me, all ye that labor and are heavy laden, and I will give you rest. 29 Take my yoke upon you, and learn of me; for

---

h See marginal note on ch. 5.46.   *i* Or, *was*   *k* Many ancient authorities read *children*: as in Lk. 7.35.   *l* Gr. *powers*.

m Many ancient authorities read *be brought down*.   *n* Or, *praise*   *o* Or, *that*

---

19. *Wisdom.* The truths announced by Jesus and John.

21. *Chorazin.* Two and a half miles north of Tell Hûm (Capernaum) on the coast of the Sea of Galilee. It has been identified with the modern Kerazeh. *Bethsaida.* Near the northern extremity of the Sea of Galilee. The five thousand were fed there. *Tyre and Sidon.* Phœnician cities on the coast of the Mediterranean Sea.

25. *Father.* Jesus in this prayer of thanksgiving and worship addresses God as Father before ascribing to Him the sovereignty of heaven and earth. *From the wise and understanding.* The simple tidings of Christ's message were hidden from the proud and self-sufficient Pharisees and scribes, but they were revealed to babes, that is, to the humble and unlearned who received them gladly.

27. *All things have been delivered unto me.* Jesus, who prayed to God as Father and Lord of heaven and earth, now affirms that he has equal authority with the Father. *No one knoweth the Son, save the Father.* The person and office of the Son are not to be understood in their fullness by man. *He to whomsoever the Son willeth.* Jesus not only knows the Father as no one else can know Him, but he alone can make known the Father. Only Jesus Christ can reveal God to man.

28. *Come unto me.* Having declared that he alone can reveal the Father, Jesus freely invites all who find life to be a struggle and a burden to test his power and willingness to give rest and peace.

29. *My yoke.* My commands; the self-denials necessary as my followers. *I am meek and lowly in heart.* Jesus thus makes himself

I am meek and lowly in heart: and ye shall find rest unto your souls. 30 For my yoke is easy, and my burden is light.

12 At that season Je'sus went on the sabbath day through the grainfields; and his disciples were hungry and began to pluck ears and to eat. 2 But the Phar'i-sees, when they saw it, said unto him, Behold, thy disciples do that which it is not lawful to do upon the sabbath. 3 But he said unto them, *a*Have ye not read what David did, when he was hungry, and they that were with him; 4 how he entered into the house of God, and *b*ate the showbread, which it was not lawful for him to eat, neither for them that were with him, but only for the priests? 5 Or have ye not read in the law, *c*that on the sabbath day the priests in the temple profane the sabbath, and are guiltless? 6 But I say unto you, that *d*one greater than the temple is here. 7 But if ye had known what this meaneth, *e*I desire mercy, and not sacrifice,

ye would not have condemned the guiltless. 8 For the Son of man is lord of the sabbath.

9 And he departed thence, and went into their synagogue: 10 and behold, a man having a withered hand. And they asked him, saying, Is it lawful to heal on the sabbath day? that they might accuse him. 11 And he said unto them, **What man shall there be of you, that shall have one sheep, and if this fall into a pit on the sabbath day, will he not lay hold on it, and lift it out?** 12 How much then is a man of more value than a sheep! Wherefore it is lawful to do good on the sabbath day. 13 Then saith he to the man, **Stretch forth thy hand.** And he stretched it forth; and it was restored whole, as the other. 14 But the Phar'i-sees went out, and took counsel against him, how they might destroy him.

15 And Je'sus perceiving *it* withdrew from thence: and many followed him; and he healed them all, 16 and charged

---

a 1 S. xxi. 6.   *b* Some ancient authorities read *they ate.*   *c* Num. xxviii. 9, 10.   *d* Gr. *a greater thing.*   *e* Hos. vi. 6.

---

the divine example of the humility necessary in learning about God.

30. *My burden.* Self-surrender to Christ, whatever sufferings may result, is a light burden compared with the heavy penalties of sin.

CHAPTER 12

3. *What David did.* The Pharisees could not resist the force of this illustration. One of the greatest heroes and saints in Israel had been turned against them. David's hunger, like that of the disciples, was a sufficient excuse. See 1 Sam. 21.6.

4. *The showbread.* Twelve loaves of bread continually kept on a table in the holy place of the temple.

They were arranged in two piles or rows and were changed every Sabbath. They were a symbol of communion between God and man.

6. *Greater than the temple.* Jesus himself, who had power to authorize his disciples to pluck the ears of grain, just as the law absolved the priests from guilt when they did certain work in the temple. The lesson was that works of necessity and mercy were to be allowed on the Sabbath. This holds true no less of the Christian Sunday. Works of mercy are illustrated in ver. 13.

15. *Withdrew.* That he might not waste time in opposing the Pharisees. See ch. 10.22.

them that they should not make him known: 17 that it might be fulfilled which was spoken through I-sa′iah the prophet, saying,

*18 Behold, my *servant whom I have chosen;
My beloved in whom my soul is well pleased:
I will put my Spirit upon him,
And he shall declare judgment to the *Gen′tiles.

19 He shall not strive, nor cry aloud;
Neither shall any one hear his voice in the streets.

20 A bruised reed shall he not break,
And smoking flax shall he not quench,
Till he send forth judgment unto victory.

21 And in his name shall the *Gen′tiles hope.

22 Then was brought unto him *one possessed with a *demon, blind and dumb: and he healed him, insomuch that the dumb

man spake and saw. 23 And all the multitudes were amazed, and said, Can this be the son of David? 24 But when the Phar′-i-sees heard it, they said, This man doth not cast out demons, but *by *Be-el′ze-bub the prince of the demons. 25 And knowing their thoughts he said unto them, **Every kingdom divided against itself is brought to desolation; and every city or house divided against itself shall not stand: 26 and if Satan casteth out Satan, he is divided against himself; how then shall his kingdom stand? 27 And if I *by *Be-el′ze-bub cast out demons, *by whom do your sons cast them out? therefore shall they be your judges. 28 But if I *by the Spirit of God cast out demons, then is the kingdom of God come upon you. 29 Or how can one enter into the house of the strong *man,* and spoil his goods, except he first bind the strong *man?* and then he will spoil his house. 30 He that is**

---

f Is. xlii. 1 ff. *g* See marginal note on Acts 3.13. *h* See marginal note on ch.

4.15. *i* Or, *a demoniac* *k* Or, *in* *l* Gr. *Beelzebul.*

---

20. *A bruised reed.* A repentant sinner. *Smoking flax.* A lamp wick whose flame has almost gone out. So long as any desire for righteousness remains God will deal compassionately with the sinner.

24. *The prince of the demons.* Beelzebub is identified by Jesus with Satan (Mk. 3.23; Lk. 11.18).

25. *Every kingdom divided against itself.* The Pharisees, having accused Jesus of being in league with Satan, are refuted out of their own mouths. According to their contention Satan was consenting to the overthrow of his own kingdom of evil.

27. *Your sons.* Disciples of the Pharisees. If casting out demons proved Jesus to be in league with

Beelzebub, the same was true of these disciples. *Be your judges.* They will indignantly deny the truth of your accusation that casting out of demons is done by the powers of evil.

28. *Then is the kingdom of God come upon you.* Ver. 25–27 were a preparation for this. What the Pharisees meant when they accused Jesus was that there was only one way of casting out demons, namely, by the power of God.

29. *Bind the strong man.* Jesus, having overcome Satan himself, could spoil his goods and his house, that is, destroy his kingdom.

30. *He that is not with me is against me.* Between the service of Christ and that of the world there

31

not with me is against me; and he that gathereth not with me scattereth. 31 Therefore I say unto you, Every sin and blasphemy shall be forgiven unto men; but the blasphemy against the Spirit shall not be forgiven. 32 And whosoever shall speak a word against the Son of man, it shall be forgiven him; but whosoever shall speak against the Holy Spirit, it shall not be forgiven him, neither in this ᵐworld, nor in that which is to come. 33 Either make the tree good, and its fruit good; or make the tree corrupt, and its fruit corrupt: for the tree is known by its fruit. 34 Ye offspring of vipers, how can ye, being evil, speak good things? for out of the abundance of the heart the mouth speaketh. 35 The good man out of his good treasure bringeth forth good things: and the evil man out of his evil treasure bringeth forth evil things. 36 And I say unto you, that every idle word that men shall speak, they shall give account thereof in the day of judgment. 37 For by thy words thou shalt be justified, and by thy words thou shalt be condemned.

38 Then certain of the scribes and Phar'i-sees answered him, saying, Teacher, we would see a sign from thee. 39 But he answered and said unto them, An evil and adulterous generation seeketh after a sign; and there shall no sign be given to it but the sign of Jo'nah the prophet: 40 for as Jo'nah was three days and three nights in the belly of the ⁿwhale; so shall the Son of man be three days and three nights in the heart of the earth. 41 The men of Nin'e-veh shall stand up in the judgment with this generation, and shall condemn it: for they repented at the preaching of Jo'nah; and behold, ᵒa greater than Jo'nah is here. 42 The queen of the south shall rise up in the judgment with this generation, and shall condemn it: for she came from the ends of the earth to hear the wisdom of Sol'o-mon; and behold, ᵒa greater than Sol'o-mon is here. 43 But the unclean spirit, when

---

m Or, *age*   *n* Gr. *sea-monster.*

o Gr. *more than.*

---

is no defensible middle course. No one can righteously be neutral. .

31. *Blasphemy against the Spirit.* The Pharisees had committed this sin by attributing the acts of Jesus to Satanic agency.

33. *Either make the tree good,* etc. A keen reproof of the wilful misrepresentation and illogical reasoning of the Pharisees.

39. *An evil and adulterous generation.* The request for a sign was an insult, because Jesus had just been charged with working miracles by the power of an unclean spirit. Moreover a sign, in the sense of a miracle, was only

given to the devout and sincere inquirer after the truth. These scribes and Pharisees were sneering enemies, and were rebuked by Christ as belonging to an 'evil and adulterous generation.' 'Adulterous' here means apostates from God. *The sign of Jonah the prophet.* The death and resurrection of Jesus as typified in the history of Jonah.

40. *Three days and three nights.* According to a custom of Jewish reckoning.

42. *Queen of the south.* The Queen of Sheba (1 Kings 10.1).

43. *The man.* A symbol of the Jewish people.

*p*he is gone out of the man, passeth through waterless places, seeking rest, and findeth it not. 44 Then *p*he saith, I will return into my house whence I came out; and when *p*he is come, *p*he findeth it empty, swept, and garnished. 45 Then goeth *p*he and taketh with *q*himself seven other spirits more evil than *q*himself, and they enter in and dwell there: and the last state of that man becometh worse than the first. Even so shall it be also unto this evil generation.

46 While he was yet speaking to the multitudes, behold, his mother and his brethren stood without, seeking to speak to him. 47 *r*And one said unto him, Behold, thy mother and thy brethren stand without, seeking to speak to thee. 48 But he answered and said unto him that told him, Who is my mother? and who are my brethren? 49 And he stretched forth his hand towards his disciples, and said, Behold, my mother and

my brethren! 50 For whosoever shall do the will of my Father who is in heaven, he is my brother, and sister, and mother.

13 On that day went Je′sus out of the house, and sat by the sea side. 2 And there were gathered unto him great multitudes, so that he entered into a boat, and sat; and all the multitude stood on the beach. 3 And he spake to them many things in parables, saying, Behold, the sower went forth to sow; 4 and as he sowed, some *seeds* fell by the way side, and the birds came and devoured them: 5 and others fell upon the rocky places, where they had not much earth: and straightway they sprang up, because they had no deepness of earth: 6 and when the sun was risen, they were scorched; and because they had no root, they withered away. 7 And others fell upon the thorns; and the thorns grew up and choked them: 8 and others fell upon the good ground, and

---

p Or, *it*   *q* Or, *itself*   *r* Some ancient | authorities omit ver. 47.

44. *Garnished.* Adorned so as to be attractive.

48. *My brethren.* Jesus had four brothers: James, Joseph (Joses), Simon, Judas (not Iscariot); and at least two sisters (ch. 13.55).

50. *For whosoever shall do the will of my Father.* Love of man to God creates a spiritual relation to Him higher than all family ties.

CHAPTER 13

3. *Many things in parables.* The parables of our Lord were stories picturing imaginary actions or incidents, such as might naturally occur in every-day life, and uttered to explain and enforce spiritual truths. This was a form of teach-

ing familiar to the Jews. Probably not all the parables spoken on this occasion were recorded. Matthew gives seven, Mark four, and Luke two. They all relate to the kingdom of heaven. *The sower.* This parable was the first of four spoken to the multitudes, the other three being the parables of the tares, the mustard seed and the leaven. Then follow those of the hid treasure, the pearl and the net, spoken to the disciples as a more discerning audience, better fitted to understand the mysteries of the kingdom of heaven. See ver. 13–23 for the meaning of the parable of the sower. Comp. Mk. 4.13–20; Lk. 8.11–15.

yielded fruit, some a hundred-fold, some sixty, some thirty. 9 He that hath ears[a], let him hear.

10 And the disciples came, and said unto him, Why speakest thou unto them in parables? 11 And he answered and saith unto them, Unto you it is given to know the mysteries of the kingdom of heaven, but to them it is not given. 12 For whosoever hath, to him shall be given, and he shall have abundance: but whosoever hath not, from him shall be taken away even that which he hath. 13 Therefore speak I to them in parables; because seeing they see not, and hearing they hear not, neither do they understand. 14 And unto them is fulfilled the prophecy of I-sa′iah, which saith,

[b]By hearing ye shall hear, and shall in no wise understand;

And seeing ye shall see, and shall in no wise perceive:

15 For this people's heart is waxed gross,

And their ears are dull of hearing,

And their eyes they have closed;

Lest haply they should perceive with their eyes,

And hear with their ears,

And understand with their heart,

And should turn again,

And I should heal them.

16 But blessed are your eyes, for they see; and your ears, for they hear. 17 For verily I say unto you, that many prophets and righteous men desired to see the things which ye see, and saw them not; and to hear the things which ye hear, and heard them not. 18 Hear then ye the parable of the sower. 19 When any one heareth the word of the kingdom, and understandeth it not, then cometh the evil one, and snatcheth away that which hath been sown in his heart. This is he that was sown by the way side. 20 And he that was sown upon the rocky places, this is he that heareth the word, and straightway with joy receiveth it; 21 yet hath he not root in himself, but endureth for a while; and when tribulation or persecution ariseth because of the word, straightway he stumbleth. 22 And he that was sown among the thorns, this is he that heareth the word; and the care of the [c]world, and the deceitfulness of riches,

---

a Some ancient authorities add here, and in ver. 43, *to hear*: as in Mk. 4.9; Lk. 8.8.

b Is. vi. 9.10. *c* Or, *age*

11. *The mysteries of the kingdom of heaven.* The inner truths, which only the most spiritually enlightened of the apostles and disciples could understand.

12. *Whosoever hath.* Those who have the desire to search for the truths of the Spirit hidden in these parables shall grow rich in the knowledge of them; but those who have not will, in listening, become

more indifferent or hostile than before. See ch. 25.29.

13. *Seeing they see not,* etc. Christ had spoken the truth plainly, but through malice, blind prejudice and indifference many of his hearers had rejected it. Now he speaks in parables to compel their attention. He arouses their curiosity, so that they must now take trouble to find out his meaning.

34

choke the word, and he becometh unfruitful. 23 And he that was sown upon the good ground, this is he that heareth the word, and understandeth it; who verily beareth fruit, and bringeth forth, some a hundredfold, some sixty, some thirty.

24 Another parable set he before them, saying, The kingdom of heaven is likened unto a man that sowed good seed in his field: 25 but while men slept, his enemy came and sowed ᵈtares also among the wheat, and went away. 26 But when the blade sprang up and brought forth fruit, then appeared the tares also. 27 And the ᵉservants of the householder came and said unto him, Sir, didst thou not sow good seed in thy field? whence then hath it tares? 28 And he said unto them, ᶠAn enemy hath done this. And the ᵉservants say unto him,

Wilt thou then that we go and gather them up? 29 But he saith, Nay; lest haply while ye gather up the tares, ye root up the wheat with them. 30 Let both grow together until the harvest: and in the time of the harvest I will say to the reapers, Gather up first the tares, and bind them in bundles to burn them; but gather the wheat into my barn.

31 Another parable set he before them, saying, The kingdom of heaven is like unto a grain of mustard seed, which a man took, and sowed in his field: 32 which indeed is less than all seeds; but when it is grown, it is greater than the herbs, and becometh a tree, so that the birds of the heaven come and lodge in the branches thereof.

33 Another parable spake he unto them; The kingdom of heaven is like unto leaven,

---

d Or, *darnel* *e* Gr. *bondservants.* | *f* Gr. *A man* that is *an enemy.*

25. *His enemy came and sowed tares.* Tares, or darnel, are very like wheat in appearance and hard to distinguish from the latter. This suggests the difficulty of separating the evil from the good when the outward resemblance between them is strong, and foreshadows the confusion and loss resulting from the attempt. Yet the tares, the evil, are to be taken out finally from the wheat and are to be burned. They will not be gathered as wheat. They who try to gain the kingdom of heaven under cover of associating with the righteous cannot hope to succeed, whether members of the visible church or not. See explanation in ver. 37–43.

31. *A grain of mustard seed.* The mustard seed was proverbial for smallness, and though not actually the least of seeds it was commonly thought to be. It was the smallest in proportion to the plant growing

from it. It sometimes attained to a height of seven or eight feet, though this was exceptional. In this parable the kingdom of heaven, which is likened to a mustard seed, is considered as an organization of small beginnings, but with an ever-increasing power of life and growth. Jesus foresaw the immense extent and influence of the kingdom founded by him in an obscure province of Palestine. He knew the secret of its abounding strength to be in the need of the human heart. See Mk. 4.30–32; Lk. 13.18, 19.

33. *Like unto leaven.* See Lk. 13.20, 21. Yeast was put into new dough to cause it to ferment, a small amount being sufficient to change the condition of a very large quantity of dough. This parable typified the secret and pervasive power of Christ's person and teaching throughout the world.

which a woman took, and hid in three *g*measures of meal, till it was all leavened.

34 All these things spake Je'sus in parables unto the multitudes; and without a parable spake he nothing unto them: 35 that it might be fulfilled which was spoken through the prophet, saying,

*h*I will open my mouth in parables;
I will utter things hidden from the foundation *i*of the world.

36 Then he left the multitudes, and went into the house: and his disciples came unto him, saying, Explain unto us the parable of the tares of the field. 37 And he answered and said, He that soweth the good seed is the Son of man; 38 and the field is the world; and the good seed, these are the sons of the kingdom; and the tares are the sons of the evil *one*; 39 and the enemy that sowed them is the devil: and the harvest is *k*the end of the world; and the reapers are angels. 40 As therefore the tares are gath-

ered up and burned with fire; so shall it be in the *k*end of the world. 41 The Son of man shall send forth his angels, and they shall gather out of his kingdom all things that cause stumbling, and them that do iniquity, 42 and shall cast them into the furnace of fire: there shall be the weeping and the gnashing of teeth. 43 Then shall the righteous shine forth as the sun in the kingdom of their Father. He that hath ears*l* let him hear.

44 The kingdom of heaven is like unto a treasure hidden in the field; which a man found, and hid; and *m*in his joy he goeth and selleth all that he hath, and buyeth that field.

45 Again, the kingdom of heaven is like unto a man that is a merchant seeking goodly pearls: 46 and having found one pearl of great price, he went and sold all that he had, and bought it.

47 Again, the kingdom of heaven is like unto a *n*net, that was cast into the sea, and gath-

---

q The word in the Greek denotes the Hebrew seah, a measure containing nearly a peck and a half.   *h* Ps. lxxviii. 2.   *i* Many ancient authorities omit *of the* *world.*   *k* Or, *the consummation of the age* *l* See ver. 9.   *m* Or, *for joy thereof*   *n* Gr. *drag-net.*

---

44. *A treasure hidden in the field.* This parable of the hidden treasure, and also those of the pearl of great price and of the net, are recorded only by Matthew. All three were spoken to the disciples only. The treasure hidden is the truth of Christ; and the lesson to be taken to heart is the joy of finding this truth, a joy so great that the finder is willing to part with all that he has in order to secure the treasure.

45. *Like unto a man that is a merchant seeking goodly pearls.* Having found the pearl of great

price, he values it above all else and parts with all he has to possess it.

47. *Like unto a net.* A drag-net, or a seine, which was operated from the shore, to which one part of it was fastened, while the other was taken out to sea in a boat and after a time hauled in again on shore. All kinds of fishes were caught in it, the valuable and worthless. This parable resembles that of the tares, in which good and evil are found together. In both the good are separated from the bad.

ered of every kind: 48 which,
when it was filled, they drew
up on the beach; and they sat
down, and gathered the good
into vessels, but the bad they
cast away. 49 So shall it be
in [o]the end of the world: the angels shall come forth, and sever
the wicked from among the
righteous, 50 and shall cast
them into the furnace of fire:
there shall be the weeping and
the gnashing of teeth.

51 Have ye understood all
these things? They say unto
him, Yea. 52 And he said unto
them, **Therefore every scribe
who hath been made a disciple
to the kingdom of heaven is like
unto a man that is a householder,
who bringeth forth out of his
treasure things new and old.**

53 And it came to pass, when
Je'sus had finished these parables, he departed thence.

54 And coming into his own
country he taught them in their
synagogue, insomuch that they
were astonished, and said,
Whence hath this man this wisdom, and these [p]mighty works?
55 Is not this the carpenter's
son? is not his mother called
Mary? and his brethren, [q]James,
and Joseph, and Si'mon, and
Ju'das? 56 And his sisters, are
they not all with us? Whence
then hath this man all these
things? 57 And they were [r]of-
fended in him. But Je'sus said
unto them, **A prophet is not
without honor, save in his own
country, and in his own house.**
58 And he did not many [p]mighty
works there because of their
unbelief.

14 At that season Her'od the
tetrarch heard the report
concerning Je'sus, 2 and said
unto his servants, This is John
the Bap'tist; he is risen from the
dead; and therefore do these
powers work in him. 3 For
Her'od had laid hold on John,
and bound him, and put him in
prison for the sake of He-ro'di-as,
his brother Philip's wife. 4 For
John said unto him, It is not
lawful for thee to have her.
5 And when he would have put
him to death, he feared the
multitude, because they counted
him as a prophet. 6 But when
Her'od's birthday came, the
daughter of He-ro'di-as danced
in the midst, and pleased Her'od.

---

[o] Or, *the consummation of the age* [p] Gr. *powers.* [q] Or, *Jacob* [r] Gr. *caused to stumble.*

---

52. *Made a disciple to the kingdom of heaven*. etc. That is, the disciples who had listened to these parables and were instructed in the truth of the Master were in the position of a householder who bountifully provides for those in his care. They were to give freely of their treasures of truth, whenever and wherever required. They were to be new scribes of the kingdom in a higher sense than the scribes of the Jewish law.

54. *His own country*. This was his second visit to Nazareth (Mk. 6.1).

CHAPTER 14

1. *Herod the tetrarch*. Herod Antipas, son of Herod the Great.

3. *Herodias*. She had been the wife of Herod's half-brother, Herod Philip, who lived in Rome. Herod married her after divorcing his first wife. Not only John the Baptist, but orthodox Jews, were bitterly offended by Herod's conduct.

6. *The daughter of Herodias*. Salome, who afterwards married her uncle Philip, the tetrarch of the country east of Galilee. A tetrarch

7 Whereupon he promised with an oath to give her whatsoever she should ask. 8 And she, being put forward by her mother saith, Give me here on a platter the head of John the Bap'tist. 9 And the king was grieved; but for the sake· of his oaths and of them that sat at meat with him, he commanded it to be given; 10 and he sent and beheaded John in the prison. 11 And his head was brought on a platter, and given to the damsel: and she brought it to her mother. 12 And his disciples came, and took up the corpse, and buried him; and they went and told Je'sus.

13 Now when Je'sus heard *it*, he withdrew from thence in a boat, to a desert place apart: and when the multitudes heard *thereof*, they followed him *a*on foot from the cities. 14 And he came forth, and saw a great multitude, and he had compassion on them, and healed their sick. 15 And when even was come, the disciples came to him, saying, The place is desert, and the time is already past; send the multitudes away, that they may go into the villages, and buy themselves food. 16 But Je'sus said unto them, **They have no need to go away; give ye them to eat.** 17 And they say unto him, We have here but five loaves, and two fishes. 18 And he said, **Bring them hither to me.** 19 And he commanded the multitudes to *b*sit down on the grass; and he took the five loaves, and the two fishes, and looking up to heaven, he blessed, and brake and gave the loaves to the disciples, and the disciples to the multitudes. 20 And they all ate, and were filled: and they took up that which remained over of the broken pieces, twelve baskets full. 21 And they that did eat were about five thousand men, besides women and children.

22 And straightway he constrained the disciples to enter

---

a Or, *by land*

b Gr. *recline.*

---

was the ruler of one-fourth of a country or province.

8. *Being put forward by her mother.* Herodias eagerly seized this opportunity of revenge upon John.

9. *The king was grieved.* Because he could not help admiring the noble character of John, whose denunciation of his (Herod's) wickedness, emphasized by the great power of a prophet with the people, naturally made the Baptist a difficult person for the king to deal with.

10. *In the prison.* At Machærus. See note on ch. 11.2.

12. *His disciples came,* etc. Herod could have prevented the last rites for John, and his not doing so suggests some feeling of respect and regard for the murdered prophet.

13. *When Jesus heard it, he withdrew.* Probably because he was waiting to see if Herod intended any opposition to him. He went to the city of Bethsaida Julias, just east of the Sea of Galilee, in the tetrarchy of Philip (Lk. 9.10).

21. *They that did eat were about five thousand men, besides women and children.* The feeding of the five thousand is the only miracle recorded by all four evangelists. All mention five thousand as the number of the men, while Matthew alone says there were also women and children.

22. *Straightway.* Immediately. Jesus wished to leave the multi-

into the boat, and to go before him unto the other side, till he should send the multitudes away. 23 And after he had sent the multitudes away, he went up into the mountain apart to pray: and when even was come, he was there alone. 24 But the boat [c]was now in the midst of the sea, distressed by the waves; for wind was contrary. 25 And in the fourth watch of the night he came unto them, walking upon the sea. 26 And when the disciples saw him walking on the sea, they were troubled, saying, It is a ghost; and they cried out for fear. 27 But straightway Je'sus spake unto them, saying, **Be of good cheer; it is I; be not afraid.** 28 And Peter answered him and said, Lord, if it be thou, bid me come unto thee upon the waters. 29 And he said, **Come.** And Peter went down from the boat, and walked upon the wa-

ters [d]to come to Je'sus. 30 But when he saw the [e]wind, he was afraid; and beginning to sink, he cried out, saying, Lord, save me. 31 And immediately Je'sus stretched forth his hand, and took hold of him, and saith unto him, **O thou of little faith, wherefore didst thou doubt?** 32 And when they were gone up into the boat, the wind ceased. 33 And they that were in the boat [f]worshipped him, saying, Of a truth thou art the Son of God.

34 And when they had crossed over, they came to the land, unto Gen-nes'a-ret. 35 And when the men of that place knew him, they sent into all that region round about, and brought unto him all that were sick; 36 and they besought him that they might only touch the border of his garment: and as many as touched were made whole.

---

c Some ancient authorities read *was many furlongs distant from the land.* d Some ancient authorities read *and came.* e Many

ancient authorities add *strong.* f See marginal note on ch. 2.2.

---

tudes, as in their excitement they were planning to make him a king (Jn. 6.14, 15).

23. *He went up into the mountain apart to pray.* To commune with the Father. He was weary and the people did not understand him as their spiritual deliverer. Jesus often went apart and prayed in solitude. At this time the increased importunity of the people possibly added to the burden of his weariness.

25. *The fourth watch of the night.* Three o'clock in the morning. *Walking upon the sea.* This miracle, like that of the feeding of the five thousand, was a direct control of the powers of nature. See Mk. 6.47–51; Jn. 6.18–21.

28. *Lord, if it be thou, bid me come.* Peter's impulsiveness interfered

with the calm trust that was necessary.

29. *Walked upon the waters.* It is significant that as long as Peter's faith lasted he was enabled to perform a miracle also, but when he began to fear he began to sink.

33. *The Son of God.* The true Messiah. For the first time Jesus was here spontaneously acknowledged by men to be the Son of God. John's confession was part of his divinely ordained mission (Jn. 1.33, 34; 3.35, 36).

34. *Unto Gennesaret.* A district on the north-western shore of the Sea of Galilee, which was also called the Lake of Gennesaret. The climate was genial and the land was level and fertile. Its modern name is ElGhuweir.

36. *Only touch.* See ch. 9.20.

15 Then there come to Je'sus from Je-ru'sa-lem Phar'i-sees and scribes, saying, 2 Why do thy disciples transgress the tradition of the elders? for they wash not their hands when they eat bread. 3 And he answered and said unto them, Why do ye also transgress the commandment of God because of your tradition? 4 For God said, [a]Honor thy father and thy mother: and, [b]He that speaketh evil of father or mother, let him [c]die the death. 5 But ye say, Whosoever shall say to his father or his mother, That wherewith thou mightest have been profited by me is given *to God*; 6 he shall not honor his father[d]. And ye have made void the [e]word of God because of your tradition. 7 Ye hypocrites, well did I-sa'iah prophesy of you, saying, 8 [f]This people honoreth me with their lips;

But their heart is far from me. 9 But in vain do they worship me,

Teaching *as their* doctrines the precepts of men. 10 And he called to him the multitude, and said unto them. Hear, and understand: 11 Not that which entereth into the mouth defileth the man; but that which proceedeth out of the mouth, this defileth the man. 12 Then came the disciples, and said unto him, Knowest thou that the Phar'i-sees were [g]offended, when they heard this saying? 13 But he answered and said, Every [h]plant which my heavenly Father planted not, shall be rooted up. 14 Let them alone: they are blind guides. And if the blind guide the blind, both shall fall into a pit. 15 And Peter answered and said unto him, Declare unto us the parable. 16 And he said, Are ye

a Ex. xx. 12; Dt. v. 16. b Ex. xxi. 17; Lev. xx. 9. c Or, *surely die* d Some ancient authorities add *or his mother.* e Some ancient authorities read *law.* f Is. xxix. 13. g Gr. *caused to stumble.* h Gr. *planting.*

CHAPTER 15

2. *The tradition of the elders.* The Pharisees and scribes, who had probably come from Jerusalem for the purpose, now attacked Jesus over the heads of his disciples by charging the latter with violating the oral traditions of the elders. They were bigoted defenders of these traditions, which in some cases they even put above the Mosaic law. They had popular sympathy with them in this respect, and herein lay the danger of their charge against Jesus. They strove to undermine his power with the people. *They wash not.* It was a serious matter to offend in this respect. See Mk. 7.3.

3. *Why do ye also transgress,* etc. Ignoring the charge against his disciples, Jesus suddenly brings a far more serious charge against his accusers—that of transgressing a commandment of God by their tradition. He does not condemn their tradition in itself, but the misuse of it by which they had made void the law of God to 'honor thy father and thy mother.'

11. *Not that which entereth into the mouth defileth.* Our Lord here expands the questions of form and ceremony, of secret intention and outward act, beyond their local application to the Pharisees and lays down the universal truth that the only defilement or impurity to be dreaded comes from within the heart. Forms and ceremonies as such cannot be either pure or impure; only the thought and will behind them.

12. *The Pharisees were offended.* They were more than offended. They were silenced, put to rout.

also even yet without understanding? 17 Perceive ye not, that whatsoever goeth into the mouth passeth into the belly, and is cast out into the draught? 18 But the things which proceed out of the mouth come forth out of the heart; and they defile the man. 19 For out of the heart come forth evil thoughts, murders, adulteries, fornications, thefts, false witness, railings: 20 these are the things which defile the man; but to eat with unwashen hands defileth not the man.

21 And Je'sus went out thence, and withdrew into the parts of Tyre and Si'don. 22 And behold, a Ca-naan-i'tish woman came out from those borders, and cried, saying, Have mercy on me, O Lord, thou Son of David; my daughter is grievously vexed with a demon. 23 But he answered her not a word. And his disciples came and besought him, saying, Send her away; for she crieth after us. 24 But he answered and said, I was not sent but unto the lost sheep of the house of Is'ra-el. 25 But she came and [i]worshipped him, saying, Lord, help me. 26 And he answered and said, It is not meet to take the children's [k]bread and cast it to the dogs. 27 But she said, Yea, Lord: for even the dogs eat of the crumbs which fall from their masters' table. 28 Then Je'sus answered and said unto her, O woman, great is thy faith: be it done unto thee even as thou wilt. And her daughter was healed from that hour.

29 And Je'sus departed thence, and came nigh unto the sea of Gal'i-lee; and he went up into the mountain, and sat there. 30 And there came unto him great multitudes, having with them the lame, blind, dumb, maimed, and many others, and they cast them down at his feet: and he healed them: 31 inso-

---

[i] See marginal note on ch. 2.2.

[k] Or, loaf

21. *Parts of Tyre and Sidon.* Jesus went north-westerly from upper Galilee into Phœnicia, the country of Tyre and Sidon.

22. *A Canaanitish woman.* The Phœnicians were descendants of the old Canaanites. This woman was a heathen, but she had evidently heard of the miracles of Jesus and believed in him.

23. *Answered her not a word.* A test of her faith. *Send her away.* Get rid of her by curing her daughter.

24. *The lost sheep of the house of Israel.* Jesus further tests the woman's faith by reminding her that she is not of the Jews and therefore she has no right to ask for mercy.

26. *The children's bread.* The children are the Jews. *The dogs.* The Gentiles.

27. *Even the dogs eat of the crumbs.* Her great humility, her willingness to be accounted among the 'dogs,' proved her deep sincerity. She allowed no reproaches, no objections to stand in the way of her appeal to Christ. The 'crumbs' were probably the soft pieces of bread upon which, according to the custom at table, the hands were then thrown to the dogs to eat.

29. *Departed thence.* Having found no rest and quiet in the borders of Phœnicia he returned to the district east of the Sea of Galilee.

30. *He healed them.* A work of grace to many, and undisturbed by the Pharisees and scribes.

31. *Glorified the God of Israel.*

much that the multitude wondered, when they saw the dumb speaking, the maimed whole, and the lame walking, and the blind seeing: and they glorified the God of Is'ra-el.

32 And Je'sus called unto him his disciples, and said, **I have compassion on the multitude, because they continue with me now three days and have nothing to eat: and I would not send them away fasting, lest haply they faint on the way.** 33 And the disciples say unto him, Whence should we have so many loaves in a desert place as to fill so great a multitude? 34 And Je'sus said unto them, **How many loaves have ye?** And they said, Seven, and a few small fishes. 35 And he commanded the multitude to sit down on the ground; 36 and he took the seven loaves and the fishes; and he gave thanks and brake, and gave to the disciples, and the disciples to the multitudes. 37 And they all ate,

and were filled: and they took up that which remained over of the broken pieces, seven baskets full. 38 And they that did eat were four thousand men, besides women and children. 39 And he sent away the multitudes, and entered into the boat, and came into the borders of Mag'a-dan.

16 And the Phar'i-sees and Sad'du-cees came, and trying him asked him to show them a sign from heaven. 2 But he answered and said unto them, *a*When it is evening, ye say, *It will be* fair weather: for the heaven is red. 3 And in the morning, *It will be* foul weather to-day: for the heaven is red and lowering. Ye know how to discern the face of the heaven; but ye cannot *discern* the signs of the times. 4 An evil and adulterous generation seeketh after a sign; and there shall no sign be given unto it, but the sign of Jo'nah. And he left them, and departed.

---

a The following words, to the end of ver. 3, are omitted by some of the most ancient and other important authorities.

Indicating that the majority of the multitude were not Jews.

37. *And they all ate and were filled.* This miracle is not to be mistaken for the feeding of the five thousand. The two resemble each other in some ways but differ widely in others. The numbers fed are different, and so are the numbers and kinds of baskets filled with the fragments. Moreover, our Lord refers to the two miracles in ch. 16.9, 10 and in Mk. 8.19, 20.

39. *The borders of Magadan.* The exact location of Magadan is unknown, but it was west of the Sea of Galilee.

CHAPTER 16
1. *Pharisees and Sadducees.* An

unusual and unnatural combination, one that could only have been brought about by their common hatred of Jesus. Sadducees are here seen acting against him for the first time. See ch. 3.7. *A sign from heaven.* As if his great miracles were not signs from heaven. They wanted something more brilliant in a material sense, something visible in the sky. It was commonly believed that when the Messiah came some sign from heaven would mark the event.

3. *The signs of the times.* The meaning of Christ's preaching and miracles.

4. *The sign of Jonah.* See ch. 12. 39, 40.

5 And the disciples came to the other side and forgot to take *b*bread. 6 And Je'sus said unto them, **Take heed and beware of the leaven of the Phar'i-sees and Sad'du-cees.** 7 And they reasoned among themselves, saying, *c*We took no *b*bread. 8 And Je'sus perceiving it said, **O ye of little faith, why reason ye among yourselves, because ye have no *b*bread? 9 Do ye not yet perceive, neither remember the five loaves of the five thousand, and how many *d*baskets ye took up? 10 Neither the seven loaves of the four thousand, and how many *d*baskets ye took up? 11 How is it that ye do not perceive that I spake not to you concerning *b*bread? But beware of the leaven of the

Phar'i-sees and Sad'du-cees.** 12 Then understood they that he bade them not beware of the leaven of *b*bread, but of the teaching of the Phar'i-sees and Sad'du-cees.

13 Now when Je'sus came into the parts of Cæs-a-re'a Phi-lip'pi, he asked his disciples, saying, **Who do men say *e*that the Son of man is?** 14 And they said, Some *say* John the Bap'tist; some, E-li'jah; and others, Jer-e-mi'ah, or one of the prophets. 15 He saith unto them, **But who say ye that I am?** 16 And Si'mon Peter answered and said, Thou art the Christ, the Son of the living God. 17 And Je'sus answered and said unto him, **Blessed art thou, Si'mon Bar-Jo'nah: for flesh and blood hath not revealed it

---

b Gr. *loaves.* *c* Or, It is *because we took no bread.* *d Basket* in ver. 9 and 10 represents different Greek words. *e* Many

ancient authorities read *that I the Son of man am.* See Mk. 8.27; Lk. 9.18.

---

5. *The other side.* The east side.

6–12. *The leaven of the Pharisees and Sadducees.* The miracles of feeding the five thousand and the four thousand, taken with the parable of the leaven, ought to have familiarized the disciples with the meaning of this saying of Jesus. Beware of the deadly permeating influence of the hypocrisy, formalism and deceit of the Pharisees and Sadducees, was what Jesus meant. Thus he condemned both the great Jewish parties alike. See Mk. 8. 14–21; Lk. 12.1.

13. *Cæsarea Philippi.* A city built by Philip the Tetrarch. It was situated at the foot of Mount Hermon at the upper source of the river Jordan. It was surrounded by hills, except from the west. The city was named after Tiberius Cæsar. Jesus and his disciples visited it, and it was the most northerly point in Palestine reached by them.

14. *Elijah.* Believed by the Jews to be a forerunner of the Messiah. *Jeremiah.* It was also a popular belief that this prophet would prepare the way for the Messiah.

15. *Who say ye that I am?* Jesus sought to put to proof the spiritual insight of his disciples. At this time the people had begun to give up hope that he was the Messiah because he did not declare himself to be their political deliverer from the Romans.

16. *Thou art the Christ, the Son of the living God.* Peter's confession means: (1) Jesus is the Messiah; (2) the Messiah is the divine Son of God. The words 'Christ' and 'Messiah' are from the Greek and Hebrew respectively, and mean 'the Anointed.' But the words 'the Son of the living God' declare the divine nature of the Messiah. He is the ruler of the spiritual kingdom.

17. *Simon Bar-Jonah.* Simon, son of Jonah. The Aramaic name of Peter.

unto thee, but my Father who is in heaven. 18 And I also say unto thee, that thou art *f*Peter, and upon this *g*rock I will build my church; and the gates of Ha'des shall not prevail against it. 19 I will give unto thee the keys of the kingdom of heaven: and whatsoever thou shalt bind on earth shall be bound in heaven; and whatsoever thou shalt loose on earth shall be loosed in heaven. 20 Then charged he the disciples that they should tell no man that he was the Christ.

21 From that time began *h*Je'sus to show unto his disciples, that he must go unto Je-ru'sa-lem, and suffer many things of the elders and chief priests and scribes, and be killed, and the third day be raised up. 22 And Peter took him, and began to rebuke him, saying, *i*Be it far from thee, Lord: this shall never be unto thee. 23 But he turned, and said unto Peter, **Get thee behind me, Satan: thou art a stumbling-block unto me: for** thou mindest not the things of God, but the things of men. 24 Then said Je'sus unto his disciples, If any man would come after me, let him deny himself, and take up his cross, and follow me. 25 For whosoever would save his life shall lose it: and whosoever shall lose his life for my sake shall find it. 26 For what shall a man be profited, if he shall gain the whole world, and forfeit his life? or what shall a man give in exchange for his life? 27 For the Son of man shall come in the glory of his Father with his angels; and then shall he render unto every man according to his *k*deeds. 28 Verily I say unto you, There are some of them that stand here, who shall in no wise taste of death, till they see the Son of man coming in his kingdom.

17 And after six days Je'sus taketh with him Peter, and *a*James, and John his brother, and bringeth them up into a high mountain apart:

---

f Gr. *Petros*. *g* Gr. *petra*. *h* Some ancient authorities read *Jesus Christ*. *i* Or, God *have mercy on thee* *k* Gr. *doing* *a* Or, *Jacob*

---

18. *Thou art Peter.* Jesus had already called the apostle 'Cephas,' which is an Aramaic word of the same meaning as Peter, a rock or stone. He now repeats the name of Peter, implying that the apostle had proved himself worthy of it by his decision of character. *Upon this rock.* Not Peter, but the truth of his confession. *My church.* Believers in Jesus Christ as their spiritual head throughout the world, and who work to advance his kingdom by means of a visible organization. *The gates of Hades.* The Greek 'Hades' has the same meaning as the Hebrew 'Sheol,' the abode of departed spirits.

19. *The keys of the kingdom of heaven.* The power of the apostles to exercise government and discipline over the visible church.
20. *That they should tell no man.* Lest the people should again try to make him king.
21. *From that time.* That is, after Peter's confession of Jesus as the Messiah, when the disciples became better fitted to understand him.

CHAPTER 17

1. *Six days.* After Peter's confession. Luke says 'about eight days after' (9.28). This would be according to the Jewish custom whereby each part of a day is

2 and he was transfigured before them; and his face did shine as the sun, and his garments became white as the light. 3 And behold, there appeared unto them Mo'ses and E-li'jah talking with him. 4 And Peter answered, and said unto Je'sus, Lord, it is good for us to be here: if thou wilt, I will make here three *b*tabernacles; one for thee, and one for Mo'ses, and one for E-li'jah. 5 While he was yet speaking, behold, a bright cloud overshadowed them: and behold, a voice out of the cloud, saying, This is my beloved Son, in whom I am well pleased; hear ye him. 6 And when the disciples heard it, they fell on their face, and were sore afraid. 7 And Je'sus came and touched them and said, **Arise, and be not afraid.** 8 And lifting up their eyes, they saw no one, save Je'sus only.

9 And as they were coming down from the mountain, Je'sus commanded them, saying, **Tell the vision to no man, until the Son of man be risen from the dead.** 10 And his disciples asked him, saying, Why then say the scribes that E-li'jah must first come? 11 And he answered and said, **E-li'jah indeed cometh, and shall restore all things: 12 but I say unto you, that E-li'jah is come already, and they knew him not, but did unto him whatsoever they would. Even so shall the Son of man also suffer of them.** 13 Then understood the disciples that he spake unto them of John the Bap'tist.

14 And when they were come to the multitude, there came to him a man, kneeling to him, and saying, 15 Lord, have mercy on my son: for he is epileptic, and suffereth grievously; for oft-times he falleth into the fire, and oft-times into the water. 16 And I brought him to thy disciples, and they could not cure him. 17 And Je'sus answered and said, **O faithless and perverse generation, how long shall I be with you? how long shall I bear with you? bring him hither to me.** 18 And Je'sus rebuked him; and the

---

b Or, *booths*

counted as a day. *A high mountain apart.* Probably Mount Hermon, near Cæsarea Philippi. It is 9,000 feet high.

3. *Moses and Elijah.* The law and the prophets were represented in these two.

5. *Hear ye him.* A command to hear and obey Jesus the Christ, the Son of God, rather than the law and the prophets. The old dispensation had given place to the new.

9. *Tell the vision to no man.* The vision, literally, the thing seen. Peter, James, and John were chosen to see the glory of Christ because they were the most spiritually enlightened of the apostles. The others were not advanced enough, while the multitudes, if told of the glory on the mountain, would have tried to make Christ their earthly king. *Risen from the dead.* The resurrection distinctly foretold.

15. *Epileptic.* Jesus healed the epileptic immediately after coming down from the mountain of transfiguration. He thus set the example of refusing to permit even the most exalted spiritual enjoyments to delay attention to duty.

16. *Thy disciples.* The nine apostles were among them, the other three having been with Jesus on the mountain.

45

demon went out of him: and the boy was cured from that hour.

19 Then came the disciples to Je'sus apart, and said, Why could not we cast it out? 20 And he saith unto them, Because of your little faith: for verily I say unto you, If ye have faith as a grain of mustard seed, ye shall say unto this mountain, Remove hence to yonder place; and it shall remove; and nothing shall be impossible unto you*c*.

22 And while they *d*abode in Gal'i-lee, Jesus said unto them, The Son of man shall be *e*delivered up into the hands of men; 23 and they shall kill him, and the third day he shall be raised up. And they were exceeding sorry.

24 And when they were come to Ca-per'na-um, they that re-ceived the *f*half-shek'el came to Peter, and said, Doth not your teacher pay the *f*half-shek'el? 25 He saith, Yea. And when he came into the house, Je'sus spake first to him, saying, What thinkest thou, Simon? the kings of the earth, from whom do they receive toll or tribute? from their sons, or from strangers? 26 And when he said, From strangers, Je'sus said unto him, Therefore the sons are free. 27 But, lest we cause them to stumble, go thou to the sea, and cast a hook, and take up the fish that first cometh up; and.when thou hast opened his mouth, thou shalt find a *g*shek'el: that take, and give unto them for me and thee.

18 In that hour came the disciples unto Je'sus, saying, Who then is *a*greatest in the

---

c Many authorities, some ancient, insert ver. 21 *But this kind goeth not out save by prayer and fasting.* See Mk. 9.29. *d* Some ancient authorities read *were gathering themselves together.*   *e* See ch. 10.4.   *f* Gr. *didrachma.* Comp. marginal note on Lk. 15.8.   *g* Gr. *stater.*   *a* Gr. *greater.*

---

20. *If ye have faith as a grain of mustard seed.* That is, the smallest degree of faith, which like the mustard seed is living and capable of great growth. *Ye shall say unto this mountain,* etc. Jesus employs this strong proverbial expression to illustrate the tremendous importance of faith (ch. 21.21).

23. *They were exceeding sorry.* The disciples, not yet fully understanding the meaning of Christ's foretold death and resurrection, easily fell into despondency over the prospect of losing his affectionate guidance and protection. Three of them, Peter, James and John, who had witnessed the transfiguration, may have gained from it an idea of Christ's glory and power which enabled them to think of the resurrection hopefully; but the others were probably without this consolation.

24. *They that received the half-shekel.* Officers of the Jewish authorities, whose duty it was to collect the annual tax for the support of the Te _ _le services. Every male Jew above twenty years of age had to pay the half-shekel, whose value was about thirty or thirty-five cents. Jesus had been absent from Capernaum for some time and the tax was overdue.

26. *The sons are free.* Meaning, the Son of God is rightly free from a tax for the services of his Father's temple.

27. *Lest we cause them to stumble.* That is, lest a wrong impression of the unwillingness of Jesus to pay the tax should be made.

CHAPTER 18

1. *Who then is greatest in the kingdom of heaven?* The form of the question shows that it was asked under the impression of a coming kingdom that was to be earthly,

kingdom of heaven? 2 And he called to him a little child, and set him in the midst of them, 3 and said, Verily I say unto you, Except ye turn, and become as little children, ye shall in no wise enter into the kingdom of heaven. 4 Whosoever therefore shall humble himself as this little child, the same is the ᵃgreatest in the kingdom of heaven. 5 And whoso shall receive one such little child in my name receiveth me: 6 but whoso shall cause one of these little ones that believe on me to stumble, it is profitable for him that ᵇa great millstone should be hanged about his neck, and *that* he should be sunk in the depth of the sea.

7 Woe unto the world because of occasions of stumbling! for it must needs be that the occasions come; but woe to that man through whom the occasion cometh! 8 And if thy hand or

thy foot causeth thee to stumble, cut it off, and cast it from thee: it is good for thee to enter into life maimed or halt, rather than having two hands or two feet to be cast into the eternal fire. 9 And if thine eye causeth thee to stumble, pluck it out, and cast it from thee: it is good for thee to enter into life with one eye, rather ,than having two eyes to be cast into the ᶜhell of fire. 10 See that ye despise not one of these little ones: for I say unto you, that in heaven their angels do always behold the face of my Father who is in heavenᵈ. 12 How think ye? if any man have a hundred sheep, and one of them be gone astray, doth he not leave the ninety and nine, and go unto the mountains, and seek that which goeth astray? 13 And if so be that he find it, verily I say unto you, he rejoiceth over it more than

---

a Gr. *greater.* *b* Gr. *a millstone turned by an ass.* *c* Gr. *Gehenna of fire.* *d* Many authorities, some ancient, insert ver. 11

For the Son of man came to save that which was lost. See Lk. 19.10.

---

not heavenly. Peter's prominence had perhaps caused a feeling of rivalry among the disciples and they had thought much, some of them probably with growing envy, about their future position under Christ's leadership. The reply showed them the sin of their self-seeking and taught the lesson of spiritual humility. See Mk. 9.33–37; Lk. 9.46–48.

3. *Ye shall in no wise enter.* Jesus showed them that their mental attitude shut them out from the kingdom of heaven. Their question as to who is greatest was entirely out of place.

7. *Woe to that man through whom the occasion cometh!* The man who puts temptation as a stumbling-block in the way of others.

8. *And if thy hand or thy foot offend thee,* etc. Having pronounced

a woe on the tempter who gives occasion for stumbling, Jesus appeals to the individual to remove from within himself all ˙causes of stumbling, whatever the sacrifice may be. An earthly life maimed, so to speak, by self-denial or heroic suffering and privation is well worth if by means of it one gain the life eternal.

10. *These little ones.* The humble disciples of Christ. They are not to be despised, for they are honored in heaven by angels who minister in their behalf.

12. *Seek that which goeth astray.* Here the parable of the lost sheep, which is also given in Lk. 15.4–7, teaches the disciples the importance of each one of the 'little ones,' since it is not God's will that one of them should perish.

47

over the ninety and nine which have not gone astray. 14 Even so it is not *e*the will of *f*your Father who is in heaven, that one of these little ones should perish.

15 And if thy brother sin *g*against thee, go, show him his fault between thee and him alone: if he hear thee, thou hast gained thy brother. 16 But if he hear *thee* not, take with thee one or two more, that at the mouth of two witnesses or three every word may be established. 17 And if he refuse to hear them, tell it unto the *h*church: and if he refuse to hear the *h*church also, let him be unto thee as the Gen'tile and the *i*publican. 18 Verily I say unto you, What things soever ye shall bind on earth shall be bound in heaven; and what things soever ye shall loose on earth shall be loosed in heaven. 19 Again I say unto you, that if two of you shall agree on earth as touching anything that they shall ask, it *k*shall be done for them of my Father who is in heaven. 20 For where two or three are gathered together in my name, there am I in the midst of them.

21 Then came Peter and said to him, Lord, how oft shall my brother sin against me, and I forgive him? until seven times? 22 Je'sus saith unto him, I say not unto thee, Until seven times; but, Until *l*seventy times seven. 23 Therefore is the kingdom of heaven likened unto a certain king, who would

---

e Gr. *a thing willed before your Father.*
f Some ancient authorities read *my.*
g Some ancient authorities omit *against*

thee. h Or, *congregation* i See marginal note on ch. 5.46. k Gr. *shall become.* l Or, *seventy times and seven*

---

15. *Show him his fault.* Convince him by reasoning in a friendly spirit that he is wrong. *Between thee and him alone.* For sake of the privacy which keeps the fault from being known and prevents scandal. *Gained thy brother.* Gained him back to righteousness and to thyself.
17. *Tell it unto the church.* Unto the congregation of Christian believers, a public step necessary after the failure of private attempts to settle the dispute. *As the Gentile and the publican.* Outside of Christian fellowship while unrepentant.
18. *Verily I say unto you.* The power of binding and loosing, which in ch. 16.19 is given to Peter as representative of the apostles, is here given to the apostles collectively. 'Binding and loosing' means the power of deciding questions of faith and morals in the visible church. The words, derived from the Aramaic, meant in that dialect the power of deciding what was lawful or unlawful to be done according to Jewish law, and what

was right or not right to be believed. This power was conferred upon a rabbi or scribe at his ordination ceremony. To bind was to prohibit; to loose was to permit.
20. *Where two or three.* The presence of Christ among two or three is promised only when they are gathered together in his name. His presence, as that of the Son of God, assures an answer to their prayers. The first small meetings of Christians, surrounded by strangers and enemies, needed this encouragement.
22. *Until seven times.* The questions in ver. 21 show that Peter was learning slowly. The rabbis held that no one ought to be forgiven more than three times. Peter thought he was generous in asking more than doubling the number. Jesus rebukes him by affirming that one should forgive another seventy times seven, in other words, as often as forgiveness is asked
23. *A certain king.* An eastern king looked upon his governors and

48

make a reckoning with his
^mservants. 24 And when he had
begun to reckon, one was
brought unto him, that owed
him ten thousand ⁿtalents.
25 But forasmuch as he had
not *wherewith* to pay, his lord
commanded him to be sold,
and his wife, and children, and
all that he had, and payment
to be made. 26 The ^oservant
therefore fell down and ^pwor-
shipped him, saying, Lord, have
patience with me, and I will
pay thee all. 27 And the lord
of that ^oservant, being moved
with compassion, released him,
and forgave him the ^qdebt.
28 But that ^oservant went out,
and found one of his fellow-servants, who owed him a hundred
^rshillings: and he laid hold on
him, and took *him* by the throat,
saying, Pay what thou owest.
29 So his fellow-servant fell
down and besought him, saying,
Have patience with me, and I

will pay thee. 30 And he would
not: but went and cast him into
prison, till he should pay that
which was due. 31 So when his
fellow-servants saw what was
done, they were exceeding sorry,
and came and told unto their
lord all that was done. 32 Then
his lord called him unto him,
and saith to him, Thou wicked
^oservant, I forgave thee all that
debt, because thou besoughtest
me: 33 shouldest not thou also
have mercy on thy fellow-
servant, even as I had mercy
on thee? 34 And his lord was
wroth, and delivered him to
the tormentors, till he should
pay all that was due. 35 So
shall also my heavenly Father
do unto you, if ye forgive not
every one his brother from
your hearts.

19 And it came to pass
when Je'sus had finished
these words, he departed from
Gal'i-lee, and came into the

---

m Gr. *bondservants.*   *n* This talent was
probably worth about £200, or $1000.
o Gr. *bondservant.*   *p* See marginal note on

ch. 2.2.   *q* Gr. *loan.*   *r* The word in the
Greek denotes a coin worth about eight
pence half-penny or nearly seventeen cents.

---

satraps as his servants, and one of
his greatest difficulties was to get
from them an honest accounting as
to the revenues for which they were
responsible. In this parable the
king is represented as merciful, like
the Heavenly Father.

24. *Ten thousand.* The sum in
the parable is enormous, about
$10,000,000, so as to suggest the
incalculable spiritual debt of a
sinner to God.

25. *Commanded him to be sold.*
This was permitted by the law of
Moses (Lev. 25.39; 2 Kings 4.1).
The debtor's wife and children were
also allowed to be sold, as they were
regarded as the debtor's property.
This was gradually modified by
later custom into a more merciful
sentence.

27. *Forgave him the debt.* This

servant asked only for time, but his
lord gave him far more—he forgave
him his debt.

28. *He laid hold on him.* The
forgiven servant now reveals his
ingratitude and mercilessness. He
was forgiven a debt of ten thousand
talents; he refuses to forgive a debt
of a hundred shillings.

34. *And his lord was wroth.* God
does not and cannot forgive the
unforgiving. *The tormentors.* Those
who tortured the debtors to discover whether they were concealing
any money or other valuables.

CHAPTER 19

1. *He departed from Galilee.* This
was the end of his ministry in that
province. *Borders of Judæa beyond
the Jordan.* Peræa.

borders of Ju-dæ'a beyond the Jordan; 2 and great multitudes followed him; and he healed them there.

3 And there came unto him [a]Phar'i-sees, trying him, and saying, Is it lawful *for a man* to put away his wife for every cause? 4 And he answered and said, Have ye not read, [b]that he who [c]made *them* from the beginning made *them* male and female, 5 and said, [d]For this cause shall a man leave his father and mother, and shall cleave to his wife; and the two shall become one flesh? 6 So that they are no more two, but one flesh. What therefore God hath joined together, let not man put asunder. 7 They say unto him, [e]Why then did Mo'ses command to give a bill of divorcement, and to put *her* away? 8 He saith unto them, Mo'ses for your hardness of heart suffered you to put away your wives: but from the beginning it hath not been so. 9 And I say unto you, Whosoever shall put away his wife, [f]except for fornication, and shall marry another, committeth adultery: [g]and he that marrieth her when she is put away committeth adultery. 10 The disciples say unto him, If the case of the man is so with his wife, it is not expedient to marry. 11 But he said unto them, Not all men

---

[a]Many authorities, some ancient, insert *the.* b Gen. i. 27; v. 2. c Some ancient authorities read *created.* d Gen. ii. 24. e Dt. xxiv. 1–4. f Some ancient authorities read *saving for the cause of fornication.*

maketh her an adulteress: as in ch. 5.32. g The following words, to the end of the verse, are omitted by some ancient authorities.

---

3. *There came unto him Pharisees, trying him.* Matthew here resumes the narrative, after omitting nearly six months in the ministry of Jesus. Luke and John give an account of what took place in the interval. The Pharisees were active against Jesus even in Peræa. They sought to entrap him into making some statement that would form the basis of a charge against him. *For every cause.* The followers of Hillel, the great doctor of the law at Jerusalem in the time of King Herod, held that a man might divorce his wife for every cause, while the followers of Shammai, Hillel's great rival and contemporary, allowed it for adultery only.

6. *What therefore God hath joined together.* Jesus did not give the Pharisees the answer they hoped for. He ignored the disputes between the schools of Hillel and Shammai as to the causes of divorce. He took the whole question away from local and party points of view and went even beyond the law of Moses to the purpose of God in making mankind male and female; one for one. This was why he said, 'let not man put asunder,' forbidding divorce except for adultery.

8. *For your hardness of heart.* Their moral standard as to the sacredness of marriage was low. Moses did not command, he permitted, a man to put away his wife, but only to save her from prolonged ill-treatment in case a bill of divorce were not granted. Instead of replying to the Pharisees from the point of view of the Mosaic law, Jesus reminds them that the law itself was less perfect in regard to marriage than it was 'from the beginning,' and he sternly rebukes the hardness of heart which had caused this change.

10. *It is not expedient to marry.* The disciples, brought up under the Mosaic law, were themselves astonished at the pure ideal of marriage put before them by Jesus. They could not see how it was possible to realize it.

11. *This saying.* That it is not expedient to marry.

can receive this saying, but they to whom it is given. 12 For there are eunuchs, that were so born from their mother's womb: and there are eunuchs, that were made eunuchs by men: and there are eunuchs, that made themselves eunuchs for the kingdom of heaven's sake. He that is able to receive it, let him receive it.

13 Then were there brought unto him little children, that he should lay his hands on them, and pray: and the disciples rebuked them. 14 But Je'sus said, Suffer the little children, and forbid them not, to come unto me: for *h*to such belongeth the kingdom of heaven. 15 And he laid his hands on them, and departed thence.

16 And behold, one came to him and said, *i*Teacher, what good thing shall I do, that I may have eternal life? 17 And he said unto him, *k*Why askest thou me concerning that which is good? One there is who is

good: but if thou wouldest enter into life, keep the commandments. 18 He saith unto him, Which? And Je'sus said, *l*Thou shalt not kill, Thou shalt not commit adultery, Thou shalt not steal, Thou shalt not bear false witness, 19 Honor thy father and thy mother; and, *m*Thou shalt love thy neighbor as thyself. 20 The young man saith unto him, All these things have I observed: what lack I yet? 21 Je'sus said unto him, If thou wouldest be perfect, go, sell that which thou hast, and give to the poor, and thou shalt have treasure in heaven: and come, follow me. 22 But when the young man heard the saying, he went away sorrowful; for he was one that had great possessions.

23 And Je'sus said unto his disciples, Verily I say unto you, It is hard for a rich man to enter into the kingdom of heaven. 24 And again I say unto you, It is easier for a

---

h Or, *of such is* *i* Some ancient authorities read *Good Teacher.* See Mk. 10.17; Lk. 18.18. *k* Some ancient authorities read *Why callest thou me good? None is* *good save one,* even *God.* See Mk. 10.18; Lk. 18.19. *l* Ex. xx. 12–16; Dt. v. 16–20. *m* Lev. xix. 18.

---

13. *Then were there brought unto him little children.* Jewish parents ordinarily brought their infant children to the synagogue to receive the rabbi's blessing.

14. *For to such belongeth the kingdom of heaven.* To such as are children in spirit (ch. 18.1–14; Mk. 10.15; Lk. 18.17).

16. *One came.* Luke speaks of him as a ruler (ch. 18.18). *What good thing shall I do.* Evidently the rich young man's moral ideal was the doing of good things. The difficulty was that his doing was largely formal and external. It had not plucked up all the roots of selfishness from within him.

21. *If thou wouldest be perfect.* Jesus reveals the young man's lack, his love of riches, as the real barrier to his being good as well as doing good in the highest sense.

24. *Easier for a camel to go through a needle's eye.* A saying which is literally true if by a rich man is meant one who puts his trust in riches (Mk. 10.24, 25). Such an one cannot enter the kingdom of God while that trust remains. There seems to be no convincing authority for some interpretations of this passage. A needle's eye is not here to be identified with a small city gate through which a camel could not go. Jesus spoke after the

camel to go through a needle's eye, than for a rich man to enter into the kingdom of God. 25 And when the disciples heard it, they were astonished exceedingly, saying, Who then can be saved? 26 And Je′sus looking upon *them* said to them, With men this is impossible; but with God all things are possible. 27 Then answered Peter and said unto him, Lo, we have left all, and followed thee; what then shall we have? 28 And Je′sus said unto them, Verily I say unto you, that ye who have followed me, in the regeneration when the Son of man shall sit on the throne of his glory, ye also shall sit upon twelve thrones, judging the twelve tribes of Is′ra-el. 29 And every one that hath left houses, or brethren, or sisters, or father, or mother, [n]or children, or lands, for my name's sake, shall receive [o]a hundredfold, and shall inherit eternal life. 30 But many shall be last *that are* first; and first *that are* last. 1 For the kingdom 20 of heaven is like unto a man that was a householder, who went out early in the morning to hire laborers into his vineyard. 2 And when he had agreed with the laborers for a [a]shilling a day, he sent them into his vineyard. 3 And he went out about the third hour, and saw others standing in the marketplace idle; 4 and to them he said, Go ye also into the vineyard, and whatsoever is right I will give you. And they went their way. 5 Again he went out about the sixth and the ninth hour, and did likewise. 6 And about the eleventh *hour* he went out, and found others standing; and he saith unto

---

n Many ancient authorities add *or wife:* as in Lk. 18.29.   o Some ancient authorities read *manifold.*   a See marginal note on ch. 18.28.

---

manner of the East in saying that some difficult things are impossible. He emphasized the power of faith in a similar way (ch. 17.20).

25. *They were astonished.* Because they were accustomed to look upon the rich as specially favored by God. *Who then can be saved?* If it is so hard for the rich, how much harder, thought the disciples, must it be for the poor! Even the disciples were slow in casting off the prejudices of their early training. They had been taught to believe that the poor had fewer chances of entering the kingdom of heaven than the rich.

27. *What then shall we have?* Peter's question showed that he still looked for a reward that was in part earthly.

28. *In the regeneration.* The spiritual renewal of the world. *The twelve tribes of Israel.* Not to be understood literally, because the Jews rejected Jesus. It means all believers in Christ over whom he shall rule in the regeneration of which he speaks (Rev. 7.9).

CHAPTER 20

1. *Like unto a man that was a householder.* This parable of the laborers in the vineyard must be considered in connection with ver. 28–30 of the preceding chapter. It was spoken only to the disciples, in whose behalf Peter had asked Christ what their reward would be. Our Lord's answer in ver. 28, 29 mentioned the reward, but in ver. 30 he hinted that there would be disappointments, that many who considered themselves first would be last and that many of whom the disciples had never heard would be among the first.

3. *The third hour.* Nine o'clock in the morning, the busiest time in the market-place.

them, Why stand ye here all the day idle? 7 They say unto him, Because no man hath hired us. He saith unto them, Go ye also into the vineyard. 8 And when even was come, the lord of the vineyard saith unto his steward, Call the laborers, and pay them their hire, beginning from the last unto the first. 9 And when they came that *were hired* about the eleventh hour, they received every man a *b*shilling. 10 And when the first came, they supposed that they would receive more; and they likewise received every man a *b*shilling. 11 And when they received it, they murmured against the householder, 12 saying, These last have spent *but* one hour, and thou hast made them equal unto us, who have borne the burden of the day and the *c*scorching heat. 13 But he answered and said to one of them, Friend, I do thee no wrong: didst not thou agree with me for a *b*shilling? 14 Take up that which is thine, and go thy way; it is my will to give unto this last, even as unto thee. 15 Is it not lawful for me to do what I will with mine own? or is thine eye evil, because I am good? ' 16 So the last shall be first, and the first last.

17 And as Je'sus was going up to Je-ru'sa-lem, he took the twelve disciples apart, and on the way he said unto them, 18 Behold, we go up to Je-ru'sa-lem; and the Son of man shall be *d*delivered unto the chief priests and scribes; and they shall condemn him to death, 19 and shall deliver him unto the Gen'tiles to mock, and to scourge, and to crucify: and the third day he shall be raised up.

20 Then came to him the mother of the sons of Zeb'e-dee with her sons, *e* worshipping *him*, and asking a certain thing of him. 21 And he said unto her, What wouldest thou? She saith unto him, Command that these my two sons may sit, one on thy right hand, and one on thy left hand, in thy kingdom. 22 But

---

b see marginal note on ch. 18.28.   *c* Or, hot wind

d See ch. 10.4.   *e* See marginal note on ch. 2.2.

---

15. *Is thine eye evil, because I am good?* Because I am liberal art thou envious?

16. *So the last shall be first.* This saying opens and closes the parable. The fact that the laborers hired at the eleventh hour received as much as those hired early in the morning shows that length of time in service does not necessarily bring the greatest reward, either in worldly or spiritual concerns. Nor do those called first thereby obtain the highest reward. Priority in time is not essential. Paul, though called to be an apostle later than the others, did not receive less honor.

18. *They shall condemn him to death.* In this verse Jesus foretells

his death and resurrection for the third time (chs. 16.21; 17.22, 23). This prediction is more detailed than the two preceding. It mentions mocking, scourging and crucifixion.

20. *The mother of the sons of Zebedee.* Salome. Comp. ch. 27.56 with Mk. 15.40. She is generally believed to have been the sister of the Virgin Mary.

21. *Command that these my two sons.* The ambitious desire of James and John to have the highest places in the coming kingdom prompted this request. It was a painful proof that the spiritual meaning of Christ's words was not yet understood by them.

53

Je'sus answered and said, Ye know not what ye ask. Are ye able to drink the cup that I am about to drink? They say unto him, We are able. 23 He saith unto them, My cup indeed ye shall drink: but to sit on my right hand, and on *my* left hand, is not mine to give; but *it is for them* for whom it hath been prepared of my Father. 24 And when the ten heard it, they were moved with indignation concerning the two brethren. 25 But Je'sus called them unto him, and said, Ye know that the rulers of the Gen'tiles lord it over them, and their great ones exercise authority over them. 26 Not so shall it be among you: but whosoever would become great among you shall be your *f* minister; 27 and whosoever would be first among you shall be your *g* servant: 28 even as the Son of man came not to be ministered unto, but to minister, and to give his life a ransom for many.

29 And as they went out from Jer'i-cho, a great multitude followed him. 30 And behold, two blind men sitting by the way side, when they heard that Je'sus was passing by, cried out, saying, Lord, have mercy on us, thou son of David. 31 And the multitude rebuked them, that they should hold their peace: but they cried out the more, saying, Lord, have mercy on us, thou son of David. 32 And Je'sus stood still, and called them, and said, What will ye that I should do unto you? 33 They say unto him, Lord, that our eyes may be opened. 34 And Je'sus, being moved with compassion, touched their eyes; and straightway they received their sight, and followed him.

21 And when they drew nigh unto Je-ru'sa-lem,

---

f Or, *servant*   *g* Gr. *bondservant.*

23. *My cup indeed ye shall drink.* James died as a martyr (Acts 12.2). John lived to an advanced age, but experienced much persecution and physical torture in behalf of the truth. He died a natural death. *Is not mine to give.* The two sons of Zebedee regarded the subject of their request as if they had a right to ask it as a personal favor. They forgot that the greatest place demands the greatest qualifications.

26. *Not so shall it be among you.* In Christ's kingdom greatness is measured not by rank but by service.

28. *Ransom.* The price paid for a life destroyed or for redeeming a slave from captivity. Its meaning is illustrated in Rom. 3.24; 1 Cor. 6.20; 1 Pet. 1.18, 19. *For many.* Literally, in place of many. 'Many' here is equivalent to 'all' (1 Tim. 2.6).

29. *Jericho.* A city in the valley of the Jordan, west of the river and about six miles north of the Dead Sea.

30. *Two blind men.* Only one blind man, Bartimæus, is mentioned in Mark and Luke (Mk. 10. 46; Lk. 18.35). He was probably the better known of the two. *Son of David.* The Messiah.

34. *Touched their eyes.* Only Matthew mentions this.

CHAPTER 21

1. *When they drew nigh unto Jerusalem.* The distance between Jericho and Jerusalem was between seventeen and twenty miles. *Bethphage.* It is not certain whether it was a village or a district; but most probably it was a village between Bethany and Jerusalem, and on the eastern slope of the Mount of Olives.

and came unto Beth'pha-ge,
unto the mount of Ol'ives,
then Je'sus sent two disciples,
2 saying unto them, Go into the
village, that is over against you,
and straightway ye shall find an
ass tied, and a colt with her:
loose *them*, and bring *them* unto
me. 3 And if any one say aught
unto you, ye shall say, The Lord
hath need of them; and straightway he will send them. 4 Now
this is come to pass, that it
might be fulfilled which was
spoken through the prophet,
saying,

5 [a]Tell ye the daughter of Zi'on,
Behold, thy King cometh
unto thee,
Meek, and riding upon an
ass,
And upon a colt the foal of
of an ass.

6 And the disciples went, and

did even as Je'sus appointed
them, 7 and brought the ass, and
the colt, and put on them their
garments; and he sat thereon.
8 And the most part of the
multitude spread their garments
in the way; and others cut
branches from the trees, and
spread them in the way. 9 And
the multitudes that went before
him, and that followed, cried,
saying, Ho-san'na to the son of
David: Blessed *is* he that
cometh in the name of the Lord;
Ho-san'na in the highest. 10 And
when he was come into Je-ru'-
sa-lem, all the city was stirred,
saying, Who is this? 11 And
the multitudes said, This is the
prophet, Je'sus, from Naz'a-reth
of Gal'i-lee.

12 And Je'sus entered into the
temple [b]of God, and cast out all
them that sold and bought in

---

a Is. lxii. 11; Zech. ix. 9.   *b* Many ancient authorities omit *of God*.

The latter was separated from
Jerusalem by the valley of the
Kidron.
  2. *An ass tied, and a colt.* Mark
and Luke mention only the colt.
The latter would be more suitable
for this occasion. See Mk. 11.2;
1 Sam. 6.7.
  3. *Straightway he will send them.*
Most probably the owner of the
two animals was a secret disciple
of Jesus.
  5. *Riding upon an ass.* After the
manner of a king of peace. In
selecting an ass whereon to ride
Jesus consciously fulfilled the prophecy of Zechariah.
  7. *He sat thereon.* On the garments or clothes placed upon the
back of the colt.
  8. *Spread their garments.* An
unusual tribute of admiration and
devotion, such as was sometimes
paid to great religious teachers
among the Jews, or to great rulers.
  9. *Hosanna.* The Greek form
of a Hebrew word meaning 'save
now' (Ps. 118.25). It had come to

be an expression meaning 'praise'
or 'honor.' *To the Son of David.*
A joyous acknowledgment that
Jesus was the Messiah.
  10. *When he was come into Jerusalem.* The triumphal entry into
Jerusalem took place on the ninth
day of Nisan, the first month of the
Jewish year, and nearly corresponding to our April. The day is known
to Christians as Palm Sunday.
  12. *Jesus entered into the temple.*
This took place on the day following the entry into the city (Mk.
11.11). *All them that sold and
bought.* There was a market in the
Court of the Gentiles for the sale
of sheep and oxen and whatever
else was necessary for the Temple
sacrifices and service. *The tables
of the money-changers.* The money
tribute of a half-shekel due at
this time from male Israelites had
to be paid in Jewish coins. Roman
and other coins were exchanged for
these, and the amount of the commission profits had grown into an
abuse.

the temple, and overthrew the tables of the money-changers, and the seats of them that sold the doves; 13 and he saith unto them, It is written, *c*My house shall be called a house of prayer: *d*but ye make it a den of robbers. 14 And the blind and the lame came to him in the temple; and he healed them. 15 But when the chief priests and the scribes saw the wonderful things that he did, and the children that were crying in the temple and saying, Ho-san'na to the son of David; they were moved with indignation, 16 and said unto him, Hearest thou what these are saying? And Je'sus saith unto them, Yea: did ye never read, *e*Out of the mouth of babes and sucklings thou hast perfected praise? 17 And he left them, and went forth out of the city to Beth'a-ny, and lodged there.

18 Now in the morning as he returned to the city, he hungered. 19 And seeing *f*a fig tree by the way side, he came to it, and found nothing thereon, but leaves only; and he saith unto it, Let there be no fruit from

thee henceforward for ever. And immediately the fig tree withered away. 20 And when the disciples saw it, they marvelled, saying, How did the fig tree immediately wither away? 21 And Je'sus answered and said unto them, Verily I say unto you, If ye have faith, and doubt not, ye shall not only do what is done to the fig tree, but even if ye shall say unto this mountain, Be thou taken up and cast into the sea, it shall be done. 22 And all things, whatsoever ye shall ask in prayer, believing, ye shall receive.

23 And when he was come into the temple, the chief priests and the elders of the people came unto him as he was teaching, and said, By what authority doest thou these things? and who gave thee this authority? 24 And Je'sus answered and said unto them, I also will ask you one *g*question, which if ye tell me, I likewise will tell you by what authority I do these things. 25 The baptism of John, whence was it? from heaven or from men? And they reasoned with themselves, saying, If we

---

c Is. lvi. 7.   d Jer. vii. 11.   e Ps. viii. 2.

f Or, *a single*   g Gr. *word.*

15. *The children.* Only Matthew mentions this.

19. *Immediately the fig tree withered.* According to Mark this miracle was performed on Monday morning, but the disciples did not see the withered tree until the following morning (Mk. 11.12–14; 20.21). Those who see in this an evidence of Christ's anger apparently forget that it was wrought upon a tree, while his miracles of deliverance and compassion were all wrought in behalf of mankind.

21. *Be thou taken up.* It was the oriental way of speaking: an emphatic expression for something very difficult. See ch. 17.20; Lk. 17.6; 1 Cor. 13.2.

23. *By what authority.* Jesus had not been ordained as a rabbi. *These things.* His triumphal entry into the city, the driving out of the money-changers and the miracles of healing the lame and blind, etc. The question also referred to the claim of Jesus as Messiah and to the whole character of his mission and teaching.

shall say, From heaven; he will say unto us, Why then did ye not believe him? 26 But if we shall say, From men; we fear the multitude; for all hold John as a prophet. 27 And they answered Je′sus, and said, We know not. He also said unto them, Neither tell I you by what authority I do these things. 28 But what think ye? A man had two [h]sons; and he came to the first, and said, [i]Son, go work to-day in the vineyard. 29 And he answered and said, I will not: but afterward he repented himself, and went. 30 And he came to the second, and said likewise. And he answered and said, I *go*, sir: and went not. 31 Which of the two did the will of his father? They say, The first. Je′sus saith unto them, Verily I say unto you, that the [k]publicans and the harlots go into the kingdom of God before you. 32 For John came unto you in the way of righteousness, and ye believed him not; but the [k]publicans and the harlots believed him: and ye, when ye saw it, did not even repent yourselves afterward, that ye might believe him.

33 Hear another parable: There was a man that was a householder, who planted a vineyard, and set a hedge about it, and digged a winepress in it, and built a tower, and let it out to husbandmen, and went into another country. 34 And when the season of the fruits drew near, he sent his [l]servants to the husbandmen, to receive [m]his fruits. 35 And the husbandmen took his [l]servants, and beat one, and killed another, and stoned another. 36 Again, he sent other [l]servants more than the first: and they did unto them in like manner. 37 But afterward he sent unto them his son, saying, They will reverence my son. 38 But the husbandmen, when they saw the son, said among themselves, This is the heir; come, let us kill him, and take his inheritance. 39 And they took him, and cast him forth out of the vineyard, and killed him. 40 When therefore the lord of the vineyard shall come, what will he do unto those husbandmen? 41 They say unto him, He will miserably destroy those miserable men, and will let out the vineyard unto other husbandmen, who shall render him the fruits in their seasons. 42 Je′sus saith unto them, Did ye never read in the scriptures,

h Gr. *children.* i Gr. *Child.* k See marginal note on ch. 5.46.   l Gr. *bondservants.*   m Or, *the fruits of it*

27. *We know not.* A humiliating confession of ignorance from those whose duty it was to be able to answer such a question. They were expected, as members of the Sanhedrin, to decide between true and false prophets.

32. *In the way of righteousness.* Of the righteousness of the law, and as such not objectionable to the Pharisees.

33-44. *Hear another parable.* The parable of the wicked husbandmen was a direct reproof to the chief priests and elders as conspirators who were seeking the death of Christ. In it the householder represents God; the son, Christ; the servants, Moses and the prophets; the husbandmen, the Pharisees and scribes, teachers of the people. Christ as the son of the householder,

[n]The stone which the builders rejected,
The same was made the head of the corner;
This was from the Lord,
And it is marvellous in our eyes?

43 Therefore say I unto you, The kingdom of God shall be taken away from you, and shall be given to a nation bringing forth the fruits thereof. 44 [o]And he that falleth on this stone shall be broken to pieces: but on whomsoever it shall fall, it will scatter him as dust. 45 And when the chief priests and the Phar'i-sees heard his parables, they perceived that he spake of them. 46 And when they sought to lay hold on him, they feared the multitudes, because they took him for a prophet.

22 And Je'sus answered and spake again in parables unto them, saying, 2 The kingdom of heaven is likened unto a certain king, who made a marriage feast for his son, 3 and sent forth his [a]servants to call them that were bidden to the marriage feast: and they would not come. 4 Again he sent forth other [a]servants, saying, Tell them that are bidden, Behold, I have made ready my dinner; my oxen and my fatlings are killed, and all things are ready: come to the marriage feast. 5 But they made light of it, and went their ways, one to his own farm, another to his merchandise; 6 and the rest laid hold on his [a]servants, and treated them shamefully, and killed them. 7 But the king was wroth; and he sent his armies, and destroyed those murderers, and burned their city. 8 Then saith he to his [a]servants, The wedding is ready, but they that were bidden were not worthy. 9 Go ye therefore unto the partings of the highways, and as many as ye shall find, bid to the marriage feast. 10 And those [a]servants went out into the highways, and gathered together all as many

---

n Ps. cxviii. 22 f.   o Some ancient authorities omit ver. 44.

a Gr. bondservants.

---

claims to be the Son of God, thus giving his accusers the final answer to their question as to the authority by which he preached and wrought miracles. *They say.* Here the accusers of Jesus in their own answer acknowledged the punishment that was coming upon them and the Jewish nation.

46. *When they sought to lay hold on him.* Indicating their fixed purpose to kill him, since they could neither diminish the enthusiasm for him among the multitudes nor silence him by argument. They were undoubtedly acting for the Sanhedrin, whose object was to seize Jesus as quickly as possible and as quietly, for the vengeance of Christ's Galilean followers was feared. This was why they made use of the treachery of Judas.

CHAPTER 22

2. *A certain king.* In this parable of the royal marriage feast (ver. 1–14) Jesus repeats the truths and warnings of the preceding one. God is meant by 'a certain king;' the 'servants' are the apostles; the 'rest,' or the remnant, are the chief priests, scribes and Pharisees.

7. *Burned their city.* Jerusalem is meant.

9. *The partings of the highways.* The territory of the Gentiles. Since the Jews, the bidden guests, would not come to the marriage feast, the servants were to invite as many as they could find, both bad and good.

as they found, both bad and good: and the wedding was filled with guests. 11 But when the king came in to behold the guests, he saw there a man who had not on a wedding-garment: 12 and he saith unto him, Friend, how camest thou in hither not having a wedding-garment? And he was speechless. 13 Then the king said to the. [b]servants, Bind him hand and foot, and cast him out into the outer darkness; there shall be the weeping and the gnashing of teeth. 14 For many are called, but few chosen.

15 Then went the Phar'i-sees, and took counsel how they might ensnare him in *his* talk. 16 And they sent to him their disciples, with the He-ro'di-ans, saying, Teacher, we know that thou art true, and teachest the

way of God in truth, and carest not for any one: for thou regardest not the person of men. 17 Tell us therefore, What thinkest thou? Is it lawful to give tribute unto Cæ'sar, or not? 18 But Je'sus perceived their wickedness, and said, Why make ye trial of me, ye hypocrites? 19 Show me the tribute money. And they brought unto him a [c]denarius. 20 And he saith unto them, Whose is this image and superscription? 21 They say unto him, Cæ'sar's. Then saith he unto them, Render therefore unto Cæ'sar the things that are Cæ'sar's; and unto God the things that are God's. 22 And when they heard it, they marvelled, and left him, and went away.

23 On that day there came to him Sad'du-cees, [d]they that say

---

b Or, *ministers*   *c* See marginal note on ch. 18.28.

d Many ancient authorities read *saying.*

---

11. *A man who had not on a wedding-garment.* A serious offence according to eastern etiquette, and in the parable one that could easily have been avoided, as the king had provided a wedding-garment for each of his guests. The meaning is plain. The wedding-garment is a righteous life, which alone gives the right to appear at the wedding feast. The guests were judged. Those who had the garment were accepted; he who was without it was condemned.

14. *Many are called, but few chosen.* Referring most probably to the Jews of Christ's time. Few were chosen because few responded to the call. See ch. 20.16.

15. *Took counsel.* Our Lord's replies were so exasperating to his accusers that the latter were resolved at all hazards to exhaust their ingenuity before giving up the attempt to entrap him in his own words.

16. *The Herodians.* Partisans of

the royal family of Herod. They naturally strove to please the Romans and were unfriendly to the Pharisees. Nevertheless the latter called them to their aid as being especially serviceable in case Jesus should give an entangling answer to a political question.

21. *Render therefore unto Cæsar the things,* etc. An argument against the union of church and state. Each has its own rights and its own duties and these are to be kept apart. The Jews were commanded to obey Cæsar in political matters, but to worship God in their religion. In the latter respect Jesus defied Cæsar, as in the former he upheld his authority.

22. *Marvelled, and left him.* The reply was altogether above and beyond their petty religious and political notions. It showed how a universal religion could be made possible by separating it from any narrow national restrictions.

that there is no resurrection: and they asked him, 24 saying, Teacher, Mo'ses said, [e]If a man die, having no children, his brother [f]shall marry his wife, and raise up seed unto his brother. 25 Now there were with us seven brethren: and the first married and deceased, and having no seed left his wife unto his brother; 26 in like manner the second also, and the third, unto the [g]seventh. 27 And after them all, the woman died. 28 In the resurrection therefore whose wife shall she be of the seven? for they all had her. 29 But Je'sus answered and said unto them, Ye do err, not knowing the scriptures, nor the power of God. 30 For in the resurrection they neither marry, nor are given in marriage, but are as angels[h] in heaven. 31 But as touching the resurrection of the dead, have ye not read that which was spoken unto you by God, saying, 32 [i]I am the God of Abraham, and the God of I'saac, and the God of Jacob? God is not *the God* of the dead, but of the living. 33 And when the multitudes heard it, they were astonished at his teaching.

34 But the Phar'i-sees, when they heard that he had put the Sad'du-cees to silence, gathered themselves together. 35 And one of them, a lawyer, asked him a question, trying him: 36 Teacher, which is the great commandment in the law? 37 And he said unto him, [k]Thou shalt love the Lord thy God with all thy heart, and with all they soul, and with all thy mind. 38 This is the great and first commandment. 39 [l]And a second *like unto it* is this, [m]Thou shalt love thy neighbor as thyself. 40 On these two commandments the whole law hangeth, and the prophets.

41. Now while the Phar'i-sees were gathered together, Je'sus asked them a question, 42 saying, What think ye of the Christ? whose son is he? They say unto him, *The son* of David. 43 He saith unto them How then doth David in the Spirit call him Lord, saying, 44 [n]The Lord said unto my Lord,

---

e Dt. xxv. 5.   f Gr. *shall perform the duty of a husband's brother to his wife.*   g Gr. *seven.*   h Many ancient authorities add *of God.*   i Ex. iii. 6.   k Dt. vi. 5.   l Or, *And a second is like unto it, Thou shalt love &c.*   m Lev. xix. 18.   n Ps. cx. 1.

29. *Ye do err, not knowing the scriptures.* The Sadducees, disbelieving in the resurrection, naturally sought to make light of it. They were mistaken in supposing that if persons rose from the dead they would meet with conditions similar to those of the earthly life.

30. *As angels.* This was a rebuke to the Sadducees in their denial of the existence of angels (Acts 23.8). See Lk. 20.36.

31. *Spoken unto you by God.* That is, in the book of Exodus, a part of the Mosaic law in which they believed.

38. *The great and first commandment.* It is probable that the Pharisee who asked this question did not do so in a hostile spirit. At least it does not appear so from Mk. 12.28 and Lk. 10.25. Most likely it was intended as a fair test. The reply of Jesus in Mk. 12.34 shows that he was pleased with his questioner.

39. *Love thy neighbor as thyself.* Not as a man ordinarily does love himself, that is, selfishly, but as he should love himself.

42. *The Christ.* The Messiah.

44. *Lord.* God or Jehovah. *My*

Sit thou my on right hand,
Till I put thine enemies
underneath thy feet?
45 If David then calleth him
Lord, how is he his son? 46 And
no one was able to answer him
a word, neither durst any man
from that day forth ask him
any more questions.

23 Then spake Je'sus to
the multitudes and to his
disciples, 2 saying, The scribes
and the Phar'i-sees sit on Moses'
seat: 3 all things therefore whatsoever they bid you, *these* do and
observe: but do not ye after
their works; for they say, and
do not. 4 Yea, they bind heavy
burdens *a*and grievous to be

borne, and lay them on men's
shoulders; but they themselves
will not move them with their
finger. 5 But all their works
they do to be seen of men: for
they make broad their phylacteries, and enlarge the borders *of their garments*, 6 and love
the chief place at feasts, and the
chief seats in the synagogues,
7 and the salutations in the
marketplaces, and to be called
of men, Rab'bi. 8 But be not
ye called Rab'bi: for one is your
teacher, and all ye are brethren.
9 And call no man your father
on the earth: for one is your
Father, *b*even he who is in heaven.
10 Neither be ye called masters:

---

a Many ancient authorities omit *and*

grievous to be borne.   *b* Gr. *the heavenly.*

Lord. The Lord of David, the
Messiah that was to come.

45. *How is he his son?* The reply
of the Pharisees, acknowledging
that the Christ, or Messiah, was the
Son of David, was only partly
acceptable to Jesus. The psalm
quoted by him in ver. 44 implies
that the Christ is also Lord of David
and that he has a right to sit at the
right hand of God. Thus did Jesus
prove to the Pharisees the divine
authority of the Christ as Messiah
from a psalm which they fully
accepted as Messianic.

CHAPTER 23

2. *Sit on Moses' seat.* Referring
to the power of judging and teaching, which they received by the
laying on of hands at their ordination ceremony.

3. *All things therefore.* Jesus
recognizes the right of the scribes
and Pharisees to be loyally obeyed
until the incoming of the new dispensation.

4. *Heavy burdens.* Minute and
perplexing interpretations of the
law. See ch. 11.30.

5. *Phylacteries.* Small boxes
made out of calfskin, containing
little rolls on which were written
these four portions of the Mosaic

law: Ex. 13.1–10; 11–16; Deut.
4.4–9; 11.13–21. They were attached to a broad strip of leather or
other material, and were used at
prayer-time. One was worn on the
brow between the eyes and in each
of its four small compartments one
of the four passages from the law
was enclosed, inscribed on a bit of
parchment. The other was worn
on the inside of the left arm, and
hidden by the sleeve. The scripture
passages in this were on a single
roll. Making broad the phylacteries came to be known as an external sign of piety. Jesus rebukes
the scribes and Pharisees for their
pretentious use of them. *The
borders.* The fringes on the cloak or
outer garment, and fastened to it
by a blue ribbon. See Num. 15.38.
The Pharisees wore the fringes
wider than others.

7. *Rabbi.* Aramaic for 'My Master,' the usual manner of addressing a scribe or teacher of the law

9. *Father.* This was also a title
sometimes given to the scribes.
'Father' and 'master' are not condemned by Jesus as names. He
denounces the spiritual arrogance
and conceit of the religious leaders
who shelter themselves under such
names.

for one is your master, *even* the Christ. 11 But he that is *c*greatest among you shall be your *d*servant. 12 And whosoever shall exalt himself shall be humbled; and whosoever shall humble himself shall be exalted.

13 But woe unto you, scribes and Phar'i-sees, hypocrites! because ye shut the kingdom of heaven *e*against men: for ye enter not in yourselves, neither suffer ye them that are entering in to enter.*f*

15 Woe unto you, scribes and Phar'i-sees, hypocrites! for ye compass sea and land to make one proselyte; and when he is become so, ye make him twofold more a son of *g*hell than yourselves.

16 Woe unto you, ye blind guides, that say, Whosoever shall swear by the *h*temple, it is nothing; but whosoever shall swear by the gold of the *h*temple, he is *i*a debtor. 17 Ye fools and blind: for which is greater, the gold, or the *h*temple that hath sanctified the gold? 18 And, Whosoever shall swear by the altar, it is nothing; but whoso-

ever shall swear by the gift that is upon it, he is *i*a debtor. 19 Ye blind: for which is greater, the gift, or the altar that sanctifieth the gift? 20 He therefore that sweareth by the altar, sweareth by it, and by all things thereon. 21 And he that sweareth by the *h*temple, sweareth by it, and by him that dwelleth therein. 22 And he that sweareth by the heaven, sweareth by the throne of God, and by him that sitteth thereon.

23 Woe unto you, scribes and Phar'i-sees, hypocrites! for ye tithe mint and *k*anise and cummin, and have left undone the weightier matters of the law, justice, and mercy, and faith: but these ye ought to have done, and not to have left the other undone. 24 Ye blind guides, that strain out the gnat, and swallow the camel!

25 Woe unto you, scribes and Phar'i-sees, hypocrites! for ye cleanse the outside of the cup and of the platter, but within they are full from extortion and excess. 26 Thou blind Phar'i-see, cleanse first the inside of the

---

c Gr. *greater.* *d* Or, *minister* *e* Gr. *before.*
f Some authorities insert here, or after ver. 12, ver. 14 *Woe unto you, scribes and Pharisees, hypocrites! for ye devour widows' houses, even while for a pretence ye make*

13. *Because ye shut the kingdom of heaven against men.* The first of the seven woes against the scribes and Pharisees. It alludes to the hiding of the truth by outward ceremonies and false teaching, thereby keeping men out of the kingdom of heaven.
15. *Compass.* Travel over or about (chs. 4.23; 9.35). *Proselyte.* A new convert.
16. *The gold of the temple.* Gold brought as an offering or gift; the 'Corban' or 'devoted,' the saying

long prayers: therefore ye shall receive greater condemnation. See Mk. 12.40; Lk. 20.47. *g* Gr. *Gehenna.* *h* Or, *sanctuary:* as in ver. 35. *i* Or, *bound* by his oath *k* Or, *dill*

of which word bound the giver as by an oath.
23. *Tithe mint and anise and cummin.* The Jews were commanded to give a tenth part of the fruit of the field and the trees as an offering (Lev. 27.30). The small and unimportant garden herbs were likewise included in the tithe by the Pharisees in their excessive zeal for minute regulations. Cummin was used as a spice in cooking.
24. *Strain out the gnat.* Out of the wine that was to be drunk.

cup and of the platter, that the outside thereof may become clean also.

27 Woe unto you, scribes and Phar'i-sees, hypocrites! for ye are like unto whited sepulchres, which outwardly appear beautiful, but inwardly are full of dead men's bones, and of all uncleanness. 28 Even so ye also outwardly appear righteous unto men, but inwardly ye are full of hypocrisy and iniquity.

29 Woe unto you, scribes and Phar'i-sees, hypocrites! for ye build the sepulchres of the prophets, and garnish the tombs of the righteous, 30 and say, If we had been in the days of our fathers, we should not have been partakers with them in the blood of the prophets. 31 Wherefore ye witness to yourselves, that ye are sons of them that slew the prophets. 32 Fill ye up then the measure of your fathers. 33 Ye serpents, ye offspring of vipers, how shall ye escape the judgment of *l*hell? 34 Therefore, behold, I send unto you prophets, and wise men,

and scribes: some of them shall ye kill and crucify; and some of them shall ye scourge in your synagogues, and persecute from city to city: 35 that upon you may come all the righteous blood shed on the earth, from the blood of Abel the righteous unto the blood of Zach-a-ri'ah son of Bar-a-chi'ah, whom ye slew between the sanctuary and the altar. 36 Verily I say unto you, All these things shall come upon this generation.

37 O Je-ru'sa-lem, Je-ru'sa-lem, that killeth the prophets, and stoneth them that are sent unto her! how often would I have gathered thy children together, even as a hen gathereth her chickens under her wings, and ye would not! 38 Behold, your house is left unto you *m*desolate. 39 For I say unto you, Ye shall not see me henceforth, till ye shall say, Blessed *is* he that cometh in the name of the Lord.

24 And Je'sus went out from the temple, and was going on his way; and his dis-

---

l Gr. Gehenna.

m Some ancient authorities omit *desolate.*

---

27. *Whited sepulchres.* The Jews whitewashed the graves of their dead in order to avoid the ceremonial defilement resulting from walking over them.

31. *Ye witness to yourselves.* If those whom Jesus rebuked had lived in the time of their fathers, they would have slain the prophets as their fathers did.

32. *Fill ye up then.* Proceed with your evil designs, as your fathers did, and slay also this prophet sent to you from God.

34. *I send unto you prophets,* etc. Here Jesus refers to his apostles, prophets, teachers and evangelists, but he gives them Jewish titles. See Lk. 11.49–51.

35. *Upon you.* Upon the scribes and Pharisees as leaders of the people. *All the righteous blood.* The penalty for shedding it.

37. *How often.* The words suggest that Jesus had frequently preached and ministered in Jerusalem.

38. *Your house.* The city itself.

39. *Till ye shall say, Blessed is he that cometh.* The verse closes the last public discourse of Jesus.

CHAPTER 24

1. *The buildings of the temple.* Herod's Temple had not at this time been completed (Jn. 2.20).

ciples came to him to show him the buildings of the temple. 2 But he answered and said unto them, See ye not all these things? verily, I say unto you, There shall not be left here one stone upon another, that shall not be thrown down.

3 And as he sat on the mount of Ol'ives, the disciples came unto him privately, saying, Tell us, when shall these things be? and what *shall be* the sign of thy *ᵃ*coming, and of *ᵇ*the end of the world? 4 And Je'sus answered and said unto them, Take heed that no man lead you astray. 5 For many shall come in my name, saying, I am the Christ; and shall lead many astray. 6 And ye shall hear of wars and rumors of wars; see that ye be not troubled: for *these things* must needs come to pass; but the end is not yet. 7 For nation shall rise against nation, and kingdom against kingdom; and there shall be famines and earthquakes in divers places. 8 But all these things are the beginning of travail. 9 Then shall they deliver you up unto tribulation, and shall kill you: and ye shall be hated of all the nations for my name's sake. 10 And then shall many stum-ble, and shall *ᶜ*deliver up one another, and shall hate one another. 11 And many false prophets shall arise, and shall lead many astray. 12 And because iniquity shall be multiplied, the love of the many shall wax cold. 13 But he that endureth to the end, the same shall be saved. 14 And *ᵈ*this gospel of the kingdom shall be preached in the whole *ᵉ*world for a testimony unto all the nations; and then shall the end come.

15 When therefore ye see the abomination of desolation, which was *ᶠ*spoken of through Dan'iel the prophet, standing in *ᵍ*the holy place (let him that readeth understand), 16 then let them that are in Ju-dæ'a flee unto the mountains: 17 let him that is on the housetop not go down to take out the things that are in his house: 18 and let him that is in the field not return back to take his cloak. 19 But woe unto them that are with child and to them that give suck in those days! 20 And pray ye that your flight be not in the winter, neither on a sabbath: 21 for then shall be great tribulation, such as hath not been from the beginning of the world until now, no, nor ever shall be. 22 And

---

a Gr. *presence.* *b* Or, *the consummation of the age.* *c* See ch. 10.4. *d* Or, *these good tidings* *c* Gr. *inhabited earth.* *f* Dan. ix. 27; xi. 31; xii. 11. *g* Or, *a holy place*

2. *One stone.* The prediction of the Temple's destruction was literally fulfilled. The whole building was laid even with the ground.

3. *Came unto him privately.* Peter, James, John and Andrew are meant (Mk. 13.3).

4. *Take heed.* This warning opens a didactic discourse to the disciples which is concluded at the end of ch. 25.

5. *Shall come in my name.* Among such pretenders who appeared before the destruction of Jerusalem were Simon Magus, Dositheus and Menander.

16. *Flee unto the mountains.* Many Christians fled to Pella in Peræa during the siege of Jerusalem.

22. *Those days.* The days of the siege, whose horrors were so great

except those days had been shortened, no flesh would have been saved: but for the elect's sake those days shall be shortened. 23 Then if any man shall say unto you, Lo, here is the Christ, or, Here; believe *h*it not. 24 For there shall arise false Christs, and false prophets, and shall show great signs and wonders; so as to lead astray, if possible, even the elect. 25 Behold, I have told you beforehand. 26 If therefore they shall say unto you, Behold, he is in the wilderness; go not forth: Behold, he is in the inner chambers; believe *i*it not. 27 For as the lightning cometh forth from the east, and is seen even unto the west; so shall be the *k*coming of the Son of man. 28 Wheresoever the carcase is, there will the *l*eagles be gathered together.

29 But immediately after the tribulation of those days the sun shall be darkened, and the moon shall not give her light, and the stars shall fall from heaven, and the powers of the heavens shall be shaken: 30 and then shall appear the sign of the Son of man in heaven: and then shall all the tribes of the earth mourn, and they shall see the Son of man coming on the clouds of

heaven with power and great glory. 31 And he shall send forth his angels *m*with *n*a great sound of a trumpet, and they shall gather together his elect from the four winds, from one end of heaven to the other.

32 Now from the fig tree learn her parable: when her branch is now become tender, and putteth forth its leaves, ye know that the summer is nigh; 33 even so ye also, when ye see all these things, know ye that *o*he is nigh, *even* at the doors. 34 Verily I say unto you, This generation shall not pass away, till all these things be accomplished. 35 Heaven and earth shall pass away, but my words shall not pass away. 36 But of that day and hour knoweth no one, not even the angels of heaven, *p*neither the Son, but the Father only. 37 And as *were* the days of Noah, so shall be the *k*coming of the Son of man. 38 For as in those days which were before the flood they were eating and drinking, marrying and giving in marriage, until the day that Noah entered into the ark, 39 and they knew not until the flood came, and took them all away; so shall be the *k*coming of the Son of man. 40 Then

---

h Or, him   *i* Or, them   *k* Gr. *presence.*
l Or, *vultures*   *m* Many ancient authorities read *with a great trumpet, and they shall*

gather &c.   *n* Or, *a trumpet of great sound*   *o* Or, *it*   *p* Many authorities, some ancient, omit *neither the Son.*

---

that only their being shortened allowed any to escape. Jerusalem was captured by the Romans on August 10, A.D. 70.

26. *In the wilderness.* A false Christ or prophet might strive to lure people after him by an ascetic life.

29. *The sun shall be darkened,* etc. The striking and figurative

expressions contained in ver. 29–31 are characteristic of scripture prophecy, especially in the Old Testament.

32. *From the fig tree.* This parable has been interpreted to mean the coming of the kingdom of heaven.

37. *As were the days of Noah.* See Lk. 17.27–29.

shall two men be in the field; one is taken, and one is left: 41 two women *shall be* grinding at the mill; one is taken, and one is left. 42 Watch therefore: for ye know not on what day your Lord cometh. 43 ^qBut know this, that if the master of the house had known in what watch the thief was coming, he would have watched, and would not have suffered his house to be ^rbroken through. 44 Therefore be ye also ready; for in an hour that ye think not the Son of man cometh.

45 Who then is the faithful and wise ^sservant, whom his lord hath set over his household, to give them their food in due season? 46 Blessed is that ^sservant, whom his lord when he cometh shall find so doing. 47

Verily I say unto you, that he will set him over all that he hath. 48 But if that evil ^sservant shall say in his heart, my lord tarrieth; 49 and shall begin to beat his fellow-servants, and shall eat and drink with the drunken; 50 the lord of that ^sservant shall come in a day when he expecteth not, and in an hour when he knoweth not, 51 and shall ^tcut him asunder, and appoint his portion with the hypocrites: there shall be the weeping and the gnashing of teeth.

25 Then shall the kingdom of heaven be likened unto ten virgins, who took their ^alamps, and went forth to meet the bridegroom. 2 And five of them were foolish, and five were wise. 3 For the foolish, when they took their ^alamps, took no

---

^q Or, *But this ye know*   ^r Gr. *digged through.*   ^s Gr. *bondservant.*

^t Or, *severely scourge him*   ^a Or, *torches*

---

41. *Two women shall be grinding.* The custom of women grinding grain with hand-mills is alluded to. In Palestine these mills are still in common use where there are no mill streams.

42. *Watch therefore: for ye know not on what day.* An argument as well as a command. The uncertainty of the Lord's coming will not permit any lack of vigilance.

43. *If the master of the house had known.* The bitter reflection of all who neglect their duty and lament the resulting loss and punishment. This truth is brought home by three parables: the wise servant, the ten virgins and the talents.

45. *Whom his lord hath set over his household.* This was a servant who was promoted to be a steward, a reward of fidelity and discretion. The position called for the ability of a manager and the honesty of a faithful trustee.

47. *Over all that he hath.* Still further promotion; he now has charge of all his lord's affairs.

48. *Shall say in his heart.* In the promptings of a heart that is unfaithful begins the failure of watchfulness. The evil servant thought he could speculate on the time of his lord's return. He was in danger from the moment when he said, My Lord tarrieth.

CHAPTER 25

1. *Then.* In the time of the judgment. This is another parable about watchfulness. *To meet the bridegroom.* It was the custom at a Jewish wedding for the bridegroom's friends to escort the bride to the threshold of her husband's home. When the threshold was reached, the bridegroom led the bride across it. In this parable the bridegroom himself went to bring his bride, and the virgins awaited his return.

2. *Were wise.* Here the wisdom was shown in a form of watchfulness, a preparation for meeting the bridegroom in the proper manner when he came.

oil with them: 4 but the wise took oil in their vessels with their *a*lamps. 5 Now while the bridegroom tarried, they all slumbered and slept. 6 But at midnight there is a cry, Behold, the bridegroom! Come ye forth to meet him. 7 Then all those virgins arose, and trimmed their *a*lamps. 8 And the foolish said unto the wise, Give us of your oil; for our *a*lamps are going out. 9 But the wise answered, saying, Peradventure there will not be enough for us and you: go ye rather to them that sell, and buy for yourselves. 10 And while they went away to buy, the bridegroom came; and they that were ready went in with him to the marriage feast: and the door was shut. 11 Afterward came also the other virgins, saying, Lord, Lord, open to us. 12 But he answered and said, Verily I say unto you, I know you not. 13 Watch therefore, for ye know not the day nor the hour.

14 For *it is* as *when* a man, going into another country, called his own *b*servants, and delivered unto them his goods. 15 And unto one he gave five talents, to another two, to another one; to each according to his several ability; and he went on his journey. 16 Straightway he that received the five talents went and traded with them, and made other five talents. 17 In like manner he also that *received* the two gained other two. 18 But he that received the one went away and digged in the earth, and hid his lord's money. 19 Now after a long time the lord of those *b*servants cometh, and maketh a reckoning with them. 20 And he that received the five talents came and brought other five talents, saying, Lord, thou deliveredst unto me five talents: lo, I have gained other five talents. 21 His lord said unto him, Well done, good and faithful *c*servant: thou hast been faithful over a few things, I will set thee over many things; enter thou into the joy of thy lord. 22 And he also that *received* the two talents came and said, Lord, thou deliveredst unto me two

---

a Or, *torches*   *b* Gr. *bondservants.*   *c* Gr. *bondservant.*

9. *There will not be enough for us and you.* The foolish virgins had some oil, that is, a certain degree of preparation; they lacked the thoroughness and persistence that fully provided for the coming event.

10. *While they went away to buy.* The test of watchfulness came in the very moment when they were hurrying to make good their lack of prudence.

15. *Five talents.* The parable of the talents is only in the Gospel according to Matthew. Like the two preceding, it is a parable of watchfulness, but there are also thoughts on the use of time while waiting and watching. The fact is emphasized that difference in natural gifts is less important than the careful cultivation by each one of such talents as have been bestowed. See Lk. 19.11–28 for differences between the parable of the talents and the parable of the pounds.

18. *He that received the one went away.* His thought was similar to that of the evil servant in the parable of the wise steward. He had put out of his mind the need of watchful provision against his lord's return. He did worse, in deliberately neglecting the trust reposed in him.

talents: lo, I have gained other two talents. 23 His lord said unto him, Well done, good and faithful ᶜservant: thou hast been faithful over a few things, I will set thee over many things; enter thou into the joy of thy lord. 24 And he also that had received the one talent came and said, Lord, I knew thee that thou art a hard man, reaping where thou didst not sow, and gathering where thou didst not scatter; 25 and I was afraid, and went away and hid thy talent in the earth: lo, thou hast thine own. 26 But his lord answered and said unto him, Thou wicked and slothful ᶜservant, thou knewest that I reap where I sowed not, and gather where I did not scatter; 27 thou oughtest therefore to have put my money to the bankers, and at my coming I should have received back mine own with interest. 28 Take ye away therefore the talent from him, and give it unto

him that hath the ten talents. 29 For unto every one that hath shall be given, and he shall have abundance: but from him that hath not, even that which he hath shall be taken away. 30 And cast ye out the unprofitable ᶜservant into the outer darkness: there shall be the weeping and the gnashing of teeth.

31 But when the Son of man shall come in his glory, and all the angels with him, then shall he sit on the throne of his glory: 32 and before him shall be gathered all the nations: and he shall separate them one from another, as the shepherd separateth the sheep from the goats; 33 and he shall set the sheep on his right hand, but the goats on the left. 34 Then shall the King say unto them on his right hand, Come, ye blessed of my Father, inherit the kingdom prepared for you from the foundation of the world: 35 for I was hungry, and ye gave me to eat; I was

ᶜ Gr. bondservant.

23. *Enter thou into the joy of thy lord.* Partake of the happiness of thy lord, the reward which thy faithfulness has earned.

24. *Lord I knew thee that thou art a hard man.* His excuse begins with a falsehood which proves to be a trap, for his lord takes him at his word and condemns him because he did not prepare to meet the requirements of a hard man who reaped where he sowed not. It was easy for this servant to have intrusted his lord's money to responsible persons.

28. *Take ye away therefore.* Gifts unused become worthless. This is the lesson of the lord's sentence upon the slothful servant. It holds good in all walks of life.

33. *The sheep.* The righteous, set on the right hand. The words 'right' and 'left' in this connection

have the same meaning in the Hebrew and Greek languages. Those on the right are the righteous; those on the left, the wicked. See Deut. 33.2; Prov. 3.16. *The goats.* The wicked.

34. *The King.* Christ. Afterward he also acknowledges himself king before Pilate (ch. 27.11). *Inherit the kingdom.* As sons of God coming to their own.

35. *For I was hungry.* Christ, the judge of those before him, rewards them according to their acts. It has often been pointed out that the good deeds for which Christ rewards his faithful increase in their self-sacrificing quality up to the last of those here enumerated. To satisfy hunger and thirst, or to give lodging to a stranger is the mark of a charitable and well-disposed person; but, though mer-

thirsty, and ye gave me drink; I was a stranger, and ye took me in; 36 naked, and ye clothed me; I was sick, and ye visited me; I was in prison, and ye came unto me. 37 Then shall the righteous answer him, saying, Lord, when saw we thee hungry, and fed thee? or athirst, and gave thee drink? 38 And when saw we thee a stranger, and took thee in? or naked, and clothed thee? 39 And when saw we thee sick, or in prison, and came unto thee? 40 And the King shall answer and say unto them, Verily I say unto you, Inasmuch as ye did it unto one of these my brethren, *even* these least, ye did it unto me. 41 Then shall he say also unto them on the left hand, *d*Depart from me, ye cursed, into the eternal fire which is prepared for the devil and his angels: 42 for I was hungry, and ye did not give me to eat; I was thirsty, and ye gave me no drink; 43 I was a stranger, and ye took me not in; naked, and ye clothed me not; sick, and in prison, and ye visited me not. 44 Then shall they also answer, saying, Lord,

when saw we thee hungry, or athirst, or a stranger, or naked, or sick, or in prison, and did not minister unto thee? 45 Then shall he answer them, saying, Verily I say unto you, Inasmuch as ye did it not unto one of these least, ye did it not unto me. 46 And these shall go away into eternal punishment: but the righteous into eternal life.

26 And it came to pass, when Je′sus had finished all these words, he said unto his disciples, 2 Ye know that after two days the passover cometh, and the Son of man is *a*delivered up to be crucified. 3 Then were gathered together the chief priests, and the elders of the people, unto the court of the high priest, who was called Ca′ia-phas; 4 and they took counsel together that they might take Je′sus by subtlety, and kill him. 5 But they said, Not during the feast, lest a tumult arise among the people.

6 Now when Je sus was in Beth′a-ny, in the house of Si′mon the leper, 7 there came unto him a woman having *b*an alabaster cruse of exceeding precious oint-

---

d Or, *Depart from me under a curse*

a See ch. 10.4.   *b* Or, *a flask*

---

itorious, it calls for less self-denial than clothing the naked or visiting those who are sick and in prison.

40. *Inasmuch as ye did it unto one of these.* Here is declared the great distinctive motive of Christian service. The things done for mankind, even the least of men and women and children, are done for Christ and are so accepted by him.

CHAPTER 26

2. *The Son of man is delivered up.* An emphatic prediction of the betrayal found only in Matthew.

3. *Then were gathered together.*

Probably an informal gathering of the great council, the Sanhedrin. *The court of the high priest.* The central quadrangle around which the palace was built. *Caiaphas.* Joseph Caiaphas, son-in-law of Annas. He was appointed high priest in A.D. 26 by the Roman procurator Valerius Gratus.

6. *Simon the leper.* Simon's disease must have been cured, otherwise he would not have been allowed to have guests in his house.

7. *A woman having an alabaster cruse.* Mary, the sister of Lazarus (Jn. 12.2, 3). The cruse was a vase

ment, and she poured it upon his head, as [c]he sat at meat.
8 But when the disciples saw it, they had indignation, saying, To what purpose is this waste? 9 For this *ointment* might have been sold for much, and given to the poor. 10 But Je'sus perceiving it said unto them, Why trouble ye the woman? for she hath wrought a good work upon me. 11 For ye have the poor always with you; but me ye have not always. 12 For in that she [d]poured this ointment upon my body, she did it to prepare me for burial. 13 Verily I say unto you, Wheresoever [e]this gospel shall be preached in the whole world, that also which this woman hath done shall be spoken of for a memorial of her.

14 Then one of the twelve, who was called Ju'das Is-car'i-ot, went unto the chief priests, 15 and said, What are ye willing to give me, and I will [f]deliver him unto you? And they weighed unto him thirty pieces of silver. 16 And from that time he sought

opportunity to [f]deliver him *unto them.*

17 Now on the first *day* of unleavened bread the disciples came to Je'sus, saying, Where wilt thou that we make ready for thee to eat the passover? 18 And he said, Go into the city to such a man, and say unto him, The Teacher saith, My time is at hand; I keep the passover at thy house with my disciples. 19 And the disciples did as Je'sus appointed them; and they made ready the passover.

20 Now when even was come, he was [g]sitting at meat with the twelve [h]disciples; 21 and as they were eating, he said, Verily I say unto you, that one of you shall [i]betray me. 22 And they were exceeding sorrowful, and began to say unto him every one, Is it I, Lord? 23 And he answered and said, He that dipped his hand with me in the dish, the same shall [i]betray me. 24 The Son of man goeth, even as it is written of him: but woe unto that man through whom the Son of man is [i]betrayed! good

---

c Or, *reclined at table*   d Gr. *cast.*
e Or, *these good tidings*   f See ch. 10.4.
g Or, *reclining at table*   h Many authorities, some ancient, omit *disciples.*
i See marginal note on ch. 10.4.

---

with a long neck. *Exceeding precious.* The ointment was worth about $150.

12. *To prepare me for burial.* Another prediction of his death.

13. *That also which this woman hath done.* Mary's act won higher praise from Jesus than any other mentioned in the New Testament. It was a most touching proof of devotion, and a sign of recognition of Christ's true nature and work. The anointing has had a place in the Christian consciousness ever since and will have unto the end of time.

15. *Willing to give.* The motive was greed. See Jn. 12.6.

17 *On the first day of unleavened bread.* The Feast of Unleavened Bread began on the 14th of Nisan, the first month of the Jewish year, in the evening, that is, in the beginning of the 15th day. It was popularly identified with the Passover.

18. *Such a man.* Probably a disciple who had been informed and who was ready and willing to do what was required of him. *My time is at hand.* The time of his betrayal and crucifixion.

24. *Good were it for that man,* etc. An expression often used among the Jews in condemnation of one who

were it *k*for that man if he had not been born. 25 And Ju'das, who *l*betrayed him, answered and said, Is it I, Rab'bi? He saith unto him, Thou hast said.

26 And as they were eating, Je'sus took *m*bread, and blessed, and brake it; and he gave to the disciples, and said, Take, eat; this is my body. 27 And he took *n*a cup, and gave thanks, and gave to them, saying, Drink ye all of it; 28 for this is my blood of the *o*covenant, which is poured out for many unto remission of sins. 29 But I say unto you, I shall not drink henceforth of this fruit of the vine, until that day when I drink it new with you in my Father's kingdom.

30 And when they had sung a hymn, they went out into the mount of Ol'ives.

31 Then saith Je'sus unto them, All ye shall be offended in me this night: for it is written, *p*I will smite the shepherd, and the sheep of the flock shall be scattered abroad. 32 But after I am raised up, I will go before you into Gal'i-lee. 33 But Peter answered and said unto him, If all shall be *q*offended in thee, I will never be *q*offended. 34 Je'sus said unto him, Verily I say unto thee, that this night, before the cock crow, thou shalt deny me thrice. 35 Peter saith unto me, Even if I must die with thee, *yet* will I not deny

---

k Gr. *for him if that man.* *l* See marginal note on ch. 10.4. *m* Or, *a loaf* *n* Some ancient authorities read *the cup.* *o* Many ancient authorities insert *new.* *p* Zech. xiii. 7. *q* Gr. *caused to stumble.*

---

knew the law, and did not obey it.

25. *Thou hast said.* A common form of assent in Palestine.

26. *And as they were eating, Jesus took the bread.* The institution of the Last Supper is recorded in ver. 26–29. See Mk. 14.22; Lk. 22.19; 1 Cor. 11.23–25. It was on the 14th, which began after sunset on the 13th of Nisan. In ver. 18 the words 'I keep the passover at thy house' may be taken as spoken by our Lord with the intention of following the ritual of the Passover as far as possible. That would be according to his declaration that he came to fulfil the law; but on the other hand he was instituting a new rite to be observed by his followers for all time, so that the Passover ritual would, if necessary, be modified. Some think there was no paschal lamb, Christ himself being offered as a sacrifice, doing away forever with the necessity of the typical lamb without blemish.

28. *This is my blood.* The wine poured from the cup was a symbol of the blood shed for the remission of sins. *For many.* Mankind.

30. *When they had sung a hymn.*

The second part of the Hallel (Ps. 115–118). 'Hallel', meaning praise, was a term of the Hebrew religious service applied to certain psalms, especially to those above indicated.

32. *I will go before you into Galilee.* That is, I will lead you as a shepherd into Galilee. Jesus after again predicting his resurrection, continues in these words the figure of a shepherd going before his flock, in harmony with Zechariah's prophecy quoted in ver. 31. The disciples were to meet in Galilee. See ch. 28.16; Jn. 21; 1 Cor. 15.6.

33. *But Peter answered.* Impulsive arrogance here characterized the words of Peter as on former occasions. He declared in effect that his loyalty and affection for his Master were deeper than those of the other apostles.

34. *Before the cock crow.* Before dawn. Mark says: Before the cock crow twice (ch. 14.30). The two expressions practically mean the same, as the cock crows at frequent intervals in the early morning.

35. *Even if I must die with thee,* etc. Peter's sinful presumption and

71

thee. Likewise also said all the disciples.

36 Then cometh Je'sus with them unto ᵣa place called Geth-sem'a-ne, and saith unto his disciples, **Sit ye here, while I go yonder and pray.** 37 And he took with him Peter and the two sons of Zeb'e-dee, and began to be sorrowful and sore troubled. 38 Then saith he unto them, **My soul is exceeding sorrowful, even unto death: abide ye here, and watch with me.** 39 And he went forward a little, and fell on his face, and prayed, saying, **My Father, if it be possible, let this cup pass away from me: nevertheless, not as I will, but as thou wilt.** 40 And he cometh unto the disciples, and findeth them sleeping, and saith unto Peter, **What, could ye not watch with me one hour?** 41 ˢ**Watch and pray, that ye enter not into**

temptation: **the spirit indeed is willing, but the flesh is weak.** 42 Again a second time he went away, and prayed, saying, **My Father, if this cannot pass away, except I drink it, thy will be done.** 43 And he came again and found them sleeping, for their eyes were heavy. 44 And he left them again, and went away, and prayed a third time, saying again the same words. 45 Then cometh he to the disciples, and saith unto them, ᵗ**Sleep on now, and take your rest: behold, the hour is at hand, and the Son of man is** ᵘ**betrayed into the hands of sinners.** 46 **Arise, let us be going: behold, he is at hand that** ᵘ**betrayeth me.**

47 And while he yet spake, lo, Ju'das, one of the twelve, came, and with him a great multitude with swords and staves, from the chief priests and elders of the

---

ᵣ Gr. *an enclosed piece of ground.*   ˢ Or, *Watch ye, and pray that ye enter not*   ᵗ Or,

ᵗ *Do ye sleep on, then, and take your rest?*
ᵘ See marginal note on ch. 10.4

---

audacity increased even after Jesus warned him. Hence the humiliation of his denial was correspondingly deep.

36. *Gethsemane.* Literally, 'the oil press'. It was at the foot of the western slope of the Mount of Olives, and was probably an olive yard. Like all the other gardens of Jerusalem, it was outside the city walls.

37. *Peter and the two sons of Zebedee.* Peter, James and John were closest to Jesus and were better fitted than the others to witness his agony in the garden. They had been with him on the Mount of the Transfiguration.

39. *Not as I will.* The human nature of our Lord sought deliverance from his coming trial, yet he submitted to the will of his Father.

40. *Saith unto Peter.* As Peter was first in professing loyalty so he first received the rebuke of Jesus

for failure to act according to his profession.

44. *A third time, saying again the same words.* A proof of his intense earnestness and anguish. Contrast this with the 'vain repetitions' of ch. 6.7.

46. *Let us be going.* To meet those who were coming to take him. It was impossible that the disciples should sleep on. The sudden appearance of Judas and those with him prevented it.

47. *A great multitude.* It was composed of part of the Jewish Temple guard (Lk. 22.52), a detachment of Roman soldiers (Jn. 18.3, 12), servants of the high priest (ver. 51) and probably some of the more bigoted among the elders and chief priests. The size of the crowd indicated that the power of Jesus was feared. It was necessary for the Jews to make the Roman governor believe that they were arresting a dangerous political agitator.

people. 48 Now he that 'betrayed him gave them a sign, saying, Whomsoever I shall kiss, that is he: take him. 49 And straightway he came to Je'sus, and said, Hail, Rab'bi; and ᵛkissed him. 50 And Je'sus said unto him, **Friend, do** that for which thou art come. Then they came and laid hands on ¹Je'sus, and took him. 51 And behold, one of them that were with Je'sus stretched out his hand, and drew his sword, and smote the ˣservant of the high priest, and struck off his ear. 52 Then saith Je'sus unto him, **Put up again thy sword into its place: for all they that take the sword shall perish with the sword. 53 Or thinkest thou that I cannot beseech my Father, and he shall even now send me more than twelve legions of angels? 54 How then should the scriptures be fulfilled, that thus it must be?** 55 In that hour said Je'sus to the multitudes, **Are ye come out as against a robber with swords and staves to seize me? I saf daily in the temple teaching, and ye took me not.** 56 But all this is come to pass, that the scriptures of the prophets might be fulfilled. Then all the disciples left him, and fled.

57 And they that had taken Je'sus led him away to *the house of* Ca'ia-phas the high priest, where the scribes and the elders were gathered together. 58 But Peter followed him afar off, unto the court of the high priest, and entered in, and sat with the officers, to see the end. 59 Now the chief priests and the whole council sought false witness against Je'sus, that they might put him to death; 60 and they found it not, though many false witnesses came. But afterward came two, 61 and said, This man said, I am able to destroy the ᵛtemple of God, and

---

v Gr. *kissed him much.*   *x* Gr. *bondserv-*   *ant.*   *y* Or, *sanctuary:* as in ch. 23.35; 27.5.

---

48. *Whomsoever I shall kiss.* The kiss, thus debased by Judas to a sign of treachery, was sometimes given by a pupil to a master but more often by a master to a pupil. In addressing our Lord as Rabbi, or Master, Judas showed that he intended to avail himself of this custom.

50. *Friend.* The Greek word stands for an expression of civility rather than for friendliness. It was a word often used in reply by a rabbi to a pupil.

51. *One of them.* Peter. See Jn. 18.10). *The servant.* Malchus (Jn. 18.10).

52. *All they that take the sword,* etc. In his most perilous hour Jesus fearlessly affirmed in effect that warfare in his behalf must be carried on by the power of the Spirit.

53. *Twelve legions of angels.* Our Lord could have invoked almighty power to save himself, but obediently fulfilled his Father's will as revealed in the Scriptures.

58. *Peter followed him afar off.* He was evidently the first of the disciples to recover from the terror caused by the arrest of Jesus. *Unto the court of the high priest.* Outside the room into which Jesus was taken for examination.

59. *Sought false witness against Jesus.* It was illegal for judges to seek any witness, but to seek a false witness was infamous. Both the spirit and the letter of Jewish law were ignored in the proceedings before the Sanhedrin. Murder was in the hearts of its members.

61. *I am able to destroy,* etc. These witnesses did not report the words of our Lord correctly. See Jn. 2.19–21.

to build it in three days. 62 And the high priest stood up, and said unto him, Answerest thou nothing? what is it which these witness against thee? 63 But Je'sus held his peace. And the high priest said unto him, I adjure thee by the living God, that thou tell us whether thou art the Christ, the Son of God. 64 Je'sus saith unto him, **Thou hast said: nevertheless I say unto you, Henceforth ye shall see the Son of man sitting at the right hand of Power, and coming on the clouds of heaven.** 65 Then the high priest rent his garments, saying, He hath spoken blasphemy: what further need have we of witnesses? behold, now ye have heard the blasphemy: 66 what think ye? They answered and said, He is *z*worthy of death. 67 Then did they spit in his face and buffet him: and

some smote him *a*with the palms of their hands, 68 saying, Prophesy unto us, thou Christ: who is he that struck thee?

69 Now Peter was sitting without in the court: and a maid came unto him, saying, Thou also wast with Je'sus the Gal-i-læ'an. 70 But he denied before them all, saying, I know not what thou sayest. 71 And when he was gone out into the porch, another *maid* saw him, and saith unto them that were there, This man also was with Je'sus of Naz'a-reth. 72 And again he denied with an oath, I know not the man. 73 And after a little while they that stood by came and said to Peter, Of a truth thou also art *one* of them; for thy speech maketh thee known. 74 Then began he to curse and to swear, I know not the man. And straightway the cock crew.

---

z Gr. liable to.   a Or, with rods

---

63. *Tell us whether thou art the Christ, the Son of God.* The attempt to obtain an answer from Jesus having failed through the latter's silence, the high priest asked him the most searching and decisive question that was possible, an affirmative answer to which made any further proof unnecessary.

64. *Thou hast said.* See note on ver. 25.

65. *Rent his garments.* This was according to custom, on proof of a charge of blasphemy. It would have been contrary to the hostile intention of the high priest or of the Sanhedrin to take any honest step towards investigating the claim of Jesus to be the Christ, the Messiah.

66. *He is worthy of death.* This condemnation was illegal because passed on the same day as the trial. Jewish law required a delay of one day in such cases. The trial itself

was informal, and it was also illegal because held at night on the eve of the Passover feast.

68. *Prophesy.* At this moment Jesus was blindfolded (Lk. 22.64).

70. *He denied before them all.* See Mk. 14.66–72; Lk. 22.55–62; Jn. 18.15–18; 25–27. The denials of Peter that are recorded by the other three evangelists do not differ from these in essential points. There are only variations of minor detail, such as would appear in the accounts of witnesses who were intent upon the main issue and the most striking scenes, and therefore not careful about those of less importance.

71. *Into the porch.* The entrance hall from the street. Beyond this was the court or quadrangle, open to the sky, and around which were built the different rooms of the house of the high priest.

73. *Thy speech maketh thee known.* Peter's Galilean dialect.

75 And Peter remembered the word which Je'sus had said, Before the cock crow, thou shalt deny me thrice. And he went out, and wept bitterly.

27 Now when morning was come, all the chief priests and the elders of the people took counsel against Je'sus to put him to death: 2 and they bound him, and led him away, and delivered him up to Pi'late the governor.

3 Then Ju'das, who *a*betrayed him, when he saw that he was condemned, repented himself, and brought back the thirty pieces of silver to the chief priests and elders, 4 saying, I have sinned in that I *a*betrayed *b*innocent blood. But they said,

What is that to us? see thou *to it.* 5 And he cast down the pieces of silver into the sanctuary, and departed; and he went away and hanged himself. 6 And the chief priests took the pieces of silver, and said, It is not lawful to put them into the *c*treasury, since it is the price of blood. 7 And they took counsel, and bought with them the potter's field, to bury strangers in. 8 Wherefore that field was called, The field of blood, unto this day. 9 Then was fulfilled that which was spoken through Jer-e-mi'ah the prophet, saying, *d*And *e*they took the thirty pieces of silver, the price of him that was priced, *f*whom *certain* of the children of Is'ra-el did price; 10 and *g*they

a See marginal note on ch. 10.4. *b* Many ancient authorities read *righteous.* *c* Gr. *corbanas,* that is, *sacred treasury.* Comp. Mk. 7.11. *d* Zech. xi. 12, 13. *e* Or, *I*

took f Or, *whom they priced on the part of the sons of Israel g* Some ancient authorities read *I gave.*

75. *Peter remembered.* See Mk. 14.72; Lk. 22.61. *He went out, and wept bitterly.* Out from the porch or entrance passage into the street. Repentance and remorse drove him away from the throng.

CHAPTER 27

1. *When morning was come.* This was a formal meeting of the *e* San-hedrin, held to ratify what had been done at the earlier one and also to consider the execution of the sentence. The power of life and death was in the Roman authorities.

3. *Repented himself.* Judas repented, but not so as to change his character. The word used here signifies remorse, not the acceptance of new motives of action.

4. *What is that to us?* The question indicates an abrupt dismissal of Judas as of one who had been hired and paid for his crime, and therefore had no right to reproach his fellow-criminals. The chief priests and elders had done with Judas. His remorse was his

own affair, not theirs. But his appearance must have made them extremely uncomfortable. It was like a threat to reveal their complicity in a disgraceful plot. They wanted Jesus to be condemned by Pilate without inquiry. Had Judas been so minded, he might have made serious trouble for them with the Roman governor.

5. *Into the sanctuary.* The holy place where none but priests had a right to enter. *Went away and hanged himself.* This account of the end of Judas apparently differs in some respects from that given in Acts 1.18; but the two accounts are not necessarily inconsistent, although the materials for reconciling them are lacking.

7. *The potter's field.* According to tradition it was in the valley of Hinnom, south of Jerusalem.

9. *Through Jeremiah the prophet.* The quotation is from Zech. 11.12, 13; but it is said to be from Jeremiah because that prophet's name heads the list of prophetical books from which it was taken.

75

gave them for the potter's field, as the Lord appointed me.

11 Now Je'sus stood before the governor: and the governor asked him, saying, Art thou the King of the Jews? And Je'sus said unto him, **Thou sayest.** 12 And when he was accused by the chief priests and elders, he answered nothing. 13 Then saith Pi'late unto him, Hearest thou not how many things they witness against thee? 14 And he gave him no answer, not even to one word: insomuch that the governor marvelled greatly. 15 Now at ^{h}the feast the governor was wont to release unto the multitude one prisoner, whom they would. 16 And they had then a notable prisoner, called Bar-ab'bas. 17 When therefore they were gathered together, Pi'late said unto them, Whom will ye that I release unto you? Bar-ab'bas, or Je'sus who is called Christ? 18 For he knew that for envy they had delivered him up. 19 And while he was sitting on the judgment-seat, his wife sent unto him, saying, Have thou nothing to do with that righteous man; for I have suffered many things this day in a dream because of him. 20 Now the chief priests and the elders persuaded the multitudes that they should ask for Bar-ab'bas, and destroy Je'sus. 21 But the governor answered and said unto them, Which of the two will ye that I release unto you? And they said, Bar-ab'bas. 22 Pi'late saith unto them, What then shall I do unto Je'sus who is called Christ? They all say, Let him be crucified. 23 And he said, Why, what evil hath he done? But they cried out exceedingly, saying, Let him be crucified. 24 So when Pi'late saw that he prevailed nothing, but rather that a

---

^{h} Or, a feast

11. *Jesus stood before the governor.* The narrative of the trial before Pilate given by Matthew is practically the same as that by Mark. Luke and John, though substantially agreeing with the first two evangelists, add several features. Luke emphasizes the political charges, John the conversations between Jesus and Pilate. *Art thou the King of the Jews?* See Jn. 18. 33–37.

15. *Was wont to release.* A custom of the Feast of the Passover, which recalled the deliverance of the Jews from bondage. See Jn. 18.39. There is no known Jewish authority for the custom, even although it was in connection with the Passover; but it was probably established by Herod the Great in imitation of the Roman practice of liberating prisoners at certain festivals.

16. *Barabbas.* He had committed a murder during a political insurrection of which he was leader (Mk. 15.7; Lk. 23.19).

19. *His wife.* Claudia Procula or Procla was her name according to tradition. *In a dream because of him.* The dream of Pilate's wife is given by Matthew only.

20. *Persuaded the multitudes.* The chief priests and elders feared the popularity of Jesus, especially the Galileans. Hence they sought to discredit him with the people.

22. *Let him be crucified.* A brutal cry for vengeance. The Jewish leaders had been first in their desire to kill our Lord and now they had induced the mob, or the majority of the mob, to join them.

24. *Washed his hands.* This is only in Matthew. It was a Jewish custom which Pilate knew that all would understand.

tumult was arising, he took water, and washed his hands before the multitude, saying, I am innocent *of the blood of this righteous man; see ye *to it.* 25 And all the people answered and said, His blood *be* on us, and on our children. 26 Then released he unto them Barab'bas; but Je'sus he scourged and delivered to be crucified.

27 Then the soldiers of the governor took Je'sus into the *k*Præ-to'ri-um, and gathered unto him the whole *l*band. 28 And they *m*stripped him, and put on him a scarlet robe. 29 And they platted a crown of thorns and put it upon his head, and a reed in his right hand; and they kneeled down before him, and mocked him,

saying, Hail, King of the Jews! 30 And they spat upon him, and took the reed and smote him on the head. 31 And when they had mocked him, they took off from him the robe, and put on him his garments, and led him away to crucify him.

32 And as they came out, they found a man of Cy-re'ne, Si'mon by name: him they *n*compelled to go *with them,* that he might bear his cross.

33 And when they were come unto a place called Gol'go-tha, that is to say, The place of a skull, 34 they gave him wine to drink mingled with gall: and when he had tasted it, he would not drink. 35 And when they had crucified him, they parted his garments among them, cast-

---

i Some ancient authorities read *of this blood: see ye &c.*   *k* Or, *palace* See Mk.   15.16.   *l* Or, *cohort*   *m* Some ancient authorities read *clothed.*   *n* Gr. *impressed.*

---

25. *His blood be on us, and on our children.* They knew not what they said in uttering these words. In one sense the sufferings of the Jews ever since have been witness that the prophecy has been terribly fulfilled.

26. *Jesus he scourged.* That is, caused to be scourged. According to a Roman custom, scourging preceded crucifixion. The scourge was made of leather thongs, to which were attached sharp pieces of metal or other hard substance.

28. *A scarlet robe.* A sign of royalty. Mark and John call it purple.

29. *A reed.* A symbol of the kingly sceptre.

31. *To crucify him.* Crucifixion was the most painful and degrading form of punishment known. It was a custom of the Romans and was introduced by them among the Jews. The cross was commonly formed of two pieces of wood, one a pole or stake from nine to twelve feet long and fixed in the ground, the other shorter. The victim's hands were usually nailed to the

shorter piece and then he was raised and fastened to the upright stake. The suffering often lasted for days, death resulting from exhaustion. See Mk. 15.20, 21; Lk. 23.26–32; Jn. 19.16, 17.

32. *A man of Cyrene. Simon by name.* He was a Jew and the city from which he came was in North Africa. It contained a large colony of Jews. Simon was the father of Alexander and Rufus, afterwards known in the early church. *That he might bear his cross.* There is a tradition that our Lord fainted under his burden. Such may have been partly the effect of the scourging, when Simon was compelled to take up the cross. Mark would seem to indicate that Jesus was exhausted when brought to the place of crucifixion (Mk. 15.21–23).

33. *Golgotha.* Aramaic for skull. This name was given to it either because of the skulls found there, or because the shape of the hill was like that of a skull.

35. *When they had crucified him.* The cross on which our Lord suf-

ing lots; 36 and they sat and
watched him there. 37 And
they set up over his head his
accusation written, THIS IS
JE'SUS THE KING OF THE
JEWS. 38 Then are there crucified with him two robbers,
one on the right hand and one
on the left. 39 And they that
passed by railed on him, wagging their heads, 40 and saying,
Thou that destroyest the [o]tem-
ple, and buildest it in three
days, save thyself: if thou art
the Son of God, come down
from the cross. 41 In like manner also the chief priests mocking *him*, with the scribes and
elders, said, 42 He saved others;
[p]himself he cannot save. He is
the King of Is'ra-el; let him now
come down from the cross, and
we will believe on him. 43 He
trusteth on God; let him deliver
him now, if he desireth him:
for he said, I am the Son of God.
44 And the robbers also that
were crucified with him cast
upon him the same reproach.
45 Now from the sixth hour
there was darkness over all
the [q]land until the ninth hour.
46 And about the ninth hour
Je'sus cried with a loud voice,
saying, [r]**E'li, E'li, la'ma sa-bach-
tha'ni?** that is, My God, my God,
[s]why hast thou forsaken me?
47 And some of them that
stood there, when they heard
it, said, This man calleth
E-li'jah. 48 And straightway
one of them ran, and took a
sponge, and filled it with vinegar,
and put it on a reed, and gave him
to drink. 49 And the rest said,
Let be; let us see whether E-li'jah
cometh to save him.[t] 50 And
Je'sus cried again with a loud
voice, and yielded up his spirit.
51 And behold, the veil of the
[o]temple was rent in two from
the top to the bottom; and the

o Or, *sanctuary* *p* Or, *can he not save himself?* *q* Or, *earth* *r* Ps. xxii. 1. *s* Or, *why didst thou forsake me?* *t* Many ancient authorities add *And another took a spear and pierced his side, and there came out water and blood.* See Jn. 19.34.

fered was of the kind usually shown in illustrations, namely, that in which the shorter beam or stake crosses the longer at right angles and about half way between the top and the center. This is indicated by the fact that the inscription was put above his head. Christ was placed upon the cross at the third hour (Mk. 15.25), or nine o'clock in the morning. *They parted his garments*, etc. The garments of a victim of the death sentence were given to his executioners. Lots were cast because of the seamless coat which the Roman soldiers did not wish to rend (Jn. 19.24).

37. *His accusation written.* The name and crime of an accused person were written on a placard above his head. In the case of our Lord it was in Hebrew, Greek and Latin (Jn. 19.20).

40. *Thou that destroyest the temple.* See Jn. 2.21.

42. *King of Israel.* A title given to Jesus only here and in Mk. 15.32.

43. *He trusteth on God.* This is nearly identical with the language of Ps. 22.8.

45. *Now from the sixth hour.* From twelve or noon until three in the afternoon.

46. *Eli.* This is the Hebrew form; the Aramaic is given in Mk. 15.34. This is the fourth of the Seven Words from the cross. The first is from Lk. 23.34; the second, Lk. 23.43; the third, Jn. 19.26, 27; the fifth, Jn. 19.28; the sixth, Jn. 19.30; the seventh, Lk. 23.46; Ps. 31.5.

47. *Calleth Elijah.* This was probably spoken in derision.

earth did quake; and the rocks were rent; 52 and the tombs were opened; and many bodies of the saints that had fallen asleep were raised; 53 and coming forth out of the tombs after his resurrection they entered into the holy city and appeared unto many. 54 Now the centurion, and they that were with him watching Je'sus, when they saw the earthquake, and the things that were done, feared exceedingly, saying, Truly this was ᵘthe Son of God. 55 And many women were there beholding from afar, who had followed Je'sus from Gal'i-lee, ministering unto him: 56 among whom was Mary Mag-da-le'ne, and Mary the mother of ᵛJames and Jo'ses, and the mother of the sons of Zeb'e-dee.

57 And when even was come, there came a rich man from Ar-i-ma-thæ'a, named Joseph, who also himself was Je'sus' disciple: 58 this man went to Pi'late, and asked for the body of Je'sus. Then Pi'late commanded it to be given up. 59 And Joseph took the body,

and wrapped it in a clean linen cloth, 60 and laid it in his own new tomb, which he had hewn out in the rock: and he rolled a great stone to the door of the tomb, and departed. 61 And Mary Mag-da-le'ne was there, and the other Mary, sitting over against the sepulchre.

62 Now on the morrow, which is *the day* after the Preparation, the chief priests and the Phar'i-sees were gathered together unto Pi'late, 63 saying, Sir, we remember that that deceiver said while he was yet alive, After three days I rise again. 64 Command therefore that the sepulchre be made sure until the third day, lest haply his disciples come and steal him away, and say unto the people, He is risen from the dead: and the last error will be worse than the first. 65 Pi'late said unto them, ˣYe have a guard: go, ᵛmake it *as* sure as ye can. 66 So they went, and made the sepulchre sure, sealing the stone, the guard being with them.

28 Now late on the sabbath day, as it began to dawn

ᵘ Or. *a son of God*   ᵛ Or, *Jacob*   ˣ Or.   *Take a guard*   ᵞ Gr. *make it sure, as ye know.*

51. *Rent in two.* The veil between the holy place and the holy of holies. See Heb. 10.19, 20.

53. *After his resurrection.* Though the tombs had been opened by the earthquake, the dead did not rise from them until after the resurrection of Jesus.

54. *The centurion.* He commanded the four Roman soldiers who were the guard at the crucifixion. See Lk. 23.47. *Mary Magdalene.* The same who had been cured of demoniacal possession (Lk. 8.2). See Mk. 15.40, 41; Jn. 19.25.

57. *A rich man from Arimathæa, named Joseph.* A secret follower

of Jesus who was a member of the Sanhedrin, but had not taken any part in condemning his Master (Lk. 23.50, 51).

60. *Rolled a great stone.* Nicodemus helped Joseph in this (Jn. 19.39–42).

61. *The other Mary.* The mother of Joses and James the Less (Mk. 15.47).

62. *The Preparation.* Friday, the day before the Sabbath.

64. *Error.* Deceit.

CHAPTER 28

1. *As it began to dawn.* At sunrise (Mk. 16.2).

toward the first *day* of the week, came Mary Mag-da-le'ne and the other Mary to see the sepulchre. 2 And behold, there was a great earthquake, for an angel of the Lord descended from heaven, and came and rolled away the stone, and sat upon it. 3 His appearance was as lightning, and his raiment white as snow: 4 and for fear of him the watchers did quake, and became as dead men. 5 And the angel answered and said unto the women, Fear not ye; for I know that ye seek Je'sus, who hath been crucified. 6 He is not here; for he is risen, even as he said. Come, see the place *a*where the Lord lay. 7 And go quickly, and tell his disciples, He is risen from the dead; and lo, he goeth before you into Gal'i-lee; there shall ye see him: lo, I have told you. 8 And they departed quickly from the tomb with fear and

great joy, and ran to bring his disciples word. 9 And behold, Je'sus met them, saying, All hail. And they came and took hold of his feet, and *b*worshipped him. 10 Then saith Je'sus unto them, Fear not: go tell my brethren that they depart into Gal'i-lee, and there shall they see me.

11 Now while they were going, behold, some of the guard came into the city, and told unto the chief priests all the things that were come to pass. 12 And when they were assembled with the elders, and had taken counsel, they gave much money unto the soldiers, 13 saying, Say ye, His disciples came by night, and stole him away while we slept. 14 And if this *c*come to the governor's ears, we will persuade him, and rid you of care. 15 So they took the money, and did as they were taught: and this saying

---

a Many ancient authorities read *where he lay.*   *b* See marginal note on ch. 2.2.

c Or, *come to a hearing before the governor*

2. *A great earthquake.* Mentioned only by Matthew. *An angel of the Lord.* See Lk. 24.4; Jn. 20.12.

4. *The watchers.* The guard of soldiers.

6. *He is not here, for he is risen.* This was clear and decisive as well as joyful news to the wondering women. The accounts of the other evangelists show that it was hard to convince some of the saddened followers of the Lord that he was indeed risen. See Jn. 20.2, 15; 25–29; Lk. 24.34–43.

7. *He goeth before you into Galilee.* Jesus had promised this to his disciples (Mk. 14.28).

8. *Ran to bring his disciples word.* The sequence of events concerning the appearance of Jesus to the women was probably as follows: After Mary Magdalene and the other Mary had been spoken to by

the angel they ran to tell the disciples. Peter and John hurried to the tomb and returned. Then Mary Magdalene, who had also returned to the tomb, lingered after they departed and did not know Jesus when she saw him, mistaking him for the gardener; then Jesus appeared to Mary Magdalene a second time, when she was with other women.

10. *Go tell my brethren that they depart into Galilee.* Tell them of my resurrection in order that they may prepare to meet me in Galilee according to my words.

12. *They gave much money unto the soldiers.* The bribery of the guard by the chief priests and elders is told only by Matthew.

14. *We will persuade him.* In the same way as they had persuaded the soldiers—by bribes.

was spread abroad among the Jews, *and continueth* until this day.

16 But the eleven disciples went into Gal'i-lee, unto the mountain where Je'sus had appointed them. 17 And when they saw him, they [d] worshipped *him*; but some doubted. 18 And Je'sus came to them and spake unto them, saying, **All** authority hath been given unto me in heaven and on earth. 19 Go ye therefore, and make disciples of all the nations, baptizing them into the name of the Father and of the Son and of the Holy Spirit: 20 teaching them to observe all things whatsoever I commanded you: and lo, I am with you [e]always, even unto the [f]end of the world.

---

[d] See marginal note on ch. 2.2.   [e] Gr. *all* the days.   [f] Or, *the consummation of the age.*

16. *Unto the mountain.* It was probably near Capernaum. Not only the eleven, but all the disciples of Jesus who were told of his resurrection were most likely gathered there. It has been held that the words 'my brethren' in ver. 10 apply generally to all the disciples who could be assembled to meet the Lord. This appearance of Jesus is therefore that mentioned in 1 Cor. 15.6.

18. *All authority hath been given* unto me. A sublime affirmation of the victory won through his resurrection.

20. *Lo, I am with you always.* Jesus after his resurrection had proved by his different appearances how he could be with his disciples and yet unseen by them. After he had triumphed over death they could not doubt his promise to be with them at all times, even unto the end of their lives and of the world.

CALENDAR (JEWISH).

BY PROFESSOR JOHN D. DAVIS, PRINCETON.

MONTH.	NEARLY.	FESTIVAL.	SEASON.
1. ABIB or NISAN. (Ex. 23. 15 ; Neh. 2. 1.)	April.	14. Passover (Ex. 12. 18, 19 ; 13. 3-10) introducing	Latter or spring rains. Jordan in flood (Josh. 3. 15).
		15-21. Feast of Unleavened Bread (Lev. 23. 6).	Barley ripe in lowlands.
		16. Sheaf of firstfruits of the harvest presented (Lev. 23. 10-14 ; cf. Josh. 5. 11).	Wheat partly in ear.
2. ZIV or IYAR.* 1 Kings 6. 1, 37.)	May.		Early figs in the mountains of Northern Galilee.
		14. Passover for those who could not keep the regular one (Num. 9. 10, 11).	Barley harvest in the hill country.
			Wheat harvest in the lower districts.
3. SIVAN. (Esth. 8. 9.)	June.	6. Pentecost, or Feast of Weeks, or of Harvest, or Day of Firstfruits. Loaves as firstfruits of gathered harvest presented (Ex. 23. 16 ; 34. 22 ; Lev. 23. 17, 20 ; Num. 28. 26 ; Deut. 16. 9, 10).	Apples on sea-coast. Almonds ripe.
4. TAMMUZ.*	July.		Dry season from late April to early October. Wheat harvest in higher mountains.
5. AB.*	August.		First ripe grapes.
6. ELUL. (Neh. 6. 15.)	September.		Olives in the lowlands. Summer figs.
7. ETHANIM or TISHRI.* (1 Kings 8. 2.)	October.	1. Feast of Trumpets (Num. 29. 1).	Grape-gathering general.
		10. Day of Atonement (Lev. 16. 29).	Pomegranates ripe.
		15-21. Feast of Ingathering or Tabernacles. Firstfruits of wine and oil (Ex. 23. 16 ; Lev. 23. 34 ; Deut. 16. 13).	Season changing to winter (*Antiq.* III. x. 4). Former or early rains begin.
		22. Great day (Lev. 23. 36 ; Num. 29. 35 ; Neh. 8. 18 ; John 7. 37).	Ploughing and sowing.
8. BUL or MARCHESH-VAN.* (1 Kings 6. 38.)	November.		Olives gathered in Northern Galilee.
9. CHISLEU. (Zech. 7. 1.)	December.	25. Feast of Dedication (1. Macc. 4. 52 ; John 10. 22).	Winter figs on the trees.
10. TEBETH. (Esth. 2. 16.)	January.		Hail. Snow on higher hills, and occasionally at Jerusalem. In the lowlands grain-fields and green pastures, wild flowers abundant.
11. SHEBAT. (Zech. 1. 7.)	February.		
12. ADAR. (Esth. 3. 7.)	March.		Oranges and lemons ripe in the lowlands.
		14, 15. Feast of Purim (Esth. 9. 21-28).	Barley ripe at Jericho.

* Name does not occur in the Bible.

THE GOSPEL ACCORDING TO MARK

INTRODUCTION BY PROFESSOR M. B. RIDDLE, D.D., LL.D.

The Writer.—Mark, or John Mark (Acts 12.12, 25; 15.37), was the son of Mary, at whose house in Jerusalem the early Christians seem to have found a home (Acts 12.12). Probably a native of that city, possibly the "young man" present at the capture of Jesus (Mark 14. 51, 52), he was undoubtedly a cousin of Barnabas (Col. 4.10, *A . S . V .*), and the attendant of the two Christian preachers in Paul's first missionary journey. But he became the occasion of "sharp contention" between Paul and Barnabas (Acts 15. 36-40), in consequence of his leaving them at Perga. Afterwards, however, he was with the apostle Paul during his first imprisonment at Rome (Col. 4.10; Philem. 24). The apostle Peter refers to Mark as with him when he wrote his first epistle, probably at Babylon. Evidently the evangelist made a journey to the east about 63 A.D., and he was at Ephesus with Timothy shortly before the death of Paul (2 Tim. 4.11). Trustworthy details of his later life are wanting. He is spoken of as the "interpreter" of Peter, and, according to tradition, was the founder of the Church at Alexandria.

Design and Character of the Gospel.—The presence in this Gospel of Latin terms and also of Aramaic words, which are translated into Greek, points to a Gentile circle of readers, probably in Rome, as is generally held. It exhibits Christ in His power, as a worker of miracles, producing amazement and fear. The discourses are reported very briefly; events are noted in their exact sequence; many vivid details of gesture and action are introduced. All these peculiarities suggest that an eye-witness was the source of information. From the days of Papias it has been believed that Peter was this source, and internal phenomena favor this view. No direct supervision by that apostle can be affirmed, though Eusebius asserts, on the authority of Clement of Alexandria, that it was submitted to him for approval.

This Gospel contains few passages (two miracles, one parable, and the story of the young man near Gethsemane) peculiar to itself, but many details are mentioned which are not found elsewhere. Our Lord's gestures are noted; prominence is given to His power over evil spirits; the withdrawals are more frequently indicated.

The style is vivacious; the present tense is often used in narrative; the word "straightway" occurs more than forty times. This Gospel could not have been an abridgment of that of Matthew, since it bears all the marks of originality.

Time and Place of Writing.—Early tradition assigns Rome as the place, and this accords with the fact that Mark was in that city at the time of Paul's imprisonment. The *date* was certainly

before the destruction of Jerusalem, probably before the death of
Peter and Paul. As Mark seems to have been with the apostle
Peter about 62 A.D., the Gospel may have been written immediately after, between 63-66 A.D., internal evidence pointing to the
earlier date. Some authorities agree, however, that the Gospel
according to Mark was written before the narratives of Matthew
and Luke.

Summary.—Omitting all reference to the early history of our
Lord, the Gospel begins with the appearance of John the Baptist.

1. The preaching of the forerunner (1.1-8).
2. The baptism and temptation (1.9-13).
3. The early ministry in Galilee (1.14 to 6.13).

Here the order is chronological, with the exception of 2.15-22,
which, in order of time, should be placed between 5.21 and 22.

4. From the death of John the Baptist to the close of the Galilæan ministry (6.14 to 9.50).
5. The close of the Peræan ministry and the final journey to
Jerusalem (10).
6. The final conflicts at Jerusalem (11-13).
7. The Passover, and subsequent events in Gethsemane; the
death and burial (14, 15).
8. The resurrection (16).

The passage 16.9-20 stands in a peculiar relation to the preceding narrative. It is not found in the two earliest manuscripts;
and while it presents an authentic statement of facts, there is a
strong probability that it was not written by Mark as a conclusion
to the Gospel.

ACCORDING TO MARK

1 The beginning of the *a*gospel of Je′sus Christ, *b*the Son of God.

2 Even as it is written *c*in I-sa′iah the prophet,

*d*Behold, I send my messenger before thy face,

Who shall ′prepare thy way;

3 *e*The voice of one crying in the wilderness,

Make ye ready the way of the Lord,

Make his paths straight;

4 John came, who baptized in the wilderness and preached the baptism of repentance unto remission of sins. 5 And there went out unto him all the country of Ju-dæ′a, and all they of Je-ru′sa-lem; and they were baptized of him in the river Jordan, confessing their sins. 6 And John was clothed with camel's hair, and *had* a leathern girdle about his loins, and did eat locusts and wild honey. 7 And he preached, saying, There cometh after me he that is mightier than I, the latchet of whose shoes I am not *f*worthy to stoop down and unloose. 8 I baptized you *g*in water: but he shall baptize you *g*in the Holy Spirit.

9 And it came to pass in those days, that Je′sus camé from Naz′a-reth of Gal′i-lee, and was baptized of John *h*in the Jordan. 10 And straightway coming up out of the water, he saw the heavens rent asunder, and the Spirit as a dove descending upon him: 11 and a voice came out of the heavens, Thou art my beloved Son, in thee I am well pleased.

12 And straightway the Spirit driveth him forth into the wilderness. 13 And he was in the wilderness forty days tempted

---

a Or, *good tidings*: and so elsewhere.
b Some ancient authorities omit *the Son of God*. c Some ancient authorities read *in*
the prophets. d Mal. iii. 1. e Is. xl. 3
f Gr. *sufficient*. g Or, *with* h Gr. *into*.

CHAPTER 1

1. *The beginning.* The opening of Mark's narrative is not concerned with the birth and genealogy of Jesus but with his public ministry. *Son of God.* Mark wrote for the Gentiles; Matthew for the Jews. Hence the latter sought to prove the Davidic descent of our Lord. Mark in describing Jesus as the Son of God has the point of view of directly presenting him as the Saviour of the world.

4. *In the wilderness.* Between Hebron and the Dead Sea.

5. *All the country.* All classes of the people: Pharisees and Sadducees (Mt. 3.7.), publicans or tax-collectors (Lk. 3.12.), rich and poor (Lk. 3. 10.) and soldiers (Lk. 3.14.).

10. *He saw.* While praying (Lk. 3. 21).

13. *Tempted of Satan.* 'Satan'

85

of Satan; and he was with the wild beasts; and the angels ministered unto him.

14 Now after John was delivered up, Je′sus came into Gal′ilee, preaching the *gospel of God, 15 and saying, **The time is fulfilled, and the kingdom of God is at hand: repent ye, and believe in the** *gospel.

16 And passing along by the sea of Gal′i-lee, he saw Si′mon and Andrew the brother of Si′mon casting a net in the sea; for they were fishers. 17 And Je′sus said unto them, **Come ye after me, and I will make you to become fishers of men.** 18 And straightway they left the nets, and followed him. 19 And going on a little further, he saw *k*James the *son* of Zeb′edee, and John his brother, who also were in the boat mending

the nets. 20 And straightway he called them: and they left their father Zeb′e-dee in the boat with the hired servants, and went after him.

21 And they go into Ca-per′na-um; and straightway on the sabbath day he entered into the synagogue and taught. 22 And they were astonished at his teaching: for he taught them as having authority, and not as the scribes. 23 And straightway there was in their synagogue a man with an unclean spirit; and he cried out, 24 saying, What have we to do with thee, Je′sus thou Naz-a-rene′? art thou come to destroy us? I know thee who thou art, the Holy One of God. 25 And Je′sus rebuked *l*him, saying, **Hold thy peace and come out of him.** 26 And the unclean

---

i Or, *good tidings*: and so elsewhere. *k* Or, *Jacob*   *l* Or, *it*

means enemy. In Matthew and Luke he was tempted of the 'devil,' which word means slanderer or false accuser. *With the wild beasts.* This feature of the temptation is mentioned by Mark only.

.14. *Was delivered up.* Imprisoned by Herod. See ch. 6.17. *Came into Galilee.* The opening of the Galilean ministry.

16. *The sea of Galilee.* Its other names are the Sea of Tiberias and the Lake of Gennesaret. In the Old Testament it is called the Sea of Chinnereth or Cinneroth. It is twelve and three-fourths miles long by seven and a half miles wide. The water is fresh and clear and fish abound. The sea is notable for its low level, being 682.5 feet beneath that of the Mediterranean. It is liable to sudden and violent storms. *Simon.* Afterwards called Peter. It is significant that Peter's call to be a disciple of Jesus is recorded thus early by Mark. This gospel was founded mainly on Peter's reminiscences. Peter and his brother

Andrew lived at Bethsaida on the north shore of the Sea of Galilee. See Mt. 4.18–22.

19. *With the hired servants.* Zebedee was not a poor man. It is a mistake to suppose that the occupation of a fisherman in Galilee in the time of Christ indicated any unusual poverty or ignorance.

21. *Capernaum.* See note on Mt. 4.13.

22. *As having authority.* The teaching of Jesus completely reversed the method of the scribes. The latter narrowly interpreted the letter of the law; Jesus affirmed principles by which even the law itself was to be judged. See note on Mt. 7.29.

23. *Their synagogue.* See note on Mt. 4.23. *A man with an unclean spirit.* Literally, in an unclean spirit. In Luke he is spoken of as having the spirit of an unclean demon (4.33).

24. *I know thee.* A clear recognition of Jesus as the Messiah.

spirit, [m]tearing him and crying with a loud voice, came out of him. 27 And they were all amazed, insomuch that they questioned among themselves, saying, What is this? a new teaching! with authority he commandeth even the unclean spirits, and they obey him. 28 And the report of him went out straightway everywhere into all the region of Gal'i-lee round about.

29 And straightway, [n]when they are come out of the synagogue, they came into the house of Si'mon and Andrew, with [o]James and John. 30 Now Si'mon's wife's mother lay sick of a fever; and straightway they tell him of her: 31 and he came and took her by the hand, and raised her up; and the fever left her, and she ministered unto them.

32 And at even, when the sun did set, they brought unto him all that were sick, and them that were [p]possessed with de-

mons. 33 And all the city was gathered together at the door. 34 And he healed many that were sick with divers diseases, and cast out many demons; and he suffered not the demons to speak, because they knew him[q].

35 And in the morning, a great while before day, he rose up and went out, and departed into a desert place, and there prayed. 36 And Si'mon and they that were with him followed after him; 37 and they found him, and say unto him, All are seeking thee. 38 And he saith unto them, **Let us go elsewhere into the next towns, that I may preach there also; for to this end came I forth.** 39 And he went into their synagogues throughout all Gal'i-lee, preaching and casting out demons.

40 And there cometh to him a leper, beseeching him, [r]and kneeling down to him, and saying unto him, If thou wilt,

m Or, *convulsing*. n Some ancient authorities read *when he was come out of the synagogue, he came &c.* o Or, *Jacob* p Or, *demoniacs* q Many ancient authorities add *to be Christ.* See Lk. 4.41. r Some ancient authorities omit *and kneeling down to him.*

29. *They.* The four who had been called (ver. 16–20).

30. *Sick of a fever.* A dangerous and violent malady, as seems to be indicated by Lk. 4.38.

32. *When the sun did set.* After the heat of the day when the sick could be brought more comfortably to Jesus.

33. *At the door.* Of Peter's house. Peter and his brother Andrew, whose permanent home was Bethsaida, were at that time living in Capernaum.

35. *A great while before day.* At the earliest dawn. *Into a desert place, and there prayed.* A season of solitary communion with God naturally following a day of self-denying labor. It was our Lord's habit to prepare by prayer for the work that lay before him. Many of these holy

seasons of quiet were spent by him around the shores of the Sea of Galilee, where desert places were near.

38. *Into the next towns.* At this time there was a crowded population in Galilee. The towns and cities were numerous. Chorazin, Bethsaida, Magdala and many other populous places were not far from Capernaum. Jesus could not submit to excessive calls upon his miraculous powers at any one place when multitudes elsewhere needed his preaching. *For to this end came I forth.* Note the emphasis of his preaching, a greater work than performing miracles.

40. *There cometh to him a leper.* In the East leprosy was the most terrible of diseases, incurable then as now. The nature of his affliction compelled him to wander about

thou canst make me clean.
41 And being moved with compassion, he stretched forth his hand, and touched him, and saith unto him, I will; be thou made clean. 42 And straightway the leprosy departed from him, and he was made clean. 43 And he *strictly charged him, and straightway sent him out, 44 and saith unto him, See thou say nothing to any man: but go show thyself to the priest, and offer for thy cleansing the things which Mo'ses 'commanded, for a testimony unto them. 45 But he went out, and began to publish it much, and to spread abroad the "matter, insomuch that "Je'sus could no more openly enter into ᶻa city, but was without in desert places: and they came to him from every quarter.

2 And when he entered again into Ca-per'na-um after some days, it was noised that he was ᵃin the house, 2 And many were gathered together, so that there was no longer room for them, no, not even about the door: and he spake the word unto them. 3 And they come,

bringing unto him a man sick of the palsy, borne of four. 4 And when they could not ᵇcome nigh unto him for the crowd, they uncovered the roof where he was: and when they had broken it up, they let down the ᶜbed whereon the sick of the palsy lay. 5 And Je'sus seeing their faith saith unto the sick of the palsy, ᵈSon, thy sins are forgiven. 6 But there were certain of the scribes sitting there, and reasoning in their hearts, 7 Why doth this man thus speak? he blasphemeth: who can forgive sins but one, even God? 8 And straightway Je'sus perceiving in his spirit that they so reasoned within themselves, saith unto them, Why reason ye these things in your hearts? 9 Which is easier, to say to the sick of the palsy, Thy sins are forgiven; or to say, Arise, and take up thy ᶜbed, and walk? 10 But that ye may know that the Son of man hath authority on earth to forgive sins (he saith to the sick of the palsy), 11 I say unto thee, Arise, take up thy ᶜbed, and go unto thy house. 12 And he

---

s Or, sternly   t Lev. xiii. 49; xiv. 2 ff.
u Gr. word.   v Gr. he.   x Or, the city
a Or, at home

b Many ancient authorities read bring him unto him.   c Or, pallet   d Gr. Child.

---

alone, shunned like a wild beast. See note on Mt. 8.2-4.

45. Began to publish it much. The astounding cure of the leper could not be kept secret, and the news spread so rapidly that the eager crowds made it appear as if some political agitator required the notice of the authorities. Jesus wished to avoid this, as at that time Galilee was in a turbulent and rebellious condition.

CHAPTER 2

2. Spake the word. Was teaching.

4. Uncovered the roof. The dwelling houses of Palestine usually had a flight of stone steps built on the outside and leading to the roof. In this case the four who carried the paralytic in his bed up to the roof lifted enough of the thin stone tiling to lower the bed through the opening.

5. Thy sins are forgiven. See note on Mt. 9.2-5.

12. Before them all. As if the crowd had been awed by the miracle that had been performed and in-

arose, and straightway took up the *e*bed, and went forth before them all; insomuch that they were all amazed, and glorified God, saying, We never saw it on this fashion.

13 And he went forth again by the sea side; and all the multitude resorted unto him, and he taught them. 14 And as he passed by, he saw Le'vi the *son* of Al-phæ'us sitting at the place of toll and he saith unto him, **Follow me.** And he arose and followed him.

15 And it came to pass, that he was sitting at meat in his house, and many *f*publicans and sinners sat down with Je'sus and his disciples: for there were many, and they followed him. 16 And the scribes *g*of the Phar'i-sees, when they saw that he was eating with the sinners and *f*publicans, said unto his disciples, *hHow is it* that he eateth *i*and drinketh with *f*publicans and sinners? 17 And

when Je'sus heard it, he saith unto them, **They that are *k*whole have no need of a physician, but they that are sick: I came not to call the righteous, but sinners.**

18 And John's disciples and the Phar'i-sees were fasting: and they come and say unto him, Why do John's disciples and the disciples of the Phar'i-sees fast, but thy disciples fast not? 19 And Je'sus said unto them, **Can the *l*sons of the bridechamber fast, while the bridegroom is with them? as long as they have the bridegroom with them, they cannot fast. 20 But the days will come when the bridegroom shall be taken away from them, and then will they fast in that day. 21 No man seweth a piece of undressed cloth on an old garment: else that which should fill it up taketh from it, the new from the old, and a worse rent is made. 22 And no man put-**

---

e Or, *pallet* *f* That is, *collectors or renters of Roman taxes. g* Some ancient authorities read *and the Pharisees. h* Or, *He eateth . . .*

sinners. i Some ancient authorities omit *and drinketh. k* Gr. *strong. l* That is, *companions of the bridegroom.*

stinctively made way for the healed man. *On this fashion.* Jesus had astonished the crowd by healing the paralytic; but more especially were the scribes confounded by his assumption of the power to forgive sins. He challenged them to deny this, in effect declaring that it was as easy for him to forgive sins as it was to cure disease.

14. *Levi.* See note on Mt. 9.9. 'Matthew', or 'Mattathias', means the gift of God.

15. *Many publicans and sinners.* Matthew himself having been a publican, it was natural that publicans should be among his guests. Their reputation may be guessed from the fact that they and sinners are mentioned in the same breath.

The publicans here spoken of were the lesser native collectors of taxes, subject to Roman officials. They were notorious for merciless greed.

16. *Said unto his disciples,* etc. It was significant that this objection by the scribes was made to the disciples and not to their Master. Jesus had just vindicated his claims in a manner that discouraged interference. It was easier to annoy his disciples.

18. *John's disciples and the Pharisees.* See note on Mt. 9.14.

19. *While the bridegroom is with them.* See note on Mt. 9.15.

20. *Then will they fast.* See note on Mt. 9.15.

21. *Undressed cloth.* See note on Mt. 9.16.

teth new wine into old ᵐwine-skins; else the wine will burst the skins, and the wine perisheth, and the skins: but *they put* new wine into fresh wine-skins.

23 And it came to pass, that he was going on the sabbath day through the grainfields; and his disciples ⁿbegan, as they went, to pluck the ears. 24 And the Phar′i-sees said unto him, Behold, why do they on the sabbath day that which is not lawful? 25 And he said unto them, ᵒDid ye never read what David did, when he had need, and was hungry, he, and they that were with him? 26 How he entered into the house of God ᵖwhen A-bi′a-thar was high priest, and ate the show-bread, which it is not lawful to eat save for the priests, and gave also to them that were with him? 27 And he said unto them, The sabbath was made for man, and not man for the sabbath: 28 so that the Son of man is lord even of the sabbath.

3 And he entered again into the synagogue; and there was a man there who had his hand withered. 2 And they watched him, whether he would heal him on the sabbath day; that they might accuse him. 3 And he saith unto the man that had his hand withered, ᵃStand forth. 4 And he saith unto them, **Is it lawful on the sabbath day to do good, or to do harm? to save a life, or to kill?** But they held their peace. 5 And when he had looked round about on them with anger, being grieved at the hardening of their heart, he saith unto the man, **Stretch forth thy hand.** And he stretched it forth; and his hand was restored. 6 And the Phar′i-sees went out, and straightway with the He-ro′di-ans took counsel against him, how they might destroy him.

7 And Je′sus with his disciples withdrew to the sea: and a great multitude from Gal′i-lee followed; and from Ju-dæ′a, 8 and from Je-ru′sa-lem, and

---

m That is, *skins used as bottles.*   *n* Gr. *began to make their way plucking.*   *o* 1 S. xxi. 6.   *p* Some ancient authorities read *in the days of Abiathar the high priest.*   *a* Gr. *Arise into the midst.*

---

25. *What David did.* See note on Mt. 12.3.

26. *The showbread.* See note on Mt. 12.4.

CHAPTER 3

1. *A man there who had his hand withered.* Luke says it was his right hand (ch. 6.6).

2. *They watched him.* They had followed and closely observed him for some time with the design of securing grounds of legal accusation against him.

5. *Looked round about on them with anger.* Implying a deliberate and penetrating gaze that was intended for each and all. The anger

was that of holy indignation deeply touched with grief. *Being grieved.* Though righteously angry, our Lord yet had the deepest compassion for their hardness of heart, a condition more hopeless than they realized.

6. *With the Herodians took counsel.* The Herodians were political adherents of Herod the Great and his successors. The Pharisees were bitterly hostile to them, and the willingness of the former to join thus with their enemies shows how deep was their hatred of Jesus.

7. *Withdrew.* See note on Mt. 12.15.

8. *Idumæa.* The district south of Judæa and the Dead Sea. *Be-*

from Id-u-mæ'a, and beyond the Jordan, and about Tyre and Si'don, a great multitude, hearing [b]what great things he did, came unto him. 9 And he spake to his disciples, that a little boat should wait on him because of the crowd, lest they should throng him: 10 for he had healed many; insomuch that as many as had [c]plagues [d]pressed upon him that they might touch him. 11 And the unclean spirits, whensoever they beheld him, fell down before him, and cried, saying, Thou art the Son of God. 12 And he charged them much that they should not make him known.

13 And he goeth up into the mountain, and calleth unto him whom he himself would; and they went unto him. 14 And he appointed twelve,[e] that they might be with him, and that he might send them forth to preach, 15 and to have authority to cast out demons: 16 [f]and Si'mon he surnamed Peter; 17 and [g]James the son of Zeb'e-dee, and John the brother of [g]James; and them he surnamed Bo-a-ner'ges, which is, Sons of thunder: 18 and Andrew, and Philip, and Bar-thol'o-mew, and Mat'thew, and Thomas, and [g]James the son of Al-phæ'us, and Thaddæ'us, and Si'mon the [h]Ca-nanæ'an, 19 and Ju'das Is-car'i-ot, who also [i]betrayed him.

And he cometh [k]into a house. 20 And the multitude cometh together again, so that they could not so much as eat bread. 21 And when his friends heard it, they went out to lay hold on him: for they said, He is beside himself. 22 And the scribes that came down from Je-ru'salem said, He hath [l]Be-el'ze-bub, and, [m]By the prince of the demons casteth he out the demons. 23 And he called them unto him, and said unto them in parables, **How can Satan cast out Satan? 24 And if a kingdom be divided against itself, that kingdom cannot stand. 25 And**

---

b Or, *all the things that he did   c* Gr. *scourges.   d* Gr. *fell.   e* Some ancient authorities add *whom also he named apostles.* See Lk. 6.13; comp. ch. 6.30.   *f* Some

yond Jordan. This district was Gentile with a mixed population.

11. *Thou art the Son of God.* The Messiah. *That they should not make him known.* The fame of his teaching and miracles had so spread that the people were likely to be attracted to him as a political deliverer. The thought of Jesus was far from this. Besides, he was about to appoint the twelve apostles.

17. *Boanerges.* James and John were men of exceptional force of character and eloquence. The former was sometimes called James the Great.

18. *Bartholomew.* Nathanael of Cana of Galilee (Jn. 1.45; 21.2). *The son of Alphæus.* James the son

ancient authorities insert *and he appointed twelve.   g* Or, *Jacob   h* Or, *Zealot.* See Lk. 6.15; Acts. 1.13.   *i* Or, *delivered him up   k* Or, *home   l* Gr. *Beelzebul.   m* Or, *In*

of Alphæus was called James the Less or the Little. *Thaddæus.* This was his surname. In Luke he is mentioned as Judas the son of James (ch. 6.16).

20. *So much as eat bread.* This is a graphic detail that was most probably taken by Mark from Peter's reminiscences.

21. *He is beside himself.* His friends thought that his excessive zeal in his work was likely to deprive him of self-control.

22. *The scribes.* The same enemies who had been watching him for days. *The prince of the demons.* See note on Mt. 12.24.

24. *If a kingdom be divided against itself.* See note on Mt. 12.25.

if a house be divided against itself, that house will not be able to stand. 26 And if Satan hath risen up against himself, and is divided, he cannot stand, but hath an end. 27 But no one can enter into the house of the strong *man*, and spoil his goods, except he first bind the strong *man*; and then he will spoil his house. 28 Verily I say unto you, All their sins shall be forgiven unto the sons of men, and their blasphemies wherewith soever they shall blaspheme: 29 but whosoever shall blaspheme against the Holy Spirit hath never forgiveness, but is guilty of an eternal sin: 30 because they said, He hath an unclean spirit.

31 And there come his mother and his brethren; and, standing without, they sent unto him, calling him. 32 And a multitude was sitting about him; and they say unto him, Behold, thy mother and thy brethren without seek for thee. 33 And he answereth them, and saith, Who is my mother and my brethren? 34 And looking round on them that sat round about him, he saith, Behold, my mother and my brethren! 35 For whosoever shall do the will of God, the same is my brother, and sister, and mother.

4 And again he began to teach by the sea side. And there is gathered unto him a very great multitude, so that he entered into a boat, and sat in the sea; and all the multitude were by the sea on the land. 2 And he taught them many things in parables, and said unto them in his teaching, 3 Hearken: Behold, the sower went forth to sow: 4 and it came to pass, as he sowed, some *seed* fell by the way side, and the birds came and devoured it. 5 And other fell on the rocky *ground*, where it had not much earth; and straightway it sprang up, because it had no deepness of earth: 6 and when the sun was risen, it was scorched: and because it had no root, it withered away. 7 And other fell among the thorns, and the thorns grew up, and choked it, and it yielded no fruit. 8 And others fell into the good ground, and yielded fruit, growing up and increasing; and brought forth, thirtyfold, and sixtyfold, and a hundredfold. 9 And he said, Who hath ears to hear let him hear.

10 And when he was alone, they that were about him with the twelve asked of him the parables. 11 And he said unto them, Unto you is given the mystery of the kingdom of God: but unto them that are without, all things are done in parables: 12 that seeing they may see, and not perceive; and hearing they

27. *Except he first bind the strong man.* See note on Mt. 12.29.

29. *Shall blaspheme against the Holy Spirit.* See note on Mt. 12.31.

31. *His brethren.* See ch. 6.3; Mt. 13.55.

35. *For whosoever shall do the will of God.* See note on Mt. 12.50.

CHAPTER 4

2. *Many things in parables.* See notes on Mt. 13.3.

3. *The sower.* See notes on Mt.13.3.

11. *The mystery of the kingdom of God.* See note on Mt. 13.11.

12. *That seeing they may see.* 'See-

may hear, and not understand; lest haply they should turn again, and it should be forgiven them. 13 And he saith unto them, Know ye not this parable? and how shall ye know all the parables? 14 The sower soweth the word. 15 And these are they by the way side, where the word is sown; and when they have heard, straightway cometh Satan, and taketh away the word which hath been sown in them. 16 And these in like manner are they that are sown upon the rocky *places*, who, when they have heard the word, straightway receive it with joy; 17 and they have no root in themselves, but endure for a while; then, when tribulation or persecution ariseth because of the word, straightway they stumble. 18 And others are they that are sown among the thorns; these are they that have heard the word, 19 and the cares of the *a*world, and the deceitfulness of riches, and the lusts of other things entering in, choke the word, and it becometh unfruitful. 20 And those are they that were sown upon the good ground;

such as hear the word, and accept it, and bear fruit, thirty-fold, and sixtyfold, and a hundredfold.

21 And he said unto them, Is the lamp brought to be put under the bushel, or under the bed, *and* not to be put on the stand? 22 For there is nothing hid, save that it should be manifested; neither was *anything* made secret, but that it should come to light. 23 If any man hath ears to hear, let him hear. 24 And he said unto them, Take heed what ye hear: with what measure ye mete it shall be measured unto you; and more shall be given unto you. 25 For he that hath, to him shall be given: and he that hath not, from him shall be taken away even that which he hath.

26 And he said, So is the kingdom of God, as if a man should cast seed upon the earth; 27 and should sleep and rise night and day, and the seed should spring up and grow, he knoweth not how. 28 The earth *b*beareth fruit of herself; first the blade, then the ear, then the full grain in the ear. 29 But

---

a Or, *age* | *b* Or, *yieldeth*

---

ing they see not.' See note on Mt. 13.13.

13. *Know ye not this parable?* As if it were not easily understood without an interpretation.

14. *The sower soweth the word.* Christ, the sower of the seed of divine truth.

15. *The way side.* The hard, trodden road.

21. *The lamp.* See note on Mt. 5. 15. *The bushel.* See note on Mt. 5.15.

24. *With what measure ye mete.* Ye shall increase in spiritual knowledge according to your attentiveness and diligence.

25. *He that hath not.* See note on Mt. 25.28.

26. *As if a man should cast seed upon the earth.* Mark is the only one of the evangelists who records this parable. 'A man' here means Christ, and 'the earth' is the spiritual nature and needs of man.

27. *He knoweth not how.* He does not understand the unseen power by which the seed grows, and which is constantly taking effect.

28. *First the blade.* The gradual unfolding of the plant counsels patience in the development of character.

when the fruit cis ripe, straightway he dputteth forth the sickle, because the harvest is come.

30 And he said, How shall we liken the kingdom of God? or in what parable shall we set it forth? 31 eIt is like a grain of mustard seed, which, when it is sown upon the earth, though it be less than all the seeds that are upon the earth, 32 yet when it is sown, groweth up and becometh greater than all the herbs, and putteth out great branches; so that the birds of the heaven can lodge under the shadow thereof.

33 And with many such parables spake he the word unto them, as they were able to hear it; 34 and without a parable spake he not unto them: but privately to his own disciples he expounded all things.

35 And on that day, when even was come, he saith unto them, Let us go over unto the other side. 36 And leaving the multitude, they take him with them, even as he was, in the boat. And other boats were with him. 37 And there ariseth a great storm of wind, and the waves beat into the boat, insomuch that the boat was now filling. 38 And he himself was in the stern, asleep on the cushion: and they awake him,

and say unto him, Teacher, carest thou not that we perish? 39 And he awoke, and rebuked the wind, and said unto the sea, Peace, be still. And the wind ceased, and there was a great calm.   40 And he said unto them, Why are ye fearful? have ye not yet faith? 41 And they feared exceedingly, and said one to another, Who then is this, that even the wind and the sea obey him?

5 And they came to the other side of the sea, into the country of the Ger'a-senes'. 2 And when he was come out of the boat, straightway there met him out of the tombs a man with an unclean spirit, 3 who had his dwelling in the tombs: and no man could any more bind him, no, not with a chain; 4 because that he had been often bound with fetters and chains, and the chains had been rent asunder by him, and the fetters broken in pieces: and no man had strength to tame him. 5 And always, night and day, in the tombs and in the mountains, he was crying out, and cutting himself with stones.   6 And when he saw Je'sus from afar, he ran and aworshipped him; 7 and crying out with a loud voice, he saith, What have I to do with thee, Je'sus, thou Son

---

c Or, alloweth d Or, sendeth forth e Gr. As unto. a The Greek word denotes an act of reverence, whether paid to a crea-

ture (see Mt. 4.9; 18.26) or to the Creator (see Mt. 4.10).

31. Like a grain of mustard seed. See note on Mt. 13.31.

35. The other side. The east side of the Sea of Galilee.

38. Carest thou not that we perish? See note on Mt. 8.25.

CHAPTER 5

1. The Gerasenes. Or Gadarenes. See notes on Mt. 8.28.

2. Out of the tombs. See notes on Mt. 8.28.

7. Jesus, thou Son of the Most High

of the Most High God? I adjure thee by God, torment me not. 8 For he said unto him, **Come forth, thou unclean spirit, out of the man.** 9 And he asked him, **What is thy name?** And he saith unto him, My name is Legion; for we are many. 10 And he besought him much that he would not send them away out of the country. 11 Now there was there on the mountain side a great herd of swine feeding. 12 And they besought him, saying, Send us into the swine, that we may enter into them. 13 And he gave them leave. And the unclean spirits came out, and entered into the swine: and the herd rushed down the steep into the sea, *in number* about two thousand; and they were drowned in the sea. 14 And they that fed them fled, and told it in the city, and in the country. And they came to see what it was that had come to pass. 15 And they come to Je'sus, and behold *b*him that was possessed with demons sitting, clothed and in

his right mind, *even* him that had the legion: and they were afraid. 16 And they that saw it declared unto them how it befell *b*him that was possessed with demons, and concerning the swine. 17 And they began to beseech him to depart from their borders. 18 And as he was entering into the boat, *b*he that had been possessed with demons besought him that he might be with him. 19 And he suffered him not, but saith unto him, **Go to thy house unto thy friends, and tell them how great things the Lord hath done for thee, and** *how* **he had mercy on thee.** 20 And he went his way, and began to publish in De-cap'o-lis how great things Je'sus had done for him: and all men marvelled.

21 And when Je'sus had crossed over again in the boat unto the other side, a great multitude was gathered unto him; and he was by the sea. 22 And there cometh one of the rulers of the synagogue, Ja-i'rus by name; and seeing him, he

---

b Or, *the demoniac*

God. See notes on Mt. 8.29. *Torment me not.* See notes on Mt.8.29.

9. *My name is Legion.* The word 'Legion' is used because it expressed the popular idea of great numbers. In the New Testament period a Roman legion included ten cohorts of six centuries each. A cohort contained six hundred men; a century, one hundred men.

11. *A great herd of swine feeding.* As swine were an abomination to the Jews, the fact that there was such a herd at large suggests the wild and uncivilized nature of the district.

15. *Clothed and in his right mind.* The man was naked when Jesus commanded the unclean spirit to leave him (Lk. 8.27).

17. *To depart from their borders.* Probably among those who besought him to depart were the owners of the swine, who were troubled over their loss.

18. *Besought him that he might be with him.* This appeal of the man who was now restored to reason was unspeakably pathetic. No wonder that he wished to be with his divine Deliverer.

20. *Decapolis.* See note on Mt. 4. 25. Decapolis was a district containing the following ten cities: Damascus, Philadelphia, Raphana, Scythopolis, Gadara, Hippus, Dium, Pella, Gerasa, Canatha.

22. *One of the rulers of the synagogue.* See note on Mt. 9.18.

falleth at his feet, 23 and be-
seecheth him much, saying, My
little daughter is at the point of
death: *I pray thee*, that thou
come and lay thy hands on her,
that she may be ᶜmade whole,
and live. 24 And he went with
him; and a great multitude
followed him, and they thronged
him.

25 And a woman, who had an
issue of blood twelve years, 26
and had suffered many things of
many physicians, and had spent
all that she had, and was nothing
bettered, but rather grew worse,
27 having heard the things concerning Je'sus, came in the
crowd behind, and touched his
garment. 28 For she said, If I
touch but his garments, I shall
be made whole.   29 And
straightway the fountain of her
blood was dried up; and she felt
in her body that she was healed
of her ᵈplague. 30 And straightway Je'sus, perceiving in himself
that the power *proceeding* from
him had gone forth, turned him
about in the crowd, and said,
Who touched my garments? 31
And his disciples said unto him,

Thou seest the multitude throng-
ing thee, and sayest thou, Who
touched me? 32 And he looked
round about to see her that had
done this thing. 33 But the
woman fearing and trembling,
knowing what had been done to
her, came and fell down before
him, and told him all the truth.
34 And he said unto her, **Daughter, thy faith hath** ᵉ**made thee
whole; go in peace, and be whole**
of thy ᵈplague.

35 While he yet spake, they
come from the ruler of the synagogue's *house*, saying, Thy
daughter is dead: why troublest
thou the Teacher any further?
36 But Je'sus, ᶠnot heeding the
word spoken, saith unto the
ruler of the synagogue, **Fear not,
only believe.** 37 And he suffered
no man to follow with him, save
Peter, and ᵍJames, and John the
brother of ᵍJames. 38 And they
come to the house of the ruler of
the synagogue; and he beholdeth
a tumult, and *many* weeping and
wailing greatly. 39 And when
he was entered in, he saith unto
them, **Why make ye a tumult,
and weep? the child is not dead,**

---

c Or, *saved*   d Gr. *scourge*.   e Or, *saved* | thee   f Gr. *overhearing*.   g Or, *Jacob*

25. *A woman, who had an issue of
blood twelve years.* While Jesus was
on his way to the bedside of the
daughter of Jaïrus, he was timidly
approached by this woman, whose
meekness and modesty would not
permit her to press forward boldly
toward him. Her touch of humble,
quiet faith contrasts with the crowd-
ing of the throng.

29. *And straightway.* She was
healed even before Jesus spoke to
her. See note on Mt. 9.20.

32. *And he looked round about to
see.* He looked round in expectant
love to see her who so humbly
trusted in him. Not long before he

had looked round in holy indignation, yet in compassionate grief,
upon the hard-hearted Pharisees
(ch. 3.5).

36. *Fear not, only believe.* In his
miracles our Lord insists with tremendous force upon the necessity of
faith for those who would be healed.
So here he ignores the report of the
death of the ruler's little daughter and turns to the ruler himself,
concerned only about the latter's
faith.

39. *Why make ye a tumult, and
weep?* Part of the tumult and weeping did not signify real grief. See
note on Mt. 9.23.

but sleepeth. 40 And they laughed him to scorn. But he, having put them all forth, taketh the father of the child and her mother and them that were with him, and goeth in where the child was. 41 And taking the child by the hand, he saith unto her, Tal'i-tha cu'mi; which is, being interpreted, Damsel, I say unto thee, Arise. 42 And straightway the damsel rose up, and walked; for she was twelve years old. And they were amazed straightway with a great amazement. 43 And he charged them much that no man should know this: and he commanded that *something* should be given her to eat.

6 And he went out from thence; and he cometh into his own country; and his disciples follow him. 2 And when the sabbath was come, he began to teach in the synagogue: and ªmany hearing him were astonished, saying, Whence hath this man these things? and, What is the wisdom that is given unto

this man, and *what mean* such ᵇmighty works wrought by his hands? 3 Is not this the carpenter, the son of Mary, and brother of ᶜJames, and Jo'ses, and Ju'das, and Si'mon? and are not his sisters here with us? And they were ᵈoffended in him. 4 And Je'sus said unto them, **A prophet is not without honor, save in his own country, and among his own kin, and in his own house.** 5 And he could there do no ᵉmighty work, save that he laid his hands upon a few sick folk, and healed them. 6 And he marvelled because of their unbelief.

And he went round about the villages teaching.

7 And he calleth unto him the twelve, and began to send them forth by two and two; and he gave them authority over the unclean spirits; 8 and he charged them that they should take nothing for *their* journey, save a staff only; no bread, no wallet, no ᶠmoney in their ᵍpurse; 9 but *to go* shod with sandals: and,

---

a Some ancient authorities insert *the.*
b Gr. *powers.*   *c* Or, *Jacob*   *d* Gr. *caused*

to stumble.   *e* Gr. *power.*   *f* Gr. *brass.*
g Gr. *girdle.*

40. *They laughed him to scorn.* See note on Mt. 9.24.

41. *Talitha cumi.* This and other expressions in Aramaic, a Hebrew dialect, go to show that it was the language commonly spoken by our Lord. See ch. 7.34; Mt. 27.46.

42. *They were amazed straightway.* The word 'amazed' here expresses an almost helpless wonder. It was a wholesome reaction from the jeering scorn and doubt with which they had at first greeted our Lord.

CHAPTER 6

1. *His own country.* His second visit to Nazareth. He was treated in the same manner on his first visit

(Lk. 4.16–30). There is no record of his ever having been in Nazareth again.

3. *Is not this the carpenter,* etc. The description of our Lord as 'the carpenter' is peculiar to Mark. In Matthew he is spoken of as 'the carpenter's son' (ch. 13.55). There is an old tradition that Jesus made yokes and ploughs.

7. *Authority over the unclean spirits.* To that extent he imparted to his disciples his power of working miracles.

8. *Wallet.* Made of leather to contain food, and carried over the shoulder.

9. *Sandals.* Made of bark, usually of the palm tree.

said he, put not on two coats.
10 And he said unto them,
**Wheresoever ye enter into a
house, there abide till ye depart
thence.** 11 **And whatsoever
place shall not receive you, and
they hear you not, as ye go forth
thence, shake off the dust that
is under your feet for a testimony
unto them.** 12 And they went
out, and preached that *men*
should repent. 13 And they cast
out many demons, and anointed
with oil many that were sick,
and healed them.

14 And king Her'od heard
thereof; for his name had become
known: and [h]he said, John the
Bap-ti'zer is risen from the dead,
and therefore do these powers
work in him. 15 But others said,
It is E-li'jah. And others said,
It is a prophet, *even* as one of the
prophets. 16 But Her'od, when
he heard *thereof*, said, John,
whom I beheaded, he is risen.
17 For Her'od himself had sent
forth and laid hold upon John,
and bound him in prison for the
sake of He-ro'di-as, his brother
Philip's wife; for he had married
her. 18 For John said unto

Her'od, It is not lawful for thee
to have thy brother's wife. 19
And He-ro'di-as set herself
against him, and desired to kill
him; and she could not; 20 for
Her'od feared John, knowing
that he was a righteous and holy
man, and kept him safe. And
when he heard him, he [i]was much
perplexed; and he heard him
gladly. 21 And when a convenient day was come, that
Her'od on his birthday made a
supper to his lords, and the
[k]high captains, and the chief
men of Gal'i-lee; 22 and when
[l]the daughter of He-ro'di-as herself came in and danced, [m]she
pleased Her'od and them that
sat at meat with him; and the
king said unto the damsel, Ask
me whatsoever thou wilt, and I
will give it thee. 23 And he
sware unto her, Whatsoever thou
shalt ask of me, I will give it thee,
unto the half of my kingdom.
24 And she went out, and said
unto her mother, What shall I
ask? And she said, The head of
John the Bap-ti'zer. 25 And she
came in straightway with haste
unto the king, and asked, saying,

---

h Some ancient authorities read *they*.
i Many ancient authorities read *did many
things*. k Or, *military tribunes* Gr. *chili-*

archs. l Some ancient authorities read *his
daughter Herodias.* m Or, *it*

---

10. *Wheresoever ye enter.* They
were to abide in the house which
received them. Matthew adds that
they were to salute it (ch. 10.12).
11. *Shake off the dust that is under
your feet.* This was to be a witness
against those who rejected Christ.
See note on Mt. 10.14. Paul did
this on two notable occasions. See
Acts 13.51; 18.6.
14. *King Herod.* Herod Antipas,
tetrarch of Ituræa and Peræa. He
was the son of Herod the Great.
16. *John, whom I beheaded, he is
risen.* Superstition and remorse led

Herod to believe that the man whom
he had murdered had risen from the
dead. As a thoroughgoing Sad-
ducee in his sympathy Herod did
not believe in the resurrection, but
his troubled conscience overcame
his disbelief.
17. *For the sake of Herodias.* See
note on Mt. 14.3.
22. *Daughter of Herodias.* Salome.
See note on Mt. 14.6.
24. *What shall I ask?* This was
the opportunity for revenge that
Herodias longed for. See notes on
Mt. 14.3, 6, 8.

I will that thou forthwith give me on a platter the head of John the Bap'tist. 26 And the king was exceeding sorry; but for the sake of his oaths, and of them that sat at meat, he would not reject her. 27 And straightway the king sent forth a soldier of his guard, and commanded to bring his head: and he went and beheaded him in the prison, 28 and brought his head on a platter, and gave it to the damsel; and the damsel gave it to her mother. 29 And when his disciples heard *thereof*, they came and took up his corpse, and laid it in a tomb.

30 And the apostles gather themselves together unto Je'sus; and they told him all things, whatsoever they had done, and whatsoever they had taught. 31 And he saith unto them, **Come ye yourselves apart into a desert place, and rest a while.** For there were many coming and going, and they had no leisure so much as to eat. 32 And they went away in the boat to a

desert place apart. 33 And *the people* saw them going, and many knew *them*, and they ran together there [n]on foot from all the cities, and outwent them. 34 And he came forth and saw a great multitude, and he had compassion on them, because they were as sheep not having a shepherd: and he began to teach them many things. 35 And when the day was now far spent, his disciples came unto him, and said, The place is desert, and the day is now far spent; 36 send them away, that they may go into the country and villages round about, and buy themselves somewhat to eat. 37 But he answered and said unto them, **Give ye them to eat.** And they say unto him, Shall we go and buy two hundred [o]shillings' worth of bread, and give them to eat? 38 And he saith unto them, **How many loaves have ye? go** *and* **see.** And when they knew, they say, Five, and two fishes. 39 And he commanded them that all should [p]sit down by

n Or, *by land* *o* The word in the Greek denotes a coin worth about eight pence

26. *The king was exceeding sorry.* A proof of his high regard for John. Though depraved himself, he recognized the strength and loftiness of the prophet's character. See note on Mt. 14.9.

27. *In the prison.* At Machærus, where a fort and prison had been built. It was about five miles east of the Dead Sea.

30. *And the apostles gather themselves together.* This was their return to Capernaum to tell the Master about the results of their first mission.

31. *No leisure so much as to eat.* Besides those assembled to hear our Lord and to be healed, Capernaum was now crowded with pilgrims on

half-penny, or nearly seventeen cents. *p* Gr. *recline.*

their way to the Passover feast at Jerusalem (Jn. 6.4). From the excessive toil thus caused Jesus called the apostles to rest themselves.

32. *To a desert place apart.* Near Bethsaida Julias, a few miles northeast of the Sea of Galilee. This town was originally called Bethsaida. It had been greatly improved and enlarged by the tetrarch Herod Philip, who gave it the additional name of Julias in honor of the daughter of the Roman emperor.

35. *The place is desert.* It was probably uninhabited, but not all sandy waste. See ver. 39.

38. *Five, and two fishes.* They found that a lad had five barley loaves and two small fishes (Jn. 6.9).

companies upon the green grass. 40 And they sat down in ranks, by hundreds, and by fifties. 41 And he took the five loaves and the two fishes, and looking up to heaven, he blessed, and brake the loaves; and he gave to the disciples to set before them; and the two fishes divided he among them all. 42 And they all ate, and were filled. 43 And they took up broken pieces, twelve basketfuls, and also of the fishes. 44 And they that ate the loaves were five thousand men.

45 And straightway he constrained his disciples to enter into the boat, and to go before *him* unto the other side to Beth-sa'i-da, while he himself sendeth the multitude away. 46 And after he had taken leave of them, he departed into the mountain to pray. 47 And when even was come, the boat was in the midst of the sea, and he alone on the land. 48 And seeing them distressed in rowing, for the wind was contrary unto them, about the fourth watch of the night he

cometh unto them, walking on the sea; and he would have passed by them: 49 but they, when they saw him walking on the sea, supposed that it was a ghost, and cried out; 50 for they all saw him, and were troubled. But he straightway spake with them, and saith unto them, **Be of good cheer: it is I; be not afraid.** 51 And he went up unto them into the boat; and the wind ceased: and they were sore amazed in themselves; 52 for they understood not concerning the loaves, but their heart was hardened.

53 And when they had qcrossed over, they came to the land unto Gen-nes'a-ret, and moored to the shore. 54 And when they were come out of the boat, straightway *the people* knew him, 55 and ran round about that whole region, and began to carry about on their rbeds those that were sick, where they heard he was. 56 And wheresoever he entered, into villages, or into cities, or into the country, they laid the

---

q Or. *crossed over to the land they came*   *unto Gennesaret*   r Or, *pallets*

---

40. *In ranks.* In groups.

44. *Were five thousand men.* Matthew says, 'about five thousand men, besides women and children.' See note on Mt. 14.21. According to custom the women and children would stand or sit separate from the men.

45. *And straightway he constrained his disciples.* No time was to be lost in preventing the multitude, who were astounded by this miracle, from forcibly attempting to make him king. See Jn. 6.14, 15. Therefore he sent the disciples by boat across the lake while he dispersed the people. *Bethsaida.* Not Bethsaida Julias, but a place west of Capernaum (Jn. 6.17).

46. *Into the mountain to pray.* See note on Mt. 14.23.

47. *In the midst of the sea.* The contrary winds prevented them from sailing more than half way across (Jn. 6.19).

48. *The fourth watch.* Three o'clock in the morning. *Walking on the sea.* Like the feeding of the five thousand, this miracle was a direct mastery of the powers of nature.

51. *And the wind ceased.* Matthew's account of this miracle includes Peter's attempt to walk upon the sea (ch. 14.28–30).

53. *The land unto Gennesaret.* On the northwestern shore of the Sea of Galilee. It is a plain, three miles long by one wide and remarkably fertile.

sick in the marketplaces, and besought him that they might touch if it were but the border of his garment: and as many as touched ˢhim were made whole.

7 And there are gathered together unto him the Phar'i-sees, and certain of the scribes, who had come fron Je-ru'sa-lem, 2 and had seen that some of his disciples ate their bread with ᵃdefiled, that is, unwashen, hands. 3 (For the Phar'i-sees, and all the Jews, except they wash their hands ᵇdiligently, eat not, holding the tradition of the elders; 4 and *when they come* from the marketplace, except they ᶜbathe themselves, they eat not; and many other things there are, which they have received to hold, ᵈwashings of cups, and pots, and brasen vessels ᵉ.) 5 And the Phar'i-sees and the scribes ask him, Why walk not thy disciples according to the tradition of the elders, but eat their bread with ᵃdefiled hands? 6 And he said unto them, Well did I-sa'iah prophesy of you hypocrites, as it is written,

ᶠThis people honoreth **me** with their lips, But their heart is far from me. 7 But in vain do they worship me, Teaching *as their* doctrines the precepts of men.

8 Ye leave the commandment of God, and hold fast the tradition of men. 9 And he said unto them, Full well do ye reject the commandment of God, that ye may keep your tradition. 10 For Mo'ses said, ᵍHonor thy father and thy mother; and, He that speaketh evil of father or mother, let him ʰdie the death: 11 but ye say, If a man shall say to his father or his mother, That wherewith thou mightest have been profited by me is Cor'ban, that is to say, Given *to God*; 12 ye no longer suffer him to do aught for his father or his mother; 13 making void the word of God by your tradition, which ye have delivered: and many such like things ye do. 14 And he called to him the multitude again, and said unto them, Hear me all of you, and

s Or, *it* a Or, *common* b Or, *up to the elbow* Gr. *with the fist.* c Gr. *baptize.* Some ancient authorities read *sprinkle themselves.* d Gr. *baptizings.* e Many

ancient authorities add *and couches.* f Is. xxix. 13. g Ex. xx. 12; Dt. v. 16; Ex. xxi. 17; Lev. xx. 9. h Or, *surely die*

CHAPTER 7

1. *Who had come from Jerusalem.* The Pharisees and scribes had been keeping the Passover feast and now returned to watch Jesus.

2. *Unwashen hands.* That is, not washed according to the ceremonial manner practised by the Pharisees. It does not mean that the disciples failed in the cleanliness resulting from the ordinary Jewish custom of washing by pouring water upon the hands.

3. *The tradition of the elders.* The Pharisees sometimes set the tradi-

tion of the elders above the law itself. See note on Mt. 15.2.

8. *The commandment of God.* Jesus answered their accusation of violating the tradition of the elders by charging them with rejecting the command-ment of God. See note on Mt. 15.3.

13. *By your tradition.* The un-written law, or tradition, was de-rived from the elders, to whom it was said to have been given in charge by Moses. Moses was said to have received it orally from God. The Pharisees had in this case (ver. 11, 12.) so exalted tradition that the word of God had been made void.

101

understand: 15 there is nothing from without the man, that going into him can defile him; but the things which proceed out of the man are those that defile the man.ⁱ 17 And when he had entered into the house from the multitude, his disciples asked of him the parable. And he saith unto them, Are ye so without understanding also? Perceive ye not, that whatsoever from without goeth into the man, *it* cannot defile him; 19 because it goeth not into his heart, but into his belly, and goeth out into the draught? *This he said,* making all meats clean. 20 And he said, That which proceedeth out of the man, that defileth the man. 21 For from within, out of the heart of men, ᵏevil thoughts proceed, fornications, thefts, murders, adulteries, 22 covetings, wickednesses, deceit, lasciviousness, an evil eye, railing, pride, foolishness: 23 all these evil things proceed from within, and defile the man.

24 And from thence he arose, and went away into the borders of Tyre ˡand Si'don. And he entered into a house, and would have no man know it; and he could not be hid. 25 But straightway a woman, whose little daughter had an unclean spirit, having heard of him, came and fell down at his feet. 26 Now the woman was a ᵐGreek, a Sy-ro-phœ-ni'cian by race. And she besought him that he would cast forth the demon out of her daughter. 27 And he said unto her, Let the children first be filled: for it is not meet to take the children's ⁿbread and cast it to the dogs. 28 But she answered and saith unto him, Yea, Lord; even the dogs under the table eat of the children's crumbs. 29 And he said unto her, For this saying go thy way; the demon is gone out of thy daughter. 30 And she went away unto her house, and found the child laid upon the bed, and the demon gone out.

ⁱ Many ancient authorities insert ver. 16 *If any man hath ears to hear, let him hear.* See ch. 4.9. 23.   k Gr. *thoughts that are evil.*   l Some ancient authorities omit *and Sidon.*   m Or, *Gentile*   n Or, *loaf*

---

15. *There is nothing from without,* etc. Our Lord here contrasts external form and ceremony with the secret thoughts of the heart. See note on Mt. 15.11.

22. *An evil eye.* The disposition that is revealed in the look of jealous hatred.

24. *He arose, and went away.* The bitter opposition of the Pharisees and scribes caused him to do so. He had to seek a more fruitful field of labor. Accordingly he left the district around Capernaum and went north-westerly into the borders of Phœnicia.

25. *Having heard of him.* There was hardly any inhabited district of Palestine, and but few on its borders, into which the fame of Jesus had not gone. See ch. 3.7, 8.

26. *A Syrophœnician by race.* That is, a Phœnician belonging to the Roman province of Syria. See note on Mt. 15.22.

27. *The children.* The Jews. *The dogs.* Or little dogs. The term applied by the Jews to the heathen. An epithet commonly used by Mohammedans to-day against Christians is, 'dog of an infidel.'

28. *Even the dogs.* The woman, believing in Jesus and thinking only of her daughter's affliction, willingly accepts this description of her race, not knowing that her faith was being tested.

30. *And the demon gone out.* This miracle was one of those in which the person cured was distant. See Lk. 7.6; Jn. 4.46–54.

31 And again he went out from the borders of Tyre, and came through Si'don unto the sea of Gal'i-lee, through the midst of the borders of De-cap'o-lis. 32 And they bring unto him one that was deaf, and had an impediment in his speech; and they beseech him to lay his hand upon him. 33 And he took him aside from the multitude privately, and put his fingers into his ears, and he spat, and touched his tongue; 34 and looking up to heaven, he sighed, and saith unto him, **Eph'pha-tha,** that is, Be opened. 35 And his ears were opened, and the bond of his tongue was loosed, and he spake plain. 36 And he charged them that they should tell no man: but the more he charged them, so much the more a great deal they published it. 37 And they were beyond measure astonished, saying, He hath done all things well; he maketh even the deaf to hear, and the dumb to speak.

8 In those days, when there was again a great multitude, and they had nothing to eat, he called unto him his disciples, and saith unto them, 2 **I have compassion on the multitude, because they continue with me now three days, and have nothing to eat:** 3 **and if I send them away fasting to their home, they will faint on the way;** and some of them are come from far. 4 And his disciples answered him, Whence shall one be able to fill these men with ªbread here in a desert place? 5 And he asked them, **How many loaves have ye?** And they said, Seven. 6 And he commandeth the multitude to sit down on the ground: and he took the seven loaves, and having given thanks, he brake, and gave to his disciples, to set before them; and they set them before the multitude. 7 And they had a few small fishes: and having blessed them, he commanded to set these also before them. 8 And they ate, and were filled: and they took up, of broken pieces that remained over, seven baskets.

---

a Gr. *loaves.*

---

32. *Deaf, and had an impediment in his speech.* Though deaf, the man was not entirely dumb. *They beseech.* The afflicted man was brought to Jesus by his friends, who had to make a way for him through the crowd and speak for him. See ch. 2.3–5.

33. *Put his fingers into his ears, and he spat.* This was evidently done to help the man understand that his cure was being effected. He could only be made to comprehend by signs. It was only after this that Jesus cured him.

34. *Ephphatha.* See note on ch. 5.41.

CHAPTER 8

1. *Again a great multitude,* etc.

Brought together by the fame of the miracles. That the multitude was mainly heathen is evident from the known race and religion of the De-capolis district, and also from the expression 'they glorified the God of Israel' in Mt. 15.31.

4. *Whence shall one be able.* A strange and careless question for the disciples to ask, especially after the feeding of the five thousand.

6. *He commandeth the multitude to sit down.* In a desert place on the east side of the Sea of Galilee. See Mt. 15.33.

8. *They ate and were filled.* For comparison with the miracle of feeding the five thousand see note on Mt. 15.37.

9 And they were about four thousand: and he sent them away. 10 And straightway he entered into the boat with his disciples, and came into the parts of Dal-ma-nu′tha.

11 And the Phar′i-sees came forth, and began to question with him, seeking of him a sign from heaven, trying him. 12 And he sighed deeply in his spirit, and saith, Why doth this generation seek a sign? verily I say unto you, There shall no sign be given unto this generation. 13 And he left them, and again entering into *the boat* departed to the other side.

14 And they forgot to take bread; and they had not in the boat with them more than one loaf. 15 And he charged them, saying, Take heed, beware of the leaven of the Phar′i-sees and the leaven of Her′od. 16 And they reasoned one with another, *b*say-ing, *c*We have no bread. 17 And

Je′sus perceiving it saith unto them, Why reason ye, because ye have no bread? do ye not yet perceive, neither understand? have ye your heart hardened? 18 Having eyes, see ye not? and having ears, hear ye not? and do ye not remember? 19 When I brake the five loaves among the five thousand, how many *d*baskets full of broken pieces took ye up? They say unto him, Twelve. 20 And when the seven among the four thousand, how many *d*basketfuls of broken pieces took ye up? And they say unto him, Seven. 21 And he said unto them, Do ye not yet understand?

22 And they come unto Beth-sa′i-da. And they bring to him a blind man, and beseech him to touch him. 23 And he took hold of the blind man by the hand, and brought him out of the village; and when he had spit on his eyes, and laid his hands upon him, he asked him, Seest

b Some ancient authorities read *because they had no bread.*   *c* Or, It is *because we have no bread*   *d Basket* in ver. 19 and 20 represents different Greek words.

10. *Into the parts of Dalmanutha.* The region about Magdala on the western shore of the Sea of Galilee.

11. *And the Pharisees came forth.* They had evidently been waiting for his return. They wished to resume their malicious questioning with a view to silencing him. This time some Sadducees joined them (Mt. 16.1). *A sign from heaven.* Jesus had confounded them by his miracles of healing; now they wanted to test him in a different way. They asked for some appearance in the sky, some portentous and dazzling wonder such as Elijah and Samuel had wrought by God's power.

12. *He sighed deeply.* In mingled grief and compassion over their willful blindness and hardness of

heart. *There shall no sign be given.* He looked upon their question as a temptation and refused to consider it. See Mt. 12.39–41.

13. *The other side.* The eastern side of the Sea of Galilee.

15. *The leaven of the Pharisees.* Hypocrisy and deceit. *The leaven of Herod.* Worldliness. See note on Mt. 16.6–12.

21. *Do ye not yet understand?* Can ye not interpret my words spiritually?

22. *Bethsaida.* Bethsaida Julias.

23. *He took hold of the blind man.* Jesus led him apart from the crowd and wrought the cure gradually, as he did in the case of the deaf man with the impediment in his speech. The man's friends had besought Jesus to heal him by a touch, but this was denied.

thou aught? 24 And he looked up, and said, I see men; for I behold *them* as trees, walking. 25 Then again he laid his hands upon his eyes; and he looked stedfastly, and was restored, and saw all things clearly. 26 And he sent him away to his home, saying, Do not even enter into the village.

27 And Je'sus went forth, and his disciples, into the villages of Cæs-a-re'a Phi-lip'pi: and on the way he asked his disciples, saying unto them, Who do men say that I am? 28 And they told him, saying, John the Bap'tist; and others, E-li'jah; but others, One of the prophets. 29 And he asked them, But who say ye that I am? Peter answereth and saith unto him, Thou art the Christ. 30 And he charged them that they should tell no man of him.

31 And he began to teach them, that the Son of man must suffer many things, and be rejected by the elders, and the chief priests, and the scribes, and be killed, and after three days rise again. 32 And he spake the saying openly. And Peter took him, and began to rebuke him. 33 But he turning about, and seeing his disciples, rebuked Peter, and saith, **Get thee behind me, Satan; for thou mindest not the things of God, but the things of men.** 34 And he called unto him the multitude with his disciples, and said unto them, **If any man would come after me, let him deny himself, and take up his cross, and follow me. 35 For whosoever would save his life shall lose it; and whosoever shall lose his life for my sake and the ᵉgospel's shall save it. 36 For what doth it profit a man, to gain the whole world, and forfeit his life? 37 For what should a man give in exchange for his life? 38 For whosoever shall be ashamed of me and of my words in this adulterous and sinful generation, the Son of man also shall be ashamed of him, when he cometh in the glory of his Father with**

e See marginal note on ch. 1.1.

27. *The villages of Cæsarea Philippi.* The parts or regions. See note on Mt. 16.13.
28. *Elijah.* See note on Mt. 16.14.
29. *But who say ye that I am?* A test of the spiritual insight of his disciples. See note on Mt. 16.15. *Thou art the Christ.* The great fact of Peter's confession is here given more briefly than in Mt. 16.16, and Lk. 9.20. It is noteworthy that Mark, who wrote under the guidance of Peter, omits any reference to the latter's being the rock on which Christ's church was to be built. See note on Mt. 16.16.
31. *That the Son of man must suffer many things.* It was new and strange teaching for the disciples. Thus far, although there had been

toil, privation and persecution, victory had always been on the side of the Master. Now he began to talk to them in a way that, to their inadequate foresight, suggested defeat. They could not understand him and were troubled.
33. *Get thee behind me, Satan.* Our Lord looked upon Peter's well-meant but presumptuous words as a temptation. The words ' turning about, and seeing his disciples' indicate that the manner of the rebuke was open and deliberate, as its language was severe.
34. *And take up his cross.* See note on Mt. 10.38.
35. *Shall lose it.* See note on Mt. 10.39. *Shall save it.* See note on Mt. 10.39.

9 the holy angels. 1 And he said unto them, **Verily I say unto you, There are some here of them that stand *by*, who shall in no wise taste of death, till they see the kingdom of God come with power.**

2 And after six days Je'sus taketh with him Peter and *a*James, and John, and bringeth them up into a high mountain apart by themselves: and he was transfigured before them; 3 and his garments became glistering, exceeding white, so as no fuller on earth can whiten them. 4 And there appeared unto them E-li'jah with Mo'ses: and they were talking with Je'sus. 5 And Peter answereth and saith to Je'sus, Rab'bi, it is good for us to be here: and let us make three *b*tabernacles; one for thee, and one for Mo'ses, and one for E-li'jah. 6 For he knew not what to answer; for they became sore afraid. 7 And there came a cloud overshadowing them: and there came a voice out of the cloud, This is my beloved Son: hear ye him. 8 And suddenly looking round about, they saw no one any more, save Je'sus only with themselves.

9 And as they were coming down from the mountain, he charged them that they should tell no man what things they had seen, save when the Son of man should have risen again from the dead. 10 And they kept the saying, questioning among themselves what the rising again from the dead should mean. 11 And they asked him, saying, *c*How *is it* that the scribes say that E-li'jah must first come? 12 And he said unto them, **E-li'jah indeed cometh first and restoreth all things: and how is it written of the Son of man, that he should suffer many things and be set at nought?** 13 **But I say unto you, that E-li'jah is come, and they have also done unto him whatsoever they would, even as it is written of him.**

14 And when they came to the disciples, they saw a great multitude about them, and

a Or, *Jacob*   b Or, *booths*   c Or, *The*   scribes say . . . come.

CHAPTER 9

2. *After six days.* After Peter's confession; but see Lk. 9.28. *A high mountain apart.* See notes on Mt. 17.1. *He was transfigured before them.* That they might see him in his majesty and glory and be thereby comforted at the time of his humiliation and death.

4, 5. *Elijah with Moses.* Representing the law and the prophets. *Were talking with Jesus.* The facts that he was seen by the three apostles at once, and that he was also heard talking with them, prove the reality of the event. *Let us make three tabernacles.* Peter said this in his usual impulsive way. He was awed by the vision, and wished to take some action in order that its beauty and glory might remain.

7. *Hear ye him.* To him is committed all authority. See note on Mt. 17.5.

10. *Questioning among themselves.* Mark alone of the evangelists mentions this debate among the three. They were troubled only about the death and resurrection of their Master. Jesus had already told them of his approaching sufferings. Immediately after this vision of surpassing glory he had spoken of his rising again from the dead. The words added to their perplexity.

13. *Elijah is come.* In the person of John the Baptist (Mt. 17.13).

106

scribes questioning with them. 15 And straightway all the multitude, when they saw him, were greatly amazed, and running to him saluted him. 16 And he asked them, **What question ye with them?** 17 And one of the multitude answered him, Teacher, I brought unto thee my son, who hath a dumb spirit; 18 and wheresoever it taketh him, it ᵈdasheth him down: and he foameth, and grindeth his teeth, and pineth away: and I spake to thy disciples that they should cast it out; and they were not able. 19 And he answereth them and saith, **O faithless generation, how long shall I be with you? how long shall I bear with you? bring him unto me.** 20 And they brought him unto him: and when he saw him, straightway the spirit ᵉtare him grievously; and he fell on the ground, and wallowed foaming. 21 And he asked his father, **How long time is it since this hath come unto him?** And he said, From a child. 22 And oft-times it hath cast him both into the fire and

into the waters, to destroy him: but if thou canst do anything, have compassion on us, and help us. 23 And Je'sus said unto him, **If thou canst! All things are possible to him that believeth.** 24 Straightway the father of the child cried out, and saidᶠ, I believe; help thou mine unbelief. 25 And when Je'sus saw that a multitude came running together, he rebuked the unclean spirit, saying unto him, **Thou dumb and deaf spirit, I command thee, come out of him, and enter no more into him.** 26 And having cried out, and ᵉtorn him much, he came out: and *the boy* became as one dead; insomuch that the more part said, He is dead. 27 But Je'sus took him by the hand, and raised him up; and he arose. 28 And when he was come into the house, his disciples asked him privately, ᵍ*How is it* that we could not cast it out? 29 And he said unto them, **This kind can come out by nothing, save by prayer**ʰ.

30 And they went forth from

---

d Or, *rendeth him* See Mt. 7. 6. *e* Or, *convulsed* See ch. 1. 26. *f* Many ancient authorities add *with tears.* *g* Or, *saying,* *We could not cast it out.* *h* Many ancient authorities add *and fasting.*

15. *Were greatly amazed.* As if the glory of his transfiguration was yet visible in his countenance.

17. *My son, who hath a dumb spirit.* He was an only son (Lk. 9.38). His affliction was epilepsy, a disease of the brain, which causes persons affected with it to fall down suddenly. See note on Mt. 17.15.

18. *They were not able.* The humiliation of their failure must have been deepened by the fact that the scribes were present.

19. *O faithless generation.* Our Lord meant not only those before him, but the Jews of his time.

23. *If thou canst!* Not an expression of anger, but spoken to remind the father of the epileptic that doubt was not permissible if a cure was looked for. *All things,* etc. Another of the many solemn affirmations of Jesus as to the necessity of faith.

28. *Asked him privately.* They were sorely perplexed, for Jesus had given them power to do that which in this case they had failed to do. See Mt. 10.1; Lk. 9.1.

29. *This kind.* Our Lord replied in effect that some forms of demoniac possession were more malignant and difficult than others. The disciples had not sufficiently considered this.

thence, and passed through Gal'i-lee; and he would not that any man should know it. 31 For he taught his disciples, and said unto them, The Son of man is *delivered up into the hands of men, and they shall kill him; and when he is killed, after three days he shall rise again. 32 But they understood not the saying, and were afraid to ask him.

33 And they came to Ca-per'-na-um: and when he was in the house he asked them, What were ye reasoning on the way? 34 But they held their peace: for they had disputed one with another on the way, who *was* the *kgreatest*. 35 And he sat down, and called the twelve; and he saith unto them, If any man would be first, he shall be last of all, and *lservant of all. 36 And he took a little child, and set him in the midst of them: and taking him in his arms, he said unto them, 37

Whosoever shall receive one of such little children in my name, receiveth me: and whosoever receiveth me, receiveth not me, but him that sent me.

38 John said unto him, Teacher, we saw one casting out demons in thy name; and we forbade him, because he followed not us. 39 But Je'sus said, Forbid him not: for there is no man who shall do a *mmighty work in my name, and be able quickly to speak evil of me. 40 For he that is not against us is for us. 41 For whosoever shall give you a cup of water to drink, *nbecause ye are Christ's, verily I say unto you, he shall in no wise lose his reward. 42 And whosoever shall cause one of these little ones that believe *oon me to stumble, it were better for him if *pa great millstone were hanged about his neck, and he were cast into the sea. 43 And if thy hand cause thee to stumble, cut it

---

i See ch. 3.19.   *k* Gr. *greater*.   *l* Or, *minister*   *m* Gr. *power*.   *n* Gr. *in name that ye are*.   *o* Many ancient authorities omit *on me*.   *p* Gr. *a millstone turned by an ass*.

---

30. *They went forth from thence.* From the region of Mount Hermon in the north down through upper Galilee on the way to Capernaum. They went as privately as possible on account of the watchfulness of the scribes and Pharisees.

31. *The Son of man is delivered up.* The prediction of his suffering, death and resurrection.

32. *Were afraid to ask him.* Through grief and dismay at the disappointment of all their hopes. They did not expect that his Messiahship would lead to his death.

35. *If any man would be first.* The fact that Peter, James and John had been selected to witness the transfiguration was not without its natural effect upon them. They disputed as to who was the greatest.

Jesus decided by reproving them because of the wrong principle of ambition which actuated them. He taught them to measure greatness by the test of devoted, humble service. See note on Mt. 18.1.

38. *We saw one casting out demons.* A private and unknown disciple of Jesus, whose faith had been so strengthened by the example of the Master that he was able to perform this miracle in his name.

39. *Forbid him not.* Christ's words are a rebuke to the spirit of narrow exclusiveness in the exercise of spiritual gifts. The disciples should have welcomed the man as a brother worker instead of showing jealousy of his success.

42. *These little ones.* See note on Mt. 18.10.

off: it is good for thee to enter into life maimed, rather than having thy two hands to go into *q*hell, into the unquenchable fire.*r* 45 And if thy foot cause thee to stumble, cut it off: it is good for thee to enter into life halt, rather then having thy two feet to be cast into *q*hell. 47 And if thine eye cause thee to stumble, cast it out: it is good for thee to enter into the kingdom of God with one eye, rather than having two eyes to be cast into *q*hell; 48 where their worm dieth not, and the fire is not quenched. 49 For every one shall be salted with fire*s*. 50 Salt is good: but if the salt have lost its saltness, wherewith will ye season it? Have salt in yourselves, and be at peace one with another.

10 And he arose from thence, and cometh into the borders of Ju-dæ′a and beyond the Jordan: and multitudes come together unto him again; and, as he was wont, he taught them again.

2 And there came unto him Phar′i-sees, and asked him, Is it lawful for a man to put away *his* wife? trying him. 3 And he answered and said unto them, *a*What did Mo′ses command you? 4 And they said, Mo′ses suffered to write a bill of divorcement, and to put her away. 5 But Je′sus said unto them, For your hardness of heart he wrote you this commandment. 6 But from the beginning of the creation, Male and female made he them. 7 For this cause shall a man leave his father and mother, *b*and shall cleave to his wife; 8 and the two shall become one flesh: so that they are no more two, but one flesh. 9 What therefore God hath joined together, let not man put asunder. 10 And in the house the disciples asked him again of this matter. 11 And he saith unto them, Whosoever shall put away his wife, and marry another, committeth adultery against her: 12 and if she herself shall put away her hus-

---

q Gr. *Gehenna*. *r* Ver 44 and 46 (which are identical with ver. 48) are omitted by the best ancient authorities. *s* Many ancient authorities add *and every sacrifice*

shall be salted with salt. See Lev. 2.13. *a* Dt. xxiv. 1, 3. *b* Some ancient authorities omit *and shall cleave to his wife.*

---

48. *Where their worm dieth not.* The remorse and torment of the ungodly.
49. *Every one shall be salted with fire.* Shall be preserved and purified by a life of spiritual endeavor and achievement, or, on the other hand, shall be compelled to endure the salt of affliction and retribution for persistence in evil ways.

CHAPTER 10
1. *Beyond the Jordan.* Peræa. Between the end of ch. 9 and the beginning of ch. 10 Mark omits several events. See note on Mt. 19.3.
2. *Is it lawful*, etc. See note on Mt. 19.3.

5. *For your hardness of heart.* Christ rebukes their false standard as to the sacredness of the marriage relation. See note on Mt. 19.8.
9. *What therefore God hath joined together.* See note on Mt. 19.6.
10. *And in the house.* Perplexed by the moral rigor and purity of Christ's commands, the disciples sought more light on the question. They had already done so on more than one occasion (ch. 9.28, 29: 9.33–37). They themselves had been brought up in a more lax view of marriage than that announced authoritatively by our Lord. See note on Mt. 19.10.

band, and marry another, she committeth adultery.

13 And they were bringing unto him little children, that he should touch them: and the disciples rebuked them. 14 But when Je'sus saw it, he was moved with indignation, and said unto them, **Suffer the little children to come unto me; forbid them not: for** *c***to such belongeth the kingdom of God. 15 Verily I say unto you, Whosoever shall not receive the kingdom of God as a little child, he shall in no wise enter therein.** 16 And he took them in his arms, and blessed them, laying his hands upon them.

17 And as he was going forth *d*into the way, there ran one to him, and kneeled to him, and asked him, Good Teacher, what shall I do that I may inherit eternal life? 18 And Je'sus said unto him, **Why callest thou me good? none is good save one, even God. 19 Thou knowest the commandments,** *e***Do not kill, Do not commit adultery, Do not steal, Do not bear false witness, Do not defraud, Honor thy father and mother.** 20 And

he said unto him, Teacher, all these things have I observed from my youth. 21 And Je'sus looking upon him loved him, and said unto him, **One thing thou lackest: go, sell whatsoever thou hast, and give to the poor, and thou shalt have treasure in heaven: and come, follow me.** 22 But his countenance fell at the saying, and he went away sorrowful: for he was one that had great possessions.

23 And Je'sus looked round about, and saith unto his disciples, **How hardly shall they that have riches enter into the kingdom of God!** 24 And the disciples were amazed at his words. But Je'sus answereth again, and saith unto them, **Children, how hard is it** *f***for them that trust in riches to enter into the kingdom of God! 25 It is easier for a camel to go through a needle's eye, than for a rich man to enter into the kingdom of God.** 26 And they were astonished exceedingly, saying *g*unto him, Then who can be saved? 27 Je'sus looking upon them saith, **With men it is impossible,**

---

c Or, *of such is* *d* Or, *on his way* *e* Ex. xx. 12–16; Dt. v. 16–20. *f* Some ancient authorities omit *for them that trust in*

riches. *g* Many ancient authorities read *among themselves.*

---

13. *Bringing unto him little children.* According to custom. See notes on Mt. 19.13, 14.

17. *There ran one to him.* The rich young man who had kept the commandments, but lacked the courage to sell all he had and give to the poor. See notes on Mt. 19.16, 21.

24. *How hard is it for them that trust in riches.* This utterance of our Lord regarding the destructive power of riches on the spiritual life is even more emphatic than the words in Mt. 19.23–25, or in Lk. 18. 24, 25. It points out the reason why

it is so difficult for a rich man to enter the kingdom of God—because his trust is in his riches. See notes on Mt. 19.16–24.

26. *They were astonished exceedingly.* The compassion of Jesus for all who suffered, and his tender care of his disciples, often seemed to the latter in sharp contrast to the inflexible severity of his moral principles and commands. But when they were thus astonished and perplexed, he was always ready to point out the way of escape, as in ver. 27. See notes on Mt. 19.25.

but not with God: for all things are possible with God. 28 Peter began to say unto him, Lo, we have left all, and have followed thee. 29 Je'sus' said, Verily I say unto you, There is no man that hath left house, or brethren, or sisters, or mother, or father, or children, or lands, for my sake, and for the *h*gospel's sake, 30 but he shall receive a hundredfold now in this time, houses, and brethren, and sisters, and mothers, and children, and lands, with persecutions; and in the *i*world to come eternal life. 31 But many *that are* first shall be last; and the last first.

32 And they were on the way, going up to Je-ru'sa-lem; and Je'sus was going before them: and they were amazed; and they that followed were afraid. And he took again the twelve, and began to tell them the things that were to happen unto him, 33 *saying,* Behold, we go up to Je-ru'sa-lem; and the Son of man shall be delivered unto the chief priests and the scribes; and they shall condemn him to death, and shall deliver him unto the Gen'tiles: 34 and they shall mock him, and shall spit upon him, and shall scourge him, and shall kill him; and after three days he shall rise again.

35 And there come near unto him *k*James and John, the sons of Zeb'e-dee, saying unto him, Teacher, we would that thou shouldest do for us whatsoever we shall ask of thee. 36 And he said unto them, What would ye that I should do for you? 37 And they said unto him, Grant unto us that we may sit, one on thy right hand, and one on *thy* left hand, in thy glory. 38 But Je'sus said unto them, Ye know not what ye ask. Are ye able to drink the cup that I drink? or to be baptized with the baptism that I am baptized with? 39 And they said unto him, We are able. And Je'sus said unto them, The cup that I drink ye shall drink; and with the baptism that I am baptized withal shall ye be baptized: 40 but to sit on my right hand or on *my* left hand is not mine to give; but *it is for them* for whom it hath been prepared.

---

h See marginal note on ch. 1.1.   *i* Or, *age*   *k* Or, *Jacob*

28. *Peter began to say.* Peter's words here seem to indicate that he too was not free from the taint of undue love of riches. He asked, evidently not with the highest motive, 'what then shall we have?' (Mt. 19.27). The reply of Jesus affirms all the fulness of earthly as well as heavenly reward for those who are true to him; but he adds, 'with persecutions.'

32. *On the way.* The main road that led to Jerusalem. *Was going before them.* In the position of authority as well as danger—leader, guide, shepherd. He was proceed-

ing to the scene of his suffering and death.

33. *Shall deliver him unto the Gentiles.* It was the Roman power that carried out the sentence of death. See note on Mt. 20.18.

37. *Grant unto us.* See notes on Mt. 20.20, 21.

39. *The cup that I drink ye shall drink.* Foretelling their sufferings in his service. See notes on Mt. 20.23.

40. *For whom it hath been prepared.* That is, the question you ask does not now concern your position and your needs and will be finally decided in due time.

41 And when the ten heard it, they began to be moved with indignation concerning *l*James and John. 42 And Je′sus called them to him, and saith unto them, **Ye know that they who are accounted to rule over the Gen′tiles lord it over them; and their great ones exercise authority over them.** 43 **But it is not so among you: but whosoever would become great among you, shall be your** *m*minister; 44 **and whosoever would be first among you, shall be** *n*servant **of all.** 45 **For the Son of man also came not to be ministered unto, but to minister, and to give his life a ransom for many.**

46 And they come to Jer′i-cho: and as he went out from Jer′i-cho, with his disciples and a great multitude, the son of Ti-mæ′us, Bar-ti-mæ′us, a blind beggar, was sitting by the way side. 47 And when he heard that it was Je′sus the Naz-a-rene′, he began to cry out, and say, Je′sus, thou son of David, have mercy on me. 48 And many rebuked him, that he should hold his peace: but he cried out the more a great deal, Thou son of David, have mercy on me. 49 And Je′sus stood still, and said, **Call ye him.** And they call the blind man, saying unto him, Be of good cheer: rise, he calleth thee. 50 And he, casting away his garment, sprang up, and came to Je′sus. 51 And Je′sus answered him, and said, **What wilt thou that I should do unto thee?** And the blind man said unto him, *o*Rab-bo′ni, that I may receive my sight. 52 And Je′sus said unto him, **Go thy way; thy faith hath** *p*made **thee whole.** And straightway he received his sight, and followed him in the way.

11 And when they draw nigh unto Je-ru′sa-lem, unto Beth′pha-ge and Beth′a-ny, at the mount of Ol′ives, he sendeth two of his disciples, 2 and saith unto them, **Go your way into the village that is over against you: and straightway as ye enter into it, ye shall find a colt tied,**

---

l Or, *Jacob* *m* Or, *servant* *n* Gr. *bond-servant.* *o* See John 20.16. *p* Or, *saved thee*

---

41. *Began to be moved with indignation.* At the presumption of James and John in trying to secure the highest position for themselves. Their father Zebedee was wealthier than the parents of the other apostles, and probably they considered that they had stronger claims to advancement.

43. *It is not so among you.* You are not to imitate the cruel pride of force and brutal authority which obtains among the Gentiles. You are under a higher law, the law of unselfish service.

45. *A ransom for many.* The supreme proof of his right to be ruler in the kingdom of God. He gave most for us, therefore most righteously does he rule over us. See notes on Mt. 20.28.

46. *Bartimæus, a blind beggar.* Matthew says there were two blind men. Only one is mentioned here, probably because he was better known. See notes on Mt. 20.29, 30, 34.

CHAPTER 11

1. *He sendeth two of his disciples.* It is not certain who they were; but the details given indicate an attentive eye-witness. Most probably Peter, on whom Mark depended for his narrative, was one, and the other may have been James or John. 2-9. *A colt.* See notes on Mt. 21.2, 3, 5, 7-9, 10.

whereon no man ever yet sat; loose him, and bring him. 3 And if any one say unto you, Why do ye this? say ye, The Lord hath need of him; and straightway he [a]will send him [b]back hither. 4 And they went away, and found a colt tied at the door without in the open street; and they loose him. 5 And certain of them that stood there said unto them, What do ye, loosing the colt? 6 And they said unto them even as Je'sus had said: and they let them go. 7 And they bring the colt unto Je'sus, and cast on him their garments; and he sat upon him. 8 And many spread their garments upon the way; and others [c]branches, which they had cut from the fields. 9 And they that went before, and they that followed, cried, Ho-san'na; Blessed is he that cometh in the name of the Lord: 10 Blessed is the kingdom that cometh, the kingdom of our father David: Ho-san'na in the highest.

11 And he entered into Je-ru'-sa-lem, into the temple; and when he had looked round about upon all things, it being now eventide, he went out unto Beth'a-ny with the twelve.

12 And on the morrow, when they were come out from Beth'-a-ny, he hungered. 13 And seeing a fig tree afar off having leaves, he came, if haply he might find anything thereon: and when he came to it he found nothing but leaves; for it was not the season of figs. 14 And he answered and said unto it, **No man eat fruit from thee henceforward for ever.** And his disciples heard it.

15 And they come to Je-ru'-sa-lem: and he entered into the temple, and began to cast out them that sold and them that bought in the temple, and overthrew the tables of the money-changers, and the seats of them that sold the doves; 16 and he would not suffer that any man should carry a vessel through the temple. 17 And he taught, and said unto them, Is it not written, [d]**My house shall be called a house of prayer for all the nations?** [e]**but ye have made it a den of robbers.** 18 And the chief priests and the scribes heard it, and sought how they might destroy him: for they feared

---

a Gr. *sendeth.* *b* Or, *again* *c* Gr. *layers of leaves.* *d* Is. lvi. 7. *e* Jer. vii. 11.

10. *The kingdom of our father David.* A proof that they were entirely ignorant, perhaps with the exception of a few, of the true character of the Messiah. They still thought that Jesus intended to restore the earthly kingdom of David.

11. *He entered into Jerusalem.* The city was thronged in the streets and on the housetops. The scribes and Pharisees, and all the friends of the party of Herod and the Sadducees, must have fully realized at last the great power of Jesus over the multitude. They must have feared deeply for the safety of the beliefs and institutions which they championed. *Into the temple.* But before this he uttered his lament over the beloved and doomed city (Lk. 19.41–44).

14. *No man eat fruit from thee.* See Mt. 21.19 and note thereon.

15. *He entered into the temple.* This is to be distinguished from the entry into the Temple recorded in ver. 11. See notes on Mt. 21.12.

18. *All the multitude was astonished.* They were on the verge of

him, for all the multitude was astonished at his teaching.

19 And ᶠevery evening ᵍhe went forth out of the city.

20 And as they passed by in the morning, they saw the fig tree withered away from the roots. 21 And Peter calling to remembrance saith unto him, Rab′bi, behold, the fig tree which thou cursedst is withered away. 22 And Je′sus answering saith into them, **Have faith in God.** 23 **Verily I say unto you, Whosoever shall say unto this mountain, Be thou taken up and cast into the sea; and shall not doubt in his heart, but shall believe that what he saith cometh to pass; he shall have it. 24 Therefore I say unto you, All things whatsoever ye pray and ask for, believe that ye ʰreceive them, and ye shall have them. 25 And whensoever ye stand praying, forgive, if ye have aught against any one; that your Father also who is in heaven may forgive you your trespasses.** ⁱ

27 And they come again to Je-ru′sa-lem: and as he was walking in the temple there come to him the chief priests, and the scribes, and the elders; 28 and they said unto him, By what authority doest thou these things? or who gave thee this authority to do these things? 29 And Je′sus said unto them, **I will ask of you one ᵏquestion, and answer me, and I will tell you by what authority I do these things. 30 The baptism of John, was it from heaven, or from men? answer me.** 31 And they reasoned with themselves, saying, If we shall say, From heaven; he will say, Why then did ye not believe him? 32 ˡBut should we say, From men—they feared the people: ᵐfor all verily held John to be a prophet. 33 And they answered Je′sus and say, We know not. And Je′sus saith unto them, **Neither tell I you by what authority I do these things.**

ᶠ Gr. *whenever evening came.* ᵍ Some ancient authorities read *they.* ʰ Gr. *received.* ⁱ Many ancient authorities add ver. 26 *But if ye do not forgive, neither will your Father who is in heaven forgive your trespasses.* Comp. Mt. 6.15; 18.35. ᵏ Gr. *word.* ˡ Or, *But shall we say, From men?* ᵐ Or. *for all held John to be a prophet indeed*

making a great public demonstration in his behalf. This explains the fear of the chief priests and scribes.

19. *Went forth out of the city.* Showing his perfect fearlessness in the most imminent danger.

20. *In the morning.* On Tuesday, the day following the cleansing of the temple.

23. *And shall not doubt in his heart.* Whose faith shall remain steadfast and clear, even in the inmost recesses of the soul. See Mt. 17.20; Lk. 17.6.

24. *All things whatsoever ye pray and ask for,* etc. A never-to-be-surpassed statement of the meaning of faith and prayer. It is only the union of faith with prayer that pro-

duces results. No petition made in doubt or despair can be answered. Christ himself declares that in order that we may have or possess the things we ask for, we must first believe that God grants them.

28. *By what authority doest thou these things?* There is no record that Jesus was ever ordained as a rabbi. If not, he had no official authority to teach, according to the requirements of Jewish custom. It was his authority to call himself the Son of God and to do mighty works about which his enemies questioned him. See notes on Mt. 21.23.

33. *We know not.* See note on Mt. 21.27.

12 And he began to speak unto them in parables. A man planted a vineyard, and set a hedge about it, and digged a pit for the winepress, and built a tower, and let it out to husbandmen, and went into another country. 2 And at the season he sent to the husbandmen a *a*servant, that he might receive from the husbandmen of the fruits of the vineyard. 3 And they took him, and beat him, and sent him away empty. 4 And again he sent unto them another *a*servant; and him they wounded in the head, and handled shamefully. 5 And he sent another; and him they killed: and many others; beating some, and killing some. 6 He had yet one, a beloved son: he sent him last unto them, saying, They will reverence my son. 7 But those husbandmen said among themselves, This is the heir; come, let us kill him, and the inheritance shall be ours. 8 And they took him, and killed him, and cast him forth out of the vineyard. 9 What therefore will the lord of the vineyard do? he will come and destroy the husbandmen, and will give the vineyard unto others. 10 Have ye not read even this scripture:

*b*The stone which the builders rejected,
The same was made the head of the corner;
11 This was from the Lord,
And it is marvellous in our eyes?
12 And they sought to lay hold on him; and they feared the multitude; for they perceived that he spake the parable against them: and they left him, and went away.

13 And they send unto him certain of the Phar'i-sees and of the He-ro'di-ans, that they might catch him in talk. 14 And when they were come they say unto him, Teacher, we know that thou art true, and carest not for any one; for thou regardest not the person of men, but of a truth teachest the way of God: Is it lawful to give tribute unto Cæ'sar, or not? 15 Shall we give, or shall we not give? But he, knowing their hypocrisy, said unto them, Why make ye trial of me? bring me a *c*denarius, that I may see it. 16 And they brought it. And he saith unto them, Whose is this image and superscription? And they said unto him, Cæ'sar's. 17 And Je'sus said unto them, Render unto Cæ'sar the things that

a Gr. *bondservant.*   *b* Ps. cxviii. 22 f.   *c* See marginal note on ch. 6.37.

CHAPTER 12

1. *And digged a pit for the winepress.* The pit was a hole dug in the ground and lined with masonry. Into it, through an opening, flowed the juice of the grapes which had been trodden upon in the winepress over the pit. *Let it out to husbandmen.* See note on Mt. 21.33–44.

12. *They sought to lay hold on him.* See note on Mt. 21.46.

13. *Certain of the Pharisees and of the Herodians.* The Pharisees were probably selected for their ability and willingness to make the attempt to ensnare Jesus by some hoped-for admission on his part. With regard to the Herodians, see note on Mt. 22.16.

17. *Render unto Cæsar,* etc. See note on Mt. 22.21. *And they marvelled greatly.* See note on Mt. 22.22.

are Cæ'sar's, and unto God the things that are God's. And they marvelled greatly at him.

18 And there come unto him Sad'du-cees, who say that there is no resurrection; and they asked him, saying, 19 Teacher, Mo'ses wrote unto us, *d*If a man's brother die, and leave a wife behind him and leave no child, that his brother should take his wife, and raise up seed unto his brother. 20 There were seven brethren: and the first took a wife, and dying left no seed; 21 and the second took her, and died, leaving no seed behind him; and the third likewise: 22 and the seven left no seed. Last of all the woman also died. 23 In the resurrection whose wife shall she be of them? for the seven had her to wife. 24 Je'sus said unto them, Is it not for this cause that ye err, that ye know not the scriptures, nor the power of God? 25 For when they shall rise from the dead, they neither marry, nor are given in marriage; but are as angels in heaven. 26 But as touching the dead, that they are raised; have ye not read in the book of Mo'ses, in *the place concerning* the Bush, how God spake unto him, saying, *e*I *am* the God of Abraham, and the God of I'saac, and the God of Jacob? 27 He is not the God of the dead, but of the living: ye do greatly err.

28 And one of the scribes came, and heard them questioning together, and knowing that he had answered them well, asked him, What commandment is the first of all? 29 Je'sus answered, The first is, *f*Hear, O Is'ra-el; *g*The Lord our God, the Lord is one: and thou shalt love the Lord thy God *h*with all thy heart, and with all thy soul, and *h*with all thy mind, and *h*with all thy strength. 31 The second is this, *i*Thou shalt love thy neighbor as thyself. There is none other commandment greater than these. 32 And the scribe said unto him, Of a truth, Teacher, thou hast well said that he is one; and there is none other but he: 33 and to love him with all the heart, and with all the understanding, and with all the strength, and to love his neighbor as himself, is much more than all whole burnt-offerings and sacrifices. 34 And when Je'sus saw that he answered

---

d Dt. xxv. 5.   *e* Ex. iii. 6.   *f* Dt. vi. 4 ff.   *g* Or, *The Lord is our God; the Lord is one*   *h* Gr. *from.*   *i* Lev. xix. 18.

---

18. *There come unto him Sadducees.* Hitherto they had not been active in their hostility to Jesus, as the Pharisees had been. They had the chief places in Jewish society, and were worldly-minded and indifferent to religious agitation. But now they deemed it prudent to take at least an intellectual, if not a critical, interest in the teaching of our Lord.

24. *For this cause that ye err.* See note on Mt. 22.29.

25. *As angels in heaven.* See note on Mt. 22.30.

28. *One of the scribes.* He was a Pharisee and a lawyer (Mt. 22.34, 35). *What commandment is the first of all?* This questioner, who was fair-minded, had been moved to admiration by the replies of Jesus to those who had tried to entangle him in an argument.

29–34. *The first is,* etc. See notes on Mt. 22.38, 39.

discreetly, he said unto him, Thou art not far from the kingdom of God. And no man after that durst ask him any question.

35 And Je'sus answered and said, as he taught in the temple, How say the scribes that the Christ is the son of David? 36 David himself said in the Holy Spirit,

^kThe Lord said unto my Lord,
Sit thou on my right hand,
Till I make thine enemies
^lthe foot-stool of thy feet.

37 David himself calleth him Lord; and whence is he his son? And ^mthe common people heard him gladly.

38 And in his teaching he said, Beware of the scribes, who desire to walk in long robes, and *to have* salutations in the marketplaces, 39 and chief seats in the synagogues, and chief places at feasts: 40 they that devour widows' houses, ⁿand for a pretence make long pray-

ers; these shall receive greater condemnation.

41 And he sat down over against the treasury, and beheld now the multitude cast ^omoney into the treasury: and many that were rich cast in much. 42 And there came ^pa poor widow, and she cast in two mites, which make a farthing. 43 And he called unto him his disciples, and said unto them, Verily I say unto you, This poor widow cast in more than all they that are casting into the treasury: 44 for they all did cast in of their superfluity; but she of her want did cast in all that she had, *even* all her living.

13 And as he went forth out of the temple, one of his disciples saith unto him, Teacher, behold, what manner of stones and what manner of buildings! 2 And Je'sus said unto him, Seest thou these great buildings? there shall not be left here one stone upor

---

k Ps. cx. 1. *l* Some ancient authorities read *underneath thy feet.* m Or, *the great multitude* n Or, *even while for a pretence they make* o Gr. *brass.* p Gr. *one.*

35. *How say the scribes that the Christ is the son of David?* Jesus here introduced a topic with which every Jew was more or less familiar. He who claimed to be the Christ, or Messiah, had first of all to prove his Davidic descent. That the Christ must be the son of David was not only a prevalent religious belief, but it was patriotic politics.

36, 37. *The Lord said,* etc. See notes on Mt. 22.42–44, 45.

38–40. *Beware,* etc. See notes on Mt. 23.2, 3, 4, 5, 7. The denunciation of the scribes here is not so severe as in Matthew, but has the same general meaning and object.

42. *There came a poor widow.* Jesus had just spoken (ver. 40) about the scribes who devoured widows' houses, that is, abused the confidence of poor widows of whose

property they were legal guardians; and now the sight of this widow casting into the treasury all she had moved him to profound sympathy. *Two mites.* About equal to three-tenths of a cent; but this would not be a reliable indication of their purchasing power in our Lord's time.

43. *Cast in more than all,* etc. A righteous and final estimate of her pious act.

CHAPTER 13

1. *What manner of buildings!* An expression of admiration at their beauty and massiveness. Most of the 'stones' or blocks, which were of marble, were thirty-seven and a half feet long, eighteen feet wide and twelve feet thick. See note on Mt. 24.1.

2. *There shall not be left here one stone.* See note on Mt. 24.2.

MARK 13.3—13.22   The Destruction of Jerusalem

another, which shall not be thrown down.

3 And as he sat on the mount of Ol'ives over against the temple, Peter and ^aJames and John and Andrew asked him privately, 4 Tell us, when shall these things be? and what *shall be* the sign when these things are all about to be accomplished? 5 And Je'sus began to say unto them, Take heed that no man lead you astray. 6 Many shall come in my name, saying, I am *he*; and shall lead many astray. 7 And when ye shall hear of wars and rumors of wars, be not troubled: *these things* must needs come to pass; but the end is not yet. 8 For nation shall rise against nation, and kingdom against kingdom; there shall be earthquakes in divers places; there shall be famines: these things are the beginning of travail.

9 But take ye heed to yourselves: for they shall deliver you up to councils; and in synagogues shall ye be beaten; and before governors and kings shall ye stand for my sake, for a testimony unto them. 10 And the ^bgospel must first be preached unto all the nations. 11 And when they lead you *to judgment*, and deliver you up, be not anxious beforehand what ye shall speak: but whatsoever shall be given you in that hour, that speak ye; for it is not ye that speak, but the Holy Spirit. 12 And brother shall ^cdeliver up brother to death, and the father his child; and children shall rise up against parents, and ^dcause them to be put to death. 13 And ye shall be hated of all men for my name's sake: but he that endureth to the end, the same shall be saved.

14 But when ye see the abomination of desolation standing where he ought not (let him that readeth understand), then let them that are in Ju-dæ'a flee unto the mountains: 15 and let him that is on the housetop not go down, nor enter in, to take anything out of his house: 16 and let him that is in the field not return back to take his cloak. 17 But woe unto them that are with child and to them that give suck in those days! 18 And pray ye that it be not in the winter. 19 For those days shall be tribulation, such as there hath not been the like from the beginning of the creation which God created until now, and never shall be. 20 And except the Lord had shortened the days, no flesh would have been saved; but for the elect's sake, whom he chose, he shortened the days. 21 And then if any man shall say unto you, Lo, here is the Christ; or, Lo, there; believe ^eit not: 22 for there shall arise false Christs and false prophets,

---

a Or, *Jacob*   *b* See marginal note on ch. 1.1.

c See ch. 3.19.   *d* Or, *put them to death*
e Or, *him*

---

6. *Many shall come in my name.*
See note on Mt. 24.5.
14. *Flee unto the mountains.* See note on Mt. 24.16.

20. *Except the Lord had shortened the days.* The days of the siege of Jerusalem. See note on Mt. 24.22.

and shall show signs and wonders that they may lead astray, if possible, the elect. 23 But take ye heed: behold, I have told you all things beforehand.

24 But in those days, after that tribulation, the sun shall be darkened, and the moon shall not give her light, 25 and the stars shall be falling from heaven, and the powers that are in the heavens shall be shaken. 26 And then shall they see the Son of man coming in clouds with great power and glory. 27 And then shall he send forth the angels, and shall gather together his elect from the four winds, from the uttermost part of the earth to the uttermost part of heaven.

28 Now from the fig tree learn her parable: when her branch is now become tender, and putteth forth its leaves, ye know that the summer is nigh; 29 even so ye also, when ye see these things coming to pass, know ye that *f*he is nigh *even* at the doors. 30 Verily I say unto you, This generation shall not pass away, until all these things be accomplished. 31 Heaven and earth shall pass away: but my words shall not pass away. 32 But of that day or that hour knoweth no one, not even the angels in heaven, neither the Son, but the Father. 33 Take ye heed, watch *g*and pray: for ye know not when the

time is. 34 *It is* as *when* a man, sojourning in another country, having left his house, and given authority to his *h*servants, to each one his work, commanded also the porter to watch. 35 Watch therefore: for ye know not when the lord of the house cometh, whether at even, or at midnight, or at cockcrowing, or in the morning; 36 lest coming suddenly he find you sleeping. 37 And what I say unto you I say unto all, Watch.

14 Now after two days was *the feast of* the passover and the unleavened bread: and the chief priests and the scribes sought how they might take him with subtlety, and kill him: 2 for they said, Not during the feast, lest haply there shall be a tumult of the people.

3 And while he was in Beth'-a-ny in the house of Si'mon the leper, as he sat at meat, there came a woman having *a*an alabaster cruse of ointment of *b*pure nard very costly; *and* she brake the cruse, and poured it over his head. 4 But there were some that had indignation among themselves, *saying*, To what purpose hath this waste of the ointment been made? 5 For this ointment might have been sold for above three hundred *c*shillings, and given to the poor. And they murmured against her. 6 But Je'sus said, Let her alone; why trouble ye

---

f Or, *it*   *g* Some ancient authorities omit *and pray.*   *h* Gr. *bondservants.*   *a* Or,

a flask   *b* Or, *liquid nard*   *c* See marginal note on ch. 6.37.

24. *The sun shall be darkened.* See note on Mt. 24.29.

33. *For ye know not when the time is.* See note on Mt. 24.42.

CHAPTER 14

3–9. *While he was in Bethany in the house of Simon the leper.* See notes on Mt. 26.6, 7, 12, 13.

119

her? she hath wrought a good work on me. 7 For ye have the poor always with you, and whensoever ye will ye can do them good: but me ye have not always. 8 She hath done what she could; she hath anointed my body beforehand for the burying. 9 And verily I say unto you, Wheresoever the ^dgospel shall be preached throughout the whole world, that also which this woman hath done shall be spoken of for a memorial of her.

10 And Ju'das Is-car'i-ot, ^ehe that was one of the twelve, went away unto the chief priests, that he might ^fdeliver him unto them. 11 And they, when they heard it, were glad, and promised to give him money. And he sought how he might conveniently ^fdeliver him *unto them*.

12 And on the first day of unleavened bread, when they sacrificed the passover, his disciples say unto him, Where wilt thou that we go and make ready that thou mayest eat the passover? 13 And he sendeth two of his disciples, and saith unto them, Go into the city, and there shall meet you a man

bearing a pitcher of water: follow him; 14 and wheresoever he shall enter in, say to the master of the house, The Teacher saith, Where is my guest-chamber, where I shall eat the passover with my disciples? 15 And he will himself show you a large upper room furnished *and* ready: and there make ready for us. 16 And the disciples went forth, and came into the city, and found as he had said unto them: and they made ready the passover.

17 And when it was evening he cometh with the twelve. 18 And as they ^gsat and were eating, Je'sus said, Verily I say unto you, One of you shall ^hbetray me, *even* he that eateth with me. 19 They began to be sorrowful, and to say unto him one by one, Is it I? 20 And he said unto them, *It is* one of the twelve, he that dippeth with me in the dish. 21 For the Son of man goeth, even as it is written of him: but woe unto that man through whom the Son of man is ^hbetrayed! good were it for ⁱthat man if he had not been born.

22 And as they were eating, he took ^kbread, and when he

---

d See marginal note on ch. 1.1.   e Gr. *the one of the twelve.*   f See ch. 3.19.   g Gr. re-clined.   h See marginal note on ch. 3.19.   i Gr. *for him if that man.*   k Or, *a loaf*

11. *They, when they heard it, were glad.* This was for them a happy escape from the difficulty of taking Jesus captive ' with subtlety.' With one of the apostles turned traitor, it was easy for them to devise some scheme to attain their object.

12. *On the first day.* See note on M[·]. 26.17.

13. *Two of his disciples.* Peter and John. *There shall meet you a man*, etc. This description is more detailed than in Mt. 26.18.

16. *They made ready the Passover.* It was necessary to procure for the meal the unleavened bread, the cups of red wine mixed with water, and the bitter herbs. The preparation did not, however, resemble those of the Passover feast in all respects.

21. *Good were it for that man.* See note on Mt. 26.24.

22. *And as they were eating, he took bread.* The institution of the Last Supper is recorded in ver.

had blessed, he brake it, and gave to them, and said, **Take ye: this is my body.** 23 And he took a cup, and when he had given thanks, he gave to them: and they all drank of it. 24 And he said unto them, **This is my blood of the** *l* **covenant, which is poured out for many.** 25 Verily I say unto you, I shall no more drink of the fruit of the vine, until that day when I drink it new in the kingdom of God.

26 And when they had sung a hymn, they went out unto the mount of Ol'ives.

27 And Je'sus saith unto them, **All ye shall be** *m* **offended: for it is written,** *n* **I will smite the shepherd, and the sheep shall be scattered abroad. 28 Howbeit, after I am raised up, I will go before you into Gal'i-lee.** 29 But Peter said unto him, Although all shall be *m* offended, yet will not I. 30 And Je'sus saith unto him, **Verily I say unto thee that thou to-day,** *even* **this night, before the cock crow twice, thou shalt deny me thrice.** 31 But he spake exceeding vehemently, If I must die with thee, I will not deny thee. And in like manner also said they all.

32 And they come unto *o* a place which was named Geth-sem'a-ne: and he saith unto his disciples, **Sit ye here, while I pray.** 33 And he taketh with him Peter and *p* James and John, and began to be greatly amazed, and sore troubled. 34 And he saith unto them, **My soul is exceeding sorrowful even unto death: abide ye here, and watch.** 35 And he went forward a little, and fell on the ground, and prayed that, if it were possible, the hour might pass away from him. 36 And he said, **Ab'ba, Father, all things are possible unto thee; remove this cup from me: howbeit not what I will, but what thou wilt.** 37 And he cometh, and findeth them sleeping, and saith unto Peter, **Si'mon, sleepest thou? couldest thou not watch one hour? 38** *q* **Watch and pray, that ye enter not into temptation: the spirit indeed is willing, but the flesh is weak.** 39 And again he went away, and prayed, saying the same words. 40 And again he came, and found them sleeping, for their eyes were very heavy; and they knew not what to answer him. 41 And he com-

---

l Some ancient authorities insert *new.* *m* Gr. *caused to stumble.* n Zech. xiii. 7.

o Gr. *an enclosed piece of ground.* *p* Or, *Jacob* *q* Or, *Watch ye, and pray that ye enter not*

22–25. See notes on Mt. 26.26, 28.
26. *When they had sung a hymn.* The second part of the Hallel. See note on Mt. 26.30.
28. *I will go before you into Galilee.* A promise to precede the disciples as leader and guide. See note on Mt. 26.32.
29–31. See notes on Mt. 26.33, 34, 35.
32. *Gethsemane.* The word means oil press. See note on Mt. 26.36.
34. *Abide ye here, and watch.* It

was the expression of the human yearning of Christ in his anguish for the close sympathy of the three, Peter, James and John.
36. *Abba.* The Aramaic word for father. *Howbeit not what I will.* His human weakness and sense of limitation at first began to be overpowered, but he did not yield to fear. He triumphed in submitting to the will of his Father.
37–42. *Findeth them sleeping.* See notes on Mt. 26.40, 44, 46.

eth the third time, and saith unto them, ʳSleep on now, and take your rest: it is enough; the hour is come; behold, the Son of man is ˢbetrayed into the hands of sinners. 42 Arise, let us be going: behold, he that ˢbetrayeth me is at hand.

43 And straightway, while he yet spake, cometh Ju'das, one of the twelve, and with him a multitude with swords and staves, from the chief priests and the scribes and the elders. 44 Now he that ˢbetrayed him had given them a token, saying, Whomsoever I shall kiss, that is he; take him, and lead him away safely. 45 And when he was come, straightway he came to him, and saith, Rab'bi; and ᵗkissed him. 46 And they laid hands on him, and took him. 47 But a certain one of them that stood by drew his sword, and smote the ᵘservant of the high priest, and struck off his ear. 48 And Je'sus answered and said unto them, Are ye come out, as against a robber, with swords and staves to seize me? 49 I was daily with you in the temple teaching, and ye took me not: but this is done that the scriptures might be fulfilled. 50 And they all left him, and fled.

51 And a certain young man followed with him, having a linen cloth cast about him, over his naked body: and they lay hold on him; 52 but he left the linen cloth, and fled naked.

53 And they led Je'sus away to the high priest: and there come together with him all the chief priests and the elders and the scribes. 54 And Peter had followed him afar off, even within, into the court of the high priest; and he was sitting with the officers, and warming himself in the light of the fire. 55 Now the chief priests and the whole council sought witness against Je'sus to put him to death; and found it not. 56 For many bare false witness against him, and their witness agreed not together. 57 And there stood up certain, and bare false witness against him, saying, 58 We heard him say, I will destroy this ᵛtemple that is made with hands, and in three days I will build another made without hands. 59 And not even so did their witness agree together. 60 And the high priest stood up in the midst, and asked Je'sus, saying, Answerest thou nothing? what is it which these witness against thee? 61 But he held his peace, and answered nothing. Again the high priest asked him, and saith unto him, Art thou the Christ, the Son of the Blessed? 62 And Je'sus said, I am: and ye shall see the Son of man sitting at

---

r Or, Do ye sleep on, then, and take your rest?   s See marginal note on ch. 3.19.

t Gr. kissed him much.   u Gr. bondservant.
v Or, sanctuary

---

43. A multitude. Chiefly Roman and Jewish soldiers, elders and chief priests. See note on Mt. 26.47.

44–50. A token, etc. See notes on Mt. 26.48, 51–53.

51. A certain young man. Most probably Mark himself. He was living in Jerusalem at that time. A linen cloth. A night garment.

53–65. They led, etc. See notes on Mt. 26.58, 59, 61, 63–66, 68.

the right hand of Power, and coming with the clouds of heaven. 63 And the high priest rent his clothes, and saith, What further need have we of witnesses? 64 Ye have heard the blasphemy: what think ye? And they all condemned him to be [u]worthy of death. 65 And some began to spit on him, and to cover his face, and to buffet him, and to say unto him, Prophesy: and the officers received him with [v]blows of their hands.

66 And as Peter was beneath in the court, there cometh one of the maids of the high priest; 67 and seeing Peter warming himself, she looked upon him, and saith, Thou also wast with the Naz-a-rene', *even* Je'sus. 68 But he denied, saying, [w]I neither know, nor understand what thou sayest: and he went out into the [x]porch; [y]and the cock crew. 69 And the maid saw him, and began again to say to them that stood by, This is *one* of them. 70 But he again denied it. And after a little while again they that stood by said to Peter, Of a truth thou art *one* of them; for thou art a Gal-i-læ'an. 71 But he began to curse, and to swear, I know not this man of whom ye speak. 72 And straightway the second time the cock crew. And Peter called to mind the word, how that Je'sus said

unto him, Before the cock crow twice, thou shalt deny me thrice. [z]And when he thought thereon, he wept.

15 And straightway in the morning the chief priests with the elders and scribes, and the whole council, held a consultation, and bound Je'sus, and carried him away, and delivered him up to Pi'late. 2 And Pi'late asked him, Art thou the King of the Jews? And he answering saith unto him, **Thou sayest.** 3 And the chief priests accused him of many things. 4 And Pi'late again asked him, saying, Answerest thou nothing? behold how many things they accuse thee of. 5 But Je'sus no more answered anything; insomuch that Pi'late marvelled.

6 Now at [a]the feast he used to release unto them one prisoner, whom they asked of him. 7 And there was one called Bar-ab'bas, *lying* bound with them that had made insurrection, men who in the insurrection had committed murder. 8 And the multitude went up and began to ask him *to do* as he was wont to do unto them. 9 And Pi'late answered them, saying, Will ye that I release unto you the King of the Jews? 10 For he perceived that for envy the chief priests had delivered him up. 11 But the chief priests stirred up the mul-

---

u Gr. *liable to.*   *v* Or, *strokes of rods*
w Or, *I neither know, nor understand: thou, what sayest thou?*   *x* Gr. *forecourt.*   *y* Many

66–72. *And as Peter,* etc. See notes on Mt. 26.70, 71, 73, 75.

CHAPTER 15

1. *In the morning.* See note on

ancient authorities omit *and the cock crew.*   *z* Or, *And he began to weep*   *a* Or, *a feast*

Mt. 27.1.   *Pilate.*   Pontius Pilate was fifth Roman procurator of Judæa, Samaria, and Idumæa (26–36 A.D.).

2–15. *Thou sayest.* See notes on Mt. 27.11, 15, 16, 20, 22, 26.

titude, that he should rather release Bar-ab'bas unto them. 12 And Pi'late again answered and said unto them, What then shall I do unto him whom ye call the King of the Jews? 13 And they cried out again, Crucify him. 14 And Pi'late said unto them, Why, what evil hath he done? But they cried out exceedingly, Crucify him. 15 And Pi'late, wishing to content the multitude, released unto them Bar-ab'bas, and delivered Je'sus, when he had scourged him, to be crucified.

16 And the soldiers led him away within the court, which is the ^b Præ-to'ri-um; and they call together the whole ^c band. 17 And they clothe him with purple, and platting a crown of thorns, they put it on him; 18 and they began to salute him, Hail, King of the Jews! 19 And they smote his head with a reed, and spat upon him, and bowing their knees ^d worshipped him. 20 And when they had mocked him, they took off from him the purple, and put on him his garments. And they lead him out to crucify him.

21 And they ^e compel one passing by, Si'mon of Cy-re'ne, coming from the country, the father of Al-ex-an'der and Ru'fus, to go *with them*, that he might bear his cross.

22 And they bring him unto the place Gol'go-tha, which is, being interpreted, The place of a skull. 23 And they offered him wine mingled with myrrh: but he received it not. 24 And they crucify him, and part his garments among them, casting lots upon them, what each should take. 25 And it was the third hour, and they crucified him. 26 And the superscription of his accusation was written over, THE KING OF THE JEWS. 27 And with him they crucify two robbers; one on his right hand, and one on his left.^f 29 And they that passed by railed on him, wagging their heads, and saying, Ha! thou that destroyest the ^g temple, and buildest it in three days, 30 save thyself, and come down from the cross. 31 In like manner also the chief priests mocking *him* among themselves with the scribes said, He saved others; ^h himself he cannot save. 32 Let the Christ, the King of Is'ra-el, now come down from the cross, that we may see and believe. And they that were crucified with him reproached him.

33 And when the sixth hour was come, there was darkness over the whole ^i land until the ninth hour. 34 And at the ninth hour Je'sus cried with a loud voice, **E-lo'i, E-lo'i, la'ma sa-bach-tha'ni?** which is, being interpreted, ^k My God, my God, ^l why hast thou forsaken me? 35 And some of them that stood by, when they heard it, said, Be-

b Or, *palace*   *c* Or, *cohort*   *d* See marginal note on ch. 5.6.   *e* Gr. *impress.*   *f* Many ancient authorities insert ver. 28 *And the scripture was fulfilled, which* saith, *And he was reckoned with transgressors.* See Lk. 22.37.   *g* Or, *sanctuary*   *h* Or, *can he not save himself?*   *i* Or, *earth*   *k* Ps. xxii. 1.   *l* Or, *why didst thou forsake me?*

16–21. *Led him away,* etc. See notes on Mt. 27.28–32.
22–32. *The place Golgotha.* See notes on Mt. 27.33, 35, 37, 40, 42.
33–41. *The sixth hour.* See notes on Mt. 27.45–47, 51, 54,56.

hold, he calleth E-li'jah. 36 And one ran, and filling a sponge full of vinegar, put it on a reed, and gave him to drink, saying, Let be; let us see whether E-li'jah cometh to take him down. 37 And Je'sus uttered a loud voice, and gave up the ghost. 38 And the veil of the *m*temple was rent in two from the top to the bottom. 39 And when the centurion, who stood by over against him, saw that he *n*so gave up the ghost, he said, Truly this man was *o*the Son of God. 40 And there were also women beholding from afar: among whom *were* both Mary Mag-da-le'ne, and Mary the mother of *p*James the *q*less and of Jo'ses, and Sa-lo'me; 41 who, when he was in Gal'i-lee, followed him, and ministered unto him; and many other women that came up with him unto Je-ru'sa-lem.

42 And when even was now come, because it was the Preparation, that is, the day before the sabbath, 43 there came Joseph of Ar-i-ma-thæ'a, a councillor of honorable estate, who also himself was looking for the kingdom of God; and he boldly went in unto Pi'late, and asked for the body of Je'sus. 44 And Pi'late

marvelled if he were already dead: and calling unto him the centurion, he asked him whether he *r*had been any while dead. 45 And when he learned it of the centurion, he granted the corpse to Joseph. 46 And he bought a linen cloth, and taking him down, wound him in the linen cloth, and laid him in a tomb which had been hewn out of a rock; and he rolled a stone against the door of the tomb. 47 And Mary Mag-da-le'ne and Mary the *mother* of Jo'ses beheld where he was laid.

16 And when the sabbath was past, Mary Mag-da-le'ne, and Mary the *mother* of *a*James, and Sa-lo'me, bought spices, that they might come and anoint him. 2 And very early on the first day of the week, they come to the tomb when the sun was risen. 3 And they were saying among themselves, Who shall roll us away the stone from the door of the tomb? 4 and looking up, they see that the stone is rolled back: for it was exceeding great. 5 And entering into the tomb, they saw a young man sitting on the right side, arrayed in a white robe; and they were amazed. 6 And he saith unto

---

m Or, *sanctuary*   *n* Many ancient authorities read *so cried out, and gave up the ghost.* *o* Or, *a son of God* *p* Or, *Jacob*

q Gr. *little.*   *r* Many ancient authorities read *were already dead.*   *a* Or, *Jacob*

---

43. *Joseph of Arimathæa.* Arimathæa was probably the same as Ramathaim in Ephraim, in Canaan as divided among the twelve tribes. See note on Mt. 27.57.

44. *If he were already dead.* Sometimes a criminal hung on the cross for several days before death took place. Pilate could hardly believe that Jesus was dead after being on the cross only a few hours.

46. *Rolled a stone against the door.* See note on Mt. 27.60.

47. *Mary the mother of Joses.* See note on Mt. 27.61.

CHAPTER 16

4. *They see that the stone is rolled back.* See notes on Mt. 28.2.

5. *A young man.* Luke says two. See notes on Mt. 28.2.

6–8. *Ye seek,* etc. See Mt. 28.6–8.

them, Be not amazed: ye seek Je'sus, the Naz-a-rene', who hath been crucified: he is risen; he is not here: behold, the place where they laid him! 7 But go, tell his disciples and Peter, He goeth before you into Gal'i-lee: there shall ye see him, as he said unto you. 8 And they went out, and fled from the tomb; for trembling and astonishment had come upon them: and they said nothing to any one; for they were afraid.

9 *b*Now when he was risen early on the first day of the week, he appeared first to Mary Mag-da-le'ne, from whom he had cast out seven demons. 10 She went and told them that had been with him, as they mourned and wept. 11 And they, when they heard that he was alive, and had been seen of her, disbelieved.

12 And after these things he was manifested in another form unto two of them, as they walked, on their way into the country. 13 And they went away and told it unto the rest: neither believed they them.

14 And afterward he was manifested unto the eleven themselves as they sat as meat; and he upbraided them with their unbelief and hardness of heart, because they believed nòt them that had seen him after he was risen.   15 And he said unto them, **Go ye into all the world, and preach the *c*gospel to the whole creation. 16 He that believeth and is baptized shall be saved; but he that disbelieveth shall be condemned. 17 And these signs shall accompany them that believe: in my name shall they cast out demons; they shall speak with *d*new tongues; 18 they shall take up serpents, and if they drink any deadly thing, it shall in no wise hurt them; they shall lay hands on the sick, and they shall recover.**

19 So then the Lord Je'sus, after he had spoken unto them, was received up into heaven, and sat down at the right hand of God. 20 And they went forth, and preached everywhere, the Lord working with them, and confirming the word by the signs that followed.   A-men'.

---

b The two oldest Greek manuscripts, and some other authorities, omit from ver. 9 to the end.   Some other authorities have a different ending to the Gospel. *c* See marginal note on ch. 1.1.   *d* Some ancient authorities omit *new*.

---

12. *Unto two of them.* As they walked to Emmaus.   They were Cleopas, and another whose name is unknown.   See Lk. 24.13.

15. *Go ye unto all the world*, etc. See Mt. 28.19; Lk. 24.47; Acts. 1.8.

17. *With new tongues.* As on the day of Pentecost.   See Acts 2.4; 10.46; 19.6.

18. *They shall take up serpents.* As Paul did out of the bundle of sticks on the fire in the island of Malta (Act 28.3–6).   *Lay hands on the sick.*   Peter healed the lame man at the Temple gate (Acts 3.7) and Paul cured the father of the Roman official Publius in Malta (Acts 28.8).

THE GOSPEL ACCORDING TO LUKE

INTRODUCTION BY PROFESSOR M. B. RIDDLE, D.D., LL.D.

The Writer.—Luke was a Gentile, as appears from a comparison of Col. 4.11 and 14. Eusebius says he was a native of Antioch, but this is uncertain. He was a physician, an educated man, familiar with the eastern Mediterranean and adjacent countries. Tradition claims that he was a painter. In the Acts he appears as the companion of Paul, from Troas to Philippi (16.10-17), where he probably remained from 52 to 58 A.D., rejoining the apostle at that place, and continuing with him to the time when the narrative closes (58 to 63 A.D.). In 2 Tim. 2.11 he is referred to as being with Paul. Hence the evangelist must have been in Palestine during the two years of Paul's imprisonment at Cæsarea (58-60 A.D.), and must have had opportunity of making the research of which he writes in the opening verses of the Gospel (1.1-4). As he was not himself an "eye-witness," he cannot have been one of the seventy, or one of the two disciples that walked to Emmaus. Of his later life nothing is known.

Design.—The Gospel was primarily intended for the instruction of "Theophilus" (1.3). It is most probable that an individual of that name is addressed, of whom, however, nothing further is known, though it was held by some Fathers that he lived at Antioch. But internal evidence from both the Gospel and the Acts favors the view that his home was in Italy. As he seems to have been a Gentile, the Gospel is designed for that class of readers. There is, however, no evidence that it was intended to uphold Gentile Christianity in opposition to Jewish Christianity. It presents Christ as the Saviour of men of every nation, giving prominence to His real humanity and to "the healing nature of His redeeming work," thus indicating a writer who was a physician.

Characteristics.—The Gospel is not so strictly chronological as those of Mark and John. The writer arranges his material "in order" (1.3), but groups details in the historical method, carrying out to a conclusion one series of events, and then proceeding to another. The style is that of an educated man. In ch. 1, 2, there are many Hebraisms, which may be accounted for by the nature of the facts or by the source of information. The accuracy of the writer has been abundantly verified. The two "treatises" refer to many details of contemporary history, of topography, etc., which have been proved correct, even where error was alleged. That the human, tender, all-embracing compassion of our Lord is made prominent appears from the narrative itself, especially from the passages found only in this Gospel. Nearly one-third of the matter is peculiar to this Gospel. While many new details are given in the account of incidents recorded by the other evangelists, Luke alone narrates the events in ch. 1, 2; the first rejection at Nazareth; the miraculous draught of fishes; the raising of the widow's son; the anointing by the sinful woman; the mission of the seventy; the parable of the Good Samaritan; the visit to Martha and Mary; the importunate neighbor; the barren fig-tree; the Lord at the house of a Pharisee; the prodigal son; the unjust steward; Dives and Lazarus; the ten lepers; the importunate widow; the Pharisee and the publican; the visit to Zacchæus; the parable of the pounds; the mockery by Herod; the penitent robber; the walk to Emmaus; and the Ascension.

Time and Place of Writing.—The Gospel was probably written at Rome, about 63 A.D. At that time "eye-witnesses" were still living; but there would be a desire for written records, to give "certainty" to Theophilus and others respecting the facts they had learned by oral instruction (1.4).

The Gospel must have been written before the destruction of Jerusalem. In 21.24 it is stated that our Lord predicted that Jerusalem "shall be trodden down of the Gentiles." This has been used to prove that the Gospel was written after the city was destroyed. But such an argument implies that the writer wilfully misreported our Lord's prediction. Aside from the insuperable moral objection to this view, there is a literary difficulty. If the writer purposely inserted this clause because Jerusalem had already been destroyed, he would certainly have modified more of the discourse for the same reason. The date assigned above agrees with the view that the Synoptic Gospels are independent narratives, written within the limit of a few years.

Summary.—1. The prologue; the birth of John the Baptist; the birth at Bethlehem and the boyhood of Jesus (1, 2).

2. The baptism and temptation (3 to 4.13).

3. The ministry in Galilee (4.14 to 9.50).

The order in the early part of this division agrees with that of Mark, though many of the incidents are not narrated by the latter. The period of opposition in Galilee, fully detailed by Matthew and Mark, is very briefly referred to in this Gospel.

4. The Peræan ministry (9.51 to 18.34).

This part of the narrative is almost entirely peculiar to this Gospel. Some of the incidents, especially those recorded in 11.14 to 13.9, may belong to the Galilæan ministry. With the blessing of the little children (18.15), the three accounts become parallel.

5. Events at Jericho (18.35 to 19.28).

6. The final conflicts at Jerusalem (19.29 to 21.38).

7. The Passover, and subsequent events; the death and burial (22.1 to 23.56).

8. The resurrection and ascension (24).

ACCORDING TO LUKE

Preface

1 Forasmuch as many have taken in hand to draw up a narrative concerning those matters which have been [a]fulfilled among us, 2 even as they delivered them unto us, who from the beginning were eyewitnesses and ministers of the word, 3 it seemed good to me also, having traced the course of all things accurately from the first, to write unto thee in order, most excellent The-oph′i-lus; 4 that thou mightest know the certainty concerning the [b]things [c]wherein thou wast instructed.

5 There was in the days of Her′od, king of Ju-dæ′a, a certain priest named Zach-a-ri′as, of the course of A-bi′jah: and he had a wife of the daughters of Aar′on, and her name was E-lis′a-beth. 6 And they were both righteous before God, walking in all the commandments and ordinances of the Lord blameless. 7 And they had no

---

a Or, *fully established* b Gr. *words.*
c Or, *which thou wast taught by word of mouth*

CHAPTER 1

1. *Forasmuch as many have taken in hand,* etc. A proof that many attempts to give an account of what our Lord did and said had already been made. Though, from Luke's point of view, these early narratives were inadequate and incomplete, his language suggests that they were substantially accurate as sources of information. Among them, most probably, were fragmentary accounts that were highly important and useful, such as collections of our Lord's sayings, especially the parables and discourses. Many Biblical scholars think that the Gospel according to Mark was written before Luke began his narrative and that it was one of Luke's sources. The fact that no mention is made of Mark does not indicate the contrary, as the custom of the time permitted it.

2. *Even as they delivered them unto us, who from the beginning were eyewitnesses.* The reader is liable to misapprehend this passage on account of the position of 'who,' which immediately follows 'us.' It

is not meant that Luke and his friends or companions were eyewitnesses of the doings of our Lord. The eyewitnesses and ministers were chiefly the apostles and disciples.

3. *To write unto thee in order.* That is, to give a connected historical account in which what precedes prepares for and explains what follows. *Most excellent Theophilus.* Theophilus (beloved of God) was probably a prominent Roman citizen who had become a Christian convert. 'Most excellent' was the form of address due to one of his knightly rank. The same title was given to Felix and Festus (Acts 23.26; 26.25).

5. *Of the course of Abijah.* A 'course' was a selected number or group of priests to whom was assigned in rotation the conduct of the Temple services for a week. There were twenty-four courses, of which Abijah's was the eighth. *Elizabeth.* Or, Elisheba (one whose oath is by God).

6. *Righteous before God.* Not without sin, but righteous according to the requirements of the Mosaic law.

7. *They had no child.* Childless-

child, because that E-lis'a-beth was barren, and they both were now *d*well stricken in years.

8 Now it came to pass, while he executed the priest's office before God in the order of his course, 9 according to the custom of the priest's office, his lot was to enter into the *e*temple of the Lord and burn incense. 10 And the whole multitude of the people were praying without at the hour of incense. 11 And there appeared unto him an angel of the Lord standing on the right side of the altar of incense. 12 And Zach-a-ri'as was troubled when he saw *him*, and fear fell upon him. 13 But the angel said unto him, Fear not, Zach-a-ri'as: because thy supplication is heard, and thy wife E-lis'a-beth shall bear thee a son, and thou shalt call his name John. 14 And thou shalt have joy and gladness; and many shall rejoice at his birth.

15 For he shall be great in the sight of the Lord, and he shall drink no wine nor *f*strong drink; and he shall be filled with the Holy Spirit, even from his mother's womb. 16 And many of the children of Is'ra-el shall he turn unto the Lord their God. 17 And he shall *g*go before his face in the spirit and power of E-li'jah, to turn the hearts of the fathers to the children, and the disobedient *to walk* in the wisdom of the just; to make ready for the Lord a people prepared *for him*. 18 And Zach-a-ri'as said unto the angel, Whereby shall I know this? for I am an old man, and my wife *h*well stricken in years. 19 And the angel answering said unto him, I am Ga'bri-el, that stand in the presence of God; and I was sent to speak unto thee, and to bring thee these good tidings. 20 And behold, thou shalt be silent and

---

d Gr. *advanced in their days.*   *e* Or, *sanctuary*   *f* Gr. *sikera.*   *g* Some ancient authorities read *come nigh before his face.*   *h* Gr. *advanced in her days.*

---

ness was looked upon among the Jews not only as a misfortune, but also as a reproach. The childless family could never hope to give the Messiah to the world.

9. *His lot.* He was chosen by lot. *And burn incense.* The incense altar, which was made of acacia wood thickly plated with gold, was before the veil of the Holy of Holies. To burn incense upon the altar was the highest and most prized priestly function. It signified that the prayers of the people had found favor with God.

10. *The people were praying without.* The Temple was less used for prayer than for the various sacrificial offerings.

11. *The right side.* Or, the south side. The right side was traditionally associated with righteousness and with good tidings or other good fortune. See Mt. 25.33; Mk. 16.5.

13. *John.* (Jehovah is gracious.)

15. *He shall drink no wine nor strong drink.* John was a life member of the Nazirites, a Jewish order consecrated to the service of God. They wore their hair long, abstained from strong drink and kept themselves free from ceremonial defilement under the Mosaic law.

17. *He shall go before his face.* That is, he shall be the forerunner of the Messiah.

19. *Gabriel.* (The mighty man of God). One of the two angels named in the New Testament, the other being Michael (who is like God?). See Jude *v*; Rev. 12.7. *That stand in the presence of God.* Or, one of the angels of the presence. See Mt. 18.10; Rev. 8.2.

20. *Thou shalt be silent.* This was the angel's answer to the question of Zacharias in ver. 18. The priest, doubting, had asked for a sign,

not able to speak, until the day that these things shall come to pass, because thou believedst not my words, which shall be fulfilled in their season. 21 And the people were waiting for Zach-a-ri'as, and they marvelled ⁱwhile he tarried in the ᵏtemple. 22 And when he came out, he could not speak unto them: and they perceived that he had seen a vision in the ᵏtemple: and he continued making signs unto them, and remained dumb. 23 And it came to pass, when the days of his ministration were fulfilled, he departed unto his house.

24 And after these days E-lis'-a-beth his wife conceived; and she hid herself five months, saying, 25 Thus hath the Lord done unto me in the days wherein he looked upon *me*, to take away my reproach among men.

26 Now in the sixth month the angel Ga'bri-el was sent from

God unto a city of Gal'i-lee, named Naz'a-reth, 27 to a virgin betrothed to a man whose name was, Joseph, of the house of David; and the virgin's name was Mary. 28 And he came in unto her, and said, Hail, thou that art ˡhighly favored, the Lord *is* with theeᵐ. 29 But she was greatly troubled at the saying, and cast in her mind what manner of salutation this might be. 30 And the angel said unto her, Fear not, Mary: for thou hast found ⁿfavor with God. 31 And behold, thou shalt conceive in thy womb, and bring forth a son, and shalt call his name JE'SUS. 32 He shall be great, and shall be called the Son of the Most High: and the Lord God shall give unto him the throne of his father David: 33 and he shall reign over the house of Jacob ᵒfor ever; and of his kingdom there shall be no end. 34 And

<hr>

ⁱ Or, *at his tarrying*　　ᵏ Or, *sanctuary*
ˡ Or, *endued with grace*　ᵐ Many ancient authorities add *blessed* art *thou among*　*women.* See ver. 42.　ⁿ Or, *grace*　ᵒ Gr. *unto the ages.*

<hr>

which was given him as a penalty in the form of his own dumbness.

21. *Marvelled while he tarried.* They wondered why his ministrations at the altar of incense lasted so long, and they feared that he had incurred the divine displeasure by some neglect or imperfect performance of his duties.

22. *When he came out, he could not speak.* Being dumb, he was unable to pronounce the priestly blessing for which the people were waiting.

23. *The days of his ministration.* The week chosen for the priests of Abijah's course.

26. *In the sixth month.* After the conception of John the Baptist. *Named Nazareth.* See note on Mt. 2.23. The word 'named' suggests that Luke wrote for readers who knew little about Palestine.

27. *Betrothed.* The betrothal of a

Jewish maiden was more binding and significant than a similar ceremony is with us. It implied that the bridegroom had paid to the father of the prospective bride a sum of money, by which payment the control of the father over his daughter had passed to the bridegroom. Betrothal ordinarily took place a year before marriage. *Mary.* The same name as Miriam and Marah.

31. *Shalt call his name Jesus.* 'Jesus' was the Greek form of the Hebrew Joshua, Jeshua, or Jehosua (Jehovah is salvation). See Mt. 1.21.

32. *He shall be great,* etc. Mary at this time could not have understood the sublime meanings of the angel's message, known to the world as the Annunciation; but she received the message in humble and obedient faith, being in this respect in marked contrast to the aged priest Zacharias (ch. 1.18).

Mary said unto the angel, How shall this be, seeing I know not a man? 35 And the angel answered and said unto her, The Holy Spirit shall come upon thee, and the power of the Most High shall overshadow thee: wherefore also ᵖthe holy thing which is begotten qshall be called the Son of God. 36 And behold, E-lis'a-beth thy kinswoman, she also hath conceived a son in her old age; and this is the sixth month with her that ʳwas called barren. 37 For no word from God shall be void of power. 38 And, Mary said, Behold, the ˢhandmaid of the Lord; be it unto me according to thy word. And the angel departed from her.

39 And Mary arose in these days and went into the hill country with haste, into a city of Ju'dah; 40 and entered into the house of

Zach-a-ri'as and saluted E-lis'a-beth. 41 And it came to pass, when E-lis'a-beth heard the salutation of Mary, the babe leaped in her womb; and E-lis'a-beth was filled with the Holy Spirit; 42 and she lifted up her voice with a loud cry, and said, Blessed *art* thou among women, and blessed *is* the fruit of thy womb. 43 And whence is this to me, that the mother of my Lord should come unto me? 44 For behold, when the voice of thy salutation came into mine ears, the babe leaped in my womb for joy. 45 And blessed *is* she that ᵗbelieved; for there shall be a fulfilment of the things which have been spoken to her from the Lord. 46 And Mary said,

My soul doth magnify the Lord,
47 And my spirit hath rejoiced
    in God my Saviour.

---

p Or, *that which is to be born shall be called holy, the Son of God* q Some ancient

authorities insert *of thee.* r Or, *is* s Gr. *bondmaid.* t Or, *believed that there shall be*

36. *Thy kinswoman.* The degree of relationship is unknown.

39. *In these days.* Probably within a few weeks after the angel had departed. *Into the hill country.* The elevated parts of Judæa, Samaria and lower Galilee. In Canaan as divided among the twelve tribes the hill country included the mountainous districts of Ephraim, Benjamin and Judah. *With haste.* As Mary was now betrothed to Joseph, her sudden departure from her home in Nazareth, where by Jewish custom she was bound to remain apart from her future husband until her marriage, could only result from her knowledge that the angel's prediction was true. *Into a city of Judah.* 'Judah' here means Judæa; but the name of the city is unknown. Some scholars have conjectured that it was Juttah, one of the cities set apart for the priesthood.

43. *The mother of my Lord.* Elizabeth knew that the Son born to Mary would be the Messiah.

46. *My soul doth magnify the Lord.* These and the following words of ver. 46–55 constitute the historic Christian hymn known as the Magnificat, an utterance of praise and thanksgiving by the Virgin Mary for the blessing and honor vouchsafed to her by God in the conception and birth of Jesus Christ. It has been used in public church services since the sixth century. Although a Christian hymn, its devotional feeling and spiritual outlook are Jewish. Mary was far from fully comprehending the truth of which she was the vehicle. Only the life and death of Jesus, and the Christian experience of all succeeding ages, could reveal the full meaning of her words.

47. *God my Saviour.* That is, Jehovah, Saviour not only from sin, but Deliverer from the Roman empire or other foreign power. Much spiritual growth was needed before she knew her Son to be the Saviour of the world.

48 For he hath looked upon the low estate of his *handmaid: For behold, from henceforth all generations shall call me blessed.

49 For he that is mighty hath done to me great things; And holy is his name.

50 And his mercy is unto generations and generations On them that fear him.

51 He hath showed strength with his arm; He hath scattered the proud ᵘin the imagination of their heart.

52 He hath put down princes from *their* thrones, And hath exalted them of low degree.

53 The hungry he hath filled with good things; And the rich he hath sent empty away.

54 He hath given help to Is'ra-el his servant, That he might remember mercy

55 (As he spake unto our fathers) Toward Abraham and his seed for ever.

56 And Mary abode with her about three months, and returned unto her house.

57 Now E-lis'a-beth's time was fulfilled that she should be delivered; and she brought forth a son. 58 And her neighbors and her kinsfolk heard that the Lord had magnified his mercy towards her; and they rejoiced with her. 59 And it came to pass on the eighth day, that they came to circumcise the child; and they would have called him Zach-a-ri'as, after the name of his father. 60 And his mother answered and said, Not so; but he shall be called John. 61 And they said unto her, There is none of thy kindred that is called by this name. 62 And they made signs to his father, what he would have him called. 63 And he asked for a writing tablet, and wrote, saying, His name is John.

s Gr. *bondmaid.*   *u* Or, *by*

48. *All generations shall call me blessed.* Spoken as a prophecy, which has been in part fulfilled.

49. *Holy is his name.* These words close the first or personal part of the hymn, Mary's praise and thanks.

52. *He hath put down princes from their thrones.* He hath made nought of the physical force commanded by the rulers of the earth. *Hath exalted them of low degree.* Hath put into the places of power those who are 'meek and lowly of heart.' See Mk. 10.42-45.

54. *He hath given help to Israel,* etc. Here are manifest the Jewish and patriotic, though limited, character and application of Mary's words. So far, apparently, she had no thought of Jehovah as God of the Gentiles. Nevertheless the latter part of the hymn, ver. 50-55, taken as a whole, declares unmistakably that the kingdom of the Spirit—the rule of divine mercy, justice and truth—had forever displaced the kingdom of worldly pride and strength.

56. *Returned unto her house.* It was not until after Mary's return to Nazareth that Joseph discovered the reason for her long absence. See Mt. 1.18-25.

59. *The eighth day.* According to the Mosaic law the rite of circumcision was performed upon Jewish male children on the eighth day after birth. The rite was a symbol of purification, by which the child was prepared for the privileges of a member of the Jewish community. He was also named at this time.

63. *A writing tablet.* Wooden, and covered with wax or sand.

And they marvelled all. 64 And his mouth was opened immediately, and his tongue *loosed*, and he spake, blessing God. 65 And fear came on all that dwelt round about them: and all these sayings were noised abroad throughout all the hill country of Ju-dæ′a. 66 And all that heard them laid them up in their heart saying, What then shall this child be? For the hand of the Lord was with him.

67 And his father Zach-a-ri′as was filled with the Holy Spirit, and prophesied, saying,

68 Blessed *be* the Lord, the God of Is′ra-el;

For he hath visited and wrought redemption for his people,

69 And hath raised up a horn of salvation for us

In the house of his servant David

70 (As he spake by the mouth of his holy prophets that have been from of old),

71 Salvation from our enemies, and from the hand of all that hate us;

72 To show mercy towards our fathers,

And to remember his holy covenant;

73 The oath which he sware unto Abraham our father,

74 To grant unto us that we being delivered out of the hand of our enemies

Should serve him without fear,

75 In holiness and righteousness before him all our days.

76 Yea and thou, child, shalt be called the prophet of the Most High:

For thou shalt go before the face of the Lord to make ready his ways;

77 To give knowledge of salvation unto his people

In the remission of their sins,

---

68. *Blessed be the Lord, the God of Israel*, etc. These and the following words of ver. 68-79 are known as the Benedictus, which takes its name from the Latin word for ‘blessed.’ The Benedictus is a Christian hymn which has been used in public church services probably since the sixth century. The prophet Zacharias, freed from the dumbness imposed upon him for his doubt, spoke in a strain of mingled blessing and prophecy. The first part of his utterance, ver. 68-75, is an offering of praise and thanks to God for the fulfilment of His covenant in the birth of the Messiah; the second part, ver. 76-89, is in honor of his son, afterward known as John the Baptist, who was to be the Messiah's forerunner and the preacher of repentance as a preparation for his coming. The Benedictus, like the Magnificat, is thoroughly Jewish in feeling and outlook. Zacharias had only a dim apprehension of the far-reaching significance of his words. He had no more thought of the Gentiles than had Mary, and he was the unconscious instrument of divine purposes which embraced all mankind.

69. *A horn of salvation.* A figure of speech often used to symbolize strength, and here applied to the Messiah.

71. *Salvation from our enemies.* According to the Jewish belief, this would mean deliverance from political as well as spiritual enemies.

76. *Before the face of the Lord.* An announcement of John's mission as the forerunner of Jesus.

77. *To give knowledge of salvation*, etc. The ‘knowledge’ of salvation was communicated to the Jews in John's prophetic declaration that the kingdom of heaven was at hand; but it was fully realized only by those who repented, thereby obtaining the remission of their sins.

78 Because of the ᵛtender mercy
  of our God,
  ˣWhereby the dayspring from
    on high ʸshall visit us,
79 To shine upon them that sit
    in darkness and the shadow
    of death;
  To guide our feet into the way
    of peace.
80 And, the child grew, and
waxed strong in spirit, and was
in the deserts till the day of his
showing unto Is'ra-el.

2 Now it came to pass in
  those days, there went out a
decree from Cæ'sar Au-gus'tus,
that all ᵃthe world should be
enrolled. 2 This was the first
enrolment made when Qui-rin'-
i-us was governor of Syr'i-a.
3 And all went to enrol themselves, every one to his own city.
4 And Joseph also went up from
Gal'i-lee, out of the city of Naz'a-

reth, into Ju-dæ'a, to the city of
David, which is called Beth'le-
hem, because he was of the house
and family of David; 5 to enrol
himself with Mary, who was
betrothed to him, being great
with child. 6 And it came to
pass, while they were there, the
days were fulfilled that she
should be delivered. 7 And she
brought forth her firstborn son;
and she wrapped him in swaddling clothes, and laid him in a
manger, because there was no
room for them in the inn.
  8 And there were shepherds in
the same country abiding in the
field, and keeping ᵇwatch by
night over their flock. 9 And an
angel of the Lord stood by them,
and the glory of the Lord shone
round about them: and they were
sore afraid. 10 And the angel
said unto them, Be not afraid;

ᵛ Or, heart of mercy   ˣ Or, Wherein
ʸ Many ancient authorities read hath

viisited us. ᵃ Gr. the inhabited earth. ᵇ Or,
night-watches

---

78. *The dayspring.* The dawn.
79. *The way of peace.* The true
aim and end of the Messianic kingdom; the way of spiritual as well as
of earthly peace.

CHAPTER 2

1. *Cæsar Augustus.* The first
Roman emperor, who reigned from
31 B. C. to 14 A. D. *That all the
world should be enrolled.* That is,
a census of the inhabitants of the
Roman empire.
2. *When Quirinius was governor
of Syria.* Quirinius was at this time
a special legate or commissioner of
Augustus to carry on a war against
a rebellious tribe, the Homona-
denses. As such he was military
governor of Syria and director of
its foreign policy, while the civil administration was in the hands of
Varus.
3. *To enrol themselves, every one to
his own city.* This enrolment, so far
as it concerned the Jews, was specially designed to avoid giving of-

fence to them. It was conducted
according to their own system of
tribes and households.
4. *The city of David, which is
called Bethlehem.* See notes on Mt.
2.1.
7. *No room for them in the inn.*
The crowds who responded to the
summons for enrolment could not
be accommodated as on ordinary
occasions. Joseph and Mary, who
were in humble circumstances, had
no means of obtaining good lodging
in such an emergency. After the
enrolment was over they took a
home in Bethlehem with the intention of living there. See Mt. 2.11.
8. *There were shepherds.* His
birth was in a stable; it was first
made known to shepherds. The
earthly circumstances of the birth
of Jesus were in harmony with the
poverty and obscurity of the common lot. The Bethlehem shepherds
had charge of the sheep reserved for
the sacrifices in the Temple.
10. *To all the people.* The Jews.

for behold, I bring you good tidings of great joy which shall be to all the people: 11 for there is born to you this day in the city of David a Saviour, who is *c*Christ the Lord. 12 And this *is* the sign unto you: Ye shall find a babe wrapped in swaddling clothes, and lying in a manger. 13 And suddenly there was with the angel a multitude of the heavenly host praising God, and saying,

14 Glory to God in the highest, And on earth *d*peace among *e*men in whom he is well pleased.

15 And it came to pass, when the angels went away from them into heaven, the shepherds said one to another, Let us now go even unto Beth'le-hem, and see this *f*thing that is come to pass, which the Lord hath made known unto us. 16 And they came with haste, and found both Mary and Joseph, and the babe lying in the manger. 17 And when they saw it, they made known concerning the saying which was spoken to them about this child. 18 And all that heard it wondered at the things which were spoken unto them by the shepherds. 19

But Mary kept all these *g*sayings, pondering them in her heart. 20 And the shepherds returned, glorifying and praising God for all the things that they had heard and seen, even as it was spoken unto them.

21 And when eight days were fulfilled for circumcising him, his name was called JE'SUS, which was so called by the angel before he was conceived in the womb.

22 And when the days of their purification *h*according to the law of Mo'ses were fulfilled, they brought him up to Je-ru'sa-lem, to present him to the Lord 23 (as it is written in the law of the Lord, *i*Every male that openeth the womb shall be called holy to the Lord), 24 and to offer a sacrifice according to that which is said in the law of the Lord, *k*A pair of turtledoves, or two young pigeons. 25 And behold, there was a man in Je-ru'sa-lem, whose name was Sim'e-on; and this man was righteous and devout, looking for the consolation of Is'ra-el: and the Holy Spirit was upon him. 26 And it had been revealed unto him by the Holy Spirit, that he should not

---

c Or, *Anointed Lord*   *d* Many ancient authorities read *peace, good pleasure among men.*   *e* Gr. *men of good pleasure.*   *f* Or, *saying*   *g* Or, *things*   *h* Lev. xii. 2–6.   *i* Ex. xiii. 2, 12.   *k* Lev. xii. 8; v. 11.

---

11. *A Saviour.* 'Saviour' is to be understood in a spiritual sense, the deliverer from sin and death.

14. The words of this verse have been known for centuries as the Gloria in excelsis (Glory in the highest), one of the historic hymns of the Christian Church. It is sung at morning services.

21. *Eight days.* The rite of circumcision was performed eight days after birth. *His name was called Jesus.* The Jewish male child was

named at the time of circumcision, just as the Christian child is named at baptism. 'Jesus' means Saviour.

25. *Looking for the consolation of Israel.* The coming of the Messiah. Men like Simeon were humbly waiting for a more spiritual manifestation of religion than was seen in the services and sacrifices of the Temple. They knew that these were only a preparation for the advent of Christ.

see death, before he had seen the Lord's Christ. 27 And he came in the Spirit into the temple: and when the parents brought in the child Je′sus, that they might do concerning him after the custom of the law, 28 then he received him into his arms, and blessed God, and said,

29 Now lettest thou thy *l*ser-
    vant depart, *m*Lord,
    According to thy word, in
      peace;
30 For mine eyes have seen thy
    salvation,
31 Which thou hast prepared be-
    fore the face of all peoples;
32 A light for *n*revelation to the
    Gen′tiles,
    And the glory of thy people
      Is′ra-el.

33 And his father and his mother were marvelling at the things which were spoken concerning

him; 34 and Sim′e-on blessed them, and said unto Mary his mother, Behold, this *child* is set for the falling and the rising of many in Is′ra-el; and for a sign which is spoken against; 35 yea and a sword shall pierce through thine own soul; that thoughts out of many hearts may be re-vealed. 36 And there was one Anna, a prophetess, the daughter of Phan′u-el, of the tribe of Ash′er (she was *o*of a great age, having lived with a husband seven years from her virginity, 37 and she had been a widow even unto fourscore and four years), who departed not from the temple, worshipping with fastings and supplications night and day. 38 And coming up at that very hour she gave thanks unto God, and spake of him to all them that were looking for

---

l Gr. *bondservant.*   *m* Gr. *Master.*   *n* Or, *the unveiling of the Gentiles*

o Gr. *advanced in many days.*

29–32. *Now lettest thou thy servant depart, Lord.* These and the re-maining words of ver. 29–32 are known as the Nunc dimittis, a hymn which has been used in church evening services since the fifth cen-tury. Its opening words are Sime-on's prayer to be allowed to die in peace since the promise and revela-tion vouchsafed to him in ver. 26 had been fulfilled. He had seen Jesus, the Messiah, and was content to depart in the peace of God. *Thy salvation.* Jesus the Christ, the Saviour of mankind. *Of all peoples.* These words sound the note of uni-versal salvation for all tribes and nations and races. In the song of Mary (the Magnificat) and of the priest Zacharias (the Benedictus) no mention was made of peoples out-side of Israel. There was no thought apparently of a Saviour for all man-kind. The Messiah was to be a Jew-ish Saviour. Neither Mary nor Zacharias had the larger view or the larger hope, though each was true

to the allotted measure of light. *For revelation to the Gentiles.* The gift of the Messiah was peculiarly the national possession, the sacred pride of the Jews, the treasured hope long dreamed of and spirit-ually dwelt upon; but the promises connected with it were new to the rest of the world. Outside peoples only vaguely yearned for a Deliverer from sin and wretchedness; yet when he appeared they knew him better than did his own people.

34. *For the falling and the rising of many in Israel.* The message and claims of Jesus were to divide the people. Some would accept him. Many would reject him. *For a sign which is spoken against.* In his earthly life a mark for public de-rision and hatred. Words of scorn and contempt were to be applied to him and his followers.

35. *A sword shall pierce through thine own soul.* The sufferings of our Lord's mother were foretold at the same time.

the redemption of Je-ru'sa-lem.
39 And when they had accomplished all things that were according to the law of the Lord,
they returned into Gal'i-lee, to
their own city Naz'a-reth.
40 And the child grew, and
waxed strong, [p]filled with wisdom: and the grace of God was
upon him.
41 And his parents went every
year to Je-ru'sa-lem at the feast
of the passover. 42 And when
he was twelve years old, they
went up after the custom of the
feast; 43 and when they had fulfilled the days, as they were returning, the boy Je'sus tarried
behind in Je-ru'sa-lem; and his
parents knew it not; 44 but supposing him to be in the company,
they went a day's journey; and
they sought for him among their
kinsfolk and acquaintance: 45
and when they found him not,
they returned to Je-ru'sa-lem,
seeking for him. 46 And it came
to pass, after three days they
found him in the temple, sitting
in the midst of the [q]teachers,
both hearing them and asking
them questions: 47 and all that

p Gr. *becoming full of wisdom.*

q Or, *doctors* See ch. 5.17; Acts. 5.34.

40. *And the child grew, and waxed strong.* In this verse the description of the early growth of Jesus in mind and body is that of a normal, healthy human being. It has been rightly said that his doing nothing wonderful was itself a kind of wonder.

41. *His parents went every year.* Mary was not legally required to go up to the Passover feasts, but did so from pious motives.

42. *When he was twelve years old.* At this age, according to the law, the youth of a Jewish boy ended. In his thirteenth year he became a 'son of the law' and began to assume the necessary duties and responsibilities. He was presented before the authorities of the synagogue and given his phylacteries to wear. See note on Mt. 23.5. The ceremony had a meaning similar to that of confirmation or reception into membership in Christian churches. The boy Jesus, if not previously presented at the Nazareth synagogue, was most probably taken up to Jerusalem for that ceremony in the Temple. While there he could see the Jewish great world for himself and begin to be familiar with the national headquarters of the law, written and unwritten, and with its rabbis, teachers, and copyists.

44. *Supposing him to be in the company.* They may have thought that he was in one of the caravans behind them. As the distances were short and kinsfolk were numerous, the presumption was that he would be found amond the latter. It was only after the preliminary search proved fruitless that his parents became alarmed.

46. *In the temple, sitting in the midst of the teachers.* Some scholars have thought that the scene took place in a synagogue specially designed for instructing Jewish youths, and situated within the walls of the Temple enclosure; others that Jesus was within one of the chambers that surrounded the main building. *Hearing them and asking them questions.* The attitude of Jesus as indicated here was teachable and respectful. In the course of instruction the Jewish boy had a right to ask questions.

47. *Amazed at his understanding and his answers.* This effect could only have been produced by the spiritual insight of Jesus, his original grasp of principles. It could not have been his vast knowledge of the law that astonished them. That would have been an empty wonder and beyond the normal acquirement of a youth. The teachers must have been led by his questions to ask questions in return. Among them may been have some learned rabbis and well-known members of the Sandhedrin, such as Shammai, Hillel, Gamaliel, Joseph of Arimathæa and Caiaphas.

heard him were amazed at his understanding and his answers. 48 And then they saw him, they were astonished; and his mother said unto him, 'Son, why hast thou thus dealt with us? behold, thy father and I sought thee sorrowing. 49 And he said unto them, **How is it that ye sought me? knew ye not that I must be ˢin my Father's house?** 50 And they understood not the saying which he spake unto them. 51 And he went down with them, and came to Naz'a-reth; and he was subject unto them: and his mother kept all *these* ᵗsayings in her heart.

52 And Je'sus advanced in wisdom and ᵘstature, and in ᵛfavor with God and men.

3 Now in the fifteenth year of the reign of Ti-be'ri-us Cæ-sar, Pon'tius Pi'late, being governor of Ju-dæ'a, and Her'od being tetrarch of Gal'i-lee, and his brother Philip tetrarch of the region of It-u-ræ'a and Trach-o-ni'tis, and Ly-sa'ni-as tetrarch of Ab-i-le'ne, 2 in the high-priesthood of An'nas and Ca'iaphas, the word of God came unto John the son of Zach-a-ri'as in the wilderness. 3 And he came into all the region round about the Jordan, preaching the baptism of repentance unto remission of sins; 4 as it is written in the book of the words of I-sa'iah the prophet,

ᵃThe voice of one crying in the wilderness,

ᵗ Gr. *Child.*   ˢ Or, *about my Father's business*   Gr. *in the things of my Father.*

ᵗ Or, *things*   ᵘ Or, *age*   ᵛ Or, *grace*   ᵃ Is. xl. 3 ff.

49. *Knew ye not that I must be in my Father's house?* As if it were unreasonable to expect that he would be found in any other place.

50. *They understood not the saying.* The words 'my Father's' were too mysterious for them. His intuition of his divine sonship was very far beyond their comprehension.

51. *Came to Nazareth; and he was subject unto them.* A dutiful return to Nazareth, and submission to Joseph and Mary, were not ordinarily to be expected from a youth who had confounded the learned doctors of the law at Jerusalem; but they illustrate the perfect example of Jesus in the filial relation. His unique spiritual greatness was, in part, his humility (Mt. 11.29); therefore he was an obedient son. He was consistent alike in youth and manhood.

52. *Advanced in wisdom and stature.* History is silent as to the eighteen years between the return to Nazareth and the beginning of his ministry. Whether he lived with his parents all that time is not certainly known. It is at least probable that he frequently visited Jerusalem; but there is no hint that he ever studied with any of the rabbis or doctors of the law, or that he ever received ordination from them by the laying on of hands.

CHAPTER 3

1. *In the fifteenth year,* etc. A. D. 26. *Pontius Pilate.* Fifth Roman procurator of Judæa, Samaria and Idumæa (26–31 A. D.). *Herod.* Herod Antipas, son of Herod the Great. *His brother Philip.* A mild and just prince, who ruled for thirty-eight years. *Abilene.* A district whose chief city was Abila, on the river Abana, eighteen miles from Damascus and thirty-eight from Baalbec.

2. *High-priesthood of Annas and Caiaphas.* This would seem to imply that they were both occupants of the same office at the same time. Luke gives both names because Annas was much more influential than his successor; besides, many Jews believed that he had been wrongfully deposed and had a right to the title. *The word of God.* A call from God.

Make ye ready the way of
the Lord,
Make his paths straight.
5 Every valley shall be filled,
And every mountain and hill
shall be brought low;
And the crooked shall become
straight,
And the rough ways smooth;
6 And all flesh shall see the
salvation of God.

7 He said therefore to the
multitudes that went out to be
baptized of him, Ye offspring of
vipers, who warned you to flee
from the wrath to come? 8
Bring forth therefore fruits
worthy of [b]repentance, and begin not to say within yourselves,
We have Abraham to our father:
for I say unto you, that God is
able of these stones to raise up
children unto Abraham. 9 And
even now the axe also lieth at
the root of the trees: every tree
therefore that bringeth not forth
good fruit is hewn down, and
cast into the fire. 10 And the
multitudes asked him, saying,
What then must we do? 11 And
he answered and said unto them,
He that hath two coats, let him
impart to him that hath none;
and he that hath food, let him
do likewise. 12 And there came
also [c]publicans to be baptized,
and they said unto him, Teacher,
what must we do? 13 And he
said unto them, Extort no more
than that which is appointed
you. 14 And [d]soldiers also asked
him, saying, And we, what must
we do? And he said unto them,
Extort from no man by violence,
neither accuse any one wrongfully; and be content with your
wages.

15 And as the people were in
expectation, and all men reasoned in their hearts concerning
John, whether haply he were the
Christ; 16 John answered, saying unto them all, I indeed
baptize you with water; but
there cometh he that is mightier
than I, the latchet of whose
shoes I am not [e]worthy to unloose: he shall baptize you [f]in
the Holy Spirit and in fire: 17
whose fan is in his hand, thoroughly to cleanse his threshing-
floor, and to gather the wheat into
his garner; but the chaff he will
burn up with unquenchable fire.

b Or, your repentance   c That is, collectors or renters of Roman taxes.   d Gr. soldiers on service.   e Gr. sufficient.   f Or,
with

8. We have Abraham to our father.
This was the time-worn excuse of
the Jews for hoping and believing
that their privileges as descendants
of Abraham would exempt them
from the penalties visited upon
other peoples. They thought that
God ought certainly to spare a son
of Abraham, as he was better than
anybody else.

10-14. What then must we do?
How can we escape the punishments
coming upon us? See notes on Mt.
3.7; Jn. 8.32-36. Extort no more
than that which is appointed you.
Advice that cut through the habitual fault of publicans at its root.
They had the right to collect a certain amount in taxes; but they
habitually exceeded this amount.
From no man by violence. This command to soldiers was both practical
and radical. It condemned lawless
robbery and bloodshed, false swearing to get money and the desire to
break their contract. The Baptist
did not condemn the life of a soldier, but he insisted that it should
be lived honorably.

15-17. Concerning John, whether
haply he were the Christ. See Mt.
3.11, 12; Jn. 1.6-8.

140

18 With many other exhortations therefore preached he *g*good tidings unto the people; 19 but Her′od the tetrarch, being reproved by him for He-ro′di-as his brother′s wife, and for all the evil things which Her′od had done, 20 added this also to them all, that he shut up John in prison.

21 Now it came to pass, when all the people were baptized, that, Je′sus also having been baptized, and praying, the heaven was opened, 22 and the Holy Spirit descended in a bodily form, as a dove, upon him, and a voice came out of heaven, Thou art my beloved Son; in thee I am well pleased.

23 And Je′sus himself, when he began *to teach,* was about thirty years of age, being the son (as was supposed) of Joseph, the *son* of He′li, 24 the *son* of Mat′that, the *son* of Le′vi, the *son* of Mel′chi, the *son* of Jan′na-i, the *son* of Joseph, 25 the *son* of Mat-ta-thi′as, the *son* of A′mos, the *son* of Na′hum, the *son* of Es′li, the *son* of Nag′ga-i, 26 the *son* of Ma′ath, the *son* of Mat-ta-thi′as, the *son* of Sem′e-in, the *son* of Jo′sech, the *son* of Jo′da, 27 the *son* of Jo-an′an, the *son* of Rhe′sa, the *son* of Ze-rub′ba-bel, the *son* of *h*She-al′ti-el, the *son* of Ne′ri, 28 the *son* of Mel′chi, the *son* of Ad′di, the *son* of Co′sam, the *son* of El-ma′dam, the *son* of Er, 29 the *son* of Je′sus, the *son* of E-li-e′zer, the *son* of Jo′rim, the *son* of Mat′that, the *son* of Le′vi, 30 the *son* of Sym′e-on, the *son* of Ju′das, the *son* of Joseph, the *son* of Jo′nam, the *son* of E-li′a-kim, 31 the *son* of Me′le-a, the *son* of Men′na, the *son* of Mat′-ta-tha, the *son* of Na′than, the *son* of David, 32 the *son* of Jes′se, the *son* of O′bed, the *son* of Bo′az, the *son* of *i*Sal′mon, the *son* of Nah′shon, 33 the *son* of Am-min′a-dab, *k*the *son* of *l*Ar′ni, the *son* of Hez′ron, the *son* of Pe′rez, the *son* of Ju′dah, 34 the *son* of Jacob, the *son* of I′saac, the *son* of Abraham, the *son* of Te′rah, the *son* of Na′hor, 35 the *son* of Se′rug, the *son* of Re′u, the *son* of Pe′leg, the *son* of E′ber, the *son* of She′lah, 36 the *son* of Ca-i′nan, the *son* of Ar-phax′ad, the *son* of Shem, the *son* of Noah, the *son* of La′mech, 37 the *son* of Me-thu′se-lah, the *son* of E′noch, the *son* of Ja′red, the *son* of Ma-ha′la-le-el, the *son* of Ca-i′nan, 38 the *son* of E′nos, the *son* of Seth, the *son* of Adam, the *son* of God.

---

g Or, *the gospel*   *h* Gr. *Salathiel.*
i Some ancient authorities write *Sala.*
k Many ancient authorities insert *the* son of *Admin*: and one writes *Admin* for *Amminadab.*   *l* Some ancient authorities write *Aram.*

---

20. *Shut up John in prison.* See note on Mt. 14.3.
21. *When all the people were baptized.* This seems to show that Jesus was the last one to accept the rite. Luke says nothing about John's unwillingness to baptize our Lord. See note on Mt. 3.15.
22. *In a bodily form, as a dove.*

See note on Mt. 3.16.
23–38. *About thirty years of age.* The age required by law for a Levite to begin his ministry. Matthew, writing specially for the Jews, traces the descent of Jesus from Abraham through David. Luke, writing for Gentiles, takes the broader view and traces the descent from Adam.

4 And Je'sus, full of the Holy Spirit, returned from the Jordan, and was led in the Spirit in the wilderness 2 during forty days, being tempted of the devil. And he did eat nothing in those days: and when they were completed, he hungered. 3 And the devil said unto him, If thou art the Son of God, command this stone that it become ªbread. 4 And Je'sus answered unto him, **It is written, ᵇMan shall not live by bread alone.** 5 And he led him up, and showed him all the kingdoms of ᶜthe world in a moment of time. 6 And the devil said unto him, To thee will I give all this authority, and the glory of them: for it hath been delivered unto me; and to whomsoever I will I give it. 7 If thou therefore wilt ᵈworship before me, it shall all be thine. 8 And Je'sus answered and said unto him, **It is written, Thou shalt worship the Lord thy God, and him only shalt thou serve.** 9 And he led him to Je-ru'sa-lem, and set him on the ᵉpinnacle of the temple, and said unto him, If thou art the Son of God, cast thyself down from hence: 10 for it is written,

ᶠHe shall give his angels charge concerning thee, to guard thee:

11 and,

On their hands they shall bear thee up,

Lest haply thou dash thy foot against a stone.

12 And Je'sus answering said unto him, **It is said, ᵍThou shalt not make trial of the Lord thy God.**

13 And when the devil had completed every temptation, he departed from him ʰfor a season.

14 And Je'sus returned in the power of the Spirit into Gal'i-lee: and a fame went out concerning him through all the region round about. 15 And he taught in their synagogues, being glorified of all.

16 And he came to Naz'a-reth, where he had been brought up: and he entered, as his custom was, into the synagogue on the sabbath day, and stood up to read. 17 And there was delivered unto him ⁱthe book of the prophet I-sa'iah. And he

---

a Or, *a loaf*   *b* Dt. viii. 3.   *c* Gr. *the inhabited earth.*   *d* The Greek word denotes an act of reverence, whether paid to a creature, or to the Creator (comp. marginal note on Mt. 2.2)   *e* Gr. *wing.*   *f* Ps. xci. 11, 12.   *g* Dt. vi. 16.   *h* Or, *until.*   *i* Or, *a roll*

CHAPTER 4

1–13. *Was led in the Spirit in the wilderness.* Luke's narrative differs from that of Matthew in changing the order of the second and third temptations. See notes on Mt. 4. 1–3, 5,6–9. The one truth which solves all mysteries of the temptation of Jesus in the mind of the earnest believer is, that he was tempted as the rest of mankind in order that, by victory, he might be their perfect example. *For a season.* Until Gethsemane. Then an angel, as in the temptation, was near to comfort him.

14. *Returned in the power of the Spirit unto Galilee.* See notes on Mt. 4.12, 13.

15. *Taught in their synagogues.* See notes on Mt. 4.23.

16. *Stood up to read.* Readers of the law and the prophets in synagogues were required to stand.

17. *There was delivered unto him.* By the chazzan or attendant. *The book.* Or roll.

opened the ^kbook, and found the place where it was written,

18 ^lThe Spirit of the Lord is upon me,

^mBecause he anointed me to preach ⁿgood tidings to the poor:

He hath sent me to proclaim release to the captives,

And recovering of sight to the blind,

To set at liberty them that are bruised,

19 To proclaim the acceptable year of the Lord.

20 And he closed the ^kbook, and gave it back to the attendant, and sat down: and the eyes of all in the synagogue were fastened on him. 21 And he began to say unto them, To-day hath this scripture been fulfilled in your ears. 22 And all bare him witness, and wondered at the words of grace which proceeded out of his mouth: and they said, Is not this Joseph's son? 23

And he said unto them, Doubtless ye will say unto me this parable, Physician, heal thyself: whatsoever we have heard done at Ca-per'na-um, do also here in thine own country. 24 And he said, Verily I say unto you, No prophet is acceptable in his own country. 25 But of a truth I say unto you, There were many widows in Is'ra-el in the days of E-li'jah, when the heaven was shut up three years and six months, when there came a great famine over all the land; 26 and unto none of them was E-li'jah sent, but only to ^o Zar'e-phath, in the land of Si'don, unto a woman that was a widow. 27 And there were many lepers in Is'ra-el in the time of E-li'sha the prophet; and none of them was cleansed, but only Na'a-man the Syr'i-an. 28 And they were all filled with wrath in the synagogue, as they heard these things; 29 and they rose up, and

k Or, *roll*   l Is. lxi. 1   f.   m Or, *Where-* | *fore*   n Or, *the gospel*   o Gr. *Sarepta.*

18. *He anointed me.* Jesus gives to the words of Isaiah, meant to comfort the Jewish exiles in Babylon, a wider and more spiritual application. The baptism of Jesus was his anointing to preach the gospel to the poor. *Release to the captives.* Meaning the captives of sin and wretchedness, to whom the message of Jesus was release, if they accepted it.

19. *The acceptable year of the Lord.* In Isaiah this means the return of the Jews from their captivity; Jesus meant his own ministry.

20. *Sat down.* Having read while standing, he sat down according to custom to preach the sermon.

21. *To-day hath this scripture been fulfilled.* This was an emphatic assertion of his divine power and message. The glorious note of all that he had read was deliverance. Instead of release to the Babylonian

captives, he proclaimed freedom from the limitations of sin and guilt to the whole world.

22. *Is not this Joseph's son?* How is it possible that one we knew not long ago as a common worker with ourselves should presume to speak with such authority and power? Preposterous! Why, we often saw him at the carpenter's bench! However, if he is really what he claims to be, let him perform here some miracles like those at Capernaum that we heard about. Then we may believe him, but not till then.

25–27. *In the days of Elijah.* In these verses Jesus compares himself to Elijah and Elisha who, like him, were not accepted in their own country but were honored by foreigners.

28. *All filled with wrath.* Because he had dared to think of himself as worthy to be mentioned along with two great prophets.

cast him forth out of the city, and led him unto the brow of the hill whereon their city was built, that they might throw him down headlong. 30 But he passing through the midst of them went his way.

31 And he came down to Ca-per'na-um, a city of Gal'i-lee. And he was teaching them on the sabbath day: 32 and they were astonished at his teaching; for his word was with authority. 33 And in the synagogue there was a man, that had a spirit of an unclean demon; and he cried out with a loud voice, 34 ᵖAh! what have we to do with thee, Je'sus thou Naz-a-rene'? art thou come to destroy us? I know thee who thou art, the Holy One of God. 35 And Je'sus re-buked him, saying, **Hold thy peace, and come out of him.** And when the demon had thrown him down in the midst, he came out of him, having done him no hurt. 36 And amazement came upon all, and they spake together, one with another, say-ing, What is ᵠthis word? for with authority and power he commandeth the unclean spirits, and they come out. 37 And there went forth a rumor con-cerning him into every place of the region round about.

38 And he rose up from the synagogue, and entered into the house of Si'mon. And Si'mon's wife's mother was holden with a great fever; and they besought him for her. 39 And he stood over her, and rebuked the fever; and it left her: and immediately she rose up and ministered unto them.

40 And when the sun was set-ting, all they that had any sick with divers diseases brought them unto him; and he laid his hands on every one of them, and healed them. 41 And demons also came out from many, cry-ing out, and saying, Thou art the Son of God. And rebuking them, he suffered them not to speak, because they knew that he was the Christ.

42 And when it was day, he came out and went into a des-ert place: and the multitudes sought after him, and came unto him, and would have stayed him, that he should not go from them. 43 But he said unto them, **I must preach** ʳ**the good tidings of the kingdom of God to the other cities also: for therefore was I sent.**

44 And he was preaching in the synagogues of ˢGal'i-lee.

5 Now it came to pass, while the multitude pressed

---

p Or, *Let alone*   q Or, *this word, that with authority . . . come out?*   r Or, *the gospel*

s Very many ancient authorities read *Judæa.*

---

29. *That they might throw him down headlong.* As a punishment for what they looked upon as blasphemy.

30. *Went his way.* Their violent attempt was hindered, either mirac-ulously or by the calm majesty of his person and demeanor. It is not known that he ever visited Naz-areth again.

31. *Came down to Capernaum.*

See note on Mt. 4.13.

33–37. *Had a spirit of an unclean demon.* See notes on Mk. 1.23, 24.

38–41. *Simon's wife's mother.* See note on Mt. 8.15.

42–44. *Went into a desert place.* See notes on Mt. 4.23, 25.

CHAPTER 5

1. *Lake of Gennesaret.* Also called

upon him and heard the word of God, that he was standing by the lake of Gen-nes'a-ret; 2 and he saw two boats standing by the lake: but the fishermen had gone out of them, and were washing their nets. 3 And he entered into one of the boats, which was Si'mon's, and asked him to put out a little from the land. And he sat down and taught the multitudes out of the boat. 4 And when he had left speaking, he said unto Si'mon, **Put out into the deep, and let down your nets for a draught.** 5 And Si'mon answered and said, Master, we toiled all night, and took nothing: but at thy word I will let down the nets. 6 And when they had done this, they inclosed a great multitude of fishes; and their nets were breaking; 7 and they beckoned unto their partners in the other boat, that they should come and help them. And they came, and filled both the boats, so that they began to sink. 8 But Si'mon Peter, when he saw it, fell down at Je'sus' knees, saying, Depart from me; for I am a sinful man, O Lord. 9 For he was amazed, and all that were with him, at the draught of the fishes which they

had taken; 10 and so were also ªJames and John, sons of Zeb'e-dee, who were partners with Si'mon. And Je'sus said unto Si'mon, **Fear not; from henceforth thou shalt** ᵇ**catch men.** 11 And when they had brought their boats to land, they left all, and followed him.

12 And it came to pass, while he was in one of the cities, behold, a man full of leprosy: and when he saw Je'sus, he fell on his face, and besought him, saying, Lord, if thou wilt, thou canst make me clean. 13 And he stretched forth his hand, and touched him, saying, **I will; be thou made clean.** And straightway the leprosy departed from him. 14 And he charged him to tell no man: but go thy way, and show thyself to the priest, and offer for thy cleansing, ᶜaccording as Mo'ses commanded, for a testimony unto them. 15 But so much the more went abroad the report concerning him: and great multitudes came together to hear, and to be healed of their infirmities. 16 But he withdrew himself in the deserts, and prayed.

17 And it came to pass on one of those days, that he was teaching; and there were Phar'isees

---

a Or, *Jacob* b Gr. *take alive.*

c Lev. xiii. 49; xiv. 2 ff.

Lake of Tiberias and Sea of Galilee. See note on Mk. 1.16.

8. *Depart from me; for I am a sinful man, O Lord.* Peter's impulsive nature was as capable of quick self-condemnation and repentance as of arrogant conceit and forwardness. On this occasion the holiness and power of Jesus were in such contrast to his own weak faith that he knelt in remorse and besought his Master to leave him.

12–16. *A man full of leprosy.* See notes on Mt. 8.2–4; Mk. 1.40, 45; Lk. 17.12–19.

17. *Pharisees and doctors of the law sitting by.* A proof that the effect of the teaching and miracles of Jesus had gone beyond the multitude and had influenced the leaders of Jewish thought. The Pharisees and doctors of the law mentioned were so interested that they came from all parts of Judæa and Galilee;

and doctors of the law sitting by, who were come out of every village of Gal'i-lee and Ju-dæ'a and Je-ru'sa-lem: and the power of the Lord was with him [d]to heal. 18 And behold, men bring on a bed a man that was palsied: and they sought to bring him in, and to lay him before him. 19 And not finding by what *way* they might bring him in because of the multitude, they went up to the housetop, and let him down through the tiles with his couch into the midst before Je'sus. 20 And seeing their faith, he said, **Man, thy sins are forgiven thee.** 21 And the scribes and the Phar'i-sees began to reason, saying, Who is this that speaketh blasphemies? Who can forgive sins, but God alone? 22 But Je'sus perceiving their [e]reasonings, answered and said unto them, [f]**Why reason ye in your hearts? 23 Which is easier, to say, Thy sins are forgiven thee; or to say, Arise and walk? 24 But that ye may know that the Son of man hath authority on earth to forgive sins** (he said unto him that was palsied), **I say unto thee, Arise, and take up thy couch, and go unto thy house.** 25 And immediately he rose up before them, and took up that whereon he lay, and departed to his house, glorifying

God. 26 And amazement took hold on all, and they glorified God; and they were filled with fear, saying, We have seen strange things to-day.

27 And after these things he went forth, and beheld a [g]publican, named Le'vi, sitting at the place of toll, and said unto him, **Follow me.** 28 And he forsook all, and rose up and followed him.

29 And Le'vi made him a great feast in his house: and there was a great multitude of [g]publicans and of others that were sitting at meat with them. 30 And [h]the Phar'i-sees and their scribes murmured against his disciples, saying, Why do ye eat and drink with the [g]publicans and sinners? 31 And Je'sus answering said unto them, **They that are [i]in health have no need of a physician; but they that are sick. 32 I am not come to call the righteous but sinners to repentance.**

33 And they said unto him, The disciples of John fast often, and make supplications; likewise also the *disciples* of the Phar'i-sees; but thine eat and drink. 34 And Je'sus said unto them, **Can ye make the [k]sons of the bride-chamber fast, while the bridegroom is with them? 35 But the days will come; and**

---

d Gr. *that he should heal.* Many ancient authorities read *that he should heal them.* *e* Or, *questionings*   *f* Or, *What*   *g* See marginal note on ch. 3.12.   *h* Or, *the*

but apparently they were not yet actively hostile.
18–26. *A man that was palsied.* See notes on Mt. 9.2, 3, 5; Mk. 2.4, 12.
27. *And beheld a publican, named Levi.* See note on Mt. 9.9.

Pharisees and the scribes among them *i* Gr. *sound.* *k* That is, *companions of the bridegroom.*

29. *Publicans and of others that were sitting at meat with them.* See note on Mk. 2.15.
30. *Murmured against his disciples.* See note on Mk. 2.16.
33–38. *The disciples of John fast often.* See notes on Mt. 9.14–16.

when the bridegroom shall be taken away from them, then will they fast in those days. 36 And he spake also a parable unto them: No man rendeth a piece from a new garment and putteth it upon an old garment; else he will rend the new, and also the piece from the new will not agree with the old. 37 And no man putteth new wine into old *l*wine-skins; else the new wine will burst the skins, and itself will be spilled, and the skins will perish. 38 But new wine must be put into fresh wine-skins. 39 And no man having drunk old *wine* desireth new; for he saith, The old is *m*good.

6 Now it came to pass on a *a*sabbath, that he was going through the grainfields; and his disciples plucked the ears, and did eat, rubbing them in their hands. 2 But certain of the Phar'i-sees said, Why do ye that which it is not lawful to do on the sabbath day? 3 And Je'sus answering them said, *b*Have ye not read even this, what David did, when he was hungry, he, and they that were with him; 4 how he entered into the house of God, and took and ate the showbread, and gave also to them that were with him; which it is not lawful to eat save for the priests alone? 5 And he said unto them, The Son of man is lord of the sabbath.

6 And it came to pass on another sabbath, that he entered into the synagogue and taught: and there was a man there, and his right hand was withered. 7 And the scribes and the Phar'i-sees watched him, whether he would heal on the sabbath; that they might find how to accuse him. 8 But he knew their thoughts; and he said to the man that had his hand withered, Rise up, and stand forth in the midst. And he rose and stood forth. 9 And Je'sus said unto them, I ask you, Is it lawful on the sabbath to do good, or to do harm? to save a life, or to destroy it? 10 And he looked round about on them all, and said unto him, Stretch forth thy hand. And he did *so*: and his hand was restored. 11 But they were filled with *c*madness; and communed one with another what they might do to Je'sus.

---

l That is, *skins used as bottles.*   *m* Many ancient authorities read *better.*   *a* Many ancient authorities insert *second - first.*   *b* 1 S. xxi. 6.   *c* Or, *foolishness*

---

39. *No man having drunk old wine desireth new.* No man accustomed to old beliefs and practices is likely to find any attraction in new ones. *For he saith, The old is good.* That is, what he finds agreeable he probably thinks right and needs no change, at least not without the strongest and most urgent reason. Jesus meant that the disciples of John and of the Pharisees could not be expected to receive without misgiving and opposition doctrines which were so radically different from the Mo-saic law, especially in its narrow interpretation.

CHAPTER 6

1–5. *He was going through the grain-fields.* See notes on Mt. 12.3, 4.

6–10. *A man there, and his right hand was withered.* See notes on Mk. 3.1, 2, 5.

11. *They were filled with madness.* Enraged because of the exposure of their hypocrisy. *Communed one with another what they might do to Jesus.* See note on Mk. 3.6.

12 And it came to pass in these days, that he went out into the mountain to pray; and he continued all night in prayer to God. 13 And when it was day, he called his disciples; and he chose from them twelve, whom also he named apostles: 14 Si'mon, whom he also named Peter, and Andrew his brother, and ᵈJames and John, and Philip and Bar-thol'o-mew, 15 and Mat'thew and Thomas, and ᵈJames the son of Al-phæ'us, and Si'mon who was called the Zealot, 16 and Ju'das the ᵉson of ᵈJames, and Ju'das Is-car'i-ot, who became a traitor; 17 and he came down with them, and stood on a level place, and a great multitude of his disciples,

and a great number of the people from all Ju-dæ'a and Je-ru'sa-lem, and the sea coast of Tyre and Si'don, who came to hear him, and to be healed of their diseases; 18 and they that were troubled with unclean spirits were healed. 19 And all the multitude sought to touch him; for power came forth from him, and healed them all.

20 And he lifted up his eyes on his disciples, and said, Blessed are ye poor: for yours is the kingdom of God. 21 Blessed are ye that hunger now: for ye shall be filled. Blessed are ye that weep now: for ye shall laugh. 22 Blessed are ye, when men shall hate you, and when they shall separate you from their company, and reproach

---

d Or, Jacob   e Or, brother   See Jude 1.

---

12. *He went out into the mountain to pray.* Luke emphasizes more frequently than the other evangelists the prayers of Jesus. The mountain here referred to is commonly known as that on which the Sermon on the Mount was preached. Tradition since the 13th century has identified it with the Kurn Hattin, a double-peaked hill sixty ft. high and two hours' journey west of Tiberias, on the western shore of the Sea of Galilee. Some Biblical scholars agree with this view; but others think that 'the mountain' means the high land near the northwest shore, just behind Tell Hûm, near the site of Capernaum.

13. *He chose from them twelve, whom also he named apostles.* To be a disciple of Christ was not in itself sufficient to qualify for an apostle. The latter was one who, according to the meaning of the word, could be 'sent forth,' as an authoritative messenger of Christ, a preacher and expounder of his principles and precepts, an organizer of the spiritual kingdom in its earthly relations and requirements.

14–19. *Simon, whom he also named*

Peter, etc. See notes on Mt. 10.1. 2, 5, 7, 8, 11, 12, 14, 15; Mk. 3.17, 18.

20. *And he lifted up his eyes on his disciples, and said.* Ver. 20–49 which follow are practically the same Sermon on the Mount that is given in Mt. 5–7. It was delivered immediately after the choice of the twelve apostles, Luke, however, gives the sermon in abridged form, though in about the same order as Matthew. The sermon is Christ's exposition of the kingdom of heaven. *Blessed are ye poor.* See note on Mt. 5.3.

21. *Blessed are ye that hunger now.* See note on Mt. 5.6. *Blessed are ye that weep now.* See note on Mt. 5.4.

22. *Blessed are ye, when men shall hate you.* See note on Mt. 5.10. Only those who are hated for righteousness' sake shall share this blessing. *Shall separate you,* etc. This refers to social ostracism and the penalties of exclusion from the synagogue and Temple. *For the Son of man's sake.* Faith in and suffering endured for the sake of Christ and the truth spoken by him were required.

you, and cast out your name as evil, for the Son of man's sake. 23 Rejoice in that day, and leap *for joy*: for behold, your reward is great in heaven; for in the same manner did their fathers unto the prophets. 24 But woe unto you that are rich! for ye have received your consolation. 25 Woe unto you, ye that are full now! for ye shall hunger. Woe *unto you*, ye that laugh now! for ye shall mourn and weep. 26 Woe *unto you*, when all men shall speak well of you! for in the same manner did their fathers to the false prophets.

27 But I say unto you that hear, Love your enemies, do good to them that hate you, 28 bless them that curse you, pray for them that despitefully use you. 29 To him that smiteth thee on the *one* cheek offer also the other; and from him that taketh away thy cloak withhold not thy coat also. 30 Give to every one that asketh thee; and of him that taketh away thy goods ask them not again. 31 And as ye would that men should do to you, do ye also to them likewise. 32 And if ye love them that love you, what thank have ye? for even sinners love those that love them. 33 And if ye do good to them that do good to you, what thank have ye? for even sinners do the same. 34 And if ye lend to them of whom ye hope to receive, what

---

24. *Woe unto you that are rich!* The 'woes' included in ver. 24–26 are found only in Luke. They heighten the contrast to the beatitudes, showing how righteousness and blessedness are inseparable on the one hand, and sin and misery on the other. The rich in ver. 24 are not the rich who are just, generous and merciful, but those who put their trust in riches. See notes on Mt. 19.24, 25; Mk. 10.24, 26. Comp. the woes pronounced on the scribes and Pharisees (Mt. 23.13–36).

25. *Ye shall hunger.* Famish in spiritual poverty. *Ye that laugh now!* Those that are derisively contemptuous of the righteous.

26. *When all men shall speak well of you!* A divine warning as to the deceiving nature of human praise. It suggests the question, What is the moral standard of such praise? It implies the command, Bring human approbation to the test of the righteousness of Christ.

27. *Love your enemies.* This not only negatives the Mosaic law of retaliation, but positively forbids hate. It prevents this sin at its source in the erring spirit. See note on Mt. 5.44.

28. *Pray for them that despitefully*

use you. Jesus gave the greatest example of this on the cross (ch. 23.34).

29. *Offer also the other.* A form of speech which illustrates in the most forcible manner and in the most uncompromising spirit the duty of forgiveness. *Taketh away thy cloak.* See note on Mt. 5.40.

30. *Give to every one that asketh thee.* Jesus does not intend that we should give without knowing what we do. See note on Mt. 5.42.

31. *As ye would that men should do to you.* The Golden Rule in Luke is without the reason for it given in Mt. 7.12: 'For this is the law and the prophets.' Jesus spoke these words in harmony with his saying that he came not to destroy the law or the prophets, but to fulfil. Matthew, writing for Jews, naturally emphasized an utterance that would reconcile them to accepting a principle which not only contained all that was best in their own religious thought, but went far beyond it. Luke, writing for Gentiles, omitted any reference to the law or the prophets. See note on Mt. 7.12.

32–36. *What thank have ye?* A rebuke to those whose love springs from self-interest. See notes on Mt. 5.42, 44, 48.

149

thank have ye? even sinners lend to sinners, to receive again as much. 35 But love your enemies, and do *them* good, and lend, *f*never despairing; and your reward shall be great, and ye shall be sons of the Most High: for he is kind toward the unthankful and evil. 36 Be ye merciful, even as your Father is merciful. 37 And judge not, and ye shall not be judged: and condemn not, and ye shall not be condemned: release, and ye shall be released: 38 give, and it shall be given unto you; good measure, pressed down, shaken together, running over, shall they give into your bosom. For with what measure ye mete it shall be measured to you again.

39 And he spake also a parable unto them, Can the blind guide the blind? shall they not both fall into a pit? 40 The disciple is not above his teacher: but every one when he is perfected shall be as his teacher. 41 And why beholdest thou the mote that is in thy brother's eye, but considerest not the beam that is in thine own eye? 42 Or how canst thou say to thy brother, Brother, let me cast out the mote that is in thine eye, when thou thyself beholdest not the beam that is in thine own eye? Thou hypocrite, cast out first the beam out of thine own eye, and then shalt thou see clearly to cast out the mote that is in thy brother's eye. 43 For there is no good tree that bringeth forth corrupt fruit; nor again a corrupt tree that bringeth forth good fruit. 44 For each tree is known by its own fruit. For of thorns men do not gather figs, nor of a bramble bush gather they grapes. 45 The good man out of the good treasure of his heart bringeth forth that which is good; and the evil *man* out of the evil *treasure* bringeth forth that which is evil: for out of the abundance of the heart his mouth speaketh.

46 And why call ye me, Lord, Lord, and do not the things which I say? 47 Every one that cometh unto me, and heareth my words, and doeth them, I will show you to whom he is like: 48 he is like a man building a house, who digged and went deep, and laid a foundation upon the rock: and when a flood arose, the stream brake against that house, and could not shake it: *g*because it had been well

---

f Some ancient authorities read *despairing of no man.*   *g* Many ancient authorities read *for it had been founded upon the rock*: as in Mt. 7.25.

37. *Judge not.* See note on Mt. 7.1.

38. *Shall they give into your bosom.* Alluding to the fold of the robe in front, in which things were carried. Pockets were unknown. *Mete.* Measure.

39. *Can the blind guide the blind?* Are they who are ignorant and heedless of their own faults competent to advise others?

40. *When he is perfected shall be as his teacher.* With Christ as teacher, this promise guarantees an incalculable growth in purity and power to the obedient and persevering disciple.

41. *The mote.* 'Mote' and 'beam' were common terms in Jewish controversy. They signified little and serious faults respectively. See notes on Mt. 7.3.

43–45. *There is no good tree that bringeth forth corrupt fruit.* See notes on Mt. 7.16, 19.

46—49. *Lord.* See notes on Mt. 7.21, 24, 26.

builded. 49 But he that *h*heareth, and *i*doeth not, is like a man that built a house upon the earth without a foundation; against which the stream brake, and straightway it fell in; and the ruin of that house was great.

7 After he had ended all his sayings in the ears of the people, he entered into Ca-per'na-um.

2 And a certain centurion's *a*servant, who was *b*dear unto him, was sick and at the point of death. 3 And when he heard concerning Je'sus, he sent unto him elders of the Jews, asking him that he would come and save his *a*servant. 4 And they, when they came to Je'sus, besought him earnestly, saying, He is worthy that thou shouldest do this for him; 5 for he loveth our nation, and himself built us our synagogue. 6 And Je'sus went with them. And when he was now not far from the house, the centurion sent friends to him, saying unto him, Lord, trouble not thyself; for I am not *c*worthy that thou shouldest come under my roof: 7 wherefore neither thought I myself worthy to come unto thee: but say *d*the word, and my *e*servant shall be healed. 8 For I also am a man set under authority, having under myself soldiers: and I say to this one, Go, and he goeth; and to another, Come, and he cometh; and to my *a*servant, Do this, and he doeth it. 9 And when Je'sus heard these things, he marvelled at him, and turned and said unto the multitude that followed him, **I say unto you, I have not found so great faith, no, not in Is'ra-el.** 10 And they that were sent, returning to the house, found the *a*servant whole.

11 And it came to pass *f*soon afterwards, that he went to a city called Na'in; and his disciples went with him, and a great multitude. 12 Now when he drew near to the gate of the city, behold, there was carried out one that was dead, the only son of his mother, and she was a widow: and much people of the city was with her. 13 And when the Lord saw her, he had compassion on her, and said unto her, Weep not. 14 And he came nigh and touched the bier: and the bearers stood still. And he said, **Young man, I say unto thee, Arise.** 15 And he that was dead sat up, and began to speak. And he gave him to his mother. 16 And fear took hold on all: and

---

h Gr. *heard.* *i* Gr. *did not.* *a* Gr. *bondservant.* *b* Or, *precious to him* Or, *honorable with him* *c* Gr. *sufficient.* *d* Gr. *with a word.* *e* Or, *boy* *f* Many ancient authorities read *on the next day.*

CHAPTER 7

2–10. *A certain centurion's servant.* See notes on Mt. 8.5, 6, 8.

11. *Nain.* 'Nain' means beautiful. The city was twenty-five miles southwest of Capernaum.

12. *When he drew near to the gate.* No burial was allowed within the walls of a Jewish city. In this case the funeral procession had passed out through the city gate. *Much people of the city.* An evidence of the deep sympathy felt for the loss of her only son. See Jn. 11.19.

13. *Weep not.* Jesus was moved to the deepest compassion by grief for bereavement. He wept with Mary and Martha because of the death of their brother Lazarus.

16. *And fear took hold on all.* The people present were apparently as

they glorified God, saying, A great prophet is arisen among us: and, God hath visited his people. 17 And this report went forth concerning him in the whole of Ju-dæ´a, and all the region round about.

18 And the disciples of John told him of all these things. 19 And John calling unto him ᵍtwo of his disciples sent them to the Lord, saying, Art thou he that cometh, or look we for another? 20 And when the men were come unto him, they said, John the Bap´tist hath sent us unto thee, saying, Art thou he that cometh, or look we for another? 21 In that hour he cured many of diseases and ʰplagues and evil spirits; and on many that were blind he bestowed sight. 22 And he answered and said unto them, Go and tell John the things which ye have seen and heard; the blind receive their sight, the lame walk, the lepers are cleansed, and the deaf hear, the dead are raised up, the poor

have ⁱgood tidings preached to them. 23 And blessed is he, whosoever shall find no occasion of stumbling in me.

24 And when the messengers of John were departed, he began to say unto the multitudes concerning John, What went ye out into the wilderness to behold? a reed shaken with the wind? 25 But what went ye out to see? a man clothed in soft raiment? Behold, they that are gorgeously apparelled, and live delicately, are in kings' courts. 26 But what went ye out to see? a prophet? Yea, I say unto you, and much more than a prophet. 27 This is he of whom it is written,

ᵏBehold, I send my messenger before thy face,
Who shall prepare thy way before thee.

28 I say unto you, Among them that are born of women there is none greater than John: yet he that is ˡbut little in the kingdom of God is greater than he.

---

g Gr. *certain two.*   *h* Gr. *scourges.*   *i* Or, *the gospel.*   *k* Mal. iii. 1.   *l* Gr. *lesser.*

much struck with wonder and amazement as a modern crowd would have been. *A great prophet.* That is, a prophet upon whom God had bestowed exceptional power, one of Messianic rank. Christ's miracles may have suggested to the spectators that Elijah or Elisha had returned.

17. *Judæa, and all the region round about.* The fame of miracles in which Jesus raised the dead is invariably represented as of the widest and most convincing kind. His power over death seemed greater than any other manifestation by which the favor of God was made known through him.

18–23. *The disciples of John told him of all these things.* John the Baptist was at this time in prison at

Machærus. See note on Mt. 11.2. Rumors must have reached him which made him wish to know at first hand who the person was about whom his disciples had brought disquieting news. This by no means implies that John ever doubted that Jesus was the Messiah, but the way in which Jesus was laying the foundations of the Messianic kingdom may have been different from John's expectations. See notes on Mt. 11.3, 6.

24–28. *A reed shaken with the wind?* The convincing reply of Jesus to the disciples of John was immediately followed by the greatest tribute of praise that was ever paid to any human being. Jesus here more than vindicated the character and claims of the Baptist. See notes on Mt. 11.7, 12.

29 And all the people when they
heard, and the [m]publicans, justified God, [n]being baptized with
the baptism of John. 30 But the
Phar′i-sees and the lawyers rejected for themselves the counsel of God, [o]being not baptized
of him. 31 **Whereunto then
shall I liken the men of this generation, and to what are they
like?** 32 **They are like unto children that sit in the marketplace, and call one to another;
who say, We piped unto you,
and ye did not dance; we wailed,
and ye did not weep.** 33 **For
John the Bap′tist is come eating
no bread nor drinking wine; and
ye say, He hath a demon.** 34
**The Son of man is come eating
and drinking; and ye say, Behold, a gluttonous man, and a
winebibber, a friend of [m]publicans
and sinners!** 35 **And wisdom [p]is
justified of all her children.**

36 And one of the Phar′i-sees
desired him that he would eat
with him. And he entered into
the Phar′i-see's house, and [q]sat
down to meat. 37 And behold, a
woman who was in the city, a
sinner; and when she knew that
he was [r]sitting at meat in the
Phar′i-see's house, she brought
[s]an alabaster cruse of ointment,
38 and standing behind at his
feet, weeping, she began to wet
his feet with her tears, and
wiped them with the hair of her
head, and [t]kissed his feet, and
anointed them with the ointment. 39 Now when the Phar′i-
see that had bidden him saw it,
he spake within himself, saying,
This man, if he were [u]a prophet,
would have perceived who and
what manner of woman this is
that toucheth him, that she is
a sinner. 40 And Je′sus answering said unto him, **Si′mon, I
have somewhat to say unto thee.**
And he saith, Teacher, say on. 41
**A certain lender had two debtors:
the one owed five hundred [v]shil-**

m See marginal note on ch. 3.12. *n* Or, *having been* *o* Or, *not having been* *p* Or, *was* *q* Or, *reclined at table* *r* Or, *reclining at table* *s* Or, *a flask* *t* Gr. *kissed much.*

u Some ancient authorities read *the prophet.* See Jn. 1.21, 25. *v* The word in the Greek denotes a coin worth about eight pence half-penny, or nearly seventeen cents.

32–35. *They are like unto children.* A reproof of the Jews, who in their fickleness and triviality are likened to children playing games. See notes on Mt. 11.16, 19.

36. *Into the Pharisee's house, and sat down to meat.* A proof that Jesus was not yet wholly out of favor with the Pharisees. Had he been publicly denounced as their enemy he could hardly have been received as a guest at one of their houses.

37. *A woman who was in the city, a sinner.* Not Mary Magdalene, still less Mary, the sister of Lazarus, whose home was at Bethany. Besides, the woman described as a sinner was only such in the estimation of the Pharisee and his guests, except Jesus. She was no longer a sinner, having been led to a new life by the forgiveness of our Lord.

38. *Standing behind at his feet.* Jesus was reclining at table and his feet were stretched out on the couch behind him. The woman could easily approach and anoint his feet.

39. *This man, if he were a prophet,* etc. There speaks the hardened and formal Pharisee! His idea of a prophet was that of a moral detective, of a searcher out and punisher of crime. A prophet whose nature was to love and bless and forgive, was beyond his mental routine and conventional sympathies.

40. *Simon.* To be distinguished from Simon the leper, at whose house the other anointing by Mary, sister of Lazarus, took place.

lings, and the other fifty. 42 When they had not *wherewith* to pay, he forgave them both. Which of them therefore will love him most? 43 Si'mon answered and said, He, I suppose, to whom he forgave the most. And he said unto him, Thou hast rightly judged. 44 And turning to the woman, he said unto Si'mon, Seest thou this woman? I entered into thy house, thou gavest me no water for my feet: but she hath wetted my feet with her tears, and wiped them with her hair. 45 Thou gavest me no kiss: but she, since the time I came in, hath not ceased to *kiss my feet. 46 My head with oil thou didst not anoint: but she hath anointed my feet with ointment. 47 Wherefore I say unto thee, Her sins, which are many, are forgiven; for she loved much: but to whom little is forgiven, *the same* loveth little. 48 And he said unto her, Thy sins are forgiven. 49 And

they that *sat at meat with him began to say *within themselves, Who is this that even forgiveth sins? 50 And he said unto the woman, Thy faith hath saved thee; go in peace.

8 And it came to pass soon afterwards, that he went about through cities and villages, preaching and bringing the *good tidings of the kingdom of God, and with him the twelve, 2 and certain women who had been healed of evil spirits and infirmities: Mary that was called Mag-da-le'ne, from whom seven demons had gone out, 3 and Jo-an'na the wife of Chu'zas Her'od's steward, and Su-san'na, and many others, who ministered unto *them of their substance.

4 And when a great multitude came together, and they of every city resorted unto him, he spake by a parable: 5 The sower went forth to sow his seed: and as he sowed, some fell by the way side; and it was trodden under

---

x Gr. *kiss much.*   *y* Gr. *reclined.*   *z* Or, *among*

a Or, *gospel*   *b* Many ancient authorities read *him.*

---

44. *No water for my feet.* A mark of disrespect, showing the patronizing frame of mind in which he had received Jesus.

46. *My head with oil thou didst not anoint.* The contrast between the slighting attitude of the Pharisee and the adoring gratitude of the forgiven woman is brought out by emphasizing the difference between their outward greetings respectively. The Pharisee did not even anoint the head of Jesus with oil, which was cheap; while the woman anointed the feet of Jesus with ointment, which was very dear.

47. *Her sins, which are many, are forgiven.* The forgiveness of her sins, which was the cause of her reverent love, opened up to her in its beauty a new world, the life of the

spirit. She was not only forgiven, but converted.

CHAPTER 8

2. *Certain women.* The women who ministered to Jesus in his journeys through Galilee. *From whom seven demons had gone out.* 'Seven' indicates only the severe nature of her bodily afflictions.

3. *Chuzas, Herod's steward.* Manager of the palace and estates of Herod Antipas. It has been conjectured by some scholars that Luke obtained from Joanna, Chuzas' wife, who was familiar with the life of Herod's court, much of his knowledge of the Herodian family as well as this account of the ministering women. These were evidently women of wealth.

5–15. *The sower went forth to sow.*

foot, and the birds of the heaven devoured it. 6 And other fell on the rock; and as soon as it grew, it withered away, because it had no moisture. 7 And other fell amidst the thorns; and the thorns grew with it, and choked it. 8 And other fell into the good ground, and grew, and brought forth fruit a hundredfold. As he said these things, he cried, He that hath ears to hear, let him hear.

9 And his disciples asked him what this parable might be. 10 And he said, Unto you it is given to know the mysteries of the kingdom of God: but to the rest in parables; that seeing they may not see, and hearing they may not understand. 11 Now the parable is this: The seed is the word of God. 12 And those by the way side are they that have heard; then cometh the devil, and taketh away the word from their heart, that they may not believe and be saved. 13 And those on the rock *are* they who, when they have heard, receive the word with joy; and these have no root, who for a while believe, and in time of temptation fall away. 14 And that which fell among the thorns, these are they that have heard, and as they go on their way they are choked with cares and riches and pleasures of *this*

life, and bring no fruit to perfection. 15 And that in the good ground, these are such as in an honest and good heart, having heard the word, hold it fast, and bring forth fruit with ᶜpatience.

16 And no man, when he hath lighted a lamp, covereth it with a vessel, or putteth it under a bed; but putteth it on a stand, that they that enter in may see the light. 17 For nothing is hid, that shall not be made manifest; nor *anything* secret, that shall not be known and come to light. 18 Take heed therefore how ye hear: for whosoever hath, to him shall be given; and whosoever hath not, from him shall be taken away even that which ʰe ᵈthinketh he hath.

19 And there came to him his mother and brethren, and they could not come at him for the crowd. 20 And it was told him, Thy mother and thy brethren stand without, desiring to see thee. 21 But he answered and said unto them, My mother and my brethren are these that hear the word of God, and do it.

22 Now it came to pass on one of those days, that he entered into a boat, himself and his disciples; and he said unto them, Let us go over unto the other side of the lake: and they launched forth. 23 But as they sailed he fell asleep: and there

---

See notes on Mt. 13.3, 11–13; Mk. 4.13–15.

16. *A lamp.* See note on Mt. 5. 15.

17. *Nothing is hid, that shall not be made manifest.* This refers to the truths that Jesus came to reveal. At first they were the possession of

the few; but their wide and ever growing recognition is inevitable.

18. *Whosoever hath.* See note on Mt. 13.12.

19–21. *His mother and brethren.* See notes on Mt. 12.48, 50.

23–25. *There came down a storm of wind on the lake.* Then as now the

came down a storm of wind on the lake; and they were filling *with water*, and were in jeopardy. 24 And they came to him, and awoke him, saying, Master, master, we perish.   And he awoke, and rebuked the wind and the raging of the water: and they ceased, and there was a calm. 25 And he said unto them, **Where is your faith?** And being afraid they marvelled, saying one to another, Who then is this, that he commandeth even the winds and the water, and they obey him?

26 And they arrived at the country of the *e*Ger′a-senes′, which is over against Gal′i-lee. 27 And when he was come forth upon the land, there met him a certain man out of the city, who had demons; and for a long time he had worn no clothes, and abode not in *any* house, but in the tombs. 28 And when he saw Je′sus, he cried out, and fell down before him, and with a loud voice said, What have I to do with thee, Je′sus, thou Son of the Most High God? I beseech thee, torment me not. 29 For he was commanding the unclean spirit to come out from the man. For *f*oftentimes it had seized him: and he was kept under guard, and bound with chains and fetters; and breaking the bands asunder, he was driven of the demon into the deserts. 30 And Je′sus asked him, **What is** thy name? And he said, Legion; for many demons were entered into him. 31 And they entreated him that he would not command them to depart into the abyss. 32 Now there was there a herd of many swine feeding on the mountain: and they ·entreated him that he would ·give them leave to enter into them.   And he gave them leave. 33 And the demons came out from the man, and entered into the swine: and the herd rushed down the steep into the lake, and were drowned. 34 And when they that fed them saw what had come to pass, they fled, and told it in the city and in the country. 35 And they went out to see what had come to pass; and they came to Je′sus, and found the man, from whom the demons were gone out, sitting, clothed and in his right mind, at the feet of Je′sus: and they were afraid. 36 And they that saw it told them how he that was possessed with demons was *g*made whole. 37 And all the people of the country of the Ger′a-senes′ round about asked him to depart from them; for they were holden with great fear: and he entered into a boat, and returned. 38 But the man from whom the demons were gone out prayed him that he might be with him: but he sent him away, saying, 39 **Return** **to thy house, and declare how** **great things God hath done for**

---

e Many ancient authorities read *Gergesenes*; others, *Gadarenes*: and so in

Sea of Galilee was swept by frequent wind-storms coming down from the snow-capped Mount Hermon. See note on Mt. 8.25.

ver. 37.   *f* Or, *of a long time*   *g* Or, *saved*

26–39. *At the country of the Gerasenes, which is over against Galilee.* See notes on Mt. 8.28, 29; Mk. 5.9, 11, 15, 17, 18.

thee. And he went his way, publishing throughout the whole city how great things Je′sus had done for him.

40 And as Je′sus returned, the multitude welcomed him; for they were all waiting for him. 41 And behold, there came a man named Ja-ï′rus, and he was a ruler of the synagogue: and he fell down at Je′sus′ feet, and besought him to come into his house; 42 for he had an only daughter, about twelve years of age, and she was dying. But as he went the multitudes thronged him.

43 And a woman having an issue of blood twelve years, who ᵸhad spent all her living upon physicians, and could not be healed of any, 44 came behind him, and touched the border of his garment: and immediately the issue of her blood stanched. 45 And Je′sus said, Who is it that touched me? And when all denied, Peter said, ⁱand they that were with him, Master, the multitudes press thee and crush thee. 46 But Je′sus said, Some one did touch me; for I perceived that power had gone forth from me. 47 And when the woman saw that she was not hid, she came trembling, and falling down before him declared in the presence of all the people for what cause she

touched him, and how she was healed immediately. 48 And he said unto her, Daughter, thy faith hath ᵏmade thee whole; go in peace.

49 While he yet spake, there cometh one from the ruler of the synagogue's *house*, saying, Thy daughter is dead; trouble not the Teacher. 50 But Je′sus hearing it, answered him, Fear not: only believe, and she shall be ˡmade whole. 51 And when he came to the house, he suffered not any man to enter in with him, save Peter, and John, and James, and the father of the maiden and her mother. 52 And all were weeping, and bewailing her: but he said, Weep not; for she is not dead, but sleepeth. 53 And they laughed him to scorn, knowing that she was dead. 54 But he, taking her by the hand, called, saying, Maiden, arise. 55 And her spirit returned, and she rose up immediately: and he commanded that *something* be given her to eat. 56 And her parents were amazed: but he charged them to tell no man what had been done.

9 And he called the twelve together, and gave them power and authority over all demons, and to cure diseases. 2 And he sent them forth to preach the kingdom of God, and

---

h Some ancient authorities omit *had spent all her living upon physicians, and.*

43–48. *A woman having an issue of blood.* See notes on Mk. 5.25, 29.
49–56. *Thy daughter is dead; trouble not the Teacher.* Jesus, while on his way to the house of Jaïrus, a ruler of the synagogue, had stopped to heal the woman with

i Some ancient authorities omit *and they that were with him.* *k* Or, *saved thee* *l* Or, *saved*

the issue of blood. See notes on Mt. 9.24; Mk. 5.36, 39, 41, 42.

CHAPTER 9

1. *Gave them power and authority.* See note on Mt. 10.1.
2–6. *To preach the kingdom of God.*

to heal *a*the sick. 3 And he said unto them, **Take nothing for your journey, neither staff, nor wallet, nor bread, nor money; neither have two coats.** 4 **And into whatsoever house ye enter, there abide, and thence depart.** 5 **And as many as receive you not, when ye depart from that city, shake off the dust from your feet for a testimony against them.** 6 And they departed, and went throughout the villages, preaching the *b*gospel, and healing everywhere.

7 Now Her'od the tetrarch heard of all that was done: and he was much perplexed, because that it was said by some, that John was risen from the dead; 8 and by some, that E-li'jah had appeared; and by others, that one of the old prophets was risen again. 9 And Her'od said, John I beheaded: but who is this, about whom I hear such things? And he sought to see him.

10 And the apostles, when they were returned, declared unto him what things they had done. And he took them, and withdrew apart to a city called Beth-sa'i-da. 11 But the multitudes perceiving it followed him: and he welcomed them, and spake to them of the kingdom of God,

and them that had need of healing he cured. 12 And the day began to wear away; and the twelve came, and said unto him, Send the multitude away, that they may go into the villages and country round about, and lodge, and get provisions: for we are here in a desert place. 13 But he said unto them, **Give ye them to eat.** And they said, We have no more than five loaves and two fishes; except we should go and buy food for all this people. 14 For they were about five thousand men. And he said unto his disciples, **Make them *c*sit down in companies, about fifty each.** 15 And they did so, and made them all *c*sit down. 16 And he took the five loaves and the two fishes, and looking up to heaven, he blessed them, and brake; and gave to the disciples to set before the multitude. 17 And they ate, and were all filled: and there was taken up that which remained over to them of broken pieces, twelve baskets.

18 And it came to pass, as he was praying apart, the disciples were with him: and he asked them, saying, **Who do the multitudes say that I am?** 19 And they answering said, John the Bap'tist; but others *say*, E-li'jah;

---

a Some ancient authorities omit *the sick.*   *b* Or, *good tidings*   *c* Gr. *recline.*

See notes on Mt. 10.7, 11, 12, 14; Mk. 6.7–11.

7. *Herod the tetrarch heard of all that was done.* Herod Antipas, son of Herod the Great.

8. *That Elijah had appeared.* The word 'appeared' is in significant contrast to 'risen' in ver. 7. Elijah had been translated.

9. *John I beheaded.* See note on Mk. 6.16.

10–17. *Withdrew apart to a city*

called Bethsaida. A desert place near the city of Bethsaida Julias. See notes on Mt. 14.13, 21; Mk. 6.32, 35, 38, 40, 44.

18. *Praying apart.* Only Luke mentions that Jesus was praying alone. *Who do the multitudes say that I am?* That is, the crowds that were following Jesus about.

19–27. *And they answering said.* See notes on Mt. 16.14–20; Mk. 8.29.

158

and others, that one of the old prophets is risen again. 20 And he said unto them, But who say ye that I am? And Peter answering said, The Christ of God. 21 But he charged them, and commanded *them* to tell this to no man; 22 saying, The Son of man must suffer many things, and be rejected of the elders and chief priests and scribes, and be killed, and the third day be raised up. 23 And he said unto all, If any man would come after me, let him deny himself, and take up his cross daily, and follow me. 24 For whosoever would save his life shall lose it; but whosoever shall lose his life for my sake, the same shall save it. 25 For what is a man profited, if he gain the whole world, and lose or forfeit his own self? 26 For whosoever shall be ashamed of me and of my words, of him shall the Son of man be ashamed, when he cometh in his own glory, and *the glory* of the Father, and of the holy angels. 27 But I tell you of a truth, There are some of them that stand here, who shall in no wise taste of death, till they see the kingdom of God.

28 And it came to pass about eight days after these sayings, that he took with him Peter and John and James, and went up into the mountain to pray. 29 And as he was praying, the fashion of his countenance was altered, and his raiment *became* white *and* dazzling. 30 And behold, there talked with him two men, who were Mo'ses and E-li'jah; 31 who appeared in glory, and spake of his ᵈdecease which he was about to accomplish at Je-ru'sa-lem. 32 Now Peter and they that were with him were heavy with sleep: but ᵉwhen they were fully awake, they saw his glory, and the two men that stood with him. 33 And it came to pass, as they were parting from him, Peter said unto Je'sus, Master, it is good for us to be here: and let us make three ᶠtabernacles; one for thee, and one for Mo'ses, and one for E-li'jah: not knowing what he said. 34 And while he said these things, there came a cloud, and overshadowed them: and they feared as they entered into the cloud. 35 And a voice came out of the cloud, saying, This is ᵍmy Son, my chosen: hear ye him. 36 And when the voice ʰcame, Je'sus was found alone. And they held their peace, and told no man in those days any of the things which they had seen.

37 And it came to pass, on the next day, when they were come down from the mountain, a great multitude met him. 38 And behold, a man from the multitude cried, saying, Teacher,

d Or, *departure*   e Or, *having remained awake*   f Or, *booths*   g Many ancient authorities read *my beloved Son*. See Mt. 17.5; Mk. 9.7.   h Or, *was past*

28–36. *He took with him Peter and John and James.* To witness his transfiguration. See notes on Mt. 17.1, 3, 5, 9; Mk. 9.2, 4, 7.
37–43. *When they were come down from the mountain.* They came from the vision of Christ in the glory of his transfiguration to meet the distress of the epileptic boy. See notes on Mt. 17.15, 16; Mk. 9.17–19, 23.

I beseech thee to look upon my son; for he is mine only child: 39 and behold, a spirit taketh him, and he suddenly crieth out; and it *teareth him that he foameth, and it hardly departeth from him, bruising him sorely. 40 And I besought thy disciples to cast it out; and they could not. 41 And Je′sus answered and said, **O faithless and perverse generation, how long shall I be with you, and bear with you? bring hither thy son.** 42 And as he was yet a coming, the demon *k*dashed him down, and *l*tare *him* grievously. But Je′sus rebuked the unclean spirit, and healed the boy, and gave him back to his father. 43 And they were all astonished at the majesty of God.

But while all were marvelling at all the things which he did, he said unto his disciples, 44 Let these words sink into your ears: for the Son of man shall be *m*delivered up into the hands of men. 45 But they understood not this saying, and it was concealed from them, that they should not perceive it; and they were afraid to ask him about this saying.

46 And there arose a *n*reasoning among them, which of them was the *o*greatest. 47 But when Je′sus saw the *n*reasoning of their heart, he took a little child, and set him by his side, 48 and said unto them, **Whosoever shall receive this little child in my name receiveth me: and whosoever shall receive me receiveth him that sent me: for he that is *p*least among you all, the same is great.**

49 And John answered and said, Master, we saw one casting out demons in thy name; and we forbade him, because he followeth not with us. 50 But Je′sus said unto him, **Forbid *him* not: for he that is not against you is for you.**

51 And it came to pass, when the days *q*were well-nigh come that he should be received up, he

---

i Or, *convulseth* *k* Or, *rent him* *l* Or, *convulsed* *m* Or, *betrayed* *n* Or, *question-* *ing* *o* Gr. *greater*. *p* Gr. *lesser*. *q* Gr. *were being fulfilled*.

44. *The Son of man shall be delivered up.* A saddening contrast to the expected glory of his Messianic power.

45. *And they understood not this saying.* They could not grasp the meaning of Christ's prediction of his death on the cross and of his resurrection. They were both saddened and confused by it; but after he was crucified and risen, they were as courageous in their action, as clear in their conviction and self-denying in their devotion as formerly they had been fearful and irresolute. Their changed attitude is a convincing proof that Jesus died and rose again.

46–48. *Which of them was the greatest.* See notes on Mt. 18.1; Mk. 9.35.

49, 50. *Casting out demons in thy name.* See notes on Mk. 9.38, 39.

51. *When the days were well-nigh come.* This verse begins a section of ten chapters, extending to ch. 19.28, and including the events in what is generally called the Peræan ministry of Jesus, although the scene of that ministry was partly in Judæa. In this section, which is peculiar to Luke, there is described the progress of our Lord on his last solemn journey to Jerusalem. It contains a much greater number of events, and demands a much longer time, than the corresponding narratives by Matthew and Mark. A part of this journey is given in Mt. 18–20.1–16 and Mk. 10.1–31.

stedfastly set his face to go to Je-ru'sa-lem, 52 and sent messengers before his face: and they went, and entered into a village of the Sa-mar'i-tans, to make ready for him. 53 And they did not receive him, because his face was *as though he were* going to Je-ru'sa-lem. 54 And when his disciples James and John saw *this*, they said, Lord, wilt thou that we bid fire to come down from heaven, and consume them[r]? 55 But he turned, and rebuked them[s]. 56 And they went to another village.

57 And as they went on the way, a certain man said unto him, I will follow thee whithersoever thou goest. 58 And Je'sus said unto him, **The foxes have holes, and the birds of the heaven *have* 'nests; but the Son** of man hath not where to lay his head. 59 And he said unto another, **Follow me.** But he said, Lord, suffer me first to go and bury my father. 60 But he said unto him, **Leave the dead to bury their own dead; but go thou and publish abroad the kingdom of God.** 61 And another also said, I will follow thee, Lord; but first suffer me to bid farewell to them that are at my house. 62 But Je'sus said unto him, **No man, having put his hand to the plow, and looking back, is fit for the kingdom of God.**

10 Now after these things the Lord appointed seventy [a]others, and sent them two and two before his face into every city and place, whither he himself was about to come. 2 And

---

[r] Many ancient authorities add *even as Elijah did.* Comp. 2 K. 1.10–12. [s] Some ancient authorities add *and said, Ye know not what manner of spirit ye are of.* Some, but fewer, add also *For the Son of*

---

52. *And sent messengers.* They were probably disciples. *To make ready for him.* To provide food and lodging, as there were with him other disciples and followers than the twelve apostles.

53. *They did not receive him, because*, etc. The inhabitants of this Samaritan village were swayed by race jealousy because Jesus appeared to them as a leader, possibly of a Messianic movement, who clashed with their views. The face of our Lord 'was as though he were going to Jerusalem'; but the Samaritans looked upon their holy mountain, Gerizim, as the place where the Messiah ought to go.

57–60. *I will follow thee whithersoever thou goest.* See notes on Mt. 8.19, 20, 22.

61, 62. *Another also said, I will follow thee, Lord.* The 'certain man' of ver. 57, the man who wished first to go and bury his father, and he who asked first to bid farewell to

---

man came not to destroy men's lives but to save them. Comp. ch. 19.10; Jn. 3.17; 12.47. [t] Gr. *lodging-places.* [a] Many ancient authorities add *and two*: and so in ver. 17.

---

his household, were all examples of the impulsive follower or believer who does not count the cost. Jesus means by his reply in each case that full devotion to him must, if necessary, instantly abandon the concerns and attractions of the moment, sever family ties and accept work and responsibility.

CHAPTER 10

1. *After these things.* After his departure from Galilee and the beginning of his journey through Peræa. *The Lord appointed seventy others.* He had already promised the twelve that they should sit on thrones judging the twelve tribes of Israel. He now sends out on a special mission a number of disciples equal to that of the Sanhedrin. It is significant that he used numbers identified with the institutions of the old dispensation to shadow forth the new.

2–16. *The harvest indeed is plenteous.* Our Lord's charge to the

he said unto them, The harvest indeed is plenteous, but the laborers are few: pray ye therefore the Lord of the harvest, that he send forth laborers into his harvest. 3 Go your ways; behold, I send you forth as lambs in the midst of wolves. 4 Carry no purse, no wallet, no shoes; and salute no man on the way. 5 And into whatsoever house ye shall *b*enter, first say, Peace *be* to this house. 6 And if a son of peace be there, your peace shall rest upon *c*him: but if not, it shall turn to you again. 7 And in that same house remain, eating and drinking such things as they give: for the laborer is worthy of his hire. Go not from house to house. 8 And into whatsoever city ye enter, and they receive you, eat such things as are set before you: 9 and heal the sick that are therein, and say unto them, The kingdom of God is come nigh unto you. 10 But into whatsoever city ye shall enter, and they receive you not, go out into the streets thereof and say, 11 Even the dust from your city, that cleaveth to our feet, we wipe off against you: nevertheless know this, that the kingdom of God is come nigh. 12 I say unto you, It shall be more tolerable in that day for Sod'om, than for that city. 13 Woe unto thee, Cho-ra'zin! woe unto thee, Beth-sa'i-da! for if the *d*mighty works had been done in Tyre and Si'don, which were done in you, they would have repented long ago, sitting in sackcloth and ashes. 14 But it shall be more tolerable for Tyre and Si'don in the judgment, than for you. 15 And thou, Ca-per'na-um, shalt thou be exalted unto heaven? thou shalt be brought down unto Ha'des. 16 He that heareth you heareth me; and he that rejecteth you rejecteth me; and he that rejecteth me rejecteth him that sent me.

17 And the seventy returned with joy, saying, Lord, even the demons are subject unto us in thy name. 18 And he said unto them, I beheld Satan fallen as lightning from heaven. 19 Behold, I have given you authority to tread upon serpents and scorpions, and over all the power of the enemy: and nothing shall in any wise hurt you. 20 Nevertheless in this rejoice not, that

---

b Or, *enter first, say*   *c* Or, *it*

d Gr. *powers.*

---

seventy is briefer than that to the twelve, but otherwise is practically the same. See notes on Mt. 9.37; 10.12, 14–16, 40; 11.21, 22.

18. *I beheld Satan fallen as lightning from heaven.* Alluding to the victory of the seventy over the demons in his name, and comparing the defeat of Satan therein to his original fall from heaven.

20. *Nevertheless in this rejoice not.* That is, they were to rejoice less in their power over the enemy, Satan, and over all evil spirits, than in the great fact that the Spirit of God was dwelling within them, whereby their names were written in heaven. The occurrence of the word 're-joice' twice in this verse is noteworthy. The word in the original Greek is even stronger; it means 'exult.' All through the Christian ages there has been a weakening tendency to dwell too much upon our Lord's life as that of the Man of Sorrows, whereas his chief manifestation was exultant spiritual joy and thankfulness. See Phil. 4.4–7.

the spirits are subject unto you; but rejoice that your names are written in heaven.

21 In that same hour he rejoiced *e*in the Holy Spirit, and said, I *f*thank thee, O Father, Lord of heaven and earth, that thou didst hide these things from the wise and understanding, and didst reveal them unto babes: yea, Father; *g*for so it was well-pleasing in thy sight. 22 All things have been delivered unto me of my Father: and no one knoweth who the Son is, save the Father; and who the Father is, save the Son, and he to whomsoever the Son willeth to reveal *him*. 23 And turning to the disciples, he said privately, Blessed *are* the eyes which see the things that ye see: 24 for I say unto you, that many prophets and kings desired to see the things which ye see, and saw them not; and to hear the things which ye hear, and heard them not.

25 And behold, a certain lawyer stood up and made trial of him, saying, Teacher, what shall I do to inherit eternal life? 26 And he said unto him, **What** is written in the law? how readest thou? 27 And he answering said, *h*Thou shalt love the Lord thy God *i*with all thy heart, and with all thy soul, and with all thy strength, and with all thy mind; *k*and thy neighbor as thyself. 28 And he said unto him, Thou hast answered right: **this** do, and thou shalt live. 29 But he, desiring to justify himself, said unto Je′sus, And who is my neighbor? 30 Je′sus made answer and said, **A certain man was** going down from Je-ru′sa-lem to Jer′i-cho; and he fell among robbers, who both stripped him and beat him, and departed, leaving him half dead. 31 And by chance a certain priest was going down that way: and when he saw him, he passed by on the other side. 32 And in like man-

<hr>

e Or, *by*   *f* Or, *praise*   *g* Or, *that*   *h* Dt. vi. 5.   *i* Gr. *from*.   *k* Lev. xix. 18.

21, 22. *I thank thee, O Father, Lord of heaven and earth.* See notes on Mt. 11.25, 27.

23, 24. *Which see the things that ye see.* The mysteries of the kingdom of heaven, explained to the disciples by Jesus the Messiah, as well as his miracles and ministrations of mercy; things which many prophets and kings desired in vain to see.

25–28. *What shall I do to inherit eternal life?* The lawyer mentioned in ver. 25 is not the same as in Mt. 22.35; but the question he asked brings out in the same way the first and greatest commandment. See notes on Mt. 22.38, 39.

29. *And who is my neighbor?* The answer to this is the parable of the Good Samaritan, ver. 30–37. In this parable the Jewish conception of a neighbor, limited by the

sympathies of the tribe and nation, is forever superseded by the divine ideal portrayed in the words of Jesus.

30. *Jericho* (city of palm trees). The road from Jerusalem to Jericho was a rapid and winding descent. It was dangerous, then as now, to travelers on account of marauding Arabs. It is about twenty-one miles long. Jericho, one of the priestly cities, was about fifteen miles northeast of Jerusalem. On its site is the small village of Riha. See note on Mt. 20.29.

31. *Passed by on the other side.* This priest, whose office implied not only the duty of kindness but the responsibility of being an example, ignored the helpless plight of his own countryman.

32. *And in like manner a Levite also.* This Levite, lower in rank than the priest, being an assistant

ner a Le've Levite also, when he came to the place, and saw him, passed by on the other side. 33 But a certain Sa-mar'i-tan, as he journeyed, came where he was: and when he saw him, he was moved with compassion, 34 and came to him, and bound up his wounds, pouring on *them* oil and wine; and he set him on his own beast, and brought him to an inn, and took care of him. 35 And on the morrow he took out two *l*shillings, and gave them to the host, and said, Take care of him; and whatsoever thou spendest more, I, when I come back again, will repay thee. 36 Which of these three, thinkest thou, proved neighbor unto him that fell among the robbers? 37 And he said, He that showed mercy on him.   And Je'sus said unto him, Go, and do thou likewise.

38 Now as they went on their way, he entered into a certain village: and a certain woman named Martha received him into her house. 39 And she had a sister called Mary, who also sat at the Lord's feet, and heard his word. 40 But Martha was *m*cumbered about much serving; and she came up to him, and said, Lord, dost thou not care that my sister did leave me to serve alone? bid her therefore that she help me. 41 But the Lord answered and said unto her, *n*Martha, Martha, thou art anxious and troubled about many things: 42 *o*but one thing is needful: for Mary hath chosen the good part, which shall not be taken away from her.

---

l See marginal note on ch. 7. 41. *m* Gr. *distracted.* *n* A few ancient authorities read *Martha, Martha, thou art troubled;*

Mary hath chosen &c. *o* Many ancient authorities read *but few things are needful, or one.*

---

who could not enter the sanctuary of the Temple, was as deficient in sympathy as his superior, though perhaps less blameworthy.

33. *A certain Samaritan.* In thus selecting as an example of pure neighborliness a member of a community to whom the Jews denied all neighborliness, our Lord implied a serious rebuke to the questioning lawyer and his nation.

34. *Oil and wine.* The usual remedies of that time.

37. *Go and do thou likewise.* Jesus immediately enforces by a command the admission of the truth. The lawyer was fortunate in hearing the parable, but could be blessed only in acting up to the spirit of it.

38. *A certain village.* Bethany.

39. *Sat at the Lord's feet, and heard his word.* The account of the little household at Bethany, composed of Lazarus, Martha and Mary, is peculiar to Luke. Mary, though not more hospitable than Martha, was more spiritually con-

templative.   It was a natural difference between the characters of the two sisters which led one to emphasize unduly the details of housekeeping, and the other to treasure up the words of Jesus.

41. *Martha, Martha, thou art anxious and troubled.* The repetition of her name by our Lord shows that in his gentle reproof of Martha there was tender consideration. *About many things.* Which were not important enough to call for excessive attention or worry.

42. *But one thing is needful.* This contrasts the central fact of spiritual insight and instruction with the fleeting and distracting variety of concerns purely earthly. *Hath chosen the good part.* Both sisters had reverent love for our Lord, but not in equal measure, for Mary better understood him. Still, she was commended for choosing the good part, and Christ's reproof of Martha was meant to incline her choice likewise.

11 And it came to pass, as he was praying in a certain place, that when he ceased, one of his disciples said unto him, Lord, teach us to pray, even as John also taught his disciples. 2 And he said unto them, When ye pray, say, *a*Father, Hallowed be thy name. Thy kingdom come.*b* 3 Give us day by day *c*our daily bread. 4 And forgive us our sins; for we ourselves also forgive every one that is indebted to us. And bring us not into temptation*d*.

5 And he said unto them, Which of you shall have a friend, and shall go unto him at midnight, and say to him, Friend, lend me three loaves; 6 for a friend of mine is come to me from a journey, and I have nothing to set before him; 7 and he from within shall answer and say, Trouble me not: the door is now shut, and my children are with me in bed; I cannot rise and give thee? 8 I say unto you, Though he will not rise and give him because he is his friend, yet because of his importunity he will arise and give him *e*as many as he needeth. 9 And I say unto you, Ask, and it shall be given you; seek, and ye shall find; knock, and it shall be opened unto you. 10 For every one that asketh receiveth; and he that seeketh findeth; and to him that knocketh it shall be opened. 11 And of which of you that is a father shall his son ask *f*a loaf, and he give him a stone? or a fish, and he for a fish give him a

---

a Many ancient authorities read *Our Father, who art in heaven.* See Mt. 6.9. *b* Many ancient authorities add *Thy will be done, as in heaven, so on earth.* See Mt. 6.10. *c* Gr. *our bread for the coming day.* Or, *our needful bread:* as in Mt. 6.11.

d Many ancient authorities add *but deliver us from the evil* one (or, *from evil*). See Mt. 6.13. *e* Or, *whatsoever things* *f* Some ancient authorities omit *a loaf, and he give him a stone?* or.

CHAPTER 11

1–4. *Lord, teach us to pray.* In the Lord's Prayer as recorded by Luke two petitions given by Matthew are omitted: 'Thy will be done,' etc., and 'but deliver us from the evil one.' Luke has 'Father,' 'sins,' where Matthew has 'Our Father,' etc., and 'debts.' See notes on Mt. 6.9–13.

5. *Which of you shall have a friend*, etc. This parable, which immediately follows the Prayer spoken by Jesus for imitation by his disciples in all ages after him, teaches unfailing perseverance in prayer and the certainty of its power to obtain an answer. *At midnight.* A time often favorable for traveling in the East, on account of the heat in daytime.

7. *Trouble me not: the door is now shut.* A forbidding and irritating reply, discouraging to the ordinary seeker, but only intended here to teach the discipline and resolution that overcome spiritual as well as material obstacles.

8. *Because of his importunity.* That is, his daring, unyielding, almost impudent persistence in asking for what he wanted for a legitimate purpose.

9, 10. *Ask, and it shall be given you; seek,* etc. The words of these two verses, uttered by Jesus Christ for the universal use of mankind, are a statement of the law of attraction in spiritual things. The law of gravitation in the physical universe is no more certain in its operation than the law of spiritual gravitation, a manifestation of the nature of God whereby they who seek Him shall surely find him. See note on Mt. 7.7.

11. *Shall his son ask a loaf, and he give him a stone?* Shall a father give his son that which is a mockery of his request?

165

serpent? 12 Or *if* he shall ask an egg, will he give him a scorpion? 13 If ye then, being evil, know how to give good gifts unto your children, how much more shall *your* heavenly Father give the Holy Spirit to them that ask him?

14 And he was casting out a demon *that was* dumb. And it came to pass, when the demon was gone out, the dumb man spake; and the multitudes marvelled. 15 But some of them said, *g*By *h*Be-el'ze-bub the prince of the demons casteth he out demons. 16 And others, trying *him*, sought of him a sign from heaven. 17 But he, knowing their thoughts, said unto them, Every kingdom divided against itself is brought to desolation; *i*and a house *divided* against a house falleth. 18 And if Satan also is divided against himself, how shall his kingdom stand? because ye say that I cast out demons *g*by *h*Be-el'ze-bub. 19 And if I *g*by *h*Be-el'ze-bub cast out demons, by whom do your sons cast them out? therefore shall they be your judges. 20 But if I by the finger of God cast out demons, then is

the kingdom of God come upon you. 21 When the strong *man* fully armed guardeth his own court, his goods are in peace: 22 but when a stronger than he shall come upon him, and overcome him, he taketh from him his whole armor wherein he trusted, and divideth his spoils. 23 He that is not with me is against me; and he that gathereth not with me scattereth. 24 The unclean spirit when *k*he is gone out of the man, passeth through waterless places, seeking rest, and finding none, *k*he saith, I will turn back unto my house whence I came out. 25 And when *k*he is come, *k*he findeth it swept and garnished. 26 Then goeth *k*he, and taketh *to him* seven other spirits more evil than *l*himself; and they enter in and dwell there: and the last state of that man becometh worse than the first.

27 And it came to pass, as he said these things, a certain woman out of the multitude lifted up her voice, and said unto him, Blessed is the womb that bare thee, and the breasts which thou didst suck. 28 But he said,

---

g Or, *In*   *h* Gr. *Beelzebul.*   *i* Or, *and*   *house falleth upon house*   *k* Or, *tt*   *l* Or, *itself*

13. *Shall your heavenly Father give the Holy Spirit.* Our Lord prescribes a form of universal prayer, encourages persistence in prayer by a parable, declares in striking though familiar speech the law whereby an answer to prayer is always gained, and illustrates by examples the different objects of a request and the different values of a gift—all in order to set before us the supreme duty of asking for the gift of the Holy Spirit, and the supreme felicity of receiving it.

14. *A demon that was dumb.* The

word 'dumb' here may also mean a deaf mute.

15. *By Beelzebub the prince of the demons.* See note on Mt. 9.34.

16. *Sought of him a sign from heaven.* See notes on Mt. 12.39, 40.

17–23. *Every kingdom divided against itself,* etc. See notes on Mt. 12.25, 27–30.

24. *The man.* A symbol of the Jewish people.

25. *Garnished.* Adorned so as to be attractive.

28. *Yea rather.* The first of these words expresses an assent, but the

Yea rather, blessed are they that hear the word of God, and keep it.

29 And when the multitudes were gathering together unto him, he began to say, This generation is an evil generation: it seeketh after a sign; and there shall no sign be given to it but the sign of Jo'nah. 30 For even as Jo'nah became a sign unto the Nin'e-vites, so shall also the Son of man be to this generation. 31 The queen of the south shall rise up in the judgment with the men of this generation, and shall condemn them: for she came from the ends of the earth to hear the wisdom of Sol'o-mon; and behold, [m]a greater than Sol'o-mon is here. 32 The men of Nin'e-veh shall stand up in the judgment with this generation, and shall condemn it: for they repented at the preaching of Jo'nah; and behold, [m]a greater than Jo'nah is here.

33 No man, when he hath lighted a lamp, putteth it in a cellar, neither under the bushel, but on the stand, that they which enter in may see the light.

34 The lamp of thy body is thine eye: when thine eye is single, thy whole body also is full of light; but when it is evil, thy body also is full of darkness. 35 Look therefore whether the light that is in thee be not darkness. 36 If therefore thy whole body be full of light, having no part dark, it shall be wholly full of light, as when the lamp with its bright shining doth give thee light.

37 Now as he spake, a Phar'i-see asketh him to [n]dine with him: and he went in, and sat down to meat. 38 And when the Phar'i-see saw it, he marvelled that he had not first bathed himself before [n]dinner. 39 And the Lord said unto him, Now ye the Phar'i-sees cleanse the outside of the cup and of the platter; but your inward part is full of extortion and wickedness. 40 Ye foolish ones, did not he that made the outside make the inside also? 41 But give for alms those things which [o]are within; and behold, all things are clean unto you.

42 But woe unto you Phar'i-

---

m Gr. *more than*

n Gr. *breakfast.*   *o* Or, *ye can*

second a preference which our Lord was careful to emphasize when his mother was mentioned. See ch. 8. 21; Mt. 12.46–50.

29–32. *An evil generation: it seeketh after a sign.* See notes on Mt. 12.39; 16.1, 4.

33–36. *No man, when he hath lighted a lamp.* The binding truths taught in these three verses are: (1) the duty of letting one's light shine for others, of using any talent or advantage for the public good; (2) when conscience, the inner light, is pure, it is a safe guide; (3) be sure that this light *is* pure, and watchful that it may so remain. One

must guard against self-deception.

38. *Marvelled that he had not first bathed himself.* That is, washed his hands according to the particular custom of the Pharisees. See note on Mk. 7.2.

41. *But give for alms those things which are within.* Let your giving be inspired by the best that is within you, the loving sympathy that thinks not of reward. *And behold, all clean things are clean unto you.* The pure motive makes clean every act proceeding from it and does away with false distinctions between the clean and unclean.

42. *Ye tithe mint and rue.* Rue

sees! for ye tithe mint and rue and every herb, and pass over justice and the love of God: but these ought ye to have done, and not to leave the other undone. 43 Woe unto you Phar′i-sees! for ye love the chief seats in the synagogues, and the salutations in the marketplaces. 44 Woe unto you! for ye are as the tombs which appear not, and the men that walk over *them* know it not.

45 And one of the lawyers answering saith unto him, Teacher, in saying this thou reproachest us also. 46 And he said, Woe unto you lawyers also! for ye load men with burdens grievous to be borne, and ye yourselves touch not the burdens with one of your fingers. 47 Woe unto you! for ye build the tombs of the prophets, and your fathers killed them. 48 So ye are witnesses and consent unto the works of your fathers: for they killed them, and ye build *their tombs.*

49 Therefore also said the wisdom of God, I will send unto them prophets and apostles; and *some* of them they shall kill and persecute; 50 that the blood of all the prophets, which was shed from the foundation of the world, may be required of this generation; 51 from the blood of A′bel unto the blood of Zach-a-ri′ah, who perished between the altar and the ᵖsanctuary: yea, I say unto you, it shall be required of this generation.   52 Woe unto you lawyers! for ye took away the key of knowledge: ye entered not in yourselves, and them that were entering in ye hindered.

53 And when he was come out from thence, the scribes and the Phar′i-sees began to ᵠpress upon *him* vehemently, and to provoke him to speak of ʳmany things; 54 laying wait for him, to catch something out of his mouth.

12 In the mean time, when ᵃthe many thousands of the multitude were gathered to-

---

p Gr. *house.*   *q* Or, *set themselves vehemently against* him

r Or, *more*   *a* Gr. *the myriads of.*

---

was a medicinal herb. See note on Mt. 23.23.

44. *Ye are as the tombs which appear not.* It was customary among the Jews to whitewash the graves of the dead, so that people would notice them and avoid walking over them. If they walked over them, they were thereby ceremonially defiled. The Pharisees, by their hypocrisy, concealed their corrupting character to the unwary.

46. *Burdens grievous to be borne.* Minute and exacting interpretations of the Mosaic law.

47–51. *Ye build the tombs of the prophets.* See notes on Mt. 23.31, 32, 34, 35.

52. *Ye took away the key of knowledge.* The lawyers' key of knowledge was their practical monopoly of legal interpretation. Their nar-

row and vexatious application of the law not only hid the truth from themselves but hindered the people even from making an honest attempt to get at it. See notes on Mt. 23.13.

CHAPTER 12

1. *Many thousands of the multitude.* The gathering together of the crowds was a natural result of the now open hate and malicious opposition of the scribes and Pharisees. The people, most of whom sympathized with Jesus, were roused against their former spiritual guides. *The leaven of the Pharisees, which is hypocrisy.* Our Lord denounced hypocrisy as the comprehensive sin which explained the dearth of spirituality among his countrymen. It was the main burden of the woes he

gether, insomuch that they trod one upon another, he began to [b]say unto his disciples first of all, Beware ye of the leaven of the Phar'i-sees, which is hypocrisy. 2 But there is nothing covered up, that shall not be revealed; and hid, that shall not be known. 3 Wherefore whatsoever ye have said in the darkness shall be heard in the light; and what ye have spoken in the ear in the inner chambers shall be proclaimed upon the housetops. 4 And I say unto you my friends, Be not afraid of them that kill the body, and after that have no more that they can do. 5 But I will warn you whom ye shall fear: Fear him, who after he hath killed hath [c]power to cast into [d]hell; yea, I say unto you, Fear him. 6 Are not five sparrows sold for two pence? and not one of them is forgotten in the sight of God. 7 But the very hairs of your head are all numbered. Fear not: ye are of more value than many sparrows. 8 And I say unto you, Every one who shall confess [e]me before men, [f]him shall the Son of man also confess before the angels of God: 9 but he that denieth me in the presence of men shall be denied in the presence of the angels of God. 10 And every one who shall speak a word against the Son of man, it shall be forgiven him: but unto him that blasphemeth against the Holy Spirit it shall not be forgiven. 11 And when they bring you before the synagogues, and the rulers, and the authorities, be not anxious how or what ye shall answer, or what ye shall say: 12 for the Holy Spirit shall teach you in that very hour what ye ought to say.

13 And one out of the multitude said unto him, Teacher, bid my brother divide the inheritance with me. 14 But he said unto him, Man, who made me a judge or a divider over you? 15 And he said unto them, Take heed, and keep yourselves from all covetousness: [g]for a man's life consisteth not in the abun-

---

b Or, *say unto his disciples. First of all beware ye* *c* Or, *authority* *d* Gr. *Gehenna.* *e* Gr. *in me.* *f* Gr. *in him.* *g* Or, *for even* *in a man's abundance his life is not from the things which he possesseth*

---

pronounced upon their leaders. It was the leaven whose ferment of evil poisoned the great mass of Jewish life.

2–9. *Nothing covered up, that shall not be revealed.* A warning of the utter uselessness of concealment in the final accounting of the finite spirit to its Maker. *Yea, I say unto you, Fear him.* God, not Satan. See Mt. 10.28.

10. *Unto him that blasphemeth against the Holy Spirit.* See note on Mt. 12.31.

11. *The rulers, and the authorities.* As Paul was brought before the governor, Festus, and King Agrippa.

12. *The Holy Spirit shall teach you in that very hour.* Shall speak in and through you with infallible wisdom and power. See Acts 6.8, 10; 2 Tim. 4.17.

14. *Who made me a judge or a divider over you?* The attitude of Jesus with regard to this questioner was the same as in the case of the Pharisees and Herodians who asked him if it was lawful to give tribute unto Cæsar (Mt. 22.17). He declined to assume the function of a judge or arbitrator. The division of an inheritance was a legal function of the local synagogue, and to the synagogue he left it.

15. *For a man's life consisteth not,*

dance of the things which he possesseth. 16 And he spake a parable unto them, saying, The ground of a certain rich man brought forth plentifully: 17 and he reasoned within himself, saying, What shall I do, because I have not where to bestow my fruits? 18 And he said, This will I do: I will pull down my barns, and build greater; and there will I bestow all my grain and my goods. 19 And I will say to my [h]soul, [h]Soul, thou hast much goods laid up for many years; take thine ease, eat, drink, be merry. 20 But God said unto him, Thou foolish one, this night [i]is thy [h]soul required of thee; and the things which thou hast prepared, whose shall they be? 21 So is he that layeth up treasure for himself, and is not rich toward God.

22 And he said unto his disciples, Therefore I say unto you, Be not anxious for *your* [k]life, what ye shall eat; nor yet for your body, what ye shall put on. 23 For the [k]life is more than the food, and the body than the raiment. 24 Consider the ravens, that they sow not, neither reap; which have no store-chamber nor barn; and God feedeth them: of how much more value are ye than the birds! 25 And which of you by being anxious can add a cubit unto [l]the measure of his life? 26 If then ye are not able to do even that which is least, why are ye anxious concerning the rest? 27 Consider the lilies, how they grow: they toil not, neither do they spin; yet I say unto you, Even Sol'o-mon in all his glory was not arrayed like one of these. 28 But if God doth so clothe the grass in the field, which to-day is, and to-morrow is cast into the oven; how much more *shall he clothe* you, O ye of little faith? 29 And seek not ye what ye shall eat, and what ye shall drink, neither be ye of doubtful mind. 30 For all these things do the nations of the world seek after: but your Father knoweth that ye have need of these things. 31 Yet seek ye [m]his kingdom, and these things shall be added unto you. 32 Fear not, little flock; for it is your Father's good pleasure to give you the

---

h Or, *life*   *i* Gr. *they require thy soul.*
k Or, *soul*   *l* Or, *his stature*   *m* Many ancient authorities read *the kingdom of God.*

---

etc. This challenge of Jesus to the power of riches has become a watchword to those who would live by the power of the Spirit. A man's life consists not in what he has, but in what he is. The character of his living is expressed in his habitual preferences. A man may have few worldly goods, but he may desire them so engrossingly that his life may be nothing but a fruitless want, as materialistic in its way as the riotous, short-lived abundance of a spendthrift.

16–21. *And he spake a parable unto them.* To warn them of the sin of covetousness. *Soul, thou hast much goods.* This man spoke to his soul as if he had always mistaken it for his body. He had never sought to come to the consciousness of his higher self.

22–31. *Be not anxious for your life.* See notes on Mt. 6.25, 27, 28, 30, 32–34.

32. *Fear not, little flock.* An affectionate encouragement of his disciples. *To give you the kingdom.* If it was their Father's good pleasure to do this, all lesser gifts would be included therein, such as food and raiment.

kingdom. 33 Sell that which ye have, and give alms; make for yourselves purses which wax not old, a treasure in the heavens that faileth not, where no thief draweth near, neither moth destroyeth. 34 For where your treasure is, there will your heart be also.

35 Let your loins be girded about, and your lamps burning; 36 and be ye yourselves like unto men looking for their lord, when he shall return from the marriage feast; that, when he cometh and knocketh, they may straightway open unto him. 37 Blessed are those [n]servants, whom the lord when he cometh shall find watching; verily I say unto you, that he shall gird himself, and make them sit down to meat, and shall come and serve them. 38 And if he shall come in the second watch, and if in the third, and find *them* so, blessed are those *servants*. 39 [o]But know this, that if the master of the house had known in what hour the thief was coming,

he would have watched, and not have left his house to be [p]broken through. 40 Be ye also ready: for in an hour that ye think not the Son of man cometh.

41 And Peter said, Lord, speakest thou this parable unto us, or even unto all? 42 And the Lord said, Who then is [q]the faithful and wise steward, whom his lord shall set over his household, to give them their portion of food in due season? 43 Blessed is that [r]servant, whom his lord when he cometh shall find so doing. 44 Of a truth I say unto you, that he will set him over all that he hath. 45 But if that [r]servant shall say in his heart, My lord delayeth his coming; and shall begin to beat the menservants and the maidservants, and to eat and drink, and to be drunken; 46 the lord of that [r]servant shall come in a day when he expecteth not, and in an hour when he knoweth not, and shall [s]cut him asunder, and appoint his portion with the unfaithful. 47 And that [r]servant,

---

n Gr. *bondservants*. o Or, *But this ye know* p Gr. *digged through*. q Or, *the faithful steward, the wise man whom &c.* r Gr. *bondservant*. s Or, *severely scourge him*

33. *Sell that which ye have, and give alms*. This was a command to those who had been chosen to go forth and preach the truth.

34. *Where your treasure is, there will your heart be*. The lesson of this truth is the right choice of a treasure, whose quality determines what the heart shall be. See note on Mt. 6.21.

35, 36. *Let your loins be girded*. A warning to be in vigilant readiness, in view of the uncertain times at which the divine call for service or accounting may come.

37–40. *I say unto you, that he shall gird himself*. There are tremendous meanings in this verse. The master of these watchful and

ready servants changes places with them, as it were, and girds himself to serve them. In obeying his commands they win his love, and he no longer appears to them as master, but as equal, friend, brother. If we willingly obey the laws of God our hold on Him is as strong as His hold on us, and the relation of master and servant will be finally merged in the perfect love which casts out fear. See note on Mt. 24.43.

41. *Unto us, or even unto all?* Primarily unto the apostles and disciples, but the lesson is for all.

42–46. *Who then is the faithful and wise steward*, etc. [*]See notes on Mt. 24.45, 47, 48.

47. *Shall be beaten with many*

who knew his lord's will, and made not ready, nor did according to his will, shall be beaten with many *stripes*; 48 but he that knew not, and did things worthy of stripes, shall be beaten with few *stripes*. And to whomsoever much is given, of him shall much be required: and to whom they commit much, of him they will ask the more.

49 I came to cast fire upon the earth; and *t*what do I desire, if it is already kindled! 50 But I have a baptism to be baptized with; and how am I straitened till it be accomplished! 51 Think ye that I am come to give peace in the earth? I tell you, Nay; but rather division: 52 for there shall be from henceforth five in one house divided, three against two, and two against three. 53 They shall be divided, father against son, and son against father; mother against daughter, and daughter against her mother; mother in law against her daughter in law, and daughter in law against her mother in law.

---

t Or, *how would I that it were already kindled!*

---

54 And he said to the multitudes also, When ye see a cloud rising in the west, straightway ye say, There cometh a shower; and so it cometh to pass. 55 And when *ye see* a south wind blowing, ye say, There will be a *u*scorching heat; and it cometh to pass. 56 Ye hypocrites, ye know how to *v*interpret the face of the earth and the heaven; but how is it that ye know not how to *v*interpret this time? 57 And why even of yourselves judge ye not what is right? 58 For as thou art going with thine adversary before the magistrate, on the way give diligence to be quit of him; lest haply he drag thee unto the judge, and the judge shall deliver thee to the *x*officer, and the *x*officer shall cast thee into prison. 59 I say unto thee, Thou shalt by no means come out thence, till thou have paid the very last mite.

13 Now there were some present at that very season who told him of the Gal-i-læ'ans, whose blood Pi'late had mingled

---

u Or, *hot wind*   *v* Gr. *prove.*   *z* Gr. *exactor.*

---

stripes. For the presumptuous ignoring of his lord's will.

48. *With few stripes.* Ignorance partly blameless shall lighten his punishment.

49–53. *I came to cast fire upon the earth.* Jesus more than once told his hearers that his truth would stir up strife, sundering even the closest family ties. See notes on Mt. 10.34, 37. *What do I desire,* etc. What can I long more for than the fulfilling of my Father's will? *How am I straitened!* Oppressed by the burden of the world's redemption. See notes on Mt. 10.34, 37.

54–59. *Straightway ye say, There cometh a shower.* They could easily read the meaning of weather signs.

Ye know not how to interpret this time. The spiritual signs of that time were as clear as the weather signs. They were the preaching and miracles of Jesus. See notes on Mt. 16.1, 3. *Even of yourselves.* A rebuke to his listeners for not using their common sense in spiritual things. *Give diligence to be quit of him.* Lose no time in coming to good terms with him. See note on Mt. 5.25.

CHAPTER 13

1. *Galilæans, whose blood Pilate had mingled,* etc. They had been slain by Pilate's order while sacrificing in the Temple.

172

with their sacrifices. 2 And he answered and said unto them, Think ye that these Gal-i-læ′ans were sinners above all the Gal-i-læ′ans, because they have suffered these things? 3 I tell you, Nay: but, except ye repent, ye shall all in like manner perish. 4 Or those eighteen, upon whom the tower in Si-lo′am fell, and killed them, think ye that they were ⁿoffenders above all the men that dwell in Je-ru′sa-lem? 5 I tell you, Nay: but, except ye repent, ye shall all likewise perish.

6 And he spake this parable; A certain man had a fig tree planted in his vineyard; and he came seeking fruit thereon, and found none. 7 And he said unto the vinedresser, Behold, these three years I come seeking fruit on this fig tree, and find none: cut it down; why doth it also cumber the ground? 8 And he answering saith unto him, Lord, let it alone this year also, till I shall dig about it, and dung it: 9 and if it bear fruit thenceforth, *well*; but if not, thou shalt cut it down.

10 And he was teaching in one of the synagogues on the sabbath day. 11 And behold, a woman that had a spirit of infirmity eighteen years; and she was bowed together, and could in no wise lift herself up. 12 And when Je′sus saw her, he called her, and said to her, Woman, thou art loosed from thine infirmity. 13 And he laid his hands upon her: and immediately she was made straight, and glorified God. 14 And the ruler of the synagogue, being moved with indignation because Je′sus had healed on the sabbath, answered and said to the multitude, There are six days in which men ought to work: in them therefore come and be

---

a Gr. *debtors.*

---

2. *Because they have suffered these things.* Jesus condemned the belief held by the Jews that great suffering or calamity is to be considered a proof of great sin. They were in danger of a more serious penalty, the spiritual death, unless they repented.

4. *The tower in Siloam.* Probably a work connected with the aqueduct to the Pool of Siloam.

6–9. *A certain man had a fig tree planted.* In this parable the fig tree is the Jewish nation, God the owner, Christ the vinedresser. The fig tree is condemned to be cut down for its barrenness, but the vinedresser intercedes, asking for more time and attention to the tree, in order that it may yet bear fruit. If it does not bear fruit,—that is, if the Jewish or any other nation or any individual fails to bear fruit in that righteousness which exalts and preserves,—then it is to be destroyed.

12. *Woman, thou art loosed from thine infirmity.* This miraculous cure was unasked by the woman or by any one in her behalf.

14–17. *The ruler of the synagogue, being moved with indignation.* This miracle was the occasion of a great lesson in love and mercy to the sabbatic formalists who made even the day of rest an engine of cruelty and oppression. The ruler of the synagogue was willing to see human beings suffer grievously on that day, because it was *work* to relieve them *then*, while it was in accordance with sabbatic *rest* to loose an ox from his stall to lead him away to watering! Our Lord here reaffirmed the truth he vindicated when his disciples plucked the ears of grain (Mk. 2.27). *His adversaries were put to shame.* The rebuke of Jesus gave them a flash of insight into the wretched perversion of their own consciences. They saw the truth, and it shamed them.

healed, and not on the day of the sabbath. 15 But the Lord answered him, and said, Ye hypocrites, doth not each one of you on the sabbath loose his ox or his ass from the *b*stall, and lead him away to watering? 16 And ought not this woman, being a daughter of Abraham, whom Satan had bound, lo, *these* eighteen years, to have been loosed from this bond on the day of the sabbath? 17 And as he said these things, all his adversaries were put to shame: and all the multitude rejoiced for all the glorious things that were done by him.

18 He said therefore, Unto what is the kingdom of God like? and whereunto shall I liken it? 19 It is like unto a grain of mustard seed, which a man took, and cast into his own garden; and it grew, and became a tree; and the birds of the heaven lodged in the branches thereof.

20 And again he said, Whereunto shall I liken the kingdom of God? 21 It is like unto leaven, which a woman took and hid in three *c*measures of meal, till it was all leavened.

22 And he went on his way through cities and villages, teaching, and journeying on unto Je-ru′sa-lem. 23 And one said unto him, Lord, are they few that are saved? And he said unto them, 24 Strive to enter in by the narrow door: for many, I say unto you, shall seek to enter in, and shall not be *d*able. 25 When once the master of the house is risen up, and hath shut to the door, and ye begin to stand without, and to knock at the door, saying, Lord, open to us; and he shall answer and say to you, I know you not whence ye are; 26 then shall ye begin to say, We did eat and drink in thy presence, and thou didst teach in our streets; 27 and he shall say, I tell you, I know not whence ye are; depart from me, all ye workers of iniquity. 28 There shall be the weeping and the gnashing of teeth, when ye shall see Abraham, and I′saac, and Jacob, and all the prophets, in the kingdom of God, and yourselves cast forth without. 29 And they shall come from the east and west, and from the north and south, and shall *e*sit down in the kingdom of God. 30 And behold, there are last who shall be first, and there are first who shall be last.

31 In that very hour there came certain Phar′i-sees, saying to him, Get thee out, and go hence: for Her′od would fain kill

---

b Gr. *manger*.   *c* See marginal note on Mt. 13.33.

d Or, *able, when once*   *e* Gr. *recline*.

18–21. Unto what is the kingdom of God like? The parables of the mustard seed and the leaven are here given. See notes on Mt. 13.31, 33.

23–30. Are they few that are saved? The answer of Jesus, given in the form of a parable, encourages the questioner, while pointing out the difficulty of living so as to be saved.

Our Lord more especially condemns the rejection of his message by his own people. See notes on Mt. 7.13, 23; 8.11, 12; 20.16; 25.10.

31. For Herod would fain kill thee. The Pharisees who said this were not telling the truth. There was no reason for thinking that Herod, although a man of base character, wished to kill Jesus.

174

thee. 32 And he said unto them,
Go and say to that fox, Behold, I
cast out demons and perform
cures to-day and to-morrow, and
the third *day* I *f*am perfected.
33 Nevertheless I must go on
my way to-day and to-morrow
and the *day* following: for it cannot be that a prophet perish out
of Je-ru′sa-lem. 34 O Je-ru′sa-
lem, Je-ru′sa-lem, that killeth
the prophets, and stoneth them
that are sent unto her! how often
would I have gathered thy children together, even as a hen
gathereth her own brood under
her wings, and ye would not! 35
Behold, your house is left unto
you *desolate*: and I say unto you,
Ye shall not see me, until ye
shall say, Blessed *is* he that
cometh in the name of the Lord.

14 And it came to pass, when
he went into the house of one
of the rulers of the Phar′i-sees on
a sabbath to eat bread, that they
were watching him. 2 And behold, there was before him a certain man that had the dropsy.
3 And Je′sus answering spake
unto the lawyers and Phar′i-sees,
saying, Is it lawful to heal on the
sabbath, or not? 4 But they
held their peace. And he took
him, and healed him, and let him
go. 5 And he said unto them,
Which of you shall have *a*an ass
or an ox fallen into a well, and
will not straightway draw him up
on a sabbath day? 6 And they
could not answer again unto
these things.

7 And he spake a parable unto
those that were bidden, when he

---

f Or, *end my course*   *a* Many ancient authorities read *a son.* See ch. 13.15.

32. *That fox.* A term of contempt for the mingled cunning and
cowardice of Herod. *Behold, I cast
out demons,* etc. That is, I proceed
with this work of my Father until
it is finished and I am perfected by
my death and resurrection. Nothing can shorten or lengthen my appointed time.

33. *Out of Jerusalem.* As if Jerusalem, where so many prophets had
been killed, were the only fitting
place for the violent death of Jesus
himself. The latter part of ver. 33
is an utterance of terrible irony,
heightened by the outburst of mingled anguish and grief that immediately follows.

34, 35. *Jerusalem, that killeth the
prophets.* See notes on Mt. 23.37,
38.

CHAPTER 14

1. *On a sabbath to eat bread.*
Feasts and good cheer at table on
the Sabbath were an honored custom among the Jews. *Were watching
him.* They had most probably invited him as part of a plan to trap
him.

2. *A certain man that had the dropsy.* It was permissible for outsiders to enter a house while a feast
was in progress; but other schemes
of the Pharisees on like occasions
make it very probable that the Pharisees had purposely placed the drop-
sical man where Jesus could not fail
to notice him. This would challenge
a cure, and a possible failure, or afford reasons for a prosecution before
the Sanhedrin.

3. *Jesus answering spake.* Our
Lord instantly saw the meaning of
the situation and utilized it before
his enemies had time to interfere.
He confounded them by bringing
the lawfulness of sabbatic healing to
them for an opinion before they
could bring it for him to decide.

4. *They held their peace.* They
were outwitted and helpless because
he had first asked *them* the question
they expected to ask *him.*

7-11. *A parable unto those that
were bidden.* It was spoken to them
by reason of their unseemly haste in
the choice of places. Our Lord had
healed the man with the dropsy and
the dinner was about to be begun.

marked how they chose out the chief seats; saying unto them, 8 When thou art bidden of any man to a marriage feast, *b*sit not down in the chief seat; lest haply a more honorable man than thou be bidden of him, 9 and he that bade thee and him shall come and say to thee, Give this man place; and then thou shalt begin with shame to take the lowest place. 10 But when thou art bidden, go and sit down in the lowest place; that when he that hath bidden thee cometh, he may say to thee, Friend, go up higher: then shalt thou have glory in the presence of all that *c*sit at meat with thee. 11 For every one that exalteth himself shall be humbled; and he that humbleth himself shall be exalted.

12 And he said to him also that had bidden him, When thou makest a dinner or a supper, call not thy friends, nor thy brethren,

nor thy kinsmen, nor rich neighbors; lest haply they also bid thee again, and a recompense be made thee. 13 But when thou makest a feast, bid the poor, the maimed, the lame, the blind: 14 and thou shalt be blessed; because they have not *where-with* to recompense thee: for thou shalt be recompensed in the resurrection of the just.

15 And when one of them that *d*sat at meat with him heard these things, he said unto him, Blessed is he that shall eat bread in the kingdom of God. 16 But he said unto him, A certain man made a great supper; and he bade many: 17 and he sent forth his *e*servant at supper time to say to them that were bidden, Come; for *all* things are now ready. 18 And they all with one *consent* began to make excuse. The first said unto him, I have bought a field, and I must needs go out and see

---

b Gr. *recline not.*   *c* Gr. *recline.* Comp. ch. 7.36, 37, marg.   *d* Gr. *reclined.*

Comp. ch. 7.36, 37, marg.   *e* Gr. *bond-servant.*

The chief seats. Struggles for precedence on social occasions were encouraged often by the example of the the rabbis. Rabbi Simeon ben Shetah was invited to dinner by King Jannæus (104–79 B. C.), and seated himself, unasked, between the king and queen. When rebuked he quoted in his defence from Ecclesiasticus: 'Exalt wisdom and she shall exalt thee, and make thee to sit among princes.' Christ's parable enforces the lesson of humility and consideration for others.

12–14. *To him also that had bidden him.* Jesus had a lesson for the host as well as for the inconsiderate guests. The former was warned, though in a friendly and gracious manner, against the narrow hospitality which entertains only from motives of self-interest. He was told to express sympathy with and to show practical kindness to all,

including those who could not recompense him.

15. *Eat bread in the kingdom of God.* That true Messianic kingdom which, according to Jewish belief, would begin with 'the resurrection of the just' spoken of in ver. 14. See note on Mt. 8.11.

16–24. *A certain man made a great supper.* Comp. the parable of the royal marriage feast (Mt. 22.1–10). In the parable of the great supper he who invites the many is God; the servant is Jesus Christ; the many are the rulers of the Jews, who, refusing or ignoring the invitation for various trifling or unworthy reasons, are sent away and in their place the great mass of the people, including the poor and maimed and blind and lame, are invited. *That my house may be filled.* Showing the kindness and compassion which would save all, not only the few.

it; I pray thee have me excused.
19 And another said, I have
bought five yoke of oxen, and I
go to prove them; I pray thee
have me excused. 20 And another said, I have married a wife,
and therefore I cannot come. 21
And the ᵉservant came, and told
his lord these things. Then the
master of the house being angry
said to his ᵉservant, Go out
quickly into the streets and lanes
of the city, and bring in hither
the poor and maimed and blind
ɩnd lame. 22 And the ᵉservant
said, Lord, what thou didst command is done, and yet there is
room. 23 And the lord said unto
the ᵉservant, Go out into the
highways and hedges, and con-
strain *them* to come in, that my
house may be filled. 24 For I
say unto you, that none of those
men that were bidden shall taste
of my supper.

25 Now there went with him
great multitudes: and he turned,
and said unto them, 26 If any
man cometh unto me, and hateth
not his own father, and mother,
and wife, and children, and
brethren, and sisters, yea, and
his own life also, he cannot be my
my disciple. 27 Whosoever doth

not bear his own cross, and come
after me, cannot be my disciple. 28 For which of you,
desiring to build a tower, doth
not first sit down and count the
cost, whether he have *wherewith* to complete it? 29 Lest
haply, when he hath laid a foundation, and is not able to finish,
all that behold begin to mock
him, 30 saying, This man began
to build, and was not able to finish. 31 Or what king, as he
goeth to encounter another king
in war, will not sit down first and
take counsel whether he is able
with ten thousand to meet him
that cometh against him with
twenty thousand? 32 Or else,
while the other is yet a great way
off, he sendeth an ambassage,
and asketh conditions of peace.
33 So therefore whosoever he be
of you that renounceth not all
that he hath, he cannot be my
disciple. 34 Salt therefore is
good: but if even the salt have
lost its savor, wherewith shall it
be seasoned? 35 It is fit neither
for the land nor for the dunghill:
men cast it out. He that hath
ears to hear, let him hear.

15 Now all the ᵃpublicans
and sinners were drawing

---

e Gr. *bondservant.*

a See marginal note on ch. 3.12.

26. *And hateth not his own father,*
etc. Our Lord warned the multitudes who were following him (ver.
25) lest they should mistake the nature of his Messiahship. Many expected some reward or advantage of
a material kind. Jesus tells them
they can not follow him unless they
are prepared to leave their nearest
relatives if these stand in the way
of duty. See Mt. 10.37, 38. The
word 'hateth' in this connection
means the readiness to oppose
even one's dearest earthly rela-

tives, if the higher love requires it.
28–33. *First sit down and count
the cost.* The first illustration, that
of the man who attempts to build a
tower, is adapted to everyday life;
the second, that of a king going
forth to war with another king,
would appeal more strongly to the
class called the 'rulers of the Jews,'
men conversant with larger affairs.
34. *Salt therefore is good.* 'Salt'
here means the tried and proved
character of a Christian believer.

near unto him to hear him. 2 And both the Phar'i-sees and the scribes murmured, saying, This man receiveth sinners, and eateth with them.

3 And he spake unto them this parable, saying, 4 What man of you, having a hundred sheep, and having lost one of them, doth not leave the ninety and nine in the wilderness, and go after that which is lost, until he find it? 5 And when he hath found it, he layeth it on his shoulders, rejoicing. 6 And when he cometh home, he calleth together his friends and his neighbors, saying unto them, Rejoice with me, for I have found my sheep which was lost. 7 I say unto you, that even so there shall be joy in heaven over one sinner that repenteth, *more* than over ninety and nine righteous persons, who need no repentance.

8 Or what woman having ten *b*pieces of silver, if she lose one piece, doth not light a lamp, and

---

b Gr. *drachma*, a coin worth about eight

sweep the house, and seek diligently until she find it? 9 And when she hath found it, she calleth together her friends and neighbors, saying, Rejoice with me, for I have found the piece which I had lost. 10 Even so, I say unto you, there is joy in the presence of the angels of God over one sinner that repenteth.

11 And he said, A certain man had two sons: 12 and the younger of them said to his father, Father, give me the portion of *c*thy substance that falleth to me. And he divided unto them his living. 13 And not many days after, the younger son gathered all together and took his journey into a far country; and there he wasted his substance with riotous living. 14 And when he had spent all, there arose a mighty famine in that country; and he began to be in want. 15 And he went and joined himself to one of the citizens of that country; and he sent him into his fields

---

pence, or sixteen cents.   *c* Gr. *the.*

CHAPTER 15

2–7. *Receiveth sinners, and eateth with them.* In answer to the murmuring of the Pharisees and scribes Jesus spoke the parable of the lost sheep, which teaches the love of God for the lost and repentant sinner. See notes on Mt. 18.10, 12. *The ninety and nine in the wilderness.* Those that are safe and do not need the immediate care of the chief shepherd, especially in view of the divine pity which seeks to recover the one lost sheep.

8–10. *Having ten pieces of silver, if she lose one.* The parable of the lost coin has the same application as the previous one—compassion and unselfish seeking for the lost one, with joy, both in earth and heaven, over his repentance. *Until*

she find it. God will never abandon one of his children so long as the possibility of repentance remains.

11–32. *A certain man had two sons.* The parable of the prodigal son, like the two immediately preceding it, teaches the infinite compassion of God for the sinning and guilty soul that feels the touch of remorse and desires to return to righteousness. It speaks, in language to which the Christian world has never ceased to listen, of the joy with which such a soul will be welcomed back by the Father from whose home it has wilfully strayed. *Father, give me the portion.* Onethird, according to Jewish law. *When he came to himself.* The supreme moment in which the soul, recognizing its degradation, turns to God for help. *While he was yet*

to feed swine. 16 And he would fain *d*have filled his belly with *e*the husks that the swine did eat: and no man gave unto him. 17 But when he came to himself he said, How many hired servants of my father's have bread enough and to spare, and I perish here with hunger! 18 I will arise and go to my father, and will say unto him, Father, I have sinned against heaven, and in thy sight: 19 I am no more worthy to be called thy son: make me as one of thy hired servants. 20 And he arose, and came to his father. But while he was yet afar off, his father saw him, and was moved with compassion, and ran, and fell on his neck, and *f*kissed him. 21 And the son said unto him, Father, I have sinned against heaven, and in thy sight: I am no more worthy to be called thy son*g*. 22 But the father said to his *h*servants, Bring forth quickly the best robe, and put it on him; and put a ring on his hand, and shoes on his feet: 23 and bring the fatted calf, *and* kill it, and let us eat, and make merry: 24 for this my son was dead, and is alive again; he was lost, and is found. And they began to be merry. 25 Now his elder son was in the field: and as he came and drew nigh to the house, he heard music and dancing. 26 And he called to him one of the servants, and inquired what these things might be. 27 And he said unto him, Thy brother is come; and thy father hath killed the fatted calf, because he hath received him safe and sound. 28 But he was angry, and would not go in: and his father came out, and entreated him. 29 But he answered and said to his father, Lo, these many years do I serve thee, and I never transgressed a commandment of thine; and *yet* thou never gavest me a kid, that I might make merry with my friends: 30 but when this thy son came, who hath devoured thy living with harlots, thou killedst for him the fatted calf. 31 And he said unto him, *i*Son, thou art ever with me, and all that is mine is thine. 32 But it was meet to make merry and be glad: for this thy brother was dead, and is alive *again*; and *was* lost, and is found.

16 And he said also unto the disciples, There was a certain rich man, who had a steward; and the same was accused unto him that he was wasting his goods. 2 And he called him, and said unto him, What is this that I hear of thee? render the account of thy stewardship; for thou canst be no longer steward. 3 And the steward said within himself,

---

d Many ancient authorities read *have been filled.* *e* Gr. *the pods of the carob tree.* *f* Gr. *kissed him much.* See ch. 7.38, 45.

g Some ancient authorities add *make me as one of thy hired servants.* See ver. 19. *h* Gr. *bondservants.* *i* Gr. *Child.*

afar off. The father's love had watched and waited for the son's repentance and return. *Bring forth quickly.* The father did not delay to examine the reasons for the prodigal's contrite humility.

CHAPTER 16

3. *What shall I do,* etc. The note of vigilant thoughtfulness is heard in this question. The steward did not deny the charge of dishonesty,

What shall I do, seeing that my lord taketh away the stewardship from me? I have not strength to dig; to beg I am ashamed. 4 I am resolved what to do, that, when I am put out of the stewardship, they may receive me into their houses. 5 And calling to him each one of his lord's debtors, he said to the first, How much owest thou unto my lord? 6 And he said, A hundred *a*measures of oil. And he said unto him, Take thy *b*bond, and sit down quickly and write fifty. 7 Then said he to another, And how much owest thou? And he said, A hundred *c*measures of wheat. He saith unto him, Take thy *b*bond, and write fourscore. 8 And his lord commended *d*the unrighteous steward because he had done wisely: for the sons of this *e*world are for their own generation wiser than the sons of the light. 9 And I say unto you, Make to yourselves friends *f*by means of the mammon of un-

righteousness; that, when it shall fail, they may receive you into the eternal tabernacles. 10 He that is faithful in a very little is faithful also in much: and he that is unrighteous in a very little is unrighteous also in much. 11 If therefore ye have not been faithful in the unrighteous mammon, who will commit to your trust the true *riches*? 12 And if ye have not been faithful in that which is another's, who will give you that which is *g*your own? 13 No *h*servant can serve two masters: for either he will hate the one, and love the other; or else he will hold to one, and despise the other. Ye cannot serve God and mammon.

14 And the Phar'-i-sees, who were lovers of money, heard all these things; and they scoffed at him. 15 And he said unto them, Ye are they that justify yourselves in the sight of men; but God knoweth your hearts: for

---

a Gr. *baths*, the bath being a Hebrew measure. See Ezek. 45.10, 11, 14.   *b* Gr. *writings*.   *c* Gr. *cors*, the cor being a Hebrew measure. See Ezek. 45.14.   *d* Gr.

the steward of unrighteousness.   *e* Or. *age*   *f* Gr. *out of.*   *g* Some ancient authorities read *our own.*   *h* Gr. *household-servant.*

---

but he prepared to meet the consequences in a way that would at least gain him food and shelter. He made the best of a bad situation. If he lost his lord's friendship, he would gain that of his lord's debtors, even by trickery.

6. *A hundred measures of oil.* Nine hundred gallons.

7. *A hundred measures of wheat.* Eleven hundred bushels.

8. *Commended the unrighteous steward.* For his prudence only. *Wiser than the sons of the light.* Even the dishonest who manage their worldly affairs so as to take full advantage of every opportunity are often wiser in their way than are the honest and upright who

mismanage their spiritual affairs.

9. *By means of the mammon of unrighteousness.* A direction to use worldly-wise means for spiritual ends; for example, the prudent use of wealth in good works. *That, when it shall fail,* etc. When wealth is taken away from its possessor, the good done by it nevertheless endures and has its part in securing for the doer the gracious rewards of eternity.

11. *Who will commit to your trust the true riches?* If men are unfaithful in the use of money, what hope is there that they will be wise stewards of spiritual gifts?

13. *No servant can serve two masters.* See note on Mt. 6.24.

that which is exalted among men is an abomination in the sight of God. 16 The law and the prophets *were* until John: from that time the ⁱgospel of the kingdom of God is preached, and every man entereth violently into it. 17 But it is easier for heaven and earth to pass away, than for one tittle of the law to fall.

18 Every one that putteth away his wife, and marrieth another, committeth adultery: and he that marrieth one that is put away from a husband committeth adultery.

19 Now there was a certain rich man, and he was clothed in purple and fine linen, ᵏfaring sumptuously every day: 20 and a certain beggar named Laz'a-rus was laid at his gate, full of sores, 21 and desiring to be fed with the *crumbs* that fell from the rich man's table; yea, even the dogs came and licked his sores. 22 And it came to pass, that the beggar died, and that he was carried away by the angels into Abraham's bosom: and the rich man also died, and was buried. 23 And in Ha'des he lifted up his eyes, being in torments, and seeth Abraham afar off, and Laz'a-rus in his bosom. 24 And he cried and said, Father Abraham, have mercy on me, and send Laz'a-rus, that he may dip the tip of his finger in water, and cool my tongue; for I am in anguish in this flame. 25 But Abraham said, ⁱSon, remember that thou in thy lifetime receivedst thy good things, and Laz'a-rus in like manner evil things: but now here he is comforted, and thou art in anguish. 26 And ᵐbesides all this, between us and you there is a great gulf fixed, that they that would pass from hence to you may not be able, and that none

---

i Or, *good tidings*: comp. ch. 3.18.   *k* Or, *living in mirth and splendor every day*   *l* Gr. *Child*.   *m* Or, *in all these things*

---

16. *The law and the prophets were until John.* There was better excuse for spiritual failure before John's coming, when the true kingdom of heaven was set forth. See note on Mt. 11.12.

18. *Putteth away his wife, and marrieth another.* See note on Mt. 5.32.

19–21. *There was a certain rich man.* The parable of Dives (rich man) and Lazarus (helped of God) was a lesson to selfish and irreligious money lovers. The rich man was one to whom material enjoyment was the chief end of life. He stands for that class whose pleasure in riches is morally purposeless. Lazarus was destitute of all worldly goods, but he is not commended for his destitution any more than the rich man is condemned for the mere possession of wealth. What redeemed the one was his feeling for that which is above and beyond the fleeting pleasures of the earthly life; what ruined the other was the blind selfishness which saw nothing beyond those pleasures and closed his heart against the poor. *Purple and fine linen.* 'Purple' was a rich cloth dyed with the liquid obtained from a species of shell-fish. Fine linen was also very costly. *Even the dogs.* His wretched plight was made more so by the humiliation of contact with animals regarded in the East as unclean.

22–31. *Into Abraham's bosom.* A Jewish expression for Paradise. It was a figure of speech for fellowship with the departed righteous and faithful who await judgment. *Hades.* Used here to signify the intermediate state between death and judgment. The rich man had not, therefore, received his final sentence. According to Jewish belief

may cross over from thence to us. 27 And he said, I pray thee therefore, father, that thou wouldest send him to my father's house; 28 for I have five brethren; that he may testify unto them, lest they also come into this place of torment. 29 But Abraham saith, They have Mo'-ses and the prophets; let them hear them. 30 And he said, Nay, father Abraham: but if one go to them from the dead, they will repent. 31 And he said unto him, If they hear not Mo'ses and the prophets, neither will they be persuaded, if one rise from the dead.

17 And he said unto his disciples, It is impossible but that occasions of stumbling should come; but woe unto him, through whom they come! 2 It were well for him if a millstone were hanged about his neck, and he were thrown into the sea, rather than that he should cause one of these little ones to stumble. 3 Take heed to yourselves: if thy brother sin, rebuke him; and if he repent, forgive him. 4 And if he sin against thee seven times in the day, and seven times turn again to thee, saying, I repent; thou shalt forgive him.

5 And the apostles said unto the Lord, Increase our faith. 6 And the Lord said, If ye had faith as a grain of mustard seed, ye would say unto this sycamine tree, Be thou rooted up, and be thou planted in the sea; and it would obey you. 7 But who is there of you, having a *servant plowing or keeping sheep, that will say unto him, when he is come in from the field, Come straightway and sit down to meat; 8 and will not rather say unto him, Make ready wherewith I may sup, and gird thyself, and serve me, till I have eaten and drunken; and afterward thou shalt eat and drink? 9 Doth he thank the *servant because he did the things that were commanded? 10 Even so ye also, when ye shall have done all the things that are commanded you, say, We are unprofitable *bservants; we have done that which it was our duty to do.

11 And it came to pass, *cas they were on the way to Je-ru'-

---

a Gr. *bondservant.*   *b* Gr. *bondservants.*   *c* Or, *as he was*

both happiness and torment might exist in the condition between death and the judgment. *Anguish in this flame.* The torments of the rich man are described by words which must be taken figuratively, since he was now a disembodied spirit.

CHAPTER 17

1. *Occasions of stumbling.* See note on Mt. 18.7.
2. *One of these little ones.* See note on Mt. 18.10.
3. *If thy brother sin, rebuke him.* See notes on Mt. 18.15, 17, 22.
6. *This sycamine tree.* A species

of mulberry. *Be thou rooted up.* A figurative expression used in Jewish controversies. Rabbis of intellectual eminence were often called 'uprooters of mountains' in allusion to their power of solving difficult questions. See note on Mt. 17.20.

7–10. *Who is there of you, having a servant plowing,* etc. The parable of the plowing servant rebukes the self-satisfied Christian who thinks that in obeying God he has done something especially meritorious. Jesus points out to his disciples that even faithful servants have only done their duty.

sa-lem, that he was passing ^dalong the borders of Sa-ma'ri-a and Gal'i-lee. 12 And as he entered into a certain village, there met him ten men that were lepers, who stood afar off: 13 and they lifted up their voices, saying, Je'sus, Master, have mercy on us. 14 And when he saw them, he said unto them, Go and show yourselves unto the priests. And it came to pass, as they went, they were cleansed. 15 And one of them, when he saw that he was healed, turned back, with a loud voice glorifying God; 16 and he fell upon his face at his feet, giving him thanks: and he was a Sa-mar'i-tan. 17 And Je'sus answering said, Were not the ten cleansed? but where are the nine? 18 ^eWere there none found that returned to give glory to God, save this ^fstranger? 19 And he said unto him, Arise, and go thy way: thy faith hath ^gmade thee whole.

20 And being asked by the Phar'i-sees, when the kingdom of God cometh, he answered them and said, The kingdom of God cometh not with observation: 21 neither shall they say, Lo, here! or, There! for lo, the kingdom of God is ^hwithin you.

22 And he said unto the disciples, The days will come, when ye shall desire to see one of the days of the Son of man, and ye shall not see it. 23 And they shall say to you, Lo, there! Lo, here! go not away, nor follow after *them:* 24 for as the lightning, when it lighteneth out of the one part under the heaven, shineth unto the other part under heaven; so shall the Son of man be ⁱin his day. 25 But first must he suffer many things and be rejected of this generation. 26 And as it came to pass in the days of Noah, even so shall it be also in the days of the Son of man. 27 They ate, they drank, they married, they were

---

d Or, *through the midst of &c.*   e Or, *There were none found . . . save this stranger.*   f Or, *alien*   g Or, *saved thee*   h Or, *in the*

midst of you   i Some ancient authorities omit *in his day.*

12–19. *Ten men that were lepers.* The leprosy of the Bible included under that name a group of diseases; but modern leprosy is defined by medical science as an affection producing nodules or rounded little masses of diseased flesh on the eyelids, cheeks, nose, ears, hands and feet. It eats into the joints of the hands and feet. It is caused by a functional degeneration of the nerves of the skin. Jewish law prescribed tests by which the disease was recognized (Lev. 13.3, 8, 14), and if the priest declared the symptoms leprous, the person brought before him was pronounced unclean. In Palestine leprosy was incurable. See note on Mt. 8.2. *And he was a Samaritan.* It is interesting that the

facts of this healing suggest some parts of the parable of the Good Samaritan. The one grateful leper was a Samaritan, a stranger; the nine ungrateful were, presumably, Jews. Their ingratitude seems to have made a sorrowful impression upon the Divine Healer.

20. *The kingdom of God cometh not with observation.* It has not the visible signs of an earthly kingdom. Its coming is not spectacular. The ordinary observer does not know how or where to look for it with the trained physical eye.

21. *The kingdom of God is within you.* The reign of righteousness, within the heart.

22–37. *The days will come,* etc. See notes on Mt. 24.37, 41.

given in marriage, until the day that Noah entered into the ark, and the flood came, and destroyed them all. 28 Likewise even as it came to pass in the days of Lot; they ate, they drank, they bought, they sold, they planted, they builded; 29 but in the day that Lot went out from Sod'om it rained fire and brimstone from heaven, and destroyed them all: 30 after the same manner shall it be in the day that the Son of man is revealed. 31 In that day, he that shall be on the housetop, and his goods in the house, let him not go down to take them away: and let him that is in the field likewise not return back. 32 Remember Lot's wife. 33 Whosoever shall seek to gain his life shall lose it: but whosoever shall lose *his life* shall *k*preserve it. 34 I say unto you, In that night there shall be two men on one bed; the one shall be taken, and the other shall be left. 35 There shall be two women grinding together; the one shall

be taken, and the other shall be left*l*. 37 And they answering say unto him, Where, Lord? And he said unto them, Where the body *is*, thither will the *m*eagles also be gathered together.

18 And he spake a parable unto them to the end that they ought always to pray, and not to faint; 2 saying, There was in a city a judge, who feared not God, and regarded not man: 3 and there was a widow in that city; and she came oft unto him, saying, *a*Avenge me of mine adversary. 4 And he would not for a while: but afterward he said within himself, Though I fear not God, nor regard man; 5 yet because this widow troubleth me, I will avenge her, *b*lest she *c*wear me out by her continual coming. 6 And the Lord said, Hear what *d*the unrighteous judge saith. 7 And shall not God avenge his elect, that cry to him day and night, *e*and *yet* he is longsuffering over them? 8 I say unto you, that

k Gr. *save it alive.* *l* Some ancient authorities add ver. 36 *There shall be two men in the field; the one shall be taken, and the other shall be left.* Mt. 24.40. *m* Or, *vultures* *a* Or, *Do me justice of:* and so in

ver. 5, 7, 8. *b* Or, *lest at last by her coming she wear me out* *c* Gr. *bruise.* *d* Gr. *the judge of unrighteousness.* *e* Or, *and is he slow to punish on their behalf?*

CHAPTER 18

1. *That they ought always to pray, and not to faint.* Continual, unwearied prayer which Jesus urged upon his disciples was contrary to the teaching of the Jewish rabbis. They thought that if God was approached in prayer too often, He resented it as familiar and annoying. Christ's command implies the natural need of the soul, as if it could not live apart from God and had its only home in Him.

2–8. *A judge, who feared not God.* This parable of the unjust judge il-

lustrates by a striking contrast the willingness of God to answer persistent prayer. *A widow.* Belonging to a class especially in need of judicial protection against unprincipled persons. *Lest she wear me out.* No feeling for justice, no compassion for the helpless, no sense of personal honor animated this judge. He granted the widow's prayer to get rid of a nuisance. *Shall not God avenge his elect?* If the unjust judge for his own comfort avenged the widow, how much more readily will the heavenly Father in love hear and answer the petitions of those who love Him.

he will avenge them speedily. Nevertheless, when the Son of man cometh, shall he find ʲfaith on the earth?

9 And he spake also this parable unto certain who trusted in themselves that they were righteous, and set ᵍall others at nought: 10 Two men went up into the temple to pray; the one a Phar'i-see, and the other a ʰpublican. 11 The Phar'i-see stood and prayed thus with himself, God, I thank thee, that I am not as the rest of men, extortioners, unjust, adulterers, or even as this ʰpublican. 12 I fast twice in the week; I give tithes of all that I get. 13 But the ʰpublican, standing afar off, would not lift up so much as his eyes unto heaven, but smote his breast, saying, God, ⁱbe thou merciful to me ᵏa sinner. 14 I say unto you, This man went down to his house justified rather than the other: for every one that exalteth himself shall be humbled; but he that humbleth himself shall be exalted.

15 And they were bringing unto him also their babes, that he should touch them: but when the disciples saw it, they rebuked them. 16 But Je'sus called them unto him, saying, Suffer the little children to come unto me,

and forbid them not: for ˡto such belongeth the kingdom of God. 17 Verily I say unto you, Whosoever shall not receive the kingdom of God as a little child, he shall in no wise enter therein.

18 And a certain ruler asked him, saying, Good Teacher, what shall I do to inherit eternal life? 19 And Je'sus said unto him, Why callest thou me good? none is good, save one, *even* God. 20 Thou knowest the commandments, ᵐDo not commit adultery, Do not kill, Do not steal, Do not bear false witness, Honor thy father and mother. 21 And he said, All these things have I observed from my youth up. 22 And when Je'sus heard it, he said unto him, One thing thou lackest yet: sell all that thou hast, and distribute unto the poor, and thou shalt have treasure in heaven: and come, follow me. 23 But when he heard these things, he became exceeding sorrowful; for he was very rich. 24 And Je'sus seeing him said, How hardly shall they that have riches enter into the kingdom of God! 25 For it is easier for a camel to enter in through a needle's eye, than for a rich man to enter into the kingdom of God. 26 And they that heard it said, Then who

---

ʲ Or, *the faith*   ᵍ Gr. *the rest.*   ʰ See marginal note on ch. 3.12.   ⁱ Or, *be*   *thou propitiated*   ᵏ Or, *the sinner*   ˡ Or, *of such is*   ᵐ Ex. xx. 12–16; Dt. v. 16–20.

9–14. *Unto certain who trusted in themselves.* This parable, which illustrates the duty of humility in prayer, may have been addressed to some of his disciples. *Into the temple to pray.* The Temple was originally for sacrifice rather than prayer, but with the growth of spirituality the custom of resorting thither to pray had become firmly established.

15–17. *Were bringing unto him also their babes.* See notes on Mt. 19.13, 14. *As a little child.* With teachable humility.

18–30. *What shall I do to inherit eternal life?* See notes on Mt. 19.16, 21, 24, 25, 27, 28.

can be saved? 27 But he said, The things which are impossible with men are possible with God. 28 And Peter said, Lo, we have left [n]our own, and followed thee. 29 And he said unto them, Verily I say unto you, There is no man that hath left house, or wife, or brethren, or parents, or children, for the kingdom of God's sake, 30 who shall not receive manifold more in this time, and in the [o]world to come eternal life.

31 And he took unto him the twelve, and said unto them, Behold, we go up to Je-ru'sa-lem, and all the things that are written through the prophets shall be accomplished unto the Son of man. 32 For he shall be [p]delivered up unto the Gen'-tiles, and shall be mocked, and shamefully treated, and spit upon: 33 and they shall scourge and kill him: and the third day he shall rise again. 34 And they understood none of these things; and this saying was hid from them, and they perceived not the things that were said.

35 And it came to pass, as he drew nigh unto Jer'i-cho, a certain blind man sat by the way side begging: 36 and hearing a multitude going by, he inquired what this meant. 37 And they told him, that Je'sus of Naz'a-reth passeth by. 38 And he cried, saying, Je'sus, thou son of David, have mercy on me. 39 And they that went before rebuked him, that he should hold his peace: but he cried out the more a great deal, Thou son of David, have mercy on me. 40 And Je'sus stood, and commanded him to be brought unto him: and when he was come near, he asked him, 41 What wilt thou that I should do unto thee? And he said, Lord, that I may receive my sight. 42 And Je'sus said unto him, Receive thy sight: thy faith hath [q]made thee whole. 43 And immediately he received his sight, and followed him, glorifying God: and all the people, when they saw it, gave praise unto God.

19 And he entered and was passing through Jer'i-cho. 2 And behold, a man called by name Zac-chæ'us; and he was a chief publican, and he was rich. 3 And he sought to see Je'sus who he was; and could not for the crowd, because he was little of stature. 4 And he ran on before,

---

n Or, *our own* homes   See Jn. 19.27.

o Or, *age*   p Or, *betrayed*   q Or, *saved thee*

31–34. *All the things that are written through the prophets shall be accomplished.* Jesus on his final journey to Jerusalem foretold to his disciples his coming death and resurrection. It grieved and perplexed them because such an ending to our Lord's life dashed their Messianic hopes and thoughts and left him an apparent failure. See note on Mat. 20.18. It was in some respects strange that the twelve did not understand this prediction. It was the third time Jesus had told them about his coming passion. His words were too clear to be mistaken.

35–43. *A certain blind man sat by the way side begging.* See notes on Mt. 20.29, 30.

CHAPTER 19

2. *Zacchæus; and he was a chief publican.* Or chief tax-gatherer. Most probably he was head of the custom house at Jericho, a rich trading as well as a priestly city.

4. *Climbed up into a sycomore tree.* Not sycamore, but a tree deriving

and climbed up into a sycomore tree to see him: for he was to pass that way. 5 And when Je'sus came to the place, he looked up, and said unto him, **Zac-chæ'us, make haste, and come down; for to-day I must abide at thy house.** 6 And he made haste, and came down, and received him joyfully. 7 And when they saw it, they all murmured, saying, He is gone in to lodge with a man that is a sinner. 8 And Zac-chæ'us stood, and said unto the Lord, Behold, Lord, the half of my goods I give to the poor; and if I have wrongfully exacted aught of any man, I restore fourfold. 9 And Je'sus said unto him, **To-day is salvation come to this house, forasmuch as he also is a son of Abraham. 10 For the Son of man came to seek and to save that which was lost.**

11 And as they heard these things, he added and spake a parable, because he was nigh to Je-ru'sa-lem, and *because* they supposed that the kingdom of God was immediately to appear. 12 He said therefore, **A certain nobleman went into a far country, to receive for himself a kingdom, and to return.** 13 **And he called ten** *a*servants of his, and gave them ten *b*pounds, and said unto them, Trade ye *herewith* till I come. 14 But his citizens hated him, and sent an ambassage after him, saying, We will not that this man reign over us. 15 And it came to pass, when he was come back again,

---

a Gr. *bondservants.*   *b Mina,* here translated a pound, is equal to one hundred drachmas. See ch. 15.8.

---

its name from its fig-like fruit. Its leaves resembled those of the mulberry tree.

5. *I must abide at thy house.* In saying this Jesus disregarded the deep-seated hatred of publicans as a class and the special aversion which the people of Jericho must have had to Zacchæus. There were great opportunities for extortion in connection with the balsam export duties. The chief tax-gatherer's subsequent offer to restore fourfold the amount of possible wrongful exactions suggests that he may have taken advantage of his position.

6. *Received him joyfully.* He, an object of bitter dislike and contempt, was very glad to be thus singled out as host by one who was known and honored as a great prophet.

7. *When they saw it, they all murmured.* The visit of our Lord to the despised household of the publican had its natural result. There was a clamorous outburst of feeling against him.

8. *Zacchæus stood, and said,* etc. We do not know what Jesus said to Zacchæus while he was being entertained, but the result was a complete change in the host's spiritual outlook. Springs of generosity were opened in the heart of the greedy tax-gatherer. He had learned something about social justice. *The half of my goods I give to the poor.* Much of his great wealth was doubtless fairly earned; to give half to the poor was all that could have been expected. He also promised to restore fourfold the amount of whatever wrongful exactions he might have made. This was what Jewish law required of a detected thief. The remorse of Zacchæus for past misdeeds was so keen that he did not hesitate to meet the penalty due to a convicted criminal. The genuineness of his conversion was proved by his immediate acts.

9. *Is a son of Abraham.* In spirit as well as by descent. The Jews denied the right of a publican to be considered a son of Abraham.

11–27. *Spake a parable, because he was nigh to Jerusalem.* Many of his disciples and followers were rapidly growing more excited, because

having received the kingdom, that he commanded these [b]servants, unto whom he had given the money, to be called to him, that he might know what they had gained by trading. 16 And the first came before him, saying, Lord, thy pound hath made ten pounds more. 17 And he said unto him, Well done, thou good [c]servant: because thou wast found faithful in a very little, have thou authority over ten cities. 18 And the second came, saying, Thy pound, Lord, hath made five pounds. 19 And he said unto him also, Be thou also over five cities. 20 And [d]another came, saying, Lord, behold, *here is* thy pound, which I kept laid up in a napkin: 21 for I feared thee, because thou art an austere man: thou takest up that which thou layedst not down, and reapest that which thou didst not sow. 22 He saith unto him, Out of thine own mouth will I judge thee, thou wicked [c]servant. Thou knewest that I am an austere man, taking up that which I laid not down, and reaping that which I did not sow? 23 then wherefore gavest thou not my money into the bank, and [e]I at my coming should have required it with interest? 24 And he said unto

them that stood by, Take away from him the pound, and give it unto him that hath the ten pounds. 25 And they said unto him, Lord, he hath ten pounds. 26 I say unto you, that unto every one that hath shall be given; but from him that hath not, even that which he hath shall be taken away from him. 27 But these mine enemies, that would not that I should reign over them, bring hither, and slay them before me.

28 And when he had thus spoken, he went on before, going up to Je-ru′sa-lem.

29 And it came to pass, when he drew nigh unto Beth′pha-ge and Beth′a-ny, at the mount that is called Ol′i-vet, he sent two of the disciples, 30 saying, Go your way into the village over against *you;* in which as ye enter ye shall find a colt tied, whereon no man ever yet sat: loose him and bring him. 31 And if any one ask you, Why do ye loose him? thus shall ye say, The Lord hath need of him. 32 And they that were sent went away, and found even as he had said unto them. 33 And as they were loosing the colt, the owners thereof said unto them, Why loose ye the colt? 34 And they said, The Lord hath need of him.

---

b Gr. *bondservants.*   *c* Gr. *bondservant.*
d Gr. *the other.*

e Or, *I should have gone and required*

---

the nearer he approached Jerusalem the nearer, they believed, was the manifestation of his power as the Messiah. This parable of the pounds was spoken to recall them from false notions and fix their thoughts on patient work done with a sense of responsibility. *Pounds.* A pound was worth about sixteen

dollars. *An ambassage.* Or embassy, persons entrusted with a public message. *Be thou also over five cities.* The rewards in the parable are proportioned to the services. See notes on Mt. 25.15, 18, 24, 28.

28–40. *He went on before, going up to Jerusalem.* After this parable Jesus, at the head of the apostles and

35 And they brought him to Je'sus: and they threw their garments upon the colt, and set Je'sus thereon. 36 And as he went, they spread their garments in the way. 37 And as he was now drawing nigh, *even* at the descent of the mount of Ol'ives, the whole multitude of the disciples began to rejoice and praise God with a loud voice for all the *f*mighty works which they had seen; 38 saying, Blessed *is* the King that cometh in the name of the Lord: peace in heaven, and glory in the highest. 39 And some of the Phar'i-sees from the multitude said unto him, Teacher, rebuke thy disciples. 40 And he answered and said, I tell you that, if these shall hold their peace, the stones will cry out.

41 And when he drew nigh, he saw the city and wept over it, 42 saying, *g*If thou hadst known in *h*this day, even thou, the things which belong unto *i*peace! but now they are hid from thine eyes. 43 For the days shall come upon thee, when thine enemies shall cast up a *k*bank about thee, and compass thee round, and keep thee in on every side, 44 and shall dash thee to the ground, and thy children within thee; and they shall not leave in thee one stone upon another; because thou knewest not the time of thy visitation.

45 And he entered into the temple, and began to cast out them that sold, 46 saying unto them, It is written, *l*And my house shall be a house of prayer: but *m*ye have made it a den of robbers.

47 And he was teaching daily in the temple. But the chief priests and the scribes and the principal men of the people sought to destroy him: 48 and they could not find what they might do; for the people all hung upon him, listening.

20 And it came to pass, on one of the days, as he was teaching the people in the temple, and preaching the *a*gospel, there came upon him the chief priests and the scribes with the elders; 2 and they spake, saying unto him, Tell us: By what authority doest thou these

---

f Gr. *powers.*   *g* Or, *O that thou hadst known   h* Some ancient authorities read *this thy day.   i* Some ancient authorities read *thy peace.   k* Gr. *palisade.   l* Is. lvi. 7.   *m* Jer. vii. 11.   *a* Or, *good tidings:* comp. ch. 3.18.

disciples and the multitude, journeyed to Jerusalem and made his triumphal entry. See notes on Mt. 21.1, 2, 5, 7–9.

41. *He saw the city and wept over it.* The view referred to was most probably at the beginning of the descent of the Mount of Olives. The city is seen at this point with great distinctness. In Christ's time Jerusalem with the magnificent temple, the Roman fortress and other buildings, and the background of gardens and suburban villages, must have been a vision of exceeding beauty as they lay in the valley below.

43. *Thine enemies.* The Romans. *Shall cast up a bank about thee.* A palisade surrounding the city, which kept out all supplies of food.

44. *The time of thy visitation.* The time of Christ's preaching and miracles.

45, 46. *Began to cast out them that sold.* This was the second and final cleansing of the temple. See notes on Mt. 21.12. The first cleansing was at the beginning of his ministry (Jn. 2.14–17).

CHAPTER 20

2–8. *By what authority doest thou*

things? or who is he that gave thee this authority? 3 And he answered and said unto them, I also will ask you a *b*question; and tell me: 4 The baptism of John, was it from heaven, or from men? 5 And they reasoned with themselves, saying, If we shall say, From heaven; he will say, Why did ye not believe him? 6 But if we shall say, From men; all the people will stone us: for they are persuaded that John was a prophet. 7 And they answered, that they knew not whence *it was.* 8 And Je′sus said unto them, Neither tell I you by what authority I do these things.

9 And he began to speak unto the people this parable: A man planted a vineyard, and let it out to husbandmen, and went into another country for a long time. 10 And at the season he sent unto the husbandmen a *c*servant, that they should give him of the fruit of the vineyard: but the husbandmen beat him, and sent him away empty. 11 And he sent yet another *c*servant: and him also they beat, and handled him shamefully, and sent him away empty. 12 And he sent yet a third: and him also they wounded, and cast him forth. 13 And the lord of the vineyard said, What shall I do?

I will send my beloved son; it may be they will reverence him. 14 But when the husbandmen saw him, they reasoned one with another, saying, This is the heir; let us kill him, that the inheritance may be ours. 15 And they cast him forth out of the vineyard, and killed him. What therefore will the lord of the vineyard do unto them? 16 He will come and destroy these husbandmen, and will give the vineyard unto others. And when they heard it, they said, *d*God forbid. 17 But he looked upon them, and said, What then is this that is written,

*e*The stone which the builders rejected,
The same was made the head of the corner?

18 Every one that falleth on that stone shall be broken to pieces; but on whomsoever it shall fall, it will scatter him as dust.

19 And the scribes and the chief priests sought to lay hands on him in that very hour; and they feared the people: for they perceived that he spake this parable against them. 20 And they watched him, and sent forth spies, who feigned themselves to be righteous, that they might take hold of his speech, so as to deliver him up to the *f*rule and to the authority of the governor.

---

b Gr. *word.* *c* Gr. *bondservant.* *d* Gr. *Be tt not so.* *e* Ps. cxviii. 22. *f* Or, *ruling power*

these things? See notes on Mt. 21. 23, 27.

9–18. *Planted a vineyard, and let it out to husbandmen.* This is the parable of the wicked husbandmen. See notes on Mt. 21.33, 41.

19–26. *Sought to lay hands on him in that very hour.* The scribes and Pharisees, though seeking to lay hands on him, feared a riot if they attempted physical violence. Therefore all their power was exerted in framing questions which were intended to be legal traps, excuses for his authorized arrest and appearance before the Sanhedrin. One of

21 And they asked him, saying, Teacher, we know that thou sayest and teachest rightly, and acceptest not the person *of any,* but of a truth teachest the way of God: 22 Is it lawful for us to give tribute unto Cæ'sar, or not? 23 But he perceived their craftiness, and said unto them, 24 Show me a *ᵍ*denarius. Whose image and superscription hath it? And they said, Cæ'sar's. 25 And he said unto them, Then render unto Cæ'sar the things that are Cæ'sar's, and unto God the things that are God's. 26 And they were not able to take hold of the saying before the people: and they marvelled at his answer, and held their peace.

27 And there came to him certain of the Sad'du-cees, they that say that there is no resurrection; 28 and they asked him, saying, Teacher, *ʰ*Mo'ses wrote unto us, that if a man's brother die, having a wife, and he be childless, his brother should take the wife, and raise up seed unto his brother. 29 There were therefore seven brethren: and the first took a wife, and died childless; 30 and the second: 31 and the third took her; and likewise the seven also left no children, and died. 32 Afterward the woman also died. 33 In the resurrection therefore whose wife of them shall she be? for the seven had her to wife. 34 And Je'sus said unto them, The sons of this *ⁱ*world marry, and are given in marriage: 35 but they that are accounted worthy to attain to that *ⁱ*world, and the resurrection from the dead, neither marry, nor are given in marriage: 36 for neither can they die any more: for they are equal unto the angels; and are sons of God, being sons of the resurrection. 37 But that the dead are raised, even Mo'ses showed, in *ᵏthe place concerning* ⁱthe Bush, when he calleth the Lord the God of Abraham, and the God of I'saac, and the God of Jacob. 38 Now he is not the God of the dead, but of the living: for all live unto him. 39 And certain of the scribes answering said, Teacher, thou hast well said. 40 For they durst not any more ask him any question.

41 And he said unto them, How say they that the Christ is David's son? 42 For David himself saith in the book of Psalms, *ⁱ*The Lord said unto my Lord, Sit thou on my right hand, 43 Till I make thine enemies the footstool of thy feet. 44 David therefore calleth him Lord, and how is he his son? 45 And in the hearing of all

---

g See marginal note on ch. 7.41.   *h* Dt. xxv. 5.   *i* Or, *age*   *k* Ex. iii. 6.   *l* Ps. cx. 1.

the most memorable of these questions concerned the lawfulness of giving tribute unto Cæsar. See notes on Mt. 22.15, 21, 22.

27–40. *That say that there is no resurrection.* Christ's rebuke and instruction of the Sadducees, who denied the resurrection from the dead, were in effect an affirmation of the immortality of the soul, which also they denied. See notes on Mt. 22. 29–31. *Neither can they die any more.* Therefore the earthly institution of marriage had no function in the spiritual state.

41–44. *How say they that the Christ is David's son?* See notes on Mt. 22.42, 44, 45.

the people he said unto his disciples, 46 **Beware of the scribes, who desire to walk in long robes, and love salutations in the marketplaces, and chief seats in the synagogues, and chief places at feasts; 47 who devour widows' houses, and for a pretence make long prayers: these shall receive greater condemnation.**

21 And he looked up, *a*and saw the rich men that were casting their gifts into the treasury. 2 And he saw a certain poor widow casting in thither two mites. 3 And he said, Of a truth I say unto you, This poor widow cast in more than they all: 4 for all these did of their superfluity cast in unto the gifts; but she of her want did cast in all the living that she had.

5 And as some spake of the temple, how it was adorned with goodly stones and offerings, he said, 6 As for these things which ye behold, the days will come, in which there shall not be left here one stone upon another, that shall not be thrown down. 7 And they asked him, saying, Teacher, when therefore shall these things be? and what *shall*

be the sign when these things are about to come to pass? 8 And he said, Take heed that ye be not led astray: for many shall come in my name, saying, I am *he;* and, The time is at hand: go ye not after them. 9 And when ye shall hear of wars and tumults, be not terrified: for these things must needs come to pass first; but the end is not immediately.

10 Then said he unto them, Nation shall rise against nation, and kingdom against kingdom; 11 and there shall be great earthquakes, and in divers places famines and pestilences; and there shall be terrors and great signs from heaven. 12 But before all these things, they shall lay their hands on you, and shall persecute you, delivering you up to the synagogues and prisons, *b*bringing you before kings and governors for my name's sake. 13 It shall turn out unto you for a testimony. 14 Settle it therefore in your hearts, not to meditate beforehand how to answer: 15 for I will give you a mouth and wisdom, which all your adversaries shall not be able to withstand or to gainsay. 16 But ye shall be

---

a Or, *and saw them that . . . treasury, and* *they were rich*   *b* Gr. *you being brought.*

46. *Beware of the scribes.* See notes on Mt. 23.2–5, 7–9.
47. *Devour widows' houses.* See Mk. 12.40.

CHAPTER 21

1–4. *Casting their gifts into the treasury.* The treasury of the Temple was in the Court of the Women, but the name 'treasury' was also applied to the colonnade around this court, in which were placed con-

tribution-boxes shaped like trumpets. According to the text it would seem that the widow who cast two mites into the treasury did so in one of these boxes, along with the rich men who were contributing. See notes on Mk. 12.42, 43.

6–36. *There shall not be left here one stone upon another.* The fall of Jerusalem and the second coming of Christ are predicted in these verses. *For a testimony.* For an opportunity to bear witness and suf-

192

^cdelivered up even by parents, and brethren, and kinsfolk, and friends; and *some* of you ^dshall they cause to be put to death. 17 And ye shall be hated of all men for my name's sake. 18 And not a hair of your head shall perish. 19 In your ^epatience ye shall win your ^fsouls.

20 But when ye see Je-ru'sa-lem compassed with armies, then know that her desolation is at hand. 21 Then let them that are in Ju-dæ'a flee unto the mountains; and let them that are in the midst of her depart out; and let not them that are in the country enter therein. 22 For these are days of vengeance, that all things which are written may be fulfilled. 23 Woe unto them that are with child and to them that give suck in those days! for there shall be great distress upon the ^gland, and wrath unto this people. 24 And they shall fall by the edge of the sword, and shall be led captive into all the nations: and Je-ru'sa-lem shall be trodden down of the Gen'tiles, until the times of the Gen'tiles be fulfilled.

25 And there shall be signs in sun and moon and stars; and upon the earth distress of nations, in perplexity for the roaring of the sea and the billows; 26 men ^hfainting for fear, and for expectation of the things which are coming on ⁱthe world: for the powers of the heavens shall be shaken. 27 And then shall they see the Son of man coming in a cloud with power and great glory. 28 But when these things begin to come to pass, look up, and lift up your heads; because your redemption draweth nigh.

29 And he spake to them a parable: Behold the fig tree, and all the trees: 30 when they now shoot forth, ye see it and know of your own selves that summer is now nigh. 31 Even so ye also, when ye see these things coming to pass, know ye that the kingdom of God is nigh. 32 Verily I say unto you, This generation shall not pass away, till all things be accomplished. 33 Heaven and earth shall pass away: but my words shall not pass away.

34 But take heed to yourselves, lest haply your hearts be overcharged with surfeiting, and drunkenness, and cares of this life, and that day come on you suddenly as a snare: 35 for *so* shall it come upon all them that dwell on the face of all the earth. 36 But watch ye at every season, making supplication, that ye may prevail to escape all these things that shall come to pass, and to stand before the Son of man.

37 And every day he was teaching in the temple; and every night he went out, and lodged in the mount that is called Ol'i-vet. 38 And all the people came early in the morn-

c Or, *betrayed*   d Or, *shall they put to death*   e Or, *stedfastness*   f Or, *lives*   g Or, *earth*   h Or, *expiring*   i Gr. *the inhabited earth.*

fer for the truth's sake.   *Mouth.*
Words.   *Compassed with armies.*
The Roman legions.   *The times of* the Gentiles. Their period of power and prosperity.   See notes on Mt. 24.1–5, 16, 29, 32.

ing to him in the temple, to hear him.

22 Now the feast of unleavened bread drew nigh, which is called the Passover. 2 And the chief priests and the scribes sought how they might put him to death; for they feared the people.

3 And Satan entered into Ju'das who was called Is-car'i-ot, being of the number of the twelve. 4 And he went away, and communed with the chief priests and captains, how he might *a*deliver him unto them. 5 And they were glad, and covenanted to give him money. 6 And he consented, and sought opportunity to *a*deliver him unto them *b*in the absence of the multitude.

7 And the day of unleavened bread came, on which the passover must be sacrificed. 8 And he sent Peter and John, saying, Go and make ready for us the passover, that we may eat. 9 And they said unto him, Where wilt thou that we make ready? 10 And he said unto them, Behold, when ye are entered into the city, there shall meet you a man bearing a pitcher of water; follow him into the house whereinto he goeth. 11 And ye shall say unto the master of the house, The Teacher saith unto thee, Where is the guest-chamber, where I shall eat the passover with my disciples? 12 And he will show you a large upper room furnished: there make ready. 13 And they went, and found as he had said unto them: and they made ready the passover.

14 And when the hour was come, he sat down, and the apostles with him. 15 And he said unto them, With desire I have desired to eat this passover with you before I suffer: 16 for I say unto you, I shall not eat it, until it be fulfilled in the kingdom of God. 17 And he received a cup, and when he had given thanks, he said, Take this, and divide it among yourselves: 18 for I say unto you, I shall not drink from henceforth of the fruit of the vine, until the kingdom of God shall come. 19 And he took *c*bread, and when he had given thanks, he brake it, and gave to them, saying, This is

---

a Or, *betray*   *b* Or, *without tumult*

c Or, *a loaf*

CHAPTER 22

1–6. *Which is called the Passover.* The word 'called' is a concession to the Gentile readers for whom Luke wrote. The feast of unleavened bread was not the same as the Passover, which began on the 14th of Nisan, while the feast of unleavened bread began a day later. The name 'Passover' was popularly applied to the whole two feasts, from the 14th of Nisan to the end of the seven days after the 15th. *How they might put him* to death. Either by some device secretly carried into effect, or by the direct aid of the Roman authorities. *Captains.* The Temple guard of Levites. See notes on Mt. 26.3, 15.

7–13. *On which the passover must be sacrificed.* Alluding to the custom of killing the paschal lamb, which was eaten at the feast. See notes on Mt. 26.17, 18.

14–23. *When the hour was come.* These verses contain the narrative of the institution of the Last Supper and the denunciation of Judas. See notes on Mt. 26.24–26, 28.

my body ᵈwhich is given for you: this do in remembrance of me. 20 And the cup in like manner after supper, saying, This cup is the new covenant in my blood, *even* that which is poured out for you. 21 But behold, the hand of him that ᵉbetrayeth me is with me on the table. 22 For the Son of man indeed goeth, as it hath been determined: but woe unto that man through whom he is ᵉbetrayed! 23 And they began to question among themselves, which of them it was that should do this thing.

24 And there arose also a contention among them, which of them was accounted to be ᶠgreatest. 25 And he said unto them, The kings of the Gen'tiles have lordship over them; and they that have authority over them are called Benefactors. 26 But ye *shall* not *be* so: but he that is the greater among you, let him ʻbecome as the younger; and he that is chief, as he that doth serve. 27 For which is greater, he that ᵍsitteth at meat, or he that serveth? is not he that ᵍsitteth at meat?

but I am in the midst of you as he that serveth. 28 But ye are they that have continued with me in my temptations; 29 and ʰI appoint unto you a kingdom, even as my Father appointed unto me, 30 that ye may eat and drink at my table in my kingdom; and ye shall sit on thrones judging the twelve tribes of Is'ra-el.

31 Si'mon, Si'mon, behold, Satan ⁱasked to have you, that he might sift you as wheat: 32 but I made supplication for thee, that thy faith fail not; and do thou, when once thou hast turned again, establish thy brethren. 33 And he said unto him, Lord, with thee I am ready to go both to prison and to death. 34 And he said, I tell thee, Peter, the cock shall not crow this day, until thou shalt thrice deny that thou knowest me.

35 And he said unto them, When I sent you forth without purse, and wallet, and shoes, lacked ye anything? And they said, Nothing. 36 And he said unto them, But now, he that hath a purse, let him take it, and

---

d Some ancient authorities omit *which is given for you . . . which is poured out for you.* *e* See ver. 4. *f* Gr. *greater.* *g* Gr. *reclineth.*

h Or, *I appoint unto you, even as my Father appointed unto me a kingdom, that ye may eat and drink &c.* *i* Or, *obtained you by asking*

24–30. *There arose also a contention among them.* Although Luke places this dispute immediately after the supper it was probably at the beginning. See note on Jn. 13.4. *The kings of the Gentiles.* See notes on Mt. 20.21, 23, 26, 28; 19.27, 28.

31–34. *Simon, behold, Satan asked to have you.* Peter's fitful ambition and his times of weakened allegiance to Jesus, notwithstanding the rock-like faith of which he was capable, made him an object of our Lord's solicitude and prayer. Here the great apostle is addressed in lan-

guage of sorrowful reproof; yet he is signally honored by being commanded to establish his brethren, after his own faith is made firm. See notes on Mt. 26.33–35.

35. *Lacked ye anything?* Did ye really need any worldly aids and precautions when I sent you forth at first without purse, and wallet, and shoes? Were ye not well able to do without them?

36. *But now.* The times were changed; there were special reasons why they should be prudent and protect themselves. This need was

likewise a wallet; [k]and he that hath none, let him sell his cloak, and buy a sword. 37 For I say unto you, that this which is written must be fulfilled in me, [l]And he was reckoned with transgressors: for that which concerneth me hath [m]fulfilment. 38 And they said, Lord, behold, here are two swords. And he said unto them, It is enough.

39 And he came out, and went, as his custom was, unto the mount of Ol'ives; and the disciples also followed him. 40 And when he was at the place, he said unto them, 'Pray that ye enter not into temptation. 41 And he was parted from them about a stone's cast; and he kneeled down and prayed, 42 saying, Father, if thou be willing, remove this cup from me: nevertheless not my will, but thine, be done. 43 [n]And there appeared unto him an angel from heaven, strengthening him. 44 And being in an agony he prayed more earnestly; and his

sweat became as it were great drops of blood falling down upon the ground. 45 And when he rose up from his prayer, he came unto the disciples, and found them sleeping for sorrow, 46 and said unto them, Why sleep ye? rise and pray, that ye enter not into temptation.

47 While he yet spake, behold, a multitude, and he that was called Ju'das, one of the twelve, went before them; and he drew near unto Je'sus to kiss him. 48 But Je'sus said unto him, Ju'das, [o]betrayest thou the Son of man with a kiss? 49 And when they that were about him saw what would follow, they said, Lord, shall we smite with the sword? 50 And a certain one of them smote the [p]servant of the high priest, and struck off his right ear. 51 But Je'sus answered and said, Suffer ye *them* thus far. And he touched his ear, and healed him. 52 And Je'sus said unto the chief priests, and captains of the temple, and elders, that were come against

---

k Or, *and he that hath no sword, let him sell his cloak, and buy one. l* Is. liii. 12. *m* Gr. end.   *n* Many ancient authorities omit ver. 43, 44.   *o* See ver. 4.   *p* Gr. *bondservant.*

---

emphasized figuratively by our Lord's telling them to buy a sword. The apostles strangely misunderstood his meaning.

37. *That which concerneth me hath fulfilment.* His foretold death and resurrection.

38. *Here are two swords.* As if two sharpened pieces of metal carried in the hands would have been any protection against thousands of enemies! *It is enough.* A sudden rebuke to their stupidity in taking his words in a literal sense.

39–46. *Unto the mount of Olives.* He went across the ravine through which the brook Kidron had formerly flowed, then up the slope beyond it to the foot of the mountain, where was the garden or little farm of Gethsemane (oil press). *The disciples.* Peter, James and John. *An angel from heaven, strengthening him.* For the first known time since the temptation (Mt. 4.11). *As it were great drops of blood.* Luke is the only evangelist who records this. Extreme mental anguish has been known to produce a like effect. The qualifying words 'as it were' should be noted. See notes on Mt. 26.36, 37, 39, 40, 44.

47–53. *Drew near unto Jesus to kiss him.* Judas knew that the Master with his disciples had gone to Gethsemane, and was thus enabled

him, Are ye come out, as against a robber, with swords and staves? 53 When I was daily with you in the temple, ye stretched not forth your hands against me: but this is your hour, and the power of darkness.

54 And they seized him, and led him *away*, and brought him into the high priest's house. But Peter followed afar off. 55 And when they had kindled a fire in the midst of the court, and had sat down together, Peter sat in the midst of them. 56 And a certain maid seeing him as he sat in the light *of the fire*, and looking stedfastly upon him, said, This man also was with him. 57 But he denied, saying, Woman, I know him not. 58 And after a little while another saw him, and said, Thou also art *one* of them. But Peter said, Man, I am not. 59 And after the space of about one hour another confidently affirmed, saying, Of a truth this man also was with him; for he is a Gal-i-læ'an. 60 But Peter said, Man, I know not what thou sayest. And immediately, while he yet

spake, the cock crew. 61 And the Lord turned, and looked upon Peter. And Peter remembered the word of the Lord, how that he said unto him, Before the cock crow this day thou shalt deny me thrice. 62 And he went out, and wept bitterly.

63 And the men that held *qJe'sus* mocked him, and beat him. 64 And they blindfolded him, and asked him, saying, Prophesy: who is he that struck thee? 65 And many other things spake they against him, reviling him.

66 And as soon as it was day, the assembly of the elders of the people was gathered together, both chief priests and scribes; and they led him away into their council, saying, 67 If thou art the Christ, tell us. But he said unto them, **If I tell you, ye will not believe: 68 and if I ask *you*, ye will not answer. 69 But from henceforth shall the Son of man be seated at the right hand of the power of God.** 70 And they all said, Art thou then the Son of God? And he said unto them, *r*Ye say that I am. 71 And they

q Gr. *him.* *r* Or, *Ye say* it, *because I am*

to plan the betrayal and arrest (Jn. 18.2). *Your hour, and the power of darkness.* The hour in which the temporal triumph of your evil designs, and of the power of Satan, is permitted. See notes on Mt. 26.47, 48, 50, 51–53.

54–62. Brought him into the high priest's house. The narrative of Peter's denials is given in these verses. See notes on Mt. 26.58, 59, 70, 73, 75.

66–71. They led him away into their council. This trial, held before the regularly assembled Sanhedrin at dawn, was the last of three attempts by the Jewish authorities

which ended in the unlawful conviction of Jesus. He was first taken bound before Annas (Jn. 18.12, 13); afterwards before Caiaphas and an informal gathering of members of the Sanhedrin. These two attempts were not only illegal in form, but were designed to affect injuriously the case of Jesus before the full court. If his first appearance before the aged and powerfully influential Annas were unfavorable, his appearance before the bigoted son-in-law Caiaphas and the hostile members of the council would be more so. With two irregular and prejudicial proceedings already against him, he

said, What further need have we of witness? for we ourselves have heard from his own mouth.

23 And the whole company of them rose up, and brought him before Pi'late. 2 And they began to accuse him, saying, We found this man perverting our nation, and forbidding to give tribute to Cæ'sar, and saying that he himself is Christ a king. 3 And Pi'late asked him, saying, Art thou the King of the Jews? And he answered him and said, **Thou sayest.** 4 And Pi'late said unto the chief priests and the multitudes, I find no fault in this man. 5 But they were the more urgent, saying, He stirreth up the people, teaching throughout all Ju-dæ'a, and beginning from Gal'i-lee even unto this place. 6 But when Pi'late heard it, he asked whether the man were a Gal-i-læ'an. 7 And when he knew that he was of Her'od's jurisdiction, he sent him unto Her'od, who himself also was at Je-ru'salem in these days.

8 Now when Her'od saw Je'-

rus, he was exceeding glad: for he was of a long time desirous to see him, because he had heard concerning him; and he hoped to see some *a*miracle done by him. 9 And he questioned him in many words; but he answered him nothing. 10 And the chief priests and the scribes stood, vehemently accusing him. 11 And Her'od with his soldiers set him at nought, and mocked him, and arraying him in gorgeous apparel sent him back to Pi'late. 12 And Her'od and Pi'late became friends with each other that very day: for before they were at enmity between themselves.

13 And Pi'late called together the chief priests and the rulers and the people, 14 and said unto them, Ye brought unto me this man, as one that perverteth the people: and behold, I, having examined him before you, found no fault in this man touching those things whereof ye accuse him: 15 no, nor yet Her'od: for *b*he sent him back unto us; and behold, nothing worthy of death

---

a Gr. *sign.*   *b* Many ancient authorities read *I sent you to him.*

would of course be unjustly convicted before the Sanhedrin in the morning. Luke alone notices the trial before Herod, which interrupted that before Pilate.

CHAPTER 23

1–5. *Brought him before Pilate.* To procure the execution of the death sentence. The Romans had deprived the Sanhedrin of the power of life and death. But it was necessary to change the nature of the accusation against Jesus. The Jewish sentence was for blasphemy; a sentence by Pilate could only result from a conviction for treason to the

Roman emperor. See notes on Mt. 27.11.

6–12. *Whether the man were a Galilæan.* The report that Jesus was a Galilæan enabled Pilate temporarily to put the responsibility of the trial, from which he strongly desired to escape, upon Herod and to make friendly advances to that ruler, with whom he had quarreled. *Herod's jurisdiction.* Which included Galilee and Peræa. *At Jerusalem.* To keep the Passover. *Exceeding glad.* But not righteously so. It was the pleasure of gratifying his curiosity.

13–25. *Pilate called together the chief priests and the rulers.* He was compelled to do so by Herod's fail-

hath been done by him. 16 I will therefore chastise him, and release him.ᶜ 18 But they cried out all together, saying, Away with this man, and release unto us Bar-ab′bas:—19 one who for a certain insurrection made in the city, and for murder, was cast into prison. 20 And Pi′late spake unto them again, desiring to release Je′sus; 21 but they shouted, saying, Crucify, crucify him. 22 And he said unto them the third time, Why, what evil hath this man done? I have found no cause of death in him: I will therefore chastise him and release him. 23 But they were urgent with loud voices, asking that he might be crucified. And their voices prevailed. 24 And Pi′late gave sentence that what they asked for should be done. 25 And he released him that for insurrection and murder had been cast into prison, whom they asked for; but Je′sus he delivered up to their will.

26 And when they led him away, they laid hold upon one Si′mon of Cy-re′ne, coming from the country, and laid on him the cross, to bear it after Je′sus.

27 And there followed him a great multitude of the people, and of women who bewailed and lamented him. 28 But Je′sus turning unto them said, **Daughters of Je-ru′sa-lem, weep not for me, but weep for yourselves, and for your children. 29 For behold, the days are coming, in which they shall say, Blessed are the barren, and the wombs that never bare, and the breasts that never gave suck. 30 Then shall they begin to say to the mountains, Fall on us; and to the hills, Cover us. 31 For if they do these things in the green tree, what shall be done in the dry?**

32 And there were also two others, malefactors, led with him to be put to death.

33 And when they came unto the place which is called ᵈThe skull, there they crucified him, and the malefactors, one on the right hand and the other on the left.   34 ᵉAnd Je′sus said, **Father, forgive them; for they know not what they do.** And parting his garments among them, they cast lots. 35 And the people stood beholding. And the rulers also scoffed at him, saying, He saved others; let him save himself, if this is the Christ of God, his chosen.   36 And the soldiers also mocked him, coming to him, offering him

---

c Many ancient authorities insert ver. 17 *Now he must needs release unto them at the feast one* prisoner. Comp. Mt. 27. 15; Mk. 15.6; Jn. 18.39. Others add the same words after ver. 19. d According to

ure to assume any authority over the proceedings against Jesus. See notes on Mt. 27.15, 16, 20, 22.

26–32. *One Simon of Cyrene.* See notes on Mt. 27.32. *Weep for yourselves.* For the destruction which shall come upon yourselves and Jerusalem.

the Latin, *Calvary,* which has the same meaning. e Some ancient authorities omit *And Jesus said, Father, forgive them; for they know not what they do.*

33–38. *There they crucified him, and the malefactors.* See notes on Mt. 27.33, 35. *Father, forgive them; for they know not what they do.* The first of the Seven Words from the Cross. See note on Mt. 27.46. *A superscription.* See note on Mt. 27.37.

199

vinegar, 37 and saying, If thou
art the King of the Jews, save
thyself. 38 And there was also
a superscription over him, THIS
IS THE KING OF THE JEWS.

39 And one of the malefactors
that were hanged railed on him,
saying, Art not thou the Christ?
save thyself and us. 40 But the
other answered, and rebuking
him said, Dost thou not even
fear God, seeing thou art in the
same condemnation? 41 And
we indeed justly; for we receive
the due reward of our deeds:
but this man hath done nothing
amiss. 42 And he said, Je'sus,
remember me when thou comest
*in thy kingdom. 43 And he
said unto him, **Verily I say unto
thee, To-day shalt thou be with
me in Paradise.**

44 And it was now about the
sixth hour, and a darkness came
over the whole *land until the
ninth hour, 45 *the sun's light
failing: and the veil of the *temple was rent in the midst. 46
*And Je'sus, crying with a loud
voice, said, **Father, into thy
hands I commend my spirit:** and
having said this, he gave up the
ghost. 47 And when the centurion saw what was done, he
glorified God, saying, Certainly
this was a righteous man. 48

And all the multitudes that came
together to this sight, when they
beheld the things that were done,
returned smiting their breasts.
49 And all his acquaintance, and
the women that followed with
him from Gal'i-lee, stood afar
off, seeing these things.

50 And behold, a man named
Joseph, who was a councillor, a
good and righteous man 51 (he
had not consented to their
counsel and deed), *a man of
Ar-i-ma-thæ'a, a city of the
Jews, who was looking for the
kingdom of God: 52 this man
went to Pi'late, and asked for
the body of Je'sus. 53 And he
took it down, and wrapped it in
a linen cloth, and laid him in a
tomb that was hewn in stone,
where never man had yet lain.
54 And it was the day of the
Preparation, and the sabbath
*drew on. 55 And the women,
who had come with him out of
Gal'i-lee, followed after, and
beheld the tomb, and how his
body was laid. 56 And they
returned, and prepared spices
and ointments.

24 And on the sabbath they
rested according to the
commandment. 1 But on
the first day of the week, at
early dawn, they came unto the

---

f Some ancient authorities read *this thy
kingdom.* *g* Or, *earth* *h* Gr. *the sun failing.* *i* Or, *sanctuary* *k* Or, *And when*

*Jesus had cried with a loud voice, he said
l* Gr. *began to dawn.*

39–43. *One of the malefactors.*
Both thieves at first railed upon him
(Mt. 27.44). *Jesus, remember me
when thou comest in thy kingdom.* A
sublime act of faith by one who
hitherto had shown no faith in either
God or man, yet on the cross turned
in repentant prayer to one who was
apparently as helpless and wretched
as himself. *With me in Paradise.*

The answer of Jesus was ready and
plenteously merciful; he granted
more than was asked.

44–56. *A darkness came over the
whole land.* See notes on Mt. 27.45–
47, 52–54, 57, 60–62.

CHAPTER 24

1–12. *At early dawn, they came
unto the tomb.* Matthew and John

tomb, bringing the spices which they had prepared. 2 And they found the stone rolled away from the tomb. 3 And they entered in, and found not the body *a*of the Lord Je'sus. 4 And it came to pass, while they were perplexed thereabout, behold, two men stood by them in dazzling apparel: 5 and as they were affrighted and bowed down their faces to the earth, they said unto them, Why seek ye *b*the living among the dead? 6 *c*He is not here, but is risen: remember how he spake unto you when he was yet in Gali'ilee, 7 saying that the Son of man must be delivered up into the hands of sinful men, and be crucified, and the third day rise again. 8 And they remembered his words, 9 and returned *d*from the tomb, and told all these things to the eleven, and to all the rest. 10 Now they were Mary Mag-da-le'ne, and Jo-an'na, and Mary the *mother* of James: and the other women with them told these things unto the apostles. 11 And these words appeared in their sight as idle talk; and they disbelieved them. 12 *e*But Peter arose, and ran unto the tomb; and stooping and looking in, he

seeth the linen cloths by themselves; and he *f*departed to his home, wondering at that which was come to pass.

13 And behold, two of them were going that very day to a village named Em-ma'us, which was threescore furlongs from Je-ru'sa-lem. 14 And they communed with each other of all these things which had happened. 15 And it came to pass, while they communed and questioned together, that Je'sus himself drew near, and went with them. 16 But their eyes were holden that they should not know him. 17 And he said unto them, *g*What communications **are these that ye have one with another, as ye walk?** And they stood still, looking sad. 18 And one of them, named Cle'o-pas, answering said unto him, *h*Dost thou alone sojourn in Je-ru'sa-lem and not know the things which are come to pass there in these days? 19 And he said unto them, **What things?** And they said unto him, The things concerning Je'sus the Naz-a-rene', who was a prophet mighty in deed and word before God and all the poeple: 20 and how the chief priests and our rulers de-

---

a Some ancient authorities omit *of the Lord Jesus*. *b* Gr. *him that liveth*. *c* Some ancient authorities omit *He is not here, but is risen*. *d* Some ancient authorities omit *from the tomb*. *e* Some ancient

authorities omit ver. 12. *f* Or, *departed, wondering with himself* *g* Gr. *What words are these that ye exchange one with another.* *h* Or, *Dost thou sojourn alone in Jerusalem, and knowest thou not the things*

---

practically agree (Mt. 28.1; Jn. 20.1), while Mark is more explicit. According to his narrative the sun had begun to rise before they arrived at the tomb (ch. 16.2). See notes on Mt. 28.1, 2, 4, 6–8; Jn. 20.1–10. *Peter arose, and ran into the tomb.* See Jn. 20.3–10.

13. *Two of them.* They were not apostles. See ver. 33. *Emmaus.*

Probably a village of that name mentioned by the historian Josephus. It was seven miles west of Jerusalem.

16. *That they should not know him.* There were other occasions when Jesus was not recognized after his resurrection. See ver. 37; Mt. 28.18; Jn. 20.14; 21.4.

18. *Cleopas.* Apart from this event nothing is known of him.

livered him up to be condemned to death, and crucified him. 21 But we hoped that it was he who should redeem Is'ra-el. Yea and besides all this, it is now the third day since these things came to pass. 22 Moreover certain women of our company amazed us, having been early at the tomb; 23 and when they found not his body, they came, saying, that they had also seen a vision of angels, who said that he was alive. 24 And certain of them that were with us went to the tomb, and found it even so as the women had said: but him they saw not. 25 And he said unto them, O foolish men, and slow of heart to believe ¹in all that the prophets have spoken! 26 Behooved it not the Christ to suffer these things, and to enter into his glory? 27 And beginning from Mo'ses and from all the prophets, he interpreted to them in all the scriptures the things concerning himself. 28 And they drew nigh unto the village, whither they were going: and he made as though he would

i Or, *after*

go further. 29 And they constrained him, saying, Abide with us; for it is toward evening, and the day is now far spent. And he went in to abide with them. 30 And it came to pass, when he had sat down with them to meat, he took the ᵏbread and blessed; and breaking *it* he gave to them. 31 And their eyes were opened, and they knew him; and he vanished out of their sight. 32 And they said one to another, Was not our heart burning within us, while he spake to us in the way, while he opened to us the scriptures? 33 And they rose up that very hour, and returned to Je-ru'salem, and found the eleven gathered together, and them that were with them, 34 saying, The Lord is risen indeed, and hath appeared to Si'mon. 35 And they rehearsed the things *that happened* in the way, and how he was known of them in the breaking of the bread.

36 And as they spake these things, he himself stood in the midst of them, ¹and saith unto

k Or, *loaf*   l Some ancient authorities omit *and saith unto them, Peace be unto you.*

21. *Who should redeem Israel.* They had the notion of a Messiah who was expected to be an earthly ruler. *Now the third day.* They evidently remembered the prophecy of his resurrection and were waiting for the event.

26. *To suffer these things, and to enter into his glory.* Do ye not see that the things which have saddened you were my appointed lot by the will of the Father?

31. *Their eyes were opened, and they knew him.* Apparently both their failure to know Jesus while walking with him, and their sudden recognition of him in the breaking of the bread, were according to his

will. The appearance of his risen body was in some way unfamiliar to them until he chose to reveal himself. *Vanished out of their sight.* The risen body of Jesus was under the complete control of spirit. It was superior to the laws of ordinary matter. It could be made to appear suddenly as well as to vanish. See ver. 36 and Jn. 20.19.

36—43. *He himself stood in the midst of them.* This was while the apostles were at supper with the doors closed. They did not recognize him. *See my hands and my feet, that it is I myself.* The spiritual body in which Jesus here manifested himself suddenly to the apostles was

202

them, **Peace** *be* **unto you.** 37 But they were terrified and affrighted, and supposed that they beheld a spirit. 38 And he said unto them, **Why are ye troubled? and wherefore do questionings arise in your heart?** 39 **See my hands and my feet, that it is I myself: handle me, and see; for a spirit hath not flesh and bones, as ye behold me having.** 40 [m]**And when he** had said this, he showed them his hands and his feet. 41 And while they still disbelieved for joy, and wondered, he said unto them, **Have ye here anything to eat?** 42 And they gave him a piece of a broiled fish[n]. 43 And he took it, and ate before them.

44 And he said unto them, **These are my words which I spake unto you, while I was yet with you, that all things must needs be fulfilled, which are**

written in the law of Mo'ses, and the prophets, and the psalms, concerning me. 45 Then opened he their mind, that they might understand the scriptures; 46 and he said unto them, **Thus it is written, that the Christ should suffer, and rise again from the dead the third day;** 47 **and that repentance** [o]**and remission of sins should be preached in his name unto all the** [p]**nations, beginning from Je-ru'sa-lem.** 48 **Ye are witnesses of these things.** 49 **And behold, I send forth the promise of my Father upon you: but tarry ye in the city, until ye be clothed with power from on high.**

50 And he led them out until *they were* over against Beth'a-ny: and he lifted up his hands, and blessed them. 51 And it came to pass, while he blessed them, **he** parted from them, [q]**and was**

---

m Some ancient authorities omit ver. 40. *n* Many ancient authorities add *and a honeycomb.* *o* Some ancient authorities read *unto.* *p* Or, nations. *Beginning from Jerusalem, ye are witnesses* *q* Some ancient authorities omit *and was carried up into heaven.*

---

made to assume material conditions. His power over that body enabled him to present it to them as physically identical with the body in which he was before, during and after the crucifixion, and which was laid in the tomb. His object was to show them that he was the same Jesus who was crucified for them, 'that it is I myself.' They needed to be convinced through the medium of the senses.

41. *While they still disbelieved for joy.* An emotional failure of faith such as has always done much harm. There are great numbers of people who refuse to believe and act because they think the result would be too good to be true. This is as wrong and disastrous in its way as the contrary habit of excessive presumption. *Have ye anything to eat?* The question was intended to dispel any remaining doubt as to the com-

plete identity of the risen Jesus with the Master they had previously followed.

43. *And ate before them.* If he had not eaten, some would not have fully believed.

44–49. *Which I spake unto you, while I was yet with you.* These verses contain a brief explanation of the meaning of all that was said to the apostles during the forty days between his resurrection and ascension. *The law of Moses, and the prophets, and the psalms.* The Jewish division of the Old Testament. *Then opened he their mind.* That they might spiritually discern the truth about him in the Scriptures.

50–53. *Over against Bethany.* The traditional place of the ascension is the Mount of Olives. At least it was some place near Bethany. *Returned to Jerusalem with great joy.* The evidence of entire, triumphant

carried up into heaven. 52 And they 'worshipped him, and returned to Je-ru'sa-lem with great joy: 53 and were continually in the temple, blessing God.

---

r Some ancient authorities omit *worshipped*

him, and. See marginal note on ch. 4.7.

faith which merged the sadness of their earthly parting from him in the assurance of his spiritual presence evermore.

204

THE GOSPEL ACCORDING TO JOHN

INTRODUCTION BY PROFESSOR M. B. RIDDLE, D.D., LL.D.

The Writer.—The Fourth Gospel has, from the earliest notice of it, been attributed to the apostle John, the younger son of Zebedee and Salome. His mother was probably the sister of our Lord's mother (19.25). The historical evidence has been strengthened by recent discoveries. It is now quite certain that this Gospel was used by Justin Martyr; that it was one of the four combined in the Diatessaron of Tatian (about 170| A.D.). It was accepted by Irenæus, the pupil of Polycarp, himself the friend and pupil of John. The internal evidence is equally strong. Though the apostle does not name himself, he indicates that he is the writer. Hence to deny that he wrote it is to assert that this book, so spiritual in tone, is a forgery.

The New Testament history is silent respecting this apostle after the council at Jerusalem (50 A.D.), but he was undoubtedly in Ephesus during his later years. Banished thence to Patmos, presumably in the reign of Domitian, he returned to Ephesus, and there lived to an extreme old age, the last survivor of the Twelve. To this fact the last chapter of the Gospel refers, and the incidents there recorded seem to have been appended in view of the approaching death of the aged apostle. He is often styled "the Apostle of Love," but his writings, and the notices of him in the other Gospels, reveal a man of strong character. His "love" implied hatred of evil, and his writings denounce it.

Time and Place of Writing.—At Ephesus, as is generally held, not long before the death of the apostle, and probably at the request of Christians in that city. Ch. 21.24 ("and we know that his witness is true") suggests that others desired to attest the truth of the record as coming from the apostle. This late date, nearly a generation after the writing of the other Gospels, shows that the leading facts about Jesus Christ were already known to Christians. This Gospel is therefore, in a certain sense, supplementary; but there is no evidence that it was chiefly intended to supply omissions in the other narratives. The design is stated in the book itself, and the many events and discourses found only in this Gospel are in accordance with it.

Purpose and Plan of the Gospel.—The purpose is stated in ch. 20.31: "But these are written, that ye may believe that Jesus is the Christ, the Son of God; and that believing, ye may have life through his name." The facts are selected with this design—to present our Lord as an object of faith and the source of life. But the contents of the Gospel show that the selection has also been made to contrast the unbelief and the faith which met the Incarnate Word when He "dwelt among us." In the prologue the plan of the

Gospel is at least suggested (1.11-14). "The Word became flesh": of this the proof is given. "He came unto his own, and they that were his own received him not": thus the unbelief of the Jews is indicated. "But as many as received him, to them gave he the right to become children of God, even to them that believe on his name": here the blessed results of faith are set forth. Accordingly the Gospel emphasizes the three great truths: the person of Christ; the rejection of this incarnate Saviour; the new life granted to believers as children of God.

Summary.—1. Prologue (1.1-18): the pre-existent Word; witness of John the Baptist; the incarnate Word declaring the Father; rejected by "his own," and received by believers.

2. The opening manifestation of Jesus to His disciples and to the Jews (1.19 to 4): the testimony of John the Baptist (1.19-34); the manifestation to the first disciples (1.35-51); the first sign at Cana (2.1-12); the first cleansing of the Temple (2.13-17); the first public manifestation at the Passover (2.18-25); the interview with Nicodemus (3.1-21), the ministry in Judæa (3.22-36); the brief ministry in Samaria (4.1-42); the second sign (4.46-54).

3. The growing unbelief and opposition (5-12): the Sabbath miracle at Jerusalem, and the persecution which followed (5); the feeding of the five thousand, and the discourse at Capernaum, resulting in the withdrawal of most of the disciples (6); the conflict at Jerusalem at the Feast of Tabernacles (7, 8); the healing of the man born blind (9 to 10.21); the Feast of Dedication, and the withdrawal to Peræa (10.22-42); the raising of Lazarus at Bethany, and the withdrawal to Ephraim (11); the public entry to Jerusalem, and the unbelief of the Jews (12).

4. Jesus reveals Himself to the faith of His disciples (13-17): at the last supper (13); in the last discourse, promising the Comforter (14-16); in the "high-priestly" prayer (17).

5. The apparent victory of unbelief (18, 19): in Gethsemane; before the Jewish rulers; in the denial by Peter, and before Pilate (18); in the mockery, the death, and the burial (19).

6. The real victory of Jesus the Christ, the Son of God (20): His appearance to Mary Magdalene, to the disciples, and a week later to the eleven, when Thomas confessed Him (20.1-29); the purpose of the Gospel (20.30, 31).

7. Epilogue (21): the appearance by the Sea of Galilee to seven disciples; the promise to the beloved disciple (21.1-23); final attestation and comment (21.24, 25).

[While this Gospel in its design is less of a historical narrative than the Synoptic Gospels, it gives more notices of time than they do. A historical outline of our Lord's ministry can only be constructed by arranging the events in accordance with the feasts mentioned by John.]

ACCORDING TO JOHN

The Prologue

1 In the beginning was the Word, and the Word was with God, and the Word was God. 2 The same was in the beginning with God. 3 All things were made through him; and without him *a*was not anything made that hath been made. 4 In him was life; and

a Or, *was not anything made.   That which hath been made was life in him; and the life &c.*

CHAPTER 1

1. *In the beginning.* Not the beginning of time, but before time was. *Was the Word.* 'Was' here implies not the creation, but the eternal existence of the Word. 'Word' is a title of Jesus Christ which is peculiar to John's writings. The meaning of the Greek term (Logos) of which it is a translation is, reason expressed in speech; and as applied by the apostle to our Lord signifies that from all eternity he was the divine reason, and after his incarnation became its expression in human form. But in John's use of 'Word' there is more than this. It implies, in addition to the visible expression of the divine reason in Jesus Christ, the manifestation also of the divine will and purpose in him. The latter meaning may be traced to the Hebrew term Memra, or Word, which was frequently employed in the Aramaic translations of the Old Testament and denoted an intermediate agency through which Jehovah made known His will in the world. John considered these meanings in the light of his own experience in describing Jesus Christ as the Word, who 'became flesh and dwelt among us'. *Was with God.* In communion with the Father. *Was God.* Was as divine as God, and therefore to be worshipped as God.

3. *All things were made through him.* John is the only evangelist who declares that Jesus Christ is the creator of the universe. But see Col. 1.16; 1 Cor. 8.6; Heb. 1.2, 10.

The word 'through', while implying the agency of Jesus Christ in creating the world, does not mean that he was inferior to God. The same word is used in regard to the Father, 'through whom ye are called' (1 Cor. 1.9).

4. *In him was life.* Jesus Christ, the Word, was the source of life in all things created, and of the kinds and degrees of life which they manifest. The life of Christ among men has clarified and enriched all ideas of life. Many things are commonly though erroneously said to be dead; and those who speak of 'dead' matter often mistake absence of visible motion for absence of life. *The life was the light of men.* The life of the Word is not only the source of all forms of physical life, but is also the light of men. 'Light' here stands for the truth, and more especially spiritual truth, revealing and directing the conscience of a person, the highest of the various degrees of life thus far attained in the world. Its significance in this connection comes largely from its contrast to those kinds of life in which there is little or no light at all. A seed, a blade of grass, a rose, an oak—all have life but not light, which is given only with intelligence. The animal world, in part, has but little of this light; and its true life can increase only with increasing power of thought. The 'light of men' is the greater measure of ruling intelligence and spiritual life given by the Word to those of his creatures who are most like unto him. It may also be considered in

the life was the light of men. 5 And
the light shineth in the darkness;
and the darkness ᵇapprehended
it not. 6 There came a man, sent
from God, whose name was John.
7 The same came for witness,
that he might bear witness of
the light, that all might believe
through him. 8 He was not the
light, but *came* that he might
bear witness of the light. 9
ᶜThere was the true light, *even
the light* which lighteth ᵈevery
man, coming into the world.
10 He was in the world, and the
world was made through him,
and the world knew him not.
11 He came unto ᵉhis own, and
they that were his own received
him not. 12 But as many as received him, to them gave he the
right to become children of God,
even to them that believe on his
name: 13 who were ᶠborn, not
of ᵍblood, nor of the will of the
flesh, nor of the will of man, but
of God. 14 And the Word became flesh, and ʰdwelt among us
(and we beheld his glory, glory
as of ⁱthe only begotten from
the Father), full of grace and
truth. 15 John beareth witness

b Or, *overcame* See ch. 12.35 (Gr.).
c Or, *the true light, which lighteth every man,
was coming* *d* Or, *every man as he cometh*
e Gr. *his own things.* *f* Or, *begotten*
g Gr. *bloods.* *h* Gr. *tabernacled.* *i* Or, *an
only begotten from a father* Comp. Heb.
11.17.

a special sense the historical manifestation of Christ's example.

5. *The darkness apprehended it
not.* The moral darkness of those
who rejected or did not receive the
spiritual light given them.

6. *A man, sent from God, whose
name was John.* 'Sent from God'
indicates the person and function
of a prophet. John the Baptist is
here meant. Although often mentioned in this narrative, the Baptist
is never so named but is simply called
John.

7. *Came for witness.* This reference to the Baptist was introduced
to prevent any misapprehension as
to his true mission, that of a witness.
It was a divinely authorized mission
so far as it went, but was accomplished by one who was to prepare
the way for a greater than he.

9. *Which lighteth every man, coming into the world.* This refers to
the spiritual light given by the Word
to each and every human being at
birth. It is the light of conscience,
the recognition of a difference between right and wrong. All relig-
ions, therefore, have some truth.

10. *He was in the world.* Before
he was incarnated.

11. *Unto his own.* His own
nation, his home and land of Palestine. *His own received him not.*
His own people, the Jews.

12. *The right to become children of
God.* 'Right' here denotes a higher
degree of favor with God than is
enjoyed by one who, even though
living according to his best natural
light, has not received Christ. Any
normal person has at birth the capacity to receive spiritual truth,
and thus to become a child of God.
This is true because of the light
'which lighteth every man coming
into the world'; but when Christ is
consciously received there is conferred in a special sense the right
to become a true child of God.
That believe on his name. As the
Son of God and Saviour of mankind.

13. *Nor of the will of man, but of
God.* The right to become a child
of God is a free gift from Him, not
dependent upon family relationship
or racial origin.

14. *The Word became flesh.* Took
human form and life, tempted and
suffering therein, though without
yielding to sin. *We beheld.* John's
claim to be an eye-witness. *His
glory.* His ministry of love and
good works, his transfiguration, his
ascension, the unique majesty of
his character and example. *Full
of grace.* Kindliness, love. *Truth.*
Light.

15. *He that cometh after me.* Jesus
Christ began his ministry later than
John the Baptist. *Is become before*

of him, and crieth, saying, *k*This was he of whom I said, He that cometh after me is become before me: for he was *l*before me. 16 For of his fulness we all received, and *m*grace for grace. 17 For the law was given through Mo'ses; grace and truth came through Je'sus Christ. 18 No man hath seen God at any time; *n*the only begotten Son, who is in the bosom of the Father, he hath declared *him.*

19 And this is the witness of John, when the Jews sent unto him from Je-ru'sa-lem priests and Le'vites to ask him, Who art thou? 20 And he confessed, and denied not; and he confessed, I am not the Christ. 21 And they asked him, What then? Art thou E-li'jah? And he saith, I am not. Art thou the prophet? And he answered, No. 22 They said therefore unto him, Who art thou? that we may give an answer to them that sent us. What sayest thou of thyself? 23 He said, I am the voice of one crying in the wilderness, Make straight the way of the Lord, as *o*said I-sa'iah the prophet. 24 *p*And they had been sent from the Phar'i-sees. 25 And they asked him, and said unto him, Why then baptizest thou, if thou art not the Christ, neither E-li'jah, neither the prophet?

k Some ancient authorities read (*this was he that said*). *l* Gr. *first in regard of me. m* Or. *grace upon grace n* Many very ancient authorities read *God only begotten. o* Is. xl. 3. *p* Or, *And certain had been sent from among the Phari*sees.

me. But at once took rank immeasurably above him. *For he was before me.* Existed from all eternity. The Baptist's words were quoted to prove, probably to some whose faith in his mission was unsound or exaggerated, the rightful precedence and authority of Christ.

16. *Of his fulness.* The fulness of his attributes as perfect God and perfect man. 'For in him dwelleth all the fulness of the Godhead bodily' (Col. 2.9). *We all received, and grace for grace.* These are the evangelist's words. They express the inexhaustible store of the divine power, justice and mercy, on which all the rightfully disposed and obedient are privileged to draw. One grace or favor is granted after another. The gifts of God increase in number and preciousness according to the faith and persistence of the seeker. All true Christian experience confirms this.

17. *The law was given through Moses.* To prevent sin by penalty. *Grace and truth came through Jesus Christ.* They were inherent in Jesus Christ, who came to impart them to believers so that by receiving them the sinful nature might be changed. The law was force; the grace and truth of Jesus Christ are love and light.

18. *No man hath seen God at any time.* By this is meant that the Father reveals Himself to men only through Jesus Christ. This verse closes the preface of John's narrative, in which he affirms the central truths more elaborately set forth hereafter.

19–28. *This is the witness of John.* These verses contain the public testimony of John the Baptist to the Jewish religious and ecclesiastical leaders regarding the Divine Messiahship of Jesus. *Priests and Levites.* The full hierarchy, the priests being superior in authority in the religious services, the Levites assisting them. Together they were a delegated body of official inquiry to find out who John the Baptist was and what his claims were. *Why then baptizest thou?* John, in the opinion of the investigating deputation, was acting irregularly, that is, baptizing those who were not proselytes. He apparently had no credentials. *Bethany beyond the Jordan.* Probably a ford on the river about fourteen miles south of the Sea of Galilee, and now called 'Abarah' (passing over).

26 John answered them, saying, I baptize *q*in water: in the midst of you standeth one whom ye know not, 27 *even* he that cometh after me, the latchet of whose shoe I am not worthy to unloose. 28 These things were done in 'Beth'a-ny beyond the Jordan, where John was baptizing.

29 On the morrow he seeth Je'sus coming unto him, and saith, Behold, the Lamb of God, that *s*taketh away the sin of the world! 30 This is he of whom I said, After me cometh a man who is become before me: for he was *t*before me. 31 And I knew him not; but that he should be made manifest to Is'ra-el, for this cause came I baptizing *q*in water. 32 And John bare witness, saying, I have

beheld the Spirit descending as a dove out of heaven; *and* it abode upon him. 33 And I knew him not: but he that sent me to baptize *q*in water, he said unto me, Upon whomsoever thou shalt see the Spirit descending, and abiding upon him, the same is he that baptizeth *q*in the Holy Spirit. 34 And I have seen, and have borne witness that this is the Son of God.

35 Again on the morrow John was standing, and two of his disciples; 36 and he looked upon Je'sus as he walked, and saith, Behold, the Lamb of God! 37 And the two disciples heard him speak, and they followed Je'sus. 38 And Je'sus turned, and beheld them following, and saith unto them, What seek ye?

q Or, *with*   *r* Many ancient authorities read *Bethabarah,* some *Betharabah.* Comp.

Josh. 15.6, 61; 18.22.   *s* Or, *beareth the sin*   *t* Gr. *first in regard of me.*

29–34. *The Lamb of God.* An expression most probably suggested by the lamb mentioned in Isa. 53.7. These verses record the Baptist's testimony to the people concerning the Divine Messiahship of Jesus. It was no less emphatic than his testimony to the hierarchy. Its decisive feature was a promised deliverance from sin in place of the expected national and political deliverance from the Romans. Its contradiction of popular beliefs was startling and humiliating. The 'Lamb of God, that taketh away the sin of the world' was adoringly announced to the Jews as their Messiah by a lonely, ascetic prophet in the desert, instead of the triumphant 'Lion of the tribe of Judah' who was looked for to head an army, sweep the foreigner out of Palestine and revive the ancient glories of David and Solomon. Yet the Baptist, in thus placing holiness and humility above earthly greatness as the Jewish ideal to be realized, was only true to his appointed function of Messianic forerunner. When Jesus at the head of his apos-

tles and disciples was making his last journey to Jerusalem, his prediction of his sufferings, death and resurrection was in exact agreement with the character of Messiahship here declared by John. *I knew him not.* That is, did not at first view recognize him definitely as Messiah. Not until the sign of the Spirit's descent in the form of a dove was John fully convinced.

35–37. *John was standing, and two of his disciples.* Having testified to the priests and Levites, and then to the people, the Baptist further testified in the same manner to two of his own disciples, Andrew and John, the son of Zebedee, thus resigning in favor of Jesus all claim to be their finally authoritative teacher. The singleness of his loyal love and self-abnegation is an example to all time. *They followed Jesus.* They were the first known disciples of the Master, and both afterward became apostles. This first following of Jesus has been called the beginning of the Christian Church.

38. *What seek ye?* This implies that they had not yet actually been

And they said unto him, Rab′bi (which is to say, being interpreted, Teacher), where abidest thou? 39 He saith unto them, **Come, and ye shall see.** They came therefore and saw where he abode; and they abode with him that day: it was about the tenth hour. 40 One of the two that heard John *speak*, and followed him, was Andrew, Si′mon Peter's brother. 41 He findeth first his own brother Si′mon, and saith unto him, We have found the Mes-si′ah (which is, being interpreted, ᵘChrist). 42 He brought him unto Je′sus. Je′sus looked upon him, and said, **Thou art Si′mon the son of** ᵛ**John: thou shalt be called Ce′phas** (which is by interpretation, ˣPeter).

43 On the morrow he was minded to go forth into Gal′i-lee, and he findeth Philip: and Je′sus saith unto him, **Follow me.** 44 Now Philip was from Beth-sa′i-da, of the city of Andrew and Peter. 45 Philip findeth Na-than′a-el, and saith unto him, We have found him, of whom Mo′ses in the law, and the prophets, wrote, Je′sus of Naz′a-reth, the son of Joseph. 46 And Na-than′a-el said unto him, Can any good thing come out of Naz′a-reth? Philip saith unto him, Come and see. 47 Je′sus saw Na-than′a-el coming to him, and saith of him, **Behold, an Is′ra-el-ite indeed, in whom is no guile!** 48 Na-than′a-el saith unto him, Whence knowest thou me? Je′sus answered and

---

ᵘ That is, *Anointed.* Comp. Ps. 2.2.
ᵛ Gr. *Joanes:* called in Mt. 16.17, *Jonah.*

ˣ That is, *Rock* or *Stone.*

---

accepted as disciples, but were disposed to become such and were inquiring about the truth.

39. *It was about the tenth hour.* About four o'clock in the afternoon.

40–51. *One of the two.* The unnamed one was John the son of Zebedee. In these verses the testimony of the Baptist's disciples concerning the Messiahship of Jesus is given. In them also is narrated the call of Andrew, John, Peter, Philip and Nathanael (Bartholomew) to be disciples. All afterward became apostles. This call was not the same as that referred to in the other evangelists (Mt. 4.18–22; Mk. 1.16–20; Lk. 5.7–11). It was informal and preparatory, the beginning of their discipleship, which gradually led them finally to decide to follow Jesus. It explains the readiness with which they obeyed his later summons, as illustrated by the words 'straightway' and 'left all' (Mt. 4.20, 22; Mk. 1.18; Lk. 5.11). *Jesus looked upon him.* A look that infallibly divined Peter's character. *Bethsaida.* Bethsaida (house of fish) on the western shore of the Sea of Galilee. Bethsaida Julias, named after Julia, daughter of the Roman Emperor Augustus, was near the northern extremity of the Sea. *Nathanael.* Commonly identified with Bartholomew, since Matthew, Mark and Luke never mention Nathanael, while John does not mention Bartholomew. The latter name means 'son of Tolmai'. *An Israelite indeed, in whom is no guile.* Alluding to a characteristic defect of the Israelites, as typified in the deceitfulness of Jacob. *The Son of God.* In Nathanael's confession these words are not to be taken in the highest sense, but according to the Jewish custom in the Old Testament, in which the Messiah is thus entitled, though 'Son of David' is more frequently used. *King of Israel.* The title proves that Nathanael shared the popular hope of a political Messiah. *Angels of God ascending and descending.* Jesus probably alluded to the vision of Jacob's ladder, on which angels were ascending and descending between earth and heaven, thus typifying the union

said unto him, **Before Philip called thee, when thou wast under the fig tree, I saw thee.** 49 Na-than′a-el answered him, **Rab′bi, thou art the Son of God; thou art King of Is′ra-el.** 50 Je′sus answered and said unto him, **Because I said unto thee, I saw thee underneath the fig tree, believest thou? thou shalt see greater things than these.** 51 And he saith unto him, **Verily, verily, I say unto you, Ye shall see the heaven opened, and the angels of God ascending and descending upon the Son of man.**

2 And the third day there was a marriage in Ca′na of Gal′i-lee; and the mother of Je′sus was there: 2 and Je′sus also was bidden, and his disciples, to the marriage. 3 And when the wine failed, the mother of Je′sus saith unto him, **They have no wine.** 4 And Je′sus saith unto her, **Woman, what have I to do with thee? mine**

hour is not yet come. 5 His mother saith unto the servants, **Whatsoever he saith unto you, do it.** 6 Now there were six waterpots of stone set there after the Jews' manner of purifying, containing two or three firkins apiece. 7 Je′sus saith unto them, **Fill the waterpots with water.** And they filled them up to the brim. 8 And he saith unto them, **Draw out now, and bear unto the** *a*ruler **of the feast.** And they bare it. 9 And when the ruler of the feast tasted the water *b*now become wine, and knew not whence it was (but the servants that had drawn the water knew), the ruler of the feast calleth the bridegroom, 10 and saith unto him, Every man setteth on first the good wine; and when *men* have drunk freely, *then* that which is worse: thou has kept the good wine until now. 11 This beginning of his signs did Je′sus in Ca′na of Gal′i-lee,

---

a Or, *steward*   *b* Or, *that it had become*

between heaven and earth to be accomplished by his power and life. *Son of man.* See note on Mt. 8.20.

CHAPTER 2

1. *The third day.* The third day from 'the morrow' when Philip was called (ver. 43).

2. *Cana of Galilee.* Now commonly identified with Kana-el-Jehil, a small village nine miles northwest of Nazareth.

4. *Woman, what have I to do with thee.* A mild rebuke to his mother for interfering with him in the course of his ministry, on which he had now entered. *Mine hour is not yet come.* The hour for manifesting his power through a miracle.

5. *Do it.* The answer of the mother of Jesus shows that she understood his rebuke and accepted it.

6. *Purifying.* Washing the hands

before dinner. See notes on Mk. 7.2, 3 ; Mt. 15.2, 3, 11. *Two or three firkins apiece.* A firkin was about nine gallons. As the stone waterpots held from eighteen to twenty-seven gallons each, the six would contain together from one hundred and six to one hundred and sixty-two gallons.

11. *This beginning of his signs did Jesus.* In John's narrative the miracles of Jesus are spoken of as signs. This agrees with the spiritual and allegorical character of his writing, which aims to express the deeper meanings of the words and acts of our Lord. 'Sign' stands not only for the miracle, but for its inner significance. The changing of the water into wine may be considered as typifying the power of Christ over matter, the introduction of a new authority greater than the Mosaic law, the inferiority of the

212

and manifested his glory; and his disciples believed on him.

12 After this he went down to Ca-per'na-um, he, and his mother, and *his* brethren, and his disciples; and there they abode not many days.

13 And the passover of the Jews was at hand, and Je'sus went up to Je-ru'sa-lem. 14 And he found in the temple those that sold oxen and sheep and doves, and the changers of money sitting: 15 and he made a scourge of cords, and cast all out of the temple, both the sheep and the oxen; and he poured out the changers' money, and overthrew their tables; 16 and to them that sold the doves he said, **Take these things hence; make not my Father's house a house of merchandise.** 17 His disciples remembered that it was written, *c*Zeal for thy house shall eat me up. 18 The Jews therefore answered and said unto him, What

sign showest thou unto us, seeing that thou doest these things? 19 Je'sus answered and said unto them, **Destroy this *d*temple, and in three days I will raise it up.** 20 The Jews therefore said, Forty and six years was this *d*temple in building, and wilt thou raise it up in three days? 21 But he spake of the *d*temple of his body. 22 When therefore he was raised from the dead, his disciples remembered that he spake this; and they believed the scripture, and the word which Je'sus had said.

23 Now when he was in Je-ru'-sa-lem at the passover, during the feast, many believed on his name, beholding his signs which he did. 24 But Je'sus did not trust himself unto them, for that he knew all men, 25 and because he needed not that any one should bear witness concerning *e*man; for he himself knew what was in man.

---

c Ps. lxix. 9. *d* Or, *sanctuary*   *e* Or, *a man; for . . . the man.*

---

water of the old Jewish dispensation compared with the new wine of the Gospel.

12. *Capernaum.* On the northern shore of the Sea of Galilee. Its site was near the modern Tell-Hûm, where the remains of a synagogue have been found.

13. *The passover.* An annual Jewish feast to commemorate the deliverance from Egypt. See note on Mt. 26.17; Lk. 22.1. This Passover was the first in Christ's ministry.

14–17. *He found in the temple those that sold oxen,* etc. This was the first cleansing of the Temple. See notes on Mt. 21.12.

18. *What sign showest thou unto us,* etc. They asked for some visible proof of this authority, some evidence apart from his own words, preferably some omen or appearance in the sky.

20. *Forty and six years was this temple in building.* This was the Temple begun by Herod the Great in 20 B. C. and finished by Herod Agrippa in 64 A. D. At the time of this incident the building operations had apparently been stopped, to be resumed before long. Like its two predecessors Solomon's Temple and Zerubbabel's Temple, it was situated on Mount Moriah. On its site is the Mosque of Omar.

21. *He spake of the temple of his body.* The reply of Jesus was a prediction of his own death and resurrection, which the Jews at that time could not have understood, a sign in entire contrast to the one they sought. The answer given in ver. 19 was afterward quoted against our Lord when he was brought before Caiaphas the high priest (Mt. 26.61).

3 Now there was a man of the Phar'i-sees, named Nic-o-de'mus, a ruler of the Jews: 2 the same came unto him by night, and said to him, Rab'bi, we know that thou art a teacher come from God; for no one can do these signs that thou doest, except God be with him. 3 Je'-sus answered and said unto him, Verily, verily, I say unto thee, Except one be born *a*anew, he cannot see the kingdom of God. 4 Nic-o-de'mus saith unto him, How can a man be born when is is old? can he enter a second time into his mother's womb, and be born? 5 Je'sus answered, Verily, verily, I say unto thee, Except one be born of water and the Spirit, he cannot enter into the kingdom of God. 6 That which is born of the flesh is flesh; and that which is born of the Spirit is spirit. 7 Marvel not that I said unto thee, Ye must be born *a*anew. 8 *b*The wind bloweth where it will, and thou hearest the voice thereof, but knowest not whence it cometh, and whither it goeth: so is every one that is born of the Spirit. 9 Nic-o-de'mus answered and said unto him, How can these things be? 10 Je'sus answered and said unto him, Art thou the teacher of Is'ra-el, and understandest not these things? 11 Verily, verily, I say unto thee, We speak that which we know, and bear witness of that which we have. seen; and ye receive not our witness. 12 If I told you earthly things and ye believe not, how shall ye believe if I tell you heavenly things? 13 And no one hath ascended into heaven, but he that descended out of heaven, *even* the Son of man, *c*who is in heaven. 14 And

a Or, *from above* See ver. 31; ch. 19. 11; Jas. 1.17; 3.15, 17. *b* Or, *The Spirit* *breatheth* *c* Many ancient authorities omit *who is in heaven.*

CHAPTER 3

1. *A ruler of the Jews.* A member of the Sanhedrin.

2. *Came unto him by night.* Most probably because night would afford a better opportunity for conversation with Jesus.

4. *Nicodemus saith unto him.* The questions which follow show that Nicodemus was embarrassed by what was to him, as well as to most other leaders of Jewish opinion a new problem, that of being born of the Spirit.

5. *Except one be born of water and the Spirit.* Jesus here insists upon the spiritual nature of the new birth, of which baptism is the outward sign. The efficacy of the rite is dependent upon and accompanied by a change of heart. *He cannot enter the kingdom of God.* Cannot qualify to exercise its powers or enjoy its privileges. Sincere repentance, humble trust and willingness to love all, ene-mies as well as friends, are requirements for entrance into the kingdom of God.

7. *Marvel not.* As if Nicodemus, a member of the Sanhedrin and a religious leader of his people, should wonder at the elementary truth that a spiritual birth is necessary for a spiritual life and growth.

11. *We.* Some of the disciples may have been present.

12. *Earthly things.* The visible, understandable facts of the religious life which has its source from above. *Heavenly things.* The deeper mysteries which are beyond human comprehension.

13. *No one hath ascended into heaven but he,* etc. The meaning is that only Jesus Christ, who was in heaven with the Father before his incarnation, immediately comprehends the heavenly things mentioned in ver. 12.

14. *The serpent in the wilderness.* A lesson in the rudiments of faith

214

as Mo'ses lifted up the serpent in the wilderness, even so must the Son of man be lifted up; 15 that whosoever ᵈbelieveth may in him have eternal life.

16 For God so loved the world, that he gave his only begotten Son, that whosoever believeth on him should not perish, but have eternal life. 17 For God sent not the Son into the world to judge the world; but that the world should be saved through him. 18 He that believeth on him is not judged: he that believeth not hath been judged already, because he hath not believed on the name of the only begotten Son of God. 19 And this is the judgment, that the light is come into the world, and men loved the darkness rather than the light; for their

works were evil. 20 For every one that ᶜdoeth evil hateth the light, and cometh not to the light, lest his works should be ᶠreproved. 21 But he that doeth the truth cometh to the light, that his works may be made manifest, ᵍthat they have been wrought in God.

22 After these things came Je'sus and his disciples into the land of Ju-dæ'a; and there he tarried with them, and baptized. 23 And John also was baptizing in Æ'non near to Sa'lim, because there ʰwas much water there: and they came, and were baptized. 24 For John was not yet cast into prison. 25 There arose therefore a questioning on the part of John's disciples with a Jew about purifying. 26 And they came unto John, and said

---

d Or, believeth in him may have

e Or, practiseth f Or, convicted g Or, because h Gr. were many waters.

---

was given to the children of Israel by commanding those who were bitten by the fiery serpents to look upon the brazen model of a serpent held up before them. They were cured by obedience. See Num. 21.6–9. *Even so must the Son of man be lifted up.* So that mankind by looking to him in faith may be healed of sin and receive eternal life.

16. *God so loved the world.* The Gentiles equally with the Jews. *Whosoever believeth.* The free offer of salvation by faith.

17. *That the world should be saved through him.* Again salvation is put before the penalty of judgment. The latter was much emphasized by the narrow Jewish leaders, who believed that severe judgments would be visited upon the Gentiles.

21. *Doeth the truth.* Much more vital than merely believing it in the sense of intellectual assent. To do the truth as Jesus announced it is the perfection of Christian life.

22. *Into the land of Judæa.*

Went from Jerusalem to preach and baptize in the rural parts of the province. Jesus personally did not baptize (ch. 4.2).

23. *Ænon* (full of springs). The location is uncertain. Some scholars think it is a valley extending from Mount Ebal to the Jordan.

24. *John was not yet cast into prison.* Which proves that the ministry of Jesus was for some time in progress along with that of John. It is a mistake to suppose that Jesus did not begin his ministry until after the imprisonment of the Baptist. The latter was evidently waiting for the declared Messiah to assume a more prominent public position, and while waiting continued his preaching and baptism of repentance, though it was then no less than before a work of preparation for Christ.

25. *About purifying.* But judging from the following five verses, a question arose as to whether the baptism of Jesus was superior to that of John.

215

to him, Rab′bi, he that was with thee beyond the Jordan, to whom thou hast borne witness, behold, the same baptizeth, and all men come to him. 27 John answered and said, A man can receive nothing, except it have been given him from heaven. 28 Ye yourselves bear me witness, that I said, I am not the Christ, but, that I am sent before him. 29 He that hath the bride is the bridegroom: but the friend of the bridegroom, that standeth and heareth him, rejoiceth greatly because of the bridegroom's voice: this my joy therefore is made full. 30 He must increase, but I must decrease.

31 He that cometh from above is above all: he that is of the earth is of the earth, and of the earth he speaketh: ′he that cometh from heaven is above all.

i Some ancient authorities read *he that cometh from heaven beareth witness of what*

27–30. *A man can receive nothing,* etc. An implied admission by the Baptist that no rivalry or other obstacle of any kind could interfere with the heaven-bestowed power and the heaven-sent mission of the Christ. *Bear me witness, that I said.* John repeats his testimony already publicly given. This time he wishes to make it clear beyond all possibility of doubt. *The friend of the bridegroom, that standeth and heareth him, rejoiceth,* etc. A beautiful illustration, drawn from the heart of Jewish social life, of the loyal care and devotion of one friend, who is glad to acknowledge himself the lesser, to another who is indisputably the greater. It befitted the occasion of a marriage that the bridegroom's friend should find his own joy in serving the bridegroom. Among the Jews he was much more important than the 'best man' is with us. He had entire charge of the ceremony, as well as the marriage agreement

32 What he hath seen and heard, of that he beareth witness; and no man receiveth his witness. 33 He that hath received his witness hath set his seal to *this,* that God is true. 34 For he whom God hath sent speaketh the words of God: for he giveth not the Spirit by measure. 35 The Father loveth the Son, and hath given all things into his hand. 36 He that believeth on the Son hath eternal life; but he that ᵏobeyeth not the Son shall not see life, but the wrath of God abideth on him.

4 When therefore the Lord knew that the Phar-i′sees had heard that Je′sus was making and baptizing more disciples than John 2 (although Je′sus himself baptized not, but his disciples), 3 he left Ju-dæ′a, and departed again into Gal′i-lee. 4 And

he hath seen and heard.   k Or, *believeth not*

beforehand. In this illustration John, the bridegroom's friend, has by his preaching and testimony prepared for the marriage of the bridegroom, Christ, with his bride, the Jewish people, and finds his usefulness solely in that work.

31–36. *He that cometh from above.* Christ, whose teaching must therefore prevail. John bears witness that, as he is of the earth and Christ is from above, there can be no comparison between them. *No man receiveth his witness.* That is, few or none in comparison with the vast numbers who ought to have received it. *Hath eternal life.* A present possession, not one to be bestowed in an indefinite future. The believer in Christ must strive to keep what he has. In these six verses John the Baptist bears his final recorded testimony to the majesty and power of Jesus, the Messiah.

CHAPTER 4

4. *Samaria.* A province of Pal-

216

he must needs pass through Sa-ma'ri-a. 5 So he cometh to a city of Sa-ma'ri-a, called Sy'char, near to the parcel of ground that Jacob gave to his son Joseph: 6 and Jacob's *a*well was there. Je'sus therefore, being wearied with his journey, sat *b*thus by the *a*well. It was about the sixth hour. 7 There cometh a woman of Sa-ma'ri-a to draw water: Je'sus saith unto her, Give me to drink. 8 For his disciples were gone away into the city to buy food. 9 The Sa-mar'i-tan woman therefore saith unto him, How is it that thou, being a Jew, askest drink of me, who am a Sa-mar'i-tan woman? *c*(For Jews have no dealings with Sa-mar'i-tans.) 10 Je'sus answered and said unto her, If thou knewest the gift of God, and who it is that saith to thee, Give me to drink; thou wouldest have asked of him, and he would have given thee living water. 11 The woman saith unto him, *d*Sir, thou hast nothing to draw with, and the well is deep; whence then hast thou that living water? 12 Art thou greater than our father Jacob, who gave us the well, and drank thereof himself, and his sons, and his cattle? 13 Je'sus answered and said unto her, Every one that drinketh of this water shall thirst again: 14 but whosoever drinketh of the water that I shall give him shall never thirst; but the water that I shall give him shall become in him a well of water springing up unto eternal life. 15 The woman saith unto him, *d*Sir, give me this water,

---

a Gr. *spring*: and so in ver. 14; but not in ver. 11, 12. *b* Or. *as he was* Comp. ch. 13.25. *c* Some ancient authorities omit

For Jews have no dealings with Samaritans.
d Or, *Lord*

---

estine between Galilee on the north and Judæa on the south. Its greatest length is about forty miles and its greatest width about forty-five miles. Its western boundary is the Mediterranean Sea and its eastern the River Jordan. The Samaritans were a mixed race, but with a considerable Jewish element. In the time of our Lord they worshipped mainly according to the Jewish faith, but rejected the Old Testament with the exception of the first five books or Pentateuch. They believed that the only place of the Temple was on Mount Gerizim. This was a prominent cause of their dislike of the Jews, who despised them.

5. *A city of Samaria, called Sychar.* Now identified by some scholars with Askar, near Shechem.

6. *Jacob's well was there.* It is there still. *Being wearied.* His human nature, though without sin, was touched with our infirmities. *The sixth hour.* About noon.

9. *No dealings.* That is, no important or intimate communications. This was particularly true of the Jews of Judæa. Our Lord's disciples, being Galileans, were less prejudiced. Hence they went to a Samaritan town to buy food. Jesus himself had spoken in a friendly manner to the woman, before he began to reprove her for her manner of life. His ministry in Samaria was as full of love and compassionate warning as it was in any other part of Palestine.

11. *Whence then hast thou that living water?* The woman had taken his words literally, thinking he meant spring water as purer than the water in the well.

14. *A well of water springing up unto everlasting life.* A fountain of spiritual power, satisfying every righteous aspiration and hunger of the soul.

15. *The woman saith unto him.* It is difficult to say whether sincerity or mockery prompted her reply.

that I thirst not, neither come all the way hither to draw. 16 Je′sus saith unto her, **Go, call thy husband, and come hither.** 17 The woman answered and said unto him, I have no husband. Je′sus saith unto her, **Thou saidst well, I have no husband: 18 for thou hast had five husbands; and he whom thou now hast is not thy husband: this hast thou said truly.** 19 The woman saith unto him, ᵈSir, I perceive that thou art a prophet. 20 Our fathers worshipped in this mountain; and ye say, that in Je-ru′sa-lem is the place where men ought to worship. 21 Je′sus saith unto her, **Woman, believe me, the hour cometh, when neither in this mountain, nor in Je-ru′sa-lem, shall ye worship the Father. 22 Ye worship that which ye know not: we worship that which we know; for salvation is from the Jews. 23 But the hour cometh, and now is, when the true worshippers shall worship the Father in spirit and truth: ᵉfor such doth the Father seek to be his worshippers. 24 ᶠGod is a Spirit: and they that worship him must worship in spirit and truth.** . 25 The woman saith unto him, I know that Mes-si′ah cometh (he that is called Christ): when he is come, he will declare unto us all things. 26 Je′sus saith unto her, **I that speak unto thee am he.**

---

d Or, Lord e Or, for such the Father also seeketh f Or, God is spirit

---

16. *Go, call thy husband.* This command of Jesus suddenly revealed the woman's frailty and compelled her alarmed attention. He wished to convince her of sin and show her the way to righteousness. Her trifling answers were no longer possible.

17. *I have no husband.* A true answer, literally taken, though given with an intention to deceive.

18. *Whom thou now hast is not thy husband.* Jesus reveals her past life, but there is no word of severe reproof. He was always gentle and compassionate with sinners of her class. See ch. 8.3–11; Lk. 7.37–50.

19. *Thou art a prophet.* The woman felt that concealment was vain. In addressing Jesus as a prophet she also saw a chance to avoid further humiliation by suggesting a different subject.

20. *Worshipped in this mountain.* The Samaritans believed that Mount Gerizim was the proper place for the Temple. This was a standing dispute between them and the Jews. Doubtless the woman thought that Jesus would have something important to say about it.

21. *Woman, believe me.* Seeing that she was ashamed, Jesus permitted her to forget her fault for the moment and proceeded to instruct her. *The hour cometh, and now is,* etc. A blessed and glorious prophecy, in whose fulfilment all the strife and pettiness proceeding from unessential and limiting forms of worship shall pass away for ever. Christ shows the woman that in that time there shall be no exclusive place of worship, though for her and in her time Jerusalem is better than Mount Gerizim. 'Now is' refers to the few who already worshipped the Father in spirit and in truth, valuing symbols for their educational uses, and seeing through incense and the smoke of sacrifice to the heart of the holy mystery of religion.

22. *Salvation is from the Jews.* Through the promises of God to Abraham (Gen. 12.3; 18.18; 22.18) and Isaac (Gen. 26.4) and David (2 Sam. 7.11–13, 16; Ps. 89.3, 4; 132.11). Moreover, Christ himself declared that 'repentance and remission of sins should be preached in his name unto all the nations, beginning from Jerusalem' (Lk. 24.47).

26. *I that speak unto thee am he.* Christ's willingness in making himself known as Messiah to the woman was in marked contrast to his refusal

218

27 And upon this came his disciples; and they marvelled that he was speaking with a woman; yet no man said, What seekest thou? or, Why speakest thou with her? 28 So the woman left her waterpot, and went away into the city, and saith to the people, 29 Come, see a man, who told me all things that *ever* I did: can this be the Christ? 30 They went out of the city, and were coming to him. 31 In the mean while the disciples prayed him, saying, Rab'bi, eat. 32 But he said unto them, I have meat to eat that ye know not. 33 The disciples therefore said one to another, Hath any man brought him *aught* to eat? 34 Je'sus saith unto them, My meat is to do the will of him that sent me, and to accomplish his work. 35 Say not ye, There are yet four months, and *then* cometh the harvest? behold, I say unto you, Lift up your eyes, and look on the fields, that they are *g*white already unto harvest.

36 He that reapeth receiveth wages, and gathereth fruit unto life eternal; that he that soweth and he that reapeth may rejoice together. 37 For herein is the saying true, One soweth, and another reapeth. 38 I sent you to reap that whereon ye have not labored: others have labored, and ye are entered into their labor.

39 And from that city many of the Sa-mar'i-tans believed on him because of the word of the woman, who testified, He told me all things that *ever* I did. 40 So when the Sa-mar'i-tans came unto him, they besought him to abide with them: and he abode there two days. 41 And many more believed because of his word; 42 and they said to the woman, Now we believe, not because of thy speaking: for we have heard for ourselves, and know that this is indeed the Saviour of the world.

43 And after the two days he went forth from thence into

---

g Or, *white unto harvest. Already he that reapeth &c.*

to permit a similar declaration among the Jews. But the Samaritans looked for a religious deliverer and had no political hopes. Even if they had known that he who thus spoke to the woman was the Messiah, they would not have interrupted his spiritual mission to make him king.

27. *Speaking with a woman.* The disciples marvelled because it was not customary for a Jewish rabbi to speak to a woman publicly.

35. *Say not ye, There are yet four months,* etc. This reference to the harvest, which is not figurative, indicates that the time was about the middle of December, as harvest did not begin until about the middle of April. *Look on the fields,* etc. Alluding most probably to the Sa-

maritans who were coming from all sides to hear him.

37. *One soweth, and another reapeth.* Christ sowed the seed; the apostles and all generations after them were to reap the grain.

38. *Others.* Meaning Christ himself.

42. *The Saviour of the world.* The reasons for this conviction are clear. The Samaritans were not looking for a deliverer from the Romans and were therefore more disposed to listen to the words of one who spoke only of spiritual things. The conversion of the woman led many to seek him. In simple faith they accepted him as the Saviour of the world because they believed him to be their Messiah.

43. *He went forth from thence into*

Gal'i-lee. 44 For Je'sus himself testified, that a prophet hath no honor in his own country. 45 So when he came into Gal'i-lee, the Gal-i-læ'ans received him, having seen all the things that he did in Je-ru'sa-lem at the feast: for they also went unto the feast.

46 He came therefore again unto Ca'na of Gal'i-lee, where he made the water wine. And there was a certain ʰnobleman, whose son was sick at Ca-per'-na-um. 47 When he heard that Je'sus was come out of Ju-dæ'a into Gal'i-lee, he went unto him, and besought *him* that he would come down, and heal his son; for he was at the point of death. 48 Je'sus therefore said unto him, **Except ye see signs and wonders, ye will in no wise believe.** 49 The ʰnobleman saith unto him, ⁱSir, come down ere my child die. 50 Je'sus saith unto him, **Go thy way; thy son liveth.** The man believed the word that Je'sus spake unto him, and he went his way. 51 And as he was now going down, his ᵏservants met him, saying, that his son lived. 52 So he inquired of them the hour when he began to amend. They said therefore unto him, Yesterday at the seventh hour the fever left him. 53 So the father knew that *it was* at that hour in which Je'sus said unto him, Thy son liveth: and himself believed, and his whole house. 54 This is again the second sign that Je'sus did, having come out of Ju-dæ'a into Gal'i-lee.

5 After these things there was ᵃa feast of the Jews; and Je'sus went up to Je-ru'sa-lem.

2 Now there is in Je-ru'sa-lem by the sheep *gate* a pool, which

h Or, *king's officer*   i Or, *Lord*
k Gr. *bondservants.*   a Many ancient authorities read *the feast.* (Comp. ch. 2. 13?)

Galilee. This was the beginning of his Galilean ministry. His previous appearance at Cana in Galilee was an episode of his Judæan ministry.

44. *In his own country.* Judæa, the country of his birth.

46–54. *A certain nobleman, whose son was sick.* The miracle of the healing of the nobleman's son is narrated in these verses. *Capernaum.* About twenty miles from Cana. *Except ye see signs and wonders,* etc. These words were spoken to test the nobleman's faith. He seemed to think it necessary for Jesus to be present at the bedside of his son in order to heal him. He asked Jesus the second time to go down to Capernaum. *Go thy way; thy son liveth.* A critical instant for the distressed father. If he had hesitated, his son might have died. *The man believed.* His faith must have been immediate and entire; he showed this by starting on his return apparently without a word. But the strongest proof of it was the testimony of his servants that the fever left his son at the time when Jesus spoke the healing word. The man's faith thought not of distance or of any limitation. *The seventh hour.* One o'clock in the afternoon.

CHAPTER 5

1. *There was a feast of the Jews.* The Feast of Purim, in memory of the deliverance in 473 B. C. of the Jews in Persia from Haman, who conspired to exterminate them. It was held annually in the month Adar (March), about a month before the Passover. See Esther 3.7; 9.24, 26, 28.

2. *The sheep gate.* Probably so named because near it sheep were sold for the Temple sacrifices. *Bethesda.* Meaning house of mercy or house of the stream. Some scholars have identified it with the Fountain of the Virgin, a spring

is called in Hebrew ᵇBe-thes'da, having five porches. 3 In these lay a multitude of them that were sick, blind, halt, withered ᶜ. 5 And a certain man was there, who had been thirty and eight years in his infirmity. 6 When Je'sus saw him lying, and knew that he had been now a long time *in that case*, he saith unto him, **Wouldest thou be made whole?** 7 The sick man answered him, ᵈSir, I have no man, when the water is troubled, to put me into the pool: but while I am coming, another steppeth down before me. 8 Je'sus saith unto him, **Arise, take up thy ᵉbed, and walk.** 9 And straightway the man was made whole, and took up his ᵉbed and walked.

Now it was the sabbath on that day. 10 So the Jews said unto him that was cured, It is the sabbath, and it is not lawful for thee to take up thy ᵉbed. 11 But he answered them, He that made me whole, the same said unto me, Take up thy ᵉbed, and walk. 12 They asked him, Who is the man that said unto thee, Take up *thy* ᵉ*bed*, and walk? 13 But he that was healed knew not who it was; for Je'sus had conveyed himself away, a multitude being in the place. 14 Afterward Je'sus findeth him in the temple, and said unto him, **Behold, thou art made whole: sin no more, lest a worse thing befall thee.** 15 The man went away, and told the Jews that it was Je'sus who had made him whole. 16 And for this cause the Jews persecuted Je'sus, because he did these things on the sabbath. 17 But Je'sus answered them, **My Father work-**

ᵇ Some ancient authorities read *Bethsaida*, others *Bethzatha*.   ᶜ Many ancient authorities insert, wholly or in part, *waiting for the moving of the water: 4 for an angel of the Lord went down at certain seasons into the pool, and troubled the water: whosoever then first after the troubling of the water stepped in was made whole, with whatsoever disease he was holden.*   ᵈ Or, *Lord*   ᵉ Or *pallet*

---

still existing in Jerusalem. Its waters alternately flow and cease to flow. *Porches.* Colonnades to shield the sick from sun and rain.

3. *Halt.* Lame, crippled.

6. *Wouldest thou be made whole?* In this case Jesus performs a miracle without being asked, possibly because the sick man had been so long helpless that even the desire and the will to be well had become dangerously weakened.

10. *It is not lawful for thee.* Only the narrowest interpretation could be made to hold the man guilty of an unlawful act in carrying his own bed, or pallet, on the Sabbath. It was not a 'burden', within the meaning of Jer. 17.21 and Neh. 13.19.

16. *And for this cause the Jews persecuted Jesus.* The opposition of the Jews to Jesus begins at this point to be organized and continuous. More especially the scribes and Pharisees saw in his teaching and miracles a threat to their oppressive rule of Jewish opinion.

17. *My father worketh .even until now.* An utterance which warned the Jews that their rules of Sabbath rest must be set aside. Their interpretation of the Mosaic law in this respect had resulted merely in the prohibition of activity of many kinds, even when such activity was merciful and relieved suffering. Jesus told them that his Father works without ceasing. This meant that the so-called rest which fetters or forbids the doing of good deeds on the Sabbath is contrary to God's will. Let them therefore take their rest on His day by worshipping Him and proving their love for Him by works of loving kindness for men. *And I work.* Implying his equality with the Father. It was this which especially angered the Jews who

eth even until now, and I work. 18 For this cause therefore the Jews sought the more to kill him, because he not only brake the sabbath, but also called God his own Father, making himself equal with God.

19 Je'sus therefore answered and said unto them, Verily, verily, I say unto you, The Son can do nothing of himself, but what he seeth the Father doing: for what things soever he doeth, these the Son also doeth in like manner. 20 For the Father loveth the Son, and showeth him all things that himself doeth: and greater works than these will he show him, that ye may marvel. 21 For as the Father raiseth the dead and giveth them life, even so the Son also giveth life to whom he will. 22 For neither doth the Father judge any man, but he hath given all judgment unto the Son; 23 that all may honor the Son, even as they honor the Father. He that honoreth not the Son honoreth not the Father

that sent him. 24 Verily, verily, I say unto you, He that heareth my word, and believeth him that sent me, hath eternal life, and cometh not into judgment, but hath passed out of death into life. 25 Verily, verily, I say unto you, The hour cometh, and now is, when the dead shall hear the voice of the Son of God; and they that *hear shall live. 26 For as the Father hath life in himself, even so gave he to the Son also to have life in himself: 27 and he gave him authority to execute judgment, because he is a son of man. 28 Marvel not at this: for the hour cometh, in which all that are in the tombs shall hear his voice, 29 and shall come forth; they that have done good, unto the resurrection of life; and they that have *done evil, unto the resurrection of judgment.

30 I can of myself do nothing: as I hear, I judge: and my judgment is righteous; because I seek not mine own will, but the will of him that sent me. 31 If

---

f Or, hearken　　g Or, practised

heard it. They at once inferred that he made himself equal with God. Jesus, instead of contradicting them, reaffirms this truth in the most uncompromising way in ver. 21–29.

19, 20. *The Son can do nothing of himself*, etc. The thought of these verses is the filial dependence of Jesus upon the Father, his union with Him and likeness to Him.

21–29. *For as the Father raiseth the dead*, etc. As in ver. 19 the Son is declared to depend upon the Father, so in these he is declared to have full sovereignty and exercise of power with Him, whether in imparting spiritual life, in judgment, in honor, or in the resurrection of

the dead. The relation of the Son to the Father here given is also found described more briefly in the eleventh chapter of Matthew, 25–30. See notes on Mt. 11.25, 27.

30. *I can of myself do nothing.* The Son cannot act apart from the Father. *As I hear, I judge.* According to the knowledge imparted by the Father.

31. *My witness is not true.* That is, if the witness as to himself borne by the Son is any other than the witness borne by the Father. The words are also applicable to a rule of Jewish law. See ch. 8.13; Num. 35.30; Deut. 17.6. At least two witnesses, preferably three, were required in legal proceedings.

I bear witness of myself, my witness is not true. 32 It is another that beareth witness of me; and I know that the witness which he witnesseth of me is true. 33 Ye have sent unto John, and he hath borne witness unto the truth. 34 But the witness which I receive is not from man: howbeit I say these things, that ye may be saved. 35 He was the lamp that burneth and shineth; and ye were willing to rejoice for a season in his light. 36 But the witness which I have is greater than *that of* John; for the works which the Father hath given me to accomplish, the very works that I do, bear witness of me, that the Father hath sent me. 37 And the Father that sent me, he hath borne witness of me. Ye have neither heard his voice at any time, nor seen his form. 38 And ye have not his word abiding in you: for whom he sent, him ye believe not. 39 [h]Ye search the scriptures, because ye think that in them ye have eternal life; and these are they which bear witness of me; 40 and ye will not come to me, that ye may have life. 41 I receive not glory from men. 42 But I know you, that ye have not the love of God in yourselves. 43 I am come in my Father's name, and ye receive me not: if another shall come in his own name, him ye will receive. 44 How can ye believe, who receive glory one of another, and the glory that *cometh* from [i]the only God ye seek not? 45 Think not that I will accuse you to the Father: there is one that accuseth you, *even* Mo'ses, on whom ye have set your hope. 46 For if ye believed Mo'ses, ye would believe me; for he wrote of me. 47 But if ye believe not his writings, how shall ye believe my words?

6 After these things Je'sus went away to the other side of the sea of Gal'i-lee, which is

---

h Or, *Search the scriptures*   i Some ancient authorities read *the only* one.

32. *It is another that beareth witness of me.* The Father.

33-39. *Ye have sent unto John,* etc. In these verses Jesus states who are the witnesses to his person and work. He aims to convince the Jews that he is the Divine Messiah by putting before them all the evidence he had, distinguishing its values and leaving them to choose. He had already decided the question of his own witnessing to himself (ver. 31). Here he also mentions: (1) his Father; (2) John the Baptist; (3) the Scriptures; and (4) his own works. *Greater than that of John.* There could not have been a more important human witness than the Baptist; but his testimony was not enough. *The very works that I do.* His teaching, character and signs, or miracles. These,

Jesus declared, bore witness that the Father sent him. They convinced many; but some doubted. The prejudices of the scribes and Pharisees were against giving him a fair hearing. *And the Father that sent me,* etc. The Jews were not willing to believe the Father's witness to him. *Ye search the scriptures.* They also rejected the testimony of the Scriptures concerning him.

43. *If another shall come in his own name,* etc. A false Messiah. The Jews were easily duped by these deceivers. More than sixty false Messiahs appeared in Jewish history.

CHAPTER 6

1. *After these things.* Probably about a month later. *The other*

the sea of Ti-be′ri-as. 2 And a great multitude followed him, because they beheld the signs which he did on them that were sick. 3 And Je′sus went up into the mountain, and there he sat with his disciples. 4 Now the passover, the feast of the Jews, was at hand. 5 Je′sus therefore lifting up his eyes, and seeing that a great multitude cometh unto him, saith unto Philip, Whence are we to buy *a*bread, that these may eat? 6 And this he said to prove him: for he himself knew what he would do. 7 Philip answered him, Two hundred *b*shillings′ worth of ⁎bread is not sufficient for them, that every one may take a little. 8 One of his disciples, Andrew, Si′mon Peter′s brother, saith unto him, 9 There is a lad here, who hath five barley loaves, and two fishes: but what are these among so many? 10 Je′sus said,

Make the people sit down. Now there was much grass in the place. So the men sat down, in number about five thousand. 11 Je′sus therefore took the loaves; and having given thanks, he distributed to them that were set down; likewise also of the fishes as much as they would. 12 And when they were filled, he saith unto his disciples, Gather up the broken pieces which remain over, that nothing be lost. 13 So they gathered them up, and filled twelve baskets with broken pieces from the five barley loaves, which remained over unto them that had eaten. 14 When therefore the people saw the *c*sign which he did, they said, This is of a truth the prophet that cometh into the world.

15 Je′sus therefore perceiving that they were about to come and take him by force, to make

---

a Gr. *loaves.* *b* The word in the Greek denotes a coin worth about eight pence halfpenny, or nearly seventeen cents. *c* Some ancient authorities read *signs.*

---

side of the sea of Galilee. The eastern shore. *Tiberias.* A city on the western shore of the sea of Galilee. It was built by Herod Antipas about 20 A.D. and named after the Roman emperor. Its inhabitants were mostly foreigners. It became the capital of Galilee and after the fall of Jerusalem the Sanhedrin met there. Tiberias also became the seat of a famous school of Jewish learning. On its site is a town of about four thousand people, mostly Jews.

2. *A great multitude followed him.* It was a time of much excitement. The twelve apostles had just returned from their first mission and many came with them. The fame of the miracles drew others. See Lk. 9.10, 11.

4. *Now the passover, the feast of the Jews,* etc. This was the second Passover feast in our Lord′s minis-

try. The Passover was held annually to commemorate the deliverance of the Jews from their bondage in Egypt. It began on the fourteenth of Nisan, a month corresponding in part to our April.

5–14. *Whence are we to buy bread that these may eat?* The miracle of the feeding of the five thousand is here narrated. According to the evangelist′s method of considering the miracles as signs or symbols of spiritual truths, he gives an account of the feeding of the five thousand as introductory to our Lord′s discourse on the bread of life (ver. 26–40). See notes on Mt. 14.21; Mk. 6.32, 35, 38, 40, 44.

15. *To make him king.* Jesus was now at the height of his popularity. The multitudes who were astonished at his miraculous power, but who did not understand his spiritual mission, wanted to make

him king, withdrew again into the mountain himself alone.

16 And when evening came, his disciples went down unto the sea; 17 and they entered into a boat, and were going over the sea unto Ca-per′na-um. And it was now dark, and Je′sus had not yet come to them. 18 And the sea was rising by reason of a great wind that blew. 19 When therefore they had rowed about five and twenty or thirty furlongs, they behold Je′sus walking on the sea, and drawing nigh unto the boat: and they were afraid. 20 But he saith unto them, It is I; be not afraid. 21 They were willing therefore to receive him into the boat: and straightway the boat was at the land whither they were going.

22 On the morrow the multitude that stood on the other side of the sea saw that there was no other *d*boat there, save one, and that Je′sus entered not with his disciples into the boat, but *that* his disciples went away alone 23 (howbeit there came *e*boats from Ti-be′ri-as nigh unto the place where they ate the bread after the Lord had given thanks): 24 when the multitude therefore saw that Je′sus was not there, neither his disciples, they themselves got into the *e*boats, and came to Ca-per′na-um, seeking Je′sus. 25 And when they found him on the other side of the sea, they said unto him, Rab′bi, when camest thou hither? 26 Je′sus answered them and said, Verily, verily, I say unto you, Ye seek me, not because ye saw signs, but because ye ate of the loaves, and were filled. 27 Work not for the food which perisheth, but for the food which abideth unto eternal life, which the Son of man shall give unto you: for him the Father, *even* God, hath sealed. 28 They said therefore unto him, What must we do,

---

d Gr. *little boat.*　　　　*e* Gr. *little boats.*

---

him a political ruler. His sudden retirement disappointed them.

16–21. *His disciples went down unto the sea.* Here is described the miracle of walking on the sea. *About five and twenty or thirty furlongs.* Between three and four miles. See notes on Mt. 14.25. Comp. Mt. 14.22–33; Mk. 6.47–52.

22. *The other side of the sea.* The eastern side.

25. *The other side of the sea.* The multitude had now crossed in boats and were on the western side.

26. *Ye seek me, not because ye saw signs,* etc. This is the opening of Christ's discourse in the Capernaum synagogue on the bread of life. Together with the controversial interruptions of the listening Jews, some of whom believed, it is continued to ver. 66. Jesus takes the physical hunger of the multitude, their eager quest for bodily food,

as the starting point of instruction in order to create in their souls a hunger for spiritual nourishment that shall be eternally life-giving in contrast to the food which perishes.

27. *Which the Son of man shall give unto you.* As many who heard him believed him to be the Messiah, it was a mystery and a disappointment to be told that they must work for the food which abideth unto eternal life. Was this all that their expected national deliverer and king could do for them? What did it mean? *Hath sealed.* Hath testified to and authorized.

28. *What must we do, that we may work,* etc. 'Work' for 'the food which abideth' suggested to them that Jesus meant something very different from the ceremonial routine of observances and sacrifices to which they were accustomed. And so it proved.

that we may work the works of God? 29 Je′sus answered and said unto them, This is the work of God, that ye believe on him whom *f*he hath sent. 30 They said therefore unto him, What then doest thou for a sign, that we may see, and believe thee? what workest thou? 31 Our fathers ate the man′na in the wilderness; as it is written, He *g*gave them bread out of heaven to eat. 32 Je′sus therefore said unto them, Verily, verily, I say unto you, It was not Mo′ses that gave you the bread out of heaven; but my Father giveth you the true bread out of heaven. 33 For the bread of God is that which cometh down out of heaven, and giveth life unto the world. 34 They said therefore unto him, Lord, evermore give us this bread. 35 Je′sus said unto them, I am the bread of life: he that cometh to

me shall not hunger, and he that believeth on me shall never thirst. 36 But I said unto you, that ye have seen me, and yet believe not. 37 All that which the Father giveth me shall come unto me; and him that cometh to me I will in no wise cast out. 38 For I am come down from heaven, not to do mine own will, but the will of him that sent me. 39 And this is the will of him that sent me, that of all that which he hath given me I should lose nothing, but should raise it up at the last day. 40 For this is the will of my Father, that every one that beholdeth the Son, and believeth on him, should have eternal life; and *h*I will raise him up at the last day.

41 The Jews therefore murmured concerning him, because he said, I am the bread which came down out of heaven, 42 And they said, Is not this Je′sus,

---

f Or, *he sent*   *g* Neh. ix. 15; Ex. xvi. 4, 15; Ps. lxxviii. 24; cv. 40.

h Or, *that I should raise him up*

---

29. *This is the work of God.* Not *a* work, but *the* work which includes and sanctifies all other works of God. *That ye believe on him whom he hath sent.* Faith in Jesus the Messiah as the Son of God was 'the work' they were required to do. It should not have been difficult for those who had heard his words of love, authority and power and witnessed his acts of mercy and his miracles.

30, 31. *What workest thou?* What work of God canst thou do so that we may know that thou art the Son of God? What proof canst thou give that will compel us to accept thy words as our rule of life? *Our fathers ate the manna.* As if some sign like that of the manna in the wilderness (Ex. 16.4, 15) would have been received by them as convincing evidence. Their thoughts could not leave the material view of food.

32. *My father giveth you the true bread.* The manna was in no sense the spiritual food, which is the true bread from heaven.

35–40. *I am the bread of life.* All the preceding words of the discourse lead up to this. Jesus declares himself to be the sustainer of spiritual life. Coming to him and believing on him eternally satisfy the spiritual hunger and thirst for God which are the deepest need of human nature. *Raise it up at the last day.* The death of the body is no interruption of the believer's spiritual life, but on the contrary opens up before it limitless possibilities.

41. *The Jews therefore murmured.* Not all were against him, though the majority were certainly hostile; but the revelation of originality and power in his words was a challenge to take him seriously.

42. *Is not this Jesus, the son of*

the son of Joseph, whose father and mother we know? how doth he now say, I am come down out of heaven? 43 Je'sus answered and said unto them, **Murmur** not among yourselves. 44 No man can come to me, except the Father that sent me draw him: and I will raise him up in the last day. 45 It is written in the prophets, *And they shall all be taught of God. Every one that hath heard from the Father, and hath learned, cometh unto me. 46 Not that any man hath seen the Father, save he that is from God, he hath seen the Father. 47 Verily, verily, I say unto you, He that believeth hath eternal life. 48 I am the bread of life. 49 Your fathers ate the man'na in the wilderness, and they died. 50 This is the bread which cometh down out of heaven, that a man may eat thereof, and not die. 51 I am the living bread which came down out of heaven:

if any man eat of this bread, he shall live for ever: yea and the bread which I will give is my flesh, for the life of the world.

52 The Jews therefore strove one with another, saying, How can this man give us his flesh to eat? 53 Je'sus therefore said unto them, Verily, verily, I say unto you, Except ye eat the flesh of the Son of man and drink his blood, ye have not life in yourselves. 54 He that eateth my flesh and drinketh my blood hath eternal life; and I will raise him up at the last day. 55 For my flesh is *k*meat indeed, and my blood is *l*drink indeed. 56 He that eateth my flesh and drinketh my blood abideth in me, and I in him. 57 As the living Father sent me, and I live because of the Father; so he that eateth me, he also shall live because of me. 58 This is the bread which came down out of heaven: not as the fathers ate,

---

i Is. liv. 13; (Jer. xxxi. 34?).   *k* Gr. *true meat.*   *l* Gr. *true drink.*

Joseph, etc. The more narrow-minded among them raised this objection. The same feeling was behind it which would not tolerate Jesus in his own village of Nazareth. *I am come down out of heaven.* They seem to have taken this utterance literally although our Lord had spoken to them in strikingly figurative language.

44. *Except the Father that sent me draw him.* Jesus rebukes them for their murmuring by telling them, in effect, that they are against him because they resist the drawing influence, the loving invitation, of the Father.

51–58. *The bread which I will give is my flesh.* This part of the discourse is considered by many scholars as intended to prepare the minds of his hearers, more particularly the apostles and disciples, to understand the spiritual meaning of the Last

Supper which he instituted just a year afterward. Faith in Christ as the bread of life had already been set forth and urged upon them; but they are now told that this bread is his flesh, which he will give for the life of the world. By 'flesh' is meant his sinless human nature; and in order to impress upon them in the most effective manner their need of spiritual union with it he employs a figure of speech which is perhaps unique in the religious literature of the world. He tells them, 'Except ye eat the flesh of the Son of man and drink his blood, ye have not life in yourselves' (ver. 53). In other words, they must be spiritually united to his perfect human nature by faith, if they would have life. That life would be eternal (ver. 58). The truths here mentioned were made part of Christianity in the Lord's Supper.

and died; he that eateth this bread shall live for ever. 59 These things said he in *m*the synagogue, as he taught in Ca-per'na-um.

60 **Many therefore of his disciples, when they heard** *this*, **said, This is a hard saying; who can hear** *n*it? 61 **But Je'sus knowing in himself that his disciples murmured at this, said unto them, Doth this cause you to stumble?** 62 *What* **then if ye should behold the Son of man ascending where he was before?** 63 **It is the spirit that giveth life; the flesh profiteth nothing: the words that I have spoken unto you are spirit, and are life.** 64 **But there are some of you that believe not.** For Je'sus knew from the beginning who they were that believed not, and who

it was that should *o*betray him. 65 And he said, **For this cause have I said unto you, that no man can come unto me, except it be given unto him of the Father.**

66 Upon this many of his disciples went back, and walked no more with him. 67 Je'sus said therefore unto the twelve, **Would ye also go away?** 68 Si'mon Peter answered him, Lord, to whom shall we go? thou *p*hast the words of eternal life. 69 And we have believed and know that thou art the Holy One of God. 70 Je'sus answered them, **Did not I choose you the twelve, and one of you is a devil?** 71 Now he spake of Ju'das *the son* of Si'mon Is-car'i-ot, for he it was that should *o*betray him, *being* one of the twelve.

---

m Or, *a synagogue*   *n* Or, *him*

o Or, *deliver him up*   *p* Or, *hast words*

---

59. *These things said he in the synagogue.* If Tell Hûm is, as many Biblical scholars think, the site of Capernaum, it is probable that the ruins of a synagogue discovered there are those of the very building in which this sermon was delivered.

62. *What then if ye should behold the Son of man,* etc. If they found it so difficult to understand in a spiritual sense what he said about his natural body, about eating his flesh and drinking his blood, what would they think if they should see him ascending in his spiritual body? They would then know beyond all doubt that his words had a spiritual meaning.

63. *It is the spirit that giveth life.* Only spirit is creative and intelligent.

65. *No man can come unto me, except,* etc. The explanation is found in ver. 44, 45.

66. *Went back, and walked no more with him.* Some could not understand and left him in honest doubt, perhaps to be convinced later. Others understood, but were too

timid or worldly to accept the consequences of following him. Some hated his words because they saw in them a spiritualizing process whereby the Messiah popularly hoped for, the available, political Messiah who might be profitably used by his adherents, would be made entirely impossible.

67–70. *The twelve.* The apostles are here thus named for the first time. They were better grounded in faith than the other disciples and remained firm. *To whom shall we go?* Here Peter's impetuous leadership in a crisis appears again. He was the first to speak, and his words reveal the faith and insight which later came to full fruitage in his historic confession. See Mt. 16.16 and notes thereon.

71. *Judas, the son of Simon Iscariot.* 'Iscariot' means a man of Kerioth, a Judæan town. It is a striking coincidence that even in the little company of the apostles it was his own who 'received him not.' The native province of Jesus rejected him; his own Nazareth

7 And after these things Je'sus walked in Gal'i-lee: for he would not walk in Ju-dæ'a, because the Jews sought to kill him. 2 Now the feast of the Jews, the feast of tabernacles, was at hand. 3 His brethren therefore said unto him, Depart hence, and go into Ju-dæ'a, that thy disciples also may behold thy works which thou doest. 4 For no man doeth anything in secret, *and himself seeketh to be known openly. If thou doest these things, manifest thyself to the world. 5 For even his brethren did not believe on him. 6 Je'sus therefore saith unto them, My time is not yet come; but your time is always ready. 7 The world cannot hate you; but me it hateth, because I testify of it, that its works are

evil. 8 Go ye up unto the feast: I go not up *unto this feast; because my time is not yet fulfilled. 9 And having said these things unto them, he abode *still* in Gal'i-lee.

10 But when his brethren were gone up unto the feast, then went he also up, not publicly, but as it were in secret. 11 The Jews therefore sought him at the feast, and said, Where is he? 12 And there was much murmuring among the multitudes concerning him: some said, He is a good man; others said, Not so, but he leadeth the multitude astray. 13 Yet no man spake openly of him for fear of the Jews.

14 But when it was now the midst of the feast Je'sus went up into the temple, and taught. 15 The Jews therefore marvelled,

---

a Some ancient authorities read *and seeketh it to be known openly.*

b Many ancient authorities add *yet.*

would have none of him; the man who betrayed him was a Judæan. All the other apostles were Galileans.

CHAPTER 7

1. *After these things Jesus walked in Galilee.* He continued his ministry in Galilee for a period not known, then visited the country of Tyre and Sidon, the Decapolis region, and Cæsarea Philippi. During this time his popularity was waning and the opposition of the Jewish ruling classes was increasing. See notes on Mt. 4.25; 16.13. His transfiguration also took place during this period. After an interval of between five and six months following the discourse on the bread of life, his ministry in Galilee was finished and he went up to Jerusalem, at the Feast of Tabernacles.

2. *The feast of tabernacles.* This was the annual festival of the fruit, wine and oil harvest. It lasted eight days, during which the people dwelt in booths, to remind them of

their wilderness wanderings. It was the annual Jewish harvest home and the most joyous of their feasts.

3. *That thy disciples also may behold thy works.* At the Feast of Tabernacles there would be a better opportunity to make his teaching more widely known, as his disciples would gather there in large numbers.

4. *No man doeth anything in secret, and himself seeketh,* etc. A presumptuous suggestion by his brethren that he was not acting consistently. They hinted that Jesus ought to go up to Jerusalem and openly challenge attention.

6. *My time.* That is, his time according to divine appointment. See ch. 2.4.

14. *The midst of the feast.* It is uncertain on what day. Jesus, though having to come up to the feast quietly as if to avoid publicity, now appeared and taught openly.

15. *How knoweth this man letters.* His hearers wondered that a man never trained by the rabbis should

saying, How knoweth this man letters, having never learned? 16 Je'sus therefore answered them, and said, My teaching is not mine, but his that sent me. 17 If any man willeth to do his will, he shall know of the teaching, whether it is of God, or *whether* I speak from myself. 18 He that speaketh from himself seeketh his own glory: but he that seeketh the glory of him that sent him, the same is true, and no unrighteousness is in him. 19 Did not Mo'ses give you the law, and *yet* none of you doeth the law? Why seek ye to kill me? 20 The multitude answered, Thou hast a demon: who seeketh to kill thee? 21 Je'sus answered and said unto them, I did one work, and ye all marvel because thereof. 22 Mo'ses hath given you circumcision (not that it is of Mo'ses, but of the fathers); and on the sabbath ye

circumcise a man. 23 If a man receiveth circumcision on the sabbath, that the law of Mo'ses may not be broken; are ye wroth with me, because I made ᶜa man every whit whole on the sabbath? 24 Judge not according to appearance, but judge righteous judgment.

25 Some therefore of them of Je-ru'sa-lem said, Is not this he whom they seek to kill? 26 And lo, he speaketh openly, and they say nothing unto him. Can it be that the rulers indeed know that this is the Christ? 27 Howbeit we know this man whence he is: but when the Christ cometh, no one knoweth whence he is. 28 Je'sus therefore cried in the temple, teaching and saying, Ye both know me, and know whence I am; and I am not come of myself, but he that sent me is true, whom ye know not. 29 I know him; because I am

---

c Gr. *a whole man sound.*

---

be so well acquainted with the Scriptures and rabbinical learning.

16–18. *My teaching is not mine, but his that sent me.* Jesus in this utterance again affirms his union with the Father. *If any man willeth to do his will,* etc. An invitation by our Lord to any one to test and confirm his teaching by the experience of a godly life.

19. *And yet none of you doeth the law.* Their own obedience to the law of Moses was defective, as proved by their attempts to kill Jesus.

20. *Thou hast a demon.* This can only be taken as the ignorant exclamation of those who did not know of the plot to kill him. That others did know of the plot is shown in ver. 25.

21. *I did one work, and ye all marvel.* The healing of the impotent man at the pool of Bethesda. *Marvel.* Or complain that it was done on the Sabbath.

22–24. *Moses hath given you circumcision.* The thought of these verses is that if circumcision was right only when performed on the Sabbath, it was impossible for a much better deed, the making of a man every whit whole, to be wrong because done on the Sabbath.

26. *That the rulers indeed know that this is the Christ.* There were conflicting beliefs among the Jews as to knowing the Messiah when he appeared. The question asked in this verse apparently suggests that the rulers, or at least some of them, were convinced that Jesus was the Messiah, and for that reason dare not lay hands on him when he taught openly.

28. *Ye both know me, and know whence I am.* That is, they knew he was born in Bethlehem, and that he was descended from David. *Whom ye know not.* But they were far from knowing God who sent him.

230

from him, and he sent me.   30
They sought therefore to take
him: and no man laid his hand
on him, because his hour was
not yet come.   31 But of the
multitude many believed on
him; and they said, When the
Christ shall come, will he do
more signs than those which
this man hath done?   32 The
Phar'i-sees heard the multitude
murmuring these things concerning him; and the chief
priests and the Phar'i-sees sent
officers to take him.   33 Je'sus
therefore said, Yet a little while
am I with you, and I go unto
him that sent me.   34 Ye shall
seek me, and shall not find me:
and where I am, ye cannot come.

35 The Jews therefore said among
themselves, Whither will this
man go that we shall not find
him? will he go unto the Dispersion ᵈamong the Greeks, and
teach the Greeks?   36 What
is this word that he said, Ye
shall seek me, and shall not find
me; and where I am, ye cannot
come?

37 Now on the last day, the
great *day* of the feast, Je'sus
stood and cried, saying, If any
man thirst, let him come unto
me and drink.   38 He that believeth on me, as the scripture
hath said, ᵉfrom within him shall
flow rivers of living water.   39
But this spake he of the Spirit,
which they that believed on him

---

d Gr. *of.*   *e* Gr. *out of his belly.*

---

33. *Yet a little while am I with
you.* The deliberate attempt of the
scribes and Pharisees to take him he
knew to be an indication of his
approaching death. In announcing to the multitude that he would
be with them yet a little while, he
implied that his appointed task was
almost done and that his appointed
hour was near. ʿHe meant especially to remind the scribes and Pharisees of this truth, so that they might
know that no designs and acts of
their own could either hasten or
delay the approach of that hour.
34. *Ye shall seek me, and shall not
find me.* Ye shall come to know
more of him whom ye have rejected,
and shall ask his aid; but ye shall
not be able to come where ye might
find him, as ye know not the Father
who sent him.
35. *The Dispersion.* The Jews
who lived in countries outside of
Palestine. *And teach the Greeks.*
'Greeks' here means Greek-speaking Jews and also may be taken in a
wider sense to apply to the Gentile
world. The Jews outside of Palestine were chiefly in Syria, Egypt and
Babylonia. As they were mostly
engaged in commerce they spoke
Greek and thus came to be called

Hellenists or Greek-speaking Jews.
The Jews therefore who thus ignorantly asked this question suggested
for Jesus the great plan which was
actually attempted afterward by his
apostles, and most comprehensively
carried into effect by Paul.
37. *The last day, the great day of
the feast.* The eighth day, which
was kept as a Sabbath. On this
day there was a holy convocation, a
memorial celebration of the entrance
of the Israelites into Canaan.
38. *From within him shall flow
rivers of living water.* Jesus, in
teaching on the last day of the feast,
adapted his theme to the character
of the ceremonies familiar to the
people. On each of the seven days
water was publicly brought and
poured from a golden pitcher during
the morning sacrifice. In ver. 37,
38 Jesus therefore compares himself
to the living water, spiritually interpreted. It is the same teaching
that was given to the Samaritan
woman at the well of Sychar ʿ(ch.
4.5–26).
39. *Because Jesus was not yet
glorified.* The meaning of this verse
is that the Holy Spirit, the Comforter, could not be given to believers
until the time came to send Him,

were to receive: *f*for the Spirit was not yet *given*; because Je'sus was not yet glorified. 40 *Some* of the multitude therefore, when they heard these words, said, This is of a truth the prophet. 41 Others said, This is the Christ. But some said, What, doth the Christ come out of Gal'i-lee? 42 *g*Hath not the scripture said that the Christ cometh of the seed of David, and from Beth'-le-hem, the village where David was? 43 So there arose a division in the multitude because of him. 44 And some of them would have taken him; but no man laid hands on him.

45 The officers therefore came to the chief priests and Phar'i-sees; and they said unto them, Why did ye not bring him? 46 The officers answered, Never man so spake. 47 The Phar'i-sees therefore answered them, Are ye also led astray? 48 Hath any of the rulers believed on

him, or of the Phar'i-sees? 49 But this multitude that knoweth not the law are accursed. 50 Nic-o-de'mus saith unto them (he that came to him before, being one of them), 51 Doth our law judge a man, except it first hear from himself and know what he doeth? 52 They answered and said unto him, Art thou also of Gal'i-lee? Search, and *h*see that out of Gal'i-lee ariseth no prophet.

53 *a*[And they went every man
8 unto his own house: 1 but Je'sus went unto the mount of Ol'ives. 2 And early in the morning he came again into the temple, and all the people came unto him; and he sat down, and taught them. 3 And the scribes and the Phar'i-sees bring a woman taken in adultery; and having set her in the midst, 4 they say unto him, Teacher, this woman hath been taken in

f Some ancient authorities read *for the Holy Spirit was not yet given.*   *g* 2 S. vii. 12 ff.; Mic. v. 2.   *h* Or, *see: for out of*

Galilee &c.   a Most of the ancient authorities omit John 7.53–8.11.   Those which contain it vary much from each other.

that is, after the death, resurrection and ascension of Jesus Christ.

40. *This is of a truth the prophet.* The prophet of Deut. 18.15, looked upon as the Messiah's forerunner.

47. *Are ye also led astray?* Have even you, our officers, sent by the Sanhedrin to arrest this man, been so influenced by him that you have failed in your duty?

49. *This multitude that knoweth not the law.* The scribes and Pharisees apparently had deep concern when they suspected that some of their own number were converted by the teaching of Jesus; but for the mass of the people they had only contempt. *Are accursed.* The multitude are cursed for their ignorance, not their sinfulness. This saying and the incident connected with it bring out clearly that the Pharisees were as bitterly exclusive

in their control of Jewish opinion as their enemies, the Sadducees, were in control of the public offices. See note on Mt. 3.7.

51. *Doth our law judge a man,* etc. This question by Nicodemus shows a courage and insight which were less evident when he visited Jesus and asked him about the new birth (ch. 3.1–10 and notes thereon). Evidently that interview had to some extent changed his belief.

CHAPTER 8

1. *The mount of Olives.* A prominent hill east of Jerusalem, and separated from the city by the valley of the Kidron.

3. *The scribes and Pharisees bring a woman.* The forcing of this woman into the public gaze was a brutal act. The law did not require it.

4. *They say unto him, Teacher,*

adultery, in the very act. 5
*b*Now in the law Mo'ses commanded us to stone such: what then sayest thou of her? 6 And this they said, trying him, that they might have *whereof* to accuse him. But Je'sus stooped down, and with his finger wrote on the ground. 7 But when they continued asking him, he lifted up himself, and said unto them, He that is without sin among you, let him first cast a stone at her. 8 And again he stooped down, and with his finger wrote on the ground. 9 And they, when they heard it,

went out one by one, beginning from the eldest, *even* unto the last: and Je'sus was left alone, and the woman, where she was, in the midst. 10 And Je'sus lifted up himself, and said unto her, Woman, where are they? did no man condemn thee? 11 And she said, No man, Lord. And Je'sus said, .Neither do I condemn thee: go thy way; from henceforth sin no more.]

12 Again therefore Je'sus spake unto them, saying, I am the light of the world: he that followeth me shall not walk in

---

b Lev. xx. 10; Dt. xxii. 22 f.

---

etc. The bringing of the woman before Jesus for judgment was a device similar to that in which he was asked to decide about the tribute money (Mt. 22.15–22 and notes thereon). The scribes and Pharisees cared nothing about the woman, but wished either to excite the people against Jesus or to embroil him with the Roman authorities. If he judged the woman worthy of death, that would anger the people, as capital punishment for adultery was becoming very unpopular. It would also bring him to the notice of the Roman governor, whose consent was necessary to the execution of a death sentence. That would have given the scribes and Pharisees a chance to accuse him of a political offence.

6. *With his finger wrote on the ground.* A sign that he wished to have nothing to do with the matter. He had more than once showed his unwillingness to interfere with disputes within the jurisdiction of the courts (Lk. 12.13–15; ch. 18.36).

7. *Without sin.* That is, free from committing the actual sin complained of, or from the sinful thoughts which led to it.

8. *And again he stooped down,* etc. Again he was reluctant to interfere. It has been suggested by some scholars that he wrote a word

which expressed his judgment of the woman's accusers.

11. *Neither do I condemn thee.* Jesus did not condemn her under the Mosaic law. He condoned her sin because she had compassion on her suffering and knew her sincere desire to repent. 'Sin no more' was his only condemnation.

12. *I am the light of the world.* As in the sixth chapter Jesus is represented as the Bread of Life and in the seventh as the Living Water, so here he is the Light of the World. This accords with the purpose of the evangelist so to narrate the life of our Lord that he shall appear as the source and sustainer of the Christian faith and experience in all its aspects. The Bread of Life, the Living Water, the Light of the World, the Good Shepherd, the True Vine, the Resurrection and the Life, the Great High Priest, the Way, the Truth, the Comforter—these are figurative expressions of historic importance in the development of religion. They are part of the warp and woof of Christian literature. Their spiritual meanings centre in and radiate from the person of Jesus the Christ. They compass all the seeker's needs. They have diversified and enriched the believer's contemplation in all succeeding ages.

the darkness, but shall have the light of life. 13 The Phar'i-sees therefore said unto him, Thou bearest witness of thyself; thy witness is not true. 14 Je'sus answered and said unto them, Even if I bear witness of myself, my witness is true; for I know whence I came, and whither I go; but ye know not whence I come, or whither I go. 15 Ye judge after the flesh; I judge no man. 16 Yea and if I judge, my judgment is true; for I am not alone, but I and the Father that sent me. 17 Yea and in your law it is written, *c*that the witness of two men is true. 18 I am he that beareth witness of myself, and the Father that sent me beareth witness of me. 19 They said therefore unto him, Where is thy Father? Je'sus answered, Ye know neither me, nor my

Father: if ye knew me, ye would know my Father also. 20 These words spake he in the treasury, as he taught in the temple: and no man took him; because his hour was not yet come.

21 He said therefore again unto them, I go away, and ye shall seek me, and shall die in your sin: whither I go, ye cannot come. 22 The Jews therefore said, Will he kill himself, that he saith, Whither I go, ye cannot come? 23 And he said unto them, Ye are from beneath; I am from above: ye are of this world; I am not of this world. 24 I said therefore unto you, that ye shall die in your sins: for except ye believe that I am *he*, ye shall die in your sins. 25 They said therefore unto him, Who art thou? Je'sus said unto them, *d*Even that which I have

---

c Comp. Dt. xix. 15; xvii. 6.　*'d* Or, *Altogether that which I also speak unto you.*

---

13. *Thy witness is not true.* According to the Mosaic law, which required two witnesses.

14. *My witness is true*, etc. Jesus puts aside, as inapplicable to himself, the Jewish rule as to the insufficiency of one witness. That was for men, and valid in cases before the Sanhedrin or the local synagogue courts; but the witness of our Lord as to himself was a spiritual intuition, the immediate knowledge that the Father had sent him, the direct action of the Father's life in him and union with him. It was in this sense that Jesus declared that his witness as to himself is true.

18. *The Father that sent me.* Even admitting the justice of the Jewish law of two witnesses in its proper application, how much more weighty the witness of the Father and the witness of Jesus as to the latter's mission than those of any number of human witnesses!

20. *In the treasury.* In the Women's Court were thirteen brazen chests for the reception of vol-

untary offerings and the Temple dues.

21. *Whither I go, ye cannot come.* Because they did not believe in him.

22. *Will he kill himself*, etc. An insult, by which his enemies meant that Jesus intended to commit suicide.

23. *Ye are from beneath.* Your worldly natures cannot understand the truth of God.

24. *Except ye believe that I am he.* The Messiah, the Saviour of the world.

25. *That which I have also spoken unto you from the beginning.* By this reply our Lord not only reaffirms his Messiahship as implied in the words 'I am he' of ver. 24, but also the truths he had previously uttered, or accepted when uttered by others, concerning his person and mission, namely, that he is the Son of God, the Son of man (Mt. 8.20 and note thereon), Saviour of the world from sin (ch. 1.29), Light of the World, etc. (ch. 8.12 and note thereon).

also spoken unto you from the beginning. 26 I have many things to speak and to judge concerning you: howbeit he that sent me is true; and the things which I heard from him, these speak I unto the world. 27 They perceived not that he spake to them of the Father. 28 Je'sus therefore said, When ye have lifted up the Son of man, then shall ye know that ⌐I am *he*, and *that* I do nothing of myself, but as the Father taught me, I speak these things. 29 And he that sent me is with me; he hath not left me alone; for I do always the things that are pleasing to him. 30 As he spake

these things, many believed on him.

31 Je'sus therefore said to those Jews that had believed him, If ye abide in my word, *then* are ye truly my disciples; 32 and ye shall know the truth, and the truth shall make you free. 33 They answered unto him, We are Abraham's seed, and have never yet been in bondage to any man: how sayest thou, Ye shall be made free? 34 Je'sus answered them, Verily, verily, I say unto you, Every one that committeth sin is the bondservant of sin. 35 And the bondservant abideth not in the house for ever: the son abideth for

---

e Or, *I am* he: *and I do*

26–28. *Many things to speak and to judge,* etc. The meaning of these three verses is apparently this: Although Jesus had many things to speak and judge concerning the Jews, yet he looked upon his teaching of the truth to the world as a greater duty. The truth was that he came from the Father and was the Messiah. They who did not believe his words would see their truth when he was crucified, raised from the dead and ascended into heaven.

29. *I do always the things,* etc. This implies an affirmation that he is the divine Son of God, who alone can always do what is pleasing to the Father.

31. *If ye abide in my word,* etc. 'Those Jews that had believed in him' evidently did not go far enough. They accepted him as the Messiah, but not without some reserve. They were not fully prepared to set aside the Mosaic law and take him as their sole spiritual guide.

32–36. *Ye shall know the truth.* A humiliating announcement to those of his hearers, especially the Pharisees, who looked upon themselves as the favored possessors and dispensers of the truth. *The truth shall make you free.* From the limiting, debasing power of sin. *Never*

yet been in bondage to any man. By this answer the new temporary believers among the rulers and Pharisees, not yet free from class pride, meant that a son of Abraham ought never even to be considered as having been in bondage. They knew that, historically, their reply was false, because the Jews had been enslaved in Egypt and Babylon, and were even then under the heel of the Roman emperor. *How sayest thou,* etc. Some may have been dull to perceive, but others well knew, and the knowledge made them wince, that the truth and freedom spoken of by Jesus was spiritual insight to be made the rule of life, liberating them from the letter-worship of the Mosaic law without violating its spirit. They had been disciplined by a code; they were now to be guided by faith in the revealed Messiah and inspired by his example. *Every one that committeth sin,* etc. Jesus shows them that instead of enjoying the boasted freedom of sons of Abraham, they were really under a self-imposed bondage; each man's captor and enslaver was his own sin. They had not, therefore, the privileges of any son of the house; they were only bondservants in it and might be put out of it. Nor could they,

ever. 36 If therefore the Son shall make you free, ye shall be free indeed. 37 I know that ye are Abraham's seed; yet ye seek to kill me, because my word *f*hath not free course in you. 38 I speak the things which I have seen with *g*my Father: and ye also do the things which ye heard from *your* father. 39 They answered and said unto him, Our father is Abraham. Je'sus saith unto them, If ye *h*were Abraham's children, *i*ye would do the works of Abraham. 40 But now ye seek to kill me, a man that hath told you the truth, which I heard from God: this did not Abraham. 41 Ye do the works of your father. They said unto him, We were not born of fornication; we have one Father, even . God. 42 Je'sus said unto them, If God were your Father, ye would love me: for I came forth and am come from God; for neither have I come of myself, but he sent me. 43 Why do ye not *k*understand my

speech? *Even* because ye cannot hear my word. 44 Ye are of *your* father the devil, and the lusts of your father it is your will to do. He was a murderer from the beginning, and standeth not in the truth, because there is no truth in him. *l*When he speaketh a lie, he speaketh of his own: for he is a liar, and the father thereof. 45 But because I say the truth, ye believe me not. 46 Which of you convicteth me of sin? If I say truth, why do ye not believe me? 47 He that is of God heareth the words of God: for this cause ye hear *them* not, because ye are not of God. 48 The Jews answered and said unto him, Say we not well that thou art a Sa-mar'i-tan, and hast a demon? 49 Je'sus answered, I have not a demon; but I honor my Father, and ye dishonor me. 50 But I seek not mine own glory: there is one that seeketh and judgeth. 51 Verily, verily, I say unto you, If a man keep my word, he shall

---

f Or, *hath no place in you*   *g* Or, *the Father: do ye also therefore the things which ye heard from the Father.*   *h* Gr. *are.*   *i* Some ancient authorities read *ye do the*   *works of Abraham.*   *k* Or, *know*   *l* Or, *When one speaketh a lie, he speaketh of his own: for his father also is a liar.*

while slaves of sin and of the mere text of the law, be members of the Messiah's kingdom. A son of the house, however, had power to free one of its slaves. Much more could the Son of man give the liberty of the spirit to those who obeyed him.

37. *Ye are Abraham's seed.* But only nominally, else they would not have sought to kill Jesus.

41. *Fornication.* Sensual and idolatrous worship.

43. *Word.* Teaching.

46, 47. *Which of you convicteth me of sin?* Why can ye not believe the words of one whose life ye have found sinless?

48-50. *That thou art a Samaritan.* Meaning that Jesus, like the Samar-

itans, was an alien at heart and an unbeliever. *Hast a demon.* Unable to deny the miracles, the Jews attribute them to the agency of a demon. *Ye dishonor me.* By the malicious charge that he had a demon. *There is one,* etc. The Father, whose glory he sought, would judge those who had dishonored his Son.

51. *Keep my word.* Accept my teaching and live according to it. *Shall never see death.* This does not mean physical death; it is above and beyond that. It implies that the believer in Jesus Christ has eternal life now, a life which cannot be affected by the disintegration of the body.

never see death. 52 The Jews said unto him, Now we know that thou hast a demon. Abraham died, and the prophets; and thou sayest, If a man keep my word, he shall never taste of death. 53 Art thou greater than our father Abraham, who died? and the prophets died: whom makest thou thyself? 54 Je′sus answered, If I glorify myself, my glory is nothing: it is my Father that glorifieth me; of whom ye say, that he is your God; 55 and ye have not known him: but I know him; and if I should say, I know him not, I shall be like unto you, a liar: but I know him, and keep his word. 56 Your father Abraham rejoiced ᵐto see

my day; and he saw it, and was glad. 57 The Jews therefore said unto him, Thou art not yet fifty years old, and hast thou seen Abraham? 58 Je′sus said unto them, **Verily, verily, I say unto you, Before Abraham was born, I am.** 59 They took up stones therefore to cast at him: but Je′sus ⁿhid himself, and went out of the temple.ᵒ

9 And as he passed by, he saw a man blind from his birth. 2 And his disciples asked him, saying, Rab′bi, who sinned, this man, or his parents, that he should be born blind? 3 Je′sus answered, **Neither did this man sin, nor his parents: but that the works of God should be made**

---

m Or, *that he should see* n Or, *was hidden, and went &c.*, o Many ancient authorities add *and going through the midst of them went his way and so passed by.*

52. *Now we know*, etc. The Jews replied in effect: We are sure now that you are in league with Satan, for you have not only used the words 'life' and 'death' in a sense that we cannot understand, but you have dared to affirm that your teaching will keep us from ever seeing death at all. Worse than all, you have in this way presumed to assert that you have a power over death which was denied even to our father Abraham.

53. *Whom makest thou thyself?* A fierce challenge to declare himself in all the fullness of his power. The angry questioners could not longer endure the masterful and mysterious wisdom of Jesus. They wanted a positive, clear reply on the plane of their own comprehension.

54. *It is my Father that glorifieth me.* Before giving them the answer toward which the conversation was leading, our Lord further baffled them by ascribing all power of glorifying him to his Father, of Whom they said that He was their God. They dared not rebuke him for this.

56. *Abraham rejoiced to see my day.* Rejoiced on earth to know that the Messiah would come. And

he saw it, and was glad. He knew, in the world of spirit, that Jesus the Messiah had come.

57. *Fifty years old.* Not to be taken as an opinion of his questioners as to how old Jesus was; it was a conventional Jewish expression for the age of full manhood.

58. *Before Abraham was born, I am.* A sublime utterance that could proceed only from God Incarnate without transcending the human capacity for belief. 'I am' means absolute, independent being, beyond the limitations of space and time. Jesus here affirms that he exists from and throughout all eternity, is equal with God and is God.

59. *They took up stones.* They thought or pretended to think, that he was guilty of blasphemy, for which the penalty was stoning.

CHAPTER 9

2. *Who sinned, this man, or his parents.* etc. The disciples evidently shared the belief common among the Jews, that suffering and calamity were invariably proofs of sin. Jesus elsewhere rejected this belief (Lk. 13.2–5). In the opening part of ver. 3 he also rejects it.

manifest in him. 4 We must work the works of him that sent me, while it is day: the night cometh, when no man can work. 5 When I am in the world, I am the light of the world. 6 When he had thus spoken, he spat on the ground, and made clay of the spittle, *a* and anointed his eyes with the clay, 7 and said unto him, Go, wash in the pool of Si-lo'am (which is by interpretation, Sent). He went away therefore, and washed, and came seeing. 8 The neighbors therefore, and they that saw him aforetime, that he was a beggar, said, Is not this he that sat and begged? 9 Others said, It is he: others said, No, but he is like him. He said, I am *he*. 10 They said therefore unto him, How then were thine eyes opened? 11 He answered, The man that

is called Je'sus made clay, and anointed mine eyes, and said unto me, Go to Si-lo'am, and wash: so I went away and washed, and I received sight. 12 And they said unto him, Where is he? He saith, I know not.

13 They bring to the Phar'i-sees him that aforetime was blind. 14 Now it was the sabbath on the day when Je'sus made the clay, and opened his eyes. 15 Again therefore the Phar'i-sees also asked him how he received his sight. And he said unto them, He put clay upon mine eyes, and I washed, and I see. 16 Some therefore of the Phar'i-sees said, This man is not from God, because he keepeth not the sabbath. But others said, How can a man that is a sinner do such signs? And there was a division among them. 17 They

---

a Or, and with the clay thereof anointed   *his eyes*

5. *I am the light of the world.* Spoken here with reference to the opening of the eyes of the man born blind. The miracle is an object-lesson of the truth that Jesus is the Light of the World.

6. *When he had thus spoken*, etc. The means here described were to assist the man's faith. They were ordinary remedies in popular belief.

7. *Go, wash in the pool of Siloam.* To strengthen faith by a test in which the man's will took a more active part. Siloam is now known as Birket Silwan, southeast of the hill of Zion in Jerusalem. Its water supply is from the Fountain of the Virgin through a conduit underground. *Washed, and came seeing.* Apparently went among his own people. Evidently he did not recognize who his Divine Healer was, otherwise he would not have spoken of him as in ver. 11.

9. *He said, I am he.* The opening of his eyes, and the new joyful exercise of the power of sight made such a difference in his appearance

that some of his neighbors did not know him, until he assured them that it was he whom they had formerly known as blind.

13. *They.* The neighbors and friends. They brought the blind man to the Pharisees probably more from curiosity than any other motive. They wanted the wonder of the man's healing explained by those who were supposed to know.

16. *Because he keepeth not the sabbath.* At once the more narrow-minded among the Pharisees seized upon the manner of performing the miracle as an excuse for charging Jesus with breaking the law of the Sabbath. Our Lord had, in fact, authoritatively ignored the petty rule against applying on the Sabbath the popular remedy of saliva as a means of cure for the eyes. But there were those among them who were awed by the miracle, and who could not think of Jesus as a transgressor.

17. *He is a prophet.* The man to whom sight was given showed

say therefore unto the blind man again, What sayest thou of him, in that he opened thine eyes? And he said, He is a prophet. 18 The Jews therefore did not believe concerning him, that he had been blind, and had received his sight, until they called the parents of him that had received his sight, 19 and asked them, saying, Is this your son, who ye say was born blind? how then doth he now see? 20 His parents answered and said, We know that this is our son, and that he was born blind: 21 but how he now seeth, we know not; or who opened his eyes, we know not: ask him; he is of age; he shall speak for himself. 22 These things said his parents, because they feared the Jews: for the Jews had agreed already, that if any man should confess him *to be* Christ, he should be put out of the synagogue. 23 Therefore said his parents, He is of age; ask him. 24 So they called a second time the man that was blind, and said unto him, Give glory to God: we know that this man is a sinner. 25 He therefore answered, Whether he is a sinner, I know not: one thing I know, that, whereas I was blind, now I see. 26 They said therefore unto him, What did he to thee? how opened he thine eyes? 27 He answered them, I told you even now, and ye did not hear; wherefore would ye hear it again? would ye also become his disciples? 28 And they reviled him, and said, Thou art his disciple; but we are disciples of Mo'ses. 29 We know that God hath spoken unto Mo'ses: but as for this man, we know not whence he is. 30 The man answered and said unto them, Why, herein is the marvel, that ye know not whence he is, and *yet* he opened mine eyes. 31 We know that God heareth not sinners: but if any man be a worshipper of God, and do his

---

more courage and insight than any of the Pharisees. Besides, it was a challenge to them to hear Jesus called a prophet. To admit that would have nullified the charge against him of Sabbath-breaking, as a prophet was above the Sabbath law.

22. *Put out of the synagogue.* Excommunicated. At this time it was not customary to exclude an offender indefinitely, still less finally. Thirty days was the usual period, unless for a very serious offence.

24. *Give glory to God.* This command to the man was a cowardly evasion. The Pharisees could get no satisfactory evidence either from him or his parents by which to convict Jesus. Therefore they appealed to his feelings. *We know that this man is a sinner.* That is, they not only said they knew, but implied that they had the right to decide that Jesus was a sinner.

25. *Whereas I was blind, now I see.* This baffling reply rebuked the threats and anger of the Pharisees and put them back upon a consideration of the evidence.

27. *Ye did not hear.* The first indication given by the man that he saw through the deceit of the Pharisees and was willing to oppose them in behalf of Jesus.

28. *Thou art his disciple.* This was nothing but an expression of baffled rage by the Pharisees They attempted to cover their own defeat by denouncing the blind man.

29. *That God hath spoken unto Moses.* That is, that there is a dispensation and authority established by God through Moses, and by which we Jews still regulate our lives.

will, him he heareth. 32 Since the world began it was never heard that any one opened the eyes of a man born blind. 33 If this man were not from God, he could do nothing. 34 They answered and said unto him, Thou wast altogether born in sins, and dost thou teach us? And they cast him out.

35 Je′sus heard that they had cast him out; and finding him, he said, Dost thou believe on *b*the Son of God? 36 He answered and said, And who is he, Lord, that I may believe on him? 37 Je′sus said unto him, Thou hast both seen him, and he it is that speaketh with thee. 38 And he said, Lord, I believe. And he

*c*worshipped him. 39 And Je′sus said, For judgment came I into this world, that they that see not may see; and that they that see may become blind. 40 Those of the Phar′i-sees who were with him heard these things, and said unto him, Are we also blind? 41 Je′sus said unto them, If ye were blind, ye would have no sin: but now ye say, We see: your sin remaineth.

10 Verily, verily, I say unto you, He that entereth not by the door into the fold of the sheep, but climbeth up some other way, the same is a thief and a robber. 2 But he that entereth in by the door is *a*the shepherd of the sheep. 3 To him

b Many ancient authorities read *the Son of Man.* *c* The Greek word denotes an act of reverence, whether paid to a creature (as here) or to the Creator (see ch. 4. 20). *a* Or, *a shepherd*

35. *And finding him.* Jesus apparently sought the man after the Jews had cast him out of the synagogue. The sovereign compassion of the Divine Healer went much further than opening the physical eyes of the blind one, whose spiritual eyes also were opened to the light. *Dost thou believe on the Son of God?* It was in order to prepare the healed one to answer this question affirmatively that Jesus showed such tender solicitude.

38. *Lord, I believe.* This was the crowning result. Jesus sought to illumine a benighted soul through the gift of vision to sightless eyes of the flesh. It should not be forgotten that in working this great sign, in which our Lord is seen as the Light of the World, he gradually leads the man, by an ascending series of acts beginning with faith assisted by physical remedies and ending with faith assured by spiritual contact, to complete recognition of him as the Son of God.

39. *For judgment came I into this world.* Not the act of deciding, but to bring about that division and opposition among mankind which results from the acceptance of his

message by some and its rejection by others.

41. *If ye were blind, ye would have no sin.* Implying that their spiritual blindness is willful, and therefore punishable.

CHAPTER 10

1. *Verily, I say unto you.* This chapter continues the discourse to the Pharisees begun in ver. 39 of the preceding chapter. In it Jesus is represented as the Good Shepherd who offers up his life to save his sheep. The truth of self-sacrificing love set forth is enforced by the great sign of the raising of Lazarus from the dead, for which the Jews cause the arrest and crucifixion of our Lord. In these allegories of the fold and the Good Shepherd it is necessary to go beyond the literal meaning and discern the spiritual truths taught. *Entereth not by the door into the fold.* In the East sheep-folds are enclosures open to the sky. The surrounding wall has only one door, through which the flocks are driven into the fold at evening.

3. *The porter.* Who stands at the door on guard until the return of the

the porter openeth; and the sheep hear his voice: and he calleth his own sheep by name, and leadeth them out. 4 When he hath put forth all his own, he goeth before them, and the sheep follow him: for they know his voice. 5 And a stranger will they not follow, but will flee from him: for they know not the voice of strangers. 6 This *b*parable spake Je'sus unto them: but they understood not what things they were which he spake unto them.

7 Je'sus therefore said unto them again, Verily, verily, I say unto you, I am the door of the sheep. 8 All that came *c*before me are thieves and robbers: but the sheep did not hear them. 9 I am the door; by me if any man enter in, he shall be saved, and shall go in and go out, and shall find pasture. 10 The thief cometh not, but that he may steal, and kill, and destroy: I came that they may have life, and may *d*have *it* abundantly. 11 I am the good shepherd: the good shepherd layeth down his life for the sheep. 12 He that is a hireling, and not a shepherd, whose own the sheep are not, beholdeth the wolf coming, and leaveth the sheep, and fleeth, and the wolf snatcheth them, and scattereth *them*: 13 *he fleeth* because he is a hireling, and careth not for the sheep. 14 I am the good shepherd; and I know mine own, and mine own know me, 15 even as the Father knoweth me, and I know the Father; and I lay down my life for the sheep. 16 And other sheep I have, which are not of this fold: them also I must *e*bring, and they shall hear my voice; and *f*they shall become one flock, one shepherd. 17 Therefore doth the Father love me, because I lay down my life, that I may take it again. 18 No one *g*taketh it away from me, but I lay it down of myself. I have *h*power to lay it down, and I have *h*power to take it again. This commandment received I from my Father.

19 There arose a division

---

b Or, *proverb*   *c* Some ancient authorities omit *before me.*   *d* Or, *have abundance*   *e* Or, *lead*   *f* Or, *there shall be one flock*   *g* Some

ancient authorities read *took it away.*   *h* Or, *right*

---

shepherds. *By name.* A mark of complete supervision and tender care. The sheep are cared for as a flock, and each sheep in the flock is also known and watched by the shepherd.

4. *When he hath put forth all his own.* That is, when the shepherd has led all his own sheep forth from the fold. *He goeth before them.* In other words, a true shepherd is the leader of his flock. There is a lesson here for pastors, who are only truly such when they are spiritual guides.

7. *Jesus therefore said.* In order to explain the meaning of what was said in ver. 1–6. *I am the door of the sheep.* The source of authority and spiritual leadership of pastors.

8. *Thieves and robbers.* Alluding to the scribes and Pharisees, and to the false teachers who had misled the Jews since the time of the prophets.

11–18. These verses contain the allegory of the Good Shepherd. *Layeth down his life for the sheep.* A prophecy of his death. *Hireling.* Pastors for the sake of their own interests rather than those of their flocks. *The wolf.* Satan. *Other sheep.* Gentiles. *Lay down my life, that I may take it again.* The crucifixion and resurrection foretold. *Of myself.* Love for mankind from the Master of Life passing into voluntary death that they may share his life.

again among the Jews because of these words. 20 And many of them said, He hath a demon, and is mad; why hear ye him? 21 Others said, These are not the sayings of one possessed with a demon. Can a demon open the eyes of the blind?

22 ᶦAnd it was the feast of the dedication at Je-ru'sa-lem: 23 it was winter; and Je'sus was walking in the temple in Sol'o-mon's ᵏporch. 24 The Jews therefore came round about him, and said unto him, How long dost thou hold us in suspense? If thou art the Christ, tell us plainly. 25 Je'sus answered them, I told you, and ye believe not: the works that I do in my Father's name, these bear witness of me. 26 But ye believe not, because ye are not of my sheep. 27 My sheep hear my voice, and I know them, and they follow me: 28 and I give unto them eternal life; and they shall never perish, and no one

shall snatch them out of my hand. 29 ᶦMy Father, who hath given *them* unto me, is greater than all; and no one is able to snatch ᵐ*them* out of the Father's hand. 30 I and the Father are one. 31 The Jews took up stones again to stone him. 32 Je'sus answered them, Many good works have I showed you from the Father; for which of those works do ye stone me? 33 The Jews answered him, For a good work we stone thee not, but for blasphemy; and because that thou, being a man, makest thyself God. 34 Je'sus answered them, Is it not written in your law, ⁿI said, Ye are gods? 35 If he called them gods, unto whom the word of God came (and the scripture cannot be broken), 36 say ye of him, whom the Father ᵒsanctified and sent into the world, Thou blasphemest: because I said, I am *the* Son of God? 37 If I do not the works of my Father, believe me not.

---

i Some ancient authorities read *At that time was the feast.*   *k* Or, *portico*   *l* Some ancient authorities read *That which my*

Father hath given unto me.   *m* Or, aught *n* Ps. lxxxii. 6.   *o* Or, *consecrated*

---

22. *Feast of the dedication.* Held to celebrate the restoration of the true worship in the Temple (B. C. 164), after it had been desecrated by the Syrian King Antiochus Epiphanes. The feast took place two months after the Feast of Tabernacles when the blind man was healed.

23. *Solomon's porch.* A cloister on the east side of the Temple buildings.

24. *In suspense.* How long would he continue to baffle their eagerness to know from his own words just who and what he was?

25. *I told you.* He had told them that he was the Christ or Messiah in chs. 5.17–47; 7.14–39; and 10.1-18.

28. *No one shall snatch them out of my hand.* Only the voluntary

neglect or rejection of Christ can cause the weakening of his protection.

29. *Greater than all.* More powerful than any possible combination of enemies.

30. *I and the Father are one.* One in substance and spirit; one in willing and doing.

35. *If he called them gods*, etc. If the Scripture spoke of rulers as gods, because in the Old Testament time they were regarded as the representatives of God, what right had the unbelieving Jews of Christ's day to call him a blasphemer because he, whom the Father sanctified, called himself the Son of God?

37–39. *If I do not the works of my Father, believe me not.* Jesus permits them to judge him by his

242

38 But if I do them, though ye believe not me, believe the works: that ye may know and understand that the Father is in me, and I in the Father. 39 They sought again to take him: and he went forth out of their hand.

40 And he went away again beyond the Jordan into the place where John was at the first baptizing; and there he abode. 41 And many came unto him; and they said, John indeed did no sign: but all things whatsoever John spake of this man were true. 42 And many believed on him there.

11 Now a certain man was sick, Laz'a-rus of Beth'a-ny, of the village of Mary and her sister Martha. 2 And it was that Mary who anointed the Lord with ointment, and wiped his feet with her hair, whose brother Laz'a-rus was sick. 3 The sisters therefore sent unto him, saying, Lord, behold, he whom thou lovest is sick. 4 But when Je'sus heard it, he said, **This sickness is not unto death, but for the glory of God, that the Son of God may be glorified thereby.** 5 Now Je'sus loved Martha, and her sister, and Laz'-a-rus. 6 When therefore he heard that he was sick, he abode at that time two days in the place where he was. 7 Then after this he saith to the disciples, **Let us go into Ju-dæ'a again.** 8 The disciples say unto him, Rab'bi, the Jews were but now seeking to stone thee; and goest thou thither again? 9 Je'sus answered, **Are there not twelve hours in the day? If a man walk in the day, he stumbleth not, because he seeth the light of this world.** 10 But if a man walk

works, apart from the names and titles which he could rightfully claim as describing his person and mission.

40–42. These verses cover the ministry of Jesus in Peræa which lasted over three months, from the latter part of December until the middle of April. *Into the place.* Bethany or Bethabara beyond Jordan. Its location is uncertain. It is to be distinguished from Bethany near Jerusalem.

CHAPTER 11

1. *Lazarus.* (God is my help). *Bethany.* A small village at the foot of the Mount of Olives, and about two miles east of Jerusalem.

4. *But for the glory of God.* That God might be glorified by the resurrection of Lazarus.

6. *He abode at that time two days.* Our Lord purposely remained away from Bethany until the death of Lazarus in order that, by the great sign of raising his loved friend from the dead, he might be known and believed in as the resurrection and the life. He intended that the conditions under which the miracle was to be performed should produce a firm conviction of its reality. He saw that there must be no doubt as to the death of Lazarus. Therefore he did not attempt to bring him back to life until he had been pronounced dead four days (ver. 39). He saw that there must be credible witnesses of what he intended to do. His waiting allowed these witnesses to assemble. He longed that the multitude should believe (ver. 42).

9, 10. *Are there not twelve hours in the day?* The meaning of these verses apparently is, 'I must disregard all danger and continue my ministry during the remaining part of my allotted time. The twelve hours of my working day are not yet gone. The night, wherein a man stumbleth if he walk, is not yet come. While the light of day remains I must do my Father's will.'

243

in the night, he stumbleth, because the light is not in him. 11 These things spake he: and after this he saith unto them, **Our friend Laz′a-rus is fallen asleep; but I go, that I may awake him out of sleep.** 12 The disciples therefore said unto him, Lord, if he is fallen asleep, he will *a*recover. 13 Now Je′sus had spoken of his death: but they thought that he spake of taking rest in sleep. 14 Then Je′sus therefore said unto them plainly, **Laz′a-rus is dead. 15 And I am glad for your sakes that I was not there, to the intent ye may believe; nevertheless let us go unto him.** 16 Thomas therefore, who is called *b*Did′ymus, said unto his fellow-disciples, Let us also go, that we may die with him.

17 So when Je′sus came, he found that he had been in the tomb four days already. 18 Now Beth′a-ny was nigh unto Je-ru′sa-lem, about fifteen furlongs off;

19 and many of the Jews had come to Martha and Mary, to console them concerning their brother. 20 Martha therefore, when she heard that Je′sus was coming, went and met him: but Mary still sat in the house. 21 Martha therefore said unto Je′sus, Lord, if thou hadst been here, my brother had not died. 22 And even now I know that, whatsoever thou shalt ask of God, God will give thee. 23 Je′sus saith unto her, **Thy brother shall rise again.** 24 Martha saith unto him, I know that he shall rise again in the resurrection at the last day. 25 Je′sus said unto her, **I am the resurrection, and the life: he that believeth on me, though he die, yet shall he live; 26 and whosoever liveth and believeth on me shall never die. Believest thou this?** 27 She saith unto him, Yea, Lord: I have believed that thou art the Christ, the Son of God, *even* he that cometh into

---

a Gr. *be saved.*   *b* That is, *Twin.*

---

15. *Glad for your sakes.* Our Lord's great object in this miracle was to produce belief in himself as the Son of God who has the power of life. Here he implies that his absence from the death bed of Lazarus was intentional, that his disciples might believe. His absence also helped to strengthen the faith of the two sisters (ver. 22, 27, 32).

16. *That we may die with him.* They feared that he would be killed in Judæa.

17. *The tomb.* Which belonged to the family of Lazarus and indicated that they were in comfortable circumstances.

18. *Fifteen furlongs.* A little less than two miles.

19. *To console them.* Jewish mourning ceremonies were elaborate and numerously attended. At least ten persons were expected to take part in them. They were continued for about thirty days.

20. *Still sat.* The customary attitude of grief.

22. *Even now I know.* An evidence of the firmest faith.

25–27. *I am the resurrection, and the life.* For him who 'liveth and believeth' there is, in the spiritual sense, neither death nor resurrection. Our Lord himself declares that such an one 'shall never die' (ver. 26). He who has this faith has eternal life now with all the promise and power of its endless progress. Death and resurrection are no interruption of the life of the spirit. *Believest thou this?* The question asked of Martha is the test to which each one who has heard the truth must submit.

the world. 28 And when she had said this, she went away, and called Mary *c*her sister secretly, saying, The Teacher is here, and calleth thee. 29 And she, when she heard it, arose quickly, and went unto him. 30 (Now Je'sus was not yet come into the village, but was still in the place where Martha met him.) 31 The Jews then who were with her in the house, and were consoling her, when they saw Mary, that she rose up quickly and went out, followed her, supposing that she was going unto the tomb to *d*weep there. 32 Mary therefore, when she came where Je'sus was, and saw him, fell down at his feet, saying unto him, Lord, if thou hadst been here, my brother had not died. 33 When Je'sus therefore saw her *e*weeping, and the Jews *also* *e*weeping who came with her, he *f*groaned in the spirit, and *g*was troubled, 34 and said, **Where have ye laid him?** They say unto him, Lord, come and see. 35 Je'sus wept. 36 The Jews therefore said, Behold how he loved him! 37 But some of them said, Could not this man, who opened the eyes of him that was blind, have caused that this man also should not die? 38 Je'sus therefore again *h*groaning in himself cometh to the tomb. Now it was a cave, and a stone lay *i*against it. 39 Je'sus saith, **Take ye away the stone.** Martha, the sister of him that was dead, saith unto him, Lord, by this time *k*the body decayeth; for he hath been *dead* four days. 40 Je'sus saith unto her, **Said I not unto thee, that, if thou believedst, thou shouldest see the glory of God?** 41 So they took away the stone. And Je'sus

---

c Or, *her sister, saying secretly*   *d* Gr. *wail.*   *e* Gr. *wailing.*   *f* Or, *was moved with indignation in the spirit*   *g* Gr. *troubled*   *h* Or, *being moved with indignation in himself*   *i* Or, *upon*   *k* Gr. *he stinketh.*

---

31. *The Jews.* Some of them were hostile to Jesus. See ver. 37.

33. *He groaned in the spirit.* Not only with tender sympathy for the sisters, but with sorrowful anger at the power of evil to cause such misery.

35. *Jesus wept.* These precious words are both a consolation and an argument. They reveal the Saviour in his human sympathy with grief. The weeping of Jesus as he walked to the tomb of Lazarus is a pledge of his spiritual presence with sorrowing ones at the open grave of every believer since that memorable burial. Yet these human tears were shed by one who in a few moments was most signally to exercise the prerogative of God. The evangelist shows us the might of the Master of Life, of the Word who was with God and was God, wielded to restore life in order that sorrow might be turned into joy. He who knew the human nature of our Lord more intimately than any other disciple affirmed most strongly that Jesus Christ is God.

37. *Some of them.* Some were hostile; some probably only curious. Possibly some who wondered why Jesus allowed Lazarus to die also doubted whether he had really healed the man born blind.

38. *Now it was a cave.* There is shown at the present time in Bethany as the grave of Lazarus a deep cave, hewn out of rock, to which one may descend by twenty-six steps.

41. *Father, I thank thee that thou heardest me.* These words of Jesus fulfil the law of prayer declared by him elsewhere (Mk. 11.24, 25). He himself set the example of the perfect faith which he required of others. Even while he prayed he thanked the Father because he knew that he had been heard and that the

lifted up his eyes, and said, **Father, I thank thee that thou heardest me.** 42 **And I knew that thou hearest me always: but because of the multitude that standeth around I said it, that they may believe that thou didst send me.** 43 And when he had thus spoken, he cried with a loud voice, **Laz′a-rus, come forth.** 44 He that was dead came forth, bound hand and foot with *l*grave-clothes; and his face was bound about with a napkin. Je′sus saith unto them, **Loose him, and let him go.**

45 Many therefore of the Jews, who came to Mary and beheld *m*that which he did, believed on him. 46 But some of them went away to the Phar′i-sees, and told them the things which Je′sus had done.

47 The chief priests therefore and the Phar′i-sees gathered a council, and said, What do we? for this man doeth many signs. 48 If we let him thus alone, all men will believe on him: and the Romans will come and take away both our place and our nation. 49 But a certain one of them, Ca′ia-phas, being high priest that year, said unto them, Ye know nothing at all, 50 nor do ye take account that it is expedient for you that one man should die for the people, and that the whole nation perish not. 51 Now this he said not of him-

---

l Or, *grave-bands*   *m* Many ancient authorities read *the things which he did.*

---

power to raise Lazarus had been granted to him. See note on Mk. 11.24.

42. *I said it.* That is, gave thanks publicly because the Father had heard him.

44. *Loose him.* A command to untie the grave-clothes.

46. *Went away to the Pharisees, and told them.* Probably they did not go in a hostile mood, but rather to witness in favor of Jesus.

47. *The chief priests therefore and the Pharisees.* Apparently the Sadducees, of whom the chief priests were leaders, were more active than the Pharisees in persecuting Jesus when the critical hour arrived. As the monopolists of high office and submissive allies of the Romans, they were fearful lest any political movement in his favor should endanger their position. As compared with the Pharisees, they were indifferent as to his moral teaching. *This man doeth many signs.* A very significant statement. 'Signs' here means miracles. Even the selfish and hostile Sadducees and Pharisees, assembled in the Sanhedrin, are compelled to admit that Jesus performed miracles and that the popular effect of those miracles was

not only to endanger the confidence of the Romans in the leadership of the Jewish upper classes, but the national existence of the Jewish people.

50. *That one man should die for the people.* Caiaphas saw that the teaching and miracles of Jesus would so influence the people that they would accept him as Messiah. He knew also that our Lord did not countenance the Messianic hopes that were cherished by the scribes and Pharisees. If Jesus succeeded, it meant the extinction of those hopes and a continuance of Roman rule. It was strictly true, therefore, that his death was regarded by Caiaphas as politically 'expedient.' *That the whole nation perish not.* That is, that the nation may not have its hope of political freedom quenched forever.

51. *Being high priest that year, he prophesied,* etc. The evangelist here implies that Caiaphas by virtue of his office foretold the death of Jesus. This does not contradict the fact that the high priest's envenomed prejudice and aroused fears found satisfaction in the letter of his prophecy. In former times the prophetic gift, as one of the high-

self: but being high priest that year, he prophesied that Je'sus should die for the nation; 52 and not for the nation only, but that he might also gather together into one the children of God that are scattered abroad. 53 So from that day forth they took counsel that they might put him to death.

54 Je'sus therefore walked no more openly among the Jews, but departed thence into the country near to the wilderness, into a city called E'phra-im; and there he tarried with the disciples. 55 Now the passover of the Jews was at hand: and many went up to Je-ru'sa-lem out of the country before the passover, to purify themselves. 56 They sought therefore for Je'sus, and spake one with another, as they stood in the temple, What think ye? That he will not come to the feast? 57 Now the chief priests and the Phar'i-sees had given

commandment, that, if any man knew where he was, he should show it, that they might take him.

12 Je'sus therefore six days before the passover came to Beth'a-ny, where Laz'a-rus was, whom Je'sus raised ᶠrom the dead. 2 So they made him a supper there: and Martha served; but Laz'a-rus was one of them that ᵃsat at meat with him. 3 Mary therefore took a pound of ointment of ᵇpure nard, very precious, and anointed the feet of Je'sus, and wiped his feet with her hair: and the house was filled with the odor of the ointment. 4 But Ju'das Is-car'i-ot, one of his disciples, that should ᶜbetray him, saith, 5 Why was not this ointment sold for three hundred ᵈshillings, and given to the poor? 6 Now this he said, not because he cared for the poor; but because he was a thief, and having the ᵉbag ᶠtook away what was put

---

a Gr. reclined.   b Or. liquid nard   c Or. deliver him up   d See marginal note on ch.

6.7.   e Or. box   f Or. carried what was put therein

---

priestly functions, was actively exercised; but it had fallen into comparative disuse.

52. *That he might also gather into one*, etc. The meaning is, that this would be the result of the high priest's action and advice, though by no means so intended. Caiaphas is here spoken of as an unconscious instrument in the hand of God.

54. *Walked no more openly.* Because the Sanhedrin had ordered his arrest (ver. 57). *Ephraim.* The location is uncertain, but most probably it was between eight and twenty miles northeast of Jerusalem.

CHAPTER 12

1. *Six days before the passover.* On the eighth of Nisan, after sunset and on the beginning of the Sabbath.

The Jewish day was reckoned from sunset to sunset. *Bethany.* A village about two miles from Jerusalem, at the foot of the Mount of Olives. *Where Lazarus was.* Added emphasis as to the truth of the resurrection of Lazarus, which had already been related in detail by the evangelist (ch. 11.1-44).

2. *They made him a supper there.* It was at the house of Simon the leper (Mt. 26.6; Mk. 14.3).

3. *A pound.* Twelve ounces. *Nard.* A fragrant ointment made from a kind of bearded grass found in India.

5. *Three hundred shillings.* About fifty dollars of our money.

6. *The bag.* In which the money needed by the apostles was carried. Judas was the keeper or treasurer of this fund. One bag or cash-box for the whole company implies that no

therein. 7 Je'sus therefore said, *Suffer her to keep it against the day of my burying. 8 For the poor ye have always with you; but me ye have not always.

9 The common people therefore of the Jews learned that he was there: and they came, not for Je'sus' sake only, but that they might see Laz'a-rus also, whom he had raised from the dead. 10 But the chief priests took counsel that they might put Laz'a-rus also to death; 11 because that by reason of him many of the Jews went away, and believed on Je'sus.

12 On the morrow *a great multitude that had come to the feast, when they heard that Je'sus was coming to Je-ru'sa-lem, 13 took the branches of the palm trees, and went forth to meet him, and cried out, Ho-san'na: Blessed *is* he that cometh in the name of the Lord, even the King of Is'ra-el. 14 And Je'sus, having found a

young ass, sat thereon; as it is written, 15 *Fear not, daughter of Zi'on: behold, thy King cometh, sitting on an ass's colt. 16 These things understood not his disciples at the first: but when Je'sus was glorified, then remembered they that these things were written of him, and that they had done these things unto him. 17 The multitude therefore that was with him when he called Laz'a-rus out of the tomb, and raised him from the dead, bare witness. 18 For this cause also the multitude went and met him, for that they heard that he had done this sign. 19 The Phar'i-sees therefore said among themselves, *Behold how ye prevail nothing; lo, the world is gone after him.

20 Now there were certain Greeks among those that went up to worship at the feast: 21 these therefore came to Philip, who was of Beth-sa'i-da of Gal'i-lee, and asked him, saying, Sir,

---

g Or, *Let her alone:* it was *that she might keep it*   *h* Some ancient authorities read the common people. See ver. 9.   *i* Zech. ix. 9.   *k* Or, *Ye behold*

one member of it had exclusive ownership of any part of the money.

7. *Keep it against the day of my burying.* That is, keep what is left for the anointing of my body on my burial day, which is near.

10. *That they might put Lazarus also to death.* They feared the effect of the miracle on the great mass of people. Multitudes might acclaim Jesus both as political and religious leader. Also the chief priests, most of whom were Sadducees, were angered by the thought of Lazarus raised from the dead, because denial of the resurrection was with them an important doctrine.

11. *Went away, and believed on Jesus.* Renounced Judaism and accepted Jesus as their Saviour.

12–19. *On the morrow a great multitude,* etc. The evangelist's

account of the triumphal entry of Jesus into Jerusalem shows that inhabitants of the city as well as the great multitude of Galileans that had come to the feast, welcomed Jesus as the Messiah (ver. 17, 18). The 'morrow' of ver. 12 was what is now called Palm Sunday. *Palm trees.* Palm branches were commonly considered as symbols of triumph and rejoicing. See notes on Mt. 21.1, 2, 3, 5, 7–10; Mk. 11.1, 10, 11.

20. *Greeks.* Gentiles. They went up to worship at the feast, not because they were in full sympathy with the Jewish ritual, but by reason of their devout belief in one God. They were 'proselytes of the gate,' not received into full membership in the Jewish community, but willing to accept some of its rules.

we would see Je′sus. 22 Philip cometh and telleth Andrew: Andrew cometh, and Philip, and they tell Je′sus. 23 And Je′sus answereth them, saying, **The hour is come, that the Son of man should be glorified.** 24 **Verily, verily, I say unto you, Except a grain of wheat fall into the earth and die, it abideth by itself alone; but if it die, it beareth much fruit.** 25 **He that loveth his** ᶦ**life loseth it; and he that hateth his** ᶦ**life in this world shall keep it unto** ᵐ**life eternal.** 26 **If any man serve me, let him follow me; and where I am, there shall also my servant be: if any man serve me, him will the Father honor.** 27 **Now is my soul troubled; and what shall I say? Father, save me from this** ⁿ**hour. But for this cause came I unto this hour.** 28 **Father,**

glorify thy name. There came therefore a voice out of heaven, *saying,* I have both glorified it, and will glorify it again. 29 The multitude therefore, that stood by, and heard it, said that it had thundered: others said, An angel hath spoken to him. 30 Je′sus answered and said, **This voice hath not come for my sake, but for your sakes.** 31 **Now is** ᵒ**the judgment of this world: now shall the prince of this world be cast out.** 32 **And I, if I be lifted up** ᵖ**from the earth, will draw all men unto myself.** 33 But this he said, signifying by what manner of death he should die. 34 The multitude therefore answered him, We have heard out of the law that the Christ abideth for ever: and how sayest thou, The Son of man must be lifted up? who is this Son of man?

---

l m life in these places represents two different Greek words.   *n* Or, *hour?*

o Or, *a judgment*   *p* Or, *out of*

---

22. *Philip.* Both 'Philip' (lover of horses) and 'Andrew' (manly) were Greek names. Both apostles were from Bethsaida, on the shore of the Sea of Galilee.

23. *Should be glorified.* By his suffering and death.

24. *If it die, it beareth much fruit.* Jesus, teaching these Gentiles, likens his coming crucifixion and its results to a process of nature. As a grain of wheat can only impart its latent power of life and growth to the new plant by decaying and dying under the ground, so must the Son of man give up his human body to the operation of physical death, in order that his divine life and teaching may spring up into the bloom and fruitage of the Spirit for all mankind.

25. *He that loveth his life loseth it.* See notes on Mt. 10.39.

26. *Let him follow me.* Jesus plainly tells the enquiring Gentiles that they too may hope to gain the larger life only by losing the smaller.

The life of worldly satisfaction and advantage must give way to the life of self-sacrifice, which they can know by following him.

27. *Now is my soul troubled.* The despair and anguish of his human nature.

28. *Father, glorify thy name.* By the passion, death and resurrection of Jesus.

30. *For your sakes.* That they might believe that Jesus came from God.

31. *The judgment of this world.* The responsibility of accepting or rejecting Christ incurred by those who were soon to know of his death and resurrection. *The prince of this world.* Satan.

32. *And I, if I be lifted up from the earth,* etc. Sympathy and love for an unselfish life and unselfish suffering, together with the hope of eternal life springing up in mankind as the result of a divine example of power over death, find their central attraction, their abiding assurance, in the Cross of Christ.

35 Je'sus therefore said unto them, **Yet a little while is the light ^qamong you. Walk while ye have the light, that darkness overtake you not: and he that walketh in the darkness knoweth not whither he goeth. 36 While ye have the light, believe on the light, that ye may become sons of light.**

These things spake Je'sus, and he departed and ^rhid himself from them. 37 But though he had done so many signs before them, yet they believed not on him: 38 that the word of I-sa'iah the prophet might be fulfilled, which he spake,

> ^sLord, who hath believed our report?
> And to whom hath the arm of the Lord been revealed?

39 For this cause they could not believe, for that I-sa'iah said again,

40 'He hath blinded their eyes, and he hardened their heart;

> Lest they should see with their eyes, and perceive with their heart,
> And should turn,
> And I should heal them.

41 These things said I-sa'iah, because he saw his glory; and he spake of him. 42 Nevertheless even of the rulers many believed on him; but because of the Phar'i-sees they did not confess ^uit, lest they should be put out of the synagogue: 43 for they loved the glory *that is* of men more than the glory *that is* of God.

44 And Je'sus cried and said, **He that believeth on me, believeth not on me, but on him that sent me. 45 And he that beholdeth me beholdeth him that sent me. 46 I am come a light into the world, that whosoever believeth on me may not abide in the darkness. 47 And if any man hear my sayings, and keep them not, I judge him not: for I came not to judge the world, but to save the world. 48 He that rejecteth me, and receiveth not my sayings, hath one that judgeth him: the word that I spake, the same shall judge him in the last day. 49 For I spake not from myself; but the Father that sent me, he hath given me a commandment, what I should say, and what I should speak.**

---

q Or, *in*   *r* Or, *was hidden from them*   *s* Is. liii. 1.   *t* Is. vi. 10.   *u* Or, *him*

---

35. *Jesus therefore said,* etc. He does not give the questioners a direct reply; but he merges all needless controversy in the affirmation that he is the light, and that they must believe in it and walk in it while they have it. This was, in effect, telling him that he was the Messiah.

36. *Hid himself.* Most probably he went to Bethany.

41. *His glory.* The glory of Christ.

42. *Even of the rulers many believed.* Nicodemus and Joseph of Arimathæa are the only known ones. They did not openly profess their faith in Christ until after the crucifixion.

44–50. *And Jesus cried and said,* etc. The words of Jesus contained in these verses are not a continuation of his last public discourse (ver. 23–36), but are recorded here for the purpose of strengthening what the evangelist had written about our Lord's life and work in ver. 37–43. *Believeth not on me, but on him that sent me.* Christ in these words about his person and mission directly declares that he came from the Father Who sent him. *He that beholdeth me,* etc. 'He that hath

250

50 And I know that his commandment is life eternal; the things therefore which I speak, even as the Father hath said unto me, so I speak.

13 Now before the feast of the passover, Je'sus knowing that his hour was come that he should depart out of this world unto the Father, having loved his own that were in the world, he loved them *a*unto the end. 2 And during supper, the devil having already put into the heart of Ju'das Is-car'i-ot, Si'mon's *son*, to *b*betray him, 3 Je'sus, knowing that the Father had given all things into his hands, and that he came forth from God, and goeth unto God, 4 riseth from supper, and

layeth aside his garments; and he took a towel, and girded himself. 5 Then he poureth water into the basin, and began to wash the disciples' feet, and to wipe them with the towel wherewith he was girded. 6 So he cometh to Si'mon Peter. He saith unto him, Lord, dost thou wash my feet? 7 Je'sus answered and said unto him, **What I do thou knowest not now; but thou shalt understand hereafter.** 8 Peter saith unto him, Thou shalt never wash my feet. Je'sus answered him, **If I wash thee not, thou hast no part with me.** 9 Si'mon Peter saith unto him, Lord, not my feet only, but also my hands and my head. 10 Je'sus saith to him, **He that is**

---

a Or, *to the uttermost.*   *b* Or, *deliver*   *him up*

---

seen me hath seen the Father' (ch. 14.9). *The word that I spake.* And which the hearer had power to accept or reject. *His commandment is life eternal.* Because they who obey it become thereby partakers of His nature.

CHAPTER 13

1. *Before the feast of the passover.* This would indicate that the supper referred to in ver. 2 was not the Jewish Passover, but was a Christian feast, although Jewish forms may have been observed in part. See notes on Mt. 26.17, 26, 28.

2. *And during supper.* The Last Supper is meant, although the evangelist does not here describe its institution, because it was his purpose to supply the omissions of Matthew, Mark and Luke rather than to repeat what they had written.

4. *Ariseth from supper, and layeth aside his garments.* The minute details suggest that the evangelist was an eye-witness. According to Luke (22.24) there was a dispute among the disciples as to which was the greatest, and apparently (Lk. 22.27) no one of them was willing to begin

to serve at supper, for fear that it would be regarded as a confession of inferiority. Their Lord and Master therefore rose first, setting the example of humility and brotherly love.

5. *Began to wash the disciples' feet.* A still more striking example of the love which prompts to service.

7. *What I do thou knowest not now.* Peter erred presumptuously in implying that Jesus in washing the feet of a disciple, condescended too much. He was rebuked by being told that he did not then understand what was being done.

8. *If I wash thee not, thou hast no part with me.* Our Lord again rebuked Peter in words that suggested the possibility of a spiritual separation between them, unless the disciple obeyed the Master.

9. *Not my feet only, but also my hands and my head.* Once more Peter impulsively goes too far, though prompted by affection. Warned by the Lord's words, and remembering past sins, he mistakenly concludes that he is totally unclean.

10. *He that is bathed needeth not save to wash his feet.* 'Bathed' is taken to mean a nature spiritually clean or purified, yet which may be

bathed needeth not ^csave to wash his feet, but is clean every whit: and ye are clean, but not all. 11 For he knew him that should ^bbetray him; therefore said he, Ye are not all clean.

12 So when he had washed their feet, and taken his garments, and ^dsat down again, he said unto them, Know ye what I have done to you? 13 Ye call me, Teacher, and, Lord: and ye say well; for so I am. 14 If I then, the Lord and the Teacher, have washed your feet, ye also ought to wash one another's feet. 15 For I have given you an example, that ye also should do as I have done to you. 16 Verily, verily, I say unto you, A ^eservant is not greater than his lord; neither ^fone that is sent greater than he that sent him. 17 If ye know these things, blessed are ye if ye do them. 18 I speak not of you all: I know whom I ^ghave chosen: but that the scripture may be fulfilled,

^hHe that eateth ⁱmy bread lifted up his heel against me. 19 From henceforth I tell you before it come to pass, that, when it is come to pass, ye may believe that I am *he*. 20 Verily, verily, I say unto you, He that receiveth whomsoever I send receiveth me; and he that receiveth me receiveth him that sent me.

21 When Je′sus had thus said, he was troubled in the spirit, and testified, and said, Verily, verily, I say unto you, that one of you shall ^kbetray me. 22 The disciples looked one on another, doubting of whom he spake. 23 There was at the table reclining in Je′sus' bosom one of his disciples, whom Je′sus loved. 24 Si′mon Peter therefore beckoneth to him, and saith unto him, Tell *us* who it is of whom he speaketh. 25 He leaning back, as he was, on Je′sus' breast saith unto him, Lord, who is it? 26 Je′sus therefore answereth, He it is, for whom I shall dip the

---

b Or, *deliver him up* *c* Some ancient authorities omit *save*, and *his feet*. *d* Gr. *reclined*. *e* Gr. *bondservant*. *f* Gr. *an apostle*. *g* Or, *chose* *h* Ps. xli. 9. *i* Many ancient authorities read *his bread with me*. *k* Or, *deliver me up*

---

more or less tarnished afterward by occasional sins. Prayer, repentance and good works in behalf of these sins are here symbolized by the washing of the feet, representing the necessary cleansing of a part, after which the spiritual nature is wholly pure again.

16. *A servant is not greater than his lord*. A lesson in the humility of love to the disciples, whose Lord and Master, through love of them, became as their servant. See note on Lk. 12.37.

18. *I speak not of you all*. There was one, Judas Iscariot, who had no disposition to be worthy of the blessedness mentioned in ver. 17.

19. *From henceforth I tell you*. Jesus did not reveal the traitorous character of Judas until after every opportunity of repentance had been

rejected. While still sharing in the benefit of the washing of the disciples' feet, Judas harbored the intention and design of the betrayal.

21. *One of you shall betray me*. Our Lord now decides that the true nature of Judas shall be made known to the other apostles.

23. *One of his disciples, whom Jesus loved*. John, the son of Zebedee. The apostles reclined on couches, resting the head upon the left hand.

26. *The sop*. Or morsel. The offering of the dipped morsel to Judas was the last sign to him of Christ's good will and forgiving love; yet he remained fixed in his evil purpose. It is to be noted that our Lord did not reveal the wickedness of Judas to the outside world, but only to the apostles. According to the evan-

sop, and give it him. So when
he had dipped the sop, he taketh
and giveth it to Ju′das, *the son*
of Si′mon Is-car′i-ot. 27 And
after the sop, then entered Satan
into him. Je′sus therefore saith
unto him, **What thou doest, do
quickly.** 28 Now no man at the
table knew for what intent he
spake this unto him. 29 For
some thought, because Ju′das
had the *l*bag, that Je′sus said
unto him, Buy what things we
have need of for the feast; or,
that he should give something
to the poor. 30 He then having received the sop went out
straightway: and it was night.

31 When therefore he was gone
out, Je′sus saith, **Ncw** *m*is the

Son of man glorified, and God
*m*is glorified in him; 32 and God
shall glorify him in himself, and
straightway shall he glorify him.
33 Little children, yet a little while
I am with you. Ye shall seek
me: and as I said unto the Jews,
Whither I go, ye cannot come; so
now I say unto you. 34 A new
commandment I give unto you,
that ye love one another; *n*even
as I have loved you, that ye also
love one another. 35 By this shall
all men know that ye are my disciples, if ye have love one to another.

36 Si′mon Peter saith unto
him, Lord, whither goest thou?
Je′sus answered, **Whither I go,
thou canst not follow me now;
but thou shalt follow afterwards.**

---

l Or, *box*   *m* Or, *was*   *n* Or, *even as I*   *loved you, that ye also may love one another*

gelist, even to the apostles the fact
was made known only privately.

30. *It was night.* His time of active treason was in the darkness, as
his secret thoughts had been.

31. *Jesus saith.* Here begin the
last discourses of Jesus to his disciples. They end with the last verse
of the seventeenth chapter. In
them are recorded his deeper
thoughts, uttered in part in the upper room after the institution of the
Last Supper. Judas had left them,
so that the bond of love and confidence between them and the Master
was now entire. *Now is the Son of
man glorified.* Or, about to be glorified, by his death, which had been
plotted and was very near.

32. *God shall glorify him.* By his
resurrection and ascension. *In himself.* See ch. 17.5.

33. *Little children.* An expression
of endearment found nowhere else
in the evangelists. The disciples
were soon to be parted from the
earthly presence of their Lord. *As I
said unto the Jews,* etc. See note on
ch. 7.34. There is an important difference between what he said to the
Jews and what he said to the disciples. The Jews would seek him
and not be able to find him; not so

the disciples. They would find him
abundantly in doing his will, and although they could not come immediately where he was about to go, they
could come hereafter, for he went to
prepare a place for them (ch. 14.2).

34. *That ye love one another.* This
was not literally a new commandment, because the Mosaic law had
said, 'thou shalt love thy neighbor
as thyself' (Lev. 19.18). But it was
new in the sense that Jesus Christ
himself had won the right to send
it forth to all the world under the
sanction of his own example. The
reason for 'love one another' is
'even as I have loved you.'

35. *By this shall all men know.*
Our Lord here tells his disciples in
effect that the unfailing sign of his
followers, the unfailing sign of Christians at any time and everywhere,
shall be their love one to another.
Whatever value there is in creeds,
confessions, formularies, rituals, or
in any other external note of the
churchly growth and order is due to
the spiritual bond of love declared by
Christ to be the heart of his teaching.

36. *Thou shalt follow afterwards.*
Referring probably to Peter's martyrdom by crucifixion. See ch.
21.18, 19.

37 Peter saith unto him, Lord, why cannot I follow thee even now? I will lay down my life for thee. 38 Je'sus answereth, Wilt thou lay down thy life for me? Verily, verily, I say unto thee, The cock shall not crow, till thou hast denied me thrice.

14 Let not your heart be troubled: ^abelieve in God, believe also in me. 2 In my Father's house are many ^bmansions; if it were not so, I would have told you; for I go to prepare a place for you. 3 And if I go and prepare a place for you, I come again, and will receive you unto myself; that where I am, *there* ye may be also. 4 ^cAnd whither I go, ye know the way. 5 Thomas saith unto him, Lord, we know not whither thou goest; how know we the way? 6 Je'sus saith unto him, I am the way, and the truth, and the life: no one cometh unto the Father, but ^dby me. 7 If ye had known me, ye would have known my Father also: from henceforth ye know him, and have seen him. 8 Philip saith unto him, Lord, show us the Father, and it sufficeth us. 9 Je'sus saith unto him, Have I been so long time with you, and dost thou not know me, Philip? he that hath seen me hath seen the Father; how sayest thou, Show us the Father? 10 Believest thou not that I am in the Father, and the Father in me? the words that I say unto you I speak not from myself: but the Father abiding in me doeth his works. 11 Believe me that I am in the Father, and the Father in me: or else believe me for the very works' sake. 12 Verily, verily, I say unto you, He that believeth on me, the works that I do shall

---

a Or, *ye believe in God*   *b* Or, *abiding-places*   *c* Many ancient authorities read *And whither I go ye know, and the way ye know.*   *d* Or, *through*

38. *The cock shall not crow, till thou hast denied me thrice.* See Mt. 26. 33–35; Mk. 14.29–31; Lk. 22.31–34.

CHAPTER 14

1. *Let not your heart be troubled.* They were in doubt and despair over the betrayal and Christ's own prediction of his death.

2. *My Father's house.* Heaven. *Many mansions.* Implying more than abundance of opportunity and scope for activity and joy in heaven among the faithful.

4. *Ye know the way.* Belief in and obedience to Christ. It was more important for them to know the way by which they were to follow him than to question him about the place.

6. *No one cometh unto the Father, but by me.* Nevertheless all they who would have been willing to accept Christ in the flesh, if they had known him, may be said to have come to the Father, through His Son. See Rom. 2.14–16.

7. *Have seen him.* That is, have seen the Father's nature as revealed in Jesus Christ (ch. 6.46; ver. 9).

8. *Show us the Father, and it sufficeth us.* Philip aspired in good faith to know if it were possible to see the Father with the eyes of the flesh. He probably wanted a distinct vision of the Father resembling the vision of Christ vouchsafed to Peter, James and John in the Transfiguration. He was not satisfied with seeing the revelation of the Father's nature in Jesus Christ; but our Lord tells him in effect that he must be content with that revelation only. See ver. 9-11.

12. *Greater works than these shall he do, because,* etc. That is, the work of his disciples would be more important after he had gone to the Father than it could be while he remained in the flesh. The apostles would proclaim the message and win

he do also; and greater *works* than these shall he do; because I go unto the Father. 13 And whatsoever ye shall ask in my name, that will I do, that the Father may be glorified in the Son. 14 If ye shall ask *e*anything in my name, that will I do. 15 If ye love me, ye will keep my commandments. 16 And I will *f*pray the Father, and he shall give you another *g*Comforter, that he may be with you for ever, 17 *even* the Spirit of truth: whom the world cannot receive; for it beholdeth him not, neither knoweth him: ye know him; for he abideth with you, and shall be in you. 18 I will not leave you *h*desolate: I come unto you. 19 Yet a little while, and the world beholdeth me no more;

but ye behold me: because I live, *i*ye shall live also. 20 In that day ye shall know that I am in my Father, and ye in me, and I in you. 21 He that hath my commandments, and keepeth them, he it is that loveth me: and he that loveth me shall be loved of my Father, and I will love him, and will manifest myself unto him. 22 Ju'das (not Is-car'i-ot) saith unto him, Lord, what is come to pass that thou wilt manifest thyself unto us, and not unto the world? 23 Je'sus answered and said unto him, If a man love me, he will keep my word: and my Father will love him, and we will come unto him, and make our abode with him. 24 He that loveth me not keepeth not my words: and

---

e Many ancient authorities add *me-*
f Gr. *make request of.*   *g* Or, *Advocate* Or,

Helper Gr. *Paraclete.*   *h* Or. *orphans*
i Or, *and ye shall live.*

---

disciples not only in Palestine but in the Roman Empire, and future believers would spread his truth throughout the world. They would do this because the inspiration of the Holy Spirit, as Comforter, which he would send them, would be more powerful in their behalf than his own presence with them on earth.

13. *In my name.* A command to approach the Father in prayer only in the name of His Son, Jesus Christ.

14. *Anything in my name, that will I do.* There are certain qualifications righteously required of those who pray. They must have faith (Mt. 21.22); they must forgive the trespasses of others (Mt. 6.14); and they must obey the commandments of God (1. Jn. 3.22). 'That will I do' means that Christ himself will grant the petition made to the Father in his name. Prayer can be made to the Father in the name of Christ; and also directly to Christ himself. See Acts 7.59; 9.14, 21; 1. Cor. 1.2.

16. *Another Comforter.* The Holy Spirit.

17. *The Spirit of truth.* The Spirit

that reveals, commands and sanctions truth in the individual conscience, in the individual intellect, in the family and in all other social relations.

18. *I come unto you.* In the gift of the Holy Spirit.

20. *In that day.* At Pentecost and after.

22. *Judas (not Iscariot).* Also called Tháddæus or Lebbæus, and to be distinguished from Jude, the half-brother of our Lord. *Unto us, and not unto the world.* The question could only have been asked on the supposition that Jesus was to manifest himself as a worldly, political Messiah. Judas wanted to know why our Lord intended to restrict that manifestation to the eleven, instead of making it to the world. It was the old Jewish way of looking at the question.

23, 24. *If a man love me, he will keep my word.* Our Lord in his reply to Judas ignores the whole question of an earthly Messiah, and instructs him as to manifestations only on the spiritual plane. He speaks of men keeping his word through love of

255

the word which ye hear is not mine, but the Father's who sent me.

25 These things have I spoken unto you, while *yet* abiding with you. 26 But the *k*Comforter, *even* the Holy Spirit, whom the Father will send in my name, he shall teach you all things, and bring to your remembrance all that I said unto you. 27 Peace I leave with you; my peace I give unto you: not as the world giveth, give I unto you. Let not your heart be troubled, neither let it be fearful. 28 Ye heard how I said to you, I go away, and I come unto you. If ye loved me, ye would have rejoiced, because I go unto the Father: for the Father is greater than I. 29 And now I have told you before it come to pass, that, when it is come to pass, ye may believe. 30 I will no more speak much with you, for the prince of the world cometh: and he hath nothing *l*in me; 31 but that the world may know that I love the Father, and as the Father gave me commandment, even so I do. Arise, let us go hence.

15 I am the true vine, and my Father is the husband-

---

k Or, *Advocate*   Or, *Helper*   Gr. *Paraclete.*

l Or, *in me.* 31 *But that &c. . . . I do. arise &c.*

him, and tells of the Father's love and of His coming with Jesus to take up their joint abode in the believer's heart. Thus Philip's wrong desire for an unnecessary vision of God, and the wrong notion of Judas about Christ's manifestation, were both corrected.

26. *Will send in my name.* As the representative of Jesus Christ, fully empowered to carry on his work. *Teach you all things.* Even truths which Jesus did not teach them because they could not then bear them (ch. 16.12). But the Holy Spirit as the representative of the ascended Christ would illumine throughout all time the minds and hearts of believers in meeting new perplexities and emergencies. *Bring to your remembrance.* That is, bring out more clearly in the minds of the apostles and disciples the meaning of what Jesus had told them. Many scholars have noticed how aptly this truth is illustrated in the narrative of this evangelist.

27. *My peace.* The peace of God through Christ; the power to make peace for and within one's self, as well as the disposition to promote peace between others. See note on Mt. 5.9. *Not as the world giveth.* That is, not selfishly, expecting a return; but as the Father who sendeth His rain upon the just and the unjust. See note on Mt. 5.48.

28. *Rejoiced, because I go unto the Father.* If they had loved him more understandingly and obediently they would have rejoiced at his going unto the Father, to be exalted at His right hand with the glory which he had with Him before the world was (ch. 17.5). Only then could he send the Holy Spirit, the Comforter, and thus endow his followers with greater power than before to carry on his work. *The Father is greater than I.* Greater than His son, Jesus Christ, during the latter's time on earth in 'the humiliation of the flesh.'

30. *The prince of the world.* Satan. *Hath nothing in me.* No power over me. Jesus implies his own sinlessness.

31. *Arise, let us go hence.* Some scholars think that the words of the three following chapters were spoken after Jesus and the eleven had arisen from the table in the upper room where the Last Supper took place; others, while our Lord was walking with the eleven toward the Mount of Olives. The latter is the more probable view.

CHAPTER 15

1. *I am the true vine.* The ideal, perfect vine, symbol of the spiritual life which Christ imparts to believers, who are the branches. During the Last Supper he spoke of the

man. 2 Every branch in me that beareth not fruit, he taketh it away: and every *branch* that beareth fruit, he cleanseth it, that it may bear more fruit. 3 Already ye are clean because of the word which I have spoken unto you. 4 Abide in me, and I in you. As the branch cannot bear fruit of itself, except it abide in the vine; so neither can ye, except ye abide in me. 5 I am the vine, ye are the branches: He that abideth in me, and I in him, the same beareth much fruit: for apart from me ye can do nothing. 6 If a man abide not in me, he is cast forth as a branch, and is withered; and they gather them, and cast them into the fire, and they are burned. 7 If ye abide in me, and my words abide in you, ask whatsoever ye will, and it shall be done unto you. 8 Herein [a]is my Father glorified, [b]that ye bear much fruit; and *so* shall ye be my disciples. 9 Even as the Father hath loved me, I also have loved you: abide ye in my love. 10 If ye keep my commandments, ye shall abide in my love; even as I have kept my Father's commandments, and abide in his love. 11 These things have I spoken unto you, that my joy may be in you, and *that* your joy may be made full. 12 This is my commandment, that ye love one another, even as I have loved you. 13 Greater love hath no man than this, that a man lay down his life for his friends. 14 Ye are my friends, if ye do the things which I command you. 15 No longer do I call you [c]servants; for the [d]servant knoweth not what his lord doeth: but I have called you friends; for all things that I heard from my Father I have made known unto you. 16 Ye did not choose me, but I chose you, and appointed you, that ye

a Or, *was*   *b* Many ancient authorities read *that ye bear much fruit, and be my disciples.*   *c* Gr. *bondservants.*   *d* Gr. *bondservant.*

'fruit of the vine' (Mt. 26.29), and this most probably suggested the allegory of the true vine which illustrates the union of believers with Christ. The Last Supper was instituted to instil this truth in the hearts of all Christians. *My Father is the husbandman.* In these words the husbandman, the Father, not only cares for the vine but owns the vineyard.

2. *Every branch.* Every person. *He cleanseth it.* They who would remain steadfast must submit to the discipline of effort and suffering necessary to their perfecting in the faith.

3. *The word.* The teaching.

4. *Except ye abide in me.* Implying that every branch of the vine, each individual believer, has the power either to remain a partaker of Christ's life or to reject it.

6. *They gather them,* etc. Those who were once fruitful believers but afterward became spiritually dead are cast forth, like dead branches, as useless into the place of destruction.

11. *That your joy may be made full.* That their joy in him might be made as full as his joy in the Father.

12. *That ye love one another.* See note on ch. 13.34.

15. *No longer do I call you servants.* See notes on Lk. 12.37-40. *All things that I heard from my Father,* etc. That is, all things that were then necessary for them to know. He had already promised to send the Holy Spirit for their future instruction and guidance (ch. 14.26). And before his last discourses to them were ended he reminds them that they were not able to bear certain things (ch. 16.12).

16. *That your fruit should abide.* The results of the apostles' work are

257

should go and bear fruit, and *that* your fruit should abide: that whatsoever ye shall ask of the Father in my name, he may give it you. 17 These things I command you, that ye may love one another. 18 If the world hateth you, *e*ye know that it hath hated me before *it hated* you. 19 If ye were of the world, the world would love its own: but because ye are not of the world, but I chose you out of the world, therefore the world hateth you. 20 Remember the word that I said unto you, A *f*servant is not greater than his lord. If they persecuted me, they will also persecute you; if they kept my word, they will keep yours also. 21 But all these things will they do unto you for my name's sake, because they know not him that sent me. 22 If I had not come and spoken unto them, they had not had sin: but now they have no excuse for their sin. 23 He that hateth me hateth my Father also. 24 If I had not

done among them the works which none other did, they had not had sin: but now have they both seen and hated both me and my Father. 25 But *this cometh to pass*, that the word may be fulfilled that is written in their law. *g*They hated me without a cause. 26 But when the *h*Comforter is come, whom I will send unto you from the Father, *even* the Spirit of truth, which *i*proceedeth from the Father, he shall bear witness of me: 27 *k*and ye also bear witness, because ye have been with me from the beginning.

16 These things have I spoken unto you, that ye should not be caused to stumble. 2 They shall put you out of the synagogues: yea, the hour cometh, that whosoever killeth you shall think that he offereth service unto God. 3 And these things will they do, because they have not known the Father, nor me. 4 But these things have I spoken unto you, that when

---

e Or, *know ye   f* Gr. *bondservant.   g* Ps. xxxv. 19; lxix. 4.   *h* Or, *Advocate* Or,

Helper Gr. *Paraclete.   i* Or, *goeth forth from   k* Or, *and bear ye also witness*

---

embodied in the Christian Church, whose aggressive vitality is still unimpaired. *In my name*. See notes on ch. 14.13, 14.

18–21. *Ye know that it hath hated me*. Jesus, after enlightening his apostles as to the nature of their union with him, contrasts with it the hatred of the world for him and them. He comforts them by showing how he has experienced this hatred, thus enabling them to be their guide in overcoming it. Moreover, the world's hatred brought them closer to him. They were his not only by reason of his love for them, but because the world, in its alienation from the truth, drove them to him as their refuge.

22. *Now they have no excuse*. Be-

cause they sinned against the light of his word and works.

25. *Their law*. The Old Testament Scriptures.

26. *The Spirit of truth*. The Holy Spirit as revealer of the truth in word and deed. See note on ch. 14.17.

27. *Ye also*. The apostles.

CHAPTER 16

1. *These things*. Christ's teaching.

2. *Put you out*. Excommunicate you.

3. *Have not known the Father*. Did not know that He must be worshipped in spirit and truth. They were in bondage to the forms and ceremonies of the Mosaic law.

4. *Their hour*. The hour in which

their hour is come, ye may remember them, how that I told you. And these things I said not unto you from the beginning, because I was with you. 5 But now I go unto him that sent me; and none of you asketh me, Whither goest thou? 6 But because I have spoken these things unto you, sorrow hath filled your heart. 7 Nevertheless I tell you the truth: It is expedient for you that I go away; for if I go not away, the *Comforter will not come unto you; but if I go, I will send him unto you. 8 And he, when he is come, will convict the world in respect of sin, and of righteousness, and of judgment: 9 of sin, because they believe not on me; 10 of righteousness, because I go to the Father, and ye behold me no more; 11 of judgment, because the prince of this world hath been judged. 12 I have yet many things to say unto you,

but ye cannot bear them now. 13 Howbeit when he, the Spirit of truth, is come, he shall guide you into all the truth: for he shall not speak from himself; but what things soever he shall hear, *these* shall he speak: and he shall declare unto you the things that are to come. 14 He shall glorify me: for he shall take of mine, and shall declare *it* unto you. 15 All things whatsoever the Father hath are mine: therefore said I, that he taketh of mine, and shall declare *it* unto you. 16 A little while, and ye behold me no more; and again a little while, and ye shall see me. 17 *Some* of his disciples therefore said one to another, What is this that he saith unto us, A little while, and ye behold me not; and again a little while, and ye shall see me: and, Because I go to the Father? 18 They said therefore, What is this that he saith, A little while?

---

a Or, *Advocate*   Or, *Helper*   Gr. *Para-* | clete.

the enemies of Jesus apparently triumphed and when his sayings would comfort the persecuted apostles and disciples. *Because I was with you.* While he was with them he protected them; these warnings were given that they might prepare for the time when his bodily presence would be withdrawn.

5. *None of you asketh me,* etc. In their sorrow for the Master's approaching death and in fear of their own future, the apostles forgot about the glory of Christ's return to the Father.

7–15. *Expedient for you that I go away.* So that the Comforter could come in Christ's name and continue his work in larger measure than before. *In respect of sin.* Showing man's sinful nature and the need of the Holy Spirit to purify it. *Of righteousness.* Showing the world that in rejecting Christ it also re-

jected the righteous one sent by the Father. *Of judgment.* Judging the world, more particularly the Jewish world, by the bad results of its formalism and lack of spiritual worship. *Spirit of truth.* See notes on ch. 15.26. *Things that are to come.* Things that must be known and done in order that the work of Christ may be continued and perfected in the world. *For he shall take of mine.* The Holy Spirit sent by Christ and representing him. *Whatsoever the Father hath are mine.* Christ sent by the Father and exercising all the Father's power. Thus the Holy Spirit's influence comes from the Father through Christ.

16. *Ye behold me no more.* Alluding to the withdrawal of his bodily presence. *A little while, and ye shall see me.* Recognize his spiritual presence at Pentecost and after. See notes on Acts 2.1–4.

We know not what he saith. 19 Je'sus perceived that they were desirous to ask him, and he said unto them, Do ye inquire among yourselves concerning this, that I said, A little while, and ye behold me not, and again a little while, and ye shall see me? 20 Verily, verily, I say unto you, that ye shall weep and lament, but the world shall rejoice: ye shall be sorrowful, but your sorrow shall be turned into joy. 21 A woman when she is in travail hath sorrow, because her hour is come: but when she is delivered of the child, she remembereth no more the anguish, for the joy that a man is born into the world. 22 And ye therefore now have sorrow: but I will see you again, and your heart shall rejoice, and your joy no one taketh away from you. 23 And in that day ye shall [b]ask me no question. Verily, verily, I say unto you, If ye shall ask anything of the Father, he will give it you in my name. 24 Hitherto have ye asked nothing in my name: ask, and ye shall receive, that your joy may be made full.

25 These things have I spoken unto you in [c]dark sayings: the hour cometh, when I shall no more speak unto you in [c]dark sayings, but shall tell you plainly of the Father. 26 In that day ye shall ask in my name: and I say not unto you, that I will [d]pray the Father for you; 27 for the Father himself loveth you, because ye have loved me, and have believed that I came forth from the Father. 28 I came out from the Father, and am come into the world: again, I leave the world, and go unto the Father 29 His disciples say, Lo, now speakest thou plainly, and speakest no [e]dark saying. 30 Now know we that thou knowest all things, and needest not that any man should ask thee: by this we believe that thou camest forth from God. 31 Je'sus answered them, Do ye now believe? 32 Behold, the hour cometh, yea, is

---

b Or, ask me nothing   Comp. ver. 26; ch. 14.13, 20.

c Or, parables
e Or, parable

d Gr. make request of.

---

20.   The world shall rejoice. The exultation of his enemies who thought that his influence died with him on the cross.

22.   Ye therefore now have sorrow. It was necessary for them to grieve over his departure before they could have the joy which he promised them.   I will see you again. At his resurrection and various times during the forty days afterwards. Also the coming of the Holy Spirit was his return to them in greater power than before.

23.   In that day. At Pentecost and after.   Ye shall ask me no question. That is, all doubt shall then be cleared away. Ye shall then understand the things which perplex you now.

24.   Hitherto have ye asked nothing in my name. Before they prayed to the Father in his name it was necessary for him to be glorified by his death, resurrection and ascension.

25.   These things. His teaching.

26.   In that day. Pentecost and after.

27.   For the Father himself loveth you. Therefore they could approach the Father directly in his name.

30.   Thou knowest all things. He had divined their thoughts and dispelled their doubts.   By this we believe. Because of his infallible spiritual insight, proving that he came forth from the Father.

32.   Shall leave me alone. See Mt. 26.31; Mk. 14.27.   And yet I am not alone. The teaching and miracles

260

come, that ye shall be scattered, every man to his own, and shall leave me alone: and *yet* I am not alone, because the Father is with me. 33 These things have I spoken unto you, that in me ye may have peace. In the world ye have tribulation: but be of good cheer; I have overcome the world.

17 These things spake Je'-sus; and lifting up his eyes to heaven, he said, Father, the hour is come; glorify thy Son, that the Son may glorify thee: 2 even as thou gavest him authority over all flesh, that *a*to all whom thou hast given him, he should give eternal life. 3 And this is life eternal, that they should know thee the only true God, and him whom thou didst send, *even* Je'sus Christ. 4 I glorified thee on the earth, hav-

ing accomplished the work which thou hast given me to do. 5 And now, Father, glorify thou me with thine own self with the glory which I had with thee before the world was. 6 I manifested thy name unto the men whom thou gavest me out of the world: thine they were, and thou gavest them to me; and they have kept thy word. 7 Now they know that all things whatsoever thou hast given me are from thee: 8 for the words which thou gavest me I have given unto them; and they received *them*, and knew of a truth that I came forth from thee, and they believed that thou didst send me. 9 I *b*pray for them: I *b*pray not for the world, but for those whom thou hast given me; for they are thine: 10 and all things that are mine are

---

a Gr. *whatsoever thou hast given him, to*   *them he &c.*   *b* Gr. *make request.*

of Christ presupposed the presence of the Father. His consciousness of that presence was never interrupted except during the brief, dreadful interval on the cross. See note on Mt. 27.46.

33. *I have overcome the world.* A victory won in order that disciples and believers might follow him in a like victory over temptation and sin.

CHAPTER 17

1. *Lifting up his eyes to heaven, he said.* The words of Jesus in this chapter have often been called his high-priestly prayer. In it he assumes the high-priestly office and function, but in a unique sense, offering himself as a sacrifice for the sins of the world. *Glorify thy Son, that the Son may glorify thee.* He prays that the Father may glorify him by accepting the offering of his life and may raise him from the dead in order that, risen and ascended, he may show forth the glory of the

Father by the regeneration of mankind.

3. *This is life eternal.* The knowledge of God and Jesus Christ which is here declared to be eternal life is that which becomes the inspiration and spiritual guide of the believer's life.

4. *I glorified thee on the earth.* By an obedience that was perfect.

5. *Which I had with thee before the world was.* Implying the deity of Jesus. Ver. 1–5 contain the prayer of Jesus for himself.

6. *Manifested thy name.* Jesus Christ was God 'manifested in the flesh' (1 Tim. 3.16). *The men.* The apostles. *Kept thy word.* Thy commands expressed in my teaching.

9. *I pray for them.* Ver. 6–19 contain Christ's prayer for his apostles. *Not for the world.* His prayer for the world is in ver. 20–26.

10. *All things that are mine are thine,* etc. The words of this verse are an unqualified affirmation of the equality of Jesus Christ with God.

261

thine, and thine are mine: and I am glorified in them. 11 And I am no more in the world, and these are in the world, and I come to thee. Holy Father, keep them in thy name which thou hast given me, that they may be one, even as we *are*. 12 While I was with them, I kept them in thy name which thou hast given me: and I guarded them, and not one of them perished, but the son of perdition; *c*that the scripture might be fulfilled. 13 But now I come to thee; and these things I speak in the world, that they may have my joy made full in themselves. 14 I have given them thy word, and the world hated them, because they are not of the world, even as I am not of the world. 15 I *d*pray not that thou shouldest take them *e*from the world,

but that thou shouldest keep them *e*from *f*the evil *one*. 16 They are not of the world, even as I am not of the world. 17 *g*Sanctify them in the truth: thy word is truth. 18 As thou didst send me into the world, even so sent I them into the world. 19 And for their sakes I *g*sanctify myself, that they themselves also may be sanctified in truth. 20 Neither for these only do I *d*pray, but for them also that believe on me through their word; 21 that they may all be one; even as thou, Father, *art* in me, and I in thee, that they also may be in us: that the world may believe that thou didst send me. 22 And the glory which thou hast given me I have given unto them; that they may be one, even as we *are* one; 23 I in them, and thou in me, that they may be perfected

---

c Ps. xii. 9?   *d* Gr. *make request.*   *e* Gr.   *f* Or, *evil*   *g* Or, *Consecrate*

---

11. *In thy name.* By thy power keep them in love and obedience.

12. *The son of perdition.* Judas Iscariot. 'Iscariot' means a man of Kerioth, a town of Judæa.

13. *That they may have my joy.* That they, by my teaching and example, may fully partake with me in the joy I have in Thee.

14. *I have given them thy word.* I have manifested Thy nature unto them in my life and work.

15. *Not that thou shouldest take them from the world.* It was necessary for the apostles to remain and carry on the work; but therein were their discipline and spiritual strengthening. *Keep them from the evil one.* That they might effectually do what was commanded them. Temptations were to be avoided, but when met with, overcome; persecution was to be endured without weakening their faith.

16. *They are not of the world.* As believers in him they shared the world's hatred of him.

17. *Sanctify them in the truth.*

out of.   Consecrate them to the truth, to the work of preaching the gospel I have declared unto them and to the world, and to the organization of the kingdom in its earthly relations and requirements.

19. *For their sakes I sanctify myself.* By the offering of himself, the high priest of humanity, in voluntary sacrifice for the sins of mankind and an abiding example unto their salvation.

20. *Neither for these only do I pray.* Ver. 20–26 contain Christ's prayer for believers and the world generally.

21. *That they may all be one,* etc. The outstanding fact of our Lord's prayer for the unity of believers is that it may be spiritual, in the Father through him.

22. *The glory which thou hast given me,* etc. The glory which he has by being one with the Father they also have by being one with the Father through him.

23. *That the world may know.* May be convinced of the truth by the

into one; that the world may know that thou didst send me, and lovedst them, even as thou lovedst me. 24 Father, *h*I desire that they also whom thou hast given me be with me where I am, that they may behold my glory, which thou hast given me: for thou lovedst me before the foundation of the world. 25 O righteous Father, the world knew thee not, but I knew thee; and these knew that thou didst send me; 26 and I made known unto them thy name, and will make it known; that the love wherewith thou lovedst me may be in them, and I in them.

18 When Je′sus had spoken these words, he went forth with his disciples over the *a*brook *b*Kid′ron, where was a garden, into which he entered, himself and his disciples. 2 Now Ju′das also, who *c*betrayed him, knew the place: for Je′sus oft-times resorted thither with his disciples. 3 Ju′das then, having received the *d*band *of soldiers*, and officers from the chief priests and the Phar′i-sees, com-

eth thither with lanterns and torches and weapons. 4 Je′sus therefore, knowing all the things that were coming upon him, went forth, and saith unto them, Whom seek ye? 5 They answered him, Je′sus of Naz′a-reth. Je′sus saith unto them, **I am *he*.** And Ju′das also, who *c*betrayed him, was standing with them. 6 When therefore he said unto them, I am *he*, they went backward, and fell to the ground. 7 Again therefore he asked them, Whom seek ye? And they said, Je′sus of Naz′a-reth. 8 Je′sus answered, I told you that I am *he*: if therefore ye seek me, let these go their way: 9 that the word might be fulfilled which he spake, Of those whom thou hast given me I lost not one. 10 Si′mon Peter therefore having a sword drew it, and struck the high priest's *e*servant, and cut off his right ear. Now the *e*servant's name was Mal′chus. 11 Je′sus therefore said unto Peter, **Put up the sword into the sheath: the cup which the Father hath given me, shall I not drink it?**

h Gr. *that which thou hast given me, I desire that where I am, they also may be with me, that &c.* *a* Or. *ravine* Gr. *winter-torrent.*

b Or. *of the Cedars*   *c* Or. *delivered him up* *d* Or *cohort*   *e* Gr. *bondservant.*

spiritual unity of the followers of Je-sus Christ.

24. *May behold my glory.* As he prayed that those whom his Father had given him might be with him where he was, they would not only behold his glory but be partakers thereof.

26. *Made known unto them thy name.* Manifested Thy nature.

CHAPTER 18

1–11. *Over the brook Kidron.* A deep ravine separating Jerusalem, on the east side, from the Mount of Olives. In ver. 1–11 the betrayal

cf Christ is narrated. *A garden.* Gethsemane. See note on Mt. 26. 36. *Jesus oft-times resorted thither.* See note on Lk. 22.39. *Band of soldiers.* Part of the Roman cohort of six hundred men. The reason for so considerable a number was that the arrest of Jesus was expected to cause political trouble. *Officers.* The Levitical guard of the Temple, together, probably, with Sanhedrin officials. *Fell to the ground.* This proof of his power shows that Christ might have resisted his arrest. See ch. 10.18. *Which he spake.* See ch. 17.2. *Put up the sword.* See note on Mt. 26.52. *The cup.* A hint of the

12 So the ƒband and the
ᵍchief captain, and the officers
of the Jews, seized Je′sus and
bound him, 13 and led him to
An′nas first; for he was father
in law to Ca′ia-phas, who was
high priest that year. 14 Now
Ca′ia-phas was he that gave
counsel to the Jews, that it was
expedient that one man should
die for the people.

15 And Si′mon Peter followed
Je′sus, and *so did* another disciple. Now that disciple was
known unto the high priest, and
entered in with Je′sus into the
court of the high priest; 16 but
Peter was standing at the door
without. So the other disciple,
who was known unto the high
priest, went out and spake unto
her that kept the door, and
brought in Peter. 17 The maid
therefore that kept the door
saith unto Peter, Art thou also
one of this man's disciples? He
saith, I am not. 18 Now the
ʰservants and the officers were

standing *there*, having made ⁱa
fire of coals; for it was cold; and
they were warming themselves:
and Peter also was with them,
standing and warming himself.

19 The high priest therefore
asked Je′sus of his disciples, and
of his teaching. 20 Je′sus answered him, **I have spoken
openly to the world; I ever
taught in ᵏsynagogues, and in
the temple, where all the Jews
come together; and in secret
spake I nothing. 21 Why askest
thou me? ask them that have
heard *me*, what I spake unto
them: behold, these know the
things which I said.** 22 And
when he had said this, one of
the officers standing by struck
Je′sus ˡwith his hand, saying,
Answerest thou the high priest
so? 23 Je′sus answered him, **If
I have spoken evil, bear witness
of the evil: but if well, why
smitest thou me?** 24 An′nas
therefore sent him bound unto
Ca′ia-phas the high priest.

ƒ Or, *cohort* ᵍ Or, *military tribune* Gr.
chiliarch. ʰ Gr. *bondservants.* ⁱ Gr. a

fire of charcoal. ᵏ Gr. *synagogue.* ˡ Or,
with a rod

agony in Gethsemane. See Mt. 26.
39; Mk. 14.36; Lk. 22.42.
12–14. *Seized Jesus and bound
him.* The arrest of our Lord and
the taking him for trial before Annas are here narrated. *Annas.* He
was very influential. Many Jews
thought that he had been illegally
deposed and was therefore still rightful high priest. *Caiaphas.* See
notes on ch. 11.50; Lk. 22.66–71.
15–19. *Simon Peter followed Jesus.* In these verses is recorded Peter's first denial of Jesus. *Another
disciple.* John the son of Zebedee.
It was John's acquaintance with the
family of Annas that procured admission for Peter into the court of
the high priest. *Coals.* Charcoal.
19–24. *The high priest therefore
asked Jesus.* Annas informally
questioned our Lord before sending

him to Caiaphas for formal examination. He was doubtless in complete sympathy with, and by reason
of his shrewdness and influence possibly inspired, the plot to kill Jesus,
and his object here was to beguile
his captive into making incriminat-
ing admissions. Our Lord's reply
was a challenge which closed the
interview. Neither Annas nor any
of those with him could make head-
way against a bold appeal to the
people as to the character of the
teaching. *In secret spake I nothing.*
Which suggests that one of the accusations against him was that of
founding a secret organization, which
of course would have brought him to
the notice of the Roman governor
and subjected his apostles and disciples to imprisonment or death.
Struck Jesus. See Lk. 22.63.

25 Now Si'mon Peter was standing and warming himself. They said therefore unto him, Art thou also *one* of his disciples? He denied, and said, I am not. 26 One of the ᵐservants of the high priest, being a kinsman of him whose ear Peter cut off, saith, Did not I see thee in the garden with him? 27 Peter therefore denied again: and straightway the cock crew.

28 They lead Je'sus therefore from Ca'ia-phas into the ⁿPræto'ri-um: and it was early; and they themselves entered not into the ⁿPræ-to'ri-um, that they might not be defiled, but might eat the passover. 29 Pi'late therefore went out unto them, and saith, What accusation bring ye against this man? 30 They answered and said unto him, If this man were not an evil-doer, we should not have delivered him up unto thee. 31 Pi'late therefore said unto them, Take him yourselves, and judge him according to your law. The Jews said unto him, It is not lawful for us to put any man to death: 32 that the word of Je'sus might be fulfilled, which he spake, signifying by what manner of death he should die.

33 Pi'late therefore entered again into the ⁿPræ-to'ri-um, and called Je'sus, and said unto him, Art thou the King of the Jews? 34 Je'sus answered, **Sayest thou this of thyself, or did others tell it thee concerning me?** 35 Pi'late answered, Am I a Jew? Thine own nation and the chief priests delivered thee unto me: what hast thou done?

---

m Gr. bondservants.   *n Or, palace*

25–27. *Simon Peter.* The second and third denials of Peter are contained in these verses. *The cock crew.* The time of cock-crow began about three o'clock in the morning.

28. *The Prætorium.* The official residence of Pilate, the Roman governor. Most probably it was part of the Roman fortress of Antonia, not far from the Temple. *Early.* Between four and five o'clock in the morning. *Might eat the passover.* As the fortress was a Gentile building and presumably had not been searched for unleavened bread, no orthodox Jew could enter such a place without being defiled. The expression 'might eat the passover' apparently refers to the following day and indicates that according to this evangelist the Jewish Passover was on Friday evening, instead of Thursday evening as is implied by Matthew, Mark and Luke. The Last Supper had already taken place. As an explanation of the difficulty it has been suggested that the expression refers only to the sacrifice on the morning following the Passover.

30. *If this man were not an evil-doer,* etc. The Jews may have been confused as to what to say at this moment. The Roman authorities had no interest in offences against Jewish law; hence the only effective accusation was a political one.

32. *That the word of Jesus might be fulfilled.* He had foretold his death by crucifixion; death by stoning for blasphemy, even if permitted to be carried into effect, would have been contrary to that prediction. The Sanhedrin could sentence a man to death, but could not execute the sentence without permission of the Roman governor.

33–38. *Entered again into the Prætorium.* This evangelist alone records the conversations between our Lord and Pilate. The latter's question, 'Art thou the King of the Jews?' was probably asked in entire confidence that Jesus was not implicated in a political plot. The cynical and experienced politician could easily recognize the imprint and power of goodness in the man before him. But the governor had to dis-

36 Je'sus answered, **My kingdom is not of this world: if my kingdom were of this world, then would my °servants fight, that I should not be delivered to the Jews: but now is my kingdom not from hence.** 37 Pi'late therefore said unto him, Art thou a king then? Je'sus answered, *p*Thou sayest that I am a king. To this end have I been born, and to this end am I come into the world, that I should bear witness unto the truth. Every one that is of the truth heareth my voice. 38 Pi'late saith unto him, What is truth?

And when he had said this, he went out again unto the Jews, and saith unto them, I find no crime in him. 39 But ye have a custom, that I should

o Or, *officers*: as in ver. 3, 12, 18. 22.
p Or, *Thou sayest it, because I am a king.*

release unto you one at the passover: will ye therefore that I release unto you the King of the Jews? 40 They cried out therefore again, saying, Not this man, but Bar-ab'bas. Now Bar-ab'bas was a robber.

19 Then Pi'late therefore took Je'sus, and scourged him. 2 And the soldiers platted a crown of thorns, and put it on his head, and arrayed him in a purple garment; 3 and they came unto him, and said, Hail, King of the Jews! and they struck him °with their hands. 4 And Pi'late went out again, and saith unto them, Behold, I bring him out to you, that ye may know that I find no crime in him. 5 Je'sus therefore came out, wearing the crown of thorns

a Or, *with rods*

charge his official duty, and this was satisfied in part by the question and the answer given to it. This was, that although Jesus was rightfully a king, yet his kingdom was spiritual. *Witness unto the truth.* The mention of truth by our Lord opened a subject for which Pilate had neither inclination nor ability. If his reply was not a jest, it was at least a confession of ignorance. Nothing in his Roman education or official experience had taught him anything of moral or religious value on the question of truth. He had probably heard debaters wrangle over it in Rome, but without result. The words of Jesus most likely made the Roman feel that behind them was the purpose of a pure and sincere character. The troubled conscience, the indecision, the genuine desire to free Jesus from the Jews all point to the conclusion that Pilate recognized, however imperfectly, the moral greatness of the blameless and mysterious accused one.

39, 40. *Ye have a custom.* As soon as Pilate went out again from the Prætorium into the open air, the

clamor of the malignant Jews began injuriously to affect his executive discretion. He wanted to see an easy way out of the difficulty; he was a moral coward. See notes on Mt. 27.11, 15, 16, 19, 20, 22, 24, 25; on Lk. 23.1-5.

CHAPTER 19

1. *Took Jesus, and scourged him.* Pilate did this with the intention of finding out whether a moderate punishment of Jesus would satisfy the Jews. He wished earnestly to avoid inflicting the penalty of death (Lk. 23.16). The same wish is evident in ver. 4.

5. *Behold, the man!* Words of sympathy with the sufferer, yet unwittingly spoken to designate, with Roman brevity, the central figure of the race, the one who is most truly 'the man' whom to 'behold' in steadfast faith is life. This utterance of the Roman governor, though a mere fleeting breath of administrative incident, was yet to live long after the empire whose servant he was had been sealed in the sepulchre of history. Its destiny has

and the purple garment. And Pi'late saith unto them, Behold, the man! 6 When therefore the chief priests and the officers saw him, they cried out, saying, Crucify *him*, crucify *him*! Pi'late saith unto them, Take him yourselves, and crucify him: for I find no crime in him. 7 The Jews answered him, We have a law, and by that law he ought to die, because he made himself the Son of God. 8 When Pi'late therefore heard this saying, he was the more afraid; 9 and he entered into the *b*Præ-to'ri-um again, and saith unto Je'sus, Whence art thou? But Je'sus gave him no answer. 10 Pi'late therefore saith unto him, Speakest thou not unto me? knowest

thou not that I have *c*power to release thee, and have *c*power to crucify thee? 11 Je'sus answered him, **Thou wouldest have no *c*power against me, except it were given thee from above: therefore he that delivered me unto thee hath greater sin.** 12 Upon this Pi'late sought to release him: but the Jews cried out, saying, If thou release this man, thou art not Cæ'sar's friend: every one that maketh himself a king *d*speaketh against Cæ'sar. 13 When Pi'late therefore heard these words, he brought Je'sus out, and sat down on the judgment-seat at a place called The Pavement, but in Hebrew, Gab'-ba-tha. 14 Now it was the

---

b Or, *palace*

c Or, *authority*   *d* Or, *opposeth Cæsar*

---

been unexampled among the recorded sayings of the public men of the ancient world. The words of a heathen have been the text of innumerable discourses to proclaim the divine majesty and authority of him who was led forth as a prisoner of expediency, placed on view as an object of pity, troublesome enough to scourge, too harmless to crucify.

6. *Take him yourselves.* Pilate was weak and wicked enough to allow others to treat as a criminal one whom he knew to be without offence.

8. *He was the more afraid.* Perplexed and mystified. He did not understand the enmity and fear of the Jewish leaders: he knew little of the moral and religious issues at stake. He was swayed at one moment by sympathy with his prisoner and by his contempt for the Jews, at another by official prudence. The consideration that troubled him most was, What will they think of me in Rome?

11. *He that delivered me unto thee.* Caiaphas. *Hath greater sin.* Caiaphas aided the attempt to play upon Pilate's fears by misrepresenting Jesus as a political offender. He knew

perfectly that his intended victim was morally upright. He could not, in face of the evidence, deny the astounding miracle of the raising of Lazarus. He could easily have known that Jesus had no political ambition and had often rejected the notion of a Jewish kingship. But he recognized and feared the spiritual power of the new leader and the shock it would give to the religious externalism and prestige of the Jewish ruling classes. He was a custodian of the existing order and accordingly hated its disturber.

12. *Cæsar's friend.* Tiberius was then emperor. *A king.* The Jews knew well the falsehood implied in this use of the word 'king:' but it had weight with Pilate. The mere suspicion of a charge of disloyalty heard at Rome touched the weakest joint in his moral anatomy. See notes on ch. 18.33–38.

13. *On the judgment-seat.* In the open air. *Hebrew.* Aramaic. *Gabbatha.* A rounded height.

14. *The Preparation.* The day preceding. *Behold, your King!* Words less expressive of contempt for Jesus than for those who were clamoring for his life. At this mo-

Preparation of the passover: it was about the sixth hour. And he saith unto the Jews, Behold, your King! 15 They therefore cried out, Away with *him*, away with *him*, crucify him! Pi'late saith unto them, Shall I crucify your King? The chief priests answered, We have no king but Cæ'sar. 16 Then therefore he delivered him unto them to be crucified.

17 They took Je'sus therefore: and he went out, bearing the cross for himself, unto the place called The place of a skull, which is called in Hebrew Gol'go-tha: 18 where they crucified him, and with him two others, on either

side one, and Je'sus in the midst. 19 And Pi'late wrote a title also, and put it on the cross. And there was written, JE'SUS OF NAZ'A-RETH, THE KING OF THE JEWS. 20 This title therefore read many of the Jews, *for the place where Je'sus was crucified was nigh to the city; and it was written in Hebrew, *and* in Latin, *and* in Greek. 21 The chief priests of the Jews therefore said to Pi'late, Write not, The King of the Jews; but, that he said, I am King of the Jews. 22 Pi'late answered, What I have written I have written.

23 The soldiers therefore, when

---

e Or, *for the place of the city where Jesus was crucified was nigh at hand*

---

ment our Lord presented both to Roman and Jew a spectacle of pitiful contrast to worldly position and importance. The sting of Pilate's irony was in the fact that this man, robed and crowned in mockery, represented in the weakness and apparent disgrace of his appearance the punished rebel whom every ardent Roman would have wished a Jew to be. Behold your King, ye Jews! A king who looks like this is good enough for a people like you! 15. *No king but Cæsar.* A degrading admission for the chief priests, who were supposed to acknowledge only God as ruler; but it is partly explained by the fact that most of them were Sadducees, who sought the favor of Rome. 16. *He delivered him unto them.* Pilate delivered Jesus to the chief priests with the design of fixing upon them the infamy of his crucifixion, but he quieted his own political doubts by sending Roman soldiers to perform the act. It should be noted that Pilate did not formally pronounce sentence of death on Jesus; but nevertheless he thought it prudent that a man suspected of kingly aspirations, or even widely reported to have them, should not be saved from death by the intervention of a Roman official.

17-22. *They took Jesus therefore.* In these verses the crucifixion is narrated. As compared with Matthew, Mark and Luke this evangelist omits the bearing of the cross by Simon of Cyrene and the prayer or first 'word' from the cross in Lk. 23. 34; but he adds the request of the chief priests that the inscription on the cross be changed (ver. 21). *For himself.* Until relieved by Simon of Cyrene (Mt. 27.32; Mk. 15.21; Lk. 23.26). *Golgotha.* See note on Mt. 27.33. *Two others.* The two malefactors. See notes on Lk. 23.39-43. *Pilate wrote a title.* The written title was meant especially to emphasize the contempt for the Jews which Pilate had already expressed in the exclamation, 'Behold, your King!' (ver. 14). That the inscription on the cross was thought to be an insult to the Jewish nation is clear from the request of the chief priests to have it removed. *What I have written I have written.* The crucifixion was now almost accomplished; it was useless to hedge and too late to weigh chances. so Pilate's natural stubbornness had its way. See notes on Mt. 27.28, 31-33, 35, 37, 40, 42, 43-46.
23. *His garments.* Head-dress; cloak or outer garment; girdle; shoes; coat or inner garment. *Four parts.*

they had crucified Je′sus, took his garments and made four parts, to every soldier a part; and also the *f*coat: now the *f*coat was without seam, woven from the top throughout. 24 They said therefore one to another, Let us not rend it, but cast lots for it, whose it shall be: that the scripture might be fulfilled, which saith,

*g*They parted my garments among them,
And upon my vesture did they cast lots.

25 These things therefore the soldiers did. But there were standing by the cross of Je′sus his mother, and his mother's sister, Mary the *wife* of Clo′pas, and Mary Mag-da-le′ne. 26 When Je′sus therefore saw his

mother, and the disciple standing by whom he loved, he saith unto his mother, **Woman, behold, thy son!** 27 Then saith he to the disciple, **Behold, thy mother!** And from that hour the disciple took her unto his own *home.*

28 After this Je′sus, knowing that all things are now finished, *h*that the scripture might be accomplished, saith, **I thirst.** 29 There was set there a vessel full of vinegar: so they put a sponge full of the vinegar upon hyssop, and brought it to his mouth. 30 When Je′sus therefore had received the vinegar, he said, **It is finished:** and he bowed his head, and gave up his spirit.

31 The Jews therefore, because

---

f Or, *tunic*   *g* Ps. xxii. 18.   *h* Ps. lxix. 21.

One of the above, in the order mentioned, to each of the soldiers, which would leave the coat to be divided. The clothes of an executed offender belonged by custom to the executioners.

25. *His mother's sister.* Salome, mother of John the apostle, the son of Zebedee. Thus there were four women near the cross.

26. *Whom he loved.* John, the son of Zebedee. *Woman, behold, thy son!* This, and 'Behold, thy mother!' of ver. 27, are the third 'word' from the cross. John was nephew of the Virgin Mary. Being the son of well-to-do parents, he had his own house in Jerusalem. His residence there in comfortable circumstances would account for his acquaintance with the family of Annas. His influence with Annas enabled Peter to enter the court of the high priest after the arrest of Jesus (ch. 18.16). The fact that our Lord did not mention the name of Joseph indicates that the latter was not then living. Nor is it remarkable that he passed over his own brethren if, as some scholars think, they were Joseph's children by a

former marriage. Still less would he consent to commit his mother to their care if they were not believers. They certainly were not at a time of special stress and danger in his ministry (ch. 7.5). Apparently they were not convinced until after the resurrection (Acts 1.14).

28. *I thirst.* The fifth 'word' from the cross. It explains why Jesus was offered a sponge filled with vinegar to drink, as recorded in Mt. 27.48; Mk. 15.36; and Lk. 23.36.

29. *Vinegar.* A kind of sour wine. *Hyssop.* It is not certain what species of plant is meant. It is the 'reed' mentioned by the other three evangelists in their account of the crucifixion.

30. *It is finished.* The sixth 'word' from the cross. See note on Mt. 27.46. The seventh 'word', spoken immediately after and recorded by Luke, is 'Father, into thy hands I commend my spirit' (Lk. 23.46). These words, indicating that our Lord freely and willingly resigned his life, confirm the truth of the declaration in ch. 10.18.

31. *The Preparation.* The day before the Sabbath. *The bodies.* The

it was the Preparation, that the bodies should not remain on the cross upon the sabbath (for the day of that sabbath was a high *day*), asked of Pi'late that their legs might be broken, and *that* they might be taken away. 32 The soldiers therefore came, and brake the legs of the first, and of the other that was crucified with him: 33 but when they came to Je'sus, and saw that he was dead already, they brake not his legs: 34 howbeit one of the soldiers with a spear pierced his side, and straightway there came out blood and water. 35 And he that hath seen hath borne witness, and his witness is true: and he knoweth that he saith true, that ye also may believe. 36 For these things came to pass, *i*that the scripture might be fulfilled, A bone of him shall not be *k*broken. 37 And again another scripture saith, *l*They shall look on him whom they pierced.

38 And after these things Joseph of Ar-i-ma-thæ'a, being a disciple of Je'sus, but secretly for fear of the Jews, asked of Pi'late that he might take away the body of Je'sus: and Pi'late gave *him* leave. He came therefore, and took away his body. 39 And there came also Nic-o-de'mus, he who at the first came to him by night, bringing a *m*mixture of myrrh and aloes, about a hundred pounds. 40 So they took the body of Je'sus, and bound it in linen cloths with the spices, as the custom of the Jews is to bury. 41 Now in the place where he was crucified there was a garden; and in the garden a new tomb wherein was never man yet laid. 42 There then because of the Jews' Preparation (for the tomb was nigh at hand) they laid Je'sus.

20 Now on the first *day* of the week cometh Mary Mag-da-le'ne early, while it was

---

i Ex. xii. 46; Num. ix. 12; Ps. xxxiv.
20.   *k* Or, *crushed*   *l* Zech. xii. 10.

m Some ancient authorities read *roll*.

Jewish law commanded the removal of a criminal's body before night (Dt. 21.22, 23). *A high day.* That Sabbath was also the first day of the feast of unleavened bread. *Their legs might be broken.* To hasten death. It was the Roman custom to leave bodies to rot upon the cross.

34. *With a spear pierced his side.* To make his death certain. In this case the piercing of his side made the truth of the resurrection all the more convincing.

35. *Hath borne witness.* The evangelist bears specially emphatic testimony to the truth of what he had seen with his own eyes. *His witness is true.* That is, both credible and sufficient; satisfying the requirements of good evidence.

38–42. *Joseph of Arimathæa.* In these verses the burial of Jesus is described.   Joseph of Arimathæa

now came boldly and claimed the body. See notes on Mt. 27.57; Mk. 15.43. *Nicodemus.* Who came to assist in the burial. See notes on ch. 3.2, 4, 5, 7. Nicodemus, like Joseph, was a member of the Sanhedrin. *Myrrh and aloes.* Myrrh was a resinous gum, which when mixed with crushed or pounded aloe-wood, was used for embalming. It was placed between the bandages as they were wound about the body. The aloe is an evergreen shrub found in tropical countries. *A hundred pounds.* About seventy-five pounds, avoirdupois weight. *A garden.* This evangelist alone tells us that the tomb was near the place of crucifixion. *Preparation.* See note on ver. 31.

CHAPTER 20

1–10. *Cometh Mary Magdalene.* The

yet dark, unto the tomb, and seeth the stone taken away from the tomb. 2 She runneth therefore, and cometh to Si'mon Peter, and to the other disciple whom Je'sus loved, and saith unto them, They have taken away the Lord out of the tomb, and we know not where they have laid him. 3 Peter therefore went forth, and the other disciple, and they went toward the tomb. 4 And they ran both together: and the other disciple outran Peter, and came first to the tomb; 5 and stooping and looking in, he seeth the linen cloths lying; yet entered he not in. 6 Si'mon Peter therefore also cometh, following him, and entered into the tomb; and he beholdeth the linen cloths lying, 7 and the napkin, that was upon his head, not lying with the linen cloths, but rolled up in a place by itself. 8 Then entered in therefore the other disciple also, who came first to the tomb, and he saw, and believed. 9 For as yet they knew not the scripture, that he must rise again from the dead. 10 So the disciples went away again unto their own home.

11 But Mary was standing without at the tomb weeping: so, as she wept, she stooped and looked into the tomb; 12 and she beholdeth two angels in white sitting, one at the head, and one at the feet, where the body of Je'sus had lain. 13 And they say unto her, Woman, why weepest thou? She saith unto them, Because they have taken away my Lord, and I know not

---

four narratives of the resurrection agree in regard to the early visit of the women to the tomb, the removal of the stone, and the appearance of angels before the risen Jesus was seen. This evangelist omits, in harmony with his general plan, certain details of the resurrection supplied by the other three, but adds details which they omit. As to the omissions, see notes on Mt. 28, Mk. 16, Lk. 24. *The other disciple.* John, son of Zebedee. *We.* Implying that other women also were concerned to know where the body of Jesus was. *Seeth the linen cloths lying.* John and Peter, in going to and entering the tomb, acted in a characteristic manner. Peter, the bolder and more impulsive, entered first; but there is nothing to show that his mind grasped the meaning of what he saw. The more observant and reflective John, entering later, intently noticed the condition of the linen cloths and the napkin. He saw that they lay unwound, and in the form in which they had enclosed Christ's body, which had disappeared. The encasing garments had been left empty.

John believed that Jesus had risen. Why? (1) Because the appearance of the linen cloths and the napkin convinced him that no human hands from outside the tomb had entered it and touched the sacred body or the enclosing garments; (2) only Christ's power over death and his own body could have effected a release from which all purely human aid or agency had been manifestly excluded; (3) John's belief resulting from an examination of the external facts was strengthened by remembering Christ's prediction that he would die and be raised from the dead. He had faith in the words of Jesus.

11-18. *Mary was standing without.* That the first appearance of Jesus after the resurrection was to Mary Magdalene is evident from Mk. 16.9. The details are, however, given only by the fourth evangelist. *Knew not that it was Jesus.* Because of the greater beauty and majesty of his spiritual body. *The gardener.* Because of the early hour. *Rabboni.* Galilean for 'Rabbi.' *Touch me not.* Behind the various

where they have laid him. 14 When she had thus said, she turned herself back, and beholdeth Je'sus standing, and knew not that it was Je'sus. 15 Je'sus saith unto her, **Woman, why weepest thou? whom seekest thou?** She, supposing him to be the gardener, saith unto him, Sir, if thou hast borne him hence, tell me where thou hast laid him, and I will take him away. 16 Je'sus saith unto her, **Mary.** She turneth herself, and saith unto him in Hebrew, Rab-bo'ni; which is to say, Teacher. 17 Je'sus saith to her, [a]**Touch me not; for I am not yet ascended unto the Father: but go unto my brethren, and say to them, I ascend unto my Father and your Father, and my God and your God.** 18 Mary Mag-da-le'ne cometh and telleth the disciples, I have seen the Lord; and *that* he had said these things unto her.

19 When therefore it was evening, on that day, the first *day* of the week, and when the doors were shut where the disciples were, for fear of the Jews, Je'sus came and stood in the midst, and saith unto them, **Peace** *be* **unto you.** 20 And when he had said this, he showed unto them his hands and his side. The disciples therefore were glad, when they saw the Lord. 21 Je'sus therefore said to them again, **Peace** *be* **unto you: as the Father hath sent me, even so send I you.** 22 And when he had said this, he breathed on them, and saith unto them, **Receive ye the Holy Spirit: 23 whose soever sins ye forgive, they are forgiven unto them; whose soever** *sins* **ye retain, they are retained.**

24 But Thomas, one of the twelve, called [b]Did'y-mus, was not with them when Je'sus came. 25 The other disciples therefore said unto him, We have seen the Lord. But he said unto them, Except I shall see in his hands the print of the nails, and put my finger into the print of the

---

a Or, *Take not hold on me.*

b That is, *Twin.*

interpretations of these words the main truth is that the days of friendship and communion with Christ as he was on earth in the flesh, were to be considered ended. Mary Magdalene was to wait for the time when her faith would bring her into the deeper spiritual communion with her Risen Master after his ascension. *My Father, and your Father.* The distinction implied is that Christ's relation to his Father is special. God is his Father in a different sense from that in which He is Father to the individual human believer. Jesus himself never prayed to God as 'Our Father,' though he taught the disciples so to pray.

19-23. *When the doors were shut.* These verses describe the appearance of Jesus to the disciples in the evening. The great truth implied is the power of the spiritual body over matter. *Peace be unto you.* The usual Jewish greeting; but now under circumstances that enlarged and infinitely enriched its significance. The peace now won by him through his example of living self-sacrifice and voluntary death was for the benefit of the whole world. *He breathed on them.* To signify that the inspiration and power of the Holy Spirit proceeded from him. *Whose soever sins ye forgive,* etc. The words stand for the delegation by Christ of ministerial powers to the visible church over its members. See note on Mt. 18.18. It is the power of deciding questions of faith and morals in the visible church.

nails, and put my hand into his side, I will not believe.

26 And after eight days again his disciples were within, and Thomas with them. Je'sus cometh, the doors being shut, and stood in the midst, and said, **Peace** *be* **unto you.** 27 Then saith he to Thomas, **Reach hither thy finger, and see my hands; and reach** *hither* **thy hand, and put it into my side: and be not faithless, but believing.** 28 Thomas answered and said unto him, My Lord and my God. 29 Je'sus saith unto him, **Because thou hast seen me,** *c* **thou hast believed: blessed** *are* **they that have not seen, and** *yet* **have believed.**

30 Many other signs therefore

did Je'sus in the presence of the disciples, which are not written in this book: 31 but these **are** written, that ye may believe that Je'sus is the Christ, the Son of God; and that believing ye may have life in his name.

21 After these things Je'sus manifested himself again to the disciples at the sea of Ti-be'-ri-as; and he manifested *himself* on this wise. 2 There were together Si'mon Peter, and Thomas called *a* Did'y-mus, and Na-than'a-el of Ca'na in Gal'i-lee and the *sons* of Zeb'e-dee, and two other of his disciples. 3 Si'mon Peter saith unto them, I go a fishing. They say unto him, We also come with thee. They went forth, and entered

---

c Or, *hast thou believed?*   *a* That is, *Twin.*

---

26. *After eight days.* The first Sunday after the resurrection. *The doors being shut, and stood in the midst.* See notes on parts of 1–10 and 19–23.

28. *My Lord and my God.* The key to the mental limitations of Thomas, and to the quality of his doubt, is supplied by the facts that finally convinced him. Only the pierced hands and side of his Master brought him to his knees. In his attempts to measure truth he was a materialist. His spiritual intuitions were not strong enough, without other aids, to keep him in the path of discipleship. If he had possessed an enlightened faith in Jesus before the crucifixion, he would not have doubted so persistently after the resurrection. He would have recalled the miracles and pondered their meaning. Among his own remembered experiences were marvels not less difficult for a natural sceptic than was the resurrection of the Lord. He was present when Lazarus came forth from the grave (ch. 11.16), yet that glorious manifestation did not teach him that Christ's power could be exercised on any human body, including that which

was laid in the new tomb of Joseph of Arimathæa. Like most of his kind he was prompt to ask for evidence, provided a narrow notion of evidence be allowed; but his faith seemed unable to reach beyond his eyesight. He had forgotten the predicted cross and sepulchre and raising from the dead. Even in Christ's acceptance of his confession there was no blessing (ver. 29).

29. *That have not seen, and yet have believed.* All believers since the resurrection, and those of the present time, share the blessing.

30. *His name.* His person and teaching.

CHAPTER 21

1. *Sea of Tiberias.* Also called Sea of Galilee and Lake of Gennesaret. See note on Mk. 1.16. As to the city of Tiberias, see notes on ch. 6.1.

2. *Nathanael of Cana.* Otherwise known as Bartholomew. See note thereon in ch. 1.40-51. *Sons of Zebedee.* James and John, apostles.

3. *I go a fishing.* Peter's remark, together with that of the others who agreed to go with him, indicates that in the interval of anxious wait-

into the boat; and that night they took nothing. 4 But when day was now breaking, Je'sus stood on the beach: yet the disciples knew not that it was Je'sus. 5 Je'sus therefore saith unto them, **Children, have ye aught to eat?** They answered him, No. 6 And he said unto them, **Cast the net on the right side of the boat, and ye shall find.** They cast therefore, and now they were not able to draw it for the multitude of fishes. 7 That disciple therefore whom Je'sus loved saith unto Peter, It is the Lord. So when Si'mon Peter heard that it was the Lord, he girt his coat about him (for he [b]was naked), and cast himself into the sea. 8 But the other disciples came in the little boat (for they were not far from the land, but about two hundred cubits off), dragging

the net *full* of fishes. 9 So when they got out upon the land, they see [c]a fire of coals there, and [d]fish laid thereon, and [e]bread. 10 Je'sus saith unto them, **Bring of the fish which ye have now taken.** 11 Si'mon Peter therefore went [f]up, and drew the net to land, full of great fishes, a hundred and fifty and three: and for all there were so many, the net was not rent. 12 Je'sus saith unto them, **Come *and* break your fast.** And none of the disciples durst inquire of him, Who art thou? knowing that it was the Lord. 13 Je'sus cometh, and taketh the [g]bread, and giveth them, and the fish likewise. 14 This is now the third time that Je'sus was manifested to the disciples, after that he was risen from the dead.

15 So when they had broken their fast, Je'sus saith to Si'mon

---

b Or, *had on his undergarment only* Comp. ch. 13.4; Is. 20.2; Mic. 1.8, 11.

c Gr. *a fire of charcoal.* d Or, *a fish a loaf* f Or, *aboard* e Or, g Or, *loaf*

ing for the appearance of Jesus the disciples had returned to their usual occupation. *That night.* Their failure to catch anything at night was the more remarkable since night was the best time, as the fish then went blindly into the nets.

4. *Knew not that it was Jesus.* For the same reason which explains the failure of Mary to recognize him after his resurrection, namely, the greater beauty and majesty of his spiritual body. See ch. 20.11–18 and notes thereon.

7. *It is the Lord.* John was not only the first to believe that Christ had risen, but the first to recognize him as he stood on the beach of the Sea of Tiberias. *Cast himself into the sea.* In an overmastering impulse of affection, mingled with grief for his denials. His heart was true to his Lord and he hastened with passionate eagerness to be reconciled to him.

8. *Two hundred cubits.* Three hundred feet.

9. *Coals.* Charcoal. *Fish laid thereon, and bread.* A meal prepared by Christ as a means of impressing upon his disciples, then and forever afterward, the truth that he is the true spiritual sustenance of mankind, the divine source and nourisher of life.

11. *The net was not rent.* Some scholars think that this is intended by the evangelist to represent the church triumphant in heaven, which cannot lose any of its members by reason of the imperfections which characterize the visible church on earth.

14. *The third time.* For the two previous appearances see ch. 20.19–23, 26–29.

15. *Lovest thou me,* etc. Jesus, before restoring Peter to his former position as an apostle, required a threefold confession, not of belief, as

Peter, Si'mon, *son* of [h]John, [i]lovest thou me more than these? He saith unto him, Yea, Lord; thou knowest that I [k]love thee. He saith unto him, **Feed my lambs.** 16 He saith to him again a second time, Si'mon, *son* of [h]John, [i]lovest thou me? He saith unto him, Yea, Lord; thou knowest that I [k]love thee. He saith unto him, **Tend my sheep.** 17 He saith unto him the third time, Si'mon, *son* of [h]John, [k]lovest thou me? Peter was grieved because he said unto him the third time, [k]Lovest thou me? And he said unto him, Lord, thou knowest all things; thou [l]knowest that I [k]love thee. Je'sus saith unto him, **Feed my sheep.** 18 Verily, verily, I say unto thee, **When thou wast young, thou girdedst thyself, and walkedst whither thou wouldest: but when thou shalt be old, thou shalt stretch forth thy hands, and another shall gird thee, and carry thee whither thou wouldest not.** 19 Now this he spake, signifying by what manner of death he should glorify God. And when he had spoken this, he saith unto him, **Follow me.** 20 Peter, turning about, seeth the disciple whom Je'sus loved following; who also leaned back on his breast at the supper, and said, Lord, who is he that [m]betrayeth thee? 21 Peter therefore seeing him saith to Je'sus, Lord, [n]and what shall this man do? 22 Je'sus saith unto him, **If I will that he tarry till I come, what** *is that* **to thee? follow thou me.** 23 This saying therefore went forth among the brethren, that that disciple should not die: yet Je'sus said not unto him, that he should not die; but, If I will that he tarry

---

[h] Gr. *Joanes.* See ch. 1.42. margin. [i] [k] *Love* in these places represents two different Greek words. [l] Or, *perceivest*

[m] Or, *delivereth thee up* [n] Gr. *and this man, what?*

---

on a former memorable occasion (Mt. 16.16), but of love. *Feed my lambs.* Peter's confession of love, given three times, was immediately followed each time by Christ's command of service. 'Feed my lambs,' 'Tend my sheep' (ver. 16), and 'Feed my sheep' (ver. 17) were to be binding, irrevocable tests of the restored apostle's sincerity.

18, 19. *When thou wast young, thou girdedst thyself.* Peter's martyrdom is foretold in these verses. Jesus contrasts the free activity of his apostle's youth with the painful and tragic constraint which was to overtake him at the time of martyrdom. *Another shall gird thee.* The executioner, who would compel Peter to 'stretch forth' his hands and would fasten him to the cross. *Follow me.* To be understood figuratively, as a call to Peter for his devoted service.

20. *Following.* Walking after him. Peter, looking round, saw John following and probably supposed that he wanted to go along, sharing the lot and the service to which the Lord had just called him (Peter). He may have resented John's supposed attempt to emulate him. *What shall this man do?* Is he to become a rival? Will he share my triumph? Is he also to be a martyr like me?

22. *Jesus saith unto him,* etc. The reply of our Lord was a rebuke to Peter for his presumptuous and wrong-headed notion of John's act. *Follow thou me.* Attend to my command, without permitting anything to interfere with your duty.

23. *That that disciple should not die.* The words 'tarry till I come' had been wrongly taken to mean that John would live until Christ's return.

till I come, what *is that* to thee?

24 This is the disciple that beareth witness of these things, and wrote these things: and we know that his witness is true.

25 And there are also many other things which Je'sus did, the which if they should be written every one, I suppose that even the world itself would not contain the books that should be written.

THE ACTS OF THE APOSTLES

INTRODUCTION BY PROFESSOR W. M. RAMSAY, D.C.L., LL.D.

The "Acts of the Apostles" is, in the strictest sense, the second book of an historical work, of which the "Gospel according to Luke" forms the first book. The second book takes up the subject from the death and resurrection of the Saviour, and describes the great steps and critical stages by which Christianity spread over the world, and was at the same time formed into an organized and universal church. But the author's conception of "the world" was practically confined to the Roman world: in Luke 2.1 he uses the expression "all the world" to indicate the Roman empire, and so also in Acts 11.28. Hence, when he describes the spread of the gospel, he never alludes to the steps by which it spread from the Holy Land to the south and the east, but carefully describes those by which it spread towards the west over the Roman world; and yet there is no reason to doubt that the baptism of the Ethiopian (Acts 8.27 ff.), and the presence of many Christians in Damascus (9.2, 10, 19), are signs of a process by which the religion diffused itself southwards and eastwards. There can, indeed, be no doubt that the author of these two books considered Christianity to be given to the whole world, Jew and Greek, barbarian and Scythian; but the development of the church seemed to him to have been determined by its history in the Roman world (i.e. the civilized part of the world), and hence, in practice, he describes that history alone.

The history follows the stages of development.

1. The Primitive Church in Jerusalem, ch. 1–5.— In the first place, the state of the church at the ascension is described; then follows the account of the quickening of the church at Pentecost. The brethren, depressed for the time at the loss of their leader, became conscious for the first time of a new spirit and new power; and their changed and ennobled nature soon impressed with wonder even their opponents (4.13). The general condition of the first simple community—its unselfish spirit, the voluntary offering by many of their whole property for the benefit of the poor, and the existence within it, even at that time, of false and unworthy members—is described in considerable detail. The presence of divine grace and favor in the community is attested by the power over disease granted to Peter and John (3.1 ff.).

2. Stephen, ch. 6–7.— The apostles found that the superintendence of the poor required too much time, and seven deacons (the noun is not used here, but the cognate verb) were appointed for the purpose. Among them Stephen was distinguished by his bold preaching. This stirred up a persecution, in which Stephen

277

was stoned, and the brethren scattered as far as Damascus, Cyprus, Phœnicia, and Antioch. The result was that the gospel was preached far more widely. Saul here enters on the scene, having probably now reached the age for public life (the thirtieth year). He took a rather prominent part in the murder of Stephen.

3. **The Dispersion, ch. 8-9.** — Philip, one of the deacons, founded at Samaria the first church outside of Jerusalem. The apostles, who had remained in Jerusalem during the persecution, sanctioned this new foundation by Peter and John, who visited Samaria. On their way back to Jerusalem, they preached in many villages; while Philip preached in the cities of the coast, going as far north as Cæsarea, the Roman capital of Palestine. Saul went to Damascus with authority to bring back as prisoners the Jewish Christians who had settled there; but, as he approached Damascus, Jesus appeared to him by the way, and he was converted. A long process of peaceful development, with the foundation of new congregations throughout all Judæa and Samaria and Galilee, then took place (9.31). The development is not described in detail, but it evidently lasted for many years, and Peter was very active in it, "went throughout all parts" (9.32). It continued without any interruption until the persecution by Herod in the spring of 44 A.D. (12.1 ff.).

4. **Peter and Cornelius, ch. 10.** — During this period Peter, ordered by a special revelation, went from Joppa to Cæsarea, and admitted into the Christian brotherhood the first uncircumcised Gentile — namely, a Roman centurion called Cornelius. This important step in the widening of the church provoked opposition in Jerusalem, where the Jews at first blamed him, but accepted his argument that God had ordered the action.

5. **The Church in Antioch, ch. 11.** — Antioch, the great metropolis of Syria, and even Cyprus, were affected by the dispersion. The congregation in Antioch was marked out from all other congregations by the admission of Greeks. The importance of this new church was felt in Jerusalem, and Barnabas was sent to Antioch; he associated Saul with himself, and they consolidated the congregation during 43 A.D. The nickname "Christians," first applied to the Antiochian brethren by the pagan population, was soon accepted by the adherents of the new religion as their regular name. The charity which, as the result of divine revelation (11.28), was extended by the richer brethren of Antioch to the poor sufferers in Jerusalem during the great famine that occurred in 45 and 46 A.D., had an important effect in uniting and consolidating the churches in Syria and in Judæa. Barnabas and Saul administered the charity in Jerusalem (12.25).

6. **Paul.** — From this point the further development of the Christian church centres in the activity of the apostle Saul, who is

henceforth called by his Greek (or Roman) name Paul, while he appears mainly in Greek (or Roman) surroundings. By a series of three wonderful journeys, he planted Christianity first in the southern cities of the Roman province of Galatia (ch. 13, 14, 16.1-5); next, led by the divine revelation along a strange road (16.6-9), in the provinces of Macedonia and Achaia (ch. 16-18); and finally in the province of Asia (ch. 19). To consolidate his new congregations, and bring them into close union with Jerusalem as the centre of the whole church, he instituted on this third journey a general contribution in the four provinces for the benefit of the poor Christians in Jerusalem (Acts 24.17; Rom. 15.26; 1 Cor. 16.1; 2 Cor. 8.19 to 9.1 ff.). He ordered the money to be set apart week by week by each member in each church; and at last he sailed for Palestine with a numerous body of delegates, in charge of the whole sum (20.4). His intention now was to leave the work in these eastern provinces to others (20.25), while he himself went on to Rome (19.21), and thereafter to Spain, the great seat of Roman civilization in the west (Rom. 15.24). These intentions point unmistakably to a scheme already mapped out in Paul's mind for the evangelization of the Roman empire. His first intention was to reach Jerusalem in time for the Passover of 57 A.D.; but, in order to avoid a conspiracy against his life, he postponed the journey so as to arrive in time for Pentecost, May 28, 57 A.D. (though many authorities prefer the date 58 A.D.).

7. **The Trial of Paul,** ch. 20-28.—At this point the narrative becomes far more minute and detailed, marking that the author considered this part of his subject to be specially important. Not merely the stages of the trial at Jerusalem and Cæsarea, with the speeches of Paul in his own defence, but also the previous voyage to Palestine and the subsequent voyage by Crete and Malta to Rome, are described very fully. Further, whereas very little is said about the conduct of the Palestinian Christians towards Paul, the relations into which he was brought with the various Roman officials, Lysias, Felix, Festus, Julius, and with the crew of the ship bound for Rome, are stated very clearly. This would suggest that the author was concerned to bring out that there had existed at first no antagonism between the Roman government and the Christians; and that the trial of Paul at Rome resulted in his acquittal which implied that evangelization was not illegal. Many authorities have concluded from the abruptness of the ending of the book that it was never completed by the author; and this opinion may be regarded as highly probable, for the description of the final trial and acquittal of Paul before the supreme court in Rome is required in order to complete and explain the plan of the work.

Date and Author.—Many characteristics suggest that the date of this history belongs to the period following 75 A.D. There were

THE ACTS OF THE APOSTLES

already in existence many histories of the Saviour (Luke 1.1) when the plan of this history was conceived, and it has been suggested that the dates in Luke 3.1 were calculated between 79 and 81 A.D. The marked insistence on the fact that Jesus and afterwards Paul were repeatedly pronounced by Roman officials to be guiltless of any crime against the Roman law (Luke 23.2, 4, 14, 22; Acts 18. 16; 24.23; 25.25; 26.31; 27.3; 28.31, and presumably in the final trial at Rome), taken in connection with the fact that the Acts was composed in a time of persecution (14.22), after Christianity had been declared by the government to be illegal and a capital offence, would lead to the belief that the author was guided to a certain degree by the desire to "appeal to the truth of history against the immoral and ruinous policy" of persecution. The book, then, was intended to contain among other things "a temperate and solemn record of the facts concerning the formation of the church, its unswerving loyalty to the Roman government, its friendly reception by many of the Romans, and its triumphant vindication in the first great trial at Rome." Further, if the book is unfinished, the reason may probably lie in the death of the writer; perhaps an incident of the persecution.

With regard to the author, his personal acquaintance with many of the facts and personages of the history is shown by the marvellous vividness and accuracy of the narrative, especially where the scene lies in Greek lands or seas. The term "we" often occurs in the narrative of ch. 16, 20, 21, 27, 28, marking that the author was personally engaged in the incidents there described. His tastes and ideas (so far as they are disclosed under the veil of anonymity and impersonality in which he shrouded himself) are of the Greek type, and he certainly had no liking for the Jews. He was evidently a man of good education, and possessed a considerable range of knowledge and reading. Many little touches show an interest in medical details. All these characteristics agree with and confirm the very early tradition that the author was Luke, the friend and "the beloved physician" of Paul (Col. 4.14; 2 Tim. 4.11).

MIRACLES OF THE APOSTLES.

AFTER PROFESSOR W. M. RAMSAY, D.C.L., LL.D.

In Jesus' lifetime	Mat. 10.1, 8; Luke 10.9, 17.	Dorcas restored to life	Acts 9.40.
Lame man at Temple gate	Acts 3.2.	Peter delivered from prison	Acts 12.6.
Death of Ananias	Acts 5.5.	Elymas smitten with blindness	Acts 13.11.
Death of Sapphira	Acts 5.10.	Crippled healed at Lystra	Acts 14.8.
Many sick healed	Acts 5.16.	Damsel with spirit of divination	Acts 16.16
Apostles delivered from prison	Acts 5.19.	Special miracles through Paul	Acts 19.11. cf. 2 Cor. 12.12.
Great miracles of Stephen	Acts 6.8.		
Miracles of Philip	Acts 8.6.		
Saul's blindness	Acts 9.3.	Eutychus restored to life	Acts 20.10.
Ananias recovers Saul	Acts 9.17.	Viper's bite harmless	Acts 28.5.
Peter heals Æneas	Acts 9.34.	Publius' father healed	Acts 28.8

THE ACTS

The Introduction

1 The *a*former treatise I made, O The-oph'i-lus, concerning all that Je'sus began both to do and to teach, 2 until the day in which he was received up, after that he had given commandment through the Holy Spirit unto the apostles whom he had chosen: 3 to whom he also *b*showed himself alive after his passion by many proofs, appearing unto them by the space of forty days, and speaking the things concerning the kingdom of God: 4 and, *c*being assembled together with them, he charged them not to depart from Je-ru'sa-lem, but to wait for the promise of the Father, which, *said he*, ye heard from me: 5 for John indeed baptized with water; but ye shall be baptized *d*in the Holy Spirit not many days hence.

6 They therefore, when they were come together, asked him, saying, Lord, dost thou at this time restore the kingdom to Is'ra-el? 7 And he said unto them, It is not for you to know times or seasons, which the Father hath *e*set within his own authority. 8 But ye shall receive power, when the Holy Spirit is come upon you: and ye shall be my witnesses both in Je-ru'sa-lem, and in all Ju-dæ'a and Sa-ma'ri-a, and unto the

---

a Gr. *first.* *b* Gr. *presented.* *c* Or, *eating* *d* Or, *with* *e* Or, *appointed by*

CHAPTER 1

1. *Treatise.* The Gospel according to Luke. *Theophilus* (beloved of God). Mentioned also as 'most excellent Theophilus' (Lk. 1.3). This form of address, which is applied also to Felix (Acts 23.26; 24. 3) and to Festus (Acts 26.25) suggests that Theophilus was a man of rank, most probably a Roman official. He was a believer in Christ. *Began both to do and to teach,* etc. This refers to the work of Jesus on earth and in the flesh until Ascension Day, when he was received up into heaven. His work as recorded in Acts is carried on by the power of the Holy Spirit.

3. *Passion.* Literally, after he had suffered. *Many.* A word which strengthens belief in the resurrection by implying more appearances of Jesus than the few recorded in Luke's narrative.

4. *Jerusalem.* They were to remain together so that the apostles might receive the gift of the Holy Spirit at one time and place.

6. *Israel.* This shows how hard it was even for the apostles to give up the narrow idea of the earthly kingdom which Jesus had taught them not to expect.

7. *It is not for you.* Jesus discouraged their questions when not directly concerned with the advancement of his spiritual kingdom.

8. *Samaria.* Jesus had formerly forbidden the apostles to enter into any city of the Samaritans (Mt. 10. 5). He here revokes this command, thereby making known that the kingdom is not meant for Israel

uttermost part of the earth. 9 And when he had said these things, as they were looking, he was taken up; and a cloud received him out of their sight. 10 And while they were looking stedfastly into heaven as he went, behold two men stood by them in white apparel; 11 who also said, Ye men of Gal'i-lee, why stand ye looking into heaven? this Je'sus, who was received up from you into heaven, shall so come in like manner as ye beheld him going into heaven.

12 Then returned they unto Je-ru'sa-lem from the mount called Ol'i-vet, which is nigh unto Je'ru-sa-lem, a sabbath day's journey off. 13 And when they were come in, they went up into the upper chamber, where they were abiding; both Peter and John and *f*James and Andrew, Philip and Thomas, Bar-thol'o-mew and Mat'thew, *f*James *the son* of Al-phæ'us, and Si'mon the Zealot, and Ju'das *the gson* of *f*James. 14 These all with one accord continued stedfastly in prayer, *h*with the women, and Mary the mother of Je'sus, and with his brethren.

15 And in these days Peter stood up in the midst of the brethren, and said (and there was a multitude of *i*persons *gathered* together, about a hundred and twenty), 16 Brethren, it was needful that the scripture should be fulfilled, which the Holy Spirit spake before by the mouth of David concerning Ju'das, who was guide to them

---

f Or, *Jacob*   *g* Or, brother   See Jude 1.
h Or, *with certain women*

i Gr. *names*.   See Rev. 3.4.

---

only, but is to be gradually extended from Jerusalem to include the whole earth.

10. *Two men.* Angels, as is shown by the expression 'white apparel,' and also by the 'dazzling apparel' mentioned in Lk. 24.4.

11. *Why stand ye.* An emphatic call to waste no time in wondering, but to return to the Master's work.

12. *Olivet.* The Mount of Olives, east of Jerusalem, the scene of Jesus' agony in the garden of Gethsemane, of his betrayal, and lastly of his ascension. *Sabbath day's journey off.* Two thousand cubits, or three-fourths of a mile.

13. *Upper chamber.* Most probably the room in which the Last Supper was held. *Peter,* etc. The names of the apostles are here given for the fourth time in the New Testament. *Simon the Zealot.* Called Simon the Canenæan (Mt. 10.4; Mk. 3.18). The Zealots were the strictest observers of the Mosaic law.

14. *With one accord.* An expression repeated nine times in Acts and occurring but once elsewhere in the New Testament (Rom. 15.6). There is no sign of division, but only loyal obedience, among Christians recorded in Acts. *Women.* Their mention here is proof of the higher position given to women by Christianity. They were not allowed to pray or worship on an equality with men either in the Jewish Temple or in the synagogue, but were kept apart by themselves. See Mt. 28.1; Mk. 16.1; Lk. 23.55; Jn. 19.25. *Mary, the mother of Jesus.* The last mention of her in the New Testament. *His brethren.* James, Joseph (or Joses), Simon and Judas.

15. *These days.* The ten days of waiting after the Ascension and until the gift of the Holy Spirit. *Peter stood up.* His force of character made him leader. The special duty of the apostles was to proceed in filling the vacant place caused by the crime of Judas.

16. *Should be fulfilled.* Referring to the prophecies in the Psalms quoted from in ver. 20.

that took Je′sus. 17 For he was numbered among us, and received his *k*portion in this ministry. 18 (Now this man obtained a field with the reward of his iniquity; and falling headlong, he burst asunder in the midst, and all his bowels gushed out. 19 And it became known to all the dwellers at Je-ru′salem; insomuch that in their language that field was called A-kel′da-ma, that is, The field of blood.) 20 For it is written in the book of Psalms,

*l*Let his habitation be made desolate,

And let no man dwell therein: and,

*m*His *n*office let another take. 21 Of the men therefore that have companied with us all the time that the Lord Je′sus went in and went out *o*among us, 22 beginning from the baptism of John, unto the day that he was received up from us, of these must one become a witness with

us of his resurrection. 23 And they put forward two, Joseph called Bar′sab-bas, who was surnamed Jus′tus, and Mat-thi′-as. 24 And they prayed, and said, Thou, Lord, who knowest the hearts of all men, show of these two the one whom thou hast chosen, 25 to take the place in this ministry and apostleship from which Ju′das fell away, that he might go to his own place. 26 And they gave lots *p*for them; and the lot fell upon Mat-thi′as; and he was numbered with the eleven apostles.

2 And when the day of Pen′-te-cost *a*was now come, they were all together in one place. 2 And suddenly there came from heaven a sound as of the rushing of a mighty wind, and it filled all the house where they were sitting. 3 And there appeared unto them tongues *b*parting asunder, like as of fire; and it sat upon each one of them. 4 And they were all filled with the Holy

---

k Or, *lot*   *l* Ps. lxix. 25.   *m* Ps. cix. 8.
n Gr. *overseership.*   *o* Or, *over*   *p* Or, *unto*

a Gr. *was being fulfilled.*   *b* Or, *parting among them*   Or, *distributing themselves*

17. *Us.* The apostles.

19. *Their language.* Aramaic, a dialect of the ancient Hebrew.

21. *Of the men.* Ver. 21, 22 state the necessary qualifications for an apostle to succeed Judas: (1) The candidate must have been a disciple of Jesus from the time of his baptism by John; (2) he must have witnessed the resurrection.

23. *Put forward two.* A free choice of candidates, whether by the eleven, or by the eleven after consulting all the rest, is not certain; but most probably the latter.

24. *They prayed.* The first Christian prayer found in the New Testament. *Thou, Lord.* God only was to decide finally.

25. *To his own place.* The punishment fitted for such a crime.

26. *They gave lots.* A revival of

an old custom. The descent of the Holy Spirit as Guide and Comforter forever ended this use of the lot among true Christian believers.

CHAPTER 2

1. *The day of Pentecost.* The fiftieth day after the Feast of the Passover. The Feast of Pentecost was instituted to commemorate the gift of the law on Mount Sinai on the fiftieth day after the departure of the Jews from Egypt and also as the occasion of the annual offering of the first fruits of the harvest. It was a fitting day for the gift of the Holy Spirit to the church, as at this time many Jews from abroad visited Jerusalem.

4. *Other tongues.* Foreign languages. The power of the Holy

Spirit, and began to speak with other tongues, as the Spirit gave them utterance.

5 Now there were dwelling at Je-ru′sa-lem Jews, devout men, from every nation under heaven. 6 And when this sound was heard, the multitude came together, and were confounded, because that every man heard them speaking in his own language. 7 And they were all amazed and marvelled, saying, Behold, are not all these that speak Gal-i-læ′ans? 8 And how hear we, every man in our own language wherein we were born? 9 Par′thi-ans and Medes and E′lam-ites, and the dwellers in Mes-o-po-ta′mi-a, in Ju-dæ′a and Cap-pa-do′ci-a, in Pon′tus and A′si-a, 10 in Phryg′i-a and Pam-phyl′i-a, in E′gypt and the parts of Lib′y-a about Cy-re′ne, and sojourners from Rome, both Jews and proselytes, 11 Cre′tans and A-ra′bi-ans, we hear them speaking in our tongues the mighty works of God. 12 And they were all amazed, and were perplexed, saying one to another, What meaneth this? 13 But others mocking said, They are filled with new wine.

14 But Peter, standing up with the eleven, lifted up his voice, and spake forth unto them, *saying*, Ye men of Ju-dæ′a, and all ye that dwell at Je-ru′sa-lem, be this known unto you, and give ear unto my words. 15 For these are not drunken, as ye suppose; seeing it is *but* the third hour of the day; 16 but this is that which hath been spoken through the prophet Jo′el:

17 ᶜAnd it shall be in the last days, saith God,
I will pour forth of my Spirit upon all flesh:
And your sons and your daughters shall prophesy,
And your young men shall see visions,
And your old men shall dream dreams:

---

c Joel ii. 28 ff.

Spirit enabled them to know and understand each other notwithstanding differences of race and speech. In the confusion of tongues at the tower of Babel men were separated (Gen. 11.6–9).

5. *From every nation.* The love of the Jews for their holy city and the Temple worship brought some of them to Jerusalem from all foreign lands. Many came to pass the remainder of their lives there.

9–11. *Parthians and Medes and Elamites.* These were men of Jewish descent who came to Jerusalem either as pilgrims to the festival or as permanent residents. Parthia was a land south of the Caspian Sea; Media was a part of what is now Persia; and Elam was a region east of Babylonia. *Mesopotamia.* The region between the rivers Euphrates and Tigris, bounded by a mountain range on the north and by the Syro-Arabian desert on the south. *Cappadocia, in Pontus and Asia, in Phrygia and Pamphylia,* etc. Cappadocia, Pontus, Phrygia and Pamphylia were parts of the Roman province of Asia Minor. Libya was a region of North Africa. Crete was an island in the Mediterranean Sea. The Arabians were men of Jewish descent who came from Arabia.

15. *The third hour.* Nine o'clock in the morning.

17–21. *I will pour forth of my Spirit.* In these verses the words of the prophet Joel are quoted by Peter as being fulfilled in the experience of those who spoke with tongues at Pentecost. The prophecy, however, includes a wider range of spiritual manifestation than speaking with tongues, and its figurative expressions imply that even when the

18 Yea and on my *d*servants and
     on my *e*handmaidens in
     those days
     Will I pour forth of my Spirit;
       and they shall prophesy.
19 And I will show wonders in
     the heaven above,
     And signs on the earth be-
     neath;
     Blood, and fire, and vapor of
     smoke:
20 The sun shall be turned into
     darkness,
     And the moon into blood,
     Before the day of the Lord
     come,
     That great and notable *day*:
21 And it shall be, that whoso-
     ever shall call on the name
     of the Lord shall be saved.
22 Ye men of Is'ra-el, hear these
words: Je'sus of Naz'a-reth, a
man approved of God unto you
by *f*mighty works and wonders
and signs which God did by him
in the midst of you, even as ye
yourselves know; 23 him, being
delivered up by the determinate
counsel and foreknowledge of
God, ye by the hand of *g*lawless
men did crucify and slay: 24
whom God raised up, having
loosed the pangs of death: because it was not possible that he
should be holden of it. 25 For
David saith concerning him,

*h*I beheld the Lord always
     before my face;
     For he is on my right hand,
       that I should not be moved:
26 Therefore my heart was glad,
     and my tongue rejoiced;
     Moreover my flesh also shall
     *i*dwell in hope:
27 Because thou wilt not leave
     my soul unto Ha'des,
     Neither wilt thou give thy
     Holy One to see corrup-
     tion.
28 Thou madest known unto me
     the ways of life;
     Thou shalt make me full of
     gladness *k*with thy coun-
     tenance.

29 Brethren, I may say unto
you freely of the patriarch David, that he both died and was
buried, and his tomb is with us
unto this day. 30 Being therefore a prophet, and knowing that
God had sworn with an oath to
him, that of the fruit of his loins
*l*he would set *one* upon his
throne; 31 he foreseeing *this*
spake of the resurrection of the
Christ, that neither was he left
unto Ha'des, nor did his flesh
see corruption. 32 This Je'sus
did God raise up, *m*whereof we
all are witnesses. 33 Being
therefore *n*by the right hand of
God exalted, and having re-

---

d Gr. *bondmen.*   *e* Gr. *bondmaidens.*
f Gr. *powers.*   *g* Or, *men without the law*
See Rom. 2.12.

h Ps. xvi. 8 ff.   *i* Or, *tabernacle*   *k* Or,
in thy presence   *l* Or, one *should sit*   *m* Or,
of whom   *n* Or, *at*

---

kingdom of Christ shall have become
established in the world, difficulties
and tribulations shall still afflict
mankind.

22–28. *Men of Israel, hear these
words.* Peter in his sermon im-
presses upon his hearers the fact
that all these manifestations at
Pentecost find their explanation and
meaning in Jesus the Christ, whom

God raised from the dead. What
they now saw and heard and wondered at was the pouring forth of
the Holy Spirit, which Christ had
received of the Father and had now
imparted (ver. 33). *Thy Holy One.*
Jesus, raised from the dead according to the prophecy of David.

29–36. *The patriarch David,* etc.
Peter's thought in these verses is to

ceived of the Father the promise of the Holy Spirit, he hath poured forth this, which ye see and hear. 34 For David ascended not into the heavens: but he saith himself,

*o*The Lord said unto my Lord, Sit thou on my right hand,

35 Till I make thine enemies the footstool of thy feet.

36 Let *p*all the house of Is'ra-el therefore know assuredly, that God hath made him both Lord and Christ, this Je'sus whom ye crucified.

37 Now when they heard *this*, they were pricked in their heart, and said unto Peter and the rest of the apostles, Brethren, what shall we do? 38 And Peter *said* unto them, Repent ye, and be baptized every one of you in the name of Je'sus Christ unto the

remission of your sins; and ye shall receive the gift of the Holy Spirit. 39 For to you is the promise, and to your children, and to all that are afar off, *even* as many as the Lord our God shall call unto him. 40 And with many other words he testified, and exhorted them, saying, Save yourselves from this crooked generation. 41 They then *q*that received his word were baptized: and there were added *unto them* in that day about three thousand souls. 42 And they continued stedfastly in the apostles' teaching and *r*fellowship, in the breaking of bread and the prayers.

43 And fear came upon every soul: and many wonders and signs were done through the apostles *s*. 44 And all that believed were together, and had all

o Ps. cx. 1.   *p* Or, *every house*   *q* Or, *having received*   *r* Or, *in fellowship*   *s* Many ancient authorities add *in Jerusalem; and great fear was upon all.*

present Jesus to his hearers as Lord and the Christ, or the Divine Messiah, who was raised from the dead according to prophecy. *His tomb.* The tombs of the House of David were one of the notable features of interest in Jerusalem. *We all.* The apostles.

37. *Pricked in their heart.* Remorse on account of their consent to the crucifixion of Christ, and for failing to accept him as the Messiah. Among Peter's hearers there were probably some who had witnessed the triumphal entry of Jesus into Jerusalem, heard his preaching in the Temple and stood idly by while he was being led forth to die on the cross. *What shall we do?* The question implied a sincere desire for a better life of which Jesus should be the inspiration.

38. *Repent ye, and be baptized.* Peter's promptness turned their remorse to immediate account. In this reply he strove to obey one of the final commands of Jesus (Mt.

28.19). The gift of the Holy Spirit. See chs. 8.17; 10.47.

39. *All that are afar off.* The Gentiles. Peter saw this truth clearly enough; but it required the vision of the let-down sheet, with its lesson, to compel him to act according to his knowledge (ch. 10.9–16).

42–47. *Stedfastly in the apostles' teaching and fellowship.* These verses describe the religious life of the first converts to Christianity. We learn that (1) they accepted the teaching of the apostles in regard to Jesus, (2) they continued in the apostles' fellowship; (3) they partook of the Lord's Supper; (4) they joined with the apostles in the services of prayer, which were both public and private. Nevertheless they attended the services in the Temple, which shows that they had not yet entirely broken away from their ancestral faith, Judaism. The great change for them, from the point of view of religious practice and administration, was in accepting the spiritual

things common; 45 and they
sold their possessions and goods,
and parted them to all, according as any man had need. 46
And day by day, continuing
stedfastly with one accord in the
temple, and breaking bread at
home, they took their food with
gladness and singleness of heart,
47 praising God, and having
favor with all the people. And
the Lord added 'to them day by
day those that "were saved.

3 Now Peter and John were
going up into the temple at
the hour of prayer, *being* the
ninth *hour*. 2 And a certain
man that was lame from his
mother's womb was carried,
whom they laid daily at the door
of the temple which is called
Beautiful, to ask alms of them
that entered into the temple;
3 who seeing Peter and John

t Gr. together. u Or, were being saved

about to go into the temple,
asked to receive an alms. 4 And
Peter, fastening his eyes upon
him, with John, said, Look on
us. 5 And he gave heed unto
them, expecting to receive something from them. 6 But Peter
said, Silver and gold have I
none; but what I have, that give
I thee. In the name of Je'sus
Christ of Naz'a-reth, walk. 7
And he took him by the right
hand, and raised him up: and
immediately his feet and his
ankle-bones received strength.
8 And leaping up, he stood, and
began to walk; and he entered
with them into the temple, walking, and leaping, and praising
God. 9 And all the people saw
him walking and praising God:
10 and they took knowledge of
him, that it was he that sat for
alms at the Beautiful Gate of

leadership of the apostles instead of
that of the scribes and Pharisees.
Had all things common. A temporary and voluntary arrangement,
made because some of the new converts were poor, and therefore the
more easily gave up their small
property to the common fund along
with the worldly goods of their
richer brethren, in whom they had
complete confidence. The new converts did this of their own accord,
and doubtless were in large measure
thus influenced because many of
them believed that Jesus would soon
return, which naturally made comparatively unimportant all considerations about property. There was
no communism, so-called, about this
arrangement, because the individual
property rights of some members
had not been given up (ch. 12.12).
No further mention of incidents in
connection with the common fund
occurs after ch. 6.1, 2. *Breaking
bread at home.* This could not be
done in the Temple, but had to take
place privately. The distinctively

Christian institution of the Lord's
Supper is of course meant by 'breaking bread;' but it is to be distinguished from the meal, called the
love-feast, which at that time preceded it. The sacrament exactly
followed this order. The love-feast
and the sacrament together were
known as the Lord's Supper. After
a time, owing to certain abuses
which arose, the two began to be
separated (1 Cor. 11.20, 21, 25).
In 150 A.D. they were entirely so.

CHAPTER 3

1. *The ninth hour.* Three o'clock
in the afternoon. The other hours
of prayer were nine o'clock in the
forenoon, and twelve o'clock noon.
2–10. *A certain man that was lame.*
In these verses the healing of the
lame man by Peter is narrated.
Beautiful. The splendid Gate of
Nicanor, facing the east. It was
built of Corinthian brass and orna-
mented with silver and gold. *In the
name of Jesus Christ.* Peter's faith

the temple; and they were filled with wonder and amazement at that which had happened unto him.

11 And as he held Peter and John, all the people ran together unto them in the *porch that is called Sol'o-mon's, greatly wondering. 12 And when Peter saw it, he answered unto the people, Ye men of Is'ra-el, why marvel ye at this *bman? or why fasten ye your eyes on us, as though by our own power or godliness we had made him to walk? 13 The God of Abraham, and of I'saac, and of Jacob, the God of our fathers, hath glorified his *cServant Je'sus; whom ye delivered up, and denied before the face of Pi'late, when he had determined to release him. 14 But ye denied the Holy and Righteous One, and asked for a murderer to be granted unto you, 15 and killed the *dPrince of life; whom God raised from the dead; *ewhereof we are witnesses. 16 And *fby faith in his name hath his name made this man strong, whom ye behold and know: yea, the faith which is through him hath given him this perfect soundness in the presence of you all. 17 And now, brethren, I know that in ignorance ye did it, as did also your rulers. 18 But the things which God foreshowed by the mouth of all the prophets, that his Christ should suffer, he thus fulfilled. 19 Repent ye therefore, and turn again, that your sins may be blotted out, that so there may come seasons of refreshing from the presence of the Lord; 20 and that he may send the Christ who hath been appointed for you, *even Je'sus; 21 whom the heaven must receive until the times of restoration of all things, whereof God spake by the mouth of his holy prophets that have been from of old. 22 Mo'ses indeed said, *gA prophet shall the Lord God raise up unto you from among your brethren, *hlike unto me; to him shall ye hearken in all

---

a Or. *portico*   b Or, *thing*   c Or, *Child* See Mt. 12.18; Is. 42.1; 52.13; 53.11.   d Or,

Author   e Or, *of whom*   f Or, *on the ground of*   g Dt. xviii. 15.   h Or, *as he raised up me*

in Christ was no longer to be shaken. Its strength enabled him to heal the lame man. He and the other apostles never attempted to perform a miracle except in the name of Jesus Christ.

11. *The porch that is called Solomon's.* A cloister on the east side of the Temple buildings.

13. *The God of Abraham,* etc. A form of speech well adapted to win the confidence of the Jews. It was their God who had done this miracle through His Servant, Jesus Christ. But these conciliating words were immediately followed by a severe rebuke in ver. 13–15.

15. *Whereof we are witnesses.* A challenge to his hearers and to all other Jews to test the credibility of

Peter and the other apostles as witnesses of the resurrection.

16. *By faith in his name.* In his person, teaching and power.

17. *In ignorance ye did it.* A concession which made Peter's appeal more effective. See Lk. 23.24. *Your rulers.* They were more guilty than the people, yet even their ignorance is considerably judged.

18. *That his Christ should suffer.* See Ps. 22; Isa. 50.6; 53.5; Dan. 9. 26; Lk. 24.26; Jn. 13.18.

21. *Must receive.* Or, retain. *Restoration of all things.* The perfecting of mankind through complete acceptance of Christ and his kingdom.

22. *Like unto me,* etc. The coming and power of Jesus Christ foretold.

things whatsoever he shall speak unto you. 23 ʲAnd it shall be, that every soul that shall not hearken to that prophet, shall be utterly destroyed from among the people. 24 Yea and all the prophets from Sam′u-el and them that followed after, as many as have spoken, they also told of these days. 25 Ye are the sons of the prophets, and of the covenant which God ᵏmade with your fathers, saying unto Abraham, ˡAnd in thy seed shall all the families of the earth be blessed. 26 Unto you first God, having raised up his ᵐServant, sent him to bless you, in turning away every one of you from your iniquities.

4 And as they spake unto the people, ᵃthe priests and the captain of the temple and the Sad′du-cees came upon them,

2 being sore troubled because they taught the people, and proclaimed in Je′sus the resurrection from the dead. 3 And they laid hands on them, and put them in ward unto the morrow: for it was now eventide. 4 But many of them that heard the word believed; and the number of the men came to be about five thousand.

5 And it came to pass on the morrow, that their rulers and elders and scribes were gathered together in Je-ru′sa-lem; 6 and An′nas the high priest *was there*, and Ca′ia-phas, and John, and Al-ex-an′der, and as many as were of the kindred of the high priest. 7 And when they had set them in the midst, they inquired, By what power, or in what name, have ye done this? 8 Then Peter, filled with the Holy Spirit, said

---

ʲ Dt. xviii. 19. ᵏ Gr. *covenanted.* ˡ Gen. xii. 3; xxii. 18; xxvi. 4; xxviii. 14. *m* Or, *Child* See Mt. 12.18; Is. 42.1; 52.13;

53.11. *a* Some ancient authorities read *the chief priests.*

---

26. *You first.* The Jews first; afterward the Gentiles.

CHAPTER 4

1. *Captain of the temple.* Chief officer of the Temple guard of priests and Levites. *The Sadducees.* This Jewish party was especially angered because the apostles preached the resurrection.
2. *Sore troubled.* The preaching of Peter and the rapid increase of converts were amazing and ominous facts for the Jewish religious leaders. They thought that the crucifixion of Jesus had silenced a dangerous agitation. They were bitterly undeceived.
3. *In ward.* In prison. *Now eventide.* It was not legal to hold a judicial inquiry at night.
5. *Rulers and elders and scribes.* That is, the Sanhedrin, the supreme Jewish council. See note on Mt. 2.
4. The rulers were the chief priests,

those who had held the office of high priest. The scribes were the lawyers or rabbis, trained expounders of the law. The elders were not professionally trained, but were Jews of sufficient general prominence to entitle them to seats in the Sanhedrin. They corresponded to prominent laymen elected or appointed to the governing councils of modern Christian denominations. *Were gathered together.* The Sanhedrin met formally to try Peter and the other apostles.
6. *Annas.* See notes on Jn. 18. 12–14. He was so powerful that he practically controlled the decisions of the Sanhedrin. *Caiaphas.* Son-in-law of Annas. *John.* Some scholars think he was the same as Jonathan, son of Annas and successor of Caiaphas as high priest. *Alexander.* Not otherwise mentioned.
8–12. *Then Peter, filled with the Holy Spirit.* This affords an inspir-

unto them, Ye rulers of the people, and elders, 9 if we this day are examined concerning a good deed done to an impotent man, *b*by what means this man is made whole; 10 be it known unto you all, and to all the people of Is'ra-el, that in the name of Je'sus Christ of Naz'a-reth, whom ye crucified, whom God raised from the dead, *even* in *c*him doth this man stand here before you whole. 11 He is *d*the stone which was set at nought of you the builders, which was made the head of the corner. 12 And in none other is there salvation: for neither is there any other name under heaven, that is given among men, wherein we must be saved.

13 Now when they beheld the boldness of Peter and John, and had perceived that they were unlearned and ignorant men, they marvelled; and they took knowledge of them, that they had been with Je'sus. 14 And seeing the man that was healed standing with them, they could say nothing against it. 15 But when they had commanded them to go aside out of the council, they conferred among themselves, 16 saying, What shall we do to these men? for that indeed a notable *e*miracle hath been wrought through them, is manifest to all that dwell in Je-ru'sa-lem; and we cannot deny it. 17 But that it spread no further among the people, let us threaten them, that they speak henceforth to no man in this name. 18 And they called them, and charged them not to speak at all nor teach in the name of Je'sus. 19 But Peter and John answered and said unto them, Whether it is right in the sight of God to hearken unto you rather than unto God, judge ye: 20 for we cannot but speak the things which we saw and heard. 21 And they, when they had further threatened them, let them go, finding nothing how they might punish them, because of the people; for all men glorified God for that which was done. 22 For the man was more than forty years old, on whom this *e*miracle of healing was wrought.

---

b Or, *in whom*   *c* Or, *this name*   *d* Ps. cxviii. 22.   *e* Gr. *sign.*

ing view of the spiritually transformed apostle, who was now fixed and fearless in faith, at last true to the meaning of his name of 'rock.' Every word of his speech before the Sanhedrin was uncompromisingly in honor of Jesus Christ. *You all, and to all the people.* A challenge to the whole Jewish world, in Palestine and abroad. *In the name.* By the power. *In none other is there salvation.* That is, no other means of salvation for those to whom the knowledge of Jesus Christ has been brought.

13. *Unlearned and ignorant men.* That is, unlearned, common and ignorant according to the qualifications required by the Jewish religious system. Yet it must have entered somewhat into the thought of the Sanhedrin to respect the spiritual strength of men who had been taught by Jesus. Otherwise it is difficult to explain their concern about the miracle referred to in ver. 14. *Took knowledge,* etc. Took notice, probably for future identification. They might have to deal judicially with Peter and John later. Probably some of them had already seen the two apostles with Jesus when he was brought before Caiaphas and Pilate.

23 And being let go, they came to their own company, and reported all that the chief priests and the elders had said unto them. 24 And they, when they heard it, lifted up their voice to God with one accord, and said, O *f*Lord, *g*thou that didst make the heaven and the earth and the sea, and all that in them is: 25 *h*who by the Holy Spirit, *by* the mouth of our father David thy servant, didst say,

*i*Why did the *k*Gen'tiles rage,
And the peoples *l*imagine vain things?

26 The kings of the earth set themselves in array,
And the rulers were gathered together,
Against the Lord, and against his *m*Anointed:

27 for of a truth in this city against thy holy *n*Servant Je'sus, whom thou didst anoint, both Her'od and Pon'tius Pi'late, with the *k*Gen'tiles and the peoples of Is'ra-el, were gathered together, 28 to do whatsoever thy hand and thy counsel foreordained to come to pass. 29 And now, Lord, look upon their threatenings: and grant unto thy *o*servants to speak thy word with all boldness, 30 while thou stretchest forth thy hand to heal; and that signs and wonders may be done through the name of thy holy *n*Servant Je'sus. 31 And when they had prayed, the place was shaken wherein they were gathered together; and they were all filled with the Holy Spirit, and they spake the word of God with boldness.

32 And the multitude of them that believed were of one heart and soul: and not one *of them* said that aught of the things which he possessed was his own; but they had all things common. 33 And with great power gave the apostles their witness of the resurrection of the Lord Je'sus*p*:

---

f Gr. *Master.* *g* Or, *thou* art *he that did make* *h* The Greek text in this clause is somewhat uncertain. *i* Ps. ii. 1, 2. *k* Gr. *nations.* *l* Or, *meditate* *m* Gr. *Christ.*

n Or, *Child* See marginal note on ch. 3. 13. *o* Gr. *bondservants.* *p* Some ancient authorities add *Christ.*

---

27. *Herod.* Herod Antipas, son of Herod the Great. He was tetrarch or ruler of Galilee and Peræa. When Pilate knew that Jesus had lived in Galilee and was probably within Herod's jurisdiction, he sent him to Herod for trial, as the latter was then in Jerusalem. See notes on Lk. 23.6–12. *Pontius Pilate.* Sixth Roman procurator of Judæa. His official term was A.D. 25–36. In the latter year he was sent to Rome to answer a charge brought against him by the Samaritans. There is no historic account of his subsequent life.

29. *Look upon their threatenings.* A prayer to be shielded from their threatenings.

30. *While thou stretchest forth thy hand,* etc. A prayer to God to continue, in behalf of the apostles, the signs and wonders which Jesus had wrought.

31. *The place was shaken,* etc. Manifestations in part like those at Pentecost occurred. *Spake the word.* Proceeded with their preaching and teaching, regardless of the warnings and threats of the Sanhedrin.

32–37. *One heart and soul.* In these verses is described the operation of the voluntary and temporary expedient of the common fund referred to in ch. 2.44. See notes on ch. 2.42–47. *Not one of them said,* etc. Showing clearly that individual rights of property were reserved. The fact was, that owners of property treated their possessions, for the time being—that is, during the temporary needs of the first Chris-

and great grace was upon them all. 34 For neither was there among them any that lacked: for as many as were possessors of lands or houses sold them, and brought the prices of the things that were sold, 35 and laid them at the apostles' feet: and distribution was made unto each, according as any one had need.

36 And Joseph, who by the apostles was surnamed Bar′na-bas (which is, being interpreted, Son of *q*exhortation), a Le′vite, a man of Cy′prus by race, 37 having a field, sold it, and brought the money and laid it at the apostles' feet.

5 But a certain man named An-a-ni′as, with Sap-phi′ra his wife, sold a possession, 2 and kept back *part* of the price, his wife also being privy to it, and brought a certain part, and laid it at the apostles' feet. 3 But Peter said, An-a-ni′as, why hath Satan filled thy heart to *a*lie to the Holy Spirit, and to keep

q Or. consolation   See Lk. 2.25; ch. 9.31; 15.31; 2 Cor. 1.3–7, in the Gr.

back *part* of the price of the land? 4 While it remained, did it not remain thine own? and after it was sold, was it not in thy power? How is it that thou hast conceived this thing in thy heart? thou hast not lied unto men, but unto God. 5 And An-a-ni′as hearing these words fell down and gave up the ghost: and great fear came upon all that heard it. 6 And the *b*young men arose and wrapped him round, and they carried him out and buried him.

7 And it was about the space of three hours after, when his wife, not knowing what was done, came in. 8 And Peter answered *√*unto her, Tell me whether ye sold the land for so much. And she said, Yea, for so much. 9 But Peter *said* unto her, How is it that ye have agreed together to try the Spirit of the Lord? behold, the feet of them that have buried thy husband are at the door, and

a Or, deceive   *b Gr. younger.*

tian Church at Jerusalem—as if they were common property. They forbore to assert their right to those possessions. *Any that lacked.* The needy did not suffer for want of worldly goods. *A Levite.* The Levites assisted the priests in the Temple services and performed the more menial tasks. *Cyprus.* An island in the Mediterranean Sea, sixty miles from the coast of Syria and forty-five miles from the coast of Asia Minor. Its area is 3,584 square miles. In Christ's time there were large numbers of Jews in the island. Christianity was established there shortly after the death of Stephen.

CHAPTER 5

1. *Ananias* (the graciousness of Jehovah). Sapphira (beautiful).

3–6. *But Peter said.* Peter's immediate knowledge and rebuke of the hypocrisy and falsehood of Ananias were inspired by God. The punishment of death immediately inflicted upon Ananias was the act of God. *Lie to the Holy Spirit.* Said because Ananias had committed a sin which directly tended to overthrow the work of the Holy Spirit, whose power had just descended upon the earliest builders, under divine guidance, of the infant church. The introduction of falsehood and deception at this juncture would have ruined the work of the apostles. *Thine own.* Another proof that the individual right of property had not been given up. See notes on ch. 2.42–47.

9. *Ye have agreed together.* The answer of Sapphira, given in ver. 8,

they shall carry thee out. 10 And she fell down immediately at his feet, and gave up the ghost: and the young men came in and found her dead, and they carried her out and buried her by her husband. 11 And great fear came upon the whole church, and upon all that heard these things.

12 And by the hands of the apostles were many signs and wonders wrought among the people: and they were all with one accord in Sol'o-mon's ᶜporch. 13 But of the rest durst no man join himself to them: howbeit the people magnified them; 14 ᵈand believers were the more added to the Lord, multitudes both of men and women: 15 insomuch that they even carried out the sick into the streets, and laid them on beds and ᵉcouches, that, as Peter came by, at the least his shadow might overshadow some one of them. 16 And there also came together the multitude from the cities round

about Je-ru'sa-lem, bringing sick folk, and them that were vexed with unclean spirits: and they were healed every one.

17 But the high priest rose up, and all they that were with him (which is the sect of the Sad'du-cees), and they were filled with jealousy, 18 and laid hands on the apostles, and put them ịn public ward. 19 But an angel of the Lord by night opened the prison doors, and brought them out, and said, 20 Go ye, and stand and speak in the temple to the people all the words of this Life. 21 And when they heard *this*, they entered into the temple about daybreak, and taught. But the high priest came, and they that were with him, and called the council together, and all the senate of the children of Is'ra-el, and sent to the prison-house to have them brought. 22 But the officers that came found them not in the prison; and they returned, and told, 23 saying, The prison-

---

c Or, *portico*   d Or, *and there were the more added* to them, *believing on the Lord*

e Or, *pallets*

proved that she had knowledge of her husband's deceit and was equally guilty with him.

12. *In Solomon's porch.* The apostles and their followers resorted to this place daily for their public meetings. See note on ch. 3.11.

13. *Of the rest.* The non-believers.

15. *His shadow.* A touch of superstition is evident here. See ch. 19.12.

17. *Filled with jealousy.* The warning given to the apostles by the Sanhedrin having been disregarded, the high priest and his Sadducean supporters imprisoned Peter and John a second time. See note on Mt. 3.7.

20. *The words of this Life.* The spiritual life brought to mankind by the teaching, death and resurrection of Jesus.

21. *The council together, and all the senate*, etc. 'Council' and 'senate' both refer to the Sanhedrin, the supreme Jewish legislative and administrative body. Some scholars have suggested that 'senate of the children of Israel' was added by Luke for the benefit of Theophilus to whom he wrote and who, though a Roman official, was probably a Greek by birth and would more readily understand the nature of the Jewish Sanhedrin by speaking of it as a senate. Another explanation is that 'council' means the smaller Sanhedrin, that is, the less numerous attendance for routine business, while 'senate' means the full Sanhedrin of seventy-one members, assembled for the most important deliberations.

house we found shut in all safety, and the keepers standing at the doors: but when we had opened, we found no man within. 24 Now when the captain of the temple and the chief priests heard these words, they were much perplexed concerning them whereunto this would grow. 25 And there came one and told them, Behold, the men whom ye put in the prison are in the temple standing and teaching the people. 26 Then went the captain with the officers, and brought them, *but* without violence; for they feared the people, lest they should be stoned. 27 And when they had brought them, they set them before the council. And the high priest asked them, 28 saying, We strictly charged you not to teach in this name: and behold, ye have filled Je-ru'sa-lem with your teaching, and intend to bring this man's blood upon us. 29 But Peter and the apostles answered and said, We must

obey God rather than men. 30 The God of our fathers raised up Je'sus, whom ye slew, hanging him on a tree. 31 Him did God exalt *f*with his right hand *to be* a Prince and a Saviour, to give repentance to Is'ra-el, and remission of sins. 32 And we are witnesses*g* of these *h*things; *i*and *so is* the Holy Spirit, whom God hath given to them that obey him.

33 But they, when they heard this, were cut to the heart, and were minded to slay them. 34 But there stood up one in the council, a Phar'i-see, named Ga-ma'li-el, a doctor of the law, had in honor of all the people, and commanded to put the men forth a little while. 35 And he said unto them, Ye men of Is'ra-el, take heed to yourselves as touching these men, what ye are about to do. 36 For before these days rose up Theu'das, giving himself out to be somebody; to whom a number of men, about four hundred, joined

---

f Or, *at in him.*   *g* Some ancient authorities add   *h* Gr. *sayings.*   *i* Some ancient

authorities read *and God hath given the Holy Spirit to them that obey him.*

---

24. *Captain of the temple.* See note on ch. 4.1.

28. *Bring this man's blood upon us.* The speech of men who had learned to look upon themselves as culprits, and who feared righteous vengeance. See Mt. 27.25 and note thereon.

29–32. *Peter and the apostles answered*, etc. Peter's speech contains the substance of what he had already said. See chs. 3.12–26; 4.8–12.

33. *Were cut to the heart.* Not with remorse, but with greater anger than before.

34. *Gamaliel.* The most distinguished rabbi then living and the teacher of the apostle Paul. He was the grandson of Hillel, the great doctor of the law who was the rival of Shammai. Hillel and Shammai

were the leaders respectively of the liberal and the conservative schools of Jewish legal interpretation.

35–39. *Ye men of Israel, take heed,* etc. The discreet moderation of Gamaliel may have been due in part to a latent sympathy with the Christian doctrine of the resurrection. As a leader of the Pharisees, he could not wish that doctrine to be discredited by the victory of the Sadducees, who denied it. As a great scholar and teacher and member of the Sanhedrin, he must have reflected deeply upon the new Christian sect, weighing its political chances, noting its fundamental beliefs, and estimating the character of its apostles and adherents. He had probably learned much about

themselves: who was slain; and all, as many as obeyed him, were dispersed, and came to nought. 37 After this man rose up Ju'das of Gal'i-lee in the days of the enrolment, and drew away *some of the* people after him: he also perished; and all, as many as obeyed him, were scattered abroad. 38 And now I say unto you, Refrain from these men, and let them alone: for if this counsel or this work be of men, it will be overthrown: 39 but if it is of God, ye will not be able to overthrow them; lest haply ye be found even to be fighting against God. 40 And to him they agreed: and when they had called the apostles unto them, they beat them and charged them not to speak in the name of Je'sus, and let them go. 41 They therefore departed from the presence of the council, re-

joicing that they were counted worthy to suffer dishonor for the Name. 42 And every day, in the temple and at home, they ceased not to teach and to *k*preach Je'sus *as* the Christ.

6 Now in these days, when the number of the disciples was multiplying, there arose a murmuring of the *a*Gre'cian Jews against the Hebrews be-cause their widows were neg-lected in the daily ministration. 2 And the twelve called the multitude of the disciples unto them, and said, It is not *b*fit that we should forsake the word of God, and *c*serve tables. 3 *d*Look ye out therefore, breth-ren, from among you seven men of good report, full of the Spirit and of wisdom, whom we may appoint over this business. 4 But we will continue stedfastly in prayer, and in the ministry

---

k Gr. *bring good tidings of.* See ch. 13. 32; 14.15. a Gr. *Hellenists.* b Gr. *pleas-ing.* c Or, *minister to tables* d Some an-

cient authorities read *But, brethren, look ye out from among you.*

Jesus and his teaching before the date of this speech, which was in A.D. 35 or 36. His attitude of men-tal detachment contrasts memora-bly with that of his brother members of the council. He stood for the thoughtful minority, the saving remnant of a blindly prejudiced caste that missed its chance of spir-itual renewal. He saw that the sur-vival of the new doctrines was more likely than their defeat. He was familiar with the history of Jewish imposters; but he must have known that Jesus of Nazareth, the crucified reformer whose marvellous teaching and known life of self-sacrificing love led to an early and awful death, was not one of the false Messiahs. In his plea for delay prudence made him keep back much. Consider-ing the issue, the occasion and the temper of the Sanhedrin, Gama-liel's speech was little less than a guarded admission of the truth.

Judas of Galilee. A revolutionary leader who in A.D. 6 or 7 opposed the imposition of new taxes. *Enrolment.* A taking of the census for purposes of taxation.

40. *They beat them.* For their dis-obedience of the Sanhedrin's first command (ch. 4.18). The penalty was probably thirty-nine stripes. See 2 Cor. 11.24.

CHAPTER 6

1. *Grecian Jews.* Greek-speaking Jews. Their widows suffered in the distribution (ministration) of food, receiving less than their Aramaic-speaking sisters.
2. *Serve tables.* Distribute the food; or, perhaps, attend to the tables where the money was given to applicants.
3. *Wisdom.* Practical ability and tact.

of the word. 5 And the saying pleased the whole multitude: and they chose Ste'phen, a man full of faith and of the Holy Spirit, and Philip, and Proch'o-rus, and Ni-ca'nor, and Ti'mon, and Par'me-nas, and Nic-o-la'üs a proselyte of An'ti-och; 6 whom they set before the apostles: and when they had prayed, they laid their hands upon them.

7 And the word of God increased; and the number of the disciples multiplied in Je-ru'-sa-lem exceedingly; and a great company of the priests were obedient to the faith.

8 And Ste'phen, full of grace and power, wrought great wonders and signs among the people. 9 But there arose certain of them that were of the synagogue called *the synagogue* of the 'Lib'er-tines, and of the Cy-re'-ni-ans, and of the Al-ex-an'dri-ans, and of them of Ci-li'ci-a and A'si-a, disputing with Ste'phen. 10 And they were not able to withstand the wisdom and the Spirit by which he spake. 11 Then they suborned men, who said, We have heard him speak blasphemous words against Mo'-ses, and *against* God. 12 And they stirred up the people, and the elders, and the scribes, and came upon him, and seized him, and brought him into the council, 13 and set up false witnesses, who said, This man ceaseth not to speak words against this holy place, and the law: 14 for we

e Or, Freedmen

5, 6. *They chose Stephen*, etc. The names of the chosen seven are Greek, and probably the majority of them were Greek-speaking Jews. This would imply a disposition to trust the latter to distribute the supplies so as to remedy the abuse which had arisen (ver. 1). Excepting Stephen and Philip nothing is afterward recorded of the seven. Philip subsequently preached in Samaria (ch. 8.5). This popular choice or election of the seven was the origin of the grade of church officers afterward known as the diaconate. The number of the first deacons was fixed at seven, following the Jewish custom of choosing seven for civic, legal and religious service in the towns. Thus the local courts were in charge of seven elders. Since the protest of Greek-speaking, or Hellenistic Jews, was the cause of this development in the organization of the early Church, it should be noted that they were, as a class, more cultured and tolerant than their Hebrew or Aramaic-speaking brethren. They were born or had lived abroad among Gentiles and were more kindly disposed toward them. They read the Old Testament in Greek, in the famous Septuagint, a translation of the Hebrew Scriptures said to have been made by about seventy scholars at Alexandria in 270 or 280 B.C. by order of Ptolemy Philadelphus, King of Egypt.

7. *A great company of the priests.* Their conversion was far more significant than that of the ordinary Jew. They had to bear the full brunt of hatred and persecution from those they left.

8–15. *Wrought great wonders and signs*, etc. In these verses the preaching, miracles and arrest of Stephen are recorded. *Libertines.* These were the descendants of Jewish prisoners in Rome who had subsequently achieved their freedom. *Cyrenians.* Jews from Cyrene, a city of North Africa. See note on Mt. 27.32. *Alexandrians.* Jews from Alexandria, a city of Egypt founded by Alexander the Great in 332 B.C. The Jewish population was large. *Cilicia.* The southeastern portion of Asia Minor. *Asia.* The Roman province of that name. It contained the cities of Ephesus, Smyrna and Pergamos. *Suborned men.* Procured false wit-

296

have heard him say, that this Je'sus of Naz'a-reth shall destroy this place, and shall change the customs which Mo'ses delivered unto us. 15 And all that sat in the council, fastening their eyes on him, saw his face as it had been the face of an angel.

7 And the high priest said, Are these things so? 2 And he said,

Brethren and fathers, hearken: The God of glory appeared unto our father Abraham, when he was in Mes-o-po-ta'mi-a, before he dwelt in Ha'ran, 3 and said unto him, Get thee out of thy land, and from thy kindred, and come into the land which I shall show thee. 4 Then came he out of the land of the Chal-dæ'ans, and dwelt in Ha'ran: and from thence, when his father was dead, *God* removed him into this land, wherein ye now dwell: 5 and he gave him none inheritance in it, no, not so much as to set his foot on: and he promised that he would give it to him in possession, and to his seed after him, when *as yet* he had no child. 6 And God spake on this wise, that his seed should sojourn in a strange land, and that they should bring them into bondage, and treat them ill, four hundred years. 7 And the nation to which they shall be in bondage will I judge, said God: and after that shall they come forth, and serve me in this place. 8 And he gave him the covenant of circumcision: and so *Abraham* begat I'saac, and circumcised him the eighth day; and I'saac *begat* Jacob, and Jacob the twelve patriarchs. 9 And the patriarchs, moved with jealousy against Joseph, sold him into E'gypt: and God was with him, 10 and delivered him out of all

---

nesses. *Holy place.* The Temple. *Change the customs.* From Stephen's subsequent defence it may be inferred that he had said that God was not always to be worshipped at Jerusalem as an exclusive centre. This was falsely reported so as to give color to a charge of blasphemy, not only against the holiness of which the Temple was a symbol, but against the whole Jewish system, of which Jehovah was the founder. *The face of an angel.* Evidence of the calm spiritual triumph and peace with God.

CHAPTER 7

2. *Brethren and fathers.* Fellow-Israelites and members of the Sanhedrin. The defence of Stephen occupies nearly all of this chapter, and is concluded in ver. 53. It is not a specific answer to the accusation made against him in ch. 6.14. The anger of his hearers did not permit him to say all that he intended to say; otherwise he would surely have denied the charge that Jesus intended to destroy the Temple or change the customs which Moses delivered unto the Jews. The false witnesses had perverted the words of Jesus. If Stephen's defence had not been interrupted so tragically, he might have told the Sanhedrin that unless the Jews accepted Jesus as the Messiah foretold by Moses and the prophets, both their Temple and their city would be destroyed. *Mesopotamia.* See notes on ch. 2.9–11. *Haran.* A city of northern Mesopotamia.

4. *Chaldæans.* A Semitic people that occupied the seacoast region of South Babylonia in the twelfth century B.C.

7. *In this place.* Canaan.

8. *The covenant of circumcision.* See Gen. 17.9–14.

9. *Moved with jealousy against Joseph,* etc. See Gen. 37.4.

his afflictions, and gave him favor and wisdom before Pha'-raoh king of E'gypt; and he made him governor over E'gypt and all his house. 11 Now there came a famine over all E'gypt and Ca'naan, and great affliction: and our fathers found no sustenance. 12 But when Jacob heard that there was grain in E'gypt, he sent forth our fathers the first time. 13 And at the second time Joseph was made known to his brethren; and Joseph's race became manifest unto Pha'raoh. 14 And Joseph sent, and called to him Jacob his father, and all his kindred, threescore and fifteen souls. 15 And Jacob went down into E'gypt; and he died, himself and our fathers; 16 and they were carried over unto She'chem, and laid in the tomb that Abraham bought for a price in silver of the sons of *a*Ha'mor in She'chem. 17 But as the time of the promise drew nigh which God vouch-safed unto Abraham, the people grew and multiplied in E'gypt, 18 till there arose another king over E'gypt, who knew not Joseph. 19 The same dealt craftily with our race, and ill-treated our fathers, that *b*they should cast out their babes to the end they might not *c*live. 20 At which season Mo'ses was born, and was *d*exceeding fair; and he was nourished three months in his father's house: 21 and when he was cast out, Pha'raoh's daughter took him up, and nourished him for her own son. 22 And Mo'ses was instructed in all the wisdom of the E'gyp-tians; and he was mighty in his words and works. 23 But when he was wellnigh forty years old, it came into his heart to visit his brethren the children of Is'ra-el. 24 And see-ing one *of them* suffer wrong, he defended him, and avenged him that was oppressed, smiting the E-gyp'tian: 25 and he supposed that his brethren understood that God by his hand was giving them *e*deliverance; but they understood not. 26 And the day following he appeared unto them as they strove, and would have set them at one again, saying, Sirs, ye are brethren; why do ye wrong one to another? 27 But he that did his neighbor wrong thrust him away, saying, Who made thee a ruler and a judge over us? 28 Wouldest thou kill me, as thou killedst the E-gyp'-tian yesterday? 29 And Mo'ses fled at this saying, and became a sojourner in the land of Mid'i-an, where he begat two sons. 30 And when forty years were fulfilled, an angel appeared to him in the wilderness of mount Si'nai, in a flame of fire in a bush. 31 And when Mo'ses saw it, he wondered at the sight: and as

a Gr. *Emmor.*   *b* Or, *he*   *c* Gr. *be pre-served alive.*   *d* Or, *fair unto God*   Comp.
2 Cor. 10.4.   *e* Or, *salvation*

18. *Who knew not Joseph.* Had no appreciation of his beneficent work in behalf of Egypt, and therefore no sense of obligation toward the Hebrew race to which he belonged.

22. *The wisdom of the Egyptians.* The knowledge under control of the priestly caste. It included mathe-matics, natural science, astronomy, magic, medicine and astrology.

29. *Midian.* Northwest Arabia.

he drew near to behold, there came a voice of the Lord, 32 I am the God of thy fathers, the God of Abraham, and of I'saac, and of Jacob. And Mo'ses trembled, and durst not behold. 33 And the Lord said unto him, Loose the shoes from thy feet: for the place whereon thou standest is holy ground. 34 I have surely seen the affliction of my people that is in E'gypt, and have heard their groaning, and I am come down to deliver them: and now come, I will send thee into E'gypt. 35 This Mo'ses whom they refused, saying, Who made thee a ruler and a judge? him hath God sent *to be* both a ruler and a *f*deliverer with the hand of the angel that appeared to him in the bush. 36 This man led them forth, having wrought wonders and signs in E'gypt, and in the Red sea, and in the wilderness forty years. 37 This is that Mo'ses, who said unto the children of Is'ra-el, *g*A prophet shall God raise up unto you from among your brethren, *h*like unto me. 38 This is he that was in the *i*church in the wilderness with the angel that spake to him in the mount Si'nai, and with our fathers: who received living oracles to give unto us:

39 to whom our fathers would not be obedient, but thrust him from them, and turned back in their hearts unto E'gypt, 40 saying unto Aar'on, Make us gods that shall go before us: for as for this Mo'ses, who led us forth out of the land of E'gypt, we know not what is become of him. 41 And they made a calf in those days, and brought a sacrifice unto the idol, and rejoiced in the works of their hands. 42 But God turned, and gave them up to serve the host of heaven; as it is written in the book of the prophets,

*k*Did ye offer unto me slain beasts and sacrifices
Forty years in the wilderness, O house of Is'ra-el?

43 And ye took up the tabernacle of Mo'loch,
And the star of the god Re'phan,
The figures which ye made to worship them:
And I will carry you away beyond Bab'y-lon.

44 Our fathers had the tabernacle of the testimony in the wilderness, even as he appointed who spake unto Mo'ses, that he should make it according to the figure that he had seen. 45 Which also our fathers, in their

---

f Gr. *redeemer.* *g* Dt. xviii. 15. *h* Or, *as* he raised up *me* *i* Or, *congregation*

k Amos v. 25 ff.

---

37. *Like unto me.* Moses was like unto Jesus, in that he was a lawgiver, prophet and deliverer or saviour, a type of the Saviour, the divine Messiah, that was to come.

38. *Living oracles.* The revelations and commands received by Moses on Mount Sinai.

39. *Unto Egypt.* Unto the worship of Egyptian idols.

42. *The host of heaven.* The stars.

See 2 Kings 17.16.

43. *Moloch.* A god of the Ammonites. Children were offered to him as sacrifices. *Rephan.* The planet Saturn.

44. *Tabernacle of the testimony.* Literally 'tent of meeting,' the tent where God met his people. It contained the Ark and the two tables on which the ten commandments were written.

turn, brought in with [l]Josh'u-a
when they entered on the possession of the [m]nations, that God
thrust out before the face of our
fathers, unto the days of David;
46 who found favor in the sight
of God, and asked to find a
habitation for the God of Jacob.
47 But Sol'o-mon built him a
house. 48 Howbeit the Most
High dwelleth not in *houses* made
with hands; as saith the prophet,
49 [n]The heaven is my throne,
   And the earth the footstool
      of my feet:
   What manner of house will
      ye build me? saith the
      Lord:
   Or what is the place of my
      rest?
50 Did not my hand make all
   these things?

51 Ye stiffnecked and uncircumcised in heart and ears, ye
do always resist the Holy Spirit:
as your fathers did, so do ye.

52 Which of the prophets did
not your fathers persecute? and
they killed them that showed
before of the coming of the
Righteous One; of whom ye have
now become betrayers and murderers; 53 ye who received the
law [o]as it was ordained by
angels, and kept it not.

54 Now when they heard these
things, they were cut to the
heart, and they gnashed on him
with their teeth. 55 But he,
being full of the Holy Spirit,
looked up stedfastly into heav-
en, and saw the glory of God,
and Je'sus standing on the right
hand of God, 56 and said, Behold, I see the heavens opened,
and the Son of man standing
on the right hand of God. 57
But they cried out with a loud
voice, and stopped their ears,
and rushed upon him with one
accord; 58 and they cast him
out of the city, and stoned him:

---

l Gr. *Jesus.* Comp. Heb. 4.8. *m* Or,
Gentiles Comp. ch. 4.25. *n* Is. lxvi. 1 f.

o Or, *as the ordinance of angels* Gr. *unto
ordinances of angels.*

---

46. *To find a habitation.* See 2
Sam. 7.16, 17; Ps. 132.5.
48. *Not in houses made with hands.*
This was a direct intimation by
Stephen that the Temple was not to
be the permanent centre of divine
worship. It was a challenge to the
Sanhedrin, who could not let it pass
unregarded. See note on Jn. 4.21.
51. *Ye stiffnecked and uncircumcised in heart*, etc. Stephen, pas-
sionately determined to declare and
defend the truth, suddenly dared all
consequences. Such words, spoken
by an unknown and obscure man to
the supreme Jewish council, expressed the very height of fearlessness and provoked the sharpest
vengeance. Apparently the Sanhedrin had not yet, however, resolved
to kill him.
53. *And kept it not.* A charge of
disobedience of the law made
against those who were its traditional guardians and interpreters.

56. *The Son of man.* The only
instance in the New Testament
where this title is applied to Jesus
by a believer. See Mt. 26.64.
Standing. As if rising to welcome
his first martyr.
57. *Stopped their ears.* Undoubtedly they were shocked by what
appeared to them as blasphemy.
Rushed upon him. Mob violence by
members of the supreme Jewish
council, men upon whom there was
the highest obligation to set the
example of order in administration
of the law. In this case sentence of
death by stoning, the penalty for
blasphemy, was not legally pronounced, nor did the Sanhedrin obtain the necessary permission of the
Roman governor to execute a capital
offender. *The witnesses.* They were
legally required to cast the first
stones at the offender (Deut. 17.7).
58. *Saul* (one asked for). Born
of Jewish parents in comfortable

and the witnesses laid down their garments at the feet of a young man named Saul. 59 And they stoned Ste'phen, calling upon *the Lord*, and saying, Lord Je'sus, receive my spirit. 60 And he kneeled down, and cried with a loud voice, Lord, lay not this sin to their charge. And when he had said this, he fell **8** asleep. 1 And Saul was consenting unto his death.

And there arose on that day a great persecution against the church which was in Je-ru'sa-lem; and they were all scattered abroad throughout the regions of Ju-dæ'a and Sa-ma'ri-a, except the apostles. 2 And devout men buried Ste'phen, and made great lamentation over him. 3 But Saul laid waste the church, entering into every house, and dragging men and women committed them to prison.

4 They therefore that were scattered abroad went about *a*preaching the word. 5 And Philip went down to the city of Sa-ma'ri-a, and proclaimed unto them the Christ. 6 And the

multitudes gave heed with one accord unto the things that were spoken by Philip, when they heard, and saw the signs which he did. 7 *b*For *from* many of those that had unclean spirits, they came out, crying with a loud voice: and many that were palsied, and that were lame, were healed. 8 And there was much joy in the city.

9 But there was a certain man, Si'mon by' name, who beforetime in the city used sorcery, and amazed the *c*people of Sa-ma'ri-a, giving out that himself was some great one: 10 to whom they all gave heed, from the least to the greatest, saying, This man is'that power of God which is called Great. 11 And they gave heed to him, because that of long time he had amazed them with his sorceries. 12 But when they believed Philip *a*preaching good tidings concerning the kingdom of God and the name of Je'sus Christ, they were baptized, both men and women. 13 And Si'mon also himself believed: and being baptized, he continued with Philip;

---

a Comp. marg. note on ch. 5.42.   *b* Or, *For many of those that had unclean spirits*   *c* Gr. *nation.*

that cried with a loud voice came forth

circumstances at Tarsus, Cilicia. By birth he was a Roman citizen and by trade a tent-maker. He was trained for the position of a rabbi under Gamaliel at Jerusalem. Tarsus was a city noted for its culture. Jewish, Greek and Roman influences surrounded Saul in his youth, but under Gamaliel's teaching he had become a strict Pharisee. The name of Paul first appears in ch. 13.9.

59. *Lord Jesus, receive my spirit.* A prayer implying the belief of Stephen in the divinity of Jesus.

60. *Lord, lay not this sin to their charge.* A prayer for his enemies, like that of Jesus on the cross (Lk. 23.34).

CHAPTER 8

5. *Philip.* Not the apostle, but one of the seven deacons mentioned in ch. 6.5. He now became an evangelist. *Samaria.* The capital city of the province of that name.

9. *Simon.* A Samaritan by birth. He was an indefatigable enemy of both Peter and Paul. He was a sorcerer and conjurer.

13. *Simon also himself believed.* But it was not a sincere belief in Jesus Christ, whom Philip had preached to the people. It was rather a belief in the superior power which had made Philip a better worker of miracles than he (Simon)

and beholding signs and great ^{d}miracles wrought, he was amazed.

14 Now when the apostles that were at Je-ru'sa-lem heard that Sa-ma'ri-a had received the word of God, they sent unto them Peter and John: 15 who, when they were come down, prayed for them, that they might receive the Holy Spirit: 16 for as yet it was fallen upon none of them: only they had been baptized into the name of the Lord Je'sus. 17 Then laid they their hands on them, and they received the Holy Spirit. 18 Now when Si'mon saw that through the laying on of the apostles' hands the ^{e}Holy Spirit was given, he offered them money, 19 saying, Give me also this power, that on whomsoever I lay my hands, he may receive the Holy Spirit. 20 But Peter said unto him, Thy silver perish with thee, because thou hast thought to obtain the gift of God with money. 21 Thou hast neither part nor lot in this ^{f}matter: for thy heart is not right before God. 22 Repent therefore of this thy wickedness, and pray the Lord, if perhaps the thought of thy heart shall be forgiven thee. 23 For I see that thou ^{g}art in the gall of bitterness and in the bond of iniquity. 24 And Si'mon answered and said, Pray ye for me to the Lord, that none of the things which ye have spoken come upon me.

25 They therefore, when they had testified and spoken the word of the Lord, returned to Je-ru'sa-lem, and ^{h}preached the gospel to many villages of the Sa-mar'i-tans.

26 But an angel of the Lord spake unto Philip, saying, Arise, and go ^{i}toward the south unto the way that goeth down from Je-ru'sa-lem unto Ga'za: the same is desert. 27 And he arose

---

d Gr. *powers.* e Some ancient authorities omit *Holy.* f Gr. *word.* g Or, *wilt become gall* (or, *a gall root*) *of bitterness and a bond* *of iniquity.* Comp. Dt. 29.18; Heb. 12.15. h Gr. *brought good tidings.* Comp. ch. 5.42. i Or, *at noon* Comp. ch. 22.6.

---

was. The Samaritan conjurer was amazed and humiliated by one to whom the power of healing was after all but one of the consequences of his faith in the risen Christ.

14–17. *Sent unto them Peter and John.* In other words, they formally accepted the converted Samaritans as duly accredited followers of Jesus. The new converts were considered by Jews almost as idolaters on account of their heathen origin. It was the first step towards bringing the great outside world of Gentiles into the Christian Church.

18. *He offered them money.* The hypocrisy and love of notoriety which were at the bottom of Simon's 'belief' were revealed in this offer. He had been waiting and watching all the time to learn the secret of Philip's power of working miracles.

It occurred to him that Philip might sell the secret. The laying on of hands he evidently looked upon as a conjurer's trick. His brazen materialism brought upon him a deserved rebuke.

24. *Pray ye for me.* A request which at least implied a prudent fear of the Power which had enabled Philip to do so much. It went no further than that. There was no real sorrow or repentance behind it.

26. *Gaza.* It had been destroyed in 96 B.C., but was afterward rebuilt on a site nearer the seacoast. It was the most southerly of the five principal cities of the Philistines. *The same is desert.* This refers to the desert country on either side of the road to Gaza which Philip was directed to take.

27. *Ethiopia.* That is, the king-

and went: and behold, a man of E-thi-o′pi-a, a eunuch of great authority under Can-da′ce, queen of the E-thi-o′pi-ans, who was over all her treasure, who had come to Je-ru′sa-lem to worship; 28 and he was returning and sitting in his chariot, and was reading the prophet I-sa′iah. 29 And the Spirit said unto Philip, Go near, and join thyself to this chariot. 30 And Philip ran to him, and heard him reading I-sa′iah the prophet, and said, Understandest thou what thou readest? 31 And he said, How can I, except some one shall guide me? And he besought Philip to come up and sit with him. 32 Now the passage of the scripture which he was reading was this,

k He was led as a sheep to the slaughter;

And as a lamb before his shearer is dumb,

So he openeth not his mouth:

33 In his humiliation his judgment was taken away:

His generation who shall declare?

For his life is taken from the earth.

34 And the eunuch answered Philip, and said, I pray thee, of whom speaketh the prophet this? of himself, or of some other? 35 And Philip opened his mouth, and beginning from this scripture, *l* preached unto him Je′sus. 36 And as they went on the way, they came unto a certain water; and the eunuch saith, Behold, *here is* water; what doth hinder me to be baptized?*m* 38 And he commanded the chariot to stand still: and they both went down into the water, both Philip and the eunuch; and he baptized him. 39 And when they came up out of the water, the Spirit of the Lord caught away Philip;

---

k Is. liii. 7 f.   *l* See marg. note on ch. 5.42.   *m* Some ancient authorities insert, wholly or in part, ver. 37 *And Philip said,*

If thou believest with all thy heart, thou mayest. And he answered and said, I believe that Jesus Christ is the Son of God.

---

dom of Meroe, south of Egypt. *Candace.* Meroe was ruled by queens whose dynastic name was Candace, just as the Egyptian kings of that time were called Ptolemies. *To Jerusalem to worship.* He was a proselyte or convert.

32, 33. *He was led,* etc. The Servant of Jehovah, whose sufferings are described in these verses, is identified with Jesus Christ in ver. 35. *In his humiliation.* He was cruelly prejudged, and thus humiliated, by the Jew; he was carelessly considered, and thus humiliated, by the Roman. *His judgment was taken away.* That is, justice was denied him by the bitter prejudice of the Sanhedrin and the weakness and dishonesty of Pilate. *His generation.* The contemporaries of Jesus. By 'who shall declare' is meant that it would be difficult

adequately to describe the wickedness of those who were resolved upon his death. *His life is taken from the earth.* That is, he was put to death on the cross.

36. *As they went on the way.* It took time and great discretion for Philip to impart the necessary instruction. Most probably his eminent pupil had already heard much about Jesus and the new sect, for he had likely been in Jerusalem before; but Jewish sources of information would be prejudiced and Philip had to correct wrong notions. It is clear that Philip told him not only about the life and death and general teaching of Jesus, but explained the sacrament of baptism, and, most probably, that of the Lord's Supper. *To be baptized.* That every doubt had been removed is hereby shown.

39. *Caught away Philip.* That is,

and the eunuch saw him no more, for he went on his way rejoicing. 40 But Philip was found at A-zo'tus: and passing through he ⁿpreached the gospel to all the cities, till he came to Cæs-a-re'a.

9 But Saul, yet breathing threatening and slaughter against the disciples of the Lord, went unto the high priest, 2 and asked of him letters to Da-mas'-

n See marg. note on ch. 5.42.

cus unto the synagogues, that if he found any that were of the Way, whether men or women, he might bring them bound to Je-ru'sa-lem. 3 And as he journeyed, it came to pass that he drew nigh unto Da-mas'cus: and suddenly there shone round about him a light out of heaven: 4 and he fell upon the earth, and heard a voice saying unto him, **Saul, Saul, why persecutest**

most probably, inspired him suddenly to leave to continue his work elsewhere, beginning at Azotus.

40. *Azotus.* One of the five principal Philistine cities. It was twenty miles north of Gaza. *All the cities.* Including Jamnia, Joppa and Lydda. *Cæsarea.* A city on the coast of Palestine. It was built by Herod the Great in 12 B.C. on the site of a small town called Strato's Tower and renamed Cæsarea Augusta after Augustus Cæsar. It was an important city until about 1300 A.D. It inhabitants were chiefly Greeks and Jews. After 6 A.D. it became the residence of the Roman procurators, whose authority extended over all Palestine.

CHAPTER 9

2. *Damascus.* Often said by scholars to be the oldest city in the world. It was the ancient capital of Syria, and is situated on the river Abana (Barada) amid the gardens and orchards of a fertile plain. It existed in the days of Abraham (Gen. 14.15) and was identified from the earliest times with Jewish history. Its name is found on monuments as early as 1600 B.C., but it is very much older. Its situation between Palestine and Chaldæa made it a great trade centre, and it is an important commercial city to-day, with a population of a quarter of a million. It was brought under the rule of Solomon about 1000 B.C. After his death it became the chief city of the Syrian dynasty for several centuries. It was afterward conquered by Alexander the Great,

and in 65 B.C. became subject to Rome. It was long the capital of the Roman province of Syria. Since 624 A.D. it has been under Mohammedan rule. In Paul's time it contained a large Jewish population. At the present time the Christians, Jews and Mohammedans respectively occupy distinct portions of the city. *Unto the synagogues.* The fact that Saul was in angry haste to search for believers in Jesus in these synagogues proves that in Damascus the Christians had not yet dared to assemble in separate meetings. *The Way.* Employed in Acts as a name for the Christian religion. See chs. 16.17; 18.25, 26; 19.9, 23; 22.4; 24.14, 22.

3. *A light out of heaven.* There is evidence as to the nature of this light and the time of its appearance. It was 'above the brightness of the sun' 'at midday' (ch. 26.13). Elsewhere also we learn that it appeared 'about noon' (ch. 22.6). Its brightness so far exceeded that of the sun at noon that Saul was overcome and fell to the ground (chs. 22.7; 26.14). When he arose he was blind and had to be led by the hand (ver. 8; ch. 22. 11). What did he see in the light? He declares that he saw Jesus (1 Cor. 15.8). The light was thus carefully distinguished by Saul from daylight or sunlight and, by inference, from lightning. That it was seen also by his companions appears from ch. 26. 14. The fact to be noted is that in the light Saul saw the risen and glorified Jesus Christ. None of his companions had this vision.

4. *Heard a voice, saying,* etc. He not only heard a voice, but the

304

thou me? 5 And he said, Who art thou, Lord? And he *said*, I am Je′sus whom thou persecutest: 6 but rise, and enter into the city, and it shall be told thee what thou must do. 7 And the men that journeyed ·with him stood speechless, hearing the *a*voice, but beholding no man. 8 And Saul arose from the earth; and when his eyes were opened, he saw nothing; and they led him by the hand, and brought him into Da-mas′cus. 9 And he was three days without sight, and did neither eat nor drink.

10 Now there was a certain disciple at Da-mas′cus, named An-a-ni′as; and the Lord said unto him in a vision, An-a-ni′as. And he said, Behold, I *am here*, Lord. 11 And the Lord *said* unto him, Arise, and go to the street which is called Straight, and inquire in the house of Ju′das for one named Saul, a man of Tar′sus: for behold, he

prayeth; 12 and he hath seen a man named An-a-ni′as coming in, and laying his hands on him, that he might receive his sight. 13 But An-a-ni′as answered, Lord, I have heard from many of this man, how much evil he did to thy saints at Je-ru′sa-lem: 14 and here he hath authority from the chief priests to bind all that call upon thy name. 15 But the Lord said unto him, Go thy way: for he is a *b*chosen vessel unto me, to bear my name before the Gen′tiles and kings, and the children of Is′ra-el: 16 for I will show him how many things he must suffer for my name's sake. 17 And An-a-ni′as departed, and entered into the house; and laying his hands on him said, Brother Saul, the Lord, *even* Je′sus, who appeared unto thee in the way which thou camest, hath sent me, that thou mayest receive thy sight, and be filled with the Holy Spirit. 18 And straightway there fell from

---

a Or, *sound*

b Gr. *vessel of election.*

words that were spoken. Saul's companions also heard the voice, or, according to the alternative reading, the sound; but they heard not the words. This is what is meant in ch. 22.9. The 'voice' heard by Saul means both sound and words; the voice heard by the companions means only the sound.

7. *Hearing the voice.* See note on ver. 4.

9. *Three days.* Saul was blind and fasting for three days. It was a period of sorrowful penitence and deep meditation. While in this condition it was revealed to him that Ananias would come to him (ver. 12).

10. *Ananias.* Evidently one of the leaders, possibly the leader, of the Christians at Damascus. See ch. 22.12.

11. *The street which is called*

Straight. Some scholars think that the 'Straight' street mentioned in this verse still exists. At the present time there is a long straight street which runs through the city.

14. *To bind all that call upon thy name.* So that they might be taken to Jerusalem, and judged by the Sanhedrin. In cases of this kind the Roman authorities allowed Jewish law to govern, even outside of Palestine.

15. *Before the Gentiles.* The Gentiles are here preferred to the children of Israel in describing Saul's future work. *Kings.* See ch. 26.1, 32.

18. *Was baptized.* With his baptism Saul became a known and accredited follower of Jesus. His conversion is one of the greatest decisive events in the history of Christianity. It was of immediate

his eyes as it were scales, and he received his sight; and he arose and was baptized; 19 and he took food and was strengthened.

And he was certain days with the disciples that were at Da-mas'cus. 20 And straightway in the synagogues he proclaimed Je'sus, that he is the Son of God. 21 And all that heard him were amazed, and said, Is not this he that in Je-ru-sa'lem made havoc of them that called on this name? and he had come hither for this intent, that he might bring them bound before the chief priests. 22 But Saul increased the more in strength, and confounded the Jews that dwelt at Da-mas'cus, proving that this is the Christ.

23 And when many days were fulfilled, the Jews took counsel together to kill him: 24 but their plot became known to Saul. And they watched the gates also day and night that they might kill him: 25 but his disciples took him by night, and let him down through the wall, lowering him in a basket.

26 And when he was come to Je-ru'sa-lem, he assayed to join himself to the disciples: and they were all afraid of him, not believing that he was a disciple. 27 But Bar'na-bas took him, and brought him to the apostles, and declared unto them how he had seen the Lord in the way, and that he had spoken to him, and how at Da-mas'cus he had

---

practical advantage to the infant community of believers, for Saul was of more social consequence than any of the other apostles, as he was also far more learned and cultured than any of them. Even his fanatical devotion to the Jewish code and tradition had a beneficent reaction; in other words, his eager emphasis of the ceremonial law drove him, under the new light, the more rapidly to see that its day had gone forever. He knew that he had been saved not as one of the chosen race, but as a sinful man; this swept away forever from his religious consciousness the barrier between Jew and Gentile. His new and glad spiritual freedom irresistibly prompted him to strike the universal note in his preaching of the gospel. From this sprang the urgency that impelled him to become 'all things to all men' that he might gain some for Christ. He was the first Christian to say in his heart, 'My mission field is the world,' and the first immediately to plan and act in harmony with the thought. By early education the strictest of Jews, he became by conversion the great apostle to the Gentiles. He had not all the qualifications for apostleship that were re-

quired at the election of Matthias (ch. 1.21–23 and notes thereon). He had not been a follower of Jesus on earth; but he had, like the eleven, seen the risen Christ (ver. 3 and notes thereon). Moreover, Jesus had appointed him to be an apostle (ch. 22.21) and this was proved to the world by the results (2 Cor. 12.12).

20. *Straightway in the synagogues*. The synagogues offered the best opportunities for preaching and for securing new converts. *The Son of God*. The divine Messiah, the Saviour from sin; not the political deliverer and king that the Jew commonly expected.

22. *The Christ*. Or, the Messiah.

23. *When many days were fulfilled*, etc. It is not certain what period is covered by the expression 'many days.' Not long after his baptism Saul left Damascus and retired into Arabia for a time, then returned to Damascus, after which hostile Jews sought to kill him. The governor of the city knew of the plot and permitted it (2 Cor. 11.32).

25. *Through the wall*. Through a window or aperture in the wall (2 Cor. 11.33). *Basket*. Of the large sort used for carrying merchandise overland.

preached boldly in the name of Je'sus. 28 And he was with them going in and going out at Je-ru'-sa-lem, 29 preaching boldly in the name of the Lord: and he spake and disputed against the ^cGre'cian Jews; but they were seeking to kill him. 30 And when the brethren knew it, they brought him down to Cæs-a-re'a, and sent him forth to Tar'sus.

31 So the church throughout all Ju-dæ'a and Gal'i-lee and Sa-ma-ri'a had peace, being ^dedified; and, walking ^ein the fear of the Lord and ^ein the comfort of the Holy Spirit, was multiplied.

32 And it came to pass, as Peter went throughout all parts, he came down also to the saints that dwelt at Lyd'da. 33 And there he found a certain man named Æ'ne-as who had kept his bed eight years; for he was palsied. 34 And Peter said unto him, Æ'ne-as, Je'sus Christ healeth thee: arise, and make thy bed. And straightway he

arose. 35 And all that dwelt at Lyd'da and in Shar'on saw him, and they turned to the Lord.

36 Now there was at Jop'pa a certain disciple named Tab'i-tha, which by interpretation is called ^fDor'cas: this woman was full of good works and almsdeeds which she did. 37 And it came to pass in those days, that she fell sick, and died: and when they had washed her, they laid her in an upper chamber. 38 And as Lyd'da was nigh unto Jop'pa, the disciples, hearing that Peter was there, sent two men unto him, entreating him, Delay not to come on unto us. 39 And Peter arose and went with them. And when he was come, they brought him into the upper chamber: and all the widows stood by him weeping, and showing the coats and garments which Dor'cas made, while she was with them. 40 But Peter put them all forth, and kneeled down, and prayed; and turning to the body, he said,

---

c Gr. Hellenists.   d Gr. builded up.   e Or, by   f That is, Gazelle.

28. *He was with them.* Saul remained in Jerusalem fifteen days, and of the apostles saw only Peter and James, the Lord's brother (Gal. 1.18, 19).

29. *Grecian Jews.* Greek-speaking Jews.

30. *Cæsarea.* See notes on ch. 8. 40. *Tarsus.* The chief city of Cilicia, a province of Asia Minor. Paul the apostle was born here. Tarsus was situated on the river Cydnus, and in Paul's time was famous as a seat of learning and culture, being exceeded in these respects only by Athens and Alexandria. It was also a centre of trade between Asia Minor, Syria and the Far East.

31. *Had peace.* Because the Jews were intensely excited at this time

by reason of the proposal of the Roman emperor, Caligula, to have his statue placed in the Temple at Jerusalem. They had neither inclination nor leisure to persecute Christians while this outrage was being attempted.

32. *Lydda.* A city in the Sharon plain, ten miles southeast of Joppa. It was on the route between Joppa and Jerusalem.

36. *Joppa.* The port of Jerusalem and the only seaport of Judæa, situated on the coast of the Mediterranean Sea, thirty-four miles northwest of Jerusalem. It is the modern Jaffa, with a population of about 40,000. It is connected by railway with Jerusalem.

39. *The widows.* Those associated with Dorcas in good works.

Tab'i-tha, arise. And she opened her eyes; and when she saw Peter, she sat up. 41 And he gave her his hand, and raised her up; and calling the saints and widows, he presented her alive. 42 And it became known throughout all Jop'pa: and many believed on the Lord. 43 And it came to pass, that he abode many days in Jop'pa with one Si'mon a tanner.

10 Now *there was* a certain man in Cæs-a-re'a, Cor-ne'-li-us by name, a centurion of the ᵃband called the I-tal'ian *band*, 2 a devout man, and one that feared God with all his house, who gave much alms to the people, and prayed to God always. 3 He saw in a vision openly, as it were about the ninth hour of the day, an angel of God coming in unto him, and saying to him, Cor-ne'li-us. 4 And he, fastening his eyes upon him, and being affrighted, said, What is it, Lord? And he said unto him, Thy prayers and thine alms are gone up for a memorial before God. 5 And now send men to Jop'pa, and fetch one Si'mon, who is surnamed Peter:

6 he lodgeth with one Si'mon a tanner, whose house is by the sea side. 7 And when the angel that spake unto him was departed, he called two of his household-servants, and a devout soldier of them that waited on him continually; 8 and having rehearsed all things unto them, he sent them to Jop'pa.

9 Now on the morrow, as they were on their journey, and drew nigh unto the city, Peter went up upon the housetop to pray, about the sixth hour: 10 and he became hungry, and desired to eat: but while they made ready, he fell into a trance; 11 and he beholdeth the heaven opened, and a certain vessel descending, as it were a great sheet, let down by four corners upon the earth: 12 wherein were all manner of four-footed beasts and creeping things of the earth and birds of the heaven. 13 And there came a voice to him, Rise, Peter; kill and eat. 14 But Peter said, Not so, Lord; for I have never eaten anything that is common and unclean. 15 And a voice *came* unto him again the second time, What God hath cleansed, make not thou com-

---

a Or, *cohort*

---

43. *Simon a tanner.* The Jews despised tanners, as belonging to a disreputable trade. The fact that Peter abode with Simon shows that he had begun to disregard Jewish prejudices.

CHAPTER 10

1. *Cæsarea.* See note on ch. 8.40. *Centurion.* Commander of a hundred men. *Italian band.* Probably recruited in Italy.

2. *A devout man.* A sincere believer in God, observing as far as possible the Jewish religious customs, such as the prayer hours and almsgiving, but, owing to lack of circumcision, not an accredited member of the Jewish religious community.

3. *Ninth hour.* Three o'clock in the afternoon.

9. *The housetop.* The roofs of oriental houses are flat, and convenient for prayer and meditation. They could be reached by an outside staircase. *Sixth hour.* Noon.

10. *A trance.* A state in which the soul seems to have left the body, and during a temporary absence has visions of spiritual realities.

mon. 16 And this was done thrice: and straightway the vessel was received up into heaven.

17 Now while Peter was much perplexed in himself what the vision which he had seen might mean, behold, the men that were sent by Cor-ne'li-us, having made inquiry for Si'mon's house, stood before the gate, 18 and called and asked whether Si'mon, who was surnamed Peter, were lodging there. 19 And while Peter thought on the vision, the Spirit said unto him, Behold, three men seek thee. 20 But arise, and get thee down, and go with them, nothing doubting: for I have sent them. 21 And Peter went down to the men, and said, Behold, I am he whom ye seek: what is the cause wherefore ye are come? 22 And they said, Cor-ne'li-us a centurion, a righteous man and one that feareth God, and well reported of by all the nation of the Jews, was warned *of God* by a holy angel to send for thee into his house, and to hear words from thee. 23 So he called them in and lodged them.

And on the morrow he arose and went forth with them, and certain of the brethren from Jop'pa accompanied him. 24 And on the morrow ᵇthey entered into Cæs-a-re'a. And Cor-ne'li-us was waiting for them, having called together his kinsmen and his near friends. 25 And when it came to pass that Peter entered, Cor-ne'li-us met him, and fell down at his feet, and ᶜworshipped him. 26 But Peter raised him up, saying, Stand up; I myself also am a man. 27 And as he talked with him, he went in, and findeth many come together: 28 and he said unto them, Ye yourselves know ᵈhow it is an unlawful thing for a man that is a Jew to join himself or come unto one of another nation; and *yet* unto me hath God showed that I should not call any man common or unclean: 29 wherefore also I came without gainsaying, when I was sent for. I ask therefore with what intent ye sent for me. 30 And Cor-ne'li-us said, Four days ago, until this hour, I was keeping the ninth hour of prayer in my house; and behold, a man stood before me in bright apparel, 31 and saith, Cor-ne'li-us, thy prayer is heard, and thine alms are had in remembrance in the sight of God. 32 Send therefore to Jop'pa, and call unto thee Si'mon, who is surnamed Peter; he lodgeth in the house of Si'mon a tanner, by the sea side. 33 Forthwith therefore I sent to thee; and thou hast well done that thou art come. Now there-

---

ᵇ Some ancient authorities read *he.* ᶜ The Greek word denotes an act of reverence.

whether paid to a creature or to the Creator. ᵈ Or, *how unlawful it is for a man &c.*

16. *Thrice.* For emphasis and warning.

26. *Raised him up, saying,* etc. See Rev. 19.10.

28. *Yet unto me hath God showed,* etc. The meaning of the vision, which had perplexed Peter (ver. 17), was now clear to him—the Jewish

distinction between clean and unclean meats was abolished in order that he and all the other apostles and disciples of Jesus might see that there was to be no like distinction between Jew and Gentile, that no man was to be considered 'common or unclean.'

fore we are all here present in the sight of God, to hear all things that have been commanded thee of the Lord. 34 And Peter opened his mouth, and said,

Of a truth I perceive that God is no respecter of persons: 35 but in every nation he that feareth him, and worketh righteousness, is acceptable to him. 36 *e*The word which he sent unto the children of Is'ra-el, preaching *f*good tidings of peace by Je'sus Christ (he is Lord of all)—37 that saying ye yourselves know, which was published throughout all Ju-dæ'a, beginning from Gal'-i-lee, after the baptism which John preached; 38 *even* Je'sus of Naz'a-reth, how God anointed him with the Holy Spirit and with power: who went about doing good, and healing all that were oppressed of the devil; for God was with him. 39 And we are witnesses of all things which he did both in the country of the Jews, and in Je-ru'sa-lem; whom also they slew, hanging him on a tree. 40 Him God raised up the third day, and gave him to be made manifest, 41 not to all the people, but unto witnesses that were chosen before of God, *even* to us, who ate and drank with him after he rose from the dead. 42

And he charged us to preach unto the people, and to testify that this is he who is ordained of God *to be* the Judge of the living and the dead. 43 To him bear all the prophets witness, that through his name every one that believeth on him shall receive remission of sins.

44 While Peter yet spake these words, the Holy Spirit fell on all them that heard the word. 45 And they of the circumcision that believed were amazed, as many as came with Peter, because that on the Gen'tiles also was poured out the gift of the Holy Spirit. 46 For they heard them speak with tongues, and magnify God. Then answered Peter, 47 Can any man forbid the water, that these should not be baptized, who have received the Holy Spirit as well as we? 48 And he commanded them to be baptized in the name of Je'sus Christ. Then prayed they him to tarry certain days.

11 Now the apostles and the brethren that were in Ju-dæ'a heard that the Gen'tiles also had received the word of God. 2 And when Peter was come up to Je-ru'sa-lem, they that were of the circumcision contended with him, 3 saying,

---

e Many ancient authorities read *He sent the word unto.* *f* Or, *the gospel*

34. *No respecter of persons.* Peter's first thought was naturally a re-statement of the new truth that had been revealed to him (ver. 28).

41. *Unto witnesses that were chosen.* See Jn. 17.6. *Ate and drank with him.* See Lk. 24.41–43 and notes thereon.

43. *Bear all the prophets witness.* See ch. 3.24; 26.22; Isa. 49.6; Joel 2.32.

46. *With tongues.* See note on ch. 2.4.

47. *The water.* That is, the rite of baptism.

CHAPTER 11

2. *They that were of the circumcision.* They who opposed the admission of uncircumcised Gentiles into Christian fellowship. They were the Judaizing party within the church.

Thou wentest in to men uncircumcised, and didst eat with them. 4 But Peter began, and expounded *the matter* unto them in order, saying, 5 I was in the city of Jop'pa praying: and in a trance I saw a vision, a certain vessel descending, as it were a great sheet let down from heaven by four corners; and it came even unto me: 6 upon which when I had fastened mine eyes, I considered, and saw the fourfooted beasts of the earth and wild beasts and creeping things and birds of the heaven. 7 And I heard also a voice saying unto me, Rise, Peter; kill and eat. 8 But I said, Not so, Lord: for nothing common or unclean hath ever entered into my mouth. 9 But a voice answered the second time out of heaven, What God hath cleansed, make not thou common. 10 And this was done thrice: and all were drawn up again into heaven. 11 And behold, forthwith three men stood before the house in which we were, having been sent from Cæs-a-re'a unto me. 12 And the Spirit bade me go with them, making no distinction. And these six brethren also accompanied me; and we entered into the man's house: 13 and he told us how he had seen the angel standing in his house, and saying, Send to Jop'pa, and fetch Si'mon, whose surname is Peter; 14 who shall speak unto thee words, whereby thou shalt be saved, thou and all thy house. 15 And as I began to speak, the Holy Spirit fell on them, even as on us at the beginning. 16 And I remembered the word of the Lord, how he said, John indeed baptized with water; but ye shall be baptized *a*in the Holy Spirit. 17 If then God gave unto them the like gift as *he did* also unto us, when we believed on the Lord Je'sus Christ, who was I, that I could withstand God? 18 And when they heard these things, they held their peace, and glorified God, saying, Then to the Gen'tiles also hath God granted repentance unto life.

19 They therefore that were scattered abroad upon the tribulation that arose about Ste'phen travelled as far as Phœ-ni'ci-a, and Cy'prus, and An'ti-och, speaking the word to none

a Or, *with*

19. *Phœnicia*. A country lying along the Mediterranean coast north of Mount Carmel. Its length was one hundred and twenty miles and its average breadth about twenty miles. Its chief cities were Tyre, Sidon, Gebal and Arvad. It was a great commercial and colonizing power, its chief colony, Carthage, having been able for a time to defy the power of the Roman empire. Its commerce was chiefly maritime and its fleets of merchant ships sailed to all the main seaports of the known world. *Cyprus*. See notes on ch. 4.32–37. *Antioch*. The capital of the Roman province of Syria, and the residence of its governor. It was situated on the river Orontes, about sixteen miles from the Mediterranean seacoast. Although its population was mainly Syrian, it became a centre of the Greek language and culture. Its commerce and industry were very important. At the height of its prosperity its inhabitants numbered 400,000 and it was the third largest city in the Roman empire, ranking next to Alexandria. At Antioch the disciples of Jesus were first called Christians (ver. 26). From this city

save only to Jews. 20 But there were some of them, men of Cy'prus and Cy-re'ne, who, when they were come to An'ti-och, spake unto the [b]Greeks also, [c]preaching the Lord Je'-sus. 21 And the hand of the Lord was with them: and a great number that believed turned unto the Lord. 22 And the report concerning them came to the ears of the church which was in Je-ru'sa-lem: and they sent forth Bar'na-bas as far as An'ti-och: 23 who, when he was come, and had seen the grace of God, was glad; and he exhorted them all, [d]that with purpose of heart they would cleave unto the Lord: 24 for he was a good man, and full of the Holy Spirit and of faith: and much people was added unto the Lord. 25 And he went forth to Tar'sus to seek for Saul; 26 and when he had found him, he brought him

unto An'ti-och. And it came to pass, that even for a whole year they were gathered together [e]with the church, and taught much people; and that the disciples were called Chris'tians first in An'ti-och.

27 Now in these days there came down prophets from Je-ru'sa-lem unto An'ti-och. 28 And there stood up one of them named Ag'a-bus, and signified by the Spirit that there should be a great famine over all [f]the world: which came to pass in the days of Clau'di-us. 29 And the disciples, every man according to his ability, determined to send [g]relief unto the brethren that dwelt in Ju-dæ'a: 30 which also they did, sending it to the elders by the hand of Bar'na-bas and Saul.

12 Now about that time Her'od the king put forth his hands to afflict certain of the

---

b Many ancient authorities read *Grecian Jews.* See ch. 6.1. c See marginal note on ch. 5.42. d Some ancient authorities read

also Paul began each of his three missionary journeys. It was the chief centre from which Christianity spread to the Gentiles.

20. *Cyrene.* A city of the Roman province of Cyrenaica, North Africa. It contained a large Jewish population. *Spake unto the Greeks also.* That is, unto the Greek-speaking Jews.

27. *Prophets.* See note on ch. 13.1.

28. *Agabus.* See ch. 21.10. *In the days of Claudius.* There was a famine in 45 A.D. in this Roman emperor's reign (41–54 A.D.).

30. *The elders.* Or presbyters. A body of local rulers of the churches, whose duties were chiefly pastoral—that is, involving moral supervision. They were chosen by the church and were required to have certain qualifications fixed by the apostles. They were of higher

that they would cleave unto the purpose of their heart in the Lord. e Gr. *in.* f Gr. *the inhabited earth* g Gr. *for ministry.* Comp. ch. 6.1.

rank than those now commonly called deacons, but were subject to the supervision of the apostles. Though sometimes called bishops (ch. 20.28), they did not exercise the authority of a bishop as that term is now understood. 'Pastor,' 'bishop,' and 'elder' in the earliest Christian community had practically the same meaning, that is, an elected church officer of local supervisory and administrative functions. Local church government by elders was adopted from the constitution of the synagogues. The earliest followers of Christ, being Jews, naturally followed the plan of the organization in which they had been brought up.

CHAPTER 12

1. *About that time.* Probably 43 A.D. *Herod the king.* Herod Agrippa I, son of Aristobulus and grandson

church. 2 And he killed James the brother of John with the sword. 3 And when he saw that it pleased the Jews, he proceeded to seize Peter also. And *those* were the days of unleavened bread. 4 And when he had taken him, he put him in prison, and delivered him to four quaternions of soldiers to guard him; intending after the Passover to bring him forth to the people. 5 Peter therefore was kept in the prison: but prayer was made earnestly of the church unto God for him. 6 And when Her'od was about to bring him forth, the same night Peter was sleeping between two soldiers, bound with two chains: and guards before the door kept the prison. 7 And behold, an angel of the Lord stood by him, and a light shined in the cell: and he smote Peter on the side, and awoke him, saying, Rise up quickly. And his chains fell off from his hands. 8 And the angel said unto him, Gird thyself, and bind on thy sandals. And he did so. And he saith unto him, Cast thy garment about thee, and follow me. 9 And he went out, and followed; and he knew not that it was true which was done *a*by the angel, but thought he saw a vision. 10 And when they were past the first and the second guard, they came unto the iron gate that leadeth into the city; which opened to them of its own accord: and they went out, and passed on through one street; and straightway the angel departed from him. 11 And when Peter was come to himself, he said, Now I know of a truth, that the Lord hath sent forth his angel and delivered me out of the hand of Her'od, and from all the expectation of the people of the Jews. 12 And when he had considered *the thing*, he came to the house of Mary the mother of John whose surname was Mark; where many were gathered to-

---

a Gr. *through.*

---

of Herod the Great. To gain the favor of the Jews was one of the chief objects of his policy. He was careful to humor as far as possible the prejudices of the popular or Pharisaic party, and in the appointment of the high priest did the least possible injury to their feelings. In this way he had gained great popularity, which he sought to increase by persecuting the Christians.

2. *James the brother of John.* One of the sons of Zebedee, commonly called James the Great.

3. *Proceeded to seize Peter also.* Thinking, perhaps, that the death of Peter, the most prominent of the apostles, might result in the extinction of the new sect. These attempts by Herod were the last of the means of Jewish persecution then available. The struggling com-

munity of believers had first to meet the enmity of the chief priests and Sadducees, then of the Pharisees, and, later, of Herod. Roman persecution came after the spread of Christianity in the Gentile world. *The days of unleavened bread.* Commonly identified with the Feast of the Passover, which began on the 14th of Nisan, the first month of the Jewish year. See note on Mt. 26.17.

4. *Four quaternions.* A quaternion of soldiers was a party of four. There were four of such parties set to guard Peter.

12. *Mark.* The evangelist. Mark's mother, Mary, was aunt of Barnabas, who was therefore Mark's cousin. She was well-to-do, having sufficient means to place her house at the disposal of the earliest Christians as a meeting-place.

gether and were praying. 13 And when he knocked at the door of the gate, a maid came to answer, named Rho'da. 14 And when she knew Peter's voice, she opened not the gate for joy, but ran in, and told that Peter stood before the gate. 15 And they said unto her, Thou art mad. But she confidently affirmed that it was even so. And they said, It is his angel. 16 But Peter continued knocking: and when they had opened, they saw him, and were amazed. 17 But he, beckoning unto them with the hand to hold their peace, declared unto them how the Lord had brought him forth out of the prison. And he said, Tell these things unto James, and to the brethren. And he departed, and went to another place. 18 Now as soon as it was day, there was no small stir among the soldiers, what was become of Peter. 19 And when Her'od had sought for him, and found him not, he examined the guards, and commanded that they should be *b*put to death.

And he went down from Ju-dæ'a to Cæs-a-re'a, and tarried there.

20 Now he was highly displeased with them of Tyre and Si'don: and they came with one accord to him, and, having made Blas'tus the king's chamberlain their friend, they asked for peace, because their country was fed from the king's country. 21 And upon a set day Her'od arrayed himself in royal apparel, and sat on the *c*throne, and made an oration unto them. 22 And the people shouted, *saying*, The voice of a god, and not of a man. 23 And immediately an angel of the Lord smote him, because he gave not God the glory: and he was eaten of worms, and gave up the ghost.

24 But the word of God grew and multiplied.

25 And Bar'na-bas and Saul returned *d*from Je-ru'sa-lem, when they had fulfilled their ministration, taking with them John whose surname was Mark.

13 Now there were at An'-ti-och, in the church that

---

b Gr. *led away to death.*   *c* Or, *judg-ment-seat*   See Mt. 27.19.   *d* Many ancient authorities read *to Jerusalem.*

---

15. *It is his angel.* That is, his guardian angel, according to the Jewish belief. See also note on Mt. 18.10.

17. *Tell these things unto James.* As unto one who had the right to know. It was an implied recognition by Peter of the authority of the apostle James as head of the church at Jerusalem.

19. *Cæsarea.* See note on ch. 8.40.

20. *Displeased with them of Tyre and Sidon.* Because of some alleged unfairness on their part in regard to the trade between Phœnicia and Palestine. *They asked for peace, because,* etc. They sought to appease Herod's anger. They knew he had the power to divert trade from his own dominions to other ports than Tyre and Sidon. These depended chiefly upon Palestine for their grain and provisions.

21. *A set day.* A festival day appointed in honor of the Roman emperor. Herod, who reigned by favor of the emperor, was careful to celebrate the day with all due ceremony.

23. *An angel of the Lord smote him,* etc. This account of the death of Herod is confirmed in many respects by the Jewish historian Josephus in his work, *The Jewish Antiquities,* XIX. 8.2.

CHAPTER 13

1. *Prophets.* The inspired utterances of these prophets, as of others

314

was *there*, prophets and teachers, Bar′na-bas, and Sym′e-on that was called Ni′ger, and Lu′cius of Cy-re′ne, and Man′a-en the foster-brother of Her′od the tetrarch, and Saul. 2 And as they ministered to the Lord, and fasted, the Holy Spirit said, Separate me Bar′na-bas and Saul for the work whereunto I have called them. 3 Then, when they had fasted and prayed and laid their hands on them, they sent them away.

4 So they, being sent forth by the Holy Spirit, went down to Se-leu′ci-a; and from thence they sailed to Cy′prus. 5 And when they were at Sal′a-mis, they proclaimed the word of God in the synagogues of the Jews: and they had also John as their attendant. 6 And when they had gone through the whole island unto Pa′phos, they found a certain ᵃsorcerer, a false prophet, a Jew, whose name was Bar-Je′sus; 7 who was with the pro-

---

a Gr. *Magus*: as in Mt. 2.1, 7, 16.

---

in New Testament times, included the foretelling of events, but were mainly exhortations to righteousness. Certain ministers in whom the gift appeared in a high degree were officially recognized as prophets. They were next in authority to the apostles. *Teachers.* Those who were able to help inquirers to solve difficult religious questions. Our Lord himself was addressed as 'Teacher' on some notable occasions when the questioners either sought for light or tried to entangle him (Jn. 3.2; Mk. 12.14). Teachers in the church at Antioch were mentioned along with prophets, and elsewhere they are placed side by side with apostles, prophets and evangelists (Eph. 4.11). Thus their rank was high, and with the growth of the early church they became a distinct official class and were so recognized during the second century. Their duties and methods were defined. *Symeon that was called Niger.* 'Symeon' was a Jewish name, and 'Niger,' meaning black, was Roman. A Jew at Antioch, mixing with various nationalities, would find some convenience in having two such names. It was a Jewish custom in places outside of Palestine. *Lucius of Cyrene.* He also was probably a Jew with a Roman name. Cyrene, in North Africa, was a city with a large Jewish population. *Manaen.* Or Menahem. The name is Jewish. *Herod the tetrarch.* Herod Antipas, the son of Herod the Great.

2. *Ministered to the Lord.* Performed public worship.
4. *Seleucia.* The seaport of Antioch at the mouth of the river Orontes. *Cyprus.* See notes on ch. 4.32–37. In ch. 13.4–14, 28 are narrated the first missionary journey of Paul. Sailing from Seleucia, the seaport of the Syrian capital, Antioch, he came to Salamis in Cyprus. Traversing that island, he arrived at Paphos on the west coast, whence he sailed northwesterly to Perga, a town of Pamphylia, situated not far from the mouth of the river Cestrus. From this place he proceeded north to Antioch in Pisidia, thence to Iconium, Lystra and Derbe. From the last mentioned city he returned to Lystra, Iconium and Antioch in Pisidia, through which district he came south to Perga in Pamphylia, thence again to Attalia, sailing from that seaport to Antioch in Syria.
5. *Salamis.* A town on the southeast coast of Cyprus. It was successively under the dominion of the Assyrians, Egyptians, Persians and Greeks, and in 58 B.C. came under the sway of Rome. That is, John Mark, the evangelist and cousin of Barnabas.
6. *Paphos.* The capital city of Cyprus and residence of the Roman governor. *Sorcerer.* One who exercised or pretended to exercise magical powers, especially by the aid of evil spirits.
7. *The proconsul.* The official title of the governor of a senatorial, as distinguished from an impera-

consul, Ser'gi-us Pau'lus, a man of understanding. The same called unto him Bar'na-bas and Saul, and sought· to hear the word of God. 8 But El'y-mas the *sorcerer (for so is his name by interpretation) withstood them, seeking to turn aside the proconsul from the faith. 9 But Saul, who is also *called* Paul, filled with the Holy Spirit, fastened his eyes on him, 10 and said, O full of all guile and all villany, thou son of the devil, thou enemy of all righteousness, wilt thou not cease to pervert the right ways of the Lord? 11 And now, behold, the hand of the Lord is upon thee, and thou shalt be blind, not see-

ing the sun *b*for a season. And immediately there fell on him a mist and a darkness; and he went about seeking some to lead him by the hand. 12 Then the proconsul, when he saw what was done, believed, being astonished at the teaching of the Lord.

13 Now Paul and his company set sail from Pa'phos, and came to Per'ga in Pam-phyl'i-a: and John departed from them and returned to Je-ru'sa-lem. 14 But they, passing through from Per'ga, came to An'ti-och of Pi-sid'i-a; and they went into the synagogue on the sabbath day, and sat down. 15 And after the reading of the law and the proph-

---

a Gr. *Magus:* as in Mt. 2.1, 7, 16.   *b* Or, *until*

torial, province. The governor of the latter was a propraetor. The main distinction between an imperatorial and a senatorial province was that in the former troops were specially needed to maintain order. *Sergius Paulus.* Luke's mention of him as proconsul has been verified by an inscription found since the British occupation of Cyprus in 1878.

8. *Elymas.* An Arabian name meaning wise. 'Bar-Jesus' was his Jewish name.

9. *Saul, who is also called Paul.* The name by which the great apostle is universally known appears here for the first time. He was called Paul, probably, in part, because of the Jewish custom of assuming an additional name when living in foreign lands, but more especially because it was a well-known Roman name and he had now become a militant advocate of Christ in the Gentile world, the best part of which was included in the Roman empire.

13. *Perga.* The capital city of the province of Pamphylia. *Pamphylia.* This province occupied the southern and central part of Asia Minor. It came under the sway of Rome in 133 B.C. The population was originally barbarian, but Greek colonists

planted their language and civilization there. *John departed.* John Mark, the evangelist. The reason for his departure is not given, but it was one that did not please Paul (ch. 15.38).

14. *Antioch of Pisidia.* So-called to distinguish it from Antioch in Syria. It was not actually within the district of Pisidia, but on its border, a distinction that was indicated in its Latin name, 'Antiochia ad Pisidiam' or 'Antioch toward Pisidia.' It was made a Roman colony in 6 B.C. and in Paul's time was a military and governmental centre in the southern part of the province of Galatia. Some scholars think that Paul suffered from a serious illness in Perga and came north to Antioch on account of its healthier climate. See Gal. 4.13. *Pisidia.* A district of southern Asia Minor, and immediately north of Pamphylia. It was a wild, mountainous country, with a population that was lawless until brought under the power of Rome in 25 B.C., though even afterward brigands infested the northerly parts. Some biblical writers have suggested that the dangers of travel through Pisidia are referred to by Paul in an expression 'perils of robbers' in one of his epistles (2 Cor. 11.26).

ets the rulers of the synagogue sent unto them, saying, Brethren, if ye have any word of exhortation for the people, say on. 16 And Paul stood up, and beckoning with the hand said,

Men of Is'ra-el, and ye that fear God, hearken: 17 The God of this people Is'ra-el chose our fathers, and exalted the people when they sojourned in the land of E'gypt, and with a high arm led he them forth out of it. 18 And for about the time of forty years [c]as a nursing-father bare he them in the wilderness. 19 And when he had destroyed seven nations in the land of Ca'naan, he gave *them* their land for an inheritance, for about four hundred and fifty years: 20 and after these things he gave *them* judges until Sam'u-el the prophet. 21 And afterward they asked for a king: and God gave unto them Saul the son of Kish, a man of the tribe of Ben'ja-min, for the space of forty years. 22 And when he had removed him, he raised up David to be their king; to whom also he bare witness and said, [d]I have found David the son of

Jes'se, a man after my heart, who shall do all my [e]will. 23 Of this man's seed hath God according to promise brought unto Is'ra-el a Saviour, Je'sus; 24 when John had first preached [f]before his coming the baptism of repentance to all the people of Is'ra-el. 25 And as John was fulfilling his course, he said, What suppose ye that I am? I am not *he*. But behold, there cometh one after me the shoes of whose feet I am not worthy to unloose. 26 Brethren, children of the stock of Abraham, and those among you that fear God, to us is the word of this salvation sent forth. 27 For they that dwell in Je-ru'sa-lem, and their rulers, because they knew him not, nor the voices of the prophets which are read every sabbath, fulfilled *them* by condemning *him*. 28 And though they found no cause of death *in him*, yet asked they of Pi'late that he should be slain. 29 And when they had fulfilled all things that were written of him, they took him down from the tree, and laid him in a tomb. 30 But God raised him from the

---

c Many ancient authorities read *suffered he their manners in the wilderness.* See Dt.

9.7.   d 1 S. xiii. 14; Ps. lxxxix. 20.   e Gr. *wills.*   f Gr. *before the face of his entering in.*

16. *Men of Israel, and ye that fear God.* In his salutation Paul naturally places Jews before proselytes and devout Gentiles. His sermon in the synagogue of Pisidian Antioch is included in ver. 16–41.

17–25. *Chose our fathers,* etc. In the introductory part of the sermon the elect position and importance of the Jewish people are emphasized by Paul in order to commend more invitingly to his hearers the claims of the Messiah, who issued from this divinely appointed order and the historic line of[f] Jewish kings. *Destroyed seven nations.* See Deut. 7.1.

26–29. *To us is the word of this sal-*

vation. The special favor shown the Jews in their original selection by God as His chosen people is here declared to be extended to both Jews and Gentiles, the latter being included in the words 'us' and 'those among you that fear God.' Both Jews and Gentiles were in the audience. *The voice of the prophets.* That bore witness to the coming of Jesus.

30. *But God raised him from the dead.* This liberating announcement of a Messiah whom God had raised from the dead could be appreciated only by a few, if any, of Paul's hearers. It went far beyond the

dead: 31 and he was seen for many days of them that came up with him from Gal'i-lee to Je-ru'-sa-lem, who are now his witnesses unto the people. 32 And we bring you good tidings of the promise made unto the fathers, 33 that God hath fulfilled the same unto our children, in that he raised up Je'sus; as also it is written in the second psalm, *g*Thou art my Son, this day have I begotten thee. 34 And as concerning that he raised him up from the dead, now no more to return to corruption, he hath spoken on this wise, *h*I will give you the holy and sure *blessings* of David. 35 Because he saith also in another *psalm*, *i*Thou wilt not give thy Holy One to see corruption. 36 For David, after he had *k*in his own generation served the counsel of God, fell asleep, and was laid unto his fathers, and saw corruption: 37 but he whom God raised up saw no corruption. 38 Be it known unto you therefore, brethren, that through this man is proclaimed unto you remission of sins: 39 and by him every one that believeth is justified from all things, from which ye could not be justified by the law of Mo'ses. 40 Beware therefore, lest that come upon *you* which is spoken in the prophets:

41 *l*Behold, ye despisers, and wonder, and *m*perish;

For I work a work in your days,

A work which ye shall in no wise believe, if one declare it unto you.

42 And as they went out, they besought that these words might be spoken to them the next sabbath. 43 Now when the synagogue broke up, many of the

---

g Ps. ii. 7.   *h* Is. lv. 3.   *i* Ps. xvi. 10. *k* Or, *served his own generation by the counsel of God, fell asleep* Or, *served his own generation, fell asleep by the counsel of God* *l* Hab. i. 5.   *m* Or, *vanish away* Jas. 4.14.

---

commonly received notion of a temporal deliverer. It said nothing about a free and independent nation. Nor was it instantly to be seen, except by the thoughtfully prepared, how only a risen and spiritual Saviour could fulfill the promises that God had made to Abraham and David, from whom was to spring one in whom all the nations of the earth would be blessed and whose throne would be established forever (Gen. 26.4; 2 Sam. 7. 12–16).

39. *By him every one that believeth is justified*, etc. A truth which at once superseded the Mosaic law, and its outgrowth of tradition and interpretation, in favor of the Messiah, the ruler of the spiritual kingdom. This did not mean that what was good in the existing system would be destroyed (Mt. 5.17), but that the way of approach to God would be changed from the discipline of a national code to the spiritual contact of mankind with Him through faith in Jesus Christ. All who had this faith would be justified, that is, free from sin, in a sense which could not be realized under the law of Moses. The law, and the works under it, had been necessary; but the machinery of rules and penalties at length threatened the free growth of the individual spirit. The incalculable importance of this freedom Jesus had recognized when he said, 'The kingdom of heaven is within you,' that is, to be sought for and realized in the soul. That it could be thus realized only by faith in the risen Messiah was announced in effect by Paul in this sermon.

40. *Which is spoken in the prophets*. Alluding to the destruction brought upon the Jews by the Babylonians under King Nebuchadnezzar.

318

Jews and of the devout prose-lytes followed Paul and Bar'na-bas; who, speaking to them, urged them to continue in the grace of God.

44 And the next sabbath almost the whole city was gathered together to hear the word of [n]God. 45 But when the Jews saw the multitudes, they were filled with jealousy, and contradicted the things which were spoken by Paul, and [o]blasphemed. 46 And Paul and Bar'na-bas spake out boldly, and said, It was necessary that the word of God should first be spoken to you. Seeing ye thrust it from you, and judge yourselves unworthy of eternal life, lo, we turn to the Gen'tiles. 47 For so hath the Lord commanded us, *saying*,

  [p]I have set thee for a light of the Gen'tiles,

That thou shouldest be for salvation unto the uttermost part of the earth.

48 And as the Gen'tiles heard this, they were glad, and glorified the word of [n]God: and as many as were ordained to eternal life believed. 49 And the word of the Lord was spread abroad throughout all the region. 50 But the Jews urged on the devout women of honorable estate, and the chief men of the city, and stirred up a persecution against Paul and Bar'na-bas, and cast them out of their borders. 51 But they shook off the dust of their feet against them, and came unto I-co'ni-um. 52 And the disciples were filled with joy and with the Holy Spirit.

14 And it came to pass in I-co'ni-um that they entered together into the synagogue of the Jews, and so spake that a great multitude both of Jews and of Greeks believed. 2 But the Jews that were disobedient stirred up the souls of the Gen'tiles, and made them evil affected against the brethren. 3 Long time therefore they tarried *there* speaking boldly in the Lord, who bare witness unto the word of his grace, granting signs and wonders to be done by their hands. 4 But the multitude of the city was divided; and part held with the Jews, and part with

---

[n] Many ancient authorities read *the*   Lord.   [o] Or. *railed*   [p] Is. xlix. 6.

---

45. *Filled with jealousy*. Because Paul had declared the law of Moses insufficient and had preached in favor of admitting the Gentiles to all the privileges of salvation on the same footing as the Jews.

50. *Devout women*. Women of good position who had become converts to Judaism, and who naturally could be influenced to resent outside interference with the orderly proceedings of the synagogue.

51. *Shook off the dust of their feet.* See Mt. 10.14 and note thereon. *Iconium.* The capital city of Lycaonia, a district of the Roman province of Galatia in Asia Minor. It

was situated in a fertile plain. Its modern name is Konieh.

52. *Filled with joy*. As Christ commanded his persecuted disciples. See Mt. 5.12.

CHAPTER 14

1. *Greeks*. Greek-speaking Jews, or, possibly, referring to the Gentile population of the city.

3. *Granting signs and wonders*. In confirmation of their apostleship. See Rom. 15.18, 19; 2 Cor. 12.12.

4. *The apostles*. Paul and Barnabas are here called apostles for the first time after their separation unto the work of God (ch. 13.2, 3).

the apostles. 5 And when there was made an onset both of the Gen'tiles and of the Jews with their rulers, to treat them shamefully and to stone them, 6 they became aware of it, and fled unto the cities of Lyc-a-o'ni-a, Lys'tra and Der'be, and the region round about: 7 and there they*preached the gospel.

8 And at Lys'tra there sat a certain man, impotent in his feet, a cripple from his mother's womb, who never had walked. 9 The same heard Paul speaking: who, fastening his eyes upon him, and seeing that he had faith to be made whole, 10 said with a loud voice, Stand upright on thy feet. And he leaped up and walked. 11 And when the multitude saw what Paul had done, they lifted up their voice, saying in the speech of Lyc-a-o'ni-a, The gods are come down to us in the likeness of men. 12 And they called Bar'na-bas, *b*Ju'pi-ter; and Paul, *c*Mer'cu-ry, because he was the chief speaker. 13 And the priest of *b*Ju'pi-ter whose *temple* was before the city, brought oxen and garlands unto the gates, and would have done sacrifice with the multitudes. 14 But when the apostles, Bar'na-bas and Paul, heard of it, they rent their garments, and sprang forth among the multitude, crying out 15 and saying, Sirs, why do ye these things? We also are men of like *d*passions with you, and bring you good tidings, that ye should turn from these vain things unto a living God, who made the heaven and the earth and the sea, and all that in them

---

a See marginal note on ch. 5.42.   *b* Gr. *Zeus.*   *c* Gr. *Hermes.*   *d* Or, *nature*

---

6. *Lystra.* A city which had been made a Roman colony in 6 B.C. Its population was mainly heathen. It was the home of Timothy (ch. 16.1), with whose parents, in the opinion of some scholars, Paul and Barnabas lived during their visit. *Derbe.* A city which came under Roman rule in 25 B.C. It was twice visited by Paul, the first time (ver. 6, 20) about 46 A.D. The second visit is referred to in Acts 16.1.

9. *Heard Paul speaking.* The apostle's custom was first to go to a synagogue in the various cities visited by him. No mention is made of a synagogue at Lystra, and it is not probable that the city contained one, as there were few Jews.

11. *The speech of Lycaonia.* A rude dialect of which the apostles were ignorant.

12. *Jupiter.* The Latin name for the supreme god in the Greek mythology. *Mercury.* Or Hermes, the spokesman and messenger of the Greek gods. The crowd naturally gave this title to Paul, as he was the chief speaker. The beliefs of the Greek religion prevailed at Lystra and the surrounding region. The people thought that the gods sometimes came down to the earth in human form.

14. *Heard of it.* The apostles did not at first understand, owing to their ignorance of the popular dialect, what was being done in their honor. *Rent their garments.* A sign of horror and dismay at what they looked upon as blasphemy. See note on Mt. 26.65.

15–18. *From these vain things unto a living God,* etc. From foolish idolatry to the spiritual worship of the Supreme Being. Paul's speech to the multitude at Lystra was a good example of his facility in adapting his preaching to the needs and capacity of his hearers. He had not here to confront stubborn and prejudiced Jews who refused to welcome Gentiles on equal terms as fellow-worshippers of the true God. He had to warn and instruct simple-minded heathen who were elated to find in their city a wonder-working man, and who for that reason were

is: 16 who in the generations gone by suffered all the ᶜnations to walk in their own ways. 17 And yet he left not himself without witness, in that he did good and gave you from heaven rains and fruitful seasons, filling your hearts with food and gladness. 18 And with these sayings scarce restrained they the multitudes from doing sacrifice unto them.

19 But there came Jews thither from An'ti-och and I-co'-ni-um: and having persuaded the multitudes, they stoned Paul, and dragged him out of the city, supposing that he was dead. 20 But as the disciples stood round about him, he rose up, and entered into the city: and on the morrow he went forth with Bar'na-bas to Der'be. 21 And when they had ᶠpreached the gospel to that city, and had made many disciples, they returned to Lys'tra, and to I-co'ni-um, and to An'ti-och, 22 confirming the souls of the disciples,

exhorting them to continue in the faith, and that through many tribulations we must enter into the kingdom of God. 23 And when they had appointed for them elders in every church, and had prayed with fasting, they commended them to the Lord, on whom they had believed. 24 And they passed through Pi-sid'i-a, and came to Pam-phyl'i-a. 25 And when they had spoken the word in Per'ga, they went down to At-ta-li'a; 26 and thence they sailed to An'ti-och, from whence they had been committed to the grace of God for the work which they had fulfilled. 27 And when they were come, and had gathered the church together, they rehearsed all things that God had done with them, and that he had opened a door of faith unto the Gen'tiles. 28 And they tarried no little time with the disciples.

15 And certain men came down from Ju-dæ'a and

ᵉ Or, *Gentiles.* See ch. 4.25.   ᶠ Gr. *brought the good tidings.* Comp. ch. 5.42.

quite as liable to go to a new extreme of idolatry as to be moved to sober thought. He therefore condemned their worship of many gods by declaring that there was only One, Who, as they could see, was kind (ver. 17). He showed them how the goodness of God was evident in nature: but he said nothing about the risen Messiah or of the revelation that had been made to a chosen people. If the onset of persecuting Jews from Antioch and Iconium had been delayed, he would have duly preached Christ to them. His argument at Lystra was more fully set forth on Mars' Hill (ch. 17. 22–31).

19. *Having persuaded the multitudes, they stoned Paul.* Doubtless the fickle crowd was turned against the apostle by the ready malignity which ascribed his healing of the

cripple to the aid of evil spirits.

20. *He rose up, and entered into the city.* The stoning of Paul at Lystra, which came near to being one of the greatest of tragedies, is narrated with the colorless brevity of a concise official report. It is highly probable that Timothy was one of the disciples who 'stood round about' the prostrate body of the apostle.

23. *Elders in every church.* See note on ch. 11.30.

25. *Attalia.* The seaport of Perga.

26. *Antioch.* Their starting-point, from which they had been absent about a year and a half.

CHAPTER 15

1. *Certain men came down from Judæa,* etc. These belonged to the Judaizing party within the church. They contended that Gentiles

321

taught the brethren, *saying*, Except ye be circumcised after the custom of Moses, ye cannot be saved. 2 And when Paul and Bar′na-bas had no small dissension and questioning with them, *the brethren* appointed that Paul and Bar′na-bas, and certain other of them, should go up to Je-ru′sa-lem unto the apostles and elders about this question. 3 They therefore, being brought on their way by the church, passed through both Phœ-ni′ci-a and Sa-ma′ri-a, declaring the conversion of the Gen′tiles: and they caused great joy unto all the brethren. 4 And when they were come to Je-ru′sa-lem, they were received of the church and the apostles and the elders, and they rehearsed all things that God had done with them. 5 But there rose up certain of the sect of the Phar′i-sees who believed, saying, It is needful to circumcise them, and to charge them to keep the law of Mo′ses.

6 And the apostles and the elders were gathered together to consider of this matter. 7 And when there had been much questioning, Peter rose up, and said unto them,

Brethren, ye know that *a* a good while ago God made choice among you, that by my mouth the Gen′tiles should hear the word of the *b* gospel, and believe. 8 And God, who knoweth the heart, bare them witness, giving them the Holy Spirit, even as he did unto us; 9 and he made no distinction between us and them, cleansing their hearts by faith. 10 Now therefore why make ye trial of God, that ye should put a yoke upon the neck of the dis-

---

a Gr. *from early days.*   *b* Or, *good tidings*

---

should not be admitted to membership without being circumcised, and were highly offended because Paul during his first missionary journey had baptized uncircumcised converts. They came from Judæa resolved to compel the Christians at Antioch to accept the chief rite of Judaism as the distinctive requirement for admission to the church. Their Christian experience had not been deep enough to drive out the spirit of Jewish exclusiveness.

3. *Declaring the conversion of the Gentiles.* Affirming that the gospel was for all mankind, and telling how they had baptized Gentiles without Jewish rites. Naturally during his progress through Phœnicia and Samaria the majority received him gladly. The dissatisfied Christians were in Judæa.

4. *Received of the church and the apostles,* etc. This indicates the general greeting that was given to Paul as the returned hero of a great mission to the Gentiles. In this the whole church, with its officials, joined. There were at Jerusalem, waiting to be edified by Paul's recital, more important interests than those of the Judaizers, who were not numerous, even in the holy city.

5. *Pharisees who believed.* Who had been Pharisees before their conversion to Christianity. They brought into the church much of the bigotry which had characterized them as a Jewish party. They were of those who had believed in a spiritual Messiah, and who after the crucifixion of Jesus had been convinced that he was the predicted of the prophets. They were attracted also by the Christian belief in the resurrection. They nevertheless persisted in their Judaizing attempts during the rest of Paul's life.

6. *To consider of this matter.* To decide whether Gentile converts were to be circumcised.

7–11. *Peter rose up,* etc. Peter's speech was a direct rebuke to the Judaizing Pharisees and their sympathizers. It upheld the action of

322

ciples which neither our fathers nor we were able to bear? 11 But we believe that we shall be saved through the grace of the Lord Je′sus, in like manner as they.

12 And all the multitude kept silence; and they hearkened unto Bar′na-bas and Paul rehearsing what signs and wonders God had wrought among the Gen′tiles through them. 13 And after they had held their peace, James answered, saying,

Brethren, hearken unto me: 14 Sym′e-on hath rehearsed how first God visited the ^cGen′tiles, to take out of them a people for his name. 15 And to this agree the words of the prophets; as it is written,

16 ^dAfter these things I will return,

And I will build again the

tabernacle of David, which is fallen;

And I will build again the ruins thereof,

And I will set it up:

17 That the residue of men may seek after the Lord,

And all the ^cGen′tiles, upon whom my name is called,

18 Saith the Lord, ^ewho maketh these things known from of old.

19 Wherefore my judgment is, that we trouble not them that from among the Gen′tiles turn to God; 20 but that we ^fwrite unto them, that they abstain from the pollutions of idols, and from fornication, and from what is strangled, and from blood. 21 For Mo′ses from generations of old hath in every city them that preach him, being read in the synagogues every sabbath.

---

c See marginal note on ch. 4.25.   d Am. ix. 11, 12.   e Or, *who doeth these things*   which were *known &c.*   f Or, *enjoin them*

Paul, affirming salvation by grace through faith.

13–21. *James answered, saying,* etc. James, as head of the church at Jerusalem, summed up the arguments that had been presented, and gave judgment in favor of Paul on the general question of admitting uncircumcised Gentiles. *Symeon.* The old Hebrew form of Peter's name. *Build again the tabernacle of David.* Repair the injured fortunes of the royal house. *That we trouble not,* etc. That is, that Gentile converts be not burdened with the observance of unfamiliar Jewish rites and ceremonies. *That they abstain.* The judgment of the apostle James in favor of the uncircumcised converts was qualified by prohibitions which were not only just concessions to Jewish prejudices, but essential to the harmonious working together of Jews and Gentiles in the church. The latter were of heathen origin. Their social customs and domestic habits were tainted by idolatrous associations. These could not be permitted to break through the safeguards of social purity evolved by the Jews through long ages of effort and suffering. If Jewish exclusiveness had to give way, it was only just that Gentile lawlessness and coarseness should be curbed. This was the object of the letter proposed by James. *Pollutions of idols.* The buying or the eating of flesh that had been sacrificed to idols. *Fornication.* A sin that was regarded much more lightly among the heathen than among Jews. Some of the former had actually been accustomed to think of it in connection with their temple worship. *What is strangled.* Gentile converts were not to be allowed to eat the flesh of strangled animals from which the blood had not been removed. *From blood.* A prohibition which included the preceding one. Blood as food had been forbidden from almost the earliest period of Jewish civilization (Gen. 9.4).

22 Then it seemed good to the apostles and the elders, with the whole church, to choose men out of their company, and send them to An'ti-och with Paul and Bar'-na-bas; *namely*, Ju'das called Bar'sab-bas, and Si'las, chief men among the brethren: 23 and they wrote *thus* by them, ^gThe apostles and the elders, brethren, unto the brethren who are of the Gen'tiles in An'ti-och and Syr'i-a and Ci-li'ci-a, greeting: 24 Forasmuch as we have heard that certain ^hwho went out from us have troubled you with words, subverting your souls; to whom we gave no commandment; 25 it seemed good unto us, having come to one accord, to choose out men and send them unto you with our beloved Bar'na-bas and Paul, 26 men that have hazarded their lives for the name of our Lord Je'sus Christ. 27 We have sent therefore Ju'das and Si'las, who themselves also shall tell you the same things by word of mouth. 28 For it seemed good to the Holy Spirit, and to us, to lay upon you no greater burden than these necessary things: 29 that ye abstain from things sacrificed to idols, and from blood, and from things strangled, and from fornication; from which if ye keep yourselves, it shall be well with you. Fare ye well.

30 So they, when they were dismissed, came down to An'ti-och; and having gathered the multitude together, they delivered the epistle. 31 And when they had read it, they rejoiced for the ⁱconsolation. 32 And Ju'das and Si'las, being themselves also prophets, ^kexhorted the brethren with many words, and confirmed them. 33 And after they had spent some time *there*, they were dismissed in peace from the brethren unto those that had sent them forth.^l 35 But Paul and Bar'na-bas tarried in An'ti-och, teaching and ^mpreaching the word of the Lord, with many others also.

36 And after some days Paul said unto Bar'na-bas, Let us return now and visit the brethren

---

g Or, *The apostles and the elder brethren* *h* Some ancient authorities omit *who went out.* *i* Or, *exhortation* *k* Or, *comforted* *l* Some ancient authorities insert, with variations, ver. 34 *But it seemed good unto Silas to abide there.* *m* Comp. marginal note on ch. 5.42.

22. *Judas called Barsabbas.* Probably a brother of the Barsabbas mentioned in ch. 1.23. The latter was a candidate for the vacancy in the apostolate caused by the death of Judas Iscariot. *Silas.* Otherwise known as Silvanus. He was a companion of Paul (2 Cor. 1.19) and afterward of Peter (1 Pet. 5.12).

23–29. *And they wrote thus by them.* The letter contained in these verses sets forth the terms on which future harmony between Jewish and Gentile followers of Christ was to be assured. It embodies the conclusions previously announced in the decision by James; but its prohibitions are gently imposed. Its brotherly greeting, its farewell, its tender solicitude lest any one, especially from Jerusalem, should mislead a converted Gentile soul, its tribute of honor in the appointment of special ambassadors to deliver the message from the apostles and elders—all these tactful and considerate precautions did not fail of their intended effect (ver. 31).

36. *Let us return now and visit the brethren*, etc. In this verse is indicated the beginning of Paul's second missionary journey, which included not only the revisiting of the churches founded during the

in every city wherein we proclaimed the word of the Lord, *and see* how they fare. 37 And Bar'na-bas was minded to take with them John also, who was called Mark. 38 But Paul thought not good to take with them him who withdrew from them from Pam-phyl'i-a, and went not with them to the work. 39 And there arose a sharp contention, so that they parted asunder one from the other, and Bar'na-bas took Mark with him, and sailed away unto Cy'prus: 40 but Paul chose Si'las, and went forth, being commended by the brethren to the grace of the Lord. 41 And he went through Syr'i-a and Ci-li'ci-a, confirming the churches.

16 And he came also to Der'be and to Lys'tra: and behold, a certain disciple was

there, named Tim'o-thy, the son of a Jewess that believed; but his father was a Greek. 2 The same was well reported of by the brethren that were at Lys'tra and I-co'ni-um. 3 Him would Paul have to go forth with him; and he took and circumcised him because of the Jews that were in those parts: for they all knew that his father was a Greek. 4 And as they went on their way through the cities, they delivered them the decrees to keep which had been ordained of the apostles and elders that were at Je-ru'sa-lem. 5 So the churches were strengthened ᶜin the faith, and increased in number daily.

6 And they went through ᵇthe region of Phyrg'i-a and Ga-la'-ti-a, having been forbidden of the Holy Spirit to speak the word in A'si-a; 7 and when they were

---

a Or, *in faith*   *b* Or, *Phrygia and the region of Galatia*

first journey, but also the European cities of Philippi, Thessalonica, Berœa, Athens and Corinth, from which last mentioned place the apostle returned to Antioch in Syria. The second journey is narrated in chs. 15.36–18.22.

37. *Barnabas was minded*, etc. Naturally, as John Mark, the evangelist, was his cousin.

38. *Went not with them to the work.* Paul had reason for his refusal to take Mark with him. He did not wish to risk another defection at an urgent moment (ch. 13.13).

CHAPTER 16

1. *Timothy.* His mother, Eunice, was a Jewess and a widow; his father was a Greek. His grandmother Lois brought him up in the Jewish faith, though he had not been circumcised. Probably the reason for this was his mixed parentage. There were few Jews in Lystra and no synagogue.

3. *Because of the Jews.* The coun-

cil at Jerusalem had now decided that Gentiles need not be circumcised, but the rule did not apply to a man born of a Jewish mother, more especially if that man, as in the case of Timothy, was being prepared as a teacher of Christians among whom Jews were to be found. The latter would have reproached him and could have seriously hindered his ministry.

4. *The decrees.* Containing the regulations in the apostolic letter from Jerusalem.

6. *Phrygia.* An inland district of Asia Minor, west of Galatia. *Galatia.* An inland Roman province of Asia Minor, inhabited in early times by Celts (Galli). Paul was detained in this province by sickness (Gal. 4.13). The Epistle to the Galatians was probably written after a second visit (Acts 18.23). *Asia.* A Roman province of Asia Minor.

7. *Mysia.* A country in the northwestern part of Asia Minor. *Bithynia.* A Roman province in the

come over against My'si-a, they assayed to go into Bi-thyn'i-a; and the Spirit of Je'sus suffered them not; 8 and passing by My'-si-a, they came down to Tro'as. 9 And a vision appeared to Paul in the night: There was a man of Mac-e-do'ni-a standing, beseeching him, and saying, Come over into Mac-e-do'ni-a, and help us. 10 And when he had seen the vision, straightway we sought to go forth into Mac-e-do'ni-a, concluding that God had called us to ᶜpreach the gospel unto them.

11 Setting sail therefore from Tro'as, we made a straight course to Sam'o-thrace, and the day following to Ne-ap'o-lis; 12 and from thence to Phi-lip'pi, which is a city of Mac-e-do'ni-a, the first of the district, a *Roman* colony: and we were in this city tarrying certain days. 13 And on the sabbath day we went forth without the gate by a river side, ᵈwhere we supposed there was a place of prayer; and we sat down, and spake unto the women that were come together. 14 And a certain woman named Lyd'i-a, a seller of purple, of the city of Thy-a-ti'ra, one that worshipped God, heard us: whose heart the Lord opened to give heed unto the things which were spoken by Paul. 15 And when she was baptized, and her household, she besought us, saying, If ye have judged me to be faithful to the Lord, come into my house, and abide *there*. And she constrained us.

16 And it came to pass, as we were going to the place of prayer, that a certain maid having ᵉa spirit of divination met us, who brought her masters much gain

northwestern part of Asia Minor, bounded by the Black Sea on the north and by the Sea of Marmora on the west. *The Spirit of Jesus suffered them not.* A proof of belief in the divinity of Jesus.

8. *Troas.* A city on the west coast of Asia Minor. It was the chief port of Mysia.

9. *Macedonia.* The northern Roman province of Greece. It was visited a second time by Paul (Acts 20.1–6).

10. *We.* Indicating that Luke, the writer of this narrative, was now journeying with Paul.

11. *Samothrace.* An island midway between Neapolis and Troas. *Neapolis.* The seaport of Philippi.

12. *Philippi.* A city of the Roman province of Macedonia. It was named after King Philip of Macedon. *A Roman colony.* That is, a city inhabited by colonists sent out by Italy, who retained their Latin rights, spoke the Latin language and were entirely independent of the provincial governor. A colony of this kind was intended to be a protection to the Roman interests, watchful of the governors, and faithfully modeled on the Roman rule and life which it represented. Its magistrates were always sent from Rome.

13. *A place of prayer.* Used by resident Jews in cities where there was no synagogue.

14. *Lydia.* A wealthy and charitable woman of Thyatira, who had been converted to Judaism. *Thyatira.* A city of Lydia, a country of Asia Minor. It was situated on the river Lycus, and was famed for its dyed garments, or purple goods, of which Lydia was a seller.

16. *A spirit of divination.* The maid was gifted with a certain degree of spiritual insight, as was shown by her perception of the character and mission of Paul and his companions. *Her masters.* Who profitably employed her as a clairvoyant or fortune teller.

by soothsaying. 17 The same following after Paul and us cried out, saying, These men are *f*servants of the Most High God, who proclaim unto you *g*the way of salvation. 18 And this she did for many days. But Paul, being sore troubled, turned and said to the spirit, I charge thee in the name of Je'sus Christ to come *h*ut of her. And it came out that very hour.

19 But when her masters saw that the hope of their gain was *h*gone, they laid hold on Paul and Si'las, and dragged them into the marketplace before the rulers, 20 and when they had brought them unto the *i*magistrates, they said, These men, being Jews, do exceedingly trouble our city, 21 and set forth customs which it is not lawful for us to receive, or to observe, being Romans. 22 And the multitude rose up together against them: and the *i*magistrates rent their garments off them, and commanded to beat them with rods. 23 And when they had laid many stripes

upon them, they cast them into prison, charging the jailor to keep them safely: 24 who, having received such a charge, cast them into the inner prison, and made their feet fast in the stocks. 25 But about midnight Paul and Si'las were praying and singing hymns unto God, and the prisoners were listening to them; 26 and suddenly there was a great earthquake, so that the foundations of the prison-house were shaken: and immediately all the doors were opened; and every one's bands were loosed. 27 And the jailor, being roused out of sleep and seeing the prison doors open, drew his sword and was about to kill himself, supposing that the prisoners had escaped. 28 But Paul cried with a loud*/*voice, saying, Do thyself no harm: for we are all here. 29 And he called for lights and sprang in, and, trembling for fear, fell down before Paul and Si'las, 30 and brought them out and said, Sirs, what must I do to be saved? 31 And they said; Believe

f Gr. *bondservants.* *g* Or, *a way* *h* Gr. *come out.*

i Gr. *prætors*: comp. ver. 22, 35, 36, 38.

19. *Silas.* A companion and friend of Paul; most probably the same person as Silvanus, afterward mentioned in Paul's epistles. (2 Cor. 1.19.)

20. *The magistrates.* Two prætors, the chief authorities of a Roman colony. *Being Jews.* The masters of the soothsaying woman knew that Paul and his companions were Jews by race, but knew nothing of their Christian belief.

27. *Drew his sword,* etc. A Roman jailor whose prisoner escaped was liable to forfeit his life.

30. *What must I do to be saved?* The unhappy jailor must have heard something about Paul and known why he was imprisoned. He

had been thrown suddenly into despair by a medley of amazing occurrences, of which Paul's behavior was not the least confusing. Here was a captive who, when he had a chance, did not attempt to escape from a Roman dungeon! The benign and enraptured countenance of the apostle, to whom the shaken foundations were only an answering deliverance, first abashed the jailor, then reassured him. He naturally linked the possibility of his own immediate salvation from the earthquake or the executioner's axe, to Paul's good will and the salvation he had been heard to proclaim. He did not at first realize what he most needed.

on the Lord Je'sus, and thou shalt be saved, thou and thy house. 32 And they spake the word of [k]the Lord unto him, with all that were in his house. 33 And he took them the same hour of the night, and washed their stripes; and was baptized, he and all his, immediately. 34 And he brought them up into his house, and set [l]food before them, and rejoiced greatly, with all his house, [m]having believed in God.

35 But when it was day, the [n]magistrates sent the [o]serjeants, saying, Let those men go. 36 And the jailor reported the words to Paul, *saying,* The [n]magistrates have sent to let you go: now therefore come forth, and go in peace. 37 But Paul said unto them, They have beaten us publicly, uncondemned, men that are Romans, and have cast us into prison; and do they now cast us out privily? nay verily; but let them come themselves

and bring us out. 38 And the [o]serjeants reported these words unto the [n]magistrates: and they feared when they heard that they were Romans; 39 and they came and besought them; and when they had brought them out, they asked them to go away from the city. 40 And they went out of the prison, and entered into *the house of* Lyd'i-a: and when they had seen the brethren, they [p]comforted them, and departed.

17 Now when they had passed through Am-phip'-o-lis and Ap-ol-lo'ni-a, they came to Thes-sa-lo-ni'ca, where was a synagogue of the Jews: 2 and Paul, as his custom was, went in unto them, and for three [a]sabbath days reasoned with them from the scriptures, 3 opening and alleging that it behooved the Christ to suffer, and to rise again from the dead; and that this Je'sus, whom, *said he,* I proclaim

---

k Some ancient authorities read *God.*
l Gr. *a table.* *m* Or, *having believed God*

n Gr. *prætors.* See ver. 20. *o* Gr. *lictors.*
p Or. *exhorted* *a* Or, *weeks*

---

32. *Spake the word of the Lord unto him.* Explained how God had revealed Himself in Jesus Christ for the spiritual salvation of mankind. This was a truth to which the Roman civilization, with all its achievements and resources, was absolutely foreign.

35. *The serjeants.* The attendants upon the magistrates.

37. *Men that are Romans.* It is difficult to believe that Paul failed to demand the protection of his Roman citizenship before he and his companions were beaten with rods. The sudden rush and cries of the mob for vengeance probably drowned any protest that was made. In Paul's time Roman citizenship conferred freedom from corporal punishment, the right of appeal to the emperor against the sentences of magistrates, the right to hold

office, and exemption from direct taxation.

CHAPTER 17

1. *Amphipolis.* A city of Thrace, situated on the river Strymon. *Apollonia.* A city of Macedonia. It was thirty miles west of Amphipolis and thirty-eight miles east of Thessalonica. *Thessalonica.* The capital city of the province of Macedonia. It was a Roman colony and a great trade centre, with a considerable Jewish population. It is now Saloniki, one of the largest cities in the Turkish Empire.

3. *Is the Christ.* Paul's invariable custom in the cities with a Jewish population, was to go first to the synagogue and convince its congregation that Jesus was the Messiah.

unto you, is the Christ. 4 And some of them were persuaded, and consorted with Paul and Si'-las; and of the devout Greeks a great multitude, and of the chief women not a few. 5 But the Jews, being moved with jealousy, took unto them certain vile fellows of the rabble, and gathering a crowd, set the city on an uproar; and assaulting the house of Ja'son, they sought to bring them forth to the people. 6 And when they found them not, they dragged Ja'son and certain brethren before the rulers of the city, crying, These that have turned *the world upside down are come hither also; 7 whom Ja'-son hath received: and these all act contrary to the decrees of Cæ'sar, saying that there is another king, *one* Jesus. 8 And they troubled the multitude and the rulers of the city, when they heard these things. 9 And when they had taken security from

Ja'son and the rest, they let them go.

10 And the brethren immediately sent away Paul and Si'las by night unto Be-rœ'a: who when they were come thither went into the synagogue of the Jews. 11 Now these were more noble than those in Thes-sa-lo-ni'ca, in that they received the word with all readiness of mind, examining the scriptures daily, whether these things were so. 12 Many of them therefore believed; also of the Greek women of honorable estate, and of men, not a few. 13 But when the Jews of Thes-sa-lo-ni'ca had knowledge that the word of God was proclaimed of Paul at Be-rœ'a also, they came thither likewise, stirring up and troubling the multitudes. 14 And then immediately the brethren sent forth Paul to go as far as to the sea: and Si'las and Tim'o-thy abode there still. 15 But they that conducted Paul

---

b Gr, the inhabited earth.

4. *Devout Greeks.* Greek-speaking Gentiles who had accepted the Jewish faith and worshipped in the synagogue.

5. *Jason.* A Jew in whose house Paul and his companions were entertained.

6. *Rulers of the city.* The Greek word for 'rulers' employed by Luke is found in an inscription in the modern city of Saloniki on an arch which has been preserved since Paul's time.

7. *Another king, one Jesus.* The hostile Jews thought that they could get rid of Paul and his friends most speedily by involving them in a charge of treason. The mere mention of the name of Jesus in connection with his kingdom, even though a spiritual kingdom, would afford a pretext for such a charge.

9. *Had taken security from Jason.* That is, had made him legally

responsible for future good behavior. It was probably stipulated that Paul should leave the city and not return to it.

10. *Berœa.* A city of Macedonia, fifty miles southwest of Thessalonica. It was destroyed by an earthquake in 900 A.D. On its site is the modern town of Verria.

14. *To go as far as to the sea.* Paul waited on the seacoast whence he was taken by ship to Athens.

15. *Athens.* A city of the Roman province of Achaia. Its glory had in large measure departed; but it was still the intellectual and artistic centre of the world. In Paul's time the more gifted Athenians were indifferent to religion; but the mass of the people were superstitious, and their artistic temperament strongly influenced the expression of their religious feeling. Hence their streets were adorned with numerous

brought him as far as Ath'ens: and receiving a commandment unto Si'las and Tim'o-thy that they should come to him with all speed, they departed.

16 Now while Paul waited for them at Ath'ens, his spirit was provoked within him as he beheld the city full of idols. 17 So he reasoned in the synagogue with the Jews and the devout persons, and in the marketplace every day with them that met him. 18 And certain also of the Ep-i-cu-re'an and Sto'ic philosophers encountered him. And some said, What would this babbler say? others, He seemeth to be a setter forth of *strange *d*gods:

because he *preached Je'sus and the resurrection. 19 And they took hold of him, and brought him *unto *g*the Ar-e-op'a-gus, saying, May we know what this new teaching is, which is spoken by thee? 20 For thou bringest certain strange things to our ears: we would know therefore what these things mean. 21 (Now all the A-the'ni-ans and the strangers sojourning there *h*spent their time in nothing else, but either to tell or to hear some new thing.) 22 And Paul stood in the midst of the Ar-e-op'a-gus, and said,

Ye men of Ath'ens, in all things I perceive that ye are

---

c Or, *foreign divinities*   *d* Gr. demons.
e See marginal note on ch. 5.42.

f Or, *before*   *g* Or, *the hill of Mars*
h Or, *had leisure for nothing else*

---

statues, temples and altars. Athens was also the educational centre of the Roman empire. Many students from Rome came to gain the unrivalled advantages of Athenian instruction in philosophy and art.

16. *His spirit was provoked*, etc. Paul's Jewish training had taught him the gross impiety of representing the divine being in material form.

17. *In the synagogue.* Paul's line of argument with the Jews here was the same as in other synagogues, namely, that Jesus was the Christ or Messiah. *In the marketplace.* Here he had to argue with all who chose to question him; but his aim at first was to discredit atheism, materialism and idolatry. Thus he prepared to preach Jesus and the resurrection (ver. 18).

18. *Epicurean and Stoic philosophers.* The Epicureans were named after their founder Epicurus (341–270 B.C.). They believed that the happiness of mankind was most effectively promoted by striving for pleasure, by which was meant bodily and mental states free from pain. They did not commend unreservedly the lower kinds of pleasure. They had no faith in Divine Providence, but held that the world was

under the power of chance. The Stoics believed that human happiness was best attained by the practice of virtue as indicated by the law of nature. They believed also in Divine Providence, but only as superintending in a general way the structure of the world, leaving the individual to the subordinate operation of unalterable natural laws. This part of their system contrasted most strongly with the doctrine of Christ, that not one sparrow fell to the ground unnoticed by the Father, and that the very hairs of the head were numbered (Mt. 10.29, 30). *This babbler.* That is, a gatherer of words and phrases. The term expressed the fine scorn which Athenian philosophers and men of the world felt for any outsider who dared to come into their marketplace and talk philosophy.

19. *Areopagus.* The meeting-place of the Athenian council or court of the Areopagus. It was on a hill to the west of the Acropolis. Paul was taken to it in a spirit of indulgent curiosity, in order that he might have a better chance to speak.

22–31. *And Paul stood in the midst*, etc. These verses contain the apostle's speech on Mars' Hill. Whatever may have been his dis-

'very religious. 23 For as I passed along, and observed the objects of your worship, I found also an altar with this inscription, To an Unknown God. What therefore ye worship in ignorance, this I set forth unto you. 24 The God that made the world and all things therein, he, being Lord of heaven and earth, dwelleth not in *k*temples made with hands; 25 neither is he served by men's hands, as though he needed anything, seeing he himself giveth to all life, and breath, and all things; 26 and he made of one every nation of men to dwell on all the face of the earth, having determined *their* appointed seasons, and the bounds of their habitation; 27 that they should seek God, if haply they might feel after him and find him, though he is not far from each one of us: 28 for in him we live, and move, and have our being; as certain even of your own poets have said,

For we are also his offspring. 29 Being then the offspring of God, we ought not to think that *l*the Godhead is like unto gold, or silver, or stone, graven by art and device of man. 30 The times of ignorance therefore God overlooked; but now he *m*commandeth men that they should all everywhere repent: 31 inasmuch as he hath appointed a day in which he will judge *n*the world in righteousness *o*by *p*the man whom he hath ordained; whereof he hath given assurance unto all men, in that he hath raised him from the dead.

32 Now when they heard of the resurrection of the dead, some mocked; but others said, We will hear thee concerning this yet again. 33 Thus Paul went out from among them. 34 But certain men clave unto him, and believed: among whom also was Di-o-nys'i-us the Ar-e-op'a-gite, and a woman named Dam'a-ris, and others with them.

---

i Or, *somewhat superstitious*   *k* Or, *sanctuaries*   *l* Or, *that which is divine*   *m* Some ancient authorities read *declareth to men.*   *n* Gr. *the inhabited earth.*   *o* Gr. *in.*   *p* Or. *a man*

---

cussions with individual Stoics and Epicureans in the marketplace, the greater part of Paul's argument in the Areopagus was directed against the popular worship of idols, the main thought being that the inscription to an unknown God suggested the deepest need of the people. Paul told the Athenians in effect that they did not know the true God; that He was Spirit, the origin of all life, and could not be likened unto images; that in Him mankind dwell and have their being; that they should seek after Him, and that He ordained the man Jesus Christ, whom He raised from the dead, and by whom He will judge the world in righteousness. The apostle talked of judgment so that repentance might be hastened.

Certain even of your own poets. Aratus, a Greek poet of Cilicia. He was a Stoic
32. *Some mocked.* It was not a philosophical argument for the resurrection which was laughed at by the cynical listeners, but the statement that God had raised a man from the dead. *'Yet again.* Probably they wished to hear more about the circumstances under which the resurrection of Jesus took place.
34. *Dionysius the Areopagite.* A member of the Court of the Areopagus, or upper Athenian council. It was the governing power of the city, and was composed of those who had been important officers of state. No one under sixty years of age could be a member. The court

18 After these things he departed from Ath′ens, and came to Cor′inth. 2 And he found a certain Jew named Aq′-ui-la, a man of Pon′tus by race, lately come from It′a-ly, with his wife Pris-cil′la, because Clau′di-us had commanded all the Jews to depart from Rome: and he came unto them; 3 and because he was of the same trade, he abode with them, and they wrought; for by their trade they were tentmakers. 4 And he reasoned in the synagogue every sabbath, and *a*persuaded Jews and Greeks.

5 But when Si′las and Tim′o-thy came down from Mac-e-do′ni-a, Paul was constrained by the word, testifying to the Jews that Je′sus was the Christ. 6 And when they opposed themselves and *b*blasphemed, he shook out his raiment and said unto them, Your blood *be* upon your own heads; I am clean: from henceforth I will go unto the Gen′tiles. 7 And he departed thence, and went into the house of a certain man named Ti′tus Jus′tus, one that worshipped God, whose house joined hard to the synagogue. 8 And Cris′pus, the ruler of the synagogue, *c*believed in the Lord with all his house; and many of the Co-rin′thi-ans hearing believed, and were baptized. 9 And the Lord said unto Paul in the night by a vision, **Be not afraid, but speak and hold not thy peace: 10 for I am with thee, and no man shall set on thee to harm thee: for I have much people in this city.** 11 And he dwelt *there* a year and six months, teaching the word of God among them.

12 But when Gal′li-o was proconsul of A-cha′ia, the Jews with one accord rose up against Paul and brought him before the judg-

---

a Gr. *sought to persuade.*   *b* Or, *railed*   *c* Gr. *believed the Lord.*

---

had jurisdiction in criminal and political cases, as well as those affecting the public morals.

CHAPTER 18

1. *Corinth.* The capital city of the Roman province of Achaia. Its situation on the isthmus made it the chief commercial centre, as it commanded all the traffic between the isthmus and the rest of Achaia, while its two ports Cenchreæ and Lechæum attracted to it the maritime trade respectively of east and west. Corinth in Paul's time was a Roman colony and the residence of the Roman proconsul. The morals of the city were very low. Paul remained there for a year and a half (ver. 11). From Corinth he wrote his two epistles to the Thessalonians.

2. *Aquila.* The name is Roman. *Pontus.* A Roman province of Asia Minor. *Priscilla.* Aquila and Priscilla entertained Paul during his stay at Corinth. They were probably converted Jews of the Dispersion. They worked heartily with the apostle in his evangelism, and were important aids to him in Ephesus (ver. 26; 1 Cor. 16.19).

7. *Titus Justus.* Probably a member of the Roman colony in the city. Corinth, which had been completely destroyed by the Roman general Mummius in B.C. 146, was rebuilt as a Roman colony by Julius Cæsar in 46 B.C.

8. *Crispus.* One of Paul's converts. See 1 Cor. 1.14.

12. *Gallio was proconsul.* Gallio was a brother of the philosopher Seneca, Nero's tutor, and an uncle of the poet Lucan. He had been consul at Rome, and was afterward sent out to rule in Achaia. The title 'proconsul' proves that Achaia was a province belonging to the

ment-seat, 13 saying, This man persuadeth men to worship God contrary to the law. 14 But when Paul was about to open his mouth, Gal′li-o said unto the Jews, If indeed it were a matter of wrong or of wicked villany, O ye Jews, reason would that I should bear with you: 15 but if they are questions about words and names and your own law, look to it yourselves; I am not minded to be a judge of these matters. 16 And he drove them from the judgment-seat. 17 And they all laid hold on Sos′the-nes, the ruler of the synagogue, and beat him before the judgment-seat. And Gal′li-o cared for none of these things.

18 And Paul, having tarried after this yet many days, took his leave of the brethren, and sailed thence for Syr′i-a, and with him Pris-cil′la and Aq′ui-la: having shorn his head in Cen′-chre-æ; for he had a vow. 19 And they came to Eph′e-sus, and he left them there: but he himself entered into the synagogue, and reasoned with the Jews. 20 And when they asked him to abide a longer time, he consented not; 21 but taking his leave of them, and saying, I will return again unto you if God will, he set sail from Eph′e-sus.

22 And when he had landed at Cæs-a-re′a, he went up and saluted the church, and went down to An′ti-och. 23 And having spent some time *there*, he departed, and went through the region of Ga-la′ti-a, and Phryg′i-a,

Roman senate, not to the emperor. See note on ch. 13.7.

13. *Law.* Jewish law.

14. *Gallio said*, etc. He determined to have nothing to do with the complaint of the Jews, even before Paul was heard. He was contemptuously indifferent to Jewish laws and customs.

17. *Sosthenes.* The crowd thought that a Jew could be safely beaten after the Roman proconsul had decided that a Jewish wrangle was not worth bothering about. *For none of these things.* That is, neither for the unjust assault upon Sosthenes and the complaint against Paul, nor the general question of Jewish religious rights and privileges.

18. *For he had a vow.* Probably the vow of a Nazirite (Num. 6.1–21). It was taken in gratitude for deliverance from sickness or other misfortune. The hair of the head was shaved and then allowed to grow, and after a certain period the person went to Jerusalem and made an offering of the hair which had grown in the interval. Then the head was again shaved.

19. *Ephesus.* The capital city of the Roman province of Asia. It was celebrated for its temple of Diana and for its theatre, which seated 24,500. In Paul's time its population of 225,000 made it next to Alexandria in size among the cities of the East. From about 300 A.D. it became a great centre of Christian pilgrimage because of its association with Paul, Timothy, and the apostle John who died there in 100 A.D.

22. *Cæsarea.* See notes on ch. 8.40. *Antioch.* See notes on ch. 11.19.

23. *Galatia, and Phrygia.* See notes on ch. 16.6. Paul's third missionary journey is narrated in chs. 18.23–21.17. Starting again from Antioch in Syria, he revisited the churches founded in the cities of his first journey, namely, Derbe, Lystra, Iconium, and Antioch in Pisidia; thence he proceeded to the churches in the northerly cities of Galatia. Returning he crossed through Phrygia and Lydia to Ephesus, where he remained two years. From Ephesus he sailed north to the coast of Macedonia, revisiting the churches and going south by land through Greece as

in order, establishing all the disciples.

24 Now a certain Jew named A-pol'los, an Al-ex-an'dri-an by race, [d]an eloquent man, came to Eph'e-sus; and he was mighty in the scriptures. 25 This man had been [e]instructed in the way of the Lord; and being fervent in spirit, he spake and taught accurately the things concerning Je'sus, knowing only the baptism of John: 26 and he began to speak boldly in the synagogue. But when Pris'cil-la and Aq'ui-la heard him, they took him unto them, and expounded unto him the way of God more accurately. 27 And when he was minded to pass over into A-cha'ia, the brethren encouraged him, and wrote to the disciples to receive him: and when he was come, he [f]helped them much that had believed through grace; 28 for he powerfully confuted the Jews, [g]and that publicly, showing by the scriptures that Je'sus was the Christ.

19 And it came to pass, that, while A-pol'los was at Cor'inth, Paul having passed through the upper country came to Eph'e-sus, and found certain

disciples: 2 and he said unto them, Did ye receive the Holy Spirit when ye believed? And they said unto him, Nay, we did not so much as hear whether [a]the Holy Spirit was given. 3 And He said, Into what then were ye baptized? And they said, Into John's baptism. 4 And Paul said, John baptized with the baptism of repentance, saying unto the people that they should believe on him that should come after him, that is, on Je'sus. 5 And when they heard this, they were baptized into the name of the Lord Je'sus. 6 And when Paul had laid his hands upon them, the Holy Spirit came on them; and they spake with tongues, and prophesied. 7 And they were in all about twelve men.

8 And he entered into the synagogue, and spake boldly for the space of three months, reasoning and persuading as to the things concerning the kingdom of God. 9 But when some were hardened and disobedient, speaking evil of the Way before the multitude, he departed from them, and separated the disciples, reasoning daily in the school of Ty-ran'nus. 10 And this continued for the

---

d Or, *a learned man*   *e* Gr. *taught by word of mouth.*   *f* Or, *helped much through grace them that had believed*   *g* Or, *showing publicly*   *a* Or, *there is a Holy Spirit*

---

far as Corinth. Hearing of a plot against him by the Jews, he determined to return home by way of Macedonia, sailing from Philippi to Troas, Assos, Mytelene, Chios, Samos, Miletus, Cos, Rhodes, and Patara; thence direct to Tyre on the Phœnician coast. From Tyre he went to Ptolemais and Cæsarea, and thence to Jerusalem.

24. *Apollos.* Or Apollonius.

26. *Expounded unto him,* etc. An important and timely help, greatly

strengthening the usefulness of Apollos. He knew Jesus as the Messiah, as the Saviour of the world from sin; but how much more he must have learned from his two friends, who had been instructed by Paul!

CHAPTER 19

9. *The Way.* Christianity. *Ty-rannus.* Head of a school of philosophic disputants.

10. *Two years.* During which the

space of two years; so that all they that dwelt in A′si-a heard the word of the Lord, both Jews and Greeks. 11 And God wrought special [b]miracles by the hands of Paul: 12 insomuch that unto the sick were carried away from his body handkerchiefs or aprons, and the diseases departed from them, and the evil spirits went out. 13 But certain also of the strolling Jews, exorcists, took upon them to name over them that had the evil spirits the name of the Lord Je′sus, saying, I adjure you by Je′sus whom Paul preacheth. 14 And there were seven sons of one Sce′va, a Jew, a chief priest, who did this. 15 And the evil spirit answered and said unto them, Je′sus I [c]know, and Paul I know, but who are ye? 16 And the man in whom the evil spirit was leaped on them, and mastered both of them, and prevailed against them, so that they fled out of that house naked and wounded. 17 And this became known to all, both Jews and Greeks, that dwelt at Eph′e-sus; and fear fell upon them all, and the name of the Lord Je′sus was magnified. 18 Many also of them that had believed came, confessing, and declaring their deeds. 19 And not a few of them that practised magical arts brought their books together and burned them in the sight of all; and they counted the price of them, and found it fifty thousand pieces of silver. 20 So mightily grew the word of the Lord and prevailed.

21 Now after these things were ended, Paul purposed in the spirit, when he had passed through Mac-e-do′ni-a and A-cha′ia, to go to Je-ru′sa-lem, saying, After I have been there, I must also see Rome. 22 And having sent into Mac-e-do′ni-a two of them that ministered unto him, Tim′o-thy and E-ras′-tus, he himself stayed in A′si-a for a while.

23 And about that time there arose no small stir concerning the Way. 24 For a certain man named De-me′tri-us, a silversmith, who made silver shrines of [d]Di-a′na, brought no little business unto the craftsmen; 25 whom he gathered together, with the workmen of like occupation, and said, Sirs, ye know that by this business we have our wealth. 26 And ye see and hear, that not alone at Eph′e-sus, but almost throughout all A′si-a, this Paul hath persuaded and turned away much people, saying that they are no gods, that are made with hands: 27 and not only is there danger that this our trade come

---

b Gr. powers.   c Or. recognize

seven churches of Asia were founded. *Asia.* That is, the Roman province of Asia, otherwise called Proconsular Asia. See Rev. 1.11.

13. *Exorcists.* Who pretended to expel the evil spirits by uttering certain words alleged to have a magical effect.

19. *Fifty thousand pieces of silver.* Fifty thousand drachmas. Equal to about ten thousand dollars.

---

d Gr. Artemis.

22. *Timothy.* See notes on ch. 16.1   *Erastus.* Afterward mentioned by Paul (2 Tim. 4.20).

24. *Diana.* A goddess personifying the fruitful powers of nature.

25. *Workmen of like occupation.* Those who were employed in the procuring and preparation of the materials used in the manufacture of the shrines.

27. *All Asia.* Contributions for

into disrepute; but also that the temple of the great goddess *Di-a'na* be made of no account, and that she should even be deposed from her magnificence whom all A'si-a and *the world worship-peth. 28 And when they heard this they were filled with wrath, and cried out, saying, Great *is* *Di-a'na* of the E-phe'sians. 29 And the city was filled with the confusion: and they rushed with one accord into the theatre, having seized Ga'ius and Ar-is-tar'chus, men of Mac-e-do'ni-a, Paul's companions in travel. 30 And when Paul was minded to enter in unto the people, the disciples suffered him not. 31 And certain also of the *A'si-archs*, being his friends, sent unto him and besought him not to adventure himself into the theatre. 32 Some therefore cried one thing, and some another: for the assembly was in confusion; and the more part knew not wherefore they were come together. 33 *And they brought Al-ex-an'der out of the multitude, the Jews putting him forward. And Al-ex-an'der beckoned with the hand, and would have made a

defence unto the people. 34 But when they perceived that he was a Jew, all with one voice about the space of two hours cried out, Great *is* *Di-a'na* of the E-phe'-sians. 35 And when the town-clerk had quieted the multitude, he saith, Ye men of Eph'e-sus, what man is there who knoweth not that the city of the E-phe'si-ans is temple-keeper of the great *Di-a'na, and of the *image* which fell down from *Jupiter? 36 Seeing then that these things cannot be gainsaid, ye ought to be quiet, and to do nothing rash. 37 For ye have brought *hither* these men, who are neither robbers of temples nor blasphemers of our goddess. 38 If therefore De-me'tri-us, and the craftsmen that are with him, have a matter against any man, *the courts are open, and there are proconsuls: let them accuse one another. 39 But if ye seek anything about other matters, it shall be settled in the regular assembly. 40 For indeed we are in danger to be *accused concerning this day's riot, there being no cause *for it*: and as touching it we shall not be able to give account of this con-

---

d Gr. *Artemis.* *e* Gr. *the inhabited earth.*
f That is, officers having charge of festivals &c. in the Roman province of Asia. *g* Or,

the Temple were sent in from all parts of the province of Asia.

33. *Alexander.* Who was chosen as a representative Jew to convince the crowd that the Jews of Ephesus had no sympathy with Paul and his preaching.

35. *The town-clerk.* He kept the city records, received public communications, sent replies in his name in the city's behalf, and was the presiding officer at the regular popular assemblies. He also put in writing and affixed his seal to laws

And some *of the multitude instructed Alexander* *h* Or, *heaven* *i* Or, *court* days *are kept* *k* Or, *accused of riot concerning this day*

of the city. *Fell down from Jupiter.* This was said to quiet the crowds. If the image fell down from Jupiter, that is, had a supernatural origin, what harm could possibly befall it by reason of this disturbance? Jupiter, the king of their gods, could take care of his own.

38. *Proconsuls.* There was only one proconsul in the province of Asia; but the town-clerk meant to refer generally to courts and proconsuls to settle disputes. See notes on ch. 13.7.

course. 41 And when he had thus spoken, he dismissed the assembly.

20 And after the uproar ceased, Paul having sent for the disciples and exhorted them, took leave of them, and departed to go into Mac-e-do′-ni-a. 2 And when he had gone through those parts, and had given them much exhortation, he came into Greece. 3 And when he had spent three months *there*, and a plot was laid against him by the Jews as he was about to set sail for Syr′i-a, he determined to return through Mac-e-do′ni-a. 4 And there accompanied him *a*as far as A′si-a, Sop′a-ter of Be-rœ′a, *the son* of Pyr′rhus; and of the Thes-sa-lo′ni-ans, Ar-is-tar′-chus and Se-cun′dus; and Ga′ius of Der′be, and Tim′o-thy; and of A′si-a, Tych′i-cus and Troph′-i-mus. 5 But these *b*had gone before, and were waiting for us at Tro′as. 6 And we sailed away from Phi-lip′pi after the days of unleavened bread, and came unto them to Tro′as in five days; where we tarried seven days.

7 And upon the first day of the week, when we were gathered together to break bread, Paul discoursed with them, intending to depart on the morrow; and prolonged his speech until midnight. 8 And there were many lights in the upper chamber where we were gathered together. 9 And there sat in the window a certain young man named Eu′ty-chus, borne down with deep sleep; and as Paul discoursed yet longer, being borne down by his sleep he fell down from the third story, and was taken up dead. 10 And Paul went down, and fell on him, and embracing him said, Make ye no ado; for his life is in him. 11 And when he was gone up, and had broken the bread, and eaten, and had talked with them a long while, even till break of day, so he departed.

a Many ancient authorities omit *as far as Asia.*

b Many ancient authorities read *came, and were waiting.*

CHAPTER 20

2. *Gone through those parts.* Revisited the churches at Philippi, Thessalonica and Berœa.

3. *Three months.* At Corinth. *A plot.* To murder him on shipboard after he had sailed for Syria.

4. *Aristarchus.* The same who was seized with Gaius (ch. 19.29). He was a faithful companion of Paul, and afterwards fellow-prisoner with him at Rome. *Tychicus and Trophimus.* Tychicus was fellow-prisoner with Paul at Rome during the apostle's first imprisonment. See also Eph. 6.21, 22; Col. 4.7, 8; 2 Tim. 4.12; Tit. 3.12. Trophimus also travelled much with Paul. He is mentioned in 2 Tim. 4.20.

5. *Troas.* See notes on ch. 16.8.

6. *Philippi.* See note on ch. 16.12.

Unleavened bread. Paul readily joined with the Christians at Philippi in the Passover feast, under which name the Feast of Unleavened Bread was popularly included. The apostle clung tenaciously to the customs of his people when they did not directly conflict with his Christian belief. At all events it was more agreeable to celebrate the feast at Philippi than at Jerusalem.

7. *The first day of the week.* Which had now come to be kept as a holy day; the Lord's Day. See 1 Cor. 16.2. *We.* Luke, the writer of this narative, was taken on board at Philippi (ver. 6). *Break bread.* To celebrate the Lord's Supper.

10. *Paul went down.* By the staircase built, according to the custom of the East, around the outside of the house.

12 And they brought the lad alive, and were not a little comforted.

13 But we, going before to the ship, set sail for As'sos, there intending to take in Paul: for so had he appointed, intending himself to go ᶜby land. 14 And when he met us at As'sos, we took him in, and came to Mit-y-le'ne. 15 And sailing from thence, we came the following day over against Chi'os; and the next day we touched at Sa'mos; and ᵈthe day after we came to Mi-le'tus. 16 For Paul had determined to sail past Eph'e-sus, that he might not have to spend time in A'si-a; for he was hastening, if it were possible for him, to be at Je-ru'sa-lem the day of Pen'te-cost.

17 And from Mi-le'tus he sent to Eph'e-sus, and called to him the ᵉelders of the church. 18 And when they were come to him, he said unto them,

Ye yourselves know, from the first day that I set foot in A'si-a, after what manner I was with you all the time, 19 serving the Lord with all lowliness of mind, and with tears, and with trials which befell me by the plots of the Jews; 20 how I shrank not from declaring unto you anything that was profitable, and teaching you publicly, and from house to house, 21 testifying both to Jews and to Greeks repentance toward God, and faith toward our Lord Je'sus ᶠChrist. 22 And now, behold, I go bound in the spirit unto Je'ru-sa-lem, not knowing the things that shall befall me there: 23 save that the Holy Spirit testifieth unto me in every city, saying that bonds and afflictions abide me. 24 But I hold not my life of any account as dear unto myself, ᵍso that I may accomplish my course, and the ministry which I received from the Lord Je'sus, to testify the ʰgospel of the grace of God. 25 And now, behold, I know that

---

c Or, *on foot* *d* Many ancient authorities insert *having tarried at Trogyllium.* *e* Or, *presbyters* *f* Many ancient authorities omit *Christ.* *g* Or, *in comparison of accomplishing my course* *h* Or, *good tidings*

---

12. *Brought the lad alive.* It is a mistake to suppose that the words 'for his life is in him' (ver. 10) indicate that the youth was not killed by the fall. That is contradicted by the words of this verse.

13. *Assos.* A town on the coast of Mysia. A Roman road led to it from Troas.

14. *Mitylene.* The capital city of the island of Lesbos.

15. *Chios.* An island south of Lesbos and about five miles from the coast of Asia Minor. *Samos.* An island southwest of Chios, and a few miles off the coast of the mainland. *Miletus.* A seaport on the coast of Caria.

16. *To be at Jerusalem the day of the Pentecost.* To meet the Christian brethren, relate the story of his missionary labors and bring the contributions which had been entrusted to him by the members of the churches outside of Jerusalem. The Feast of Pentecost, or of the harvest, or weeks, was the second of the great annual feasts of the Jews. It was held on the fiftieth day after the beginning of harvest. The day was observed as a Sabbath.

17. *The elders.* See note on ch. 11.30. The difference between the elders of the Sanhedrin and those who were pastors of Christian congregations should be kept in mind. See notes on ch. 4.5.

25. *Shall see my face no more.* A presentiment that may not have proved true. Paul certainly afterwards visited both Miletus and

ye all, among whom I went about preaching the kingdom, shall see my face no more. 26 Wherefore I testify unto you this day, that I am pure from the blood of all men. 27 For I shrank not from declaring unto you the whole counsel of God. 28 Take heed unto yourselves, and to all the flock, in which the Holy Spirit hath made you *bishops, to feed the church of *the Lord which he *purchased with his own blood. 29 I know that after my departing grievous wolves shall enter in among you, not sparing the flock; 30 and from among your own selves shall men arise, speaking perverse things, to draw away the disciples after them. 31 Wherefore watch ye, remembering that by the space of three years I ceased not to admonish every one night and day with tears. 32 And now I commend you to *God, and to the word of his grace, which is able to build *you* up, and to give *you* the inheritance among all them that are sanctified. 33 I coveted no man's silver, or gold, or apparel. 34 Ye yourselves know that these

hands ministered unto my necessities, and to them that were with me. 35 In all things I gave you an example, that so laboring ye ought to help the weak, and to remember the words of the Lord Je'sus, that he himself said, It is more blessed to give than to receive.

36 And when he had thus spoken, he kneeled down and prayed with them all. 37 And they all wept sore, and fell on Paul's neck and kissed him, 38 sorrowing most of all for the word which he had spoken, that they should behold his face no more. And they brought him on his way unto the ship.

21 And when it came to pass that we were parted from them and had set sail, we came with a straight course unto Cos, and the next day unto Rhodes, and from thence unto Pat'a-ra: 2 and having found a ship crossing over unto Phœ-ni'-ci-a, we went aboard, and set sail. 3 And when we had come in sight of Cy'prus, leaving it on the left hand, we sailed unto Syr'i-a, and landed at Tyre; for there the

---

i Or, *overseers*   *k* Some ancient authorities, including the two oldest manuscripts,

read *God*. *l* Gr. *acquired*. *m* Some ancient authorities read *the Lord*.

Ephesus, whether the elders then saw him or not. See 2 Tim. 4.20; 1 Tim. 1.3; 3.14.

28. *Bishops*. Overseers or elders.
34. *These hands*, etc. Alluding to Paul's supporting himself by working at his trade of tent-maker.

CHAPTER 21

1. *Cos*. A small island near the coast of Asia Minor. *Rhodes*. A large island lying south of Caria. Its capital city was of the same name, and was celebrated for its great Temple of the Sun, and the Colossus, the famous statue at the

entrance to the harbor. The latter was one hundred and five feet high. and was a representation of the Sun-god. *Patara*. A city on the coast of Lycia.

3. *Cyprus*. See notes on ch. 4.32–37. *Tyre*. The greatest of maritime cities in ancient times. Its fleets of merchant ships once far exceeded those of any other nation. It was famed for its manufacture of purple dye and glass. Its sailors were capable and daring, and its trade was carried to and from all the countries of the civilized world. In Paul's time it had lost much of

ship was to unlade her burden. 4 And having found the disciples, we tarried there seven days: and these said to Paul through the Spirit, that he should not set foot in Je-ru'sa-lem. 5 And when it came to pass that we had accomplished the days, we departed and went on our journey; and they all, with wives and children, brought us on our way till we were out of the city: and kneeling down on the beach, we prayed, and bade each other farewell; 6 and we went on board the ship, but they returned home again.

7 And when we had finished the voyage from Tyre, we arrived at Ptol-e-ma'is; and we saluted the brethren, and abode with them one day. 8 And on the morrow we departed, and came unto Cæs-a-re'a: and entering into the house of Philip the evangelist, who was one of the seven, we abode with him. 9 Now this man had four virgin daughters, who prophesied. 10 And as we tarried there some days, there came down from Ju-dæ'a a certain prophet, named Ag'a-bus. 11 And coming to us, and taking Paul's girdle, he bound his own feet and hands, and said, Thus saith the Holy Spirit, So shall the Jews at Je-ru'sa-lem bind the man that owneth this girdle, and shall deliver him into the hands of the Gen'tiles. 12 And when we heard these things, both we and they of that place besought him not to go up to Je-ru'sa-lem. 13 Then Paul answered, What do ye, weeping and breaking my heart? for I am ready not to be bound only, but also to die at Je-ru'sa-lem for the name of the Lord Je'sus. 14 And when he would not be persuaded, we ceased, saying, The will of the Lord be done.

15 And after these days we ᵃtook up our baggage and went up to Je-ru'sa-lem. 16 And there went with us also *certain* of the disciples from Cæs-a-re'a, ᵇbringing *with them* one Mna'son of Cy'prus, an early disciple, with whom we should lodge.

17 And when we were come to Je-ru'sa-lem, the brethren received us gladly. 18 And the day following Paul went in with us unto James; and all the elders were present. 19 And when he had saluted them, he rehearsed one by one the things which God had wrought among the Gen'tiles through his ministry.

---

a Or, *made ready*　　　　*b* Or, *bringing* us to *one Mnason &c.*

its ancient glory, though it was still important.

5. *Accomplished the days.* The seven days of their stay at Tyre.

7. *Ptolemais.* Named after Ptolemy Philadelphus, king of Egypt. Its first name was Acco (Judges 1.31). It is now called Acre.

8. *Cæsarea.* See notes on ch. 8.40. *Philip the evangelist.* See ch. 6.5, 6 and notes thereon.

9. *Who prophesied.* That is, preached the gospel, as did their father. The word 'prophesy' has only comparatively recently been restricted in meaning to 'predict,' in the sense of foretelling the future.

10. *Agabus.* See ch. 11.28.

17. *Jerusalem.* In chs. 21.17—23.31 are narrated Paul's experience in Jerusalem after his return from his third missionary journey.

18. *James.* The half-brother of our Lord, and head of the church in Jerusalem.

340

20 And they, when they heard
it, glorified God; and they said
unto him, Thou seest, brother,
how many ^cthousands there are
among the Jews of them that
have believed; and they are all
zealous for the law: 21 and they
have been informed concerning
thee, that thou teachest all the
Jews who are among the Gen'tiles
to forsake Mo'ses, telling them
not to circumcise their children,
neither to walk after the customs.
22 What is it therefore? they will
certainly hear that thou art
come. 23 Do therefore this that
we say to thee: We have four
men that have a vow on them;
24 these take, and purify thyself
with them, and be at charges for
them, that they may shave their
heads: and all shall know that
there is no truth in the things
whereof they have been informed
concerning thee; but that thou
thyself also walkest orderly,
keeping the law. 25 But as
touching the Gen'tiles that have
believed, we ^dwrote, giving judgment that they should keep themselves from things sacrificed to
idols, and from blood, and from
what is strangled, and from fornication. 26 Then Paul ^etook
the men, and the next day purifying himself with them went
into the temple, declaring the
fulfilment of the days of purification, until the offering was
offered for every one of them.

27 And when the seven days
were almost completed, the Jews
from A'si-a, when they saw him
in the temple, stirred up all the
multitude and laid hands on him,
28 crying out, Men of Is'ra-el,
help: This is the man that teacheth all men everywhere against
the people, and the law, and this
place; and moreover he brought
Greeks also into the temple, and
hath defiled this holy place.
29 For they had before seen with
him in the city Troph'i-mus the
E-phe'sian, whom they supposed
that Paul had brought into the
temple. 30 And all the city was
moved, and the people ran together; and they laid hold on
Paul, and dragged him out of the
temple: and straightway the
doors were shut. 31 And as they
were seeking to kill him, tidings
came up to the ^fchief captain of
the ^gband, that all Je-ru'sa-lem
was in confusion. 32 And forth-
with he took soldiers and centurions, and ran down upon
them: and they, when they saw
the ^fchief captain and the soldiers, left off beating Paul. 33
Then the ^fchief captain came

c Gr. myriads. d Or. enjoined Many ancient authorities read sent. e Or, took the men

the next day, and purifying himself &c. f Or,
military tribune Gr. chiliarch. g Or, cohort

23. *Four men.* Nazirites. See
note on ch. 18.18.
26. *Paul took the men,* etc. He
did this in accordance with the rec-
ommendation of James and the
elders, in order to show that he was
a good Jew in keeping the law, and
to ward off controversial discord
over the question of his advising
his Gentile converts to ignore the
Jewish customs.

27. *The Jews from Asia.* That
is, those who had known or heard
of him during his missionary labors
in the province of Asia.
31. *The chief captain of the band.*
The commander of the Roman
garrison in the fortress of Antonia.
32. *Left off beating Paul.* A
beneficent interference that probably saved the apostle's life.

341

near, and laid hold on him, and commanded him to be bound with two chains; and inquired who he was, and what he had done.   34 And some shouted one thing, some another, among the crowd: and when he could not know the certainty for the uproar, he commanded him to be brought into the castle.   35 And when he came upon the stairs, so it was that he was borne of the soldiers for the violence of the crowd; 36 for the multitude of the people followed after, crying out, Away with him.

37 And as Paul was about to be brought into the castle, he saith unto the [h]chief captain, May I say something unto thee? And he said, Dost thou know Greek? 38 Art thou not then the E-gyp'-tian, who before these days stirred up to sedition and led out into the wilderness the four thousand men of the Assassins? 39 But Paul said, I am a Jew, of Tar'sus in Ci-li'ci-a, a citizen of no mean city: and I beseech thee, give me leave to speak unto the people.   40 And when he had given him leave, Paul, standing on the stairs, beckoned with the

hand unto the people; and when there was made a great silence, he spake unto them in the He-brew language, saying,

22 Brethren and fathers, hear ye the defence which I now make unto you.

2 And when they heard that he spake unto them in the He-brew language, they were the more quiet: and he saith,

3 I am a Jew, born in Tar'sus of Ci-li'ci-a, but brought up in this city, at the feet of Ga-ma'li-el, instructed according to the strict manner of the law of our fathers, being zealous for God, even as ye all are this day: 4 and I persecuted this Way unto the death, binding and delivering into prisons both men and wom-en.   5 As also the high priest doth bear me witness, and all the estate of the elders: from whom also I received letters unto the brethren, and journeyed to Da-mas'cus to bring them also that were there unto Je-ru'sa-lem in bonds to be punished.   6 And it came to pass, that, as I made my journey, and drew nigh unto Da-mas'cus, about noon, suddenly there shone from heaven a great

---

h Or. *military tribune* Gr. *chiliarch*

38. *The Egyptian.* One of the imposters and rebels of that time. *The Assassins.* Or the Sicarii. Men armed with daggers, who mixed with crowds, wounded some by stabbing them, and then pretended to join in the hunt for the guilty ones.   In this way they often evaded arrest.

39. *Tarsus.* See notes on ch. 7.58.

40. *The Hebrew language.* That is, Aramaic, the vernacular, which was a dialect of Hebrew.

CHAPTER 22

3. *Brought up in this city.* He was

sent to Jerusalem to be educated. *At the feet of Gamaliel.* See note on ch. 5.34.

4. *This Way.* The Christian re-ligion.

5. *The high priest doth bear me witness,* etc. Paul here declares in effect that he can prove the truth of his statement, that he persecuted Christians, by the testimony of the high priest and the records of the Sanhedrin.   He could not have gone on his persecuting way with-out express authority.

6. *A great light round about me.* See notes on ch. 9.3.

342

light round about me. 7 And I
fell unto the ground, and heard a
voice saying unto me, **Saul, Saul,
why persecutest thou me?** 8
And I answered, Who art thou,
Lord? And he said unto me, **I am
Je′sus of Naz′a-reth, whom thou
persecutest.** 9 And they that
were with me beheld indeed the
light, but they heard not the
voice of him that spake to me.
10 And I said, What shall I do,
Lord? And the Lord said unto
me, **Arise, and go into Da-mas′-
cus; and there it shall be told
thee of all things which are appointed for thee to do.** 11 And
when I could not see for the
glory of that light, being led by
the hand of them that were with
me I came into Da-mas′cus. 12
And one An-a-ni′as, a devout
man according to the law, well
reported of by all the Jews that
dwelt there, 13 came unto me,
and standing by me said unto
me, Brother Saul, receive thy
sight. And in that very hour I
*a*looked up on him. 14 And he
said, The God of our fathers
hath appointed thee to know his
will, and to see the Righteous
One, and to hear a voice from his
mouth. 15 For thou shalt be a
witness for him unto all men of
what thou hast seen and heard.
16 And now why tarriest thou?
arise, and be baptized, and wash
away thy sins, calling on his
name. 17 And it came to pass,

that, when I had returned to Je-
ru′sa-lem, and while I prayed in
the temple, I fell into a trance,
18 and saw him saying unto me,
**Make haste, and get thee quick-
ly out of Je-ru′sa-lem; because
they will not receive of thee testimony concerning me.** 19 And
I said, Lord, they themselves
know that I imprisoned and beat
in every synagogue them that
believed on thee: 20 and when
the blood of Ste′phen thy witness was shed, I also was standing by, and consenting, and keeping the garments of them that
slew him. 21 And he said unto
me, **Depart: for I will send thee
forth far hence unto the Gen′-
tiles.**

22 And they gave him audience unto this word; and they
lifted up their voice, and said,
Away with such a fellow from
the earth: for it is not fit that he
should live. 23 And as they
cried out, and threw off their
garments, and cast dust into the
air, 24 the *b*chief captain commanded him to be brought into
the castle, bidding that he should
be examined by scourging, that
he might know for what cause
they so shouted against him.
25 And when they had tied him
up *c*with the thongs, Paul said
unto the centurion that stood by,
Is it lawful for you to scourge a
man that is a Roman, and uncondemned? 26 And when the cen-

---

a Or, *received my sight* and looked upon
him.

11. *When I could not see,* etc. See
notes on ch. 9.8, 9.
22. *Unto this word.* That is, up
to the point at which he mentioned
that he was to be sent far hence
unto the Gentiles.

b Or, *military tribune* Gr. *chiliarch*
c Or, *for*

24. *Examined by scourging.* Subjected to torture until he confessed.
The chief captain resorted to this
legal device in default of knowing
what else to do.

turion heard it, he went to the ^dchief captain and told him, saying, What art thou about to do? for this man is a Roman. 27 And the ^dchief captain came and said unto him, Tell me, art thou a Roman? And he said, Yea. 28 And the ^dchief captain answered, With a great sum obtained I this citizenship. And Paul said, But I am a Roman born. 29 They then that were about to examine him straightway departed from him: and the ^dchief captain also was afraid when he knew that he was a Roman, and because he had bound him.

30 But on the morrow, desiring to know the certainty wherefore he was accused of the Jews, he loosed him, and commanded the chief priests and all the council to come together, and brought Paul down and set him before them.

23 And Paul, looking stedfastly on the council, said, Brethren, I have lived before God in all good conscience until this day. 2 And the high priest An-a-ni'as commanded them that stood by him to smite him on the mouth. 3 Then said Paul unto him, God shall smite thee, thou whited wall: and sittest thou to judge me according to the law, and commandest me to be smitten contrary to the law? 4 And they that stood by said, Revilest thou God's high priest? 5 And Paul said, I knew not, brethren, that he was high priest: for it is written, ^aThou shalt not speak evil of a ruler of thy people. 6 But when Paul perceived that the one part were Sad'ducees and the other Phar'i-sees, he cried out in the council, Brethren, I am a Phar'i-see, a son of Phar-i-sees: touching the hope and resurrection of the dead I am

---

d Or. military tribune Gr. chiliarch

a Ex. xxii. 28.

28. *I am a Roman born.* Paul's family at Tarsus possessed Roman citizenship at the time of his birth. See note ch. 16.37.

CHAPTER 23

1. *And Paul, looking stedfastly on the council,* etc. Twenty years before he was the fanatical servant of the Sanhedrin members; now he was their chastened, enlightened, irresistible accuser, who had left their tribal narrowness far behind, and who saw their weakness and impending fate. So far as known the Sanhedrin had not changed, except for the protest of Gamaliel (ch. 5.34 and note thereon), from the spirit which condemned Jesus to death. If it had, the bigoted high priest Ananias would not have dared to command that Paul should be smitten on the mouth (ver. 2). Ananias was high priest during 47–59 A.D.

3. *Thou whited wall.* Thou hypocrite. *Contrary to the law.* Because Paul had not yet been allowed to speak in his own behalf. See Jn. 7.51.

6. *When Paul perceived that the one part were Sadducees,* etc. This perception, and the use Paul made of it, cut the ground from under any further humiliation of him before the Sanhedrin. To set the Pharisees and Sadducees at each others' throats, so to speak, was masterly tactics, and it was quite natural that the master tactician should escape in the resulting confusion and excitement. Paul well knew that to proclaim himself a Pharisee, at the same time announcing himself as on the defensive in behalf of the doctrine of the resurrection, would split the Sanhedrin into two warring factions, one of whom would side with him.

344

called in question. 7 And when he had so said, there arose a dissension between the Phar'i-sees and Sad'du-cees; and the assembly was divided. 8 For the Sad'du-cees say that there is no resurrection, neither angel, nor spirit; but the Phar'i-sees confess both. 9 And there arose a great clamor: and some of the scribes of the Phar'i-sees' part stood up, and strove, saying, We find no evil in this man: and what if a spirit hath spoken to him, or an angel? 10 And when there arose a great dissension, the *b*chief captain, fearing lest Paul should be torn in pieces by them, commanded the soldiers to go down and take him by force from among them, and bring him into the castle.

11 And the night following the Lord stood by him, and said, **Be of good cheer: for as thou hast testified concerning me at Je-ru'sa-lem, so must thou bear witness also at Rome.**

12 And when it was day, the Jews banded together, and bound themselves under a curse, saying that they would neither eat nor drink till they had killed Paul. 13 And they were more than forty that made this conspiracy. 14 And they came to the chief priests and the elders, and said, We have bound ourselves under a great curse, to taste nothing until we have killed Paul. 15 Now therefore do ye with the council signify to the *b*chief captain that he bring him down unto you, as though ye would judge of his case more exactly: and we, before he comes near, are ready to slay him. 16 But Paul's sister's son heard of their lying in wait, *c*and he came and entered into the castle and told Paul. 17 And Paul called unto him one of the centurions, and said, Bring this young man unto the *b*chief captain; for he hath something to tell him. 18 So he took him, and brought him to the*b*chief captain, and saith, Paul the prisoner called me unto him, and asked me to bring this young man unto thee, who hath something to say to thee. 19 And the *b*chief captain took him by the hand, and going aside asked him privately, What is it that thou hast to tell

---

b Or, *military tribune*. Gr. *chiliarch.*   *c* Or, *having come in* upon them, *and he entered &c.*

11. *So must thou bear witness also at Rome.* A testimony at the centre of the civilized world, and which would prove to be the crown of his life work, completing his mission as the great apostle to the Gentiles. Rome, as the capital of the Gentile world, must have been often in Paul's thought. It was the logical place for his martyrdom. It was his natural bent to seek the chief place of crucial test in obedience to the risen Christ who appeared to him on the Damascus road. He was as daringly defiant in service and suffering for the liberating truth revealed, as he had first been in behalf of the narrow, partial truth inherited.

13. *More than forty.* It was probably thought that the conspiring murderers, in the event of success, were numerous and influential enough to prevent punishment. At least it was hoped that the Roman governor would not go to great lengths to avenge the slaying of a troublesome Jew like Paul. The conspirators probably did not know that the apostle's Roman citizenship would have brought vengeance upon them for its violation.

me? 20 And he said, The Jews have agreed to ask thee to bring down Paul to-morrow unto the council, as though thou wouldest inquire somewhat more exactly concerning him. 21 Do not thou therefore yield unto them: for there lie in wait for him of them more than forty men, who have bound themselves under a curse, neither to eat nor to drink till they have slain him: and now are they ready, looking for the promise from thee. 22 So the *d*chief captain let the young man go, charging him, Tell no man that thou hast signified these things to me. 23 And he called unto him two of the centurions, and said, Make ready two hundred soldiers to go as far as Cæs-a-re'a,

and horsemen threescore and ten, and spearmen two hundred, at the third hour of the night: 24 and *he bade them* provide beasts, that they might set Paul thereon, and bring him safe unto Felix the governor. 25 And he wrote a letter after this form: 26 Clau'di-us Lys'i-as unto the most excellent governor Felix, greeting. 27 This man was seized by the Jews, and was about to be slain of them, when I came upon them with the soldiers and rescued him, having learned that he was a Roman. 28 And desiring to kncw the cause wherefore they accused him, *e*I brought him down unto their council: 29 whom I found to be accused about questions of their law, but

d Or, *military tribune* Gr. *chiliarch.*

e Some ancient authorities omit *I brought him down unto their council.*

---

23. *Make ready two hundred soldiers*, etc. The whole course of this commander of the Antonia garrison is an impressive proof of the impartial majesty of the Roman sway and its beneficent effect upon the progress of early Christianity. It was at this time the austere protector, just, though despising, of the struggling Christians against Jewish enemies who would gladly have exterminated them. The chief captain saved Paul when the savage mob of Jews at Jerusalem dragged him out of the Temple and first sought to kill him (ch. 21.30). He saved him again when the vindictive persecutors tried to lay violent hands on Paul while he was being taken up the stairs of the castle (ch. 21.35). For the third time he interfered in the apostle's behalf at the enforced conclusion of his speech on the stairs (ch. 22. 24). For the fourth time he saved his captive when the latter finished his defence before the Sanhedrin (ch. 23.10). Then, after the forty and more plotters had done their best, the chief captain for the fifth time rescued his prisoner by pro-

viding a military escort (ch. 23.23). The subsequent persecution of Christians by degenerate, cruel or ignorant emperors might dim the glory of heathen Rome in having been in earlier times the just though grim guardian of Christian truth. *Third hour of the night.* Nine o'clock.

24. *Felix the governor.* Procurator of Judæa (A.D. 52–58). He took the severest measures against the Zealots or Cananæans, a violently nationalistic and revolutionary party. This severity gave rise to an organization of assassins called the Sicarii. See note on ch. 21.38. Felix proved to be an inefficient and cruel ruler and left Judæa more disturbed than he found it.

26–30. *Unto the most excellent governor Felix.* The letter of Lysias the chief captain is more plausible than accurate. Although he protected Paul at Jerusalem, he failed to give a true account of what had taken place. The explanation is to be found in the wholesome fear lest he, an official subordinate, should be found inflicting a degrading punishment upon a Roman citizen.

to have nothing laid to his charge worthy of death or of bonds. 30 And when it was shown to me that there would be a plot *against the man, I sent him to thee forthwith, charging his accusers also to speak against him before thee.*

31 So the soldiers, as it was commanded them, took Paul and brought him by night to An-tip'a-tris. 32 But on the morrow they left the horsemen to go with him, and returned to the castle: 33 and they, when they came to Cæs'a-re'a and delivered the letter to the governor, presented Paul also before him. 34 And when he had read it, he asked of what province he was; and when he understood that he was of Ci-li'ci-a, 35 I will hear thee fully, said he, when thine accusers also are come: and he commanded him to be kept in Her'od's *palace.

24 And after five days the high priest An-a-ni'as came down with certain elders, and with an orator, one Ter-tul'lus; and they informed the governor against Paul. 2 And when he was called, Ter-tul'lus began to accuse him, saying,

Seeing that by thee we enjoy much peace, and that by thy providence evils are corrected for this nation, 3 we accept it in all ways and in all places, most excellent Felix, with all thankfulness. 4 But, that I be not further tedious unto thee, I entreat thee to hear us of thy clemency a few words. 5 For we have found this man a pestilent fellow, and a mover of insurrections among all the Jews throughout *the world, and a ringleader of the sect of the Naz-a-renes': 6 who moreover assayed to profane the temple: on whom also we laid hold:* 8 from whom thou wilt be able, by examining him thyself, to take knowledge of all these things whereof we accuse him. 9 And the Jews also joined in the charge, affirming that these things were so.

---

f Many ancient authorities read *against the man on their part, I sent him to thee, charging &c.* *g* Many ancient authorities add *Farewell.* *h* Gr. *Prœtorium.* *a* Gr. *the inhabited earth.* *b* Some ancient author-

ities insert *and we would have judged him according to our law. 7 But the chief captain Lysias came, and with great violence took him away out of our hands, 8 commanding his accusers to come before thee.*

Lysias is careful not to mention that he was about to scourge Paul before he knew that he was a Roman, and he is equally careful to say that he rescued him, 'having learned that he was a Roman.'

31. *Antipatris.* A city on the main road leading from Cæsarea. It was twenty-six miles from the latter city and forty-two miles from Jerusalem. Herod the Great rebuilt it and named it after his father Antipater.

CHAPTER 24

1. *Tertullus.* The advocate hired by the accusing Jews to represent them before Felix.

2. *By thee we enjoy much peace.* A compliment to Felix for his repression of the Zealots and the revolt headed by the Egyptian false prophet (ch. 21.38).

5. *A mover of insurrections.* This charge, though false, would most readily be heard by the governor. It concerned the security and majesty of Roman rule. *A ringleader of the sect of the Nazarenes.* The most contemptuous words that could be found to express an opinion of Paul and his belief. Everything from Nazareth was despised. By Nazarenes in this verse is meant followers of the man of Nazareth, or Christians.

10 And when the governor had beckoned unto him to speak, Paul answered,

Forasmuch as I know that thou hast been of many years a judge unto this nation, I cheerfully make my defence: 11 seeing that thou canst take knowledge that it is not more than twelve days since I went up to worship at Je-ru′sa-lem: 12 and neither in the temple did they find me disputing with any man or stirring up a crowd, nor in the synagogues, nor in the city. 13 Neither can they prove to thee the things whereof they now accuse me. 14 But this I confess unto thee, that after the Way which they call a sect, so serve I the God of our fathers, believing all things which are according to the law, and which are written in the prophets; 15 having hope toward God, which these also themselves clook for, that there shall be a resurrection both of the just and unjust. 16 dHerein I also exercise myself to have a conscience void of offence toward God and men always. 17 Now after some years I came to bring alms to my nation, and offerings: 18eamidst which they found me purified in the temple, with no crowd, nor yet with tumult: but *there were* certain Jews from A′si-a—19 who ought to have been here before thee, and to make accusation, if they had aught against me. 20 Or else let these men themselves say what wrong-doing they found when I stood before the council, 21 except it be for this one voice, that I cried standing among them, Touching the resurrection of the dead I am called in question before you this day.

22 But Felix, having more exact knowledge concerning the Way, deferred them, saying, When Lys′i-as the fchief captain

---

c Or, *accept*   d Or, *On this account*
e Or, *in* presenting *which*

f Or, *military tribune* Gr. *chiliarch.*

10–21. *I cheerfully make my defence.* Paul's answer to the charges made against him denied that he had made any disturbance. Ignoring the accusation of being a ring-leader of the sect of Nazarenes, he acknowledged that he served 'the God of our fathers' after the way of that sect, that is, according to their principles; but that he did not thereby depart from his ancestral faith. He still believed in the law and the prophets and hoped for a resurrection. Finally he denied that he had desecrated the Temple (ver. 18).

22. *More exact knowledge concerning the Way.* Felix had more than one reason for stopping the proceedings until the arrival of Lysias, the chief captain. He knew that Paul was a Roman citizen and, mindful of that status, he saw that no charge against him, of whatever kind, could be a safe basis of conviction unless supported by strong evidence. Again, he probably knew something of the Way, or Christianity, as a religious movement that might be made use of by revolutionaries. Moreover the chief captain had been silent in his letter as to the 'questions of their law' concerning which Paul had been accused by the Jews. Felix probably recognized that the prosecutors were most actively hostile to Paul on account of his religious opinions. As a Roman governor, and apart from any political consideration, he could have little sympathy with the Jews in the attempted vindication of their religion. But he had a Jewish wife, Drusilla, a daughter of Herod Agrippa I., and she may have given him an account of the new sect which made him interested to hear Paul's exposition of its principles.

shall come down, I will determine your matter. 23 And he gave order to the centurion that he should be kept in charge, and should have indulgence; and not to forbid any of his friends to minister unto him.

24 But after certain days, Felix came with Dru-sil'la, *his wife, who was a Jewess, and sent for Paul, and heard him concerning the faith in Christ Je'sus. 25 And as he reasoned of righteousness, and self-control, and the judgment to come, Felix was terrified, and answered, Go thy way for this time; and when I have a convenient season, I will call thee unto me. 26 He hoped withal that money would be given him of Paul: wherefore also he sent for him the oftener, and communed with him. 27 But when two years were fulfilled, Felix was succeeded by Por'cius Fes'tus; and desiring to

gain favor with the Jews, Felix left Paul in bonds.

25 Fes'tus therefore, *having come into the province, after three days went up to Je-ru'sa-lem from Cæs-a-re'a. 2 And the chief priests and the principal men of the Jews informed him against Paul; and they besought him, 3 asking a favor against him, that he would send for him to Je-ru'sa-lem; laying a plot to kill him on the way. 4 Howbeit Fes'tus answered, that Paul was kept in charge at Cæs-a-re'a, and that he himself was about to depart *thither* shortly. 5 Let them therefore, saith he, that are of power among you go down with me, and if there is anything amiss in the man, let them accuse him.

6 And when he had tarried among them not more than eight or ten days, he went down unto Cæs-a-re'a; and on the morrow

25. *Felix was terrified.* He may have expected to hear Paul describe Christianity in general terms, or at least talk entertainingly about the resurrection and the judgment. He heard instead an uncompromising statement of faith in Christ in its relation to the individual life, a statement which searched out and laid bare his own sins in all their hideousness. The 'righteousness, and self-control, and the judgment to come' of which Paul reasoned were ominous contrasts to his own life. He feared for the future.

26. *That money would be given him of Paul.* Felix was accustomed to bribery. The most reasonable explanation of his hope of receiving money from Paul was that the latter was known to have brought a fund of contributions for the church at Jerusalem. Felix doubtless thought that there was more to be had from the source of that fund.

27. *Porcius Festus.* Appointed procurator of Judæa by Nero in A.D. 60. He was a man of good character and tried to rule wisely. *Left Paul bound.* Nothing definite and certain is known as to how Paul employed his time during his two years of imprisonment in Cæsarea. The epistles thought by some to have been written there were likely composed in Rome.

CHAPTER 25

5. *Let them accuse him.* They must accuse him at Cæsarea not at Jerusalem. It was another memorable instance of the beneficent intervention of Roman authority at a crisis in the history of Christianity. The official dignity of Festus which was not to be too soon and too eagerly approached by troublesome Jews, foiled their plot and prevented the murder of Paul.

349

he sat on the judgment-seat, and commanded Paul to be brought. 7 And when he was come, the Jews that had come down from Je-ru'sa-lem stood round about him, bringing against him many and grievous charges which they could not prove; 8 while Paul said in his defence, Neither against the law of the Jews, nor against the temple, nor against Cæ'sar, have I sinned at all. 9 But Fes'tus, desiring to gain favor with the Jews, answered Paul and said, Wilt thou go up to Je-ru'sa-lem, and there be judged of these things before me? 10 But Paul

said, I am standing before Cæ'-sar's judgment-seat, where I ought to be judged: to the Jews have I done no wrong, as thou also very well knowest. 11 If then I am a wrong-doer, and have committed anything worthy of death, I refuse not to die; but if none of those things is *true* whereof these accuse me, no man can *b*give me up unto them. I appeal unto Cæ'sar. 12 Then Fes'tus, when he had conferred with the council, answered, Thou hast appealed unto Cæ'sar: unto Cæ'sar shalt thou go.

13 Now when certain days

b Gr. *grant me by favor.*

9. *Desiring to gain favor with the Jews*, etc. Festus was prudent in not ignoring entirely the persistent attempts of the Jewish leaders to gain possession of Paul. The Sanhedrin was a power to be reckoned with, the interpreter of Jewish law and custom, and if its members knew that Festus was befriending Paul unduly, they could bring charges of maladministration against him after his term of office had expired. The delinquent governor of a province always had before him the fear of justice in Rome at the hand of his emperor. *Wilt thou go up to Jerusalem*, etc. It was clear that Festus saw no proof that the apostle had committed a political offence. There remained only the charges of violating Jewish law and profaning the Temple. Would Paul go up to Jerusalem and face the Sanhedrin if he, Festus, went with him to see that justice was done? The question was plausible and correct; but Festus had only a surface acquaintance with the motives and purposes of the accusers.

10, 11. *I am standing before Cæsar's judgment-seat, where I ought to be judged.* An affirmation which disposed of official doubt and Jewish clamor in one breath. Wherever there was a Roman hall of justice, whether in the imperial city or at the remotest frontier, there was

Cæsar's judgment-seat. A Roman citizen taken from Jerusalem to Cæsarea, as Paul was taken, had a right to be judged at Cæsarea unless he chose to be sent to Rome on appeal to the emperor. At this crucial moment a false step might have changed the whole subsequent course of Christianity. But Paul knew his rights and how to maintain them. He saw that condemnation and death were prepared for him by the Sanhedrin. 'The chief priests and principal men of the Jews' who belonged to it perfectly understood that one formidable life still threatened their supremacy. They supposed that it had been safeguarded by the crucifixion. They saw with profound alarm that Paul kept alive the belief in Jesus as the Messiah, and this was the reason for their hatred. The apostle's safety was in his Roman citizenship with its right of appeal. This right he instantly asserted, thereby saving the remainder of his life for Christian service. His grand character and subtle intellect were more than equal to the crisis. He saw its pitfalls at a glance. Saint, scholar, missionary, logician, statesman, man of the world—he was all these in resourcefulness of spirit, whether he fought enemies or persuaded judges and kings.

13. *Agrippa the king.* Herod

were passed, A-grip'pa the king and Ber-ni'ce arrived at Cæs-a-re'a, *and saluted Fes'tus. 14 And as they tarried there many days, Fes'tus laid Paul's case before the king, saying, There is a certain man left a prisoner by Felix; 15 about whom, when I was at Je-ru'sa-lem, the chief priests and the elders of the Jews informed *me*, asking for sentence against him. 16 To whom I answered, that it is not the custom of the Romans to *d*give up any man, before that the accused have the accusers face to face, and have had opportunity to make his defence concerning the matter laid against him. 17 When therefore they were come together here, I made no delay, but on the next day sat on the judgment-seat, and commanded the man to be brought. 18 Concerning whom, when the accusers stood up, they brought no charge of such evil things as I supposed; 19 but had certain questions against him of their own *e*religion, and of one Je'sus, who was dead, whom Paul affirmed to be alive. 20 And I, being perplexed how to inquire concerning these things, asked whether he would go to Je-ru'sa-lem and there be judged of these matters. 21 But when Paul had appealed to be kept for the decision of *f*the emperor, I commanded him to be kept till I should send him to Cæ'sar. 22 And

A-grip'pa *said* unto Fes'tus, I also *g*could wish to hear the man myself. To-morrow, saith he, thou shalt hear him.

23 So on the morrow, when A-grip'pa was come, and Ber-ni'ce, with great pomp, and they were entered into the place of hearing with the *h*chief captains and the principal men of the city, at the command of Fes-tus Paul was brought in. 24 And Fes'tus saith, King A-grip'pa, and all men who are here present with us, ye behold this man, about whom all the multitude of the Jews made suit to me, both at Je-ru'sa-lem and here, crying that he ought not to live any longer. 25 But I found that he had committed nothing worthy of death: and as he himself appealed to *f*the emperor I determined to send him. 26 Of whom I have no certain thing to write unto my lord. Wherefore I have brought him forth before you, and specially before thee, king A-grip'pa, that, after examination had, I may have somewhat to write. 27 For it seemeth to me unreasonable, in sending a prisoner, not withal to signify the charges against him.

26 And A-grip'pa said unto Paul, Thou art permitted to speak for thyself. Then Paul stretched forth his hand, and made his defence:

2 I think myself happy, king A-grip'pa, that I am to make

---

c Or, *having saluted*   *d* Gr. *grant me by favor.*   *e* Or, *superstition*   *f* Gr. *the* Augustus.   *g* Or, *was wishing*   *h* Or, *military tribunes* Gr. *chiliarchs.*

Agrippa II., son of Herod Agrippa I., and great grandson of Herod the Great. *Bernice.* Sister of King Herod Agrippa II.

CHAPTER 26

2. *I think myself happy,* etc. Because Paul knew that Agrippa, who

my defence before thee this day touching all the things whereof I am accused by the Jews: 3 [a]especially because thou art expert in all customs and questions which are among the Jews: wherefore I beseech thee to hear me patiently. 4 My manner of life then from my youth up, which was from the beginning among mine own nation and at Je-ru'sa-lem, know all the Jews; 5 having knowledge of me from the first, if they be willing to testify, that after the straitest sect of our religion I lived a Phar'i-see. 6 And now I stand *here* to be judged for the hope of the prom-

ise made of God unto our fathers; 7 unto which *promise* our twelve tribes, earnestly serving *God* night and day, hope to attain. And concerning this hope I am accused by the Jews, O king! 8 Why is it judged incredible with you, if God doth raise the dead? 9 I verily thought with myself that I ought to do many things contrary to the name of Je'sus of Naz'a-reth. 10 And this I also did in Je-ru'sa-lem: and I both shut up many of the saints in prisons, having received authority from the chief priests, and when they were put to death I gave my vote against them. 11 And

---

a Or, *because thou art especially expert*

---

was popular with the Jews and familiar with their social customs and habits of thought, would understand, as no Roman could, arguments designed to justify the apostle before an audience largely composed of Jews and their sympathizers. Agrippa, though careful to make himself outwardly acceptable to the Jews, had no real sympathy with their religion; he was an admirer and patron of Greek culture. Nevertheless his worldly indifference and mental detachment were valuable to Paul, whose defence was replete with reasons historically and philosophically interesting to the king. The apostle's argument, which occupies the entire chapter, was chiefly a recital of his experience, and the belief which it compelled. The coming of Jesus as the Messiah, and the religious community based on faith in him, were nothing less than the fulfillment of what had been predicted in the Scriptures: they were completed Judaism. All that Paul preached was contained in Moses and the prophets. How could he be condemned by Jews?

5. *I lived a Pharisee.* See note on ch. 23.6; also notes on Mt. 3.7.

6. *The promise made of God to our fathers.* That they would be

blessed in Abraham's seed, the Messiah. See Gen. 22.18.

7. *Our twelve tribes.* A patriotic Jew always loved to speak of his race as it was in the days of its greatest power. He would instinctively refuse to think less of it because it had been divided into the two kingdoms of Israel and Judah, or because of the captivity in Babylon. To an Israelite of the Dispersion, who lived outside of Palestine, Jerusalem was always the Holy City. At home or abroad, no Jew could be free from his consciousness of an elect and divinely designated membership in the chosen people.

8. *Why is it judged incredible,* etc. The question was suggested by 'this hope' in the preceding verse. The hope could only be realized by the advent of a spiritual Messiah whom God would raise from the dead in order that he might be the spiritual Saviour of his people.

9. *Contrary to the name,* etc. Contrary to the teaching and divine authority of Jesus of Nazareth.

10. *I gave my vote against them.* He consented, that is, gave his vote for the stoning of Stephen, the first Christian martyr (ch. 8.1); but according to this verse he had also helped to put others to death for their faith in Jesus.

11. *Foreign cities.* Cities outside

punishing them oftentimes in all the synagogues, I strove to make them blaspheme; and being exceedingly mad against them, I persecuted them even unto foreign cities. 12 *b*Whereupon as I journeyed to Da-mas'cus with the authority and commission of the chief priests, 13 at midday, O king, I saw on the way a light from heaven, above the brightness of the sun, shining round about me and them that journeyed with me. 14 And when we were all fallen to the earth, I heard a voice saying unto me in the Hebrew language, Saul, Saul, why persecutest thou me? it is hard for thee to kick against *c*the goad. 15 And I said, Who art thou, Lord? And the Lord said, I am Je'sus whom thou persecutest. 16 But arise, and stand upon thy feet: for to this end have I appeared unto thee, to appoint thee a minister and a witness both of the things *d*wherein thou hast seen me, and of the things wherein I will appear unto thee; 17 delivering thee from the people, and from the Gen'tiles, unto whom I send

thee, 18 to open their eyes, *e*that they may turn from darkness to light and from the power of Satan unto God, that they may receive remission of sins and an inheritance among them that are sanctified by faith in me. 19 Wherefore, O king A-grip'pa, I was not disobedient unto the heavenly vision: 20 but declared both to them of Da-mas'cus first, and at Je-ru'sa-lem, and throughout all the country of Ju-dæ'a, and also to the Gen'tiles, that they should repent and turn to God, doing works worthy of *f*repentance. 21 For this cause the Jews seized me in the temple, and assayed to kill me. 22 Having therefore obtained the help that is from God, I stand unto this day testifying both to small and great, saying nothing but what the prophets and Mo'ses did say should come; 23 *g*how that the Christ *h*must suffer, *and g*how that he first by the resurrection of the dead should proclaim light both to the people and to the Gen'tiles.

24 And as he thus made his defence, Fes'tus saith with a loud

---

b Or, *On which errand*   *c* Gr. *goads.* *d* Many ancient authorities read *which thou hast seen.*   *e* Or, *to turn them*   *f* Or, *their repentance* *g* Or, *if* Or, *whether* *h* Or, *is subject to suffering*

of Palestine. Damascus was only one of the places he had visited in his persecuting zeal. Paul evidently intended the listening Jews to know that, during the time of his hatred of Jesus, he was a sincere and relentless enemy of the sect to which he now belonged. If honest then, could they refuse to believe at least that he was honest in his reasons for the great change that had since been wrought in him?

12–18. *As I journeyed to Damascus,* etc. See notes on ch. 9.2–4, 15, 18, 20, 22. *Goad.* A stick used for driving beasts, and pointed with metal.

23. *How that the Christ must suffer.* See Isa. 53; Lk. 24.26, 46. The belief that the Christ or Messiah must suffer was not held by all the Jews. Many thought that suffering and humiliation were incompatible with the glory and power of the Messiahship. See Jn. 12.34. *That he first by the resurrection,* etc. That is, the Messiah's manifested power over death would first reveal the light of his everlasting truth to his own people, the Jews, and to the rest of the world.

24. *Thy much learning is turning thee mad.* The 'learning' was

voice, Paul, thou art mad; thy much learning ⁱis turning thee mad. 25 But Paul saith, I am not mad, most excellent Fes′tus; but speak forth words of truth and soberness. 26 For the king knoweth of these things, unto whom also I speak freely: for I am persuaded that none of these things is hidden from him; for this hath not been done in a corner. 27 King A-grip′pa, believest thou the prophets? I know that thou believest. 28 And A-grip′pa *said* unto Paul, ᵏWith but little persuasion thou wouldest fain make me a Chris′tian. 29 And Paul *said,* I would to God, that ˡwhether with little or with much, not thou only, buₜ

also all that hear me this day, might become such as I am, except these bonds.

30 And the king rose up, and the governor, and Ber-ni′ce, and they that sat with them: 31 And when they had withdrawn, they spake one to another, saying, This man doeth nothing worthy of death or of bonds. 32 And A-grip′pa said unto Fes′tus, This man might have been set at liberty, if he had not appealed unto Cæ′sar.

27 And when it was determined that we should sail for It′a-ly, they delivered Paul and certain other prisoners to a centurion named Ju′li-us, of the Au-gus′tan ᵃband. 2 And em-

---

ⁱ Gr. *turneth thee to madness.*   ᵏ Or, *In a little* time *thou &c.*   ˡ Or, *both in little* *and in great,* i.e., in all respects   ᵃ Or, *cohort*

Paul's familiarity with and powerful reasoning from the Scriptures of the Old Testament. It was not remarkable that an affirmation that Jesus—crucified within the recollection of some then present—was alive and that he was the Messiah of the Jews, should seem to Festus like the raving of a person of unsound mind. Still more so would seem Paul's serious statements about the resurrection. These were the very height of presumption to the governor, trained as he was in the hard, prudential maxims of Roman official life, of which religion was only a department, and not the most important one. Roman literature contained little that was memorable about life and death, and it is not certain that Festus knew that little. How strange to him must have seemed Paul's inspired certainty of the stupendous fact about which Roman philosophers reasoned in the dark!

26. *For the king knoweth of these,* etc. On the judgment-ʲseat with Festus was the king to whom the apostle turned for confirmation of the reasonableness of his words. It was a compliment which Agrippa

did not decline, though guarding against a hurtful interpretation of it.

28. *With but little persuasion,* etc. Agrippa's reply was half truth, half embarrassment. Paul's argument was strong; but strong also was the king's desire to remain popular with the Jews. It would probably have cost him his crown if he had declared himself a believer in Jesus and the resurrection.

31. *Doeth nothing worthy of death or of bonds.* Agrippa saw that Paul had done nothing contrary to Jewish law and that his argument was permissible because drawn from the Scriptures. The Jews were able controversialists, as their opposing rabinnical schools testify. Paul had done no act which either Festus or Agrippa could pronounce a legal offence.

CHAPTER 27

1. *They.* The soldiers, by order of the governor. *Centurion.* See note on Mt. 8.5. *The Augustan band.* One of the five cohorts of imperial troops stationed at Cæsarea. A cohort contained six hundred men.

2. *Adramyttium.* A seaport of

barking in a ship of Ad-ra-myt'ti-um, which was about to sail unto the places on the coast of A'si-a, we put to sea, Ar-is-tar'chus, a Mac-e-do'ni-an of Thes-sa-lo-ni'-ca, being with us. 3 And the next day we touched at Si'don: and Ju'li-us treated Paul kindly, and gave him leave to go unto his friends and [b]refresh himself. 4 And putting to sea from thence, we sailed under the lee of Cy'prus, because the winds were contrary. 5 And when we had sailed across the sea which is off Ci-li'ci-a and Pam-phyl'i-a, we came to My'ra, *a city* of Ly'ci-a. 6 And there the centurion found a ship of Al-ex-an'dri-a sailing for It'a-ly; and he put us therein. 7 And when we had sailed slowly many days, and were come with difficulty over against Cni'dus, the wind not [c]further suffering us, we sailed under the lee of Crete, over against Sal-mo'ne; 8 and with difficulty coasting along it we came unto a certain place called Fair Havens; nigh whereunto was the city of La-se'a.

9 And when much time was spent, and the voyage was now dangerous, because the Fast was now already gone by, Paul admonished them, 10 and said unto them, Sirs, I perceive that the voyage will be with injury and much loss, not only of the lading and the ship, but also of our lives. 11 But the centurion gave more heed to the master and to the owner of the ship, than to those things which were spoken by Paul. 12 And because the haven was not commodious to winter in, the more part advised to put to sea from thence, if by any means they could reach Phœ'nix, and winter *there; which is* a haven of Crete, looking [d]north-east and south-east. 13 And when the south wind blew softly, supposing that they had obtained their purpose, they weighed anchor and sailed along Crete, close in shore. 14 But

---

b Gr. *receive attention.*   *c* Or, *suffering us to get there*

d Gr. *down the south-west wind and down the north-west wind.*

Mysia. *Asia.* The Roman province of Asia. *Aristarchus.* See ch. 19.29; 20.4. *Thessalonica.* See note on ch. 17.1.

3. *Sidon.* A seaport on the coast of Phœnicia, twenty miles north of Tyre.

4. *Under the lee of Cyprus.* On the side of the island which was sheltered from the wind. See note on ch. 13.4.

5. *Cilicia and Pamphylia.* See note on ch. 15.23. *Myra.* Situated on the river Andriacus, two and a half miles from the coast. It was an important port in the grain trade.

6. *A ship.* Laden with wheat (ver. 38).

7. *Cnidus.* A seaport of Caria. *Crete.* See note on ver. 4, and on ch. 2.11. *Salmone.* The eastern extremity of Crete.

8. *Fair Havens.* A bay on the southern coast of Crete. It still retains its ancient name. *Lasea.* A city about four miles east of Fair Havens. Its ruins were discovered in 1856. Neither Fair Havens nor Lasea is known to have been mentioned by any other writer than the writer of Acts.

9. *The Fast.* That was observed on the Day of Atonement, the tenth day of Tishri, the seventh month of the Jewish year, about the same as the latter part of September and the first part of October. Storms were then to be expected.

10. *Lading.* Cargo.

11. *Master.* The sailing-master or captain.

12. *Phœnix.* The modern port of Loutro.

14. *Euraquilo.* A northeast wind.

after no long time there beat down from it a tempestuous wind, which is called Eu-raq'ui-lo: 15 and when the ship was caught, and could not face the wind, we gave way *to it*, and were driven. 16 And running under the lee of a small island called ᵉCau'da, we were able, with difficulty, to secure the boat: 17 and when they had hoisted it up, they used helps, under-girding the ship; and, fearing lest they should be cast upon the Syr'tis, they lowered the gear, and so were driven. 18 And as we labored exceedingly with the storm, the next day they began to throw *the freight* overboard; 19 and the third day they cast out with their own hands the ᶠtackling of the ship. 20 And when neither sun nor stars shone upon *us* for many days, and no small tempest lay on *us*, all hope that we should be saved was now taken away. 21 And when they had been long without food, then Paul stood forth in the midst of them, and said, Sirs, ye should have hearkened unto me, and not have set sail from Crete, and have gotten this injury and loss. 22 And now I exhort you to be of good cheer; for there shall be no loss of life among you, but *only* of the ship. 23 For there stood by me this night an angel of the God whose I am, whom also I serve, 24 saying, Fear not, Paul; thou must stand before Cæ'sar: and lo, God hath granted thee all them that sail with thee. 25 Wherefore, sirs, be of good cheer: for I believe God, that it shall be even so as it hath been spoken unto me. 26 But we must be cast upon a certain island.

27 But when the fourteenth night was come, as we were driven to and fro in the *sea of* A'dri-a, about midnight the sailors surmised that they were drawing near to some country: 28 and they sounded, and found twenty fathoms; and after a little space, they sounded again, and found fifteen fathoms. 29 And fearing lest haply we should be cast ashore on rocky ground, they let go four anchors from the stern, and ᵍwished for the day. 30 And as the sailors were seeking to flee out of the ship, and had lowered the boat into the sea, under color as though they would lay out anchors from the foreship, 31 Paul said to the centurion and to the soldiers, Except these abide in the ship, ye cannot be saved.

ᵉ Many ancient authorities read *Clauda*.   ᶠ Or. *furniture*   ᵍ Or. *prayed*

16. *Under the lee.* See note on ver. 4. *Cauda.* Twenty-three miles south of Phœnix.

17. *Under-girding the ship.* Passing strong ropes or cables around the hull, in order to keep the timbers in place. *Syrtis.* Quicksands to the southwest of Cauda. *Lowered the gear.* Let down some one of the sails, probably the mainsail.

24. *Stand before Cæsar.* That is, go to Rome and be heard by the emperor. He was to bear heroic witness for Christ in the capital of the Roman empire.

26. *We must be cast,* etc. A prediction which was fulfilled (ver. 44; ch. 28.1).

27. *The fourteenth night.* After they had sailed from Fair Havens. *The sea of Adria.* That part of the Mediterranean Sea which is between Italy, Greece and Africa.

28. *Twenty fathoms.* One hundred and twenty feet. *Fifteen fathoms.* Ninety feet.

32 Then the soldiers cut away the ropes of the boat, and let her fall off. 33 And while the day was coming on, Paul besought them all to take some food, saying, This day is the fourteenth day that ye wait and continue fasting, having taken nothing. 34 Wherefore I beseech you to take some food: for this is for your safety: for there shall not a hair perish from the head of any of you. 35 And when he had said this, and had taken bread, he gave thanks to God in the presence of all; and he brake it, and began to eat. 36 Then were they all of good cheer, and themselves also took food. 37 And we were in all in the ship two hundred threescore and sixteen souls. 38 And when they had eaten enough, they lightened the ship, throwing out the wheat into the sea. 39 And when it was day, they knew not the land: but they perceived a certain bay with a beach, and they took counsel whether they could [h]drive the ship upon it. 40 And casting off the anchors, they left them in the sea, at the same time loosing the bands of the rudders; and hoisting up the foresail to the wind, they made for the beach. 41 But lighting upon a place where two seas met, they ran the vessel aground; and the foreship struck and remained unmoveable, but the stern began to break up by the violence *of the waves*. 42 And the soldiers' counsel was to kill the prisoners, lest any *of them* should swim out, and escape. 43 But the centurion, desiring to save Paul, stayed them from their purpose; and commanded that they who could swim should cast themselves overboard, and get first to the land; 44 and the rest, some on planks, and some on *other* things from the ship. And so it came to pass, that they all escaped safe to the land.

28 And when we were escaped, then we knew that the island was called [a]Mel'i-ta. 2 And the barbarians showed us no common kindness: for they kindled a fire, and received us all, because of the present rain, and because of the cold. 3 But when Paul had gathered a bundle of sticks and laid them on the fire, a viper came out [b]by reason of the heat, and fastened on his hand. 4 And when the barbari-

---

h Some ancient authorities read *bring the ship safe to shore.* a Some ancient authorities read *Melitene.* b Or, *from the heat*

40. *The bands of the rudders.* That is, lowering the rudders again into the water so that the ship could be steered safely. The ships of ancient times had two large oar-shaped rudders, which in this case had been raised out of the water and tied fast while the ship was drifting, so that they might not be destroyed.

41. *Where two seas meet.* A narrow strait between the coast of Malta and the small island of Salmonetta.

CHAPTER 28

1. *Melita.* Malta. The scene of Paul's shipwreck is, according to tradition, St. Paul's Bay, about eight miles northwest of Valetta, the capital of the island.

2. *Barbarians.* Those who were not Greeks and Romans were called barbarians.

4. *Justice.* The goddess of justice, according to the idolatrous notions of the natives.

ans saw the *venomous* creature hanging from his hand, they said one to another, No doubt this man is a murderer, whom, though he hath escaped from the sea, yet Justice hath not suffered to live. 5 Howbeit he shook off the creature into the fire, and took no harm. 6 But they expected that he would have swollen, or fallen down dead suddenly: but when they were long in expectation and beheld nothing amiss come to him, they changed their minds, and said that he was a god.

7 Now in the neighborhood of that place were lands belonging to the chief man of the island, named Pub'li-us; who received us, and entertained us three days courteously. 8 And it was so, that the father of Pub'li-us lay sick of fever and dysentery: unto whom Paul entered in, and prayed, and laying his hands on him healed him. 9 And when this was done, the rest also that had diseases in the island came, and were cured: 10 who also honored us with many honors; and when we sailed, they put on board such things as we needed.

11 And after three months we set sail in a ship of Al-ex-an'dri-a which had wintered in the island, whose sign was *c*The Twin Brothers. 12 And touching at Syr'acuse, we tarried there three days. 13 And from thence we *d*made a circuit and arrived at Rhe'gium: and after one day a south wind sprang up, and on the second day we came to Pu-te'o-li; 14 where we found brethren, and were entreated to tarry with them seven days: and so we came to Rome. 15 And from thence the brethren, when they heard of us, came to meet us as far as The Market of Ap'pi-us and the Three Taverns; whom when Paul saw, he thanked God, and took courage.

16 And when we entered into Rome, *e*Paul was suffered to abide by himself with the soldier that guarded him.

17 And it came to pass, that after three days he called together *f*those that were the chief of the Jews: and when they were come together, he said unto them, I, brethren, though I had done nothing against the people, or the customs of our fathers, yet was

---

c Gr. *Dioscuri.* *d* Some ancient authorities read *cast loose.* *e* Some ancient authorities insert *the centurion delivered the prisoners to the Chief of the camp: but &c.* *f* Or, *those that were of the Jews first*

---

6. *Said that he was a god.* As they did at Lystra. See ch. 14.11 and notes thereon.

7. *The chief man.* An inscription since discovered verifies this title.

11. *Whose sign,* etc. Meaning the figurehead. *Twin Brothers.* Castor and Pollux. In Roman mythology they were sons of Jupiter. They were the favoring gods of sailors.

12. *Syracuse.* Capital city of the island of Sicily. It was at this time a Roman colony, and was a hundred miles north of Malta. For explana-

tion of a Roman colony see note on ch. 16.12.

13. *Rhegium.* A city at the southern extremity of Italy, on the Straits of Messina. Its modern name is Reggio. *Puteoli.* Then the chief port of Rome. It was on the north shore of the Bay of Naples.

15. *The Market of Appius.* A town on the Appian Way, and forty-three miles from Rome. It was a great resort for sailors. *The Three Taverns.* A place about ten miles nearer Rome than the Market of Appius.

delivered prisoner from Je-ru′sa-lem into the hands of the Romans: 18 who, when they had examined me, desired to set me at liberty, because there was no cause of death in me. 19 But when the Jews spake against it, I was constrained to appeal unto Cæ′sar; not that I had aught whereof to accuse my nation. 20 For this cause therefore did I *g*entreat you to see and to speak with *me*: for because of the hope of Is′ra-el I am bound with this chain. 21 And they said unto him, We neither received letters from Ju-dæ′a concerning thee, nor did any of the brethren come hither and report or speak any harm of thee. 22 But we desire to hear of thee what thou thinkest: for as concerning this sect, it is known to us that everywhere it is spoken against.

23 And when they had appointed him a day, they came to him into his lodging in great number; to whom he expounded *the matter*, testifying the kingdom of God, and persuading them concerning Je′sus, both from the law of Mo′ses and from the prophets, from morning till evening. 24 And some believed the things which were spoken, and some disbelieved. 25 And when they agreed not among themselves, they departed after that Paul had spoken one word, Well spake the Holy Spirit through I-sa′iah the prophet unto your fathers, 26 saying,

*h*Go thou unto this people, and say,
By hearing ye shall hear, and shall in no wise understand;
And seeing ye shall see, and shall in no wise perceive:
27 For this people's heart is waxed gross,
And their ears are dull of hearing,
And their eyes they have closed;
Lest haply they should per-*i*ceive with their eyes,
And hear with their ears,
And understand with their heart,
And should turn again,
And I should heal them.

28 Be it known therefore unto you, that this salvation of God is sent unto the Gen′tiles: they will also hear.*i*

30 And he abode two whole years in his own hired dwelling, and received all that went in unto him, 31 preaching the kingdom of God, and teaching the things concerning the Lord Je′sus Christ with all boldness, none forbidding him.

g Or, call for you, to see and to speak with you   h Is. vi. 9, 10.   i Some ancient authorities insert ver. 29 And when he had said these words, the Jews departed, having much disputing among themselves.

CHRONOLOGY OF THE ACTS AND OF THE EPISTLES

AFTER PROFESSOR W. M. RAMSAY, D.C.L., LL.D.

A.D.	EVENTS.	EMPERORS OF ROME AND PROCURATORS OF JUDÆA.
30	Crucifixion. Pentecost, May 26.	Tiberius, Emperor. *Pontius Pilate, Procurator.*
32, 33	Martyrdom of Stephen. Conversion of Saul.	
35	First visit of Saul to Jerusalem.	
37		Caligula, Emperor.
41	Herod Agrippa I. King of Judæa and Samaria.	Claudius, Emperor.
43	Saul brought to Antioch by Barnabas.	
44	Death of Herod.	*Cuspius Fadus, Procurator.*
45 (46)	Saul and Barnabas visit Jerusalem with relief for the brethren in time of famine.	
46	The famine at its worst.	*Tiberius Alexander, Procurator.*
47	First Missionary Journey of Saul and Barnabas.	
48		*Ventidius Cumanus and Felix, Joint Procurators.**
49	(Autumn). Return to Antioch.	
49	Council at Jerusalem.	
50	Second Missionary Journey, with Silas. Expulsion of Jews from Rome.	
51, 52	Paul at Athens and Corinth.	*Felix, sole Procurator (52).*
51	Epistles to the Thessalonians.	
53	Paul leaves Corinth, and visits Jerusalem (March). Antioch. Epistle to the Galatians. Third Missionary Journey. Ephesus.	
53–56	At Ephesus.	
54		Nero, Emperor.
55	First Epistle to the Corinthians.	
56	Leaves Ephesus, and visits Macedonia and Corinth.	
56	Second Epistle to the Corinthians, from Macedonia.	
57	Epistle to the Romans, from Corinth. Leaves Corinth for Jerusalem. Arrest in the Temple.	
57–59	At Cæsarea.	*Porcius Festus, Procurator.*
59	Paul sails for Rome.	
59	(October). Sails from Fair Havens. Shipwreck at Malta.	
60	(March). Reaches Rome.	
61, 62	Epistles to Philemon, Colossians, Ephesians, and Philippians.	
62	Paul tried and acquitted, early in the year.	*Albinus, Procurator.*
63–66	Journeys in Macedonia, Asia Minor, Crete, and perhaps Spain. First Epistle to Timothy. Epistle to Titus.	
64		
66	Winters at Nicopolis. Sent to Rome.	*Gessius Florus, Procurator.*
67	Second trial at Rome. Second Epistle to Timothy. Martyrdom of Paul, in the thirty-fifth year of conversion and sixty-eighth of age	
68		Galba, Emperor.

*Tacitus says that Cumanus ruled only in Galilee; Josephus, that he was Procurator of all Palestine, and that Felix succeeded him in 52.

THE EPISTLES OF PAUL*

INTRODUCTION BY PROFESSOR MARCUS DODS, D.D.

Paul contrived, in a remarkable degree, to maintain a connection with the churches he founded. The care of all the Gentile churches (2 Cor. 11.28) he exercised not merely by occasionally revisiting them, but by letter. Of the letters thus produced we possess thirteen. The originals have indeed naturally disappeared; they were written by amanuenses, and authenticated by the addition of a paragraph in Paul's own writing (Gal. 6.11), or by his signature (2 Thes. 3.17). With the exception of the three pastoral epistles to Timothy and Titus, which are still questioned by some critics, the epistles ascribed to Paul in our New Testament are generally and justly received as his.

These thirteen epistles all belong to the later half of Paul's ministry. The first eighteen years after his conversion give us not one epistle.

In the year 52 or 53 A.D. the two epistles to the Thessalonians were written.

Then follows another blank period till 58, when, within the space of one year, the four great epistles to the Corinthians, Galatians, and Romans were produced.

Again there occurs an interval of five years till 63, when the four "prison Epistles" appeared: Philippians, Ephesians, Colossians and Philemon.

And finally, yet another gap, until 66-68 A.D., when he sent the pastoral letters to Timothy and Titus.

In the character of these groups there is a marked difference, while within each group the epistles belonging to it resemble one another. In the earliest group there is a reflection of Paul's preaching to the heathen, in which the second coming and the kingdom of Christ are in the foreground. The second group exhibits the doctrines of grace in conflict with Judaism, and also shows us in detail the difficulties Christianity had to overcome in the social ideas and customs of the Roman world. The third group is characterized by a calmer spirit, a higher reach of Christian thought, more constructive statements regarding Christ's person. In the fourth group we have chiefly instructions regarding church order, interspersed with passages of remarkable beauty and richness.

* Conybeare and Howson date Paul's Epistles as follows:—Thessalonians, 52, 53 A.D.; Galatians, 57; Corinthians, 57; Romans, 58; Philemon, Colossians, Ephesians, and Philippians, 62; 1 Timothy and Titus, 67; 2 Timothy, 68.

THE EPISTLE TO THE ROMANS

INTRODUCTION BY PROFESSOR MARCUS DODS, D.D.

Its Date.—Although this epistle stands first among the Pauline letters, this position has been accorded to it, not because it is the earliest in point of time, but partly owing to its doctrinal importance, and mainly on account of its being addressed to the metropolis of the world. Its probable date is the early spring of the year 58 A.D. The previous winter months had been spent by Paul in Greece (Acts 20.2, 3); and while in Corinth he was the guest of Gaius, in whose house this letter was written (16.23; 1 Cor. 1.14). He must have written it a week or two before leaving; for at the time of writing he intended to sail direct from Greece to Syria (15.25), to hand over to the authorities at Jerusalem the funds he had collected among his Gentile churches in aid of the poor Jews. But at the last moment he altered his route to baffle certain Jews who had laid a plot against him (Acts 20.3). The letter may have been entrusted to Phœbe, a deaconess of Cenchreæ, who was traveling to Rome (16.1), but between Corinth and the metropolis there can have been no lack of persons coming and going.

Its Purpose.—Paul's primary purpose in writing to the Romans was to explain why during the many years of his missionary journeyings he had never yet reached Rome, and to pave the way for his intended visit. He had many friends among the Christians of Rome (ch. 16); and it is likely that in a friendly way they had been chiding him with attending so much to others and so little to them. He assures them that this was due to no oblivion of the claims of Rome, nor to any intentional neglect on his part. On the contrary he, himself a Roman citizen, had intensely felt the attraction of Rome, and had "oftentimes" (1.13) purposed to visit it, and had only been hindered by work from which he could not escape. "Paul had conceived the great idea of Christianity as the religion of the Roman world," and finding that wherever he went there was a constant reference to the great centre and source of law and government and unity, he could not but be continually possessed with the thought: "I must also see Rome" (Acts 19.21).

Paul takes the opportunity of presenting an exposition of his "gospel" more systematic than we have in any other of his letters. Why, if he expected so soon to see his friends in Rome? Possibly because it was said that he shrank from bringing his bare and simple gospel into the trying light of the metropolis. It is not this, he says, that hinders him from coming to Rome. "I am not ashamed of the gospel of Christ" (1.16). And having good reason to know the precariousness of life, and the delays which may hinder and retard the best intentions, he at once proceeds to give the main out-

362

THE EPISTLE TO THE ROMANS

line of his habitual teaching. It was natural that, while proposing greatly to extend his mission, he should wish to make clear to the church of the imperial city, the centre of the Gentile world, what his gospel was, and that it was applicable to Gentiles as well as to Jews, to metropolitans as well as to provincials. The letter is a justification of his mission to the Gentiles.

Origin and Composition of the Roman Church.—The precise form which this exposition took was partly determined by the character of the church addressed. The origin of the church in Rome is obscure. Jews had been numerous in Rome for a hundred years before the date of this letter. Under Augustus they formed a colony on the farther side of the Tiber. Under Nero they had several synagogues, and outside the walls the remains of more than one Jewish cemetery have been discovered. But the number of Christian Jews must have been small, or they cannot have detached themselves from the synagogue; for when Paul visited the city, their leading men declared they had never heard of him, and knew nothing of Christianity save by vague rumor (Acts 28.21, 22). Yet that there were some Jews in the Roman church appears from the salutations (ch. 16), where such names as Mary, Apelles, Aquila, and Priscilla, and those of Paul's "kinsmen" appear (cf. 2.17, ff.). In the main, however, the church was composed of Gentiles. This appears not merely from the names in ch. 16, but from such expressions as, "I speak to you that are Gentiles" (11.13). Some of the names are those borne by slaves and freedmen; and yet there are indications that the church even then contained some persons of culture (Philologus) and standing. Rome, whither all things drifted, could not fail to hear of the Christ. Whether by persons present at the first Pentecost or by those who had met Paul in Ephesus or in Corinth, the gospel had been carried thither, and had borne fruit.

Contents of the Epistle.—The epistle may be divided as follows:—

1. An epistolary introduction, 1.1-15.
2. The theme stated, 1.16, 17.
3. Proof of the universality of guilt, 1.18 to 3.20.
4. Righteousness is God's gift received by faith, 3.21 to 5.11.
5. The relation of Christ and His righteousness to all men, 5.12-21.
6. Those who participate in Christ's death participate also in His life, 6-8.
7. The relation of Israel to the salvation of the Gentiles, 9-11.
8. Resulting duties as individuals and as members of society, the state, and the church, 12.1 to 15.13.
9. Epistolary conclusion, salutations, and benedictions, 15.14 to 16.27.

The theme of the epistle is this: The Gospel is the power of God unto salvation, because it proclaims a righteousness furnished by God, and therefore satisfactory to God, and which man has not to earn but only to receive. What comes of man's conduct, and what likelihood there is of his working out a righteousness for himself, have been sufficiently manifested in the ungodly and immoral condition of the empire. This state of things has evoked the wrath of God. But the Jews are as decisively condemned by their law as the Gentiles are by their conscience. All alike are guilty, and unable to earn righteousness. Gentile and Jew alike must accept God's favor as a gift, if they are to have it at all—must believe that, irrespective of their merit or demerit, God loves them, and claims them as His children. Thus was Abraham himself justified. In Christ this undeserved love or grace is revealed. And it need not surprise any person that by the righteousness of one many should be blessed, for by the sin of one many were made sinners. And the abandonment of the idea that we must earn God's favor will not make us indifferent to holiness. On the contrary, dying with Christ, we shall with Him rise to newness of life, to God, and to all the hope and glory that come of fellowship with God.

But the very triumph Paul feels in depicting a salvation so perfect and so applicable to Gentiles fills him with pity for his own countrymen, and in ch. 9-11 he aims at showing that their refusal of the gospel and their consequent rejection have been the occasion of the ingathering of the Gentiles: if "the casting away of them be the reconciling of the world, what shall the receiving of them be but life from the dead?" He cannot think their rejection is final. Then he gives in detail a wonderfully rich exhibition of the conduct appropriate to those in whom works the power of God to salvation.

THE EPISTLE OF PAUL TO THE

ROMANS

Salutation.   Personal Explanations

1 Paul, a *a*servant of Je'sus Christ, called *to be* an apostle, separated unto the *b*gospel of God, 2 which he promised afore through his prophets in the holy scriptures, 3 concerning his Son, who was born of the seed of David according to the flesh, 4 who was *c*declared *to be* the Son of God *d*with power, according to the spirit of holiness, by the resurrection *e*from the dead; *even* Je'sus Christ our Lord, 5 through whom we received grace and apostleship, unto obedience *f*of faith among all the *g*nations, for his name's sake; 6 among whom are ye also, called *to be* Je'sus Christ's: 7 to all that are in Rome, beloved of God, called *to be* saints: Grace to you and peace from God our Father and the Lord Je'sus Christ.

8 First, I thank my God through Je'sus Christ for you all,

---

a Gr. *bondservant.*   *b* Gr. *good tidings:* and so elsewhere.   See marginal note on | Mt. 4.23.   *c* Gr. *determined.*   *d* Or. *tn*   *e* Or. *of the dead*   *f* Or. *to the faith*   *g* Or, *Gentiles*

CHAPTER 1

1. *Paul, a servant of Jesus Christ,* etc.   The salutation in ver. 1–7 is remarkable as a disclosure of Paul's spiritual experience and beliefs.   It contains an affirmation of his apostleship, his message of good tidings concerning the Son of God, the fulfilment of Old Testament prophecy in the coming of Christ (ver. 2, 3), and the divinity of Jesus the Messiah as manifested by the resurrection (ver. 4).   As to the name of the apostle, see notes on Acts 7.58; 13.9.   *Called.*   Chosen by Jesus Christ while Paul, then a persecuting Pharisee, was journeying to Damascus.   See Acts 26.12–18; also notes on Acts 9.2–4, 15, 18, 20, 23.   *Apostle.*   See note on Mt. 10.2.   *Separated.*   See Acts 9.15; 13.2; Gal. 1.15, 16.

3. *Of the seed of David.*   See Isa. 11.1; Mk. 12.35; Jn. 7.42; also note on Mt. 1.1.

4. *According to the spirit of holiness.*   Or, in respect of the divine, as opposed to the human, nature of our Lord.

5. *Grace.*   The favor of God shared by all believers in Jesus Christ.   *Unto obedience of faith.*   That is, unto submission, in the spirit of Christian humility, which is essential to faith.   *All the nations.*   The Gentiles.

6. *Called to be Jesus Christ's.*   All who sincerely believe in Jesus Christ are called by him and belong to him.

7. *Saints.*   Christians, consecrated to the service of God.   In this sense all such Christians may be said to be saints.   The term does not imply perfection or entire holiness in believers, but that they shall become such by the will and under the guidance of God.   *Grace.*   The Greek form of salutation.   *Peace.*   The Hebrew form of salutation.

8. *That your faith is proclaimed.*   There was special importance in the

ʰthat your faith is proclaimed throughout the whole world. 9 For God is my witness, whom I serve in my spirit in the ⁱgospel of his Son, how unceasingly I make mention of you, always in my prayers 10 making request, if by any means now at length I may be prospered ᵏby the will of God to come unto you. 11 For I long to see you, that I may impart unto you some spiritual gift, to the end ye may be established; 12 that is, that I with you may be comforted ⁱin you, each of us by the other's faith, both yours and mine. 13 And I would not have you ignorant, brethren, that oftentimes I purposed to come unto you (and was hindered hitherto), that I might

have some fruit ⁱin you also, even as ⁱin the rest of the Gen'-tiles. 14 I am debtor both to Greeks and to Barbarians, both to the wise and to the foolish. 15 So, as much as in me is, I am ready to ᵐpreach the gospel to you also that are in Rome.

16 For I am not ashamed of the ⁱgospel: for it is the power of God unto salvation to every one that believeth; to the Jew first, and also to the Greek. 17 For therein is revealed a righteousness of God from faith unto faith: as it is written, ⁿBut the righteous shall live ᵒby faith.

18 For ᵖthe wrath of God is revealed from heaven against all ungodliness and unrighteousness of men, who ᵠhinder the truth

h Or, because   i Gr. good tidings: and so elsewhere. See marginal note on Mt. 4.23.   k Gr. in.   l Or, among   m Gr. bring good tidings.   Comp. ch. 10.15 f. n Hab. ii. 4.   o Gr. from.   p Or, a wrath   q Or, hold the truth   Comp. 1 Cor. 7.30 (Gr.).

strength of Christian faith at Rome, the capital of the empire and centre of its power. The cities of the provinces would be likely to follow such an example.

11. *Some spiritual gift.* That is, any spiritual advantage which his visit to Rome would enable Paul to confer.

13. *Was hindered hitherto.* See Acts 16.6, 7.

14. *Greeks and to Barbarians.* A division of mankind according to language. 'Greeks' here includes the Romans, as the majority of educated Romans spoke Greek. In Paul's time all nations other than the Greeks and Romans were called barbarians, a term originally applied to those who could not speak a language intelligible to a Greek. *To the wise and to the foolish.* The educated and the uneducated.

15. *To you also that are in Rome.* To you that are in the world's chief city, where the claims of the gospel will be most severely scrutinized, if not contemptuously rejected; where all the imperial pride and power will

be confronted by a religion whose founder died on the cross.

16. *Salvation.* That is, eternal life. Nothing less than this expresses the full meaning of salvation. It implies final deliverance from all foes and perils, temporal and spiritual. *To every one that believeth.* A free offer of salvation to all who accept Jesus Christ as Saviour and Lord. *The Jew first.* According to promise. *Greek.* Gentiles. Paul here divides mankind into Jew and Greek, or Gentile, according to religion.

17. *A righteousness of God.* That is, the grace or favor of God toward mankind through faith in Jesus Christ. *From faith unto faith.* In other words, one must have faith in order to receive and benefit by the divine favor, and this in turn increases faith.

18. *The wrath of God.* The eternal and unalterable opposition of His nature to sin. *Is revealed.* By the misery, loss and destruction which result from disobedience of His laws.

in unrighteousness; 19 because that which is known of God is manifest in them; for God manifested it unto them. 20 For the invisible things of him since the creation of the world are clearly seen, being perceived through the things that are made, *even* his everlasting power and divinity; ʳthat they may be without excuse: 21 because that, knowing God, they glorified him not as God, neither gave thanks; but became vain in their reasonings, and their senseless heart was darkened. 22 Professing themselves to be wise, they became fools, 23 and changed the glory of the incorruptible God for the likeness of an image of corruptible man, and of birds, and four-footed beasts, and creeping things.

24 Wherefore God gave them up in the lusts of their hearts unto uncleanness, that their bodies should be dishonored among themselves: 25 for that they exchanged the truth of God for a lie, and worshipped and served the creature rather than the Creator, who is blessed ˢfor ever. A-men'.

26 For this cause God gave them up unto ᵗvile passions: for their

women changed the natural use into that which is against nature: 27 and likewise also the men, leaving the natural use of the woman, burned in their lust one toward another, men with men working unseemliness, and receiving in themselves that recompense of their error which was due.

28 And even as they ᵘrefused to have God in *their* knowledge, God gave them up unto a reprobate mind, to do those things which are not fitting; 29 being filled with all unrighteousness, wickedness, covetousness, maliciousness; full of envy, murder, strife, deceit, malignity; whisperers, 30 backbiters, ᵛhateful to God, insolent, haughty, boastful, inventors of evil things, disobedient to parents, 31 without understanding, covenant-breakers, without natural affection, unmerciful: 32 who, knowing the ordinance of God, that they that practise such things are worthy of death, not only do the same, but also consent with them that practise them.

2 Wherefore thou art without excuse, O man, whosoever thou art that judgest: for

---

ʳ Or, *so that they are*   ˢ Gr. *unto the ages.*   ᵗ Gr. *passions of dishonor.*   ᵘ Gr. *did not approve.*   ᵛ Or, *haters of God*

19. *That which is known of God.* That which mankind has learned about God. *Is manifest in them.* Is known through the light of conscience in each normal person.

20. *For the invisible things of him,* etc. The meaning is that the power and wisdom of God are and have always been abundantly revealed in nature. *Without excuse.* Conscience and intelligence have enabled them to see the power and goodness of God in His works; they are

barred from pleading ignorance.

23. *Changed the glory of the incorruptible God,* etc. Those who had this light from God in nature nevertheless disregarded it and dishonored their Maker by turning to idolatry in its grossest forms. Birds, beasts and even insects were worshipped as deities. The heathen world in Paul's day was full of the proofs of this wandering away from the spiritual apprehension and worship of the true God.

367

wherein thou judgest *a*another, thou condemnest thyself; for thou that judgest dost practise the same things. 2 *b*And we know that the judgment of God is according to truth against them that practise such things. 3 And reckonest thou this, O man, who judgest them that practise such things, and doest the same, that thou shalt escape the judgment of God? 4 Or despisest thou the riches of his goodness and forbearance and longsuffering, not knowing that the goodness of God leadeth thee to repentance? 5 but after thy hardness and impenitent heart treasurest up for thyself wrath in the day of wrath and revelation of the righteous judgment of God; 6 who will render to every man according to his works: 7 to them that by *c*patience in well-doing seek for glory and honor and incorruption, eternal life: 8 but unto them that are factious, and obey not the truth, but obey unrighteousness, *shall be* wrath and indignation, 9 tribulation and anguish, upon every soul of man that worketh evil, of the Jew first, and also of the Greek; 10 but glory and honor and peace to every man that worketh good, to the Jew first, and also to the Greek: 11 for there is no respect of persons with God. 12 For as many as *d*have sinned without the law shall also perish without the law: and as many as *d*have sinned under the law shall be judged by the law; 13 for not the hearers of the law are *e*just before

---

a Gr. *the other.*   *b* Many ancient authorities read *For.*

c Or, *stedfastness*   *d* Gr. *sinned.*   *e* Or, *righteous*

CHAPTER 2

2. *According to truth.* According to the degree of spiritual enlightenment and responsibility of each person.

3. *O man, who judgest them that practise such things,* etc. The apostle means his countrymen, the Jews, and his aim is to convince them that, as they have sinned, they have no right to judge and condemn the wickedness of Gentiles.

5. *After.* According to. *The day of wrath,* etc. The day of God's judgment upon the unrighteous (Amos 5.18; Isa. 2.12; Mt. 3.7).

8. *Factious.* Resisting the divine authority.

9. *Every soul of man,* etc. Alluding to the penalty suffered by man's spiritual nature through disobedience.

11. *No respect of persons with God.* No partiality or favor given on account of external advantages, apart from character.

12. *Sinned without the law.* That is, without knowing that they were acting unlawfully in the sight of

God. *Shall also perish without the law.* This means that such transgressors shall suffer only for the violation of their consciences, but that they shall not suffer the penalties of a law of which they were ignorant. *Under the law.* 'The law' here means law which is clearly revealed and known, and whose penalties inevitably fall upon those who disobey.

13. *The doers of the law shall be justified.* The apostle here contrasts hearers with doers of the law. Jews thought that merely hearing the law made them better than Gentiles. Paul means to remind them that only doers of the law, if any, shall be justified at all, that is, judged righteous according to the law and free from its penalties. That the apostle does this only to heighten the contrast between living sincerity and dead formalism, is evident from his own showing that no one has fully obeyed the law (whether the law of conscience or the law of Moses) and therefore never has been justified or acquitted by God. But 'justified' in this verse is not to be taken in the sense

God, but the doers of the law shall be *justified; 14 (for when Gen'tiles that have not the law do by nature the things of the law, these, not having the law, are the law unto themselves; 15 in that they show the work of the law written in their hearts, their conscience bearing witness therewith, and *their *thoughts one with another accusing or else excusing *them*); 16 in the day when God *shall judge the secrets of men, according to my *gospel, by Je'sus Christ.

17 But if thou bearest the name of a Jew, and restest upon the law, and gloriest in God, 18 and knowest *his will, and *approvest the things that are excellent, being instructed out of the law, 19 and art confident that thou thyself art a guide of the blind, a light of them that are in darkness, 20 *a corrector of the

foolish, a teacher of babes, having in the law the form of knowledge and of the truth; 21 thou therefore that teachest another, teachest thou not thyself? thou that preachest a man should not steal, dost thou steal? 22 thou that sayest a man should not commit adultery, dost thou commit adultery? thou that abhorrest idols, dost thou rob temples? 23 thou who gloriest in the law, through thy transgression of the law dishonorest thou God? 24 For the name of God is blasphemed among the Gen'tiles because of you, *even as it is written. 25 For circumcision indeed profiteth, if thou be a doer of the law: but if thou be a transgressor of the law, thy circumcision is become uncircumcision. 26 If therefore the uncircumcision keep the ordinances of the law, shall not his uncircumcision be

---

f Or, *accounted righteous: and so elsewhere.* *g* Or, *their thoughts accusing or else excusing* them *one with another* *h* Or, *reasonings* 2 Cor. 10.5. *i* Or, *judgeth*

k See marginal note on ch. 1.1. *l* Or, *the Will* *m* Or, *dost distinguish the things that differ* *n* Or, *an instructor* *o* Is. iii. 5.

---

of 'justification by faith' (ch. 5.1). That is the believer's acceptance with God through faith in Jesus Christ. It comes through a 'law of faith' (ch. 3.27 and note thereon).

14. *Are the law unto themselves.* Gentiles, not being under the Mosaic law, governed their thoughts and acts according to the light of conscience.

15. *The work of the law written in their hearts.* Its work or effect was to make men think and act with reference to the distinction between right and wrong. *Their conscience bearing witness therewith.* But an imperfect or misleading witness unless directed and enlightened by communion with God. As to the corruption and blindness of conscience see 1 Cor. 8.7, 10; Tit. 1.15; Mt. 6.23.

16. *My gospel.* Paul's message to Jew and Gentile. *By Jesus Christ.*

The appointed agent of God in judgment.

17. *And restest upon the law.* Upon its possession, instead of active obedience to it.

20, 21. *A corrector of the foolish,* etc. The apostle condemns the Jews because of their failure to live up to the truth known to them as favored possessors of the law. Their special danger was a false sense of security. *Thou that preachest,* etc. It was well known that many faithful observers of the ceremonial law were immoral in their private lives.

25. *Thy circumcision is become uncircumcision.* Thy special light and privilege, when disregarded, place thee spiritually among the heathen.

26. *Be reckoned for circumcision.* If the uncircumcised Gentile, in following the natural light of his conscience, does those things which

reckoned for circumcision? 27 and shall not the uncircumcision which is by nature, if it fulfil the law, judge thee, who with the letter and circumcision art a transgressor of the law? 28 For he is not a Jew who is one outwardly; neither is that circumcision which is outward in the flesh: 29 but he is a Jew who is one inwardly; and circumcision is that of the heart, in the spirit not in the letter; whose praise is not of men, but of God.

3 What advantage then hath the Jew? or what is the profit of circumcision? 2 Much every way: first of all, that they were intrusted with the oracles of God. 3 For what if some were without faith? shall their want of faith make of none effect the faithfulness of God? 4 ᵃGod forbid: yea, let God be found true, but every man a liar; as it is written,

ᵇThat thou mightest be justified in thy words,
And mightest prevail when thou comest into judgment.

a Gr. Be it not so: and so elsewhere.
b Ps. li. 4.

are commanded by the Mosaic law, he shall be counted as one of those who possess the law.

CHAPTER 3

1. *What advantage then hath the Jew?* Having shown that both Jew and Gentile have sinned and are equally under condemnation, the apostle reverts to the special advantage they still possess as being entrusted with the 'oracles of God,' the words and promises of God in the Scriptures, the Old Testament. There were other privileges. See ch. 9.4, 5; 11.28–32. These privileges gave to the Jews the opportunity of leadership in spreading the truth among the Gentiles.

5 But if our unrighteousness commendeth the righteousness of God, what shall we say? Is God unrighteous who visiteth with wrath? (I speak after the manner of men.) 6 ᵃGod forbid: for then how shall God judge the world? 7 ᶜBut if the truth of God through my lie abounded unto his glory, why am I also still judged as a sinner? 8 and why not (as we are slanderously reported, and as some affirm that we say), Let us do evil, that good may come? whose condemnation is just.

9 What then? are we better than they? No, in no wise: for we before laid to the charge both of Jews and Greeks, that they are all under sin; 10 as it is written,

ᵈThere is none righteous, no, not one;
11 There is none that understandeth,
There is none that seeketh after God;
12 They have all turned aside, they are together become unprofitable;

c Many ancient authorities read For.
d Ps. xiv. 1 ff.; liii. 1 ff.

6. *For then how shall God judge the world?* The apostle says in effect:
There would be no judgment of sin at all if the arguments of some unbelieving Jews were sound. They urge that the rejection of Jesus as Messiah only makes the faithfulness of God more clear; therefore it accomplished a certain good and cannot be so wicked. Paul answers that their reasoning, if true, would sweep away the distinction between right and wrong and leave the world in moral darkness.
8. *Whose condemnation is just.* The condemnation of those who are so blind and wilful as to say, 'Let us do evil that good may come.'

There is none that doeth good,
no, not so much as one:

13 *Their throat is an open
sepulchre;
With their tongues they have
used deceit:
*The poison of asps is under
their lips:

14 *Whose mouth is full of cursing and bitterness:

15 *Their feet are swift to shed
blood;

16 Destruction and misery are in
their ways;

17 And the way of peace have
they not known:

18 *There is no fear of God before their eyes.

19 Now we know that what
things soever the law saith, it
speaketh to them that are under
the law; that every mouth may

be stopped, and all the world
may be brought under the judgment of God: 20 because *by
*the works of the law shall no
flesh be *justified in his sight;
for *through the law *cometh* the
knowledge of sin.

21 But now apart from the
law a righteousness of God hath
been manifested, being witnessed
by the law and the prophets; 22
even the righteousness of God
through faith *in Je'sus Christ
unto all *them that believe; for
there is no distinction; 23 for all
*have sinned, and fall short of
the glory of God; 24 being justified freely by his grace through
the redemption that is in Christ
Je'sus: 25 whom God set forth
to be a propitiation, through
faith, in his blood, to show his

e Ps. v. 9.   f Ps. cxl. 3.   g Ps. x. 7.
h Is. lix. 7 f.   { Ps. xxxvi. 1.   k Gr. out of.
l Or. works of law   m Or. accounted right-

eous   n Or. through law   o Or. of   p Some
ancient authorities add and upon all.   q Gr.
sinned.   r Or. to be propitiatory

19. *The law.* The Mosaic law.
Them that are under the law. The Jews.

20. *The works of the law,* etc. Acts done as tasks in obedience to a command; in other words, laboring for salvation without faith. *Through the law cometh the knowledge of sin.* That is, through the law as a power of punishment. Law is an educator; it sets up a standard, develops conscience and helps a man to discern between right and wrong. He who violates law becomes increasingly conscious of its authority and of the danger of disregarding it. He learns more about the disastrous effects of sin.

21. *But now apart from the law,* etc. Paul does not mean to disparage the idea of law in general, but to say that the righteousness of God, in other words, the acceptance of the believer by God through faith in Jesus Christ, establishes the law (ver. 31). *Hath been manifested.* In Christ. This righteousness is therefore a gift from God, and the believer is not entitled to claim any

merit in enjoying its benefits. *Witnessed by the law and the prophets.* The faith of Abraham, the chief of the race for whom the Mosaic law had been given as a discipline, was accounted as righteousness. Therefore even in the beginning of Jewish history faith was supreme in the religious life. See Gen. 15.6.

22. *Unto all them that believe.* All they who accept Jesus Christ as Saviour and Lord have this righteousness.

24. *Being justified freely.* Only those who believe are justified (ver. 22). *The redemption.* The deliverance. The idea was developed from the ancient practice of redeeming, or delivering from bondage, a slave or captive by the payment of a ransom or price. Christ's voluntary death is here represented, in language borrowed from the customs of war and the market-place, as the price he paid to bring us into favor with God. See Mk. 10.45; 1 Cor. 6.20; 1 Tim. 2.6.

25. *A propitiation.* That which wins favor. *Of the sins done afore-*

righteousness because of the passing over of the sins done aforetime, in the forbearance of God; 26 for the showing, *I say*, of his righteousness at this present season: that he might himself be *s*just, and the *s*justifier of him that *t*hath faith *u*in Je'sus. 27 Where then is the glorying? It is excluded. By what manner of law? of works? Nay: but by a law of faith. 28 *v*We reckon therefore that a man is justified by faith apart from *w*the works of the law. 29 Or is God *the God* of Jews only? is he not *the God* of Gen'tiles also? Yea, of Gen'-tiles also: 30 if so be that God is one, and he shall justify the circumcision *x*by faith, and the uncircumcision *v*through faith.

31 Do we then make *z*the law of none effect *v*through faith? God forbid: nay, we establish *z*the law.

4 What then shall we say *a*that Abraham, our *b*forefather, hath found according to the flesh? 2 For if Abraham was justified *x*by works, he hath whereof to glory; but not toward God. 3 For what saith the scripture? *c*And Abraham believed God, and it was reckoned unto him for righteousness. 4 Now to him that worketh, the reward is not reckoned as of grace, but as of debt. 5 But to him that worketh not, but believeth on him that justifieth the ungodly, his faith is reckoned for righteousness. 6 Even as David also pronounceth

---

s See ch. 2.13. marg.   *t* Gr. *is of faith.* *u* Or, *of*   *v* Many ancient authorities read *For we reckon.*   *w* Or, *works of law*   *x* Gr. *out of.*   Gal. 3.8.   *y* Or, *through the faith*

Gal. 2.16.   *z* Or, *law*   *a* Some ancient authorities read *of Abraham, our forefather according to the flesh?*   *b* Or, *our forefather according to the flesh hath found?*   *c* Gen. xv. 6.

---

time. The times of ignorance, in which God did not punish sin, 'passing over' it, or temporarily delaying the judgment and penalty.

27. *A law of faith.* The requirement of faith in God's goodness, which brings the believer into intimate communion with Him. By 'law of faith' Paul means the condition or means whereby man comes into acceptance with God; the law of faith is the way of faith.

28. *Is justified by faith apart*, etc. This is true only when living faith is contrasted with works done as tasks to gain merit. But a living faith naturally results in good works; works are the thermometer of faith and measure its sincerity and fervor.

30. *He shall justify the circumcision*, etc. A contrast between Jewish and Gentile Christians is indicated here. The former thought that they were justified by faith because they already had circumcision and obeyed the Mosaic law; but they also thought that Gentile Christians could not be justified until, in addition to faith, they observed

the Mosaic law and were circumcised. Paul here reminds both that they are wrong, that justification is by faith.

CHAPTER 4

1. *Hath found according to the flesh.* The meaning is, what special benefit had Abraham by being circumcised?

3. *For what saith the scripture?* The apostle, who is here speaking to the Jews, shows them that justification by faith is found in their Scriptures; that it is as old as Abraham, to whom his faith was accounted righteousness before God. Paul's line of argument brings out the fact that the Jews did not understand the inner meaning of the revelation God had made to them.

4. *To him that worketh*, etc. Referring to the wages of the daily toiler, which are paid to him as a debt.

5. *That justifieth the ungodly.* Accepting the faith even of the wicked who turn to Him. The thought is that the ungodly, through faith, may be brought into acceptance

blessing upon the man, unto whom God reckoneth righteousness apart from works, 7 *saying*,
  *d*Blessed are they whose iniquities are forgiven,
  And whose sins are covered.
8 Blessed is the man to whom the Lord will not reckon sin. 9 Is this blessing then pronounced upon the circumcision, or upon the uncircumcision also? for we say, To Abraham his faith was reckoned for righteousness. 10 How then was it reckoned? when he was in circumcision, or in uncircumcision? Not in circumcision, but in uncircumcision: 11 and he received the sign of circumcision, a seal of the righteousness of the faith which he had while he was in uncircumcision: that he might be the father of all them that believe, though they be in uncircumcision, that righteousness might be reckoned unto them; 12 and the father of circumcision to them who not only are of the circum-

cision, but who also walk in the steps of that faith of our father Abraham which he had in uncircumcision. 13 For not *e*through the law was the promise to Abraham or to his seed that he should be heir of the world, but through the righteousness of faith. 14 For if they that are of the law are heirs, faith is made void, and the promise is made of none effect: 15 for the law worketh wrath; but where there is no law, neither is there transgression. 16 For this cause *it is* of faith, that *it may be* according to grace; to the end that the promise may be sure to all the seed; not to that only which is of the law, but to that also which is of the faith of Abraham, who is the father of us all 17 (as it is written *f*A father of many nations have I made thee) before him whom he believed, *even* God, who giveth life to the dead, and calleth the things that are not, as though they were. 18 Who in hope be-

---

d Ps. xxxii. 1 f.   *e* Or, *through law*   *f* Gen. xvii. 5.

---

with God without works, and apart from works. But see note on ch. 3.28.

10. *In uncircumcision.* The faith of Abraham long preceded his circumcision. See Gen. 15.6; 17.10, 24.

11. *A seal.* Completing, or in token of, his acceptance through faith. *The father of all them that believe.* The supreme example of the power of faith among men.

12. *The father of circumcision,* etc. The apostle intends here to emphasize, for the benefit of his own race, the true view of circumcision. Abraham was not the father of circumcision in the traditional Jewish sense of the term; he was the father only of the circumcised who had faith. See ch. 2.28, 29.

13. *Heir of the world.* See Gen. 12.2–4; 22.17–19.

14. *Faith is made void,* etc. The

meaning of the verse is, that faith is necessary to heirship.

15. *The law worketh wrath.* See ch. 3.20 and note thereon.

16. *For this cause.* That is, since 'the law worketh wrath' and there is no hope for mankind by reason of their wilful persistence in breaking the law. *It is of faith.* Since the law has failed, salvation must be by faith, a free gift to those who believe. *May be sure to all the seed.* Salvation must be by faith, on the believer's part, and 'according to grace' or the favor of God, in order that the promise may be 'sure,' by a power above the law (whether the law of Moses or the law of conscience) which is constantly being broken; and sure 'to all the seed,' all those who have faith. 'Seed' means here both Jewish and Gentile

lieved against hope, to the end that he might become a father of many nations, according to that which had been spoken, *g*So shall thy seed be. 19 And without being weakened in faith he considered his own body *h*now as good as dead (he being about a hundred years old), and the deadness of Sarah's *i*womb; 20 yet, looking unto the promise of God, he wavered not through unbelief, but waxed strong through faith, giving glory to God, 21 and being fully assured that what he had promised, he was able also to perform. 22 Wherefore also it was reckoned unto him for righteousness. 23 Now it was not written for his sake alone, that it was reckoned unto him; 24 but for our sake also, unto whom it shall be reckoned, who believe on him that raised Je′sus our Lord from the dead, 25 who was

delivered up for our trespasses, and was raised for our justification.

5 Being therefore justified *a*by faith, *b*we have peace with God through our Lord Je′sus Christ; 2 through whom also we have had our access *c*by faith into this grace wherein we stand; and *d*we *e*rejoice in hope of the glory of God. 3 And not only so, but *f*we also *e*rejoice in our tribulations: knowing that tribulation worketh stedfastness; 4 and stedfastness, approvedness; and approvedness, hope: 5 and hope putteth not to shame; because the love of God hath been *g*shed abroad in our hearts through the Holy Spirit which was given unto us. 6 For while we were yet weak, in due season Christ died for the ungodly. 7 For scarcely for a righteous man will one die: for peradventure for the

g Gen. xv. 5.   *h* Many ancient authorities omit *now*.   *i* Or, *womb: yea, &c.*   *a* Gr. *out of.*   *b* Many ancient authorities read *let us have.*   *c* Some an-

cient authorities omit *by faith.*   *d* Or, *let us rejoice*   *e* Gr. *glory.* Ver. 11; Heb. 3.6.   *f* Or, *let us also rejoice*   *g* Gr. *poured out.*

believers, all who, like Abraham, had faith.
18. *Who.* Abraham.
25. *Delivered up.* By the Father (ch. 8.32); nevertheless the death of Christ was voluntary; he delivered up himself (Gal. 2.20; Eph. 5.2). *Raised for our justification.* For our justification by faith. If Christ had not been raised from the dead, faith in him, as emphasized by the apostle, would have had no beginning and no purpose or end to which it could have been directed. See Acts 17.31. Without the resurrection the gospel message, through which justification by faith is given, would never have been proclaimed.

CHAPTER 5

1–11. *Peace with God.* The first and greatest consequence of justification by faith. It includes all the

blessings specified by the apostle in these verses. *This grace.* This favor. *Rejoice in our tribulations.* Peace with God warrants rejoicing under all circumstances. See Phil. 4.4–7. *Weak.* Through sinfulness. *A righteous man.* A just, upright, moral man. A 'righteous' man in this sense might not inspire such affection and devotion as would cause one to die for him. One would 'scarcely' die for a man whose righteousness made him appear self-sufficient. *The good man.* 'Good' is here intended to represent a more lovable kind of man than 'righteous.' *Christ died for us.* The apostle here brings out the contrast between the timid, halting selfishness of those who would refuse to die even for the 'righteous' or the 'good,' and the compassionate self-surrender of Christ, who died for sinners. *By his life.* By union of

good man some one would even dare to die. 8 But God commendeth his own love toward us, in that, while we were yet sinners, Christ died for us. 9 Much more then, being now justified *h*by his blood, shall we be saved from the wrath *of God* through him. 10 For if, while we were enemies, we were reconciled to God through the death of his Son, much more, being reconciled, shall we be saved *h*by his life; 11 and not only so, *i*but we also rejoice in God through our Lord Je'sus Christ, through whom we have now received the reconciliation.

12 Therefore, as through one man sin entered into the world, and death through sin; and so death passed unto all men, for that all sinned:—13 for until the law sin was in the world; but sin is not imputed when there is no law. 14 Nevertheless death reigned from Adam until Mo'ses, even over them that had not sinned after the likeness of Adam's transgression, who is a figure of him that was to come. 15 But not as the trespass, so also *is* the free gift. For if by the trespass of the one the many died, much more did the grace of God, and the gift by the grace of the one man, Je'sus Christ, abound unto the many. 16 And not as through one that sinned, *so* is the gift: for the judgment *came* of one unto condemnation, but the free gift *came* of many trespasses unto *k*justification. 17 For if, by the trespass of the one, death reigned through the one; much more shall they that receive the abundance of grace and *l*of the gift of righteousness reign in life through the one, *even* Je'sus Christ. 18 So then as through one trespass *the judgment came* unto all men to condemnation;

---

h Gr. *in.* *i* Gr. *but also glorying.* Comp. ver. 2. *k* Gr. *an act of righteousness.* Rev.

15.4; 19.8. *l* Some ancient authorities omit *of the gift.*

the believer's life with the life of the risen Christ.

12. *As through one man sin entered,* etc. Entered the world through man's inheriting a sinful tendency.

13. *Until the law sin was in the world.* The Mosaic law is here meant. Sin, the violation of God's command, was in the world 'until,' that is, before the law of Moses was given. *But sin is not imputed,* etc. That is, the transgressions of God's law committed by those who were not fully conscious of what they were doing, did not merit the same penalty as that incurred by wilful transgressors against the clearer light under the law.

14. *Even over them,* etc. Even over those who had not, like Adam, continuously sinned. *Figure.* Type. *Him that was to come.* Christ.

15–17. *But not as the trespass, so also is the free gift.* The apostle in these verses emphasizes the life-giving work of Christ as compared with the death-bringing transgression of Adam. On the one side are trespass, sin, judgment, death; on the other, free gift, grace, justification, righteousness, life. In ver. 14 Adam was the type of Christ in the sense that he so lived and sinned that he brought death on mankind without their fault; in ver. 15–17 Christ, the last Adam, is represented as so living and suffering that he brought eternal life to mankind without their merit. Adam is represented as the type of Christ only in so far as to heighten the stupendous contrast between the life and work of each.

18. *One act of righteousness.* The meaning here is, the justification obtained by Jesus Christ for mankind. It does not refer only to the death of Christ. *Justification of*

even so through one act of righteousness *the free gift came* unto all men to justification of life. 19 For as through the one man's disobedience the many were made sinners, even so through the obedience of the one shall the many be made righteous. 20 And ᵐthe law came in besides, that the trespass might abound; but where sin abounded, grace did abound more exceedingly: 21 that, as sin reigned in death, even so might grace reign through righteousness unto eternal life through Je′sus Christ our Lord.

6 What shall we say then? Shall we continue in sin, that grace may abound? 2 God forbid. We who died to sin, how shall we any longer live therein? 3 Or are ye ignorant that all we who were baptized into Christ Je′sus were baptized into his death? 4 We were buried therefore with him through baptism into death: that like as Christ was raised from the dead through the glory of the Father, so we also might walk in newness of life. 5 For if we have become ᵃunited with *him* in the likeness of his death, we shall be also *in the likeness* of his resurrection; 6 knowing this, that our old man was crucified with *him*, that the body of sin might be done away, that so we should no longer be in bondage to sin; 7 for he that hath died is ᵇjustified from sin. 8 But if we died with Christ, we believe that we shall also live with him; 9 knowing that Christ being raised from the dead dieth no more; death no more hath dominion over him. 10 For ᶜthe death that he died, he died unto sin ᵈonce: but ᶜthe life that he liveth, he liveth unto God. 11 Even so reckon ye also yourselves to be dead unto sin, but alive unto God in Christ Je′sus.

12 Let not sin therefore reign in your mortal body, that ye should obey the lusts thereof: 13 neither present your members

---

m Or, *law* *a* Or, *united with the likeness*
... with the likeness *b* Or, *released*

Comp. Ecclus. 26.29 (Gr.); ch. 7.1. *c* Or, in that *d* Gr. *once for all*. Heb. 7.27.

life. Justification whose effect is life.

20. *The law came in besides*. Came in as an afterthought. *That the trespass might abound.* That is, that sin might multiply in order to show the failure of the law to uproot it.

21. *Reigned in death*. Reigned as a tyrant in the midst of the ruin he had caused. Sin is here personified.

CHAPTER 6

3. *Into his death*. Into the death to sin obtained for the believer by Christ's voluntary sacrifice of himself.

4. *We were buried therefore*, etc. The apostle means to emphasize the idea that the true believer is so inseparably united by faith to Jesus Christ, the slain and risen Saviour, that he shares both the grave and the resurrection glory with him. *Newness of life.* A life free from the trammels and dangers of the old experience, even as the life of Christ after the resurrection was more free and glorious than his life on earth.

6. *Our old man*. Our old self. Comp. ch. 7.22; 2 Cor. 4.16; Eph. 3.16; 4.22, 24; Col. 3.9; 1 Pet. 3.4. *The body of sin*. The body considered as the instrument or servant of sin (Col. 2.11–13).

7 *He that hath died*. He who has died in Christ; he who has shared in Christ's death to sin.

10. *Liveth unto God*. For evermore.

13. *As alive from the dead*. **As in**

376

unto sin *as* ⁶instruments of un-righteousness; but present your-selves unto God, as alive from the dead, and your members *as* ⁶instruments of righteousness unto God. 14 For sin shall not have dominion over you: for ye are not under law, but under grace.

15 What then? shall we sin, because we are not under law, but under grace? God forbid. 16 Know ye not, that to whom ye present yourselves *as* ᶠserv-ants unto obedience, his ᶠserv-ants ye are whom ye obey; whether of sin unto death, or of obedience unto righteousness? 17 But thanks be to God, ᵍthat, whereas ye were ᶠservants of sin, ye became obedient from the heart to that ʰform of teaching whereunto ye were delivered; 18 and being made free from sin, ye became ᶠservants of righteous-

ness. 19 I speak after the man-ner of men because of the in-firmity of your flesh: for as ye presented your members *as* serv-ants to uncleanness and to in-iquity unto iniquity, even so now present your members *as* serv-ants to righteousness unto sanc-tification. 20 For when ye were ᶠservants of sin, ye were free in regard of righteousness. 21 What fruit then had ye at that time in the things whereof ye are now ashamed? for the end of those things is death. 22 But now being made free from sin and become servants to God, ye have your fruit unto sanctification, and the end eternal life. 23 For the wages of sin is death; but the free gift of God is eternal life in Christ Je'sus our Lord.

7 Or are ye ignorant, breth-ren (for I speak to men who know ᵃthe law), that the law

---

e Or, *weapons*   Comp. 2. Cor. 10.4.   *f* Gr. *bondservants.*   *g* Or, *that ye were. . . but ye became*   *h* Or, *pattern*   *a* Or. *law*

the possession of eternal life. See note on Jn. 11.25–27.

14. *Not under law, but under grace.* That is, under law in the wider sense of the term; any code of rules. *Under grace.* In a state of acceptance with God; justified by faith.

16. *Servants unto obedience.* Serv-ants who really obey. The apostle takes his illustration from slavery, because only slavery, where the master has absolute power over the life and liberty of the slave, could here adequately represent the truth about man's position and dangers under the power of sin. Each per-son must choose his or her master, must take a line of conduct which leads either to spiritual freedom (life), or to spiritual slavery and denial of life (death).

17. *That form of teaching,* etc. Their lessons in Christian faith and practice. See Acts 2.42.

19. *I speak after the manner of men,* etc.   The apostle illustrated

the fact of the deliverance of the Corinthian Christians from sin by employing the language of the slave-market, with which they were famil-iar. *Righteousness unto sanctifica-tion.* They had chosen the right Master, Christ; let them now pro-ceed, by growth in the spiritual life, unto sanctification.

20. *Were free in regard of righteous-ness.* In other words, they knew nothing about it.

22. *Ye have your fruit unto sancti-fication,* etc. Paul here contrasts the shame and humiliation due to fleeting, sinful pleasures, with the blessedness and eternal life resulting from acceptance of Jesus Christ as the gift of God.

CHAPTER 7

1. *Or are ye ignorant, brethren,* etc. The question is asked with the ob-ject of explaining how Christians are not under the law. Had his

hath dominion over a man for so long time as he liveth? 2 For the woman that hath a husband is bound by law to the husband while he liveth; but if the husband die, she is discharged from the law of the husband. 3 So then if, while the husband liveth, she be joined to another man, she shall be called an adulteress: but if the husband die, she is free from the law, so that she is no adulteress, though she be joined to another man. 4 Wherefore, my brethren, ye also were made dead to the law through the body of Christ; that ye should be joined to another, *even* to him who was raised from the dead, that we might bring forth fruit unto God. 5 For when we were in the flesh, the *b*sinful passions, which were through the law, wrought in our members to bring forth fruit unto death. 6 But now we have been discharged from the law, having died to that wherein we were held; so that we serve in newness of the spirit, and not in oldness of the letter.

7 What shall we say then? Is the law sin? God forbid. Howbeit, I had not known sin, except through *c*the law: for I had not known *d*coveting, except the law had said, *e*Thou shalt not *d*covet: 8 but sin, finding occasion, wrought in me through the commandment all manner of *d*coveting: for apart from *c*the law sin *is* dead. 9 And I was alive apart

---

b Gr. *passions of sins.*   *c* Or, *law*   *d* Or, *lust*   *e* Ex. xx. 17; Dt. v. 21.

Jewish converts forgotten that the power of law over a person ends with the latter's death? Had he not made clear to them that a believer who becomes dead to sin with Christ is thereby released from the power of law, having been saved by faith? There was evidently some lingering confusion of thought on the subject, which the apostle sought to remove by an illustration taken from the law of marriage (ver. 2, 3). *Men who know the law.* 'Law' is here used in the wider sense of the term; law in general.

4. *Wherefore, my brethren, ye also were made dead to the law,* etc. The apostle here extends the argument from the law of marriage, to the law which, when broken, results in sin and death. As the woman was released from the marriage law by the death of her husband, so the Christian is released from the law of sin by the death of his old self, through his union with the crucified and risen Christ.

5. *The sinful passions, which were through the law.* 'Sinful passions,' those which have led to wrong indulgence through yielding to temptation. Nevertheless the tempted one's failure came through the existence of the law (ver. 7).

6. *Newness of the spirit.* Newness of motive, intention and outlook, resulting from the ascent to a higher plane of life.

7. *Not known sin, except through the law.* The apostle means that the law gave him the occasion for sin and brought down the penalties of transgression upon him. 'Known' is here practically equivalent to 'committed.' In ch. 2.20 there is a somewhat different meaning. The 'knowledge of sin' is there equivalent to the discovery or detection of sin. In ver. 7–25 the apostle most probably outlines his own experience before he found deliverance from the law by faith in the risen Christ. He means to record his experience as typical of that of the average person.

8. *Finding occasion.* Through the law. *Apart from the law sin is dead.* The consciousness of wrongdoing first comes from the shock of broken law, from the check to natural inclinations.

9. *Alive apart from the law once.* During the time of undeveloped conscience, when he was happily un-

from *f* the law once: but when the commandment came, sin revived, and I died; 10 and the commandment, which *was* unto life, this I found *to be* unto death: 11 for sin, finding occasion, through the commandment beguiled me, and through it slew me. 12 So that the law is holy, and the commandment holy, and righteous, and good. 13 Did then that which is good become death unto me? God forbid. But sin, that it might be shown to be sin, by working death to me through that which is good;—that through the commandment sin might become exceeding sinful. 14 For we know that the law is spiritual: but I am carnal, sold under sin. 15 For that which I *g* do I know not: for not what I

would, that do I practise; but what I hate, that I do. 16 But if what I would not, that I do, I consent unto the law that it is good. 17 So now it is no more I that *g* do it, but sin which dwelleth in me. 18 For I know that in me, that is, in my flesh, dwelleth no good thing: for to will is present with me, but to *g* do that which is good *is* not. 19 For the good which I would I do not: but the evil which I would not, that I practise. 20 But if what I would not, that I do, it is no more I that *g* do it, but sin which dwelleth in me. 21 I find then *h* the law, that, to me who would do good, evil is present. 22 For I delight *i* in the law of God after the inward man: 23 but I see a different law in my members,

---

f Or. *law* *g* Gr. *work.* *h* Or, *in regard of the law* Comp. ver. 12, 14. *i* Gr. *with.*

---

conscious of any disobedience of the law. It may have been in his youth, or even in the period of his Pharisaic self-satisfaction and persecution of the Christians. *Sin revived..* By the knowledge that law had been violated. *Died.* Felt condemned.

10. *The commandment, which was unto life.* See ch. 10.5; Lev. 18.5. *Found to be unto death.* By reason of his inability to obey it.

11. *Beguiled me.* Signifying the deceiving allurements of sin. The sinner, by breaking the moral law, does not really obtain what he expected; the fancied pleasure or gain turns to ashes, so to speak, in his possession or seems worse than worthless by reason of the loss and suffering it brings back upon him. In this sense a breaker of the law is always 'beguiled' or deceived. See Gen. 3.13; 2 Cor. 11.3; 1 Tim. 2.14. *Slew me.* With the realized feeling of guilt.

12. *The law is holy.* The apostle emphasizes the holiness of the law in contrast to the degrading results of sin. He had spoken so often about deliverance from sin and law

that a critical Jew might have objected that the two terms were intended to mean the same thing. But Paul, while admitting that the law is the occasion of sin, and even provokes sin, is careful to prevent any confusion of thought by affirming that the law is holy.

13. *But sin.* The meaning becomes clear by adding, 'became death unto me.

14. *The law is spiritual.* Requires the control of the flesh by the spirit. *Am carnal, sold under sin.* Am therefore unable to obey the law.

16. *I consent unto the law.* Unto its authority, the rightful rule of the spirit over the flesh.

17. *No more I.* 'I' here is the higher self. See ver. 20.

18. *Flesh.* The higher self gone wrong. *To will is present with me.* The wish to do right is ever before me. *To do that which is good is not.* The wish fails to result in actually doing good.

22. *The inward man.* The light of conscience and reason.

23. *But I see a different law in my members.* 'I,' the higher self, am

warring against the law of my mind, and bringing me into captivity *k*under the law of sin which is in my members. 24 Wretched man that I am! who shall deliver me out of *l*the body of this death? 25 *m*I thank God through Je'sus Christ our Lord. So then I of myself with the mind, indeed, serve the law of God; but with the flesh the law of sin.

8 There is therefore now no condemnation to them that are in Christ Je'sus. 2 For the law of the Spirit of life in Christ Je'sus made me free from the law of sin and of death. 3 For what the law could not do, *a*in that it was weak through the flesh, God, sending his own Son in the like-

ness of *b*sinful flesh *c*and for sin, condemned sin in the flesh: 4 that the *d*ordinance of the law might be fulfilled in us, who walk not after the flesh, but after the Spirit. 5 For they that are after the flesh mind the things of the flesh; but they that are after the Spirit the things of the Spirit. 6 For the mind of the flesh is death; but the mind of the Spirit is life and peace: 7 because the mind of the flesh is enmity against God; for it is not subject to the law of God, neither indeed can it be: 8 and they that are in the flesh cannot please God. 9 But ye are not in the flesh but in the Spirit, if so be that the Spirit of God dwelleth in you. But if any man hath not the

---

k Gr. *in.* Many ancient authorities read *to.* *l* Or, *this body of death* *m* Many ancient authorities read *But thanks be to God.* Comp. ch. 6.17. *a* Or, *wherein*

b Gr. *flesh of sin.* *c* Or, *and as an offering for sin* Lev. 7.37 &c. Heb. 10.6. &c. *d* Or, *requirement*

conscious that the delight of the inward man in the law of God cannot be realized, owing to 'a different law,' the power of sin, 'in my members,' or, over the flesh. *The law of my mind.* See note on ver. 22.

24. *The body of this death.* The sinful tendency of the unregenerate self. See ch. 6.6 and notes thereon.

25. *I thank God.* Because of the deliverance from 'the body of this death' through faith in Jesus Christ. *So then I of myself,* etc. These and the remaining words of the verse indicate that, although the law of God is uppermost in the mind of him who has been delivered from sin by accepting Christ, yet the deliverance is only fully and finally realized by continuing the inward struggle between the spirit and the flesh.

CHAPTER 8

1. *In Christ Jesus.* Justified and sanctified by faith in him and union with him. In this chapter the apostle outlines the results of faith in the spiritual life and joy of the believer.

2. *The law of the Spirit of life.* The way or process of the Spirit of life. See note on ch. 3.27. *Made me free,* etc. The power of the Spirit of life destroys the power of sin and death.

3. *What the law could not do.* What it was powerless to do. *In that it was weak through the flesh.* Because it was unable to regenerate and sanctify. The nature of the 'flesh,' or the unregenerate self, could not be changed by the law. *God, sending his own Son.* The sinless life of Jesus in the flesh 'condemned sin in the flesh.'

4. *That the ordinance of the law might be fulfilled in us.* The law itself was utterly powerless to vindicate its ordinance, or requirement, of holiness; but faith in Christ enables the believer to do this, that is, to fulfil the holiness of the law not by a perfect obedience, but by a continued inner conflict with sin inevitably resulting in final victory through faith.

8. *In the flesh.* Ruled by the flesh.

9. *In the Spirit, if so be,* etc. Showing the power and glory of the

Spirit of Christ, he is none of his. 10 And if Christ is in you, the body is dead because of sin; but the spirit is life because of righteousness. 11 But if the Spirit of him that raised up Je'sus from the dead dwelleth in you, he that raised up Christ Je'sus from the dead 'shall give life also to your mortal bodies ʿthrough his Spirit that dwelleth in you.

12 So then, brethren, we are debtors, not to the flesh, to live after the flesh: 13 for if ye live after the flesh, ye must die; but if by the Spirit ye put to death the ʃdeeds of the body, ye shall live. 14 For as many as are led

by the Spirit of God, these are sons of God. 15 For ye received not the spirit of bondage again unto fear; but ye received the spirit of adoption, whereby we cry, Ab'ba, Father. 16 The Spirit himself beareth witness with our spirit, that we are children of God: 17 and if children, then heirs; heirs of God, and joint-heirs with Christ; if so be that we suffer with *him*, that we may be also glorified with *him*.

18 For I reckon that the sufferings of this present time are not worthy to be compared with the glory which shall be revealed to us-ward. 19 For the earnest ex-

_e_ Many ancient authorities read _be-cause of._   _f_ Gr. _doings._

Spirit from the moment of its dwelling in the believer's heart. This was not to be won by effort, but received through faith.

10. *The body is dead.* The physical body doomed to die as the punishment of sin. *The spirit is life because of righteousness.* The human spirit in whom the Divine Spirit has begun to dwell through faith in Christ. 'Life' here means eternal life, which results from the righteousness made possible by Christ.

12–17. *So then, brethren, we are debtors*, etc. In these verses Christians are urged to live according to their privileges as sons and heirs of God. *Not to the flesh*. But to the Spirit, who alone can deliver from the rule of the flesh. *Ye must die.* Because the way of the flesh, or the sinning self, leads to destruction. *Sons of God.* Fully conscious of their rights and privileges, as compared with children under guardianship and tutelage. *The spirit of bondage.* The feeling of servile subjection and liability to punishment. *The spirit of adoption.* Fatherly love attracting filial devotion. 'Adoption' derives special force in this passage by reason of its contrast to fatherhood and sonship in the ordinary sense. Among the Greeks and Romans one who was entirely unrelated to the family could be

made a son by legal process. Here the Father is represented as willing to accept, or adopt, as sons those who are alien to him as slaves to sin. See Gal. 4.5, 6. *Abba, Father.* 'Abba' is Chaldee for 'father.' Both words, though they have the same meaning, are used by the apostle according to a custom which had obtained among Gentile converts. Our Lord used the same expression (Mk. 14.36). *Beareth witness with our spirit.* The human spirit is conscious of and testifies to the approval of the Divine Spirit. *Joint-heirs.* See ver. 29.

18. *For I reckon that the sufferings of this present time*, etc. In ver. 18–25 the believer is exhorted to remain stedfast and to consider his sufferings as of no account in view of the glory that shall be revealed. The apostle reckons or counts the gains as compared with the losses in accepting Christ, but finds the glory to come incalculably greater than the sufferings of the present. The 'glory' is companionship with the risen Christ, the being made more perfect with him in heaven after suffering on earth in obedience to him.

19. *The earnest expectation of the creation waiteth*, etc. 'Creation' here means nature as commonly understood; all life as well as things

pectation of the creation waiteth for the revealing of the sons of God. 20 For the creation was subjected to vanity, not of its own will, but by reason of him who subjected it, *g*in hope 21 that the creation itself also shall be delivered from the bondage of corruption into the liberty of the glory of the children of God. 22 For we know that the whole creation groaneth and travaileth in pain *h*together until now. 23 And not only so, but ourselves also, who have the firstfruits of the Spirit, even we ourselves groan within ourselves, waiting for *our* adoption, *to wit*, the redemption of our body. 24 For *i*in hope were we saved: but hope that is seen is not hope: *k*for who *l*hopeth for that which he seeth? 25 But if we hope for that which

we see not, *then* do we with *m*patience wait for it.

26 And in like manner the Spirit also helpeth our infirmity: for we know not how to pray as we ought; but the Spirit himself maketh intercession for *us* with groanings which cannot be uttered; 27 and he that searcheth the hearts knoweth what is the mind of the Spirit, *n*because he maketh intercession for the saints according to *the will of* God. 28 And we know that to them that love God *o*all things work together for good, *even* to them that are called according to *his* purpose. 29 For whom he foreknew, he also foreordained *to be* conformed to the image of his Son, that he might be the first-born among many brethren: 30 and whom he foreordained, them he also called:

---

g Or, *in hope; because the creation &c.* *h* Or, *with us* *i* Or, *by* *k* Many ancient authorities read *for what a man seeth, why doth he yet hope for?* *l* Some ancient au-thorities read *awaiteth.* *m* Or, *stedfastness* *n* Or, *that o* Some ancient authorities read *God worketh all things with them for good.*

---

without life. It is poetically conceived of by the apostle as sharing in the higher life which man shall attain to by faith in Jesus Christ. *The sons of God.* See notes on ver. 12–17; 1 Cor. 15.51–53; 1 Thess. 4.16, 17.

20. *Was subjected.* See Gen. 3.17–19. *Vanity.* Evil, loss, delusion. See Eph. 4.17; 2 Pet. 2.18. *Him who subjected it.* God.

21. *The bondage of corruption.* The processes of physical decay, disintegration and death. *The liberty of the glory,* etc. The free development of the spiritual and mental powers.

22. *Now.* The time of deliverance which had just come through the truths of the gospel.

23. *The firstfruits of the Spirit.* The pledge of the spiritual harvest to come. See ch. 11.16; 16.5; 1 Cor. 15.20. *Redemption of our body.* Release from physical decay and death.

24. *Hope that is seen is not hope.*

When the thing hoped for is seen, it then ceases to be an object of hope.

26. *Our infirmity.* Human weakness and limitations, especially, in this connection, inability 'to pray as we ought.'

27. *He that searcheth the hearts knoweth,* etc. God, the Father. *The mind of the Spirit.* The intention. *The saints.* Consecrated believers in Christ. See note on ch. 1.7.

28. *All things.* Earthly trials and misfortunes as well as rewards and successes. *His purpose.* Which is to have mercy upon all (ch. 11.32). This contradicts the idea that God intends to save some and reject others.

29, 30. *Foreknew.* See note on ch. 11.2. *Foreordained.* See Acts 4.28; 1 Cor. 2.7; Eph. 1.5, 11. *Conformed.* Made essentially similar. *Called . . . Justified . . . Glorified.* There is nothing in these two verses which contradicts the truth that God's foreknowledge and foreordination

382

and whom he called, them he also justified: and whom he justified, them he also glorified.

31 What then shall we say to these things? If God *is* for us, who *is* against us? 32 He that spared not his own Son, but delivered him up for us all, how shall he not also with him freely give us all things? 33 Who shall lay anything to the charge of God's elect? *p*It is God that justifieth; 34 who is he that condemneth? *q*It is Christ Je′sus that died, yea rather, that was raised from the dead, who is at the right hand of God, who also maketh intercession for us. 35 Who shall separate us from the love *r*of Christ? shall tribulation, or anguish, or persecution, or famine, or nakedness, or peril, or sword? 36 Even as it is written,

*s*For thy sake we are killed all the day long;

We were accounted as sheep for the slaughter.

37 Nay, in all these things we are more than conquerors through him that loved us. 38 For I am persuaded, that neither death, nor life, nor angels, nor principalities, nor things present, nor things to come, nor powers, 39 nor height, nor depth, nor any other *t*creature, shall be able to separate us from the love of God, which is in Christ Je′sus our Lord.

9 I say *t*he truth in Christ, I lie not, my conscience bearing witness with me in the Holy Spirit, 2 that I have great sorrow and unceasing pain in my heart. 3 For I could *a*wish that I myself were an-ath′e-ma from

---

p Or, *Shall God that justifieth?* *q* Or, *Shall Christ Jesus that died,...us?* *r* Some ancient authorities read *of God.* *s* Ps. xliv. 22. *t* Or, *creation* *a* Or, *pray*

are in harmony with his gracious purpose to have mercy upon all (ver. 28).

31. *If God is for us, who is against us?* A question equivalent to the strongest affirmation of the safety of Christian believers. This safety is the theme of the remaining verses of the chapter.

33. *Elect.* See ver. 29, 30 and notes thereon. *It is God that justifieth.* On account of Christ's life, death and resurrection.

34. *Intercession.* See Heb. 7.25; 1 Tim. 2.1.

37. *More than conquerors.* Not only victorious over all enemies, but stronger in faith and knowledge through the intensity of the struggle (2 Cor. 4.17).

38, 39. *For I am persuaded,* etc. Or, I am confident. *Neither death, nor life.* Neither the terrors of death, which are certain, nor the changing allurements and uncertainties of life. *Angels.* Paul's mention of angels was intended as a condemnation of Jewish extrava-

gant beliefs in them and worship of them. In the earlier history of the Jews angels were considered as messengers of God to men, but after the Babylonian captivity the belief in evil angels became widespread. The latter are meant in ver. 38. *Principalities.* A Jewish title for a high rank in the hierarchy of angels. *Powers.* To be taken in the same sense as principalities. *Nor height, nor depth.* An expression for the immensity of space. *Any other creature.* All else not already mentioned.

CHAPTER 9

2–5. *I have great sorrow,* etc. Paul's grief over the exclusion of the Jews from the Messianic kingdom impelled him all the more keenly to refute Jewish reasons against Christianity that were based on that exclusion. He maintained that Christianity was the fulfilment of the Messianic kingdom; but Jewish objectors replied that this could not be true if their race was shut out

383

Christ for my brethren's sake, my kinsmen according to the flesh: 4 who are Is'ra-el-ites; whose is the adoption, and the glory, and the covenants, and the giving of the law, and the service *of God*, and the promises; 5 whose are the fathers, and of whom is Christ as concerning the *b*flesh, who is over all, God blessed *c*for ever. A-men'.

6 But *it is* not as though the word of God hath come to nought. For they are not all Is'ra-el, that are of Is'ra-el: 7 neither, because they are Abraham's seed, are they all children: but, *d*In I'saac shall thy seed be called. 8 That is, it is not the children of the flesh that are children of God; but the children of the promise are reckoned for a seed. 9 For this is a word of promise, *e*According to this season will I come, and Sarah shall have a son. 10 And not only so; but Re-bec'ca also having conceived by one, *even* by our father I'saac—11 for *the children* being not yet born, neither having done anything good or bad, that the purpose of God according to election might stand, not of works, but of him that calleth, 12 it was said unto her, *f*The elder shall serve the younger. 13 Even as it is written, *g*Jacob I loved, but E'sau I hated.

---

b Or, *flesh; he who is over all, God*, be *blessed for ever*　*c* Gr. *unto the ages.*　*d* Gen. xxi. 12.　*e* Gen. xviii. 10.　*f* Gen. xxv. 23.　*g* Mal. i. 2 f.

---

from that kingdom. The apostle, in an argument extending through this and the two following chapters, shows how God freely chooses such peoples and spiritual agencies as suit His purpose; that because the Jews rejected Christ God admitted the Gentiles to that position in the Messianic kingdom which the Jews might have obtained. Moreover, it is in the power of those who have been chosen or elected by God to reject the benefits of His grace. The Jews were chosen and fell away because of their refusal to accept the gospel, and Gentiles who are chosen may also fall away; but the purpose of God through the chastisement of disobedience is to be merciful to all, both Jew and Gentile (ch. 11.32). *Anathema.* Devoted to ruin. *Is-raelites.* The God-governed people. 'Hebrew' refers to the language; 'Jew' to the racial contrast between the chosen people and Gentiles. *Adoption.* Of Israelites as God's chosen (Ex. 4.22). *Glory.* God's presence as manifested on the mercy-seat. See Ex. 25.22; Lev. 16.2. *Covenants.* With Abraham, Isaac and Jacob. *Service.* Of the Tabernacle and the Temple. *Promises.* Of the coming of the Messiah (ch.

1.2; Gal. 3.19; Heb. 6.12; 11.13). *God.* See Jn. 1.1; 10.30; Col. 2.9.

6. *Not all Israel, that are of Israel.* Not all who are descended from Israel shall inherit the promises.

7. *Neither, because they are Abraham's seed,* etc. Those who are Abraham's children by natural descent shall not for that reason alone inherit the promises.

8. *Children of the flesh.* By natural descent. *Children of the promise.* Children born in fulfilment of the divine promise. See Gal. 4.23.

11. *The purpose of God.* To save mankind (ch. 8.28; Eph. 1.9–11). *Not of works, but of him that calleth.* Free choice by God, apart from human merit.

13. *Hated.* Rejected. The apostle, in quoting from the prophet Malachi, does not mean the individuals Jacob and Esau but the nations, Judah and Edom, of which they respectively were ancestors. Paul here opposes the Jewish claim of exclusiveness on the ground of physical descent, and in the course of his argument contrasts the destiny of Israel with that of other nations. Throughout chs. 9–11 the apostle considers chiefly nations, not individuals, as affected by the purposes of God.

14 What shall we say then? Is there unrighteousness with God? God forbid. 15 For he saith to Mo'ses, [h]I will have mercy on whom I have mercy, and I will have compassion on whom I have compassion. 16 So then it is not of him that willeth, nor of him that runneth, but of God that hath mercy. 17 For the scripture saith unto Pha'raoh, [i]For this very purpose did I raise thee up, that I might show in thee my power, and that my name might be published abroad in all the earth. 18 So then he hath mercy on whom he will, and whom he will he hardeneth.

19 Thou wilt say then unto me, Why doth he still find fault? For who withstandeth his will? 20 Nay but, O man, who art thou that repliest against God? Shall the thing formed say to him that formed it, Why didst thou make me thus? 21 Or hath not the potter a right over the clay, from the same lump to make one part a vessel unto honor, and another unto dishonor? 22 What if God, [k]willing to show his wrath, and to make his power known, endured with much long-suffering vessels of wrath fitted unto destruction: 23 [l]and that he might make known the riches

---

h Ex. xxxiii. 19.   i Ex. ix. 16.

k Or, *although willing*   l Some ancient authorities omit *and*.

---

14. *With God.* The words are used with reference to God as a righteous judge, implying that there cannot be injustice in His court, or toward those who appear at His bar.

15. *For he saith to Moses*, etc. The meaning is: God cannot have been unjust in preferring one nation to another because, with regard to Judah and Edom, He did the same as He did with regard to Moses, whom He also chose freely, apart from any merit in the chosen one. Nor was God's choice arbitrary; His supreme will and purpose in choosing were to be taken as final, in accordance with His nature.

16. *Runneth.* As in a race. Neither man's power of will nor his most strenuous action can have merit in claiming God's favor.

17. *The scripture saith.* Here equivalent to 'God saith.' *Did I raise thee up.* Pharaoh was chosen that he might be an everlasting example of divine justice.

19. *Thou wilt say then.* The apostle often wrote as if in the presence of opponents who must be refuted.

20, 21. *Nay but, O man, who art thou*, etc. 'Man' represents the Jewish people. Paul addresses them as objecting on the ground that, if God hardened their hearts as he hardened the heart of Pharaoh, they

were blameless. Even in their rejection of Christ, therefore, they were fulfilling God's purpose and were not accountable. The apostle rebukes them because of their presumption in finding fault with their Maker, from whom their being is derived. The illustration of the potter and clay has often been too narrowly considered. Nothing more is meant than the selection of certain nations for certain tasks, and the implied rejection of others. There could be no intention to doom any one nation to final dishonor or destruction, as that would contradict the gracious purpose of God to have mercy upon all (ch. 11.32).

22. *Endured with much longsuffering.* The apostle shows how God, far from arbitrarily punishing the Jews, had borne patiently with their shortcomings and sins. Jewish history had, in fact, been a record of His mercy. *Vessels of wrath.* Deserving wrath and punishment. *Fitted unto destruction.* Fitted for it by their own unwillingness to be moulded into vessels of honor. Scholars have noticed the significant absence of 'He' from before 'fitted.'

23. *Vessels of mercy.* Vessels receiving and enjoying His mercy. The figure of the potter and the clay

of his glory upon vessels of mercy, which he afore prepared unto glory, 24 *even* us, whom he also called, not from the Jews only, but also from the Gen'tiles? 25 As he saith also in Ho-se'a,

*m*I will call that my people, which was not my people; And her beloved, that was not beloved.

26 *n*And it shall be, *that* in the place where it was said unto them, Ye are not my people,

There shall they be called sons of the living God.

27 And I-sa'iah crieth concerning Is'ra-el, *o*If the number of the children of Is'ra-el be as the sand of the sea, it is the remnant that shall be saved: 28 for the Lord will execute *his* word upon the earth, finishing it and cutting it short. 29 And, as I-sa'iah hath said before,

*p*Except the Lord of Sa-ba'-oth had left us a seed, We had become as Sod'om, and had been made like unto Go-mor'rah.

30 What shall we say then? That the Gen'tiles, who followed not after righteousness, attained to righteousness, even the righteousness which is of faith: 31 but Is'ra-el, following after a law of righteousness, did not arrive at *that* law. 32 Wherefore? *q*Because *they sought it* not by faith, but as it were by works. They stumbled at the stone of stumbling; 33 even as it is written,

*r*Behold, I lay in Zi-on a stone of stumbling and a rock of offence: And he that believeth on *s*him shall not be put to shame.

10 Brethren, my heart's *a*desire and my supplica-

---

m Hos. ii. 23. *n* Hos. i. 10. *o* Is. x. 22 f.
p Is. i. 9. *q* Or, *Because,* doing it *not by*

faith, but as it were by works, they stumbled
r Is. xxviii. 16. *s* Or, *it a* Gr. *good pleasure.*

---

is continued; but the average reader often forgets that if God is the potter, man is the clay made in God's image and therefore free to be moulded into the image of God, or to reject His grace.

24. *Also from the Gentiles.* Not only had the Gentiles been chosen as a result of the rejection of Christ by the Jews, but they had been included in the mercy of God from the beginning.

28. *Finishing it and cutting it short.* In Isa. 10.22, 23, here quoted, it is shown that the judgment of the Lord will be summary and decisive.

29. *Sabaoth.* Hosts. *Sodom.* See Gen. 18, 19; Mt. 11.23, 24; Lk. 10.12.

30. *What shall we say then?* What then shall we conclude? *Who followed not after righteousness.* The Gentiles had not, like the Jews, an ideal set before them by revelation. *Righteousness which is of faith.* The

righteousness of God, as revealed in the gospel; the state of acceptance with God.

31. *A law of righteousness.* Here the Mosaic law. *Did not arrive at that law.* Did not arrive at, or fulfil, the purpose of that law. They missed the goal of true righteousness by working along the line of precepts and minute observances. They had not the faith of their father Abraham which was accounted unto him for righteousness.

32. *The stone of stumbling.* The truth in which they would not believe; their wrong attitude toward faith was the cause of their stumbling.

33. *A stone of stumbling and a rock of offence.* Jesus Christ (Mt. 21.42; 1 Cor. 1.23).

CHAPTER 10

1. *For them.* Israel.

tion to God is for them, that they may be saved. 2 For I bear them witness that they have a zeal for God, but not according to knowledge. 3 For being ignorant of God's righteousness, and seeking to establish their own, they did not subject themselves to the righteousness of God. 4 For Christ is the end of the law unto righteousness to every one that believeth. 5 For Mo'ses writeth that *b*the man that doeth the righteousness which is of the law shall live thereby. 6 But the righteousness which is of faith saith thus, *c*Say not in thy heart, Who shall ascend into heaven? (that is, to bring Christ down:) 7 or, Who shall descend into the abyss? (that is, to bring Christ up from the dead.) 8 But what saith it?

*d*The word is nigh thee, in thy mouth, and in thy heart: that is, the word of faith, which we preach: 9 *e*because if thou shalt *f*confess with thy mouth Je'sus *as* Lord, and shalt believe in thy heart that God raised him from the dead, thou shalt be saved: 10 for with the heart man believeth unto righteousness; and with the mouth confession is made unto salvation. 11 For the scripture saith, *g*Whosoever believeth on him shall not be put to shame. 12 For there is no distinction between Jew and Greek: for the same *Lord* is Lord of all, and is rich unto all that call upon him: 13 for, *h*Whosoever shall call upon the name of the Lord shall be saved. 14 How then shall they call on him in whom they have not believed? and how

---

b Lev. xviii. 5. *c* Dt. xxx. 12 f. *d* Dt.xxx. 14. *e* Or, *that* *f* Some ancient authorities read *confess the word with thy mouth, that Jesus is Lord*. *g* Is. xxviii. 16. *h* Joel ii. 32.

---

2. *I bear them witness.* Paul had once shared their unbelief and now understood its limitations. *Not according to knowledge.* Lacking spiritual insight (Col. 1.9).

3. *God's righteousness.* The righteousness as revealed in the gospel. See ch. 9.30, 31 and notes thereon. *Did not subject themselves to the righteousness of God.* Did not submit to God in humble faith.

4. *For Christ is the end of the law.* The termination of the Mosaic law, which came to a close when Christ appeared. *Unto righteousness.* Acceptance with God through faith in Christ.

5. *The righteousness which is of the law.* A perfect obedience to which none attained (ch. 7.14, 15). *Shall live thereby.* Shall live in happiness in this world and hereafter.

6. *The righteousness which is of faith.* The righteousness of God. See notes on ch. 9.30, 31. This righteousness is here personified.

7. *The abyss.* Hades, the abode of departed spirits. See Acts 2.27; 1 Pet. 3.19; 4.6.

8. *The word of faith.* Which demands faith as the way of salvation. *Which we preach.* Which was therefore already known to many Jews.

9. *Because if thou shalt confess,* etc. The apostle here explains the conditions of salvation as implied in the preceding verse and follows the order there indicated, thus making confession first and faith second. His meaning is that faith, which is really first, is valueless unless it results in confession.

10. *The heart.* The seat of the inward thoughts and affections. *Unto righteousness.* Resulting in righteousness. *Salvation.* Eternal life. See note on ch. 1.16.

12. *Lord of all.* With power to save all. See 1 Cor. 12.5; Acts 10.36; Phil. 2.10, 11. *Rich.* In the gifts and blessings of the Spirit (Eph. 3.8). *Unto all that call upon him.* Who invoke him in prayer, thus recognizing his divinity (1 Cor. 1.2).

14, 15. *In whom they have not believed.* An argument for the conversion of the heathen. In these verses

shall they believe in him whom they have not heard? and how shall they hear without a preacher? 15 and how shall they preach, except they be sent? even as it is written, *How beautiful are the feet of them that bring *glad tidings of good things!

16 But they did not all hearken to the *glad tidings. For I-sa'iah saith, *Lord, who hath believed our report? 17 So belief *cometh* of hearing, and hearing by the word of Christ. 18 But I say, Did they not hear? Yea, verily,

*Their sound went out into all the earth,
And their words unto the ends of *the world.

19 But I say, Did Is'ra-el not know? First Mo'ses saith,

*I will provoke you to jealousy with that which is no nation,
With a nation void of understanding will I anger you.

20 And I-sa'iah is very bold, and saith,

*I was found of them that sought me not;
I became manifest unto them that asked not of me.

21 But as to Is'ra-el he saith, *All the day long did I spread out my hands unto a disobedient and gainsaying people.

11 I say then, Did God cast off his people? God forbid. For I also am an Is'ra-el-ite, of the seed of Abraham, of the tribe of Ben'ja-min. 2 God did not cast off his people which he foreknew. Or know ye not what the scripture *saith *of E-li'jah? how he pleadeth with God against Is'ra-el: 3 Lord, they have killed thy prophets, they have digged down thine altars; and I am left alone, and they seek my life. 4 But what *saith the answer of God unto him? I have left for myself seven thousand men, who have not bowed the knee to Ba'al. 5 Even

---

t Is. lii. 7.   *k* Or, *a gospel*   *l* Or, *gospel*
m Is. liii. 1.   *n* Ps. xix. 4.   *o* Gr. *the inhabited earth.*   *p* Dt. xxxii. 21.

q Is. lxv. 1.   *r* Is. lxv. 2.   *a* 1 K. xix. 10.   *b* Or, *in*   Comp. Mk. 12.26.   *c* 1 K. xix. 18.

---

the apostle meant to emphasize the truth that the Jews themselves ought to have sent missionaries to proclaim the Messiah to Gentiles.

17. *The word of Christ.* See note on ver. 8.

18. *But I say, Did they not hear?* At this time the gospel message had been proclaimed in all the chief cities of the Roman empire which had a Jewish population.

19. *But I say, Did Israel not know?* Had Israel not received prophetic warning that the Gentiles would accept the Messiah, and that the Jews themselves would reject him? Both Moses and Isaiah proved the contrary.

20. *Isaiah is very bold.* Very certain and specific.

CHAPTER 11

1. *The tribe of Benjamin.* The tribes of Judah and Benjamin remained faithful to the House of David. Jerusalem was in the territory of the tribe of Benjamin.

2. *Which he foreknew.* And included in His purpose to have mercy upon all (ch. 11.32). See notes on ch. 8.28, 30, 31.

4. *Baal.* The Sun-god or chief deity of the Canaanites. 'Baal' means lord. Each locality had its special Baal, and the various local Baals were summed up under the name of Baalim, 'lords.'

5. *Remnant.* The Jews who had accepted Christ. Paul aims in this chapter to show that the rejection

so then at this present time also there is a remnant according to the election of grace. 6 But if it is by grace, it is no more of works: otherwise grace is no more grace. 7 What then? That which Is'ra-el seeketh for, that he obtained not; but the election obtained it, and the rest were hardened: 8 according as it is written, *d*God gave them a spirit of stupor, eyes that they should not see, and ears that they should not hear, unto this very day. 9 And David saith,

*e*Let their table be made a snare, and a trap,

And a stumblingblock, and a recompense unto them:

10 Let their eyes be darkened, that they may not see,

And bow thou down their back always.

11 I say then, Did they stumble that they might fall? God forbid: but by their *f*fall salvation *is come* unto the Gen'tiles, to provoke them to jealousy. 12 Now if their fall is the riches of the world, and their loss the riches of the Gen'tiles; how much more their fulness? 13 But I speak to you that are Gen'tiles. Inasmuch then as I am an apostle of Gen'tiles, I glorify my ministry; 14 if by any means I may provoke to jealousy *them that are* my flesh, and may save some of them. 15 For if the casting away of them *is* the reconciling of the world, what *shall* the receiving *of them be*, but life from the dead? 16 And if the firstfruit is holy,

---

d Is. xxix. 10; Dt. xxix. 4.   *e* Ps. lxix. 22 f.   *f* Or, *trespass* Comp. ch. 5.15 ff.

---

of the Jews was only temporary. Some had been faithful and even the great majority, though they had rejected Christ, were not finally cast off. The Gentiles had been admitted to the place in God's favor which the chosen people might have had. Influenced by Gentile example, the Jews would yet accept Christ. *The election of grace.* Chosen by the favor of God apart from merit or works.

6. *Otherwise grace is no more grace.* That is, if it can be earned and demanded as a debt.

7. *That which Israel seeketh for, that he obtained not.* Because righteousness was attempted as a task instead of being accepted by faith as the gift of God. *Election.* See ver. 5. *Were hardened.* By their own faults.

8. *A spirit of stupor.* By their failure in faith they had become spiritually insensible.

9. *A snare, and a trap.* The spiritual self-sufficiency, ending in unbelief and worldliness, which had resulted from the Jews trusting in the mere possession of the law and its

ordinances. *Recompense.* Penalty.

11. *Did they stumble that they might fall?* The question here implies that the stumbling did not and could not end in a final fall; their temporary fall due to their rejection of Christ resulted in the salvation of the Gentiles. *Jealousy.* Ending in the desire to emulate the Gentiles in willingness to accept Christ.

12. *Their fulness.* The salvation by faith of the whole Jewish people.

13, 14. *I speak to you that are Gentiles.* In these two verses Paul's intention is to remind the Gentiles that what he wrote about the Jews has an application to them also. He rejoices in the probability that, by reason of the Gentiles, people of his own race may be saved.

15. *Reconciling of the world.* See 2 Cor. 5.18, 19; Col. 1.20. *Life from the dead.* Their salvation by faith would be spiritual life, or as a resurrection from the dead compared with their former condition.

16. *Firstfruit.* See Num. 15.19–21. The firstfruits were Abraham and the other Jewish patriarchs. *Holy.* Here to be taken in the sense

so is the lump: and if the root is holy, so are the branches. 17 But if some of the branches were broken off, and thou, being a wild olive, wast grafted in among them, and didst become partaker with them *g*of the root of the fatness of the olive tree; 18 glory not over the branches: but if thou gloriest, it is not thou that bearest the root, but the root thee. 19 Thou wilt say then, Branches were broken off, that I might be grafted in. 20 Well; by their unbelief they were broken off, and thou standest by thy faith. Be not high-minded, but fear: 21 for if God spared not the natural branches, neither will he spare thee. 22 Behold then the goodness and severity of God: toward them that fell, severity; but toward thee, God's goodness, if thou continue in his goodness: otherwise thou also shalt be cut off. 23 And they also, if they continue not in their unbelief, shall be grafted in: for God is able to graft them in again. 24 For if thou wast cut out of that which is by nature a wild olive tree, and wast grafted contrary to nature into a good olive tree; how much more shall these, which are the natural *branches*, be grafted into their own olive tree?

25 For I would not, brethren, have you ignorant of this mystery, lest ye be wise in your own conceits, that a hardening in part hath befallen Is'ra-el, until the fulness of the Gen'tiles be come in; 26 and so all Is'ra-el shall be saved: even as it is written,

*h*There shall come out of Zi'on the Deliverer;
He shall turn away *i*ungodliness from Jacob:
27 *k*And this is *l*my covenant unto them,
When I shall take away their sins.

28 As touching the *m*gospel, they are enemies for your sake: but as touching the election, they are beloved for the fathers' sake. 29 For the gifts and the calling of God are not repented of. 30 For as ye in time past were disobe-

---

g Many ancient authorities read *of the root and of the fatness.* *h* Is. lix. 20 f. *i* Gr. *ungodlinesses.* *k* Is. xxvii. 9. *l* Gr. *the covenant from me.* *m* See ch. 10.15, 16, and marginal note on ch. 1.1.

of being set apart, dedicated to God.

17. *Thou, being a wild olive,* etc. Referring to the Gentiles, who were without the special favor which God had shown to the Jews, and were therefore a worthless branch of wild olive in comparison with the real olive tree.

18. *Glory not over the branches.* Do not be proud and scornful toward the Jews because you have gained their place in God's favor.

21. *Neither will he spare thee.* A warning to the Gentiles in the church at Rome and other places to continue in faith.

23. *Shall be grafted in.* Saved by faith.

26. *The Deliverer.* See 1 Thess. 1.10.

27. *When I shall take away their sins.* A covenant of forgiveness of sins as contrasted with a covenant under which laws were to be obeyed.

28. *As touching the gospel.* In regard to God's purpose in spreading the gospel. *Enemies.* Punished as enemies for their rejection of Christ. *Election.* God's favor to them as the chosen people. *The fathers' sake.* The patriarchs; the great ancestors.

29. *Not repented of.* That is, God's purpose of mercy in regard to Jews remains the same.

30, 31. *But now have obtained mercy.* The disobedience of both Jews and Gentiles is emphasized in

dient to God, but now have obtained mercy by their disobedience, 31 even so have these also now been disobedient, that by the mercy shown to you they also may now obtain mercy. 32 For God hath shut up all unto disobedience, that he might have mercy upon all.

33 O the depth ⁿof the riches ᵒboth of the wisdom and the knowledge of God! how unsearchable are his judgments, and his ways past tracing out! 34 For who hath known the mind of the Lord? or who hath been his counsellor? 35 or who hath first given to him, and it shall be recompensed unto him again? 36 For of him, and through him, and unto him, are all things. To

---

n Or, of the riches and the wisdom &c. o Or, both of wisdom &c. p Gr. unto the ages. a Gr. well-pleasing. b Gr. belonging

---

him *be* the glory ᵖfor ever. A-men'.

12 I beseech you therefore, brethren, by the mercies of God, to present your bodies a living sacrifice, holy, ᵃacceptable to God, *which is* your ᵇspiritual ᶜservice. 2 And be not fashioned according to this ᵈworld: but be ye transformed by the renewing of your mind, that ye may prove what is ᵉthe good and ᵃacceptable and perfect will of God.

3 For I say, through the grace that was given me, to every man that is among you, not to think of himself more highly than he ought to think; but so to think as to think soberly, according as God hath dealt to each man a

---

to the reason.   c Or, worship   d Or, age e Or, the will of God, even the thing which is good and acceptable and perfect

---

order to bring out more clearly their deliverance through God's mercy. The fact that Jews were especially favored did not in this respect put them in a more advantageous position than Gentiles.

32. *God hath shut up all unto disobedience.* 'All' here has no reference to individuals, but to the great mass of Jews and Gentiles, collectively considered, who have rejected God's goodness. *That he might have mercy upon all.* Here appears the divine purpose from the beginning. The penalties of disobedience were inflicted only to make the divine mercy supremely manifest. The Jews were first favored by God, but fell away from Him; the Gentiles had also fallen away through neglecting the light of conscience within them, but afterwards heard the divine message and received salvation. But in all God's discipline of both Jews and Gentiles His supreme purpose was to have mercy upon them.

33. *Unsearchable.* Not to be fully understood and explained.

35. *Who hath first given to him,* etc. Who hath laid God under any

obligation? God's mercy without man's merit is the underlying truth.

CHAPTER 12

1. *I beseech you therefore, brethren,* etc. In chs. 12, 13 the apostle gives the practical application to all Christian life of the truths set forth in the preceding chapters. 'Therefore' implies a brief review of and conclusion from the considerations through which the goodness and mercy of God have been made clear, so that believers might promptly act conformably thereto. *A living sacrifice.* In contrast to the dead bodies of beasts sacrificed under the Mosaic law.

2. *Transformed.* The word has the same meaning as in Mt. 17.2; 2 Cor. 3.18.

3. *Through the grace that was given me.* By virtue of which he exercised the authority of an apostle (ch. 1.5). *A measure of faith.* According to which each believer was also to exercise the gift and perform the task allotted to him.

measure of faith. 4 For even as we have many members in one body, and all the members have not the same office: 5 so we, who are many, are one body in Christ, and severally members one of another. 6 And having gifts differing according to the grace that was given to us, whether prophecy, *let us prophesy* according to the proportion of our faith; 7 or ministry, *let us give ourselves* to our ministry; or he that teacheth, to his teaching; 8 or he that exhorteth, to his exhorting: he that giveth, *let him do it* with *f*liberality; he that ruleth, with diligence; he that showeth mercy, with cheerfulness.

9 Let love be without hypocrisy. Abhor that which is evil; cleave to that which is good. 10 In love of the brethren be tenderly affectioned one to another; in honor preferring one another; 11 in diligence not slothful; fervent in spirit; serving *g*the Lord; 12 rejoicing in hope; patient in tribulation; continuing stedfastly in prayer; 13 communicating to the necessities of the saints; *h*given to hospitality. 14 Bless them that persecute you; bless, and curse not. 15 Rejoice with them that rejoice; weep with them that weep. 16 Be of the same mind one toward another. Set not your mind on high things, but *i*condescend to *k*things that are lowly. Be not wise in your own conceits. 17 Render to no man evil for evil. Take thought for things honorable in the sight of all men. 18 If it be possible, as much as in you lieth, be at peace with all men. 19 Avenge not yourselves, beloved, but give place unto *l*the wrath *of God*: for it is written, *m*Vengeance belongeth unto me; I will recompense, saith the Lord. 20 But *n*if thine enemy hunger, feed him; if he thirst, give him to drink: for in so doing thou shalt heap coals of fire upon his head. 21 Be not overcome of evil, but overcome evil with good.

13 Let every soul be in subjection to the higher powers: for there is no power

f Gr. *singleness. g* Some ancient authorities read *the opportunity.*

h Gr. *pursuing. i* Gr. *be carried away with. k* Or, *them l* Or, *wrath m* Dt. xxxii. 35. *n* (Prov. xxv. 21 f.)

5. *One body in Christ.* Through union with him. See 1 Cor. 12–14; Eph. 4.15, 16; Col. 1.18.

7. *Ministry.* Service, practical Christian work. *He that teacheth.* An expounder of Christian truth. See 1 Cor. 12.28; Eph. 4.11.

8. *He that exhorteth.* A variety of teaching, more especially with reference to encouraging and consoling those oppressed by difficulties. *He that ruleth.* One in any position of authority.

13. *Communicating to the necessities of the saints.* Freely relieving their poverty and distress. See Acts 2.42, 45.

14. *Bless.* See Mt. 5.44.

15. *Rejoice with them that rejoice.* etc. Show sympathy under all circumstances, whether joyful or sorrowful; as Jesus did at the Cana marriage feast and on the way with the mourners to the tomb of Lazarus. See note on Jn. 11.35.

16. *Be of the same mind.* Have stedfast confidence in and unchanging kindness toward one another.

17. *Render to no man evil for evil.* See Mt. 5.39; 1 Thess. 5.15.

CHAPTER 13

1. *The higher powers.* The state; civil authority. The apostle in this

but of God; and the *powers* that be are ordained of God. 2 Therefore he that resisteth the power, withstandeth the ordinance of God: and they that withstand shall receive to themselves judgment. 3 For rulers are not a terror to the good work, but to the evil. And wouldest thou have no fear of the power? do that which is good, and thou shalt have praise from the same: 4 for *a*he is a minister of God to thee for good. But if thou do that which is evil, be afraid; for *a*he beareth not the sword in vain: for *a*he is a minister of God, an avenger for wrath to him that doeth evil. 5 Wherefore *ye* must

needs be in subjection, not only because of the wrath, but also for conscience' sake. 6 For for this cause ye pay tribute also; for they are ministers of God's service, attending continually upon this very thing. 7 Render to all their dues: tribute to whom tribute is *due*; custom to whom custom; fear to whom fear; honor to whom honor.

8 Owe no man anything, save to love one another: for he that loveth *b*his neighbor hath fulfilled the law. 9 For this, *c*Thou shalt not commit adultery, Thou shalt not kill, Thou shalt not steal, Thou shalt not covet, and if there be any other command-

---

a Or, *it*

b Gr. *the other.* Comp. 1 Cor. 6.1; 10.24; Gal. 6.4. *c* Ex. xx. 13 ff; Dt. v. 17 ff.

chapter speaks of the Christian's duty to civil rulers. No reference is made to any particular form of government; but obedience is commanded to civil government in general, or 'the powers that be,' which 'are ordained of God.' Religious principle therefore sanctions obedience to the civil power. These instructions to Christians in Rome were urgently needed, especially by the Jewish converts. The Jewish population of Rome at that time was turbulent. It was in every way desirable that Christians should appear law-abiding. Paul's Roman citizenship, and the protection he had received from it against his own countrymen, had large part in determining his attitude on the relation of subjects to rulers. His principles are true and applicable at all times, and agree with those laid down by Christ himself when he was asked for opinions on or to interfere in legal and political matters. Christ always upheld the civil power by precept and example. See Mt. 17. 24-27; 22.21; 26.52; Lk. 12.14.

3. *For rulers are not a terror to the good work,* etc. Here the root of the difficulty is indicated with regard to obeying rulers. The individual's

moral and mental attitude toward lawful authority decides whether he shall be a free, loyal, honorable citizen or a criminal. Does he look upon the ruler as his friend or as his enemy? The apostle says in effect that the ruler is not only his protector and friend, but a minister of God to him for good: therefore he is to be cheerfully accepted as well as obeyed. The Christian is to think of lawful rulers rightly so that it will be easier to obey them.

4. *He beareth not the sword in vain.* Not content with persuading the Christians at Rome to be friendly and loyal to rulers, he warns in regard to their power of punishment, accentuating his warning by an illustration of convincing force. The sword used in beheading a criminal was sometimes borne before a magistrate in token of his authority.

6. *Tribute.* Taxes paid by a subject people to a ruling state (Lk. 20.22).

7. *Custom.* Tax on merchandise (Mt. 17.25). *Fear.* Strict obedience. *Honor.* Respect for authority.

8. *Hath fulfilled the law.* Has done all that the law commands. See Mt. 22.40.

ment, it is summed up in this word, namely, Thou shalt love thy neighbor as thyself. 10 Love worketh no ill to his neighbor: love therefore is the fulfilment of the law.

11 And this, knowing the season, that already it is time for you to awake out of sleep: for now is ᵈsalvation nearer to us than when we *first* believed. 12 The night is far spent, and the day is at hand: let us therefore cast off the works of darkness, and let us put on the armor of light. 13 Let us walk becomingly, as in the day; not in revelling and drunkenness, not in chambering and wantonness, not in strife and jealousy. 14 But put ye on the Lord Je′sus Christ, and make not provision for the flesh, to *fulfil* the lusts *thereof.*

14 But him that is weak in faith receive ye, *yet* not ᵃfor decision of scruples. 2 One man hath faith to eat all things: but he that is weak eateth herbs. 3 Let not him that eateth set at nought him that eateth not; and let not him that eateth not judge him that eateth: for God hath received him. 4 Who art thou that judgest the ᵇservant of another? to his own lord he standeth or falleth. Yea, he shall be made to stand; for the Lord hath power to make him stand. 5 One man esteemeth one day above another: another esteemeth every day *alike*. Let each man be fully assured in his own mind. 6 He that regardeth the day, regardeth it unto the Lord: and he that eateth, eateth unto the Lord, for he giveth God thanks; and he that eateth not, unto the Lord he eateth not, and giveth God thanks. 7 For none of us liveth to himself, and none dieth to himself. 8 For whether we live, we live unto the Lord; or whether we die, we die unto the Lord: whether we live therefore, or die, we are the Lord's. 9 For to this end Christ died and lived *again*, that he might be Lord of both the dead and the living.

---

d Or, our salvation nearer than when &c.
a Or, to doubtful disputations

b Gr. household-servant.

11–14. And this, knowing the season, etc. The meaning is: Do this —all I have advised and warned you to do—for the time of Christ's second coming is near; there is not much time left for the works of light; let us therefore 'cast off the works of darkness.' *Salvation.* Which would be complete when Christ came. *Walk becomingly.* Upright conduct. The explanation of ver. 11–14 is found in the belief of early Christians that Christ's second coming was very near.

CHAPTER 14

1. *Decision of scruples.* The believer whose faith was weak was to be made to feel that differences with the church authorities on minor points should not be allowed to prejudice him, provided he held the essential truths of the gospel. In this chapter the apostle considers the doubts of some Christians in regard to food and other matters. This was necessary only because they were weak in faith, and if their scruples were not judiciously dealt with they might desert their stronger brethren. These latter were too well established in the faith to be troubled with doubts on comparatively unimportant questions.

5. *Assured.* Sincere.
6. *Eateth.* Meat.
9. *Lord of both the dead and the living.* Master of the believer both on earth and in heaven.

10 But thou, why dost thou judge thy brother? or thou again, why dost thou set at nought thy brother? for we shall all stand before the judgment-seat of God. 11 For it is written,

<blockquote>
^cAs I live, saith the Lord, to me every knee shall bow,
And every tongue shall ^dconfess to God.
</blockquote>

12 So then each one of us shall give account of himself to God.

13 Let us not therefore judge one another any more: but judge ye this rather, that no man put a stumblingblock in his brother's way, or an occasion of falling. 14 I know, and am persuaded in the Lord Je'sus, that nothing is unclean of itself: save that to him who accounteth anything to be unclean, to him it is unclean. 15 For if because of meat thy brother is grieved, thou walkest no longer in love. Destroy not with thy meat him for whom Christ died. 16 Let not then your good be evil spoken of: 17 for the kingdom of God is not eating and drinking, but righteousness and peace and joy in the Holy Spirit. 18 For he that herein serveth Christ is well-pleasing to God, and approved of men. 19 So then ^elet us follow after things which make for peace, and things whereby we may edify one another. 20 Overthrow not for meat's sake the work of God. All things indeed are clean; howbeit it is evil for that man who eateth with offence. 21 It is good not to eat flesh, nor to drink wine, nor *to do anything* whereby thy brother stumbleth^f. 22 The faith which thou hast, have thou to thyself before God. Happy is he that judgeth not himself in that which he ^gapproveth. 23 But he that doubteth is condemned if he eat, because *he eateth* not of faith; and whatsoever is not of faith is sin^h.

15 Now we that are strong ought to bear the infirmities of the weak, and not to please ourselves. 2 Let each one of us please his neighbor for that which is good, unto edifying. 3 For Christ also pleased not himself; but, as it is written, ^aThe reproaches of them that

---

^c Is. xlv. 23.   ^d Or, *give praise*   ^e Many ancient authorities read *we follow.*   ^f Many ancient authorities add *or is offended, or*

^g Or, *putteth to the test*   ^h Many authorities, some ancient, insert here ch. 16.25—27.   ^a Ps. lxix. 9.

---

10. *Why dost thou judge thy brother?* Why dost thou judge thy brother, when thou knowest that thou also shalt be judged?

15. *Thy meat.* Thy prejudice about so small a matter as the food a Christian ought to eat.

16. *Your good.* The Christian enlightenment and freedom which make you spiritually strong and useful.

17. *The kingdom of God.* The reign of Christ in the heart in this world and the world to come.

22. *Have thou to thyself before God.* Be strictly accountable for it to God alone. *That judgeth not himself.*

That hath not occasion to rebuke himself for wrong indulgence.

CHAPTER 15

1. *Ought to bear the infirmities of the weak,* etc. In chs. 14, 15 the apostle considers the church at Rome as divided into the strong and the weak, placing upon the strong the responsibility of setting a good example to the weak.

2. *Unto edifying.* The upbuilding of Christian character, both in the individual and the community. The verse implies a warning against going too far to please our neighbor

reproached thee fell upon me.
4 For whatsoever things were
written aforetime were written
for our learning, that through
*b*patience, and through comfort
of the scriptures we might have
hope. 5 Now the God of *b*patience and of comfort grant you
to be of the same mind one
with another according to Christ
Je'sus: 6 that with one accord ye
may with one mouth glorify *c*the
God and Father of our Lord Je'sus Christ. 7 Wherefore receive
ye one another, even as Christ
also received *d*you, to the glory
of God. 8 For I say that Christ
hath been made a minister of the
circumcision for the truth of God,
that he might confirm the promises *given* unto the fathers, 9 and
that the Gen'tiles might glorify
God for his mercy; as it is written,
  *e*Therefore will I *f*give praise
    unto thee among the *g*Gen'tiles,
  And sing unto thy name.
10 And again he saith,
  *h*Rejoice, ye *g*Gen'tiles, with
    his people.
11 And again,
  *i*Praise the Lord, all ye *g*Gen'tiles;

And let all the peoples praise
  him.
12 And again, I-sa'iah saith,
  *k*There shall be the root of
    Jes'se,
  And he that ariseth to rule
    over the *g*Gen'tiles;
  On him shall the *g*Gen'tiles
    hope.
13 Now the God of hope fill you
with all joy and peace in believing, that ye may abound in hope,
in the power of the Holy Spirit.

14 And I myself also am persuaded of you, my brethren, that
ye yourselves are full of goodness,
filled with all knowledge, able
also to admonish one another.
15 But I write the more boldly
unto you in some measure, as
putting you again in remembrance, because of the grace that
was given me of God, 16 that I
should be a minister of Christ
Je'sus unto the *g*Gen'tiles, *l*ministering the *m*gospel of God, that
the offering up of the Gen'tiles
might be made acceptable, being
sanctified by the Holy Spirit.
17 I have therefore my glorying
in Christ Je'sus in things pertaining to God. 18 For I will
not dare to speak of any *n*things
save those which Christ wrought

---

b Or, *stedfastness*   *c* Or, *God and the Father* So 2 Cor. 1.3; 11.31; Eph. 1.3; 1 Pet. 1.3.   *d* Some ancient authorities read *us*.   *e* Is. xviii. 49 (or 2 S. xxii. 50). *f* Or, *confess*   *g* Gr. *nations.* Comp. Mt.

4.15.   *h* Dt. xxxii. 43.   *i* Ps. cxvii. 1. *k* Is. xi. 10.   *l* Gr. *ministering in sacrifice.* *m* See marginal note on ch. 1.1.   *n* Gr. *of those things which Christ wrought not through me.*

even in that which is good. The restriction is, unto the good which edifies.
  4. *Learning.* Instruction.
  8. *A minister of the circumcision.* Under the old covenant, in order that he might show himself to the Jews as their promised Messiah. See Mt. 15.24.
  9. *That the Gentiles might glorify*

God for his mercy. The Gentiles were included in the promises made to Abraham by reason of his faith, and before he was circumcised.
  15. *The grace that was given me of God.* Through which he became an apostle to the Gentiles (ch. 1.5).
  16. *The offering up of the Gentiles.* The giving themselves up as a willing sacrifice. See Heb. 10.10.

through me, for the obedience of the [o]Gen'tiles, by word and deed, 19 in the power of signs and wonders, in the power of [p]the Holy Spirit; so that from Je-ru-sa'lem, and round about even unto Illyr'i-cum, I have [q]fully preached the [r]gospel of Christ; 20 yea, [s]making it my aim so to [t]preach the gospel, not where Christ was already named, that I might not build upon another man's foundation; 21 but, as it is written,

[u]They shall see, to whom no tidings of him came,
And they who have not heard shall understand.

22 Wherefore also I was hindered these many times from coming to you: 23 but now, having no more any place in these regions, and having these many years a longing to come unto you, 24 whensoever I go unto Spain (for I hope to see you in my journey, and to be brought on my way thitherward by you, if first in some measure I shall have been satisfied with your company)—25 but now, *I say*, I go unto Je-ru'sa-lem, ministering unto the saints. 26 For it hath been the good pleasure of Mac-e-do'ni-a and A-cha'ia to make a certain contribution for the poor among the saints that are at Je-ru'sa-lem. 27 Yea, it hath been their good pleasure; and their debtors they are. For if the Gen'tiles have been made partakers of their spiritual things, they owe it *to them* also to minister unto them in carnal things. 28 When therefore I have accomplished this, and have sealed to them this fruit, I will go on by you unto Spain. 29 And I know that, when I come unto you, I shall come in the fulness of the blessing of Christ.

30 Now I beseech you, brethren, by our Lord Je'sus Christ,

---

o Gr. *nations.* Comp. Mt. 4.15. *p* Many ancient authorities read *the Spirit of God.* One reads *the Spirit.* *q* Gr. *fulfilled.* Comp. Col. 1.25. *r* See marginal note on ch. 1.1.

s Gr. *being ambitious.* 2 Cor. 5.9.; 1 Thess. 4.11. *t* See marginal note on ch. 1.15. *u* Is. lii. 15.

---

19. *Illyricum.* The Roman name of the extensive province lying along the east coast of the Adriatic Sea, north of Macedonia and west of Thrace. It thus contained all or parts of modern Croatia, Dalmatia, Bosnia, Albania, and Montenegro. There is no mention of this province in Acts, and it is probable that the apostle means 'unto the borders of Illyricum.' See Acts 20.1, 2.

20. *Upon another man's foundation.* See 2 Cor. 10.12–16.

21. *To whom no tidings of him came,* etc. These words were spoken of the suffering Servant of Jehovah. Paul quotes them as expressing a motive and a purpose similar to those which actuated him in preaching the gospel where it had never been heard before.

22. *From coming to you.* Paul had long intended to visit Rome (Acts 19.21).

23. *These regions.* That part of the Roman empire in Europe which was east of the Adriatic Sea.

24. *Whensoever I go unto Spain.* Some scholars think that this journey was accomplished.

25. *Ministering unto the saints.* That is, presenting to the church at Jerusalem the contribution from Gentile churches.

26. *Macedonia.* See note on Acts 16.9. *Achaia.* The name of Greece as a Roman province after its conquest.

27. *Carnal things.* Meaning here the bodily necessities for which contributions were sent (ver. 25).

28. *And have sealed to them this fruit.* And have publicly borne witness that the contributions brought

and by the love of the Spirit, that ye strive together with me in your prayers to God for me; 31 that I may be delivered from them that are disobedient in Ju-dæ'a, and *that* my ministration which *I have* for Je-ru'sa-lem may be acceptable to the saints; 32 that I may come unto you in joy through the will of God, and together with you find rest. 33 Now the God of peace be with you all. A-men'.

16 I commend unto you Phœ'be our sister, who is a *a*servant of the church that is at Cen'chre-æ: 2 that ye receive her in the Lord, worthily of the saints, and that ye assist her in whatsoever matter she may have need of you: for she herself also hath been a helper of many, and of mine own self.

3 Salute Pris'ca and Aq'ui-la my fellow-workers in Christ

Je'sus, 4 who for my life laid down their own necks; unto whom not only I give thanks, but also all the churches of the Gen'tiles: 5 and *salute* the church that is in their house. Salute Ep-æ-ne'tus my beloved, who is the firstfruits of A'si-a unto Christ. 6 Salute Mary, who bestowed much labor on you. 7 Salute An-dro-ni'cus and *b*Ju'ni-as, my kinsmen, and my fellow-prisoners, who are of note among the apostles, who also have been in Christ before me. 8 Salute Am'pli-a-tus my beloved in the Lord. 9 Salute Ur-ba'nus our fellow-worker in Christ, and Sta'chys my beloved. 10 Salute A-pel'les the approved in Christ. Salute them that are of the *household* of Ar-is-to-bu'lus. 11 Salute He-ro'di-on my kinsman. Salute them of the *household* of Nar-cis'sus, that are in the Lord.

---

a Or, *deaconess* | *b* Or, *Junia*

to Jerusalem have become the property of the receivers.

31. *Them that are disobedient.* The Judaizers within the church. They had opposed Paul from the beginning of his apostleship, maintaining that Gentiles were not to be accepted as Christians unless they were circumcised. They also disapproved of Paul's devotion to the Gentiles, striving unceasingly to restrict his work and influence to the furtherance of Judaism.

CHAPTER 16

1. *Cenchreæ.* The eastern part of Corinth. See note on Acts 18.1.

3. *Prisca and Aquila.* See Acts 18.2, 18, 26. Paul first knew them at Corinth, and went with them a year and a half later to Ephesus, where they helped to correct certain errors in the beliefs of Apollos. When Paul wrote this epistle they were in Rome. They were last

known to be in Ephesus (2 Tim. 4.19).

5. *Epænetus.* Not mentioned elsewhere in the New Testament. *Asia.* The Roman province of that name. See notes on Acts 6.8–15; 19.10.

6. *Mary.* Probably a Gentile convert.

7. *Andronicus and Junias.* The first is a Greek name, the second is Latin; but both men were Jews. It was the custom of Jews who travelled or engaged in commerce to assume Latin or Greek names. These two probably belonged, as did Paul, to the tribe of Benjamin, but there is no evidence that they were closely related to Paul. The only relative mentioned is his nephew (Acts 23.16).

8–10. *Ampliatus . . . Urbanus.* Latin names. *Stachys...Apelles... Aristobulus.* Greek names.

11. *Herodion, my kinsman.* A Greek name. See note on ver. 7.

12 Salute Try-phæ'na and Try-pho'sa, who labor in the Lord. Salute Per'sis the beloved, who labored much in the Lord. 13 Salute Ru'fus the chosen in the Lord, and his mother and mine. 14 Salute A-syn'cri-tus, Phle'-gon, Her'mes, Pat'ro-bas, Her'mas, and the brethren that are with them. 15 Salute Phi-lol'o-gus and Ju'li-a, Ne'reus and his sister, and O-lym'pas, and all the saints that are with them. 16 Salute one another with a holy kiss. All the churches of Christ salute you.

17 Now I beseech you, brethren, mark them that are causing the divisions and occasions of stumbling, contrary to the ᶜdoctrine which ye learned: and turn away from them. 18 For

they that are such serve not our Lord Christ, but their own belly; and by their smooth and fair speech they beguile the hearts of the innocent. 19 For your obedience is come abroad unto all men. I rejoice therefore over you: but I would have you wise unto that which is good, and simple unto that which is evil. 20 And the God of peace shall bruise Satan under your feet shortly.

The grace of our Lord Je'sus Christ be with you.

21 Tim'o-thy my fellow-worker saluteth you; and Lu'-cius and Ja'son and So-sip'a-ter, my kinsmen. 22 I Ter'tius, ᵈwho write the epistle, salute you in the Lord. 23 Ga'ius my host, and of the whole church,

---

c Or. teaching   d Or. who | write the epistle in the Lord, salute you

---

Narcissus. Supposed to be a well-known Roman freedman.

12. Tryphæna and Tryphosa. Probably two sisters. Their names are Greek, as is also that of Persis.

13. Rufus. A Latin name. This Rufus may have been the same as he who is mentioned in Mk. 15.21. The chosen in the Lord. He who by his faith and example is honored for his work in the Lord.

14. Asyncritus, etc. The names are all Greek.

15. Philologus, etc. All the names are Greek, except 'Julia,' a Latin name. Julia was probably either the wife or sister of Philologus (lover of wisdom).

17. Them that are causing the divisions, etc. The Judaizing teachers within the church (ch. 15.31). Some scholars think that other forms of error were meant.

18. Their own belly. Their objectionable religious notions and schemes. See Phil. 3.17–20; Col. 2.20–23.

19. Your obedience is come abroad, etc. Your loyalty to Christian truth is everywhere known. Simple

unto that which is evil. Uncontaminated by evil, though knowing its danger.

20. The God of peace. Invoked by the apostle with reference to the strife and divisions of which he had just spoken. Shall bruise Satan. Shall enable you to triumph over him. Shortly. In view of the expected second coming of Christ (ch. 13.11, 12).

21. Timothy. See note on Acts 16.1. Lucius. Possibly the same as Lucius of Cyrene, in North Africa. See Acts 13.1. Jason. Possibly the Jason mentioned in Acts 17.5, 6, 7, 9. Sosipater. Possibly Sopater the Berœan (Acts 20.4). My kinsman. See note on ver. 7.

22. Tertius. Paul's amanuensis, who wrote the apostle's letters from dictation. His sudden interruption here in order to add his own name to those who wished to salute his Christian brethren in Rome is dramatic.

23. Gaius. The same name as the Latin Caius. It is not certain that he was the same as the Caius referred to in Acts 19.29; or as the

saluteth you. E-ras'tus the treasurer of the city saluteth you, and Quar'tus the brother.*

25 *Now to him that is able to establish you according to my *gospel and the preaching of Je'sus Christ, according to the revelation of the mystery which hath been kept in silence through times eternal, 26 but now is manifested, and *by the scriptures of the prophets, according to the commandment of the eternal God, is made known unto all the *nations unto obedience *of faith: 27 to the only wise God, through Je'sus Christ, *to whom be the glory *for ever. A-men'.

---

* Some ancient authorities insert here ver. 24 *The grace of our Lord Jesus Christ be with you all. Amen,* and omit the like words in ver. 20. *f* Some ancient authorities omit ver. 25–27.

Comp. the end of ch. 14. *g* See marginal note on ch. 1.1. *h* Gr. *through.* *i* Or, *Gentiles* *k* Or, *to the faith* *l* Some ancient authorities omit *to whom.* *m* Gr. *unto the ages.*

Gaius of Derbe (Acts 20.4); or of 3 Jn. 1. *Erastus.* A Greek name. *City.* Corinth. *Quartus.* A Latin name.

25. *To establish you.* Make firm and stedfast. *My gospel.* Paul's teaching of the salvation by faith for Jew and Gentile. *The preaching of Jesus Christ.* The preaching done in the name of Jesus Christ by Paul and the other apostles. *The revelation of the mystery.* The making known of the secret purpose of God was followed by the proclamation of the gospel.

26. *Unto obedience of faith.* The humble submission which faith implies.

THE FIRST EPISTLE TO THE CORINTHIANS

INTRODUCTION BY PRINCIPAL T. C. EDWARDS, D.D.

Corinth and Its Church.—The Corinth known to the apostle Paul was not the wealthy Greek city of Homer and Thucydides. Destroyed by the Romans in 146 B.C., it was rebuilt by Julius Cæsar exactly a hundred years afterwards, and peopled by a colony of veterans and others, on the same isthmus which has always formed the highway of commerce between Asia and Italy. It became the metropolis of the Roman province of Achaia. In Corinth the social forces of the age met, and all the licentiousness that had been the shame or the religion of other lands.

That the Christian church in Corinth was founded by Paul is abundantly evident from 1 Cor. 3.6; 4.15; 2 Cor. 1.19; 10.10. He came to Corinth from Athens on his second missionary journey (Acts 18.1-2). He began his work by preaching in the synagogue. Driven thence, he resumed it in the house of a proselyte named Justus, who, with Crispus, a ruler of the synagogue, believed that Jesus was the Christ. He made many converts, mostly persons of low birth and the greater part Gentiles (1 Cor. 12.2). Before he left for Jerusalem, he wrote the two epistles to the Thessalonians.

We next hear of the arrival of Apollos from Ephesus. He was then personally unknown to the apostle, but already in part convinced of the truth of the gospel by what he had heard of the baptism of John, and more fully taught by Aquila and Priscilla (Acts 18.24). We are prepared to hear of a new phase of Christianity, in great measure independent of Pauline doctrine, consisting of Alexandrian theosophy combined with a belief in the Messiahship of Jesus.

In less than a twelvemonth news of a distressing character comes to the apostle's ears. The church is torn by factions, one party giving itself the name of Paul, another that of Apollos, another putting forward the still greater name of the apostle Peter, and another not fearing to appropriate the highest name, that of Christ Himself. Scandalous immorality of various kinds is suffered without rebuke. Disorder prevails in the assemblies. The apostle makes no delay to send Timotheus from Ephesus to admonish the Corinthian church. Not long after, messengers are sent to seek the apostle's advice on some matters of practical difficulty. Our first epistle is his reply.

Authorship and Date.—That the epistle is written by Paul is beyond a doubt. *External* evidence of its genuineness is abundant. It will suffice to mention the words of Clement of Rome, who, in his epistle to the same church, written probably between 93 and 97 A.D., refers to our epistle more than once as the apostle's. The *internal* evidence is of the strongest kind. The writer of the epistle and the missionary apostle of the Acts present similar features—the same combination of vehement energy and intellectual keenness, the same effective use of superlative verbs, the same proneness "to go off on a word," the same doctrinal basis, the same play upon words and allusions to his own life.

The epistle was undoubtedly written from Ephesus (1 Cor. 16.8, 19). The subscription in the King James Version, "from Philippi," is an error. The time of writing can be inferred approximately, according as we suppose, from the words of Tacitus and Josephus, that Festus entered on his procuratorship at Cæsarea in 60 or 61 A.D.; for the apostle's imprisonment there began two years before the accession of Festus (Acts 24.27), therefore in 58 or 59 A.D.

Contents of the Epistle.—We may divide it into eight main divisions:—

1. The factions in the church. First argument: The gospel is essentially the proclamation of salvation through Christ. This is proved from the nature of the message, from the character of the church, and from the power of the ministry. Second argument: The gospel is a divine revelation through the Spirit. Third argument: God has appointed teachers, and defined their work (ch. 1 to 4).

2. Church discipline: The case of incest; the practice of going to law before heathen tribunals. A statement of the difference between actions indifferent and actions in their very nature sinful (5, 6).

3. Marriage and celibacy; application of the Christian doctrine to particular cases. Digression on Christian liberty, with special reference to circumcision and slavery (7).

4. Concerning the eating of meats offered to idols. Reconciliation of the two opposite Christian conceptions of liberty and love, exemplified in the apostle's own conduct; the dangers to which the Corinthians exposed themselves by partaking of the idol feasts shown by the example of the Israelites, and such partaking explained to be inconsistent with partaking of the Lord's Supper (8 to 10).

5. Abuses in the church assemblies, in reference to men praying with their heads covered and women with their heads uncovered, and in reference to the Lord's Supper (11).

6. The spiritual gifts (12 to 14).

7. The resurrection of the dead: (a) The gospel which the apostle preached rested on the facts, proved by eye-witnesses, of Christ's death and resurrection. (b) The denial of the resurrection of the dead involves the denial of the resurrection of Christ. (c) Direct proof: The resurrection of the dead is the realization of the Christian order of the subjection of all things to Christ. The proof confirmed by analogies and from Scripture. Refrain of triumph (15).

8. Sundry personal and incidental matters (16).

THE FIRST EPISTLE OF PAUL TO THE

CO-RIN'THI-ANS

Salutation.

1 Paul, called *to be* an apostle of Je'sus Christ through the will of God, and Sos'the-nes *a*our brother, 2 unto the church of God which is at Cor'inth, *even* them that are sanctified in Christ Je'sus, called *to be* saints, with all that call upon the name of our Lord Je'sus Christ in every place, their *Lord* and ours: 3 Grace to you and peace from God our Father and the Lord Je'sus Christ.

Thanksgiving

4 I thank *b*my God always concerning you, for the grace of God which was given you in Christ Je'sus; 5 that in everything ye were enriched in him, in all *c*utterance and all knowledge; 6 even as the testimony of Christ was confirmed in you: 7 so that ye come behind in no gift; waiting for the revelation of our Lord Je'sus Christ; 8 who shall also confirm you unto the end, *that ye be* unreprovable in the day of

---

a Gr. *the brother.* *b* Some ancient authorities omit *my.* *c* Gr. *word.*

CHAPTER 1

1. *Called to be an apostle.* An apostle by divine calling. 'Called' has the same sense in ver. 2, 24. Paul was not one of the twelve, called by Jesus at the opening of his ministry (Mt. 10.1-4); hence his title to the apostleship could not rest upon an original divine call, such as had been given the other apostles. *Sosthenes.* Supposed by some, but without sufficient evidence, to be the chief ruler of the synagogue mentioned in Acts 28.17, with the assumption that he was afterwards converted. He must have been a person of much consideration to be joined with Paul in the salutation.

2. *The church of God which is at Corinth.* See 'Corinth and Its Church' in the introduction to the first epistle to the Corinthians. *Sanctified.* Made holy. 'Sanctified' is here applied to all true believers in the church; sanctification was the object for which they were

called, and was then begun, even if not completed in them. *Called.* See note on ver. 1. *Saints.* 'Saints' in the New Testament denotes not persons of rare and exceptional piety, but all true believers; holiness of life was the purpose of their divine calling in Christ. *With all that call,* etc. That is, directly invoke Jesus Christ in prayer, as the exalted Redeemer (Acts 7.59). *In every place.* The apostolic epistles were passed from church to church (Col. 4.16). In Corinth, a great commercial centre, there were likely to be believers from many parts of the civilized world, who would thus be included in the greeting.

5. *That in everything ye were enriched.* The members of the Corinthian church had begun the Christian life with an abundant supply of spiritual blessings.

6, 8. *Confirmed.* The meaning of 'confirmed' and 'confirm' in these two verses is 'made firm, stable, stedfast.'

403

our Lord Je′sus Christ. 9 God is faithful, through whom ye were called into the fellowship of his Son Je′sus Christ our Lord.

10 Now I beseech you, brethren, through the name of our Lord Je′sus Christ, that ye all speak the same thing, and *that* there be no *ᵈ*divisions among you; but *that* ye be perfected together in the same mind and in the same judgment. 11 For it hath been signified unto me concerning you, my brethren, by them *that are of the household* of Chlo′e, that there are contentions among you. 12 Now this I mean, that each one of you

saith, I am of Paul; and I of A-pol′los; and I of Ce′phas; and I of Christ. 13 *ᵉ*Is Christ divided? was Paul crucified for you? or were ye baptized into the name of Paul? 14 *ᶠ*I thank God that I baptized none of you, save Cris′pus and Ga′ius; 15 lest any man should say that ye were baptized into my name. 16 And I baptized also the household of Steph′a-nas: besides, I know not whether I baptized any other. 17 For Christ sent me not to baptize, but to *ᵍ*preach the gospel: not in wisdom of words, lest the cross of Christ should be made void.

18 For the word of the cross

---

d Gr. *schisms.*   e Or, *Christ is divided! Was Paul crucified for you?*   f Some ancient authorities read *I give thanks that.*   g Gr. *bring good tidings.* Comp. Mt. 11. 5.

9. *God is faithful.* To comfort and sustain believers.

10. *Divisions.* Into parties, resulting in contentions such as those indicated in ver. 11, 12.

11. *Chloe.* Not elsewhere noticed, but so well known to the Corinthians that it was sufficient to mention her name without description.

12. *Apollos.* See Acts 18.24-28. At the writing of this epistle Apollos was with or near Paul, and it is evident that there was perfect harmony between them, from Paul's words, 'as touching Apollos the brother, I besought him much to come unto you with the brethren.' But the apostle adds, 'it was not at all his will to come now' (ch. 16.12). It seems clear that Apollos had been made by his admirers, against his own will, the leader of a party against Paul, and on discovering this had taken the surest way to quench the rivalry by absenting himself from the church and joining the apostle. There is no evidence that he ever revisited Corinth. There is cordial mention of Apollos in Tit. 3.13. *Cephas.* Peter, who was the nominal head of the party with Judaizing tendencies (Gal. 2.11, 14). It is not probable that Peter him-

self had anything to do with the contest in Corinth. *Of Christ.* Those who called themselves 'of Christ' were doubtless some who had attended the ministry of Jesus or who had been directly instructed by some of his immediate followers.

14. *Crispus.* The converted ruler of the synagogue at Corinth (Acts 18.8). *Gaius.* Doubtless the same person mentioned in Rom. 16.23. Others of the name are mentioned (Acts 19.29; 20.4; 3 Jn. 1.1).

16. *The household of Stephanas.* Stephanas was the first Corinthian convert under Paul's ministry (ch. 16.15), and was with the apostle at the time (ch. 16.17). Of whom his household consisted we are not informed, but we learn from ch. 16.15 that they have set themselves to minister to the saints. *I know not,* etc. The apostle declares himself not sure whether the list, evidently supplied from memory, is complete.

17. *Not to baptize,* etc. Baptism could be performed by any qualified administrator, but preaching was Paul's special work. (Acts 9.15; 22.15, 16; 26.16.) *Lest the cross,* etc. Lest human systems, logic, or eloquence should lead the minds of men away from the simplicity of

is to them that [h]perish foolishness; but unto us who [i]are saved it is the power of God. 19 For it is written,

[k]I will destroy the wisdom of the wise,

And the discernment of the discerning will I bring to nought.

20 Where is the wise? where is the scribe? where is the disputer of this [l]world? hath not God made foolish the wisdom of the world? 21 For seeing that in the wisdom of God the world through its wisdom knew not God, it was God's good pleasure through the foolishness of the [m]preaching to save them that believe. 22 Seeing that Jews ask for signs, and Greeks seek after wisdom: 23 but we preach [n]Christ crucified, unto Jews a stumblingblock, and unto Gen'tiles foolishness; 24 but unto [o]them that are called, both Jews and Greeks, Christ the power of God, and the wisdom of God. 25 Because the foolishness of God is wiser than men; and the weakness of God is stronger than men.

26 For [p]behold your calling, brethren, that not many wise after the flesh, not many mighty, not many noble, *are called*: 27 but God chose the foolish things of the world, that he might put to shame them that are wise; and God chose the weak things of the world, that he might put to shame the things that are strong; 28 and the base things of the world, and the things that are despised, did God choose, *yea* [q]and the things that are not, that he might bring to nought the things that are: 29 that no flesh should glory before God. 30 But of him are ye in Christ Je'sus, who was made unto us wisdom from God, [r]and righteousness and sanctification, and redemption: 31 that, according as it is written, [s]He that glorieth, let him glory in the Lord.

2 And I, brethren, when I came unto you, came not with excellency of [a]speech or of wisdom, proclaiming to you the [b]testimony of God. 2 For I determined not to know anything among you, save Je'sus Christ,

---

[h] Or, *are perishing* [i] Or, *are being saved* [k] Is. xxix. 14. [l] Or, *age* [m] Gr. *thing preached.* [n] Or, *a Messiah* [o] Gr. *the called themselves.* [p] Or, *ye behold*

[q] Many ancient authorities omit *and.* [r] Or, *both righteousness and sanctification and redemption* s Jer. ix. 23 f. [a] Or, *word* [b] Many ancient authorities read *mystery.*

---

the gospel message. This thought is the key to all the verses that follow in this chapter.

19. *For it is written*, etc. The quotation is taken freely from the Septuagint, the Greek version of the Old Testament. See note on Acts 6.5, 6.

20. *Where is the wise*, etc. Where, as regards the redemption of man?

21. *In the wisdom of God.* By His providence. *Knew not God.* Whatever the world's wisdom in ante-Christian days had attained, it had not known God in his spirituality, purity, and love as revealed in Christ.

25. *The foolishness of God.* The

divine teaching which the world deems foolish. *The weakness of God.* The divine method which the world deems weak, as not employing arms, political power, or learned research. The highest example: a Saviour 'crucified through weakness' (2 Cor. 13.4).

CHAPTER 2

1. *And I, brethren*, etc. Paul's action was in accordance with this view of the divine simplicity of the Gospel.

2. *Not to know anything*, etc. Greek art, poetry, and philosophy,

and him crucified. 3 And I was
with you in weakness, and in
fear, and in much trembling.
4 And my ^cspeech and my
^dpreaching were not in persua-
sive words of wisdom, but in
demonstration of the Spirit and
of power: 5 that your faith
should not ^estand in the wisdom
of men, but in the power of God.

6 We speak wisdom, however,
among them that are fullgrown:
yet a wisdom not of this ^fworld,
nor of the rulers of this ^fworld,
who are coming to nought: 7
but we speak God's wisdom in a
mystery, *even* the *wisdom* that
hath been hidden, which God
foreordained before the ^fworlds
unto our glory: 8 which none of
the rulers of this ^fworld hath
known: for had they known it,
they would not have crucified
the Lord of glory: 9 but as it
is written,

^gThings which eye saw not,
   and ear heard not,
And *which* entered not into
   the heart of man,
Whatsoever things God prepared for them that love
   him.

10 ^hBut unto us God revealed
them through the Spirit: for the
Spirit searcheth all things, yea,
the deep things of God. 11 For
who among men knoweth the
things of a man, save the spirit
of the man, which is in him?
even so the things of God none
knoweth, save the Spirit of God.
12 But we received, not the
spirit of the ^kworld, but the
spirit which is from God; that
we might know the things that
were freely given to us of God.
13 Which things also we speak,
not in words which man's wisdom
teacheth, but which the Spirit
teacheth; ^lcombining spiritual

---

c Or, *word* *d* Gr. *thing preached.* *e* Gr.
be. *f* Or, *age;* and so in ver. 7, 8; but
not in ver. 12. *g* Is. lxiv. 4; lxv. 17.

h Some ancient authorities read *For.*
i Or, it *k* See ver. 6. *l* Or, *interpreting
spiritual things to spiritual* men

Roman law, politics and conquest,
trade and commerce, and the grand
and beautiful scenery of the lands
where he labored are unmentioned
in Paul's writings and discourses.
Only once at Athens did he quote
an obscure Greek poet, whom he did
not name. See notes on Acts 17.28.
3. *Weakness.* Physical weakness
in part. See ch. 11.30; Gal. 4.13, 14.
In fear and in much trembling, not
for consequences to himself but to
his message, the truth of the gospel
(1 Thess. 2.4; Tit. 1.3); like the anxiety of a general for his army and
his cause.
4, 5. *Power.* The power that
changes hearts and lives (ch. 6.11).
Should not stand in the wisdom of men.
Not in dependence on a human
teacher, but on the divine power.
6. *Wisdom among them that are
fullgrown.* Many truths of the gospel can be appreciated only by
those of some spiritual authority

(ch. 4.1-2; Heb. 5.12-14; 1 Pet. 2.2).
7. *Mystery.* In the Scriptures denoting: (a) something above the
ordinary human understanding (Mk.
4.11); (b) something formerly hidden in the counsels of God, but
afterwards revealed, as a plan understood by its own fulfilment. Mystery ever accompanies vastness,
depth, and power.
9. *Things which eye saw not,* etc.
A free quotation from Is. 64.4. This
refers to spiritual truths and blessings not to be known through the
senses or imagination, but only
when divinely revealed.
10, 11. *Through the Spirit.* The
meaning is that man's spirit is conscious of his human thoughts, feelings, and purposes; so the divine
Spirit, of the divine thoughts, feelings, and purposes. The Spirit of
God alone can reveal them. Ver.
12-16 are a practical unfolding of
this thought.

things with spiritual *words*. 14 Now the [m]natural man receiveth not the things of the Spirit of God: for they are foolishness unto him; and he cannot know them, because they are spiritually [n]judged. 15 But he that is spiritual [o]judgeth all things, and he himself is [n]judged of no man. 16 For who hath known the mind of the Lord, that he should instruct him? But we have the mind of Christ.

3 And I, brethren, could not speak unto you as unto spiritual, but as unto carnal, as unto babes in Christ. 2 I fed you with milk, not with meat; for ye were not yet able *to bear it*: nay, not even now are ye able; 3 for ye are yet carnal: for whereas there is among you jealousy and strife, are ye not carnal, and do ye not walk after the manner of men? 4 For when one saith, I am of Paul; and another, I am of A-pol′los; are ye not men? 5 What then is A-pol′los? and what is Paul? Ministers through whom ye believed; and each as the Lord gave to him. 6 I planted, A-pol′los watered; but God gave

the increase. 7 So then neither is he that planteth anything, neither he that watereth; but God that giveth the increase. 8 Now he that planteth and he that watereth are one: but each shall receive his own reward according to his own labor. 9 For we are God's fellow-workers: ye are God's [a]husbandry, God's building.

10 According to the grace of God which was given unto me, as a wise masterbuilder I laid a foundation; and another buildeth thereon. But let each man take heed how he buildeth thereon. 11 For other foundation can no man lay than that which is laid, which is Je′sus Christ. 12 But if any man buildeth on the foundation gold, silver, costly stones, wood, hay, stubble; 13 each man's work shall be made manifest: for the day shall declare it, because it is revealed in fire; [b]and the fire itself shall prove each man's work of what sort it is. 14 If any man's work shall abide which he built thereon, he shall receive a reward. 15 If any man's work shall be burned, he

---

m Or, unspiritual   Gr. psychical.   n Or, examined   o Or, examineth

a Gr. tilled land.   b Or, and each man's work, of what sort it is, the fire shall prove it

---

14. *The natural man,* etc. The unspiritual man cannot apprehend spiritual truth.

CHAPTER 3

1. *Carnal.* Not in the modern meaning of 'sensual,' but merely earthly, secular, worldly; having the worldly spirit of partisan strife, like politicians rather than Christian disciples.

10. *Another buildeth thereon.* Apollos, or any other successor. *Buildeth.* Applied here not to the build-

ing, by each disciple, of his own Christian character, but to the building by the Christian teachers of character in others or in the church as a whole.

13. *The day.* Of judgment; the day of days. *The fire.* A figurative expression for the severity of the test. See Mt. 7.24-27.

15. *He himself shall be saved.* The teacher who has built, however imperfectly, on the true foundation, himself shall be saved. The apostle does not intend any bitter denunciation of sincerely erring teachers.

shall suffer loss: but he himself shall be saved; yet so as through fire.

16 Know ye not that ye are a [c]temple of God, and *that* the Spirit of God dwelleth in you? 17 If any man destroyeth the [c]temple of God, him shall God destroy; for the [c]temple of God is holy, [d]and such are ye.

18 Let no man deceive himself. If any man thinketh that he is wise among you in this [e]world, let him become a fool, that he may become wise. 19 For the wisdom of this world is foolishness with God. For it is written, [f]He that taketh the wise in their craftiness: 20 and again, [g]The Lord knoweth the reasonings of the wise, that they are vain. 21 Wherefore let no one glory in men. For all things are yours; 22 whether Paul, or A-pol'los, or Ce'phas, or the world, or life, or death, or things present, or things to come; all are yours; 23 and ye are Christ's; and Christ is God's.

4 Let a man so account of us, as of ministers of Christ, and stewards of the mysteries of God. 2 Here, moreover, it is required in stewards, that a man be found faithful. 3 But with me it is a very small thing that I should be [a]judged of you, or of man's [b]judgment: yea, I [c]judge not mine own self. 4 For I know nothing against myself; yet am I not hereby justified: but he that [d]judgeth me is the Lord. 5 Wherefore judge nothing before the time, until the Lord come, who will both bring to light the hidden things of darkness, and make manifest the counsels of the hearts; and then shall each man have his praise from God.

6 Now these things, brethren, I have in a figure transferred to myself and A-pol'los for your sakes; that in us ye might learn not *to go* beyond the things which are written; that no one of you be puffed up for the one against the other. 7 For who maketh thee to differ? and what hast thou that thou didst not receive? but if thou didst receive it, why dost thou glory as if

---

c Or, *sanctuary*   *d* Or, *which temple ye are*
e Or, *age*   *f* Job v. 13.   *g* Ps. xciv. 11.

16, 17. *Know ye not that ye are a temple of God*, etc. The meaning of the verses is not the same as that of ch. 6.19, 20. In ver. 16, 17 the reference is not to the body of the individual Christian as the temple, but to the whole company of believers collectively, the church, as forming a divine temple (Eph. 2.21). Divisions and contentions tend to destroy the church; hence the warning here.

18-21. *If any man thinketh that he is wise*, etc. The apostle's advice is: Be spiritually simple-minded, and so wise to follow Christ alone. Then all helpful spiritual leadership and all things else are yours in him.

---

a Or, *examined*   *b* Gr. *day.*   See ch. 3.13.
c Or, *examine*   *d* Or, *examineth*

Human and divine wisdom are distinguished here, as in 1.25-30; 2.5-14, but with new applications.

CHAPTER 4

1. *Mysteries.* See note on ch. 2.7.
5. *His praise from God.* Such praise as belongs to him in God's perfect judgment.
6. *The things which are written.* No special text, but the teaching of the Scriptures as a whole, which no leader, however gifted, may supersede.
7. *Who maketh thee to differ?* 'Thee' is general in meaning, equivalent to 'any one,' especially any one

thou hadst not received it?
8 Already are ye filled, already
ye are become rich, ye have come
to reign without us: yea and I
would that ye did reign, that we
also might reign with you. 9
For, I think, God hath set forth
us the apostles last of all, as men
doomed to death: for we are
made a spectacle unto the world,
*both to angels and men. 10 We
are fools for Christ's sake, but
ye are wise in Christ; we are
weak, but ye are strong; ye have
glory, but we have dishonor.
11 Even unto this present hour
we both hunger, and thirst, and
are naked, and are buffeted, and
have no certain dwelling-place;
12 and we toil, working with
our own hands: being reviled,
we bless; being persecuted, we
endure; 13 being defamed, we
entreat: we are made as the
*filth of the world, the offscour-
ing of all things, even until now.

14 I write not these things to
shame you, but to admonish
you as my beloved children.

15 For though ye have ten
thousand tutors in Christ, yet
have ye not many fathers; for in
Christ Je'sus I begat you through
the *gospel. 16 I beseech you
therefore, be ye imitators of me.
17 For this cause have I sent
unto you Tim'o-thy, who is my
beloved and faithful child in the
Lord, who shall put you in
remembrance of my ways which
are in Christ, even as I teach
everywhere in every church. 18
Now some are puffed up, as
though I were not coming to you.
19 But I will come to you shortly,
if the Lord will; and I will know,
not the word of them that are
puffed up, but the power. 20
For the kingdom of God is not
in word, but in power. 21 What
will ye? shall I come unto you
with a rod, or in love and a spirit
of gentleness?

5 It is actually reported
that there is fornication
among you, and such fornication
as is not even among the Gen'-

e Or, *and to angels, and to men*   *f* Or, *refuse*   *g* Gr. *good tidings.* See marginal note on Mt. 4.23.

of the opposing teachers. The English 'you' is often so used: 'you will
find,' that is, any one will find. In
this and the following verses Paul
addresses the opposing teachers,
first in the singular, then in the
plural number, as if addressing them
personally. 'Any superiority which
any of you has is but the gift of
God, not a cause of pride or parti-
sanship.'

8-13. *Already are ye filled*, etc.
Contrasting the prosperity which
these leaders enjoyed, in a church
already established and strong, with
the hardships which Paul endured
in founding it, and which he, in
common with the other apostles, in
new fields still endured. *Naked.*
Insufficiently clothed (Mt. 25.36;
Jas. 2.15). *Working with our own*

hands. As he had done in Corinth
(Acts 18.3; 20.34).
15-20. *Fathers.* Paul claims
authority as founder and 'father' of
the church at Corinth. *Not in
word, but in power.* Not in eloquent
speech, but in the leavening influence of the Spirit (ch. 2.4, 5). This
is the key to all. Through everything and against everything the
spiritual purity and power of the
church and of the Christian life
must be maintained. This opens
the way to the strictness of the next
chapter.

CHAPTER 5

1. *Fornication.* Denounced here
as especially fatal to spiritual life
in the church at Corinth, a city
with a very dissolute population.

tiles, that one *of you* hath his father's wife. 2 And *a*ye are puffed up, and *b*did not rather mourn, that he that had done this deed might be taken away from among you. 3 For I verily, being absent in body but present in spirit, have already as though I were present judged him that hath so wrought this thing, 4 in the name of our Lord Je'sus, ye being gathered together, and my spirit, *with the power of our Lord Je'sus, 5 to deliver such a one unto Satan for the destruction of the flesh, that the spirit

may be saved in the day of the Lord *c*Je'sus. 6 Your glorying is not good. Know ye not that a little leaven leaveneth the whole lump? 7 Purge out the old leaven, that ye may be a new lump, even as ye are unleavened. For our passover also hath been sacrificed, *even* Christ: 8 wherefore let us *d*keep the feast, not with old leaven, neither with the leaven of malice and wickedness, but with the unleavened bread of sincerity and truth.

9 I wrote unto you in my epistle to have no company with

---

a Or, *are ye puffed up?* *b* Or, *did ye not rather mourn, . . . you?*

c Some ancient authorities omit *Jesus.*
d Gr. *keep festival.*

The discussion of the right relation of the sexes extends through chs. 5-7, with a brief digression at ch. 6.1-9. *His father's wife.* His step-mother. Whether the father was dead or divorced, and whether the new connection was in the form of marriage or concubinage, is not certain. These considerations the apostle passed over as immaterial compared with the one fact that the woman was 'his father's wife.' That was enough.

2. *Ye are puffed up.* 'You are actually proud of such transgression.' The views and practices here condemned by the apostle evidently had the approval of the false teachers, and were undoubtedly based upon a perverted view of Christian liberty—that faith sets the Christian free from obligation to obey the moral law. Paul's opposition to such teachers was a contest for the very existence of the church as a spiritual body.

4. *Ye being gathered together.* The separation was to be by the whole assembled church, punishment inflicted by the many (2 Cor. 2.6).

5. *To deliver such a one unto Satan.* The church was a body of those redeemed from the power of Satan; formal separation from their company was regarded as a delivery back to Satan, and to the world which is under his power, as the offender had chosen his service.

The sensual vices here condemned do naturally and commonly result in the destruction of the flesh. That there was no sentence to perdition, or loss of the soul, is expressly stated in the concluding words, 'that the spirit may be saved in the day of the Lord Jesus.' See also 2 Cor. 2.6-10, with which this verse must be compared in order to be understood.

6-8. *Leaven.* Tolerated corruption will extend in the church as the action of leaven extends in meal. The purification of the church by removal of the offenders is compared to the removal of leaven from Jewish homes at the feast of the Passover (Ex. 12.15, 19; 13.3, 7).

9. *In my epistle.* Evidently referring to a previous letter. *To have no company,* etc. Ver. 9-13 explain the purpose of church discipline, the necessary separation of the obviously impure from a society that stands for purity, unless it would imperil its own existence. *Not at all, meaning,* etc. The apostle explains that his purpose is not the seclusion or separation of the disciples from the evil elements of the world in the common relations of life. He does not mean that Christians should go out of the world. See Jn. 17.15. Monastic seclusion is not for a moment contemplated. *No, not to eat.* Have no familiar intercourse. In the case

fornicators; 10 ^enot at all *meaning* with the fornicators of this world, or with the covetous and extortioners, or with idolaters; for then must ye needs go out of the world: 11 but ^fas it is, I wrote unto you not to keep company, if any man that is named a brother be a fornicator, or covetous, or an idolater, or a reviler, or a drunkard, or an extortioner; with such a one no, not to eat. 12 For what have I to do with judging them that are without? Do not ye judge them that are within? 13 But them that are without God judgeth. Put away the wicked man from among yourselves.

6 Dare any of you, having a matter against ^ahis neighbor, go to law before the unrighteous, and not before the saints? 2 Or know ye not that the saints shall judge the world? and if the world is judged by you, are ye un-

worthy ^bto judge the smallest matters? 3 Know ye not that we shall judge angels? how much more, things that pertain to this life? 4 If then ye have ^cto judge things pertaining to this life, ^ddo ye set them to judge who are of no account in the church? 5 I say *this* to move you to shame. ^eWhat, cannot there be *found* among you one wise man who shall be able to decide between his brethren, 6 but brother goeth to law with brother, and that before unbelievers? 7 Nay, already it is altogether ^fa defect in you, that ye have lawsuits one with another. Why not rather take wrong? why not rather be defrauded? 8 Nay, but ye yourselves do wrong, and defraud, and that *your* brethren. 9 Or know ye not that the unrighteous shall not inherit the kingdom of God? Be not deceived: neither fornicators, nor

---

e Or, *not altogether with the fornicators &c.*   *f* Or, *now I write*   *a* Gr. *the other.* See Rom. 13.8.   *b* Gr. *of the smallest tri-* | *bunals.*   *c* Gr. *tribunals pertaining to.*   *d* Or, *set them . . . church*   *e* Or, *Is it so, that there cannot &c.*   *f* Or, *a loss to you*

---

of one that is 'named a brother,' but is false to his profession, withdraw from all association indicating brotherhood.

13. *Put away . . from among yourselves.* The limit of church action, carrying none of the meaning that in the later times came to be attached to the word 'excommunication.'

CHAPTER 6

1-8. *Dare any of you, having a matter,* etc. Matters relating to the conduct of Christians are to be decided by Christians within the church (5.12-13). Now the apostle applies the thought to controversies or claims of any kind. These also are to be decided within the church. The objection here is against Christians appearing voluntarily before the heathen courts of that day, with their recognition of heathen

usages and divinities. When summoned before them Paul himself did not deny their authority nor refuse to plead (Acts 24.1-21; 25.6-12; 2 Tim. 4.16, 17). *Against his neighbor.* That is, one Christian against another.

4. *If then ye have to judge,* etc. This is considered by many as a command rather than a question. In either case the implication is the same, that those least esteemed in the church would be more appropriate judges of Christian matters than any heathen magistrates.

5. *To move you to shame.* There is a touch of irony here; the plea is for Christian arbitration—in modern phrase, 'settlement out of court' in such cases. The Hague Arbitral Court for national differences is here seen to emanate from Christian teaching.

idolaters, nor adulterers, nor effeminate, nor abusers of themselves with men, 10 nor thieves, nor covetous, nor drunkards, nor revilers, nor extortioners, shall inherit the kingdom of God. 11 And such were some of you: but ye *g*were washed, but ye were sanctified, but ye were justified in the name of the Lord Je'sus Christ, and in the Spirit of our God.

12 All things are lawful for me; but not all things are expedient. All things are lawful for me; but I will not be brought under the power of any. 13 Meats for the belly, and the belly for meats: but God shall bring to nought both it and them. But the body is not for fornication, but for the Lord; and the Lord for the body: 14 and God both raised the Lord, and will raise up us through his power. 15 Know ye not that your bodies are members of

Christ? shall I then take away the members of Christ, and make them members of a harlot? God forbid. 16 Or know ye not that he that is joined to a harlot is one body? for, *h*The twain, saith he, shall become one flesh. 17 But he that is joined unto the Lord is one spirit. 18 Flee fornication. Every sin that a man doeth is without the body; but he that committeth fornication sinneth against his own body. 19 Or know ye not that your body is a *i*temple of the Holy Spirit which is in you, which ye have from God? and ye are not your own; 20 for ye were bought with a price: glorify God therefore in your body.

7 Now concerning the things whereof ye wrote: It is good for a man not to touch a woman. 2 But, because of fornications,

---

g Gr. *washed yourselves.*

h Gen. ii. 24.   *i* Or, *sanctuary*

11. *Ye were washed.* Something far higher—a spiritual and divine cleansing from sin (Heb. 10.22; Rev. 7.14).

12. *All things are lawful,* etc. Paul here sets forth the doctrine of Christian liberty. The Christian is not under the bondage of the ceremonial laws of Judaism. He has freedom in the use of all the good things of God. But this liberty must be modified at times by the exigencies of situations and surroundings.

13. *Meats.* Food in general. *The belly.* The digestive tract, commonly expressed, in modern phrase, by 'the stomach.' *But the body is not,* etc. From this point the apostle returns to the subject of pure family and social relations through ch. 7.15-17.

18. *Without the body.* The body as mere material substance cannot do moral wrong.

19. *The temple of the Holy Spirit.* (2 Cor. 6.16).

20. *Price.* The voluntary death of Christ (1 Pet. 1.18; 19).

CHAPTER 7

1. *The things whereof ye wrote.* The matters dealt with in this chapter, and others later, are treated in answer to written questions which the Corinthians had sent to the apostle. The first question is concerning marriage and celibacy. The frightful dissoluteness of the heathen society of the day led many earnest Christians to seek a remedy in the absolute separation of the sexes—a tendency which resulted in the vast number of hermits, monks, and nuns of a later period. *It is good for a man,* etc. It is well in view of the social conditions prevailing and the vicissitudes that were before the church at that period (ver. 25-27). A counsel of expediency, not a rule of duty.

2. *His own wife,* etc. Forbidding both concubinage and polygamy.

let each man have his own wife, and let each woman have her own husband. 3 Let the husband render unto the wife her due: and likewise also the wife unto the husband. 4 The wife hath not power over her own body, but the husband: and likewise also the husband hath not power over his own body, but the wife. 5 Defraud ye not one the other, except it be by consent for a season, that ye may give yourselves unto prayer, and may be together again, that Satan tempt you not because of your incontinency. 6 But this I say by way of concession, not of commandment. 7 ^aYet I would that all men were even as I myself. Howbeit each man hath his own gift from God, one after this manner, and another after that.

8 But I say to the unmarried and to widows, It is good for them if they abide even as I. 9 But if they have not continency, let them marry: for it is better to marry than to burn. 10 But unto the married I give charge, *yea* not I, but the Lord, That the wife depart not from her husband 11 (but should she depart, let her remain unmarried, or else be reconciled to her husband); and that the husband leave not his wife. 12

But to the rest say I, not the Lord: If any brother hath an unbelieving wife, and she is content to dwell with him, let him not leave her. 13 And the woman that hath an unbelieving husband, and he is content to dwell with her, let her not leave her husband. 14 For the unbelieving husband is sanctified in the wife, and the unbelieving wife is sanctified in the brother: else were your children unclean; but now are they holy. 15 Yet if the unbelieving departeth, let him depart: the brother or the sister is not under bondage in such *cases*: but God hath called ^bus in peace. 16 For how knowest thou, O wife, whether thou shalt save thy husband? or how knowest thou, O husband, whether thou shalt save thy wife? 17 Only, as the Lord hath distributed to each man, as God hath called each, so let him walk. And so ordain I in all the churches. 18 Was any man called being circumcised? let him not become uncircumcised. Hath any been called in uncircumcision? let him not be circumcised. 19 Circumcision is nothing, and uncircumcision is nothing; but the keeping of the commandments of God. 20 Let each man abide in that calling wherein he was called. 21 Wast

---

a Many ancient authorities read *For.*

b Many ancient authorities read *you.*

---

7. *As I myself.* One of many passages that show the apostle Paul to have been unmarried (ch. 9.5).

10. *Not I, but the Lord.* No longer his own opinion, as in ver. 6, but the divine command of the perpetuity of marriage (Mt. 5.32; 19.4-9).

12. *I, not the Lord.* As to the special case of a Christian married to

an unbelieving husband or wife the apostle had no special divine command, but only his own Christian interpretation of the divine law.

14. *Is sanctified.* Or brought into a hallowed relation. *Your children.* They are in a like hallowed relation by their connection with the believer.

21. *A bondservant.* Slavery, which

thou called being a bondservant? care not for it: ᶜnay, even if thou canst become free, use *it* rather. 22 For he that was called in the Lord being a bondservant, is the Lord's freedman: likewise he that was called being free, is Christ's bondservant. 23 Ye were bought with a price; become not bondservants of men. 24 Brethren, let each man, wherein he was called, therein abide with God.

25 Now concerning virgins I have no commandment of the Lord: but I give my judgment, as one that hath obtained mercy of the Lord to be trustworthy. 26 I think therefore that this is good by reason of the distress that is upon us, *namely*, that it is good for a man ᵈto be as he is. 27 Art thou bound unto a wife? seek not to be loosed. Art thou loosed from a wife? seek not a wife. 28 But shouldest thou marry, thou hast not sinned; and if a virgin marry, she hath not sinned. Yet such shall have tribulation in the flesh: and I would spare you. 29 But this I say, brethren, the time ᵉis shortened, that henceforth both those that have wives may be as though they had none; 30 and those that weep, as though they wept not; and those that rejoice, as though they rejoiced not; and those that buy, as though they possessed not; 31 and those that use the world, as not using it to the full: for the fashion of this world passeth away. 32 But I would have you to be free from cares. He that is unmarried is careful for the things of the Lord, how he may please the Lord: 33 but he that is married is careful for the things of the world, how he may please his ᶠwife, 34 and is divided. *So* also the woman that is unmarried and the virgin is careful for the things of the Lord, that she may be holy both in body and in spirit: but she that is married is careful for the things of the world, how she may please

---

c Or, *but if*   *d* Gr. *so to be.*   *e* Or, *is shortened henceforth, that both those &c.*   *f* Some ancient authorities read *wife. And*

there is a difference also between the wife and the virgin. She that is unmarried is careful &c.

---

was part of the Roman political system in the apostle's time, and is impossible to abolish, is given as a strong instance to inculcate the doing of Christian duty in an existing relation.

22. *Called in the Lord.* Called into the Christian life. 'Called' has the same sense in ver. 17, 18, 20.

23. *Bought with a price.* See 6.20; 1 Pet. 1.18, 19.

25. *Virgins.* Evidently, as ver. 36, 37 show, unmarried women still in their parents' home. The Corinthians appear to have asked instruction on some cases of this kind. *I have no commandment of the Lord.* No command laid down by Christ in his earthly ministry—nor any special revelation from him.

26. *The distress that is upon us.* The unsettled conditions of the times and of the rising church, with the probability of persecution—all viewed as part of the 'tribulation.'

28. *Hast not sinned.* See Eph. 5.21; 1 Tim. 5.14; Heb. 13.4; 1 Tim. 4.3. *Tribulation in the flesh.* The special cares and sorrows which those having families are subject to in troublous times.

29-31. *The time is shortened*, etc. The controlling thought is, all that is merely earthly is brief and transitory.

31. *The fashion of this world.* This earthly scheme of things, with its buying and selling, its possessions, its joys and sorrows passeth away.

her husband. 35 And this I say for your own profit; not that I may cast a *g*snare upon you, but for that which is seemly, and that ye may attend upon the Lord without distraction. 36 But if any man thinketh that he behaveth himself unseemly toward his *h*virgin *daughter*, if she be past the flower of her age, and if need so requireth, let h n do what he will; he sinneth not; let them marry. 37 But he that standeth stedfast in his heart, having no necessity, but hath power as touching his own will, and hath determined this in his own heart, to keep his own *h*virgin *daughter*, shall do well. 38 So then both he that giveth

his own *h*virgin *daughter* in marriage doeth well; and he that giveth her not in marriage, shall do better. 39 A wife is bound for so long time as her husband liveth; but if the husband be *i*dead, she is free to be married to whom she will; only in the Lord. 40 But she is happier if she abide as she is, after my judgment: and I think that I also have the Spirit of God.

8 Now concerning things sacrificed to idols: We know that we all have knowledge. Knowledge puffeth up, but love *a*edifieth. 2 If any man thinketh that he knoweth anything, he

---

g Or, *constraint* Gr. noose. *h* Or, *virgin* (omitting daughter)

i Gr. *fallen asleep.* See Acts 7.60. *a* Gr. *buildeth up.*

36, 37. *If any man thinketh,* etc. To be understood in view of the then universal custom among Jews, Greeks, and Romans, that the father or guardian disposed of the daughter's hand.

38. *Shall do better.* In view of the troublous times, as in ver. 26. The same thought is in view throughout this entire chapter.

39, 40. *For so long time,* etc. Maintaining the widow's right of remarriage, with limitations as in ver. 26, 27, 38. *Only in the Lord.* In accordance with his Christian relations and duties. *I think that I also have,* etc. See ver. 6, 12, 25. Meant to be a mild form of asserting his assurance.

CHAPTER 8

1. *Things sacrificed to idols.* In very many sacrifices, both among the Jews and the heathen, only a portion was consumed on the altar, the greater part being retained by the worshipper and carried away to be eaten by himself and friends or guests. The eating of such sacrificial food was deemed an act of worship n honor of the divinity to

whom it had been offered (ch. 10.18, 19). In some cases the feast might be held within the Temple enclosure (ver. 10). It might also be at the worshipper's home or elsewhere. The sacrificial meat might even be 'sold in the shambles' (ch. 10.25). For such sacrificial feasts among the Jews, see Lev. 7.15, 16; 22.30; 1 Sam. 16.2-5. The eating of such food by a Christian might easily seem, either to heathen or Christian observers, a recognition of idol worship (ver. 10). *Knowledge.* Intellectual apprehension of truth and duty, which was held by many, especially among the philosophic Greeks, to be all that was required. The apostle proceeds to show that there is something higher. *Knowledge puffeth up.* Tends to self-confidence and arrogance. *Love edifieth.* As in the margin, 'buildeth up,' either the individual Christian or the church, as a whole, in Christian character and spiritual grace (ch. 14.4, 5, 12; Rom. 14.19; Eph. 4.12; 1 Thess. 5.11).

2. *If any man thinketh that he knoweth anything,* etc. He who knows the most sees most clearly how much more there is to know.

knoweth not yet as he ought to know; 3 but if any man loveth God, the same is known by him. 4 Concerning therefore the eating of things sacrificed to idols, we know that no idol is *anything* in the world, and that there is no God but one. 5 For though there be that are called gods, whether in heaven or on earth; as there are gods many, and lords many; 6 yet to us there is one God, the Father, of whom are all things, and we unto him; and one Lord, Je′sus Christ, through whom are all things, and we through him. 7 Howbeit there is not in all men that knowledge: but some, being used until now to the idol, eat as *of* a thing sacrificed to an idol; and their conscience being weak is defiled. 8 But food will not *b*commend us to God: neither,

if we eat not, *c*are we the worse; nor, if we eat, *d*are we the better. 9 But take heed lest by any means this *e*liberty of yours become a stumblingblock to the weak. 10 For if a man see thee who hast knowledge sitting at meat in an idol's temple, will not his conscience, if he is weak, *f*be emboldened to eat things sacrificed to idols? 11 For *g*through thy knowledge he that is weak perisheth, the brother for whose sake Christ died. 12 And thus, sinning against the brethren, and wounding their conscience when it is weak, ye sin against Christ. 13 Wherefore, if meat causeth my brother to stumble, I will eat no flesh for evermore, that I cause not my brother to stumble.

9 Am I not free? am I not an apostle? have I not seen Je′sus our Lord? are not ye my

---

b Gr. *present.*

c Gr. *do we lack.*   *d* Gr. *do we abound.*
e Or. *power*   *f* Gr. *be builded up.*   *g* Gr. *in.*

In the field of knowledge humility sharpens vision.

3. *If any man loveth God*, etc. Love brings the soul into touch with God who 'is love,' as no intellectual knowledge can do (1 Jn. 4.8). *Is known by him.* In recognized and approved fellowship and communion (Mt. 7.23).

4. *That no idol is anything.* Instructed Christians did not recognize idols as having any real existence, even as false divinities. Idols were but empty names.

7. *There is not in all men that knowledge.* Many new converts had not attained this clear conception. Love will care patiently and tenderly for such.

9. *Take heed lest*, etc. Love cares for the effect of one's example, especially upon those who have less knowledge, or are in any way spiritually 'weak.' *A stumblingblock.* An occasion of yielding to temptation or sin.

10. *Thee who hast knowledge.* An

enlightened Christian must make allowance for the narrowness of one who has not his knowledge, and must sometimes therefore deny himself what he sees to be only innocent and beneficial. *Sitting at meat in an idol's temple.* The strongest case cited as an example. The weak brother 'sees' the act, but cannot read the motive, which is known only to God.

13. *If meat causeth my brother to stumble*, etc. Rather than risk such a result as mentioned in ver. 11, 12, I will make any, even the uttermost, self-denial. Compare this chapter with ch. 10.18-33; also with Rom. 14, which discusses the eating of food forbidden by the Jewish ceremonial law, applying to that case the same principles.

CHAPTER 9

1. *Have I not seen Jesus our Lord*, etc. Paul here discusses his apostolic authority and conduct, evi-

work in the Lord? 2 If to others I am not an apostle, yet at least I am to you; for the seal of mine apostleship are ye in the Lord. 3 My defence to them that examine me is this. 4 Have we no right to eat and to drink? 5 Have we no right to lead about a wife that is a *a*believer, even as the rest of the apostles, and the brethren of the Lord, and Ce′-phas? 6 Or I only and Bar′na-bas, have we not a right to forbear working? 7 What soldier ever serveth at his own charges? who planteth a vineyard, and eateth not the fruit thereof? or who feedeth a flock, and eateth not of the milk of the flock? 8 Do I speak these things after the manner of men? or saith not the law also the same? 9 For it is written in the law of Mo′ses, *b*Thou shalt not muzzle the ox when he treadeth out the corn. Is it for the oxen that God careth, 10 or saith he it *c*assuredly for

our sake? Yea, for our sake it was written: because he that ploweth ought to plow in hope, and he that thresheth, *to thresh* in hope of partaking. 11 If we sowed unto you spiritual things, is it a great matter if we shall reap your carnal things? 12 If others partake of *this* right over you, do not we yet more? Nevertheless we did not use this right; but we bear all things, that we may cause no hindrance to the *d*gospel of Christ. 13 Know ye not that they that minister about sacred things eat *of* the things of the temple, *and* they that wait upon the altar have their portion with the altar? 14 Even so did the Lord ordain that they that proclaim the *d*gospel should live of the *d*gospel. 15 But I have used none of these things: and I write not these things that it may be so done in my case; for *it were* good for me rather to die, than that any man should make

---

a Gr. *sister.*   *b* Dt. xxv. 4.   *c* Or, *alto-* | *gether*   *d* See marginal note on ch. 4.15.

---

dently in answer to objections brought by some of the opposing parties mentioned in chs. 7.11, 12; 3.8-22, and perhaps mentioned in the Corinthians' letter of inquiry, 'the things whereof ye wrote.' Those who called themselves 'of Cephas' and 'of Christ' apparently objected to Paul that he was not one of the original twelve, and had not attended the personal ministry of Jesus.

2. *The seal of mine apostleship.* The fact that God had so blessed his labors as to lead the Corinthians to Christ proved Paul's call to be genuine.

3. *Defence.* Probably referring to what follows. *Them that examine me.* Those who sit in judgment on me; the opposers already mentioned.

4. *To eat and to drink.* That is, to

receive food and drink at the cost of the church; a right given by Christ himself (Mt. 10.9, 10; Lk. 10.4-8).

5. *To lead about a wife.* Not only to be married, but to be accompanied by one's wife in ministerial travels among the churches, both being supported by the church, as indicated by ver. 4. *The rest of the apostles,* etc. Plainly showing that these were married, notably Cephas or Peter (Mk. 1.30, 31).

6. *Working.* That is, for our own support, while preaching the gospel (Acts 18.3; 20.34, 35).

7-14. *What soldier ever serveth.* etc. These verses contain a defence of the right of ministerial support. Paul feared lest his example should be pleaded against that right. *Carnal things.* Earthly enjoyments and supplies.

my glorying void. 16 For if I ᵉpreach the gospel, I have nothing to glory of; for necessity is laid upon me; for woe is unto me, if I ᵉpreach not the gospel. 17 For if I do this of mine own will, I have a reward: but if not of mine own will, I have a stewardship intrusted to me. 18 What then is my reward? That, when I ᵉpreach the gospel, I may make the ᶠgospel without charge, so as not to use to the full my right in the ᶠgospel. 19 For though I was free from all *men,* I brought myself under bondage to all, that I might gain the more. 20 And to the Jews I became as a Jew, that I might gain Jews; to them that are under the law, as under the law, not being myself under the law, that I might gain them that are under the law; 21 to them that

are without law, as without law, not being without law to God, but under law to Christ, that I might gain them that are without law. 22 To the weak I became weak, that I might gain the weak: I am become all things to all men, that I may by all means save some. 23 And I do all things for the ᶠgospel's sake, that I may be a joint partaker thereof. 24 Know ye not that they that run in a ᵍrace run all, but one receiveth the prize? Even so run, that ye may attain. 25 And every man that striveth in the games exerciseth self-control in all things. Now they *do it* to receive a corruptible crown; but we an incorruptible. 26 I therefore so run, as not uncertainly; so ʰfight I, as not beating the air: 27 but I ⁱbuffet my body, and bring it into bondage: lest

---

e See marginal note on ch. 1.17.   *f* See marginal note on ch. 4.15.

g Gr. *race-course.*   *h* Gr. *box.*   *i* Gr. *bruise.* Lk. 18.5.

---

16. *Woe is unto me, if I preach not the gospel.* Not a statement of the universal ministerial call, but of the condemnation which had stricken him down as a persecutor, and of the obligation which laid upon him at his conversion the necessity of preaching the gospel.

18. *My reward.* No earthly recompense, but the privilege of giving the gospel freely to men.

20. *Became as a Jew.* In all innocent compliances.

21. *Them that are without law.* Those who are without the ceremonial law; the Gentiles. *Not being without law to God.* Never disobeying the moral law, but pushing the ceremonial law aside in order to win those who have never been bound by it.

22. *Gain the weak.* With all generous and self-denying consideration of the needs of their weakness (ch. 8.9-13).

23. *That I may be a joint partaker*

thereof. Win the gospel's glorious reward.

25. *Exerciseth self-control in all things.* The comparison is to the Isthmian games celebrated with great splendor at Corinth. The athletes of that day, as of our own, denied themselves every indulgence that would hinder them from winning the prize. *A corruptible crown.* A fading wreath. The prize in the games was a wreath of laurel, wild olive, pine, or sometimes only of parsley. *But we an incorruptible.* (1 Tim. 4.8; 1 Pet. 5.4; Rev. 2.10; 4.10).

26. *As not beating the air.* The figure changes to that of the boxer. Not like such a one 'beating the air' with empty flourishes while no antagonist is within reach.

27. *I buffet my body.* I beat down all bodily appetites and desires. *Bring it into bondage.* Reduce the physical into entire subjection to the spiritual nature. *After that I*

by any means, after that I *k*have preached to others, I myself should be rejected.

10 For I would not, brethren, have you ignorant, that our fathers were all under the cloud, and all passed through the sea; 2 and were all baptized *a*unto Mo'ses in the cloud and in the sea; 3 and did all eat the same spiritual food; 4 and did all drink the same spiritual drink: for they drank of a spiritual rock that followed them: and the rock was *b*Christ. 5 Howbeit with most of them God was not well pleased: for they were overthrown in the wilderness. 6 Now *c*these things were our examples, to the intent we should not lust after evil things, as they also lusted. 7 Neither be ye idolaters, as were some of them; as it is

written, *d*The people sat down to eat and drink, and rose up to play. 8 Neither let us commit fornication, as some of them committed, and fell in one day three and twenty thousand. 9 Neither let us make trial of the *e*Lord, as some of them made trial, and perished by the serpents. 10 Neither murmur ye, as some of them murmured, and perished by the destroyer. 11 Now these things happened unto them *f*by way of example; and they were written for our admonition, upon whom the ends of the ages are come. 12 Wherefore let him that thinketh he standeth take heed lest he fall. 13 There hath no temptation taken you but such as man can bear: but God is faithful, who will not suffer you to be tempted

---

k Or, *have been a herald*   *a* Gr. *into.* *b* Or, *the Christ* Comp. Heb. 11.26.   *c* Or, *in those things they became figures of us*

d Ex. xxxii. 6.   *e* Some ancient authorities read *Christ.*   *f* Gr. *by way of figure.*

---

have preached to others. See Mt. 7.22, 23. *Rejected.* Either as unworthy to be a preacher or unworthy of the crown of life.

CHAPTER 10

1. *Our fathers.* Many of the Corinthians were not Israelites, but the apostle Paul, as a Jew, naturally refers to the sacred history of his own people. The indication is that the Old Testament Scriptures were used in the Christian church, and that even Gentile converts were expected to be familiar with them.

2. *Baptized unto Moses.* The allusion here is to baptism in the spiritual sense, since the Israelites were not wet by the cloud or the sea (Ex. 14.19, 22). The passage of the Red Sea separated the Israelites from their slavery in Egypt, as baptism separated the believer from slavery to sin and the world.

3, 4. *Spiritual food,* etc. So-called as affording spiritual nourishment—

not mere manna (Ex. 16.14-26) nor mere water (Ex. 17.5, 6); but symbols of Jehovah's care. *A spiritual rock that followed them.* There is no evidence nor probability that the apostle here refers to an obscure and late rabbinical tradition that the rock of Ex. 17.5, 6, and of Num. 20.7-11, followed, or that the streams followed, the Israelites in their journeys. He uses the 'rock' as a symbol and type of the Angel of the Covenant that 'followed' the people, a 'spiritual rock,' and explains the statement by the words, 'that rock was Christ.'

6. *Examples.* Not for imitation, but for warning. See ver. 11.

11. *The ends of the ages.* The last days, the closing dispensation, called also the 'last time' (1 Jn. 2.18).

12. *Him that thinketh he standeth.* Directed especially against the self-confidence of many of the Corinthians, but conveying a universal warning.

above that ye are able; but will with the temptation make also the way of escape, that ye may be able to endure it.

14 Wherefore, my beloved, flee from idolatry. 15 I speak as to wise men; judge ye what I say. 16 The cup of blessing which we bless, is it not a *g*communion of the blood of Christ? The *h*bread which we break, is it not a *g*communion of the body of Christ? 17 *i*seeing that we, who are many, are one *h*bread, one body: for we all partake *k*of the one *h*bread. 18 Behold Is′ra-el after the flesh: have not they that eat the sacrifices communion with the altar? 19 What say I then? that a thing sacrificed to idols is anything, or that an idol is anything? 20 But *I say*, that the things which the Gen′tiles sacrifice, they sacrifice to demons, and not to God: and I would not that ye should have commun-

ion with demons. 21 Ye cannot drink the cup of the Lord, and the cup of demons: ye cannot partake of the table of the Lord, and of the table of demons. 22 Or do we provoke the Lord to jealousy? are we stronger than he?

23 All things are lawful; but not all things are expedient. All things are lawful; but not all things *l*edify. 24 Let no man seek his own, but *each* *m*his neighbor's *good*. 25 Whatsoever is sold in the shambles, eat, asking no question for conscience' sake; 26 for the earth is the Lord's, and the fulness thereof. 27 If one of them that believe not biddeth you *to a feast*, and ye are disposed to go; whatsoever is set before you, eat, asking no question for conscience' sake. 28 But if any man say unto you, This hath been offered in sacrifice, eat not, for his sake that showed it, and for con-

---

g Or. *participation in*   *h* Or., *loaf*   *i* Or., *seeing that there is one bread, we, who are*   *many, are one body*   *k* Gr. *from.*   *l* Gr. *build up.*   *m* Gr. *the other's.* See Rom. 13.8.

14. *Flee from idolatry.* The apostle here returns to the question of food offered to idols. See ch. 8 and notes thereon.

15-17. *The cup of blessing,* etc. The spiritual feast of the Christian, the Lord's Supper, signifies consecration to and unity with Christ (ch. 11.27-34). The reality of the sacramental gifts and blessings is also here asserted.

19. *That an idol is anything.* A question to which a negative answer is expected, equivalent to an emphatic denial.

20. *Sacrifice to demons.* The heathen divinities, impersonations of human passions, crimes, and vices raised to superhuman power, are fitly called demons. Gentiles sacrificed to divinities such as these, though they had no real existence (8.4; 10.19). *Communion with de-*

mons. The idol feast symbolized communion with the idol (demon), just as the Lord's cup and table symbolized communion with Christ.

21. *Ye cannot drink the cup,* etc. See Mt. 6.24; Lk. 16,13.

23. *All things are lawful.* etc. See ch. 6.12.

25-27. *Eat, asking no question.* The food to be partaken of is of no consequence except by the recognized significance of its associations. If no such significance is known or recognized, no harm or wrong is done; no idol worship is then symbolized. *For conscience' sake.* The Christian is not to disturb business or social usages by obtruding conscientious scruples where no moral wrong is manifest.

28. *But if any man say unto you,* etc. If others recognize the food as so dedicated that your partaking

science' sake: 29 conscience, I say, not thine own, but the other's; for why is my liberty judged by another conscience? 30 [n]If I partake with thankfulness, why am I evil spoken of for that for which I give thanks? 31 Whether therefore ye eat, or drink, or whatsoever ye do, do all to the glory of God. 32 Give no occasion of stumbling, either to Jews, or to Greeks, or to the church of God: 33 even as I also please all men in all things, not seeking mine own profit, but the *profit* of the many, that they **11** may be saved. 1 Be ye imitators of me, even as I also am of Christ.

2 Now I praise you that ye remember me in all things, and hold fast the traditions, even as

I delivered them to you. 3 But I would have you know, that the head of every man is Christ; and the head of the woman is the man; and the head of Christ is God. 4 Every man praying or prophesying, having his head covered, dishonoreth his head. 5 But every woman praying or prophesying with her head unveiled dishonoreth her head; for it is one and the same thing as if she were shaven. 6 For if a woman is not veiled, let her also be shorn: but if it is a shame to a woman to be shorn or shaven, let her be veiled. 7 For a man indeed ought not to have his head veiled, forasmuch as he is the image and glory of God: but the woman is the glory of the man. 8 For the man is not of the woman; but the woman of

---

[n] Or, *If I by grace partake*

---

would seem to approve a wrongful dedication, then abstain.

29, 30. *Why is my liberty judged*, etc. That is, why should I be obliged to use my liberty so as to come under condemnation before another's conscience? The word here translated 'judged' often has the sense of condemnatory judgment (Acts 7.7; Rom. 3.7; Heb. 13.4). *That for which I give thanks.* That which is so innocent in my view that I can even give thanks for it— why should I indulge in it, if it will cause me and my religion to be evilly spoken of?

CHAPTER 11

2. *In all things.* 'All' is often used in the New Testament in a general sense, not necessarily including every one (Mt. 3.5, 6; 21.10; Lk. 21.38). Here the apostle himself mentions some exceptions, but thoughtfully begins by commending their faithfulness on the whole or for the most part.

2. *Traditions.* Matters orally de-

livered; ordinarily meaning handed down from generation to generation; but here referring to the precepts of doctrine or duty orally delivered by the apostles to the churches in the first Christian generation.

3. *The head of every man is Christ.* There are two Greek words for 'man'; one for man as a human being; the other contrasting man with woman or child; the latter form is used for man in every instance in this chapter (ver. 3-16). Christ is normally and rightly the head of every man, actually of every Christian. *The head of the woman is the man.* More fully explained in Eph. 5.22-33. *The head of Christ is God.* Said of Christ in his mediatorial capacity (ch. 15.28; Jn. 8.29; 14.24, 28).

4-16. *Every man praying or prophesying*, etc. The propriety of covering or veiling the head is one to be understood in accordance with the customs of those countries at that period. The veil in public places was then and there the mark of honorable and modest womanhood,

the man: 9 for neither was the man created for the woman; but the woman for the man: 10 for this cause ought the woman to have *a sign of* authority on her head, because of the angels. 11 Nevertheless, neither is the woman without the man, nor the man without the woman, in the Lord. 12 For as the woman is of the man, so is the man also by the woman; but all things are of God. 13 Judge ye *a*in yourselves: is it seemly that a woman pray unto God unveiled? 14 Doth not even nature itself teach you, that, if a man have long hair, it is a dishonor to him? 15 But if a woman have long hair, it is a glory to her: for her hair is given her for a covering. 16 But if any man seemeth to be contentious, we have no such custom, neither the churches of God.

17 But in giving you this charge, I praise you not, that ye come together not for the better but for the worse. 18 For first of all, when ye come together *b*in the church, I hear that *c*divisions exist among you; and I partly believe it. 19 For there must be also *d*factions among you, that they that are approved may be made manifest among you. 20 When therefore ye assemble yourselves together, it is not possible to eat the Lord's supper: 21 for in your eating each one taketh before *other* his own supper; and one is hungry, and another is drunken. 22 What, have ye not houses to eat and to drink in? or despise ye the *e*church of God, and put them to shame that *f*have not? What shall I say to you? *g*shall I praise you? In this I praise you not. 23 For I received of the Lord that which also I delivered unto you, that the Lord Je'sus in the night in which he was *h*betrayed took bread; 24 and when he had given thanks, he brake it, and said, **This is my body, which** *i***is for you: this do in remembrance of me.** 25 In like manner also

---

a Or. *among*   *b* Or. *in congregation*
c Gr. *schisms.*   *d* Gr. *herestes.*   *e* Or, *congregation*   *f* Or, *have nothing*   *g* Or, *shall*

I praise you in this? I praise you not.
h Or, *delivered up*   *i* Many ancient authorities read *is broken for you.*

and hence not to be disregarded by the Christian woman. Other times and lands have other forms of expressing deference and modesty. Any defiance of custom, which would indicate the lack of these qualities, would be censurable still. *Every woman praying or prophesying.* This, in connection with ver. 4, seems to indicate a recognized right of woman to 'pray or prophesy' in the Christian assemblies in a decorous manner, and this was apparently a limitation upon the seemingly absolute prohibition of ch. 14.34, 35.

11. *In the Lord.* The spiritual unity of man and wife, in spite of differences of social relations and requirements, is meant (Gal. 3.28).

18, 19. *Divisions.* See ch. 1.11, 12; 3.1-4.

20-22. *When therefore ye assemble,* etc. Disorders at the Lord's Supper may have arisen from connecting it with the 'love-feasts' of the early church. See notes on Acts 2.42-47. *Have ye not houses to eat and to drink in?* The fault was in making the sacrament a supper, a mere ordinary meal. The rudeness and selfishness displayed were disgraceful incidents.

23-25. *For I received of the Lord,* etc. This is the fourth account of the institution of the Lord's Supper; the other three are in Mt. 26. 26-28; Mk. 14.22-24; Lk. 22.17-20. The repetition in all four instances of the words of institution make

the cup, after supper, saying, This cup is the new covenant in my blood: this do, as often as ye drink *it*, in remembrance of me. 26 For as often as ye eat this bread, and drink the cup, ye proclaim the Lord's death till he come. 27 Wherefore whosoever shall eat the bread or drink the cup of the Lord in an unworthy manner, shall be guilty of the body and the blood of the Lord. 28 But let a man prove himself, and so let him eat of the bread, and drink of the cup. 29 For he that eateth and drinketh, eateth and drinketh judgment unto himself, if he *k*discern not the body. 30 For this cause many among you are weak and sickly, and not a few sleep. 31 But if we *l*discerned ourselves, we

k Gr. *discriminate.*   *l* Gr. *discriminated.*

them the most absolutely certain of all the utterances of our Lord.

27. *Guilty of the body and blood of the Lord.* 'Of' has here the sense of 'in respect to'; guilty of profaning the elements used in the communion of which the Lord had said: 'This is my body; this is my blood.'

30. *Many among you are weak and sickly, and not a few sleep.* Numerous commentators regard the illness as physical, and the sleep as the sleep of death; both sent as divine judgment. Others hold that spiritual weakness and sickness and apathy or deadness (sleep) of soul are indicated.

CHAPTER 12

1. *Concerning spiritual gifts.* That is, the extraordinary gifts of the Spirit here and elsewhere referred to, the existence of which is not declared as a thing to be proved, but assumed as well known and undisputed fact (Acts 2.1-5; 16.16-18; 19.1-7). Ch. 12-14 are a continuous discussion of spiritual gifts. Ch. 13, which seems an episode, is

should not be judged. 32 But *m*when we are judged, we are chastened of the Lord, that we may not be condemned with the world. 33 Wherefore, my brethren, when ye come together to eat, wait one for another. 34 If any man is hungry, let him eat at home; that your coming together be not unto judgment. And the rest will I set in order whensoever I come.

12 Now concerning spiritual *gifts*, brethren, I would not have you ignorant. 2 Ye know that when ye were Gen'tiles *ye were* led away unto those dumb idols, howsoever ye might be led. 3 Wherefore I make known unto you, that no man speaking in the Spirit of God

m Or, *when we are judged of the Lord, we are chastened*

part of the discussion, only rising to a higher key in showing the supremacy of love.

2. *Ye were Gentiles.* Evidently the greater part of the church; therefore needing the simplest and most elementary instruction. *Dumb idols.* See ch. 8.4; 10.19.

3. *No man speaking,* etc. The supreme test of seemingly prophetic utterance — the sincere acknowledgment of the lordship of Jesus. *Saith, Jesus is anathema.* Not necessarily in those words, but what amounts to the same; denying him as Lord and Redeemer. 'Anathema' signifies 'an accursed thing,' 'an abomination.' By some authorities the phrase 'says Jesus is anathema' is taken to mean 'reviles him as an impostor, justly put to death.' There appear to have been some Jews who still denied the Messiahship of Christ; or Greeks, inflated with the philosophical 'wisdom,' ch. 1.18-22, who desired to share the spiritual freedom and privileges of the Christian church and supposed themselves or pretended to be under divine inspira-

saith, Je'sus is an-ath'e-ma; and no man can say, Je'sus is Lord, but in the Holy Spirit.

4 Now there are diversities of gifts, but the same Spirit. 5 And there are diversities of ministrations, and the same Lord. 6 And there are diversities of workings, but the same God, who worketh all things in all. 7 But to each one is given the manifestation of the Spirit to profit withal. 8 For to one is given through the Spirit the word of wisdom; and to another the word of knowledge, according to the same Spirit: 9 to another faith, in the same Spirit; and to another gifts of healings, in the one Spirit; 10 and to another workings of ªmiracles; and to another prophecy; and to another discernings of spirits: to another *divers* kinds of tongues; and to another

the interpretation of tongues: 11 but all these worketh the one and the same Spirit, dividing to each one severally even as he will.

12 For as the body is one, and hath many members, and all the members of the body, being many, are one body; so also is Christ. 13 For in one Spirit were we all baptized into one body, whether Jews or Greeks, whether bond or free; and were all made to drink of one Spirit. 14 For the body is not one member, but many. 15 If the foot shall say, Because I am not the hand, I am not of the body; it is not therefore not of the body. 16 And if the ear shall say, Because I am not the eye, I am not of the body; it is not therefore not of the body. 17 If the whole body were an eye, where were

---

ª Gr. *powers.*

---

tion while denying Christ. That denial proved them false. *Say, Jesus is Lord.* Of course with honest utterance and purpose. *But in the Holy Spirit.* To such conviction one must be divinely led (Mt. 11.25-27; 16.16, 17).

4. *Diversities of gifts, but the same Spirit.* Gifts differing according to the purpose and choice of God, but altogether making up a divine harmony (ver. 11).

7. *To profit withal.* Literally, for advantage or utility, that is, to the church, not for pride or display.

8. *Wisdom.* In this verse 'wisdom' may refer to practical duties, and 'knowledge' to the doctrinal part of the Christian system, perhaps the mysteries of ch. 13.2.

9. *Faith.* Most probably a faith remarkable in its degree, strong enough to overcome great obstacles, as compared with the simple but untried and undeveloped faith of the inexperienced believers. *Gifts of healings.* See Acts 3.6-8, 9.32-41; 19.11, 12.

10. *Workings of miracles.* Miraculous powers in general, beyond the healing of the sick. *Prophecy.* The utterance of truth under divine inspiration. The foretelling of future events might be included (Acts 20.23; 21.10, 11), but only as a small and incidental part of the prophetic gift. In ver. 28 prophecy is placed second in rank among the spiritual gifts; it is also prominently mentioned in ch. 14.1-5. *Discernings of spirits.* Power to perceive whether a profession or utterance was truly or falsely made. *Kinds of tongues.* Emotional, ecstatic utterances. See ch. 14.2 and note thereon. *Interpretation of tongues.* By one able to make intelligible the utterance which neither the speaker nor his audience could clearly understand. For the importance of this see ch. 14.13, 27, 28.

12. *The body.* The church, with its many members and their various gifts, is likened to the human body, as explained in ver. 27. See Eph. 1.22, 23; 4.15, 16; Col. 1.18.

the hearing? If the whole were hearing, where were the smelling? 18 But now hath God set the members each one of them in the body, even as it pleased him. 19 And if they were all one member, where were the body? 20 But now they are many members, but one body. 21 And the eye cannot say to the hand, I have no need of thee: or again the head to the feet, I have no need of you. 22 Nay, much rather, those members of the body which seem to be more feeble are necessary: 23 and those *parts* of the body, which we think to be less honorable, upon these we *b*bestow more abundant honor; and our uncomely *parts* have more abundant comeliness; 24 whereas our comely *parts* have no need: but God tempered the body together, giving more abundant honor to that *part* which lacked; 25 that there should be no schism

in the body; but *that* the members should have the same care one for another. 26 And whether one member suffereth, all the members suffer with it; or *one* member is *c*honored, all the members rejoice with it. 27 Now ye are the body of Christ, and *d*severally members thereof. 28 And God hath set some in the church, first apostles, secondly prophets, thirdly teachers, then *e*miracles, then gifts of healings, helps, *f*governments, *divers* kinds of tongues. 29 Are all apostles? are all prophets? are all teachers? are all *workers of e*miracles? 30 have all gifts of healings? do all speak with tongues? do all interpret? 31 But desire earnestly the greater gifts. And moreover a most excellent way show I unto you.

13 If I speak with the tongues of men and of angels, but have not love, I am become sounding brass, or a

---

b Or, *put on*

c Or, *glorified*   *d* Or, *members each in his part*   *e* Gr. *powers.*   *f* Or, *wise counsels*

---

28. *First apostles*, etc. An enumeration which begins with persons— apostles, prophets, teachers, but then passes over to the gifts exercised, showing that the main thought is of the gifts, which are mentioned in the order of their importance. We need not suppose the enumeration to be mathematically precise. The apostleship is first, as the apostles were the leaders and founders of the church; prophecy is second, for its spiritual helpfulness, as urged in ch. 14; teaching next, as giving the sure basis of accepted truth; miracles and gifts of healing follow, but in order reversed from ver. 9, 10; helps, probably the work of caring for the sick and needy (Acts 6.1-3), but not necessarily limited to the official deacons; governments, or offices of church administration; last of all, the divers

'kinds of tongues,' which the Corinthians seem to have prized so highly.

31. *A most excellent way.* A way by which to obtain and use the highest gifts.

CHAPTER 13

1. *If I speak*, etc. In this chapter the thought rises above all special manifestations of spiritual power to the pure, unselfish and perfect devotion of the soul to God, the essence of whose being is love (1 Jn. 4.8). All else is inferior to this single grace. *The tongues of men.* Of all men, of every nation. *And of angels.* There is here no declaration regarding any speech of angels, but simply a comparison carried to its highest imaginative point, even to the language which angels may be supposed to speak. *And have not*

clanging cymbal. 2 And if I have *the gift of* prophecy, and know all mysteries and all knowledge; and if I have all faith, so as to remove mountains, but have not love, I am nothing. 3 And if I bestow all my goods to feed *the poor*, and if I give my body *a*to be burned, but have not love, it profiteth me nothing. 4 Love suffereth long, *and* is kind; love envieth not; love vaunteth not itself, is not puffed up, 5 doth not behave itself unseemly, seeketh not its own, is not provoked, taketh not account of evil; 6 rejoiceth not in unrighteousness, but rejoiceth with the truth; 7 *b*beareth all things, believeth all things, hopeth all things, endureth all things. 8 Love never faileth: but whether *there be* prophecies, they shall be done away; whether *there be* tongues, they shall cease; whether *there be* knowledge, it shall be done away. 9 For we know in part, and we prophesy in part; 10 but when that which is perfect is come, that which is in part shall be done away. 11 When I was a child, I spake as a child, I felt as a child, I thought as a child: now that I am become a man, I have put away childish things.

---

a Many ancient authorities read *that I may glory.*

b Or, *covereth* Comp. 1 Pet. 4.8.

---

love. Love in its highest reach—a pure and full affection and devotion towards God and man. See Mt. 5.44; 22.37-39; Jn. 3.16; 13.1, 34; 14.15, 31; 15.9, 12, 13; 17.23-26; 1 Cor. 2.9; 8.3; Eph. 5.2; 1 Pet. 1.8; 1 Jn. 3.11, 14; 4.8, 11, 12. *Sounding brass or a clanging cymbal.* Mere empty sound.

2. *Prophecy.* See ch. 12.10 and note thereon. *Knowledge.* See ch. 12.8 and note thereon. *Faith.* See ch. 12.9 and note thereon.

3. *Bestow.* The meaning of the original word is to feed by bits or morsels, indicating the giving of all of one's means in charity to needy persons. But even such giving might be without love (Mt. 6.1, 2). *Give my body to be burned.* When martyrdom came to be esteemed glorious, there were instances of persons who met it in an unchristian spirit, as is recorded of one who on his way to the stake refused to forgive one who implored his pardon.

4. *Suffereth long.* With meek and undiscouraged patience under wrongs, like that of the suffering Christ. *Is kind.* Tenderly thoughtful and generous in word and act. *Envieth not.* Is not disturbed by any superiority of others. *Vaunteth not itself.* Is not boastful. *Is not*

puffed up. Is not vain, proud, arrogant, or haughty.

5. *Doth not behave itself unseemly.* Avoids, for the sake of others, all conduct that may seem unworthy or may be a cause of reproach, such as 'the sitting at meat' in an idol's temple. See ch. 8.10 and notes thereon. *Seeketh not its own.* Is unselfish. *Is not provoked.* Does not readily find causes of provocation; is not irritable. *Taketh not account of evil.* Does not put it on record, as in an account book, for remembrance or revenge.

6. *Rejoiceth not in unrighteousness.* Has no pleasure in prosperity or success unrighteously obtained; or, as some interpret, in hearing or telling of unrighteousness in others. *Truth.* Of doctrine, utterance, and action.

7. *All things.* That is, all that may be rightly borne, believed, hoped, or endured. See ch. 11.2 and note thereon.

8-10. *Love never faileth.* Love is immortal as part of the heavenly life, where tongues, prophecies and human knowledge shall be superseded.

11. *Childish things.* The toys, the plays, and the lessons of childhood. Like these will the highest earthly attainments seem hereafter.

12 For now we see in a mirror, ^cdarkly; but then face to face: now I know in part; but then shall I know fully even as also I was fully known. 13 But now abideth faith, hope, love, these three; and the ^dgreatest of these is love.

14 Follow after love; yet desire earnestly spiritual *gifts*, but rather that ye may prophesy. 2 For he that speaketh in a tongue speaketh not unto men, but unto God; for no man ^aunderstandeth; but in the spirit he speaketh mysteries. 3 But he that prophesieth speaketh unto men edification, and ^bexhortation, and consolation. 4 He that speaketh in a tongue ^cedifieth himself; but he that prophesieth ^cedifieth the church. 5 Now I would have you all speak with tongues, but rather that ye should prophesy: and greater is he that prophesieth

than he that speaketh with tongues, except he interpret, that the church may receive edifying. 6 But now, brethren, if I come unto you speaking with tongues, what shall I profit you, unless I speak to you either by way of revelation, or of knowledge, or of prophesying, or of teaching? 7 Even things without life, giving a voice, whether pipe or harp, if they give not a distinction in the sounds, how shall it be known what is piped or harped? 8 For if the trumpet give an uncertain voice, who shall prepare himself for war? 9 So also ye, unless ye utter by the tongue speech easy to be understood, how shall it be known what is spoken? for ye will be speaking into the air. 10 There are, it may be, so many kinds of voices in the world, and ^dno *kind* is without signification. 11 If then I know not the meaning of the voice, I shall be to him

---

c Gr. *in a riddle.* d Gr. *greater.* Comp. Mt. 18.1, 4; 23.11.

a Gr. *heareth.* b Or, *comfort* c Gr. *buildeth up.* d Or, *nothing is without voice*

12. *In a mirror.* The easily tarnished metallic mirror of ancient times.

13. *Now abideth faith, hope, love.* They are all eternal: faith, in the forever unsearchable wisdom of God; hope, in the forever increasing glory and blessedness of heaven; love, the chief of the three, as part of the divine nature.

CHAPTER 14

1. *Prophesy.* 'Prophesy' in the Scriptures signifies not merely nor chiefly foretelling the future, but uttering truth under divine inspiration. Large portions of the books of the Old Testament prophets, as Isaiah, Jeremiah, Ezekiel, etc., are devoted to the description of present or past events, advice, reproof, and the like. This sense of the word prophesy is especially promi-

nent in the New Testament (ver. 24, 25; ch. 12.10 and note thereon).

2. *He that speaketh in a tongue,* etc. Speaking in a tongue or tongues, a kind of ecstatic utterance, is in 1 and 2 Cor. different from speaking with 'other tongues,' that is, in foreign languages, as recorded in Acts 2.4. The utterance of him who spoke in a tongue might be unknown to all the hearers. See ver. 11. In Acts 2.3-13 the speaking with tongues apparently means speaking in foreign languages; but in 1 and 2 Cor. the gift is best taken to signify an ecstatic utterance, not intelligible until interpreted. See ver. 19.

4. *Edifieth himself.* He himself is supposed to understand the words he speaks.

6. *If I come unto you, speaking with tongues.* See ver. 18.

11. *A barbarian.* This had no reference to personal character or

427

that speaketh a barbarian, and he that speaketh will be a barbarian *unto me. 12 So also ye, since ye are zealous of *spiritual gifts*, seek that ye may abound unto the edifying of the church. 13 Wherefore let him that speaketh in a tongue pray that he may interpret. 14 For if I pray in a tongue, my spirit prayeth, but my understanding is unfruitful. 15 What is it then? I will pray with the spirit, and I will pray with the understanding also: I will sing with the spirit, and I will sing with the understanding also. 16 Else if thou bless with the spirit, how shall he that filleth the place of *the unlearned say the A-men' at thy giving of thanks, seeing he knoweth not what thou sayest? 17 For thou verily givest thanks well, but the other is not *edified. 18 I thank God, I speak with tongues more than you all: 19 howbeit in the church I had rather speak five words with my understanding, that I might instruct others also, than ten thousand words in a tongue.

20 Brethren, be not children in mind: yet in malice be ye babes, but in mind be *men. 21 In the law it is written, *By men of strange tongues and by the lips of strangers will I speak unto this people; and not even thus will they hear me, saith the Lord. 22 Wherefore tongues are for a sign, not to them that believe, but to the unbelieving: but prophesying *is for a sign*, not to the unbelieving, but to them that believe. 23 If therefore the whole church be assembled together and all speak with tongues, and there come in men unlearned or unbelieving, will they not say that ye are mad? 24 But if all prophesy, and there come in one unbelieving or unlearned, he is *reproved by all, he is judged by all; 25 the secrets of his heart are made manifest; and so he will fall down on his face and worship God, declaring that God is *among you indeed.

---

e Or, *in my case*   *f* Gr. *spirits.*   *g* Or, *him that is without gifts*: and so in ver. 23, 24.   *h* Gr. *builded up.*

i Gr. *of full age.* Comp. ch. 2.6.   *k* Is. xxviii. 11f.   *l* Or, *convicted*   *m* Or, *in*

---

grade of civilization. The Greeks called every one not a Greek a barbarian, that is, one who spoke an unintelligible tongue.

12. *The edifying of the church.* The purpose that should be controlling. See ver. 12, 26; ch. 8.1; 10.23; Rom. 15.2; Eph. 4.12, 16, 29.

13. *Pray that be may interpret.* The two powers of speaking in a tongue and of interpreting the utterance seem not to have been always joined in the same person.

18. *I speak with tongues more than you all.* The only definite statement that Paul possessed the gift of tongues, which he mentions here incidentally. His use of Greek to the chief captain (Acts 21.37) and of the Aramaic or 'Hebrew' (Acts 22.2) implies nothing miraculous or more than any well educated Jew of that day might have done.

23. *Men unlearned or unbelieving.* The meetings were public; unbelievers could freely come. The Christian assemblies were never secret until persecution made them so. *Say that ye are mad.* Such visitors being evidently unable to understand the utterances.

24. *He is reproved*, etc. By the power of spiritual truth spoken in a language with which he is familiar. See Jn. 16.8.

25. *Fall down on his face.* With the face near the ground or the floor,

26 What is it then, brethren? When ye come together, each one hath a psalm, hath a teaching, hath a revelation, hath a tongue, hath an interpretation. Let all things be done unto edifying. 27 If any man speaketh in a tongue, *let it be* by two, or at the most three, and *that* in turn; and let one interpret: 28 but if there be no interpreter, let him keep silence in the church; and let him speak to himself, and to God. 29 And let the prophets speak *by* two or three, and let the others ⁿdiscern. 30 But if a revelation be made to another sitting by, let the first keep silence. 31 For ye all can prophesy one by one, that all may learn, and all may be °exhorted; 32 and the spirits of

the prophets are subject to the prophets; 33 for God is not *a God* of confusion, but of peace.

As in all the churches of the saints, 34 let the women keep silence in the churches: for it is not permitted unto them to speak; but let them be in subjection, as also ᵖsaith the law. 35 And if they would learn anything, let them ask their own husbands at home: for it is shameful for a woman to speak in the church. 36 What? was it from you that the word of God went forth? or came it unto you alone?

37 If any man thinketh himself to be a prophet, or spiritual, let him take knowledge of the things which I write unto you, that they are the commandment

---

n Gr. *discriminate.*　　*o* Or, *comforted*

p Gen. iii. 16?

---

the forehead supported on clasped hands; the oriental posture of adoration and supplication. See Mt. 17.6; 26.39; Rev. 7.11.

26. *Each one hath,* etc. Abundant resources and readiness; although these might tend to confusion unless discreetly ordered. There was one rule for this: Let all things be done unto edifying.

27. *By two, or at the most three.* Paul considered the gift of speaking in a tongue a dangerous one, to be guardedly manifested. *In turn.* One at a time, indicating that two or more may have been previously allowed to speak at once, producing the 'confusion' of ver. 33. *And let one interpret.* 'That the church may receive edifying' (ver. 5).

29. *Let the prophets speak by two or three.* Two or three such exercises on one occasion, following each other in orderly sequence.

30. *But if a revelation be made,* etc. Let any speaker close his remarks if he perceives that another has received a sudden revelation.

31. *One by one.* One at a time; two or three of one kind of exercise

to be heard in immediate sequence.

32. *The spirits of the prophets are subject,* etc. Those who exercise the prophetic gift must control it.

33. *Confusion.* The apostle meant: be sure God cannot work in you in confusion, for that is not His way, and does not fittingly manifest nor can it glorify Him. *Peace.* Goes fitly with the 'love' of ch. 13. The two terms are often joined. See ch. 7.15; Jn. 14.27; 16.33; Acts 10.36; 2 Cor. 13.11; Gal. 5.22.

34, 35. *Let the women keep silence,* etc. To be read in connection with ch. 11.5, 13. In those verses praying or prophesying by women under proper conditions seems to be permitted. The force of the present passage has been much disputed, some expositors and churches holding that the prohibition is for all places and all times; others urging that it was local and temporary, for the places and the period with reference to which the apostle wrote, where the general seclusion of women would cause any public activity to be held 'shameful,' like the dispensing with the veil.

of the Lord. 38 [q]But if any man
is ignorant, let him be ignorant.
39 Wherefore, my brethren,
desire earnestly to prophesy, and
forbid not to speak with tongues.
40 But let all things be done
decently and in order.

15 Now I make known
unto you, brethren, the
[a]gospel which I [b]preached unto
you, which also ye received,
wherein also ye stand, 2 by which
also ye are saved, if ye hold fast
[c]the word which I [b]preached
unto you, except ye believed [d]in
vain. 3 For I delivered unto
you first of all that which also
I received: that Christ died for
our sins according to the scriptures; 4 and that he was buried;
and that he hath been raised on
the third day according to the
scriptures; 5 and that he appeared to Ce′phas; then to the
twelve; 6 then he appeared to
above five hundred brethren at
once, of whom the greater part
remain until now, but some are
fallen asleep; 7 then he appeared to [e]James; then to all the
apostles; 8 and last of all, as
to the *child* untimely born, he
appeared to me also. 9 For I am
the least of the apostles, that am
not meet to be called an apostle,
because I persecuted the church
of God. 10 But by the grace of
God I am what I am: and his
grace which was bestowed upon

[q] Many ancient authorities read *But if any man knoweth not, he is not known.* Comp. ch. 8.3. [a] See marginal note on ch. 4.15. [b] See marginal note on ch. 1.17. [c] Gr. *with what word.* [d] Or, *without cause* [e] Or, *Jacob*

39. *Let all things be done decently,* etc. The object of all the special instructions here given.

CHAPTER 15

3. *First of all.* Among the first and fundamental truths of the gospel. See ch. 2.2; Acts 17.31. *That which I also received.* From the other apostles (Acts 9.27, 28; Gal. 1. 18, 19). Also, direct revelation at his own conversion. *According to the Scriptures.* In fulfilment of Old Testament prophecy. See Isa. 53; Lk. 24.44–46.

4–7. *That he was buried.* An important fact, suggesting the reality of both the death and the resurrection. *Raised on the third day.* The narrative of the resurrection by the Evangelists relates what had long been orally taught, so that Paul had ‘received’ it (ver. 3). Verses 4–7 contain the first written story of the resurrection of Christ. It was written about twenty-five years after the event, that is about 55–56 A.D. The list of witnesses here given is not complete. *Cephas* (Peter). See Jn. 21.11-21. *James.* Probably the Lord's brother. See Acts 15.13; Gal. 1.19. The appearance to James is not recorded in the gospels, but Peter and James were both personally known to Paul. *Above five hundred brethren at once.* Perhaps on the mountain in Galilee. See Mt. 28.16, 17. *The greater part remain.* They were still living when Paul wrote this epistle and might be met from time to time, or sought out and talked with as witnesses. *The twelve* (ver. 5). *All the apostles* (ver. 7). Evidently two appearances. See Mt. 28.16, 17; Lk. 24.33–36; Jn. 20.26-29; Acts 1.2, 6–11.

8. *To me also.* On the road to Damascus, at his conversion. (Acts 9.3-6.) *The child untimely born.* Born out of the ordinary course of nature, since Paul did not become an apostle, as the others did, by personal attendance on the earthly ministry of Jesus and by personally witnessing the scenes of the resurrection.

9. *The least of the apostles.* As the child untimely born is small and weak; an expression of deep humility. *Because I persecuted.* The offence which he could never forgive himself. See 1 Tim. 1.13.

me was not found *f*vain; but I labored more abundantly than they all: yet not I, but the grace of God which was with me. 11 Whether then *it be* I or they, so we preach, and so ye believed.

12 Now if Christ is preached that he hath been raised from the dead, how say some among you that there is no resurrection of the dead? 13 But if there is no resurrection of the dead, neither hath Christ been raised: 14 and if Christ hath not been raised, then is our preaching *f*vain, *g*your faith also is *f*vain. 15 Yea, and we are found false witnesses of God; because we witnessed of God that he raised up *h*Christ: whom he raised not up, if so be that the dead are not

raised. 16 For if the dead are not raised, neither hath Christ been raised: 17 and if Christ hath not been raised, your faith is vain; ye are yet in your sins. 18 Then they also that are fallen asleep in Christ have perished. 19 *i*If we have only hoped in Christ in this life, we are of all men most pitiable.

20 But now hath Christ been raised from the dead, the first-fruits of them that are asleep. 21 For since by man *came* death, by man *came* also the resurrection of the dead. 22 For as in Adam all die, so also in *h*Christ shall all be made alive. 23 But each in his own order: Christ the first-fruits; then they that are Christ's, at his *k*coming.

---

f Or, *void.* *g* Some ancient authorities read our. *h* Gr. *the Christ.*

i Or, *If in this life only we have hoped in Christ &c.* *k* Gr. *presence.*

---

11. *I or they.* By the appearance of Christ to him at his conversion, Paul could be counted with the other apostles as a personal witness of the resurrection. See ch. 9.1; Acts 22.14, 18.

12. *That there is no resurrection of the dead.* Some of the Corinthians affirmed that resurrection of the dead is, on general principles, impossible. Those who took this ground were doubtless the advocates of the so-called philosophic 'wisdom' elsewhere mentioned. See ch. 1.18–25; 2.6–8; 3.19.

13. *But if there is no resurrection,* etc. The general denial of the possibility of any resurrection of the dead would imply a denial of the fact of Christ's resurrection.

14. *Then is our preaching vain.* A dead Christ cannot be our Redeemer. Throughout the Acts and the Epistles the inspiration is that of a risen and still living Christ. See Acts 2.24-32; 5.30-32; 10.38-43; 13.28-37.

15. *False witnesses of God.* Every hypothesis as to imagination, hallucination, or ecstasy is here met and set aside. The apostle main-

tains that the witnesses, of whom he was one, are competent, and if the events to which they testify did not occur, they are 'false witnesses.' He meets squarely and openly the issue which still remains to be met: Could men of such principles, who sacrificed and suffered what they did for their testimony, be 'false witnesses'?

18. *Then they also that are fallen asleep,* etc. Those who have perished include all who have died a martyr's death for Christ's sake. 'Fallen asleep' is the familiar Christian figure of speech for death. See ver. 6, 20, 51; Mt. 27.52; Mk. 5.39; Jn. 11.11; Acts 7.60; 1 Thess. 4.14.

19. *If we have only hoped in Christ in this life.* Said in view of the sacrifices and sufferings of the Christians of that day for Christ's sake. If their hope of eternal life was ill-founded, such sacrifices and sufferings were indeed 'most pitiable.' See 2 Cor. 11.23–27.

23 *Christ the first-fruits.* The pledge of the result, as the first sheaf is of the harvest. See Lev. 23.10, 11, 20.

24 Then *cometh* the end, when he shall deliver up the kingdom to *l*God, even the Father; when he shall have abolished all rule and all authority and power. 25 For he must reign, till he hath put all his enemies under his feet. 26 The last enemy that shall be abolished is death. 27 For, He put all things in subjection under his feet. *m*But when he saith, *n*All things are put in subjection, it is evident that he is excepted who did subject all things unto him. 28 And when all things have been subjected unto him, then shall the Son also himself be subjected to him that did subject all things unto him, that God may be all in all.

29 Else what shall they do that are baptized for the dead? If the dead are not raised at all, why then are they baptized for them? 30 why do we also stand in jeopardy every hour? 31 I protest by *o*that glorying which I have in Christ Je'sus our Lord, I die daily. 32 If after the manner of men I fought with beasts at Eph'e-sus, *p*what doth it profit me? If the dead are not raised, let us eat and drink, for to-morrow we die. 33 Be not deceived: Evil companionships corrupt good morals. 34 Awake to soberness righteously, and sin not; for some have no knowledge of God: I speak *this* to move you to shame.

35 But some one will say, How are the dead raised? and with what manner of body do they come? 36 Thou foolish one, that which thou thyself sowest is not quickened except it die: 37 and that which thou sowest, thou sowest not the body that shall be, but a bare grain, it may chance of wheat, or of some other kind; 38 but God giveth it a body even as it pleased him, and to each seed a body of its own. 39 All flesh is not the same flesh: but there is one *flesh* of men, and another flesh of beasts, and another flesh of birds, and

---

l Gr. *the God and Father.*   *m* Or, *But when he shall have said, All things are put in subjection (evidently excepting him that did subject all things unto him), when,* I say. *n* Ps. viii. 6.   *o* Or, *your glorying*   *p* Or, *what doth it profit me, if the dead are not raised? Let us eat &c.*   *all things &c.*

---

28. *The Son also himself be subjected.* See Jn. 14.28; 17.4, 5.

30. *Why do we also stand in jeopardy,* etc. Why, if there is nothing to hope for beyond the grave? 'We' may denote all the Christians of that day, or, preëminently, the apostles.

31. *I die daily.* I live in daily exposure to death.

32. *Fought with beasts,* etc. There is no record of any such encounter, and Paul's Roman citizenship would possibly have saved him from exposure to wild beasts in the arena. The single Greek word translated 'fought with beasts' was figuratively used for any dangerous or dreadful conflict, and this use is

here indicated by the phrase 'after the manner of men,' that is, speaking after the manner of men or using a common mode of speech. Paul's experience with the mob at Ephesus (Acts 19.23, 24) might very naturally be figuratively described. Nevertheless the literal interpretation may very easily be possible.

35-44. *How are the dead raised?* Paul here considers a materialistic objection which has sprung up anew in every age. How can the particles of this body, when once it has been disintegrated and scattered, be reassembled into the same living organism? The apostle makes no attempt to show that they ever will be, but argues for the pres-

another of fishes. 40 There are also celestial bodies, and bodies terrestrial: but the glory of the celestial is one, and the *glory* of the terrestrial is another. 41 There is one glory of the sun, and another glory of the moon, and another glory of the stars; for one star differeth from another star in glory. 42 So also is the resurrection of the dead. It is sown in corruption; it is raised in incorruption: 43 it is sown in dishonor; it is raised in glory: it is sown in weakness; it is raised in power: 44 it is sown a *q*natural body; it is raised a spiritual body. If there is a *q*natural body, there is also a spiritual *body*. 45 So also it is written, *r*The first man Adam became a living soul. The last Adam *became* a life-giving spirit.

46 Howbeit that is not first which is spiritual, but that which is *q*natural; then that which is spiritual. 47 The first man is of the earth, earthy: the second man is of heaven. 48 As is the earthy, such are they also that are earthy: and as is the heavenly, such are they also that are heavenly. 49 And as we have borne the image of the earthy, *s*we shall also bear the image of the heavenly.

50 Now this I say, brethren, that flesh and blood cannot inherit the kingdom of God; neither doth corruption inherit incorruption. 51 Behold, I tell you a mystery: *t*We all shall not sleep, but we shall all be changed, 52 in a moment, in the twinkling of an eye, at the last trump: for the trumpet shall sound, and the

---

q Gr. *psychical.*   *r* Gen. ii. 7.

s Many ancient authorities read *let us also bear.*   *t* Or, *We shall not all &c.*

---

ervation of essential identity by examples of the infinite variety of God's creative power. *A bare grain.* A naked kernel of wheat, from which there springs another body, not composed of the same particles, since all but the life germ has decayed in the ground; but the new body is far more glorious. The seed so transformed produces a body of its own, possessing not the same particles, but essential identity, wheat always producing wheat, etc. Christ uses the same figure of speech in regard to his own death (Jn. 12.24).

40, 41. *Celestial bodies and bodies terrestrial.* Alluding to the vast differences in the nature and glory of earth, sun, moon, and stars, yet all within the easy sweep of God's creative power.

42. *So also is the resurrection of the dead.* The risen body differs vastly from the buried earthly body; it contrasts corruption with power.

45. *The last Adam.* Christ. See ver. 21, 22; Rom. 5.

50. *Flesh and blood cannot inherit,* etc. Perishable combinations of matter are on a lower plane than the spiritual principle of life; they cannot 'inherit' the kingdom of God. The apostle implies that only a spiritual body, free from the limitations of the earthly body, can enter into and abide forever in the spiritual kingdom. See Jn. 3.6; 2 Cor. 5.1, 4.

51-53. *Behold.* Calling attention to something of great importance. *A mystery.* Something that can be known only by revelation, and even then cannot be fully explained to the human mind, nor understood by it in its present state. See Jn. 16.12; 2 Cor. 12.4. *We all.* This does not necessarily imply that Paul himself expected to be alive at the moment of the change mentioned. He speaks in the first person, as one of the Christian host, including all believers living or yet to live. So 'we' in ver. 52. *Changed, in a moment.* A suggestion of what such a change may be appears in accounts

dead shall be raised incorruptible, and we shall be changed. 53 For this corruptible must put on incorruption, and this mortal must put on immortality. 54 But when ᵘthis corruptible shall have put on incorruption, and this mortal shall have put on immortality, then shall come to pass the saying that is written, ᵛDeath is swallowed up ˣin victory. 55 ʸO death, where is thy victory? O death, where is thy sting? 56 The sting of death is sin; and the power of sin is the law: 57 but thanks be to God, who giveth us the victory through our Lord Je'sus Christ. 58 Wherefore, my beloved brethren, be ye stedfast, unmovable, always abounding in the work of the Lord, forasmuch as ye

know that your labor is not ᶻvain in the Lord.

16 Now concerning the collection for the saints, as I gave order to the churches of Ga-la'ti-a, so also do ye. 2 Upon the first day of the week let each one of you lay by him in store, as he may prosper, that no collections be made when I come. 3 And when I arrive, ᵃwhomsoever ye shall approve, them will I send with letters to carry your bounty unto Je-ru'sa-lem: 4 and if it be meet for me to go also, they shall go with me. 5 But I will come unto you, when I shall have passed through Mac-e-do'ni-a; for I pass through Mac-e-do'ni-a; 6 but with you it may be that I shall abide, or

---

u Many ancient authorities omit *this corruptible shall have put on incorruption, and.* v Is. xxv. 8. x Or, *victoriously* y Hos.

xiii. 14. z Or, *void* a Or, *whomsoever ye shall approve by letters, them will I send &c.*

---

of the transfigured before them. See Mt. 17.2; Mk. 9.2; Lk. 9.29.

54, 55. *But when this corruptible,* etc. The two texts, 'Death is swallowed up,' etc. and 'O death, where is thy victory,' form together what has been well called 'a song of triumph.'

58. *Wherefore, my beloved brethren,* etc. After the thanksgiving in ver. 57, an exhortation to unshaken firmness and earnest work naturally follows, since the sufferings and the labor shall not be vain in the sure triumph of the resurrection.

CHAPTER 16

1. *The collection for the saints.* Alluding to the contributions for the poor Christians of Jerusalem during a period of hardships, while the Gentile churches were, in general, wealthy by comparison. Paul had especially arranged with the other apostles for such charity (Gal. 2.10). See Acts 24.17; Rom. 15.25, 26; 2 Cor. 8 and 9.

2. *Upon the first day of the week.*

That this was then observed as the day of Christian worship is indicated in Acts. 20.7; Rev. 1.10. *Lay by him in store.* That is, at home, put into a special fund, available when needed. *That no collections be made when I come.* That it be not necessary then to take up a special collection on the spur of the moment. This verse suggests the propriety of weekly offerings, though it was written for a special occasion and purpose.

3, 4. *And when I arrive,* etc. An arrangement for the transmission of funds by accredited and responsible agents. Paul studied businesslike methods in handling benevolent funds, that all might be 'honorable not only in the sight of the Lord, but also in the sight of men.' (2 Cor. 8.19–21).

5. *For I pass through Macedonia.* Apparently a change from a previous plan, for which reason some charged the apostle with fickleness (2 Cor. 1.17, 23).

6. *It may be that I shall abide, or even winter.* This he afterwards

even winter, that ye may set me forward on my journey whithersoever I go. 7 For I do not wish to see you now by the way; for I hope to tarry a while with you, if the Lord permit. 8 But I will tarry at Eph'e-sus until Pen'tecost; 9 for a great door and effectual is opened unto me, and there are many adversaries.

10 Now if Tim'o-thy come, see that he be with you without fear; for he worketh the work of the Lord, as I also do: 11 let no man therefore despise him. But set him forward on his journey in peace, that he may come unto me: for I expect him with the brethren. 12 But as touching A-pol'los the brother, I besought him much to come unto you with the brethren: and it was not at all *his* will to come now; but he will come when he shall have opportunity.

13 Watch ye, stand fast in the faith, quit you like men, be strong. 14 Let all that ye do be done in love.

15 Now I beseech you, brethren (ye know the house of Steph'a-nas, that it is the firstfruits of A-cha'ia, and that they have set themselves to minister unto the saints), 16 that ye also be in subjection unto such, and to every one that helpeth in the work and laboreth. 17 And I rejoice at the *coming of Steph'a-nas and For-tu-na'tus and A-cha'i-cus: for that which was lacking on your part they supplied. 18 For they refreshed my spirit and yours: acknowledge ye therefore them that are such.

19 The churches of A'si-a salute you. Aq'ui-la and Pris'ca salute you much in the Lord, with the church that is in their house. 20 All the brethren salute you. Salute one another with a holy kiss.

21 The salutation of me Paul with mine own hand. 22 If any

---

b Or, God's *will that he should come now* Comp. Rom. 2.18. marg.

c Gr. *presence.* 2 Cor. 10.10.

---

found himself able to do (Acts 20.2, 3).

7. *I do not wish to see you now by the way.* That is, in a hasty visit, and before this epistle should have done its work. See 2 Cor. 1.23; 2.4.

8. *I will tarry at Ephesus.* Where he then was, indicating that this epistle was written from Ephesus. *Pentecost.* The great Jewish festival occurring in June, fifty days after the Passover. See Acts 2.1.

10. *Timothy.* See Acts 16.1–3. Timothy seems, from many references, to have been of a shy and timid nature. Hence the special commendation and charge here given. See 2 Tim. 1.4–8.

12. *Apollos.* See note on ch. 1.12. Apollos seems purposely to have remained away at this time, that his presence might not tend to

maintain a party among his admirers.

15, 17. *Stephanas.* See ch. 1.16. Stephanas had come to visit Paul at Ephesus (ver. 17), his family apparently remaining at Corinth.

19. *The church that is in their house.* It is probable that there were as yet no special buildings for Christians.

21. *The salutation of me, Paul,* etc. The previous part of the epistle had been written, as usual, by an amanuensis from dictation; this and the following verses Paul wrote with his own hand, thus authenticating the whole.

22. *Anathema,* etc. This word denotes something devoted to destruction. It is not to be understood here in the spirit of bitterness often attached to the word. See

435

man loveth not the Lord, let him be an-ath′e-ma. ^dMar′an-a′-tha. 23 The grace of the Lord

d That is, *O* (or *Our*) *Lord, come!*

note on ch. 12.3; also Rom. 9.3, where 'anathema from Christ' evidently means an outcast from his mercy and the blessings of his gospel.

Je′sus Christ be with you. 24 My love be with you all in Christ Je′sus. A-men′.

23, 24. *The grace*, etc. This closing message of love and grace shows the spirit in which ver. 22. is written.

THE SECOND EPISTLE TO THE CORINTHIANS.

INTRODUCTION BY THE REV. JAMES DENNEY, D.D.

The Occasion of the Epistle.—This epistle was written from Macedonia, where Paul met Titus returning from Corinth, and heard from him of the effect produced by the first epistle (2.12, 13; 7.5-11). The news was such as greatly to relieve and encourage him. In a serious case of discipline the church had yielded to his authority, cleared itself of complicity, and excommunicated the offender (2.5-11; 7.7-12).

Paul had had an unpleasant visit to Corinth already, and did not want another (1.23 to 2.5; 13.10); but though one possible source of unpleasantness had now been removed, there was more to amend ere he could contemplate with a light heart his purposed visit. This explains the situation in which he writes. The epistle has three great divisions: ch. 1-7; 8, 9; and 10-13.

Contents.—1. After the customary salutation, and a thanksgiving for God's consolation experienced in distress, Paul explains the change of plan which had disappointed the Corinthians of an expected and promised visit (1 Cor. 16.5). It was not due to fickleness—impossible in a minister of God's faithfulness—but to the wish to spare them. It had cost him much pain to write as he did in the first epistle; but, happily, they had acted on his word, and their condemnation of the guilty man had led to his repentance. Paul urges them now to forgive the man (2.5-11), lest sorrow become despair, and Satan rejoice over a lost soul. Then he returns to his journey from Ephesus *via* Troas and Macedonia, and thanks God for all the victories of the gospel, including this last one at Corinth (2.12-17).

With this a long digression begins on the credentials, the characteristics, and the messengers of the gospel (3.1 to 6.10). It is not irrelevant, for Paul's authority and competence as an apostle were being questioned at Corinth, and it serves directly for his vindication. The Christianity of the Corinthians is his certificate of apostleship (3.1-3). God has given him competence as a minister of the New Covenant, as his understanding of it proves; it is a dispensation of life, righteousness, and permanent and transfiguring glory (3.4-18). It is administered in all sincerity by men like him, preaching not themselves, but Christ Jesus as Lord (4.1-6).

The apostolic life is described as a true *imitatio Jesu:* Paul dies daily as Jesus died, worn out by toil and suffering; yet the life of the risen Saviour triumphs, in his mortal flesh, over human weakness, and earth is infinitely outweighed by heaven (4.7-18). The hope of immortality, guaranteed by the Spirit, does not make dying pleasant, but robs death of terror; the soul's only interest, here or there, is to please the Lord, its Judge (5.1-10). The solemnities of the judgment, and the love of Christ, are both motives of the evangelist. Christ's love is seen in His death for all, which is virtually their death; to receive that love is to become a new creature in a new universe, which, like the original one, is God's work. Reconciliation is of Him who made the sinless One to be sin for us, and sent the apostles to preach it (5.11-21). They do preach it, as God's fellow-workers, in a life which proves its power: may it not be in vain in the Corinthians (6.1-10). Here the digression ends, and the apostle reverts to his correspondents. He warns them against compromising connections with the world (6.11 to 7.1), and pleads for a full return of mutual confidence, his relations to them having been strained, though now so far restored by their obedience (7.2-16).

2. The collection for the poor Christians at Jerusalem: Paul wishes it to be ready before he arrives. He recites the examples of the Macedonians (8.1-6), and of Christ (8.9), and recalls to the Corinthians their earlier good-will (8.10). He speaks of the law of liberality, and recommends his messengers, Titus and two others (8.12-24). In ch. 9 he again urges promptitude, to save his reputation and their own (ver. 1-5), and enlarges on the rewards of liberality.

3. With ch. 10, Paul returns to the opposition at Corinth. Some one calling himself "Christ's" had hinted that Paul's ministry was illegitimate (10.7), and that he would not be so bold in Corinth as at a distance (ver. 10). Paul only wishes he may not have to exercise his legitimate power in suppressing the disorders fomented thus in the domain assigned him by the Lord (10.7-18). Jealous anxiety over them, in their wanton readiness to hearken to hostile teachers, makes him foolish (11.1-6). He had never taken support from them, as a legitimate apostle legitimately might; true, and would his rivals imitate him there? (11.7-15).

He is driven, in extravagance of folly, to boast like them, and beats them on their own ground; he has all their Jewish prerogatives, and more than all their sufferings, to justify him (11.16-33). He might boast, as none of them could, of revelations, but prefers to speak of the humbling thorn, which made Christ's grace so essential to him (12.1-10). He comes to Corinth with a clear conscience; his only apprehension is a meeting which will not be pleasant either for them or him. Let them repent, and rectify what is amiss; this is all he writes for (12.11 to 13.10). The epistle closes with salutations and a benediction.

THE SECOND EPISTLE OF PAUL TO THE

CO-RIN'THI-ANS

Salutation. "The God of all Comfort"

1 Paul, an apostle of Christ Je'sus through the will of God, and Tim'o-thy *a*our brother, unto the church of God which is at Cor'inth, with all the saints that are in the whole of A-cha'ia: 2 Grace to you and peace from God our Father and the Lord Je'sus Christ.

3 Blessed *be* *b*the God and Father of our Lord Je'sus Christ, the Father of mercies and God of all comfort; 4 who comforteth us in all our affliction, that we may be able to comfort them that are in any affliction, through the comfort wherewith we ourselves are comforted of God. 5 For as the sufferings of Christ abound unto us, even so our comfort also aboundeth through Christ. 6 But whether we are afflicted, it is for your comfort and salvation; or whether we are comforted, it is for your comfort, which worketh in the patient enduring of the same sufferings which we also suffer: 7 and our hope for you is stedfast; knowing that, as ye are partakers of the sufferings, so also are ye of the comfort. 8 For we would not have you ignorant, brethren, concerning our affliction which befell *us* in A'si-a, that we were weighed down exceedingly, beyond our power, insomuch that we despaired even of life: 9 *c*yea, we ourselves have had the *d*sentence of death within ourselves, that we should not trust in ourselves, but in God who raiseth the dead: 10 who delivered us out of so great a death, and will deliver: on

a Gr. *the brother.*   *b* Or, *God and the Father* See Rom. 15.6. marg.

c Or, *but we ourselves*   *d* Gr. *answer.*

CHAPTER 1

1. *And Timothy.* At the time of the writing of this epistle Timothy was with Paul in Macedonia. See ch. 9.2. *The whole of Achaia.* Achaia occupied the southern part of the peninsula of Greece; Macedonia the northern part.

4. *Who comforteth us.* The comfort for which Paul praises God seems to have resulted from the good reports brought from Corinth by Titus. See ch. 7.6, 7, 13.

5. *As the sufferings of Christ abound unto us.* Much of the suffering of the Man of Sorrows was due to the refusal of the world to accept his message. See Lk. 13.34. Paul suffered from the same baffled yearning. See ver. 6, 7.

8. *Our affliction which befell us in Asia.* This affliction is believed to have been a severe illness at Ephesus.

439

whom we have *set our hope that he will also still deliver us; 11 ye also helping together on our behalf by your supplication; that, for the gift bestowed upon us by means of many, thanks may be given by many persons on our behalf.

12 For our glorying is this, the testimony of our conscience, that in holiness and sincerity of God, not in fleshly wisdom but in the grace of God, we behaved ourselves in the world, and more abundantly to you-ward: 13 For we write no other things unto you, than what ye read or even acknowledge, and I hope ye will acknowledge unto the end: 14 as also ye did acknowledge us in part, that we are your glorying, even as ye also are ours, in the day of our Lord Je'sus.

15 And in this confidence I was minded to come first unto you, that ye might have a second *benefit; 16 and by you to pass into Mac-e-do'ni-a, and again from Mac-e-do'ni-a to come unto you, and of you to be set forward on my journey unto Ju-dæ'a. 17 When I therefore was thus minded, did I show fickleness? or the things that I purpose, do I purpose according to the flesh, that with me there should be the yea yea and the nay nay? 18 But as God is faithful, our word toward you is not yea and nay. 19 For the Son of God, Je'sus Christ, who was preached among you *by us, *even *by me and Sil-va'nus and Tim'o-thy, was not yea and nay, but in him is yea. 20 For how many soever be the promises of God, in him is the yea: wherefore also through him is the A-men', unto the glory of God through us. 21 Now he that establisheth us with you in Christ, and anointed us, is God; 22 *who also sealed us, and gave *us the earnest of the Spirit in our hearts.

23 But I call God for a witness upon my soul, that to spare you I forbare to come unto Cor'inth. 24 Not that we have lordship

---

e Some ancient authorities read *set our hope; and still will he deliver us.* *f* Or, *grace* Some ancient authorities read *joy.*

g Gr. *through.* *h* Gr. *into.* *i* Or, *seeing that he hath sealed us*

---

11. *The gift bestowed upon us by means of many.* The gift was Paul's health restored through the prayers of many. Paul was a firm believer in the efficacy of united prayers. See Rom. 15.30; Phil. 1.19; Philem. 22.

12. *Not in fleshly wisdom.* 'The wisdom of this world is foolishness with God' (1 Cor. 3.19).

14. *The day of our Lord Jesus.* The day when Christ shall reign supreme. See 1 Cor. 1.8; Phil. 1.6, 10; 2.16.

15. *To come first unto you.* Paul had planned to visit the Corinthians on his way to Macedonia, and again as he returned. His defense against fickleness indicates that this charge

had been brought against him. See note ver. 23.

17. *According to the flesh, . . . the yea yea and the nay nay.* This is a denial that he would say one thing meaning another.

22. *The earnest of the Spirit.* Earnest money was a small sum paid to bind a bargain. The earnest of the Spirit is a pledge of complete salvation.

23. *To spare you I forbare to come unto Corinth.* The inference must be that had Paul gone to Corinth at the time expected it would have been with a rod of correction. See 1 Cor. 4.21; also ch. 2. 1–3.

24. *Lordship over your faith.* This is a declaration of entire free-

over your faith, but are helpers of your joy: for in *faith ye stand fast. 1 *But I determined this for myself, that I would not come again to you with sorrow. 2 For if I make you sorry, who then is he that maketh me glad but he that is made sorry by me? 3 And I wrote this very thing, lest, when I came, I should have sorrow from them of whom I ought to rejoice; having confidence in you all, that my joy is *the joy* of you all. 4 For out of much affliction and anguish of heart I wrote unto you with many tears; not that ye should be made sorry, but that ye might know the love which I have more abundantly unto you.

5 But if any hath caused sorrow, he hath caused sorrow, not to me, but in part (that I press not too heavily) to you all. 6 Sufficient to such a one is this punishment which was *inflicted* by *the many; 7 so that

---

k Or. *your faith*   a Some ancient authorities read *For.*   b Gr. *the more.*   c Some ancient authorities omit *rather.*   d Some

---

dom to every man, in the working out of his own salvation (Phil. 2.12). See ch. 4.5; 1 Pet. 5.3.

CHAPTER 2

1. *With sorrow.* Paul had heard, probably from Timothy (1 Cor. 4.17), of such departure in the church from Paul's teachings that he decided not to go in person to rebuke them, with sorrow to both; but first to remedy the trouble with a letter, written 'out of much affliction and anguish of heart' (ver. 4).

6. *Inflicted by the many.* Paul's letter had wrought its intended result, and the church had purged itself. See 1 Cor. 5.1–13. Paul now counsels forgiveness (ver. 7).

9. *Obedient in all things.* This obedience was not toward Paul, but

---

contrariwise ye should *rather forgive him and comfort him, lest by any means such a one should be swallowed up with his overmuch sorrow. 8 Wherefore I beseech you to confirm *your* love toward him. 9 For to this end also did I write, that I might know the proof of you, *whether ye are obedient in all things. 10 But to whom ye forgive anything, I *forgive* also: for what I also have forgiven, if I have forgiven anything, for your sakes *have I forgiven it* in the *presence of Christ; 11 that no advantage may be gained over us by Satan: for we are not ignorant of his devices.

12 Now when I came to Tro'as for the *gospel of Christ, and when a door was opened unto me in the Lord, 13 I had no relief for my spirit, because I found not Ti'tus my brother: but taking my leave of them, I went forth into Mac-e-do'ni-a.

14 But thanks be unto God,

---

ancient authorities read *whereby.*   e Or. *person*   f Gr. *good tidings:* see marginal note on Mt. 4.23.

'obedience to Christ' (ch. 10.5, 6). See also ch. 1.24, and note thereon.

11. *That no advantage may be gained over us by Satan.* Paul feared that in the zeal of their condemnation of the sin, Satan would craftily trick them into hatred of the erring brother, to whom he beseeches them to confirm their love (ver. 8), by forgiveness and comfort (ver. 7).

13. *Because I found not Titus.* Titus had been the bearer of the letter mentioned in verse 4, and Paul's anxiety as to the outcome was so intense that he could not remain and work in Troas, where indeed he found a welcome (ver. 12). He hastened onward to meet Titus, which he did in Macedonia (ch. 7.5, 6).

who always leadeth us in triumph in Christ, and maketh manifest through us the savor of his knowledge in every place. 15 For we are a sweet savor of Christ unto God, in them that *are saved, and in them that *perish; 16 to the one a savor from death unto death; to the other a savor from life unto life. And who is sufficient for these things? 17 For we are not as the many, *corrupting the word of God: but as of sincerity, but as of God, in the sight of God, speak we in Christ.

3 Are we beginning again to commend ourselves? or need we, as do some, epistles of commendation to you or from you? 2 Ye are our epistle, written in our hearts, known and read of all men; 3 being made manifest that ye are an epistle of Christ, ministered by us, written not with ink, but with the Spirit of the living God; not in tables of stone, but in tables *that are* hearts of flesh. 4 And such confidence have we through Christ to God-ward: 5 not that we are sufficient of ourselves, to account anything as from ourselves; but our sufficiency is from God; 6 who also made us sufficient as ministers of a new covenant; not of the letter, but of the spirit: for the letter killeth, but the spirit giveth life. 7 But if the ministration of death, *written, *and* engraven on stones, came *with glory, so that the children of Is'ra-el could not look stedfastly upon the face of Mo'ses for the glory of his face; which *glory* *was passing away: 8 how shall not rather the ministration of the spirit be with glory? 9 *For if the ministration of condemnation hath glory, much rather doth the ministration of righteousness ex-

---

g Or, *are being saved* *h* Or, *are perishing*
i Or, *making merchandise of the word of God* Comp. 2 Pet. 2.3.

a Gr. *in letters.* *b* Gr. *in.* *c* Or, *was being done away* Comp. 1 Cor. 13. 8,10. *d* Many ancient authorities read *For if the ministration of condemnation is glory.*

---

15. *A sweet savor.* The expression is symbolical, borrowed from the Jewish ceremony of burnt-offerings. See Gen. 8.21; Ex. 29.18.

16. *A savor from death unto death.* The revelation of Christ in the gospel came to those dead in trespasses and sins. Those who accepted it, passed from death into life (Jn. 5.24). To those who rejected it, it became the deeper condemnation. See Jn. 9.39–41.

17. *The many.* Those Jewish teachers who were insisting that the Gentile converts must be circumcised—made into Jews—before they could be received into the church.

CHAPTER 3

3. *Tables of stone.* The Mosaic law—the law of outward behavior—was written upon tables of stone

(Ex. 24.12). The epistle written by Paul upon the hearts of the Corinthians was the law of love—of righteousness for its own sake, through the grace of Christ. See Eph. 2.8; Acts 15.11.

7. *The ministration of death.* The Mosaic law was a law of discipline, enforced by penalties, and upheld by the fear of the visitation of death upon the evil-doer through· the wrath of God. See Josh. 7.26. *For the glory of his face.* When Moses came down from Mount Sinai, with the tables of the law, 'the skin of his face shone.' See Ex. 34.29–35.

9. *The ministration of condemnation.* See note on ver. 7. Through Adam came the judgment unto condemnation (Rom. 5.16–18); but, 'there is therefore now no condemnation to them that are in Christ Jesus' (Rom. 8.1).

ceed in glory. 10 For verily that which hath been made glorious hath not been made glorious in this respect, by reason of the glory that surpasseth. 11 For if that which *passeth* away *was* *f* with glory, much more that which remaineth *is* in glory.

12 Having therefore such a hope, we use great boldness of speech, 13 and *are* not as Mo'ses, *who* put a veil upon his face, that the children of Is'ra-el should not look stedfastly *g* on the end of that which *h* was passing away: 14 . but their *i* minds were hardened: for until this very day at the reading of the old covenant the same veil *k* remaineth, it not being revealed *to them* that it is done away in Christ. 15 But unto this day, whensoever Mo'ses is read, a veil lieth upon their heart. 16 But whensoever *l* it shall turn to the Lord, the veil is taken away. 17 Now the Lord

is the Spirit: and where the Spirit of the Lord is, *there* is liberty. 18 But we all, with unveiled face *m* beholding as in a mirror the glory of the Lord, are transformed into the same image from glory to glory, even as from the Lord the Spirit.

4 Therefore seeing we have this ministry, even as we obtained mercy, we faint not: 2 but we have renounced the hidden things of shame, not walking in craftiness, nor handling the word of God deceitfully; but by the manifestation of the truth commending ourselves to every man's conscience in the sight of God. 3 And even if our *a* gospel is veiled, it is veiled in them that *b* perish: 4 in whom the god of this *c* world hath blinded the *i* minds of the unbelieving, *d* that the *e* light of the *a* gospel of the glory of Christ, who is the image of God, should not dawn *upon them*. 5 For we preach not ourselves, but Christ

e Or, *is being done away.* See ver. 7 marg. *f* Gr. *through.* *g* Or, *unto* *h* Or, *was being done away* See ver. 7 marg. *i* Gr. *thoughts.* Ch. 4.4; 11.3. *k* Or, *remaineth unlifted; which* veil *is done away*

l Or, a man *shall turn* *m* Or, *reflecting as a mirror* *a* See marginal note on ch. 2.12. *b* Or, *are perishing* *c* Or, *age* *d* Or, *that they should not see the light . . . image of God* *e* Gr. *illumination.*

13. *Who put a veil upon his face.* See Ex. 34.33, 35.

14. *The same veil remaineth.* The language is figurative: the veil which remained was the belief of the hardened Jewish heart in the sacredness of the old covenant (of the law), which prevented the realization that it had passed away under the new covenant in Christ.

15. *A veil lieth upon their heart.* Many scholars see in this passage a reference to the Jewish custom of covering the head with a four-cornered veil called the tallith, when they were in the synagogue. The tallith did not cover the eyes but hung down over the breast.

17. *Where the Spirit of the Lord*

is, *there is liberty.* The bondage under the law of the 'thou shalt' and the 'thou shalt not' disappears in the presence of the Spirit of adoption (Gal. 4.7) through which we become 'imitators of God as beloved children' (Eph. 5.1), walking in love. See Rom. 8.2.

CHAPTER 4

1. *Even as we obtained mercy.* Paul kept continually in mind the fact that he had been a persecutor of the Christians. His salvation was the greater mercy. See 1 Tim. 1.13.

3. *It is veiled in them that perish.* See notes ch. 2.16; 3.14; also 1 Cor. 1.18.

Je′sus as Lord, and ourselves as your *f*servants *o*for Je′sus' sake. 6 Seeing it is God, that said, *h*Light shall shine out of darkness, who shined in our hearts, to give the *i*light of the knowledge of the glory of God in the face of Je′sus Christ.

7 But we have this treasure in earthen vessels, that the exceeding greatness of the power may be of God, and not from ourselves; 8 *we are* pressed on every side, yet not straitened; perplexed, yet not unto despair; 9 pursued, yet not *k*forsaken; smitten down, yet not destroyed; 10 always bearing about in the body the *l*dying of Je′sus, that the life also of Je′sus may be manifested in our body. 11 For we who live are always delivered unto death *for Je′sus' sake, that the life also of Je′sus may be manifested in our mortal flesh. 12 So then death

worketh in us, but life in you. 13 But having the same spirit of faith, according to that which is written, *m*I believed, and therefore did I speak; we also believe, and therefore also we speak; 14 knowing that he that raised up *n*the Lord Je′sus shall raise up us also with Je′sus, and shall present us with you. 15 For all things *are* for your sakes, that the grace, being multiplied through *o*the many, may cause the thanksgiving to abound unto the glory of God.

16 Wherefore we faint not; but though our outward man is decaying, yet our inward man is renewed day by day. 17 For our light affliction, which is for the moment, worketh for us more and more exceedingly an eternal weight of glory; 18 while we look not at the things which are seen, but at the things which are not seen: for the things which

---

f Gr. *bondservants.* Comp. 1 Cor. 9.19. *g* Some ancient authorities read *through Jesus.* *h* Gen. i. 3. *i* Gr. *illumination.*

k Or, *left behind* *l* Gr. *putting to death.* *m* Ps. cxvi. 10. *n* Some ancient authorities omit *the Lord.* *o* Gr. *the more.*

---

7. *In earthen vessels.* The idea conveyed is that the fragile nature of the human means through which the gospel is spread only exhibits the greater power in the gospel itself which borrows nothing from its ministers. On the contrary, the vessel is exalted by the treasure it contains. See 1 Cor. 2.3–5.

10. *The dying of Jesus.* To Paul the dying of Jesus symbolized the death of the desires of the flesh toward sin. As he writes to the Romans:—'Knowing this, that our old man was crucified with him that the body of sin might be done away with.' See Rom. 6.5–7; 8.6, 10, 13. *That the life also of Jesus.* The word life here is to be construed spiritually;—the inward regeneration as manifest in the outward life in the flesh. 'It is no longer I that live, but Christ liveth in me' (Gal. 2.20). See Rom. 8.11.

12. *So then death worketh in us, but life in you.* The death as to the flesh, manifest in the apostle, became life in those who saw and believed. See Rom. 6.4.

16. *Though our outward man is decaying.* Paul is speaking of the infirmities of disease and old age; the inward man, having been begotten again of incorruptible seed is continually renewed through growth in grace. See Eph. 4.23, 24; 1 Pet. 1.23.

18. *The things which are seen are temporal.* The spiritual things are the real things. 'The world passeth away and the lust (desires) thereof' (1 Jn. 2.17). The whole structure of modern civilization, with all its achievements and so-called riches and possessions for which men strive, shall God 'bring to nought' (1 Cor. 6.13). See 1 Cor. 7.31; also Mt. 6.20; Gal. 5.22.

are seen are temporal; but the things which are not seen are eternal.

5 For we know that if the earthly house of our *a*tabernacle be dissolved, we have a building from God, a house not made with hands, eternal, in the heavens. 2 For verily in this we groan, longing to be clothed upon with our habitation which is from heaven: 3 if so be that being clothed we shall not be found naked. 4 For indeed we that are in this *a*tabernacle do groan, *b*being burdened; not for that we would be unclothed, but that we would be clothed upon, that what is mortal may be swallowed up of life. 5 Now he that wrought us for this very thing is God, who gave unto us the earnest of the Spirit. 6 Being

therefore always of good courage, and knowing that, whilst we are at home in the body, we are absent from the Lord 7 (for we walk by faith, not by *c*sight); 8 we are of good courage, I say, and are willing rather to be absent from the body, and to be at home with the Lord. 9 Wherefore also we *d*make it our aim, whether at home or absent, to be well-pleasing unto him. 10 For we must all be made manifest before the judgment-seat of Christ; that each one may receive the things done *e*in the body, according to what he hath done, whether *it be* good or bad.

11 Knowing therefore the fear of the Lord, we persuade men, but we are made manifest unto God; and I hope that we are

---

a Or, *bodily frame*   Comp. Wisd. 9. 15.
b Or, *being burdened, in that we would not be unclothed, but would be clothed upon*

c Gr. *appearance.*   d Gr. *are ambitious.* See Rom. 15.20 marg.   e Gr. *through.*

CHAPTER 5

1. *Tabernacle.* The tabernacle was a temporary tent. See Ex. 26.1. With this Paul contrasts the permanent 'habitation which is from heaven' (ver. 2), for which he longs.

4. *Being burdened.* The burden of human life is the continual warfare of the desires of the flesh against the spirit (Rom. 7.15–24). *Not for that we would be unclothed.* Paul's desire was not to escape the conflicts with the mortal body by death, but that the mortal should 'put on immortality' (1 Cor. 15.53).

5. *The earnest of the Spirit.* The intense desire unto spiritual things is an earnest of the immortal life. See note ch. 1.22.

6. *At home in the body.* The phrase signifies satisfaction with the human life—the life of the world, as compared with the ardent desire to 'lay hold on the life which is life indeed' (1 Tim. 6.19). See Phil. 3.

12, 14; Rev. 3.20. *Absent from the Lord.* Christ is indeed with us here and always; but, in the clearer vision of the life to come, our realization of his presence will make this present existence to have been absence by comparison.

10. *The judgment-seat of Christ.* The 'fulness of Christ' is the measure to which stature we must all attain (Eph. 4.13); and God 'will judge the world in righteousness by the man whom he hath ordained' (Acts 17.31). See Jn. 3.19; 9.39.

11. *The fear of the Lord.* This is the fear inspired by love, lest we should fail of reaching the stature of the fulness of Christ. See preceding note. *Made manifest also in your consciences.* Paul is confident as to his manifestation unto God, who regards not the outward appearance, but 'looketh on the heart' (1 Sam. 16.7); he hopes that his manifestation of the Christ is recognized by the Corinthians.

made manifest also in your consciences. 12 We are not again commending ourselves unto you, but *speak* as giving you occasion of glorying on our behalf, that ye may have wherewith to answer them that glory in appearance, and not in heart. 13 For whether we *f*are beside ourselves, it is unto God; or whether we are of sober mind, it is unto you. 14 For the love of Christ constraineth us; because we thus judge, that one died for all, therefore all died; 15 and he died for all, that they that live should no longer live unto themselves, but unto him who for their sakes died and rose again. 16 Wherefore we henceforth know no man after the flesh: even though we have known Christ after the flesh, yet now we know *him* so no more. 17 Wherefore if any man is in Christ, *g*he *is* a new creature: the old things are passed away; behold, they are become new. 18 But all things are of God, who

reconciled us to himself through Christ, and gave unto us the ministry of reconciliation; 19 to wit, that God was in Christ reconciling the world unto himself, not reckoning unto them their trespasses, and having *h*committed unto us the word of reconciliation.

20 We are ambassadors therefore on behalf of Christ, as though God were entreating by us: we beseech *you* on behalf of Christ, be ye reconciled to God. 21 Him who knew no sin he made *to be* sin on our behalf; that we might become the righteousness of God in him. 1 And 6 working together *with him* we entreat also that ye receive not the grace of God in vain 2 (for he saith,

*a*At an acceptable time I
  hearkened unto thee,
And in a day of salvation did
  I succor thee:

behold, now is the acceptable time; behold, now is the day of salvation): 3 giving no occasion

---

f Or, *were*   *g* Or, there is *a new creation*   *h* Or, *placed in us*   *a* Is. xlix. 8.

14. *Therefore all died.* The death all died with Christ was death as to sin under the law. As Paul says (Rom. 7.4):—'Wherefore, my brethren, ye also were made dead to the law through the body of Christ.' And again:—'It is no longer I that live, but Christ liveth in me' (Gal. 2.20). See also Rom. 6.6–11; Gal. 2.19.

18. *Who reconciled us to himself through Christ.* This reconciliation to God is explained by Paul (Rom. 5.10) as 'through the death of his Son; much more, being reconciled, shall we be saved by his life.' See following note.

21. *Him who knew no sin he made to be sin on our behalf.* Jesus came 'in the likeness of sinful flesh' (Rom. 8.3.) and was 'in all points

tempted like as we are, yet without sin' (Heb. 4.15).

CHAPTER 6

1. *Working together with him.* Paul says in 1 Cor. 1.21;—'It was God's good pleasure through the foolishness of preaching to save them that believe,' and in this work he recognized the help of the Lord. See Mk. 16.20; 1 Cor. 3.9. *Grace of God.* What the grace of God is meant to effect is clearly set forth in Titus 2.11, 12:—'For the grace of God hath appeared bringing salvation to all men, instructing us, to the intent that, denying ungodliness and worldly lusts, we should live soberly and righteously and godly in this present world.'

of stumbling in anything, that our ministration be not blamed; 4 but in everything commending ourselves, as ministers of God, in much *b*patience, in afflictions, in necessities, in distresses, 5 in stripes, in imprisonments, in tumults, in labors, in watchings, in fastings; 6 in pureness, in knowledge, in longsuffering, in kindness, in the Holy Spirit, in love unfeigned, 7 in the word of truth, in the power of God; *c*by the armor of righteousness on the right hand and on the left, 8 by glory and dishonor, by evil report and good report; as deceivers, and *yet* true; 9 as unknown, and *yet* well known; as dying, and behold, we live; as chastened, and not killed; 10 as sorrowful, yet always rejoicing; as poor, yet making many rich; as having nothing, and *yet* possessing all things.

11 Our mouth is open unto you, O Co-rin′thi-ans, our heart is enlarged. 12 Ye are not straitened in us, but ye are straitened in your own affections.

13 Now for a recompense in like kind (I speak as unto *my* children), be ye also enlarged.

14 Be not unequally yoked with unbelievers: for what fellowship have righteousness and iniquity? or what communion hath light with darkness? 15 And what concord hath Christ with *d*Be′li-al? or what portion hath a believer with an unbeliever? 16 And what agreement hath a *e*temple of God with idols? for we are a *e*temple of the living God; even as God said, *f*I will dwell in them, and walk in them; and I will be their God, and they shall be my people. 17 Wherefore

*g*Come ye out from among them, and be ye separate, saith the Lord,

And touch no unclean thing;
And I will receive you,

18 *h*And will be to you a Father,
And ye shall be to me sons and daughters,

7 saith the Lord Almighty. 1 Having therefore these promises, beloved, let us cleanse our-

---

b Or, *stedfastness*   *c* Gr. *through*   *d* Gr. *Beliar*.   *e* Or, *sanctuary*   *f* Lev. xxvi. 12;

Ex. xxix. 45; Ezek. xxxvii. 27; Jer. xxxi. 1. *g* Is. lii. 11.   *h* Hos. i. 10; Isa. xliii. 6.

4. *In everything commending ourselves.* Paul here, in the verses following, recites his record of persecutions endured and of deeds performed, as well the results of his preaching, as a truer commendation than if he had borne letters from the heads of the Judaic Christians at Rome. It was as if he had quoted the words of Jesus:—'By their fruits ye shall know them' (Mt. 7.16–20).

11. *Our mouth is open . . . our heart is enlarged.* As Paul's heart goes out toward the Corinthians in a larger flood of affection, he does not weigh his words, but writes boldly, with the power of inspiration. See ch. 7.4.

12. *Ye are not straitened in us.* If

the Corinthians were narrow or cramped in their reception of the gospel, it was not because Paul's ministry had been lacking in fulness.

14. *Be not unequally yoked with unbelievers.* There can be no real partnership when the spiritual natures are diverse. Jesus voiced the same warning in his utterance: —'Ye cannot serve God and mammon' (Mt. 6.24). Paul follows up his argument (ver. 14–16) with the exhortation:—'Come ye out from among them and be ye separate' (ver. 17). See Rev. 18.4; also 1 Cor. 5.9, 11.

15. *Belial.* The word in the Hebrew signifies 'worthlessness.' It is here used as a name for Satan.

selves from all defilement of flesh and spirit, perfecting holiness in the fear of God.

2 [a]Open your hearts to us: we wronged no man, we corrupted no man, we took advantage of no man. 3 I say it not to condemn *you*: for I have said before, that ye are in our hearts to die together and live together. 4 Great is my boldness of speech toward you, great is my glorying on your behalf: I am filled with comfort, I overflow with joy in all our affliction.

5 For even when we were come into Mac-e-do′ni-a our flesh had no relief, but *we were* afflicted on every side; without *were* fightings, within *were* fears. 6 Nevertheless he that comforteth the lowly, *even* God, comforted us by the [b]coming of Ti′tus; 7 and not by his [b]coming only, but also by the comfort wherewith he was comforted in you, while he told us your longing, your mourning, your zeal for me; so that I rejoiced yet more. 8 For though I made you sorry with my epistle, I do not regret it: though I did regret *it* ([c]for I see that that epistle made you sorry, though but for a season), 9 I now rejoice, not that ye were made sorry, but that ye were made sorry unto repentance; for ye were made sorry after a godly sort, that ye might suffer loss by us in nothing. 10 For godly sorrow worketh repentance [d]unto salvation, *a repentance* which bringeth no regret: but the sorrow of the world worketh death. 11 For behold, this selfsame thing, that ye were made sorry after a godly sort, what earnest care it wrought in you, yea what clearing of yourselves, yea what indignation, yea what fear, yea what longing, yea what zeal, yea what avenging! In everything ye approved yourselves to be pure in the matter. 12 So although I wrote unto you, *I wrote* not for his cause that did the wrong, nor for his cause that suffered the wrong, but that your earnest care for us might be made manifest unto you in the sight of God. 13 Therefore we have been comforted: and in our comfort we joyed the more exceedingly for the joy of Ti′tus, because his spirit hath been refreshed by you all. 14 For if in anything I have gloried to him on your behalf, I was not put to shame; but as we spake all things to you in truth, so our glorying also which I made before Ti′tus was found to be truth. 15 And his affection is more abundantly toward you,

---

a Gr. *Make room for us.*   *b* Gr. *presence.*
Comp. 2 Thess. 2.9.   *c* Some ancient authorities omit *for.*   *d* Or, *unto a salvation which bringeth no regret*

donia.   See note ch. 2.13; also Rom. 15.26.

CHAPTER 7

2. *Open your hearts to us.* The Corinthians had been listening to charges that Paul was not preaching the true gospel, and that he was preaching for gain. He asks a fair hearing.   See chap. 11.4, 7-9; 12.14, 17, 18.

5. *When we were come into Mace-*

12. *Your earnest care for us.* The real intent of Paul's letter of rebuke was to recall the Corinthians to loyalty to his teachings.   See 1 Cor. 5.1-7.

15. *Fear and trembling.* Anxiety that he should find them free of need for censure.

while he remembereth the obedience of you all, how with fear and trembling ye received him. 16 I rejoice that in everything I am of good courage concerning you.

8 Moreover, brethren, we make known to you the grace of God which hath been given in the churches of Mac-e-do′ni-a; 2 how that in much proof of affliction the abundance of their joy and their deep poverty abounded unto the riches of their ᵃliberality. 3 For according to their power, I bear witness, yea and beyond their power, *they gave* of their own accord, 4 beseeching us with much entreaty in regard of this grace and the fellowship in the ministering to the saints: 5 and *this*, not as we had hoped, but first they gave their own selves to the Lord, and to us through the will of God. 6 Insomuch that we exhorted Ti′tus, that as he had made a beginning before, so he would also complete in you this grace also. 7 But as ye abound in everything, *in* faith, and utterance, and knowledge, and *in* all earnestness, and *in* ᵇyour love to us, *see* that ye abound in this

grace also. 8 I speak not by way of commandment, but as proving through the earnestness of others the sincerity also of your love. 9 For ye know the grace of our Lord Je′sus Christ, that, though he was rich, yet for your sakes he became poor, that ye through his poverty might become rich. 10 And herein I give *my* judgment: for this is expedient for you, who were the first to make a beginning a year ago, not only to do, but also to will. 11 But now complete the doing also; that as *there was* the readiness to will, so *there may be* the completion also out of your ability. 12 For if the readiness is there, *it is* acceptable according as *a man* hath, not according as *he* hath not. 13 For *I* say not *this* that others may be eased *and* ye distressed; 14 but by equality: your abundance *being a supply* at this present time for their want, that their abundance also may become *a supply* for your want; that there may be equality: 15 as it is written, ᶜHe that *gathered* much had nothing over; and he that *gathered* little had no lack.

16 But thanks be to God, who

---

a Gr. *singleness.* See Rom. 12.8.   *b* Some ancient authorities read *our love to you.*

c Ex. xvi. 18.

CHAPTER 8

2. *The riches of their liberality.* The Gentile churches of Macedonia, though themselves in deep poverty, had sent a contribution to the poor Jewish Christians at Jerusalem. See Rom. 15.26. The Macedonian churches mentioned in the New Testament are those of Philippi, Thessalonica and Berœa.

6. *This grace also.* It would appear that the Corinthians were lacking in ordinary generosity. When Paul was preaching among them he was supported by funds contributed by other churches, the church at Philippi being his dependence. See Phil. 4.15. The churches in Macedonia had given of their own accord (ver. 3); the Corinthians had to be asked for their contribution by Titus.

putteth the same earnest care for you into the heart of Ti′tus. 17 For he accepted indeed our exhortation; but being himself very earnest, he went forth unto you of his own accord. 18 And we have sent together with him the brother whose praise in the *d*gospel *is spread* through all the churches; 19 and not only so, but who was also appointed by the churches to travel with us in *the matter of* this grace, which is ministered by us to the glory of the Lord, and *to show* our readiness: 20 avoiding this, that any man should blame us in *the matter of* this bounty which is ministered by us: 21 for we take thought for things honorable, not only in the sight of the Lord, but also in the sight of men. 22 And we have sent with them our brother, whom we have many times proved earnest in many things, but now much more earnest, by reason of the great confidence which *he hath* in you. 23 Whether *any inquire* about Ti′tus, *he is* my partner and *my* fellow-worker to you-ward; or our brethren, *they are* the *e*messengers of the churches, *they are* the glory of Christ. 24 *f*Show ye therefore unto them in the face of the churches the proof of your love, and of our glorying on your behalf.

9 For as touching the min-istering to the saints, it is superfluous for me to write to you: 2 for I know your readiness, of which I glory on your behalf to them of Mac-e-do′ni-a, that A-cha′ia hath been prepared for a year past; and *a*your zeal hath stirred up *b*very many of them. 3 But I have sent the brethren, that our glorying on your behalf may not be made void in this respect; that, even as I said, ye may be prepared: 4 lest by any means, if there come with me any of Mac-e-do′ni-a and find you unprepared, we (that we say not, ye) should be put to shame in this confidence. 5 I thought it necessary therefore to entreat

---

d See marginal note on ch. 2.12. *e* Gr. *apostles.* *f* Or, *Show ye therefore in the*

face . . . on your behalf unto them. —*a* Or, *emulation of you* *b* Gr. *the more part.*

18. *The brother whose praise . . . is spread through all the churches.* No clue is given as to the identity of this brother. Some commentators surmise that he was Luke; others, Tychicus, so often Paul's faithful messenger. See Acts 20.4; also note following.

22. *Our brother.* Also unknown. The two who accompanied Titus to gather the collection were proba-bly delegated by the contributing churches at Paul's request (ver. 20). One may have been Epaphroditus, the messenger of the church at Philippi to Paul at Rome. See Phil. 2.25.

24. *Our glorying on your behalf.* See ch. 7.14; 9.2. See note ch. 9.4.

CHAPTER 9

2. *Achaia hath been prepared for a year past.* Corinth was the centre of Achaian activity, and the church there had been the first to propose aiding the poor among the Jewish brethren at Jerusalem and had actually made a beginning a year previously. See ch. 8.10.

4. *If there come with me any of Macedonia.* It is evident that Paul is writing from Macedonia, and probably from Philippi, where he had been 'glorying' in the generosity of the Corinthian church. The shame would be his as much as theirs if the collection were not as freely gathered in his absence, through love of giving, as under the influence of his presence (ver. 5).

the brethren, that they would go before unto you, and make up beforehand your aforepromised ᶜbounty, that the same might be ready as a matter of bounty, and not of ᵈextortion.

6 But this *I say*, He that soweth sparingly shall reap also sparingly; and he that soweth ᵉbountifully shall reap also ᵉbountifully. 7 *Let* each man *do* according as he hath purposed in his heart: not ᶠgrudgingly, or of necessity: for God loveth a cheerful giver. 8 And God is able to make all grace abound unto you; that ye, having always all sufficiency in everything, may abound unto every good work: 9 as it is written,

ᵍHe hath scattered abroad, he hath given to the poor; His righteousness abideth for ever.

10 And he that supplieth seed to the sower and bread for food, shall supply and multiply your seed for sowing, and increase the fruits of your righteousness: 11 ye being enriched in everything unto all ʰliberality, which worketh through us thanksgiving to God. 12 For the ministration of this service not only filleth up the measure of the wants of the saints, but aboundeth also through many thanksgivings unto God; 13 seeing that through the proving *of you* by this ministration they glorify God for the obedience of your confession unto the ⁱgospel of Christ, and for the ʰliberality of *your* contribution unto them and unto all; 14 while they themselves also, with supplication on your behalf, long after you by reason of the exceeding grace of God in you. 15 Thanks be to God for his unspeakable gift.

10 Now I Paul myself entreat you by the meekness and gentleness of Christ, I who in your presence am lowly among you, but being absent am of good courage toward you: 2 yea, I beseech you, that I may not when present show courage with the confidence wherewith I count to be bold against some, who count of us as if we walked according to the flesh. 3 For

---

c Gr. *blessing.*   *d* Or, *covetousness*   *e* Gr. *with blessings.*   Comp. ver. 5.   *f* Gr. *of sorrow.*   *g* Ps. cxii. 9.   *h* Gr. *singleness.*

Comp. ch. 8.2.   *i* Gr. *good tidings.* See marginal note on ch. 2.12.

---

7. *Not grudgingly.* The grudging gift is tainted with covetousness. Only that part of a gift which is freely given is worthy to be called bounty (blessing). Paul urges the bountiful giving while warning against the hypocrisy of the grudging gift. See Phil. 4.17.

13. *Through the proving of you by this ministration.* The contributions of the Gentiles to the Jews were evidence of their unity with them in brotherly love, as one church. The establishing of this spirit of unity in Christ was greatly desired

by Paul. See 1 Cor. 10.17; 12.13; Eph. 4.5; Col. 3.11.

14. *The exceeding grace of God in you.* See 1 Cor. 1.4, 5,

CHAPTER 10

1. *Lowly among you.* Paul was slow to assume a lordship over the Corinthians (ch. 1.24) even to the extent of administering a rebuke in person. See ch. 2.1–3.

2. *Bold against some.* Paul had personal enemies in the church at Corinth who found fault with his conduct (ch. 1.17) and with his

though we walk in the flesh, we do not war according to the flesh 4 (for the weapons of our warfare are not of the flesh, but mighty before God to the casting down of strongholds); 5 casting down *a*imaginations, and every high thing that is exalted against the knowledge of God, and bringing every thought into captivity to the obedience of Christ; 6 and being in readiness to avenge all disobedience, when your obedience shall be made full. 7 *b*Ye look at the things that are before your face. If any man trusteth in himself that he is Christ's, let him consider this again with himself, that, even as he is Christ's, so also are we. 8 For though I should glory somewhat abundantly concerning our authority (which the Lord gave for building you up, and not for casting you down), I shall not be put to shame: 9 that I may not seem as if I would terrify you by my letters. 10 For, His letters, they say, are weighty and strong; but his bodily presence is weak, and his speech of no account. 11 Let such a one reckon this, that, what we are in word by letters when we are absent, such *are we* also in deed when we are present. 12 For we are not bold *c*to number or compare ourselves with certain of them that commend themselves: but they themselves, measuring themselves by themselves, and comparing themselves with themselves, are without understanding. 13 But we will not glory beyond *our* measure, but according to the measure of the *d*province which God apportioned to us as a measure, to reach even unto you. 14 For we stretch not ourselves overmuch, as though we reached not unto you: for we *e*came even as far as unto you in the *f*gospel of Christ: 15 not glorying be-

---

a Or. *reasonings* Rom. 2.15. *b* Or. *Do ye look. . .face? c* Gr. *to judge ourselves among, or to judge ourselves with. d* Or.

limtt Gr. *measuring-rod. e* Or. *were the first to come f* Gr. *good tidings.* See marginal note on ch. 2.12.

---

teachings. Against these he would be bold. See also ver. 12.

5. *Exalted against the knowledge of God.* The chief scourge of the early Christian church was the body of false teachers who sprang up and deceived many by their worldly interpretations of the gospel. See Mt. 24.24; 1 Cor. 3.18; Eph. 4.14; Col. 2.8; 1 Tim. 1.6, 7; 2 Pet. 2.1. *Into captivity to the obedience of Christ.* The false teachers seized upon Christianity as an excuse to escape obedience as to the law, and claimed freedom from sin through the sacrifice of Christ, while still remaining in unrighteousness.

7. *Ye look at the things that are before your face.* According to outward appearance.

8. *Our authority.* Paul's mission to the Gentiles rested upon a special

divine appointment. See Acts 9.15.

10. *His bodily presence is weak, and his speech of no account.* Paul was not masterful in demeanor, but lowly (ver. 1); and though noted for his eloquence (Acts 14.12), he was persuasive, not dominating (ch. 1. 24).

12. *Comparing themselves with themselves.* The value of a comparison depends upon the standard. Paul measures himself by the magnitude of the work entrusted to him.

13. *To reach even unto you.* The gospel was given primarily to the Jews only. Through the commissioning of Paul it was extended even unto the Gentiles; that is, to the whole world.

15. *Not glorying . . . in other men's labors.* The inference here is that Paul's opponents had seized upon

yond *our* measure, *that is,* in other men's labors; but having hope that, as your faith groweth, we shall be magnified in your you according to our *ᵍ*province unto *further* abundance, 16 so as to *ʰ*preach the gospel even unto the parts beyond you, *and* not to glory in another's *ᵍ*province in regard of things ready to our hand. 17 ⁱBut he that glorieth, let him glory in the Lord. 18 For not he that commendeth himself is approved, but whom the Lord commendeth.

11 Would that ye could bear with me in a little foolishness: *ᵃ*but indeed ye do bear with me. 2 For I am jealous over you with *ᵇ*a godly jealousy: for I espoused you to one husband, that I might present you *as* a pure virgin to Christ. 3 But I fear, lest by any means, as the serpent beguiled Eve in his craftiness, your *ᶜ*minds should be corrupted from the

simplicity and the purity that is toward Christ. 4 For if he that cometh preacheth another Je′sus, whom we did not preach, or *if* ye receive a different spirit, which ye did not receive, or a different *ᵈ*gospel, which ye did not accept, ye do well to bear with *him.* 5 For I reckon that I am not a whit behind *ᵉ*the very chiefest apostles. 6 But though *I be* rude in speech, yet *am I* not in knowledge; *ᶠ*nay, in every way have we made *this* manifest unto you in all things. 7 Or did I commit a sin in abasing myself that ye might be exalted, because I *ᵍ*preached to you the gospel of God for nought? 8 I robbed other churches, taking wages *of them* that I might minister unto you; 9 and when I was present with you and was in want, I was not a burden on any man; for the brethren, when they came from Mac-e-do′ni-a, supplied the measure of my want;

---

g Or, *limit* Gr. *measuring-rod.* *h* Gr. *bring good tidings.* Comp. Mt. 11.5. *i* Jer. ix. 24. *a* Or, *nay indeed bear with me* *b* Gr. *a jealousy of God.* *c* Gr. *thoughts.* See ch. 3.14.

d Gr. *good tidings.* Comp. ch. 2.12. *e* Or, *those preëminent apostles* *f* Or, *nay, in everything we have made it manifest among all men to you-ward.* *g* Gr. *brought good tidings.* See ch. 10.16.

---

the organized church at Corinth, the fruit of Paul's labors, as a ready-made field for their 'imaginations' (ver. 5). Paul suggests that there is abundant territory still untouched in 'the parts beyond you.' See ver. 16.

CHAPTER 11

1. *A little foolishness.* In stooping to meet the accusations as to his conduct 'according to the flesh' Paul places the quibble in its proper light as foolishness. Paul, while building up the church at Corinth, had supported himself with the aid of other churches (ver. 8). His enemies had craftily charged that he had not asked contributions for his support because he knew that

the gospel he preached was worthless.

5. *Not a whit behind the very chiefest apostles.* When Paul had visited Jerusalem to confer with the apostles who had been with Jesus they could add nothing to his knowledge of the gospel. See Acts 15.2; Gal. 2.6.

6. *In every way have we made this manifest.* At the gathering of the apostles and elders at Jerusalem to hear Paul, he and Barnabas recounted the 'signs and wonders' which had attended their ministry. See Acts 15.12; Jn. 4.48.

9. *And was in want.* There is a sting of reproach in this simple statement of fact. The Corinthians had not taken thought as to Paul's daily necessities while he labored

and in everything I kept myself from being burdensome unto you, and *so* will I keep *myself*. 10 As the truth of Christ is in me, no man shall stop me of this glorying in the regions of A-cha′ia. 11 Wherefore? because I love you not? God knoweth. 12 But what I do, that I will do, that I may cut off *h*occasion from them that desire an occasion; that wherein they glory, they may be found even as we. 13 For such men are false apostles, deceitful workers, fashioning themselves into apostles of Christ. 14 And no marvel; for even Satan fashioneth himself into an angel of light. 15 It is no great thing therefore if his ministers also fashion themselves as ministers of righteousness; whose end shall be according to their works.

16 I say again, Let no man think me foolish; but if *ye do*, yet as foolish receive me, that I

also may glory a little. 17 That which I speak, I speak not after the Lord, but as in foolishness, in this confidence of glorying. 18 Seeing that many glory after the flesh, I will glory also. 19 For ye bear with the foolish gladly, being wise *yourselves*. 20 For ye bear with a man, if he bringeth you into bondage, if he devoureth you, if he taketh you *captive*, if he exalteth himself, if he smiteth you on the face. 21 I speak by way of disparagement, as though we had been weak. Yet whereinsoever any is bold (I speak in foolishness), I am bold also. 22 Are they Hebrews? so am I. Are they Is′ra-el-ites? so am I. Are they the seed of Abraham? so am I. 23 Are they ministers of Christ? (I speak as one beside himself) I more; in labors more abundantly, in prisons more abundantly, in stripes above measure, in deaths oft. 24 Of the Jews

---

h Gr. *the occasion of them.*

---

among them. His wants were relieved by others; and yet they hearkened to criticism of him for bearing in silence their own shortcomings, See 1 Cor. 9.11, 12.

13. *For such men are false apostles.* The test of true fellowship in Christ, as laid down by the apostles, was the love of the brethren. See 1 Pet. 1.22; 1 Jn. 3.14, 19.

17. *I speak not after the Lord, but as in foolishness.* Paul administers a rebuke, even as he answers the charges against him:—these things were not of the Lord, therefore foolishness. But even in his conduct as to the foolish things of the flesh he glories that he has been the giver and not a dependent on unwilling bounty.

20. *For ye bear with a man*, etc. After asking that the Corinthians bear with him in his fancy of bringing them the gospel without cost

to them (1 Cor. 9.12), even though he suffered want in so doing, he offers as a reason for expecting this favor, a catalogue of the opposite characteristics of his enemy whom they had gladly received and listened to.

23. *As one beside himself.* The idea of calling such a man (ver. 20) a minister of Christ, even for the purpose of comparison, is devoid of all reason. And here the parallel breaks down, for Paul's accuser has no record of afflictions and persecutions to match the history of Paul.

24. *Forty stripes save one.* The penalty of forty stripes, under the Jewish law, was coupled with an injunction that this number should not be exceeded. Lest a mistake be made in the count it was customary to cease with the thirty-ninth stroke. See Deut. 25.3. These scourgings are not recorded in The Acts. One

five times received I forty *stripes* save one. 25 Thrice was I beaten with rods, once was I stoned, thrice I suffered shipwreck, a night and a day have I been in the deep; 26 *in* journeyings often, *in* perils of rivers, *in* perils of robbers, *in* perils from *my* [i]countrymen, *in* perils from the Gen′tiles, *in* perils in the city, *in* perils in the wilderness, *in* perils in the sea, *in* perils among false brethren; 27 *in* labor and travail, in watchings often, in hunger and thirst, in fastings often, in cold and nakedness. 28 [k]Besides those things that are without, there is that which presseth upon me daily, anxiety for all the churches. 29 Who is weak, and I am not weak? who is caused to stumble, and I burn not? 30 If I must needs glory, I will glory of the things that concern my weakness. 31 [l]The God and Father of the Lord Je′sus, he who is blessed [m]for evermore knoweth that I lie not. 32 In Da-mas′cus the [n]governor under

Ar′e-tas the king guarded the city of the Dam-a-scenes′ in order to take me: 33 and through a window was I let down in a basket by the wall, and escaped his hands.

12 [a]I must needs glory, though it is not expedient; but I will come to visions and revelations of the Lord. 2 I know a man in Christ, fourteen years ago (whether in the body, I know not; or whether out of the body, I know not; God knoweth), such a one caught up even to the third heaven. 3 And I know such a man (whether in the body, or apart from the body, I know not; God knoweth), 4 how that he was caught up into Paradise, and heard unspeakable words, which it is not lawful for a man to utter. 5 On behalf of such a one will I glory: but on mine own behalf I will not glory, save in *my* weaknesses. 6 For if I should desire to glory, I shall not be foolish; for I shall speak the truth: but I forbear, lest any man should account of

---

i Gr. *race.* Comp. Acts. 7.19.   k Or, *Besides the things which I omit*   Or, *Besides the things that come out of course*   l Or, *God and the Father*   See Rom. 15.6.

m Gr. *unto the ages.*   n Gr. *ethnarch.*   a Some ancient authorities read *Now to glory is not expedient, but I will come &c.*

---

of the beatings with rods was at Philippi (Acts 16.22), and the stoning was at Lystra (Acts 14.19).

30. *I will glory of the things that concern my weakness.* Paul's achievements, he knew, were by the power of Christ working in him (Col. 1.29). For himself all he could boast of were the sufferings he had endured in the service.

33. *Through a window was I let down in a basket.* See Acts 9.25.

CHAPTER 12

1. *I must needs glory.* The attitude of the Corinthians toward Paul's accuser forced him to recount

to them circumstances which would tend to prove his devotion to the cause of Christ. But even this he did under protest.

2. *Fourteen years ago.* The vision on the road to Damascus (Acts 9.3) had occurred about twenty years before; and it is generally believed that the vision here referred to is that in the Temple, recorded in Acts 22.17.

4. *Paradise.* The word is used to signify the heavenly abode of departed spirits. See Luke 23.43; Rev. 2.7.

6. *For I shall speak the truth.* The inference is that Paul's accuser was

me above that which he seeth
me *to be*, or heareth from me.
7 And by reason of the exceeding greatness of the [b]revelations,
that I should not be exalted overmuch, there was given to me a
[c]thorn in the flesh, a messenger
of Satan to buffet me, that I
should not be exalted overmuch.
8 Concerning this thing I besought the Lord thrice, that it
might depart from me. 9 And
he hath said unto me, **My grace
is sufficient for thee: for** *my*
**power is made perfect in weak-
ness.** Most gladly therefore will
I rather glory in my weaknesses,
that the power of Christ may
[d]rest upon me. 10 Wherefore I
take pleasure in weaknesses, in
injuries, in necessities, in persecutions, in distresses, for
Christ's sake: for when I am
weak, then am I strong.

11 I am become foolish: ye
compelled me; for I ought to
have been commended of you:
for in nothing was I behind [e]the
very chiefest apostles, though I
am nothing. 12 Truly the signs
of an apostle were wrought

among you in all [f]patience, by
signs and wonders and [g]mighty
works. 13 For what is there
wherein ye were made inferior
to the rest of the churches, except *it be* that I myself was not a
burden to you? forgive me this
wrong.

14 Behold, this is the third
time I am ready to come to you;
and I will not be a burden to you:
for I seek not yours, but you:
for the children ought not to lay
up for the parents, but the
parents for the children. 15 And
I will most gladly spend and be
[h]spent for your souls. If I love
you more abundantly, am I
loved the less? 16 But be it so,
I did not myself burden you;
but, being crafty, I caught you
with guile. 17 Did I take advantage of you by any one of
them whom I have sent unto
you? 18 I exhorted Ti'tus, and
I sent the brother with him.
Did Ti'tus take any advantage
of you? walked we not [i]in the
same spirit? *walked we* not in
the same steps?

19 [k]Ye think all this time that

---

b Some ancient authorities read *revelations—wherefore that &c.*   c Or. *stake*
d Or, *cover me*   Gr. *spread a tabernacle over
me.* See Rev. 7.15.

e Or, *those preëminent apostles*   f Or,
stedfastness   g Gr. *powers.*   h Gr. *spent
out.*   i Or, *by the same Spirit*   k Or,
Think ye . . . you?

---

not careful to restrict his boasting
to simple fact.

7. *A thorn in the flesh.* There have
been many conjectures as to the
nature of this affliction. Paul's
reference to it suggests that it was a
source of constant humiliation, lest
he be consumed with pride.

9. *My grace is sufficient for thee.*
From this it would seem that the
desired healing was denied to Paul,
and that it was shown him that the
grace of God manifest in him was
wholly sufficient to overbalance any
physical deficiency.

10. *For when I am weak, then am*

I strong. His weakness led him the
more quickly and earnestly to seek
the power of Christ.

11. *Though I am nothing.* All
glory belongs to Christ. See 1 Cor.
2.2; Phil. 3.9.

12. *By signs and wonders.* See
note on ver. 6.

14. *But the parents for the children.*
Paul stood in the place of father to
the church in Corinth (ch. 11.2).
This relation ought to be a sufficient
answer to his critics. See ver. 13;
ch. 11.7.

18. *Did Titus take any advantage
of you?* Whether a similar charge

we are excusing ourselves unto you. In the sight of God speak we in Christ. But all things, beloved, *are* for your edifying. 20 For I fear, lest by any means, when I come, I should find you not such as I would, and should myself be found of you such as ye would not; lest by any means *there should be* strife, jealousy, wraths, factions, backbitings, whisperings, swellings, *l*tumults; 21 lest again when I come my God should humble me before you, and I should mourn for many of them that have sinned heretofore, and repented not of the uncleanness and fornication and lasciviousness which they committed.

13 This is the third time I am coming to you. At the mouth of two witnesses or three shall every word be established. 2 I have said *a*beforehand, and I do say *a*beforehand, *b*as when I was present the second time, so now, being absent, to them that have sinned heretofore, and to all the rest, that, if I come again, I will not

spare; 3 seeing that ye seek a proof of Christ that speaketh in me; who to you-ward is not weak, but is powerful in you: 4 for he was crucified through weakness, yet he liveth through the power of God. For we also are weak *c*in him, but we shall live with him through the power of God toward you. 5 Try your own selves, whether ye are in the faith; prove your own selves. Or know ye not as to your own selves, that Je′sus Christ is in you? unless indeed ye be reprobate. 6 But I hope that ye shall know that we are not reprobate. 7 Now we pray to God that ye do no evil; not that we may appear approved, but that ye may do that which is honorable, *d*though we be as reprobate. 8 For we can do nothing against the truth, but for the truth. 9 For we rejoice, when we are weak, and ye are strong: this we also pray for, even your perfecting. 10 For this cause I write these things while absent, that I may not when present deal sharply, according to the au-

---

l Or. *disorders*   *a* Or. *plainly*   Comp. 1 Thess. 3.4.   *b* Or, *as if I were present the second time, even though I am now ab-*

sent   *c* Many ancient authorities read *with.*   *d* Gr. *and that.*

---

had been made against Titus or not, Paul answers it.

21. *Should humble me before you.* Through the relapsing into sinful ways, without repentance, of some of Paul's converts. This was also doubtless intended as a rebuke and warning to those who had thus fallen away.

CHAPTER 13

4. *For he was crucified through weakness.* Jesus was crucified in the weakness of his 'likeness of men' (Phil. 2.7, 8), 'being put to death in the flesh' (1 Pet. 3.18). See Rom. 8.3.

7. *Though we be as reprobate.* Paul's desire for the Corinthians is that their attainment shall be so exalted that his own shall seem reprobate in comparison. A similar meaning is apparent in ver. 9.

10. *Not for casting down.* Paul's ardent desire to forestall any need for rebuke marks his great wisdom in developing the church along the lines of love, with no display of that authority which was a prominent feature of the government of the Jewish people under the law, and which the Judaizers continued to exert.

thority which the Lord gave me for building up, and not for casting down.

11 Finally, brethren, *farewell. Be perfected; be comforted; be of the same mind; live in peace: and the God of love and peace shall be with you. 12 Salute one another with a holy kiss.

13 All the saints salute you.

14 The grace of the Lord Je'sus Christ, and the love of God, and the communion of the Holy Spirit, be with you all.

*Or, rejoice: be perfected

THE EPISTLE TO THE GALATIANS

INTRODUCTION BY PROFESSOR MARCUS DODS, D.D.

The Persons Addressed.—This alone among the Pauline epistles is addressed, not to an individual or to a single church, but to a group of churches: "unto the churches of Galatia" (1.2). The name "Galatia," however, is ambiguous. Originally it was restricted to the region possessed and inhabited by the descendants of the invading Gauls; a tract of country separated from the Black Sea by Bithynia and Paphlagonia, and bounded on the east by Pontus and Cappadocia and on the south by Phrygia. This country had been known as Galatia since the beginning of the third century B.C., when three tribes of Gauls (Galatians, Celts), who had attempted to overrun Greece, were driven back, and finally found a footing in this part of Asia Minor.

In 189 B.C., Galatia became a Roman dependency, and in 25 B.C., Augustus added to it Lycaonia, Pisidia, Pamphylia, and a large part of Phrygia, and constituted the whole into a Roman province, under the name "Galatia." And it is not easy to determine whether we are to seek for the churches here addressed among the northern Galatians, or in Antioch, Iconium, Lystra, and Derbe. Perhaps, on the whole, the evidence is somewhat in favor of the belief that Paul addresses the last-named churches. Of the founding of these we have a full account in Acts 13.13 to 14.24.

Closely as Paul was bound to all his churches, he was exceptionally sympathetic with those of Galatia. The circumstances in which he had first appeared among them could never be forgotten by him. He had intended only to pass through Galatia; but when he was seized with illness, and might have expected neglect and contempt (4.13, 14), he was hospitably entertained and cared for, and found a welcome both for himself and his message. But this former kindness lent poignancy to his grief at their declension.

Occasion and Object of the Epistle.—During the absence of Paul from the churches of Galatia, Judaizing teachers had found access to them. These persistent enemies of the apostle of the Gentiles taught his young churches that it was only through the gate of Judaism any one could enter the Christian fold. They demanded that the Gentile converts should be circumcised, and should keep the whole law. And they had much that was plausible to advance in favor of the idea. The law was a divine institution, and could not be abrogated. The promises had been made to Abraham and to his seed. The Messiah was the Messiah of the Jews. Jesus Himself had been circumcised, and had kept the whole law. The original apostles followed His example. Besides, if the Gentiles were not enjoined to keep the law, how were they to escape

THE EPISTLE TO THE GALATIANS

from the immoralities in which they had been reared? And who was Paul, that he should presume to introduce this novel doctrine? He had not known Christ while on earth. He was merely the messenger of the church at Antioch, and had no commission from the apostolic circle at Jerusalem. And vehemently as he declaimed against circumcision, he enjoined it when it suited him: witness the case of Timothy.

The very speciousness of these arguments convinced Paul that a great crisis had arrived, and that, if Christianity was to become the universal religion, and not a mere Jewish sect—if religion was to be spiritual and not mere ritual—if union with Christ really meant emancipation from bondage of every kind, then it was time that he should, once for all, make clear the relation of Christ to the law.

Contents of the Epistle.—The epistle falls into three parts—personal, doctrinal, practical.

1. In the first two chapters he disposes of the insinuations against his authority as an apostle, and the consequent disparagement of his gospel. His reply to these insinuations is threefold:—

(1.) He is an apostle, not of the church of Antioch, nor of any individual, such as Ananias, but of Christ and God; and his gospel is not "after men," but was revealed to him by Christ. His movements after his conversion were enough to prove that he could not have derived his teaching from man. He had immediately gone into Arabia; and when at length he did go to Jerusalem, it was to see Peter, not to receive instruction from him (ch. 1).

(2.) When he did confer with the Jerusalem apostles, it was after he had already been preaching for seventeen years; and even then, although there were individuals who were resolved to crush him, and compel him to circumcise Titus, he did not for one moment yield to them; and so far from being reproved or corrected in his teaching by the persons in authority, they formally signified to him their approval of his gospel, and intimated that the Gentile world could not be in better hands than in those of Paul and Barnabas (2.1-10).

(3.) He at once makes good his authority as an apostle, and the soundness of his doctrinal position, by narrating how he had rebuked even Peter when he allowed himself to be daunted by the Judaizers. Peter had habitually been eating with uncircumcised Gentiles, which no strict Jew would do; and this was to yield the whole position, for, as Paul argued, if one who was himself a Jew neglected stringent Jewish regulations, how could he require mere Gentiles to observe them? (2.11-21).

2. In chs. 3 and 4 the dogmatic significance of the demand that the Gentiles should keep the law is explained. Here the appeal is first of all to their own experience. The possession of the

460

THE EPISTLE TO THE GALATIANS

Spirit of God is salvation: how had they attained to this all-comprehending possession? Had they earned it by their observance of the law? It had been given them when they knew nothing about the law (3.1-5). Even in the case of Abraham, the typical instance of justification, it was the same. All the blessing he had was freely offered, and he received it by faith (ver. 6-9). Indeed the law has power only to curse, and this is the very significance of Christ's coming. He came to redeem us from this curse (ver. 10-14). Moreover, the promise had been made to Abraham long before the law was heard of, and could not be annulled by it. Not that the law was useless. It prepared men by consciousness of sin to long for deliverance. It was like a jailer or a tutor—a provisional arrangement till Christ came. Christ alone could receive the fulness of the promise to Abraham. He in His human nature received the full inhabitation of the Spirit, and so proved Himself "the seed" to whom the promise was made. And all who are His, incorporated into Him, are that "one seed" (ver. 15-29). By the coming of the Son of God and His reception of the Spirit, that Spirit of sonship, by forming full-grown sons, emancipates men from childhood and bondage (4.1-7). But the Galatians are carrying into manhood their childish customs, their observances, and a ritual as outward as their old pagan rites (ver. 8-11). Therefore Paul remonstrates with them (ver. 12-20), and argues that the law itself shows that only those who accept the promise, and not those who believe in the law, are Abraham's children, and free (4.21 to 5.1).

3. In the closing chapters he shows how morality is secured without law. Liberty is not license. Free from the law, Christians serve one another in love (5.1-15). It is of the nature of the Spirit, received as the inheritance by promise, to war against the flesh (ver. 16-25). It becomes those who are heirs of the Spirit to be charitable and helpful, and to be sincere in sowing to the Spirit, for what is sown will be reaped (5.26 to 6.10). The conclusion, written by Paul himself, summarily sets his gospel of freedom and spirituality in contrast to the outward character of the religion taught by the Judaizers. What do bodily marks, circumcision or uncircumcision, count for in a religion of the Spirit? Marks such as he bore, a seamed back and a scarred face—these indeed testifying to fidelity in Christ's service—are the only marks that count.

The extraordinary compression, richness in argument, and convincing character of this epistle make it a masterpiece, even among Paul's writings. His clear perception of the sufficiency of Christ for all saving purposes is unequalled, as also is his boldness in proclaiming and in carrying to its logical consequences the truth that He alone is sufficient. The freedom and the spirituality of true religion are once for all demonstrated.

THE EPISTLE OF PAUL TO THE

GA-LA'TIANS

Salutation. The Galatians' Apostasy surprising

1 Paul, an apostle (not from men, neither through *a*man, but through Je'sus Christ, and God the Father, who raised him from the dead), 2 and all the brethren that are with me, unto the churches of Ga-la'ti-a: 3 Grace to you and peace *b*from God the Father, and our Lord Je'sus Christ, 4 who gave himself for our sins, that he might deliver us out of this present evil *c*world, according to the will of *d*our God and Father: 5 to whom *be* the glory *e*for ever and ever. A-men'.

6 I marvel that ye are so quickly removing from him that called you in the grace of Christ unto a different *f*gospel; 7 *g*which is not another *gospel*: only there are some that trouble you, and would pervert the *f*gospel of Christ. 8 But though we, or an angel from heaven, should *h*preach *i*unto you any gospel *k*other - than that which we *h*preached unto you, let him be an-ath'e-ma. 9 As we have said before, so say I now again, If any man *h*preacheth unto you any gospel *k*other than that

---

a Or, *a man* b Some ancient authorities read *from God our Father, and the Lord Jesus Christ.* c Or, *age* d Or, *God and our Father* e Gr. *unto the ages of the ages.*

f Gr. *good tidings.* See marginal note on Mt. 4.23. g Or, *which is nothing else save that there &c.* h See marginal note on Mt. 11.5. i Some ancient authorities omit *unto you.* k Or, *contrary to that*

CHAPTER 1

1. *An apostle not from men, neither through man, but through Jesus Christ.* Paul did not receive his appointment from any man or any body of men, but was called on his way to Damascus by Jesus Christ and chosen by God himself (ver. 15). Paul enlarges upon his election from ch. 1.12 to ch. 2.18. *Raised from the dead.* It was the risen Lord, to whom all authority had been given, who had called Paul—a sufficient seal of his apostleship.

2. *Churches.* Local congregations in Galatia.

4. *Gave himself for our sins.* The whole epistle conveys Paul's con-

tention that the law can define and forbid sin, but cannot cure it. We are justified by faith in Christ, not by the law. *This present evil world.* The time of temptation and sin prior to the reign of Christ in the heart.

6. *I marvel that ye are so quickly removing.* Paul's rebuke at the very outset of the epistle indicates the grave danger into which the Galatians had so readily fallen. *From him that called you.* From God (Rom. 1.28).

7. *Not another gospel.* The gospel preached by Paul offered men redemption from the law. Judaizers were trying to graft the gospel *on* the law.

8. *Anathema.* Accursed.

462

which ye received, let him be
an-ath′e-ma. 10 For am I now
seeking the favor of men, or of
God? or am I striving to please
men? if I were still pleasing men,
I should not be a [l]servant of
Christ.

11 For I make known to you,
brethren, as touching the [m]gospel
which was [n]preached by me,
that it is not after man. 12 For
neither did I receive it from
[o]man, nor was I taught it, but
it came to me through revelation
of Je′sus Christ. 13 For ye have
heard of my manner of life in
time past in the Jews' religion,
how that beyond measure I persecuted the church of God, and
made havoc of it: 14 and I
advanced in the Jews' religion
beyond many of mine own age
[p]among my countrymen, being
more exceedingly zealous for the
traditions of my fathers. 15 But
when it was the good pleasure
of God, who separated me, *even*
from my mother's womb, and
called me through his grace, 16
to reveal his Son in me, that I
might [n]preach him among the
Gen′tiles; straightway I conferred not with flesh and blood:
17 neither went I up to Je-ru′-
sa-lem to them that were apostles before me: but I went away
into A-ra′bi-a; and again I returned unto Da-mas′cus.

18 Then after three years I
went up to Je-ru′sa-lem to [q]visit
Ce′phas, and tarried with him
fifteen days. 19 But other of the
apostles saw I none, [r]save
[s]James the Lord's brother. 20
Now touching the things which
I write unto you, behold, before
God, I lie not. 21 Then I came
into the regions of Syr′i-a and
Ci-li′ci-a. 22 And I was still
unknown by face unto the

l Gr. *bondservant.* *m* Gr. *good tidings* See marginal note on Mt. 4.23. *n* See marginal note on Mt. 11.5. *o* Or, *a man*
p Gr. *in my race.* Comp. 2 Cor. 11 26. *q* Or, *become acquainted with* *r* Or, *but only* *s* Or, *Jacob*

10. *Am I now seeking the favor of men?* Paul's introductory rebuke is a sufficient guaranty of his freedom from all self-seeking.

13. *Persecuted the church of God.* See Acts 8.3; 9.1.

14. *More exceedingly zealous.* See Phil. 3.4–6. *Traditions of my fathers.* Religious precepts were handed down from father to son, often orally. Jesus spoke of the Pharisees as making void the law by their traditions, which they had added to the law until it had become a burden grievous to be borne (Mt. 23.4).

15. *Separated me, even from my mother's womb.* Consecrated even before birth. Compare Isa. 49.1; Lk. 1.15.

16. *Reveal his Son in me.* The knowledge of the glory of God in the face of Jesus Christ (2 Cor. 4.6). *Among the Gentiles.* Paul, being born a Roman as well as a Jew, seems to have had a broader outlook. See ch. 2.7–9. *Conferred not with flesh and blood.* Paul did not ask instruction of the disciples at Damascus, nor even of the apostles at Jerusalem, but went into seclusion to be taught of God. See Mt. 16.17. However, from Acts 9.20, it is evident that immediately upon his conversion he proclaimed his faith publicly.

17. *Up to Jerusalem.* The word 'up' may refer to the elevation of Jerusalem, 2,593 feet above the sea. The direction from Damascus to Jerusalem was southwesterly.

18. *After three years.* This was about A.D. 40. It was not until then that Paul had met any of the apostles and compared his revelation of Jesus Christ with them. *Cephas* was Peter (Jn. 1.42).

21. *Syria and Cilicia.* These were adjoining countries. Antioch was the capital of Syria, and Tarsus, of Cilicia, was Paul's birthplace.

churches of Ju-dæ'a which were in Christ: 23 but they only heard say, He that once persecuted us now *preacheth the faith of which he once made havoc; 24 and they glorified God in me.

2 Then after the space of fourteen years I went up again to Je-ru'sa-lem with Bar'na-bas, taking Ti'tus also with me. 2 And I went up by revelation; and I laid before them the *gospel which I preach among the Gen'tiles but privately before them who *were of repute, lest by any means I should be running, or had run, in vain. 3 But not even Ti'tus who was with me, being a Greek, was compelled to be circumcised: 4 *and that because of the false brethren privily brought in, who came in privily to spy out our liberty which we have in Christ Je'sus, that they might bring us into bondage: 5 to whom we gave place in the way of subjection, no, not for an hour; that the truth of the *gospel might continue with you. 6 But from those who *were reputed to be somewhat (*whatsoever they were, it maketh no matter to me: God accepteth not man's person)—they, I say, who were of repute imparted nothing to me: 7 but contrariwise, when they saw that I had been intrusted with the *gospel of the uncircumcision, even as Peter with *the *gospel of the circumcision 8 (for he that wrought for Peter unto the apostleship of the circumcision wrought for me also unto the Gen'tiles); 9 and when they per-

t See marginal note on Mt. 11.5. *a* See marginal note on ch. 1.6. *b* Or, *are* *c* Or, *but* it was *because of they once were* *d* Or, *what*

CHAPTER 2

1. *After fourteen years.* Commentators differ as to whether this period should be counted from Paul's conversion or from his previous visit. At all events the occasion seems to be, beyond dispute, the council of the apostles and elders recorded in Acts 15.4.

2. *By revelation.* Compare Acts 16.6, 7; 19.21; 20.22, 23; 22.17, 18. *Laid before them the gospel which I preach.* Paul may have thought his teaching might be condemned by the apostles, as it had been by men from Judæa (Acts 15.1). In this private conference, however, with those who were of repute, probably James, Peter and John (ver. 9), Paul was upheld.

3. *Not even Titus who was with me,* etc. The contention of the Judaizers was that the Gentile Christians must be circumcised to partake of the gospel. Paul's argument, doubtless in the line of 1 Cor. 7.19 and Gal. 5.6, prevailed.

6. *Imparted nothing to me.* The revelation to Paul had been so complete and had been received with such faith and intelligence that even the apostles who had been personally in the company of Jesus could add nothing to his understanding of the gospel.

7. *When they saw that I had been intrusted.* As the Lord said unto Ananias (Acts 9.15), Paul was 'a chosen vessel' to bear His name 'before the Gentiles.' *Gospel of the circumcision.* The gospel to those of the circumcision, the Jews; in the words of Peter' to the elect who are sojourners of the Dispersion' (1 Pet. 1.1).

9. *James and Cephas and John.* This James was the brother of the Lord, who had taken the place of James the son of Zebedee, slain by Herod (Acts 12.2). Cephas was Peter (Jn. 1.42). John was the beloved apostle, the son of Zebedee (Mt. 4.21; 10.2). *The right hands of fellowship.* A token of agreement in the faith, and of unity of feeling and purpose.

ceived the grace that was given unto me, *James and Ce'phas and John, they who *were reputed to be pillars, gave to me and Bar'na-bas the right hands of fellowship, that we should go unto the Gen'tiles, and they unto the circumcision; 10 only *they would* that we should remember the poor; which very thing I was also zealous to do.

11 But when Ce'phas came to An'ti-och, I resisted him to the face, because he stood condemned. 12 For before that certain came from James, he ate with the Gen'tiles; but when they came, he drew back and separated himself, fearing them that were of the circumcision. 13 And the rest of the Jews dissembled likewise with him; insomuch that even Bar'na-bas was carried away with their dissimulation. 14 But when I saw that they walked not uprightly

according to the truth of the *gospel, I said unto Ce-phas before *them* all, If thou, being a Jew, livest as do the Gen'tiles, and not as do the Jews, how compellest thou the Gen'tiles to live as do the Jews? 15 We being Jews by nature, and not sinners of the Gen'tiles, 16 yet knowing that a man is not *justified by the works of the law but through faith in Je'sus Christ, even we believed on Christ Je'sus, that we might be justified by faith in Christ, and not by the works of the law: because by the works of the law shall no flesh be justified. 17 But if, while we sought to be justified in Christ, we ourselves also were found sinners, is Christ a minister of sin? God forbid. 18 For if I build up again those things which I destroyed, I prove myself a transgressor. 19 For I through the law died unto the

---

e Or, *Jacob*   f Or, *are*   g See marginal note on ch. 1.6.   h Or, *accounted right-*

eous: and so elsewhere. Comp. Rom. 2.13.

---

10. *Remember the poor.* These were evidently the poor among the Jews at Jerusalem. That the Gentiles, under Paul, did make such contributions is evident from Rom. 15.26, 27.

11. *When Cephas came to Antioch.* This is believed to have been previous to the visit of Paul to Jerusalem recounted in the preceding verses. *He stood condemned.* Peter had been taught not to make a distinction between Jews and Gentiles. See Acts 10.11–15, 26–29; also ver. 12.

12. *Ate with the Gentiles.* The Jews were restricted to certain foods (Deut. 14.3–21). The Gentiles were not under this law.

13. *Even Barnabas was carried away.* Barnabas, although the appointed assistant to Paul in the preaching of the gospel to the Gentiles (Acts 11.22), was a Jew, and a Levite (Acts 4.36). He was the cousin of Mark the evangelist.

14. *Before them all.* Paul felt that the unity of the church was imperiled by Peter's movement toward retaining the old line of separation between Jew and Gentile, and he made his remonstrance publicly. Paul's rebuke of Peter seems to end with ver. 14. The remainder of the chapter is a plea to the dissembling Jews.

18. *Those things which I destroyed.* After preaching that justification was not by the law, but through faith, Paul argues that he cannot now claim justification through the observance of Jewish customs which were a part of the law.

19. *For I through the law died unto the law.* The law was 'our tutor' to bring us to Christ (ch. 3.24). When the law, his tutor, had brought Paul to Christ, he was no longer under the tutor, but had outgrown the necessity for him.

law, that I might live unto God. 20 I have been crucified with Christ; and it is no longer I that live, but Christ liveth in me: and that *life* which I now live in the flesh I live in faith, *the faith* which is in the Son of God, who loved me, and gave himself up for me. 21 I do not make void the grace of God: for if righteousness is through the law, then Christ died for nought.

3 O foolish Ga-la'tians, who did bewitch you, before whose eyes Je'sus Christ was openly set forth crucified? 2 This only would I learn from you, Received ye the Spirit by the works of the law, or by the *a*hearing of faith? 3 Are ye so foolish? having begun in the Spirit, *b*are ye now perfected in the flesh? 4 Did ye suffer so many things in vain? if it be indeed in vain.

5 He therefore that supplieth to you the Spirit, and worketh *c*miracles *d*among you, *doeth he it* by the works of the law, or by the *a*hearing of faith? 6 Even as Abraham *e*believed God, and it was reckoned unto him for righteousness. 7 *f*Know therefore that they that are of faith, the same are sons of Abraham. 8 And the scripture, foreseeing that God *g*would justify the *h*Gen'tiles by faith, preached the gospel beforehand unto Abraham, *saying*, *i*In thee shall all the nations be blessed. 9 So then they that are of faith are blessed with the faithful Abraham. 10 For as many as are of the works of the law are under a curse: for it is written, *k*Cursed is every one who continueth not in all things that are written in the book of the law, to do them. 11 Now that no man is justified *l*by

---

a Or. *message*   *b* Or, *do ye now make an end in the flesh?*

c Gr. *powers*. *d* Or, *in* *e* Gen. xv. 6. *f* Or, *Ye perceive* *g* Gr.*justifieth*. *h* Gr. *nations*. *i* Gen. xii. 3. *k* Dt. xxvii. 26. *l* Gr. *in*.

---

20. *Crucified with Christ.* See ch. 5.24; also Rom. 6.6.
21. *Died for nought.* Paul's argument is that Christ died to redeem men from the law and its curse upon the law-breaker. But if righteousness was still a matter of justification under the law, the death of Christ had been of no avail.

CHAPTER 3

3. *Having begun in the Spirit, are ye now perfected in the flesh?* The Galatians were not turning away from Christianity, but seeking to perfect themselves therein by observing the Jewish laws and customs. Compare 2 Cor. 3.6.
5. *Worketh miracles among you.* See 1 Cor. 12.10; Heb. 2.4.
6. *Abraham believed God.* Salvation through faith is the teaching of the Old Testament as well as of the New. But the faith required then,

as now, is of the vital kind which is perfected in obedience and expressed in works. See Jas. 2.21–23.
7. *Sons of Abraham.* In the spiritual sense those who receive the faith are Abraham's sons, whether Jews or Gentiles.
8. *In thee shall all the nations be blessed.* See Gen. 12.3. Jesus Christ, of the seed of Abraham, brought salvation not only to the Jews, but to the whole world.
10. *Cursed is every one who continueth not,* etc. This is the concluding paragraph of the condemnation under the law pronounced upon the Levites from Mount Ebal (Deut. 27.26). The law demanded entire obedience. He who violated one commandment was guilty of all (Jas. 2.10). Since no man is perfect, he who abides under the law and does not keep all, abides under the curse. Justification is by faith through obedience.

466

the law before God, is evident: for, *m*The righteous shall live by faith; 12 and the law is not of faith; but, *n*He that doeth them shall live in them. 13 Christ redeemed us from the curse of the law, having become a curse for us; for it is written, *o*Cursed is every one that hangeth on a tree: 14 that upon the Gen'tiles might come the blessing of Abraham in Christ Je'sus; that we might receive the promise of the Spirit through faith.

15 Brethren, I speak after the manner of men: Though it be but a man's covenant, yet when it hath been confirmed, no one maketh it void, or addeth thereto. 16 Now to Abraham were the promises spoken, and to his seed. He saith not, And to seeds, as of many; but as of one, *p*And to thy seed, which is Christ. 17 Now this I say: A covenant confirmed beforehand by God,

the law, which came four hundred and thirty years after, doth not disannul, so as to make the promise of none effect. 18 For if the inheritance is of the law, it is no more of promise: but God hath granted it to Abraham by promise. 19 What then is the law? It was added because of transgressions, till the seed should come to whom the promise hath been made; *and it was* ordained through angels by the hand of a mediator. 20 Now a mediator is not *a mediator* of one; but God is one. 21 Is the law then against the promises of God? God forbid: for if there had been a law given which could make alive, verily righteousness would have been of the law. 22 But the scripture shut up all things under sin, that the promise by faith in Je'sus Christ might be given to them that believe.

---

m Hab. ii. 4.   *n* Lev. xviii. 5.   *o* Dt.   xxi. 23.   *p* Gen. xiii. 15; xvii. 8.

12. *Shall live in them.* 'In them' in the sense of 'by means of them.'

13. *Having become a curse for us.* Jesus came under the law and in his death paid the penalty of the law. Like the symbolic scape-goat (Lev. 16.5–26), he was the representative of the sin and the curse which it entailed.

14. *Receive the promise of the Spirit through faith.* Faith is the only channel through which the promised gift of the Spirit can be received.

16. *To Abraham were the promises spoken.* See Gen. 12.1–3; 17.2–8.

17. *Confirmed beforehand by God.* 'He is faithful that promised' (Heb. 10.23).

18. *For if the inheritance is of the law.* An inheritance founded on the law would fail through failure to keep the law. It is saved by faith in the promises and in Christ as the fulfilment of the promises.

19. *What then is the law?* It was

added because of transgressions. 'The law made nothing perfect' (Heb. 7.19), but is a guide leading unto Christ (ver. 24), who 'having been made perfect, he became unto all them that obey him the author of eternal salvation' (Heb. 5.9). *Till the seed should come.* The iniquities of the unrighteous extended to the third and fourth generations (Ex. 20.5). *Ordained through angels.* See Acts 7.53; Heb. 2.2.

20. *A mediator is not a mediator o* *one.* The offices of a mediator are needed only when the parties are divided. There was no mediato' between God and Abraham; there is no mediator between Christ and the believer.

21. *Is the law then against the promises?* The law of Moses ended in the higher law of the gospel. For Christ became 'the mediator of a better covenant' (Heb. 8.6). See also Heb. 8.7–13.

23 But before faith came, we were kept in ward under the law, shut up unto the faith which should afterwards be revealed. 24 So that the law is become our tutor *to bring us* unto Christ, that we might be justified by faith. 25 But now that faith is come, we are no longer under a tutor. 26 For ye are all sons of God, through faith, in Christ Je′sus. 27 For as many of you as were baptized into Christ did put on Christ. 28 There can be neither Jew nor Greek, there can be neither bond nor free, there can be no male and female; for ye all are one *man* in Christ Je′sus. 29 And if ye are Christ's, then are ye Abraham's seed, heirs according to promise.

4 But I say that so long as the heir is a child, he differeth nothing from a bondservant though he is lord of all; 2 but is under guardians and stewards until the day appointed of the father. 3 So we also, when we were children, were held in bondage under the *a*rudiments

of the world: 4 but when the fulness of the time came, God sent forth his Son, born of a woman, born under the law, 5 that he might redeem them that were under the law, that we might receive the adoption of sons. 6 And because ye are sons, God sent forth the Spirit of his Son into our hearts, crying, Ab′ba, Father. 7 So that thou art no longer a bondservant, but a son; and if a son, then an heir through God.

8 Howbeit at that time, not knowing God, ye were in bondage to them that by nature are no gods: 9 but now that ye have come to know God, or rather to be known by God, how turn ye back again to the weak and beggarly *b*rudiments, whereunto ye desire to be in bondage over again? 10 Ye observe days, and months, and seasons, and years. 11 I am afraid of you, lest by any means I have bestowed labor upon you in vain.

12 I beseech you, brethren, become as I *am*, for I also *am*

---

a Or, *elements* 2 Pet. 3.10, 12.

b Or, *elements* See ver. 3.

---

23. *Shut up unto the faith.* In bondage under the law, in the absence of the higher motive power of faith, until released by righteousness through faith.

24. *The law is become our tutor.* See ch. 4.1, 2.

CHAPTER 4

5. *Born under the law.* Jesus was born a Jew and so under the Jewish law as well as under the covenant with Abraham. See Lev. 26.46; 27.34.

5. *The adoption of sons.* See Rom. 8.14–17.

8. *In bondage to them that by nature are no gods.* That is, the Galatians were formerly idolaters.

9. *Rudiments.* Jewish laws and ceremonies which were but symbols of the gospel revealed in Jesus Christ, through which they were to know God as Father, and be known by Him as sons. The turning back to exalt mere forms was idolatry. See note on ver. 8.

10. *Ye observe days*, etc. The Jews held certain days sacred to certain feasts and festivals. See Col. 2.16, 17.

11. *I am afraid of you.* The expression is one of anxiety, not of fear.

12. *Become as I am.* Although a Hebrew of the Hebrews (Phil. 3.5), Paul knew that in Christ he was free of the old Jewish law. His remonstrance is the more pointed to the

become as ye *are.* Ye did me no wrong: 13 but ye know that because of an infirmity of the flesh I *c*preached the gospel unto you the *d*first time: 14 and that which was a temptation to you in my flesh ye despised not, nor *e*rejected; but ye received me as an angel of God, *even* as Christ Je′sus. 15 Where then is that gratulation *f*of yourselves? for I bear you witness, that, if possible, ye would have plucked out your eyes and given them to me. 16 So then am I become your enemy, *g*by telling you the truth? 17 They zealously seek you in no good way; nay, they desire to shut you out, that ye may seek them. 18 But it is good to be zealously sought in a good matter at all times, and not only when I am present with you. 19 My little children, of whom I am again in travail until Christ be formed in you—20 but I could wish to be present with you now, and to change my tone; for I am perplexed about you.

21 Tell me, ye that desire to be under the law, do ye not hear the law? 22 For it is written, *h*that Abraham had two sons, one by the handmaid, and one by the freewoman. 23 *i*Howbeit the *son* by the handmaid is born after the flesh; but the *son* by the freewoman *is born* through promise. 24 Which things contain an allegory: for these *women* are two covenants; one from mount Si′nai, bearing children unto bondage, which is Ha′gar. 25 *k*Now this Ha′gar is mount Si′nai in A-ra′bi-a and answereth to the Je-ru′sa-lem that now is: for she is in bondage with her children. 26 But the Je-ru′sa-lem that is above is free, which is our mother. 27 For it is written,

*l*Rejoice, thou barren that bearest not;
Break forth and cry, thou that travailest not:
For more are the children of the desolate than of her that hath the husband.

---

c See marginal note on ch. 1.8. *d* Gr. *former.* *e* Gr. *spat out.* *f* Or, *of yours* *g* Or, *by dealing truly with you*

Galatians who had never been under the law.

13. *An infirmity of the flesh.* This is understood to refer to an illness of Paul's, which was a temptation (ver. 14) to the Galatians to despise him who had wrought miracles of healing upon others, yet seemed unable to heal himself (Acts 14.8–10). *Received me as an angel.* Compare Acts 14.11–13.

17. *They desire to shut you out.* The Judaizers, by insisting upon conformity to Jewish rites and observances, aimed to shut out the whole body of Gentile believers.

19. *My little children.* This expression is one used often by John. Paul's use of it here expresses unusual tenderness. *In travail.* In

h Gen. xvi. 15. *i* Gen. xxi. 2. *k* Many ancient authorities read *For Sinai is a mountain in Arabia.* *l* Is. liv. 1.

agonizing anxiety. *Formed in you.* 'Transformed by the renewing of your mind' (Rom. 12.2).

22. *Abraham had two sons.* Ishmael, see Gen. 16.15; and Isaac, see Gen. 21.2, 3.

23. *Born through promise.* Gen. 17.16, 19, 21.

24. *Mount Sinai.* The covenant of Mount Sinai was the covenant of the law. See Ex. 34.2, 28.

25. *Jerusalem that now is.* The city then in Palestine.

26. *The Jerusalem that is above.* 'The city of the living God, the heavenly Jerusalem' (Heb. 12.22).

27. *Thou barren.* Sarah, who became the mother of Isaac, the child of promise. *More are the children.* They include all nations. In the

28 Now ^mwe, brethren, as I'-saac was, are children of promise. 29 But as then he that was born after the flesh persecuted him *that was born* after the Spirit, so also it is now. 30 Howbeit what saith the scripture? ⁿCast out the handmaid and her son: for the son of the handmaid shall not inherit with the son of the free-woman. 31 Wherefore, brethren, we are not children of a hand-maid, but of the freewoman.

5 For freedom did Christ set us free: stand fast therefore, and be not entangled again in a yoke of bondage.

2 Behold, I Paul say unto you, that, if ye receive circumcision, Christ will profit you nothing. 3 Yea, I testify again to every man that receiveth circumcision, that he is a debtor to do the whole law. 4 Ye are ^asevered from Christ, ye who would be justified by the law; ye are fallen away from grace. 5 For we through the Spirit by faith wait for the hope of righteous-ness. 6 For in Christ Je'sus neither circumcision availeth anything, nor uncircumcision; but faith ^bworking through love. 7 Ye were running well; who hindered you that ye should not obey the truth? 8 This persua-sion *came* not of him that calleth you. 9 A little leaven leaveneth the whole lump. 10 I have con-fidence to you-ward in the Lord, that ye will be none otherwise minded: but he that troubleth you shall bear his judgment, whosoever he be. 11 But I, brethren, if I still preach cir-cumcision, why am I still per-secuted? then hath the stumb-lingblock of the cross been done away. 12 I would that they that unsettle you would even ^cgo beyond circumcision.

---

m Many ancient authorities read *ye.* *n* Gen. xxi. 10, 12. *a* Gr. *brought to nought.*

Comp. Rom. 7.2, 6 (in the Gr.). *b* Or, *wrought* *c* Gr. *mutilate themselves.*

allegory the son of the bondwoman represents the bondage of the law; the son of the freewoman the free-dom which comes by faith. See Jn. 8.32–36; Rom. 8.2.

29. *But as then he that was born after the flesh.* See Gen. 21.9.

30. *Shall not inherit.* The children of the flesh, and thereby under bond-age of the law, shall not inherit with the children of the gospel, free of the law by righteousness through faith.

CHAPTER 5

1. *For freedom did Christ set us free.* See Jn. 8.36.

2. *Christ will profit you nothing.* The receiving of the outward rite of circumcision is virtually a denial of the complete sufficiency of the truth as it is in Christ.

3. *Debtor to do the whole law.* There is no middle ground. If one pro-vision of the law (circumcision) is necessary to salvation, the whole law must be necessary.

4. *Severed from Christ.* Through denial of the gospel. 'For Christ is the end of the law' (Rom. 10.4).

8. *This persuasion.* To assume the bondage of the law by making it of equal importance with the revela-tion of Jesus Christ.

9. *A little leaven.* If circumcision were accepted the whole burden of bondage to the law would be de-veloped.

10. *None otherwise minded.* Com-pare Phil. 2.5; 3.15.

11. *If I still preach circumcision.* This refers to the fact that Paul advised the circumcision of Timothy (Acts 16.3), as his mother was a Jewess. Paul had also observed other Jewish customs (Acts 21.21–26). *Stumblingblock of the cross.* The great discord was in the super-

13 For ye, brethren, were called for freedom; only *use* not your freedom for an occasion to the flesh, but through love be servants one to another. 14 For the whole law is fulfilled in one word, *even* in this: [d]Thou shalt love thy neighbor as thyself. 15 But if ye bite and devour one another, take heed that ye be not consumed one of another.

16 But I say, Walk by the Spirit, and ye shall not fulfil the lust of the flesh. 17 For the flesh lusteth against the Spirit, and the Spirit against the flesh; for these are contrary the one to the other; that ye may not do the things that ye would. 18 But if ye are led by the Spirit, ye are not under the law. 19 Now the works of the flesh are manifest, which are *these*: fornication, uncleanness, lasciviousness, 20 idolatry, sorcery, enmities, strife, jealousies, wraths, factions, divisions, [e]parties, 21 envyings, drunkenness, revellings, and such like; of which I

[f]forewarn you, even as I did [f]forewarn you, that they who practise such things shall not inherit the kingdom of God. 22 But the fruit of the Spirit is love, joy, peace, longsuffering, kindness, goodness, faithfulness, 23 meekness, self-control; against such there is no law. 24 And they that are of Christ Je'sus have crucified the flesh with the passions and the lusts thereof.

25 If we live by the Spirit, by the Spirit let us also walk. 26 Let us not become vainglorious, [g]provoking one another, envying one another.

6 Brethren, even if a man be overtaken [a]in any trespass, ye who are spiritual, restore such a one in a spirit of gentleness; looking to thyself, lest thou also be tempted. 2 Bear ye one another's burdens, and so fulfil the law of Christ. 3 For if a man thinketh himself to be something when he is nothing, he deceiveth himself. 4 But let each man prove his own work,

---

d Lev. xix. 18.   e Gr. *hereses*.   f Or, *tell you plainly*   g Or, *challenging*   a Or, *by*

seding of the discipline of the Mosaic law, with its minute and hallowed observances, by faith in the teachings of One who had died the shameful death of the cross.

13. *Use not your freedom for an occasion to the flesh.* See Rom. 6.12–15.

14. *The whole law is fulfilled in one word.* Paul is writing of the law as to the brethren. The same end was attained by faith in Christ as under the law (Lev. 19.18), but under faith the regeneration was from within, through love (ver. 13).

16. *Walk by the Spirit.* See Rom. 8.9.

17. *For the flesh lusteth against the Spirit.* See Rom. 7.14–23.

18. *Not under the law.* The observance of the law was an outward

obedience through fear. The true fulfilment of the law was in love (Rom. 13.10), through the influence of the indwelling Spirit.

24. *Have crucified the flesh.* See ch. 2.20; Rom. 6.6.

26. *Let us not become vainglorious.* Even Jesus said, 'The Son can do nothing of himself' (Jn. 5.19). See Phil. 2.13.

CHAPTER 6

1. *Spirit of gentleness.* Not with condemnation, but with meekness, as of one also subject to temptation. See Rom. 7.19.

2. *Bear ye one another's burdens.* See Rom. 15.1.

3. *Thinketh himself to be something.* See 1 Cor. 9.16; Rom. 7.24.

471

and then shall he have his glorying in regard of himself alone, and not of [b]his neighbor. 5 For each man shall bear his own [c]burden.

6 But let him that is taught in the word communicate unto him that teacheth in all good things. 7 Be not deceived; God is not mocked: for whatsoever a man soweth, that shall he also reap. 8 For he that soweth unto his own flesh shall of the flesh reap corruption; but he that soweth unto the Spirit shall of the Spirit reap eternal life. 9 And let us not be weary in well-doing: for in due season we shall reap, if we faint not. 10 So then, [d]as we have opportunity, let us work that which is good toward all men, and especially toward them that are of the household of the faith.

11 See with how large letters I [e]write unto you with mine own hand. 12 As many as desire to make a fair show in the flesh, they compel you to be circumcised; only that they may not be persecuted [f]for the cross of Christ. 13 For not even they who [g]receive circumcision do themselves keep the law; but they desire to have you circumcised, that they may glory in your flesh. 14 But far be it from me to glory, save in the cross of our Lord Je'sus Christ, through [h]which the world hath been crucified unto me, and I unto the world. 15 For neither is circumcision anything, nor uncircumcision, but a new [i]creature. 16 And as many as shall walk by this rule, peace be upon them, and mercy, and upon the Is'ra-el of God.

17 Henceforth let no man trouble me; for I bear branded on my body the marks of Je'sus.

18 The grace of our Lord Je'sus Christ be with your spirit, brethren. A-men'.

---

b Gr. the other. See Rom. 13.8.   c Or. load   d Or. while   e Or. have written

f Or. by reason of   g Some ancient authorities read have been circumcised.   h Or. whom   i Or. creation

---

8. Soweth unto his own flesh. Compare Mt. 6.19. Soweth unto the Spirit. Compare Mt. 6.33.

10. Especially toward them that are of the household of faith. Fellowship in Christ calls for special love and tenderness. Compare 1 Pet. 1.22.

11. With mine own hand. The letters of Paul were usually written by a scribe, only the closing sentences being in Paul's own hand. Compare Rom. 16.22; 1 Cor. 16.21; Col. 4.18; 2 Thess. 3.17.

13. For not even they. See ver. 15. Glory in your flesh. In the outward appearance.

15. A new creature. Compare Jn. 3.3–6; 1 Pet. 1.23.

17. Branded on my body. Paul here compares the scars of martyrdom for his faith with the empty rite of circumcision. See 2 Cor. 11. 23–25.

THE EPISTLE TO THE EPHESIANS

INTRODUCTION BY PROFESSOR MARCUS DODS, D.D.

The Persons Addressed.—Paul had resided in Ephesus for more than two years (Acts 19.8, 10), and was consequently very well acquainted with many persons in the city and neighborhood. Yet abundant as are his personal references in his other epistles, in this there are no salutations, no references to his experiences in Ephesus, nor any allusions or teaching which might indicate that a church with special and distinguishing characteristics was in view.

In the Epistle to the Galatians, and also in the Epistle to the Colossians, which was written simultaneously with that to the Ephesians, the object of writing and the character of the church addressed are at once apparent from the direct confutation of certain errors; but in this epistle the teaching is positive and general. All this tends to open the question whether the title of the epistle is correct. Marcion, early in the second century, entitled it "To the Laodicenes;" and from the best MSS. the words "at Ephesus" are wanting in the first verse. Beza suggested that the epistle was intended as a circular letter for the churches of the provinces of Asia, and this suggestion has been generally adopted. This letter would then be that which the Colossians were instructed (Col. 4.16) to receive "from Laodicea," and the address might either be left blank, or be filled up in the case of transcripts with the name of the particular churches to which it was delivered.

Contents of the Epistle.—The general subject of the letter is in obvious agreement with its supposed circular character. It is the unity of the church which is mainly in view. The unity formed by Jew and Gentile, redeemed by "one body unto God through the cross" (ch. 2.16), and thus brought into union with God, the unity of all members in the one body of Christ (4.1-16)—this is the theme of the epistle. "In Christ dwelleth all the fulness of the Godhead bodily," and as He is, as it were, the body and fulness of God, so the church is "Christ's body, the fulness of Him that filleth all in all."

"Here, for the first time [explicitly], we hear Christians throughout the world described as together making up a single Ecclesia,—*i.e.* assembly of God, or church; and here, for the first time, we find the relation of Christ to *the* or *a* church conceived as that of a Head to the body." But "the unity of which it [the epistle] speaks has in itself nothing to do with organization, though, no doubt, a sense of it might be expected to help towards the growth of organization. The units of the one church spoken of in the epistle are not churches, but individual men."

But this unity is not worked out in a dogmatic interest, but

473

THE EPISTLE TO THE EPHESIANS

to its practical issues. The epistle is ethical, not doctrinal. The real basis of unity is elaborately exhibited, that the force of the appeals to unison of spirit in all its practical manifestations may be felt. Ch. 4-6 form the real body of the epistle. In these we find its motive, its object, and its substance. There is one body and one spirit, *therefore* must all that separates man from man be put aside. Lowliness, meekness, forbearance must be cultivated (4.1-3); each man must exercise his gifts for the growth of the whole body (ver. 4-16); Gentiles must forget their upbringing in vice, and put on the new man presented in Christ (ver. 17-24); and as one member of the body cannot counterwork another member, so neither can one Christian lie, or cherish anger, or defraud or corrupt another (ver. 25-32). Love is to be the guiding principle of the new life, but not such love as leads to impurity, which ought not even to be named by the heirs of God's kingdom; persons thus dignified must be wise, and find worthy expressions of mirth (5.1-21).

In opposition to Gnostic asceticism, which taught that the radical relationships of life must be abjured if men would be holy, it is in these relationships that the highest Christian grace, the very love which Christ bore to man, is to be cultivated (5.22 to 6.9). Finally, and perhaps suggested by the presence of the armed soldier guarding him, Paul counsels them to put on the whole armor of God, and commends to them Tychicus, the bearer of the letter.

Relation to Other New Testament Literature.—That the Epistle to the Ephesians was written after, but on the same day or within the same week as that to the Colossians appears from Col. 4.7, "All my state shall Tychicus declare unto you," compared with Eph. 6.21, "But that *ye also* may know my state, and how I do, Tychicus shall make known to you," etc. Tychicus was the bearer of both letters. The similarities of thought in the two epistles are also marked and obvious. The reconcilement of all things in Christ in fulfilment of God's eternal purpose is common to the two (Eph. 1.10; Col. 1.19, 20); so too is the conception of Christ as the Head of the church (Eph. 4.15; Col. 2.19); the practical exhortations, although more compressed in the Epistle to the Colossians, yet follow the same order, and embrace similar topics.

Considering that the epistles were written at the same time, these similarities were to be expected. The differences discernible, as well as the fact that a separate epistle was addressed to the Colossians, arise from the more definite erroneous teaching which prevailed in the church of Colossæ. Hence also the calmer and more meditative style of this Ephesian epistle.

474

E-PHE'SIANS

Salutation. Blessings of Redemption

1 Paul, an apostle of Christ Je'sus through the will of God, to the saints that are *a*at Eph'e-sus, and the faithful in Christ Je'sus: 2 Grace to you and peace from God our Father and the Lord Je'sus Christ.

3 Blessed *be* *b*the God and Father of our Lord Je'sus Christ, who hath blessed us with every spiritual blessing in the heavenly *places* in Christ; 4 even as he chose us in him before the foundation of the world, that we should be holy and without blemish before *c*him in love: 5 having foreordained us unto adoption as sons through Je'sus Christ unto himself, according to the good pleasure of his will, 6 to the praise of the glory of his grace, *d*which he freely bestowed on us in the Beloved: 7 in whom we have our redemption through his blood, the forgiveness of our trespasses, according to the riches of his grace, 8 *e*which he made to abound toward us in all wisdom and prudence, 9 making known unto us the mystery of his will, according to his good pleasure which he purposed in him 10 unto a dispensation of the fulness of the *f*times, to sum up all things in Christ, the

---

a Some very ancient authorities omit *at Ephesus.* *b* Or, *God and the Father* See Rom. 15.6. marg. *c* Or, *him: having in*   *love foreordained us* *d* Or, *wherewith he endued us* *e* Or, *wherewith he abounded* *f* Gr. *seasons.*

CHAPTER 1

1. *Through the will of God.* See Acts 9.15. *The faithful in Christ Jesus.* Paul's thought while addressed to the Ephesians in particular was toward the entire body of the faithful in Christ.

3. *In the heavenly places.* In the spiritual realm.

4. *He chose us in him.* This refers not to the Jews as the 'chosen people,' but to the 'Israel of God' (Gal. 6.16). Compare Rom. 4.11, 12. *Before the foundation of the world.* As the spiritual world was before the physical world, so was God's divine plan as to man before the physical man.

5. *Unto adoption as sons.* Adoption is in itself a choosing into a new relation. Compare Gal. 4.7. Also Rom. 8.15; 9.4.

6. *The Beloved.* Compare Mt. 3.17.

7. *Through his blood.* The blood signifies the life. But the redemptive work of Jesus preceded (ver. 4) and follows (ch. 2.7) his human life.

9. *Mystery of his will.* God's will could not be understood until revealed in Christ. See ch. 3.3, 4, 9; 6.19. *His good pleasure which he purposed in him.* This refers to the divine purpose concerning salvation through Christ Jesus. See ver. 5, 11; ch. 3.11.

10. *The fulness of the times.* Through the development of the

things *in the heavens, and the things upon the earth; in him, *I say,* 11 in whom also we were made a heritage, having been foreordained according to the purpose of him who worketh all things after the counsel of his will; 12 to the end that we should be unto the praise of his glory, we who *had before hoped in Christ: 13 in whom ye also, having heard the word of the truth, the *gospel of your salvation,—in whom, having also believed, ye were sealed with the Holy Spirit of promise, 14 which is an earnest of our inheritance, unto the redemption of *God's* own possession, unto the praise of his glory.

15 For this cause I also, having heard of the faith in the Lord Je'sus which is *among you, and *the love which *ye show* toward all the saints, 16 cease not to give thanks for you, making mention *of you* in my prayers; 17 that the God of our Lord Je'sus Christ, the Father of glory, may give unto you a spirit of wisdom and revelation in the knowledge of him; 18 having the eyes of your heart enlightened, that ye may know what is the hope of his calling, what the riches of the glory of his inheritance in the saints, 19 and what the exceeding greatness of his power to us-ward who believe, according to that working of the strength of his might 20 which he wrought in Christ, when he raised him from the dead, and made him to sit at his right hand in the heavenly *places,* 21 far above all rule, and authority, and power, and dominion, and every name that is named, not only in this *world, but also in that which is to come: 22 and he put all things in subjection under his feet, and gave him to be head over all things to the church, 23 which is his body, the fulness of him that filleth all in all.

2 And you *did he make alive,* when ye were dead through your trespasses and sins, 2 wherein ye once walked according to the *course of this world, according to the prince of the

---

g Gr. *upon.*   *h* Or, *have*   *i* Gr. *good tidings.*   See marginal note on Mt. 4.23.

k Or, *in*   *l* Many ancient authorities omit *the love.*   *m* Or, *age*   *a* Gr. *age.*

ages the world was ready for the revelation.
11. *In whom also we were made a heritage.* Partakers of salvation through Christ by the grace of God.
13. *Sealed with the Holy Spirit.* The indwelling of the Holy Spirit was the seal or pledge of adoption. 'The Spirit himself beareth witness with our spirit that we are children of God' (Rom. 8.16). See also ch. 4.30; 2 Cor. 1.22.
14. *An earnest of our inheritance.* Through adoption (see note on ver. 13) we become children, 'and if children, then heirs; heirs of God, and joint-heirs with Christ' (Rom. 8.17).

18. *Having the eyes of your heart enlightened.* Compare Mt. 13.13–16.
23. *Which is his body.* Compare ch. 5.23; Col. 1.18; 2.19; John 15.5.

CHAPTER 2

1. *Did he make alive.* Jesus himself distinguished between life and mere human existence. To be dead in trespasses and sins does not mean unconsciousness or non-existence. See 1 Tim. 5.6; Rev. 3.1.
2. *Prince of the powers of the air.* This is a reference to the prevailing superstition that the air was full of evil spirits. Compare ch. 6.12; John 12.31; Acts 26.18; Col. 1.13.

*b*powers of the air, of the spirit that now worketh in the sons of disobedience; 3 among whom we also all once lived in the lusts of our flesh, doing the desires of the flesh and of the *c*mind, and were by nature children of wrath, even as the rest:—4 but God, being rich in mercy, for his great love wherewith he loved us, 5 even when we were dead through our trespasses, made us alive together *d*with Christ (by grace have ye been saved), 6 and raised us up with him, and made us to sit with him in the heavenly *places*, in Christ Je'sus: 7 that in the ages to come he might show the exceeding riches of his grace in kindness toward us in Christ Je'sus: 8 for by grace have ye been saved through faith; and that not of yourselves, *it is* the gift of God; 9 not of works, that no man should glory. 10 For we are his workmanship, created in Christ Je'sus for good works, which God afore prepared that we should walk in them.

11 Wherefore remember, that once ye, the Gen'tiles in the flesh, who are called Uncir-

cumcision by that which is called Circumcision, in the flesh, made by hands; 12 that ye were at that time separate from Christ, alienated from the commonwealth of Is'ra-el, and strangers from the covenants of the promise, having no hope and without God in the world. 13 But now in Christ Je'sus ye that once were far off are made nigh in the blood of Christ. 14 For he is our peace, who made both one, and brake down the middle wall of partition, 15 having abolished in his flesh the enmity, *even* the law of commandments *contained* in ordinances; that he might create in himself of the two one new man, *so* making peace; 16 and might reconcile them both in one body unto God through the cross, having slain the enmity thereby: 17 and he came and *e*preached peace to you that were far off, and peace to them that were nigh: 18 for through him we both have our access in one Spirit unto the Father. 19 So then ye are no more strangers and sojourners, but ye are fellow-citizens with

---

b Gr. *power.*   *c* Gr. *thoughts.*   *d* Some ancient authorities read *in Christ.*

e Gr. *brought good tidings of peace.* Comp. Mt. 11.5.

3. *Even as the rest.* Though not under the law of the Jews, the Gentiles were, by the nature of their worldly desires, equally under condemnation.

8. *By grace have ye been saved.* See Rom. 11.5-7.

9. *Not of works.* The works are the fruitage of faith; the effect of salvation, not its cause.

12. *Strangers from the covenants.* The Gentiles had not even the hope of the promises which had been made to the Jews as the chosen nation.

14. *Brake down the middle wall of*

partition. This probably is a symbolic reference to the partition in the Temple which set apart the Court of the Gentiles. Its destruction was typified in the rending of the veil of the Temple at the time of the crucifixion (Mt. 27.51).

15. *The enmity, even the law of commandments.* It was this law which separated the Jews from the Gentiles. The new covenant abolished the old. See Heb. 8.8-13.

18. *We both.* Jews and Gentiles. *Access in one Spirit.* 'The Spirit of his Son' (Gal. 4.6.). Compare Rom. 8.15.

the saints, and of the household of God, 20 being built upon the foundation of the apostles and prophets, Christ Je′sus himself being the chief corner stone; 21 in whom *f*each several building, fitly framed together, groweth into a holy *g*temple in the Lord; 22 in whom ye also are builded together *h*for a habitation of God in the Spirit.

3 For·this cause I Paul, the prisoner of Christ Je′sus in behalf of you Gen′tiles,—2 if so be that ye have heard of the *a*dispensation of that grace of God which was given me to youward; 3 how that by revelation was made known unto me the mystery, as I wrote before in few words, 4 whereby, when ye read, ye can perceive my understanding in the mystery of Christ; 5 which in other generations was not made known unto the sons of men, as it hath now been revealed unto his holy apostles and prophets in the Spirit; 6 *to wit*, that the Gen′-

tiles are fellow-heirs, and fellow-members of the body, and fellow-partakers of the promise in Christ Je′sus through the *b*gospel, 7 whereof I was made a minister, according to the gift of that grace of God which was given me according to the working of his power. 8 Unto me, who am less than the least of all saints, was this grace given, to *c*preach unto the Gen′tiles the unsearchable riches of Christ; 9 and to·*d*make all men see what is· the dispensation of the mystery which for ages hath been hid in God who created all things; 10 to the intent that now unto the principalities and the powers in the heavenly *places* might be made known through the church the manifold wisdom of God, 11 according to the *e*eternal purpose which he purposed in Christ Je′sus our Lord: 12 in whom we have boldness and access in confidence through *f*our faith in him. 13 Wherefore I ask that *g*ye may

f Gr. *every building.* *g* Or, *sanctuary* *h* Gr. *into.* *a* Or, *stewardship* *tidings.* See Mt. 4.23 marg. *good tidings of the &c.* Comp. ch. 2.17.
b Gr. *good light what is.* *c* Gr. *bring*
d Some ancient authorities read *bring to light what is.* *e* Gr. *purpose of the ages.* *f* Or, *the faith of him* *g* Or, *I*

20. *The foundation.* Compare 1 Cor. 3.10, 11; Mt. 16.18; 21.42; 1 Pet. 2.6.
22. *A habitation of God.* Compare 1 Pet. 2.5.

CHAPTER 3

1. *The prisoner of Christ Jesus.* Paul was made a prisoner in Jerusalem because he brought Gentiles (Greeks) into the Temple. See Acts 21.28. Compare 2 Tim. 1.8,16. Philemon ver. 1, 9.
2. *The dispensation . . . to youward.* Paul reminds the Gentiles that he was specially chosen to their service (Acts 9.15).
3. *The mystery.* In verse 6 this is explained to be the revelation

that the Gentiles are fellow-heirs. The meaning is that the promises were not to be fulfilled in the racial flesh of the Jews, but in the spiritual acceptance of the gospel in which 'neither is circumcision (Jew) anything, nor uncircumcision (Gentile), but a new creature' (Gal. 6.15). Compare Rom. 12.2.
8. *Less than the least.* Paul never forgot that he began his career by persecuting the Christian church. See 1 Cor.15.9. *Unsearchable.* Salvation was not discoverable by human agency. A revelation was needed.
9. *The mystery.* See note on Eph. 3.3.
10. *The principalities and the powers in the heavenly places.* Taken in

not faint at my tribulations for you, which [h]are your glory.

14 For this cause I bow my knees unto the Father, 15 from whom every [i]family in heaven and on earth is named, 16 that he would grant you, according to the riches of his glory, that ye may be strengthened with power through his Spirit in the inward man; 17 that Christ may dwell in your hearts through faith; to the end that ye, being rooted and grounded in love, 18 may be strong to apprehend with all the saints what is the breadth and length and height and depth, 19 and to know the love of Christ which passeth knowledge, that ye may be filled unto all the fulness of God.

20 Now unto him that is able to do exceeding abundantly above all that we ask or think, according to the power that worketh in us, 21 unto him *be* the glory in the church and in Christ Je'sus unto [k]all generations for'ever and ever. A-men'.

4 I therefore, the prisoner in the Lord, beseech you to walk worthily of the calling wherewith ye were called, 2 with all lowliness and meekness, with longsuffering, forbearing one another in love; 3 giving diligence to keep the unity of the Spirit in the bond of peace. 4 *There is* one body, and one Spirit, even as also ye were called in one hope of your calling; 5 one Lord, one faith, one baptism, 6 one God and Father of all, who is over all, and through all, and in all. 7 But unto each one of us was the grace given according to the measure of the gift of Christ. 8 Wherefore he saith,

[a]When he ascended on high,
     he led captivity captive,
 And gave gifts unto men.

9 (Now this, He ascended, what is it but that he also descended

---

h Or, *is*   *i* Gr. *fatherhood.*

k Gr. *all the generations of the age of the ages.*   *a* Ps. lxviii. 18.

---

connection with such passages as Col. 2.10, and Col. 2.15, the meaning is evidently the powers and influences of the human mind before it has been regenerated by the grace of Christ Jesus. See note ch. 1.3. Also ch. 6.12; Col. 1.16.

13. *That ye may not faint.* The spectacle of Paul's persecutions seemed likely to frighten weak believers away from their faith. That he stedfastly endured them was rather to their encouragement as proving his own faith unshaken.

14. *I bow my knees.* Kneeling in prayer was a posture peculiar to the Christians. The Jews prayed standing (Lk. 18.11). See Lk. 22.41; Acts 20.36.

15. *Every family.* The structure of the human family is a symbol of the divine relation of the fatherhood of God and the sonship of man

in the one family where all are joint heirs with Christ (Rom. 8.17). See also ch. 4.4–6.

16. *The inward man.* The inward man is the spiritual man—the immortal spirit—as distinguished from the outward man which decays. See 2 Cor. 4.16.

CHAPTER 4

1. *I therefore, the prisoner in the Lord.* Paul was at that time a prisoner, probably at Rome.

7. *According to the measure of the gift of Christ.* The gift of Christ was equal to all. Its acceptance was unequal, and its manifestation differed accordingly. See ver. 11; also 1 Cor. 12.4–11.

9. *What is it but that he also descended?* Paul's argument is that he who ascended must first have

ᵇinto the lower parts of the earth? 10 He that descended is the same also that ascended far above all the heavens, that he might fill all things.) 11 And he gave some *to be* apostles; and some, prophets; and some, evangelists; and some, pastors and teachers; 12 for the perfecting of the saints, unto the work of ministering, unto the building up of the body of Christ: 13 till we all attain unto the unity of the faith, and of the knowledge of the Son of God, unto a fullgrown man, unto the measure of the stature of the fulness of Christ: 14 that we may be no longer children, tossed to and fro and carried about with every wind of doctrine, by the sleight of men, in craftiness, after the wiles of error; 15 but ᶜspeaking truth in love, may grow up in all things into him, who is the head, *even* Christ; 16 from whom all the body fitly framed and knit together ᵈthrough that which every joint

supplieth, according to the working in *due* measure of each several part, maketh the increase of the body unto the building up of itself in love.

17 This I say therefore, and testify in the Lord, that ye no longer walk as the Gen'tiles also walk, in the vanity of their mind, 18 being darkened in their understanding, alienated from the life of God, because of the ignorance that is in them, because of the hardening of their heart; 19 who being past feeling gave themselves up to lasciviousness, ᵉto work all uncleanness with ᶠgreediness. 20 But ye did not so learn Christ; 21 if so be that ye heard him, and were taught in him, even as truth is in Je'sus: 22 that ye put away, as concerning your former manner of life, the old man, that waxeth corrupt after the lusts of deceit; 23 and that ye be renewed in the spirit of your mind, 24 and put on the new man, ᵍthat after God hath been created in righteousness and holiness of truth.

---

b Some ancient authorities insert *first.*
c Or, *dealing truly* *d* Gr. *through every joint of the supply.*

e Or, *to make a trade of* *f* Or, *covetousness* Comp. ch. 5.3; Col. 3.5. *g* Or, *that is after God, created &c.*

---

descended. In talking with Nicodemus Jesus declared, 'No one hath ascended into heaven but he that descended out of heaven' (Jn. 3.13). See Rom. 10.6, 7.

13. *Unto the measure of the stature of the fulness of Christ.* Paul sets the standard at the summit, as did Jesus in the Sermon on the Mount: —'Ye therefore shall be perfect, as your heavenly Father is perfect' (Mt. 5.48). See Jn. 1.16.

14. *By the sleight of men, in craftiness.* The meaning here is beyond that of simple false teaching. The deceit was intentional. See Gal. 1.7; Rom. 16.17, 18.

17. *In the vanity of their mind.* Vanity that is—'nothingness'—as

in Eccles. 1.2; not the self-conceit of the Pharisees. See Rom. 1.21.

18. *Darkened in their understanding.* Unable even to grasp the truth. In the words of Jesus: 'He that walketh in the darkness knoweth not whither he goeth' (Jn. 12.35).

19. *Being past feeling.* 'Lost to the accusations of conscience.' This condition is explained in Rom. 1.28: —'Even as they refused to have God in their knowledge, God gave them up unto a reprobate mind.' See 1 Tim. 5.6.

22. *The lusts of deceit.* The enticements of earthly pleasures and desires which lead only to ruin. See 2 Pet. 2.18, 19; Rom. 1.29; Heb. 3.13.

25 Wherefore, putting away falsehood, *h*speak ye truth each one with his neighbor: for we are members one of another. 26 *i*Be ye angry, and sin not: let not the sun go down upon your *k*wrath: 27 neither give place to the devil. 28 Let him that stole steal no more: but rather let him labor, working with his hands the thing that is good, that he may have whereof to give to him that hath need. 29 Let no corrupt‧ speech proceed out of your mouth, but such as is good for *l*edifying as the need may be, that it may give grace to them that hear. 30 And grieve not the Holy Spirit of God, in whom ye were sealed unto the day of redemption. 31 Let all bitterness, and wrath, and anger, and clamor, and railing, be put away from you, with all malice: 32 and be ye kind one to another, tenderhearted, forgiving each other, even as God also in Christ forgave *m*you.

5 Be ye therefore imitators of God, as beloved children; 2 and walk in love, even as Christ also loved you, and gave himself up for *a*us, an offering and a sacrifice to God for an odor of a sweet smell.

3 But fornication, and all uncleanness, or covetousness, let it not even be named among you, as becometh saints; 4 nor filthiness, nor foolish talking, or jesting, which are not befitting: but rather giving of thanks. 5 For this ye know of a surety, that no fornicator, nor unclean person, nor covetous man, who is an idolater, hath any inheritance in the kingdom of Christ and God. 6 Let no man deceive you with empty words: for because of these things cometh the wrath of God upon the sons of disobedience. 7 Be not ye therefore partakers with them; 8 for ye were once darkness, but are now light in the Lord: walk as children of light 9 (for the fruit

---

h Zech. viii. 16.   *i* Ps. iv. 4.   *k* Gr. *provocation.*   *l* Gr. *the building up of the* need.   *m* Many ancient authorities read *us.*   *a* Some ancient authorities read *you.*

---

26. *Be ye angry, and sin not.* The anger which is not sinful is that directed against sin, even in one's self; not against sinners, toward whom the Christly attitude is compassion. See Heb. 5.2.

29. *Corrupt speech.* It is by speech that good or evil thought becomes active. James calls the tongue, 'the world of iniquity among our members . . . full of deadly poison' (Jas. 3.6, 8). The warning of Paul is not to give utterance to a corrupting thought. See Mt. 12.34, 36; 15.18, 19.

30. *Sealed unto the day of redemption.* Circumcision is spoken of as the seal of Abraham's faith (Rom. 4.11). The seal of redemption was the indwelling of the Holy Spirit, but salvation was to be worked out

(Phil. 2.12), unto the day of complete redemption.

CHAPTER 5

2. *An offering and a sacrifice.* This reference to the ceremonial sacrifices of the ancient Jews has been variously construed as a sacrifice of consecration (Ex. 29), a peace-offering, (Lev. 3) and a sin-offering (Lev. 4).

5. *Who is an idolater.* The term idolatry is frequently used by Paul to denote devoted pursuit of earthly things, or even bondage to them;—'that by nature are no gods' (Gal. 4.8). In the first sense he uses the expression 'whose god is the belly' (Phil. 3.19). See also 1 Cor. 10.18-20.

of the light is in all goodness and righteousness and truth), 10 proving what is well-pleasing unto the Lord; 11 and have no fellowship with the unfruitful works of darkness, but rather even [b]reprove them; 12 for the things which are done by them in secret it is a shame even to speak of. 13 But all things when they are [c]reproved are made manifest by the light: for everything that is made manifest is light. 14 Wherefore *he* saith, [d]Awake, thou that sleepest, and arise from the dead, and Christ shall shine upon thee.

15 Look therefore carefully how ye walk, not as unwise, but as wise; 16 [e]redeeming the time, because the days are evil. 17 Wherefore be ye not foolish, but understand what the will of the Lord is. 18 And be not drunken with wine, wherein is riot, but be filled [f]with the Spirit; 19 speaking [g]one to another in psalms and hymns and spiritual songs, singing and making melody with your heart to the Lord; 20 giving thanks always for all things in the name of our Lord Je′sus Christ to [h]God, even the Father; 21 subjecting yourselves one to another in the fear of Christ.

22 Wives, *be in subjection* unto your own husbands, as unto the Lord. 23 For the husband is the head of the wife, as Christ also is the head of the church, *being* himself the saviour of the body. 24 But as the church is subject to Christ, [i]so *let* the wives also *be* to their husbands in everything. 25 Husbands, love your wives, even as Christ also loved the church, and gave himself up for it; 26 that he might sanctify it, having cleansed it by the [k]washing of water with the word, 27 that he might present the church to himself a glorious *church,* not having spot or wrinkle or any such thing; but that it should be holy and without blemish. 28 Even so ought husbands also to love their own wives as their own bodies. He that loveth his own wife loveth himself: 29 for no man ever hated his own flesh; but nour-

b Or, *convict*   *c* Or, *convicted*   *d* (?). Comp. 1 Tim. iii. 16.   *e* Gr. *buying up the opportunity.*   *f* Or, *in spirit*   *g* Or, *to*

yourselves   *h* Gr. *the God and Father.*   *i* Or, *so* are *the wives also*   *k* Gr. *laver.*

13. *When they are reproved.* Reproof brings a fault into the light; that is, it is seen to be a fault, and clamors for correction.

14. *Arise from the dead.* 'Passed out of death into life' is frequently used to express the change wrought by acceptance of Christ. In the same sense Paul exhorts in his letter to Timothy 'Lay hold on the life eternal' (1 Tim. 6.12). See Jn. 5.24; Col. 2.13; 1 Jn. 3.14.

21 *Subjecting yourselves one to another.* Not all grace and wisdom were given to one (1 Cor. 12.8–10). That all may 'attain unto the unity of the faith' (ch. 4.13). Paul coun-

sels lowliness and meekness (ch. 4.2) toward one another. *In the fear of Christ.* In anxiety to know all: fear lest any truth be lost.

25. *Even as Christ also loved the church.* In this and the preceding verses the true relation of husband and wife is compared to that of Christ and the church. The importance of this view leads Paul to repeat it in several different ways. See ver. 32.

26. *The washing of water with the word.* The phrase refers to the baptism of water, itself symbolical of the cleansing baptism of the Holy Spirit (Acts 1.5), unto sanctification. See Acts 22.16.

isheth and cherisheth it, even as Christ also the church; 30 because we are members of his body. 31 ¹For this cause shall a man leave his father and mother, and shall cleave to his wife; and the two shall become one flesh. 32 This mystery is great: but I speak in regard of Christ and of the church. 33 Nevertheless do ye also severally love each one his own wife even as himself; and *let* the wife *see* that she fear her husband.

6 Children, obey your parents in the Lord: for this is right. 2 ªHonor thy father and mother (which is the first commandment with promise), 3 that it may be well with thee, and thou ᵇmayest live long on the ᶜearth. 4 And, ye fathers, provoke not your children to wrath: but nurture them in the chastening and admonition of the Lord.

5 ᵈServants, be obedient unto them that according to the flesh are your ᵉmasters, with fear and trembling, in singleness of your heart, as unto Christ; 6 not in the way of eyeservice, as menpleasers; but as ᵈservants of

Christ, doing the will of God from the ʲheart; 7 with good will doing service, as unto the Lord, and not unto men: 8 knowing that whatsoever good thing each one doeth, the same shall he receive again from the Lord, whether *he be* bond or free. 9 And, ye ᵉmasters, do the same things unto them, and forbear threatening: knowing that he who is both their Master and yours is in heaven, and there is no respect of persons with him.

10 ᵍFinally, ʰbe strong in the Lord, and in the strength of his might. 11 Put on the whole armor of God, that ye may be able to stand against the wiles of the devil. 12 For our wrestling is not against ⁱflesh and blood, but against the principalities, against the powers, against the worldrulers of this darkness, against the spiritual *hosts* of wickedness in the heavenly *places*. 13 Wherefore take up the whole armor of God, that ye may be able to withstand in the evil day, and, having done all, to stand. 14 Stand therefore, having girded your loins

---

l Gen. ii. 24.   *a* Ex. xx. 12; Dt. v. 16. *b* Or, *shalt* *c* Or, *land* *d* Gr. *Bondservants.* *e* Gr. *lords.*

f Gr. *soul.* *g* Or, *Henceforth* *h* Gr. *be made powerful.* *i* Gr. *blood and flesh.*

CHAPTER 6

4. *The chastening and admonition of the Lord.* Admonition refers to the warnings as to those things which are, not to be done (1 Cor. 10.11; Tit. 3.10): chastening, to the inward training toward holiness (Heb. 12.10).

5. *That according to the flesh are your masters.* The coming of the kingdom of Christ did not work a revolution in the outward world, but it implanted the spirit of the brotherhood of man in which slavery could no more exist, and

made the masters servants in Christ to their own slaves. *With fear and trembling . . . as unto Christ.* Whole-hearted and conscientious service sums up and embodies all the Christian graces.

8. *The same shall he receive again from the Lord.* This is in effect a paraphrase of the declaration of Jesus, 'with what measure ye mete it shall be measured unto you again' (Mt. 7.2).

12. *Not against flesh and blood.* The enemy is an invisible one, the powers of evil to be met in one's own being. See Rom. 7.21-23.

with truth, and having put on the breastplate of righteousness, 15 and having shod your feet with the preparation of the [k]gospel of peace; 16 withal taking up the shield of faith, wherewith ye shall be able to quench all the fiery darts of the evil *one*. 17 And take the helmet of salvation, and the sword of the Spirit, which is the word of God: 18 with all prayer and supplication praying at all seasons in the Spirit, and watching thereunto in all perseverance and supplication for all the saints, 19 and on my behalf, that utterance may be given unto me [l]in opening my mouth, to make known with boldness the mystery of the [k]gospel, 20 for which

I am an ambassador in [m]chains; that in it I may speak boldly, as I ought to speak.

21 But that ye also may know my affairs, how I do, Tych'i-cus, the beloved brother and faithful minister in the Lord, shall make known to you all things: 22 whom I have sent unto you for this very purpose, that ye may know our state, and that he may comfort your hearts.

23 Peace be to the brethren, and love with faith, from God the Father and the Lord Je'sus Christ. 24 Grace be with all them that love our Lord Je'sus Christ [n]with *a love* incorruptible.

---

[k] Gr. *good tidings.*   See Mt. 4.23 marg.
[l] Or, *in opening my mouth with boldness.*

to make known   [m] Gr. *a chain.*   [n] Or, *in incorruption*   See Rom. 2.7.

---

20. *An ambassador in chains.* When Paul was rescued by the soldiers at Jerusalem he was bound with two chains (Acts 21.33). Paul seems touched by the irony of the chaining of an ambassador.

21. *Tychicus.* The bearer of this epistle to the Ephesians was a native of Asia (Acts 20.4) and probably an Ephesian. He is mentioned also as Paul's messenger to the Colossians (Col. 4.7). See 2 Tim. 4.12; Tit. 3.12.

THE EPISTLE TO THE PHILIPPIANS

INTRODUCTION BY PROFESSOR MARCUS DODS, D.D.

Date.—The Epistles to the Philippians, Ephesians, Colossians, and Philemon, having been written while Paul was under arrest, are designated "Prison Epistles" (Phil. 1.13-17; Eph. 3.1; Col. 4.10; Philem. 9). From the early summer of 58 A.D. to the spring of 63 A.D. he was detained a prisoner. Of this period the first two years were spent in Cæsarea, the last two in Rome, and some intervening months on shipboard. Some good critics have supposed that one or more of these epistles were written from Cæsarea. But the liberty to preach, which Paul was enjoying when he wrote them (Col. 4.3, 11; Eph. 6.19), seems to point to Rome; and it is obvious that, while at Cæsarea his expectation was to go to Rome, at the time of writing these epistles he looked forward to being in Asia Minor. The mention of Cæsar's household (Phil. 4.22) determines the place of origin of this epistle. It cannot be placed very early in the Roman imprisonment, for time must be allowed for the illness and various movements of Epaphroditus (2.25-30). On the other hand, it would seem to be earlier than the other three from Rome (*cf.* Philem. 22).

The Church at Philippi.—Philippi was a place of great importance. Surrounded by a fertile district, and possessing valuable mines, it also commanded the great highway from East to West, and was on this account attractive to Paul. The town which originally occupied the site was known as Krenides ("Fountains"); but Philip II. of Macedonia, having improved it, named it after himself. In Paul's time it was a Roman "colony" (Acts 16.12) *i.e.* a settlement of veterans who had served their time in the army. Hence it is Rome that Paul meets in Philippi (Acts 16.35; prætors, 36, 38); here that Paul's Roman citizenship can be pleaded; and here that appeal can be made to the sense of dignity associated with membership of a great community (Phil. 1.27; 3.20).

That he keenly felt the ignominious treatment to which he, a Roman citizen, was subjected in this Roman city is apparent from the narrative in Acts, and also from his reference to it in Phil. 1.30 and 1 Thes. 2.2. But apparently this maltreatment drew out more powerfully the affection of the Philippians, so that "once and again," after he left them, they sent him pecuniary aid (Phil. 4.16). The Macedonians themselves were a remarkably stanch and steadfast people, very different from their Greek neighbors; but how far the church at Philippi was Macedonian we have no means of knowing. The first converts seem to have been foreigners. That women play so large a part in the church (Acts 16.14, 40; Phil. 4.2, 3) is characteristic.

THE EPISTLE TO THE PHILIPPIANS

Occasion of the Epistle.—Epaphroditus had been the bearer of some pecuniary aid sent to Paul by the Philippians, and had thrown himself so vigorously into the work of Christ in the metropolis that he became alarmingly ill (Phil. 2.30). On recovering, and hearing how anxious his friends in Philippi were, he proposed to return to them; and Paul felt that he could not allow him to go without putting in his hands a written acknowledgment of their kindness. Hence this letter was intended to be a simple letter of friendship. Into friendly ears the apostle pours a frank account of his expectations, his present circumstances, his state of mind. But he also sought to use this opportunity of abating a spirit of rivalry and discord which apparently had manifested itself among the Philippians (1.27 to 2.11; and especially 4.2, 3).

Contents of the Epistle.—The epistle opens with the customary salutation, thanksgiving, and congratulation (1.1-11), and then passes to a description of the writer's circumstances, making light of his own troubles, and finding much food for thankfulness in the fact that the gospel was rather helped than hindered by his imprisonment. And he believes that whatever is awaiting him, whether death or acquittal, this also will work for good (1.12-26). One thing only he is anxious about, that the Philippians should live in unity, not seeking every man his own things, but the things of others, as Christ, the great example, did (1.27 to 2.11). In his absence they must learn to depend on themselves and on God, and to become lights in the world, not needing to receive from others, but themselves giving spiritual impulse (2.12-18). Then he promises to send Timothy, and does send Epaphroditus (2.19-30).

At this point in the epistle occurs a break. He seems to be closing with the words, "Finally, my brethren, rejoice in the Lord" (3.1), to which he returns in 4.4, "Rejoice in the Lord alway: again I will say rejoice." The interpolation between these two points consists of a warning against Judaizers, backed by a remarkably terse and impressive account of his own apprehension of Christ, and a contrast between those who looked for resurrection in the likeness of Christ and those whose "end is perdition." Resuming at 4.2, he rebukes the spirit of discord, naming two female members of the church, Euodias and Syntyche; and passes on to ethical exhortations which may be supposed to have been relevant to the character of the church addressed (4.2-9). The epistle concludes with a most courteous and delicately drawn reference to his condition, and to the kindness of the Philippians.

THE EPISTLE OF PAUL TO THE

PHI-LIP'PI-ANS

Salutation. Thanksgiving and Supplication

1 Paul and Tim'o-thy, ᵃservants of Christ Je'sus, to all the saints in Christ Je'sus that are at Phi-lip'pi, with the ᵇbishops and deacons: 2 Grace to you and peace from God our Father and the Lord Je'sus Christ.

3 I thank my God upon all my remembrance of you, 4 always in every supplication of mine on behalf of you all making my supplication with joy, 5 for your fellowship in furtherance of the ᶜgospel from the first day until now; 6 being confident of this very thing, that he who be-

gan a good work in you will perfect it until the day of Je'sus Christ: 7 even as it is right for me to be thus minded on behalf of you all, because ᵈI have you in my heart, inasmuch as, both in my bonds and in the defence and confirmation of the ᶜgospel, ye all are partakers with me of grace. 8 For God is my witness, how I long after you all in the tender mercies of Christ Je'sus. 9 And this I pray, that your love may abound yet more and more in knowledge and all discernment; 10 so that ye may ᵉapprove the things that are excellent; that ye may be sincere and

---

a Gr. *bondservants.*   b Or, *overseers* c Gr. *good tidings:* and so elsewhere; see marginal note on Mt. 4.23.

d Or, *ye have me in your heart*   e Or, *distinguish the things that differ*

CHAPTER 1

1. *Paul and Timothy.* The church at Philippi had been established by Paul when Timothy was with him. See Acts 16.1, 12–15.   *The saints.* Those who were 'sanctified in Christ Jesus' (1 Cor. 1.2.).   *Bishops and deacons.* The increasing number of believers made organization a necessity in the churches. See Acts 6.2, 3. The qualifications demanded of bishops and deacons are set forth in 1 Tim. 3.1–10.

5. *The first day.* The reference is to the day of Paul's first preaching in Philippi. See Acts 16.13.

6. *He who began.* 'It is God who worketh in you' (ch. 2.13).   *The day of Jesus Christ.* 'The day that

the Son of man is revealed' (Lk. 17.30).   'When the Son of man shall come in his glory' (Mt. 25.31). See ver. 10; ch. 2.16; 1 Cor. 1.8.

7. *In my bonds.* Paul was at this time in chains largely because of his association with the Gentiles. See ver. 13; Acts 21.33.

9. *Discernment.* The word thus translated is found in the New Testament only in this place. Its full meaning is 'refined spiritual insight.' See Rom. 14.1–8.

10. *The things that are excellent.* 'Whatsoever things are true, whatsoever things are honorable, whatsoever things are just, whatsoever things are pure, whatsoever things are lovely, whatsoever things are of good report' (ch. 4.8).

void of offence unto the day of Christ; 11 being filled with the *f*fruits of righteousness, which are through Je'sus Christ, unto the glory and praise of God.

12 Now I would have you know, brethren, that the things *which happened* unto me have fallen out rather unto the progress of the *g*gospel; 13 so that my bonds became manifest in Christ *h*throughout the whole præ-to'ri-an guard, and to all the rest; 14 and that most of the brethren in the Lord, *i*being confident through my bonds, are more abundantly bold to speak the word of God without fear. 15 Some indeed preach Christ even of envy and strife; and some also of good will: 16 *k*the one *do it* of love, knowing that I am set for the defence of the *g*gospel; 17 *l*but the other proclaim Christ of faction, not sincerely, thinking to raise up affliction for me in my bonds. 18 What then? only that in every way, whether in pretence or in truth, Christ is proclaimed; and therein I rejoice, yea, and

will rejoice. 19 For I know that this shall turn out to my salvation, through your supplication and the supply of the Spirit of Je'sus Christ, 20 according to my earnest expectation and hope, that in nothing shall I be put to shame, but *that* with all boldness, as always, *so* now also Christ shall be magnified in my body, whether by life, or by death. 21 For to me to live is Christ, and to die is gain. 22 *m*But if to live in the flesh,—*if* *n*this shall bring fruit from my work, then *o*what I shall choose I know not. 23 But I am in a strait betwixt the two, having the desire to depart and be with Christ; for it is very far better: 24 yet to abide in the flesh is more needful for your sake. 25 And having this confidence, I know that I shall abide, yea, and abide with you all, for your progress and joy *p*in the faith; 26 that your glorying may abound in Christ Je'sus in me through my presence with you again. 27 Only *q*let your manner of life be worthy of the *r*gospel of Christ: that, whether

f Gr. *fruit.*   *g* Gr. *good tidings:* and so elsewhere; see marginal note on Mt. 4.23. *h* Gr. *in the whole Prætorium.*   *i* Gr. *trusting in my bonds.*   *k* Or, *they that are moved by love* do it, *knowing &c.*   *l* Or, *but they that are factious proclaim Christ, not &c.* *m* Or, *But if to live in the flesh* be my lot,

this is the fruit of my work: and what I shall choose I know not.   *n* Gr. *this is for me fruit of work.*   *o* Or, *what shall I choose?*   *p* Or, *of faith*   *q* Gr. *behave as citizens worthily.* Comp. ch. 3.20.   *r* Gr. *good tidings.* See marginal note on ch. 1.5.

13. *The whole prætorian guard.* This was composed of ten thousand picked soldiers who were the personal body-guard of the emperor, and was placed in a fortified camp on the northeast of Rome. Paul made use of the publicity that came from his arrest to preach more widely the gospel of Christ.

15. *Even of envy and strife.* Those who differed from Paul seem to have seized upon his imprisonment as evidence that he had not the true doctrine. But their contentions

served to spread the knowledge of the gospel. See ver. 18. Thus God makes even the wrath of man to praise him (Ps. 76.10).

19. *My salvation.* The meaning here is release from the overwhelming influences of the flesh.

21. *To live is Christ, and to die is gain.* Life in the flesh, to Paul, meant the intense joy of spreading the gospel: death meant release not only from persecution, but also from the continual warfare with the flesh; and rest with Christ.

I come and see you or be absent, I may hear of your state, that ye stand fast in one spirit, with one soul striving *ͤfor the faith of the ͥgospel; 28 and in nothing affrighted by the adversaries: which is for them an evident token of perdition, but of your salvation, and that from God; 29 because to you it hath been granted in the behalf of Christ, not only to believe on him, but also to suffer in his behalf: 30 having the same conflict which ye saw in me, and now hear to be in me.

2 If there is therefore any exhortation in Christ, if any *ᵃconsolation of love, if any fellowship of the Spirit, if any tender mercies and compassions, 2 make full my joy, that ye be of the same mind, having the same love, being of one accord, *ᵇof one mind; 3 *doing* nothing through faction or through vainglory, but in lowliness of mind each counting other better than himself; 4 not looking each of

you to his own things, but each of you also to the things of others. 5 Have this mind in you, which was also in Christ Je'sus: 6 who, existing in the form of God, counted not the being on an equality with God a thing to be grasped, 7 but emptied himself, taking the form of a *ʳservant, *ᵈbeing made in the likeness of men; 8 and being found in fashion as a man, he humbled himself, becoming obedient *even* unto death, yea, the death of the cross. 9 Wherefore also God highly exalted him, and gave unto him the name which is above every name; 10 that in the name of Je'sus every knee should bow, of *things* in heaven and *things* on earth and *ᵉthings* under the earth, 11 and that every tongue should confess that Je'sus Christ is Lord, to the glory of God the Father.

12 So then, my beloved, even as ye have always obeyed, not *ᶠas in my presence only, but now much more in my absence,

---

s Gr. *with.*   *t* Gr. *good tidings.* See marginal note on ch. 1.5.   *a* Or, *persuasion*
b Some ancient authorities read *of the same*

mind. *c* Gr. *bondservant.* *d* Gr. *becoming in.* *e* Or, things *of the world below* *f* Some ancient authorities omit *as.*

---

28. *An evident token of perdition.* Persecutions and afflictions were esteemed a 'token of the righteous judgment of God' (2 Thess. 1.5). The opposite condition was evidence of perdition.

CHAPTER 2

1. *If there is therefore any exhortation in Christ.* The intensity of Paul's plea indicates that there was serious personal strife for place among the Philippian Christians.
3. *Lowliness of mind.* The attitude of supremacy is fatal to growth. From the day when the mother of James and John sought places of special honor for her sons (Mt. 20. 21–24), Jesus himself (Mt. 20.26),

and the apostles counseled self-denial.

7. *But emptied himself.* That is, he gave up everything and made himself of no reputation.

9. *The name which is above every name.* Christ made the supreme sacrifice. Salvation had to come from above and none other was equal to the task. It was accomplished once for all. It cannot be done again. The name of Christ must stand at the summit as the one and effectual Saviour of the world.

12. *Work out your own salvation.* Though salvation is through Christ it must be worked out by obedience. See Heb. 5.8. *With fear and trembling.* That is, earnest anxiety.

work out your own salvation with fear and trembling; 13 for it is God who worketh in you both to will and to work, for his good pleasure. 14 Do all things without murmurings and questionings: 15 that ye may become blameless and harmless, children of God without blemish in the midst of a crooked and perverse generation, among whom ye are seen as *⁰lights in the world, 16 holding forth the word of life; that I may have whereof to glory in the day of Christ, that I did not run in vain neither labor in vain. 17 Yea, and if I am ʰoffered upon the sacrifice and service of your faith, I joy, and rejoice with you all: 18 and in the same manner do ye also joy, and rejoice with me.

19 But I hope in the Lord Je′sus to send Tim′o-thy shortly unto you, that I also may be of good comfort, when I know your state. 20 For I have no man likeminded, who will care *ᶦtruly for your state. 21 For they all

seek their own, not the things of Je′sus Christ. 22 But ye know the proof of him, that, as a child *serveth* a father, *so* he served with me in furtherance of the ᵏgospel. 23 Him therefore I hope to send forthwith, so soon as I shall see how it will go with me: 24 but I trust in the Lord that I myself also shall come shortly. 25 But I counted it necessary to send to you E-paph-ro-di′tus, my brother and fellow-worker and fellow-soldier, and your ˡmessenger and minister to my need; 26 since he longed ᵐafter you all, and was sore troubled, because ye had heard that he was sick: 27 for indeed he was sick nigh unto death: but God had mercy on him; and not on him only, but on me also, that I might not have sorrow upon sorrow. 28 I have sent him therefore the more diligently, that, when ye see him again, ye may rejoice, and that I may be the less sorrowful. 29 Receive him therefore in the

---

g Gr. *luminaries.* Wisd. 13.2; comp. Rev. 21.11. *h* Gr. *poured out as a drink-offering.* *i* Gr. *genuinely.* *k* Gr. *good tidings.*

See marginal note on ch. 1.5. *l* Gr. *apostle.* *m* Many ancient authorities read *to see you all.*

---

14. *Without murmurings and questionings.* The phrase recalls the murmurings of the children of Israel against Moses and Aaron (Num. 16.41). Obedience cannot be half-hearted: it is then disobedience, and can result only in disaster.

16. *The day of Christ.* See second note, ch. 1.6.

17. *Offered upon the sacrifice.* Paul's meaning is figurative, referring in humility to his service as the drink-offering which was added to the burnt-offering of sweet savor. See Ex. 29.40.

19. *To send Timothy.* See note ch. 1.1.

20. *No man likeminded.* Timothy had a peculiar and whole-souled

interest in the church at Philippi, which would lead him to bring to Paul a more exhaustive report than he would get from any one else.

21. *For they all seek their own.* Paul's workers were too closely interested each in his own particular field to give intimate attention to the spiritual condition of the Philippians.

23. *How it will go with me.* The reference here is to the outcome of Paul's long imprisonment, and the expected trial in the near future.

25. *Epaphroditus.* He had been the bearer of gifts to Paul from the brethren at Philippi, and upon his return, Paul sends by him this epistle to the Philippians.

Lord with all joy; and hold such in honor: 30 because for the work of [n]Christ he came nigh unto death, hazarding his life to supply that which was lacking in your service toward me.

3 Finally, my brethren, rejoice in the Lord. To write the same things to you, to me indeed is not irksome, but for you it is safe. 2 Beware of the dogs, beware of the evil workers, beware of the concision: 3 for we are the circumcision, who worship by the Spirit of God, and glory in Christ Je'sus, and have no confidence in the flesh: 4 though I myself might have confidence even in the flesh: if any other man [a]thinketh to have confidence in the flesh, I yet more: 5 circumcised the eighth day, of the stock of Is'ra-el, of the tribe of Ben'ja-min, a He-

brew of Hebrews; as touching the law, a Pharisee; 6 as touching zeal, persecuting the church; as touching the righteousness which is in the law, found blameless. 7 Howbeit what things were [b]gain to me, these have I counted loss for Christ. 8 Yea verily, and I count all things to be loss for the excellency of the knowledge of Christ Je'sus my Lord: for whom I suffered the loss of all things, and do count them but refuse, that I may gain Christ, 9 and be found in him, [c]not having a righteousness of mine own, *even* that which is of the law, but that which is through faith in Christ, the righteousness which is from God [d]by faith: 10 that I may know him, and the power of his resurrection, and the fellowship of his sufferings, becoming conformed unto his death; 11 if by any

---

n Many ancient authorities read *the Lord.*
a Or, *seemeth*

b Gr. *gains.* *c* Or, *not having* as *my righteousness that which is of the law* *d* Gr. *upon.*

---

30. *That which was lacking in your service.* The most important part of the mission of Epaphroditus was not the gift he brought but the comfort and encouragement of his presence, which no gift, however costly, could supply. See ch. 4.10; 1 Cor. 16.17.

CHAPTER 3

1. *The same things.* These were repetitions of his former counsels, to be kept continually in mind on the score of safety.

2. *The dogs.* This term applies to those of unholy tastes and desires, of whom Jesus warned the multitude in the Sermon on the Mount:—'Give not that which is holy unto the dogs' (Mt. 7.6). *The concision.* The word signifies the mutilation practised by fanatics. See 1 Kings 18.28. It is here used by Paul in scorn for the circumcision of the flesh, as being of no greater spiritual importance.

3. *For we are the circumcision.* The rite of circumcision signified consecration unto God, but it was merely a symbol. The real consecration was from within. As Paul says, in Rom. 2.29, 'Circumcision is that of the heart, in the spirit not in the letter.' See Rom. 2.25-29.

7. *What things were gain to me.* In the two preceding verses Paul enumerates his superior outward qualifications as an orthodox Jew. These things, while gain from a worldly viewpoint, he counts as 'but refuse' (ver. 8) compared with the knowledge of Christ, and 'the righteousness which is from God, by faith' (ver. 9).

10. *Conformed unto his death.* Paul is not referring to the death on the cross, but that death unto the flesh which resulted in the resurrection. See Rom. 6.5-11.

11. *If by any means I may attain unto the resurrection from the dead.* This was the goal of Paul's hope,

means I may attain unto the resurrection from the dead. 12 Not that I have already obtained, or am already made perfect: but I press on, if so be that I may *lay hold on that for which also I was laid hold on by Christ Je′sus. 13 Brethren, I count not myself *yet to have laid hold: but one thing *I do*, forgetting the things which are behind, and stretching forward to the things which are before, 14 I press on toward the goal unto the prize of the *high calling of God in Christ Je′sus. 15 Let us therefore, as many as are *perfect, be thus minded: and if in anything ye are otherwise minded, this also shall God reveal unto you: 16 only, whereunto we have attained, by that same *rule* let us walk.

17 Brethren, be ye imitators

together of me, and mark them that so walk even as ye have us for an ensample. 18 For many walk, of whom I told you often, and now tell you even weeping, *that they are* the enemies of the cross of Christ: 19 whose end is perdition, whose god is the belly, and *whose* glory is in their shame, who mind earthly things. 20 For our *citizenship is in heaven; whence also we wait for a Saviour, the Lord Je′sus Christ: 21 who shall fashion anew the body of our humiliation, *that it may be* conformed to the body of his glory, according to the working whereby he is able even to subject all things unto himself.

4 Wherefore, my brethren beloved and longed for, my joy and crown, so stand fast in the Lord, my beloved.

---

e Or, *lay hold, seeing that also I was laid hold on*   *f* Many ancient authorities omit *yet.*   *g* Or, *upward*   *h* Or, *full-grown*   1 Cor. 2.6.   *i* Or, *commonwealth*

---

as it was the consummation of the human life of his Lord. See 1 Cor. 15.1–4, 12–25.

12. *Not that I have already obtained.* Paul was working out his own salvation with fear and trembling (see note ch. 2.12), and he permitted no self-confidence to deceive him.

13. *Forgetting the things which are behind.* Paul had held a position of high honor and influence among the Pharisees at Jerusalem because of his learning, both in literature and the law. In giving allegiance to Christ he became a despised outcast to his former associates. See ver. 5, 6.

17. *Imitators together of me.* The context (ver. 18, 19) shows that the imitation urged was as to Paul's attitude toward the things of the world as well as the anxious spirit in which he pressed onward.

18. *Enemies of the cross of Christ.* These were not of the unbelievers,

but some among the brethren. As the cross is the symbol of self-sacrifice, those who 'mind earthly things' (ver. 19) are at enmity to all that the cross stands for.

20. *Our citizenship is in heaven.* This illustration was drawn from the fact that the citizenship of the Philippian was in Rome. Paul voiced the same idea in Heb. 13.14:— 'For we have not here an abiding city, but we seek after the city which is to come.'

21. *The body of our humiliation.* This is the body of the flesh which so humiliated Paul, when he declared 'For the good which I would I do not: but the evil which I would not, that I practise' (Rom. 7.19). *Conformed to the body of his glory.* This may refer to the glorified body of Jesus at the transfiguration (Mt. 17.2), or to Paul's vision of him on the way to Damascus (Acts 9.3; 1 Cor. 15.8). Paul enlarges on the coming change in 1 Cor. 15.51–54.

2 I exhort Eu-o′di-a, and I exhort Syn′ty-che, to be of the same mind in the Lord. 3 Yea, I beseech thee also, true yoke-fellow, help these women, for they labored with me in the [a]gospel, with Clem′ent also, and the rest of my fellow-workers, whose names are in the book of life.

4 Rejoice in the Lord always: again I will say, Rejoice. 5 Let your [b]forbearance be known unto all men. The Lord is at hand. 6 In nothing be anxious; but in everything by prayer and supplication with thanksgiving let your requests be made known unto God. 7 And the peace of God, which passeth all under-standing, shall guard your hearts and your thoughts in Christ Je′sus.

8 Finally, brethren, whatso-ever things are true, what-soever things are [c]honorable, whatsoever things are just, what-soever things are pure, whatso-ever things are lovely, whatso-ever things are [d]of good report; if there be any virtue, and if there be any praise, [e]think on these things. 9 The things which ye both learned and received and heard and saw in me, these things do: and the God of peace shall be with you.

10 But I [f]rejoice in the Lord greatly, that now at length ye have revived your thought for me; [g]wherein ye did indeed take thought, but ye lacked oppor-tunity. 11 Not that I speak in respect of want: for I have learned, in whatsoever state I am, therein to be content. 12 I know how to be abased, and I know also how to abound: in everything and in all things have I learned the secret both to be filled and to be hungry, both to abound and to be in want. 13 I can do all things in him that strengtheneth me. 14 Howbeit ye did well that ye had fellow-ship with my affliction. 15 And ye yourselves also know, ye Phi-lip′pi-ans, that in the be-ginning of the [a]gospel, when I departed from Mac-e-do′ni-a, no church had fellowship with me in the matter of giving and

---

a Gr. *good tidings.* See ch. 1.5. b Or, *gentleness* Comp. 2 Cor. 10.1. c Gr. *rev-erend.* (Or. *gracious* e Gr. *take account of.* f Gr. *rej*. *iced.* g Or, *seeing that*

CHAPTER 4

2. *I exhort Euodia and I exhort Syntyche.* It is generally accepted that these prominent women were in marked disagreement and that Paul is urging them to find rec-onciliation in the 'mind of the Lord.'

3. *True yokefellow.* This is by some commentators believed to be Epaphroditus, the bearer of the epistle. See ch. 2.25. *They la-bored with me in the gospel.* In the early church, women were engaged as active helpers in spreading the gospel. See Acts 17.4, 12. *Whose*

names are in the book of life. It is plain that the possession of saving grace is of greater moment than a record of deeds. Jesus said, 'Re-joice not that the spirits are subject unto you; but rejoice that your names are written in heaven' (Lk. 10.20).

10. *Ye have revived your thought for me.* Paul had suffered want more than once, and the Philippians had before this contributed to his needs. See 2 Cor. 11.8, 9.

15. *In the beginning of the gospel.* When Paul first began his work among them. *When I departed from Macedonia.* See Acts 16.40.

receiving but ye only; 16 for even in Thes-sa-lo-ni'ca ye sent once and again unto my need. 17 Not that I seek for the gift; but I seek for the fruit that increaseth to your account. 18 But I have all things, and abound: I am filled, having received from E-paph-ro-di'tus the things *that came* from you, an odor of a sweet smell, a sacrifice acceptable, well-pleasing to God. 19 And my God shall supply every need of yours according to his riches in glory in Christ Je'sus. 20 Now unto ʰour God and Father *be* the glory ⁱfor ever and ever. A-men'.

21 Salute every saint in Christ Je'sus. The brethren that are with me salute you. 22 All the saints salute you, especially they that are of Cæ'sar's household. 23 The grace of the Lord Je'sus Christ be with your spirit.

ʰ Or, *God and our Father*

ⁱ Gr. *unto the ages of the ages.*

16. *Even in Thessalonica.* See Acts 17.1.
17. *Not that I seek for the gift.* The desire to give was the added 'grace' in which Paul delighted. See 2 Cor. 8.4, 7. The compassionate love of the brethren was a sign that they had 'passed from death unto life' (1 Jn. 3.14, 17).
18. *An odor of a sweet smell.* A figure of speech alluding to the ceremony of the burnt-offering. See Ex. 29.18, 25.
22. *Especially they that are of Cæsar's household.* Paul had taken advantage of his imprisonment to preach the gospel even to the soldiers who were his jailers, and they joined him in sending greeting to the Philippians. See ch. 1.13.

THE EPISTLE TO THE COLOSSIANS

INTRODUCTION BY PROFESSOR MARCUS DODS, D.D.

Colossæ and Its Church.—Colossæ was situated in Southwestern Phrygia, but within the proconsular province of Asia. It lay on the south bank of the river Lycus, and on the main road from Ephesus to the great plateau of Asia Minor. In the fifth century B.C. it was known as a great and prosperous city, but the still more advantageous position of its neighbor Laodicea, a few miles down the river, gradually told on Colossæ; and in the time of Paul, although a large number of Jews had been introduced into it, and although the city had become rather Greek than Phrygian, it yet had somewhat fallen from its former grandeur and importance. Since the twelfth century, only the ruins of the great church of St. Michael have marked its site. "So completely was Colossæ forgotten, that the idea arose that the Colossians to whom Paul wrote his epistle were Rhodians, so called from their famous Colossus."

Colossæ thus lay almost in the track of Paul's first and second great missionary journeys, but hitherto he had been prevented from visiting the prosperous cities which lay in the valley of the Lycus, and his route had passed east and north of them, so that in this letter he classes the Colossians with those "who had not seen his face in the flesh" (ch. 2.1). And yet, in writing to them, he was not breaking his rule never to build on another man's foundation; for the probability is that Epaphras, who had introduced them to the faith (1.7), although a Colossian (4.12), owed his own knowledge of the truth to Paul, whom he may have met in Ephesus. To this "beloved fellow-servant," at any rate, Paul owed his knowledge of the dangers to which the Colossian Christians were now exposed.

Earnest but misled and misleading teachers were proclaiming a method of salvation which not only promised to satisfy the hunger for righteousness, but also, by combining a philosophical scheme of the universe, flattered intellectual pride. That these teachers were Jews is apparent from their enjoining circumcision and the observance of the Mosaic ordinances (2.8, 11, 16, 20). But with their Judaism they combined a "philosophy" (2.8) which taught that angels (or principalities and powers) were mediators in the work of creation and redemption, and therefore deserving of worship (2.18; 1.16); and that sanctification could only be accomplished by ascetic neglect of the body, and by severe restrictions (2.20-23). This was taught as a mystery under the seal of secrecy (2.3) to the initiated few. These characteristics identify the teaching as the Gnostic Judaism of the first century.

Contents of the Epistle.—It was chiefly with the view of dissipating these errors that Paul wrote this epistle. And the method he pursues is to show that all the advantages which those novel representations fallaciously promise are already and really given in Christ. After the usual epistolary greeting, in which he includes Timothy along with himself, and the thanksgiving for their faith and love which so commonly forms the introduction of his letters (1.1-8), Paul prays for their growth in spiritual wisdom and the knowledge of God (1.9-13). He thus glides almost imperceptibly into the real theme of the epistle.

To the intellectual exclusiveness of the Gnostic he opposes the gospel which he preached to "every creature" (1.23), a gospel which proclaims that "every man" may become perfect, and not the few initiated only (1.28). To the Gnostic theory of intermediate beings interposed between God and the world, saving Him from the pollution of contact with matter, he opposes the sole mediation of Christ in creation and redemption. Christ is the real Mediator, being on the one hand the image of the invisible God, and on the other the firstborn of all creation. In Him were all things created, even all principalities and powers. Neither was God distributed among subordinate beings, each of whom possessed and represented some one of His attributes, but in Christ dwelt the fulness or totality of the Godhead; so that in Him all power, wisdom, and redemption can be found, and to seek help from angels is gratuitous humility (1.14-23; 2.9; 2.18).

In Christ ye are complete, he says, for He is the head of all principality and power; it is from Him they derive whatever powers they have. Hold therefore the Head (2.19) and you will lack nothing; and be not in bondage to the Mosaic ordinances, for in Christ you are emancipated from them. In Him you have a spiritual circumcision, and He has cancelled the written bond of ordinances, and has nailed it to the cross as a conqueror nails to a trophy the weapons of his slain foe (2.13-15). If you died in Christ's death, then these ordinances are for you abolished (2.23); and if with Christ you are raised again to newness of life, then this is your salvation from carnality and earthliness—this, and not any mere careful restriction of yourself from this or that. You are lifted to a new world, and your life is hid with Christ in God (2.20; 3.1-3). From this exposition of the essential principle of all holiness he passes to a warm exhortation to special virtues and particular duties (3.5 to 4.6), and concludes with some personal details and salutations.

THE EPISTLE OF PAUL TO THE

CO-LOS'SIANS

Salutation.   Thanksgiving and Prayer

1 Paul, an apostle of Christ Je'sus through the will of God, and Tim'o-thy *a*our brother, 2 *b*to the saints and faithful brethren in Christ *that are* at Co-los'sæ: Grace to you and peace from God our Father.

3 We give thanks to God the Father of our Lord Je'sus Christ, praying always for you, 4 having heard of your faith in Christ Je'sus, and of the love which ye have toward all the saints, 5 because of the hope which is laid up for you in the heavens, whereof ye heard before in the word of the truth of the *c*gospel, 6 which is come unto you; even as it is also in all the world bearing fruit and increasing, as *it doth* in you also, since the day ye heard and knew the grace of God in truth; 7 even as ye learned of Ep'a-phras our beloved fellow-servant, who is a faithful minister of Christ on *d*our behalf, 8 who also declared unto us your love in the Spirit.

9 For this cause we also, since the day we heard *it*, do not cease to pray and make request for you, that ye may be filled with the knowledge of his will

a Gr. *the brother.* *b* Or, *to those that are at Colossæ, holy and faithful brethren in Christ*

c Gr. *good tidings*: and so elsewhere; see marginal note on Mt. 4.23. *d* Many ancient authorities read *your.*

CHAPTER 1

1. *Through the will of God.* Paul keeps always in mind the fact of his conversion by the miraculous intervention of God. See Acts 9.3–22. It was not through his own will that he became an apostle.

2. *To the saints.* This name was used to signify those who were set apart or consecrated—in the world but not of the world. *At Colossæ.* Colossæ, in the time of Paul was a small town in Phrygia, Asia Minor, a few miles southeasterly from Laodicea. It is believed that Paul wrote the epistle while he was imprisoned at Rome.

7. *Of Epaphras.* Paul's endorsement of the teachings of Epaphras shows that there were false teachers among the Colossians also. These men seem to have followed the apostles about, devoting their energies to leading astray those who had already embraced Christianity.

8. *Declared unto us.* Epaphras had come to Paul with his trouble and he also was made a prisoner. See Philemon 23. *In the Spirit* has been construed as showing that Paul had not then visited the Colossians. See ch. 2.1.

9. *Wisdom and understanding.* The subtle arguments and enticements of the false teachers required of Christians a high degree of wisdom to 'prove all things; hold fast that which is good' (1 Th. 5.21).

in all spiritual wisdom and understanding, 10 to walk worthily of the Lord *e*unto all pleasing, bearing fruit in every good work, and increasing *f*in the knowledge of God; 11 *g*strengthened *h*with all power, according to the might of his glory, unto all *i*patience and longsuffering with joy; 12 giving thanks unto the Father, who made *k*us meet to be partakers of the inheritance of the saints in light; 13 who delivered us out of the power of darkness, and translated us into the kingdom of the Son of his love; 14 in whom we have our redemption, the forgiveness of our sins: 15 who is the image of the invisible God, the firstborn of all creation; 16 for in him were all things created, in the heavens and upon the earth, things visible and things invisible, whether thrones or dominions or principalities or powers; all things have been created through him, and unto him; 17 and he is before all things, and in him all things *l*consist. 18 And he is the head of the body, the church: who is the beginning, the firstborn from the dead; *m*that in all things he might have the preëminence. 19 *n*For it was the good pleasure *of the Father* that in him should all the fulness dwell; 20 and through him to reconcile all things *o*unto *p*himself, having made peace through the blood of his cross; through him, *I say*, whether things upon the earth, or things in the heavens. 21 And you, being in time past alienated and enemies in your mind in your evil works, 22 yet now *q*hath he reconciled in the body of his flesh through death, to present you holy and without blemish and unreprovable before him: 23 if so be that ye continue in the faith, grounded and stedfast, and not moved away from the hope of the *r*gospel which ye heard, which was preached in all creation under heaven; whereof I Paul was made a minister.

24 Now I rejoice in my sufferings for your sake, and fill up on

e Or, *unto all pleasing, in every good work, bearing fruit and increasing &c.* *f* Or, *by* *g* Gr. *made powerful.* *h* Or, *in* *i* Or, *stedfastness* *k* Some ancient authorities read *you.* *l* That is, *hold together.* *m* Or, *that among all he might have &c.* *n* Or, *For* ‖ *the whole fulness* of God *was pleased to dwell in him* *o* Or, *into him* *p* Or, *him* *q* Some ancient authorities read *ye have been reconciled.* *r* Gr. *good tidings;* and so elsewhere; see marginal note on Mt. 4.23.

12. *In light.* In understanding; as contrasted with the darkness of ignorance. See ver. 13; Acts 26.18; Eph. 4.18; 5.8.

15. *The firstborn of all creation.* Christ was 'before all things' (ver. 17), 'in the beginning with God' (Jn. 1.1, 2). See Jn. 8.58.

16. *Thrones or dominions or principalities or powers.* This is taken to be an allusion to the system of angel worship introduced by the false teachers in Colossæ. See Rom. 8.38; Eph. 1.21; 1 Pet. 3.22.

18. *The firstborn from the dead.* The first to experience the resurrection of the body. See Acts 26.23; 1 Cor. 15.20, 23; Rev. 1.5.

22. *Reconciled.* 'God was in Christ reconciling the world unto himself' (2 Cor. 5.19). *In the body.* Christ came 'in the likeness of sinful flesh' (Rom. 8.3), and, being without sin (Heb. 4.15), 'condemned sin in the flesh' (Rom. 8.3). See Rom. 8.10.

23. *If so be.* There was a condition upon which reconciliation became effective—continuance in the faith of the pure gospel.

24. *On my part.* Whatever lack there might be in Paul's afflictions

my part that which is lacking of the afflictions of Christ in my flesh for his body's sake, which is the church; 25 whereof I was made a minister, according to the *s*dispensation of God which was given me to you-ward, to fulfil the word of God, 26 *even* the mystery which hath been hid *t*for ages and generations: but now hath it been manifested to his saints, 27 to whom God was pleased to make known what is the riches of the glory of this mystery among the Gen'tiles, which is Christ in you, the hope of glory: 28 whom we proclaim, admonishing every man and teaching every man in all wisdom, that we may present every man perfect in Christ; 29 whereunto I labor also, striving according to his working, which worketh in me *u*mightily.

2 For I would have you know how greatly I strive for you, and for them at La-od-i-ce'a, and for as many as have not seen my face in the flesh; 2 that their hearts may be comforted, they being knit together in love, and unto all riches of the *a*full assurance of understanding, that they may know the mystery of God, *b*even Christ, 3 in whom are all the treasures of wisdom and knowledge hidden. 4 This I say, that no one may delude you with persuasiveness of speech. 5 For though I am absent in the flesh, yet am I with you in the spirit, joying and beholding your order, and the stedfastness of your faith in Christ.

6 As therefore ye received Christ Je'sus the Lord, *so* walk in him, 7 rooted and builded up in him, and established *c*in your faith, even as ye were taught, abounding *d*in thanksgiving.

8 *e*Take heed lest there shall be any one that maketh spoil of you through his philosophy and vain deceit, after the tradition of men, after the *f*rudiments of the world, and not after Christ: 9 for in him dwelleth all the

---

s Or, *stewardship* See 1 Cor. 9.17. *t* Or, *from all ages &c.* Gr. *from the ages and from the generations.* *u* Or, *in power* *a* Or, *fulness* *b* The ancient authorities vary much in the text of this passage. *c* Or, *by* *d* Some ancient authorities insert *in it.* *e* Or, *See whether* *f* Or, *elements* See Gal. 4.3 marg.

---

through continual persecution because of his faith, he made up on his own part by anxious solicitude regarding the churches. See 2 Cor. 2.4.

26. *The mystery.* To Paul the mystery of the gospel was that the Gentiles, equally with the chosen people—the Jews—should be saved; and by a salvation not through obedience to the outward ordinances of the law, but of 'Christ in you' (ver. 27); accepted by the inward man and renewing the whole being; through which they passed out of death into life (1 Jn. 3.14).

CHAPTER 2

1. *I strive.* In prayer and earnest counsel. *Laodicea.* A town near Colossæ and Hierapolis, damaged with them by an earthquake, in the time of Nero. It was a place of great wealth. See Rev. 3.17.

2. *The mystery of God.* See ch. 1.27 and note on ch. 1.26.

6. *As . . . ye received.* According to the gospel as first preached to you.

8. *Spoil.* Or *booty*; in the sense of leading captive your understanding through deceitful reasonings. See 2 Pet. 2.1, 19. *The rudiments of the world.* The elementary forces of the life of the flesh; the powers of darkness. See ch. 1.13; Gal. 4.3, 9.

fulness of the Godhead bodily, 10 and in him ye are made full, who is the head of all principality and power: 11 in whom ye were also circumcised with a circumcision not made with hands, in the putting off of the body of the flesh, in the circumcision of Christ; 12 having been buried with him in baptism, wherein ye were also raised with him through faith in the working of God, who raised him from the dead. 13 And you, being dead through your trespasses and the uncircumcision of your flesh, you, *I say*, did he make alive together with him, having forgiven us all our trespasses; 14 having blotted out the *g*bond written in ordinances that was against us, which was contrary to us: and he hath taken it out of the way, nailing it to the cross; 15 *h*having despoiled the principalities

and the powers, he made a show of them openly, triumphing over them in it.

16 Let no man therefore judge you in meat, or in drink, or in respect of a feast day or a new moon or a sabbath day: 17 which are a shadow of the things to come; but the body is Christ's. 18 Let no man rob you of your prize *i*by a voluntary humility and *k*worshipping of the angels, *l*dwelling in the things which he hath *m*seen, vainly puffed up by his fleshly mind, 19 and not holding fast the Head, from whom all the body, being supplied and knit together through the joints and bands, increaseth with the increase of God.

20 If ye died with Christ from the *n*rudiments of the world, why, as though living in the world, do ye subject yourselves to ordinances, 21 Handle not,

---

g Or, *the bond that was against us by its ordinances*   *h* Or, *having put off from himself the principalities &c.*   *i* Or, *of his own mere will, by humility &c.*   *k* The Greek word denotes an act of reverence, whether paid to a creature, or to the Creator. *l* Or, *taking his stand upon*   *m* Many authorities, some ancient, insert *not.*   *n* Or, *elements*   See Gal. 4.3 marg.

---

11. *Made with hands.* The circumcision among the Jews was a seal of the old covenant. Under the new covenant the circumcision of Christ was the putting off of the body of the flesh:—that is, the whole carnal nature. See Rom. 2.29; 6.6, 11; Gal. 5.24.

13. *The uncircumcision.* This does not refer to the Jewish rite, but is in the sense given in the note on ver. 11. See Rom. 2.26, 27.

14. *In ordinances.* The Jewish law. *Against us.* The law was against the nature of the people. Through regeneration by the Spirit the nature was changed to work righteousness regardless of the law which was thus blotted out. See Rom. 10.4; Eph. 2.15.

15. *Principalities,* etc. The invisible 'spirits of the air,' believed in as mediators and avengers.

Christ did his work openly, in the sight of all men. See Eph. 2.2; 6.12.

16. *Judge you.* Comdemn you— because of eating or not eating; keeping a feast day, or not keeping it. See Rom. 14.1–23; 1 Chron. 23.31.

18. *Voluntary humility.* Some of the false teachers made a show of humility by dressing in rags and scourging themselves with whips. See ver. 23.

19. *Holding fast the Head.* 'If a man abide not in me, he is cast forth as a branch, and is withered' (Jn. 15.6). *The increase of God.* That growth 'in the grace and knowledge of our Lord and Saviour Jesus Christ' (2 Pet. 3.18), through which 'we all attain . . . unto the measure of the stature of the fulness of Christ' (Eph. 4.13, 16).

nor taste, nor touch 22 (all which things are to perish with the using), after the precepts and doctrines of men? 23 Which things have indeed a show of wisdom in will-worship, and humility, and severity to the body; *but are* not of any *°*value against the indulgence of the flesh.

3 If then ye were raised together with Christ, seek the things that are above, where Christ is, seated on the right hand of God. 2 Set your mind on the things that are above, not on the things that are upon the earth. 3 For ye died, and your life is hid with Christ in God. 4 When Christ, *who is* *°*our life, shall be manifested, then shall ye also with him be manifested in glory.

5 Put to death therefore your members which are upon the earth: fornication, uncleanness, passion, evil desire, and covetousness, which is idolatry; 6 for which things' sake cometh the wrath of God *°*upon the sons of

disobedience: 7 *°*wherein ye also once walked, when ye lived in these things; 8 but now do ye also put them all away: anger, wrath, malice, railing, shameful speaking out of your mouth: 9 lie not one to another; seeing that ye have put off the old man with his doings, 10 and have put on the new man, that is being renewed unto knowledge after the image of him that created him: 11 where there cannot be Greek and Jew, circumcision and uncircumcision, barbarian, Scyth'i-an, bondman, freeman; but Christ is all, and in all.

12 Put on therefore, as God's elect, holy and beloved, a heart of compassion, kindness, lowliness, meekness, longsuffering; 13 forbearing one another, and forgiving each other, if any man have a complaint against any; even as *°*the Lord forgave you, so also do ye: 14 and above all these things *put on* love, which is the bond of perfectness. 15 and let the peace of Christ *°*rule in your hearts, to the which also ye were called in one body; and

---

o Or, *honor*   *a* Many ancient authorities read *your.*   *b* Some ancient authorities omit *upon the sons of disobedience.* See

Eph. 5.6.   *c* Or, *amongst whom*   *d* Many ancient authorities read *Christ.*   *e* Gr. *arbitrate.*

---

23. *Severity to the body.* Referring to the practices of scourging, or slashing the body with knives, and other self-inflictions, all equally ineffective in renewing the inner man. See Gal. 6.15; Eph. 4.24.

CHAPTER 3

3. *For ye died.* Through the crucifixion of 'the flesh with the passions and the lusts thereof' (Gal. 5.24). See Rom. 6.6; Gal. 2.20; 6.14.

5. *Your members.* Paul found in himself a law of his members warring against the law of his mind

(Rom. 7.23). It was this carnal nature that was to be put to death. The same thought was voiced by Jesus in Mt. 5.30: 'If thy right hand causeth thee to stumble, cut it off, and cast it from thee.' See also Rom. 6.13, 19; Eph. 5.5; Jas. 4.1.

11. *Greek and Jew.* The title 'Greek' ₁was used to include all Gentiles. *Scythian.* The most barbarous type of the barbarians. The new Christ-man blotted out all human classifications.

14. *Bond of perfectness.* Christian love is the one perfect bond. See Jn. 13.34.

be ye thankful. 16 Let the word of [f]Christ dwell in you [g]richly; in all wisdom teaching and admonishing [h]one another with psalms *and* hymns *and* spiritual songs, singing with grace in your hearts unto God. 17 And whatsoever ye do, in word or in deed, *do* all in the name of the Lord Je'sus, giving thanks to God the Father through him.

18 Wives, be in subjection to your husbands, as is fitting in the Lord. 19 Husbands, love your wives, and be not bitter against them. 20 Children, obey your parents in all things, for this is well-pleasing in the Lord. 21 Fathers, provoke not your children, that they be not discouraged. 22 [i]Servants, obey in all things them that are your [k]masters according to the flesh; not with eye-service, as men-pleasers, but in singleness of heart, fearing the Lord: 23 whatsoever ye do, work [l]heartily, as unto the Lord, and not unto men; 24 knowing that from the Lord ye shall receive the recompense of the inheritance: ye serve the Lord Christ. 25 For he that doeth wrong shall [m]receive again for the wrong that he hath done: and there is no respect of persons.

4 1 [k]Masters, render unto your [i]servants that which is just and [a]equal; knowing that ye also have a Master in heaven.

2 Continue stedfastly in prayer, watching therein with thanksgiving; 3 withal praying for us also, that God may open unto us a door for the word, to speak the mystery of Christ, for which I am also in bonds; 4 that I may make it manifest, as I ought to speak. 5 Walk in wisdom toward them that are without, [b]redeeming the time. 6 Let your speech be always with grace, seasoned with salt, that ye may know how ye ought to answer each one.

7 All my affairs shall Tych'icus make known unto you, the beloved brother and faithful minister and fellow-servant in the Lord: 8 whom I have sent unto you for this very purpose, that ye may know our state, and that he may comfort your hearts;

---

[f] Some ancient authorities read *the Lord*: others, *God*. [g] Or, *richly in all wisdom; teaching &c.* [h] Or, *yourselves* [i] Gr. *Bond-servants.* [k] Gr. *lords.* [l] Gr. *from the soul.* [m] Gr. *receive again the wrong.* [a] Gr. *equality.* [b] Gr. *buying up the opportunity.*

24. *Ye serve the Lord Christ.* All conscientious service done as if to Christ is in fact service of Christ.

25. *No respect of persons.* The law that 'whatsoever a man soweth, that shall he also reap,' is universal. There are no exceptions. The fruitage is in the seed itself. See Gal. 6.7, 8; Acts 10.34.

CHAPTER 4

3. *The mystery.* See note ch. 1.26. *In bonds.* The chains with which Paul was bound.

6. *Seasoned with salt.* So filled with wisdom as to be acceptable to the understanding of those to whom it was addressed.

7. *Tychicus.* The epistle to the Ephesians was also sent by Tychicus. See Acts 20.4; Eph. 6.21; 2 Tim. 4.12.

9. *Onesimus.* A fugitive slave of Philemon, one of the Colossian church. He was sent with Tychicus to Colossæ, and bore an epistle to Philemon. See Philemon 10.

502

9 together with O-nes'i-mus, the faithful and beloved brother, who is one of you. They shall make known unto you all things that *are done* here.

10 Ar-is-tar'chus my fellow-prisoner saluteth you, and Mark, the cousin of Bar'na-bas (touching whom ye received commandments; if he come unto you, receive him), 11 and Je'sus that is called Jus'tus, who are of the circumcision: these only *are my* fellow-workers unto the kingdom of God, men that have been a comfort unto me. 12 Ep'a-phras, who is one of you, a ᶜservant of Christ Je'sus, saluteth you, always striving for you in his prayers, that ye may stand perfect and fully assured in all the will of God. 13 For I

bear him witness, that he hath much labor for you, and for them in La-od-i-ce'a, and for them in Hi-e-rap'o-lis. 14 Luke, the beloved physician, and De'-mas salute you. 15 Salute the brethren that are in La-od-i-ce'a, and ᵈNym'phas, and the church that is in ᵉtheir house. 16 And when ᶠthis epistle hath been read among you, cause that it be read also in the church of the La-od-i-ce'ans; and that ye also read the epistle from La-od-i-ce'a. 17 And say to Ar-chip'pus, Take heed to the ministry which thou hast received in the Lord, that thou fulfil it.

18 The salutation of me Paul with mine own hand. Remember my bonds. Grace be with you.

---

c Gr. *bondservant.*   *d* The Greek may represent *Nympha.*   *e* Some ancient authorities read *her.*   *f* Gr. *the.*

---

10. *Aristarchus.* A Macedonian who had been a fellow-worker with Paul. He and Gaius had been seized with Paul at Ephesus, and at the time of the writing of this epistle he was a prisoner with Paul. See Acts 19.29; 20.4; 27.2. *Mark.* John Mark, the evangelist who was the cause of the separation of Paul and Barnabas. See Acts 12.12; 13.13; 15.37-39. *Receive him.* A passing endorsement of Mark, to set aside any prejudice against him because of his former trouble with Paul.
11. *Who are of the circumcision.* The only Jewish workers who were with Paul.
16. *The epistle from Laodicea.* This letter is believed to be the one now known as the Epistle to the

Ephesians. Many excellent arguments support this view, especially as the oldest copies of the epistle omit the word Ephesus in the greeting. No other epistle to Laodicea is in existence.
17. *Archippus.* Mentioned also in Philemon 2.
18. *Remember my bonds.* It was Paul's habit to have his letters written by a secretary, and to write a brief salutation at the close with his own hand to assure their authenticity. See 2 Th. 3.17. The bonds to which Paul here refers consisted of a chain joining his right hand to the left hand of a soldier. Probably it caused such a difference in his handwriting as to require this explanation.

THE FIRST EPISTLE TO THE THESSALONIANS

INTRODUCTION BY PROFESSOR MARCUS DODS, D.D.

Thessalonica and Its Church.—Thessalonica (now *Saloniki*), originally known as Emathia or Thermæ ("Wells," "Bath"), lay at the head of the Thermaic Gulf, which deeply indents the Macedonian shore, and it covered the slope which runs up from the water's edge towards the rich country inland. It was named Thessalonica by Cassander, who rebuilt it, and called it after his wife, a half-sister of Alexander the Great. In Paul's time it was a free city governed by seven politarchs (Acts 17.6, 8). Its public assembly or Demos is also mentioned in Acts 17.5. Constantine almost chose it as his new capital; and it has a population of about 170,000, an active trade, and stands next to Constantinople as the second city of Turkey in Europe.

Lying on the great Via Egnatia, which connected Rome with the East, and almost 100 miles from Philippi, it was inevitable that Paul should find his way to it. As his custom was, he first appealed to the Jews (who have now about twenty synagogues in Saloniki); but after three Sabbaths he was no longer admitted to the synagogue, and shortly after he was expelled from the city. But his preaching had not been in vain. A few Jews, a multitude of "devout Greeks," and a considerable number of women, accepted his teaching.

Purpose of the Letter.—Compelled thus suddenly to leave a church in its infancy, the apostle was naturally anxious to hear of its welfare, and as he himself was prevented from returning, he sent back Timothy (2.17; 3.2). And as soon as this messenger returned and brought back tidings of their stedfastness, Paul at once sent this letter of congratulation, thankfulness, and counsel (3.6). This gives us both the purpose and the date of the epistle; for in Acts 18.5 we are told that it was at Corinth that Timothy overtook the apostle. The letter may therefore be dated late in 52 or early in 53 A.D.

The report brought by Timothy was not wholly favorable. Insinuations against the character and motives of Paul were rife. Greek vice was following the Thessalonians into the Christian church. The persecution to which the Christians were exposed, although it did not avail to destroy their faith, made them more ready to listen to highly-colored representations of the coming of Christ. This produced in some minds the impression that ordinary occupations might be suspended, while others again were disturbed because they feared that their friends who had died before the coming of Christ, might lose the joy and glory accompanying that event. Paul's purpose in writing was therefore complex.

THE FIRST EPISTLE TO THE THESSALONIANS

Contents of the Epistle.—In the first three chapters Paul's object is to encourage the Thessalonians; and in order to do this he acknowledges with thankfulness their faith and its fruits, and reminds them that they had become exemplary to all within the two great provinces of Macedonia and Achaia and elsewhere. The faith of the Thessalonians seemed to illustrate both the power which accompanied the preaching of Paul and the unusually striking effects of it (ch. 1.1-10). In the second chapter he first expatiates on the former and then on the latter of these features. In ch. 2.1-12 he repels the insinuation of mercenary motives, and appeals to the Thessalonians themselves as witnesses of his blameless and industrious life. In ch. 2.13-16 he appeals to their stedfastness under persecution in proof that his gospel was the Word of God; and in ch. 2.17 to 3.13 he continues his self-defence, but now against the charge of fickleness or cowardice, explaining that it was from no want of will or lack of interest he had not returned to visit them.

To this is added a supplementary portion introduced by, "Finally then." And in this supplement he first warns his readers against forgetfulness of the Christian commandments, and especially against unchastity (4.1-8). He also exhorts them to diligence in their callings (4.9-12), some having been led to abandon their ordinary employments owing to their expectation of the Lord's coming, and others having been drawn into curious questionings, especially regarding the fate of those who had died before the *Parousia* (Second Coming). Paul assures them that those who have died in the Lord are at no disadvantage, and that as the time of His coming is unknown they must live as children of the light to whom the "day" is welcome (4.13 to 5.11). The epistle then passes into a series of admonitions, not as a river loses itself in a marsh, for these instructions are not made at random, but are pointedly directed against actual dangers in the Thessalonian church.

THE FIRST EPISTLE OF PAUL TO THE

THES-SA-LO'NI-ANS

Salutation.   **Thanksgiving**

1 Paul, and Sil-va'nus, and Tim'o-thy, unto the church of the Thes-sa-lo'ni-ans in God the Father and the Lord Je'sus Christ: Grace to you and peace.

2 We give thanks to God always for you all, making mention *of you* in our prayers; 3 remembering without ceasing your work of faith and labor of love and *a*patience of hope in our Lord Je'sus Christ, before *b*our God and Father; 4 knowing, brethren beloved of God, your election, 5 *c*how that our *d*gospel came not unto you in word only, but also in power, and in the Holy Spirit, and *in* much *e*assurance; even as ye know what manner of men we showed ourselves toward you for your sake. 6 And ye became imitators of us, and of the Lord, having received the word in much affliction, with joy of the Holy Spirit; 7 so that ye became an ensample to all that believe in Mac-e-do'ni-a and in A-cha'ia. 8 For from you hath sounded forth the word of the Lord, not only in Mac-e-do'ni-a and A-cha'ia, but in

---

a Or, *stedfastness*   *b* Or, *God and our Father*   *c* Or, *because our gospel &c.*   *d* Gr. *good tidings*: and so elsewhere; see marginal note on Mt. 4.23.   *e* Or, *fulness*

CHAPTER 1

1. *Silvanus.* Another name for Silas. See Acts 15.22, 40. *Timothy.* Chosen by Paul at Lystra (Acts 16.1), to accompany himself and Silas. The three labored together at Thessalonica (Acts 17.10, 14), and also at Corinth (Acts 18.5). See 2 Cor. 1.19. Thessalonica was a 'free city' as distinguished from a colony like Philippi, or Troas. As a free city it was wholly self-governing, and had no Roman garrison. This epistle was written upon the return of Timothy from Athens to Thessalonica. See ch. 3.6.

2. *We.* Although others are joined with Paul in the salutation (ver. 1), the body of the epistle shows that Paul used the plural here, as also in the epistles to the Corinthians, to designate himself alone. See ch. 3.1.

5. *In power.* The 'power of signs and wonders' (Rom. 15.19) which accompanied Paul's ministry as well as that of the other apostles. See Acts 14.3; 15.12; 2 Cor. 12.12; also Jn. 4.48; Acts 2.43; 4.30; 1 Cor. 1.22.

6. *In much affliction.* The first converts of Paul and Silas at Thessalonica were subjected to much persecution. See Acts 17.5-9.

7. *In Macedonia and in Achaia.* At this time these two provinces included all of Greece: Macedonia the northern, and Achaia the southern part.

8. *In every place.* Thessalonica was the commercial centre of a large region, and an important seaport as well. News from there would

506

every place your faith to God-ward is gone forth; so that we need not to speak anything. 9 For they themselves report concerning us what manner of entering in we had unto you; and how ye turned unto God from idols, to serve a living and true God, 10 and to wait for his Son from heaven, whom he raised from the dead, *even* Je'sus, who delivereth us from the wrath to come.

2 For yourselves, brethren, know our entering in unto you, that it hath not been found vain: 2 but having suffered before and been shamefully treated, as ye know, at Phi-lip'pi, we waxed bold in our God to speak unto you the *a*gospel of God in much conflict. 3 For our exhortation *is* not of error, nor of uncleanness, nor in guile: 4 but even as we have been approved of God to be intrusted with the *a*gospel, so we speak; not as pleasing men, but God who proveth our hearts. 5 For neither at any time were we found using words of flattery, as ye know, nor a cloak of covetous-ness, God is witness; 6 nor seeking glory of men, neither from you nor from others, when we might have *b*claimed authority as apostles of Christ. 7 But we were *c*gentle in the midst of you, as when a nurse cherisheth her own children: 8 even so, being affectionately desirous of you, we were well pleased to impart unto you, not the *a*gospel of God only, but also our own souls, because ye were become very dear to us. 9 For ye remember, brethren, our labor and travail: working night and day, that we might not burden any of you, we preached unto you the *a*gospel of God. 10 Ye are witnesses, and God *also*, how holily and righteously and unblamably we behaved ourselves toward you that believe: 11 as ye know how we *dealt with* each one of you, as a father with his own children, exhorting you, and encouraging *you*, and testifying, 12 to the end that ye should walk worthily of God, who *d*calleth you into his own kingdom and glory.

13 And for this cause we also thank God without ceasing, that,

---

a Gr. *good tidings.* See ch. 1.5.   *b* Or, *been burdensome* ver 9; comp. 1 Cor. 9.4 ff.   *c* Most of the ancient authorities read *babes.* Comp. 1 Cor. 14.20.   *d* Some ancient authorities read *called.*

---

be widespread, and the disorderly demonstrations referred to in Acts 17.5–9, would be sure to be reported with much detail.

10. *The wrath to come.* The wrath of God which falls upon the sons of disobedience (Eph. 5.6), 'is revealed from heaven against all ungodliness and unrighteousness of men' (Rom. 1.18). See Rom. 1.28, 32; 2.8, 9; Eph. 2.3; Col. 3.6.

CHAPTER 2

2. *Shamefully treated . . . at Philippi.* See Acts 16.22–24.

6. *Authority.* Paul led his converts into the truth, he did not exercise lordship over them. See 2 Cor. 1.24.

9. *Might not burden any.* One of the arguments used against Paul by his critics was the fact that he did not ask maintenance of those to whom he ministered, according to the declaration of the Lord, that 'the laborer is worthy of his hire' (Luke 10.7). At Thessalonica he worked 'night and day' to maintain himself. See Acts 18.3; 20.34; 1 Cor. 9.3–14; 2 Th. 3.8, 9.

when ye received from us *the word of the message, *even the word* of God, ye accepted *it* not *as* the word of men, but, as it is in truth, the word of God, which also worketh in you that believe. 14 For ye, brethren, became imitators of the churches of God which are in Ju-dæ'a in Christ Je'sus: for ye also suffered the same things of your own countrymen, even as they did of the Jews; 15 who both killed the Lord Je'sus and the prophets, and drove out us, and please not God, and are contrary to all men; 16 forbidding us to speak to the Gen'tiles that they may be saved; to fill up their sins always: but the wrath is come upon them to the uttermost.

17 But we, brethren, being bereaved of you for *ƒa* short season, in presence not in heart, endeavored the more exceedingly to see your face with great desire: 18 because we would fain have come unto you, I Paul once and again; and Satan hindered us. 19 For what is our hope, or joy, or crown of glory-

ing? Are not even ye, before our Lord Je'sus at his *ᵍcoming? 20 For ye are our glory and our joy.

3 Wherefore when we could no longer forbear, we thought it good to be left behind at Ath'ens alone; 2 and sent Tim'o-thy, our brother and *ᵃGod's minister in the *ᵇgospel of Christ, to establish you, and to comfort *you* concerning your faith; 3 that no man be moved by these afflictions; for yourselves know that hereunto we are appointed. 4 For verily, when we were with you, we told you *ᶜbeforehand that we are to suffer affliction; even as it came to pass, and ye know. 5 For this cause I also, when I could no longer forbear, sent that I might know your faith, lest by any means the tempter had tempted you, and our labor should be in vain. 6 But when Tim'o-thy came even now unto us from you, and brought us glad tidings of your faith and love, and that ye have good remembrance of us always, longing to see us, even as we also *to see* you; 7 for this cause,

e Gr. *the word of hearing.* Gal. 3.2, 5. ƒ Gr. *a season of an hour.* g Gr. *presence.* Comp. 2 Cor. 10.10. a Some ancient authorities read *fellow-worker with God.* b Gr. *good tidings:* see ch. 1.5. c Or, *plainly*

15. *Drove out us.* The Jews were particularly bitter against Paul because of his ministering to the Gentiles. See Acts 17.10, 14. Even the Christian Jews followed him from place to place declaiming against him and his work. See Acts 15.1; 2 Cor. 11.4; Gal. 1.7.

18. *Satan hindered.* It is surmised that illness prevented Paul's going to Thessalonica. See 2 Cor. 12.7–9.

CHAPTER 3

1. *No longer forbear.* Paul's anxiety to hear from them grew so strong as to lead him to send

Timothy, even though it left him alone. See ver. 5.

3. *We are appointed.* See Acts 9.16.

4. *As it came to pass.* See note ch. 1.6; ch. 2.14.

5. *The tempter.* When Jesus was being tempted of the devil in the wilderness the tempter's first suggestion to him was to return to the ease of worldly life by using his divine power to relieve the hunger of his body (Mt. 4.3). Paul feared lest the Thessalonians would be led back into the easier life of the world through weariness of persecutions.

brethren, we were comforted over you in all our distress and affliction through your faith: 8 for now we live, if ye stand fast in the Lord. 9 For what thanksgiving can we render again unto God for you, for all the joy wherewith we joy for your sakes before our God; 10 night and day praying exceedingly that we may see your face, and may perfect that which is lacking in your faith?

11 Now may ^dour God and Father himself, and our Lord Je′sus, direct our way unto you: 12 and the Lord make you to increase and abound in love one toward another, and toward all men, even as we also *do* toward you; 13 to the end he may establish your hearts unblamable in holiness before ^eour God and Father, at the ^fcoming of our Lord Je′sus with all his saints.^g

4 Finally then, brethren, we beseech and exhort you in the Lord Je′sus, that, as ye received of us how ye ought to walk and to please God, even as ye do walk,—that ye abound more and more. 2 For ye know what ^acharge we gave you through the Lord Je′sus. 3 For this is the will of God, *even* your sanctification, that ye abstain from fornication; 4 that each one of you know how to possess himself of his own vessel in sanctification and honor, 5 not in the passion of lust, even as the Gen′tiles who know not God; 6 that no man ^btransgress, and wrong his brother in the matter: because the Lord is an avenger in all these things, as also we ^cforewarned you and testified. 7 For God called us not for uncleanness, but in sanctification. 8 Therefore he that rejecteth, rejecteth not man, but God, who giveth his Holy Spirit unto you.

9 But concerning love of the brethren ye have no need that one write unto you: for ye yourselves are taught of God to love one another; 10 for indeed ye do it toward all the brethren that are in all Mac-e-do′ni-a. But we exhort you, brethren, that ye abound more and more; 11 and that ye ^dstudy to be quiet, and to do your own business, and to work with your hands, even as we charged you; 12 that ye may

---

d Or, *God himself and our Father* e Or, *God and our Father* f Gr. *presence.* Comp. 2 Cor. 10.10. g Many ancient authorities add *Amen.* a Gr. *charges.* b Or. *over reach* c Or, *told you plainly* d Gr. *be ambitious.* See Rom. 15.20 marg.

CHAPTER 4

3. *Even your sanctification.* Complete sanctification is impossible until the flesh is overcome with all its lusts. See Heb. 10.10; Rom. 6.12, 13.
4. *How to possess himself.* The continual struggle for this possession, or mastery of the body is pictured in Rom. 7.15–24; and is epitomized in Paul's exclamation, 'The good which I would I do not: but the evil which I would not, that I practise.'

8. *Rejecteth not man.* In rejecting Paul's message, they rejected not him, but God, whose messenger he was.
11. *To be quiet.* Paul seems to be admonishing the Thessalonians against religious excitement concerning the second coming of Christ, which they believed to be imminent. See 2 Th. 2.2; 3.11. *Work with your hands.* Paul himself had set them an example of industry. See note ch. 2.9.
12. *Becomingly.* Outward be-

walk becomingly toward them that are without, and may have need of nothing.

13 But we would not have you ignorant, brethren, concerning them that fall asleep; that ye sorrow not, even as the rest, who have no hope. 14 For if we believe that Je'sus died and rose again, even so them also that are fallen asleep *in Je'sus will God bring with him. 15 For this we say unto you by the word of the Lord, that we that are alive, that are left unto the *coming of the Lord, shall in no wise precede them that are fallen asleep. 16 For the Lord himself shall descend from heaven, with a shout, with the voice of the archangel, and with the trump of God: and the dead in Christ shall rise first; 17 then we that are alive, that are left, shall together with them be caught up in the clouds, to meet the Lord in the air: and so shall we ever be with the Lord. 18 Wherefore *comfort one another with these words.

5 But concerning the times and the seasons, brethren, ye have no need that aught be written unto you. 2 For yourselves know perfectly that the day of the Lord so cometh as a thief in the night. 3 When they are saying, Peace and safety, then sudden destruction cometh upon them, as travail upon a woman with child; and they shall in no wise escape. 4 But ye, brethren, are not in darkness, that that day should overtake you *as a thief: 5 for ye are all sons of light, and sons of the day: we are not of the night, nor of darkness; 6 so then let us not sleep, as do the rest, but let us watch and be sober. 7 For they that sleep sleep in the night; and they that are drunken are drunken in the night. 8 But let us, since we are of the day, be sober, putting on the breastplate of faith and love; and for a helmet, the hope of salvation. 9 For God appointed us not unto wrath, but unto the obtaining of sal-

---

e Gr. *through.* Or, *will God through Je'sus* f Gr. *presence.* g Or, *exhort* ch. 5.11.

a Some ancient authorities read *as thieves.*

---

havior to those who are not Christians is to be carefully guarded lest it give offense. Paul set an example in his own conduct, which he urged the Thessalonians to imitate. See 2 Th. 3.7–9. Also Rom. 14.1–7, 13, 15, 21; 15.2.

13. *As the rest.* The belief held generally by the Greeks was that there was no resurrection; that death was the end of all things.

14. *And rose again.* Paul bases his argument for the resurrection upon the resurrection. See 1 Cor. 15.12–23.

CHAPTER 5

2. *As a thief in the night.* In reminding the Thessalonians that they 'knew perfectly' that the day

of the Lord would come in this manner, Paul was doubtless referring to the words of Jesus recorded in Luke 12.39. See also Luke 21. 34, 35. The word translated 'thief,' is, more exactly, 'bandit,' a murderer as well as a thief.

4. *Darkness.* The word is used to signify ignorance as to the spiritual meaning of the gospel. See Mt. 4.16; Jn. 8.12; 12.46; 1 Jn. 2.9, 11.

5. *Sons of light.* Those whose understanding has been regenerated in Christ. See Jn. 8.12; 12.36; Eph. 5.9.

6. *The rest.* The unregenerate; the 'children of wrath' (Eph. 2.3). See Rom. 1.28–31.

9. *Obtaining of salvation.* Salvation is a gift but it must be grasped

vation through our Lord Je'sus Christ, 10 who died for us, that, whether we *b*wake or sleep, we should live together with him. 11 Wherefore *c*exhort one another, and build each other up, even as also ye do.

12 But we beseech you, brethren, to know them that labor among you, and are over you in the Lord, and admonish you; 13 and to esteem them exceeding highly in love for their work's sake. Be at peace among yourselves. 14 And we exhort you, brethren, admonish the disorderly, encourage the faint-hearted, support the weak, be longsuffering toward all. 15 See that none render unto any one evil for evil; but always follow after ,that which is good, one toward another, and toward all. 16 Rejoice always; 17 pray

without ceasing; 18 in everything give thanks: for this is the will of God in Christ Je'sus to you-ward. 19 Quench not the Spirit; 20 despise not prophesyings; 21 *d*prove all things; hold fast that which is good; 22 abstain from every form of evil.

23 And the God of peace himself sanctify you wholly; and may your spirit and soul and body be preserved entire, without blame at the *e*coming of our Lord Je'sus Christ. 24 Faithful is he that calleth you, who will also do it.

25 Brethren, pray for us*f*.

26 Salute all the brethren with a holy kiss. 27 I adjure you by the Lord that this epistle be read unto all the *g*brethren.

28 The grace of our Lord Je'sus Christ be with you.

---

b Or, *watch*   *c* Or, *comfort* ch. 4.18.   add *also*.   *g* Many ancient authorities in-
d Many ancient authorities insert *but*.   sert *holy*.
e Gr. *presence*.   *f* Some ancient authorities

to become effective. Paul exhorted the Philippians to work out their salvation 'with fear and trembling' (Phil. 2.12). See Phil. 3.12, 13; 1 Tim. 6.12, 19; Heb. 6.18.

17. *Without ceasing.* True prayer is unceasing—the earnest, ever-present desire for spiritual blessings (Eph. 1.3); by no means the long prayers of the scribes which Jesus condemned (Mk. 12.40). See ch. 2.13; Rom. 1.9; 2 Tim. 1.3.

19. *Quench not the Spirit.* Sensual and worldly living means the exclusion of the Spirit, 'for the flesh lusteth against the Spirit,' and 'these are contrary the one to the other' (Gal. 5.17). See Rom. 8.6, 13.

20. *Prophesyings.* More exactly, 'inspired preaching.' This was a common gift among the early Christians, and was subject to some abuses. See 1 Cor. 14; especially ver. 31. Also Rom. 12.6; 1 Cor. 12.10, 29; 13.2, 9.

21. *Prove all things.* This injunction to put all things to the test before accepting them as good probably relates to the prophesyings mentioned in the preceding verse. See 1 Cor. 14.24, 29.

26. *A holy kiss.* The kiss was the common form of salutation between friends. It was often insincere in that it did not express true fellowship; as the treacherous kiss of Judas.

THE SECOND EPISTLE TO THE THESSALONIANS

INTRODUCTION BY PROFESSOR MARCUS DODS, D.D.

Date and Object.—The second epistle was written in order to remove certain misunderstandings of what had been said in the first regarding the coming of the Lord. The impression had been created that "the day of the Lord is just at hand" (ch. 2.2), and Paul feels called upon to explain more accurately his meaning. The letter therefore may be placed a month or two after the first. Silas and Timothy are still with Paul, and are included with him in the opening inscription of the epistle.

Some critics have supposed that this letter was really the first; but not only does this second epistle directly refer to the first (ch. 2.15), but the first is throughout implied. In the first, the allusions to Paul's recent visit are numerous and vivid; in the second such allusions are rare. The *Parousia*, which in the first was spoken of as imminent, is in the second more guardedly spoken of.

Contents.—Encouragement is given to the Thessalonians under persecution by the assurance that their sufferings will not be forgotten, that the coming of Christ will end all injustice and oppression, and that opportunity is given them of glorifying God (1.1-12). Neither are they to be disturbed by the non-intervention of the Lord's coming and judgment, as if this had been definitely announced as speedily to take place. On the contrary, certain events must first happen; especially must lawlessness be manifested in a person before the personal coming of Christ destroys it (2.1-12). They themselves were chosen to salvation, and this they will attain by holding fast what they had been taught (2.13-17). After asking for their prayers, he concludes by giving stringent instructions regarding such members of their church as walked disorderly, being carried away by the expectation of an immediate second coming.

THE SECOND EPISTLE OF PAUL TO THE

THES-SA-LO′NI-ANS

Salutation.

1 Paul, and Sil-va′nus, and Tim′o-thy, unto the church of the Thes-sa-lo′ni-ans in God our Father and the Lord Je′sus Christ; 2 Grace to you and peace from God the Father and the Lord Je′sus Christ.

3 We are bound to give thanks to God always for you, brethren, even as it is meet, for that your faith groweth exceedingly, and the love of each one of you all toward one another aboundeth; 4 so that we ourselves glory in you in the churches of God for your *a*patience and faith in all your persecutions and in the afflictions which ye endure; 5 *which is* a manifest token of the

a Or, *stedfastness*

Thanksgiving

righteous judgment of God; to the end that ye may be counted worthy of the kingdom of God, for which ye also suffer: 6 if so be that it is a righteous thing with God to recompense affliction to them that afflict you, 7 and to you that are afflicted rest with us, at the revelation of the Lord Je′sus from heaven with the angels of his power in flaming fire, 8 rendering vengeance to them that know not God, and to them that obey not the *b*gospel of our Lord Je′sus: 9 who shall suffer punishment, *even* eternal destruction from the face of the Lord and from the glory of his might, 10 when he shall come to be glorified in his saints, and to

b Gr. *good tidings*: and so elsewhere. See marginal note on Mt. 4.23.

CHAPTER 1

1. *Silvanus, and Timothy.* Silas and Timothy were still with Paul when this epistle was written. Timothy was later at Ephesus with Paul, but meanwhile Silas had dropped out of the historical record.

3. *Your faith groweth.* The Thessalonians believed that the second coming of Christ was at hand, and under this spur their faith increased exceedingly, together with such an outpouring of brotherly love that Paul is moved to unstinted thankfulness and commendation. See ver. 4.

5. *A manifest token.* The manner

in which the Thessalonians had borne their persecutions had already brought forth fruit in a higher degree of faith and a larger measure of love among themselves.

6. *To recompense affliction.* The divine law of recompense is declared by Jesus in the words: 'For with what measure ye mete it shall be measured to you again' (Luke 6.38). Under this law every man establishes his own recompense. See Rom. 2.6; 2 Cor. 5.10.

8. *Vengeance.* The word is not used in the sense of revenge, but of just recompense. See note on ver. 6; also Rom. 12.19, 20.

be marvelled at in all them that believed (because our testimony unto you was believed) in that day. 11 To which end we also pray always for you, that our God may count you worthy of your calling, and fulfil every *c*desire of goodness and *every* work of faith, with power; 12 that the name of our Lord Je′sus may be glorified in you, and ye in him, according to the grace of our God and the Lord Je′sus Christ.

2 Now we beseech you, brethren, *a*touching the *b*coming of our Lord Je′sus Christ, and our gathering together unto him; 2 to the end that ye be not quickly shaken from your mind, nor yet be troubled, either by spirit, or by word, or by epistle as from us, as that the day of the Lord is just at hand; 3 let no man beguile you in any wise: for *it will not be,* except the falling away come first, and the man of *c*sin be revealed, the son of per-

dition, 4 he that opposeth and exalteth himself against all that is called God or *d*that is worshipped; so that he sitteth in the *e*temple of God, setting himself forth as God. 5 Remember ye not, that, when I was yet with you, I told you these things? 6 And now ye know that which restraineth, to the end that he may be revealed in his own season. 7 For the mystery of lawlessness doth already work: *f*only *there is* one that restraineth now, until' he be taken out of the way. 8 And then shall be revealed the lawless one, whom the Lord *g*Je′sus shall *h*slay with the breath of his mouth, and bring to nought by the manifestation of his *b*coming; 9 *even he,* whose *b*coming is according to the working of Satan with all *i*power and signs and lying wonders, 10 and with all deceit of unrighteousness for them that *k*perish; because they received

---

c Gr. *good pleasure of goodness.* Comp. Rom. 10.1. *a* Gr. *in behalf of.* *b* Gr. *presence.* *c* Many ancient authorities read *lawlessness.* *d* Gr. *an object of worship.* Acts. 17.23. *e* Or, *sanctuary* *f* Or, *only until he*

that now restraineth be taken &c. *g* Some ancient authorities omit *Jesus.* *h* Some ancient authorities read *consume.* *i* Gr. *power and signs and wonders of falsehood.* *k* Or, *are perishing*

---

11. *Every desire of goodness.* Progress comes through desire. Paul himself was constantly reaching forward (Phil. 3.13), and urging his hearers to higher levels. See 1 Cor. 12.31; 14.1; Eph. 5.9. *With power.* The unusual power which worked wonders. See preceding note on this verse; also Rom. 15.19; 1 Cor. 2.4; 1 Th. 1.5.

CHAPTER 2

2. *By epistle as from us.* The inference must be that a letter falsely declared to be from Paul, had been used to uphold the contention of a faction in the Thessalonian church which believed the second coming of Christ to be at hand. It is probable

that this incident, with the continued fanatical excitement of the people, led Paul to write this second epistle. See note 1 Th. 4.11.

3. *Falling away.* In the Greek, 'apostasy.' See 1 Tim. 4.1; 2 Tim. 3.1, 5. *The son of perdition.* A title also applied to Judas Iscariot. See Jn. 17.12; 6.70.

4. *He that opposeth.* See Rev. 13.5–8.

7. *One that restraineth.* Generally accepted as being the Roman government, which, for a time, protected the early Christians from the attacks of the Jews. See Acts 18. 14, 15; 21.32; 23.12–24.

9. *Lying wonders.* Some of the false Christs also worked signs and

not the love of the truth, that they might be saved. 11 And for this cause God sendeth them a working of error, that they should believe a lie: 12 that they all might be judged who believed not the truth, but had pleasure in unrighteousness.

13 But we are bound to give thanks to God always for you, brethren beloved of the Lord, for that God chose you *from the beginning unto salvation in sanctification of the Spirit and *m*belief of the truth: 14 whereunto he called you through our *n*gospel, to the obtaining of the glory of our Lord Je′sus Christ. 15 So then, brethren, stand fast, and hold ,the traditions which ye were taught, whether by word, or by epistle of ours.

16 Now our Lord Je′sus Christ himself, and God our Father who loved us and gave us eternal comfort and good hope through grace, 17 comfort your hearts and establish them in every good work and word.

3 Finally, brethren, pray for us, that the word of the Lord may run and be glorified, even as also *it is* with you; 2 and that we may be delivered from unreasonable and evil men; for all have not faith. 3 But the Lord is faithful, who shall establish you, and guard you from *a*the evil *one.* 4 And we have confidence in the Lord touching you, that ye both do and will do the things which we command. 5 And the Lord direct your hearts into the love of God, and into the *b*patience of Christ.

6 Now we command you, brethren, in the name of our Lord Je′sus Christ, that ye withdraw yourselves from every brother that walketh disorderly, and not after the tradition which *c*they received of us. 7 For yourselves know how ye ought to imitate us: for we behaved not ourselves disorderly among you; 8 neither did we eat bread for nought at any man's hand, but in labor and travail, working

---

l Many ancient authorities read *as first-fruits. m* Or, *faith   n* Gr. *good tidings:*

see ch. 1.8. *a* Or, *evil   b* Or, *stedfastness   c* Some ancient authorities read *ye.*

wonders. See Mt. 12.27; 24.24; Acts 19.13; Rev. 13.13, 14.

11. *A working of error.* The error of worldly wisdom. See Rom. 1.21, 22, 24, 25, 28. When the people harden their hearts against the truth as it is in Christ they pay the penalty of becoming victims of their own delusions.

12. *Pleasure in unrighteousness.* There were some who seized joyfully upon the doctrines of the false teachers, because they were permitted to indulge their fleshly desires under promise that all sin was already atoned for in the death of Christ. See 2 Pet. 2.1, 2, 19.

15. *Traditions.* Not the tradi-

tions of the Jewish nations, but the teachings of the apostles.

CHAPTER 3

2. *Unreasonable.* Those not controlled by reason—violent. They were probably Jews who did not accept Christianity. *Faith.* In Jesus Christ.

5. *Love of God.* Love for God. *Patience of Christ.* Using the word patience in the sense of stedfastness, Paul is urging the Thessalonians to a similar stedfastness in the face of tribulations.

6. *Walketh disorderly.* See note 1 Th. 4.11; also ver. 11.

8. *At any man's hand.* See note 1 Th. 2.9; 2 Cor. 11.7–9.

night and day, that we might not burden any of you: 9 not because we have not the right, but to make ourselves an ensample unto you, that ye should imitate us. 10 For even when we were with you, this we commanded you, If any will not work, neither let him eat. 11 For we hear of some that walk among you disorderly, that work not at all, but are busybodies. 12 Now them that are such we command and exhort in the Lord Je′sus Christ, that with quietness they work, and eat their own bread. 13 But ye, brethren, be not weary in well-doing. 14 And if any man obeyeth not our word by this epistle, note that man, that ye have no company with him, to the end that he may be ashamed. 15 And *yet* count him not as an enemy, but admonish him as a brother.

16 Now the Lord of peace himself give you peace at all times in all ways. The Lord be with you all.

17 The salutation of me Paul with mine own hand, which is the token in every epistle: so I write. 18 The grace of our Lord Je′sus Christ be with you all.

9. *The right.* With the commission to ' the seventy ' went the injunction to expect maintenance as a right from those to whom they ministered : ' for the laborer is worthy of his hire' (Lk. 10.7). See 1 Cor. 9.7–14.

THE PASTORAL EPISTLES

INTRODUCTION BY THE REV. TALBOT W. CHAMBERS, D.D.

These three epistles are so closely connected in thought, aim, and style that, as all admit, they could not have been composed at widely different intervals of time. Their genuineness and authenticity have been severely assailed, but always on internal grounds, the external evidence being conclusively in their favor. The difficulty of finding a place for them in the record of Paul's travels in the Acts has led most critics to believe that Paul was released from his first imprisonment, and after a few years of toil, during which he wrote two of these epistles, was again imprisoned at Rome, whence he sent the second letter to Timothy. The writings do not discuss doctrines, but give directions for the training and governing of churches, and the proper treatment of individual members, old and young, official and unofficial, backsliders and heretics. They are full of practical wisdom; and countless pastors through many centuries have felt the value of the guidance, warning, and encouragement here given.

FIRST TIMOTHY

Timothy was from Lystra (Acts 16.1). He was the son of a Greek father and a Jewish mother named Eunice, from whom, as also from his grandmother Lois, he had received a devout training in the Old Testament (2 Tim. 1.5; 3.14, 15). Paul calls him his "true son in the faith," whence it is inferred that he had received the gospel through Paul's preaching during his first sojourn in Lystra. At all events, on the apostle's second visit to Lystra, he found the mother and son already converted, although the father continued an unbeliever. As Timothy was well reported of by the brethren, Paul circumcised him and took him as one of his chosen companions (Acts 19.22). The connection continued intimate and unbroken till the close of the apostle's career.

The time and place of writing cannot be certainly fixed. The former must have been between the years 64 and 67 A.D. But the occasion and purport of the epistle are very plain. Heretical teachers had arisen at Ephesus, where Timothy was stationed, and the apostle gives directions which the young man required, and which have a permanent value for all youthful ministers. No systematic order of thought, such as is found in Romans and Ephesians, meets us here, but a free outpouring of the apostle's heart. The letter has been justly compared to pearls of varied size and color loosely strung on one thread.

Contents.—Ch. 1. After the usual address, the writer guards

THE PASTORAL EPISTLES—FIRST TIMOTHY

Timothy against false teachers of the law (ver. 3-11), against whom he recites his own experience of the gospel (ver. 12-17). In ch. 2 he passes to worship, and specifies the mode and subjects of prayer (ver. 1-8), adding the direction that women should be simple in attire, and "learn in quietness" (ver. 9-15). In ch. 3 he states the qualifications of a bishop or overseer (ver. 1-7), and of a deacon (ver. 8-13), adding a lofty encomium of the church. In ch. 4 he predicts the rise of a false asceticism (ver. 1-5), and urges Timothy to fortitude and diligence in his ministry (ver. 6-16). Ch. 5 prescribes his duties toward men, young or old (ver. 1), women also (ver. 2), widows, the older and the younger (ver. 3-16), elders (ver. 17-22), with some personal counsels (ver. 23-25). Ch. 6 sets forth the duties of slaves (ver. 1, 2), warns against the love of money (ver. 3-10), eloquently summons Timothy to a spotless life (ver. 11-16), says what he is to charge the rich (ver. 17-19), and ends with a renewed summons to vigilance (ver. 20, 21).

THE FIRST EPISTLE OF PAUL TO

TIM'O-THY

Salutation. Charge respecting Misuse of the Law

1 Paul, an apostle of Christ Je'sus according to the commandment of God our Saviour, and Christ Je'sus our hope; 2 unto Tim'o-thy, my true child in faith: Grace, mercy, peace, from God the Father and Christ Je'sus our Lord.

3 As I exhorted thee to tarry at Eph'e-sus, when I was going into Mac-e-do'ni-a, that thou mightest charge certain men not to teach a different doctrine, 4 neither to give heed to fables and endless genealogies, which minister questionings, rather than a *a*dispensation of God which is in faith; *so do I now.* 5 But the end of the charge is love out of a pure heart and a good conscience and faith unfeigned: 6 from which things some having *b*swerved have turned aside unto vain talking; 7 desiring to be teachers of the law, though they understand neither what they say, not whereof they confidently affirm. 8 But we know that the law is good, if a man use it lawfully, 9 as knowing this, that law is not made for a righteous man, but for the lawless and unruly, for the ungodly and sinners, for the unholy and profane, for *c*murderers of fathers and *c*murderers of mothers, for manslayers, 10 for fornicators, for abusers of themselves with men, for menstealers, for liars,

---

a Or, *stewardship* See 1 Cor. 9.17.

b Gr. *missed the mark.* ch. 6.21; 2 Tim. 2.18. *c* Or, *smiters*

CHAPTER 1

1. *The commandment.* See Acts 9.6.
2. *Unto Timothy.* Then preaching at Ephesus. The epistle seems to have been written to afford Timothy documentary proof that Paul endorsed his teachings.
3. *Ephesus.* The chief city of Asia Minor and one of the 'free' cities under the Roman empire. Here was the celebrated temple of the goddess Diana, to whose worship the city, as a whole, was devoted. See Acts 19.23–41. *Macedonia.* The northern Roman province of Greece,

the southern being Achaia. Its chief city was Philippi. See Acts 16.12; 20.1.
4. *Fables.* Fanciful traditions as to the origin of angels and their powers, and similar superstitions. See ch. 4.7; 2 Tim. 4.4; Tit. 1.14; 2 Pet. 1.16. *Genealogies . . . questionings.* Fruitless speculation on things of no importance. The one vital matter was faith in Christ Jesus.
7. *Of the law.* From the context this is accepted as being the Mosaic law, which the Judaizers were trying to impose upon the Ephesian church.

519

for false swearers, and if there be any other thing contrary to the *d*sound *e*doctrine; 11 according to the *f*gospel of the glory of the blessed God, which was committed to my trust.

12 I thank him that *g*enabled me, *even* Christ Je'sus our Lord, for that he counted me faithful, appointing me to *his* service; 13 though I was before a blasphemer, and a persecutor, and injurious: howbeit I obtained mercy, because I did it ignorantly in unbelief; 14 and the grace of our Lord abounded exceedingly with faith and love which is in Christ Je'sus. 15 Faithful is the saying, and worthy of all acceptation, that Christ Je'sus came into the world to save sinners; of whom I am chief: 16 howbeit for this cause I obtained mercy, that in me as chief might Je'sus Christ show forth all his longsuffering, for an ensample of them that

should thereafter believe on him unto eternal life. 17 Now unto the King *h*eternal, *i*immortal, invisible, the only God, *be* honor and glory *k*for ever and ever. A-men'.

18 This charge I commit unto thee, my child Tim'o-thy, according to the prophecies which led the way to thee, that by them thou mayest war the good warfare; 19 holding faith and a good conscience; which some having thrust from them made shipwreck concerning the faith: 20 of whom is Hy-me-næ'us and Al-ex-an'der; whom I delivered unto Satan, that they might be taught not to blaspheme.

2 I exhort therefore, first of all, *a*that supplications, prayers, intercessions, thanksgivings, be made for all men; 2 for kings and all that are in high place; that we may lead a tranquil and quiet life in all godliness and gravity. 3 This is good

---

d Gr. *healthful.*   *e* Or, *teaching*   *f* Gr. *good tidings.* See Mt. 4.23 marg.   *g* Some ancient authorities read *enableth.*   *h* Gr.

of the ages. Comp. Heb. 1.2· Rev. 15.3. *i* Gr. *incorruptible.*   *k* Gr. *unto the ages of the ages.*   *a* Gr. *to make supplications &c.*

---

13. *A persecutor.* See Acts 8.3; Phil. 3.6. *Injurious.* The word thus translated includes the sense of violence and outrage. *In unbelief.* Paul felt his humiliation not less because his persecutions had been carried on with a good conscience in ignorance. See Acts. 23.1.

15. *The saying.* See Mk. 2.17.

16. *An ensample.* Paul regarded himself as the chief of sinners (ver. 15), and as having received the most abounding forgiveness in the trust committed to him (ver. 11) in the great ministry to the Gentile world.

17. *King.* This title as applied to God occurs only here, in ch. 6.15, and in Mt. 5.35. See also Rev. 19.16.

18. *Prophecies.* Timothy's special fitness for the work before him was

discerned by other disciples who recommended him to Paul (Acts 16.2). In the light of his achievements their words have proved to be prophetic.

20. *Hymenæus and Alexander.* It is generally accepted that Hymenæus was the person mentioned in 2 Tim. 2.17, 18, as teaching false doctrine. Alexander was probably 'the coppersmith' spoken of in 2 Tim. 4.14, 15. *Delivered unto Satan.* That is, to the ever-increasing darkness of their own erroneous beliefs. See Rom. 1.21, 24, 28; Eph. 4.18; also 1 Cor. 5.5.

CHAPTER 2

1. *For all men.* A declaration of the virtual unity of all men in one brotherhood. See ver. 4, 6; Gal. 6.10; Col. 3.11.

and acceptable in the sight of God our Saviour; 4 who would have all men to be saved, and come to the knowledge of the truth. 5 For there is one God, one mediator also between God and men, *himself* man, Christ Je'sus, 6 who gave himself a ransom for all; the testimony *to be borne* in its own times; 7 whereunto I was appointed a *b*preacher and an apostle (I speak the truth, I lie not), a teacher of the Gen'tiles in faith and truth.

8 I desire therefore that the men pray in every place, lifting up holy hands, without wrath and *c*disputing. 9 In like manner, that women adorn themselves in modest apparel, with shamefastness and sobriety; not with braided hair, and gold or pearls or costly raiment; 10 but (which becometh women professing godliness) through good works. 11 Let a woman learn in quietness with all subjection. 12 But I permit not a woman to

teach, nor to have dominion over a man, but to be in quietness. 13 For Adam was first formed, then Eve; 14 and Adam was not beguiled, but the woman being beguiled hath fallen into transgression: 15 but she shall be saved through *d*her childbearing, if they continue in faith and love and sanctification with sobriety.

3 *a*Faithful is the saying, If a man seeketh the office of a *b*bishop, he desireth a good work. 2 The *b*bishop therefore must be without reproach, the husband of one wife, temperate, sober-minded, orderly, given to hospitality, apt to teach; 3 *c*no brawler, no striker; but gentle, not contentious, no lover of money; 4 one that ruleth well his own house, having *his* children in subjection with all gravity; 5 (but if a man knoweth not how to rule his own house, how shall he take care of the church of God?) 6 not a novice, lest being puffed up he

---

b Gr. *herald.* *c* Or, *doubting* *d* Or, *the childbearing* Comp. Gal. 4.4. *a* Some connect the words *Faithful is the saying*

with the preceding paragraph. *b* Or, *overseer* *c* Or, *not quarrelsome over wine*

---

7. *I speak the truth.* Paul was recognized as an apostle by the original twelve apostles (Acts 14. 14), although some of his enemies denied his claim. See 1 Cor. 9.1, 2; 2 Cor. 12.12; 1 Th. 2.6.

12. *I permit not a woman to teach.* Evidently this prohibition refers only to the public assembly of the churches (1 Cor. 14.34); for several passages show that women were active in the gospel work of that period. See Acts 18.26; 21.9; Rom. 16.1–3; Phil. 4.3. In making this prohibition Paul doubtless had in mind the women spoken of in ch. 5. 15, and in 2 Tim. 3.6.

15. *Her childbearing.* By some commentators this is regarded as

referring to Mary's bearing of Jesus, the Saviour of men. See Gal. 4.4. Also Gal. 3.19.

CHAPTER 3

2. *Of one wife.* Various interpretations have been placed upon this phrase. In view of the ease with which divorce was accomplished in those days it was not unusual that a man might have had several wives, in succession. It is quite probable that Paul's prohibition was directed against men of this character. *Given to hospitality.* Evidently this was not a common grace, though of great moment in a dispensation of brotherly love. See Tit. 1.8.

fall into the [d]condemnation of the devil. 7 Moreover he must have good testimony from them that are without; lest he fall into reproach and the snare of the devil. 8 Deacons in like manner *must be* grave, not double-tongued, not given to much wine, not greedy of filthy lucre; 9 holding the mystery of the faith in a pure conscience. 10 And let these also first be proved; then let them serve as deacons, if they be blameless. 11 Women in like manner *must be* grave, not slanderers, temperate, faithful in all things. 12 Let deacons be husbands of one wife, ruling *their* children and their own houses well. 13 For they that have served well as deacons gain to themselves a good standing, and great boldness in the faith which is in Christ Je'sus.

14 These things write I unto thee, hoping to come unto thee shortly; 15 but if I tarry long, that thou mayest know [e]how men ought to behave themselves in the house of God, which is the church of the living God, the pillar and [f]ground of the truth. 16 And without controversy great is the mystery of godliness;

[g]He who was manifested in the flesh,
Justified in the spirit,
Seen of angels,
Preached among the [h]nations,
Believed on in the world,
Received up in glory.

4 But the Spirit saith expressly, that in later times some shall fall away from the faith, giving heed to seducing spirits and doctrines of demons, 2 through the hypocrisy of men that speak lies, [a]branded in their own conscience as with a hot iron; 3 forbidding to marry, *and commanding* to abstain from meats, which God created to be received with thanksgiving by them that believe and know the

---

d Gr. *judgment.* e Or, *how thou oughtest to behave thyself* f Or, *stay* g The word God, in place of *He who*, rests on no suffi- cient ancient evidence. Some ancient authorities read *which* h Or, *Gentiles* a Or, *seared*

---

6. *Puffed up.* A condition of pride fatal to spiritual growth. See ch. 6.4; Rom. 1.21, 22; 1 Cor. 3. 18–20; Gal. 6.3; 2 Tim. 3.4.

7. *Them that are without.* The importance of the good opinion of outsiders is here insisted on. Paul urged the same conduct upon the Colossians (Col. 4.5), and the Thessalonians (1 Th. 4.12).

9. *The mystery.* That the Gentiles—that is, the whole world—should be saved not under the covenant of the Jewish law, but through simple faith in Christ. See Rom. 16.25; 1 Cor. 2.7; Eph. 1.9; 3.3–5.

11. *Women.* Some of the foremost scholars regard these as the deaconesses, who were appointed

to minister to the women of the church under the separation of the sexes which was then a custom.

12. *Of one wife.* See note on ver. 2.

CHAPTER 4

1. *The Spirit saith.* Some of the early Christians had the spiritual gift of prophetic utterance (1 Cor. 12.10). See Jn. 16.13; Acts 20.23; 21.11; 1 Cor. 2.9, 10. *Doctrines of demons.* The 'wisdom' which James denounced as 'earthly, sensual, devilish' (Jas. 3.15). See 2 Th. 2.9, 10; Rev. 2.24.

3. *Abstain from meats.* Paul here denounces those who, by forbidding what is acceptable to God, would encourage a false self-denial leading to harmful results.

truth. 4 For every creature of God is good, and nothing is to be rejected, if it be received with thanksgiving: 5 for it is sanctified through the word of God and prayer.

6 If thou put the brethren in mind of these things, thou shalt be a good minister of Christ Je'sus, nourished in the words of the faith, and of the good doctrine which thou hast followed *until now:* 7 but refuse profane and old wives' fables. And exercise thyself unto godliness: 8 for bodily exercise is profitable *b*for a little; but godliness is profitable for all things, having promise of the life which now is, and of that which is to come. 9 Faithful is the saying, and worthy of all acceptation. 10 For to this end we labor and strive, because we have our hope set on the living God, who is the Saviour of all men, specially of them that believe. 11 These things command and teach. 12 Let no man despise thy youth; but be thou an ensample to them that believe, in word, in manner of life, in love, in faith, in purity. 13 Till I come, give heed to reading, to

exhortation, to teaching. 14 Neglect not the gift that is in thee, which was given thee by prophecy, with the laying on of the hands of the presbytery. 15 Be diligent in these things; give thyself wholly to them; that thy progress may be manifest unto all. 16 Take heed to thyself, and to thy teaching. Continue in these things; for in doing this thou shalt save both thyself and them that hear thee.

5 Rebuke not an elder, but exhort him as a father; the younger men as brethren: 2 the elder women as mothers; the younger as sisters, in all purity. 3 Honor widows that are widows indeed. 4 But if any widow hath children or grandchildren, let them learn first to show piety towards their own family, and to requite their parents: for this is acceptable in the sight of God. 5 Now she that is a widow indeed, and desolate, hath her hope set on God, and continueth in supplications and prayers night and day. 6 But she that giveth herself to pleasure is dead while she liveth. 7 These things also command, that they may

---

b Or, *for little*

4. *With thanksgiving.* As filling a real and present need.

7. *Fables.* See note ch. 1.4.

8. *Bodily exercise.* There was a faction in the early church which sought to control the appetites of the flesh by inflicting injuries upon the body, instead of through the regeneration of the spirit. Paul urges that exercise be 'unto godliness' (ver. 7). See Col. 2.23.

12. *Thy youth.* Timothy was between 35 and 40; young for a presbyter.

14. *The gift.* Probably the gift of

inspirational teaching. See 1 Cor. 12.28; Eph. 4.11; also Acts 13. 1–3; Rom. 12.6–8.

CHAPTER 5

3. *Widows indeed.* Evidently those without relatives to support them (ver. 4). See Acts 6.1; 9.39.

4. *Let them learn.* 'Them' refers to the children and grandchildren who are to requite the care they received in childhood.

6. *Pleasure.* Satisfying oneself with worldly things. See Lk. 8.14; 2 Tim. 3.4; Jas. 5.5. *Dead.* Spirit-

be without reproach. 8 But if any provideth not for his own, and specially his own household, he hath denied the faith, and is worse than an unbeliever. 9 Let none be enrolled as a widow under threescore years old, *having been* the wife of one man, 10 well reported of for good works; if she hath brought up children, if she hath used hospitality to strangers, if she hath washed the saints' feet, if she hath relieved the •afflicted, if she hath diligently followed every good work. 11 But younger widows refuse: for when they have waxed wanton against Christ, they desire to marry; 12 having condemnation, because they have rejected their first *ª*pledge. 13 And withal they learn also *to be* idle, going about from house to house; and not only idle, but tattlers also and busybodies, speaking things which they ought not. 14 I desire therefore that the younger *ᵇwidows* marry, bear children, rule the household, give no occasion to the adversary for reviling: 15 for

already some are turned aside after Satan. 16 If any woman that believeth hath widows, let her relieve them, and let not the church be burdened; that it may relieve them that are widows indeed.

17 Let the elders that rule well be counted worthy of double honor, especially those who labor in the word and in teaching. 18 For the scripture saith, *ᶜThou shalt not muzzle the ox when he treadeth out the corn. And, The laborer is worthy of his hire.* 19 Against an elder receive not an accusation, except at *the mouth of* two or three witnesses. 20 Them that sin reprove in the sight of all, that the rest also may be in fear. 21 I charge *thee* in the sight of God, and Christ Je′sus, and the elect angels, that thou observe these things without *ᵈprejudice*, doing nothing by partiality. 22 Lay hands hastily on no man, neither be partaker of other men's sins: keep thyself pure. 23 Be no longer a drinker of water, but use a little wine for thy stom-

---

a Gr. *faith.*   *b* Or, women

c Dt. xxv. 4.   *d* Or, *preference*

---

ually dead. See Rom. 4.17: 8.13; Rev. 3.1.

10. *Washed the saints' feet.* This service was a ministration in the life of the home. See Lk. 7.44; Jn. 13.14.

11. *Wanton.* The sense is more exactly expressed by the word 'luxurious.' See Rev. 18.7, 9.

12. *Their first pledge.* When a widow was enrolled among the church widows it was with the pledge that she would devote her life to the work assigned her by the church.

15. *Turned aside.* Probably to the false teachers mentioned in ch. 1.20. See 2 Tim. 3.3.

16. *Hath widows.* Among her

relatives. *Widows indeed.* Those without any means of support. See note ver. 3.

17. *Double honor.* The elders, or aged men, among the Jews received honor. When fulfilling faithfully their appointed duties as elders in the Christian church (Acts 14.23), they were worthy of double honor.

18. *Worthy of his hire.* See Lk. 10.7.

22. *Lay hands.* In the sense of to ordain to church office. See Acts 6.6; 8.17; 13.3; 19.6. *Be partaker.* By the hasty ordination of an unfit person, Timothy would be responsible for his errors.

23. *Use a little wine.* In his desire to give no man offense (Rom. 14.3,

ach's sake and thine often infirmities. 24 Some men's sins are evident, going before unto judgment; and some men also they follow after. 25 In like manner also *there are good works that are evident; and such as are otherwise cannot be hid.

6 Let as many as are *servants under the yoke count their own masters worthy of all honor, that the name of God and the doctrine be not blasphemed. 2 And they that have believing masters, let them not despise them, because they are brethren; but let them serve them the rather, because they that *partake of the benefit are believing and beloved. These things teach and exhort.

3 If any man teacheth a different doctrine, and consenteth not to *sound words, *even the words of our Lord Je'sus Christ, and to the doctrine which is according to godliness; 4 he is puffed up, knowing nothing, but *doting about questionings and disputes of words, whereof cometh envy, strife, railings, evil surmisings, 5 wranglings of men corrupted in mind and bereft of the truth, supposing that godliness is a way of gain. 6 But godliness with contentment is great gain: 7 for we brought nothing into the world, for neither can we carry anything out; 8 but having food and covering *we shall be therewith content. 9 But they that are minded to be rich fall into a temptation and a snare and many foolish and hurtful lusts, such as drown men in destruction and perdition. 10 For the love of money is a root of all *kinds of evil: which some reaching after have been led astray from the faith, and have pierced themselves through with many sorrows.

11 But thou, O man of God, flee these things; and follow

---

e Gr. *the works that are good are evident.*   *a* Gr. *bondservants.*   *b* Or, *lay hold of*   *c* Gr.

healthful.   *d* Gr. *sick.*   *e* Or, *in these we shall have enough*   *f* Gr. *evils.*

13, 21), Timothy had denied himself needed tonic.

24. *Follow after.* Are not immediately uncovered.

CHAPTER 6

1. *Under the yoke.* As slaves; many of whom embraced Christianity. The gospel elevated slavery into the fellowship of brotherhood. However, the slave was not to presume upon this new relation, but to render his service with honor. See Eph. 6.5; Tit. 2.9; 1 Pet. 2.18. *Be not blasphemed.* The profession of a belief in Christ which did not include brotherly love expressed in cheerful service, was considered blasphemy by Paul. See Jn. 13.34; Rom. 12.10; 1 Th. 4.9; 1 Pet. 1.22.

4. *Doting.* Having an unwholesome appetite for controversy. See ch. 1.4; 2 Tim. 2.14.

5. *A way of gain.* The teaching of Jesus had been, 'Seek ye first his kingdom and his righteousness, and all these things shall be added unto you' (Mt. 6.33). There were some whose corrupted minds led them to embrace Christianity for the sake of the things they desired, and hoped would be added.

6. *Godliness with contentment.* That is, contentment with the godliness for its own sake.

10. *Money.* The term includes the love of, or desire for, those things of the world which money will buy.

12. *The good confession.* The confession of faith in the gospel of Christ. See 2 Cor. 9.13. *Manu*

after righteousness, godliness, faith, love, *p*patience, meekness. 12 Fight the good fight of the faith, lay hold on the life eternal, whereunto thou wast called, and didst confess the good confession in the sight of many witnesses. 13 I charge thee in the sight of God, who *h*giveth life to all things, and of Christ Je'sus, who before Pon'tius Pi'late witnessed the good confession; 14 that thou keep the commandment, without spot, without reproach, until the appearing of our Lord Je'sus Christ: 15 which in *i*its own times he shall show, who is the blessed and only Potentate, the King of *k*kings, and Lord of *l*lords; 16 who only hath immortality, dwelling in light unapproachable; whom no man hath seen, nor can see: to whom *b*e honor and power eternal. A-men'.

17 Charge them that are rich in this present *m*world, that they be not highminded, nor have their hope set on the uncertainty of riches, but on God, who giveth us richly all things to enjoy; 18 that they do good, that they be rich in good works, that they be ready to distribute, *n*willing to communicate; 19 laying up in store for themselves a good foundation against the time to come, that they may lay hold on the life which is *life* indeed.

20 O Tim'o-thy, guard *o*that which is committed unto *thee*, turning away from the profane babblings and oppositions of the knowledge which is falsely so called; 21 which some professing have *p*erred concerning the faith.

Grace be with you.

---

g Or, *stedfastness*   *h* Or, *preserveth all things alive*   *i* Or, *his*   *k* Gr. *them that reign as kings.*   *l* Gr. *them that rule as*

lords.   *m* Or, *age*   *n* Or, *ready to sympathize*   *o* Gr. *the deposit.*   *p* Gr. *missed the mark.*

---

witnesses. See Acts 16.2; 2 Tim. 2.2; also Rom. 10.9, 10.
14. *The commandment.* The end to be achieved is 'love out of a pure heart and a good conscience and faith unfeigned' (ch. 1.5).
15. *King of kings.* See note ch. 1.17.
16. *Who only.* God alone has immortality as the essence of His being. Those who inherit eternal life do so through faith in His only-begotten Son (Jn. 3.16), through whom we become 'heirs of God and joint-heirs with Christ' (Rom. 8.17).

No man hath seen. See Jn. 1.18; Col. 1.15; 1 Jn. 4.12.
17. *In this present world.* In the things of this life in the flesh.
19. *A good foundation.* 'Treasures in heaven' (Mt. 6.20). See Mt. 19.21; Lk. 12.33.
20. *The knowledge.* From the beginning the church has been the prey of those who distort the simple truth as given by Jesus into systems formed of their own vain imaginings. See Rom. 1.21; Eph. 4.17; Col. 2.18, 23.

SECOND TIMOTHY

INTRODUCTION BY THE REV. TALBOT W. CHAMBERS, D.D.

This epistle was written from Rome during Paul's second imprisonment, probably about 67 A.D., and is the last of his extant writings. After the address and a fervent thanksgiving for Timothy's early training (ch. 1.1-5), he exhorts him to boldness and fidelity (ver. 6-14), adducing two examples—one of desertion, the other of faithfulness (ver. 15-18); summons him to exercise fortitude (2.1-13), to reprove "profane babblings" (ver. 14-21), and to guard well his own conduct (ver. 22-26); predicts a serious outbreak of immorality covered with a show of piety (3.1-9), against which he is to be encouraged by Paul's example (ver. 10-13), and the diligent use of the Holy Scriptures (ver. 14-17); exhorts him to continuous activity (4.1-5), appealing to his own example (ver. 6-8), gives various personal directions (ver. 9-15), and concludes with an assurance of his confidence in his Lord (ver. 17, 18).

THE SECOND EPISTLE OF PAUL TO

TIM'O-THY

1 Paul, an apostle of Christ Je'sus through the will of God, according to the promise of the life which is in Christ Je'sus, 2 to Tim'o-thy, my beloved child: Grace, mercy, peace, from God the Father and Christ Je'sus our Lord.

3 I thank God, whom I serve from my forefathers in a pure conscience, how unceasing is my remembrance of thee in my supplications, night and day 4 longing to see thee, remembering thy tears, that I may be filled with *a*joy; 5 having been reminded of the unfeigned faith that is in thee; which dwelt first in thy grandmother Lo'is, and thy mother Eu-ni'ce; and, I am persuaded, in thee also. 6 For which cause I put thee in remembrance that thou *b*stir up the gift of God, which is in thee through the laying on of my hands. 7 For God gave us not a spirit of fearfulness; but of power and love and *c*discipline. 8 Be not ashamed therefore of the testimony of our Lord, nor of me his prisoner: but suffer hardship with the *d*gospel according to the power of God; 9 who saved us, and called us with a holy calling, not according to our works, but according to his own purpose and grace,

---

a Or, *joy in being reminded* *b* Gr. *stir into flame.* *c* Gr. *sobering.* *d* Gr. *good tidings:* and so elsewhere. See marginal note on Mt. 4.23.

CHAPTER 1

1. *The life.* The spiritual life, or life eternal. See Mt. 25.46; Mk. 10.30; Jn. 3.15, 16; 6.53–57.

3. *In a pure conscience.* However far from the truth Paul had been before his conversion he had lived up to the best that he knew, under the guidance of a pure conscience. See Acts 23.1; 24.14–16; 2 Cor. 1.12.

5. *Eunice.* 'A Jewess that believed' (Acts 16.1). See ch. 3.15.

6. *Laying on of my hands.* See note 1 Tim. 4.14; also Acts 8.17–20.

7. *Fearfulness.* Perhaps referring to the authority of the Jewish law which was upheld by fear of the penalties threatened. In a wider sense it may be taken as the fear of the powers of darkness (Eph. 6.12), as opposed to the power of God. See Rom. 15.19; 1 Cor. 2.4, 5; 2 Cor. 6.7; 13.4.

8. *Testimony of our Lord.* Bearing witness to faith in Christ. *His prisoner.* Paul was suffering his second imprisonment at Rome at the time this epistle was written.

9. *Before times eternal.* The grace of Christ was really bestowed upon mankind under the old covenant, but became manifest only under the new covenant of the gospel. See Tit. 1.2, 3.

which was given us in Christ Je'sus *e*before times eternal, 10 but hath now been manifested by the appearing of our Saviour Christ Je'sus, who abolished death, and brought life and *f*immortality to light through the *g*gospel, 11 whereunto I was appointed a *h*preacher, and an apostle, and a teacher. 12 For which cause I suffer also these things: yet I am not ashamed; for I know him whom I have believed, and I am persuaded that he is able to guard *i*that which I have committed unto him against that day. 13 Hold the pattern of *k*sound words which thou hast heard from me, in faith and love which is in Christ Je'sus. 14 *l*That good thing which was committed unto *thee* guard through the Holy Spirit which dwelleth in us.

15 This thou knowest, that all that are in A'si-a turned away from me; of whom are Phy-ge'lus and Her-mog'e-nes. 16 The

Lord grant mercy unto the house of On-e-siph'o-rus: for he oft refreshed me, and was not ashamed of my chain; 17 but, when he was in Rome, he sought me diligently, and found me 18 (the Lord grant unto him to find mercy of the Lord in that day); and in how many things he ministered at Eph'e-sus, thou knowest very well.

2 Thou therefore, my child, be strengthened in the grace that is in Christ Je'sus. 2 And the things which thou hast heard from me among many witnesses, the same commit thou to faithful men, who shall be able to teach others also. 3 *a*Suffer hardship with *me,* as a good soldier of Christ Je'sus. 4 No soldier on service entangleth himself in the affairs of *this* life; that he may please him who enrolled him as a soldier. 5 And if also a man contend in the games, he is not crowned, except he have contended lawfully. 6 The

---

e Or, *long ages ago*   *f* Gr. *incorruption.* See Rom. 2.7.   *g* Gr. *good tidings:* and so elsewhere. See marginal note on Mt. 4.23.   *h* Gr. *herald.*   *i* Or, *that which he*

hath committed unto me   Gr. *my deposit.* *k* Gr. *healthful.*   *l* Gr. *The good deposit.* *a* Or, *Take thy part in suffering hardship as &c.*

---

10. *Abolished death.* By his resurrection in the body Christ had proved death conquerable. See 1 Cor. 15.20, 23, 26; Heb. 2.14.

12. *That which I have committed.* The great desire of the Jews was for eternal life (Mk. 10.17; Lk. 10.25; Acts 20.32). This was Paul's supreme hope (Phil. 3.11), and in the faith that Christ was the way (Jn. 14.6), he committed his life here and hereafter wholly and unreservedly to his service. *That day.* The day of Christ's coming. See 1 Th. 1.10.

13. *The pattern.* The oft-repeated injunction of Paul to cling to the original teachings of the gospel, indicates the great variance which seemed to be continually leading

would-be followers into fatal error. See 2 Pet. 2.18; 3.16, 17.

15. *Asia.* See note on Acts 19.10.

16. *The house of Onesiphorus.* As only his house is mentioned it must be concluded that Onesiphorus himself had passed away. See ch. 4.19.

18. *Thou knowest.* Timothy had spent more time than Paul had at Ephesus.

CHAPTER 2

4. *Who enrolled him.* The soldier's allegiance is to his commander and his cause. Paul urges an undivided allegiance upon Timothy.

5. *Lawfully.* According to the rules of the game. Hardships are a part of the soldier's service.

husbandman that laboreth must be the first to partake of the fruits. 7 Consider what I say; for the Lord shall give thee understanding in all things. 8 Remember Je′sus Christ, risen from the dead, of the seed of David, according to my *b*gospel: 9 wherein I suffer hardship unto bonds, as a malefactor; but the word of God is not bound. 10 Therefore I endure all things for the elect′s sake, that they also may obtain the salvation which is in Christ Je′sus with eternal glory. 11 Faithful is the *c*saying: For if we died with him, we shall also live with him: 12 if we endure, we shall also reign with him: if we shall deny him, he also will deny us: 13 if we are faithless, he abideth faithful; for he cannot deny himself.

14 Of these things put them in remembrance, charging *them* in the sight of *d*the Lord, that they strive not about words, to no profit, to the subverting of them that hear. 15 Give diligence to present thyself approved unto God, a workman that needeth not to be ashamed, *e*handling aright the word of truth. 16 But shun profane babblings: for they will proceed further in ungodliness, 17 and their word will *f*eat as doth a gangrene: of whom is Hy-me-næ′us and Phi-le′tus; 18 men who concerning the truth have *g*erred, saying that *h*the resurrection is past already, and overthrow the faith of some. 19 Howbeit the firm foundation of God standeth, having this seal, *i*The Lord knoweth them that are his: and, *k*Let every one that nameth the name of the Lord depart from unrighteousness. 20 Now in a great house there are not only vessels of gold and of silver, but also of wood and of earth; and some unto honor, and some unto dishonor.

---

b See marginal note on ch. 1.8.   *c* Or, *saying; for if &c.*   *d* Many ancient authorities read *God.*   *e* Or, *holding a straight course in the word of truth*   Or, *rightly*
dividing the word of truth   *f* Or, *spread*   *g* Gr. *missed the mark.* 1 Tim. 1.6.   *h* Some ancient authorities read *a resurrection.*   *i* Num. xvi. 5?   *k* Is. xxvi. 13?

---

8 *Of the seed of David.* That is, Christ, a man in the flesh, and risen from the dead in the flesh.

9. *As a malefactor.* Subject to the indignity of being chained to a soldier. *The word of God is not bound.* . Even in his imprisonment Paul preached the truth to the soldiers of the guard (Phil. 1.13; 4.22), and by his letters reached a larger congregation than he could have done with his preaching.

11. *Died with him.* As to the desires of the flesh. See Rom. 6.5, 6.

12. *Reign with him.* See Rom. 5.17; 8.17.

13. *He abideth faithful.* He cannot deny his own nature; he must deny everything unlike himself. If we do not accept him we place ourselves under condemnation.

14. *About words.* The warning here is against giving such attention to the words in which the gospel is presented that its vital truth is entirely lost. The letter killeth, but the spirit giveth life (2 Cor. 3.6). See 1 Tim. 6.4; Tit. 3.9.

19. *The firm foundation.* The unchanging truth of God, 'with whom can be no variation, neither shadow that is cast by turning' (Jas. 1.17). In this connection Paul was probably speaking of the resurrection of Jesus as the foundation upon which Christianity was built. See 1 Cor. 15.14.

20. *A great house.* The parallel is drawn with the church. Not all receive the gifts of grace in equal measure. See Rom. 12.4–8.

21 If a man therefore purge himself from these, he shall be a vessel unto honor, sanctified, meet for the master's use, prepared unto every good work. 22 But flee youthful lusts, and follow after righteousness, faith, love, peace, with them that call on the Lord out of a pure heart. 23 But foolish and ignorant questionings refuse, knowing that they gender strifes. 24 And the Lord's *l*servant must not strive, but be gentle towards all, apt to teach, forbearing, 25 in meekness *m*correcting them that oppose themselves; if peradventure God may give them repentance unto the knowledge of the truth, 26 and they may *n*recover themselves out of the snare of the devil, having been *o*taken captive *p*by him unto his will.

3 But know this, that in the last days grievous times shall come. 2 For men shall be lovers of self, lovers of money, boastful, haughty, railers, disobedient to parents, unthankful, unholy, 3 without natural affection, implacable, slanderers, without self-control, fierce, no lovers of good, 4 traitors, headstrong, puffed up, lovers of pleasure rather than lovers of God; 5 holding a form of godliness, but having denied the power thereof: from these also turn away. 6 For of these are they that creep into houses, and take captive silly women laden with sins, led away by divers lusts, 7 ever learning, and never able to come to the knowledge of the truth. 8 And even as Jan'nes and Jam'bres withstood Mo'ses, so do these also withstand the truth; men corrupted in mind, reprobate concerning the faith. 9 But they shall proceed no further: for their folly shall be evident unto all men, as theirs also came to be. 10 But thou didst follow

---

l Gr. *bondservant.*   *m* Or, *instructing* *n* Gr. *return to soberness. o* Gr. *taken alive.* *p* Or, *by him, unto the will of God* Comp.

21. *From these.* Probably the false teachings spoken of in ver. 16. See 2 Pet. 2.1, 2.

23. *Ignorant questionings.* Questions which arise in a mind lacking in understanding.

25. *Give them repentance.* The consequences to those who oppose teaching, and who wilfully 'refuse to have God in their knowledge,' are described in Rom. 1.21–32. Repentance to such as these comes as the mercy of God. See 1 Tim. 1.13, 16.

26. *The snare of the devil.* In this connection the snare operated through the distorting of doctrine in men's minds, leading them through a maze of reasonings having the form of godliness but not the reality (ch. 3.5). See Eph. 4.14; 6.11; also Rom. 1.21, 25; 1 Cor. 3.19; 2 Cor. 10.5.

---

2 Cor. 10.5. Gr. *by him, unto the will of him.* In the Greek the two pronouns are different.

CHAPTER 3

1. *The last days.* The apostles seem to have expected the immediate return of Christ in glory—the second coming—in their own generation. They did not foresee the long and painful spread of the leaven of Christianity, although Jesus had warned them that only the Father had this knowledge. See Mt. 24.36; 2 Pet. 3.3.

6. *Take captive.* See note on ch. 2.26. *Silly women.* See 1 Tim. 5.6, 13.

8. *Jannes and Jambres.* The names handed down by the Jewish traditions as those of the Egyptian sorcerers who wrought wonders in opposition to Moses and Aaron. See Ex. 7.11, 12, 22; 8.7.

my teaching, conduct, purpose, faith, longsuffering, love, *a*patience; 11 persecutions, sufferings; what things befell me at An'ti-och, at I-co'ni-um, at Lys'tra; what persecutions I endured: and out of them all the Lord delivered me. 12 Yea, and all that would live godly in Christ Je'sus shall suffer persecution. 13 But evil men and impostors shall wax worse and worse, deceiving and being deceived. 14 But abide thou in the things which thou hast learned and hast *b*been assured of, knowing of *b*whom thou hast learned them; 15 and that from a babe thou hast known the sacred writings which are able to make thee wise unto salvation through faith which is in Christ Je'sus. 16 *c*Every scripture inspired of God *is* also profitable for teaching, for reproof, for correction, for *d*instruction which is in righteousness: 17 that the man of God may be complete, furnished completely unto every good work.

4 *a*I charge *thee* in the sight of God, and of Christ Je'sus,

who shall judge the living and the dead, and by his appearing and his kingdom: 2 preach the word; be urgent in season, out of season; *b*reprove, rebuke, exhort, with all longsuffering and teaching. 3 For the time will come when they will not endure the *c*sound *d*doctrine; but, having itching ears, will heap to themselves teachers after their own lusts; 4 and will turn away their ears from the truth, and turn aside unto fables. 5 But be thou sober in all things, suffer hardship, do the work of an evangelist, fulfil thy ministry. 6 For I am already being *e*offered, and the time of my departure is come. 7 I have fought the good fight, I have finished the course, I have kept the faith: 8 henceforth there is laid up for me the crown of righteousness, which the Lord, the righteous judge, shall give to me at that day; and not to me only, but also to all them that have loved his appearing.

9 Give diligence to come shortly unto me: 10 for De'mas forsook me, having loved this present *f*world, and went to

---

a Or, *stedfastness*　　*b* Gr. *what persons.*
c Or, *Every scripture* is *inspired of God, and profitable*　　*d* Or, *discipline*　　*a* Or, *I testify, in the sight . . . dead, both of his*

appearing &c.　　*b* Or, *bring to the proof*
c Gr. *healthful.*　　*d* Or, *teaching*　　*e* Gr. *poured out as a drink-offering.*　　*f* Or, *age*

---

11. *Antioch.* Antioch of Pisidia. *Iconium* (Acts 14.5). *Lystra* (Acts 14.19). *Persecutions* (2 Cor. 11. 23–27).

13. *Being deceived.* A false teacher who is himself a victim of his own delusions is the most dangerous of all, having the power added by sincerity. See Rom. 1.21; 2 Cor. 11.13; Gal. 1.7; 2 Th. 2.10; Tit. 1.10; 2 Pet. 2.1, 19; Rev. 2.2.

15. *From a babe.* See ch. 1.5.

16. *Every scripture.* The writings of the Old Testament. See Rom. 15.4; 2 Pet. 1.21.

CHAPTER 4

3. *Itching ears.* Anxious to hear teaching in accordance with their desires. See Rom. 1.24; Jas. 1.14, 15.

6. *The time of my departure.* Tradition records the death of Paul by execution in the early summer of the year 68 A.D. This second epistle to Timothy was written but a few weeks previous. It is probable that Paul had a clear premonition of his approaching end.

8. *That day.* See last note ch. 1.12.

10. *Forsook me.* It would seem

Thes-sa-lo-ni'ca; Cres'cens to *Ga-la'ti-a, Ti'tus to Dal-ma'-ti-a. 11 Only Luke is with me. Take Mark, and bring him with thee; for he is useful to me for ministering. 12 But Tych'i-cus I sent to Eph'e-sus. 13 The cloak that I left at Tro'as with Car'pus, bring when thou comest, and the books, especially the parchments. 14 Al-ex-an'der the coppersmith *did me much evil: the Lord will render to him according to his works: 15 of whom do thou also beware; for he greatly withstood our words. 16 At my first defence no one took my part, but all forsook me: may it not be laid to their account. 17 But the Lord stood by me, and *strengthened me;

that through me the *message might be fully proclaimed, and that all the Gen'tiles might hear: and I was delivered out of the mouth of the lion. 18 The Lord will deliver me from every evil work, and will save me unto his heavenly kingdom: to whom *be the glory *for ever and ever. A-men'.

19 Salute Pris'ca and Aq'ui-la, and the house of On-e-siph'o-rus. 20 E-ras'tus remained at Cor'inth: but Troph'i-mus I left at Mi-le'tus sick. 21 Give diligence to come before winter. Eu-bu'lus saluteth thee, and Pu'dens, and Li'nus, and Clau'di-a, and all the brethren.

22 The Lord be with thy spirit. Grace be with you.

---

g Or, *Gaul*   *h* Gr. *showed.*   *i* Or, *gave me power*

k Or, *proclamation*   *l* Gr. *unto the ages of the ages.*

---

that as the execution of Paul became certain, there was a scattering of some of his associates at Rome, lest they might suffer a like fate. Demas and Luke had been with Paul when he wrote the letter to the Colossians about six years previous. This was during Paul's first imprisonment. See Col. 4.14; Philemon 24. *Loved this present world.* Did not desire to suffer martyrdom. *Dalmatia.* A district of Roman Illyricum lying north of Macedonia. It was a wild and barbarous country.

14. *Did me much evil.* This apparently refers to Paul's 'first defence' (ver. 16), where Alexander

may have appeared as the accuser. It is supposed by some commentators that this Alexander is the person mentioned in 1 Tim. 1.20.

16. *No one took my part.* It was a custom in both the Roman and Greek courts to allow the friends of the accused to intercede with pleas and prayers for mercy.

17. *The mouth of the lion.* This expression may refer to the practice of throwing Christians to the wild beasts in the arena, a common penalty under Nero's rule.

19. *Prisca.* See Acts 18.2. *Onesiphorus.* See note on ch. 1.16.
20. *Erastus.* See Rom. 16.23. *Trophimus.* See Acts 20.4; 21.29.

THE EPISTLE TO TITUS

BY THE REV. TALBOT W. CHAMBERS, D.D.

Of Titus nothing is known with certainty, save that he was a Gentile, and Paul's "true son after a common faith." He is not mentioned in 1 Cor., but he is mentioned nine times in 2 Cor., and always with strong regard. This has been explained on the supposition that Titus was the bearer of the second letter to Corinth. His name does not occur in the Acts, but there is no reason to doubt that he is the Titus mentioned in Gal. 2. Paul refused to allow Titus to be circumcised, preferring to use him as a Gentile apostle to the Gentiles. When taunted by the Judaizers with inconsistency because he had circumcised Timothy, Paul replied by taking Titus with him to Galatia; and he found him a zealous helper. From Ephesus, Paul sent him to Corinth to get the contributions of the church there forwarded to the poor saints in Jerusalem. He afterward rejoined Paul in Macedonia, and cheered him with the tidings he brought from Corinth. The epistle tells us that he was left by Paul in Crete to organize the church there. That was probably on Paul's return to Asia from Rome after his first imprisonment. While in Crete he received the Epistle to Titus, written when Paul was at Nicopolis (in Epirus). The last mention of Titus is 2 Tim. 4.10, from which we learn that he had been in Rome with Paul during the second imprisonment of the latter, and that he had been sent into Dalmatia, doubtless on some important mission. There is no record either of the time or of the place of the death of Titus.

Contents.—The apostle tells Titus what sort of a man an elder required to be (1.5-9), and why such men were needed (ver. 10-16); prescribes the virtues of domestic life—namely, what belongs to aged men (2.1, 2), to aged women (ver. 3-5), to young men (ver. 6-8), to slaves (ver. 9, 10), and states as the reason that this is the design of the gospel (ver. 11-15); and adds the virtues of social life—namely, submission to civil rulers, readiness to co-operate in the general welfare, and gentle behavior toward all men (3.1-3), the reason for which is that believers were once like the heathen, but had been changed, not by themselves, but by divine grace (ver. 4-7). Then follows a charge about dealing with errors and errorists (ver. 8-12), after which come some personal directions (ver. 12-15).

THE EPISTLE OF PAUL TO

TI′TUS

Salutation. Qualifications of an Elder

1 Paul, a ᵃservant of God, and an apostle of Je′sus Christ, according to the faith of God's elect, and the knowledge of the truth which is according to godliness, 2 in hope of eternal life, which God, who cannot lie, promised ᵇbefore times eternal; 3 but in ᶜhis own seasons manifested his word in the ᵈmessage, wherewith I was intrusted according to the commandment of God our Saviour; 4 to Ti′tus, my true child after a common faith: Grace and peace from God the Father and Christ Je′sus our Saviour.

5 For this cause left I thee in Crete, that thou shouldest set in order the things that were wanting, and appoint elders in every city, as I gave thee charge; 6 if any man is blameless, the husband of one wife, having children that believe, who are not accused of riot or unruly. 7 For the ᵉbishop must be blameless, as God's steward; not self-willed, not soon angry, ᶠno brawler, no striker, not greedy of filthy lucre; 8 but given to hospitality, a lover of good, sober-minded, just, holy, self-controlled; 9 holding to the faithful word which is according to the teaching, that he may be able both to exhort in the ᵍsound ʰdoctrine, and to convict the gainsayers.

10 For there are many unruly men, vain talkers and deceivers,

---

a Gr. bondservant.   b Or. long ages ago
c Or. its   d Or. proclamation

e Or. overseer   f Or. not quarrelsome over wine   g Or. healthful.   h Or. teaching

---

CHAPTER 1

1. *God's elect.* Those whom God sealed with the earnest of the indwelling Spirit (2 Cor. 1.22). See Col. 3.12–15.

4. *My true child.* Titus was a Greek (Gal. 2.3) who had been converted by the teaching of Paul; as also Timothy. Titus is mentioned frequently in 2 Corinthians with expressions of approbation and regard.

5. *Crete.* An island in the Mediterranean Sea southeast of Greece. Paul's experience there is recorded in Acts 27.7, 8. The visit at the time he left Titus there is not recorded.

6. *Of one wife.* Of not more than one wife. See note 1 Tim. 3.2. *Or unruly.* The behavior of a man's children would be a good indication of his capacity to occupy a larger position of rule in the church. See 1 Tim. 3.12.

8. *Hospitality.* Perhaps more readily by hospitality than in any other way, the 'unfeigned love of the brethren' (1 Pet. 1.22) was manifested. See Gal. 6.10; 1 Jn. 3.14; 3 Jn. 5, 6.

10. *They of the circumcision.* That

specially they of the circumcision, 11 whose mouths must be stopped; men who overthrow whole houses, teaching things which they ought not, for filthy lucre's sake. 12 One of themselves, a prophet of their own, said,

Cre'tans are always liars,
 evil beasts, idle ⁱgluttons.

13 This testimony is true. For which cause reprove them sharply, that they may be ᵏsound in the faith, 14 not giving heed to Jewish fables, and commandments of men who turn away from the truth. 15 To the pure all things are pure: but to them that are defiled and unbelieving nothing is pure; but both their mind and their conscience are defiled. 16 They profess that they know God; but by their works they deny him, being abominable, and disobedient, and unto every good work reprobate.

2 But speak thou the things which befit the ᵃsound ᵇdoctrine: 2 that aged men be temperate, grave, sober-minded, ᵏsound in faith, in love, in ᶜpatience: 3 that aged women likewise be reverent in demeanor, not slanderers nor enslaved to much wine, teachers of that which is good; 4 that they may train the young women to love their husbands, to love their children, 5 to be sober-minded, chaste, workers at home, kind, being in subjection to their own husbands, that the word of God be not blasphemed: 6 the younger men likewise exhort to be sober-minded: 7 in all things showing thyself an ensample of good works; in thy doctrine showing uncorruptness, gravity, 8 sound speech, that cannot be condemned; that he that is of the contrary part may be ashamed, having no evil thing

---

ⁱ Gr. bellies.   ᵏ Gr. healthy.

ᵃ Gr. healthful.   ᵇ Or. teaching   ᶜ Or. stedfastness

---

faction which taught that the Gentiles must come under the Jewish law before they could receive the benefits of the gospel of Christ. See Acts 10.45; 11.2.

12. One of themselves. Epimenides, a poet, who was regarded as an oracle. He lived about 600 B.C.

15. All things are pure. The Jews 'of the circumcision' (note on ver. 10) taught the Jewish rules against eating animals which were unclean under the law. See Lev. 11.1–43. Paul goes beyond these ceremonial observances and declares that to those already defiled in mind, nothing is pure. See Rom. 14.14, 20, 23.

16. They profess. The meaning is not that of hypocritical pretense. These teachers insisted that they knew God; but their contentions were proved false by their works. See Mt. 15.8; 1 Jn. 2.4.

CHAPTER 2

1. The sound doctrine. The very simplicity of faith in Christ seems to have been a stumbling block to the Jews, accustomed as they were to an elaborate ritual. Perhaps it was for this reason that so many 'teachers' flourished, each trying to establish a system of Christianity embodying his own imaginations. See Rom. 1.21; 2 Tim. 3.13; 2 Pet. 2.1.

5. Blasphemed. See note 1 Tim. 6.1.

8. To say of us. Paul's exhortation to give due regard to the opinions of the non-Christian people, was to preserve the name of Christ free from any reproach. In this, Peter was in accord with Paul. See 1 Pet. 2.12; also Acts 28.22.

536

to say of us. 9 *Exhort* ^dservants to be in subjection to their own masters, *and* to be well-pleasing *to them* in all things; not gainsaying; 10 not purloining, but showing all good fidelity; that they may adorn the doctrine of God our Saviour in all things. 11 For the grace of God ^ehath appeared, bringing salvation to all men, 12 instructing us, to the intent that, denying ungodliness and worldly lusts, we should live soberly and righteously and godly in this present ^fworld; 13 looking for the blessed hope and appearing of the glory ^gof the great God and our Saviour Je′sus Christ; 14 who gave himself for us, that he might redeem us from all iniquity, and purify unto himself a people for his own possession, zealous of good works.

15 These things speak and exhort and reprove with all ^hauthority. Let no man despise thee.

3 Put them in mind to be in subjection to rulers, to authorities, to be obedient, to be ready unto every good work, 2 to speak evil of no man, not to be contentious, to be gentle, showing all meekness toward all men. 3 For we also once were foolish, disobedient, deceived, serving divers lusts and pleasures, living in malice and envy, hateful, hating one another. 4 But when the kindness of God our Saviour, and his love toward man, appeared, 5 not by works *done* in righteousness, which we did ourselves, but according to his mercy he saved us, through the ^awashing of regeneration ^band renewing of the Holy Spirit, 6 which he poured out upon us richly, through Je′sus Christ our Saviour; 7 that, being justified by his grace, we might be made ^cheirs according to the hope of eternal life. 8 Faithful is the saying, and concerning these things I desire that thou affirm confidently, to the end that they who have believed God may be careful to ^dmaintain good works. These things are good and prof-

d Gr. *bondservants.* e Or, *hath appeared to all men, bringing salvation* f Or, *age* g Or, *of our great God and Saviour* h Gr. *commandment.* a Or, *laver* b Or, *and through renewing* c Or, *heirs, according to hope, of eternal life* d Or, *profess honest occupations*

9. *Not gainsaying.* The Christian attitude is that of lowliness of mind and loving service. The apprehension of the truth as it is in Christ did not give the bondservant dominion over his master in the flesh, but inspired him to a more consecrated service, 'as unto the Lord' (Eph. 6.7). See Mt. 11.29; Eph. 4.2.
11. *To all men.* This declaration has been accepted as a contradiction of the factional doctrine that only the enlightened would receive salvation. See 1 Tim. 2.4.
14. *Purify unto himself.* The language of this verse relates to the Jewish ceremonial of sacrifice. See

Ex. 19.5; Deut. 14.2; 1 Pet. 2.5. The idea is expanded in Heb. 9.11–14. See also Heb. 9.23; 10.9, 10, 14.

CHAPTER 3

1. *In subjection to rulers.* Through a misapprehension as to the kind of freedom conferred by the gospel, some of the Jews became unruly and disposed to rebellion against the Roman authorities.
5. *Washing of regeneration.* A reference to the symbolism of baptism, which is a setting apart unto regeneration, a step preparatory to the 'renewing of the Holy Spirit.' See Jn. 3.5; Acts 22.16; 1 Cor. 6.11; Eph. 5.26.

itable unto men: 9 but shun foolish questionings, and genealogies, and strifes, and fightings about the law; for they are unprofitable and vain. 10 A factious man after a first and second admonition *refuse; 11 knowing that such a one is perverted, and sinneth, being self-condemned.

12 When I shall send Ar'temas unto thee, or Tych'i-cus, give diligence to come unto me to Ni-cop'o-lis: for there I have determined to winter. 13 Set forward Ze'nas the lawyer and A-pol'los on their journey diligently, that nothing be wanting unto them. 14 And let our *people* also learn to ƒmaintain good works for necessary ᵍuses, that they be not unfruitful.

15 All that are with me salute thee. Salute them that love us in faith.

Grace be with you all.

---

e Or, *avoid* | *f* Or, *profess honest occupations*   *g* Or, *wants*

9. *The law.* The Jewish ceremonial law. The Jew had been trained for centuries to the observance of this law and clung to its ceremonies. Much fruitless argument arose in the effort to preserve the law intact and graft Christianity upon it.

11. *Perverted.* The persistence in error after two admonishings showed that it sprang from inward moral darkness. The man was 'self-condemned' by his love for discord; for the true spirit of the church was unity. See 1 Cor. 12.20; also Rom. 2.8; 2 Cor. 12.20; Gal. 5.20.

12. *Nicopolis.* The city of that name in Epirus, founded by Augustus in memory of the victory of Actium.

13. *Apollos.* See Acts 18.24–28. It is supposed that Zenas and Apollos were the bearers of this epistle to Titus.

THE EPISTLE TO PHILEMON

INTRODUCTION BY PROFESSOR MARCUS DODS, D.D.

It is interesting to find this short note, on a merely domestic matter, preserved among the epistles of Paul. It was written to intercede for a runaway slave with his master, and it illustrates the multifarious services the apostle was invited to render. "It is only one sample of numberless letters which must have been written to his many friends and disciples by one of Paul's eager temperament and warm affections in the course of a long and chequered life." Philemon was resident in Colossæ (Col. 4.9). He had been brought to the faith by Paul (Philem. 19); and as it seems that as yet Paul had not visited Colossæ, it is probable that Philemon had heard him in Ephesus. He was a thorough-going Christian (4-7), loving and helpful, and the disciples in Colossæ, or a section of them, met in his house (2). Apphia was probably his wife, and Archippus his son.

Philemon's slave Onesimus (or "Profitable," a common name for a slave) had run away, not empty-handed (18); and, having found his way to Rome, and being somehow brought into contact with Paul, he was by him persuaded to abandon his old mind and his old ways (10). Paul had devoted and active friends around him in Rome; but this energetic slave, trained to watch a master's wants and to execute promptly what was intrusted to him, became almost indispensable to the apostle (11, 13). "'Profitable,' who was aforetime unprofitable to thee and to me." Paul would gladly have retained his services, but he acknowledges the claim of his master, and, besides, would not deprive Philemon of the pleasure of voluntarily sending him to minister to him (14).

The note, short as it is, is valuable in two respects:—

1. It gives us a clear view of the uprightness and courteousness of Paul. Nothing could be more winning and persuasive, nothing more sympathetic and considerate, than the terms he uses in restoring the runaway to his master's good graces.

2. But the letter shows us Christianity at work in connection with slavery. No institution was more deeply rooted in the ancient world, and none more alien to the spirit of Christ. Yet Paul does not set himself to uproot it. Rather he might seem to give it his countenance by thus restoring a runaway to his master. But Christianity (and Paul as its representative), by admitting slaves to the brotherhood of the church, and by appealing to the brotherly feeling of the masters, introduced principles which would not be stayed in their operation till slavery was seen to be unchristian, and abolished. The Christian spirit does not work the less surely because it works indirectly.

THE EPISTLE OF PAUL TO

PHI-LE'MON

1 Paul, a prisoner of Christ Je'sus, and Tim'o-thy *a*our brother, to Phi-le'mon our beloved and fellow-worker, 2 and to Ap'phi-a *b*our sister, and to Ar-chip'pus our fellow-soldier, and to the church in thy house: 3 Grace to you and peace from God our Father and the Lord Je'sus Christ.

4 I thank my God always, making mention of thee in my prayers, 5 hearing of *c*thy love, and of the faith which thou hast toward the Lord Je'sus, and toward all the saints; 6 that the fellowship of thy faith may become effectual, in the knowledge of every good thing which is in *d*you, unto Christ. 7 For I had much joy and comfort in thy love, because the hearts of the saints have been refreshed through thee, brother.

8 Wherefore, though I have all boldness in Christ to enjoin thee that which is befitting, 9 yet for love's sake I rather beseech, being such a one as Paul *e*the aged, and now a prisoner also of Christ Je'sus: 10 I beseech thee for my child, whom I have begotten in my bonds, *f*O-nes'i-mus, 11 who once was unprofitable to thee, but now is profitable to thee and to me: 12 whom I have sent back to thee in his own person, that is, my very heart: 13 whom I would fain have kept with me, that in thy behalf he might minister unto me in the bonds of the *g*gospel: 14 but without thy mind I would

---

a Gr. *the brother.* *b* Gr. *the sister.* *c* Or, *thy love and faith* *d* Many ancient authorities read *us.* *e* Or, *an ambassador, and* *now &c.* *f* The Greek word means *Helpful.* Comp. ver. 20 marg. *g* Gr. *good tidings.* See marginal note on Mt. 4.23.

1. *A prisoner.* This epistle was written at Rome during Paul's first imprisonment, nearly four years after his arrest at Jerusalem (Acts 21.33), during all of which time he had been in bonds, but permitted to preach. See Acts 28.31. *Philemon.* A member of the Christian church at Colossæ. *Apphia.* Believed to have been the wife of Philemon. *Archippus.* Probably an evangelist, and Philemon's son.

8. *To enjoin thee.* Under his apostolic authority Paul might have advised Philemon; but 'for love's sake,' he offers his request as a suppliant (ver. 9).

10. *Onesimus.* A fugitive Asiatic slave, owned by Philemon. From verse 18, it has been thought that he robbed his master before running away. He was converted at Rome under the preaching of Paul, who seems to have so highly esteemed his character and capacity, that he wished to keep him at Rome in gospel work (ver. 13).

do nothing; that thy goodness should not be as of necessity, but of free will. 15 For perhaps he was therefore parted *from thee* for a season, that thou shouldest have him for ever; 16 no longer as a [h]servant, but more than a [h]servant, a brother beloved, specially to me, but how much rather to thee, both in the flesh and in the Lord. 17 If then thou countest me a partner, receive him as myself. 18 But if he hath wronged thee at all, or oweth *thee* aught, put that to mine account; 19 I Paul write it with mine own hand, I will repay it: that I say not unto thee that thou owest to me even thine own self besides. 20 Yea, brother, let me have [i]joy of thee in the Lord: refresh my heart in Christ.

21 Having confidence in thine obedience I write unto thee, knowing that thou wilt do even beyond what I say. 22 But withal prepare me also a lodging: for I hope that through your prayers I shall be granted unto you.

23 Ep'a-phras, my fellow-prisoner in Christ Je'sus, saluteth thee; 24 *and so do* Mark, Ar-is-tar'chus, De'mas, Luke, my fellow-workers.

25 The grace of [k]our Lord Je'sus Christ be with your spirit. [l]A-men'.

---

[h] Gr. *bondservant*. [i] Or, *help* Comp. ver. 10 marg. [k] Some ancient authorities read *the*. [l] Many ancient authorities omit *Amen*.

15. *For ever.* Having accepted Christianity, Onesimus would never again desert his master, but serve him 'as unto the Lord' (Eph. 6.7). See note on Tit. 2.9.

18. *Oweth thee.* Perhaps because of absence from his duties. See also note on ver. 10.

19. *Thine own self besides.* A reminder that Philemon owes his knowledge of Christ to Paul, a much greater boon than he now asks for Onesimus.

23. *Epaphras.* A Colossian, imprisoned with Paul. See Col. 1.7.

24. *Aristarchus.* A Thessalonian, also a prisoner with Paul. See Col. 4.10; Acts 19.29; 20.4. *Demas.* See Col. 4.14; 2 Tim. 4.10. *Luke.* See Col. 4.14; 2 Tim. 4.11.

THE EPISTLE TO THE HEBREWS

INTRODUCTION BY PRINCIPAL T. C. EDWARDS

The Readers.—The earliest superscription of the epistle is "To the Hebrews." Like all the epistles of the New Testament, it was addressed to Christians (ch. 3.1). And that these were not a section of a church composed of Jews and Gentiles, but themselves constituted a purely Hebrew church, is evident from ch. 5.12; 6.10; 10.32; 12.4; 13.7-24. The epistle contains no reference to Gentile members. But these Christian Hebrews cannot be supposed to have dwelt apart, like the synagogue of the Hebrews in Rome, or like the Jewish community in Alexandria. That would have been inconsistent with their being Christians at all. If we believe the testimony of Eusebius, the church in Jerusalem had no Gentile element within it before the second century, and it was, in the later part of the apostolic age, the only well-known church in which the division into Jews and Gentiles had no place.

The words, "They of Italy salute you" (13.24) suggest that the author was in Italy when he wrote. It is true that the words may mean that there were with the author Italian Christians who sent salutation to their Hebrew brethren, but that is less probable. We are at liberty to supply from the previous sentence the word "saints," which will make it the salutation of the whole church in Italy: "The saints of Italy salute you." Assuming the probability of the epistle having been written from Italy, it follows with at least equal probability that it was sent to the church in Jerusalem. It is true that the present generation of Christians in that church "had not resisted unto blood" (12.4). But that need not allude to the absence of martyrs in the past (10.32).

It has been argued that the church in Jerusalem was not the one to which the epistle was addressed, because that church was poor, so much so, that Paul had made a collection among the Gentile Christians to help the mother church. But the words of the historian show that the occasion was a great famine in the time of Claudius Cæsar; and we infer from Rom. 15.26 that this charity was needed only by a portion of the church. Apart from these special circumstances, the epistle tells us that the wealthy members of the Jerusalem church took the spoiling of their goods with joy.

The Date of the Epistle.—Supposing that the letter was addressed to the church in Jerusalem, it must have been written between the martyrdom of James, its bishop, and the destruction of the city in 70 A.D. We infer this from the author's entire silence with regard to both events. Some, who still maintain that Paul is the author, date it during his imprisonment in Cæsarea. But that date is too early, for James was then living (Acts 21.18).

THE EPISTLE TO THE HEBREWS

The Author.—The epistle is anonymous. Not even Timothy, who was with the writer at the time (13.23), is named by him as a joint author, in the way he is sometimes named by Paul. The readers knew who the writer was.

The churches of the East, as a whole, never doubted either the canonicity or the Pauline authorship of the epistle, whereas in the West it had to maintain a struggle for its canonicity and its apostolicity.

Summary of Contents.—The author calls his epistle a "word of exhortation" (13.22). It was, indeed, the first formal treatise on Christian doctrine; but it had a practical aim, *viz.* to encourage the Hebrew Christians not to be sluggish, but to lift up the hands that hang down and the palsied knees (12.12). They were in danger of drifting away past the anchorage (2.1), and of thinking that they were already too late to enter into God's rest. Their despondency arose from their disappointment at the failure of Jesus to return and restore the kingdom to Israel. The author argues with them in the following manner:—

1. He shows that the highest revelation of God has been given in Jesus Christ, who is greater than the prophets or the angels, because He is Son (ch. 1).

2. The Old Testament itself contains a higher conception of God's purposes in the incarnation of His Son than anything attainable through Judaism, by revealing that God exalts man and sets him over the works of His hand, in and through the man Jesus (ch. 2).

3. Judaism has a spiritual side which is not made actual except in Christianity, such as the conception of the Sabbath, which, in its rudimentary form, is older than the Mosaic law, and is consummated in the spiritual blessings of the gospel; and the conception of the priest, which is older than Aaron, and is fully realized in Jesus (ch. 3-5). To this the author returns in ch. 7, after a digression in which he exhorts the readers to diligence and faith (ch. 6).

4. The prophets of Judaism themselves foretell the vanishing away of the old form of God's covenant, and the bringing in of a better (ch. 8, 9). The new covenant is typified in the old (ch. 10). The believing Jews under the old covenant exemplified the conception of faith, which is the same from Abel to Jesus Himself, as the realization of the unseen (ch. 11, 12).

5. Ch. 13 is miscellaneous, in which the treatise assumes more the form of a letter.

THE EPISTLE TO THE

HEBREWS

God's Final Word spoken through his Son, who is superior

1 God, having of old time spoken unto the fathers in the prophets by divers portions and in divers manners, 2 hath at the end of these days spoken unto us in *a*his Son, whom he appointed heir of all things, through whom also he made the *b*worlds; 3 who being the effulgence of his glory, and *c*the very image of his substance, and upholding all things by the word of his power, when he had made purification of sins, sat down on the right hand of the Majesty on high; 4 having become by so much better than the angels, as he hath inherited a more excellent name than they. 5 For unto which of the angels said he at any time,

*d*Thou art my Son,
This day have I begotten thee?

and again,

*e*I will be to him a Father,
And he shall be to me a Son?

6 *f*And when he again *g*bringeth in the firstborn into *h*the world he saith, *i*And let all the angels of God worship him. 7 And of the angels he saith,

*k*Who maketh his angels winds,
And his ministers a flame of fire:

---

a Gr. a *Son*. *b* Gr. *ages*. Comp. 1 Tim. 1.17. *c* Or, *the impress of his substance* *d* Ps. ii. 7. *e* 2 S. vii. 14. *f* Or, *And again,* *when he bringeth in* *g* Or, *shall have brought in* *h* Gr. *the inhabited earth.* *i* Dt. xxxii. 43 Sept.; comp. Ps. xcvii. 7. *k* Ps. civ. 4.

CHAPTER 1

1. *Divers portions.* The Old Testament prophets received only partial revelations from God; to none of them was given a vision of all the truth. *Divers manners.* The truth being many-sided came in many ways, directly from God or through holy men and women of different capabilities. It was revealed in dream, vision, command, prophecy, or through the instrumentality of a legal code. It sometimes came in the form of promised blessings, and of warnings. Its human agents were taken from many different positions and occupations.

2. *End of these days.* The beginning of the Christian age, the ushering in of the true Messianic kingdom. *Worlds.* All things; the material universe.

3. *Effulgence of his glory.* A new vision of the glory of God, as sunlight proceeding from the sun. *Very image of his substance.* The exact reproduction of the divine nature. *Purification.* Washing away, cleansing. See Lev. 16.30; Heb. 9.12; 10.12; 1 Pet. 2.24.

5. *Son.* No angel is ever spoken of in either the Old or the New Testament in the sense here meant in the quotation from Ps. 2.7, which applies to the Messiah, the Son of God. On the contrary, angels are commanded to worship the Son.

8 but of the Son *he saith,*
  l m Thy throne, O God, is for
    ever and ever;
  And the sceptre of uprightness
    is the sceptre of *n*thy king-
    dom.
9 Thou hast loved righteousness,
    and hated iniquity;
  Therefore God, thy God, hath
    anointed thee
  With the oil of gladness above
    thy fellows.
10 And,
  *o*Thou, Lord, in the begin-
    ning didst lay the founda-
    tion of the earth,
  And the heavens are the
    works of thy hands:
11 They shall perish; but thou
    continuest:
  And they all shall wax old
    as doth a garment;
12 And as a mantle shalt thou
    roll them up,
  As a garment, and they shall
    be changed:
  But thou art the same,
  And thy years shall not fail.

13 But of which of the angels
  hath he said at any time,
  *p*Sit thou on my right hand,
    Till I make thine enemies the
      footstool of thy feet?
14 Are they not all ministering
  spirits, sent forth to do service
  for the sake of them that shall
  inherit salvation?

2 Therefore we ought to give
  the more earnest heed to the
  things that were heard, lest
  haply we drift away *from them.*
2 For if the word spoken through
  angels proved stedfast, and every
  transgression and disobedience
  received a just recompense of
  reward; 3 how shall we escape,
  if we neglect so great a salvation?
  which having at the first been
  spoken through the Lord, was
  confirmed unto us by them that
  heard; 4 God also bearing witness
  with them, both by signs and
  wonders, and by manifold powers, and by *a*gifts of the Holy
  Spirit, according to his own will.
5 For not unto angels did he

l Ps. xlv. 6 f. *m* Or, *Thy throne is God
for &c. n* The two oldest Greek manuscripts read *his. o* Ps. cii. 25 ff. *p* Ps.
cx. 1. *a* Gr. *distributions.*

8. *Thy throne, O God, is for ever.*
In this quotation from Ps. 45 Jesus
Christ is addressed as God, and the
eternity of his dominion is contrasted with that of angels.
  9. *Anointed.* As a king. *Thy fellows.* The angels.
  12. *Thy years shall not fail.* Thou
art eternal and everlasting.
  14. *Ministering spirits.* Servants
of God and of Christ, in behalf of
those who accept salvation.

CHAPTER 2

1. *Therefore,* etc. That is, since
it is the revelation of God in Christ,
which now concerns us instead of
the former dispensation in which
angels were employed as His ministers, let us give the more earnest

heed. *To the things that were heard.*
The gospel truths.
  2. *Spoken through angels.* The
Jews considered the word of God in
the Old Testament as having been
spoken through angels as mediators.
See Deut. 33.2; Acts 7.53. The
tradition of the rabbis was that the
law came through angels. 3. *Them
that heard.* The chosen witnesses.
See Lk. 24.48; Acts 1.8, 22.
  4. *God also bearing witness.* The
divine power was manifested
through the human agent so that
the truth of the message was attested by miracles, gifts of healing,
etc. See Mk. 16.20; Acts 2.43;
19.11; Rom. 15.18, 19.
  5. *The world to come.* The new
era, the Christian ages ushered in
by the life, death, and resurrection
of Jesus.

subject [b]the world to come, whereof we speak. 6 But one hath somewhere testified, saying,

[c]What is man, that thou art mindful of him?

Or the son of man, that thou visitest him?

7 Thou madest him [d]a little lower than the angels;

Thou crownedst him with glory and honor,

[e]And didst set him over the works of thy hands:

8 Thou didst put all things in subjection under his feet.

For in that he subjected all things unto him, he left nothing that is not subject to him. But now we see not yet all things subjected to him. 9 But we behold him who hath been made [d]a little lower than the angels, *even* Je'sus, because of the suffering of death crowned with glory and honor, that by the grace of God he should taste of death for every *man.* 10 For it became him, for whom are all things, and through whom are all things, [f]in bringing many

sons unto glory, to make the [g]author of their salvation perfect through sufferings. 11 For both he that sanctifieth and they that are sanctified are all of one: for which cause he is not ashamed to call them brethren, 12 saying,

[h]I will declare thy name unto my brethren,

In the midst of the [i]congregation will I sing thy praise.

13 And again, I will put my trust in him. And again, [k]Behold, I and the children whom God hath given me. 14 Since then the children are sharers in [l]flesh and blood, he also himself in like manner partook of the same; that through death he [m]might bring to nought him that [n]had the power of death, that is, the devil; 15 and [m]might deliver all them who through fear of death were all their lifetime subject to bondage. 16 [o]For verily not to angels doth he give help, but he giveth help to the seed of Abraham. 17 Wherefore it behooved him in

---

b Gr. *the inhabited earth.* *c* Ps. viii. 4 ff. *d* Or, *for a little while lower* *e* Many authorities omit *And didst . . . hands.* *f* Or, *having brought* *g* Or, *captain* *h* Ps. xxii. 22. *i* Or, *church* *k* Is. viii. 17 f. *l* Gr. *blood and flesh,* Eph. 6.12. *m* Or, *may* *n* Or, *hath* *o* Gr. *For verily not of angels doth he take hold, but he taketh hold of &c.* Comp. Is. 41.9; Ecclus. 4.11; ch. 8.9 (in the Gr.).

---

7. *A little lower.* Man, living in a world of trial and temptation, is for a little while lower than the angels.

9. *A little lower than the angels, even Jesus.* Implying the fact of the incarnation of Christ. *Taste of death.* Through the bitterness of death Jesus became complete in his sympathy with suffering humanity.

10. *It became him,* etc. It was in harmony with the purpose of God that Christ should become the perfect Saviour of mankind through suffering.

11. *All of one.* God. Jesus, by nature the Son of God, and Chris-

tians, made holy through Christ, have one spiritual Father.

14. *Had the power of death.* Satan has the permitted, subordinate power of death in so far as he tempts men to sin, which ends in death. (Rom. 5.12; 6.23; 1 Cor. 15.56.)

16. *Help to the seed of Abraham.* But not because help was to be denied to the Gentiles. 'Help' means here that the Jews were favored by the fact that Jesus was born of their race.

17. *Merciful and faithful high priest.* When he offered himself as a voluntary sacrifice upon the cross.

all things to be made like unto his brethren, that he might become a merciful and faithful high priest in things pertaining to God, to make propitiation for the sins of the people. 18 *p*For *q*in that he himself hath suffered being tempted, he is able to succor them that are tempted.

3 Wherefore, holy brethren, partakers of a heavenly calling, consider the Apostle and High Priest of our confession, *even* Je′sus; 2 who was faithful to him that *a*appointed him, as also was Mo′ses in all *b*his house. 3 For he hath been counted worthy of more glory than Mo′ses, by so much as he that *c*built the house hath more honor than the house. 4 For every house is *c*builded by some one;

but he that *c*built all things is God. 5 And Mo′ses indeed was faithful in all *b*his house as a servant, for a testimony of those things which were afterward to be spoken; 6 but Christ as a son, over *b*his house; whose house are we, if we hold fast our boldness and the glorying of our hope firm unto the end. 7 Wherefore, even as the Holy Spirit saith,

*d*To-day if ye shall hear his voice,
8 Harden not your hearts, as in the provocation,
Like as in the day of the trial in the wilderness,
9 *e*Where your fathers tried *me* by proving *me*,
And saw my works forty years.

p Or, *For having been himself tempted in that wherein he hath suffered*   *q* Or, *wherein a Gr. made.* *b* That is, *God's house.* See

Num. 12.7. *c* Or, *established* *d* Ps. xcv. 7 ff. *e* Or, *Wherewith*

See ch. 9.24, 25 and notes thereon; also the high-priestly prayer of Jesus (Jn. 17.1–26).

CHAPTER 3

1. *Wherefore.* That is, in view of what has been already said. *Holy brethren.* See note ch. 2.11. *Heavenly calling.* To the higher life of the spirit. (Phil. 3.14; 1 Thess. 4.7.) *Apostle and High Priest.* Jesus Christ was both the Apostle, or one sent, from God to man, and the High Priest, or representative, in behalf of man before God.

2. *His house.* God's house, which in the broadest sense may be taken to mean the Church of God, the community of saints through faith in Christ. 'God's house' conveyed a familiar and suggestive meaning to the Jews, who inherited the patriarchal tradition according to which every Hebrew was named according to his father's house; for example, son of Levi. The revelation which was given through Moses to Israel as a discipline and

preparation was known as the old covenant; that which came through Christ is the new covenant. Israel entered God's house through the revelation to Moses; we must enter through Christ (Jn. 10.9).

5. *Servant.* Not to be taken in the sense of slave. It means one who willingly renders service. *Testimony.* To be a witness to the revelation made by God through the law; also as one who typified and foreshadowed the fuller revelation that was to come.

6. *Christ as a son.* Showing Christ's supremacy; the contrast is between the authority of a son, set over a house, and the dependence of a servant. *Glorying of our hope.* The Jewish converts to whom this epistle was written were in the deepest despondency and needed encouragement. The 'hope' was that Christ would soon come again.

7. *The Holy Spirit saith.* See Mk. 12.36; Acts 1.16; 2 Pet. 1.21.

8. *Provocation.* As at Meribah (Ex. 17.1–7). *Trial.* As at Massah (Num. 20.1–13).

10 Wherefore I was displeased
with this generation,
And said, They do always err
in their heart:
But they did not know my
ways;
11 [f]As I sware in my wrath,
[g]They shall not enter into
my rest.
12 Take heed, brethren, lest
haply there shall be in any one
of you an evil heart of unbelief,
in falling away from the living
God: 13 but exhort one another
day by day, so long as it is called
To-day; lest any one of you be
hardened by the deceitfulness
of sin: 14 for we are become
partakers [h]of Christ, if we hold
fast the beginning of our confidence firm unto the end: 15
while it is said,
[i]To-day if ye shall hear his
voice,
Harden not your hearts, as
in the provocation.
16 For who, when they heard,
did provoke? nay, did not all
they that came out of E'gypt by

Mo'ses? 17 And with whom was
he displeased forty years? was
it not with them that sinned,
whose [k]bodies fell in the wilderness? 18 And to whom sware he
that they should not enter into
his rest, but to them that were
disobedient? 19 And we see
that they were not able to enter
in because of unbelief.

4 Let us fear therefore, lest
haply, a promise being left
of entering into his rest, any one
of you should seem to have come
short of it. 2 For indeed we have
had [a]good tidings preached unto
us, even as also they: but the
word of hearing did not profit
them, because [b]it was not united
by faith with them that heard.
3 [c]For we who have believed do
enter into that rest; even as he
hath said,
[d] [e]As I sware in my wrath,
[g]They shall not enter into my
rest:
although the works were finished
from the foundation of the
world. 4 For he hath said some-

f Or, So g Gr. If they shall enter. h Or,
with Comp. ch. 1.9; ver. 6. i Ps. xcv. 7 f.
k Gr. limbs. a Or, a gospel b Many ancient authorities read they were. c Some
ancient authorities read We therefore. d Ps.
xcv. 11. e Or, So

11. My rest. The rest promised
by God to Israel in its earthly pilgrimage was the land of Canaan,
though the latter only symbolized
the spiritual rest for which God intended his people.

13. To-day. The day of opportunity. Deceitfulness of sin. The
false though plausible reasons by
which the Jewish converts were in
danger of being beguiled from their
belief in Christ.

16. All they that came. Caleb,
Joshua, Levites—all these entered
into the promised land. Here they
are overlooked, being so few among
the many who failed.

19. Unbelief. Which resulted in
disobedience.

CHAPTER 4

1. A promise being left. That is, a
promise of whose benefits advantage
may be taken by those who will.

2. Good tidings. The promise of
rest for Christian souls; not the
rest of inactivity but of soul peace
in the midst of world-strife; the
peace which Christians have learned
to make in and for themselves, and
which depends upon the peace of
God. See note on Mt. 5.9. Not
united by faith. The word of God
was not assimilated by them as
spiritual food, and therefore did
not strengthen or 'profit' them.

3. Works were finished. See
Gen. 2.2.

where of the seventh *day* on this wise, *f* And God rested on the seventh day from all his works;
5 and in this *place* again,

g *h* They shall not enter into my rest.

6 Seeing therefore it remaineth that some should enter thereinto, and they to whom *i* the good tidings were before preached failed to enter in because of disobedience, 7 he again defineth a certain day, To-day, saying in David so long a time afterward (even as hath been said before),

k To-day if ye shall hear his voice,

Harden not your hearts.

8 For if *l* Josh'u-a had given them rest, he would not have spoken afterward of another day.
9 There remaineth therefore a sabbath rest for the people of God. 10 For he that is entered into his rest hath himself also rested from his works, as God did from his. 11 Let us there-fore give diligence to enter into that rest, that no man fall *m* after the same example of disobedience. 12 For the word of God is living, and active, and sharper than any two-edged sword, and piercing even to the dividing of soul and spirit, of both joints and marrow, and quick to discern the thoughts and intents of the heart. 13 And there is no creature that is not manifest in his sight: but all *things* are naked and laid open before the eyes of him with whom we have to do.

14 Having then a great high priest, who hath passed through the heavens, Je'sus the Son of God, let us hold fast our con-fession. 15 For we have not a high priest that cannot be touched with the feeling of our infirmities; but one that hath been in all points tempted like as *we are, yet* without sin. 16 Let us therefore draw near with boldness unto the throne of

---

f Gen. ii. 2.   *g* Gr. *If they shall enter.*
h Ps. xcv. 11.   *i* Or, *the gospel was*   *k* Ps.

xcv. 7 f.   *l* Gr. *Jesus.* Comp. Acts 7.45.
m Or, *into* Gr. *in.*

8. *If Joshua had given them rest,* etc. If the land of Canaan had been all that was promised, David would not have spoken of a rest.

9. *A sabbath rest.* That is, there remains a rest unexhausted and un-realized, a rest of which the land of Canaan and the Sabbath are types. It begins with the spiritual peace which comes from God through faith in Christ.

12. *Word of God.* Not merely the written law, nor the 'Word' as de-scribed by the apostle John (ch. 1.1), but the spiritual power pro-ceeding from God and speaking in and to the hearts of men, as actively in the world to-day as in olden times. Like a two-edged sword it pierces through outer appearances and lays bare the inmost motives,

intentions and feelings. The reading of a single verse or of one of the gospel narratives has often changed a life.

14. *The heavens.* According to Jewish belief the blue dome of the heavens was as a curtain spread over the earth; beyond this were other heavens and the throne of the Almighty. Jesus, our high priest, is here declared to have passed through the heavens, that is, into the presence of God (ch. 9.24; 2 Cor. 12.2).

15. *Our infirmities.* However ex-alted in glory, Jesus, our great high priest, is near to us in his love and sympathy and bears with our weak-nesses, if we are trying to grow stronger.

16. *Boldness.* A rebuke to the

grace, that we may receive mercy, and may find grace to help us in time of need.

5 For every high priest, being taken from among men, is appointed for men in things pertaining to God, that he may offer both gifts and sacrifices for sins: 2 who can bear gently with the ignorant and erring, for that he himself also is compassed with infirmity; 3 and by reason thereof is bound, as for the people, so also for himself, to offer for sins. 4 And no man taketh the honor unto himself, but when he is called of God, even as was Aar'on. 5 So Christ also glorified not himself to be made a high priest, but he that spake unto him,

*a*Thou art my Son,

This day have I begotten thee:

6 as he saith also in another *place*,

*b*Thou art a priest for ever
After the order of Mel-chiz'-e-dek.

7 Who in the days of his flesh, having offered up prayers and supplications with strong crying and tears unto him that was able to save him *c*from death, and having been heard for his godly fear, 8 though he was a Son, yet learned obedience by the things which he suffered; 9 and having been made perfect, he became unto all them that obey him the *d*author of eternal salvation; 10 named of God a high priest after the order of Mel-chiz'e-dek.

11 Of *e*whom we have many things to say, and hard of interpretation, seeing ye are become dull of hearing. 12 For when by reason of the time ye ought to be teachers, ye have need again

---

a Ps. 11. 7.   *b* Ps. cx. 4.   *c* Or, *out of*   *d* Gr. *cause.*   *e* Or, *which*

timid who pray for much while expecting little, and who at times are not willing to make the sacrifice to be all that we ask God to make us.

CHAPTER 5

1. *High priest.* In Old Testament times the priest represented the people before God. He alone entered the Holy of Holies. In like manner Jesus Christ represents and intercedes for us, having entered into the immediate presence of God. *Among men.* The feeling of human brotherhood was the first necessary qualification of a Jewish high priest. In this and subsequent chapters of this epistle, the Levitical high-priesthood is compared with the eternal high-priesthood of Christ. *For men.* For the benefit of men in all that pertains to spiritual welfare.

4. *No man taketh the honor.* The sons of Aaron were priests by hereditary right. Aaron did not assume the duties of his office until he was called of God.

6. *Thou art a priest.* God ordained Jesus to his work. *After the order of Melchizedek.* This mysterious person appears but once in ancient history as both a king and a priest. He was not a Hebrew; so that his priesthood was by special divine appointment.

8. *Obedience.* Through all the experiences of his life, Christ manifested the obedience of a son who gladly surrenders his will to the will of his father (Lk. 22.42).

9. *Eternal salvation.* Jesus perfectly identified himself with us in all that we must endure, yet he sinned not. Hence he becomes the Saviour to give us help continually in every time of need. The Levitical priest could offer but momentary relief by repeated sacrifices. See ch. 9.12 and note thereon.

12. *By reason of the time.* That is, considering the length of time they had been Christians. Christ requires growth in personal religion. If we do not progress, our sincerity may well be doubted. *Oracles of*

*f*that some one teach you the rudiments of the *g*first principles of the oracles of God; and are become such as have need of milk, and not of solid food. 13 For every one that partaketh of milk is *h*without experience of the word of righteousness; for he is a babe. 14 But solid food is for *i*fullgrown men, *even* those who by reason of use have their senses exercised to discern good and evil.

6 Wherefore leaving *a*the doctrine of the first principles of Christ, let us press on unto *b*perfection; not laying again a foundation of repentance from dead works, and of faith toward God, 2 *c*of the teaching of *d*baptisms, and of laying on of hands, and of resurrection of the dead, and of eternal judgment. 3 And this will we do, if God permit.

4 For as touching those who were once enlightened *e*and tasted of the heavenly gift, and were made partakers of the Holy Spirit, 5 and *f*tasted the good word of God, and the powers of the age to come, 6 and *then* fell away, it is impossible to renew them again unto repentance; *g*seeing they crucify to themselves the Son of God afresh, and put him to an open shame. 7 For the land which hath drunk the rain that cometh oft upon it, and bringeth forth herbs meet for them for whose sake it is also tilled, receiveth blessing from God: 8 but if it beareth thorns and thistles, it is rejected and nigh unto a curse; whose end is to be burned.

9 But, beloved, we are persuaded better things of you, and things that *h*accompany salva-

---

f Or, *that one teach you which* are *the rudiments* *g* Gr. *beginning.* *h* Or, *inexperienced in* *i* Or, *perfect* *a* Gr. *the word of the beginning of Christ.* *b* Or, *full growth* *c* Some ancient authorities read, *even the*

teaching of. *d* Or, *washings* *e* Or, *having both tasted of . . . and being made . . . and having tasted &c.* *f* Or, *tasted the word of God that it is good* *g* Or, *the while* *h* Or, *belong to*

God. The truth as given to man by Christ and his apostles.

13. *Babe.* Those to whom the epistle was written had remained in spiritual infancy when they should have become fullgrown Christians, able to instruct others.

CHAPTER 6

1. *Not laying again a foundation.* Do not be content to live continually in the basement of Christian experience. Ascend the heights of faith and spiritual fruitfulness. The foundation, though necessary, is not the most useful or beautiful part of a building, and this is equally true of Christian character. *Dead works.* Without the living spirit of love; mere formal actions. 4. *Tasted of the heavenly gift.* Made it a spiritual possession by experience.

5. *The age to come.* Referring to those who had had a foretaste of

the spiritual fruition to which continual faith in God's promises would have led them.

6. *Crucify to themselves the Son of God afresh.* The actual crucifiers of Christ condemned him as a deceiver; they who continuously reject him confirm the judgment of his hating and unbelieving murderers.

7. *Bringeth forth herbs.* The fruitful field, like the fruitful Christian character, is blessed of God. Fruitfulness in Scripture is ever a symbol of blessedness.

8. *Thorns and thistles.* Better no labor and no rain than to have turned all good received to evil ends. Ver. 7, 8 contain the blessing and the warning concerning the use and misuse respectively of the gifts mentioned in ver. 4, 5. See Rom. 2.4–9.

9. *Beloved.* A warmly affectionate greeting given to remind the readers of the epistle that the rebukes and

tion, though we thus speak: 10 for God is not unrighteous to forget your work and the love which ye showed toward his name, in that ye ministered unto the saints, and still do minister. 11 And we desire that each one of you may show the same diligence unto the ⁱfulness of hope even to the end: 12 that ye be not sluggish, but imitators of them who through faith and patience inherit the promises.

13 For when God made promise to Abraham, since he could swear by none greater, he sware by himself, 14 saying, ᵏSurely blessing I will bless thee, and multiplying I will multiply thee. 15 And thus, having patiently endured, he obtained the promise. 16 For men swear by the greater: and in every dispute of theirs the oath is final for confirmation. 17 Wherein God, being minded to show more abundantly unto the heirs of the promise the immutability of his counsel, ⁱinterposed with an oath; 18 that by two immutable things, in which it is impossible for God to lie, we may have a strong encouragement, who have fled for refuge to lay hold of the hope set before us: 19 which we have as an anchor of the soul, *a hope* both sure and stedfast and entering into that which is within the veil; 20 whither as a forerunner Je′sus entered for us, having become a high priest for ever after the order of Mel-chiz′e-dek.

7 For this Mel-chiz′e-dek, king of Sa′lem, priest of God Most High, who met Abraham returning from the slaughter of the kings and blessed him, 2 to whom also Abraham divided a tenth part of all (being first, by interpretation, King of righteousness, and then also King of

---

i Or, *full assurance*   *k* Gen. xxii. 16 f.

l Gr. *mediated.*

---

warnings were only meant to bring back erring Christians to their first faith. *Accompany salvation.* Spiritual aids to salvation; the humility and obedience that lead through faith to salvation.

10. *God is not unrighteous to forget,* etc. He holds in loving remembrance the deeds done in obedience to Him. There is a conservation of virtue in the spiritual world, even as there is a conservation of energy in the natural world. See 2 Cor. 8.24; Col. 1.4.

11. *Fulness of hope.* Let your anxiety to attain fulness of spiritual maturity in your own experience equal that eagerness you have shown in ministering to others.

13. *Abraham.* See Gen. 22.16.

15. *Obtained the promise.* See Gen. 22.16–18.

18. *Immutable things.* God's promise and God's oath (ver. 13,17).

19. *Anchor of the soul.* The symbol of hope. *Within the veil.* - Just as the anchor has its holding ground in unseen depths, so the Christian's hope, his anchor, is flung out into the unseen region of eternal things. Between us and the fulfilment of our hopes there is a veil, as there was in the tabernacle of the Old Testament, beyond which the high priest passed on the Day of Atonement (Lev. 16.2, 12–17). So Jesus Christ, the eternal high priest, has entered within the veil, having risen from the dead.

CHAPTER 7

1. *Melchizedek.* The name means King of righteousness. A mysterious person appearing but once in the Old Testament (Gen. 14.18–20), here introduced as a priest of a higher order than that of Aaron. His priesthood was typical of the eternal priesthood of Christ.

Sa'lem, which is, King of peace; 3 without father, without mother, without genealogy, having neither beginning of days nor end of life, but made like unto the Son of God), abideth a priest continually.

4 Now consider how great this man was, unto whom Abraham, the patriarch, gave a tenth out of the chief spoils. 5 And they indeed of the sons of Le'vi that receive the priest's office have commandment to take tithes of the people according to the law, that is, of their brethren, though these have come out of the loins of Abraham: 6 but he whose genealogy is not counted from them hath taken tithes of Abraham, and hath blessed him that hath the promises. 7 But without any dispute the less is blessed of the better. 8 And here men that die receive tithes; but there one, of whom it is witnessed that he liveth. 9 And, so to say, through Abraham even Le'vi, who receiveth tithes, hath paid tithes; 10 for he was yet in the loins of his father, when Mel-chiz'e-dek met him.

11 Now if there was perfection through the Le-vit'ic-al priesthood (for under it hath the peo-

ple received the law), what further need *was there* that another priest should arise after the order of Mel-chiz'e-dek, and not be reckoned after the order of Aar'on? 12 For the priesthood being changed, there is made of necessity a change also of the law. 13 For he of whom these things are said *a*belongeth to another tribe, from which no man hath given attendance at the altar. 14 For it is evident that our Lord hath sprung out of Ju'dah; as to which tribe Mo'ses spake nothing concerning priests. 15 And *what we say* is yet more abundantly evident, if after the likeness of Mel-chiz'-e-dek there ariseth another priest, 16 who hath been made, not after the law of a carnal commandment, but after the power of an *b*endless life: 17 for it is witnessed *of him*,

*c*Thou art a priest for ever
    After the order of Mel-
        chiz'e-dek.

18 For there is a disannulling of a foregoing commandment because of its weakness and unprofitableness 19 (for the law made nothing perfect), and a bringing in thereupon of a better hope, through which we draw

---

a Gr. *hath partaken of.* See ch. 2.14.   *b* Gr. *indissoluble.*   *c* Ps. cx. 4.

3. *Without father, without mother.* The priestly office of the sons of Aaron and the Levites was theirs by inheritance, not by any inherent holiness of life. But Melchizedek had no priestly pedigree, and in this respect resembled Christ.

16. *Carnal commandment.* Not according to the law of natural or physical descent, as in the Aaronic priesthood. *Power of an endless life.* A sentence implying that the priesthood of Jesus is his by virtue of his be-

ing the Son of God who liveth forever.

18. *A disannulling of a foregoing commandment.* The Old Testament was a stepping stone from discipline to something new and better. The Mosaic code could not but fail to bring men into complete reconciliation with God. This could only be done by spiritual contact with God through faith in Jesus Christ.

19. *Better hope.* Historical manifestation of Christ as spiritual Saviour of mankind.

nigh unto God. 20 And inasmuch as *it is* not without the taking of an oath 21 (for they indeed have been made priests without an oath; but he with an oath *d*by him that saith *e*of him,

*f*The Lord sware and will not repent himself,

Thou art a priest for ever);
22 by so much also hath Je'sus become the surety of a better covenant. 23 And they indeed have been made priests many in number, because that by death they are hindered from continuing: 24 but he, because he abideth for ever, *g*hath his priesthood *h*unchangeable. 25 Wherefore also he is able to save *i*to the uttermost them that draw near unto God through him, seeing he ever liveth to make intercession for them.

26 For such a high priest became us, holy, guileless, undefiled, separated from sinners, and made higher than the heavens; 27 who needeth not daily,

like those high priests, to offer up sacrifices, first for his own sins, and then for the *sins* of the people: for this he did once for all, when he offered up himself. 28 For the law appointeth men high priests, having infirmity; but the word of the oath, which was after the law, *appointeth* a Son, perfected for evermore.

8 *a*Now *b*in the things which we are saying the chief point *is this*: We have such a high priest, who sat down on the right hand of the throne of the Majesty in the heavens, 2 a minister of *c*the sanctuary, and of the true tabernacle, which the Lord pitched, not man. 3 For every high priest is appointed to offer both gifts and sacrifices: wherefore it is necessary that this *high priest* also have somewhat to offer. 4 Now if he were on earth, he would not be a priest at all, seeing there are those who offer the gifts according to the law; 5 who serve *that*

---

d Or, *through*   *e* Or, *unto*   *f* Ps. cx. 4. *g* Or, *hath a priesthood that doth not pass to another*   *h* Or, *inviolable*   *i* Gr. *completely.*   *a* Or, *Now to sum up what we are saying: We have &c.*   *b* Gr. *upon.*   *c* Or, *holy things*

24. *Unchangeable.* He ever liveth to intercede for us. Our love and service vary; he abideth faithful.

25. *The uttermost.* From the lowest depths to the greatest heights; salvation from the guilt and power of sin. See Jn. 6.37–39; Rom. 8.34; Jude 24.

26. *Became us.* The Son of God met and answered the needs of those to whom he came. *Holy.* Entirely consecrated and set apart in voluntary obedience to the will of God. *Guileless.* Harmless without deceit. *Undefiled.* Pure and clean as touching the requirements of the ceremonial law.

28. *Perfected.* Christ met every test and fulfilled every requirement the law could demand. By his life,

his suffering, his death, and his resurrection he became the perfect reconciler of mankind to God, and the perfect Saviour.

CHAPTER 8

1. *Throne of the Majesty in the heavens.* An expression equivalent to 'at the right hand of God.' 'In the heavens' is 'in the highest places.' See Lk. 2.14; Eph. 1.20.

2. *True tabernacle.* The original, ideal, spiritual tabernacle, of which the tabernacle of the Old Testament was but a type, a symbol, or a shadow. God prepared the Hebrew mind for the conception of a spiritual household by a material symbol thereof.

which is a copy and shadow of
the heavenly things, even as
Mo'ses is warned *of God* when he
is about to ᵈmake the tabernacle: for, ᵉSee, saith he, that
thou make all things according
to the pattern that was showed
thee in the mount. 6 But now
hath he obtained a ministry the
more excellent, by so much as
he is also the mediator of a better
covenant, which hath been en-
acted upon better promises. 7
For if that first *covenant* had
been faultless, then would no
place have been sought for a
second. 8 For ᶠfinding fault
with them, he saith,
ᵍBehold, the days come, saith
the Lord,
That I will ʰmake a new
covenant with the house of
Is'ra-el and with the house
of Ju'dah;
9 Not according to the covenant that I made with their
fathers
In the day that I took them
by the hand to lead them
forth out of the land of
E'gypt;

For they continued not in my
covenant,
And I regarded them not,
saith the Lord.
10 For this is the covenant that
ⁱI will make with the house
of Is'ra-el
After those days, saith the
Lord;
I will put my laws into their
mind,
And on their heart also will I
write them:
And I will be to them a God,
And they shall be to me a
people:
11 And they shall not teach
every man his fellow-
citizen,
And every man his brother,
saying, Know the Lord:
For all shall know me,
From the least to the greatest
of them.
12 For I will be merciful to their
iniquities,
And their sins will I remember no more.
13 In that he saith, A new
covenant, he hath made the first
old. But that which is becoming

---

d Or, *complete* e Ex. xxv. 40. f Some
ancient authorities read *finding fault* with
it, *he saith unto them &c.* g Jer. xxxi. 31 ff.
h Gr, *accomplish.* i Gr. *I will covenant.*

6. *Better covenant.* A covenant of
universal forgiveness for mankind,
and written in the human heart, as
contrasted with a covenant of strict
obedience embodied in commandments written on tables of stone.
Under the new covenant, love to
God as revealed in Christ, gives life
to Christian service. The letter of
the old law led to dead formalism.
8. *He saith,* etc. God speaking
through his prophet Jeremiah (Jer.
31.31–34).
10. *After those days.* After the old
had been done away and Christ had
ushered in the new. *My laws into
their mind.* No longer a formal code
commanding obedience, but an inner

spirit of life. There shall be an inspiration born of love rather than a
command.
11. *They shall not teach every man.*
The old covenant was national; the
new shall be individual. Every man
shall have the new life in his heart
by faith in Jesus Christ.
12. *I will be merciful,* etc. A
gracious and free forgiveness of sins,
even the blotting out of the remembrance of them. See Rom. 11.
27, 32.
13. *A new covenant.* The prophet
saw in vision a better day, with the
old legal covenant superseded, and
the new covenant of God's grace
begun.

old and waxeth aged is nigh unto vanishing away.

9 Now even the first *covenant* had ordinances of divine service, and its sanctuary, *a sanctuary* of this world. 2 For there was a tabernacle prepared, the first, wherein *a*were the candlestick, and the table, and *b*the showbread; which is called the Holy place. 3 And after the second veil, the tabernacle which is called the Holy of holies; 4 having a golden *c*altar of incense, and the ark of the covenant overlaid round about with gold, wherein *d*was a golden pot holding the man′na, and Aar′on's rod that budded, and the tables of the covenant; 5 and above it cher′u-bim of glory overshadowing *e*the mercy-seat; of which things we cannot now speak severally. 6 Now these things having been thus pre-

pared, the priests go in continually into the first tabernacle, accomplishing the services; 7 but into the second the high priest alone, once in the year, not without blood, which he offereth for himself, and for the *f*errors of the people: 8 the Holy Spirit this signifying, that the way into the holy place hath not yet been made manifest, while the first tabernacle is yet standing; 9 which *is* a figure for the time present; according to which are offered both gifts and sacrifices that cannot, as touching the conscience, make the worshipper perfect, 10 *being* only (with meats and drinks and divers washings) carnal ordinances, imposed until a time of reformation.

11 But Christ having come a high priest of *g*the good things to come, through the greater and

a Or, are   *b* Gr. *the setting forth of the loaves.*   *c* Or, *censer*   2 Chr. 26.19; Ezek. 8.11.   *d* Or, is   *e* Gr. *the propitiatory.*   *f* Gr. *ignorances.*   Ecclus. 23.2 f.   *g* Some ancient authorities read *the good things that are come.*

CHAPTER 9

1. *Sanctuary of this world.* The holy tent of the tabernacle was an earthly sign of the heavenly, and was to symbolize divine truths. In chs. 9, 10 the contrast between the old and new covenants is further heightened.

2. *Tabernacle.* Tent. The tabernacle had an outer chamber, the Holy Place; and an inner chamber, the Holy of Holies (Ex. 26). Before each chamber there was a curtain. *Candlestick.* Lampstand (Ex. 25.31–40). *Table.* Ex. 25.23–30. *Showbread.* Bread set before the presence of God (Ex. 25.30).

3. *Second veil.* The second curtain. The first curtain being before the Holy Place.

4. *Altar of incense.* On this the high priest burned incense, without which he could not enter the Holy of Holies (Lev. 16.12). *Ark of the*

covenant. See Ex. 25.10–22. *Pot holding the manna.* See Ex. 16.32–34. *Aaron's rod.* See Num. 17. 1–10.

5. *Cherubim.* Winged figures symbolical of God's presence, which guard the place of Jehovah's glory. See Ex. 25.17–22.

6. *First tabernacle.* See note on ver. 2. Into the Holy Place the people could not enter, so that men were denied access to God except through priests.

7. *High priest alone.* To one man, the high priest, was given the privilege of beholding the Glory of God. How far separated were the common people from their God!

9. *Figure.* In time the Jews realized that all the machinery of their ritual was but a preparation for spiritual realities.

11. *Good things to come.* The eternal realities of which the old covenant was the shadow. *Not of*

more perfect tabernacle, not made with hands, that is to say, not of this creation, 12 nor yet through the blood of goats and calves, but through his own blood, entered in once for all into the holy place, having obtained eternal redemption. 13 For if the blood of goats and bulls, and the ashes of a heifer sprinkling them that have been defiled, sanctify unto the cleanness of the flesh: 14 how much more shall the blood of Christ, who through *h*the eternal Spirit offered himself without blemish unto God, cleanse *i*your conscience from dead works to serve the living God? 15 And for this cause he is the mediator of a new *k*covenant, that a death having taken place for the redemption of the transgressions that were under the first *k*covenant, they that have been called may receive the promise of the eternal inheritance. 16 For

where a *k*testament is, there must of necessity *l*be the death of him that made it. 17 For a *k*testament is of force *m*where there hath been death: *n*for it doth never avail while he that made it liveth. 18 Wherefore even the first *covenant* hath not been dedicated without blood. 19 For when every commandment had been spoken by Mo'ses unto all the people according to the law, he took the blood of the calves and the goats, with water and scarlet wool and hyssop, and sprinkled both the book itself and all the people, 20 saying, *o*This is the blood of the *k*covenant which God commanded to you-ward. 21 Moreover the tabernacle and all the vessels of the ministry he sprinkled in like manner with the blood. 22 And according to the law, I may almost say, all things are cleansed with blood, and apart from shedding of blood there is no remission.

---

h Or, his *eternal spirit* *i* Many ancient authorities read *our*. *k* The Greek word here used signifies both *covenant* and *testa-* | *ment.* *l* Gr. *be brought.* *m* Gr. *over the dead.* *n* Or, *for doth it ever . . . liveth?* *o* Ex. xxiv. 8.

this creation. The tent or sanctuary was earthly, of human manufacture.

12. *His own blood.* The high priest, cleansed symbolically by the blood of animals, entered the Holy of Holies to atone for the people. Christ by his voluntary sacrifice on the cross entered heaven, having made atonement once for all for sin. See Eph. 1.7.

14. *Dead works.* All works done in a slavish spirit, merely to comply with legal requirements, are dead.

15. *Transgressions that were under the first covenant.* God was merciful to those who died before Christ came. The virtue of his reconciling sacrifice extends back to the Old Testament saints who lived in faith, looking forward to a perfect revelation of God's love in Christ.

16. *Testament.* A will.

20. *Blood of the covenant.* Covenants sealed with blood were common in the early age of the Jewish people. Often in the Middle Ages of Europe men signed covenants with their blood. This added to the sacredness and surety of the contract. So God's covenant with his people was sealed with the blood of clean animals, symbolizing the voluntary sacrifice of Christ which sealed his final convenant with man.

22. *Shedding of blood.* Blood was the symbol of life, and underneath the whole Jewish ritual was the idea that the life of men was forfeited to God because of sin. Blood, representing life, was therefore offered in sacrifice as an atonement for sins. See Lev. 17.11; Lk. 22.20.

557

23 It was necessary therefore that the copies of the things in the heavens should be cleansed with these; but the heavenly things themselves with better sacrifices than these. 24 For Christ entered not into a holy place made with hands, like in pattern to the true; but into heaven itself, now to appear before the face of God for us: 25 nor yet that he should offer himself often, as the high priest entereth into the holy place year by year with blood not his own; 26 else must he often have suffered since the foundation of the world: but now once at the *p*end of the ages hath he been manifested to put away sin *q*by the sacrifice of himself. 27 And inasmuch as it is *r*appointed unto men once to die, and after this *cometh* judgment; 28 so

Christ also, having been once offered to bear the sins of many, shall appear a second time, apart from sin, to them that wait for him, unto salvation.

10 For the law having a shadow of the good *things* to come, not the very image of the things, *a*can never with the same sacrifices year by year, which they offer continually, make perfect them that draw nigh. 2 Else would they not have ceased to be offered? because the worshippers, having been once cleansed, would have had no more consciousness of sins. 3 But in those *sacrifices* there is a remembrance made of sins year by year. 4 For it is impossible that the blood of bulls and goats should take away sins. 5 Wherefore when he cometh into the world, he saith,

p Or, *consummation*   *q* Or, *by his sacrifice*   *r* Gr. *laid up for.* Col. 1.5;   2 Tim. 4.8.   *a* Many ancient authorities read *they can.*

23. *Heavenly things.* The spiritual sanctuary into which Christ has gone, with its heavenly realities corresponding to the symbols of the Levitical sanctuary.

24. *Before the face of God.* That is, in the immediate presence of God instead of in the Holy of Holies of an earthly and temporary tabernacle, which was only a symbol of that presence. Moreover, Christ's mediation for all mankind is continuous, eternal (ch. 7.25); the Levitical high priest appeared in behalf of the Jewish people only once a year. Humanity, therefore, is ever present in the compassionate mind of the risen Christ, who is in the eternal presence of the Father.

26. *End of the ages.* The expiration of the time during which the Levitical priesthood served as a mediator between God and the chosen people; or, from a more comprehensive point of view, the beginning of the new time when God revealed himself in Jesus Christ to

mankind (ch. 1.1, 2; 1 Cor. 10.11).

27. *Once to die.* Death ends the probationary or preparatory stage of man's career; then comes his judgment, which is here to be distinguished from the judgment of the world, mentioned in Acts 17.31.

28. *So Christ also.* Death also ended the earthly part of Christ's mission as the revealer of God to mankind and the Saviour from sin. He came first because of sin; now he awaits the fruits of his work, the defeat of sin in the lives of his people, and so apart from sin he shall come again.

CHAPTER 10

1. *Shadow.* The law was a preparation for Christ. It instilled into the minds of the Jewish people religious conceptions on which Christ could build. It was not final but a shadow, a foretaste, a beginning that was to lead men to the truth as revealed in Jesus Christ.

*b*Sacrifice and offering thou wouldest not,
But a body didst thou prepare for me;
6 In whole burnt offerings and *sacrifices* for sin thou hadst
. no pleasure:
7 Then said I, Lo, I am come
(In the roll of the book it is written of me)
To do thy will, O God.
8 Saying above, Sacrifices and offerings and whole burnt offerings and *sacrifices* for sin thou wouldest not, neither hadst pleasure therein (the which are offered according to the law), 9 then hath he said, Lo, I am come to do thy will. He taketh away the first, that he may establish the second. 10 *c*By which will we have been sanctified through the offering of the body of Je′sus Christ once for all. 11 And every *d*priest indeed standeth day by day ministering and offering oftentimes the same sacrifices, the which can never

take away sins: 12 but he, when he had offered one sacrifice for *e*sins for ever, sat down on the right hand of God; 13 henceforth expecting till his enemies be made the footstool of his feet. 14 For by one offering he hath perfected for ever them that are sanctified. 15 And the Holy Spirit also beareth witness to us; for after he hath said,
16 *f*This is the covenant that *g*I will make with them
After those days, saith the Lord:
I will put my laws on their heart,
And upon their mind also will I write them;
then saith he,
17 And their sins and their iniquities will I remember no more.
18 Now where remission of these is, there is no more offering for sin.
19 Having therefore, brethren, boldness to enter into the holy

b Ps. xl. 6 ff. *c* Or, *In* *d* Some ancient authorities read *high priest.*

e Or, *sins, for ever sat down &c.* *f* Jer. xxxi. 33 f. *g* Gr. *I will convenant.*

10. *Sanctified.* Cleansed from the impurity of sin. All believers are saints, holy, or sanctified, if considered as set apart or consecrated to the service of God (Jn. 17.19; Eph. 1.4); but from the point of view of growth in spiritual power, sanctification is progress toward perfection, and a process due to the indwelling of the Holy Spirit (Rom. 15.16). *Through the offering of the body of Jesus Christ.* This points out the reason why we also should offer our bodies 'a living sacrifice, holy, acceptable to God, which is your spiritual service' (Rom. 12.1).
11. *Day by day.* The long-continued, wearisome routine of the sacrificial system was spiritually impotent for the eradication of sin. The clear perception of this caused Paul to cry out, ' Wretched man that

I am! who shall deliver me out of the body of this death?' (Rom. 7.24).
12. *One sacrifice for sins.* A sacrifice which is pure, holy and effectual for all who accept it.
14. *Perfected.* The offering under the Levitical law was an act at a definite, prescribed time. The perfecting of men is gradual, progressing from age to age under the guidance of the Holy Spirit. See ch. 7.11, 25.
16. *My laws on their heart.* Which could only be under the covenant of forgiveness. When the laws of God are written on, and are active in, the hearts of mankind, obedience is glad and willing.
19. *Boldness.* How much of fear and trembling before God there was in the Old Testament! Mount Sinai,

place by the blood of Je'sus, 20 by the way which he dedicated for us, a new and living way, through the veil, that is to say, his flesh; 21 and *having* a great priest over the house of God; 22 let us draw near with a true heart in *h*fulness of faith, having our hearts sprinkled from an evil *i*conscience: and having our body washed with pure water, 23 let us hold fast the confession of our hope that it waver not; for he is faithful that promised: 24 and let us consider one another to provoke unto love and good works; 25 not forsaking our own assembling together, as the custom of some is, but exhorting *one another*; and so much the more, as ye see the day drawing nigh.

26 For if we sin wilfully after that we have received the knowledge of the truth, there remain-

eth no more a sacrifice for sins, 27 but a certain fearful expectation of judgment, and a *k*fierceness of fire which shall devour the adversaries. 28 A man that hath set at nought Mo'ses' law dieth without compassion on *the word of* two or three witnesses: 29 of how much sorer punishment, think ye, shall he be judged worthy, who hath trodden under foot the Son of God, and hath counted the blood of the covenant wherewith he was sanctified *l*an unholy thing, and hath done despite unto the Spirit of grace? 30 For we know him that said, *m*Vengeance belongeth unto me, I will recompense. And again, *n*The Lord shall judge his people. 31 It is a fearful thing to fall into the hands of the living God.

32 But call to remembrance the former days, in which, after

h Or, *full assurance*   i Or, *conscience, and our body washed with pure water: let us hold fast*
k Or, *jealousy*   l Gr. *a common thing.*   m Dt. xxxii. 35.   n Dt. xxxii. 36.

the place of His appearing, was wrapped in thunder clouds and illumined by lightnings. God was distant and terrible. Under the Levitical law the worshipper was not allowed to enter the Holy of Holies in the tabernacle; but the voluntary sacrifice of Jesus Christ has procured for the believer the privilege of entering, and with boldness, the Holy Place of God's presence.
22. *Our hearts sprinkled.* A sprinkling of spiritual power in contrast to the outward sprinkling of the body. The writer of the epistle here speaks as if the age of ceremonial purity in religion had passed away and a new era of inward purity had begun. See Ex. 29.21; Lev. 8.30; 1 Pet. 1.2.
23. *The confession of our hope.* The hope of eternal salvation by faith in Jesus Christ.
25. *Assembling together.* Words

which suggest that public worship is a privilege, and that Christianity is a religion for society, not thriving best in isolated lives. *The day.* The expected second coming of Christ.
26. *Sin wilfully.* The deliberate choice of sin and a persistent life of sin, which ultimately prevent the indwelling of the Holy Spirit. The words do not refer to sins done wilfully, but of which the sinner afterward repents.
29. *Trodden underfoot.* The strongest figurative expression to an oriental mind. *Done despite.* Insulted.
30. *Vengeance belongeth unto me.* God alone can punish justly. Human vengeance is often based on pride, or selfishness, or prejudice. The certainty and justice of the punishment are based on the righteous nature of God.
32. *Former days.* An appeal to

ye were enlightened, ye endured a great conflict of sufferings; 33 partly, being made a gazing-stock both by reproaches and afflictions; and partly, becoming partakers with them that were so used. 34 For ye both had compassion on them that were in bonds, and took joyfully the spoiling of your possessions, knowing that *o*ye have for your-selves a better possession and an abiding one. 35 Cast not away therefore your boldness, which hath great recompense of re-ward. 36 For ye have need of *p*patience, that, having done the will of God, ye may receive the promise.

37 *q*For yet a very little while,
He that cometh shall come,
    and shall not tarry.

38 But *r*my righteous one shall
    live by faith:

And if he shrink back, my soul hath no pleasure in him. 39 But we are not *s*of them that shrink back unto perdition; but of them that have faith unto the *t*saving of the soul.

11 Now faith is *a*assurance of *things* hoped for, a *b*con-viction of things not seen. 2 For therein the elders had witness borne to them. 3 By faith we understand that the *c*worlds have been framed by the word of God, so that what is seen hath not been made out of things which appear 4 By faith Abel offered unto God a more excel-lent sacrifice than Cain, through which he had witness borne to him that he was righteous, *d*God bearing witness *e*in respect of his gifts: and through it he being dead yet speaketh. 5 By faith E'noch was translated that he

---

o Many ancient authorities read *ye have your own selves for a better possession &c.* Comp. Lk. 9.25; 21.19. *p* Or, *stedfastness* *q* Hab. ii. 3 f. *r* Some ancient authorities read *the righteous one.* *s* Gr. *of shrinking*

back . . . but of faith. *t* Or, *gaining* *a* Or, *the giving substance to* *b* Or, *test* *c* Gr. *ages.* Comp. 1 Tim. 1.17 marg. *d* The Greek text in this clause is somewhat un-certain. *e* Or, *over his gifts*

what is best and most praiseworthy in a man's past is the best incentive to a worthy present and future.

33. *Partakers.* Sympathy and love for one another were so strong in the early church that when one suffered all suffered.

37. *Very little while.* The prophet preached that only firm confidence in God could enable a righteous man to confront life's difficulties. Here the writer of this epistle quotes from Habbakuk in order to strength-en the faith of his readers. He says in effect: As faith in God was nec-essary in the prophet's time, so it is now; but you have the hope of the near coming of Christ to help you to remain stedfast.

CHAPTER 11

1. *Assurance.* Faith, the root and inspiring principle of all true re-

ligion, is an internal confidence of the truth and reality of things hoped for. *Conviction.* Faith, or the spiritual acceptance of unseen realities, amounts to a conviction of their existence. Progress in faith intensifies this conviction. After faith has been triumphantly tested by experience, the believer has new evidence, as it were, of un-seen things. In this chapter the writer of the epistle shows how faith had been the great factor of spiritual life in the history of Israel.

2. *Elders.* The early Jewish fathers and patriarchs (ch. 1.1). *Had witness.* Commendation from God and their fellow-men.

4. *Abel.* Whose sacrifice was acceptable because it was offered in the right spirit (Gen. 4.4–7).

5. *Enoch.* Whose faith was ma-ture—full and rich by reason of his constant communion with God.

should not see death; and he was not found, because God translated him: *f*for he hath had witness borne to him that before his translation he had been well-pleasing unto God: 6 and without faith it is impossible to be well-pleasing *unto him*; for he that cometh to God must believe that he is, and *that* he is a rewarder of them that seek after him. 7 By faith Noah, being warned *of God* concerning things not seen as yet, moved with godly fear, prepared an ark to the saving of his house; through which he condemned the world, and became heir of the righteousness which is according to faith. 8 By faith Abraham, when he was called, obeyed to go out unto a place which he was to receive for an inheritance; and he went out, not knowing whither he went. 9 By faith he became a sojourner in the land of promise, as in a *land* not his own, *o*dwelling in tents, with I'saac and Jacob, the heirs with him of the same promise: 10 for he looked for the city which hath the foundations, whose *h*builder and maker is God. 11 By faith even Sarah herself received

power to conceive seed when she was past age, since she counted him faithful who had promised: 12 wherefore also there sprang of one, and him as good as dead, *so many* as the stars of heaven in multitude, and as the sand, which is by the sea-shore, innumerable.

13 These all died *i*in faith, not having received the promises, but having seen them and greeted them from afar, and having confessed that they were strangers and pilgrims on the earth. 14 For they that say such things make it manifest that they are seeking after a country of their own. 15 And if indeed they had been mindful of that *country* from which they went out, they would have had opportunity to return. 16 But now they desire a better *country*, that is, a heavenly: wherefore God is not ashamed of them, to be called their God; for he hath prepared for them a city.

17 By faith Abraham, being tried, *k*offered up I'saac: yea, he that had gladly received the promises was offering up his only begotten *son*; 18 *even he* *l*to whom it was said, *m*In I'saac

---

f Or, *for before his translation he hath had witness borne to him that he &c.* *g* Or, *having taken up his abode in tents* *h* Or, *architect* *i* Gr. *according to.* *k* Gr. *hath offered up.* *l* Or, *of* *m* Gen. xxi. 12.

---

7. *Noah.* His faith was founded on a reverential heed to God's word; it was the faith of godly fear. See Gen. 6.14–22. *Condemned the world.* By his righteous obedience, which reproved the wicked.

8. *Abraham.* His was the childlike faith of implicit trust, which grew and expanded with each new experience.

9. *Sojourner.* Realizing that he was called to a land of promise, he did not settle down and build a city.

13. *Died in faith.* Their faith remained stedfast in the hour of death, even although they had not yet received the promised fruition.

16. *Not ashamed of them.* On the contrary, God called himself the God of Abraham, Isaac and Jacob.

17. *Abraham, being tried.* Apparently to the last point of human capacity and endurance. Without this test triumphantly met he would not have been called 'father of the faithful.' His faith, at first ready

shall thy seed be called: 19 accounting that God *is* able to raise up, even from the dead; from whence he did also in a figure receive him back. 20 By faith I'saac blessed Jacob and E'sau, even concerning things to come. 21 By faith Jacob, when he was dying, blessed each of the sons of Joseph; and worshipped, *leaning* upon the top of his staff. 22 By faith Joseph, when his end was nigh, made mention of the departure of the children of Is'ra-el; and gave commandment concerning his bones. 23 By faith Mo'ses, when he was born, was hid three months by his parents, because they saw he was a goodly child; and they were not afraid of the king's commandment. 24 By faith Mo'ses, when he was grown up, refused to be called the son of Pha'raoh's daughter; 25 choosing rather to share ill treatment with the people of God, than to enjoy the pleasures of sin for a season; 26 accounting the reproach of ⁿChrist greater riches than the treasures of E'gypt: for he looked unto the recompense of reward. 27 By faith he forsook E'gypt, not fearing the wrath of the king: for he endured, as seeing him who is invisible. 28 By faith he °kept the passover, and the sprinkling of the blood, that the destroyer of the firstborn should not touch them. 29 By faith they passed through the Red sea as by dry land: which the E-gyp'-tians assaying to do were swallowed up. 30 By faith the walls of Jer'i-cho fell down, after they had been compassed about for seven days. 31 By faith Ra'hab the harlot perished not with them that were disobedient, having received the spies with peace.

32 And what shall I more say?

---

n Or, *the Christ* Comp. 1 Cor. 10.4.

o Or, *instituted* Gr. *hath made.*

and childlike, after this grew to be mature and fearless.

19. *In a figure.* Isaac was actually surrendered to death; actual death could not have increased the trial of his father's faith. Figuratively he was dead, and from death he returned.

21. *Jacob, when he was dying.* Even in extreme physical weakness his spirit, through faith, was strong and hopeful. Because of this he could transmit to his sons the blessing of God's promise not realized in his life. Three generations had elapsed since God had made this promise; no possibility of a present fulfilment appeared, and yet these faithful ones passed on to their children the blessing of the promise as of greater value than their gold and silver.

23. *A goodly child.* Because of the beauty and manifest promise of their child the parents felt that God had something great in store for him; so they dared to disobey the king.

24 *Moses.* His faith was proved by his actions. Because Israel was God's chosen people, he resigned all his honors as an Egyptian prince, and all the pleasures of a life of ease. He chose to suffer a reproach similar to that which Christ endured for the sake of saving his people. See ch. 13.13; Rom. 15.3.

28. *Passover.* See note on Mt. 26.17. Moses knew that the sprinkling of blood had no power to deliver from death, yet he obeyed God's command, believing that He would deliver his people.

31. *Rahab.* See Josh. 2.1–21; 6. 23.

32. *Gideon* (Judges 6–8); *Barak* (Judges 4, 5); *Samson* (Judges 13–16; *Jephthah* (Judges 11, 12); *David* (1 Sam. 17.45); *Samuel* (1 Sam. 7.9).

for the time will fail me if I tell of Gid'e-on, Ba'rak, Sam'son, Jeph'thah; of David and Sam'u-el and the prophets: 33 who through faith subdued king-doms, wrought righteousness, obtained promises, stopped the mouths of lions, 34 quenched the power of fire, escaped the edge of the sword, from weak-ness were made strong, waxed mighty in war, turned to flight armies of aliens. 35 Women received their dead by a res-urrection: and others were *p*tor-tured, not accepting *q*their deliverance; that they might obtain a better resurrection: 36 and others had trial of mockings and scourgings, yea, moreover of bonds and imprisonment: 37 they were stoned, they were sawn asunder, they were tempted, they were slain with the sword: they went about in sheepskins, in goatskins; being destitute, afflicted, ill-treated 38 (of whom the world was not worthy), wandering in deserts and mountains and caves, and the holes of the earth. 39 And

these all, having had witness borne to them through their faith, received not the promise, 40 God having *r*provided some better thing concerning us, that apart from us they should not be made perfect.

12 Therefore let us also, see-ing we are compassed about with so great a cloud of witnesses, lay aside every *a*weight, and the sin which *b*doth so easily beset us, and let us run with *c*patience the race that is set before us, 2 look-ing unto Je'sus the *d*author and perfecter of *our* faith, who for the joy that was set before him en-dured the cross, despising shame, and hath sat down at the right hand of the throne of God. 3 For consider him that hath en-dured such gainsaying of sinners against *e*himself, that ye wax not weary, fainting in your souls. 4 Ye have not yet resisted unto blood, striving against sin: 5 and ye have forgotten the ex-hortation which reasoneth with you as with sons,

*f*My son, regard not lightly the chastening of the Lord,

---

p Or, *beaten to death* *q* Gr. *the redemption.* *r* Or, *foreseen* *a* Or, *encumbrance* *b* Or, *doth closely cling to us* Or, *is admired*

of many *c* Or, *stedfastness* *d* Or, *captain* *e* Many ancient authorities read *themselves.* Comp. Num. 16.38. *f* Prov. iii. 11 f.

35. *Resurrection.* The widow of Sarepta (1 Kings 17.17–24) and the Shunamite (2 Kings 4.32–37) both received their dead back to life be-cause of their faith. *Others were tortured.* The writer now has in view the sufferings of the age after the Old Testament history was closed. *A better resurrection.* To eternal life, as contrasted with the resurrection to an earthly life, pre-viously mentioned in this verse.

37. *They were stoned.* Stoning was a common Jewish method of punish-ing heretics. Stephen was stoned. According to tradition Jeremiah was stoned.

CHAPTER 12

1. *Compassed about.* Referring to the illustrious heroes of faith spoken of in the preceding chapter. They had borne witness to the truth in their earthly life; they had now become heavenly witnesses, or spec-tators, of the struggles of those who were contending for the eternal re-ward.

2. *Looking unto Jesus.* Faith-fully modeling character after the perfect example of Jesus.

4. *Resisted into blood.* They had not yet faced death for the sake of holiness. Nor do men to-day face

Nor faint when thou art reproved of him;
6 For whom the Lord loveth he chasteneth,
And scourgeth every son whom he receiveth.
7 *g*It is for chastening that ye endure; God dealeth with you as with sons; for what son is there whom *his* father chasteneth not? 8 But if ye are without chastening, whereof all have been made partakers, then are ye bastards, and not sons. 9 Furthermore, we had the fathers of our flesh to chasten us, and we gave them reverence: shall we not much rather be in subjection unto the Father of *h*spirits, and live? 10 For they indeed for a few days chastened *us* as seemed good to them; but he for *our* profit, that *we* may be partakers of his holiness. 11 All chastening seemeth for the present to be not joyous but grievous; yet afterward it yieldeth peaceable fruit unto them that have been exercised thereby, *even the fruit* of righteous-

ness. 12 Wherefore *i*lift up the hands that hang down, and the palsied knees; 13 and make straight paths for your feet, that that which is lame be not *k*turned out of the way, but rather be healed.
14 Follow after peace with all men, and the sanctification without which no man shall see the Lord: 15 looking carefully *l*lest *there be* any man that *m*falleth short of the grace of God; lest any root of bitterness springing up trouble *you*, and thereby the many be defiled; 16 *l*lest *there be* any fornicator, or profane person, as E′sau, who for one mess of meat sold his own birthright. 17 For ye know that even when he afterward desired to inherit the blessing, he was *n*rejected; for he found no place for a change of mind *in his father*, though he sought it diligently with tears.
18 For ye are not come unto *o*a mount that might be touched, and that burned with fire, and unto blackness, and darkness,

---

g Or, *Endure unto chastening* *h* Or, *our spirits* *i* Gr. *make straight.* *k* Or, *put out of joint* *l* Or, *whether* *m* Or, *falleth back from* *n* Or, *rejected (for he found no place*

of repentance), &c. Or, *rejected; for . . . of repentance &c.* Comp. ch. 6.6; 2 Esdr. 9. 11; Wisd. 12.10. *o* Or, *a palpable and kindled fire*

---

death, as Christ did, for the sake of truth. Conditions have changed. The usual results of truth-speaking and of action in conformity to unwelcome truth are now ridicule, unpopularity, loss of reputation, business, wealth, social standing.
7. *Chastening.* The discipline of suffering, patiently endured and hence leading to richer and nobler character.
9. *Father of spirits.* God, the Father of our spirits. *And live.* Obedience to God is life.
12. *Lift up.* Comfort and cheer the downcast and sorrowing.
13. *Make straight paths.* Smooth,

level paths, free from obstructions that may cause to stumble those who are weaker than ourselves.
15. *Root of bitterness.* See Deut. 29.18.
16. *Profane person, as Esau.* Esau had no proper appreciation of his birthright, inasmuch as he had no thought of the spiritual blessing that accompanied it.
18. *Mount that might be touched.* Mount Sinai. See Ex. 19.12, 13, 18, 19; 20.18; Deut. 4.11. The mount that might be touched was Mount Sinai on earth. Here God was distant, fearful, the God of the thunder and the black clouds. We

and tempest, 19 and the sound of a trumpet, and the voice of words; which *voice* they that heard entreated that no word more should be spoken unto them; 20 for they could not endure that which was enjoined, *p*If even a beast touch the mountain, it shall be stoned; 21 and so fearful was the appearance, *that* Mo'ses said, *q*I exceedingly fear and quake: 22 but ye are come unto mount Zi'on, and unto the city of the living God, the heavenly Je-ru'sa-lem, *r*and to *s*innumerable hosts of angels, 23 to the general assembly and church of the firstborn who are enrolled in heaven, and to God the Judge of all, and to the spirits of just men made perfect, 24 and to Je'sus the mediator of a new covenant, and to the blood of sprinkling that speaketh better *t*than *that of* Abel. 25 See that ye refuse not him that

speaketh. For if they escaped not when they refused him that warned *them* on earth, much more *shall not* we *escape* who turn away from him *u*that *warneth* from heaven: 26 whose voice then shook the earth: but now he hath promised, saying, *v*Yet once more will I make to tremble not the earth only, but also the heaven. 27 And this *word*, Yet once more, signifieth the removing of those things that are shaken, as of things that have been made, that those things which are not shaken may remain. 28 Wherefore, receiving a kingdom that cannot be shaken, let us have *x*grace, whereby we may offer service well-pleasing to God with *y*reverence and awe: 29 for our God is a consuming fire.

13 Let love of the brethren continue. 2 Forget not to show love unto strangers: for

p Ex. xix. 12 f.   q Dt. ix. 19.   r Or, and
to innumerable hosts, the general assembly
of angels, and the church &c.   s Gr. myriads
of angels.   t Or, than that of Abel

u Or, that is from heaven   v Hag. ii. 6.
x Or, thankfulness   Comp. 1 Cor. 10.30.
y Or, godly fear   Comp. ch. 5.7.

are come up to a mountain invisible yet real, where heaven meets earth and God communes with his people.
20. *If even a beast touch the mountain*, etc. A fact which illustrated the rigor necessary in compelling reverence for sacred things, and affording a contrast between the Mosaic law and the grace and freedom which came through Christ.
21. *So fearful.* 'Fearful' is an accurate description of the Hebrew mind in its attitude toward God as revealed in the early history of Israel.
22. *Mount Zion.* The great contrast to Mount Sinai. Mount Zion is the mount of the New Testament age, and an emblem of all its spiritual blessings.
23. *General assembly and church*, etc. The gathering of all God's

children, including those in the visible church on earth and the church invisible in heaven.
24. *Better than that of Abel.* The blood of Abel spoke from the ground with a cry for vengeance; Christ's blood speaks of love, mercy, and pardon.
27. *Yet once more*, etc. The temporal things shall pass away. The eternal things shall remain.
28. *Let us have grace.* Feel and express thankfulness.

CHAPTER 13

2. *Strangers.* There was then no feeling of international brotherhood such as has since been manifested; but there was a solid preparation for it in Roman citizenship, which created a community of interest

thereby some have entertained angels unawares. 3 Remember them that are in bonds, as bound with them; them that are ill-treated, as being yourselves also in the body. 4 *Let* marriage *be* had in honor among all, and *let* the bed *be* undefiled: for fornicators and adulterers God will judge. 5 ªBe ye free from the love of money; content with such things as ye have: for himself hath said, ᵇI will in no wise fail thee, neither will I in any wise forsake thee. 6 So that with good courage we say,

ᶜThe Lord is my helper; I will not fear:

What shall man do unto me?

7 Remember them that had the rule over you, men that spake unto you the word of God; and considering the issue of their ᵈlife, imitate their faith. 8 Je´sus Christ *is* the same yesterday and to-day, *yea* and ᵉfor ever. 9 Be not carried away by divers and strange teachings: for it is good that the heart be

established by grace; not by meats, wherein they that ᶠoccupied themselves were not profited. 10 We have an altar, whereof they have no right to eat that serve the tabernacle. 11 For the bodies of those beasts whose blood is brought into the holy place ᵍby the high priest *as an offering* for sin, are burned without the camp. 12 Wherefore Je´sus also, that he might sanctify the people through his own blood, suffered without the gate. 13 Let us therefore go forth unto him without the camp, bearing his reproach. 14 For we have not here an abiding city, but we seek after *the city* which is to come. 15 Through him ʰthen let us offer up a sacrifice of praise to God continually, that is, the fruit of lips which make confession to his name. 16 But to do good and to communicate forget not: for with such sacrifices God is well pleased. 17 Obey them that have the rule over you, and sub-

---

ª Gr. Let *your turn* of mind be *free.*
ᵇ Dt. xxxi. 6; Josh. i. 5. ᶜ Ps. cxviii. 6.
ᵈ Gr. *manner of life.* ᵉ Gr. *unto the ages.*

ᶠ Gr. *walked.* ᵍ Gr. *through.* ʰ Some ancient authorities omit *then.*

---

throughout that vast empire. *Angels unawares.* See Gen. 18.2–22; Judg. 6.11.

3. *Bonds.* Already the Christians were suffering persecution.

4. *God will judge.* Alluding to the impossibility of escaping punishment for a sin which human judgment and penalty so often fail to overtake because of its secrecy.

5. *Content.* This is no condoning of indolence or lack of rightful ambition. But even trifling discontent may blind one to God's blessings, and rob one of all enjoyment.

7. *Issue of their life.* The way they kept their faith and holy living even until death.

9. *Strange teachings.* The doctrines of those who were trying to

establish in the early church certain ceremonial practices of the Mosaic law. They were probably connected with the sacrificial meals (ver. 10).

10. *No right to eat.* Referring to those who sought spiritual strength by sacrificial offerings or ceremonial purity, according to the old and superseded service of the tabernacle. These had no right to eat at the Christian altar; that is, they had not accepted the salvation by faith which came to them by the voluntary sacrifice of Christ.

12. *Without the gate.* See Jn. 19.17.

15. *A sacrifice of praise.* See Ps. 116.17; 1 Pet. 2.3, 11.

16. *Communicate.* Contribute, be generous in ministering to the necessities of the saints (Rom. 15.26).

mit *to them*: for they watch in behalf of your souls, as they that shall give account; that they may do this with joy, and not with *'*grief: for this *were* unprofitable for you.

18 Pray for us: for we are persuaded that we have a good conscience, desiring to live honorably in all things. 19 And I exhort *you* the more exceedingly to do this, that I may be restored to you the sooner.

20 Now the God of peace, who brought again from the dead the great shepherd of the sheep *k*with the blood of an eternal covenant, *even* our Lord Je'sus, 21 make you perfect in every good *l*thing to do his will, working in *m*us that which is well-pleasing in his sight, through Je'sus Christ; to whom *be* the glory *n*for ever and ever. A-men'.

22 But I exhort you, brethren, bear with the word of exhortation: for I have written unto you in few words. 23 Know ye that our brother Tim'o-thy hath been set at liberty; with whom, if he come shortly, I will see you.

24 Salute all them that have the rule over you, and all the saints. *o*They of It'a-ly salute you.

25 Grace be with you all. A-men'.

---

i Gr. *groaning.*   *k* Or, *by* Gr. *in.*   *l* Many ancient authorities read *work.*   *m* The present

ancient authorities read *you.*   *n* Gr. *unto the ages of the ages.*   *o* Or, *The* brethren *from &c.*

---

19. *Be restored.* That the present exile of the writer of the epistle from his readers may soon end.

20. *God of peace.* The God Who alone can give spiritual peace. *Brought again from the dead.* The resurrection of Jesus Christ. *With the blood of an eternal covenant.* See ch. 9.15–18.

22. *Bear with the word of exhortation.* Read and ponder patiently and prayerfully the words of this epistle.

23. *Timothy.* This is the only reference which proves that Timothy was ever imprisoned.

24. *All them.* The epistle was addressed to certain Christian communities as a whole, not to their rulers. *They of Italy.* Italian residents in the place where the writer of the epistle lived.

THE GENERAL EPISTLES

INTRODUCTION BY PROFESSOR M. B. RIDDLE, D.D., LL.D.

Seven epistles are now designated "general" or "catholic."
The term was first applied to three of these (James, 1 Peter, and
1 John), and afterwards to 2 Peter and Jude, the brief letters, 2 and
3 John, being finally classed with the five others for convenience.
The designation implies that the letter was originally addressed to
a wider circle of readers than the members of a single community
of Christians. In Greek MSS. these epistles were usually placed
immediately after the Acts of the Apostles. This group of writings
presents great variety in style and diction, in date, and in maturity
of doctrinal teaching.

THE EPISTLE OF JAMES

The Writer.—James, who wrote the General Epistle, was "the
Lord's brother," prominent in the church at Jerusalem, and referred to in the Acts and in the epistles of Paul (especially Galatians). He was not one of the Twelve, but a different person from
James the son of Alphæus. James was a "pillar" in the church
at Jerusalem (Gal. 2.9), and had probably been led to believe by a
special appearance of our Lord to him (1 Cor. 15.7). He was
recognized as a leader by the stricter Jewish Christians; but in the
council at Jerusalem he advocated the more liberal views which prevailed (Acts 15.13-29). Yet his piety was of an ascetic type and
he was called "James the Just." Remaining at Jerusalem, he was,
although a strict observer of the Mosaic law, put to death (about
63 A.D.) by the fanatical Jews.

It is natural that he would address his letter "to the twelve
tribes which are of the Dispersion" (1.1), since these Jewish Christians scattered abroad would be the objects of his special solicitude.
Though not often referred to in the New Testament, there must
have been many such.

Contents of the Epistle.—No special occasion appears for the
writing of the epistle, other than the errors of practice it rebukes.
Its teachings are mainly moral precepts, added to each other without any obvious plan. Hence it is called "The Christian Book of
Proverbs."

Summary.—Ch. 1. Address and greeting (ver. 1); the dis-
ciplinary nature of trials (ver. 2-4); the need of prayer for wisdom
(ver. 5-8); the fading away of riches (ver. 9-11); the heart the
source of temptation, not God the giver of good (ver. 12-18); pure
religion consists in doing good (ver. 19-27).

THE GENERAL EPISTLES—THE EPISTLE OF JAMES

Ch. 2. Respect of persons forbidden (ver. 1-9), since the whole law must be kept (ver. 10-13); faith apart from works is dead (ver. 14-20), illustrated by the case of Abraham and of Rahab (ver. 21-26).

Ch. 3. Warning to teachers, based upon the use of the tongue (ver. 1-12); the peaceableness of heavenly wisdom (ver. 13-18).

Ch. 4. Warnings against evil passions and the friendship of the world (ver. 1-10), against judging the brethren (ver. 11, 12), against planning without regarding God's will (ver. 13-17).

Ch. 5. Reproof of ill-gotten wealth (ver. 1-6); admonition to patience (ver. 7-11), against oaths (ver. 12); the prayer of faith illustrated by the case of Elijah (ver. 13-18). Conclusion: the blessed effect of turning another from the error of his way (ver. 19, 20).

Date of Writing.—Two views are held—(1) that the epistle was written before the council at Jerusalem 50 (A.D.); (2) that it should be dated shortly before the death of James (63 A.D.). The former view makes it the earliest written book of the New Testament, and is based upon the following reasons; exclusively Jewish Christian communities did not exist outside of Judæa after that time; the lack of fully-developed Christian doctrine points to an early date; and the trials referred to were probably incidental to the persecution in the days of Herod Agrippa. But these are not conclusive.

The errors combated point to the later date, since they indicate a perversion of the doctrine of free grace and a lax morality resulting from this, amounting to dead orthodoxy. Such a tendency, though most readily developed among Jewish Christians, would require time to reach the form of error opposed in the epistle. While this date (between 60-63 A.D.) places the letter after the earlier group of Pauline epistles, it does not necessarily involve any reference to them by James. It is generally admitted that Jerusalem was the place of writing.

THE EPISTLE OF

JAMES

Address and Greeting

1 [a]James, a [b]servant of God and of the Lord Je'sus Christ, to the twelve tribes which are of the Dispersion, [c]greeting.

2 Count it all joy, my brethren, when ye fall into manifold [d]temptations; 3 knowing that the proving of your faith worketh [e]patience. 4 And let [e]patience have *its* perfect work, that ye may be perfect and entire, lacking in nothing.

5 But if any of you lacketh wisdom, let him ask of God, who giveth to all liberally and upbraideth not; and it shall be given him. 6 But let him ask in faith, nothing doubting: for he that doubteth is like the surge of the sea driven by the wind and tossed. 7 For let not that man think [f]that he shall receive anything of the Lord; 8 a doubleminded man, unstable in all his ways.

9 But let the brother of low degree glory in his high estate: 10 and the rich, in that he is made low: because as the flower

---

a Or, *Jacob*   *b* Gr. *bondservant*.   *c* Gr. *wisheth joy*.   *d* Or, *trials*   *e* Or, *stedfastness*

f Or, *that a doubleminded man, unstable in all his ways, shall receive anything of the Lord*

CHAPTER 1

1. *A servant of God and of the Lord Jesus Christ.* The term servant is used not in any sense of servitude, but rather as expressing consecrated devotion, springing from the full acceptance of the gospel as the truth. *Dispersion.* The body of the Jews then scattered throughout the Roman Empire.

2. *Count it all joy.* The true view of temptation or trial is that it is an opportunity to gain new strength through overcoming.

3. *The proving of your faith worketh patience.* Here proving has the sense of testing; and patience implies not a mere wilted submission, but the cheerful turning to good account of every untoward circumstance and event.

4. *Perfect and entire.* The work of patience is toward completeness, as expressed in a well-rounded character.

5. *Wisdom.* The wisdom here designated is the understanding of the things of God, as distinguished from that wisdom of the world which is foolishness with God (1 Cor. 3.19). *And upbraideth not.* The text here expresses the great long-suffering of God whose giving must be limited by the degree of desire and willingness to accept on the part of those who ask.

6. *Nothing doubting.* Doubt, either as to the value of the gift or the power of the Giver, must weaken faith.

9. *Glory in his high estate.* The condition of freedom from the distractions of great possessions (Matt. 19.22), becomes a high estate through singleness of heart and purpose.

10. *And the rich, in that he is made low.* The empty vessel is pre-

of the grass he shall pass away. 11 For the sun ariseth with the scorching wind, and withereth the grass; and the flower thereof falleth, and the grace of the fashion of it perisheth: so also shall the rich man fade away in his goings.

12 Blessed is the man that endureth temptation; for when he hath been approved, he shall receive the crown of life, which *the Lord* promised to them that love him. 13 Let no man say when he is tempted, I am tempted [g]of God; for God [h]cannot be tempted with [i]evil, and he himself tempteth no man: 14 but each man is [k]tempted, when he is drawn away by his own lust, and enticed. 15 Then the lust, when it hath conceived, beareth sin: and the sin, when it is fullgrown, bringeth forth death. 16 Be not deceived, my beloved brethren. 17 Every good [l]gift and every perfect gift is from above, coming down from the Father of lights, with whom can be no variation, neither shadow that is cast by turning. 18 Of his own will he brought us forth by the word of truth, that we should be a kind of firstfruits of his creatures.

19 [m]Ye know *this*, my beloved brethren. But let every man be swift to hear, slow to speak, slow to wrath: 20 for the wrath of man worketh not the righteousness of God. 21 Wherefore putting away all filthiness and overflowing of [n]wickedness, receive with meekness the [o]implanted word, which is able to save your souls. 22 But be ye doers of the word, and not hearers only, deluding your own selves. 23 For if any one is a hearer of the word and not a doer, he is like unto a man beholding [p]his natural face in a mirror: 24 for he beholdeth himself, and goeth away, and straightway forgetteth what manner of man he was. 25 But

---

g Gr. *from.* h Or, *is untried in evil* i Gr. *evil things.* k Or, *tempted by his own lust, being drawn away* by it, *and enticed*

l Or, *giving* m Or, *Know ye* n Or, *malice* o Or, *inborn* p Gr. *the face of his birth.*

---

pared to receive the larger blessing.

11. *So also shall the rich man fade away in his goings.* The idea of possession cannot endure longer than the riches upon which it is based, and which are here compared to the grass that withereth. With the perception that his possessions are not enduring riches, the belief that he is a rich man fadeth away.

12. *The crown of life.* Life here is used in the same sense as in John 17.3: 'And this is life eternal, that they should know thee the only true God, and him whom thou didst send, *even* Jesus Christ.' The enduring of temptation advances the knowledge of God through the confirming of faith in His righteousness.

14. *Drawn away by his own lust.* The word lust has here its wider significance, of all desire toward sense gratification as used in 1 John 2.16, 17: 'For all that is in the world, the lust of the flesh and the lust of the eyes and the vainglory of life, is not of the Father, but is of the world. And the world passeth away and the lust thereof.'

17. *The Father of lights.* The source of all intelligence.

18. *A kind of firstfruits of his creatures.* In the old Jewish worship the firstfruits of the harvest were consecrated to God (Lev. 23. 10). Being brought forth by the word of truth, we are the first of God's creatures to know ourselves His children and voluntarily to consecrate ourselves the firstfruits of understanding.

25. *The law of liberty.* This dis-

he that looketh into the perfect law, the *law* of liberty, and *so* continueth, being not a hearer that forgetteth but a doer that worketh, this man shall be blessed in his doing. 26 If any man *q*thinketh himself to be religious, while he bridleth not his tongue but deceiveth his heart, this man's religion is vain. 27 Pure religion and undefiled before our God and Father is this, to visit the fatherless and widows in their affliction, *and* to keep oneself unspotted from the world.

2 My brethren, *a*hold not the faith of our Lord Je´sus Christ, *the Lord* of glory, with respect of persons. 2 For if there come into your *b*synagogue a man with a gold ring, in fine clothing, and there come in also a poor man in vile clothing; 3 and ye have regard to him that weareth the fine clothing, and say, Sit thou here in a good place; and ye say to the poor man, Stand thou there, or sit under my footstool; 4 *c*do ye not make distinctions *d*among yourselves, and become judges with evil thoughts? 5 Hearken, my beloved brethren; did not

God choose them that are poor as to the world *to be* rich in faith, and heirs of the kingdom which he promised to them that love him? 6 But ye have dishonored the poor man. Do not the rich oppress you, and themselves drag you before the judgment-seats? 7 Do not they blaspheme the honorable name *e*by which ye are called? 8 Howbeit if ye fulfil the royal law, according to the scripture, *f*Thou shalt love thy neighbor as thyself, ye do well: 9 but if ye have respect of persons, ye commit sin, being convicted by the law as transgressors. 10 For whosoever shall keep the whole law, and yet stumble in one *point*, he is become guilty of all. 11 For he that said, *g*Do not commit adultery, said also, Do not kill. Now if thou dost not commit adultery, but killest, thou art become a transgressor of the law. 12 So speak ye, and so do, as men that are to be judged by a law of liberty. 13 For judgment *is* without mercy to him that hath showed no mercy: mercy glorieth against judgment.

14 What doth it profit, my brethren, if a man say he hath

tinction is more clearly stated by Paul in Rom. 8.2: 'For the law of the Spirit of life in Christ Jesus made me free from the law of sin and death.'

CHAPTER 2

1. *The Lord of glory.* In the presence of the very Lord of glory, how utterly vain and foolish appear the honors conferred through respect of persons.

2. *A man with a gold ring.* This was a fashion borrowed from the luxurious Romans, and aping their vanity and self-importance.

5. *Poor as to the world.* The phrase means more than the mere accident of temporal poverty. It relates rather to indifference as to worldly possessions, and is qualified by the final words of the verse: 'them that love him.'

faith, but have not works? can that faith save him? 15 If a brother or sister be naked and in lack of daily food, 16 and one of you say unto them, Go in peace, be ye warmed and filled; and yet ye give them not the things needful to the body; what doth it profit? 17 Even so faith, if it have not works, is dead in itself. 18 *h*Yea, a man will say, Thou hast faith, and I have works: show me thy faith apart from *thy* works, and I by my works will show thee *my* faith. 19 Thou believest that *i*God is one; thou doest well: the demons also believe, and shudder. 20 But wilt thou know, O vain man, that faith apart from works is barren? 21 Was not Abraham our father justified by works, in that he offered up I'saac his son upon the altar? 22 *k*Thou seest that faith wrought with his works, and by works was faith made perfect; 23 and the scripture was fulfilled which saith, *l*And Abraham believed God, and it was reckoned unto him for righteousness; *m*and he was called the friend of God. 24 Ye see that by works a man is jus-

tified, and not only by faith. 25 And in like manner was not also Ra'hab the harlot justified by works, in that she received the messengers, and sent them out another way? 26 For as the body apart from the spirit is dead, even so faith apart from works is dead.

3 Be not many *of you* teachers, my brethren, knowing that we shall receive *a*heavier judgment. 2 For in many things we all stumble. If any stumbleth not in word, the same is a perfect man, able to bridle the whole body also. 3 Now if we put the horses' bridles into their mouths that they may obey us, we turn about their whole body also. 4 Behold, the ships also, though they are so great and are driven by rough winds, are yet turned about by a very small rudder, whither the impulse of the steersman willeth. 5 So the tongue also is a little member, and boasteth great things. Behold, *b*how much wood is kindled by how small a fire! 6 And the tongue is *c*a fire: *d*the world of iniquity among our members is the tongue, which defileth the

---

h Or, *But some one will say* *i* Some ancient authorities read *there is one God.* *k* Or, *Seest thou . . . perfect?* *l* Gen. xv. 6. *m* Is. xli. 8; 2 Chr. xx. 7.

---

16. *Be ye warmed and filled; and yet ye give them not the things needful.* This is a condemnation of the prayer of mere words, which stops short of the practical, effectual prayer expressed in deeds.

21. *Was not Abraham our father justified by works?* Compare Genesis 22.1–13.

25. *And in like manner was not also Rahab the harlot justified?* See Joshua 2.1–21; 6.22–25.

---

a Gr. *greater.* *b* Or, *how great a forest* *c* Or, *a fire, that world of iniquity: the tongue is among our members that which &c.* *d* Or, *that world of iniquity, the tongue, is among our members that which &c.*

CHAPTER 3

6. *Which defileth the whole body.* Compare the words of Jesus (Matt. 15.18–20): 'But the things which proceed out of the mouth come forth out of the heart; and they defile the man. For out of the heart come forth evil thoughts, murders, adulteries, fornications, thefts, false witness, railings: these are the things which defile the man.'

whole body, and setteth on fire the wheel of [e]nature, and is set on fire by [f]hell. 7 For every [g]kind of beasts and birds, of creeping things and things in the sea, is tamed, and hath been tamed [h]by [i]mankind: 8 but the tongue can no man tame; *it is* a restless evil, *it is* full of deadly poison. 9 Therewith bless we the Lord and Father; and therewith curse we men, who are made after the likeness of God: 10 out of the same mouth cometh forth blessing and cursing. My brethren, these things ought not so to be. 11 Doth the fountain send forth from the same opening sweet *water* and bitter? 12 can a fig tree, my brethren, yield olives, or a vine figs? neither *can* salt water yield sweet.

13 Who is wise and understanding among you? let him show by his good life his works in meekness of wisdom. 14 But if ye have bitter jealousy and faction in your heart, glory not and lie not against the truth. 15 This wisdom is not *a wisdom* that cometh down from above, but is earthly, [k]sensual, [l]devilish. 16 For where jealousy and faction are, there is confusion and every vile deed. 17 But the wisdom that is from above is first pure, then peaceable, gentle, easy to be entreated, full of mercy and good fruits, without [m]variance, without hypocrisy. 18 And the fruit of righteousness is sown in peace [n]for them that make peace.

4 Whence *come* wars and whence *come* fightings among you? *come they* not hence, *even* of your pleasures that war in your members? 2 Ye lust, and have not: ye kill, and [a]covet, and cannot obtain: ye fight and war; ye have not, because ye ask not. 3 Ye ask, and receive not, because ye ask amiss, that ye may spend *it* in your pleasures. 4 Ye [b]adulteresses, know ye not that the friendship of the world is enmity with God? Whosoever therefore would be a friend of the world maketh himself an enemy of God. 5 Or think ye that the scripture [c]speaketh in vain? [d]Doth the spirit which [e]he made to dwell in us long unto envying? 6 But he giveth [f]more grace. Wherefore *the scripture* saith, [g]God resisteth the proud, but giveth grace to the humble. 7 Be subject therefore unto God; but resist the devil, and he will flee from you. 8 Draw nigh to God, and he will draw nigh to you. Cleanse your hands, ye sinners; and purify your hearts, ye doubleminded. 9 Be afflicted, and mourn, and weep: let your laughter be turned to mourning,

---

e Or, *birth* *f* Gr. *Gehenna.* *g* Gr. *nature.* *h* Or, *unto* *i* Gr. *the human nature.* *k* Or, *natural* Or, *animal* *l* Gr. *demoniacal.* *m* Or, *doubtfulness* Or, *partiality* *n* Or, *by a* Gr. *are jealous.* *b* That is, *who break your marriage vow to God.* *c* Or, *saith in vain* *d* Or, *The Spirit which he made to*

dwell in us he yearneth for even unto jealous envy. Comp. Jer. 3.14; Hos. 2.19 f. Or, *That Spirit which he made to dwell in us yearneth for us even unto jealous envy.* *e* Some ancient authorities read *dwelleth in us.* *f* Gr. *a greater grace.* *g* Prov. iii. 34.

CHAPTER 4

2. *Ye kill, and covet.* The word 'kill' is to be taken in the sense of the hatred proceeding from envy, as in 1 John 3.15: 'whosoever hateth his brother is a murderer.'

and your joy to heaviness. 10 Humble yourselves in the sight of the Lord, and he shall exalt you.

11 Speak not one against another, brethren. He that speaketh against a brother, or judgeth his brother, speaketh against the law, and judgeth the law: but if thou judgest the law, thou art not a doer of the law, but a judge. 12 One *only* is the lawgiver and judge, *even* he who is able to save and to destroy: but who art thou that judgest thy neighbor?

13 Come now, ye that say, To-day or to-morrow we will go into this city, and spend a year there, and trade, and get gain: 14 whereas ye know not what shall be on the morrow. What is your life? For ye are a vapor that appeareth for a little time, and then vanisheth away. 15 *h*For that ye ought to say, If the Lord will, we shall both live, and do this or that. 16 But now ye glory in your vauntings: all such glorying is evil. 17 To him therefore that knoweth to do good, and doeth it not, to him it is sin.

5 Come now, ye rich, weep and howl for your miseries that are coming upon you. 2 Your riches are corrupted, and your garments are moth-eaten.

3 Your gold and your silver are rusted; and their rust shall be for a testimony *a*against you, and shall eat your flesh as fire. Ye have laid up your treasure in the last days. 4 Behold, the hire of the laborers who mowed your fields, which is of you kept back by fraud, crieth out: and the cries of them that reaped have entered into the ears of the Lord of Sa-ba'oth. 5 Ye have lived delicately on the earth, and taken your pleasure; ye have nourished your hearts in a day of slaughter. 6 Ye have condemned, ye have killed the righteous *one*; he doth not resist you.

7 Be patient therefore, brethren, until the *b*coming of the Lord. Behold, the husbandman waiteth for the precious fruit of the earth, being patient over it, until *c*it receive the early and latter rain. 8 Be ye also patient; establish your hearts: for the *b*coming of the Lord is at hand. 9 Murmur not, brethren, one against another, that ye be not judged: behold, the judge standeth before the doors. 10 Take, brethren, for an example of suffering and of patience, the prophets who spake in the name of the Lord. 11 Behold, we call them blessed that endured: ye have heard of the *d*patience of

---

h Gr. *Instead of your saying. a* Or, *unto* | *b* Gr. *presence. c* Or, *he d* Or, *endurance*

CHAPTER 5

3. *Your gold and your silver are rusted; and their rust shall be for a testimony against you.* The picture is drawn prophetically. The treasures of earth are described as already perished and their very corruption as evidence that they

were wrongly chosen—in that they were not of the 'perfect gifts from above.'

7. *Be patient therefore, brethren.* In this verse James turns from his accusation of the rich to exhort his fellow Christians to patience even in the face of evil conditions, which the coming of the Lord will change.

Job, and have seen the end of the Lord, how that the Lord is full of pity, and merciful.

12 But above all things, my brethren, swear not, neither by the heaven, nor by the earth, nor by any other oath: but *let your yea be yea, and your nay, nay; that ye fall not under judgment.

13 Is any among you suffering? let him pray. Is any cheerful? let him sing praise. 14 Is any among you sick? let him call for the elders of the church; and let them pray over him, *anointing him with oil in the name of the Lord: 15 and the prayer of faith shall save him that is sick, and the Lord shall raise him up; and if he have committed sins, it shall be forgiven him. 16 Con-

fess therefore your sins one to another, and pray one for another, that ye may be healed. The supplication of a righteous man availeth much in its working. 17 E-li′jah was a man of like *passions with us, and he prayed *fervently that it might not rain; and it rained not on the earth for three years and six months. 18 And he prayed again; and the heaven gave rain, and the earth brought forth her fruit.

19 My brethren, if any among you err from the truth, and one convert him; 20 *let him know, that he who converteth a sinner from the error of his way shall save a soul from death, and shall cover a multitude of sins.

---

e Or, *let yours be the yea, yea, and the nay, nay* Comp. Mt. 5.37.   *f* Or, *having*

anointed   *g* Or, *nature*   *h* Gr. *with prayer.*
i Some ancient authorities read *know ye.*

---

12. *But above all things, my brethren, swear not.* The injunction here is against a habit prevailing among the Jews of attempting to establish truth, or the appearance of truth, by an oath. See Matt. 23.16–22; Mark 14.71. The indwelling Spirit of truth (1 John 4.6) is the only and the sufficient source of right speaking.

14. *Anointing him with oil, in the name of the Lord.* The use of oil in ancient times was very common as a remedy in sickness.

16. *Pray one for another, that ye may be healed.* Lest there be any doubt as to the answering of the prayer of the righteous man, James cites the power of Elijah (1 Kings 17.1; 18.1, 42–45).

THE FIRST EPISTLE OF PETER

INTRODUCTION BY PROFESSOR M. B. RIDDLE, D.D., LL.D.

The Apostle Peter is not mentioned in the Acts after the council at Jerusalem (50 A.D.), but Gal. 2.11 refers to a subsequent visit by him to Antioch. His history after that incident has been overlaid with legends. It is impossible that he spent twenty-five years in Rome, though it is probable that his last years were passed there, and that he there suffered martyrdom. It is less probable that he and Paul were put to death at the same time. If "Babylon" (in 1 Pet. 5.13) is to be taken literally, that city was the scene of his labor during some part of the interval between the visit to Antioch and his arrival in Rome. Many hold that the term is a mystical name for the latter city, which is possible, but scarcely probable. Paul makes no reference to Peter's presence there.

Place of Writing, and Other Circumstances.—As indicated above, either Babylon or Rome was the *place* of writing, more probably the former. Mark was with the apostle when he wrote (5.13); but this fact does not decide in favor of Rome, since Mark was absent from that city at some time between 62 and 66 A.D. (*cf.* Col. 4.10 and 2 Tim. 4.11), having gone eastward. He might have been with Peter during this journey, or at an earlier period, before either visited Rome.

The *date* of the epistle is uncertain. Some place it in 61 A.D., before Paul's Roman imprisonment; others, in 63 or 64 A.D., after the release of that apostle. The probabilities are slightly in favor of the latter date. It was addressed to Christians in certain regions of Asia Minor (1.1). Strictly interpreted, the language points to Jewish Christians, but it is now generally held that all Christians are included in the address.

The *occasion* of the epistle was impending trial, probably not State persecution, but social and personal opposition and reproach. Hence the tone of consolation and encouragement, even in the exhortations. As often remarked, the keynote is "hope."

Contents.—The epistle accords with the character of the apostle. The style and language present resemblances to his speeches, as recorded in the Acts. Here also, as in the Epistle of James, the thoughts are linked together, without any obvious unity.

Summary.—Ch. 1. Address and greeting (ver. 1, 2); thanks to God for the living hope from the resurrection of Christ, to strengthen them in trial through the salvation foretold by prophets and now preached to them (ver. 3-12); exhortations to holy living, in view of the cost of redemption and the fact of regeneration (ver. 13-25).

THE FIRST EPISTLE OF PETER

Ch. 2. Patient submission to trials and wrongs, enforced by the example of Christ.

Ch. 3. Wives and husbands to live in obedience and holiness (ver. 1-7); loving and forbearing fellowship among all, from their relation to Christ, who suffered for us (ver. 8-22).

Ch. 4. For the same reason past sins should be forsaken, and lives of holiness be lived to the glory of God through Christ (ver. 1-11); fiery trials are for their profit, and may become an occasion of rejoicing (ver. 12-19).

Ch. 5. Exhortation to the elders (ver. 1-4); admonition to the younger to submit to the elder (ver. 5); all are warned to be humble, to be sober and watchful (ver. 6-10). Concluding doxology (ver. 11), followed by a reference to Silvanus, the bearer of the letter (ver. 12), salutations, and a brief benediction (ver. 13, 14).

THE FIRST EPISTLE OF

PETER

1 Peter, an apostle of Je′sus Christ, to the elect who are sojourners of the Dispersion in Pon′tus, Ga-la′ti-a, Cap-pa-do′-ci-a, A′si-a, and Bi-thyn′i-a, 2 according to the foreknowledge of God the Father, in sanctifica-

tion of the Spirit, unto obedience and sprinkling of the blood of Je′sus Christ: Grace to you and peace be multiplied.

3 Blessed *be* ᵃthe God and Father of our Lord Je′sus Christ,

---

a Or, *God and the Father* See Rom. 15.6 marg.

CHAPTER 1

1. *Elect.* Christians, or saints (Acts 9.13), because chosen or called out from the world. See Mt. 24.22, 24; Rom. 8.33; 2 Tim. 2.10. *Sojourners of the Dispersion.* An expression applied originally to Jews outside of Palestine, but in this passage referring to Christians, whether Jews or Gentiles, who had become strangers in every land. *Pontus.* A Roman province of Asia Minor, lying along the coast of the Black Sea. *Galatia.* A Roman province in the central part of Asia Minor. *Cappadocia.* An inland Roman province of Asia Minor, lying east of Galatia and south of Pontus. *Asia.* The Roman province of that name, governed by a proconsul. It lay along the coast of the Mediterranean Sea and of the Ægean Sea, and included the districts of Mysia, Lydia and Caria, together with the greater part of Phrygia. Asia contained the cities of Ephesus, Smyrna and Pergamos; and in it were the 'seven churches' mentioned in Rev. 1.4. *Bithynia.* A Roman province lying along the coast of the Black Sea, and west of Pontus.

2. *According to the foreknowledge of God the Father.* These words qualify 'elect' in ver. 1. The election or choice of the 'sojourners of the Dis-

persion' was according to the foreknowledge of God, to Whom all the events of human history, and of His universe, are known from eternity. Also Peter declared on the day of Pentecost that Jesus was 'delivered up by the determinate counsel and foreknowledge of God' (Acts 2.23). There is nothing to show that the word 'foreknowledge' had any doubtful or forbidding meaning to the early Christians, nor can it have such meaning in view of the fact that God is love (1 Jn. 4.8). The foreknowledge of God is that of the Father Whose purpose from the beginning is to love and have mercy upon mankind. *In sanctification of the Spirit.* Set apart or consecrated by the Holy Spirit. See note on Heb. 10.10. Viewed with reference to perfect holiness, sanctification is a daily growth or process. We are transformed by the renewing of our minds (Rom. 12.2), which involves obedience, to Christ's commands, complete self-surrender and the indwelling of the Holy Spirit. *Sprinkling of the blood of Jesus Christ.* This refers to the voluntary sacrifice of Jesus Christ on the cross, where his blood was shed for the remission of sins (Heb. 12.24).

3. *Begat us again unto a living hope by the resurrection.* Regenerated us in the heart by the completed work of

580

who according to his great mercy begat us again unto a living hope by the resurrection of Je′sus Christ from the dead, 4 unto an inheritance incorruptible, and undefiled, and that fadeth not away, reserved in heaven for you, 5 who by the power of God are guarded through faith unto a salvation ready to be revealed in the last time. 6 Wherein ye greatly rejoice, though now for a little while, if need be, ye have been put to grief in manifold *b*trials, 7 that the proof of your faith, *being* more precious than gold that perisheth though it is proved by fire, may be found unto praise and glory and honor at the revelation of Je′sus Christ: 8 whom not having seen ye love; on whom, though now ye see him

not, yet believing, ye rejoice greatly with joy unspeakable and *c*full of glory: 9 receiving the end of your faith, *even* the salvation of *your* souls. 10 Concerning which salvation the prophets sought and searched diligently, who prophesied of the grace that *should come* unto you: 11 searching what *time* or what manner of time the Spirit of Christ which was in them did point unto, when it testified beforehand the sufferings *d*of Christ, and the glories that should follow them. 12 To whom it was revealed, that not unto themselves, but unto you, did they minister these things, which now have been announced unto you through them that *e*preached the gospel unto you

---

Christ. It is declared that whosoever believeth that Jesus is the Christ is begotten of God (1 Jn. 5.1). Paul's definition of the gospel is, 'that Christ died for our sins according to the scriptures; and that he was buried; and that he hath been raised on the third day according to the scriptures' (1 Cor. 15.3, 4). The resurrection of Jesus Christ is the basic fact of the gospel, which is the seed sown. See 1 Pet. 1.23.

5. *Who by the power of God are guarded through faith.* See notes on Heb. 11.1. *Unto a salvation ready to be revealed in the last time.* 'Salvation' probably includes two ideas: (1) it is that salvation on which Paul had not yet laid hold (Phil. 3.12; Rom. 13.11; 1 Thess. 5.8), a complete victory over the lower self or the flesh; (2) a deliverance from trial, persecution and sorrow.

7. *Gold that perisheth though it is proved by fire.* Gold is purified by fire until the dross is burned out; Christians are thus purified by suffering and trials.

10. *Salvation the prophets sought.* The Old Testament predictions of

deliverance, glory and prosperity for Israel as found in the prophets are shown in the New Testament to refer to the salvation and blessedness of believers. *Grace that should come unto you.* The salvation through Jesus Christ.

11. *What time or what manner of time.* That is, when Christ should appear and suffer. *The Spirit of Christ which was in them.* The Holy Spirit. *When it testified beforehand the sufferings of Christ.* See Isa. 53; Mt. 8.17; 1 Pet. 2.22–24.

12. *To whom it was revealed,* etc. The prophets looked for a Messiah —a suffering Servant—and deliverance and prosperity; but they did not understand how these things were to come to pass. It remained for Jesus and his apostles to show that Jesus and his kingdom were the fulfilment of these prophecies. Thus they did not minister unto themselves but unto coming ages, even unto the present time. One of the strongest arguments for the divinity of Jesus is that he fulfilled these prophecies spoken centuries before his coming. Peter here shows the

[f]by the Holy Spirit sent forth from heaven; which things angels desire to look into.

13 Wherefore girding up the loins of your mind, be sober and set your hope perfectly on the grace that [g]is to be brought unto you at the revelation of Je'sus Christ; 14 as children of obedience, not fashioning yourselves according to your former lusts in *the time of* your ignorance: 15 but [h]like as he who called you is holy, be ye yourselves also holy in all manner of living; 16 because it is written, [i]Ye shall be holy; for I am holy. 17 And if ye call on him as Father, who without respect of persons judgeth according to each man's work, pass the time of your sojourning in fear: 18 knowing that ye were redeemed, not with corruptible things, with silver or gold, from your vain manner of life handed down from your fathers; 19 but with precious blood, as of a lamb without blemish and without spot, *even*

the blood of Christ: 20 who was foreknown indeed before the foundation of the world, but was manifested at the end of the times for your sake, 21 who through him are believers in God, that raised him from the dead, and gave him glory; so that your faith and hope might be in God. 22 Seeing ye have purified your souls in your obedience to the truth unto unfeigned love of the brethren, love one another [k]from the heart fervently: 23 having been begotten again, not of corruptible seed, but of incorruptible, through the word of [l]God, which liveth and abideth. 24 For,

[m]All flesh is as grass,
And all the glory thereof as
    the flower of grass.
The grass withereth, and the
    flower falleth:
25 But the [n]word of the Lord
    abideth for ever.
And this is the [n]word of good tidings which was [o]preached unto you.

---

f Gr. *in.*   g Gr. *is being brought.*   h Or, *like the Holy One who called you*   i Lev. xi. 44 f.; xix 2; xx. 7.   k Many ancient authorities read *from a clean heart.*   Comp.

1 Tim. 1.5.   l Or, *God who liveth*   Comp. Dan. 6.26.   m Is. xl. 6 ff.   n Gr. *saying.* o See ver. 12.

---

advantages which Christians had over the prophets of former ages. *Which things.* The things of which Peter had just written—the suffering and death of Jesus, the salvation of Jew and Gentile, etc.

13. *The revelation of Jesus Christ.* At his final advent, or, the continual revealing or unveiling of the character and glory of Jesus.

18. *Vain manner of life handed down from your fathers.* This life was a consequence of the vanity of an understanding darkened by ignorance and the hardening of the heart for many generations (Eph. 4.18).

19. *Lamb without blemish.* The

reference here is to the Paschal lamb whose blood was sprinkled upon the door posts as a testimony of obedience to the command of Jehovah, and thus a protection from the death which fell upon the Egyptians (Ex. 12.5).

20. *Who was foreknown,* etc. See notes on ch. 1.2. *At the end of the times.* The former times are now at an end because of the 'revelation of Jesus Christ' (ver. 13). 'The old times are passed away' (2 Cor. 5. 17).

22. *Unfeigned.* Genuine; without pretense. *The truth.* The example and teaching of Jesus and his apostles.

2
Putting away therefore all [a]wickedness, and all guile, and hypocrisies, and envies, and all evil speakings, 2 as newborn babes, long for the [b]spiritual milk which is without guile, that ye may grow thereby unto salvation; 3 if ye have tasted that the Lord is gracious: 4 unto whom coming, a living stone, rejected indeed of men, but with God elect, [c]precious, 5 ye also, as living stones, are built up [d]a spiritual house, to be a holy priesthood, to offer up spiritual sacrifices, acceptable to God through Je′sus Christ. 6 Because it is contained in [e]scripture,

[f]Behold, I lay in Zi′on a chief corner stone, elect, [c]precious:
And he that believeth on [g]him shall not be put to shame.

7 [h]For you therefore that believe is the [i]preciousness: but for such as disbelieve,
[k]The stone which the builders rejected,

The same was made the head of the corner;
8 and,
[l]A stone of stumbling, and a rock of offence;
[m]for they [n]stumble at the word, being disobedient: whereunto also they were appointed. 9 But ye are an elect race, a royal priesthood, a holy nation, a people for God's own possession, that ye may show forth the excellencies of him who called you out of darkness into his marvellous light: 10 who in time past were no people, but now are the people of God: who had not obtained mercy, but now have obtained mercy.

11 Beloved, I beseech you as sojourners and pilgrims, to abstain from fleshly lusts, which war against the soul; 12 having your behavior seemly among the Gen′tiles; that, wherein they speak against you as evil-doers, they may by your good works, which they behold, glorify God in the day of visitation.

---

a Or, *malice* 1 Cor. 14.20. b Gr. *belonging to the reason.* Comp. Rom. 12.1. c Or, *honorable* d Or, *a spiritual house for a holy priesthood* e Or, *a scripture* f Is. xxviii. 16. g Or, *it* h Or, *In your sight* i Or, *honor* k Ps. cxviii. 22. l Is. viii. 14. m Gr. *who.* n Or, *stumble, being disobedient to the word*

CHAPTER 2

2. *Spiritual milk.* In the explanatory rendering of the word here translated 'spiritual' the meaning is shown to be 'intellectual'; that is, appealing to the understanding. *Unto salvation.* See ch.1.5 and note thereon.

4. *Living stone.* In Peter's defence before the chief priests at Jerusalem (Acts 4.5–12) he spoke of Christ as 'the stone which was set at nought of you, the builders,' in the construction of the Jewish creed. See also Mt. 21.42; Eph. 2.20–22.

7. *For such as disbelieve,* etc. In further illustration of the contrast in this verse between those who accept and those who reject the gospel, see 2 Cor. 2.15, 16.

8. *Stumble at the word, being disobedient.* 'Word' here signifies the truth as it is in Christ. Disobedience is practically a denial of the truth, which remains unchangeable. It must humble the proud who are its enemies (Prov. 16.18).

10. *Who in time past were no people.* The Christians for whom the epistle is written are here reminded that they were once like Israel in the time of its alienation from God; or like Gentiles before they accepted Christ. See Hos. 1.6–9; 2.1, 23.

13 Be subject to every [o]ordi-
nance of man for the Lord's sake:
whether to the king, as supreme;
14 or unto governors, as sent [p]by
him for vengeance on evil-doers
and for praise to them that do
well. 15 For so is the will of
God, that by well-doing ye
should put to silence the ignorance of foolish men: 16 as free,
and not [q]using your freedom for
a cloak of [r]wickedness, but as
bondservants of God. 17 Honor
all men. Love the brotherhood.
Fear God. Honor the king.

18 [s]Servants, *be* in subjection
to your masters with all fear;
not only to the good and gentle,
but also to the froward. 19 For
this is [t]acceptable, if for conscience [u]toward God a man endureth griefs, suffering wrongfully. 20 For what glory is it, if,
when ye sin, and are buffeted
for it, ye shall take it patiently?
but if, when ye do well, and
suffer *for it*, ye shall take it
patiently, this is [t]acceptable
with God. 21 For hereunto
were ye called: because Christ
also suffered for you, leaving
you an example, that ye should
follow his steps: 22 who did no
sin, neither was guile found in
his mouth: 23 who, when he was
reviled, reviled not again; when
he suffered, threatened not; but
committed [v]*himself* to him that
judgeth righteously: 24 who his
own self [x]bare our sins in his
body upon the tree, that we,
having died unto sins, might
live unto righteousness; by
whose [y]stripes ye were healed.
25 For ye were going astray like
sheep; but are now returned
unto the Shepherd and [z]Bishop
of your souls.

3 In like manner, ye wives,
be in subjection to your own
husbands; that, even if any
obey not the word, they may
without the word be gained by
the [a]behavior of their wives; 2
beholding your chaste [a]behavior
coupled with fear. 3 Whose
adorning let it not be the outward adorning of braiding the
hair, and of wearing jewels of
gold, or of putting on apparel;

o Gr. *creation.* *p* Gr. *through.* *q* Gr. *having.* *r* Or, *malice* 1 Cor. 14.20. *s* Gr. *Household-servants.* *t* Gr. *grace.*

u Gr. *of.* *v* Or, his cause *x* Or, *carried up . . . to the tree* Comp. Col. 2:14; 1 Macc. 4.53 (Gr.). *y* Gr. *bruise.* *z* Or, *Overseer* *a* Or, *manner of life* ver. 16.

16. *As free.* That is, free from the law of Moses and the tradition of the elders, because not under the old covenant. Peter cautioned them not to use their freedom as license, since they were under the obligation of the higher law of loyalty to their master.

18. *With all fear.* Here fear does not mean terror, but deep anxiety lest in some respect service might fall short of a perfect fulfilment of each duty.

24. *Bare our sins in his body upon the tree.* This refers to the death of Jesus on the cross for the sins of the world. See Col. 1.21, 22; Isa. 53.12; Heb. 9.28. *Having died unto sins.* The phrase signifies the passing into a new life (Jn. 5.24; Rom. 6.2, 10; 1 Jn. 3.14).

CHAPTER 3

2. *Coupled with fear.* See note on ch. 2.18.

3. *Braiding the hair*, etc. This was a warning against the extravagant fashions in hair-dressing and decoration with costly jewels, prevailing among the Greeks and Romans at that period; also a reminder that the true adornment is from within.

4 but *let it be* the hidden man of the heart, in the incorruptible *apparel* of a meek and quiet spirit, which is in the sight of God of great price. 5 For after this manner aforetime the holy women also, who hoped in God, adorned themselves, being in subjection to their own *b*husbands: 6 as Sarah obeyed Abraham, calling him lord: whose children ye now are, if ye do well, and are not *c*put in fear by any terror.

7 Ye husbands, in like manner, dwell with *your wives* according to knowledge, giving honor *d*unto the woman, as unto the weaker vessel, as being also joint-heirs of the grace of life; to the end that your prayers be not hindered.

8 Finally, *be* ye all likeminded, *e*compassionate, loving as brethren, tenderhearted, humbleminded: 9 not rendering evil for evil, or reviling for reviling; but contrariwise blessing; for hereunto were ye called, that ye should inherit a blessing. 10 For,

*f*He that would love life,
And see good days,
Let him refrain his tongue from evil,

And his lips that they speak no guile:
11 And let him turn away from evil, and do good;
Let him seek peace, and pursue it.
12 For the eyes of the Lord are upon the righteous,
And his ears unto their supplication:
But the face of the Lord is upon them that do evil.

13 And who is he that will harm you, if ye be zealous of that which is good? 14 But even if ye should suffer for righteousness' sake, blessed *are ye*: and fear not their fear, neither be troubled; 15 but sanctify in your hearts Christ as Lord: *being* ready always to give answer to every man that asketh you a reason concerning the hope that is in you, yet with meekness and fear: 16 having a good conscience; that, wherein ye are spoken against, they may be put to shame who revile your good manner of life in Christ. 17 For it is better, if the will of God should so will, that ye suffer for well-doing than for evil-doing. 18 Because Christ also *g*suffered for sins once, the righteous for the unrighteous,

---

b Or. *husbands (as Sarah . . . ye are become), doing well, and not being afraid c* Or. *afraid with* d Gr. *unto the female vessel,*

as weaker. e Gr. *sympathetic.* f Ps. xxxiv. 12 ff. *g* Many ancient authorities read *died.*

---

4. *Meek and quiet spirit.* This implies meekness as toward God, the fountain of all knowledge; and perfect calmness in that knowledge, as toward men.

7. *That your prayers be not hindered.* Lest your approach to God in prayer lack humility and prove unacceptable by reason of your overbearing conduct to those who are weaker than you.

15. *Ready always to give answer.* This is an admonition toward understanding; something more than blind faith was required. *With meekness and fear.* The attitude here urged by the apostle is one devoid of boastfulness, and at the same time guarded by an anxious fear lest in the smallest particular we fail to meet fully the situation.

that he might bring us to God; being put to death in the flesh, but made alive in the spirit; 19 in which also he went and preached unto the spirits in prison, 20 that aforetime were disobedient, when the long-suffering of God waited in the days of Noah, while the ark was a preparing, *h*wherein few, that is, eight souls, were saved through water: 21 which also *i*after a true likeness doth now save you, *even* baptism, not the putting away of the filth of the flesh, but the *k*interrogation of a good conscience toward God, through the resurrection of Je'-sus Christ; 22 who is on the right hand of God, having gone into heaven; angels and authorities and powers being made subject unto him.

4 Forasmuch then as Christ suffered in the flesh, arm ye yourselves also with the same *a*mind; for he that hath suffered in the flesh hath ceased *b*from sin; 2 that *c*ye no longer should live the rest of your time in the flesh to the lusts of men, but to the will of God. 3 For the time past may suffice to have wrought the desire of the Gen'tiles, and to have walked in lasciviousness, lusts, winebibbings, revellings, carousings, and abominable idolatries: 4 wherein they think it strange that ye run not with *them* into the same *d*excess of

---

h Or, *into which few, that is, eight souls, were brought safely through water*   *i* Or, *in the antitype*   *k* Or, *inquiry* Or, *appeal*

a Or, *thought*   *b* Some ancient authorities read *unto sins.*   *c* Or, *he no longer . . . his time*   *d* Or, *flood*

19, 20. *In which also he went and preached,* etc. The interpretation of these two verses depends on whether the word 'spirit' in ver. 18 refers to the Holy Spirit, or to the eternal element in man which Jesus shared in his human nature. There are several interpretations, of which the two most important are: (1) that Christ actually descended into Hades and preached to the people who had lived in the days of Noah but were now in Hades; (2) that the Spirit of Christ preached through Noah to those who lived in Noah's time but who were in prison at the time of the writing of this epistle. Commentators differ widely as to the correct interpretation.

21. *Doth now save you, even baptism.* Noah's experience in the flood is made a type of baptism. Through faith Noah obeyed God and was saved when others were lost. Some would interpret this experience as being typical of the symbolism of baptism, while others would interpret it as meaning that we are actually saved through baptism. The verse must be interpreted in connection with other passages of Scripture. *Not the putting away,* etc. The interpretation of this passage is unusually difficult. What is the first question that a newly made believer asks? Paul asked, What shall I do, Lord? (Acts 22.10). The answer to this question is, Surrender yourself to Christ; become dead to the world and the old life. Baptism is a symbol of this surrender; it is an act of obedience. Peter emphasizes this by showing the difference between Christian baptism and the Jewish washings. The latter were for the removal of outward impurities; Christian baptism is a means ordained of God through which we testify to our faith in the resurrection (Rom. 6.2–11).

CHAPTER 4

1. *With the same mind.* Most probably this means, Look on suffering as Christ did, who was made perfect through suffering (Heb. 2. 10). *He that hath suffered in the flesh hath ceased from sin.* This teaches the moral value of suffering, in that those who have fellowship with Christ's suffering are weaned from the love of sin.

riot, speaking evil of *you*: 5 who shall give account to him that is ready to judge the living and the dead. 6 For unto this end *e*was the gospel preached even to the dead, that they might be judged indeed according to men in the flesh, but live according to God in the spirit.

7 But the end of all things is at hand: be ye therefore of sound mind, and be sober unto *f*prayer: 8 above all things being fervent in your love among yourselves; for love covereth a multitude of sins: 9 using hospitality one to another without murmuring: 10 according as each hath received a gift, ministering it among yourselves, as good stewards of the manifold grace of God; 11 if any man speaketh, *speaking* as it were oracles of God; if any man ministereth, *ministering* as of the strength which God supplieth: that in all things God may be glorified through Je'sus Christ, whose is the glory and the dominion *g*for ever and ever. A-men'.

12 Beloved, think it not strange concerning the fiery trial among you, which cometh upon you to prove you, as though a strange thing happened unto you: 13 but insomuch as ye are partakers of Christ's sufferings, rejoice; that at the revelation of his glory also ye may rejoice with exceeding joy. 14 If ye are reproached *h*for the name of Christ, blessed *are ye*; because the *Spirit* of glory and the Spirit of God resteth upon you. 15 For let none of you suffer as a murderer, or a thief, or an evil-doer, or as a meddler in other men's matters: 16 but if *a man suffer* as a Chris'tian, let him not be ashamed; but let him glorify God in this name. 17 For the time *is come* for judgment to begin at the house of God: and if *it begin* first at us, what *shall be* the end of them that obey not the *i*gospel of God? 18 And if the righteous is scarcely saved, where shall the ungodly and sinner appear? 19 Wherefore let them also that suffer according to the will of God commit their souls in well-doing unto a faithful Creator.

5 The elders therefore among you I exhort, who am a fellow-elder, and a witness of the sufferings of Christ, who am also a partaker of the glory that shall be revealed: 2 Tend the flock of God which is among you,

---

e Or, *were the good tidings preached* *f* Gr. *prayers.* *g* Gr. *unto the ages of the ages.* *h* Gr. *in.* *i* Gr. *good tidings.* See Mt. 4.23 marg.

---

7. *The end of all things is at hand.* This refers to the second coming of Christ.

10. *A gift.* Probably some gift of the Spirit. See 1 Cor. 12.4–10.

12. *The fiery trial.* Imminent persecution because of their faith in Christ.

17. *For judgment to begin at the house of God.* The sufferings of per-

secuted Christians were the beginning of judgment.

CHAPTER 5

2. *Nor yet for filthy lucre.* This injunction implies that even in the earliest days it was the custom with some of the elders to demand, or at least to accept, money in payment for such services as they rendered to the other brethren.

*exercising the oversight, not of constraint, but willingly, *b*according to *the will of* God; nor yet for filthy lucre, but of a ready mind; 3 neither as lording it over the charge allotted to you, but making yourselves ensamples to the flock. 4 And when the chief Shepherd shall be manifested, ye shall receive the crown of glory that fadeth not away. 5 *c*Likewise, ye younger, be subject unto the elder. Yea, all of you gird yourselves with humility, to serve one another: for God resisteth the proud, but giveth grace to the humble. 6 Humble yourselves therefore under the mighty hand of God, that he may exalt you in due time; 7 casting all your anxiety upon him, because he careth for you. 8 Be sober, be watchful: your adversary the devil, as a roaring lion, walketh about, seeking whom he may devour: 9 whom withstand stedfast in *d*your faith, knowing that the same sufferings are *e*accomplished in your *f*brethren who are in the world. 10 And the God of all grace, who called you unto his eternal glory in Christ, after that ye have suffered a little while, shall himself *g*perfect, establish, strengthen*h* you. 11 To him *be* the dominion *i*for ever and ever. A-men′.

12 By Sil-va′nus, *k*our faithful brother, as I account *him*, I have written unto you briefly, exhorting, and testifying that this is the true grace of God: stand ye fast therein. 13 *l*She that is in Bab′y-lon, elect together with *you*, saluteth you; and *so doth* Mark my son. 14 Salute one another with a kiss of love.

Peace be unto you all that are in Christ.

---

a Some ancient authorities omit *exercising the oversight.* *b* Some ancient authorities omit *according to* the will of God. *c* Or, *Likewise . . . elder; yea, all of you one to another. Gird yourselves with humil-*ity *d* Or, *the* *e* Gr. *being accomplished.* *f* Gr. *brotherhood.* *g* Or, *restore* *h* Many ancient authorities add *settle.* *i* Gr. *unto the ages of the ages.* *k* Gr. *the.* *l* That is, The church, or, The sister.

---

12. *Silvanus.* It is generally accepted that this was Silas, the companion of Paul in some of his journeyings, and his fellow-prisoner at Philippi (Acts 16.25).

13. *Mark my son.* The Mark here mentioned is believed to be the 'John whose surname was Mark' (Acts 12.12), the writer of the second gospel narrative.

THE SECOND EPISTLE OF PETER

INTRODUCTION BY PROFESSOR M. B. RIDDLE, D.D., LL.D.

The Genuineness of the Epistle.—The early evidence from Christian writers in support of this epistle is not so strong as in the case of most of the New Testament books. But, as it claims to be written by the "apostle" Peter, it must be regarded as genuine, or as a wilful forgery. Internal evidence disproves the latter view. It differs but slightly from the first epistle in style and language, and these slight differences can be accounted for from its purpose. The superiority to all Christian writings of the post-apostolic age is evident. A recent discovery of parts of two apocryphal books attributed to Peter shows what inferior literature the earliest forgers produced.

Two objections have been raised—that the second chapter closely resembles the Epistle of Jude; and that the epistles of Paul are referred to (3.15, 16). But even if this epistle is dependent on that of Jude, this does not disprove that Peter wrote it. Nor does the reference to Paul's epistles involve a date later than the apostolic age. It is probable that this epistle was written just before the death of the apostle (1. 13-15), about the same time as 2 Timothy (66 and 68 A.D.).

Purpose.—Apparently addressed to the same readers as the first epistle, this one has a different purpose—*viz.* to warn against teachers of error, and to enjoin an advance in knowledge as well as in holiness. The false teachers cannot be identified with those of the second century, which is another proof that Peter wrote the epistle.

Contents.—Ch. 1. A direct exhortation to advance in life and godliness (ver. 1-11); a reminder by the apostle, in view of his approaching death, that he has borne witness to the truth, with special reference to the transfiguration, which he had seen, and to prophecies thus fulfilled (ver. 12-21).

Ch. 2. Severe warnings against false teachers, their character described, their certain destruction illustrated by Old Testament examples.

Ch. 3. A reference to the previous prediction of such errors (ver. 1-7); a reminder that God's delay in judgment is not to be measured by our standard of years (ver. 8, 9); a description of the final destruction which will usher in "new heavens and a new earth" (ver. 10-13); admonition to prepare for this, since God is long-suffering in His delay, even as Paul had written, though his language had been wilfully misunderstood (ver. 14-16). Final warning and exhortation, summing up the epistle, with a brief doxology (ver. 17, 18).

THE SECOND EPISTLE OF

PETER

1 [a]Si'mon Peter, a [b]servant and apostle of Je'sus Christ, to them that have obtained [c]a like precious faith with us in the righteousness of [d]our God and *the* Saviour Je'sus Christ: 2 Grace to you and peace be multiplied in the knowledge of God and of Je'sus our Lord; 3 seeing that his divine power hath granted unto us all things that pertain unto life and godliness, through the knowledge of him that called us [e]by his own glory and virtue; 4 whereby he hath granted unto us his precious and exceeding great promises; that through these ye may become partakers of [f]the divine nature, having escaped from the corruption that is in the world by lust. 5 Yea, and for this very cause adding on your part all diligence, in your faith supply virtue; and in *your* virtue knowledge; 6 and in *your* knowledge self-control; and in *your* self-control [g]patience; and in *your* [g]patience godliness; 7 and in *your* godliness [h]brotherly kindness; and in *your* [h]brotherly kindness love. 8 For if these things are yours and abound, they make you to be not idle nor unfruitful unto the knowledge of our Lord Je'sus Christ. 9 For he that lacketh these things is blind, [i]seeing only what is near, having forgotten the cleansing from his old sins. 10 Wherefore, brethren, give the more diligence to make your calling and election sure: for if ye do these things, ye shall never stumble: 11 for thus shall be richly supplied unto you the entrance into the eternal kingdom of our Lord and Saviour Je'sus Christ.

---

a Many ancient authorities read *Symeon*. See Acts 15.14. *b* Gr. *bondservant*. *c* Gr. *an equally precious*. *d* Or, *our God and Saviour* Comp. ver. 11; 2.20; 3.18; Tit.

2.13. *e* Some ancient authorities read *through glory and virtue*. *f* Or, *a* *g* Or, *stedfastness* *h* Gr. *love of the brethren*. *i* Or, *closing his eyes*

CHAPTER 1

1. *To them that have obtained a like precious faith with us.* Those who, whether Jews or Gentiles, held a faith like that held by Peter.

2. *Knowledge of God.* In the original the word here translated 'knowledge' (epignosis) has the deeper meaning of that understanding which is developed through love. The same word occurs in verse 3.

9. *Blind, seeing only what is near.* This phrase implies a lack of perception as to spiritual things and undue attention to the allurements of the world.

10. *Your calling and election sure.* All Christians have been called, but they must work out their salvation.

590

12 Wherefore I shall be ready always to put you in remembrance of these things, though ye know them, and are established in the truth which is with *you*. 13 And I think it right, as long as I am in this tabernacle, to stir you up by putting you in remembrance; 14 knowing that the putting off of my tabernacle cometh swiftly, even as our Lord Je'sus Christ signified unto me. 15 Yea, I will give diligence that at every time ye may be able after my ᵏdecease to call these things to remembrance. 16 For we did not follow cunningly devised fables, when we made known unto you the power and ˡcoming of our Lord Je'sus Christ, but we were eyewitnesses of his majesty. 17 For he ᵐreceived from God the Father honor and glory, when there was borne such a voice to him by the Majestic Glory, This is my beloved Son, in whom I am well pleased: 18 and this voice we *ourselves* heard borne out of heaven, when we were with him in the holy mount. 19 And we have the word of prophecy *made more sure*; whereunto ye do well that ye take heed, as unto a lamp shining in a ⁿdark place, until the day dawn, and the day-star arise in your hearts: 20 knowing this first, that no prophecy of scripture is of ᵒprivate interpretation. 21 For no prophecy ever ᵖcame by the will of man: but men spake from God, being moved by the Holy Spirit.

2 But there arose false prophets also among the people, as among you also there shall be false teachers, who shall privily bring in ᵃdestructive heresies, denying even the Master that bought them, bringing upon themselves swift destruction. 2 And many shall follow their lascivious doings; by reason of whom the way of the truth shall be evil spoken of. 3 And in covetousness shall they with feigned words make merchandise of you: whose sentence now from of old lingereth not, and their destruction slumbereth not. 4 For if God spared not angels when they sinned, but ᵇcast them down to ᶜhell, and committed them to ᵈpits of darkness, to be reserved unto judgment; 5 and spared not the ancient world, but preserved Noah with seven others, ᵉa preacher of righteousness, when he brought a flood upon the world of the ungodly; 6 and turning the cities of Sod'om and Go-mor'rah

---

ᵏ Or, *departure* ˡ Gr. *presence.* ᵐ Gr. *having received.* ⁿ Gr. *squalid.* ᵒ Or, *special* ᵖ Gr. *was brought.* ᵃ Or, *sects of perdition* ᵇ Or, *cast them into dungeons* ᶜ Gr. *Tartarus.* ᵈ Some ancient authorities read *chains.* Comp. Wisd. 17.17. ᵉ Gr. *a herald.*

13. *This tabernacle.* The body. See Jn. 1.14; 2 Cor. 5.1.

17, 18. *The Majestic Glory,* etc. Peter here refers to the transfiguration, of which he was an eye-witness (Mt. 17.5).

19. *And we have the word of prophecy made more sure.* All question as to the fulfilment of the prophecies as to the coming of the Messiah in the person of Jesus were removed for Peter by the wonders of which he had been an eye-witness (verses 16–18).

CHAPTER 2

4. *Hell.* This is the only place in the New Testament where the word 'hell' is given as a translation of the Greek word 'Tartarus,' which means the lowest depth.

591

into ashes condemned them with an overthrow, having made them an example unto those that should live ungodly; 7 and delivered righteous Lot, sore distressed by the lascivious life of the wicked 8 (for that righteous man dwelling among them, in seeing and hearing, *f* vexed *his* righteous soul from day to day with *their* lawless deeds): 9 the Lord knoweth how to deliver the godly out of temptation, and to keep the unrighteous under punishment unto the day of judgment; 10 but chiefly them that walk after the flesh in the lust of defilement, and despise dominion. Daring, self-willed, they tremble not to rail at *g* dignities: 11 whereas angels, though greater in might and power, bring not a railing judgment against them before the Lord. 12 But these, as creatures without reason, born *h* mere animals *i* to be taken and destroyed, railing in matters whereof they are ignorant, shall in their *k* destroying surely be destroyed, 13 suffering wrong as the hire of wrong-doing; *men* that count it pleasure to revel in the daytime, spots and blemishes, reveling in their *l* deceivings while they feast with you; 14 having eyes full of *m* adultery, and that cannot cease from sin; enticing unstedfast souls; having a heart exercised in covetousness; children of cursing; 15 forsaking the right way, they went astray, having followed the way of Ba'laam the *son* of *n* Be'or, who loved the hire of wrong-doing; 16 but he was rebuked for his own transgression: a dumb ass spake with man's voice and stayed the madness of the prophet. 17 These are springs without water, and mists driven by a storm; for whom the blackness of darkness hath been reserved. 18 For, uttering great swelling *words* of vanity, they entice in the lusts of the flesh, by lasciviousness, those who are just escaping from them that

---

f Gr. *tormented.* *g* Gr. *glories.* *h* Gr. *natural.* *i* Or, *to take and to destroy* *k* Or, *corruption* Comp. 1 Tim. 6.9.

l Some ancient authorities read *love-feasts.* Comp. Jude 12. *m* Gr. *an adulteress.* *n* Many ancient authorities read *Bosor.*

---

9. *And to keep the unrighteous under punishment.* Implying that the unrighteous are always under punishment from the time that sin is committed, both before the judgment and after. *Day of judgment.* At the second coming of Christ. See Mt. 10.15; 11.22, 24; 1 Jn. 4.17. Even between death and the judgment there is apparently a division between the righteous and the wicked. See notes on Lk. 16.19–21; 22–31.

11. *Railing judgment.* The phrase refers to the scornful condemnation which comes only from the presumptuousness of unreason and ignorance.

12. *In their destroying surely be destroyed.* In destroying, or at-

tempting to destroy, the church by their false teachings they would surely destroy themselves.

13. *Spots and blemishes.* Referring to professing Christians who by their impure lives and their resulting bad behavior, at the love-feasts or other Christian means of grace, disgraced the name they bore.

15. *The way of Balaam.* The perverse and disobedient way. See Num. 22.7; 31.8; Rev. 2.14.

17. *Blackness of darkness.* This expression pictures the condition produced by the vanity of the thoughts of man (Ps. 94.11), as contrasted with the attitude of the meek to whom Jehovah will teach his way (Ps. 25.9).

live in error; 19 promising them liberty, while they themselves are bondservants of corruption; for of *o*whom a man is overcome, of the same is he also brought into bondage. 20 For if, after they have escaped the defilements of the world through the knowledge of *p*the Lord and Saviour Je′sus Christ, they are again entangled therein and overcome, the last state is become worse with them than the first. 21 For it were better for them not to have known the way of righteousness, than, after knowing it, to turn back from the holy commandment delivered unto them. 22 It has happened unto them according to the true proverb, *q*The dog turning to his own vomit again, and the sow that had washed to wallowing in the mire.

3 This is now, beloved, the second epistle that I write unto you; and in both of them I stir up your sincere mind by putting you in remembrance; 2 that ye should remember the words which were spoken before by the holy prophets, and the commandment of the Lord and

Saviour through your apostles: 3 knowing this first, that *a*in the last days mockers shall come with mockery, walking after their own lusts, 4 and saying, Where is the promise of his *b*coming? for, from the day that the fathers fell asleep, all things continue as they were from the beginning of the creation. 5 For this they wilfully forget, that there were heavens from of old, and an earth compacted out of water and *c*amidst water, by the word of God; 6 by which means the world that then was, being overflowed with water, perished: 7 but the heavens that now are, and the earth, by the same word have been *d*stored up for fire, being reserved against the day of judgment and destruction of ungodly men.

8 But forget not this one thing, beloved, that one day is with the Lord as a thousand years, and a thousand years as one day. 9 The Lord is not slack concerning his promise, as some count slackness; but is longsuffering to you-ward, not wishing that any should perish, but that all should come to repentance. 10 But the day of the

---

o Or, *what* *p* Many ancient authorities read *our*. *q* Prov. xxvi. 11.

a Gr. *in the last of the days.* *b* Gr. *presence.* *c* Or, *through* *d* Or, *stored with fire*

19. *Brought into bondage.* Paul says in the same sense, ' His servants ye are whom ye obey; whether of sin unto death, or of obedience unto righteousness' (Rom. 6.16).

20. *The last state is become worse,* etc. See Mt. 12.43–45.

CHAPTER 3

1. *By putting you in remembrance.* It is evident that even at this early period false teachings were so rife that Peter felt constrained to turn

back the thought of the brethren to the purity of the original word.

7. *Stored up for fire.* This verse taken with ver. 10, 12 foretell the dissolution of the earth and the heavens by the agency of heat. See Micah 1.4.

8. *One day is with the Lord,* etc. Here Peter means to caution those for whom this epistle was written against fixing upon any particular time for the second coming of Christ. The first part of ver. 10 implies the same caution.

Lord will come as a thief; in the which the heavens shall pass away with a great noise, and the *elements shall be dissolved with fervent heat, and the earth and the works that are therein shall be *burned up. 11 Seeing that these things are thus all to be dissolved, what manner of persons ought ye to be in *all* holy living and godliness, 12 looking for and *earnestly desiring the *coming of the day of God, by reason of which the heavens being on fire shall be dissolved, and the *elements shall melt with fervent heat? 13 But, according to his promise, we look for new heavens and a new earth, wherein dwelleth righteousness.

14 Wherefore, beloved, seeing that ye look for these things, give diligence that ye may be found in peace, without spot and blameless in his sight. 15 And account that the longsuffering of our Lord is salvation; even as our beloved brother Paul also, according to the wisdom given to him, wrote unto you; 16 as also in all *his* epistles, speaking in them of these things; wherein are some things hard to be understood, which the ignorant and unstedfast wrest, as *they do* also the other scriptures, unto their own destruction. 17 Ye therefore, beloved, knowing *these things* beforehand, beware lest, being carried away with the error of the wicked, ye fall from your own stedfastness. 18 But grow in the grace and knowledge of our Lord and Saviour Je'sus Christ. To him *be* the glory both now and *for ever. A-men'.

---

e Or, *heavenly bodies* *f* The most ancient manuscripts read *discovered.* *g* Or, *hasten-ing* *h* Gr. *presence.* *i* Gr. *unto the day of eternity.* Ecclus. 18.10.

13. *We look for new heavens and a new earth.* This declaration doubtless refers to the prophecy of Isaiah —'For, behold, I create new heavens and a new earth, and the former things shall not be remembered' (Isa. 65.17).

17. *The error of the wicked.* As the exhortation is to stedfastness it appears that the 'wicked' referred to are the false teachers mentioned in the beginning of ch. 2.

18. *For ever.* The glory of Christ is to be eternal.

THE FIRST EPISTLE OF JOHN

INTRODUCTION BY PROFESSOR M. B. RIDDLE, D.D., LL.D.

Circumstances of Writing.—This epistle was attributed to the apostle John by Christian writers of the succeeding generation. In thought, diction, and style it closely resembles the fourth Gospel. Whether it was written before or after the Gospel cannot be determined.

The *date* is not earlier than 90 A.D., though it may have been written some years later, the contents pointing to the close of the first century.

The *place* of writing was Ephesus, as is generally admitted.

The *occasion* was evidently the growth of error among the Christians in and about Ephesus, to whom the epistle was originally sent.

This error was twofold: first, in practice, a failure to attain unto moral fellowship with God through Jesus Christ; secondly, the source of the error in practice, *viz.* a wrong view of the person of Christ. This was a denial of the reality of the incarnation (early Docetism). Jesus and the Christ were regarded as two persons, temporarily joined together from the baptism of Jesus until the crucifixion. By presenting Jesus as the Christ, the apostle shows that we come into fellowship with God through Him, and seeks to promote living faith in the real Redeemer as a means of overcoming the practical error, which was content with "knowledge" apart from holiness, an error still more fully developed in the second century.

Contents.—The epistle is a pastoral letter, not a treatise, though the epistolary form is not strongly marked. It was not designed to be either a companion to the Gospel or a comment upon it. The purpose is set forth in ch. 5.13: "These things have I written unto you, that ye may know ye have eternal life, *even* unto you that believe on the name of the Son of God"; *cf.* 1.4. The simplest division of the epistle is as follows:—

After the introductory statement (1.1-4)—

1. God is light (1.5 to 2.28).
2. God is righteous, or, God is love (2.29 to 5.5).
3. Conclusion (5.6-21): Jesus is the Son of God; fellowship with God is through Him.

The second division is sometimes separated into two parts: God is righteous (2.29 to 4.6); God is love (4.7 to 5.5). But these are two sides of the same truth, since the apostle presents God as holy love. The whole epistle is based upon the fact that God is love, and the special aspects are indicated by the two main divisions. The two truths are illustrated by their opposites; the con-

THE FIRST EPISTLE OF JOHN

trast between believers and the world is sharply stated, for "the apostle of love" sets forth God's wrath against sin.

In this version the passage about the "heavenly witnesses" (5.7) is omitted, and no marginal notice inserted. It has no place in the epistle, except on the authority of the Latin Vulgate, and it is not found in the earliest MSS. of that version. It does not appear in any Greek MSS., save two which were written not long before the invention of printing. External and internal evidence are equally strong against it. The omission cannot affect the doctrine of the Trinity, for the Fathers who discussed and formulated the statements of that doctrine never refer to this passage.

THE FIRST EPISTLE OF

JOHN

Introduction.   "Walk in the Light"

1 That which was from the beginning, that which we have heard, that which we have seen with our eyes, that which we beheld, and our hands handled, concerning the *a*Word of life 2 (and the life was manifested, and we have seen, and bear witness, and declare unto you the life, the eternal *life*, which was with the Father, and was manifested unto us); 3 that which we have seen and heard declare we unto you also, that ye also may have fellowship with us: yea, and our fellowship is with the Father, and with his Son Je'sus Christ: 4 and these things we write, that *b*our joy may be made full.

5 And this is the message which we have heard from him and announce unto you, that God is light, and in him is no darkness at all. 6 If we say that

---

a Or, *word* Comp. Acts 5.20.

b Many ancient authorities read *your*.

CHAPTER 1

1. *That which.* The truth and purpose of God concerning the Son, Jesus Christ, who 'became flesh and dwelt among us.' *Was.* Existed from all eternity. *From the beginning.* Not the beginning of time, but .before time was. See Gen. 1.1. *That which we have heard*, etc. Referring to the companionship of John and the other apostles and disciples wíth Jesus on earth. *The word of life.* Jesus Christ. See notes on Jn. 1.1, 4.

2. *The life, the eternal life.* The eternal, life-giving power of Jesus Christ. See Jn. 1.4; 11.25–27, with notes thereon. *With the Father.* See Jn. 1.2.

3. *Fellowship with us.* Share with us the work, privilege and hope of Christian believers.

4. *That our joy may be made full.* The purpose of the apostle John was so to influence the Christians addressed that they would make sure their fellowship with him and the other apostles, so that all might together share the joy of being followers of Christ.

5. *Him.* Christ. *God is light.* 'Light' here is the truth of God, spiritual truth, which infallibly detects and is unalterably opposed to all evil. The apostle intended that his words should emphasize the difference between the light which God is and purely intellectual enlightenment so-called, and which may exist in one whose heart is corrupt. His insight into the nature of God as revealed in Christ enabled him habitually to speak of God in especially illuminating terms borrowed from external nature and the fundamental facts of spiritual life. According to him God is spirit (Jn. 4.24) and God is love (1 Jn. 4.8). He is careful to give the many points of view from which Christ is believed in as the source and sustainer of the Christian's faith and experience. See note on Jn. 8.12.

6. *Do not the truth.* Do not make

597

we have fellowship with him and walk in the darkness, we lie, and do not the truth: 7 but if we walk in the light, as he is in the light, we have fellowship one with another, and the blood of Je′sus his Son cleanseth us from all sin. 8 If we say that we have no sin, we deceive ourselves, and the truth is not in us. 9 If we confess our sins, he is faithful and righteous to forgive us our sins, and to cleanse us from all unrighteousness. 10 If we say that we have not sinned, we make him a liar, and his word is not in us.

2 My little children, these things write I unto you that ye may not sin. And if any man sin, we have an ªAdvocate

with the Father, Je′sus Christ the righteous: 2 and he is the propitiation for our sins; and not for ours only, but also for the whole world. 3 And hereby we know that we know him, if we keep his commandments. 4 He that saith, I know him, and keepeth not his commandments, is a liar, and the truth is not in him; 5 but whoso keepeth his word, in him verily hath the love of God been perfected. Hereby we know that we are in him: 6 he that saith he abideth in him ought himself also to walk even as he walked.

7 Beloved, no new commandment write I unto you, but an old commandment which ye had from the beginning: the old

---

a Or, *Comforter* Jn. 14.16. Or, *Helper*   Gr. *Paraclete.*

---

the truth, as revealed in Christ, the rule of action.

7. *Fellowship.* See note on ver 5. *Cleanseth us from all sin.* Is ever able to make us spiritually pure. To 'walk in the light' does not imply that one may not fall into sin; but saving power of faith in the voluntary sacrifice of Christ is necessary to enable the believer to walk in the light without sin.

8. *We deceive ourselves.* Because of a perverted will or of lack of moral discernment in not seeing what sin really is. The apostle was thinking of those who in his day were attempting to undermine Christian truth with the doctrine that sin has no power over those who are intellectually enlightened. See note on ver. 5.

9. *Confess.* To God and also to one another. See Jas. 5.16.

CHAPTER 2

1. *My little children.* A term of affection and fatherly oversight for all the disciples of the apostle. *Advocate.* The literal meaning of the word is, 'one who is called to the side of another to advise and assist.' Here it means either Christ

or the Holy Spirit. 'Advocate' is rendered 'Comforter' in Jn. 14.16, 25; 15.26; 16.7.

2. *Propitiation.* That which wins favor.

4. *That saith, I know him, and keepeth not,* etc. The apostle here commends only that knowledge of God which prompts to filial obedience, thereby bearing witness to the love of God in the heart. He cannot admit that an intellectual apprehension of truth about God is really knowledge of God; he refuses to consider it apart from a consecrated life. He even brands as a liar the man who says that he knows God but does not by obedience prove his sincerity.

5. *Word.* As 'word'—the revelation of the Father's will in Christ—is here a more comprehensive term than 'commandments,' so he who keeps the 'word' of God is holier, nearer the sinlessness of Jesus Christ, than he in whose obedience there is any element of fear. Perfect obedience is only possible to him from whom perfect love has cast out fear (1 Jn. 4.18).

7. *No new commandment.* 'Commandment' in this verse refers to

commandment is the word which ye heard. 8 Again, a new commandment write I unto you, which thing is true in him and in you; because the darkness is passing away, and the true light already shineth. 9 He that saith he is in the light and hateth his brother, is in the darkness even until now. 10 He that loveth his brother abideth in the light, and there is no occasion of stumbling in him. 11 But he that hateth his brother is in the darkness, and walketh in the darkness, and knoweth not whither he goeth, because the darkness hath blinded his eyes.

12 I write unto you, *my* little children, because your sins are forgiven you for his name's sake. 13 I write unto you, fathers, because ye know him who is from the beginning. I write unto you, young men, because ye have overcome the evil one. *b*I have written unto you, little children, because ye know the Father. 14 *b*I have written unto you, fathers, because ye know him who is from the beginning. *b*I have written unto you, young men, because ye are strong, and the word of God abideth in you, and ye have overcome the evil one. 15 Love not the world,

b Or, *I wrote*

---

the words of Christ, 'A new commandment I give unto you, that ye love one another.' See Jn. 13.34 and note thereon.

8. *Again, a new commandment.* The apostle employs the words 'old' and 'new' according to the light in which the commandment to love one another is considered. It was old in one sense, because Christ had spoken it many years before this epistle was written; but it was new in its constant revelations of spiritual beauty and power. *Which thing is true.* The newness of the commandment. *In him and you.* New in Christ, because it was he in whom it was first incarnated, and by whom it was first sent forth to the world by the authority of a perfect human example; new in 'you'—that is, the individual who at any time or place makes it the rule of life—because it makes all things new, brightens all personal relations with a new light, rules all motives and intentions by a new sanction, the love of Christ in us prompting to the love of mankind. *The darkness is passing away.* The old order of things, whether under the imperfect light and the hard discipline of the Mosaic law; or the ignorance and misery in the Gentile world. *The true light.* The salvation offered in Christ.

9. *And hateth his brother.* See note on ver. 4.

12-14. *I write unto you,* etc. In these verses the reasons for writing the epistle are given. *My little children.* See note on ch. 2.1. *Because your sins are forgiven you.* Through which forgiveness they had been enabled to approach God with confidence. *For his name's sake.* For the sake of the character and work of Jesus Christ. 'Name, when applied to Jesus Christ in the New Testament, always stands for what he was, and what he did for mankind. *Fathers.* Experienced Christians. *Him who is from the beginning.* Jesus Christ. See note on ch. 1.1. *Because ye have overcome.* Have been victorious over temptation. *Because ye know the Father.* The 'little children' here spoken of as knowing the Father are distinguished from more experienced Christians who had a deeper knowledge of Jesus Christ, the Son. The 'little children' had begun their Christian experience by being told of the Father, and how He could be approached through faith in Christ; later they would know more fully about Christ and his work.

15. *Love not the world.* That is, those elements in the life of the world that hinder or quench the

neither the things that are in the world. If any man love the world, the love of the Father is not in him. 16 For all that is in the world, the lust of the flesh and the lust of the eyes and the vainglory of life, is not of the Father, but is of the world. 17 And the world passeth away, and the lust thereof: but he that doeth the will of God abideth for ever.

18 Little children, it is the last hour: and as ye heard that an'ti-christ cometh, even now have there arisen many an'ti-christs; whereby we know that it is the last hour. 19 They went out from us, but they were not of us; for if they had been of us, they would have continued with us: but *they went out*, that they might be made manifest ᶜthat they all are not of us. 20 And ye have an anointing from,the Holy One, ᵈand ye know all things. 21 I have not written unto you because ye know not the truth, but because ye know it, and ᵉbecause no lie is of the truth. 22 Who is the liar but he that denieth that Je'sus is the Christ? This is the an'ti-christ *even* he that denieth the Father and the Son. 23 Whosoever denieth the Son, the same hath not the Father: he that confesseth the Son hath the Father also. 24 As for you, let that abide in you which ye heard from the beginning. If that which ye heard from the beginning abide in you, ye also shall abide in the Son, and in the Father. 25 And this is the promise which he promised ᶠ us, *even* the life eternal. 26 These things have I written

---

c Or, *that not all are of us*　d Some very ancient authorities read *and ye all know.*

e Or, *that*　f Some ancient authorities read *you.*

---

life of the Spirit (Jas. 1.27). The words do not refer to the world of mankind which God so loved that He gave His only begotten Son for it (Jn. 3.16); nor to the world of nature as ordinarily understood. *The things that are in the world.* That are of the same nature as the evil elements already mentioned.

16. *Lust.* See Jas. 1.14. *Of the flesh.* Immoderate and wrong sensual appetites of all kinds (1 Pet 2.11). *Lust of the eyes.* Wrong desire for things that appeal most strongly to human wants through the power of physical sight, morbid curiosity to see unlawful and harmful sights, for the sinful pleasure of seeing. *The vainglory of life.* Insolent pride in the enjoyment of one's position in life or in the display of one's wealth

18. *The last hour.* The expected immediate second coming of Christ to judge the world. See Jas. 5.3, 7; 1 Pet. 4.7; also note on 2 Pet. 3.8.

Antichrist cometh. 'Antichrist' is one who, pretending to be Christ, yet opposes Christ. The appearance of antichrists was regarded as a sign of the second coming of Christ.

19. *Went out from us.* These antichrists had been brought up as Christians, or had been members of the Christian community. *Were not of us.* Had not been sincere Christians.

20 *An anointing.* Which made them true Christians, as contrasted with antichrists. *The Holy One.* Christ.

23. *Hath not the Father.* Because the Sonship necessarily implies the Fatherhood and because only the Son can reveal the Father. See Jn. 15.23; 2 Jn. 9; also note on Mt. 11.27.

24. *That.* The gospel.

25. *He.* Christ. *Promised us.* 'Whosoever believeth may in him have eternal life' (Jn. 3.15).

unto you concerning them that would lead you astray. 27 And as for you, the anointing which ye received of him abideth in you, and ye need not that any one teach you; but as his anointing teacheth you concerning all things, *and is true, and is no lie, and even as it taught you, *ye abide in him. 28 And now, *my* little children, abide in him; that, if he shall be manifested, we may have boldness, and not be ashamed *before him at his *coming. 29 If ye know that he is righteous, *ye know that every one also that doeth righteousness is begotten of him.

3 Behold what manner of love the Father hath be-

g Or, *so it is true and is no lie; and even as* &c. *h* Or, *abide ye* *i* Gr. *from him.*

27. *Ye need not that any one teach you.* Because of the anointing by which they had become true Christians, endowed with spiritual insight. 'Ye know all things' (ver. 20). The apostle John wrote, not to teach them what they already knew, but to confirm them in what they already believed.

28. *If he shall be manifested.* That is, if the time of his appearing should come. This does not imply any doubt of Christ's coming, but refers only to the time.

29. *If ye know that he is righteous,* etc. They would surely know, since God is righteous, that every one also that doeth righteousness, is begotten of God.

CHAPTER 3

1. *The Father.* These words include in their meaning not only 'My Father,' as rightfully spoken in a special sense by Jesus Christ alone, but 'Our Father' of the Lord's Prayer. *World.* The evil in the world. See note on ch. 2.15. In this and the first six verses of the succeeding chapter the main theme is the righteousness of God.

stowed upon us, that we should be called children of God; and *such* we are. For this cause the world knoweth us not, because it knew him not. 2 Beloved, now are we children of God, and it is not yet made manifest what we shall be. We know that, if *he shall be manifested, we shall be like him; for we shall see him even as he is. 3 And every one that hath this hope *set* on him purifieth himself, even as he is pure. 4 Every one that doeth sin doeth also lawlessness; and sin is lawlessness. 5 And ye know that he was manifested to *take away sins; and in him is no sin. 6 Whosoever abideth in him sinneth not: whosoever sinneth hath not seen him,

k Gr. *presence.* *l* Or, *know ye* *a* Or, *it* *b* Or, *bear sins*

2. *What we shall be.* Children of God, however blessed their condition, are privileged to reach still greater spiritual heights. This is also clearly indicated by Paul, whose use of the words 'sons of God' (Rom. 8.14) implies a matured consciousness of the filial relation impossible to children under tutelage. 'Sons of God' rejoice in the liberty and glory conferred upon them. There is no limit to their spiritual attainment except perfect conformity to the image of the Son of God (Rom. 8.29).

3. *This hope.* Of becoming like God by following the example of Christ. *Set on him.* Given to him or conferred on him. Man depends upon God even for the hope of becoming like Him.

4. *Sin is lawlessness.* Because it prevents obedience to God.

6. *Sinneth not.* That is, is not and cannot be an habitual, confirmed sinner. If any man professing to abide in Christ commit sin, to that extent he does not abide in him. *Hath not seen him, neither knoweth him.* Because sin is out of all harmony with him. See note on ch. 2.1.

neither ᶜknoweth him. 7 *My* little children, let no man lead you astray: he that doeth righteousness is righteous, even as he is righteous. 8 he that doeth sin is of the devil; for the devil sinneth from the beginning. To this end was the Son of God manifested, that he might destroy the works of the devil. 9 Whosoever is begotten of God doeth no sin, because his seed abideth in him: and he cannot sin, because he is begotten of God. 10 In this the children of God are manifest, and the children of the devil: whosoever doeth not righteousness is not of God, neither he that loveth not his brother. 11 For this is the message which ye heard from the beginning, that we should love one another: 12 not as Cain was of the evil one, and slew his brother. And wherefore slew he him? Because his works were evil, and his brother's righteous.

13 Marvel not, brethren, if the world hateth you. 14 We know that we have passed out of death into life, because we love the brethren. He that loveth not abideth in death. 15 Whosoever hateth his brother is a murderer: and ye know that no murderer hath eternal life abiding in him. 16 Hereby know we love, because he laid down his life for us: and we ought to lay down our lives for the brethren. 17 But whoso hath the world's goods, and beholdeth his brother in need, and shutteth up his compassion from him, how doth the love of God abide in him? 18 *My* little children, let us not love in word, neither with the tongue; but in deed and truth. 19 Hereby shall we know that we are of the truth, and shall ᵈassure our heart ᵉbefore him: 20 because if our heart condemn us, God is greater than our heart, and knoweth all things. 21 Beloved, if our heart condemn us not, we have boldness toward God; 22 and whatsoever we ask we receive of him, because we

---

c Or, *hath known*   d Gr. *persuade.* Comp. Mt. 28.14.   e Or, *before him, whereinso-* *ever our heart condemn us; because God &c.*

7. *Even as he.* Christ.
8. *Doeth sin.*—That is, sins habitually. *Works of the devil.* The sins into which mankind has been tempted.
9. *Begotten of God.* Whosoever has been made and remains a child of God. *His seed abideth in him.* The spiritual life in him grows, and becomes more active and fruitful.
10. *That loveth not his brother.* Love for mankind, whether Christian believers or not, is the practical test of love to God.
12. *Cain.* See Heb. 11.4; Jude 11. *Of the evil one.* Inspired by the evil one.
14. *Out of death into life, because,* etc. Or, out of darkness into light (ch. 2.9–11).
15. *Whosoever hateth his brother is*
a murderer. Because murder begins, is planned and is done through hatred. See Mt. 5.22 and note thereon.
16. *Brethren.* All mankind, especially the children of God.
17. *Beholdeth.* Looks on with indifference.
19. *Hereby.* That is, because we have loved in deed and in truth (ver. 18). *Assure our heart before him.* Be comforted by trusting God for forgiveness.
20. *Greater than our heart.* More merciful than we are when our consciences condemn us through imperfect knowledge. 'For he knoweth our frame; he remembereth that we are dust' (Ps. 103.14).
22. *Whatsoever we ask we receive.* Prayer to God is answered at the

keep his commandments and do the things that are pleasing in his sight. 23 And this is his commandment, that we should ʲbelieve in the name of his Son Jeʹsus Christ, and love one another, even as he gave us commandment. 24 And he that keepeth his commandments abideth in him, and he in him. And hereby we know that he abideth in us, by the Spirit which he gave us.

4 Beloved, believe not every spirit, but prove the spirits, whether they are of God; because many false prophets are gone out into the world. 2 Hereby know ye the Spirit of God: every spirit that confesseth that Jeʹsus Christ is come

in the flesh is of God: 3 and every spirit that ᵃconfesseth not Jeʹsus is not of God: and this is the *spirit* of the anʹti-christ, whereof ye have heard that it cometh; and now it is in the world already. 4 Ye are of God, *my* little children, and have overcome them: because greater is he that is in you than he that is in the world. 5 They are of the world: therefore speak they *as* of the world, and the world heareth them. 6 We are of God: he that knoweth God heareth us; he who is not of God heareth us not. By this we know the spirit of truth, and the spirit of error.

7 Beloved, let us love one another: for love is of God; and every one that loveth is begotten of God, and knoweth God. 8 He

---

ʲ Gr. *believe the name.*   ᵃ Some ancient authorities read *annulleth Jesus.*

---

moment of asking, according to faith, but not always in the manner asked or expected. The answer may be known or seen in an instant, or it may be given through years of waiting, though in a way which makes clear the unwisdom of the first request and enhances the goodness of God. See Mk. 11.24 and note thereon. *Commandments.* Obedience to God, which is not perfect so long as it contains any element of fear. See note on ch. 2.5. *Pleasing in his sight.* Things done from love to God, a better motive than obedience strictly so-called. But love, like obedience, is imperfect so long as any fear lurks within the heart. 'He that feareth is not made perfect in love' (1 Jn. 4.8). If we are willing to hear God and to obey his voice, He will hear and grant our petition.

24. *The Spirit which he gave us.* After accepting the rule of Christ in the heart. The approval of the Spirit witnesses that God in Christ abides within us.

CHAPTER 4

1. *Prove the spirits.* By bringing them to the test of confessing that Jesus Christ is come in the flesh (ver. 2). They who would not thus confess were antichrists (ch. 2.18 and notes thereon), false prophets (ver. 1), deceivers (2 Jn. 7). *Whether they are of God.* Spirits and spiritual influences may be either good or bad. Here 'spirits' may refer either to spiritual influences from evil men; or to the miraculous powers claimed by sorcerers, false prophets, etc.

4. *He that is in the world.* The devil (Jn. 8.44; 12.31; 1 Jn. 3.10).

5. *They . . . them.* The false teachers.

7. *Every one that loveth is begotten of God.* 'Every one' here includes all the human beings in whose nature love is or ever has been, whether they ever heard of God and Christ or not; wherever human beings have loved, the love in them has come from God.

8. *God is love.* These words are the apostle's main theme from ver.

that loveth not knoweth not God; for God is love. 9 Herein was the love of God manifested *b*in us, that God hath sent his only begotten Son into the world that we might live through him. 10 Herein is love, not that we loved God, but that he loved us, and sent his Son *to be* the propitiation for our sins. 11 Beloved, if God so loved us, we also ought to love one another. 12 No man hath beheld God at any time: if we love one another, God abideth in us, and his love is perfected in us: 13 hereby we know that we abide in him and he in us, because he hath given us of his Spirit. 14 And we have beheld and bear witness that the Father hath sent the Son *to be* the Saviour of the world. 15 Whosoever shall confess that Je′sus is the Son of God, God abideth in him, and he in God. 16 And we know and have believed the love which God hath *b*in us. God is love; and he that abideth in love abideth in God, and God abideth in him. 17 Herein is love made perfect with us, that we may have boldness in the day of judgment; because as he is, even so are we in this world. 18 There is no fear in love: but perfect love casteth out fear, because fear hath punishment; and he that feareth is not made perfect in love. 19 We love, because he first loved us. 20 If a man say, I love God, and hateth his brother, he is a liar: for he that loveth not his brother whom he hath seen, *c*cannot love God whom he hath not seen. 21 And this commandment have we from him, that he who loveth God love his brother also.

5 Whosoever believeth that Je′sus is the Christ is begotten of God: and whosoever loveth him that begat loveth him also that is begotten of him. 2 Hereby we know that we love the children of God, when we love God and do his commandments. 3 For this is the love of

---

b Or, *in our case*

c Many ancient authorities read *how can he love God whom he hath not seen?*

7 to the thirteenth verse of the succeeding chapter. See notes on ch. 1.5.

9. *The world.* The evil, alienated world. See notes on ch. 2.15.

10. *But that he loved us.* His love first came to us and made possible our love for Him. *Propitiation.* See note on ch. 2.2.

12. *His love.* Our love to God, resulting from his love in our hearts.

13. *Hath given us of his Spirit.* As a witness. See note on ch. 3.24.

15. *Confess.* In all sincerity. *That Jesus is the Son of God.* Which the false teachers would not confess. See notes on ver. 1.

17. *Herein.* That is, by abiding in God. *Love.* Our love for God. *Even so are we in this world.* Thus being prepared for 'boldness in the day of judgment.'

18. *Fear hath punishment.* Is associated with the notion of punishment, and is itself a foretaste of punishment.

CHAPTER 5

1. *The Christ.* That is, Jesus of Nazareth, the divine Messiah. *Him that begat.* God. *Him also that is begotten.* Any person who accepts Christ.

3. *His commandments are not grievous.* Because love to God helps the believer to obey, and by obedience he goes on from strength unto strength. But even obedience prompted mainly by fear is far less

God, that we keep his commandments: and his commandments are not grievous. 4 For whatsoever is begotten of God overcometh the world: and this is the victory that hath overcome the world, *even* our faith. 5 And who is he that overcometh the world, but he that believeth that Je'sus is the Son of God? 6 This is he that came by water and blood, *even* Je'sus Christ; not ªwith the water only, but ªwith the water and ªwith the blood. 7 And it is the Spirit that beareth witness, because the Spirit is the truth. 8 For there are three who bear witness, the Spirit, and the water, and the blood: and the three agree in one. 9 If we receive the witness of men, the witness of God is greater: for the witness of God is this, that he hath borne witness concerning his Son. 10 He that believeth on the Son of God hath the witness in him: he

that believeth not God hath made him a liar; because he hath not believed in the witness that God hath borne concerning his Son. 11 And the witness is this, that God gave unto us eternal life, and this life is in his Son. 12 He that hath the Son hath the life; he that hath not the Son of God hath not the life.

13 These things have I written unto you, that ye may know that ye have eternal life, *even* unto you that believe on the name of the Son of God. 14 And this is the boldness which we have toward him, that, if we ask anything according to his will, he heareth us: 15 and if we know that he heareth us whatsoever we ask, we know that we have the petitions which we have asked of him. 16 If any man see his brother sinning a sin not unto death, ᵇhe shall ask, and *God* will give him life for

---

a Gr. *in.*   *b* Or, *he shall* | *ask and shall give him life, even to them &c.*

grievous than the penalty of sin: See Mt. 11.28-30 and notes thereon.

4. *Whatsoever.* The spiritual power that comes from God; it is not the person who overcomes, but God in Christ within the person. Nevertheless the person may accept or reject the grace, and therefore the power, of God unto salvation.

6. *This is he.* That is, the Jesus of whom I speak is Jesus of Nazareth, the divine Messiah. *Water and blood.* Baptism and the crucifixion. *Not with the water only.* The apostle here condemns the false teaching according to which the Christ entered the human body of Jesus of Nazareth when he was baptized by John in the river Jordan, but left it before his death on the cross. *But with the water and with the blood.* Both baptism and crucifixion were needed in Christ's redemptive work.

7. *It is the Spirit that beareth witness.* In the hearts of true believers. *Truth.* See note on Jn. 15.26.

8. *Three who bear witness.* That is, bear witness to the character and work of Christ. The three witnesses are the Spirit (ver. 7); the water, or Christ's baptism in the Jordan; and the blood, or the crucifixion. *The three agree in one.* That is, in witnessing to and confirming the teaching of Christ.

14, 15. *If we ask anything according to his will,* etc. Such prayer is inevitably answered. See ch. 3.22 and note thereon.

16. *Unto death.* Naturally resulting in death if the sinner does not turn from his downward course. 'Unto' means a tendency which may be successfully resisted; a sin unto death does not necessarily result in death. The apostle means

them that sin not unto death. There is ᶜa sin unto death: not concerning this do I say that he should make request. 17 All unrighteousness is sin: and there is ᶜa sin not unto death.

18 We know that whosoever is begotten of God sinneth not; but he that was begotten of God keepeth ᵈhimself, and the evil one toucheth him not. 19 We know that we are of God, and the whole world lieth in the evil one. 20 And we know that the Son of God is come, and hath given us an understanding, that we know him that is true, and we are in him that is true, *even* in his Son Je'sus Christ. This is the true God, and eternal life. 21 *My* little children, guard yourselves from idols.

---

c Or, *sin* d Some ancient authorities read *him*.

---

persistence in sin, the habit of sin—not any particular sin. There is no room for any division of sinful acts unto 'mortal' and 'venial.' See Heb. 6.4–6; 10.26–29.

18, 19. *The evil one.* Satan.

20. *An understanding.* Knowledge and intelligence. *Him that is true.* God. *We are in him that is true.* Here 'him' means Jesus Christ. *This is the true God.* These words also refer to Jesus Christ, and distinctly affirm his deity.

21. *Idols.* Idolatry, which still existed among the communities among whom the epistle was sent, and which might have tempted the weaker disciples.

THE SECOND EPISTLE OF JOHN

INTRODUCTION BY PROFESSOR M. B. RIDDLE, D.D., LL.D.

This and the third epistle were not so generally known and received in the early church as the other writings of the apostle, largely because of their brief, personal character. But no motive could exist for forging letters of this kind, and the internal evidence points conclusively to the apostle as the writer. As he calls himself "the elder," at one time an opinion was current that "John the Presbyter" was the writer. But it is, to say the least, doubtful whether any person of that name and title ever existed other than the apostle John.

Destination.—The second epistle is addressed "to the elect lady and her children" (ver. 1). While this might refer to a church, it is more naturally applied to an individual Christian woman. There are other views—"the lady Electa," and "the elect Kyria"; but both of these are attended with grammatical difficulties. The name of the person addressed is therefore unknown. Some of her children had met with the apostle, who rejoiced in their conduct (ver. 4). But as the error opposed in the first epistle was prevalent, he writes to warn against it, not being yet able to carry out his purpose of visiting her (ver. 12). The occasion and design thus indicated are the same, if the epistle was addressed to a church.

Contents.—Address and greeting (ver. 1-3); joy in the conduct of her sons (ver. 4); exhortation to abound in love (ver. 5, 6); warning against deceivers (ver. 7, 8), who should not be received or greeted (ver. 9-11); closing words: the hope of visiting her, the greeting from her sister's children (ver. 12, 13).

THE SECOND EPISTLE OF

JOHN

Salutation.   Farewell

1 The elder unto the elect
lady and her children, whom I
love in truth; and not I only,
but also all they that know the
truth; 2 for the truth's sake
which abideth in us, and it shall
be with us for ever: 3 Grace,
mercy, peace shall be with us,
from God the Father, and from
Je'sus Christ, the Son of the
Father, in truth and love.

4 I rejoice greatly that I have
found *certain* of thy children
walking in truth, even as we received commandment from the
Father. 5 And now I beseech
thee, *lady*, not as though I
wrote to thee a new commandment, but that which we had
from the beginning, that we love
one another. 6 And this is love,
that we should walk after his
commandments. This is the
commandment, even as ye heard
from the beginning, that ye
should walk in it. 7 For many
deceivers are gone forth into the
world, *even* they that confess
not that Je'sus Christ cometh in
the flesh. This is the deceiver
and the an'ti-christ. 8 Look to
yourselves, that ye ᵇlose not the
things which ᶜwe have wrought,
but that ye receive a full reward.
9 Whosoever ᵈgoeth onward and
abideth not in the teaching of
Christ, hath not God: he that
abideth in the teaching, the same
hath both the Father and the
Son. 10 If any one cometh unto
you, and bringeth not this teaching, receive him not into *your*
house, and give him no greeting:
11 for he that giveth him greeting partaketh in his evil works.

12 Having many things to write
unto you, I would not *write them*
with paper and ink: but I hope
to come unto you, and to speak
face to face, that your joy may
be made full. 13 The children of
thine elect sister salute thee.

---

a Or, *Cyria*

b Or, *destroy*   *c* Many ancient authorities
read *ye*. *d* Or, *taketh the lead* Comp. 3 Jn. 9.

---

1. *The elder.* The apostle John.
Elect lady. It is not certain whether
an individual or a church is meant.
Children. Members of a church, if
the latter meaning be taken. *Truth.*
The Christian teaching and practice, according to John and the
other apostles.

3. *Grace, mercy, peace.* For a
similar formula of salutation, see
1 Pet. 1.2.

7. *Deceivers.* See 1 Jn. 2.18–22,
and notes thereon.

8. *Look to yourselves,* etc. A
warning to the disciples against
false teachers who were endeavor-
ing to undermine the Christian
faith as taught by the apostles.

9. *Onward.* Away from the
Christian truth revealed and taught.
He that abideth. He who habitually
does the will of God as revealed in
Christ.

10. *Receive him not,* etc. Show no
hospitality to him who would in-
sidiously beguile you away from
your faith in Christ.

13. *Elect sister.* Either an individual or a church. See ver. 1 and
notes thereon.

THE THIRD EPISTLE OF JOHN

INTRODUCTION BY PROFESSOR M. B. RIDDLE, D.D., LL.D.

Gaius (=Caius), to whom this letter was sent, cannot be identified with any person thus named in the rest of the New Testament (Acts 19.29; 20.4; Rom. 16.23; 1 Cor. 1.14). He lived not far from Ephesus, as is indicated by the epistle, which was occasioned by his hospitality to some Christian teachers, apparently sent by the apostle (ver. 2-4). As these teachers were about to travel again, the apostle asks Gaius to continue his hospitality to them (ver. 5-8). It would appear that Diotrephes, prominent among the Christians of the place where Gaius lived, had interfered on a previous occasion, intercepting a letter from the apostle, refusing to receive the brethren, and threatening those willing to receive them (ver. 9-11). Demetrius, probably the bearer of this letter, is commended (ver. 12). The conclusion is similar to that of the second epistle.

This letter and the second also are of great historical value, revealing as they do the inner life of the Christian communities of Asia Minor at the close of the first century. There are evidences of speculative error, personal ambition, occasional insubordination to apostolic authority, and of an opposition on the part of local leaders to travelling evangelists. The recently-recovered "Teaching of the Twelve Apostles" shows a similar state of things.

THE THIRD EPISTLE OF
JOHN

Address to Gaius

1 The elder unto Ga′ius the beloved, whom I love in truth.

2 Beloved, I pray that in all things thou mayest prosper and be in health, even as thy soul prospereth. 3 For I [a]rejoiced greatly, when brethren came and bare witness unto thy truth, even as thou walkest in truth. 4 Greater joy have I none than [b]this, to hear of my children walking in the truth.

5 Beloved, thou doest a faithful work in whatsoever thou doest toward them that are brethren and strangers withal; 6 who bare witness to thy love before the church: whom thou wilt do well to set forward on their journey worthily of God: 7 because that for the sake of the Name they went forth, taking nothing of the Gen′tiles. 8 We therefore ought to welcome such, that we may be fellow-workers [c]for the truth.

9 I wrote somewhat unto the church: but Di-ot′re-phes, who loveth to have the preëminence among them, receiveth us not. 10 Therefore, if I come, I will bring to remembrance his works which he doeth, prating against us with wicked words: and not content therewith, neither doth he himself receive the brethren, and them that would he forbiddeth and casteth *them* out of the church. 11 Beloved, imitate not that which is evil, but that which is good. He that doeth good is of God: he that doeth evil hath not seen God. 12 De-me′tri-us hath the witness of all *men*, and of the truth itself: yea, we also bear witness; and thou knowest that our witness is true.

13 I had many things to write unto thee, but I am unwilling to write *them* to thee with ink and pen: 14 but I hope shortly to see thee, and we shall speak face to face. Peace *be* unto thee. The friends salute thee. Salute the friends by name.

---

a Or, *rejoice greatly, when brethren come and bear witness* b Or, *these things, that I may hear* c Or, *with*

1. *The elder.* See note on 2 Jn. 1. *Gaius.* The same as Caius, a common Roman name. It is not certain that the Caius here addressed was the same as the Gaius in Acts 19.29; 20.4; Rom. 16.23, or in 1 Cor. 1.14. *Truth.* See note on 2 Jn. 1.

5. *Them that are brethren and strangers.* Gaius is here praised for his helpfulness to Christians who were strangers, and who were comforted by his hospitality.

6. *On their journey.* The Christians aided were travelling preachers.

7. *The Name.* See notes on 1 Jn. 2.12–14.

9. *Diotrephes.* A Christian of some influence and authority in the church, but who opposed the apostle John.

10. *The brethren.* The itinerant preachers.

12. *Demetrius.* Not elsewhere mentioned. He was not the Demetrius of Acts 19.24.

14. *Friends.* The adherents of the apostle in his opposition to Diotrephes.

THE EPISTLE OF JUDE

INTRODUCTION BY PROFESSOR M. B. RIDDLE, D.D., LL.D.

The Writer.—He calls himself "brother of James," probably referring to "the Lord's brother," James the Just, the writer of the General Epistle. He does not claim apostleship. Nothing further is known of him; nor is there positive evidence as to when, where, and why the epistle was written. It is referred to by early Christian authors, but there are also early doubts respecting its place in the canon. These doubts can be accounted for, partly from the brevity of the epistle and the comparative obscurity of the writer, and partly from the contents of the letter. The resemblance to 2 Peter, and the reference to two apocryphal books ("Assumption of Moses," ver. 9; "Book of Enoch," ver. 14, 15), would naturally raise difficulties. But as the evidence in favor of the epistle is preponderant, these apparent difficulties account for the doubts, without furnishing grounds for rejecting the book. While it is general in its address, its contents indicate that it was designed for a single church, made up mainly of Jewish Christians.

Peculiarities.—As there are several references in the New Testament to uninspired, and even heathen, writers, the citation from the "Book of Enoch" and the reference to another apocryphal writing do not furnish a valid objection to the acceptance of the epistle. The evident relation to 2 Peter only calls for a discussion as to which epistle was first penned, without affecting the authority of either. The priority of Jude would probably be conceded, were it not so difficult to believe that Peter would use the work of a teacher so little known. But this objection ignores the fact that the dependence of 2 Peter upon Jude does not impugn the genuineness of the former epistle; while the dependence of Jude upon 2 Peter implies that nearly all of the briefer epistle is borrowed from the longer one.

The *date* is in doubt. If written before 2 Peter, a very early date is still improbable in view of the contents. If written after, it must have preceded the destruction of Jerusalem. The earliest probable date is 64 A.D., the latest, 67 or 68 A.D.

Contents.—Address and greeting (ver. 1, 2); occasion of writing (ver. 3, 4); condemnation of false teachers, illustrated by Biblical examples (ver. 5-7); a description of their wickedness, and a woe pronounced upon them (ver. 8-16); exhortations—to remember the teaching of the apostles foretelling such mockers (ver. 17-19), to keep themselves in the love of God (ver. 20, 21), how to deal with those who had been perverted (ver. 22, 23); and closing doxology (ver. 24, 25).

THE EPISTLE OF

JUDE

General Salutation

1 ^aJude, a ^bservant of Je′sus Christ, and brother of ^cJames, ^dto them that are called, beloved in God the Father, and kept for Je′sus Christ: 2 Mercy unto you and peace and love be multiplied.

3 Beloved, while I was giving all diligence to write unto you of our common salvation, I was constrained to write unto you exhorting you to contend earnestly for the faith which was once for all delivered unto the saints. 4 For there are certain men crept in privily, *even* they who were of old ^ewritten of beforehand unto this condemnation, ungodly men, turning the grace of our God into lasciviousness, and denying ^four only Master and Lord, Je′sus Christ.

5 Now I desire to put you in remembrance, though ye know all things once for all, that ^gthe Lord, having saved a people out of the land of E′gypt, ^hafterward destroyed them that believed not. 6 And angels that kept not their own principality, but left their proper habitation, he hath kept in everlasting bonds under darkness unto the judgment of the great day. 7 Even as Sod′om and Go-mor′rah, and the cities about them, having in

a Gr. *Judas.* *b* Gr. *bondservant.* *c* Or, *Jacob* *d* Or, *to them that are beloved in God the Father, and kept for Jesus Christ, being called* *e* Or, *set forth*

f Or, *the only Master, and our Lord Jesus Christ* *g* Many very ancient authorities read *Jesus.* *h* Gr. *the second time.*

---

1. Jude. It is generally agreed that the writer of this epistle was one of the four brothers of Jesus, named in Matt. 13.55. The similarity of many passages to the second and third chapters of the Second Epistle of Peter have led to an endeavor to discover one authorship for both, but there is no dependable evidence to support this surmise. *Them that are called.* The elect. See note, 1 Peter 1.1. Compare 1 Tim. 6.12.

3. The faith which was once for all delivered. The gospel was delivered not in part but as a complete whole—'once for all.' The verses following warn against the perversions of this 'faith' by 'certain men';—doubtless the 'false teachers' spoken of in 1 Peter 2.1.

5. To put you in remembrance, though ye know all things. Through the 'anointing from the Holy One' (1 John 2.20) the faithful believer needed not that any one teach him (1 Jn. 2.27). Jude's reminder of this is also an admonition to be stedfast.

6. Angels that kept not their own principality. It is supposed that these were the 'sons of God' mentioned in Gen. 6.2. Compare Eph. 6.12.

612

like manner with these given themselves over to fornication and gone after strange flesh, are set forth ᶦas an example, suffering the punishment of eternal fire. 8 Yet in like manner these also in their dreamings defile the flesh, and set at nought dominion, and rail at ᵏdignities. 9 But Mi′cha-el the archangel, when contending with the devil he disputed about the body of Mo′ses, durst not bring against him a railing judgment, but said, The Lord rebuke thee. 10 But these rail at whatsoever things they know not: and what they understand naturally, like the creatures without reason, in these things are they ᶦdestroyed. 11 Woe unto them! for they went in the way of Cain, and ᵐran riotously in the error of Ba′laam for hire, and perished in the gainsaying of Ko′rah. 12 These are they who are ⁿhidden rocks in your love-feasts when they feast with you, shepherds that without fear feed themselves; clouds without water, carried along by winds; autumn trees without fruit, twice dead, plucked up by the roots; 13 wild waves of the sea, foaming out their own ᵒshame; wandering stars, for whom the blackness of darkness hath been reserved for ever. 14 And to these also E′noch, the seventh from Adam, prophesied, saying, Behold, the Lord came with ᵖten thousands of his holy ones, 15 to execute judgment upon all, and to convict all the ungodly of all their works of ungodliness which they have ungodly wrought, and of all the hard things which ungodly sinners have spoken against him. 16 These are murmurers, complainers, walking after their lusts (and their mouth speaketh great swelling words), showing respect of persons for the sake of advantage.

17 But ye, beloved, remember ye the words which have been spoken before by the apostles of our Lord Je′sus Christ; 18 that they said to you, In the last time there shall be mockers, walking after ᑫtheir own ungodly lusts. 19 These are they who make separations, ʳsensual, having not the Spirit. 20 But ye, beloved, building up yourselves on your most holy faith,

---

ᶦ Or, *as an example of eternal fire, suffering punishment* k Gr. *glories.* l Or, *corrupted* Comp. 2 Pet. 2.12 marg. m Or, *cast themselves away through* n Or, *spots*

o Gr. *shames.* p Gr. *his holy myriads.* q Gr. *their own lusts of ungodliness.* r Or, *natural* Or, *animal*

---

8. *Defile the flesh, and set at nought dominion.* The great error which had come into the Christian church through false teachings seems to have been a perversion of the spiritual 'fervent love' enjoined toward the brethren (1 Pet. 1.22) into lustfulness so gross as to be comparable to the sins of Sodom and Gomorrah, and to the fall of angels from their high estate. In this condition of 'blackness of darkness' (verse 13) not only was the

flesh defiled, but spiritual dominion was set at nought, and its dignities (glories) held in contempt.

9. *But Michael the archangel when contending with the devil.* Jude here seems to refer to a familiar tradition, but no other record of it now remains.

11. *Korah.* See Num. 16.

14. *Enoch, the seventh from Adam.* The prophecy here cited is from the Apocryphal Book of Enoch in the words of an angel who thus interpreted a vision.

praying in the Holy Spirit, 21 keep yourselves in the love of God, looking for the mercy of our Lord Je′sus Christ unto eternal life. 22 *And on some have mercy, ᶠwho are in doubt; 23 and some save, snatching them out of the fire; and on some have mercy with fear; hating even the garment spotted by the flesh.

24 Now unto him that is able to guard you from stumbling, and to set you before the presence of his glory without blemish in exceeding joy, 25 to the only God our Saviour, through Je′sus Christ our Lord, *be* glory, majesty, dominion and power, before all time, and now, and ᵘfor evermore. A-men′.

---

s The Gr. text in this passage (*And . . . fire*) is somewhat uncertain. Some ancient authorities read *And some refute while they*

dispute with you. Comp. 1 Tim. 5.20; Tit. 1.9.   *t* Or, *while they dispute* with you   *u* Gr. *unto all the ages.*

---

23. *And on some have mercy with fear; hating even the garment spotted by the flesh.* An injunction to the same cau-

tion in the mental sphere as would be exercised toward the very garments of one having a contagious disease.

THE REVELATION.

INTRODUCTION BY PROFESSOR B. B. WARFIELD, D.D., LL.D.

Author.—The Book of Revelation represents itself to be written by a John so described as to be distinctly identified with the apostle John, whose long residence in Asia and banishment to Patmos by the Emperor Domitian are historically attested from the time of Justin Martyr (about 150 A.D.) onwards. After the third century, however, doubts as to the apostolic origin of the book were widely spread in the East. These doubts have been revived in modern times upon substantially the same grounds, which turn chiefly upon the unlikeness of the Revelation to John's other writings. A closer study of John's books, however, reveals a deeper resemblance between them, and leaves no reason, on such internal grounds, for setting aside the historical testimony.

Date.—Exceptionally strong and consistent historical testimony, beginning with Irenæus (about 175 A.D.), who had special opportunities for knowing the truth, assigns the book to the later years of the reign of Domitian, about 95 or 96 A.D. Nevertheless, there has existed in recent times a strong tendency to date it as early as 68 A.D. This opinion is supported chiefly by an appeal to certain passages in the book, which are supposed to imply that Jerusalem and the Temple were still undestroyed (*e.g.* 11.19), or to identify the emperor who was on the throne (13.13; 17.7–12), when the book was written; as well as to the dissimilarity of this book to John's other writings, which is supposed to be best explained by assuming a long interval between their compositions. The proposed interpretation of the passages appealed to does not seem, however, to be justified; and the differences between Revelation and the other writings of John are not such as lapse of time will account for. On the other hand, the fitness of the later date to the historical situation in the book, and to the stage of development of the churches described in its opening chapters, is becoming ever plainer as historical research proceeds.

Literary Form.—In entitling itself "The Revelation of Jesus Christ which God gave him, to show unto his servants," the book announces itself as a divine disclosure, or, in other words, as a prophetical book. It is important to observe, however, that it is a prophetical book of a particular class. This class is designated by the Greek term *Apocalypse* ("Revelation"), and is characterized by its use of symbolical visions as the vehicle of prophecy. The model for this mode of prophecy was set by the book of Daniel. In the Apocalypse of John, the Divine Spirit makes use of that literary form which had been wrought out as the natural expression of persecuted believers, in order to enhearten the suffering church.

THE REVELATION

Contents.—The woes of the churches depicted in the Revelation furnish only the starting-point for its real message. Its text may be said to be those glorious words of the departing Lord, "In the world ye shall have tribulation: but be of good cheer; I have overcome the world" (John 16.33). As the victory of Christ over the world is evinced in the triumph of that kingdom of God which He came to establish, the theme of the book comes to be the gradual triumph of the kingdom of God; and as this triumph culminates in the second coming of Christ, it is the return of the Lord in glory to which all the movement of the book advances. It may thus be conceived as the bridge cast over the chasm which divides the first and second Advents.

In Old Testament prophecy the Advent in glory was not sharply distinguished from the Advent in humiliation; and when Christ came announcing the kingdom of heaven, men looked for an immediate triumph. The contrast between these high expectations and the reality of a persecuted church, required a revelation of the real course of things to preserve the church from despair.

The Apocalypse does for the church what the spiritual vision of the love of God in Christ so often does for the individual mourner —it enables it to endure, as seeing the invisible. It is then, in the highest sense, "The Revelation": it displays before the eyes of men, blinded in the turmoil of the strife, the inner reality and the true course of events in this period between the Advents. It is the divine philosophy of history. It is the exhibition in action of Paul's two great declarations, that Christ has been made head over all things, for His church, and that all things work together for good to them that are called according to God's purpose.

Interpretation.—This general drift of the book has been perceived by most of its expositors. They have seriously differed, however, in its detailed interpretation.

Some have thought that it presents a picture, not of the whole period between the Advents, but only of its opening years; as if it were intended for the comfort of those only who met that first great crisis, and gave assurance only of the external destruction of evil as embodied in the apostate Jewish and persecuting Roman states, and of the external triumph of the church over the Jewish and Roman worlds.

Others have thought that only the closing scenes that accompany the coming of Christ in glory, and His completed victory over the world, are depicted; as if it were intended to comfort and strengthen only by revealing to those in the midst of the battle the sure and glorious end.

Others have perceived that, in the visions of this book, an inner view is given of the real nature of the whole space between the two Advents; but have mistakenly thought that it must therefore sup-

616

ply a continuous and detailed history of the course of events which fill this period, and have sought to frame from it an inspired chronicle of the history of the church or of the world.

Others still have seen that the fortunes of the church are dealt with in these visions only in broad outlines and for their ethical and spiritual ends, and not with chronological purpose or effect. They have therefore read the book, not as intended to write history beforehand, but as designed to keep steadily before the mind of the church of God the great facts that the hand of God is in all history, and that its issue is, therefore, according to His appointment and direction; and thus to strengthen it to bear all trials, and to quicken its faith and trust in God, who does all things well.

Structure.—The structure of the book is admirably adapted to serve this end. Its plan does not form a single, closed ring; nor does it advance in a continuous straight line, but, returning repeatedly on itself, it makes its progress in a sort of spiral movement towards its climax. A mode of composition like this is peculiarly accordant with Semitic literary genius and art; and in the New Testament it is specially characteristic of John, who is accustomed to present truth to his readers by turning it round and round before them in successive and yet regularly advancing aspects.

The Apocalypse, in harmony with this literary method, is found to consist of a series of parallel and yet ever-progressing sections, which bring before the reader, over and over again, but in climacteric form, the struggle of the church, and its victory over the world in its Lord. There are probably seven of these spirals, though only five are clearly marked; and it is probable that each of them consists of seven subordinate divisions, though these are distinct in only four of them. The plan of the whole is, then, something like the following:—Prologue, 1.1–8; seven parallel sections, divided at 3.22; 8.1; 11.19; 14.20; 16.21; and 19.21; Epilogue, 22.6–21.

Symbolical Language.—An Apocalypse is, before all else, a book written in symbols. The whole action of John's Apocalypse, and every detail of its representation alike, is, accordingly, wrought out not directly, but through the medium of symbolism.

The sources of this symbolism are to be sought in the prophetic books of the Old Testament and in our Lord's discourses; and the meaning of the book will become clear in proportion as the significance of these symbols is correctly ascertained. It would be idle to deny that the Revelation is a difficult book; every age of the church has found its interpretation a problem. But its difficulty will be found to arise largely from our unfamiliarity with apocalyptic writings, and it may be expected to give way in proportion as we seek consistently to interpret it as an Apocalypse, written in purely symbolical language.

THE REVELATION OF JOHN

The Revelation of Jesus Christ   To the Seven Churches

1 The Revelation of Je′sus Christ, which God *a*gave him to show unto his *b*servants, *even* the things which must shortly come to pass: and he sent and signified *c*it by his angel unto his servant John; 2 who bare witness of the word of God, and of the testimony of Je′sus Christ, *even* of all things that he saw. 3 Blessed is he that readeth, and they that hear the words of the prophecy, and keep the things that are written therein: for the time is at hand

4 John to the seven churches that are in A′si-a: Grace to you and peace, from him who is and who was and *d*who is to come; and from the seven Spirits that are before his throne; 5 and from Je′sus Christ, *who is* the faithful witness, the firstborn of the dead, and the ruler of the kings of the earth. Unto him

---

a Or, *gave unto him, to show unto his servants the things &c.*   *b* Gr. *bondservants.*

c Or, *them*   *d* Or, *who cometh*

The Book of Revelation should be read as a vision and interpretation of the problem of the struggles through which the church must pass. The church, at that time, was on the eve of a great trial which would test its faith. See Mt. 24.4–31. These visions came to John primarily for the seven churches which are named, but also, in general, for the whole church throughout all ages, to give it strength, and prepare it for what it would be called to endure.

CHAPTER 1

1–3. These three verses may be considered the title and superscription.

1. *Of Jesus.* From Jesus, the real author. *Must.* In order to fulfil divine purpose as foretold in prophecy. *Signified.* Revealed in signs and symbols; as in ch. 5–10. *John.* The apostle, son of Zebedee, author of the gospel and epistles. See Mt. 4.21.

2. *Word of God.* As received in this revelation.

3. *He that readeth.* The public reader in the assembly of the saints.

4. *Seven churches.* Those named in ver. 11. These letters were addressed to these seven churches as having individually each its own problem, and also as representative of the varying conditions and problems of the whole church. They typify the various local churches of Christendom in all ages, with their elements of strength and weakness; and there is in the message an element of progress, which seems to make them a sort of prophecy of the whole Christian age. *Asia.* The western part of what is now called Asia Minor; including: Mysia, Lydia, Caria, and part of Phrygia. *Seven Spirits.* Commentators generally agree that the term signifies the Holy Spirit in His completeness.

5. *The faithful witness.* Jesus came to bear witness unto the truth. See Jn. 18.37. *Firstborn of the dead.* The writer points out Jesus as the first victor over sin and death, the firstfruits of those who shall live and reign with him in glory. *Loveth.* A continuing action. *Loosed.* A completed act, in the

618

that loveth us, and eloosed us
from our sins fby his blood; 6
and he made us to be a kingdom,
to be priests unto ghis God and
Father; to him be the glory and
the dominion hfor ever and ever.
A-men'. 7 Behold, he cometh
with the clouds; and every eye
shall see him, and they that
pierced him; and all the tribes
of the earth shall mourn over
him. Even so, A-men'.

8 I am the Al'pha and the
O-me'ga, saith the Lord God,
iwho is and who was and iwho
is to come, the Almighty.

9 I John, your brother and
partaker with you in the tribulation and kingdom and kpa-
tience which are in Je'sus, was

in the isle that is called Pat'mos,
for the word of God and the
testimony of Je'sus. 10 I was
in the Spirit on the Lord's day,
and I heard behind me a great
voice, as of a trumpet 11 saying,
What thou seest, write in a book
and send it to the seven churches:
unto Eph'e-sus, and unto Smyr'-
na, and unto Per'ga-mum, and
unto Thy-a-ti'ra, and unto Sar'-
dis, and unto Phil-a-del'phi-a,
and unto La-od-i-ce'a. 12 And
I turned to see the voice that
spake with me. And having
turned I saw seven golden
lcandlesticks; 13 and in the
midst of the lcandlesticks one
like unto a son of man, clothed
with a garment down to the foot,

---

e Many authorities, some ancient, read
washed. Heb. 9.14; comp. ch. 7.14. f Gr.
in. g Or, God and his Father h Gr. unto
the ages of the ages. Many ancient authorities omit of the ages. i Or, he who
k Or, stedfastness l Gr. lampstands.

---

death on the cross, whereby Christ
redeemed mankind in his sublime
sacrifice. See Rom. 6.10; Heb.
7.27.

6. Priests. The kingdom is composed of those who offer spiritual
sacrifices of prayer, praise, and
service, to their Lord. See Ex. 19.6;
1 Pet. 2.5, 9.

7. With the clouds. The imagery
of the Son of man riding upon the
clouds at his second coming is frequent throughout the Scriptures.
See Dan. 7.13; Mt. 24.30; 26.64;
Acts 1.9–11. They that pierced him.
Not the Roman soldiers, but the
Jews who crucified him. See Mt.
27.25; Acts 2.23; 5.30. The verse
quotes the prophecy of Zechariah.
See Zech. 12.10.

8. The Alpha and the Omega. The
first and the last letters of the Greek
alphabet, expressing the beginning
and the end. He who speaks is the
Eternal One.

9. The tribulation. As foretold by
Jesus. See Mt. 24.9. Patmos. An
island about 10 miles long and 6
miles wide, in the Ægean Sea, about
50 miles west of Miletus. For the
word. John was probably banished

to the isle of Patmos because of his
faith in Jesus. It is possible, however, that he was bidden to go to
the isle of Patmos in order to receive the revelation.

10. In the Spirit. In a state of
prophetic illumination. See ch. 4.2;
17.3; 21.10. Peter had a like experience (Acts 10.10), and so did
Paul (2 Cor. 12.1). The Lord's day.
This may mean the first day of the
week. See Acts 20.7; 1 Cor. 16.2.
Or it may mean the final and great
day of the Lord, to which he felt
himself transported. See Joel 2.31;
Mal. 4.5. Trumpet. The sound of
the trumpet was a signal of the
divine presence. See Ex. 19.13,
16, 19; Joel 2.1; Mt. 24.31.

11. Seven churches. See notes on
ch. 2.1, 8, 12, 18; 3.1, 7, 14.

12. Seven golden candlesticks.
Representing the seven churches.
See ver. 20; also Zech. 4.2, 10.

13–20. These verses present a
picture of the glorified Christ.

13. A son of man. Having the
figure of a man. See ch. 14.14;
Dan. 7.13. Down to the foot. A
garment indicative of priestly and
regal dignity.

and girt about at the breasts with a golden girdle. 14 And his head and his hair were white as white wool, *white* as snow; and his eyes were as a flame of fire; 15 and his feet like unto burnished brass, as if it had been refined in a furnace; and his voice as the voice of many waters. 16 And he had in his right hand seven stars: and out of his mouth proceeded a sharp two-edged sword: and his countenance was as the sun shineth in his strength. 17 And when I saw him, I fell at his feet as one dead. And he laid his right hand upon me, saying, Fear not; I am the first and the last, 18 and the Living one; and I ᵐwas dead, and behold, I

am alive ⁿfor evermore, and I have the keys of death and of Ha'des. 19 Write therefore the things which thou sawest, and the things which are, and the things which shall come to pass hereafter; 20 the mystery of the seven stars which thou sawest ᵒin my right hand, and the seven golden ᵖcandlesticks. The seven stars are the angels of the seven churches: and the seven ᵖcandlesticks are seven churches.

2 To the angel of the church in Eph'e-sus write:

These things saith he that holdeth the seven stars in his right hand, he that walketh in the midst of the seven golden ᵖcandlesticks: 2 I know thy

---

m Gr. became. n Gr. unto the ages of the   *ages. o Gr. upon. p Gr. lampstands.*

---

14. *White wool.* This vision of John is similar in many details to the vision of Daniel. See Dan. 7.9; 10.6.

15. *Brass.* Either bronze, an alloy of copper and tin, or electrum —gold combined with silver, steel and bronze; brilliant when polished. *Voice of many waters.* Ezekiel also makes a like comparison of the voice of the Almighty. See Ezek. 1.24; 43.2.

16. *A sharp two-edged sword.* Figurative language to express the convincing and convicting word of the Spirit. See Heb. 4.12; Eph. 6.17; 2 Thess. 2.8.

17. *As one dead.* Overcome by fear in the presence of the divine majesty *Fear not.* John had passed through a similar experience at the transfiguration, and with almost the same words Jesus restored his confidence. See Mt. 17.6, 7. *The first and the last.* Eternal; from everlasting to everlasting. See ver. 8; Ps. 90.2; Is. 41.4.

18. *The Living one.* That is, living from all eternity, before time was, both before and after he came into the world to redeem it. *Keys of death and of Hades.* Symbols of

his authority over death and the realm of the dead.

20. *Mystery.* Truth formerly hidden, but now to be revealed. *Angels.* Symbolic representations or types of the churches themselves; or possibly the responsible heads ('bishops') of the churches.

CHAPTER 2

1. *The church in Ephesus.* The messages in this and the following chapter, while addressed to the individual historic churches, were doubtless intended to reach the whole church. *Ephesus.* The capital and chief commercial city of the Roman proconsular province of Asia. Paul regarded this city as especially advantageous for the spread of the gospel. He preached in the synagogue for three months, then taught and reasoned on gospel truth for two years in the school of Tyrannus. He was careful to send his beloved disciple Timothy to Ephesus, where a church membership composed of both Jews and Gentiles called for sound doctrine as well as the widest Christian sympathy. See Acts 19.8–10.

2. *Thy works, and thy toil and patience.* In the trial with false

620

works, and thy toil and ªpatience, and that thou canst not bear evil men, and didst try them that call themselves apostles, and they are not, and didst find them false; 3 and thou hast ªpatience and didst bear for my name's sake, and hast not grown weary. 4 But I have *this* against thee, that thou didst leave thy first love. 5 Remember therefore whence thou art fallen, and repent and do the first works; or else I come to thee, and will move thy ᵇcandlestick out of its place, except thou repent. 6 But this thou hast, that thou hatest the works of the Nic-o-la′i-tans, which I also hate. 7 He that hath an ear, let him hear what the Spirit saith to the churches. To him that overcometh, to him will I give to eat of the tree of

life, which is in the ᶜParadise of God.

8 And to the angel of the church in Smyr′na write:

These things saith the first and the last, who ᵈwas dead, and lived *again*: 9 I know thy tribulation, and thy poverty (but thou art rich), and the ᵉblasphemy of them that say they are Jews, and they are not, but are a synagogue of Satan. 10 Fear not the things which thou art about to suffer: behold, the devil is about to cast some of you into prison, that ye may be tried; ᶠand ye shall have ᵍtribulation ten days. Be thou faithful unto death, and I will give thee the crown of life. 11 He that hath an ear, let him hear what the Spirit saith to the churches. He that overcometh

---

a Or, *stedfastness* b Gr. *lampstand.*
c Or, *garden*: as in Gen. 2.8.

d Gr. *became.* e Or, *reviling* f Some ancient authorities read *and may have.*
g Gr. *a tribulation of ten days.*

---

prophets, and final withdrawal from them. *Canst not bear.* The false teachers were too heavy a burden to carry.

4. *Thy first love.* The first ardent love with which they embraced the gospel.

5. *The first works.* Such works as had followed their first love. *Move thy candlestick.* Remove the church from the circle of the seven churches, as a candlestick no longer bearing a light.

6. *Nicolaitans.* Probably a heretical sect which, claiming liberty under the gospel, committed various excesses. See ver. 14, 15; also Gal. 5.14; 2 Pet. 2.13, 14.

7. *What the Spirit saith.* Speaking through Christ to John. *The tree of life.* A symbolical reference to the tree of life in the garden of Eden. See Gen. 2.9; 3.22-24. *Paradise.* This (Persian) word occurs in only two other places in the New Testament—Lk. 23.43; 2 Cor. 12.4. Its meaning is a 'park'

or pleasure-garden, and it is used to denote the place of rest for faithful souls after death.

8. *Angel.* See note ch. 1.20. *Smyrna.* The only one of the seven cities still in existence. It was a city of wealth, a seaport fifty miles north of Ephesus. It was the home of the bishop Polycarp, and the place of his martyrdom, A.D. 155. *The first and the last.* Jesus Christ. See ch. 1.8.

9. *Thou art rich.* In spiritual things. *Say they are Jews.* Though Jews in name, they were not, in a true sense, the chosen people of God. See Rom. 2.28.

10. *That ye may be tried.* The persecutors of the Christians, in the endeavor to force them to deny Jesus, would put them to the test. *Unto death.* Even to the point of death.

11. *Second death.* The final condemnation at the judgment. See ch. 20.6, 14; 21.8.

shall not be hurt of the second death.

12 And to the angel of the church in Per'ga-mum write:

These things saith he that hath the sharp two-edged sword: 13 I know where thou dwellest, *even* where Satan's throne is; and thou holdest fast my name, and didst not deny my faith, even in the days [h]of An'ti-pas my witness, my faithful one, who was killed among you, where Satan dwelleth. 14 But I have a few things against thee, because thou hast there some that hold the teaching of Ba'laam, who taught Ba'lak to cast a stumblingblock before the children of Is'ra-el, to eat things sacrificed to idols, and to commit fornication. 15 So hast thou also some that hold the teaching of the Nic-o-la'i-tans in like manner. 16 Repent therefore; or else I come to thee quickly, and I will make war against them with the sword of my mouth. 17 He that hath an ear, let him hear what the Spirit saith to the churches. To him that overcometh, to him will I give of the hidden man'na, and I will give him a white stone, and upon the stone a new name written, which no one knoweth but he that receiveth it.

18 And to the angel of the church in Thy-a-ti'ra write:

These things saith the Son of God, who hath his eyes like a flame of fire, and his feet are like unto burnished brass: 19 I know thy works, and thy love and faith and ministry and [i]patience, and that thy last works are more than the first. 20 But I have *this* against thee, that thou

---

h The Greek text here is somewhat un-certain.   i Or, *stedfastness*

12. *Pergamum.* A city of great importance, 50 miles north of Smyrna, and about 15 miles inland from the coast. It was a city of temples devoted to pagan worship. *The sharp two-edged sword.* A symbol of the word of God as expressed in the gospel. See ch. 1.16.

13. *Satan's throne.* Probably a reference to the temple of Augustus near the top of the hill at Pergamum, where worship of the emperor was conducted. It may refer, however, to the worship of Æsculapius with its serpent symbol.

14. *Balaam.* The story of Balaam and Balak is told in Numbers, ch. 22–24; 31.8. To Balaam is attributed the plan of destroying the children of Israel through fornication and idolatry. See Num. 25.1, 2, 5; Jude 11.

16. *Repent.* The admonition is to the whole church for tolerating idolaters and fornicators within its membership.

17. *Hidden manna.* The reference

is to the pot of manna stored in the tabernacle. See Ex. 16.34; Heb. 9.4. It is used here as a symbol of the spiritual 'bread of life' (Jn. 6.31–35).

18. *Thyatira.* A place of considerable importance, with a large Greek population. Among its industries the most famous was that of dyeing. It was about 45 miles southeast of Pergamum, and 50 miles northeast of Smyrna. Lydia, one of Paul's converts, was a purple seller from Thyatira. See Acts. 16.14, 15.

19. *More than the first.* As in ver. 2.

20. *The woman Jezebel.* This perhaps refers to some woman of influence within the church, who was leading the people to licentious and idolatrous living. But more probably it is an impersonation of the powerful heathen influence which beset the church of Thyatira, as Jezebel, Ahab's queen, influenced the people of Israel. See 1 K. 21.5–16; 2 K. 9.30–37.

sufferest *k*the woman Jez′e-bel, who calleth herself a prophetess; and she teacheth and seduceth my *l*servants to commit fornication, and to eat things sacrificed to idols. 21 And I gave her time that she should repent; and she willeth not to repent of her fornication. 22 Behold, I cast her into a bed, and them that commit adultery with her into great tribulation, except they repent of *m*her works. 23 And I will kill her children with *n*death; and all the churches shall know that I am he that searcheth the reins and hearts: and I will give unto each one of you according to your works. 24 But to you I say, to the rest that are in Thy-a-ti′ra, as many as have not this teaching, who know not the deep things of Satan, as they are wont to say; I cast upon you none other burden. 25 Nevertheless that which ye have, hold fast till I come.

26 And he that overcometh, and he that keepeth my works unto the end, to him will I give authority over the *o*nations: 27 and he shall rule them with a rod of *p*iron, as the vessels of the potter are broken to shivers; as I also have received of my Father: 28 and I will give him the morning star. 29 He that hath an ear, let him hear what the Spirit saith to the churches.

3 And to the angel of the church in Sar′dis write:

These things saith he that hath the seven Spirits of God, and the seven stars: I know thy works, that thou hast a name that thou livest, and thou art dead. 2 Be thou watchful, and establish the things that remain, which were ready to die: for I have *a*found no works of thine perfected before my God. 3 Remember therefore how thou hast received and didst hear; and keep *it*, and repent. If

---

k Many authorities, some ancient, read *thy wife*. *l* Gr. *bondservants*. *m* Many ancient authorities read *their*. *n* Or, *pestilence* Sept., Ex. 5.3, &c.

o Or, *Gentiles* *p* Or, *iron; as vessels of the potter, are they broken* *a* Many ancient authorities read *not found thy works*.

---

22 *Adultery*. In the Old Testament, idolatry was often called adultery, as an abandonment of God, the husband of His people. See Deut. 31.16; Judg. 2.17; 1 Chron. 5.25.

24. *Have not this teaching*. There were some who did not follow Jezebel. *The deep things of Satan*. Probably a sarcastic reference to the pretensions of the Gnostics, a sect which had mixed some elements of Christian teaching with wild and fantastic fancies from oriental religion. The Gnostics claimed to know many mysteries of nature and of God.

28. *The morning star*. A symbol of the glory to be conferred upon those who become the children of God. See Job 38.7; 2 Cor. 3.18;

1 Jn. 3.2. *What the Spirit saith*. In this revelation.

CHAPTER 3

1. *Sardis*. About 35 miles south of Thyatira; formerly the capital of Lydia (the nation of Crœsus), and notorious for its dissolute morals. *Seven Spirits of God*. The sevenfold or complete Spirit, as in ch. 1.4. *Seven stars*. The churches. *Thy works*. As the tree is known by its fruits, the works of the church at Sardis proved that it was dead. *Be thou*. Become. *Establish the things that remain*. This church must hold on to the little Christianity it still has.

3. *As a thief*. Without warning. See ch. 16.15; Mt. 24.43; 1 Thess. 5.2, 4; 2 Pet. 3.10.

therefore thou shalt not watch, I will come as a thief, and thou shalt not know what hour I will come upon thee. 4 But thou hast a few names in Sar'dis that did not defile their garments: and they shall walk with me in white; for they are worthy. 5 He that overcometh shall thus be arrayed in white garments; and I will in no wise blot his name out of the book of life, and I will confess his name before my Father, and before his angels. 6 He that hath an ear, let him hear what the Spirit saith to the churches.

7 And to the angel of the church in Phil-a-del'phi-a write:

These things saith he that is holy, he that is true, he that hath the key of David, he that openeth and none shall shut, and that shutteth and none openeth: 8 I know thy works (behold, I have *b*set before thee a door opened, which none can shut), that thou hast a little power, and didst keep my word, and didst not deny my name. 9 Behold, I give of the synagogue of Satan, of them that say they are Jews, and they are not, but do lie; behold, I will make them to come and *c*worship before thy feet, and to know that I have loved thee. 10 Because thou didst keep the word of my *d*patience, I also will keep thee from the hour of *e*trial, that *hour* which is to come upon the whole *f*world, to *g*try them that dwell upon the earth. 11 I come quickly: hold fast that which thou hast, that no one

---

b Gr. *given.* *c* The Greek word denotes an act of reverence, whether paid to a creature, or to the Creator. *d* Or. *stedfastness* *e* Or. *temptation* *f* Gr. *inhabited earth.* *g* Or. *tempt*

---

4. *A few names.* Even in the church in Sardis, dead through luxury (idolatry of the things of the world) and sin, there were a few who were faithful to the truth they had received.

5. *White garments.* Emblematic of purity, victory, and worthiness to receive the reward. *Book of life.* A symbol to express the recording of the names of God's chosen. See ch. 13.8; 20.12, 15; 21.27; also Ex. 32.32, 33; Rom. 8.29, 30; 1 Pet. 1.1. *Confess his name.* Attest his discipleship. See Mt. 10.32; Lk. 12.8.

7. *Philadelphia.* A rich and powerful city, 28 miles southeast of Sardis. One of the letters of Ignatius (martyred about A.D. 118) was addressed to Philadelphia. *Key of David.* Emblematic of Christ's authority and power as a king, because he was the son of David. See Is. 22.22; Mt. 16.19; also Mt. 1.1; 22.42.

8. *A door opened.* For all, whether Jew or Gentile. 'Door' is a frequent figure of speech in the Bible text. See Acts 14.27; 1 Cor. 16.9; 2 Cor. 2.12; Col. 4.3. In this connection it may mean a door to everlasting life, or into the church; or perhaps a wider field of missionary usefulness. *None can shut.* It is possible that the Jews in the church in Philadelphia objected to the admission of Gentiles.

9. *Synagogue of Satan.* A satirical reference to the assembly of the Jews at Philadelphia, who claimed to belong to the synagogue of the Lord, but were bitter persecutors of the Christians. *Before thy feet.* In acknowledgment that the church at Philadelphia was a true representative of her King and Lord. See Is. 45.14; 49.23; 60.14.

10. *Word of my patience.* The teachings of Jesus which encourage and enjoin loyal endurance. *Keep thee from the hour of trial.* This does not mean kept from tribulation, but delivered from disaster in the time of trial. *The whole world.* This is the first intimation of a widespread persecution, which reaches its climax in ch. 13.

11. *That no one take thy crown.* The conqueror's reward is to him

take thy crown.   12 He that overcometh, I will make him a pillar in the ᴴtemple of my God, and he shall go out thence no more: and I will write upon him the name of my God, and the name of the city of my God, the new Je-ru′sa-lem, which cometh down out of heaven from my God, and mine own new name. 13 He that hath an ear, let him hear what the Spirit saith to the churches.

14 And to the angel of the church in La-od-i-ce′a write:

These things saith the A-men′, the faithful and true witness, the beginning of the creation of God: 15 I know thy works, that thou art neither cold nor hot: I would thou wert cold or hot.   16 So

because thou art lukewarm, and neither hot nor cold, I will spew thee out of my mouth.   17 Because thou sayest, I am rich, and have gotten riches, and have need of nothing; and knowest not that thou art the wretched one and miserable and poor and blind and naked: 18 I counsel thee to buy of me gold refined by fire, that thou mayest become rich; and white garments, that thou mayest clothe thyself, and that the shame of thy nakedness be not made manifest; and eyesalve to anoint thine eyes, that thou mayest see.   19 As many as I love, I reprove and chasten: be zealous therefore, and repent.   20 Behold, I stand at the door and knock: if any

---

h Or, sanctuary

that endureth stedfastly unto the end. See ch. 7.14.

12. *Pillar in the temple.* He that overcometh shall have a prominent place in the church. See 1 Kings 7.15, 21; Gal. 2.9. All Christians are living stones in the temple of God (1 Pet. 2.5; Eph. 2.20), but those who have endured the greater trials shall receive the more honorable place. *Thence no more.* Shall remain in the church as a pillar, both for this world and the next. *The name of my God,* etc. This inscribing makes them citizens of heaven (Phil. 3.20), who shall stand with God and the Lamb on Mount Zion forever. See ch. 14.2; 22.4. *The new Jerusalem.* The city of the elect. See ch. 21.2; Gal. 4.26. *New name.* A name in harmony with the glory of the life that is 'hid with Christ in God' (Col. 3.3). See ch. 2.17; 19.12; Is. 56.5; 62.2; 65.15.

14. *Laodicea.* One of the richest cities of Asia Minor, about 50 miles southeast of Philadelphia, and 100 miles east of Ephesus. Colossæ lay 18 miles to the southeast. It is believed by some that Paul's letter to the Ephesians was in fact

written to the Laodiceans. See Col. 4.16. *Faithful and true witness.* See note ch. 1.5; 1 Tim. 6.13. *The beginning of the creation of God.* 'All things were made through him' (Jn. 1.3). See Col. 1.15, 16; Hebrews 1.2.

15. *Neither cold nor hot.* Not actively opposing the gospel, nor ardently supporting it; a state of entire spiritual indifference. See Mt. 21.31.

16. *Because thou art lukewarm.* Alluding to the fact that lukewarm water nauseates. This strong expression is intended to show that the self-satisfied and the proud offend the divine speaker.

17. *Have need of nothing.* Riches tend to produce a fatal satisfaction with the things of this world. See Hos. 12.8; Lk. 1.53.

18. *Gold refined by fire.* The true riches out of which all dross is burned, which shall be a treasure in heaven. See Mt. 6.19, 20; Lk. 12.21.

20. *I stand at the door.* This is one of the most beautiful pictures in the whole Bible. God so respects the individuality of each person that He will not force open the door

man hear my voice and open the door, I will come in to him, and will sup with him, and he with me. 21 He that overcometh, I will give to him to sit down with me in my throne, as I also overcame, and sat down with my Father in his throne. 22 He that hath an ear, let him hear what the Spirit saith to the churches.

4 After these things I saw, and behold, a door opened in heaven, and the first voice that I heard, *a voice* as of a trumpet speaking with me, one saying, Come up hither, and I will show thee the things which must *a*come to pass hereafter. 2 Straightway I was in the Spirit: and behold, there was a throne set in heaven, and one sitting

upon the throne; 3 and he that sat *was* to look upon like a jasper stone and a sardius: and *there was* a rainbow round about the throne, like an emerald to look upon. 4 And round about the throne *were* four and twenty thrones: and upon the thrones *I saw* four and twenty elders sitting, arrayed in white garments; and on their heads crowns of gold. 5 And out of the throne proceed lightnings and voices and thunders. And *there were* seven lamps of fire burning before the throne, which are the seven Spirits of God; 6 and before the throne, as it were a *b*sea of glass like unto crystal; and in the midst *c*of the throne, and round about the throne, four living creatures full of eyes before and behind. 7 And the

---

a Or, *come to pass.*   *After these things straightway &c.*

b Or, *glassy sea*   *c* Or, *before*   See ch. 7.17; comp. 5.6.

---

of the heart of his own creature, but stands without, waiting patiently for each one to open the door and let him in. See Mt. 7.7; 13.15; Jn. 14.23.

CHAPTER 4

1. *After these things.* Here begins a second vision or group of visions, that of God's presence in Heaven, the background of all that follows. The main divisions in the Book of Revelation are marked by this phrase. See ch. 7.9; 15.5; 18.1; 19.1. *Come up hither.* John was lifted up in spirit, as was Ezekiel, to behold visions of God. See Ezek. 3.12; 8.3; 11.1.

2. *I was in the Spirit.* See ch. 1.10, and note thereon. *Set in heaven.* Already there, not placed there as a part of the vision. *One sitting.* The Eternal God. See Is. 6.1; Dan. 7.9.

3. *Like a jasper stone*, etc. These comparisons are made to suggest the splendor of the great king.

4. *Elders.* Like the elders in the

synagogues and in the early assemblies of Christians, these 'older men' are in some way representative of the church.

5. *Lightnings*, etc. Expressive of the majesty of the Most High, creating terror in the hearts of men. See Ex. 19.16; Rev. 11.19. *Seven lamps.* God's Spirit. See ch. 1.4 and notes thereon.

6. *Crystal.* Emblematic of great splendor. See 1 K. 7.23. *Living creatures.* See Is. 6.1–4; Ezek. 1.4–14. Symbolical, it would seem, of all created things. *Full of eyes.* Symbolizing the power of attention and vision. See Zech. 4.10.

7. *The first creature*, etc. In Ezekiel there are four composite figures, each having four faces. Here there are four figures, each with a different aspect. The lion is the noblest of wild beasts; the ox, the strongest of domesticated animals; and the eagle is the most wonderful of flying creatures; with them stands man, nobler and stronger and more wonderful than all. The

first creature *was* like a lion, and the second creature like a calf, and the third creature had a face as of a man, and the fourth creature *was* like a flying eagle. 8 And the four living creatures, having each one of them six wings, are full of eyes round about and within: and they have no rest day and night, saying,

Holy, holy, holy, *is* the Lord God, the Almighty, who was and who is and *d*who is to come.

9 And when the living creatures shall give glory and honor and thanks to him that sitteth on the throne, to him that liveth *e*for ever and ever, 10 the four and twenty elders shall fall down before him that sitteth on the throne, and shall worship him that liveth *e*for ever and ever, and shall cast their crowns before the throne, saying,

11 Worthy art thou, our Lord and our God, to receive the glory and the honor and

the power: for thou didst create all things, and because of thy will they were, and were created.

5 And I saw *a*in the right hand of him that sat on the throne a book written within and on the back, close sealed with seven seals. 2 And I saw a strong angel proclaiming with a great voice, Who is worthy to open the book, and to loose the seals thereof? 3 And no one in the heaven, or on the earth, or under the earth, was able to open the book, or to look thereon. 4 And I wept much, because no one was found worthy to open the book, or to look thereon: 5 and one of the elders saith unto me, Weep not; behold, the Lion that is of the tribe of Ju'dah, the Root of David, hath overcome to open the book and the seven seals thereof. 6 And I saw *b*in the midst of the throne and of the four living creatures, and in the

---

d Or, *who cometh*   e Gr. *unto the ages of the ages.*

a Gr. *on.*   b Or, *between the throne with the four living creatures, and the elders*

wings, as in Isaiah, show their readiness and power for service.

8–11. These verses present a picture of worship and humiliation before the Lord God Almighty. The song is that of the seraphim in Isaiah 6; it has passed into the worship of the Christian church.

11. *Worthy art thou.* The adoration is offered by the church and the whole creation, and is based here on the fact that God's will and His work are shown in that which He has made.

CHAPTER 5

1. *Book.* This book is a symbol of the mystery of God; the volume of His plans and purposes and works. See Ezek. 2.10. *Seven seals.* Upon

the opening of these seals is to follow the interpretation of the mystery which cannot be fully known till all are opened. See Is. 29.11; Ezek. 2.9.

3. *No one in the heaven*, etc. No one of created beings is worthy to open and read and declare the meaning of the revelation.

5. *Lion . . . of Judah.* Referring to Messianic prophecy concerning Jesus. See Gen. 49.9. *Root of David.* See Is. 11.1, 10.

6. *A Lamb.* John looks, expecting to behold a conquering lion, but sees a Lamb which shows by its wounds that it has been slain, but yet is alive. It is a symbol of the crucified and risen Lord (ch. 1.18). See Is. 53.7; Jn. 1.29, 36; Acts 8.32; 1 Pet. 1.19. *Seven horns.*

midst of the elders, a Lamb standing, as though it had been slain, having seven horns, and seven eyes, which are the *c*seven Spirits of God, sent forth into all the earth. 7 And he came, and he *d*taketh *it* out of the right hand of him that sat on the throne. 8 And when he had taken the book, the four living creatures and the four and twenty elders fell down before the Lamb, having each one a harp, and golden bowls full of incense, which are the prayers of the saints. 9 And they sing a new song, saying,

Worthy art thou to take the book, and to open the seals thereof: for thou wast slain, and didst purchase unto God with thy blood *men* of every tribe, and tongue, and people, and nation, 10 and madest them *to be* unto our God a kingdom and priests; and they reign upon the earth.

11 And I saw, and I heard a voice of many angels round about the throne and the living creatures and the elders; and the number of them was ten thousand times ten thousand, and thousands of thousands; 12 saying with a great voice,

Worthy is the Lamb that hath been slain to receive the power, and riches, and wisdom, and might, and honor, and glory, and blessing.

13 And every created thing which is in the heaven, and on the earth, and under the earth, and on the sea, and all things that are in them, heard I saying,

Unto him that sitteth on the throne, and unto the Lamb,⁻ *be* the blessing, and the honor, and the glory, and the dominion, *e*for ever and ever.

14 And the four living creatures said, A-men′. And the elders fell down and *f*worshipped.

6 And I saw when the Lamb opened one of the seven seals, and I heard one of the four

---

c Some ancient authorities omit *seven.*
d Gr. *hath taken.*

e Gr. *unto the ages of the ages.*   f See marginal note on ch. 3.9.

Symbols of power. See 1 Sam. 2.10; Ps. 112.9; 148.14; Dan. 7.7, 20. *Seven eyes.* See note on ch. 4.6. It should be remembered throughout this book, that we have not a description of real things or even of pictures, but the record of visions, as in a dream, when nothing seems impossible or incongruous.

7. *Out of the right hand.* The Father entrusts this revelation to the glorified Son, the sacrificed but living Lamb of God.

8. *Fell down before the Lamb.* The church and creation, which have praised the Father as the Creator, now praise the Son as the Redeemer and Revealer. See ch. 8.3 and notes thereon; Ps. 141.2.

9. *Didst purchase unto God.* Alluding to the redemptive blood on the cross. See Mt. 20.28; 1 Cor. 6.20; 7.23; 1 Pet. 1.18, 19; Rev. 14.3, 4. *Kingdom and priests.* As in ch. 1.6.

11. *A voice of many angels.* The worship of Him who sits on the throne, and that offered to the Lamb (ver. 12), flow into one stream, indicating very strikingly the oneness of the Son and the Father.

CHAPTER 6

1. *One of the seven seals.* Six seals are broken, in preparation for the opening of the book. They give six pictures of the preliminary

living creatures saying as with a voice of thunder, Come[a]. 2 And I saw, and behold, a white horse, and he that sat thereon had a bow; and there was given unto him a crown: and he came forth conquering, and to conquer.

3 And when he opened the second seal, I heard the second living creature saying, Come[a]. 4 And another *horse* came forth, a red horse: and to him that sat thereon it was given to take [b]peace from the earth, and that they should slay one another: and there was given unto him a great sword.

5 And when he opened the third seal, I heard the third living creature saying, Come[a]. And I saw, and behold, a black horse; and he that.sat thereon had a balance in his hand. 6 And I heard as it were a voice in the midst of the four living creatures saying, [c]A measure of wheat for a [d]shilling, and three measures of barley for a [d]shilling; and the oil and the wine hurt thou not.

7 And when he opened the fourth seal, I heard the voice of the fourth living creature saying, Come[a]. 8 And I saw, and behold, a pale horse: and he that sat upon him, his name was Death; and Ha'des followed with him. And there was given unto them authority over the fourth part of the earth, to kill with sword, and with famine, and with [e]death, and by the wild beasts of the earth.

9 And when he opened the fifth seal, I saw underneath the altar the souls of them that had been slain for the word of God, and for the testimony which they held: 10 and they cried with a great voice, saying, How long, O Master, the holy and

a Some ancient authorities add *and see.*
b Some ancient authorities read *the peace of the earth.*   *c* Or, *A choenix (i.e.* about a quart) *of wheat for a shilling*—implying great scarcity. Comp. Ezek. 4.16 f.; 5.16. *d* See marginal note on Mt. 18.28.   *e* Or, *pestilence* Comp. ch. 2.23 marg.

revelations, not all easy to interpret. *Living creatures.* See ch. 4.6–8. *Come.* This command is given successively to each of the four horses.

2. *A white horse.* Symbolic of conquest; the entry of Christ upon his victorious work and the promise of his success.

4. *A red horse.* Symbolic of slaughter. See Mt. 24.3–8; Mk. 13.7, 8. Christ's coming brings a sword.

5. *A black horse.* Symbolic of mourning or of destitution. *Had a balance.* Indicating carefulness because of scarcity. See Lev. 26.26; Ezek. 4.16.

6. *A measure of wheat.* Somewhat less than a quart, a small daily allowance for a workman, at the price of an average day's wages (Mt. 20.9–13). The language of the verse points to a time when it will not be possible to obtain more than the bare necessities of life— not a famine, but want or a scarcity of food. *Hurt thou not.* Be careful as to their use.

8. *A pale horse.* Symbolic of death. See Ezek. 14.21, where the sore judgments of God are the sword, and the famine, and the evil beasts, and pestilence as in this verse. See Mt. 24.6, 7; Lk. 21. 10, 11, 20. *Hades.* The unseen world; the abode of the dead. Thus temporal judgments move men to look for Christ's coming, and to prepare its way.

9. *Underneath the altar.* As slain victims. Martyrdom for Christ's sake is added as in Mt. 24.9. *The testimony.* See ch. 1.2, 9.

10. *How long.* See Zech. 1.12. *Master.* Expressive of God's supremacy. *Avenge our blood.* Ven-

true, dost thou not judge and avenge our blood on them that dwell on the earth? 11 And there was given them to each one a white robe; and it was said unto them, that they should rest yet for a little time, until their fellow-servants also and their brethren, who should be killed even as they were, should *have fulfilled *their* course.

12 And I saw when he opened the sixth seal, and there was a great earthquake; and the sun became black as sackcloth of hair, and the whole moon became as blood; 13 and the stars of the heaven fell unto the earth, as a fig tree casteth her unripe figs when she is shaken of a great wind. 14 And the heaven was removed as a scroll when it is rolled up; and every mountain and island were moved out of their places. 15 And the kings of the earth, and the princes, and the *g*chief captains, and the rich, and the strong, and every bondman and freeman, hid themselves in the caves and in the rocks of the mountains; 16 and they say to the mountains and to the rocks, Fall on us, and hide us from the face of him that sitteth on the throne, and from the wrath of the Lamb: 17 for the great day of their wrath is come; and who is able to stand?

7 After this I saw four angels standing at the four corners of the earth, holding the four winds of the earth, that no wind should blow on the earth, or on the sea, or upon any tree. 2 And I saw another angel ascend from

---

f Some ancient authorities read *be fulfilled* in number. 2 Esdr. 4.36.

g Or, *military tribunes* Gr. *chiliarchs.*

---

geance belongs unto God (Rom. 12.19), and He will surely avenge those who call upon Him day and night (Lk. 18.7, 8).

11. *Who should be killed.* The martyrs for the word and the testimony of Jesus are those who have overcome; and to them is given the promise (ch. 3.4, 5), and also the reward of a white robe of victory and purity. See ch. 7.9, 13–17. *They should rest.* Care should be taken here not to reason from this passage, that all shall sleep unconsciously in an intermediate world. Sleep is the symbol of rest, but it belongs to life. See 2 Thess. 1.7; Heb. 4.3; also Rev. 14.13; Dan. 12.13. *Their fellow-servants.* See ch. 11.3–13.

12. *A great earthquake.* The breaking of the sixth seal brings signs of the approaching end as often described in prophecy. See Is. 29.6; Rev. 8.5; 11.13; 16.18; Mt. 24.7. *The sun became black.* See Is. 13.10; 24.23; Ezek. 32.7, 8; Joel 2.10; 3.15; Amos 8.9. The black sun and the blood-colored moon describe the phenomenon of eclipses.

13. *The stars of the heaven fell.* See Is. 13.10; Joel 2.10; 3.15. *As a fig tree.* See Is. 34.4. Nah. 3.12; Mt. 24.32. *A great wind.* See Dan. 2.35.

14. *Every mountain,* etc. See Is. 40.15; Jer. 4.24; Hab. 3.6; Nah. 1.5.

15. *Hid themselves.* Because of fear. See Is. 2.10.

16. *Fall on us.* See Hos. 10.8; Lk. 23.30. *From the face of him.* See Ps. 34.16. *Wrath.* See Nah. 1.6; Mal. 3.2.

CHAPTER 7

In the face of impending trouble, a fixed number are sealed that they may be delivered from it, and a great multitude come out of this tribulation. The breaking of the seventh seal, and the revelation of judgment are suspended.

1. *Four corners.* The four cardinal points, north, south, east, and west.

the sunrising, having the seal of the living God: and he cried with a great voice to the four angels to whom it was given to hurt the earth and the sea, 3 saying, Hurt not the earth, neither the sea, nor the trees, till we shall have sealed the *a*servants of our God on their foreheads. 4 And I heard the number of them that were sealed, a hundred and forty and four thousand, sealed out of every tribe of the children of Is′ra-el:

5 Of the tribe of Ju′dah *were* sealed twelve thousand;

Of the tribe of Reu′ben twelve thousand;

Of the tribe of Gad twelve thousand;

6 Of the tribe of Ash′er twelve thousand;

Of the tribe of Naph′ta-li twelve thousand;

Of the tribe of Ma-nas′seh twelve thousand;

7 Of the tribe of Sim′e-on twelve thousand;

Of the tribe of Le′vi twelve thousand;

Of the tribe of Is′sa-char twelve thousand;

8 Of the tribe of Zeb′u-lun twelve thousand;

Of the tribe of Joseph twelve thousand;

Of the tribe of Ben′ja-min *were* sealed twelve thousand.

9 After these things I saw, and behold, a great multitude, which no man could number, out of every nation and of *all* tribes and peoples and tongues, standing before the throne and before the Lamb, arrayed in white robes, and palms in their hands; 10 and they cry with a great voice, saying,

Salvation unto our God who sitteth on the throne, and unto the Lamb.

11 And all the angels were standing round about the throne, and *about* the elders and the four living creatures; and they fell before the throne on their faces, and worshipped God, 12 saying, A-men′: *b*Blessing, and glory, and wisdom, and thanksgiving, and honor, and power, and might, *be* unto our God *c*for ever and ever. A-men′.

13 And one of the elders answered, saying unto me, These that are arrayed in the white robes, who are they, and whence came they? 14 And I *d*say unto him, My lord, thou knowest.

---

a Gr. *bondservants.*

b Gr. *The blessing, and the glory &c. c* Gr. *unto the ages of the ages. d* Gr. *have said.*

---

3. *Sealed the servants.* A seal put on the foreheads of the saints to preserve them through, not from, tribulations. See Ex. 12.7, 13; Ezek. 9.4; Mt. 24.31; 1 Cor. 1.22.
4. *A hundred and forty and four thousand.* Twelve times the number of the twelve tribes of Israel in′ thousands, an equal number from each tribe, seeming to mean those saved under a special covenant. See ch. 14.1–3; 21.12, 16, 17.

9. *A great multitude.* The Christian covenant is unlimited. *And palms.* Taken in connection with white robes, the palms are symbols of victory.
14. *Great tribulation.* The tribulation here spoken of is that foretold in Mt. 24.21, and may have had its first interpretation in the apostolic period, as in John 16.33, and again in Acts 14.22. But in one aspect, the whole history of the

And he said to me, These are they that come out of the great tribulation, and they washed their robes, and made them white in the blood of the Lamb. 15 Therefore are they before the throne of God; and they serve him day and night in his *temple: and he that sitteth on the throne shall spread his tabernacle over them. 16 They shall hunger no more, neither thirst any more; neither shall the sun strike upon them, nor any heat: 17 for the Lamb that is in the midst ⁱof the throne shall be their shepherd, and shall guide them unto fountains of waters of life: and God shall wipe away every tear from their eyes.

8 And when he opened the seventh seal, there followed a silence in heaven about the space of half an hour. 2 And I saw the seven angels that stand

before God; and there were given unto them seven trumpets.

3 And another angel came and stood ᵃover the altar, having a golden censer; and there was given unto him much incense, that he should ᵇadd it unto the prayers of all the saints upon the golden altar which was before the throne. 4 And the smoke of the incense, ᶜwith the prayers of the saints, went up before God out of the angel's hand. 5 And the angel ᵈtaketh the censer; and he filled it with the fire of the altar, and cast it ᵉupon the earth: and there followed thunders, and voices, and lightnings, and an earthquake.

6 And the seven angels that had the seven trumpets prepared themselves to sound.

7 And the first sounded, and there followed hail and fire, mingled with blood, and they

---

e Or. *sanctuary* *f* Or, *before* See ch. 4.6; comp. 5.6.

a Or, *at* *b* Gr. *give.* *c* Or, *for* *d* Gr. *hath taken.* *e* Or, *into*

---

church is a time of tribulation. *Washed their robes.* The startling figure, of robes washed white in blood, justifies itself in the redemption through Christ's death.

15. *Before the throne.* In a favored position because of their faithfulness. *Serve him.* Worship him.

CHAPTER 8

1. This verse concludes the record of the opening or breaking of the seals. The book of revelation may now be opened. But the seer did not look into it or hear it read. The sight of the unsealed book leads to reverential silence, and for an appreciable time the vision stops. Man cannot know yet all God's plans or the way of their fulfilment.

2. This verse begins the third part of the book, which contains the vision of the trumpets, the proclamations of God which prepare the way

of Christ and mark the progress of the church.

3. *Another angel came.* See ch. 7.2; Zech. 3.1. *Over the altar.* John has before him in his vision the temple of God in heaven patterned after the earthly temple and tabernacle of the Jews. See Ex. 25.40; 26.30; 30.1; Heb. 8.5. The altar of incense was in front of the veil behind which was the ark of the covenant with the mercy-seat and cherubim. See Heb. 9.2–5; Ex. 25.1–40; 26.1–37. *Golden censer.* The fire-pan of Ex. 27.3; 1 K. 7.50. *Prayers of all the saints.* The word 'saints' refers to Christians generally, all of whom are called to be saints (Rom 1.7), not to a distinct class of Christians. See ch. 5.8; 6.9, 10; also Lk. 18.7, 8.

5. *Upon the earth.* The worship of heaven touches the earth, and there is a vision of divine glory, as at Sinai (Ex. 19.16–21).

7. *The first sounded.* The trum-

were cast *upon the earth: and the third part of the earth was burnt up, and the third part of the trees was burnt up, and all green gráss was burnt up.

8 And the second angel sounded, and as it were a great mountain burning with fire was cast into the sea: and the third part of the sea became blood; 9 and there died the third part of the creatures which were in the sea, *even* they that had life; and the third part of the ships was destroyed.

10 And the third angèl sounded, and there fell from heaven a great star, burning as a torch, and it fell upon the third part of the rivers, and upon the fountains of the waters; 11 and the name of the star is called Wormwood: and the third part of the waters became wormwood; and many men died of the waters, because they were made bitter.

12 And the fourth angel sounded, and the third part of the sun was smitten, and the third part of the moon, and the third part of the stars; that the third part of them should be darkened, and the day should not shine for the third part of it, and the night in like manner.

13 And I saw, and I heard *f*an eagle, flying in mid heaven, saying with a great voice, Woe, woe, woe, for them that dwell on the earth, by reason of the other voices of the trumpet of the three angels, who are yet to sound.

9 And the fifth angel sounded, and I saw a star from heaven fallen unto the earth: and there was given to him the key of the pit of the abyss. 2 And he opened the pit of the abyss; and there went up a smoke out of the pit, as the smoke of a great furnace; and the sun and the air were darkened by reason of the smoke of the pit. 3 And out of the smoke came forth locusts upon the earth; and power was given them, as the scorpions of the earth have power. 4 And it was said unto them that they should not hurt the grass of the earth, neither any green thing,

---

e Or, *into*   *f* Gr. *one eagle.*

---

pets tell of judgments proclaimed and show the world ripe for punishment; they bring calamity, first on the earth, then on the sea, next on streams and fountains, and then on the lights of heaven. Everything is injured by sin, and nature itself cries out against man and thus appeals to God. *Hail and fire.* See Ex. 9.24; Ezek. 38.22.

8, 9. *Became blood.* The reference here is to two of the plagues which afflicted the Egyptians.

13. *An eagle.* A symbol of judgment. See Hos. 8.1.

CHAPTER 9
Two woe-trumpets.

1. *A star.* A personification of an

angel, supposed by some scholars to be a fallen angel. *Pit of the abyss.* The abode of evil spirits. See Lk. 8.31.

2. *Smoke of a great furnace.* See Gen. 19.28; Ex. 19.18.

3. *Came forth locusts.* They produce great desolation. See Ex. 10.12–15; Joel 1.4; 2.2–11.

4. *Neither any tree.* A third part of the trees had been burned by the plague of the first trumpet. See ch. 8.7. *As have not the seal.* See ch. 7.3; Ezek. 9.4–6. God's saints are kept safe. The disciples had power over unclean spirits (Mk. 6.7), and those who received the gospel were turned from the power of Satan unto God (Acts 26. 18).

neither any tree, but only such men as have not the seal of God on their foreheads. 5 And it was given them that they should not kill them, but that they should be tormented five months: and their torment was as the torment of a scorpion, when it striketh a man. 6 And in those days men shall seek death, and shall in no wise find it; and they shall desire to die, and death fleeth from them. 7 And the *shapes of the locusts were like unto horses prepared for war; and upon their heads as it were crowns like unto gold, and their faces were as men's faces. 8 And they had hair as the hair of women, and their teeth were as *the teeth* of lions. 9 And they had breastplates, as it were breastplates of iron; and the sound of their wings was as the sound of chariots, of many horses rushing to war. 10 And they have tails like unto scorpions, and stings; and in their tails is their power to hurt men five months. 11 They have over them as king the angel of the abyss: his name

in Hebrew is A-bad'don, and in the Greek *tongue* he hath the name *b*A-pol'ly-on.

12 The first Woe is past: behold, there come yet two Woes hereafter.

13 And the sixth angel sounded, and I heard *c*a voice from the horns of the golden altar which is before God, 14 one saying to the sixth angel that had the trumpet, Loose the four angels that are bound at the great river Eu-phra'tes. 15 And the four angels were loosed, that had been prepared for the hour and day and month and year, that they should kill the third part of men. 16 And the number of the armies of the horsemen was twice ten thousand times ten thousand: I heard the number of them. 17 And thus I saw the horses in the vision, and them that sat on them, having breastplates *as* of fire and of hyacinth and of brimstone: and the heads of the horses are as the heads of lions; and out of their mouths proceedth fire and smoke and brimstone. 18 By these

---

a Gr. *likenesses.*   *b* That is, *Destroyer.*   *c* Gr. *one voice.*

---

5. *Five months.* The period from May to September, during which locusts might work destruction. Locusts usually appear at intervals within this period, but in this vision they are continually present to torment.

6. *Shall seek death.* The utter despair of the wicked because of the torments. See Job 3.22.

7. *Horses prepared for war.* See Joel 2.4. *Crowns like unto gold.* Denoting victory. These represent the spiritual hosts of wickedness, such as are called by Paul, 'principalities,' 'powers,' and 'world-rulers of this darkness.' See Eph. 6.12; Col. 2.15.

11. *Abaddon* is the Hebrew, and *Apollyon* the Greek word for destroyer. These evil spirits are ruled by a power of malignity and ruin. *The sixth angel sounded.* The sixth trumpet proclaims destructive war. *Altar.* See ch. 8.3.

14. *River Euphrates.* From the regions of this river had come the hosts of Assyria, and the Chaldeans, to war against Israel, and into those regions God's people had been carried captives.

15. *The third part of men.* See ch. 8.7–12.

~ 18. *Fire and smoke and brimstone.* A threefold picture of the terrors of war.

three plagues was the third part of men killed, by the fire and the smoke and the brimstone, which proceeded out of their mouths. 19 For the power of the horses is in their mouth, and in their tails: for their tails are like unto serpents, and have heads; and with them they hurt. 20 And the rest of mankind, who were not killed with these plagues, repented not of the works of their hands, that they should not [d]worship demons, and the idols of gold, and of silver, and of brass, and of stone, and of wood; which can neither see, nor hear, nor walk: 21 and they repented not of their murders, nor of their sorceries, nor of their fornication, nor of their thefts.

10 And I saw another strong angel coming down out of heaven, arrayed with a cloud; and the rainbow was upon his head, and his face was as the sun, and his feet as pillars of fire; 2 and he had in his hand a little book open: and he set his right foot upon the sea, and his left upon the earth; 3 and he cried with a great voice, as a lion roareth: and when he cried, the seven thunders uttered their voices. 4 And when the seven thunders uttered *their voices*, I was about to write: and I heard a voice from heaven saying, Seal up the things which the seven thunders uttered, and write them not. 5 And the angel that I saw standing upon the sea and upon the earth lifted up his right hand to heaven, 6 and sware by him that liveth [a]for ever and ever, who created the heaven and the things that are therein, and the earth and the things that are therein, [b]and the sea and the things that are therein, that there shall be [c]delay no longer: 7 but in the days of the voice of the seventh angel, when he is about to sound, then is finished the mystery of God, according to the good tidings which he declared to his [d]servants the prophets. 8 And the voice which I heard from heaven, *I heard it* again speaking with me, and saying, Go, take the book which is open in the hand of the angel that standeth upon the sea and upon the earth. 9 And I went unto the angel, saying unto him that he

---

[d] See marginal note on ch. 3.9.   [a] Gr. *unto the ages of the ages.*   [b] Some ancient authorities omit *and the sea and the things that are therein.*   [c] Or, *time*   [d] Gr. *bondservants.*

CHAPTER 10

Between the sixth and the seventh trumpet come the visions of the 'little book' and the 'two witnesses.' They relieve the pictures of deserved judgment by telling of revelations of truth and hopes of victory.

2. *His right foot*, etc. Emblematic of power over land and sea. *Little book open.* Unsealed and also open; its contents may now be made known; the seer heard them announced as thunder; but he may not tell them yet. Still, he does announce that God will not longer delay his word.

7. *Mystery of God.* The revelation of the truth of the gospel. See Rom. 16.25, 26; Eph. 1.9; 3.3–9; Col. 1.26, 27.

8. *Take the book.* The volume is now given to the chosen man, and he is to be sent to prophesy (proclaim) from it as it becomes a part of himself.

9. *Eat it up*, etc. The reception of the revelation would bring joy, but the sorrows predicted therein

should give me the little book. And he saith unto me, Take it, and eat it up; and it shall make thy belly- bitter, but in thy mouth it shall be sweet as honey. 10 And I took the little book out of the angel's hand, and ate it up; and it was in my mouth sweet as honey: and when I had eaten it, my belly was made bitter. 11 And they say unto me, Thou must prophesy again *over many peoples and nations and tongues and kings.

11 And there was given me a reed like unto a rod: *a*and one said, Rise, and measure the *b*temple of God, and the altar, and them that worship therein. 2 And the court which is without the *b*temple *c*leave without, and measure it not; for it hath been given unto the *d*nations: and the holy city shall they tread under foot forty and two months.

3 And I will give unto my two witnesses, and they shall prophesy a thousand two hundred and threescore days, clothed in sackcloth. 4 These are the two olive trees and the two *e*candlesticks, standing before the Lord of the earth. 5 And if any man desireth to hurt them, fire proceedeth out of their mouth and devoureth their enemies; and if any man shall desire to hurt them, in this manner must he be killed. 6 These have the power to shut the heaven, that it rain not during the days of their prophecy: and they have power over the waters to turn them into blood, and to smite the earth with every plague, as often as they shall desire. 7 And when they shall have finished their testimony, the beast that cometh up out of the abyss shall make war with them, and over-

---

e Or, *concerning* Comp. Jn. 12.16. *a* Gr. *saying.* *b* Or, *sanctuary* *c* Gr. *cast*
d Or, *Gentiles* *e* Gr. *lampstands.*

---

would bring grief to a sympathetic heart.

CHAPTER 11

.The sanctuary is measured for preservation; the courts of the temple remain desolate, two witnesses appear who are killed and return to life.

1. *A reed like unto a rod.* See Ezek. 40.3; Zech. 2.1. *Measure the temple of God.* This symbolizes, as often, the faithful church, made up of God's chosen ones, preserved in spite of persecution.

2. *Court which is without.* Corresponding to the Court of the Gentiles in the Jewish Temple. See Ezek. 10.5. *The holy city.* Jerusalem. See Mt. 4.5: 27.53. *Forty and two months.* Three years and a half, 1260 days, have a symbolic meaning, which we cannot now interpret.

3. *My two witnesses.* We cannot

tell whether the words have a personal application: they certainly refer to the message of the church itself, the true witness to Christ. *Clothed in sackcloth.* Because they were to preach repentance and judgment.

4. *Two olive trees.* Supplying the lamps in the temple. See Zech. 4.3–14.

6. *To shut the heaven.* To cause a drought, as did Elijah. See 1 K. 17.1. *Over the waters,* etc. As did Moses and Aaron. See Ex. 7.17–21.

7. *Have power.* God's word is ever mighty for judgment. *The beast.* The world-power opposing the church; as prophesied ' in Daniel 7. This passage anticipates what is written in ch. 13.1, 2; 17.8. *Shall make war,* etc. Symbolic of the temporary triumph of the world-power of darkness over the church. The passage doubtless has a direct reference to the persecutions of Christians by the Roman empire.

come them, and kill them. 8 And their *dead bodies lie in the street of the great city, which spiritually is called Sod'om and E'gypt, where also their Lord was crucified 9 And from among the peoples and tribes and tongues and nations do *men* look upon their *dead bodies three days and a half, and suffer not their dead bodies to be laid in a tomb. 10 And they that dwell on the earth rejoice over them, and make merry; and they shall send gifts one to another; because these two prophets tormented them that dwell on the earth. 11 And after the three days and a half the breath of life from God entered into them, and they stood upon their feet; and great fear fell upon them that beheld them. 12 And they heard a great voice from heaven saying unto them, Come up hither. And they went up into heaven in the cloud; and their enemies beheld them. 13 And in that hour there was a great earthquake, and the tenth part of the city fell; and there were killed in the earthquake *g*seven

thousand persons: and the rest were affrighted, and gave glory to the God of heaven.

14 The second Woe is past: behold, the third Woe cometh quickly.

15 And the seventh angel sounded; and there followed great voices in heaven, and they said,

The kingdom of the world is become *the kingdom* of our Lord, and of his Christ: and he shall reign *h*for ever and ever.

16 And the four and twenty elders, who sit before God on their thrones, fell upon their faces and worshipped God, 17 saying,

We give thee thanks, O Lord God, the Almighty, who art and who wast; because thou hast taken thy great power, and didst reign. 18 And the nations were wroth, and thy wrath came, and the time of the dead to be judged, and *the time* to give their reward to thy *i*servants the prophets, and to the saints, and to

---

f Gr. *carcase.*   *g* Gr. *names of men, seven thousand.* Comp. ch. 3.4.

h Gr. *unto the ages of the ages.*   *i* Gr *bondservants.*

8. *Lie in the street.* This was a very great indignity in the eyes of the Jews. *The great city.* The last part of the verse shows that this was Jerusalem. *Sodom and Egypt.* Two names which are typical of great wickedness. In the Scriptures, Jerusalem is sometimes spoken of as Sodom. See Jer. 23.14; Ezek. 16.46–56.

10. *Prophets tormented them.* The true prophet always is a torment to those who have guilty consciences; as Elijah was to Ahab (1 K. 17; 18; 19). So also Peter, and Stephen. See Acts 5.33; 7.54.

11. *The breath of life.* See Ezek. 37.1–14; also Rom. 6.5.

15. *The seventh angel sounded.* Between the sixth and seventh trumpets is given a manifestation of Christ, with the giving of a great revelation, and the power of evil prevailing against the truth. On this follows a great victory, type of the final victory. See ch. 10.7; Mt. 24.14; Acts 2.17; Heb. 1.2; 1 Pet. 1.20.

15–18. These verses constitute a song of triumph, for God has established his kingdom and has begun to execute his judgments. Thus we

them that fear thy name, the small and the great; and to destroy them that destroy the earth.

19 And there was opened the ᵏtemple of God that is in heaven; and there was seen in his ᵏtemple the ark of his covenant; and there followed lightnings, and voices, and thunders, and an earthquake, and great hail.

12 And a great sign was seen in heaven: a woman arrayed with the sun, and the moon under her feet, and upon her head a crown of twelve stars; 2 and she was with child; and she crieth out, travailing in birth, and in pain to be delivered. 3 And there was seen another sign in heaven: and behold, a great red dragon, having

seven heads and ten horns, and upon his heads seven diadems. 4 And his tail draweth the third part of the stars of heaven, and did cast them to the earth: and the dragon standeth before the woman that is about to be delivered, that when she is delivered he may devour her child. 5 And she was delivered of a son, a man child, who is to rule all the ᵃnations with a rod of iron: and her child was caught up unto God, and unto his throne. 6 And the woman fled into the wilderness, where she hath a place prepared of God, that there they may nourish her a thousand two hundred and threescore days.

7 And there was war in heaven: Mi′cha-el and his angels *going forth* to war with the dragon; and the dragon warred and his

---

ᵏ Or, *sanctuary*

are brought to see what the end shall be.

CHAPTER 12

Series of visions. Fourth division of the Book. Clearer revelation of Christ and of his conflict with evil.

1. *A woman.* Symbolizing the church, or the ideal Christian society.

2. *Travailing in birth.* Referring to suffering which yet shall lead to life.

3. *A great red dragon.* Symbolizing the power of evil. Red probably as symbolic of bloodshed. See ver. 9. *Seven heads and ten horns.* Symbolic of great power. *Seven diadems.* Symbolic of royal claims.

4. *His tail draweth,* etc. The dragon's tail is his most destructive weapon. Thus is pictured the great destroying power of the evil one.

5. *A son, a man child.* In ch. 2.26, 27, we are told that he that overcometh shall rule with a rod of iron. This 'son' is the Messiah as coming for the church which makes

---

ᵃ Or, *Gentiles*

ready for him. But it is not amiss to consider the 'son' also as in general the seed of the church, the company of saints. *Her child was caught up.* This does not accurately describe the ascension of Jesus, but it may symbolize it, as showing his continued life and that of his people. The fact that the child was seen as 'caught up' into heaven, shows that these events occur on this earth, and not in heaven.

6. *The woman fled.* Describing first the scattering of the church from Jerusalem, because of persecution. See Mt. 24.9. In a large view the vision pictures a general scattering of those who suffer for the faith.

7. *War in heaven.* This shows a conflict in the spiritual world, such as is ever 'wrestling against the principalities, powers,' etc., mentioned in Eph. 6.12. *Michael and his angels.* Representing the powers of light. According to Jewish conception, Michael was the angel who guarded particularly the interests of the Jews. See Dan. 10.31; 12.1.

angels; 8 and they prevailed not, neither was their place found any more in heaven. 9 And the great dragon was cast down, the old serpent, he that is called the Devil and Satan, the deceiver of the whole *b*world; he was cast down to the earth; and his angels were cast down with him. 10 And I heard a great voice in heaven, saying,

*c*Now is come the salvation, and the power, and the kingdom of our God, and the authority of his Christ: for the accuser of our brethren is cast down, who accuseth them before our God day and night. 11 And they overcame him because of the blood of the Lamb, and because of the word of their testimony; and they loved not their life even unto death. 12 Therefore rejoice, O heavens, and ye that *d*dwell in them. Woe for the earth and for the sea: because the devil is gone down unto you, hav-

ing great wrath, knowing that he hath but a short time.

13 And when the dragon saw that he was cast down to the earth, he persecuted the woman that brought forth the man *child*. 14 And there were given to the woman the two wings of the great eagle, that she might fly into the wilderness unto her place, where she is nourished for a time, and times, and half a time, from the face of the serpent. 15 And the serpent cast out of his mouth after the woman water as a river, that he might cause her to be carried away by the stream. 16 And the earth helped the woman, and the earth opened her mouth and swallowed up the river which the dragon cast out of his mouth. 17 And the dragon waxed wroth with the woman, and went away to make war with the rest of her seed, that keep the commandments of God, and hold the testimony of **13** Je´sus: 1 and *a*he stood upon the sand of the sea.

---

b Gr. *inhabited earth.* *c* Or, *Now is the salvation, and the power, and the kingdom, become our God's, and the authority* is be-

come *his Christ's.* *d* Gr. *tabernacle.* *a* Some ancient authorities read *I stood &c.* connecting the clause with what follows.

8. *Neither was their place,* etc. This means that Christ and his church have already broken the power of Satan. See Is. 14.12–15.

9. *The old serpent.* See Gen. 3.1–4. *He was cast down,* etc. His struggle now is with the church on earth. A parallel passage occurs in Lk. 10.18.

10. *Saying, Now is come,* etc. The song of victory is because of the final triumph of the church and the gospel over the powers of evil.

11. *They overcame.* See ch. 3.21. *Because of the blood.* By the strength of the blood of their Lord, and for the sake of their testimony, their faith held the Christians through persecution.

12. *Rejoice, O heavens.* See Ps.

96.11; Is. 49.13. *Woe for the earth,* etc. The bitter struggle is still to go on in the world of men.

14. *Wings of the great eagle.* See Ex. 19.4.

15. *Water as a river.* The church finds refuge, though a flood—betokening a great host of adversaries—would destroy her. The host finds its ruin in the earth, which seemed its strength; but the dragon persists in his assaults. We may read here the beginning of hope, to sustain us in the sad visions which follow.

17. *The rest of her seed.* See ver. 5, and note thereon.

CHAPTER 13

1. *A beast.* A great world-power,

And I saw a beast coming up out of the sea, having ten horns and seven heads, and on his horns ten diadems, and upon his heads names of blasphemy. 2 And the beast which I saw was like unto a leopard, and his feet were as *the feet* of a bear, and his mouth as the mouth of a lion: and the dragon gave him his power, and his throne, and great authority. 3 And *I saw* one of his heads as though it had been *b*smitten unto death; and his death-stroke was healed: and the whole earth wondered after the beast; 4 and they *c*worshipped the dragon, because he gave his authority unto the beast; and they *c*worshipped the beast, saying, Who is like unto the beast? and who is able to war with him? 5 and there was given to him a mouth speaking great tnings and blasphemies; and there was given to him authority *d*to continue forty and two

months. 6 And he opened his mouth for blasphemies against God, to blaspheme his name, and his tabernacle, *even* them that *c*dwell in the heaven. 7 *f*And it was given unto him to make war with the saints, and to overcome them: and there was given to him authority over every tribe and people and tongue and nation. 8 And all that dwell on the earth shall *c*worship him, *every one* whose name hath not been *g*written from the foundation of the world in the book of life of the Lamb that hath been slain. 9 If any man hath an ear, let him hear. 10 *h*If any man *i*is for captivity, into captivity he goeth: if any man shall kill with the sword, with the sword must he be killed. Here is the *k*patience and the faith of the saints.

11 And I saw another beast coming up out of the earth; and he had two horns like unto a

b Gr. *slain.*   *c* See marginal note on ch. 3.9.   *d* Or, *to do* his works *during* See Dan. 11.28.   *e* Gr. *tabernacle.*   *f* Some ancient authorities omit *And it was given . . . overcome them.*   *g* Or, *written in the book . . .* *slain from the foundation of the world.* *h* The Greek text in this verse is somewhat uncertain.   *i* Or, leadeth *into captivity* *k* Or, *stedfastness*

hostile to the church, as the non-descript beast in Dan. 7.7. It appeared to the early church as the Roman empire, the persecuting power of the world.

2. *Leopard,* etc. The beast is a composite of all the world-powers. See Dan. 7.4–8.

3. *One of his heads,* etc. This may refer to some event in the life of Nero. At any rate, it intimates that the power of evil would seem to prevail in spite of some victories of truth; and that successful evil would be held in admiration by mankind. Men would worship Satan, because Satan maintained the power of the world.

4. *Authority unto the beast.* Satan gave his power to the world, as it was the enemy of the church.

5. *A mouth speaking,* etc. See Dan. 7.8, 20, 25; 11.36. *Forty and two months.* See ch. 11.2; 12.6; Dan. 7.25.

6. *Tabernacle, even them,* etc. The tabernacle, even more than the Temple, is a type of heaven.

7. *The saints.* The same as 'the rest of her seed' in ch. 12.17. See also note on ch. 12.5.

8. *The book of life.* See ch. 3.5, and note thereon.

10. *If any man is for captivity,* etc. See Gen. 9.6; Jer. 15.2; 43.11; Mt. 26.52. *Here is the patience.* That is, here is the reason why the saints should be 'patient' (stedfast) in tribulation.

11. *Another beast.* The earthborn beast is less repulsive than the beast which rose up from the sea.

lamb, and he spake as a dragon. 12 And he exerciseth all the authority of the first beast in his sight. And he maketh the earth and them that dwell therein to [l]worship the first beast, whose death-stroke was healed. 13 And he doeth great signs, that he should even make fire to come down out of heaven upon the earth in the sight of men. 14 And he deceiveth them that dwell on the earth by reason of the signs which it was given him to do in the sight of the beast; saying to them that dwell on the earth, that they should make an image to the beast who hath the stroke of the sword and lived. 15 And it was given *unto him* to give breath to it, *even* to the image of the beast, [m]that the image of the beast should both speak, and cause that as many as should not [l]worship the image of the beast should be killed. 16 And he causeth all, the small and the great, and the rich and the poor, and the free and the bond, that there be given them a mark on their right hand, or upon their forehead; 17 and that no man should be able to buy or to sell, save he that hath the mark, *even* the name of the beast or the number of his name. 18 Here is wisdom. He that hath understanding, let him count the number of the beast; for it is the number of a man: and his number is [n]Six hundred and sixty and six.

14 And I saw, and behold, the Lamb standing on the mount Zi'on, and with him a hundred and forty and four thousand, having his name, and the name of his Father, written on their foreheads. 2 And I heard a voice from heaven, as the voice of many waters, and as the voice of a great thunder: and the voice which I heard *was* as *the voice* of harpers harping with their harps: 3 and they sing as it were a new song before the throne, and before the four living creatures and the elders: and no man could learn the song save the hundred and forty and four thousand, *even* they that had been purchased out of the

---

l See marginal note on ch. 3.9.   *m* Some ancient authorities read *that even the image of the beast should speak; and he shall cause*

&c.   *n* Some ancient authorities read *Six hundred and sixteen.*

It would seem to be a partially Christianized, but really pagan power, deceiving man.

14. *He deceiveth them*, etc. See ch. 2.20; 2 Thess. 2.11. *Make an image.* Very probably a reference to the image of the emperor of Rome, but it means any worship of evil principles, even under the guise of right.

18. *Six hundred and sixty and six.* It seems presumptuous to attempt to explain the number 666. Probably it is a cipher, the key to which has been lost. There may have been many things in this book, which were made clear to early readers by oral interpretations now lost.

CHAPTER 14

The two chapters immediately preceding present dark pictures of the temporary triumph of the powers of evil. This chapter portrays the victory and glory that await those who overcome, the 'sealed' of chapter 7, and tells of righteous judgment.

1. *The Lamb.* As always, Christ. *The Mount Zion.* The heavenly Zion. See Ps. 2.6; Heb. 12.22.

earth. 4 These are they that were not defiled with women; for they are virgins. These *are* they that follow the Lamb whithersoever he goeth. These were purchased from among men, *to be* the firstfruits unto God and unto the Lamb. 5 And in their mouth was found no lie: they are without blemish.

6 And I saw another angel flying in mid heaven, having *a*eternal good tidings to proclaim unto them that *b*dwell on the earth, and unto every nation and tribe and tongue and people; 7 and he saith with a great voice, Fear God, and give him glory; for the hour of his judgment is come: and *c*worship him that made the heaven and the earth and sea and fountains of waters.

8 And another, a second angel, followed, saying, Fallen, fallen is Bab'y-lon the great, that hath made all the nations to drink of the wine of the wrath of her fornication.

9 And another angel, a third,

followed them, saying with a great voice, If any man *c*worshippeth the beast and his image, and receiveth a mark on his forehead, or upon his hand, 10 he also shall drink of the wine of the wrath of God, which is *d*prepared unmixed in the cup of his anger; and he shall be tormented with fire and brimstone in the presence of the holy angels, and in the presence of the Lamb: 11 and the smoke of their torment goeth up *e*for ever and ever; and they have no rest day and night, they that *c*worship the beast and his image, and whoso receiveth the mark of his name. 12 Here is the *f*patience of the saints, they that keep the commandments of God, and the faith of Je'sus.

13 And I heard a voice from heaven saying, Write, Blessed are the dead who die *g*in the Lord from henceforth: yea, saith the Spirit, that they may rest from their labors; for their works follow with them.

14 And I saw, and behold, a

---

a Or, *an eternal gospel*   *b* Gr. *sit.*   *c* See marginal note on ch. 3.9.

d Gr. *mingled.*   *e* Gr. *unto ages of ages.* *f* Or, *stedfastness* *g* Or, *in the Lord. From henceforth, yea, saith the Spirit*

Written on their foreheads. See ch. 7.3; 22.4; also ver. 9; ch. 13.16; 20.4.

4. *Not defiled.* This tells of spiritual purity of life and character. *Firstfruits unto God.* The Christians of the apostolic age and those who follow their example, the whole body of those saved in the church.

6. *Eternal good tidings.* The gospel, now to be fully proclaimed. See ch. 10.7; 1 Pet. 1.25.

7. *Fear God.* See ch. 15.4; Jer. 10.7; Acts 5.11. *The hour of his judgment.* See Acts 10.42; 17.31; 24.25.

8. *Babylon.* The great world-power of old, and the great enemy

of Israel, stands for the world-power of the later days and the great enemy of the church. Babylon cannot represent apostasy within the church. *Drink of the wine,* etc. See Jer. 51.7.

12. *Patience of the saints.* See ch. 13.10, and note thereon.

13. *Blessed.* They who die now are blessed, for they die that they may rest and are delivered from evil to come.

14. *A white cloud.* See Dan. 7.13; Mt. 24.30; Mk. 14.62. *A sharp sickle.* This verse with the two following, present a harvest scene; and ver. 17–20, a vintage scene: and these two scenes correspond to

white cloud; and on the cloud *I saw* one sitting like unto a son of man, having on his head a golden crown, and in his hand a sharp sickle. 15 And another angel came out from the [h]temple, crying with a great voice to him that sat on the cloud, Send forth thy sickle, and reap: for the hour to reap is come; for the harvest of the earth is [i]ripe. 16 And he that sat on the cloud cast his sickle upon the earth; and the earth was reaped.

17 And another angel came out from the [h]temple which is in heaven, he also having a sharp sickle. 18 And another angel came out from the altar, he that hath power over fire; and he called with a great voice to him that had the sharp sickle, saying, Send forth thy sharp sickle, and gather the clusters of the vine of the earth; for her grapes are fully ripe. 19 And the angel cast his sickle into the earth, and gathered the [k]vintage of the earth, and cast it into the winepress, the great *winepress*, of the wrath of God. 20 And the winepress was trodden without the city, and there came out blood

from the winepress, even unto the bridles of the horses, as far as a thousand and six hundred furlongs.

15 And I saw another sign in heaven, great and marvellous, seven angels having seven plagues, *which are* the last, for in them is finished the wrath of God.

2 And I saw as it were a [a]sea of glass mingled with fire; and them that come off victorious from the beast, and from his image, and from the number of his name, standing [b]by the [a]sea of glass, having harps of God. 3 And they sing the song of Mo'ses the [c]servant of God, and the song of the Lamb, saying,

Great and marvellous are thy works, O Lord God, the Almighty; righteous and true are thy ways, thou King of the [d]ages. 4 Who shall not fear, O Lord, and glorify thy name? for thou only art holy; for all the nations shall come and [e]worship before thee; for thy righteous acts have been made manifest.

5 And after these things I saw,

h Or, *sanctuary* i Gr. *become dry.* k Gr. *vine.* a Or, *glassy sea*

b Or, *upon* c Gr. *bondservant.* d Many ancient authorities read *nations.* Jer. 10.7. e See marginal note on ch. 3.9.

---

the parable of the wheat and the tares (Mt. 13.24–30, 37–43).

20. *Trodden without the city.* Identical with Sodom and Egypt in ch. 11.8. See also Lk. 21.20–24. It is a frightful picture, that the winepress runs with blood, a very deep and very wide stream. God's judgment is severe and prolonged.

CHAPTER 15

The fifth series of visions, after the record of a victor-song, tells of

the seven bowls of wrath upon the wicked.

1. *Another sign.* See ch. 12.1. *Seven angels.* See ch. 8.1, 2. *The last.* See ch. 16.17–21; 17.1; 21.9.

3. *The song of Moses.* That is, a song like that of Moses. See Ex. 15.1–18. God is blessed, as bringing deliverance through his righteous judgments.

5. *Temple.* See ch. 11.19, and note thereon. *Tabernacle of the testimony.* So-called because it contained all that was symbolized

and the *temple of the tabernacle of the testimony in heaven was opened: 6 and there came out from the *temple the seven angels that had the seven plagues, arrayed *with *precious* stone, pure *and* bright, and girt about their breasts with golden girdles. 7 And one of the four living creatures gave unto the seven angels seven golden bowls full of the wrath of God, who liveth *for ever and ever. 8 And the *temple was filled with smoke from the glory of God, and from his power; and none was able to enter into the *temple, till the seven plagues of the seven angels should be finished.

16 And I heard a great voice out of the *temple, saying to the seven angels, Go ye, and pour out the seven bowls of the wrath of God into the earth.

2 And the first went, and poured out his bowl into the earth; and *it became a noisome and grievous sore upon the men that had the mark of the beast, and that *worshipped his image.

3 And the second poured out his bowl into the sea; and *it became blood as of a dead man; and every *living soul died, *even* the things that were in the sea.

4 And the third poured out his bowl into the rivers and the fountains of the waters; *and *it became blood. 5 And I heard the angel of the waters saying, Righteous art thou, who art and who wast, thou Holy One, because thou didst thus *judge: 6 for they poured out the blood of saints and prophets, and blood hast thou given them to drink: they are worthy. 7 And I heard the altar saying, Yea, O Lord God, the Almighty, true and righteous are thy judgments.

8 And the fourth poured out his bowl upon the sun; and it was given unto *it to scorch men with fire. 9 And men were scorched with great heat: and they blasphemed the name of God who hath the power over these plagues; and they repented not to give him glory.

10 And the fifth poured out his bowl upon the throne of the beast; and his kingdom was

---

f Or, *sanctuary*   *g* Many ancient authorities read *in linen.* ch. 19.8.   *h* Gr. *unto the ages of the ages.*   *a* Or, *there came*   *j* See marginal note on ch. 3.9.

in the tabernacle of Israel (Ex. 25.40). See Acts 7.44.

7. *Seven golden bowls.* These seven bowls correspond to the seven trumpets. The first bowl affects the earth; the second, the sea; the third, the rivers and fountains; the fourth, the sun; the fifth, the throne of the beast; the sixth, the river Euphrates; the seventh, the air.

CHAPTER 16

2. *Noisome and grievous sore.*

---

c Gr. *soul of life.*   *d* Some ancient authorities read *and they became.*   *e* Or, *judge. Because they . . . prophets, thou hast given them blood also to drink*   *f* Or, *him*

Like the plague of boils upon the Egyptians. See Ex. 9.8–10.

3. *Blood as of a dead man*   See ch. 8.8, 9; Ex. 7.19–21.

4. *Rivers and the fountains.* See ch. 8.10, 11.

5. *Righteous art thou.* See Ps. 19.9; Jn. 17.25.

6. *Given them to drink.* See Mt. 23.34–37. *They are worthy.* That is, of judgment and punishment.

10. *Throne of the beast.* Satan and his angels are here tormented, as well as his subjects.

darkened; and they gnawed their tongues for pain, 11 and they blasphemed the God of heaven because of their pains and their sores; and they repented not of their works.

12 And the sixth poured out his bowl upon the great river, the *river* Eu-phra'tes; and the water thereof was dried up, that the way might be made ready for the kings that *come* from the sunrising. 13 And I saw *coming* out of the mouth of the dragon, and out of the mouth of the beast, and out of the mouth of the false prophet, three unclean spirits, as it were frogs: 14 for they are spirits of demons, working signs; which go forth *g*unto the kings of the whole *h*world, to gather them together unto the war of the great day of God, the Almighty. 15 (Behold, I come as a thief. Blessed is he that watcheth, and keepeth his garments, lest he walk naked, and they see his shame.) 16 And they gathered them together into the place which is called in Hebrew *i*Har-Ma-ged'on.

17 And the seventh poured out his bowl upon the air; and there came forth a great voice out of the *k*temple, from the throne, saying, It is done: 18 and there were lightnings, and voices, and thunders; and there was a great earthquake, such as was not since *l*there were men upon the earth, so great an earthquake, so mighty. 19 And the great city was divided into three parts, and the cities of the *m*nations fell: and Bab'y-lon the great was remembered in the sight of God, to give unto her the cup of the wine of the fierceness of his wrath. 20 And every island fled away, and the mountains were not found. 21 And great hail, *every stone* about the weight of a talent, cometh down out of heaven upon men: and men blasphemed God because of the plague of the hail; for the plague thereof is exceeding great.

17 And there came one of the seven angels that had the seven bowls, and spake with me, saying, Come hither, I will 'show thee the judgment of the

---

g Or, *upon*   *h* Gr. *inhabited earth.*   *i* Or, *Ar-Magedon.*

k Or, *sanctuary*   *l* Some ancient authorities read *there was a man.*   *m* Or, *Gentiles*

---

12. *The river Euphrates.* See ch. 9.13–19; Gen. 15.18.

13, 14. *As it were frogs.* See Ex. 8.5, 6.

16. *Har-Magedon.* That is Mount Magedon, a reference to Megiddon of the Old Testament, especially to the battle in which good King Josiah fell and lasting sorrow came to Israel. See Judg. 5.19; 2 K. 23. 29, 30; 2 Chron. 35.22.

17. *It is done.* The declaration of finality, as in our Lord's 'It is finished.'

19. *Babylon the great.* The world-power, the city of the world as opposed to the city of God; doubtless represented to the early Christians

by the city of Rome. See ch. 14.8. *Cup of the wine.* See ch. 14 10.

21. *Great hail.* See ch. 11.19; also Ex. 9.18–26. *Weight of a talent.* A Jewish 'talent' weighed more than 100 pounds.

CHAPTER 17

The sixth division of the book gives the vision of the harlot riding on the beast, and of the fall of Babylon.

1. *The great harlot.* The harlot represents the faithless church, in her submission to the world. In the prophetical sense, a harlot is one who has broken her marriage vows;

great harlot that sitteth upon many waters; 2 with whom the kings of the earth committed fornication, and they that dwell in the earth were made drunken with the wine of her fornication. 3 And he carried me away in the Spirit into a wilderness: and I saw a woman sitting upon a scarlet-colored beast, *a*full of names of blasphemy, having seven heads and ten horns. 4 And the woman was arrayed in purple and scarlet, and *b*decked with gold and precious stone and pearls, having in her hand a golden cup full of abominations, *c*even the unclean things of her fornication, 5 and upon her forehead a name written, *d*MYS-TERY, BAB′Y-LON THE GREAT, THE MOTHER OF THE HARLOTS AND OF THE ABOMINATIONS OF

THE EARTH.   6 And I saw the woman drunken with the blood of the saints, and with the blood of the *e*martyrs of Je′sus. And when I saw her, I wondered   ith a great wonder. 7 And the angel said unto me, Wherefore didst thou wonder? I will tell thee the mystery of the woman, and of the beast that carrieth her, which hath the seven heads and the ten horns. 8 The beast that thou sawest was, and is not; and is about to come up out of the abyss, *f*and to go into perdition. And they that dwell on the earth shall wonder, *they* whose name hath not been written *g*in the book of life from the foundation of the world, when they behold the beast, how that he was, and is not, and *h*shall come. 9 Here is the *i*mind that hath wisdom.

---

a Or, *names full of blasphemy* *b* Gr. *gilded.* *c* Or, *and of the unclean things* *d* Or, *a mystery, Babylon the Great*

e Or, *witnesses* See ch. 2.13. *f* Some ancient authorities read *and he goeth.* *g* Gr. *on.* *h* Gr. *shall be present.* *i* Or, *meaning*

Jerusalem and Judah thus broke their covenant vows with God. See Mt. 23.13–39. Tyre and Nineveh were both called harlots in the Old Testament. See Is. 23.17; Nah. 1.1; 3.4. *Upon many waters.* Unstable and faithless. See Jer. 51.13.

2. *Drunken with the wine.* Jer 51.7.

3. *In the Spirit.* See ch. 1.10, and note thereon. *A scarlet-colored beast.* This beast was, as before, the Roman empire, representing the world with its pomp and luxury.

4. *In purple and scarlet.* The attire of a harlot, indicating luxury and pride. Contrast this picture with the woman of ch. 12, the church in her first glory.

6. *Drunken with the blood.* Referring to the madness of persecutions. See Mt. 23.29–39; Lk. 13.33–35.

8. *Was, and is not.* This probably refers to the power of Satan himself as manifested in the world-power. He is the power of darkness (Lk. 22.53). He was in heaven (ch. 12. 3); is cast out and disappears for a

time (ch. 12.17); appears again in the beast coming up out of the sea (ch. 13.1, 2), and in the beast coming up out of the land (ch. 13.11–15). *Out of the abyss.* See ch. 9.1–11. *Go into perdition.* See Dan. 7.11; also Rev. 19.20; 20.10. *That dwell on the earth.* The ungodly shall admire and worship the pomp and pride of evil which panders to their own sin. Thus it has always been, and is today. But they whose names are written in the book of life will have their affection fixed on their Lord, and will not be deceived. *Book of life.* See ch. 13.8, and note thereon.

9. *The mind that hath wisdom.* A caution that he is speaking enigmatically, and that only the saints will be able to understand. This was probably on account of the persecutions of the church by the Jews and the Roman empire. See ch. 13.18. *Seven mountains.* This passage must have some reference to Rome, which was built upon seven hills. But it typifies all seats of evil

The seven heads are seven mountains, on which the woman sitteth: 10 and *k*they are seven kings; the five are fallen, the one is, the other is not yet come; and when he cometh, he must continue a little while. 11 And the beast that was, and is not, is himself also an eighth, and is of the seven; and he goeth into perdition. 12 And the ten horns that thou sawest are ten kings, who have received no kingdom as yet; but they receive authority as kings, with the beast, for one hour. 13 These have one mind, and they give their power and authority unto the beast. 14 These shall war against the Lamb, and the Lamb shall overcome them, for he is Lord of lords, and King of kings; and they *also shall overcome* that are with him, called and chosen and faithful. 15 And he saith unto me, The waters which thou sawest, where the harlot sitteth, are peoples, and multitudes, and nations, and tongues. 16 And the ten horns which thou sawest, and the beast, these shall hate the harlot, and shall make her desolate and naked, and shall eat her flesh, and shall burn her utterly with fire. 17 For God did put in their hearts to do his mind, and to come to one mind, and to give their kingdom unto the beast, until the words of God should be accomplished. 18 And the woman whom thou sawest is the great city, which *l*reigneth over the kings of the earth.

18 After these things I saw another angel coming down out of heaven, having great authority; and the earth was lightened with his glory. 2 And he cried with a mighty voice, saying, Fallen, fallen is Bab'y-lon the great, and is become a habitation of demons, and a *a*hold of every unclean spirit, and a *a*hold of every unclean and hateful bird. 3 For *b*by *c*the wine of the wrath of her fornication all the nations are fallen; and the kings of the earth committed fornication with her, and the merchants of the earth waxed rich by the power of her *d*wantonness.

4 And I heard another voice from heaven, saying, Come forth, my people, out of her, that ye have no fellowship with

---

k Or, *there are*   *l* Gr. *hath a kingdom.*
a Or, *prison*   *b* Some authorities read *of the wine . . . have drunk.*   *c* Some ancient authorities omit *the wine of.*   *d* Or, *luxury*

power and political influence. In this sense, the number (seven) of the mountains symbolizes universal power.

10. *Seven kings.* Probably referring to seven of the Cæsars; but the exact reference cannot be now determined.

12. *The ten horns.* Perhaps some allied powers which aided imperial Rome in warring on Christianity.

14. *These shall war,* etc. The forces of evil, arrayed against Jesus and his kingdom, shall finally turn on the church, as she has become apostate, and shall bring her to ruin.

18. *The great city.* There can hardly fail to be some reference here to Rome as the capital of the world.

CHAPTER 18

2. *Fallen, fallen,* etc. The fall and ruin of the world-power, which has opposed the kingdom of God. See Is. 21.9; Jer. 51.8; also Rev. 14.8.

3. *The wine of the wrath.* See ch. 14.8.

4. *Come forth, my people.* See Jer. 51.45; Mt. 24.16.

her sins, and that ye receive not
of her plagues: 5 for her sins
^ehave reached even unto heaven,
and God hath remembered her
iniquities. 6 Render unto her
even as she rendered, and double
unto her the double according
to her works: in the cup which
she mingled, mingle unto her
double. 7 How much soever she
glorified herself, and waxed
^fwanton, so much give her of
torment and mourning: for she
saith in her heart, I sit a queen,
and am no widow, and shall in
no wise see mourning. 8 Therefore in one day shall her plagues
come, death, and mourning, and
famine; and she shall be utterly
burned with fire; for strong is
^gthe Lord God who judged her.
9 And the kings of the earth, who
committed fornication and lived
^hwantonly with her, shall weep
and wail over her, when they
look upon the smoke of her burning, 10 standing afar off for the
fear of her torment, saying, Woe,
woe, the great city, Bab'y-lon,
the strong city! for in one hour
is thy judgment come. 11 And
the merchants of the earth weep
and mourn over her, for no man
buyeth their ⁱmerchandise any
more; 12 ⁱmerchandise of gold,
and silver, and precious stone,
and pearls, and fine linen, and
purple, and silk, and scarlet; and
all thyine wood, and every vessel
of ivory, and every vessel made
of most precious wood, and of

brass, and iron, and marble; 13
and cinnamon, and ^kspice, and
incense, and ointment, and
frankincense, and wine, and oil,
and fine flour, and wheat, and
cattle, and sheep; and *merchandise* of horses and chariots
and ^lslaves; and ^msouls of men.
14 And the fruits which thy soul
lusted after are gone from thee,
and all things that were dainty
and sumptuous are perished
from thee, and *men* shall find
them no more at all. 15 The
merchants of these things, who
were made rich by her, shall
stand afar off for the fear of her
torment, weeping and mourning;
16 saying, Woe, woe, the great
city, she that was arrayed in fine
linen and purple and scarlet, and
ⁿdecked with gold and precious
stone and pearl! 17 for in one
hour so great riches is made
desolate. And every shipmaster,
and every one that saileth any
whither, and mariners, and as
many as ^ogain their living by sea,
stood afar off, 18 and cried out
as they looked upon the smoke
of her burning, saying, What *city*
is like the great city? 19 And
they cast dust on their heads,
and cried, weeping and mourning, saying, Woe, woe, the great
city, wherein all that had their
ships in the sea were made rich
by reason of her costliness! for
in one hour is she made desolate.
20 Rejoice over her, thou heaven,
and ye saints, and ye apostles,

e Or, *clave together* f Or, *luxurious*
g Some ancient authorities omit *the Lord.*
h Or, *luxuriously* i Gr. *cargo.*

k Gr. *amomum.* l Gr. *bodies.* Gen. 36.6
(Sept.). n Or, *lives* n Gr. *gilded.* o Gr.
work the sea.

5. *Reached unto heaven.* See Jer.
51.9
7. *She saith in her heart.* See Is.
47.5, 7, 8.

9–20. For a parallel picture see
Ezek. 26.1-21; 27.1-36.
20. *Rejoice over her, thou heaven.*
See Jer. 51.48.

and ye prophets; for God hath judged your judgment on her.

21 And [p]a strong angel took up a stone as it were a great millstone and cast it into the sea, saying, Thus with a mighty fall shall Bab'y-lon, the great city, be cast down, and shall be found no more at all. 22 And the voice of harpers and minstrels and flute-players and trumpeters shall be heard no more at all in thee; and no craftsman, [q]of whatsoever craft, shall be found any more at all in thee; and the voice of a mill shall be found no more at all in thee; 23 and the light of a lamp shall shine no more at all in thee; and the voice of the bridegroom and of the bride shall be heard no more at all in thee: for thy merchants were the princes of the earth; for with thy sorcery were all the nations deceived. 24 And in her was found the blood of prophets and of saints, and of all that have been slain upon the earth.

19 After these things I heard as it were a great voice of a great multitude in heaven, saying,

Hal-le-lu'jah; Salvation, and glory, and power, belong to our God: 2 for true and righteous are his judgments; for he hath judged the great harlot, her that corrupted the earth with her fornication, and he hath avenged the blood of his [a]servants at her hand.

3 And a second time they [b]say, Hal-le-lu'jah. And her smoke goeth up [c]for ever and ever. 4 And the four and twenty elders and the four living creatures fell down and worshipped God that sitteth on the throne, saying, A-men'; Hal-le-lu'jah. 5 And a voice came forth from the throne, saying,

Give praise to our God, all ye his [a]servants, ye that fear him, the small and the great.

6 And I heard as it were the voice of a great multitude, and as the voice of many waters, and as the voice of mighty thunders, saying,

Hal-le-lu'jah: for the Lord our God, the Almighty, reigneth. 7 Let us rejoice and be exceeding glad, and let us give the glory unto him: for the marriage of the Lamb is come, and his wife

---

p Gr. one.   q Some ancient authorities omit of whatsoever craft.

a Gr. bondservants.   b Gr. have said. c Gr. unto the ages of the ages.

21. *With a mighty fall*   See Jer. 51.63, 64.

22. *The voice of harpers,* etc.   See Jer. 25.10; Ezek. 26.13.

24. *Blood of prophets.*   See Mt. 23.34, 35; Lk. 11.49–51; 13.33, 34.

CHAPTER 19

After the prophetical dirge over the fall of Babylon, the great city, the tragedy of the Book of Revelation, chapter 19 begins with a song of triumph of the redeemed, victors over the powers of darkness, the church which has thrown off the power of apostasy. See ch. 12.10, 12.

7. *Marriage of the Lamb.*   This refers to the union of Christ and his church; an action in one sense going on throughout the passing years so long as believers are united to him. The same great spiritual fact is portrayed in the Master's parables. See Mt. 22.2–13; Lk. 14.15–24. *His wife.*   The bride is the New Jerusalem—the church. See Eph. 5.23–25.

hath made herself ready.
8 And it was given unto her
that she should array herself in fine linen, bright *and*
pure: for the fine linen is the
righteous acts of the saints.
9 And he saith unto me, Write,
Blessed are they that are bidden
to the marriage supper of the
Lamb. And he saith unto me,
These are true. words of God.
10 And I fell down before his
feet to *d*worship him. And he
saith unto me, See thou do it
not: I am a fellow-servant with
thee and with thy brethren that
hold the testimony of Je′sus:
*d*worship God: for the testimony
of Je′sus is the spirit of prophecy.

11 And I saw the heaven
opened; and behold, a white
horse, and he that sat thereon
*e*called Faithful and True; and
in righteousness he doth judge
and make war. 12 And his eyes
are a flame of fire, and upon his
head *are* many diadems; and he
hath a name written which no
one knoweth but he himself.
13 And he *is* arrayed in a garment *f*sprinkled with blood: and
his name is called The Word
of God. 14 And the armies

which are in heaven followed
him upon white horses, clothed
in fine linen, white *and* pure.
15 And out of his mouth proceedeth a sharp sword, that with
it he should smite the nations:
and he shall rule them with a
rod of iron: and he treadeth the
*g*winepress of the fierceness of
the wrath of God, the Almighty.
16 And he hath on his garment
and on his thigh a name written,
KING OF KINGS, AND LORD OF
LORDS.

17 And I saw *h*an angel
standing in the sun; and he
cried with a loud voice, saying
to all the birds that fly in mid
heaven, Come *and* be gathered
together unto the great supper
of God; 18 that ye may eat the
flesh of kings, and the flesh of
*i*captains, and the flesh of mighty
men, and the flesh of horses and
of them that sit thereon, and the
flesh of all men, both free and
bond, and small and great.

19 And I saw the beast, and
the kings of the earth, and their
armies, gathered together to
make war against him that sat
upon the horse, and against his
army. 20 And the beast was

---

d See marginal note on ch. 3.9.   *e* Some
ancient authorities omit *called*.   *f* Some
ancient authorities read *dipped in*.

g Gr. *winepress of the wine of the fierceness*.   *h* Gr. *one*.   *i* Or, *military tribunes*
Gr. *chiliarchs*.

10. *Thy fellow-servant*. See ch.
22.8–11. *The testimony of Jesus*.
The word of God, especially the
New Testament.
11. The seventh section of the
revelation begins here with the clear
presentation of the millennial age—
the Messianic triumph. See 1 Cor.
15.25. *He that sat thereon*. The
Christ, on the white horse, as at the
beginning. See ch. 1.5; 3.7, 14.
13. *Garment sprinkled with blood*.
See Is. 63.1–6. *The Word of God*.
See Jn. 1.1–18.

14. *Armies*. The angelic host.
See ch. 17.14.
17. *Come and be gathered*. See
Ezek. 39.17–20.
19. *The beast*. See ch. 13.1–7.
Kings of the earth. As elsewhere, the
beast and the kings of the earth
represent the world-power which is
hostile to the Lamb.
20. *False prophet*. The beast
which came up out of the earth (ch.
13.11). See ch. 16.13. *They two
were cast alive*. See Dan. 7.11.
Lake of fire. See ch. 20.10, 14, 15;

taken, and with him the false prophet that wrought the signs in his sight, wherewith he deceived them that had received the mark of the beast and them that *k*worshipped his image: they two were cast alive into the lake of fire that burneth with brimstone: 21 and the rest were killed with the sword of him that sat upon the horse, *even the sword* which came forth out of his mouth: and all the birds were filled with their flesh.

20 And I saw an angel coming down out of heaven, having the key of the abyss and a great chain *a*in his hand. 2 And he laid hold on the dragon, the old serpent, which is the Devil and Satan, and bound him for a thousand years, 3 and cast him into the abyss, and shut *it*, and sealed *it* over him, that he should deceive the nations no more, until the thousand years should be finished: after this he must be loosed for a little time.

4 And I saw thrones, and they sat upon them, and judgment was given unto them: and *I saw* the souls of them that had been beheaded for the testimony of Je'sus, and for the word of God, and such as *k*worshipped not the beast, neither his image, and received not the mark upon their forehead and upon their hand; and they lived, and reigned with Christ a thousand years. 5 The rest of the dead lived not until the thousand years should be finished. This is the first resurrection. 6 Blessed and holy is he that hath part in the first resurrection: over these the second death hath no *b*power; but they shall be priests of God and of Christ, and shall reign with him *c*a thousand years.

7 And when the thousand years are finished, Satan shall be loosed out of his prison, 8 and shall come forth to deceive the nations which are in the four corners of the earth, Gog and

---

k See marginal note on ch. 3.9. *a* Gr. *upon.*

21.8. The same as the Gehenna of fire in Mt. 5.22; 10.28; Mk. 9.43–45, a place of utter destruction.

CHAPTER 20

The harlot, the beast, and the false prophet have been vanquished, but Christ must triumph over Satan before his victory is complete.

1. *Key of the abyss.* See ch. 9.1. *A great chain.* See 2 Pet. 2.4; Jude 6.

2. *The dragon.* See ch. 12.3–9, and notes thereon. *A thousand years.* The number, as others in this book, is symbolic (see 2 Pet. 3.8). It marks the period of the millennium, beginning with the first limiting of the power of the evil one by the incarnate Christ (see Lk.

b Or, *authority* *c* Some ancient authorities read *the.*

11.18), and continues until Christ shall have put all enemies under his feet.

4. *That had been beheaded.* Thus the Book of Revelation strengthened the faith of those who were suffering persecutions, by giving them a vision of the final triumph of Christ and the blessedness of his followers. See ch. 6.9–11; 11.11, 12; 12.5, 11. *Received not the mark,* etc. Had not devoted themselves to the services of Satan and the world. *Reigned with Christ.* Those who are truly Christians are called kings and priests, and share in Christ's power and glory. See 2 Tim. 2.11, 12.

6. *Second death.* See ver. 14; ch. 21.8; Mt. 10.28.

7. *Satan shall be loosed.* Christ's reign in his church is to be followed by a final outburst of Satan's power.

651

Ma′gog, to gather them together to the war: the number of whom is as the sand of the sea. 9 And they went up over the breadth of the earth, and compassed the camp of the saints about, and the beloved city: and fire came down ᵈout of heaven, and devoured them. 10 And the devil that deceived them was cast into the lake of fire and brimstone, where are also the beast and the false prophet; and they shall be tormented day and night ᵉfor ever and ever.

11 And I saw a great white throne, and him that sat upon it, from whose face the earth and the heaven fled away; and there was found no place for them. 12 And I saw the dead, the great and the small, standing before the throne; and books were opened: and another book was opened, which is *the book* of life: and the dead were judged out of the things which were written in the books, according

to their works. 13 And the sea gave up the dead that were in it; and death and Ha′des gave up the dead that were in them: and they were judged every man according to their works. 14 And death and Ha′des were cast into the lake of fire. This is the second death, *even* the lake of fire. 15 And if any was not found written in the book of life, he was cast into the lake of fire.

21 And I saw a new heaven and a new earth: for the first heaven and the first earth are passed away; and the sea is no more. 2 And I saw ᵃthe holy city, new Je-ru′sa-lem, coming down out of heaven from God, made ready as a bride adorned for her husband. 3 And I heard a great voice out of the throne saying, Behold, the tabernacle of God is with men, and he shall ᵇdwell with them, and they shall be his peoples, and God himself shall be with them, ᶜ*and*

ᵈ Some ancient authorities insert *from God.* ᵉ Gr. *unto the ages of the ages.*

ᵃ Or, *the holy city Jerusalem coming down new out of heaven* ᵇ Gr. *tabernacle.* ᶜ Some ancient authorities omit, and be *their God.*

---

10. *Cast into the lake of fire.* The final overthrow of Satan. See ch. 14.10, 11.

11. *A great white throne.* The throne of judgment. See Is. 6.1; Dan. 7.9.

12. *The dead.* That is, 'the rest of the dead' mentioned in ver. 5; it seems to mean those who had not their names in the book of life. *Books were opened.* See Dan. 7.10. *Book of life.* See Ex. 32.32; Ps. 56.8; 69.28; Dan. 12.1; Lk. 10.20; Phil. 4.3. *According to their works.* See Rom. 2.6; 2 Cor. 5.10.

14. *Death and Hades.* Hades signifies simply the unseen world, the 'abode of the dead.' Death shall be no more, and none shall be left in the abode of the dead, for they whose names are not written in the

book of life, shall be cast into the lake of fire. See 1 Cor. 15.26.

CHAPTER 21

1. *A new heaven.* See Is. 65.17, 18.

2. *New Jerusalem.* The old Jerusalem became one with Babylon the great, the harlot; but the new Jerusalem is the city which Paul calls the 'Jerusalem that is above' (Gal. 4.26). See also Heb. 12.22. *Bride.* The church of Christ. See Eph. 5.25–32; also ch. 19.7–9, and note thereon.

3. *Tabernacle of God.* In this tabernacle, the believer enters boldly into the holy place, by the blood of Jesus. See Heb. 10.22.

be their God: 4 and he shall wipe away every tear from their eyes; and death shall be no more; neither shall there be mourning, nor crying, nor pain, any more: the first things are passed away. 5 And he that sitteth on the throne said, Behold, I make all things new. And he saith, [d]Write: for these words are faithful and true. 6 And he said unto me, They are come to pass. I am the Al'pha and the O-me'ga, the beginning and the end. I will give unto him that is athirst of the fountain of the water of life freely. 7 He that overcometh shall inherit these things; and I will be his God, and he shall be my son. 8 But for the fearful, and unbelieving, and abominable, and murderers, and fornicators, and sorcerers, and idolaters, and all liars, their part *shall be* in the lake that burneth with fire and brimstone; which is the second death.

9 And there came one of the seven angels who had the seven bowls, who were laden with the seven last plagues; and he spake with me, saying, Come hither, I will show thee the bride, the wife of the Lamb. 10 And he carried me away in the Spirit to a mountain great and high, and showed me the holy city Je-ru'-sa-lem, coming down out of heaven from God, 11 having the glory of God: her [e]light was like unto a stone most precious, as it were a jasper stone, clear as crystal: 12 having a wall great and high; having twelve [f]gates, and at the [f]gates twelve angels; and names written thereon, which are *the names* of the twelve tribes of the children of Is'ra-el: 13 on the east were three [f]gates; and on the north three [f]gates; and on the south three [f]gates; and on the west three [f]gates. 14 And the wall of the city had twelve foundations, and on them twelve names of the twelve apostles of the Lamb. 15 And he that spake with me had for a measure a golden reed to measure the city, and the [f]gates thereof, and the wall thereof. 16 And the city lieth foursquare, and the length thereof is as great as the breadth: and he measured the city with the reed, twelve thousand furlongs: the length and the breadth and the height thereof are equal. 17 And he measured the wall thereof, a

---

d Or, *Write, These words are faithful and true.*   *e* Gr. *luminary.*   *f* Gr. *portals.*

4. *Wipe away every tear.* See ch. 7.17.

5. *He that sitteth on the throne.* See ch. 19.11–16; 20.11; 22.1.

6. *The Alpha and the Omega.* See ch. 1.8, and note thereon.

7. *Overcometh.* There are fourteen promises in the Book of Revelation, to those who overcome.

8. *The fearful.* Those who have not faith enough to endure persecution. *The lake that burneth.* See ch. 19.20, and note thereon.

9. *The seven angels.* The eighth and last vision of the revelation begins with ver. 9. See ch. 17.1. *The bride.* See Eph. 5.23–32, and above.

10. *In the Spirit.* See ch. 1.10. *To a mountain.* See Ezek. 40.2. *The holy city Jerusalem.* All that follows is in striking contrast to the great city, the mother of harlots (ch. 17.5).

12. For a parallel passage, see Ezek. 48.30–34.

17. *Measure of a man.* That is, the measure used by the angel was the same as would be used by a man.

hundred and forty and four cubits, *according to* the measure of a man, that is, of an angel. 18 And the building of the wall thereof was jasper: and the city was pure gold, like unto pure glass. 19 The foundations of the wall of the city were adorned with all manner of precious stones. The first foundation was jasper; the second, [g]sapphire; the third, chalcedony; the fourth, emerald; 20 the fifth, sardonyx; the sixth, sardius; the seventh, chrysolite; the eighth, beryl; the ninth, topaz; the tenth, chrysoprase; the eleventh, [h]jacinth; the twelfth, amethyst. 21 And the twelve [i]gates were twelve pearls; each one of the several [i]gates was of one pearl: and the street of [l]the city was pure gold, [k]as it were transparent glass. 22 And I saw no [l]temple therein: for the Lord God the Almighty, and the Lamb, are the [l]temple thereof. 23 And the city hath no need of the sun, neither of the moon, to shine upon it: for the glory of God did lighten it, [m]and the lamp thereof *is* the Lamb. 24 And the nations shall walk

[n]amidst the light thereof: and the kings of the earth bring their glory into it. 25 And the [i]gates thereof shall in no wise be shut by day (for there shall be no night there): 26 and they shall bring the glory and the honor of the nations into it: 27 and there shall in no wise enter into it anything [o]unclean, or he that [p]maketh an abomination and a lie: but only they that are written in the Lamb's book of life.

22

1 And he showed me a river of water of life, bright as crystal, proceeding out of the throne of God and of [a]the Lamb, 2 in the midst of the street thereof. And on this side of the river and on that was [b]the tree of life, bearing twelve [c]*manner of* fruits, yielding its fruit every month: and the leaves of the tree were for the healing of the nations. 3 And there shall be [d]no curse any more: and the throne of God and of the Lamb shall be therein: and his [e]servants shall serve him; 4 and they shall see his face; and his name *shall be* on their foreheads. 5 And there shall be night no more; and they need no light of lamp, neither

---

g Or, *lapis lazuli*   h Or, *sapphire*   i Gr. *portals.*   k Or, *transparent as glass*   l Or, *sanctuary*   m Or. *and the Lamb, the lamp thereof*   n Or, *by*   o Gr. *common.*   p Or, *doeth*   d Or, *the Lamb. In the midst of*

the street thereof, and on either side of the river, was the tree of life &c.   b Or, *a tree*   c Or, *crops of fruit*   d Or, *no more anything accursed*   e Gr. *bondservants.*

25. *Shall in no wise be shut.* Gates are for protection from enemies. The perpetually open gates symbolize perfect safety. See Is. 60.11.
27. *Maketh an abomination.* Probably means the practice of idolatry. See ch. 17.4; 21.8.   *The Lamb's book of life.* See ch. 3.5, and note thereon.

CHAPTER 22

1. *A river of water of life.* See

Ezek. 47.1; Zech. 14.8; Jn. 4.10, 14. See also the description of a river in the garden of Eden (Gen. 2.10).
2. *The tree of life.* See ch. 2.7; Gen. 2.9.
3. *No curse any more.* The punishment for sin—banishment from the tree of life (Gen. 3.16–19, 23)— shall be removed. All shall have access to that tree of life in the precincts of the heavenly city. See Mt. 19.29; Acts 3.25.

light of sun; for the Lord God shall give them light: and they shall reign *f*for ever and ever.

6 And he said unto me, These words are faithful and true: and the Lord, the God of the spirits of the prophets, sent his angel to show unto his *g*servants the things which must shortly come to pass. 7 And behold, I come quickly. Blessed is he that keepeth the words of the prophecy of this book.

8 And I John am he that heard and saw these things. And when I heard and saw, I fell down to *h*worship before the feet of the angel that showed me these things. 9 And he saith unto me, See thou do it not: I am a fellow-servant with thee and with thy brethren the prophets, and with them that keep the words of this book: *h*worship God.

10 And he saith unto me, Seal not up the words of the prophecy of this book; for the time is at hand. 11 He that is unrighteous, let him do unrighteousness *i*still: and he that is filthy, let him be made filthy *i*still: and he that is righteous, let him do righteous-ness *i*still: and he that is holy, let him be made holy still. 12 Behold, I come quickly; and my *k*reward is with me, to render to each man according as his work is. 13 I am the Al'pha and the O-me'ga, the first and the last, the beginning and the end. 14 Blessed are they that wash their robes, that they may have *l*the right *to come* to the tree of life, and may enter in by the *m*gates into the city. 15 Without are the dogs, and the sorcerers, and the fornicators, and the murderers, and the idolaters, and every one that loveth and *n*maketh a lie.

16 I Je'sus have sent mine angel to testify unto you these things *o*for the churches. I am the root and the offspring of Da-vid, the bright, the morning star.

17 *p*And the Spirit and the bride say, Come. And he that heareth, let him say, Come. And he that is athirst, let him come: he that will, let him take the water of life freely.

18 I testify unto every man that heareth the words of the prophecy of this book, If any man shall add *q*unto them, God shall add *q*unto him the plagues

---

f Gr. *unto the ages of the ages.* *g* Gr. *bond-servants.* *h* See marginal note on ch. 3.9. *i* Or, *yet more* *k* Or, *wages* *l* Or, *the authority over* Comp. ch. 6.8. *m* Gr. *portals.* *n* Or, *doeth* Comp. ch. 21.27. *o* Gr. *over.* *p* Or, *Both* *q* Gr. *upon.*

6. *God of the spirits,* etc. He who inspired the spirits of the prophets. The verses 6–21 form a conclusion to the whole book.

7. *I come quickly.* See Mt. 24.34–42.

11. *He that is unrighteous.* Even at the last a word of warning. See Is. 6.10; Ezek. 3.27; 20.39; Dan. 12. 10; Mt. 26.45.

14. *Right to come.* See note on ver. 3. *May enter in.* The gates are ever open to those whose names are written in the Lamb's book of life.

15. *Dogs.* The impure; lascivious persons.

16. *The root and the offspring of David.* See Is. 11.1, 10; Mt. 1.1; 22.42. *The morning star.* See ch. 2.28, and note thereon.

17. This verse is called 'the great invitation'; because of its great offer, its mercy, and its universality. *He that is athirst.* See ch. 21.6; Is. 55.1; Jn. 7.37.

which are written in this book: 19 and if any man shall take away from the words of the book of this prophecy, God shall take away his part from the tree of life, and out of the holy city, ^rwhich are written in this book.

20 He who testifieth these things saith, Yea: I come quickly. A-men': come, Lord Je'sus.

21 The grace of the Lord Je'sus ^s be ^twith the saints. A-men'.

---

r Or, even from *the things which are written*

s Some ancient authorities add *Christ.*
t Two ancient authorities read *with all.*

---

19. *This book.* The Book of the Revelation of Jesus Christ. See ver. 7, 9; ch. 1.3–11. *Take away his part.* He shall be denied access to the tree of life. See ver. 2. *The holy city.* The heavenly city, inhabited by those who have overcome.

20. *He who testifieth.* Jesus Christ. See ch. 1.2. Thus the book ends with the Lord's promise of his return, the church's prayer that it may quickly come, and (ver. 21) a benediction of grace.